ACKNOWLEDGMENTS

We gratefully acknowledge the help of our representatives for their efficient and perceptive inspection of the lodging and dining establishments listed; the establishments' proprietors for their cooperation in showing their facilities and providing information about them; the many users of previous editions of the Mobil Travel Guide who have taken the time to share their experiences; and for their time and information, the thousands of chambers of commerce, convention and visitors bureaus, city, state, and provincial tourism offices, and government agencies who assisted in our research.

The EXXON Emblem, MOBIL, and PEGASUS, the Flying Red Horse design(s) are trademarks of Exxon Mobil Corporation. All rights reserved. Reproduction by any means including but not limited to photography, electrostatic copying devices, or electronic data processing is prohibited. Use of the information contained herein for solicitation of advertising or listing in any other publication is expressly prohibited without written permission from Exxon Mobil Corporation. Violations of reserved rights are subject to prosecution.

Maps © MapQuest 2000, www.mapquest.com

Published by Publications International, Ltd.
7373 North Cicero Avenue
Lincol___od, IL 60712

_____mobiltravel.com

___o

___4-1

___hina.

2 1

Mobil
Travel Guide®

Southeast
2001

ExxonMobil Travel Publications

CONTENTS

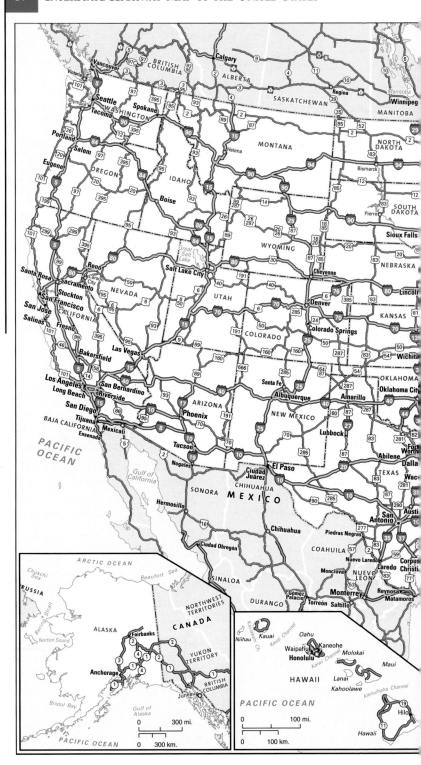

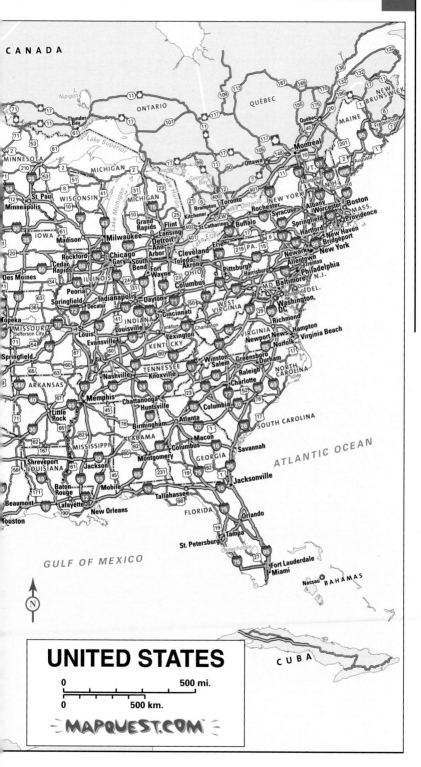

UNITED STATES

0 ——— 500 mi.

0 ——— 500 km.

MAPQUEST.COM

Distances in chart are in miles. To convert miles to kilometers, multiply the distance in miles by 1.609

Example:
New York, NY to Boston, MA = 215 miles or 346 kilometers (215 x 1.609)

	ALBUQUERQUE, NM	ATLANTA, GA	BALTIMORE, MD	BILLINGS, MT	BIRMINGHAM, AL	BISMARCK, ND	BOISE, ID	BOSTON, MA	BUFFALO, NY	BURLINGTON, VT	CHARLESTON, SC	CHARLESTON, WV	CHARLOTTE, NC	CHEYENNE, WY	CHICAGO, IL	CINCINNATI, OH	CLEVELAND, OH	DALLAS, TX	DENVER, CO	DES MOINES, IA	DETROIT, MI	EL PASO, TX	HOUSTON, TX	INDIANAPOLIS, IN	JACKSON, MS	KANSAS CITY, MO
ALBUQUERQUE, NM		1490	1902	991	1274	1333	966	2240	1808	2178	1793	1568	1649	538	1352	1409	1619	754	438	1091	1608	263	994	1298	1157	894
ATLANTA, GA	1490		679	1889	150	1559	2218	1100	910	1158	317	503	238	1482	717	476	726	792	1403	967	735	1437	800	531	386	801
BALTIMORE, MD	1902	679		1959	795	1551	2401	422	370	481	583	352	441	1665	708	521	377	1399	1690	1031	532	2045	1470	600	1032	1087
BILLINGS, MT	991	1889	1959		1839	413	626	2254	1796	2181	2157	1755	2012	455	1246	1552	1597	1433	554	1007	1534	1255	1673	1432	1836	1088
BIRMINGHAM, AL	1274	150	795	1839		1509	2170	1215	909	1241	466	578	389	1434	667	475	725	647	1356	919	734	1292	678	481	241	753
BISMARCK, ND	1333	1559	1551	413	1509		1039	1846	1388	1773	1749	1347	1604	594	838	1144	1189	1342	693	675	1126	1597	1582	1024	1548	801
BOISE, ID	966	2218	2401	626	2170	1039		2697	2239	2624	2520	2182	2375	737	1708	1969	2040	1711	833	1369	1977	1206	1952	1852	2115	1376
BOSTON, MA	2240	1100	422	2254	1215	1846	2697		462	214	1003	741	861	1961	1003	862	654	1819	2004	1326	741	2465	1890	940	1453	1427
BUFFALO, NY	1808	910	370	1796	909	1388	2239	462		375	899	431	695	1502	545	442	197	1393	1546	868	277	2039	1513	508	1134	995
BURLINGTON, VT	2178	1158	481	2181	1241	1773	2624	214	375		1061	782	919	1887	930	817	567	1763	1931	1253	652	2409	1916	878	1479	1366
CHARLESTON, SC	1793	317	583	2157	466	1749	2520	1003	899	1061		468	204	1783	907	622	724	1109	1705	1204	879	1754	1110	721	703	1102
CHARLESTON, WV	1568	503	352	1755	578	1347	2182	741	431	782	468		265	1445	506	209	255	1072	1367	802	410	1718	1192	320	816	764
CHARLOTTE, NC	1649	238	441	2012	389	1604	2375	861	695	919	204	265		1637	761	476	520	1031	1559	1057	675	1677	1041	575	625	956
CHEYENNE, WY	538	1482	1665	455	1434	594	737	1961	1502	1887	1783	1445	1637		972	1233	1304	979	100	633	1241	801	1201	1115	1382	640
CHICAGO, IL	1352	717	708	1246	667	838	1708	1003	545	930	907	506	761	972		302	346	936	1015	337	283	1543	1108	184	750	532
CINCINNATI, OH	1409	476	521	1552	475	1144	1969	862	442	817	622	209	476	1233	302		253	958	1200	599	261	1605	1079	116	700	597
CLEVELAND, OH	1619	726	377	1597	725	1189	2040	654	197	567	724	255	520	1304	346	253		1208	1347	669	171	1854	1328	319	950	806
DALLAS, TX	754	792	1399	1433	647	1342	1711	1819	1393	1763	1109	1072	1031	979	936	958	1208		887	752	1218	647	241	913	406	554
DENVER, CO	438	1403	1690	554	1356	693	833	2004	1546	1931	1705	1367	1559	100	1015	1200	1347	887		676	1284	701	1127	1088	1290	603
DES MOINES, IA	1091	967	1031	1007	919	675	1369	1326	868	1253	1204	802	1057	633	337	599	669	752	676		606	1283	992	481	931	194
DETROIT, MI	1608	735	532	1534	734	1126	1977	741	277	652	879	410	675	1241	283	261	171	1218	1284	606		1799	1338	318	960	795
EL PASO, TX	263	1437	2045	1255	1292	1597	1206	2465	2039	2409	1754	1718	1677	801	1543	1605	1854	647	701	1283	1799		758	1489	1051	1085
HOUSTON, TX	994	800	1470	1673	678	1582	1952	1890	1513	1916	1110	1192	1041	1220	1108	1079	1328	241	1127	992	1338	758		1033	445	795
INDIANAPOLIS, IN	1298	531	600	1432	481	1024	1852	940	508	878	721	320	575	1115	184	116	319	913	1088	481	318	1489	1033		675	485
JACKSON, MS	1157	386	1032	1836	241	1548	2115	1453	1134	1479	703	816	625	1382	750	700	950	406	1290	931	960	1051	445	675		747
KANSAS CITY, MO	894	801	1087	1088	753	801	1376	1427	995	1366	1102	764	956	640	532	597	806	554	603	194	795	1085	795	485	747	
LAS VEGAS, NV	578	2067	2445	965	1852	1378	760	2757	2299	2684	2371	2122	2225	843	1768	1955	2100	1331	756	1429	2037	717	1474	1843	1735	1358
LITTLE ROCK, AR	900	528	1072	1530	381	1183	1808	1493	1066	1437	900	745	754	1076	662	632	882	327	984	567	891	974	447	587	269	382
LOS ANGELES, CA	806	2237	2705	1239	2092	1702	1033	3046	2572	2957	2534	2374	2453	1116	2042	2215	2374	1446	1029	1703	2303	804	1851	1632		
LOUISVILLE, KY	1320	419	602	1547	369	1139	1932	964	545	915	610	251	464	1197	299	106	356	852	1118	595	366	1499	972	112	594	516
MEMPHIS, TN	1033	389	933	1625	241	1337	1954	1353	927	1297	760	606	614	1217	539	493	742	466	1116	720	752	1112	586	464	211	536
MIAMI, FL	2155	661	1109	2554	812	2224	2883	1529	1425	1587	583	994	730	2147	1382	1141	1507	1360	2069	1632	1401	1959	1201	1196	915	1466
MILWAUKEE, WI	1426	813	805	1175	763	767	1748	1100	642	1027	1003	601	857	1012	89	398	443	1010	1055	378	380	1617	1193	279	835	573
MINNEAPOLIS, MN	1339	1129	1121	839	1079	431	1465	1417	958	1343	1319	918	1173	881	409	714	760	999	924	246	697	1530	1240	596	1151	441
MONTRÉAL, QC	2172	1241	564	2093	1289	1685	2535	313	397	92	1145	822	1003	1799	841	815	588	1772	1843	1165	564	2363	1892	872	1514	1359
NASHVILLE, TN	1248	242	716	1648	194	1315	1976	1136	711	1066	582	387	409	1240	471	281	531	681	1162	801	287	1328	801	287	423	559
NEW ORLEANS, LA	1276	473	1142	1955	351	1734	2234	1563	1254	1588	783	926	713	1502	935	820	1070	525	1409	1117	1079	1118	360	826	185	932
NEW YORK, NY	2015	869	192	2049	985	1641	2491	215	400	299	773	515	631	1755	797	636	466	1589	1799	1121	622	2235	1660	715	1223	1202
OKLAHOMA CITY, OK	546	944	1354	1227	729	1136	1506	1694	1462	1632	1248	1022	1102	773	807	863	1073	209	681	546	1062	737	449	752	612	348
OMAHA, NE	973	989	1168	904	941	616	1234	1463	1005	1390	1290	952	1144	497	474	736	806	669	541	136	743	1236	910	618	935	188
ORLANDO, FL	1934	440	904	2333	591	2003	2662	1324	1221	1383	379	790	525	1926	1161	920	1045	1146	1847	1411	1180	1738	980	975	694	1245
PHILADELPHIA, PA	1954	782	104	2019	897	1611	2462	321	414	371	685	454	543	1725	768	576	437	1501	1744	1091	582	2157	1655	735	1135	1141
PHOENIX, AZ	466	1868	2366	1199	1723	1662	993	2706	2274	2644	2184	2035	2107	1004	1876	2085	1077	904	1558	2074	432	1188	1764	1482	1360	
PITTSBURGH, PA	1670	676	246	1719	763	1311	2161	592	217	587	642	217	438	1425	467	292	136	1246	1460	791	292	1893	1366	370	988	857
PORTLAND, ME	2338	1197	520	2352	1313	1944	2795	107	526	233	1101	839	959	2059	1101	960	751	1917	2102	1424	839	2563	1988	1038	1557	1522
PORTLAND, OR	1395	2647	2830	889	2599	1301	432	3126	2667	3052	2948	2610	2802	1166	2137	2398	2469	2140	1261	1798	2404	1754	2381	2280	2544	1805
RAPID CITY, SD	841	1511	1626	379	1463	320	930	1921	1463	1848	1824	1422	1678	305	913	1219	1264	1077	404	629	1201	1105	1318	1101	1458	710
RENO, NV	1020	2440	2623	960	2392	1372	430	2919	2460	2845	2741	2403	2595	959	1930	2162	2262	1933	1054	1591	2198	1315	2072	2073	2337	1598
RICHMOND, VA	1865	527	152	2053	678	1645	2496	572	485	630	428	317	292	1760	802	530	471	1595	1800	1151	645	1933	1330	641	914	1085
ST. LOUIS, MO	1051	549	841	1341	501	1053	1628	1181	749	1119	850	512	704	892	294	350	560	635	855	436	549	1242	863	239	505	252
SALT LAKE CITY, UT	624	1916	2100	548	1868	960	342	2395	1936	2322	2218	1880	2072	436	1406	1667	1738	1410	531	1067	1675	864	1650	1549	1813	1074
SAN ANTONIO, TX	818	1000	1671	1500	878	1599	1760	2207	1824	2310	1344	1241	1046	1270	1481	1271	1443	1099	1003	972	1486	556	200	1186	644	812
SAN DIEGO, CA	825	2166	2724	1302	2021	1765	1096	3065	2632	3020	2483	2393	2405	1179	2105	2234	2437	1375	1092	1766	2373	730	1487	2122	1780	1695
SAN FRANCISCO, CA	1111	2618	2840	1176	2472	1749	646	3135	2677	3062	2934	2620	2759	1176	2146	2407	2478	1827	1271	1807	2415	1181	1938	2290	2232	1814
SEATTLE, WA	1463	2705	2775	816	2657	1229	500	3070	2612	2997	2973	2571	2827	1234	2062	2368	2413	2208	1329	1822	2350	1944	2431	2283	2587	1842
TAMPA, FL	1949	455	960	2348	606	2018	2677	1380	1276	1438	434	845	581	1941	1176	935	1101	1161	1862	1426	1194	1753	995	990	709	1259
TORONTO, ON	1841	958	565	1762	958	1354	2204	570	106	419	1006	537	802	1468	510	484	303	1441	1512	834	233	2032	1561	541	1183	1028
VANCOUVER, BC	1597	2838	2908	949	2791	1362	633	3204	2745	3130	3106	2705	2960	1368	2196	2501	2547	2342	1463	1956	2483	2087	2583	2383	2746	2007
WASHINGTON, DC	1896	636	38	1953	758	1545	2395	458	384	517	539	346	397	1659	701	517	370	1362	1686	1025	526	2008	1630	596	996	1083
WICHITA, KS	707	989	1276	1067	838	934	1346	1616	1184	1554	1291	953	1145	613	728	785	995	367	521	390	984	898	608	674	771	192

	LOS ANGELES, CA	LOUISVILLE, KY	MEMPHIS, TN	MIAMI, FL	MILWAUKEE, WI	MINNEAPOLIS, MN	MONTRÉAL, QC	NASHVILLE, TN	NEW ORLEANS, LA	NEW YORK, NY	OKLAHOMA CITY, OK	OMAHA, NE	ORLANDO, FL	PHILADELPHIA, PA	PHOENIX, AZ	PITTSBURGH, PA	PORTLAND, ME	PORTLAND, OR	RAPID CITY, SD	RENO, NV	RICHMOND, VA	SALT LAKE CITY, UT	SAN ANTONIO, TX	SAN DIEGO, CA	SAN FRANCISCO, CA	SEATTLE, WA	ST. LOUIS, MO	TAMPA, FL	TORONTO, ON	VANCOUVER, BC	WASHINGTON, DC	WICHITA, KS
	806	1320	1033	2155	1426	1339	2172	1248	1276	2015	546	973	1934	1954	466	1670	2338	1395	841	1020	1876	1051	624	818	825	1111	1463	1949	1841	1597	1896	707
	2237	419	389	661	813	1129	1241	242	473	869	944	989	440	782	1868	676	1197	2647	1511	2440	527	549	1916	1000	2166	2168	2705	455	958	2838	636	989
	2705	602	933	1109	805	1121	564	716	1142	192	1354	1168	904	104	2366	246	520	2830	1626	2623	152	841	2100	1671	2724	2840	2775	960	565	2908	38	1276
	1239	1547	1625	2554	1175	839	2093	1648	1955	2049	1227	904	2333	2019	1199	1779	2352	889	379	960	2053	1341	548	1500	1302	1176	816	2348	1762	949	1953	1067
	2092	369	241	812	763	1079	1289	194	351	985	729	941	591	897	1723	763	1313	2599	1463	2392	678	501	1868	878	2021	2472	2657	606	958	2791	758	838
	1702	1139	1337	2224	767	431	1685	1315	1734	1641	1316	616	2003	1611	1662	1311	1944	1301	320	1372	1645	1053	960	1599	1761	1749	1229	2018	1354	1362	1545	934
	1033	1933	1954	2883	1748	1465	2535	1976	2234	2497	1506	1234	2662	2462	993	2161	2795	432	930	430	2496	1628	342	1761	1096	646	500	2677	2204	633	2395	1346
	3046	964	1353	1529	1100	1417	313	1136	1563	215	1694	1463	1324	321	2706	592	107	3126	1921	2919	572	1181	2395	2092	3065	3135	3070	1380	570	3204	458	1616
	2572	545	927	1425	642	958	397	716	1254	400	1262	1005	1221	414	2274	217	560	2667	1463	2460	485	749	1936	1665	2632	2677	2612	1276	406	2745	384	1184
	2957	915	1297	1587	1027	1343	92	1086	1588	299	1632	1390	1383	371	2644	587	233	3052	1848	2845	630	1119	2322	2036	3020	3062	2997	1438	419	3130	517	1554
	2554	610	760	583	1003	1319	1145	543	783	773	1248	1290	379	685	2184	642	1101	2948	1824	2741	428	850	2218	1310	2483	2934	2973	434	1006	3106	539	1291
	2374	251	606	994	601	918	822	395	926	515	1022	952	790	454	2055	277	839	2610	1422	2403	322	512	1880	1344	2393	2620	2571	845	337	2705	346	953
	2453	464	614	730	857	1173	1003	397	713	631	1102	1144	525	543	2107	438	959	2802	1678	2595	289	704	2072	1241	2405	2759	2827	581	802	2960	397	1145
	1116	1917	1217	2147	1012	881	1799	1240	1502	1755	773	497	1926	1725	1004	1425	2059	1166	305	959	1760	892	436	1046	1179	1176	1234	1941	1468	1368	1659	613
	2042	299	539	1382	89	409	841	474	935	797	807	474	1161	768	1819	467	1101	2137	913	1930	802	294	1406	1270	2105	2146	2052	1176	510	2196	701	728
	2215	106	493	1141	398	714	815	281	820	636	863	744	580	576	1876	292	960	2398	1219	1391	530	526	1667	1231	2234	2407	2368	935	484	2501	517	785
	2374	356	742	1250	443	760	588	531	1070	466	1073	806	1045	437	2085	136	751	2469	1264	2262	471	560	1738	1481	2437	2478	2413	1101	303	2547	370	995
	1446	852	466	1367	1010	999	1772	681	525	1589	209	669	1146	1501	1077	1246	1917	2140	1077	1933	1309	635	1410	271	1375	1827	2208	1161	1441	2342	1362	367
	1029	1118	1116	2069	1055	924	1843	1162	1409	1799	681	541	1847	1744	904	1460	2102	1261	404	1054	1688	855	531	946	1092	1271	1329	1862	1512	1463	1686	521
	1703	591	1632	378	246	1165	725	1117	1117	1121	546	1411	1091	1558	791	1424	1798	629	1591	1126	436	1067	1009	1766	1807	1822	1426	834	1956	1025	390
	2310	366	752	1401	380	697	564	541	1079	622	1062	743	1180	592	2074	292	838	2405	1201	2198	627	549	1675	1490	2373	2415	2350	1194	233	2483	526	984
	801	1499	1112	1959	1617	1530	2363	1328	1118	2235	737	1236	1738	2147	432	1893	1763	1015	1955	1242	864	556	730	1781	1944	1753	2032	2087	2008	898
	1558	972	586	1201	1193	1240	1892	801	360	1660	449	910	980	1572	1188	1366	1988	2381	1318	2072	1330	863	1650	200	1487	1938	2449	995	1561	2583	1433	608
	2104	112	464	1196	279	596	872	287	826	715	752	618	975	655	1764	370	1038	2280	1001	2073	641	239	1549	1186	2122	2290	2249	990	541	2383	596	674
	1851	594	271	915	835	1151	1514	423	185	1223	612	935	694	1315	1482	988	1550	2547	1214	2450	914	505	1813	644	1780	2232	2612	709	1283	2746	996	771
	1632	516	536	1466	573	441	1359	559	932	1202	348	188	1245	1141	1360	857	1525	1805	710	1598	1085	252	1074	812	1695	1814	1872	1259	1028	2007	1083	192
	274	1874	1611	2733	1808	1677	2596	1826	1854	2552	1124	1294	2512	2500	285	2215	2855	1188	1035	442	2444	1610	417	1272	337	575	1256	2526	2265	1390	2441	1276
	1706	526	140	1190	747	814	1446	355	455	1262	355	570	969	1175	1367	920	1590	2237	1093	2030	983	461	1507	600	1703	2012	2305	984	1115	2439	1036	464
		2126	1839	2759	2082	1951	2869	2054	1917	2820	1352	1567	2538	2760	369	2476	3144	9712	1309	519	2682	1856	691	1356	124	385	1148	2553	2538	1291	2702	1513

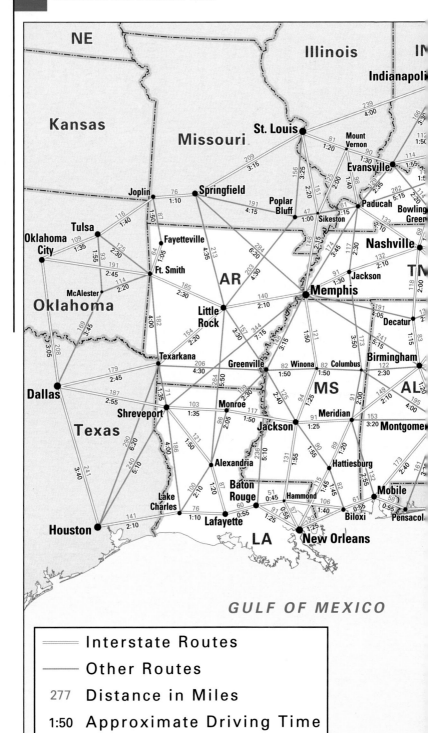

Legend:
- ══ Interstate Routes
- ── Other Routes
- 277 Distance in Miles
- 1:50 Approximate Driving Time

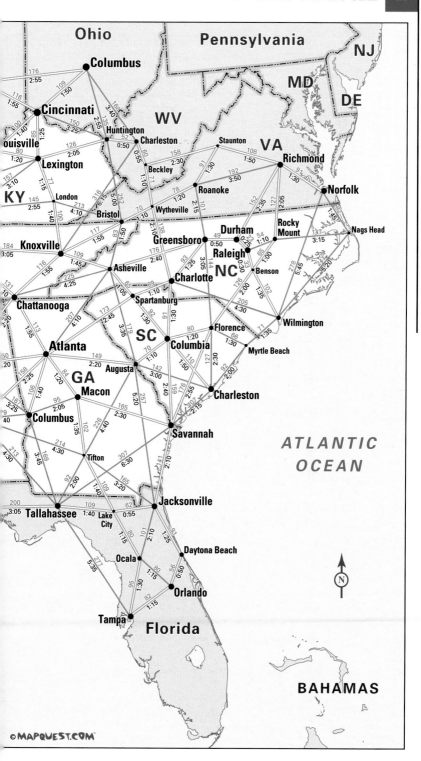

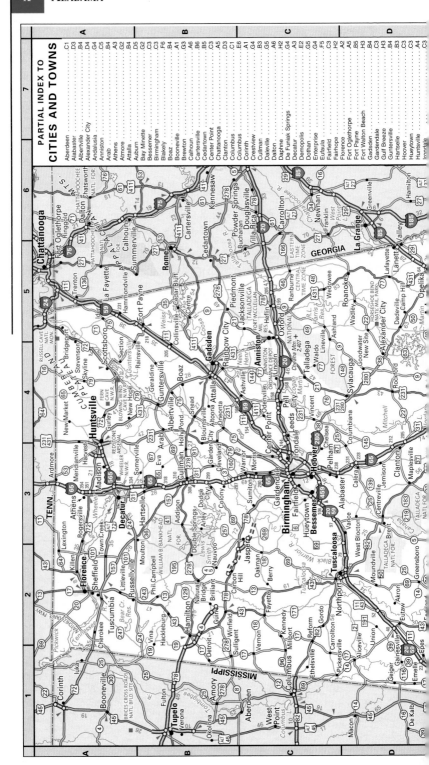

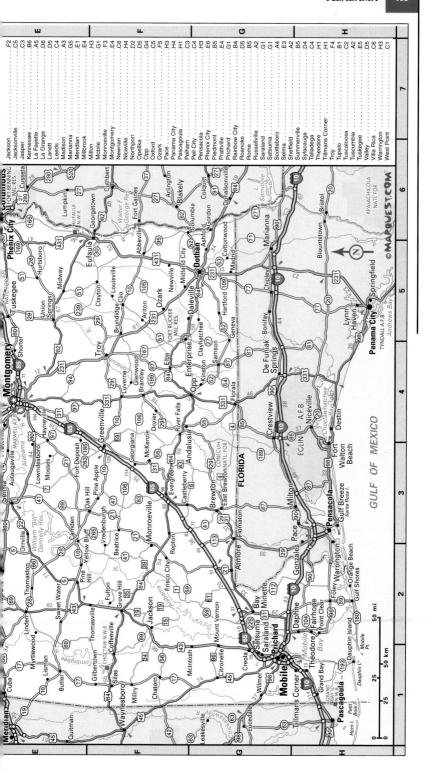

© MAPQUEST.COM

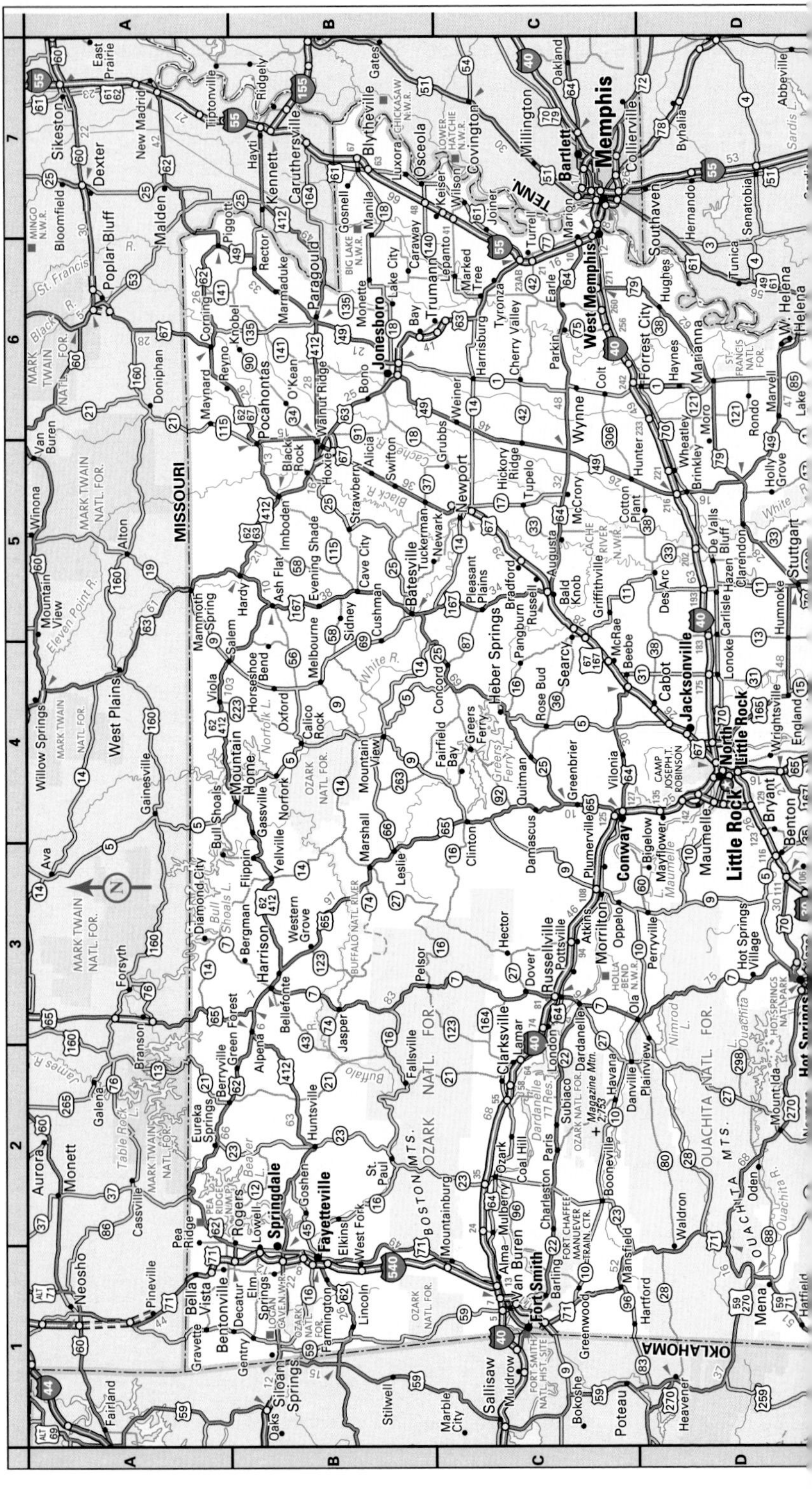
MISSOURI
OKLAHOMA
TENN.
Memphis
West Memphis
Little Rock
North Little Rock
Jacksonville
Conway
Fort Smith
Van Buren
Fayetteville
Springdale
Rogers
Bentonville
Jonesboro
Blytheville
Paragould
Batesville
Searcy
Russellville
Clarksville
Harrison
Mountain Home
Hot Springs
Benton
Bryant
Stuttgart
Forrest City
Wynne
Newport
Heber Springs
Morrilton
Pocahontas
Walnut Ridge
Osceola
Marianna
W. Helena
Mena
Poteau
Sallisaw
Siloam Springs
Eureka Springs
Berryville
Mountain View
Clinton
Marshall
Yellville
Melbourne
Salem
Ash Flat
Hardy
Piggott
Corning
Rector
Kennett
Caruthersville
Sikeston
Dexter
Poplar Bluff
Doniphan
Malden
New Madrid
West Plains
Willow Springs
Mountain Grove
Ava
Gainesville
Branson
Forsyth
Cassville
Monett
Aurora
Neosho
Pineville
Bella Vista
Millington
Bartlett
Collierville
Covington
Southaven
Hernando
Tunica
Senatobia
MARK TWAIN NATL. FOR.
OZARK NATL. FOR.
OUACHITA NATL. FOR.
BOSTON MTS.
OUACHITA MTS.
HOT SPRINGS NATL. PARK
BUFFALO NATL. RIVER

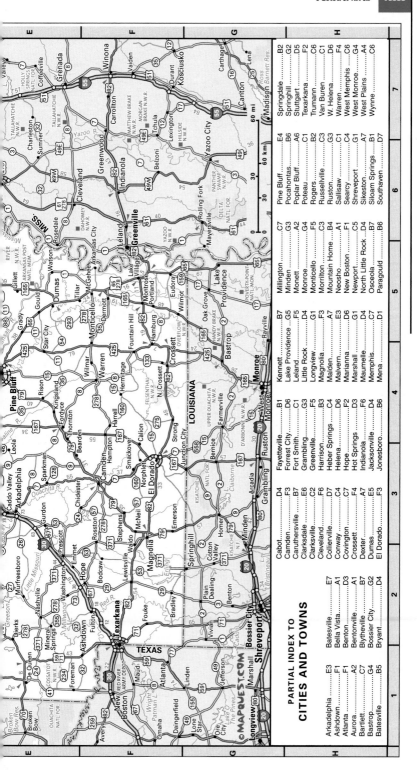

PARTIAL INDEX TO CITIES AND TOWNS

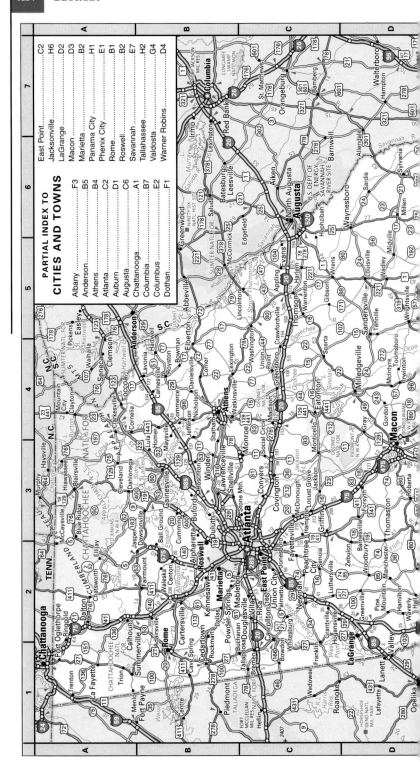

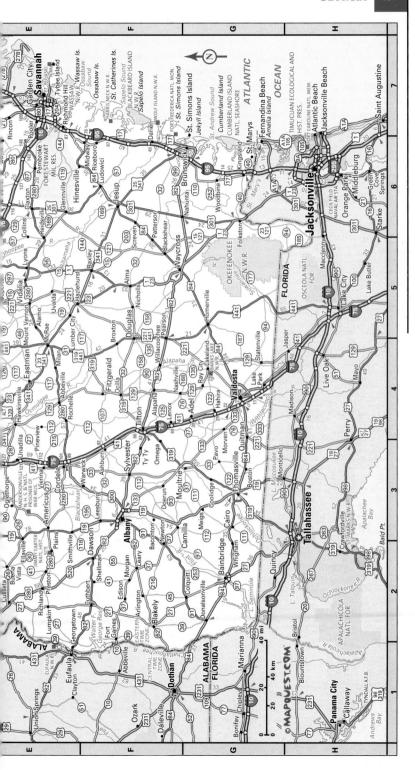

PARTIAL INDEX TO CITIES AND TOWNS

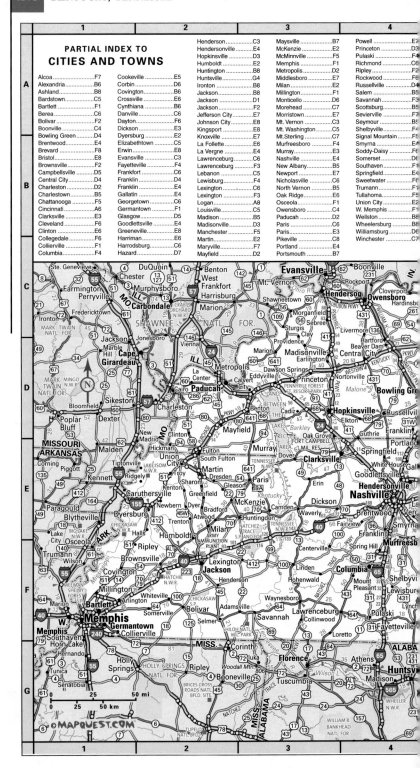

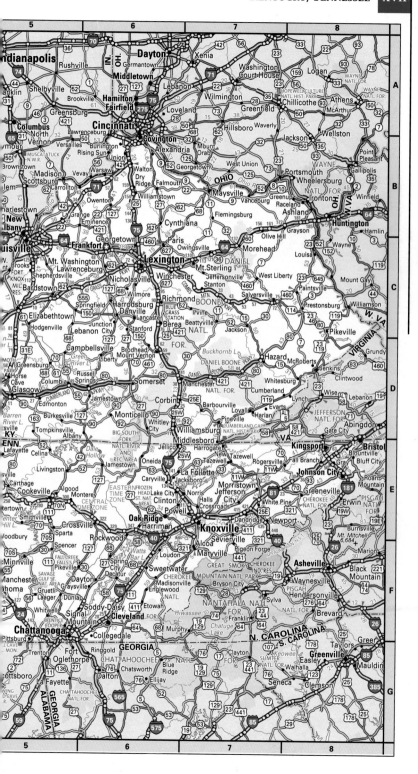

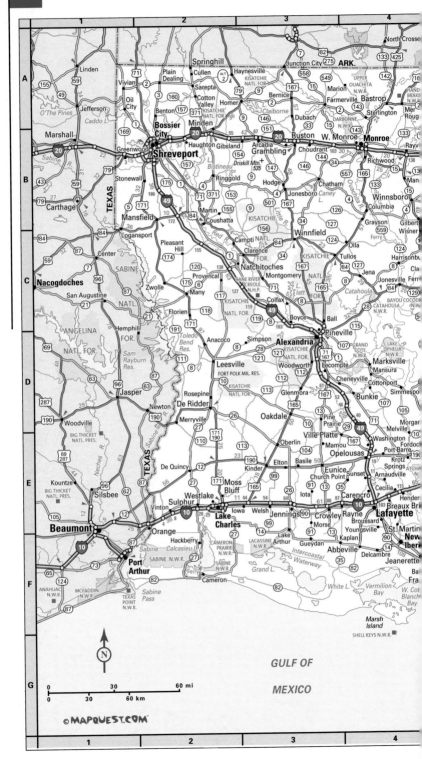

GULF OF

MEXICO

© MAPQUEST.COM

PARTIAL INDEX TO
CITIES AND TOWNS

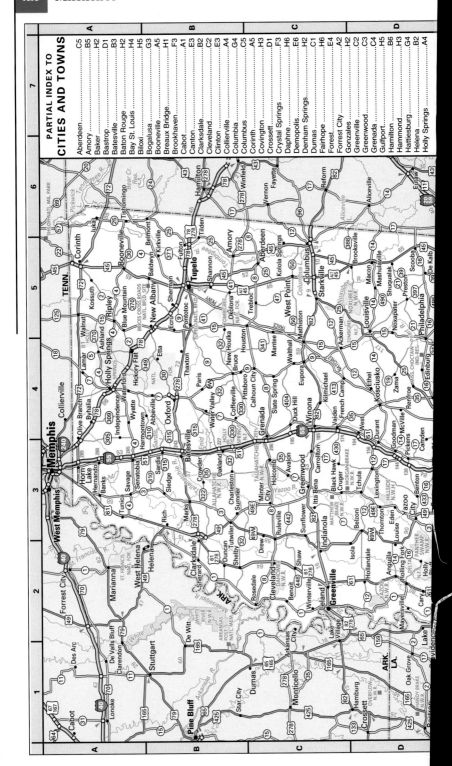

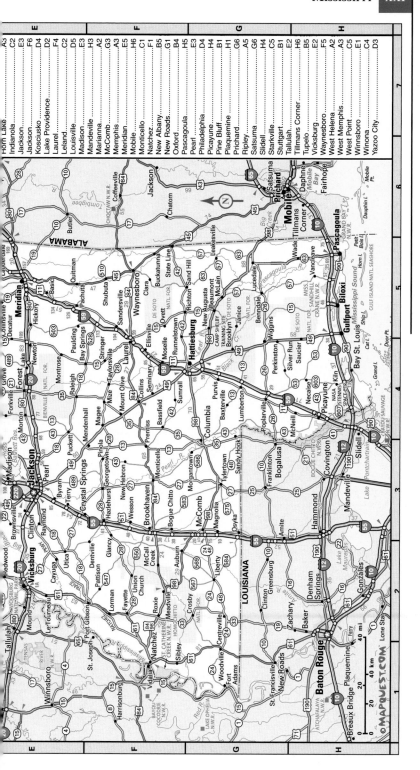

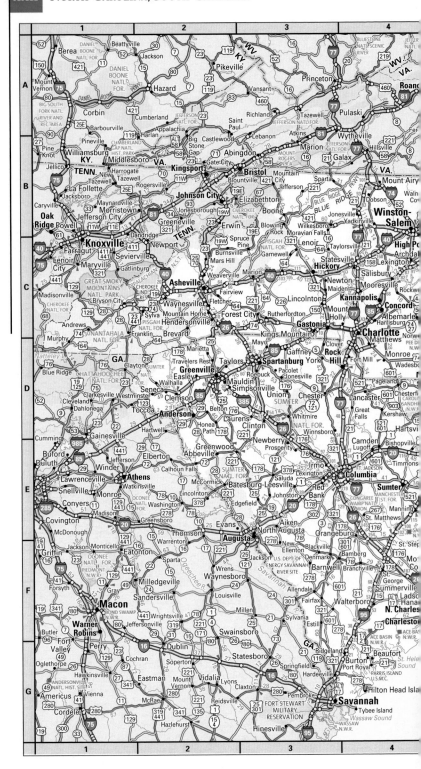

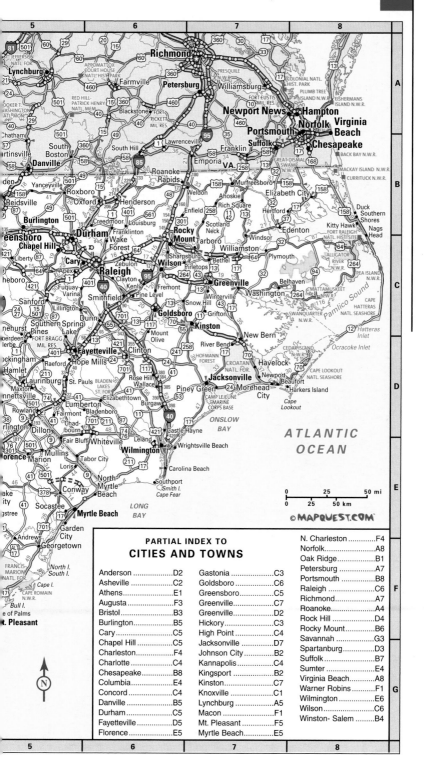

ATLANTIC OCEAN

LONG BAY

0 25 50 mi
0 25 50 km

© MAPQUEST.COM

PARTIAL INDEX TO CITIES AND TOWNS

MAP LEGEND

TRANSPORTATION

CONTROLLED ACCESS HIGHWAYS

Free

Toll; Toll Booth

Under Construction

Interchange and Exit Number

Ramp
Downtown maps only

OTHER HIGHWAYS

Primary Highway

Secondary Highway

Mutilane Divided Highway
Primary and secondary highways only

Other Paved Road

Unpaved Road
Check conditions locally

HIGHWAY MARKERS

Interstate Route

U.S. Route

State or Provincial Route

County or Other Route

Business Route

Trans-Canada Highway

Canadian Provincial Autoroute

Mexican Federal Route

OTHER SYMBOLS

Distances along Major Highways
Miles in U.S.; kilometers in Canada and Mexico

Tunnel; Pass

One-way Street

Airport

Railroad
Downtown maps only

Auto Ferry; Passenger Ferry

RECREATION AND FEATURES OF INTEREST

National Park

National Forest; National Grassland

Other Large Park or Recreation Area

Military Lands

Indian Reservation

Small State Park with and without Camping

Public Campsite

Trail

Point of Interest

Golf Course
Professional tournament location

Hospital
City maps only

Ski Area

CITIES AND TOWNS

National Capital; State or Provincial Capital

County Seat
State maps only

Cities, Towns, and Populated Places
Type size indicates relative importance

Urban Area
State and province maps only

Large Incorporated Cities

OTHER MAP FEATURES

County Boundary and Name

JEFFERSON

Time Zone Boundary

Mountain Peak; Elevation
Feet in U.S.; meters in Canada and Mexico

+ *Mt. Olympus*
7,965

Perennial; Intermittent River

Perennial; Intermittent or Dry Water Body

Dam

Swamp

WELCOME

For over 40 years, the *Mobil Travel Guide* has provided North American travelers with trusted advice on finding good value, quality service, and the distinctive attractions that give a destination its unique character. Today, the *Travel Guide* is presented by ExxonMobil and is a valued member of the ExxonMobil family of travel publications.

Although you'll notice changes in the *2001 Travel Guide* format—including introduction of the ExxonMobil name—what hasn't changed is our commitment to bring reliable lodging, dining, and sightseeing information to a broad range of travelers. Our nationwide network of professional evaluators offer you their expertise on over 22,000 properties using our 5-Star rating system that has become an industry standard. Whether you're seeking a convenient business meeting locale, an elegant 5-Star celebration, or a leisurely driving trip, it is our hope that you'll rely on the *Travel Guide* as your companion.

As we continue to enhance our products to better meet the needs of the modern traveler, we hope to hear from our most important audience—you, the traveler. Please take the time to complete the customer feedback form at the back of this book or contact us on the Internet at www.exxonmobiltravel.com. We appreciate your input and wish you safe and memorable travels.

Lee R. Raymond
Chairman
Exxon Mobil Corporation

A WORD TO OUR READERS

The exciting and complex development of the US interstate high-way system was formally—and finally—established in 1956, allow-ing Americans to take to the roads in enormous numbers. They are going on day trips, long weekends, extended family vacations, and business. Traveling across the country, stopping at National Parks, major cities, small towns, monuments, and landmarks remains a fan-tasy trip for many.

Airline travel, too, is on the increase. Whether for business or plea-sure, we can take flights between relatively close cities and from coast to coast.

You, the traveler, deserve the best food and accommodations avail-able in every city, town, or village you visit. But finding suitable accommodations can be problematic. You could try to meet and ask local residents about appropriate places to stay and eat, but that time-consuming option comes with no guarantee of getting the best advice.

That's where the *Mobil Travel Guide* comes in. This trusted, well-established tool can direct you to satisfying places to eat and stay, and to interesting events and attractions in thousands of locations across North America. Prior to the merger with Exxon Corporation, Mobil Corporation had sponsored the Mobil Travel Guide since 1958. Now ExxonMobil presents the latest edition of our annual Travel Guide series in partnership with Consumer Guide publications.

This edition has several new features. We've added driving tours, suggesting "off the beaten path" day trips (or overnight if you choose) to points of interest near a well-established destination. MapQuest has provided our maps this year, including the more-details maps for driving tours. We've also added walking tours. These allow you to stretch your legs and see the sites in and about your destination. Again, you will find maps to help you find your way to monuments, points of historic interest, and maybe even a snack.

Our three-star entries now contain more details. Clearly travelers are looking for good value, and the more information we can offer about restaurants and lodgings, the easier it will be to evaluate your many choices.

Perhaps the biggest difference this year is the addition of color to the travel guides. Pictures of places to stay, things to do, and colorful surroundings along the way might encourage you to make a stop to take your own pictures. Once a seven-volume series, The *Mobil Travel Guides* are now published as a ten book set. This allows us to add more hotel, restaurant, and attraction information, as well as several more maps in each book.

Finally, we've changed the size of the books. With more travelers carrying travel guides in their glove compartment, purse, breast pocket, or briefcase, the new size was chosen to accommodate a better fit.

The hi-tech information database that is the foundation of every title in the *Mobil Travel Guide* series is an astonishing resource: It is enormous, detailed, and continually updated, making it as accurate and useful as it can be. Highly trained field representatives, spread out across the country, generate exhaustive, computerized inspection reports. Senior staff members then evaluate these reports, along with the comments of more than 100,000 readers. All of this information is used to arrive at fair, accurate, and useful assessments of hotels, motels, and restaurants. Mobil's respected and world-famous one- to five-star rating system highlights valuable capsulized descriptions of each site. All of this dependable information, plus details about thousands of attractions and things to do, is in the dynamic Mobil database!

Space limitations make it impossible for us to include every hotel, motel, and restaurant in America. Instead, our database consists of a generous, representative sampling, with information about places that are above-average in their type. In essence, you can confidently patronize any of the restaurants, places of lodging, and attractions contained in the *Mobil Travel Guide* series.

What do we mean by "representative sampling"? You'll find that the *Mobil Travel Guide* books include information about a great variety of establishments. Perhaps you favor rustic lodgings and restaurants, or perhaps you're most comfortable with elegance and high style. Money may be no object or, like most of us, you may be on a budget. Some travelers place a high premium on 24-hour room service or special menu items. Others look for quiet seclusion. Whatever your travel needs and desires, they will be reflected in the *Mobil Travel Guide* listings.

Allow us to emphasize that we have charged no establishment for inclusion in our guides. We have no relationship with any of the businesses and attractions we list, and act only as a consumer advocate. In essence, we do the investigative legwork so you won't have to.

Look over the "How to Use This Book" section that follows. You'll discover just how simple it is to quickly and easily gather all the information you need—before your trip or while on the road. For terrific tips on saving money, travel safety, and other ways to enjoy your travels to the maximum, be sure to read our special section, "Making the Most of Your Trip."

Keep in mind that the hospitality business is ever-changing. Restaurants and places of lodging—particularly small chains or stand-alone establishments—can change management or even go out of business with surprising quickness. Although we have made every effort to double-check information during our annual updates, we nevertheless recommend that you call ahead to be sure a place you have selected is open and still offers all the features you want. Phone numbers are provided, and, when available, we also list fax and Web site information.

We hope that all your travel experiences are easy and relaxing. If any aspects of your accommodations or dining motivate you to comment, please drop us a line. We depend a great deal on our readers' remarks, so you can be assured that we will read and assimilate your comments into our research. General comments about our books are also welcome. You can write us at Mobil Travel Guide, 7373 N Cicero Ave, Lincolnwood, IL 60712, or send e-mail to info@exxonmobiltravel.com.

Take your *Mobil Travel Guide* books along on every trip. You'll be pleased by their convenience, ease of use, and breadth of dependable coverage.

Happy travels in the new millennium!

EDITORIAL CONTRIBUTORS AND CONSULTANTS FOR DRIVING TOURS, WALKING TOURS, ATTRACTIONS, EVENTS AND PHOTOGRAPHY:

Kap Stann is a travel writer and editor whose specialty is the American Southeast. She is the author of *Georgia Handbook: Including Atlanta, Savannah, and the Blue Ridge Mountains* and *South Carolina,* an online travel guide. She is also coauthor of Deep South and a contributor to USA and Road Trip USA.

W. Lynn Seldon Jr. has authored several travel titles including *Country Roads of West Virginia, Country Roads of Virginia,* and *52 Virginia Weekends.* He also contributes to several national and local travel publications including *Travel America, Ecotraveler,* and *USA Today.*

Jim Yenckel served as editor and writer for *The Washington Post* for 33 years, the last 16 of which, as their travel writer. He writes a weekly travel column for a chain of newspapers and is a regular contributor to several national magazines including *Budget Travel, Washingtonian,* and *Preservation.* He also authors and publishes the weekly newsletter *Great Getaways.*

June Naylor Rodriguez has written about travel in the U.S. for newspapers, books, and magazines since 1985. She is an award-winning author of several Texas travel guides including *Texas Off the Beaten Path* and *Quick Escapes from Dallas-Fort Worth.* She is also a food writer and restaurant critic for the *Fort-Worth Star-Telegram.*

HOW TO USE THIS BOOK

The *Mobil Travel Guide* is designed for ease of use. Each state has its own chapter. The chapter begins with a general introduction, which provides both a general geographical and historical orientation to the state; it also covers basic statewide tourist information, from state recreation areas to seatbelt laws. The remainder of each chapter is devoted to the travel destinations within the state—cities and towns, state and national parks, and tourist areas—which, like the states, are arranged alphabetically.

The following is an explanation of the wealth of information you'll find regarding those travel destinations—information on the area, on things to see and do there, and on where to stay and eat.

Maps and Map Coordinates

Next to each destination is a set of map coordinates. These are referenced to the appropriate state map in the front of this book. In addition, we have provided maps of selected larger cities and of key neighborhoods within the city sections.

Destination Information

Because many travel destinations are close to other cities and towns where visitors might find additional attractions, accommodations, and restaurants, cross-references to those places are included whenever possible. Also listed are addresses and phone numbers for travel-information resources—usually the local chamber of commerce or office of tourism—as well as pertinent vital statistics and a brief introduction to the area.

What to See and Do

Almost 20,000 museums, art galleries, amusement parks, universities, historic sites and houses, plantations, churches, state parks, ski areas, and other attractions are described in the *Mobil Travel Guides*. A white star on a black background ⭐ signals that the attraction is one of the best in the state. Since municipal parks, public tennis courts, swimming pools, and small educational institutions are common to most towns, they are generally not represented with the white star on the black background.

Following the attraction's description, you'll find the months and days it's open, address/location and phone number, and admission costs (see the inside front cover for an explanation of the cost symbols). Note that directions are given from the center of the town under which the attraction is listed, which may not necessarily be the town in which the attraction is located. Zip codes are listed only if they differ from those given for the town.

Driving and Walking Tours

New to the *Mobil Travel Guides* are the driving and walking tours. The driving tours are usually day trips—though they can be longer—that make for interesting side trips. This is a way to get off the beaten track and visit an area often overlooked. These trips frequently cover areas of natural beauty or historical significance, and a map of the tour is included with the description. The walking tours focus on a particularly interesting area of a city or town. Again, these can be a break from more everyday tourist attractions. The tours often include places to stop for a meal or snack.

Events

Events—categorized as annual, seasonal, or special—are highlighted. An annual event is one that's held every year for a period of usually no longer than a week to ten days; festivals and fairs are typical entries. A seasonal event is one that may or may not be annual and that is held for a number of weeks or months in the year, such as horse racing, summer theater, concert or opera festivals, and professional sports. Special event listings occur infrequently and mark a certain date or event, such as a centennial or other commemorative celebration.

Major Cities

Additional information on airports and ground transportation, suburbs, and neighborhoods may be included for large cities.

Lodging and Restaurant Listings

ORGANIZATION

For both lodgings and restaurants, when a property is in a town that does not have its own heading, the listing appears under the town nearest its location with the address and town in parentheses immediately after the establishment name. In large cities, lodgings located within 5 miles of major commercial airports are listed under a separate "Airport" heading, following the city listings.

LODGING CLASSIFICATIONS

Each property is classified by type according to the characteristics below. Because the following features and services are found at most motels, lodges, motor hotels, and hotels, they are not shown in those listings:

- Year-round operation with a single rate structure unless otherwise quoted
- European plan (meals not included in room rate)
- Bathroom with tub and/or shower in each room
- Air-conditioned/heated, often with individual room control
- Cots
- Daily maid service
- In-room phones
- Elevators

Motels/Motor Lodges. Accommodations are in low-rise structures with rooms easily accessible to parking (which is usually free). Properties have outdoor room entry and small, functional lobbies. Service is often limited, and dining may not be offered in lower-rated motels and lodges. Shops and businesses are found only in higher-rated properties, as are bellhops, room service, and restaurants serving three meals daily.

Lodges. These differ from motels primarily in their emphasis on outdoor recreational activities and in location. They are often found in resort and rural areas rather than in major cities or along highways.

Hotels. To be categorized as a hotel, an establishment must have most of the following facilities and services: multiple floors, a restaurant and/or coffee shop, elevators, room service, bellhops, a spacious lobby, and recreational facilities. In addition, the following features and services not shown in listings are also found:

- Valet service (one-day laundry/cleaning service)
- Room service during hours restaurant is open
- Bellhops
- Some oversize beds

Resorts. These specialize in stays of three days or more and usually offer American plan and/or housekeeping accommodations. Their emphasis is on recreational facilities, and a social director is often available. Food services are of primary importance, and guests must be able to eat three meals a day on the premises, either in restaurants or by having access to an on-site grocery store and preparing their own meals.

All Suites. All Suites' guestrooms consist of two rooms, one bedroom and one living room. Higher rated properties offer facilities and services comparable to regular hotels.

B&Bs/Small Inns. Frequently thought of as a small hotel, a Bed and Breakfast or an inn is a place of homelike comfort and warm hospitality. It is often a structure of historic significance, with an equally interesting setting. Meals are a special occasion, and refreshments are frequently served in late afternoon. Rooms are usually individually decorated, often with antiques or furnishings representative of the locale. Phones, bathrooms, or TVs may not be available in every room.

Guest Ranches. Like resorts, guest ranches specialize in stays of three days or more. Guest ranches also offer meal plans and extensive outdoor activities. Horseback riding is usually a feature; there are stables and trails on the ranch property, and trail rides and daily instruction are part of the program. Many guest ranches are working ranches, ranging from casual to rustic, and guests are encouraged to participate in ranch life. Eating is often family style and may also include cookouts. Western saddles are assumed; phone ahead to inquire about English saddle availability.

Extended Stay. These hotels specialize in stays of three days or more and usually offer weekly room rates. Service is often limited and dining might not be offered at lower-rated extended-stay hotels.

Villas/Condos. Similar to Cottage Colonies, these establishments are usually found in recreational areas. They are often separate houses, often luxuriously furnished, and rarely offer restaurants and only a small variety of services on the premises.

Conference Centers. Conference Center Hotels are hotels with extended meeting space facilities designed to house multi-day conferences and seminars. Amenities are often geared toward groups staying for longer than one night and often include restaurants and fitness facilities. Larger Conference Center Hotels are often referred to as Convention Center Hotels.

Casinos. Casino Hotels incorporate areas that offer games of chance like Blackjack, Poker, Slot machines, etc. and are only found in states that legalize gambling. Casino Hotels offer a wide range of services and amenities, comparable to regular hotels.

Cottage Colonies. These are housekeeping cottages and cabins that are usually found in recreational areas. Any dining or recreational facilities are noted in our listing.

DINING CLASSIFICATIONS

Restaurants. Most dining establishments fall into this category. All have a full kitchen and offer table service and a complete menu. Parking on or near the premises, in a lot or garage, is assumed. When a property offers valet or other special parking features, or when only street parking is available, it is noted in the listing.

Unrated Dining Spots. These places, listed after Restaurants in many cities, are chosen for their unique atmosphere, specialized menu, or local flavor. They include delis, ice-cream parlors, cafeterias, tearooms, and pizzerias. Because they may not have a full kitchen or table service, they are not given an Mobil Travel Guide rating. Often they offer extraordinary value and quick service.

QUALITY RATINGS

The *Mobil Travel Guide* has been rating lodgings and restaurants on a national basis since the first edition was published in 1958. For years the guide was the only source of such ratings, and it remains among the few guidebooks to rate restaurants across the country.

All listed establishments were inspected by experienced field representatives or evaluated by a senior staff member. Ratings are based upon their detailed inspection reports of the individual properties, on written evaluations of staff members who stay and dine anonymously, and on an extensive review of comments from our readers.

You'll find a key to the rating categories, ★ through ★★★★★, on the inside front cover, All establishments in the book are recommended. Even a ★ place is above average, usually providing a basic, informal experience. Rating categories reflect both the features the property offers and its quality in relation to similar establishments.

For example, lodging ratings take into account the number and quality of facilities and services, the luxury of appointments, and the attitude and professionalism of staff and management. A ★ establishment provides a comfortable night's lodging. A ★★ property offers more than a facility that rates one star, and the decor is well planned and integrated. Establishments that rate ★★★ are professionally managed and staffed and often beautifully appointed; the lodging experience is truly excellent and the range of facilities is extensive. Properties that have been given ★★★★ not only offer many services but also have their own style and personality; they are luxurious, creatively decorated, and superbly maintained. The ★★★★★ properties are among the best in North America, superb in every respect and entirely memorable, year in and year out.

Restaurant evaluations reflect the quality of the food and the ingredients, preparation, presentation, service levels, as well as the property's decor and ambience. A restaurant that has fairly simple goals for menu and decor but that achieves those goals superbly might receive the same number of stars as a restaurant with somewhat loftier ambitions, but the execution of which falls short of the mark. In general, ★ indicates a restaurant that's a good choice in its area, usually fairly simple and perhaps catering to a clientele of locals and families; ★★ denotes restaurants that are more highly recommended in their area; ★★★ restaurants are of national caliber, with professional and attentive service and a skilled chef in the kitchen; ★★★★ reflect superb dining choices, where remarkable food is served in equally remarkable surroundings; and ★★★★★ represent that rare group of the best restaurants in the country, where in addition to near perfection in every detail, there's that special something extra that makes for an unforgettable dining experience.

A list of the four-star and five-star establishments in each region is located just before the state listings.

Each rating is reviewed annually and each establishment must work to maintain its rating (or improve it). Every effort is made to assure that ratings are fair and accurate; the designated ratings are published purely as an aid to travelers. In general, properties that are very new or have recently undergone major management changes are considered difficult to assess fairly and are often listed without ratings.

LODGINGS

Each listing gives the name, address, directions (when there is no street address), neighborhood and/or directions from downtown (in major cities), phone number (local and 800), fax number, number and type of rooms available, room rates, and seasons open (if not year-round). Also included are details on recreational and dining facilities on the property or nearby, the presence of a luxury level, and credit card information. A key to the symbols at the end of each listing is on the inside front cover. (Note that Exxon or Mobil Corporation credit cards cannot be used for payment of meals and room charges.)

All prices quoted in the Mobil Travel Guide publications are expected to be in effect at the time of publication and during the entire year; however, prices cannot be guaranteed. In some localities there may be short-term price variations because of special events or holidays. Whenever possible, these price charges are noted. Certain resorts have complicated rate structures that vary with the time of year; always confirm listed rates when you make your plans.

RESTAURANTS

Each listing gives the name, address, directions (when there is no street address), neighborhood and/or directions from downtown (in major cities), phone number, hours and days of operation (if not open daily year-round), reservation policy, cuisine (if other than American), price range for each meal served, children's meals (if offered), specialties, and credit card information. Additionally, special features such as chef ownership, ambience, and entertainment are noted. By carefully reading the detailed restaurant information and comparing prices, you can easily determine whether the restaurant is formal and elegant or informal and comfortable for families.

TERMS AND ABBREVIATIONS IN LISTINGS

The following terms and abbreviations are used throughout the listings:

A la carte entrees With a price, refers to the cost of entrees/main dishes that are not accompanied by side dishes.

AP American plan (lodging plus all meals).

Bar Liquor, wine, and beer are served in a bar or cocktail lounge and usually with meals unless otherwise indicated (e.g., "wine, beer").

Business center The property has a designated area accessible to all guests with business services.

Business servs avail The property can perform/arrange at least two of the following services for a guest: audiovisual equipment rental, binding, computer rental, faxing, messenger services, modem availability, notary service, obtaining office supplies, photocopying, shipping, and typing.

Cable Standard cable service; "premium" indicates that HBO, Disney, Showtime, or similar cable services are available.

Ck-in, ck-out Check-in time, check-out time.

Coin lndry Self-service laundry.

Complete meal Soup and/or salad, entree, and dessert, plus nonalcoholic beverage.

Continental bkfst Usually coffee and a roll or doughnut.

Cr cds: A, American Express; C, Carte Blanche; D, Diners Club; DS, Discover; ER, enRoute; JCB, Japanese Credit Bureau; MC, MasterCard; V, Visa.

D Followed by a price, indicates room rate for a "double"—two people in one room in one or two beds (the charge may be higher for two double beds).

Downhill/X-country ski Downhill and/or cross-country skiing within 20 miles of property.

Each addl Extra charge for each additional person beyond the stated number of persons at a reduced price.

Early-bird dinner A meal served at specified hours, typically around 4:30-6:30 pm.

Exc Except.

Exercise equipt Two or more pieces of exercise equipment on the premises.

Exercise rm Both exercise equipment and room, with an instructor on the premises.

Fax Facsimile machines available to all guests.

Golf privileges Privileges at a course within 10 miles.

Hols Holidays.

In-rm modem link Every guest room has a connection for a modem that's separate from the phone line.

Kit. or **Kits.** A kitchen or kitchenette that contains stove or microwave, sink, and refrigerator and that is either part of the room or a separate room. If the kitchen is not fully equipped, the listing will indicate "no equipt" or "some equipt."

Luxury level A special section of a lodging, covering at least an entire floor, that offers increased luxury accommodations. Management must provide no less than three of these four services: separate check-in and check-out, concierge, private lounge, and private elevator service (key access). Complimentary breakfast and snacks are commonly offered.

MAP Modified American plan (lodging plus two meals).

Movies Prerecorded videos are available for rental.

No cr cds accepted No credit cards are accepted.

No elvtr In hotels with more than two stories, it's assumed there are elevators; only their absence is noted.

No phones Phones, too, are assumed; only their absence is noted.

Parking There is a parking lot on the premises.

Private club A cocktail lounge or bar available to members and their guests. In motels and hotels where these clubs exist, registered guests can usually use the club as guests of the management; the same is frequently true of restaurants.

Prix fixe A full meal for a stated price; usually one price is quoted.

Res Reservations.

S Followed by a price, indicates room rate for a "single," i.e., one person.

Serv bar A service bar, where drinks are prepared for dining patrons only.

Serv charge Service charge is the amount added to the restaurant check in lieu of a tip.

Table d'hôte A full meal for a stated price, dependent upon entree selection; no a la carte options are available.

Tennis privileges Privileges at tennis courts within 5 miles.

TV Indicates color television.

Under certain age free Children under that age are not charged if staying in room with a parent.

Valet parking An attendant is available to park and retrieve a car.

VCR VCRs in all guest rooms.

VCR avail VCRs are available for hookup in guest rooms.

Special Information for Travelers with Disabilities

The *Mobil Travel Guide* Ⓓ symbol shown in accommodation and restaurant listings indicates establishments that are at least partially accessible to people with mobility problems.

The *Mobil Travel Guide* criteria for accessibility are unique to our publication. Please do not confuse them with the universal symbol for wheelchair accessibility. When the Ⓓ symbol appears following a listing, the establishment is equipped with facilities to accommodate people using wheelchairs or crutches or otherwise needing easy access to doorways and rest rooms. Travelers with severe mobility problems or with hearing or visual impairments may or may not find facilities they need. Always phone ahead to make sure that an establishment can meet your needs.

All lodgings bearing our Ⓓ symbol have the following facilities:

- ISA-designated parking near access ramps
- Level or ramped entryways to building
- Swinging building entryway doors minimum 3900
- Public rest rooms on main level with space to operate a wheelchair; handrails at commode areas
- Elevators equipped with grab bars and lowered control buttons

- Restaurants with accessible doorways; rest rooms with space to operate wheelchair; handrails at commode areas
- Minimum 3900 width entryway to guest rooms
- Low-pile carpet in rooms
- Telephone at bedside and in bathroom
- Bed placed at wheelchair height
- Minimum 3900 width doorway to bathroom
- Bath with open sink—no cabinet; room to operate wheelchair
- Handrails at commode areas; tub handrails
- Wheelchair accessible peephole in room entry door
- Wheelchair accessible closet rods and shelves

All restaurants bearing our D symbol offer the following facilities:

- ISA-designated parking beside access ramps
- Level or ramped front entryways to building
- Tables to accommodate wheelchairs
- Main-floor rest rooms; minimum 3900 width entryway
- Rest rooms with space to operate wheelchair; handrails at commode areas

In general, the newest properties are apt to impose the fewest barriers.

To get the kind of service you need and have a right to expect, do not hesitate when making a reservation to question the management in detail about the availability of accessible rooms, parking, entrances, restaurants, lounges, or any other facilities that are important to you, and confirm what is meant by "accessible." Some guests with mobility impairments report that lodging establishments' housekeeping and maintenance departments are most helpful in describing barriers. Also inquire about any special equipment, transportation, or services you may need.

MAKING THE MOST OF YOUR TRIP

A few hardy souls might look with fondness upon the trip where the car broke down and they were stranded for a week. Or maybe even the vacation that cost twice what it was supposed to. For most travelers, though, the best trips are those that are safe, smooth, and within their budget. To help you make your trip the best it can be, we've assembled a few tips and resources.

Saving Money

ON LODGING

After you've seen the published rates, it's time to look for discounts. Many hotels and motels offer them—for senior citizens, business travelers, families, you name it. It never hurts to ask—politely, that is. Sometimes, especially in late afternoon, desk clerks are instructed to fill beds, and you might be offered a lower rate, or a nicer room, to entice you to stay. Look for bargains on stays over multiple nights, in the off-season, and on weekdays or weekends (depending on location). Many hotels in major metropolitan areas, for example, have special weekend package plans that offer considerable savings on rooms; they may include breakfast, cocktails, and meal discounts. Prices can change frequently throughout the year, so phone ahead.

Another way to save money is to choose accommodations that give you more than just a standard room. Rooms with kitchen facilities enable you to cook some meals for yourself, reducing restaurant costs. A suite might save money for two couples traveling together. Even hotel luxury levels can provide good value, as many include breakfast or cocktails in the price of the room.

State and city sales taxes, as well as special room taxes, can increase your room rates as much as 25 percent per day. We are unable to include this specific information in the listings, but we strongly urge that you ask about these taxes when placing reservations in order to understand the total cost of your lodgings.

Watch out for telephone-usage charges that hotels frequently impose on long-distance calls, credit-card calls, and other phone calls—even those that go unanswered. Before phoning from your room, read the information given to you at check-in, and then be sure to read your bill carefully before checking out. You won't be expected to pay for charges that they did not spell out. (On the other hand, it's not unusual for a hotel to bill you for your calls after you return home.) Consider using your cell phone; or, if public telephones are available in the hotel lobby, your cost savings may outweigh the inconvenience.

ON DINING

There are several ways to get a less-expensive meal at a more-expensive restaurant. Early-bird dinners are popular in many parts of the country and offer considerable savings. If you're interested in sampling a 4- or 5-star establishment, consider going at lunchtime. While the prices then are probably relatively high, they may be half of those at dinner and come with the same ambience, service, and cuisine.

ON PARK PASSES

While many national parks, monuments, seashores, historic sites, and recreation areas may be used free of charge, others charge an entrance fee (ranging from $1 to $6 per person to $5 to $15 per carload) and/or a "use fee" for special services and facilities. If you plan to make several visits to federal recreation areas, consider one of the following National Park Service money-saving programs:

Park Pass. This is an annual entrance permit to a specific unit in the National Park Service system that normally charges an entrance fee. The pass admits the permit holder and any accompanying passengers in a private noncommercial vehicle or, in the case of walk-in facilities, the holder's spouse, children, and parents. It is valid for entrance fees only. A Park Pass may be purchased in person or by mail from the National Park Service unit at which the pass will be honored. The cost is $15 to $20, depending upon the area.

Golden Eagle Passport. This pass, available to people who are between 17 and 61, entitles the purchaser and accompanying passengers in a private noncommercial vehicle to enter any outdoor National Park Service unit that charges an entrance fee and admits the purchaser and family to most walk-in fee-charging areas. Like the Park Pass, it is good for one year and does not cover use fees. It may be purchased from the National Park Service, Office of Public Inquiries, Room 1013, US Department of the Interior, 18th and C Sts NW, Washington, DC 20240, phone 202/208-4747; at any of the 10 regional offices throughout the country; and at any National Park Service area that charges a fee. The cost is $50.

Golden Age Passport. Available to citizens and permanent residents of the United States 62 years or older, this is a lifetime entrance permit to fee-charging recreation areas. The fee exemption extends to those accompanying the permit holder in a private noncommercial vehicle or, in the case of walk-in facilities, to the holder's spouse and children. The passport also entitles the holder to a 50 percent discount on use fees charged in park areas but not to fees charged by concessionaires. Golden Age Passports must be obtained in person. The applicant must show proof of age, i.e., a driver's license, birth certificate, or signed affidavit attesting to age (Medicare cards are not acceptable proof). These passports are available at most park service units where they're used, at National Park Service headquarters (see above), at park system regional offices, at National Forest Supervisors' offices, and at most Ranger Station offices. The cost is $10.

Golden Access Passport. Issued to citizens and permanent residents of the United States who are physically disabled or visually impaired, this passport is a free lifetime entrance permit to fee-charging recreation areas. The fee exemption extends to those accompanying the permit holder in a private noncommercial vehicle or, in the case of walk-in facilities, to the holder's spouse and children. The passport also entitles the holder to a 50 percent discount on use fees charged in park areas but not to fees charged by concessionaires. Golden Access Passports must be obtained in person. Proof of eligibility to receive federal benefits is required (under programs such as Disability Retirement, Compensation for Military Service-Connected Disability, Coal Mine

Safety and Health Act, etc.), or an affidavit must be signed attesting to eligibility. These passports are available at the same outlets as Golden Age Passports.

FOR SENIOR CITIZENS

Look for the senior-citizen discount symbol in the lodging and restaurant listings. Always call ahead to confirm that the discount is being offered, and be sure to carry proof of age. At places not listed in the book, it never hurts to ask if a senior-citizen discount is offered. Additional information for mature travelers is available from the American Association of Retired Persons (AARP), 601 E St NW, Washington, DC 20049, phone 202/434-2277.

Tipping

Tipping is an expression of appreciation for good service, and often service workers rely on tips as a significant part of their income. However, you never need to tip if service is poor.

IN HOTELS

Door attendants in major city hotels are usually given $1 for getting you a cab. Bellhops expect $1 per bag, usually $2 if you have only one bag. Concierges are tipped according to the service they perform. It's not mandatory to tip when you've asked for suggestions on sightseeing or restaurants or help in making reservations for dining. However, when a concierge books you a table at a restaurant known to be difficult to get into, a gratuity of $5 is appropriate. For obtaining theater or sporting event tickets, $5-$10 is expected. Maids, often overlooked by guests, may be tipped $1-$2 per days of stay.

AT RESTAURANTS

Coffee shop and counter service wait staff are usually given 8 percent–10 percent of the bill. In full-service restaurants, tip 15 percent of the bill, before sales tax. In fine restaurants, where the staff is large and shares the gratuity, 18 percent–20 percent for the waiter is appropriate. In most cases, tip the maitre d' only if service has been extraordinary and only on the way out; $20 is the minimum in upscale properties in major metropolitan areas. If there is a wine steward, tip him or her at least $6 a bottle, more if the wine was decanted or if the bottle was very expensive. If your bus person has been unusually attentive, $2 pressed into his hand on departure is a nice gesture. An increasing number of restaurants automatically add a service charge to the bill instead of a gratuity. Before tipping, carefully review your check. If you are in doubt, ask your server.

AT AIRPORTS

Curbside luggage handlers expect $1 per bag. Car-rental shuttle drivers who help with your luggage appreciate a $1 or $2 tip.

Staying Safe

The best way to deal with emergencies is to be prepared enough to avoid them. However, unforeseen situations do happen, and you can prepare for them.

IN YOUR CAR

Before your trip, make sure your car has been serviced and is in good working order. Change the oil, check the battery and belts, and make sure tires are inflated properly (this can also improve gas mileage). Other inspections recommended by the car's manufacturer should be made, too.

Next, be sure you have the tools and equipment to deal with a routine breakdown: jack, spare tire, lug wrench, repair kit, emergency tools, jumper cables, spare fan belt, auto fuses, flares and/or reflectors, flashlights, first-aid kit, and, in winter, windshield wiper fluid, a windshield scraper, and snow shovel.

Bring all appropriate and up-to-date documentation—licenses, registration, and insurance cards—and know what's covered by your insurance. Also bring an extra set of keys, just in case.

En route, always buckle up! In most states it is required by law.

If your car does break down, get out of traffic as soon as possible—pull well off the road. Raise the hood and turn on your emergency flashers or tie a white cloth to the roadside door handle or antenna. Stay near your car. Use flares or reflectors to keep your car from being hit.

IN YOUR LODGING

Chances are slim that you will encounter a hotel or motel fire. The 🔥 in a listing indicates that there were smoke detectors and/or sprinkler systems in the rooms we inspected. Once you've checked in, make sure that any smoke detector in your room is working properly. Ascertain the locations of fire extinguishers and at least two fire exits. Never use an elevator in a fire.

For personal security, use the peephole in your room's door.

PROTECTING AGAINST THEFT

To guard against theft wherever you go, don't bring anything of more value than you need. If you do bring valuables, leave them at your hotel rather than in your car, and if you have something very expensive, lock it in a safe. Many hotels have one in each room; others will store your valuables in the hotel's safe. And of course, don't carry more money than you need; use traveler's checks and credit cards, or visit cash machines.

For Travelers with Disabilities

A number of publications can provide assistance. The most complete listing of published material for travelers with disabilities is available from The Disability Bookshop, Twin Peaks Press, Box 129, Vancouver, WA 98666, phone 360/694-2462. A comprehensive guidebook to the national parks is *Easy Access to National Parks: The Sierra Club Guide for People with Disabilities* ($16), distributed by Random House.

The Reference Section of the National Library Service for the Blind and Physically Handicapped (Library of Congress, Washington, DC 20542, phone 202/707-9276 or 202/707-5100) provides information and resources for persons with mobility problems and hearing and vision impairments, as well as information about the NILS talking program (or visit your local library).

IMPORTANT TOLL-FREE NUMBERS AND ON-LINE INFORMATION

Hotels and Motels

Adam's Mark   800/444–2326
   www.adamsmark.com

Baymont Inns and Suites
   800/428–3438
   www.budgetel.com

Best Western   800/780–7234,
   TDD 800/528–2222
   www.bestwestern.com

Budget Host   800/283–4678
   www.budgethost.com

Clarion   800/252–7466

Comfort Inn   800/228–5150
   www.choicehotels.com

Courtyard by Marriott 800/321–2211
   www.courtyard.com

Days Inn   800/325–2525
   www.daysinn.com

Doubletree   800/222–8733
   www.doubletreehotels.com

Drury Inns   800/325–8300
   www.drury-inn.com

Econo Lodge   800/446–6900
   www.econolodge.com

Embassy Suites   800/362–2779
   www.embassy-suites.com

Exel Inns of America   800/356–8013
   www.exelinns.com

Fairfield Inn
by Marriott   800/228–2800
   www.fairfieldinn.com

Fairmont Hotels   800/527–4727
   www.fairmont.com

Forte   800/225–5843
   www.forte-hotels.com

Four Seasons   800/819–5053
   www.fourseasons.com

Friendship Inns   800/453–4511
   www.hotelchoice.com

Hampton Inn   800/426–7866
   www.hampton-inn.com

Hilton   800/445–8667,
   TDD 800/368–1133
   www.hilton.com

Holiday Inn   800/465–4329,
   TDD 800/238–5544
   www.holiday-inn.com

Howard Johnson   800/446–4656,
   TDD 800/654–8442
   www.hojo.com

Hyatt & Resorts   800/233–1234
   www.hyatt.com

Inns of America   800/826–0778
   www.innsamerica.com

Inter-Continental   800/327–0200
   www.interconti.com

La Quinta   800/531–5900,
   TDD 800/426–3101
   www.laquinta.com

Loews   800/235–6397
   www.loewshotels.com

Marriott   800/228–9290
   www.marriott.com

Master Hosts Inns   800/251–1962
   www.reservahost.com

Meridien   800/225–5843
   www.forte-hotels.com

Motel 6   800/466–8356
   www.motel6.com

Nikko Hotels
International   800/645–5687
   www.nikkohotels.com

Omni   800/843–6664
   www.omnihotels.com

Quality Inn   800/228–5151
   www.qualityinn.com

Radisson   800/333–3333
   www.radisson.com

Ramada   800/228–2828,
   TDD 800/228–3232
   www.ramada.com

Red Carpet Inns   800/251–1962
   www.reservahost.com

Red Lion   800/733–5466
   www.redlion.com

Red Roof Inn   800/843–7663
   www.redroof.com

Renaissance   800/468–3571
   www.renaissancehotels.com

Residence Inn
by Marriott   800/331–3131
    www.marriott.com

Ritz-Carlton   800/241–3333
    www.ritzcarlton.com

Rodeway   800/228–2000
    www.rodeway.com

Sheraton   800/325–3535
    www.sheraton.com

Shilo Inn   800/222–2244
    www.shiloinns.com

Signature Inns   800/822–5252
    www.signature-inns.com

Sleep Inn   800/753–3746
    www.sleepinn.com

Super 8   800/800–8000
    www.super8motels.com

Susse Chalet   800/524–2538
    www.sussechalet.com

Travelodge   800/578–7878
    www.travelodge.com

Vagabond Inns   800/522–1555
    www.vagabondinns.com

Westin Hotels
& Resorts   800/937–8461
    www.westin.com

Wyndham Hotels
& Resorts   800/996–3426
    www.travelweb.com

Airlines

Air Canada   800/776–3000
    www.aircanada.ca

Alaska   800/252–7522
    www.alaska-air.com

American   800/433–7300
    www.aa.com

America West   800/235–9292
    www.americawest.com

British Airways   800/247–9297
    www.british-airways.com

Canadian   800/426–7000
    www.cdnair.ca

Continental   800/523–3273
    www.flycontinental.com

Delta   800/221–1212
    www.delta-air.com

IslandAir   800/323–3345

Mesa   800/637–2247
    www.mesa-air.com

Northwest   800/225–2525
    www.nwa.com

SkyWest   800/453–9417
    www.skywest.com

Southwest   800/435–9792
    www.iflyswa.com

TWA   800/221–2000
    www.twa.com

United   800/241–6522
    www.ual.com

USAir   800/428–4322
    www.usair.com

Trains

Amtrak   800/872–7245
    www.amtrak.com

Buses

Greyhound   800/231–2222
    www.greyhound.com

Car Rentals

Advantage   800/777–5500
    www.arac.com

Alamo   800/327–9633
    www.goalamo.com

Allstate   800/634–6186
    www.bnm.com/as.htm

Avis   800/831–2847
    www.avis.com

Budget   800/527–0700
    www.budgetrentacar.com

Dollar   800/800–3665
    www.dollarcar.com

Enterprise   800/325–8007
    www.pickenterprise.com

Hertz   800/654–3131
    www.hertz.com

National   800/227–7368
    www.nationalcar.com

Payless   800/729–5377
    www.800-payless.com

Rent-A-Wreck   800/944–7501
    www.rent-a-wreck.com

Sears   800/527–0770
    www.budget.com

Thrifty   800/847–4369
    www.thrifty.com

FOUR-STAR AND FIVE-STAR ESTABLISHMENTS IN THE SOUTHEAST

Georgia
★★★★★ **Lodging**
Four Seasons Hotel, *Atlanta*
★★★★★ **Restaurants**
The Dining Room, *Atlanta*
Seeger's, *Atlanta*
★★★★ **Lodgings**
1842 Inn, *Macon*
The Cloister, *Sea Island*
The Kehoe House, *Savannah*
The Ritz-Carlton, *Atlanta*
The Ritz-Carlton Buckhead, *Atlanta*
★★★★ **Restaurants**
Bacchanalia, *Atlanta*
Bone's, *Atlanta*
Canoe, *Atlanta*
Elizabeth on 37th, *Savannah*
Nikolai's Roof, *Atlanta*
Park 75 at the Four Seasons, *Atlanta*

Kentucky
★★★★ **Lodgings**
Camberley Brown Hotel, *Louisville*
Marriott's Griffin Gate Resort, *Lexington*
The Seelbach Hilton Louisville, *Louisville*
★★★★ **Restaurant**
Lilly's, *Louisville*

Louisiana
★★★★★ **Restaurant**
Grill Room, *New Orleans*
★★★★ **Lodging**
Windsor Court Hotel, *New Orleans*
★★★★ **Restaurants**
Artesia, *Covington*
Bayona, *New Orleans*
Commander's Palace, *New Orleans*
Delmonico, *New Orleans*

Emeril's Restaurant, *New Orleans*
Lafitte's Landing, *Baton Rouge*
La Provence, *Covington*

North Carolina
★★★★★ **Lodging**
The Fearrington House, *Chapel Hill*
★★★★ **Lodgings**
Eseeola Lodge, *Linville*
The Park, *Charlotte*
Pinehurst, *Pinehurst*
Richmond Hill Inn, *Asheville*
The Swag Country Inn, *Waynesville*
Washington Duke Inn & Golf Club, *Durham*
★★★★ **Restaurants**
Angus Barn, *Raleigh*
Carolina Crossroads, *Chapel Hill*
The Fearrington House, *Chapel Hill*
La Vecchia's, *Charlotte*

South Carolina
★★★★ **Lodgings**
Charleston Place Hotel, *Charleston*
Rhett House Inn, *Beaufort*
Wild Dunes Resort, *Charleston*
Woodlands Resort & Inn, *Charleston*
★★★★ **Restaurants**
Charleston Grill, *Charleston*
The Dining Room at Woodlands, *Charleston*
Peninsula Grill, *Charleston*

Tennessee
★★★★ **Lodging**
Blackberry Farm, *Maryville*
★★★★ **Restaurants**
Chez Philippe, *Memphis*
The Wild Boar, *Nashville*

Would you like to spend less time buying gas?

 With *Speedpass,* getting gas just got a little more exciting. All you have to do is wave it at the pump, gas up and go. Fast and easy. You can link it to a major credit card or check card that you *already* have. So call our toll-free number, **1-877-MY MOBIL**, or visit www.speedpass.com to enroll. Join the millions of people who already use *Speedpass.* It's safe, secure and best of all...it's *free.*

Speedpass
Today's way to pay. Mobil

ALABAMA

From the Confederacy's first capital at
Montgomery to America's first "space
capital" at Huntsville, Alabama has successfully spanned a century that began in sec-
tional conflict but ended in a dedication to
man's quest to bridge the universe. The drive
from the business center of Birmingham to
the heart of the Cotton Kingdom surrounding Montgomery and Selma is less than 100
miles, but these miles mark one of the transi-
tions between the 19th and 20th centuries.

Harnessing the Tennessee River made it
possible to control floods and turn the
eroded soil into bountiful crop land. The
river became the South's most important
waterway, and giant Tennessee Valley
Authority (TVA) dams brought electric power
and industrialization to once-bypassed cities.
They also gave northern Alabama nationally
renowned water recreation areas.

Population: 4,369,862
Area: 51,998 square miles
Elevation: 0-2,407 feet
Peak: Cheaha Mountain
  (Cleburne County)
Entered Union: December 14,
  1819 (22nd state)
Capital: Montgomery
Motto: We Dare Defend Our
  Rights
Nickname: Heart of Dixie
Flower: Camellia
Bird: Yellowhammer
Tree: Southern Pine
Fair: 10 days mid-October,
  2001, in Birmingham
Time Zone: Central
Website: www.touralabama.org

Cotton, the traditional wealth of Alabama's rich Black Belt, fed the busy port
of Mobile until the 1870s, when Birmingham grew into an industrial center.
TVA brought the other great shift in the 1930s, culminating in new hydroelectric and steam plant power production in the 1960s.

Cotton and river waterways were the combination on which the Old South
was built. The Cotton State supreme by the 1850s, Alabama built river towns
like Selma, the old capital of "Cahawba," and Montgomery, the new capital
and "cradle of the Confederacy." The red iron ore in the northern mountains
was neglected, except for isolated forges operated by individuals, until just
before the Civil War.

On January 11, 1861 Alabama became the fourth state to secede from the
Union. Jefferson Davis was inaugurated as president of the Confederacy in
Montgomery the following month, and on April 12 he ordered General P.G.T.
Beauregard to fire on Fort Sumter. The Confederate capital was moved to Rich-
mond on May 21, 1861.

Alabama's troops fought with every active Southern force, the state contributing between 65,000 and 100,000 men from a white population of 500,000. At least 2,500 white soldiers and 10,000 black soldiers went north to support the Union. When Huntsville,

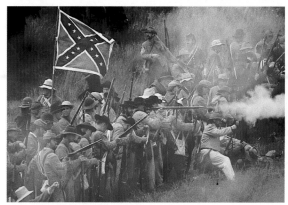
Civil War reenactment

Decatur, and Tuscumbia fell to Union forces in 1862, every male from 16 to 60 was ordered to the state's defense. Little fighting took place on Alabama's soil and water again until Admiral Farragut's Union fleet won the Battle of Mobile Bay in 1864, though the city of Mobile did not fall. Full-scale invasions by Wilson's Raiders occupied several important cities in the spring of 1865.

Reconstruction days were made bitter by carpetbaggers who supported the Republican Party. The state refused to ratify the Fourteenth Amendment, and military law was reinstated. But by the 1880s recovery was beginning. Birmingham had weathered the national panic of 1873 successfully and was producing steel in earnest.

Historic attractions are plentiful. There is the birthplace of Helen Keller at Tuscumbia (see SHEFFIELD); the unusual Ave Maria Grotto in Cullman (see), an inspiring work of faith by one Benedictine monk who built scores of miniature religious buildings; and the museum and laboratory of the great black educator and scientist George Washington Carver at the Tuskegee Institute (see TUSKEGEE).

For golf enthusiasts, the Robert Trent Jones Golf Trail has 18 championship golf courses offering a total of 324 holes located at 7 sites: Anniston/Gadsden, Auburn/Opelika, Birmingham, Dothan, Greenville, Huntsville, and Mobile (phone 800/949-4444 for more information).

On Alabama's Gulf Coast, the port city of Mobile makes a splendid entry to the whole Gulf strip between Florida and New Orleans. Mobile is famous for the Bellingrath Gardens and Home, the annual Azalea Trail and Festival, and its own Mardi Gras celebration.

When to Go/Climate

Alabama's climate is mild almost yr-round, although the extreme northern part of the state can experience cold weather and even some snow in winter. The southern part of the state can be extremely hot beginning as early as March. Fall is usually comfortable throughout the state and is generally a good time to visit.

AVERAGE HIGH/LOW TEMPERATURES (°F)

BIRMINGHAM

Jan 52/31	**May** 81/58	**Sep** 84/63
Feb 57/35	**June** 87/65	**Oct** 75/50
Mar 66/42	**July** 90/70	**Nov** 65/42
Apr 75/49	**Aug** 89/69	**Dec** 56/35

MOBILE

Jan 60/40	**May** 85/64	**Sep** 87/69
Feb 64/43	**June** 90/71	**Oct** 80/57
Mar 71/50	**July** 91/73	**Nov** 70/49
Apr 79/57	**Aug** 91/73	**Dec** 63/43

Parks and Recreation Finder

Directions to and information about the parks and recreation areas below are given under their respective town/city sections. Please refer to those sections for details.

NATIONAL PARK AND RECREATION AREAS

Key to abbreviations. I.H.S. = International Historic Site; I.P.M. = International Peace Memorial; N.B. = National Battlefield; N.B.P. = National Battlefield Park; N.B.C. = National Battlefield and Cemetery; N.C.A. = National Conservation Area; N.E.M. = National Expansion Memorial; N.F. = National Forest; N.G. = National Grassland; N.H.P. = National Historical Park; N.H.C. = National

CALENDAR HIGHLIGHTS

MARCH

Historic Mobile Tours (Mobile). Houses, buildings open to visitors. Phone 800/566-2453.

MAY

Alabama Jubilee (Decatur). Point Mallard Park. Highlight of festivities are the hot-air balloon races. Phone 800/524-6181.

JUNE

City Stages (Birmingham). Music festival of national artists. Food, dancing, children's activities, and regional craftsmen. Phone 205/251-1272.

SEPTEMBER

Big Spring Jam (Huntsville). Music festival, incl pop, rock, jazz, country, and other genres. Foods from local restaurants, shows for kids. Phone 256/551-2223.

OCTOBER

Greater Gulf State Fair (Mobile). Commercial, industrial, military, and educational exhibits; entertainment. Phone 334/344-4573.

State Fair (Birmingham). Contact Alabama State Fair Authority. Phone 205/786-8100.

Alabama Renaissance Faire (Florence). Renaissance-era arts and crafts, music, food, entertainment. Fair workers in period costumes. Phone 256/760-9648.

DECEMBER

Blue-Gray Football Classic (Montgomery). Contact Lion's Club/Blue-Gray Association. Phone 334/265-1266.

Heritage Corridor; N.H.S. = National Historic Site; N.L. = National Lakeshore; N.M. = National Monument; N.M.P. = National Military Park; N.Mem. = National Memorial; N.P. = National Park; N.Pres. = National Preserve; N.R.A. = National Recreational Area; N.R.R. = National Recreational River; N.Riv. = National River; N.S. = National Seashore; N.S.R. = National Scenic Riverway; N.S.T. = National Scenic Trail; N.Sc. = National Scientific Reserve; N.V.M. = National Volcanic Monument.

Place Name	Listed Under
Bankhead N.F.	CULLMAN
Conecuh N.F.	EVERGREEN
Horseshoe Bend N.M.P.	same
Russell Cave N.M.	same
Talladega N.F.	TALLADEGA
Tuskegee Institute N.H.S.	TUSKEGEE

STATE PARK AND RECREATION AREAS

Key to abbreviations. I.P. = Interstate Park; S.A.P. = State Archaeological Park; S.B. = State Beach; S.C.A. = State Conservation Area; S.C.P. = State Conservation Park; S.Cp. = State Campground; S.F. = State Forest; S.G. = State Garden; S.H.A. = State Historic Area; S.H.P. = State Historic Park; S.H.S. = State Historic Site; S.M.P. = State Marine Park; S.N.A. = State Natural Area; S.P. = State Park; S.P.C. = State Public Campground; S.R. = State Reserve; S.R.A. = State Recreation Area; S.Res. = State Reservoir; S.Res.P. = State Resort Park; S.R.P. = State Rustic Park.

Place Name	Listed Under
Blue Springs S.P.	OZARK
Buck's Pocket and Lake Guntersville S.P.	GUNTERSVILLE
Cheaha S.P.	TALLADEGA
Chewacla S.P.	AUBURN
Claude D. Kelley S.P.	ATMORE
DeSoto S.P.	FORT PAYNE
Gulf S.P.	GULF SHORES
Joe Wheeler S.P. (Elk River, First Creek, and Wheeler Dam units)	FLORENCE
Lake Lurleen S.P.	TUSCALOOSA
Lakepoint Resort S.P.	EUFAULA
Monte Sano S.P.	HUNTSVILLE
Oak Mountain and Rickwood Caverns S.P.	BIRMINGHAM
Paul M. Grist S.P.	SELMA
Tannehill Historical S.P.	BESSEMER
Wind Creek S.P.	ALEXANDER CITY

Water-related activities, hiking, riding, various sports, picnicking, camping, and visitor centers are available in many of these areas. Nominal entrance fees are collected at some parks. The state parks accept telephone reservations for motel rooms, cabins and improved campsites; primitive campsites are on a no-reservation basis. Fees for improved campsites are $10-$25/site/night. No pets at motels and cabins; pets on leash only at campgrounds. There are many state park fishing lakes and 12 parks that offer boat rentals and water-recreational equipment. Bait, tackle, and freshwater fishing permits are $2/day; under 13, 75 cents/day. Contact the Alabama Department of Conservation and Natural Resources, Alabama State Parks Division, 64 N Union St, Montgomery 36130; 334/242-3334 for details. For reservations phone 800/252-7275 or 334/242-3333.

SKI AREA

Place Name	Listed Under
Cloudmont Ski Resort	FORT PAYNE

FISHING AND HUNTING

More than 50,000 small ponds and lakes, incl 22 public lakes and more than ½-million acres of public impounded waters, provide ample freshwater fishing. Crappie, striped and white bass, bluegill, and redear sunfish can be caught statewide. State and national forests and state parks cater to anglers. White sandy beaches of the Gulf Coast are good for surf casting; trolling farther out in Gulf waters can hook tarpon, snapper, king mackerel, and other game fish. Largemouth bass abound from the Tennessee River to Mobile Bay. The Lewis Smith and Martin reservoirs have both largemouth and spotted bass; the Wilson and Wheeler Dam tailwaters have smallmouth bass; the East Central Alabama streams have redeye bass. Alabama has no closed season on freshwater game fish. Sportfishing licenses, nonresident: annual, $31; 7-day, $11 (includes issuance fee). The fees for reciprocal licenses for the residents of adjoining states and Louisiana vary.

Waterfowl, small game, turkey, and deer are found in the state, with state-managed and national forest wildlife areas providing hunting in season. Deer and turkey hunting require an all-game hunting license for nonresidents. Federal and State Waterfowl Stamps are required in addition to a regular hunting license when hunting waterfowl. Because nearly all lands in Alabama are under private ownership and state law requires written permission from the owner prior to hunting, persons desiring to hunt should make arrangements accordingly. Hunting licenses, nonresident: annual all-game, $202; annual small game, $42; 7-day all-game, $77; 7-day small game, $27. Management area deer and turkey licenses ($4) are required in the management areas in addition to the regular hunting license. A reciprocal agreement among Alabama and the state of Florida may alter the license fees charged residents of Florida. License costs for nonresident hunting licenses include a $2 issuance fee. For detailed information on seasons and other regulations, contact Alabama Dept of Conservation and Natural Resources, Game and Fish Division, 64 N Union St, Montgomery 36130; 334/242-3467. For information on fishing and hunting licenses, phone 334/242-3829.

Driving Information

All passengers in front seat must wear a safety belt. Children under 6 yrs must be in an approved passenger restraint anywhere in vehicle; ages 4 and 5 may use a regulation safety belt or child seat; age 3 and under must use a federally approved safety seat. For further information phone 334/242-4445.

INTERSTATE HIGHWAY SYSTEM

The following alphabetical listing of Alabama towns in *Mobil Travel Guide* shows that these cities are within 10 miles of the indicated Interstate highways. A highway map should, however, be checked for the nearest exit.

Highway Number	Cities/Towns within 10 miles
Interstate 10	Mobile.
Interstate 20	Anniston, Bessemer, Birmingham, Tuscaloosa.
Interstate 59	Bessemer, Birmingham, Fort Payne, Gadsden, Tuscaloosa.
Interstate 65	Athens, Atmore, Birmingham, Clanton, Cullman, Decatur, Evergreen, Greenville, Mobile, Montgomery.
Interstate 85	Auburn, Montgomery, Opelika, Tuskegee.

Additional Visitor Information

Travel and vacation information is offered toll-free, phone 800/ALABAMA (Mon-Fri). Travelers also may contact the Alabama Bureau of Tourism & Travel, 401 Adams Ave, PO Box 4927, Montgomery 36103; 334/242-4169 for additional information.

There are 8 welcome centers in Alabama; there visitors will find information and brochures that will help them plan stops at points of interest: Alabama (I-59S), Ardmore (I-65S), Baldwin (I-10W), Grand Bay (I-10E), Hardy (I-20W, near Heflin), Houston (US 231N), Lanett (I-85S), and Sumter (I-59N/20E); inquire locally for further information on these centers.

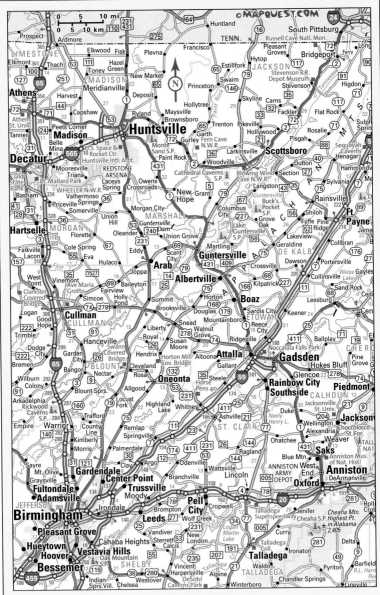

The northeastern corner of Alabama contains an attractive, remote stretch of the Cumberland Plateau that is an appealing destination for scenic drives, camping, and lake and mountain recreation. Begin in Birmingham and head northwest, stopping near Gadsden to see Noccolula Falls and Park. Continue on to DeSoto State Park, with its dramatic waterfalls and canyons, which is a popular destination on the Alabama side of the "TAG Corner," where Tennessee, Alabama, and Georgia meet. **(Approx 200 mi)**

West of Montgomery via I-85 or US 80, Selma is an important pilgrimage point for many travelers, particularly those on a tour of African-American history sites. Here, among the antebellum homes and attractive historic districts, the National Voting Rights Museum & Institute tells the story of Bloody Sunday, which took place in 1965 when marchers to Montgomery clashed with police. The Old Depot Museum relates the town's full history, including its Native American and Civil War past. **(Approx 100 mi)**

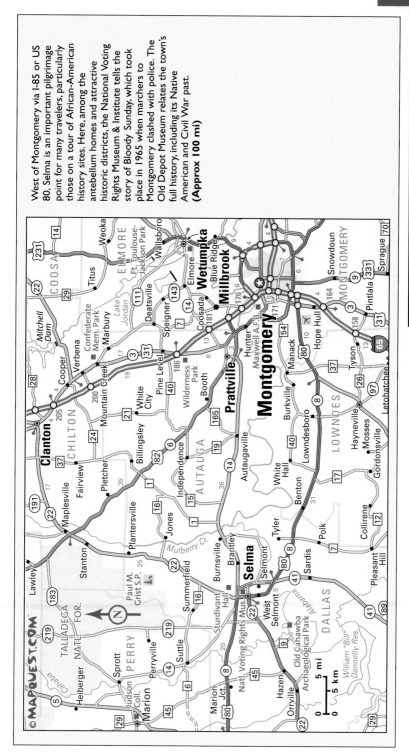

Alexander City

(D-4) *See also Sylacauga*

Settled 1836 **Pop** 14,917 **Elev** 707 ft
Area code 256 **Zip** 35010
Web www.alexandercity.com
Information Chamber of Commerce, 120 Tallapoosa St, Box 926, 35011; 256/234-3461

Martin Dam at Cherokee Bluffs not only supplies power, but also creates Lake Martin on the Tallapoosa River. Lake Martin, with a 760-mile shoreline, was the largest of its kind when it was formed in 1926. Today, it is one of the South's finest inland recreation areas.

What to See and Do

Horseshoe Bend National Military Park. (see) 13 mi NE on AL 22 to New Site, then S on AL 49.

Wind Creek State Park. A 1,445-acre wooded park on Lake Martin. Swimming beach, bathhouses, waterskiing, fishing, boating (marina, ramps); hiking, bicycling, picnic area, concessions. Improved campsites. Observation tower. Standard fees. (Daily) 7 mi SE off AL 63. Phone 256/329-0845.

Motels/Motor Lodges

★ **BEST WESTERN HORSESHOE INN.** *3146 US 280 (35010), at AL 22. 256/234-6311; fax 256/234-6314.* 90 rms. S $39-$44; D $39-$54; each addl $5. TV; cable. Pool. Restaurant opp open 24 hrs. Bar 4-10 pm, closed Sun. Ck-out 11 am. Meeting rms. Business servs avail. Cr cds: A, C, D, DS, MC, V.
🄳 ⊶ 🖂 🐾 SC

★★ **JAMESON INN.** *4335 US 280 (35010). 256/234-7099; fax 256/234-9807; toll-free 800/526-3766.* 60 rms, 2 story. S, D $48; each addl $5; suites $53-$58; under 13 free. Crib free. Pet accepted, some restrictions. TV; cable (premium). Pool. Complimentary continental bkfst. Restaurant nearby. Ck-out 11 am. Meeting rms. Exercise equipt. Some refrigerators. Cr cds: A, C, D, DS, MC, V.
🄳 🐾 ⊶ 🏋 🖂 🐾 SC

★ **SUPER 8 MOTEL.** *4000 280 Bypass (35223). 256/329-8858; fax 256/329-8858.* 44 units, 3 story. No elvtr. S, D $41.95-$48.95; each addl $5; under 12 free; wkly rates. Crib free. TV; cable (premium). Complimentary coffee in lobby. Restaurant adj 6 am-10 pm. Ck-out 11 am. Business servs avail. Cr cds: A, C, D, DS, MC, V.
🄳 🖂 🐾 SC

Restaurant

★ **CECIL'S PUBLIC HOUSE.** *243 Green St (35010). 256/329-0732.* Specializes in seafood, steak. Hrs: 11 am-2 pm, 5-9 pm; Sat from 5 pm. Closed Sun; hols. Bar. Lunch $5.50-$6.95; dinner $5.50-$14.95. Child's menu. Old house (1902); antique plate collection; stained-glass windows. Cr cds: A, MC, V.
🄳 ⊣

Anniston

(C-5) *See also Gadsden, Talladega*

Settled 1872 **Pop** 26,623 **Elev** 710 ft
Area code 205 **Zip** 36202
Web www.calhounchamber.org
Information Convention & Visitors Bureau, 14th St & Quintard Ave, PO Box 1087; 256/237-3536 or 800/489-1087

Anniston was founded by Samuel Noble, an Englishman who headed the ironworks in Rome, Georgia, and Daniel Tyler, a Connecticut capitalist. They established textile mills and blast furnaces designed to help launch the South into the industrial revolution after the devastation of the Civil War. In 1879 the owners hired accomplished Eastern architects, including the renowned Stanford White, to design and build a modern company town. The town was named after Mrs. Anne Scott Taylor (Annie's Town), wife of one of the local iron magnates. Anniston remained a private company town until 1883 when it was opened to the public. Today Anniston retains many historic structures and much of its original character.

What to See and Do

Anniston Museum of Natural History. Museum featuring Regar-Werner bird exhibit with 600 specimens including many endangered and extinct birds; reconstruction of pteranodon, a 30-ft flying dinosaur; large African animal exhibit featuring large bull elephant; Egyptian mummies; North American mammals; live reptiles; giant termite mound; replica of an Alabama cave; and changing exhibition gallery. Situated in 187-acre John B. Lagarde Environmental Interpretive Center; nature trails, picnic facilities. (Tues-Sun; closed hols) 800 Museum Dr, Lagarde Park. Phone 256/237-6766. ¢¢

Berman Museum. Collection of unique artifacts amassed by a real spy on his worldly missions. Treasures from the American West and WWII eras are featured incl a Royal Persian Scimitar encrusted with 1,295 rose-cut diamonds, 60 carats of rubies, and a single 40-carat emerald set in 3 pounds of gold. (Tues-Sun; closed hols) 840 Museum Dr, Lagarde Park. Phone 205/237-6261.

The Church of St. Michael and All Angels. Episcopal (1888) Gothic church, parish house, assembly rm, and bell tower of native stone are connected by cloisters. Twelve-foot Carrara marble altar with alabaster reredos surmounted by 7 statues of angels. Stained-glass memorial windows. Lithographs of Christian history are in assembly rm. (Daily) W 18th St & Cobb Ave. Phone 205/237-4011.

Coldwater Covered Bridge. Built before 1850; 1 of 13 restored covered bridges in Alabama. 3 mi S via US 431, 5 mi W on US 78 in Coldwater at Oxford Lake and Civic Center.

Motels/Motor Lodges

★★ **BEST WESTERN RIVERSIDE INN.** *11900 US 78 (Pell City) (35135). 205/338-3381; fax 205/338-3183; res 800/528-1234.* 70 rms, 2 story. S $35-$40; D $45-$55; each addl $6; under 12 free; race wkends 4-day min. Crib $2. Pet accepted, some restrictions. TV. Pool; wading pool. Restaurant 6 am-2 pm, 5-9 pm. Ck-out 11 am. Coin lndry. Meeting rms. Boating; waterskiing. Pier. On Logan-Martin Lake. Cr cds: A, C, D, DS, MC, V.

★★★ **HOLIDAY INN.** *US 78 & 21 S (35135), near Municipal Airport. 205/831-3410; fax 205/831-9560; toll-free 800/465-4329.* 194 rms, 2 story. S, D $68; each addl $6; suites $109; under 18 free. Crib free. TV; cable. Pool; whirlpool. Playground. Coffee in rms. Restaurant 6 am-11 am. Rm serv. Bar 11 am-11 pm. Ck-out noon. Coin lndry. Meeting rms. Business servs avail. In-rm modem link. Bellhops. Refrigerators avail. Picnic tables, grills. Cr cds: A, C, D, DS, JCB, MC, V.

Hotel

★★ **HAMPTON INN.** *1600 AL 21 (36203), 2 mi S. 256/835-1492; fax 256/835-0636; res 800/426-7866. Email anbof01@hi-hotel.com; www.swmanagement.net.* 129 rms, 2 story. Apr, June-Aug, Oct: S $64; D $74; each addl $10; under 18 free; lower rates rest of yr. Crib avail. Parking lot. Pool. TV; cable (premium). Complimentary continental bkfst, coffee in rms, newspaper, toll-free calls. Restaurant nearby. Ck-out noon, ck-in 3 pm. Meeting rm. Business center. Dry cleaning. Exercise privileges. Golf. Tennis, 2 courts. Video games. Cr cds: A, C, D, DS, MC, V.

B&B/Small Inn

★★★ **VICTORIA-A COUNTRY INN.** *1604 Quintard Ave (36201). 256/236-0503; fax 256/236-1138. Email victoria@thevictoria.com; www.thevictoria.com.* 60 units, 4 bldgs, 3 story. S $69; D $79; each addl $10; suites $129-$219; under 12 free. Crib $10. TV; cable (premium), VCR avail. Pool. Restaurant (see also THE VICTORIA). Ck-out noon, ck-in 3 pm. Business servs avail. Health club privileges. Built in 1888. Cr cds: A, C, D, DS, MC, V.

Restaurants

★ **BETTY'S BAR-B-Q.** *401 S Quintard (36201). 256/237-1411.* Specializes in barbecue, catfish, fried chicken. Hrs: 10:30 am-8:30 pm; Fri, Sat to 9 pm. Closed Sun; hols, also wk of July 4. Lunch $2.95-$5.15; dinner $5.15-$9.75. Child's menu. Antique farm implements. Family-owned. Cr cds: A, C, DS, MC, V.
D **SC**

★ ★ **THE VICTORIA.** *1604 Quintard Ave. 256/236-0503. Email thevic@mindspring.com; www.thevictoria.com.* Eclectic menu. Specializes in pasta, game, fish. Hrs: 6-9 pm; Fri, Sat to 10 pm. Closed Sun; hols. Res accepted. Bar. Dinner $13.95-$18.95. Entertainment: pianist Fri, Sat. Romantic dining experience in Victorian house. Cr cds: A, D, DS, MC, V.
D

Athens

(A-3) *See also Decatur, Huntsville*

Founded 1818 **Pop** 16,901 **Elev** 720 ft
Area code 256 **Zip** 35611
Web www.companet.net/cc/athenscc.html
Information Athens-Limestone County Chamber of Commerce, PO Box 150, 35612; 256/232-2600 or 256/232-2609

The quiet, tree-lined streets and Greek Revival houses lend an air of the old antebellum South to Athens. This was the first major Alabama town to be occupied by Union troops in the Civil War (1862). It was also the first Alabama city to get electricity (1934) from the Tennessee Valley Authority. Electrification soon spread to the surrounding area, aiding in the development of light manufacturing.

What to See and Do

Athens State College. (1822) 2,600 students. On campus is Founders Hall (1843), as well as many examples of Greek Revival architecture. On the 2nd floor of Founders Hall is the Pi Tau Chi Chapel, housing a hand-carved altar depicting scenes from New Testament. Tours of campus (academic yr, Mon-Fri). Beaty & Pryor Sts. Phone 256/233-8100.

Houston Memorial Library and Museum. Built in 1835, this house was once owned by George S. Houston, governor of Alabama and US senator. It is now maintained by the city of Athens. Meeting rms display Houston coat of arms, family portraits, and drawing-rm furniture. (Mon-Sat; closed hols) Market & Houston Sts. Phone 256/233-8770. **FREE**

Annual Events

Musical Explosion. Athens Bible School. Mostly country music, some contemporary. Phone 256/232-3525. Two wkends late Mar.

Homespun. Craft show featuring woodworking, quilting, basketmaking, and buggy rides. Phone 256/232-3525. Early May.

Tennessee Valley Old Time Fiddler's Convention. Athens State College. A wkend of traditional American music. Fiddle, mandolin, guitar, banjo, and old-time singing; also buck dancing. National and intl musicians perform; ends with the naming of the Tennessee Valley Fiddle King. Phone 256/233-8100. Fri, Sat of 1st full wkend Oct.

Motels/Motor Lodges

★ ★ **BEST WESTERN.** *1329 US 72 (35611), 2 mi E via I-65, at US 72 Exit 351. 256/233-4030; fax 256/233-4554; res 800/528-1234; toll-free 800/321-0122.* 88 rms, 2 story. S $36; D $44; each addl $4; under 12 free. Crib free. Pet accepted, some restrictions. TV; cable (premium). Pool. Complimentary continental bkfst. Restaurant opp 6 am-midnight. Ck-out noon. Picnic tables. Cr cds: A, D, DS, MC, V.
D **≈** **t** **↑** **≈** **X** **↑** **≈** **≈**

★ **BOMAR INN.** *1101 Hwy 31 S at US 72 (36203). 256/232-6944; fax 256/232-8019; toll-free 800/824-6834.* 80 rms, 1-2 story. S $38-$39; D $44-$45; each addl $5; under 12 free. Crib free. Pet accepted. TV; cable (premium). Pool. Restaurant 6 am-9 pm; Sun to 2 pm. Ck-out noon.

Meeting rms. Valet serv. Sundries. Cr cds: A, C, D, DS, JCB, MC, V.

★★ **HAMPTON INN.** *1488 Thrasher Blvd (35611), I-65 Exit 351.* 205/232-0030; fax 205/233-7006. 56 rms, 2 story. S $49.95-$59.95; D $54.95-$64.95; each addl $5; whirlpool rms $69.95; under 18 free; higher rates special events. Crib free. TV; cable (premium), VCR. Heated pool; whirlpool. Complimentary continental bkfst. Restaurant opp 6 am-10 pm. Ck-out 11 am. Meeting rm. Business servs avail. In-rm modem link. Health club privileges. Refrigerators. Cr cds: A, C, D, DS, MC, V.

★ **TRAVELODGE.** *1325 US 72E (35611), 1 mi E of jct I-65 Exit 351.* 256/233-1446; fax 256/233-1454; toll-free 800/578-7878. 60 rms, most rms with shower only, 2 story. S $33-$38; D $43-$48; each addl $5; suites, kit. units $50; under 15 free. TV; cable, VCR avail (movies). Complimentary continental bkfst, coffee in rms. Restaurant opp 24 hrs. Ck-out 11 am. Coin lndry. Business servs avail. In-rm modem link. Some refrigerators. Cr cds: A, C, D, DS, JCB, MC, V.

Atmore

(G-2) *See also Mobile*

Pop 8,046 **Elev** 287 ft **Area code** 334 **Zip** 36502
Web www.atmore.frontiernet.net/~chamber/
Information Chamber of Commerce, 501 S Pensacola Ave; 334/368-3305

What to See and Do

Claude D. Kelley State Park. A 25-acre lake is located beneath the towering pines of this 960-acre park. Swimming, fishing, boating (ramps, rentals); picnicking, primitive camping, RV hookups, cabins. Standard fees. 12 mi N of I-65, on AL 21 at Atmore Exit. Contact Rte 2, Box 77. Phone 334/862-2511.

Auburn

(D-5) *See also Opelika, Tuskegee; also see Columbus, GA*

Settled 1836 **Pop** 33,830 **Elev** 709 ft
Area code 334 **Zip** 36831
Web www.auburn-opelika.com
Information Auburn/Opelika Convention & Visitors Bureau, 714 E Glenn Ave, PO Box 2216; 334/887-8747 or 800/321-8880

Auburn took its name from the opening line in Oliver Goldsmith's poem, "The Deserted Village," which reads "Sweet Auburn, the loveliest village of the plain." Located on the southeastern slope of the Piedmont plateau, this trading and university community is graced with Greek Revival, Victorian, and early 20th-century architecture. The Tiger Trail of Auburn, granite plaques bearing the names of athletes and coaches who have brought recognition to Auburn, can be found in uptown Auburn along College Street and Magnolia Avenue.

What to See and Do

Auburn University. (1856) 22,000 students. One of the nation's earliest land-grant colleges and the first 4-yr educational institution in Alabama to admit women on an equal basis with men. A golden eagle, the university mascot, is housed on campus. Tours of campus. SW section of town off I-85, US 29, AL 14, 147. Phone 334/844-4000. Adj is

The Tiger Trail of Auburn. Granite plaques bearing the names of athletes and coaches that have brought recognition to Auburn. Uptown Auburn along College St and Magnolia Ave.

Chewacla State Park. This 696-acre park, on the fall line separating the Piedmont plateau from the coastal plain, incl a 26-acre lake. Swimming, bathhouse, fishing, boating (rentals), hiking, nature, and mountain bike trails, picnicking, playground, concession, improved camping, cabins. Standard fees. 4 mi S off US 29; 2 mi off I-85 Exit 51. Phone 334/887-5621 or 800/252-7275.

Lovelace Athletic Museum. Orange-and-blue shrine to such famous Auburn University athletes as Bo Jackson and Charles Barkley. Interactive exhibits. At Donahue Dr & Samford Ave. Phone 334/887-4750. **FREE**

Motel/Motor Lodge

★★ **QUALITY INN.** *1577 S College St (36830), I-85 Exit 51. 334/821-7001; fax 334/821-7001; res 800/282-8763.* 122 rms, 3 story. S, D $42-$69; each addl $5; suites $64-$84; under 18 free; higher rates Auburn Univ football games (2-day min). Crib free. Pet accepted. TV; cable (premium). Pool. Complimentary continental bkfst. Restaurant hrs vary. Bar 4 pm-1 am. Ck-out 11 am. Meeting rms. Business servs avail. In-rm modem link. Sundries. Exercise equipt. Refrigerators in suites. Cr cds: A, C, D, DS, JCB, MC, V.

D ⊷ ☇ ⚡ ☇ ⚡ SC

Hotel

★★★ **AUBURN UNIVERSITY HOTEL AND CONFERENCE CENTER.** *241 S College St (36830). 334/821-8200; fax 334/826-8746; toll-free 800/228-2876. Email auhotel@ mail.auburn.edu; www.auhcc.com.* 248 rms, 6 story. S, D $59-$125; each addl $10; suites $165-$250; under 18 free; higher rates football games. Crib free. Pet accepted. TV; cable. Pool. Restaurants 6:30 am-11 pm. Bar 11:30 am-11 pm. Ck-out noon. Business servs avail. In-rm modem link. Convention facilities. Gift shop. Exercise equipt. Health club privileges. Located on eastern edge of campus opp Samford Hall. Cr cds: A, C, D, DS, MC, V.

D ⊷ ☇ ⚡ ☇ ⚡ SC

B&B/Small Inn

★★ **CRENSHAW HOUSE BED & BREAKFAST.** *371 N College St (36830), I-85 Exit 51. 334/821-1131; fax 334/826-8123; toll-free 800/950-1131. Email crenshaw-gh@mindspring. com; www.auburnalabama.com.* 8 rms, 1 story, 1 suite. Feb-Jul, Sep-Nov: S

$50; D $65; each addl $10; suites $95; under 10 free; lower rates rest of yr. Crib avail, fee. Parking lot. TV; cable, VCR avail. Complimentary continental bkfst. Restaurant. Meeting rm. Business servs avail. Dry cleaning, coin lndry. Exercise privileges. Golf. Tennis. Cr cds: A, MC, V.

☇ ☇ ⚡ ☇ ⚡ ☇

Restaurant

★★ **NOODLE'S ITALIAN EATERY & GRILL.** *103 N College St (36830). 334/821-0349.* Specializes in seafood, steak. Own pasta. Hrs: 5-9 pm. Closed Sun; Thanksgiving, Dec 24, 25. Res accepted. Bar. Dinner $5-$15. Cr cds: A, D, DS, MC, V.

Bessemer

(C-3) See also Birmingham, Tuscaloosa

Founded 1887 **Pop** 33,497 **Elev** 513 ft **Area code** 205

Information Bessemer Area Chamber of Commerce, PO Box 648, 35021; 205/425-3253 or 888/423-7736

Bessemer was founded on April 12, 1887 by Henry F. DeBardeleben. It was named after Sir Henry Bessemer, inventor of the steel-making process that bears his name. As additional furnaces were built in Bessemer, the population grew. By the 1930s the town ranked second only to Birmingham as a state center for heavy industry. The factories turned out iron and steel, cast-iron pipe, steel railway cars, explosives, fertilizer, and building materials. Today various industries dominate Bessemer's economy; the medical community is among the city's largest employers.

What to See and Do

Hall of History Museum. Displays of pioneer life in Jefferson County, Mound Indians, prehistoric life, the Civil War, and Bessemer city history. (Tues-Sat; closed hols) In Southern Railway Depot, 1905 Alabama Ave. Phone 205/426-1633. **Donation**

Tannehill State Historical Park.
Restored ironworks that once produced 20 tons of pig iron a day for
the Confederacy. Iron & Steel
Museum (daily). Park features bathhouses, fishing; nature trails, picnicking, concession, camping (hookups,
dump station; fee). Park (daily). 12 mi
SW off I-59, Exit 100 at Bucksville.
Phone 205/477-5711. Day use ¢

Annual Event

Christmas Parade & Tour. Usually
2nd Sat Dec.

Motel/Motor Lodge

★★ **RAMADA INN.** *1121A 9th Ave
SW (35022), on US 11 at jct I-20, I-59.
205/424-9780; fax 205/424-9780; toll-
free 800/272-6232.* 156 rms, 2 story.
S $46-$51; D $52-$57; each addl $6;
under 12 free. Crib free. TV; cable.
Pool; wading pool. Restaurant 6-10
am, 6-9 pm. Bar 3 pm-2 am; entertainment exc Sun. Ck-out noon.
Coin lndry. Meeting rms. Business
servs avail. Some refrigerators. Cr
cds: A, D, DS, MC, V.

Restaurant

★★ **BRIGHT STAR.** *304 19th St N
(35020). 205/424-9444.* Specializes in
Greek broiled red snapper. Hrs: 10:30
am-9 pm; Thurs-Sat to 10 pm. Closed
hols. Res accepted. Bar. Lunch $4-$7;
dinner $9.95-$21.95. Child's menu.
Cr cds: A, D, DS, MC, V.

Unrated Dining Spot

BOB SYKES BAR-B-QUE. *1724 9th
Ave N (35020). 205/426-1400. Email
oink@aol.com; www.bobsykes.com.* Specializes in open pit barbecued pork,
homemade pies. Hrs: 10 am-10 pm.
Closed Sun; Jan 1, Thanksgiving, Dec
25. Lunch, dinner $2.50-$8. Family-
owned. Cr cds: A, D, DS, MC, V.

Birmingham

(C-3) *See also Bessemer, Cullman*

Founded 1871 **Pop** 265,968
Elev 601 ft **Area code** 205
Web www.birminghamal.org

Information Convention & Visitors
Bureau, 2200 9th Ave N, 35203;
205/458-8000 or 800/458-8085

A city of great industrial strength,
Birmingham once proudly called
itself the "Pittsburgh of the South."
Today Birmingham is equally proud
of its reputation as an international
medical center. Advances in medical
science through research at the University of Alabama medical complex
attract patients worldwide.

At the turn of the 19th century,
Native Americans who painted their
faces and weapons red were known
by early settlers as "Red Sticks." Even
when the red paint was found to be
hematite iron ore, it was still considered worthless, and many years
passed before Red Mountain ore
became the foundation for Birmingham's steel industry. The Confederacy's lack of iron in 1863 led to the
building of a small blast furnace
which produced cannonballs and
rifles until Wilson's Raiders destroyed
it in 1865.

Birmingham was born in 1871
when two railroads intersected. A
year later the Elyton Land Company
had sold most of its 4,150 acres at
fabulous prices. (It had bought the
land for $25 an acre.) But in 1873 a
double disaster struck. First, cholera
drove hundreds from the new city;
then, the nationwide financial panic
nearly doomed Birmingham to
extinction. Refusing to give in,
Charles Linn, a former Civil War
blockade runner who had opened a
small bank in 1871, built a grand
three-story brick bank for the huge
(at that time) sum of $36,000. He
then sent out 500 invitations to a
"Calico Ball," as he called it, to celebrate its opening. Guests came from
all over the state, women in ball
gowns and men in formal dress all

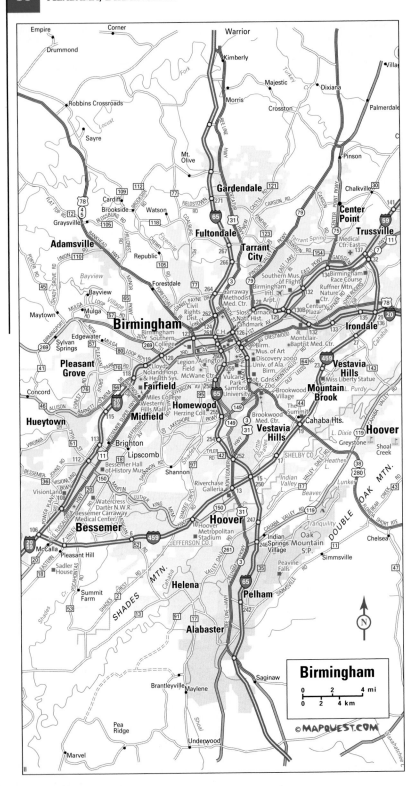

Birmingham

cut from calico. "Linn's folly" paid off—Birmingham was saved.

Today Birmingham is a modern, progressive city—one of culture as well as steel, and of education as well as the social life that began with the Calico Ball. To visitors it offers much in recreational and sightseeing opportunities. Birmingham Green, a major renaissance of the downtown area, added walkways, plantings, benches, and the DART trolley. The Five Points South area, featuring clubs with many styles of quality entertainment, plays a major role in Birmingham's nightlife. This is indeed the heart of the New South.

Transportation

Birmingham International Airport. Information 205/599-0500; lost and found 205/458-8002; weather 205/945-7000.

Car Rental Agencies. See IMPORTANT TOLL-FREE NUMBERS.

Public Transportation. Buses (Birmingham/Jefferson County Transit Authority); 205/521-0101.

Rail Passenger Service. Amtrak; 800/872-7245.

What to See and Do

Alabama Sports Hall of Fame Museum. Showcase for memorabilia of Alabama sports figures; sound-sensored displays; theater. (Daily; closed hols) Civic Center Blvd & 22nd St N. Phone 205/323-6665. ¢¢

Arlington. (ca 1850) Birmingham's last remaining antebellum house in the Greek Revival style features a diverse collection of 19th-century American decorative art. Located on a sloping hill in Elyton, the house is surrounded by shady lawns, oak and magnolia trees, and seasonal plantings. (Tues-Sun; closed hols) 331 Cotton Ave SW. Phone 205/780-5656. ¢¢

Birmingham Botanical Gardens. Incl orchids, lilies, dogwood, wildflowers, azaleas; 26-ft floral clock, conservatory, and arboretum of rare plants, shrubs, and trees. Restaurant on grounds. (Daily) 2612 Lane Park Rd. Phone 205/879-1227. **FREE** Incl

Japanese Gardens. Gardens landscaped with Asian plants, waterfalls. Also here is a bonsai

complex, Asian statuary, and a Zen garden. Gravel paths. (Daily) **FREE**

Birmingham Civil Rights Institute. Exhibits portray struggle for civil rights in Birmingham and across the nation from the 1920s to the present; multimedia presentations. (Tues-Sun; closed hols) 520 16th St N. Phone 205/328-9696. ¢

Birmingham-Jefferson Convention Complex. The entire complex covers 7 sq blks. The center contains 220,000 sq ft of exhibition space; 3,000-seat concert hall; 1,100-seat theater; 18,000-seat coliseum. Between 9th & 11th Aves N, 19th & 21st Sts. Phone 205/458-8400 for event information.

Birmingham Museum of Art. Features collections of Renaissance, Asian, and American art, incl Remington bronzes; 20th-century collection; 17th-19th-century American and European paintings and decorative arts. Also featured are pre-Columbian art and artifacts, art of the Native American, and the largest collection of Wedgwood outside of England. Changing exhibits. Multilevel sculpture garden with 2 reflecting pools and a waterfall. (Tues-Sun; closed hols) 2000 8th Ave N, across from Linn Park. Phone 205/254-2565. **FREE**

Birmingham-Southern College. (1856) 1,900 students. A 200-acre campus on wooded rolling hills. Here is the state's first planetarium (phone 205/226-4771; fee). Tours of campus. Arkadelphia Rd. Phone 205/226-4600.

Birmingham Zoo. Nearly 1,000 animals on display. Highlights incl sea lions, Siberian tiger, and the predator building. (Daily) 2630 Cahaba Rd. Phone 205/879-0409. ¢¢

DeSoto Caverns Park. (See SYLACAUGA) Approx 38 mi SE via AL 280 to AL 76.

Miles College. (1905) 700 students. Extensive collection of African-American literature; exhibits of African art forms. Two historic landmark bldgs. Tours. 5500 Myron Massey Blvd in Fairfield. Phone 205/929-1000.

Oak Mountain State Park. Peavine Falls and Gorge and 2 lakes sit amidst 9,940 acres of the state's most

Birmingham skyline at sunset

rugged mountains. Swimming, fishing, boating (marina, ramp, rentals); hiking, backpacking, and bridle trails, golf (18 holes; fee), tennis, picnicking (shelters, barbecue pits, fireplaces), concession, camping, cabins. Demonstration farm. Standard fees. 15 mi S on I-65, Exit 246, near Pelham. Phone 205/620-2524.

Red Mountain Museum and Road Cut. Natural history museum located on slopes of Red Mt. Extensive collection of fossils incl a 14-ft mosasaur (extinct marine lizard); geologic history displays and exhibits; hands-on exhibits. Walkway carved into the face of the mountain above expressway. More than 150 million yrs of geologic history are exposed for ⅓ of a mile. Picnicking. (Daily; closed hols) 1421 22nd St S. Phone 205/933-4153. ¢

Rickwood Caverns State Park. This 380-acre park offers swimming pools; hiking, carpet golf, miniature train ride, picnicking, concession, gift shop. Primitive and improved camping (standard fees). One-hr tours of cave with 260 million-yr-old limestone formations (Memorial Day-Labor Day, daily; rest of Sep-Oct and Mar-May, wkends). Park (all yr); pool (seasonal). Fee for some activities. 20 mi N on I-65 to Exit 284 (just N of Warrior) then 4 mi W on Skyline Dr to Rickwood Rd, follow state signs. Phone 205/647-9692. Park entrance ¢; Cave tour ¢¢¢

Ruffner Mountain Nature Center. 538 acres of the last undeveloped section of this area's Appalachian Mts. Displays focus on Ruffner Mt's biology, geology, and history. Wildlife refuge with nature trails. (Tues-Sun; closed hols) Fee for special

programs. 1214 81st St S. Phone 205/833-8112. **FREE**

Samford University. (1841) 4,600 students. A 172-acre campus with brick Georgian Colonial buildings. The Samford Murals on view in Rotunda, Dwight and Lucille Beeson Center for the Healing Arts. Beeson Divinity Hall Chapel is topped by a copper-clad dome that has a detailed ceiling mural on the interior (tours avail). Tours of campus. 800 Lakeshore Dr in Shades Mt section. Phone 205/870-2011 or 205/870-2921.

Sloss Furnaces National Historic Landmark. An industrial museum and site for concerts and downtown festivals. (Tues-Sun) 20 32nd St N. Phone 205/324-1911 for event and further information. **FREE**

University of Alabama at Birmingham. 16,500 students. 70-sq-blk area on S edge of downtown. **Reynolds Historical Library** in the Lister Hill Library of the Health Sciences, 1700 University Blvd, 6 blks W of US 31 and US 280, has collections of ivory anatomical manikins, original manuscripts, and rare medical and scientific books. **Alabama Museum of Health Sciences** has memorabilia of Alabama doctors, surgeons, optometrists, and other medical practitioners; reproductions of doctor and dentist turn-of-the-century offices (Mon-Fri). Phone 205/934-4475.

Vulcan. (1904) The figure of Vulcan, designed for the Louisiana Purchase Exposition in St. Louis, is one of the largest iron figures ever cast, standing 55 ft tall and weighing 60 tons. It surveys the city from a pedestal 124 ft high. Made of Birmingham iron and cast locally, Vulcan, Roman god of fire and forge, legendary inventor of smithing and metalworking, stands as a monument to the city's iron industry atop Red Mt; and since 1939, he holds a lighted torch aloft over the city. A glass-enclosed elevator takes passengers to observation deck. Vulcan's torch shines bright red when there's been a traffic fatality in the city in the previous 24 hrs. (Daily; closed Thanksgiving, Dec 25). On Valley Ave off US 31 at top of Red Mountain in Vulcan Park. Phone 205/328-6198 or 205/328-2863. ¢

Annual Events

Festival of Arts. Different country featured each yr. Mid-Apr.

City Stages. Music festival, street vendors, and regional craftsmen. Mid-June.

State Fair. Alabama State Fairgrounds. Contact Alabama State Fair Authority, 2331 Bessemer Rd, 35209; 205/786-8100. Ten days mid-late Oct.

Additional Visitor Information

Contact the Greater Birmingham Convention & Visitors Bureau, 2200 9th Ave N, 35203; 205/458-8000; or the Birmingham/Jefferson Visitor Information Center, 1201 University Blvd, 35233; 205/458-8001.

City Neighborhoods

Many of the restaurants, unrated dining establishments, and some lodgings listed under Birmingham incl neighborhoods as well as exact street addresses. Geographic descriptions of the Downtown and Five Points are given.

Downtown. S of 10th Ave N, W of 26th St, N of L & N Railroad tracks, and E of 15th St N. **N of Downtown:** N of US 20/US 59. **S of Downtown:** S of First Ave. **E of Downtown:** E of 26th St.

Five Points. Area at the intersection of 20th St S and Highland Ave.

Motels/Motor Lodges

★★ **BAYMONT INN & SUITES.** 513 Cahaba Park Cir (35242), I-459 and US 280, S of Downtown. 205/995-9990; fax 205/995-0563; res 800/301-0200. www.baymontinns.com. 102 rms, 3 story. S $41.95; D $47.95; each addl $7; suites $55.95-$62.95; under 18 free. Crib free. Pet accepted, some restrictions. TV; cable (premium). Complimentary continental bkfst. Ck-out noon. Meeting rm. Business servs avail. In-rm modem link. Cr cds: A, DS, MC, V.

[D] [symbols] [SC]

★★ **BEST WESTERN RIME GARDEN INN.** 5320 Beacon Dr (35210), I-20, Exit 133, E of Downtown. 205/951-1200; fax 205/951-1602; res 800/528-1234; toll-free 888/882-8178. www.bestwesternrime.com. 290 suites, 3 story. 1-bedrm $75; 2-bedrm $125; each addl $10; under 12 free; wkend, wkly, monthly rates. Crib free. TV; cable. Pool. Complimentary continental bkfst. Restaurant 6:30-9:30 am, 11 am-1:30 pm, 5-10 pm; wkends hrs vary. Bar 5-11 pm. Ck-out noon. Meeting rms. Business servs avail. Valet serv. Airport transportation. Tennis privileges. Private patios, balconies. Cr cds: A, C, D, DS, MC, V.

[D] [symbols]

★★ **COMFORT INN CENTRAL.** 195 Oxmoor Rd (35209), S of Downtown. 205/941-0990; fax 205/941-1527; toll-free 800/638-7949. 155 rms, 2 story. S $60; D $69; each addl $8; under 18 free. Crib free. TV; cable (premium). Pool. Complimentary continental bkfst. Restaurant adj open 24 hrs. Ck-out 11 am. Meeting rms. Business center. Valet serv. Exercise equipt. Cr cds: A, C, D, DS, JCB, MC, V.

[D] [symbols] [SC]

★★★ **COURTYARD BY MARRIOTT.** 500 Shades Creek Pkwy (35209), S via I-65. 205/879-0400; fax 205/879-6324; toll-free 800/321-2211. 140 rms, 1-3 story, 14 suites. S $86; D $98; suites $95-$110; wkend rates. Crib free. TV; cable. Pool; whirlpool. Restaurant 6:30 am-11 am; Sat, Sun from 7 am. Bar 5-11 pm. Meeting rms. Business servs avail. In-rm modem link. Guest lndry. Valet serv. Exercise equipt. Private patios, balconies. Cr cds: A, C, D, DS, MC, V.

[D] [symbols] [SC]

★ **DAYS INN AIRPORT.** 5101 Airport Hwy (35212), I-20/I-59 Airport Exit, near Municipal Airport, E of Downtown. 205/592-6110; fax 205/591-5623; res

800/329-7466. 138 rms, 5 story. S $48-$55; D $53-$61; each addl $5; under 18 free. TV; cable. Pool. Playground. Ck-out noon. Business servs avail. Airport transportation. Exercise equipt. Cr cds: A, D, DS, MC, V.

★★ **FAIRFIELD INN BY MARRIOTT.** *155 Vulcan Rd (35209), 3 mi S on I-65 Exit 256. 205/945-9600; fax 205/945-9600.* 132 rms, 3 story. S $54.95; D $65.95-$70.95; under 18 free. Crib free. TV; cable. Complimentary continental bkfst. Ck-out noon. Business servs avail. In-rm modem link. Cr cds: A, C, D, DS, MC, V.

★★ **HAMPTON INN.** *2731 US 280 (35223), S on I-65, NE on Oxmoor Rd to US 280. 205/870-7822; fax 205/871-7610; toll-free 800/426-7866.* 131 rms, 5 story. S $62; D $62-$67; under 18 free. Crib free. Pet accepted, some restrictions. TV; cable. Pool. Complimentary continental bkfst. Restaurant adj 6 am-11 pm. Ck-out noon. Meeting rm. Business servs avail. In-rm modem link. Cr cds: A, C, D, DS, MC, V.

★★ **HAMPTON INN BIRMINGHAM-EAST.** *3910 Kilgore Memorial Dr (35210), E of Downtown. 205/956-4100; fax 205/956-0906; res 800/426-7866.* 70 rms, 2 story. S $65-$69; D $69-$73; under 18 free; higher rates special events. Crib free. TV; cable (premium). Pool. Complimentary continental bkfst. Restaurant nearby. Ck-out noon. Meeting rms. Business servs avail. Health club privileges. Cr cds: A, C, D, DS, MC, V.

★★ **HAMPTON INN COLONNADE.** *3400 Colonnade Pkwy (35243), S of Downtown. 205/967-0002; fax 205/969-0901; res 800/426-7866; toll-free 800/861-7168. Email bhmco01@hi hotel.com.* 133 rms, 5 story. S $72-$88; D $81-$97; under 18 free; higher rates sports events. Crib free. TV; cable (premium). Pool. Complimentary continental bkfst. Coffee in rms. Restaurant nearby. Ck-out noon. Meeting rms. Business servs avail. In-rm modem link. Health club privileges. Cr cds: A, C, D, DS, MC, V.

★★ **HOLIDAY INN.** *5000 10th Ave N (35212), near Municipal Airport, E of Downtown. 205/591-6900; fax 205/591-2093.* 224 rms, 9 story. S, D $69. Crib free. TV; cable (premium); VCR avail (movies). Pool. Restaurant 6 am-2 pm, 5-10 pm. Bar; entertainment exc Sun. Ck-out noon. Meeting rms. Business servs avail. In-rm modem link. Bellhops. Free airport transportation. Cr cds: A, C, D, DS, MC, V.

★ **LA QUINTA MOTOR INN.** *905 11th Ct W (35212), near jct I-20, US 78, N of Downtown. 205/324-4510; fax 205/252-7972.* 106 rms, 3 story. S, D $57-$77; each addl $10; under 18 free. Crib free. Pet accepted, some restrictions. TV; cable. Pool. Complimentary continental bkfst. Restaurant adj open 24 hrs. Ck-out noon. Meeting rms. Cr cds: A, C, D, DS, MC, V.

★★ **MOTEL BIRMINGHAM.** *7905 Crestwood Blvd (35210), I-20 Montevallo Rd Exit, E of Downtown. 205/956-4440; fax 205/956-3011.* 242 rms, 1-2 story, 18 kits. (no equipt). S $48-$63; D, kit. units $58-$68; suites $95-$250; under 16 free. Crib free. Pet accepted, some restrictions; $15. TV; cable (premium). Pool. Playground. Complimentary continental bkfst. Restaurant adj open 24 hrs. Ck-out noon. Meeting rms. Business center. In-rm modem link. Valet serv. Health club privileges. Cr cds: A, C, D, DS, MC, V.

★★ **RESIDENCE INN BY MARRIOTT.** *3 Greenhill Pkwy (35242), at US 280, S of Downtown. 205/991-8686; fax 205/991-8729; toll-free 800/331-3131. www.marriott.com.* 128 kit. suites, 2 story. Kit. suites $104-$129; wkly, monthly rates. Crib free. Pet accepted; $165-$215. TV; cable. Pool; whirlpool. Complimentary continental bkfst. Ck-out noon. Coin lndry. Meeting rms. Business servs avail. Valet serv. Health club privileges. Sport court. Gas grills. Cr cds: A, C, D, DS, MC, V.

Hotels

★★★ EMBASSY SUITES. *2300 Woodcrest Pl (35051), S of Downtown. 205/879-7400; fax 205/870-4523. www.embassy-suites.com.* 243 units, 8 story. S, D $100-$150; each addl $10; under 12 free; wkend rates. Crib free. TV; cable, VCR (movies $6). Indoor pool; whirlpool. Complimentary full bkfst. Restaurant 11 am-10 pm. Bar to midnight. Ck-out noon. Meeting rms. Business servs avail. In-rm modem link. Gift shop. Free airport transportation. Sauna. Health club privileges. Refrigerators. Cr cds: A, C, D, DS, MC, V.

D ⇌ 🏋 ⊠ 🐾 SC

★★ HOLIDAY INN SOUTH ON THE LAKE. *1548 Montgomery Hwy (35216), S of Downtown. 205/822-4350; fax 205/822-0350; res 800/465-4329. Email sbruner@lodgian.com; www.holiday-inn.com/hotels/bhmso.* 164 rms, 3 story, 1 suite. Apr, Oct: S, D $59; under 18 free; lower rates rest of yr. Crib avail. Pet accepted, fee. Parking lot. Pool, whirlpool. TV; cable (premium). Complimentary coffee in rms, newspaper, toll-free calls. Restaurant 6 am-10 pm. Bar. Ck-out noon, ck-in 3 pm. Meeting rms. Business center. Dry cleaning, coin lndry. Exercise privileges. Golf. Tennis. Picnic facilities. Cr cds: A, C, D, DS, JCB, MC, V.

D 🐾 ⛷ 🏋 🎿 ⇌ 🏋 🏃 ⊠ 🐾 🎿

★★ MOUNTAIN BROOK INN. *2800 US 280 S (35223), S of Downtown. 205/870-3100; fax 205/414-2128; toll-free 800/523-7771. Email info@mountainbrookinn.com; www.chamberline.net/mountainbrookinn/.* 162 rms, 8 story. S $115; D $125; each addl $10; suites $199; under 18 free; wkend rates. Crib free. Pet accepted. TV; cable (premium). Pool. Restaurant 6:30 am-10 pm. Bar noon-2 am; entertainment. Ck-out noon. Meeting rms. Business servs avail. In-rm modem link. Free airport transportation. Health club privileges. Bathrm phones; wet bar in some suites. Cr cds: A, DS, MC, V.

D 🐾 ⇌ ⊠ 🐾 SC

★★ PICKWICK HOTEL AND CONFERENCE CENTER. *1023 20th St S (35205), Downtown. 205/933-9555; fax 205/933-6918; res 800/255-7304.* www.pickwickhotel.com. 63 rms, 8 story, 28 suites. S, D $86-$89; each addl $10; suites $109; under 12 free; wkend rates. Crib free. Pet accepted, some restrictions; $50. TV. Complimentary continental bkfst. Ck-out noon. Business servs avail. In-rm modem link. Shopping arcade. Barber, beauty shop. Free covered parking. Health club privileges. Some refrigerators. In historical area. Art Deco decor. Cr cds: A, DS, MC, V.

D 🐾 ⊠ 🐾 SC

★★★ RADISSON HOTEL. *808 S 20th St (35205), at University Blvd, opp Medical Center, S of Downtown. 205/933-9000; fax 205/933-0920. www.radisson.com.* 287 rms, 14 story. S, D $109-$119; each addl $10; suites $150-$500; family rates; some wkend rates. TV; cable. Pool. Sauna. Restaurant 6:30 am-10 pm. Bars 4 pm-midnight. Ck-out noon. Convention facilities. Business servs avail. In-rm modem link. Barber, beauty shop. Free covered parking. Airport transportation. Health club privileges. Cr cds: A, C, D, DS, ER, MC, V.

D ⇌ ⊠ 🐾 SC

★★ RAMADA INN AIRPORT. *5216 Airport Hwy (35212), I-20/I-59, Airport Exit, E of Downtown. 205/591-7900; fax 205/592-6476; toll-free 800/767-2426.* 187 rms, 4 story, 7 suites. S $74; D $82; each addl $8; suites $125; under 17 free. Crib avail. Parking lot. Pool. TV; cable (premium). Complimentary coffee in rms, newspaper, toll-free calls. Restaurant 6 am-10 pm. Bar. Ck-out noon, ck-in 3 pm. Meeting rms. Business center. Bellhops. Dry cleaning. Free airport transportation. Exercise equipt. Golf, 18 holes. Tennis, 4 courts. Video games. Cr cds: A, C, D, DS, ER, JCB, MC, V.

D 🏋 🎿 ⇌ 🏋 ✈ ⊠ 🐾 SC 🏃

★★ RED MONT BY WINDHAM. *2101 5th Ave (35203), Downtown. 205/324-2101; fax 205/324-0610.* 112 rms, 12 story. S, D $99-$109; each addl $12; suites $124-$169; under 18 free. Crib free. TV; cable (premium), VCR avail. Restaurant 6:30 am-2 pm, 5-10 pm. Bar from 4 pm. Ck-out noon. Meeting rms. Business servs avail. In-rm modem link. Concierge serv. Free airport transportation.

Health club privileges. Refrigerators. Cr cds: A, C, D, DS, JCB, MC, V.

⬛ ⬛ ⬛ 🆂🅲

★ ★ ★ **SHERATON BIRMINGHAM HOTEL.** *2101 Richard Arrington Jr. Blvd (35203), Downtown.* 205/324-5000; fax 205/307-3045; res 800/325-3535. www.sheraton.com/birmingham. 770 rms, 17 story. S, D $140; each addl $15; suites $215; under 16 free; wkend rates. Crib $15. TV; cable. Indoor pool; whirlpool. Complimentary coffee in rms. Restaurant 6 am-11 pm. Bar 11-2 am; entertainment. Ck-out noon. Convention facilities. Business center. In-rm modem link. Concierge serv. Gift shop. Valet parking. Exercise equipt; sauna, steam rm. Balconies. Cr cds: A, C, D, DS, MC, V.

⬛ ⬛ ⬛ ⬛ ⬛ ⬛ ⬛ ⬛

★ ★ **SHERATON PERIMETER PARK SOUTH.** *8 Perimeter Dr (35243), S of Downtown.* 205/967-2700; fax 205/972-8603; res 800/325-3535; toll-free 800/567-6647. www.starwood.com. 205 rms, 8 story, 2 suites. Sep-May: S $199; D $209; each addl $10; suites $500; under 17 free; lower rates rest of yr. Crib avail. Parking lot. Pool. TV; cable (premium). Complimentary coffee in rms, newspaper, toll-free calls. Restaurant 6:30 am-10 pm. Bar. Ck-out noon, ck-in 3 pm. Meeting rms. Business center. Bellhops. Concierge serv. Dry cleaning. Gift shop. Free airport transportation. Exercise privileges. Tennis. Video games. Cr cds: A, C, D, DS, ER, JCB, MC, V.

⬛ ⬛ ⬛ ⬛ ⬛ ⬛ ⬛ 🆂🅲 ⬛

★ ★ ★ **TUTWILER HOTEL.** *2021 Park Pl N (35203), Downtown.* 205/322-2100; fax 205/325-1183; toll-free 800/996-3426. 147 rms, 8 story, 52 suites. S, D $134-$154; suites $151-$178; under 12 free; wkend rates. Crib free. TV; cable (premium), VCR avail (free movies). Restaurant 6-10 am, 11 am-2 pm, 5-10 pm. Rm serv 24 hrs. Bar 11 am-midnight. Ck-out noon. Meeting rms. Business servs avail. In-rm modem link. Concierge serv. Free valet parking. Free airport, RR station, bus depot transportation. Some bathrm phones; refrigerators avail. Balconies. Luxury level. Cr cds: A, D, DS, MC, V.

⬛ ⬛ ⬛ 🆂🅲

★ ★ **WYNFREY HOTEL.** *1000 Riverchase Galleria (35244), S of Downtown.* 205/987-1600; fax 205/988-4597; toll-free 800/997-3389. www.wynfrey.com. 329 rms, 16 story. S, D $115-$219; suites $250-$825; under 12 free; wkend rates. Crib free. Valet parking $6. TV; cable (premium), VCR avail. Pool; poolside serv. Restaurant 6 am-midnight (see also WINSTON'S). Rm serv 24 hrs. Piano bar. Ck-out 11 am. Convention facilities. Business center. Concierge serv. Airport transportation. Golf privileges. Exercise equipt; steam rm. Health club privileges. Bathrm phone, refrigerator in suites. Luxury level. Elegant decor features marble, brass, and Chippendale and French Regency furnishings. Cr cds: A, C, D, DS, MC, V.

⬛ ⬛ ⬛ ⬛ ⬛ ⬛ ⬛ ⬛ ⬛

Restaurants

★ ★ **ARMAN'S.** *2117 Cahaba Rd (35223), S on I-65, NE on Oxmoor Rd to US 280.* 205/871-5551. Email armans@aol.com. Specializes in seafood, pasta. Hrs: 11 am-2 pm, 6-10 pm; Thurs-Sat to 11 pm. Closed Sun; hols. Res accepted; required Fri, Sat. Bar. Wine list. Lunch, dinner $13.95-$24.95. Valet parking. Bldg once a grocery store. Antique bar. Cr cds: A, DS, MC, V.

⬛ ⬛

★ ★ **BOMBAY CAFE.** *2839 7th Ave S (35233), S of Downtown.* 205/322-1930. Specializes in seafood, veal, lamb. Hrs: 6-9:30 pm; Fri, Sat to 10:30 pm. Closed Sun; hols. Res accepted. Bar. Dinner $14.95-$22.95. Child's menu. Valet parking. Modern decor; marble fireplace, artwork. Cr cds: A, D, DS, MC, V.

⬛ ⬛

★ ★ **BOTTEGA.** *2240 Highland Ave (35205), at Five Points.* 205/939-1000. www.bottegarestaurant.com. Specializes in veal, homemade ravioli, seafood. Hrs: 6-10 pm. Closed Sun; hols. Bar. Lunch complete meals: $3.50-$10; dinner complete meals: $5-$20. Child's menu. Valet parking. Lunch in casual cafe-style surroundings; dinner in more formal atmosphere. Cr cds: A, MC, V.

⬛

★ ★ **COBB LANE.** *1 Cobb Ln (35205), at Five Points.* 205/933-0462. Specializes in shell-crab soup, Southern cuisine, chocolate roulage. Hrs:

11 am-2:30 pm, 5-9 pm. Closed Sun. Res accepted. Bar. Lunch a la carte entrees: $6.95-$13.95; dinner a la carte entrees: $13.95-$17.95. In historic district. Cr cds: A, C, D, DS, MC, V.

[D] [⊟]

★★ **CONNIE KANAKIS' CAFE.** *3423 Colonade Pkwy (35243), in shopping center, S of Downtown.* 205/967-5775. *Email ckanakis1@aol.com.* Specializes in seafood, steak. Hrs: 11 am-10 pm; Sat 5-11 pm. Closed Sun; hols. Res accepted. Bar. Lunch $4-$9.50; dinner $7.95-$27.95. Child's menu. Cr cds: A, C, D, DS, MC, V.

[D]

★ **FORMOSA CHINESE RESTAURANT.** *2109 Lorna Ridge Ln (35216), S on I-65 to Hoover Exit, then 1 mi W to Lorna Ridge Ln.* 205/979-6684. Specializes in egg rolls, Mongolian beef, sesame chicken. Hrs: 11 am-2:30 pm, 5-9:30 pm; Fri, Sat to 10:30 pm. Closed July 4, Thanksgiving, Dec 25. Res accepted. Bar. Lunch $5-$6; dinner $6.25-$25. Chinese decor. View of flower garden. Cr cds: A, D, MC, V.

[⊟]

★ **GOLDEN CITY CHINESE RESTAURANT.** *4647 Hwy 280 (35242), in Riverhills Shopping Center, S of Downtown.* 205/991-3197. Specializes in Mongolian beef, chicken with vegetables. Hrs: 11 am-2:30 pm, 5-9:30 pm. Closed hols. Res accepted. Bar. Lunch á la carte entrees: $3.99-$5.46; dinner á la carte entrees: $6.40-$18. Asian decor. Cr cds: A, D, MC, V.

[⊟]

★★ **GRADY'S AMERICAN GRILL.** *3470 Galleria Cir (35244), adj to Galleria Mall, S of Downtown.* 205/985-4663. Specializes in prime rib, seafood, mesquite-grilled chicken. Hrs: 11 am-10 pm; Fri, Sat to 11 pm. Closed Thanksgiving, Dec 25. Bar. Lunch $5-$15; dinner $5-$15. Child's menu. Cr cds: A, D, DS, MC, V.

[D]

★★★ **HIGHLANDS.** *2011 11th Ave S (35205), at Five Points.* 205/939-1400. *www.highlandsbarandgrill.com.* Specializes in seafood, grain-fed beef. Own pastries, desserts, ice cream.

Hrs: 6-10 pm; Fri, Sat to 10:30 pm. Closed Sun, Mon; hols. Res accepted. Bar. Wine list. Dinner a la carte entrees: $17-$22. Valet parking. Cr cds: A, MC, V.

[D]

★ **LA PAREE.** *2013 5th Ave N (35203), near Civic Center, Downtown.* 205/251-5936. Specializes in fresh gulf seafood, steak, lamb. Hrs: 6:30 am-2:30 pm. Closed Sat, Sun; hols. Bkfst $2.75-$6.95; lunch $4.95-$7.25. Child's menu. Family-owned. Cr cds: D, MC, V.

[⊟]

★★ **NIKI'S WEST.** *233 Finley Ave W (35204), N of Downtown.* 205/252-5751. Specializes in fish, chicken. Hrs: 6 am-9:30 pm. Closed Sun; hols. Res accepted. Bkfst $4-$8.25; lunch $4.75-$9; dinner $7.25-$13.50. Nautical decor. Family-owned. Cr cds: A, D, MC, V.

[D] [⊟]

★★ **ROSSI'S.** *2737 US 280 (35216).* 205/879-2111. Specializes in seafood, steak, Italian dishes. Hrs: 11 am-10 pm; Sat from 5 pm. Closed Sun; hols. Res accepted. Bar. Lunch complete meals: $4.95-$9.95; dinner complete meals: $7.95-$22.95. Child's menu. Cr cds: A, C, D, DS, MC, V.

[D] [SC] [⊟]

★★★ **WINSTON'S.** *1000 Riverchase Galleria.* 205/987-1600. *www.wynfrey hotel.com.* Specializes in seafood, steak. Own baking. Hrs: 6-10 pm. Closed Sun. Bar. Wine list. Dinner á la carte entrees: $17-$28. Valet parking. English decor. Cr cds: A, D, DS, MC, V.

[D]

Clanton

(D-3) *See also Montgomery*

Founded 1873 **Pop** 7,669 **Elev** 599 ft **Area code** 205 **Zip** 35045

Information Chamber of Commerce, PO Box 66; 205/755-2400 or 800/553-0493

A peach and truck farming area, Clanton also caters to fishermen along the Coosa River and its tributaries. Lay and Mitchell dams, to the north and east respectively, are backed by lakes and furnish power to the region. Clanton is the seat of Chilton County.

What to See and Do

Confederate Memorial Park. Two Confederate cemeteries are located on 100 acres that once were the grounds of the Confederate Soldiers Home of Alabama. Museum contains mementos of Alabama's role in the Civil War as well as artifacts, records, documents, and photographs. Also hiking trails, picnicking (shelters). (Daily; closed Jan 1, Dec 25) 10 mi S via US 31 in Marbury. Phone 205/755-1990. **FREE**

Lay Dam. Hydroelectric generating plant offers 30-min guided tours (Daily). Plant (daily). 12 mi NE via AL 145, County 55. Phone 205/755-4520. **FREE**

Motels/Motor Lodges

★ **DAYS INN.** *I-65 & US 31 (35045), 3 mi SE at jct US 31, AL 22, and I-65.* 205/755-0510; fax 205/755-0510; toll-free 800/329-7466. 100 rms, 2 story. S, D $45-$56; each addl $5; under 19 free. Crib free. Pet accepted. TV. Pool; wading pool. Restaurant 6 am-2 pm, 5-10 pm. Bar 4-11 pm, closed Sun. Ck-out noon. Meeting rms. Business servs avail. In-rm modem link. Valet serv. Free airport transportation. Cr cds: A, C, D, DS, MC, V.

★ **KEY WEST INN CLANTON.** *2045 7th Ave S (35045), I-65 Exit 205.* 205/755-8500; fax 205/280-0044. 43 rms, 2 story. S $42; D $46; each addl $5; under 18 free; higher rates fishing tournaments. Crib free. Pet accepted. TV; cable. Complimentary coffee in lobby. Restaurant nearby. Ck-out noon. Coin lndry. Business servs avail. In-rm modem link. Totally nonsmoking. Cr cds: A, C, D, DS, MC, V.

Cullman

(B-3) *See also Birmingham, Decatur*

Founded 1873 **Pop** 13,367 **Elev** 799 ft
Area code 256
Information Cullman Area Chamber of Commerce, 211 Second Ave NE, PO Box 1104, 35056; 205/734-0454

Cullman was founded by Colonel John G. Cullmann, an immigrant whose dream was to build a self-sustaining colony of other German refugees and immigrants. In 1873, five German families settled on the 5,400 square miles of land he purchased from the Louisville & Nashville Railroad. He also laid out the town. Cullman's residents still enjoy the 100-foot-wide streets. In 1880 there were 6,300 people, many of them Germans, in the county that had already been named for Cullmann by the legislature. Located on the Cumberland Plateau, the area is rich in timber and coal. Today Cullman is one of the main centers for agriculture and poultry production.

What to See and Do

✪ **Ave Maria Grotto.** Brother Joseph Zoettl, a Benedictine monk, spent nearly 50 yrs building some 150 miniature replicas of famous churches, buildings, and shrines, incl Bethlehem, Nazareth, Jerusalem, the Basilica of St. Peter, and the California missions, using such materials as cement, stone, bits of jewelry, and marble. The miniatures cover 4 acres of a terraced, landscaped garden. Free picnic grounds adj to parking lot. (Daily; closed Dec 25) I-65 Exit 308. Phone 256/734-4110. ¢¢

Clarkson Covered Bridge. (1904) One of the largest covered bridges in Alabama, the truss-styled Clarkson is 270 ft long and 50 ft high. Also here are a dogtrot cabin and gristmill. Nature trail. Picnic facilities. 9 mi W via US 278W. Phone 256/739-3530. **FREE**

Cullman County Museum. Large 8-rm museum features items related to the origin and history of Cullman.

(Sun-Fri; closed hols) 211 2nd Ave NE. Phone 256/739-1258. ¢

Hurricane Creek Park. Gorge with observation platform; trail over swinging bridge; unusual rock formations, earthquake fault, and waterfalls. Picnic tables. (Daily) 6 mi N on US 31, near Vinemont. Phone 256/734-2125. ¢¢

Sportsman Lake Park. Stocked with bream, bass, catfish, and other fish. Miniature golf; kiddie rides. Picnicking, concession. Camping. (Apr-Sep, daily) Fee for some activities. N off US 31. Phone 256/734-3052. **FREE**

William B. Bankhead National Forest. This 180,684-acre forest incl the Sipsey Wilderness Area, which contains the last remaining stand of old-growth hardwood in the state. Swimming, fishing (bass, bream), boating; hunting (deer, turkey, squirrel), hiking, horseback riding. Fee for some activities. Contact District Ranger, PO Box 278, Double Springs 35553. 25 mi W on US 278. Phone 256/489-5111.

Motels/Motor Lodges

★ **DAYS INN.** *1841 4th St. SW (35055), jct I-65 and US 278. 256/739-3800; fax 256/739-3800; toll-free 800/329-7466.* 117 rms, 2 story. S, D $41-$52; each addl $5; family, wkly rates. Crib free. Pet accepted; $3. TV; cable (premium). Pool. Playground. Complimentary full bkfst. Restaurant 6 am-8 pm. Ck-out noon. Meeting rms. Business servs avail. In-rm modem link. Sundries. Picnic tables. Cr cds: A, C, D, DS, MC, V.
🐾 ➰ 🏊 ⛰ SC

★★ **RAMADA INN.** *1600 County Rd 437 (36301), I-65 and AL 69 W, ¼ mi E of I-65 Cullman-Good Hope Exit. 205/734-8484; fax 205/739-4126; toll-free 800/272-6232.* 126 rms, 1-2 story. S, D $40-$60; each addl $5; under 18 free. Crib free. Pet accepted. TV; cable (premium). Indoor pool; whirlpool. Restaurant 6 am-2 pm, 5-10 pm. Ck-out noon. Coin lndry. Meeting rms. In-rm modem link. Cr cds: A, C, D, DS, JCB, MC, V.
D 🐾 ➰ 🏊 ⛰ SC

Restaurant

★★ **ALL STEAK.** *314 2nd Ave SW (35055). 256/734-4322.* Specializes in steak, seafood. Own baking. Hrs: 6:30 am-9 pm; Thurs-Sat to 10 pm; Sun to 3 pm. Closed hols. Bkfst $2.50-$4.50; lunch $3.98-$5.50; dinner $5-$26. Child's menu. Cr cds: MC, V.
D

Dauphin Island

(H-I) *See also Mobile*

Pop 824 **Elev** 10 ft **Area code** 334 **Zip** 36528

Dauphin Island is rich in history. Spaniards visited and mapped it in the 16th century. Pierre le Moyne, Sieur d'Iberville, used the island as his base for a short time in 1699. Native Americans left a bit of their past with the "Shell Mound," an ancient monument. Today the island is part of Mobile County and a playground for Mobile's citizens. It is also a haven for birds; a 60-acre sanctuary is home to many local and migratory species.

The Battle of Mobile Bay began on the island on August 5, 1864. Admiral David G. Farragut assembled a fleet of Union warships near the mouth of the bay and faced crossfire from Fort Morgan to his east and Fort Gaines, on Dauphin Island, to his west. He proved successful; both forts were captured, and the port of Mobile was blocked.

Dauphin Island is reached from the north on AL 193, via a four-mile-long, high-rise bridge and causeway, which crosses Grants Pass. The island also has a 3,000-foot paved airstrip. A ferry service to Fort Morgan operates year-round.

What to See and Do

Fort Gaines. This 5-sided fort was begun in 1821 and completed in the 1850s. It was held by Confederate forces from 1861 until its capture by Union land troops on Aug 23, 1864. Museum. (Daily; closed Thanksgiving, Dec 25) At E end of island. Phone 334/861-6992. ¢¢ Nearby is

Dauphin Island Campground. Private path to secluded Gulf beaches, fishing piers, boat launches; hiking trail to Audubon Bird Sanctuary, recreation areas, camping, tent and trailer sites. Phone 334/861-2742 for fee information.

Decatur

(A-3) *See also Athens, Cullman, Huntsville*

Founded 1820 **Pop** 48,761 **Elev** 590 ft
Area code 256
Web www.decaturcvb.org
Information Convention & Visitors Bureau, 719 6th Ave SE, PO Box 2349, 35602; 256/350-2028 or 800/524-6181

Decatur, center of northern Alabama's mountain lakes recreation area, is a thriving manufacturing and market city with historic districts and sprawling public parks.

The town site was selected by President Monroe in 1820. The Surveyor General was instructed to reserve the area near an old Tennessee River crossing. The place was already a settlement called Rhodes Ferry, named for pioneer Dr. Henry Rhodes' ferry business; the new town was named for Commodore Stephen Decatur.

The Civil War placed Decatur in a constant seesaw between invasion and resistance. It was continually attacked and abandoned; in fact, only five buildings were left standing at war's end.

The TVA brought industry to Decatur by creating a nine-foot deep channel in the Tennessee River, making it a port for vessels from as far away as Minneapolis. Wheeler Lake, formed by the TVA's Wheeler Dam (see FLORENCE) downstream, offers fishing, boating, and other recreational activities.

What to See and Do

Cook's Natural Science Museum. Extensive collection of insects; rocks, minerals, coral, sea shells. Mounted wildlife. (Daily; closed hols) 412 13th St SE. Phone 256/350-9347. **FREE**

Mooresville. State's oldest incorporated town is preserved as a living record of 19th-century life. Features the house of Andrew Johnson, who was a tailor's apprentice here; community brick church (ca 1840); frame Church of Christ (1854) in which James Garfield is said to have preached during the Civil War; antebellum houses (private); also the oldest stage coach tavern in the state (1825). Details at Mooresville Post Office, which has original wooden call boxes (1830), mail hand-stamped. (Mon-Sat; closed hols) 6 mi E on AL 20. **FREE**

Old Decatur & Albany historic districts. Walking tour of Victorian neighborhood begins at restored Old Bank on historic Bank St; incl 3 antebellum and 194 Victorian structures. Contact Convention & Visitors Bureau.

Point Mallard Park. A 749-acre park on the Tennessee River. Incl swimming pool, wave pool, water slide, beach (mid-May-Labor Day); hiking and bicycle trails, 18-hole golf course, tennis courts, outdoor ice rink (mid-Nov-mid-Mar), camping (hookups), recreation center. Fee for activities. 1800 Point Mallard Dr SE. Phone 256/351-7777 or 800/669-9283.

Princess Theatre. Renovated Art Deco-style theater featuring children's theater, dramatic and musical groups. 112 2nd Ave NE. Phone 256/340-1778.

Wheeler National Wildlife Refuge. Alabama's oldest and largest (34,500 acres) wildlife refuge. Wintering ground for waterfowl and home to numerous species of animal and plant life. Fishing, boating; hunting (limited, permit required for hunting), picnicking. Bird study and photography. Wildlife Visitor Center and Waterfowl Observation Building. (Mar-Oct, Wed-Sun; rest of yr, daily) 2 mi E via AL 67. Phone 256/350-6639. **FREE**

Annual Events

Alabama Jubilee. Point Mallard Park (see). Highlight of festivities is the hot-air balloon races. Memorial Day wknd.

Spirit of America Festival. Point Mallard Park (see). Games, contests, beauty pageant, concerts, exhibits, fireworks. Early July.

Civil War Reenactment/September Skirmish. Point Mallard Park (see). Re-creates camp life of soldiers; features skirmishes led by General "Fighting Joe" Wheeler. Labor Day wkend.

Racking Horse World Celebration. Southeastern Sports Arena. Well-known event features gaited horses. Last full wk Sep.

Southern Wildlife Festival. Competition and exhibits of wildlife carvings, art work, photography, and duck calling. Third wkend Oct.

All Suite

★★★ COUNTRY INN & SUITES BY CARLSON. *807 Bank St NE (35601), 4 blks W of jct AL 72, US 31.* 256/355-6800; fax 256/350-0965; res 800/456-4000; toll-free 800/288-7332. www.countryinns.com. 3 story, 110 suites. Mar-Sep: S $70; D $80; each addl $10; suites $80; under 15 free; lower rates rest of yr. Crib avail. Parking lot. Pool, whirlpool. TV; cable (premium), VCR avail. Complimentary continental bkfst, coffee in rms, newspaper, toll-free calls. Restaurant nearby 11 am-10 pm. Bar. Ck-out noon, ck-in 3 pm. Meeting rms. Business center. Dry cleaning, coin lndry. Exercise privileges, sauna. Golf, 18 holes. Tennis, 4 courts. Cr cds: A, C, D, DS, ER, JCB, MC, V.

Restaurant

★★ SIMP MCGHEE'S. *725 Bank St (35601).* 256/353-6284. Specializes in seafood, grilled prime rib, Cajun dishes. Hrs: 11 am-1:30 pm, 5:30-10 pm. Closed Sun; hols. Bar. Lunch, dinner $13.95-$19.95. Child's menu. In 1890s dry goods bldg; many antiques. Cr cds: A, C, D, DS, MC, V.

Demopolis (E-2)

Founded 1817 **Pop** 7,512 **Elev** 125 ft
Area code 334 **Zip** 36732
Web www.chamber.demopolis.al.us

Information Demopolis Area Chamber of Commerce, 102 E Washington, PO Box 667; 334/289-0270

Visions of French-made wines and olive oil prompted the first European settlements in this region. The name, meaning "city of the people," is all that remains of the first settlers, a group of French exiles who were, for the most part, habituées of the French court and officers of Napoleon's armies. In July 1817, they were granted four townships by Congress as the "French Emigrants for the Cultivation of the Vine and Olive." In the end, the colonists failed to cope with the wilderness, and by the mid-1820s they had scattered.

Americans came afterward to settle on the banks of the Tombigbee River. They established flourishing cotton plantations in this Black Belt area, and many of their fine Greek Revival mansions still can be seen. Agriculture, beef and dairy cattle, as well as a diversified industry, support Demopolis today.

What to See and Do

Bluff Hall. (1832) Restored antebellum mansion built by the slaves of Allen Glover, a planter and merchant, as a wedding gift for his daughter. The interior has Corinthian columns in drawing rm, period furniture, many marble mantels. Also clothing museum and craft shop. (Tues-Sun; closed hols) 405 N Commissioners St. Phone 334/289-1666. ¢¢

Forkland Park. This park is on 10,000-acre Lake Demopolis, which was formed by a 40-ft-high dam on the Tombigbee River. Waterskiing, fishing, boating (ramp); camping (hookups, dump station; fees). (Mid-Mar-mid-Dec, daily) 12 mi N on US 43, 1 mi W of Forkland on River Rd. Phone 334/289-3540 or 334/289-5530.

Foscue Creek Park. On Lake Demopolis. Boating (ramps); trails, picnic area, pavilion, playground, ballfields, camping (hookups, dump station; fees). (Daily) 2 mi W via US 80W, Exit Maria St, on Lock & Dam Rd. Phone 334/289-3540 or 334/289-5535.

Gaineswood. (1860) Restored 20-rm Greek Revival mansion furnished with many original pieces. (Daily;

closed hols) 805 S Cedar St. Phone 334/289-4846. ¢¢

Magnolia Grove. (1840) Built for wealthy planter Col Isaac Croom, Magnolia Grove was also the home of the builder's nephew, Richmond Pearson Hobson, congressman and admiral who was responsible for sinking the *Merrimac* and for blockading the Spanish fleet in Santiago Harbor in June 1898. Greek Revival house features an unsupported winding stairway; original furnishings. (Tues-Sun) 2 mi S on US 43, then 3 mi E on US 80, then 15 mi NE on AL 69; at 1002 Hobson St in Greensboro. Phone 334/624-8618. ¢¢

Annual Event

Christmas on the River. Children's parade, eve river boat parade, fireworks, arts and crafts. First Sat Dec.

Motels/Motor Lodges

★★ **BEST WESTERN.** *1034 Hwy 80 E (36732).* 334/289-5772; fax 334/289-5772; res 800/528-1234; toll-free 800/438-8141. 70 rms. S $45.95; D $49.95; each addl $2; under 12 free; wkly rates. Crib free. Pet accepted. TV; cable, VCR avail (movies $6). Pool. Complimentary continental bkfst. Ck-out 11 am. Meeting rms. Business center. In-rm modem link. Exercise equipt. Health club privileges. Refrigerators. Cr cds: A, C, D, DS, ER, JCB, MC, V.

★ **DAYS INN.** *1005 Hwy 80 E (36732).* 334/289-2500; fax 334/289-9351; res 800/DAYSINN. 42 rms, 2 story. S $37; D $40; each addl $5; under 12 free; higher rates special events. Crib $1. TV; cable (premium). Pool. Complimentary continental bkfst, coffee in rms. Restaurant nearby. Ck-out 11 am. Coin lndry. Business servs avail. In-rm modem link. Refrigerators. Cr cds: A, C, D, DS, ER, JCB, MC, V.

★ **WINDWOOD INN OF DEMOPOLIS.** *628 Hwy 80 E (36732).* 334/289-1760; fax 334/289-1768; toll-free 800/233-0841. 90 units, 2 kits. S $29-$32; D $31-$35; each addl $5; kit. units $34-$43; under 12 free. Crib free. Pet accepted. TV; cable (premium). Pool. Restaurant adj 5 am-10 pm. Ck-out

11 am. Meeting rm. Business servs avail. Some refrigerators. Cr cds: A, C, D, DS, MC, V.

Restaurant

★ **ELLIS V.** *708 US 80 E (36732).* 334/289-3446. Specializes in steak, catfish. Salad bar. Hrs: 11 am-10 pm; Sun-Tues to 9 pm. Closed hols. Bar. Lunch $4.95-$7.25; dinner $6.95-$15.95. Cr cds: A, D, MC, V.

Dothan

(G-5) *See also Ozark*

Settled 1858 **Pop** 53,589 **Elev** 326 ft
Area code 334
Web www.dothanalcvb.com

Information Dothan Area Convention & Visitors Bureau, 3311 Ross Clark Circle NW, PO Box 8765, 36304; 334/794-6622

This marketing center in the "wiregrass" section of Alabama's southeastern corner is the seat of Houston County. Local agricultural products include peanuts, soybeans, corn, and cattle. Dothan is also a retail center.

The town had a lusty start. It was a rough pioneer settlement full of lumberjacks and turpentine workers in 1889 when the first railroad reached it. As the railroads developed, Dothan's population grew rapidly. The city owes a large part of its growth to its strategic location—almost equidistant from Atlanta, Birmingham, Jacksonville, and Mobile.

What to See and Do

Adventureland Theme Park. Park incl two 10-hole miniature golf courses, a go-cart track, bumper boats, and a game rm. Snack bar. (Daily) Charge for each separate activity. 3738 W Main St. Phone 334/793-9100. ¢¢

Landmark Park. This 60-acre park features an 1890s living-history farm, natural science and history center, planetarium; nature trails, picnic area. (Daily; closed Jan 1, Dec 25) US 431 N. Phone 334/794-3452. ¢

Opera House. (1915) Refurbished historical theater; 590 seats. (Daily) Appt recommended. 115 N St. Andrews St. Phone 334/793-0127. **FREE**

Westgate Park. Recreation facility incl Water World, with child's pool, wave pool, and giant slide (early May-Labor Day, daily; fee); recreation center with indoor pool, tennis, racquetball, basketball courts, and ball fields. (Daily; fee for various activities) Choctaw St & Westgate Pkwy off Ross Clark Circle. Phone 334/793-0221 or 334/793-0297.

Annual Events

Azalea Dogwood Festival. Marked route through residential areas at peak of bloom. Late Mar or early Apr.

National Peanut Festival. Houston County Farm Center. Livestock exhibits, sports events, arts and crafts, midway, beauty pageants, parade. Phone 334/793-4323. Late Oct-early Nov.

Motels/Motor Lodges

★★ **BEST WESTERN DOTHAN INN & SUITES.** 3285 Montgomery Hwy (36303). 334/793-4376; fax 334/793-7720; res 800/528-1234. www.bestwesterndothan.com. 120 rms, 2 story, 30 suites. S, D $57; each addl $5; suites $92; under 12 free. Crib avail. Parking lot. Pool. TV; cable (premium). Complimentary continental bkfst, coffee in rms, newspaper, toll-free calls. Restaurant noon-midnight. Ck-out 11 am, ck-in 1 pm. Business servs avail. Dry cleaning. Free airport transportation. Exercise privileges. Golf. Picnic facilities. Cr cds: A, C, D, DS, JCB, MC, V.

★ **DAYS INN DOTHAN.** 2841 Ross Clark Cir (36301). 334/793-2550; fax 334/793-7962; res 800/329-7466; toll-free 800/544-1448. 120 units, 2 story. S $31-$38; D $36-$48; each addl $5; family rates; some wkend rates. Crib free. Pet accepted; $5. TV; cable (premium). Pool. Coffee in rms. Restaurant adj open 24 hrs. Ck-out noon.

Business servs avail. In-rm modem link. Cr cds: A, D, DS, MC, V.

★★ **HOLIDAY INN SOUTH.** 2195 Ross Clark Cir SE (36301). 334/794-8711; fax 334/671-3781; toll-free 800/777-6611. 144 rms, 2 story. S $50-$56; D $56-$62; each addl $6; under 18 free; suites $64-$74. Pet accepted. TV; cable. Pool. Complimentary full bkfst., coffee in lobby. Restaurant 6 am-9:30 pm; Sun from 7 am. Rm serv (limited hrs). Bar 2:30 pm-2 am. Ck-out noon. Meeting rms. Business servs avail. In-rm modem link. Cr cds: A, C, D, DS, JCB, MC, V.

★★ **HOLIDAY INN WEST.** 3053 Ross Clark Cir (36301). 334/794-6601; fax 334/794-9032. 102 rms, 2 story, 44 suites. S, D $57-$62; suites $66-$71; under 18 free; wkend rates. Crib free. Pet accepted. TV; cable (premium). Pool; wading pool. Restaurant 6 am-9 pm. Bar 5 pm-1 am. Ck-out noon. Meeting rms. Business center. In-rm modem link. Bellhops. Valet serv. Refrigerators avail. Cr cds: A, C, D, DS, MC, V.

★ **MOTEL 6.** 2907 Ross Clark Cir SW (36301). 334/793-6013; fax 334/793-2377. 102 rms, 2 story. S, D $28.99-$34.99; each addl $5-$6; under 17 free. Crib free. Pet accepted. TV; cable. Pool. Coffee in lobby. Ck-out noon. In-rm modem link. Cr cds: A, C, D, DS, MC, V.

Hotels

★★★ **COMFORT INN.** 3593 Ross Clark Cir (36303). 334/793-9090; fax 334/793-4367; res 800/228-5150; toll-free 800/474-7298. 114 rms, 5 story, 8 suites. Jul, Oct: S $80; D $86; each addl $6; suites $94; under 18 free; lower rates rest of yr. Crib avail. Pet accepted, some restrictions. Parking lot. Pool. TV; cable (premium), VCR avail. Complimentary continental bkfst, coffee in rms, newspaper, toll-free calls. Restaurant. Ck-out 1 pm, ck-in 2 pm. Meeting rm. Business center. Dry cleaning. Exercise privileges. Golf. Tennis. Cr cds: A, C, D, DS, JCB, MC, V.

★★★ **RAMADA INN.** *3011 Ross Clark Cir (36301). 334/792-0031; fax 334/794-3134; res 800/272-6232. Email susanramada@aol.com; www. ramada.com.* 114 rms, 2 story, 4 suites. July: S $57; D $67; suites $89; under 10 free; lower rates rest of yr. Crib avail. Valet parking avail. Pool, lap pool, children's pool. TV; cable (DSS), VCR avail. Complimentary full bkfst, coffee in rms, newspaper, toll-free calls. Restaurant 6 am-10 pm. Bar. Ck-out noon, ck-in 3 pm. Meeting rms. Business center. Concierge serv. Dry cleaning, coin lndry. Exercise privileges. Golf. Tennis. Supervised children's activities. Cr cds: A, C, D, DS, MC, V.

Eufaula (F-5)

Settled 1823 **Pop** 13,220 **Elev** 257 ft
Area code 334 **Zip** 36027
Information Chamber of Commerce, 102 N Orange St, PO Box 697, 36027-0697; 334/687-6664 or 334/687-6665

This city stands on a bluff rising 200 feet above Lake Eufaula, a 45,000-acre impoundment of the Chattahoochee River known throughout the area for its excellent bass fishing.

What to See and Do

Eufaula National Wildlife Refuge. Partially located in Georgia and superimposed on the Walter F. George Reservoir, the refuge was established to provide a feeding and resting area for waterfowl migrating between the Tennessee Valley and the Gulf Coast. Ducks, geese, egrets, and herons are among the 281 species of birds found at the refuge; beaver, fox, bobcat, and deer are among the 16 species of mammals. Observation tower, nature trail; hunting; photography. (Daily) Contact Refuge Manager, 509 Old Hwy 165; 10 mi N on US 431, AL 165. Phone 334/687-4065. **FREE**

Hart House. (ca 1850) Single-story Greek Revival white frame structure with fluted Doric columns on porch serves as headquarters for the Historic Chattahoochee Commission and Visitor Information Center for the Chattahoochee Trace of Alabama and Georgia. (Mon-Fri) 211 N Eufaula Ave. Phone 334/687-9755 or 334/687-6631. **FREE**

Lakepoint Resort State Park. A 1,220-acre picturesque park on the shores of the 45,200-acre Lake Eufaula. Swimming, fishing, boating (marina); hiking, 18-hole golf (fee), tennis, picnicking, concession, restaurant, resort inn. Camping, cottages. Standard fees. 7 mi N off US 431. Phone 334/687-6676 or 334/687-8011.

Shorter Mansion. Neoclassical mansion built in 1906; 2 floors contain antique furnishings, Confederate relics, and memorabilia of 6 state governors from Barbour County. (Daily; closed hols) Mini-tour by appt (fee). 340 N Eufaula Ave. Phone 334/687-3793. ¢¢ Mansion is headquarters for the Eufaula Heritage Association and is part of

Seth Lore and Irwinton Historic District. Second-largest historic district in Alabama, with approx 582 registered landmarks. Mixture of Greek Revival, Italianate, and Victorian houses, churches, and commercial structures built between 1834-1911. Many are private. Obtain driving tour brochure from the Chamber of Commerce or Eufaula Heritage Association, PO Box 486.

Annual Events

Eufaula Pilgrimage. Daytime and candlelight tours of antebellum houses and churches, antique show and sales, historic reenactments, and Civil War displays. Phone 334/687-3793. First or 2nd wkend Apr.

Indian Summer Days. Festival incl arts and crafts, music, food, children's activities. Phone 334/687-6664. First or 2nd wkend Oct.

Motels/Motor Lodges

★★ **BEST WESTERN EUFAULA INN.** *1375 US 431 S (36027), on Dothan Hwy (US 431 S). 334/687-3900; fax 334/687-6870; res 800/528-*

1234. 42 rms, 2 story. S $38-$42; D $42-$48; each addl $4; under 12 free; higher rates: Eufaula Pilgrimage, wkend of July 4. Crib free. TV; cable, VCR avail (movies). Pool. Complimentary continental bkfst. Restaurant opp 10 am-10 pm. Ck-out 11 am. Business servs avail. In-rm modem link. Some refrigerators. Cr cds: A, D, DS, MC, V.

★★ **RAMADA INN.** *US 82 and Riverside Dr (36027). 334/687-2021; fax 334/687-2021; res 800/272-6232. www.ramada.com.* 96 rms, 2 story. S $44.50-$55; D $49.50-$66.50; each addl $5; suites $61.50-$65.50; under 18 free; golf plans. Crib free. Pet accepted. TV; cable (premium). Pool. Restaurant 6 am-10 pm. Bar 4 pm-midnight. Ck-out noon. Meeting rms. Business servs avail. In-rm modem link. Bellhops. On lake. Cr cds: A, C, D, DS, ER, JCB, MC, V.

Resort

★★ **LAKEPOINT RESORT.** *US 431 N PO Box 267 (36072), 7 mi N. 334/687-8011; fax 334/687-3273; res 800/ALAPARK; toll-free 800/544-5253. www.dcnr.state.al.us.* 89 rms, 2 story, 6 suites. Mar-Oct: S $49; D $58; each addl $5; suites $116; lower rates rest of yr. Parking lot. Pool, lifeguard. TV; cable (DSS). Restaurant 7 am-10 pm. Bar. Ck-out 11 am, ck-in 1 pm. Meeting rms. Business servs avail. Coin lndry. Gift shop. Golf, 18

Great Blue Heron

holes. Tennis, 6 courts. Beach access. Hiking trail. Picnic facilities. Cr cds: A, MC, V.

Evergreen (F-3)

Pop 3,911 **Elev** 367 ft **Area code** 334 **Zip** 36401
Web www.evergreen@alabama-net.com

Information Chamber of Commerce, 100 Depot Square; 334/578-1707

The seat of Conecuh County, this town is appropriately named for its abundance of evergreens. Each year carloads of Christmas trees and other evergreen products for use as decoration are shipped from the town.

What to See and Do

Conecuh National Forest. This 84,400-acre forest, mostly of southern pine, offers swimming (at Blue Pond, fee per vehicle), fishing, boating; hunting, hiking incl 20 mi of the Conecuh Tr, campsites at Open Pond only (fee for overnight). Contact District Ranger, US Forest Service, Rte 5, Box 157, Andalusia 36420. 25 mi E on US 84, then 11 mi S on US 29. Phone 334/222-2555 or Supervisor, 2946 Chestnut St, Montgomery 36107; 334/832-4470.

Motels/Motor Lodges

★★ **COMFORT INN.** *I-65/83 Bates Rd (36401), 1 blk W on AL 83 Business, I-65 Exit 96. 334/578-4701; fax 334/578-3180; res 800/228-5150. www.tourist hotelinternational.com.* 58 rms, 2 story. S $38; D $50; each addl $5. Crib $5. Pet accepted; $5. TV; cable (premium). Pool. Restaurant adj open 24 hrs. Ck-out 11 am. Business servs avail. In-rm modem link. Cr cds: A, C, D, DS, JCB, MC, V.

★ **DAYS INN.** *Rte 2 Box 389 (36401), I-65 and US 83, Exit 96.* 334/578-2100; fax 334/578-2100; res 800/329-7466. www.daysinn.com. 40 rms, 2 story, 4 suites. Mid-June-Labor Day: S, D $48; each addl $5; suites $55-$60; under 12 free; lower rates rest of yr. Crib free. Pet accepted, some restrictions; $5. TV; cable (premium). Complimentary continental bkfst. Ck-out 11 am. Cr cds: A, C, D, DS, JCB, MC, V.

D ◀ 🐾 💺 🏊 🏃

Florence

(A-2) *See also Russellville*

Settled 1779 **Pop** 36,426 **Elev** 541 ft
Area code 205 **Zip** 35630
Web www.flo-tour.org
Information Florence/Lauderdale Tourism, One Hightower Place; 256/740-4141 or 888/356-8687

First settled as a trading post, Florence is still the trading center of a large area. With Sheffield, Tuscumbia, and Muscle Shoals, Florence lies along the Tennessee River's famous shoals area near Wilson Dam. Inexpensive TVA power helped to bring a number of industries to the town.

What to See and Do

Alabama Music Hall of Fame. Celebrates the state's contribution to American popular music, with artifacts from Toni Tenille's bell-bottoms to the group Alabama's tour bus. Also exhibits on the local recording studios made famous for such Southern Soul classics as "When a Man Loves a Woman" by Percy Sledge and hits by Wilson Pickett, Aretha Franklin, and even the Rolling Stones. (Daily) Hosts Harvest Jam 2nd wkend Sep. On Hwy 72 in Tuscumbia. Phone 205/381-4417. ¢¢

Indian Mound and Museum. Largest ceremonial mound in the Tennessee Valley. Museum has large collection of Native American artifacts. (Tues-Sat; closed hols) S Court St. Phone 256/760-6427. ¢

Ivy Green. Helen Keller was born here in 1880. Deaf and blind from the age of 19 months, she learned to speak her first words at the water pump out back from her teacher Annie Sullivan, events recounted in the story *The Miracle Worker.* (Daily) 300 W North Commons, Tuscumbia. Phone 205/383-4066. ¢¢

Joe Wheeler State Park. Named for Confederate General Joseph Wheeler of the Army of Tennessee, the 2,550-acre park is divided into 3 parts.

Wheeler Dam. Swimming, fishing (daily), boat liveries, and harbor; tennis, picnic facilities, cabins (res through Park Manager). 18 mi E on US 72, then 4 mi S on AL 101. Phone 205/685-3306.

First Creek. Beachfront swimming, boating (marina); nature and hiking trails, 18-hole golf, tennis, picnicking, camping (primitive and improved). Resort lodge overlooking the Tennessee River (see RESORT). 2 mi W of Rogersville via US 72. Phone 205/247-5466 (office), 205/247-1184 (campground).

Elk River. Fishing, boating (launch); picnic facilities, playground, concession. Group lodge. (Daily) Standard fees. 15 mi W of Athens (see). Phone 205/247-5466.

Pope's Tavern. (1830) General Andrew Jackson stayed in this stage stop, which served as a hospital for both Union and Confederate soldiers during the Civil War. (Tues-Sat; closed hols) 203 Hermitage Dr. Phone 205/760-6439. ¢

Renaissance Tower. One of the tallest structures in the state; offers magnificent view of the Tennessee River and Wilson Dam. Aquarium with more than 60 exhibits (fee). Restaurant. (Daily; closed Jan 1, Dec 25) 1 Hightower Place. Phone 205/764-5900. ¢

University of North Alabama. (1830) 5,600 students. Tours. University Art Gallery (Mon-Fri), Planetarium-Observatory (by appt). Wesleyan Ave. Phone 205/760-4284.

W.C. Handy Home, Museum, and Library. Restored birthplace of famous composer and "father of the blues" contains hand written sheet music, personal papers, trumpet, and piano on which he composed "St. Louis Blues." (Tues-Sat; closed hols)

620 W College St. Phone 205/760-6434. ¢

Wheeler Dam. Part of the Muscle Shoals complex, this is a multipurpose TVA dam chiefly built for navigation. It is 72 ft high and 6,342 ft long, impounding a lake 74 mi long. Lobby (daily). 18 mi E on US 72 to Elgin, then 4 mi S on AL 101. **FREE**

Wilson Dam. This dam is the foundation stone of the Tennessee Valley Authority. For many yrs the Muscle Shoals area of the Tennessee River had been discussed as a source of power, and in 1918 the War Department began construction of Wilson Dam as a source of power for making munitions. The dam was completed in 1924, but little use was made of its generating capacity until the TVA took over in 1933. Today it has the largest generating capacity (630,000 kilowatts) of any TVA dam; its main lock (completed Nov 1959) is 110 ft by 600 ft and lifts vessels 100 ft, one of the world's highest single lift locks. The treacherous Muscle Shoals are no longer a bottleneck to shipping. The dam, 4,541 ft long and 137 ft high, is one of the many TVA dams that prevents floods, provides 650 mi of navigable channel, and produces electricity for the area's residents, farms, and industry. 5 mi E on US 72, then 2 mi S on AL 133. **FREE**

Wilson Lake. Extends more than 15 mi upstream to Wheeler Dam. Swimming, fishing, boating.

Annual Events

Tennessee River Fiddler's Convention. McFarland Park. Traditional fiddlers and bluegrass competition. First wkend May.

Helen Keller Days. Three-day celebration with music, arts and crafts, and parade. Last full wkend June.

W.C. Handy Music Festival. Wk-long celebration of the musical contribution of the "father of the blues." Jazz, blues, gospel concerts, street celebration, running events, bike rides. First full wk Aug.

Alabama Renaissance Faire. Renaissance-era arts and crafts, music, food, entertainment. Fair workers in period costumes. Oct.

Festival of the Singing River. McFarland Park. Honors the history and culture of Native Americans. Traditional dance competition, arts and crafts. Phone 888/356-8687. Oct.

Motels/Motor Lodges

★★ **COMFORT INN.** *400 S Court St (35630).* 205/760-8888; fax 205/760-8888; toll-free 800/638-7949. 88 rms, 5 story. S $44-$49; D $49-$54; each addl $5; suites $98; under 18 free. Crib free. TV; cable (premium). Complimentary continental bkfst. Ck-out 11 am. Meeting rms. In-rm modem link. Refrigerator in suites. Cr cds: A, DS, MC, V.

★ **DAYS INN.** *2700 Woodward Ave (35661), S on US 43, then E on AL 133.* 256/383-3000; fax 256/383-3000; toll-free 800/329-7466. 77 rms, 2 story. S $44; D $50; each addl $5; under 12 free; wkly rates. TV; cable (premium). Pool. Complimentary continental bkfst, coffee in rms. Restaurant opp 6-1 am. Bar 11-2 am. Ck-out noon. Cr cds: A, C, D, DS, MC, V.

★ **HOMESTEAD EXECUTIVE INN.** *505 S Court St (35630).* 256/766-2331; fax 256/766-3567; toll-free 800/248-5336. 120 rms, 2 story. S, D $51-$56; each addl $5; under 12 free. Crib free. Pet accepted, some restrictions. TV; cable (premium), VCR avail (movies). Pool; poolside serv. Restaurant 6 am-10 pm; Sat, Sun from 7 am. Bar 4 pm-1 am; closed Sun. Ck-out noon. Coin lndry. Meeting rms. Business servs avail. Cr cds: A, C, D, DS, MC, V.

Resort

★★ **JOE WHEELER STATE RESORT LODGE.** *4401 McLain Dr (35652), 20 mi E on US 72, then 4 mi S.* 256/247-5461; fax 256/247-5471; toll-free 800/544-5639. 75 rms, 3 story. S $58-$61; D $63-$68; each addl $5; suites $78-$119; under 12 free; golf plans. Crib free. TV; VCR avail. Pool; wading pool. Playground. Dining rm 7 am-9 pm. Ck-out 11 am, ck-in 3 pm. Coin lndry. Meeting rms. Business servs avail. Sundries. Lighted tennis. 18-hole golf, greens fee, pro, putting green, driving range. Private beach, marina, boat rentals. Hiking trails. Some refrigerators; wet bar in suites. Private patios, balconies. Picnic tables, grills. State-owned; facilities of park avail. Cr cds: A, MC, V.

Fort Payne

(B-5) *See also Gadsden*

Pop 11,838 **Elev** 899 ft **Area code** 256
Zip 35968
Web www.hsr.tis.net/~dekbtour
Information DeKalb County Tourist Assoc, 2201-J Gault Ave N, PO Box 681165; 256/845-3957

The county seat and market town of DeKalb County, Fort Payne is in an area famed for natural wonders and Native American history. Sequoyah, who invented the Cherokee alphabet, lived in Will's Town, a Cherokee settlement located near Fort Payne.

What to See and Do

Cloudmont Ski Resort. Two pony lifts; patrol, school, rentals; 100% snowmaking; concession area, snack bar. Chalets. Longest run 1,000 ft; vertical drop 150 ft. (Mid-Dec-early-Mar, daily) Summer activities incl swimming, fishing, hiking, and 9-hole golf. 5 mi NE via I-59, Exit 231 off AL 117 on County Rd 89. Phone 256/634-4344. ¢¢¢¢

DeSoto State Park. The 5,067-acre park incl Lookout Mt, Little River Canyon, and DeSoto Falls and Lake. The area, rich in Cherokee lore, was a base of military operations before the Trail of Tears. The park is noted for its variety of plant life, incl spring-blooming rhododendrons, wild azaleas, and mountain laurel. Songbirds abound. A scenic drive skirts the canyon, and 20 mi of hiking trail crosses the mountain top. Swimming pool, bathhouse, fishing; hiking trail, tennis, picnicking, playground, restaurant, country store, resort inn. Nature center. Camping (all yr), cabins (res required for both). Standard fees. 8 mi NE on County

89. Phone 256/845-5380 (cabins) or 256/845-5075 (campground).

Fort Payne Opera House. (1889) Alabama's oldest opera house still in use today. Restored and reopened in 1970 as a cultural arts center. Tours of theater incl historic murals (by appt). 510 Gault Ave N. Phone 256/845-2741. **Donation**

Landmarks of DeKalb Museum. (1891) The museum, Richardsonian Romanesque in style, features Native American artifacts from several different tribes; turn-of-the-century house and farm items; railroad memorabilia; photographs and art work of local historical significance. Special rotating exhibits. (Mon, Wed, Fri, also Sun afternoons; closed hols) 105 5th St NE. Phone 256/845-5714.
FREE

Sequoyah Caverns. Thousands of formations, reflecting lakes, and rainbow falls with indirect lighting; level walkways. Cave temperature 60° F all year. Rainbow trout pools, deer, buffalo. Swimming pool. Picnic area. Camping. Guided tours. (Mar-Nov, daily; rest of yr, wknds) 16 mi N off US 11, I-59. Phone 256/635-0024. ¢¢¢

Annual Event

DeKalb County VFW Agricultural Fair. VFW Fairgrounds, 18th St NW. Phone 256/845-4752. Early Oct.

Motels/Motor Lodges

★ **FORT PAYNE TRAVELODGE.** *1828 Gault Ave N (35967), 1½ mi S of jct I-59, US 11. 256/845-0481; fax 256/845-6152; res 800/578-7878. www.travelodge.com.* 68 rms, 1-2 story. S $35-$45; D $45-$55; under 18 free. Crib $6. Pet accepted. TV; cable (premium), VCR avail. Pool. Restaurant 5 am-9 pm. Ck-out noon. Meeting rms. Business servs avail. Free airport transportation. Downhill ski 10 mi. Cr cds: A, D, DS, MC, V.

★★ **QUALITY INN.** *1412 Glenn Blvd SW (35967). 256/845-4013; fax 256/845-2344; res 800/228-5151. www.qualityinn.com.* 79 rms, 2 story. S $38-$42; D $42-$45; each addl $5; under 16 free; higher rates hols. Crib free. Pet accepted, some restrictions. TV; cable (premium), VCR avail.

Pool; wading pool. Complimentary coffee in lobby. Ck-out 11 am. Coin lndry. Meeting rms. Business servs avail. Cr cds: A, C, D, DS, MC, V.

Gadsden

(B-4) *See also Anniston, Fort Payne, Guntersville*

Founded 1840 **Pop** 42,523 **Elev** 554 ft
Area code 205
Web www.cybrtyme.com/tourism
Information Gadsden-Etowah Tourism Board, PO Box 8267, 35902; 205/549-0351

The town was named for James Gadsden, the man who negotiated the purchase of Arizona and New Mexico in 1853. Today it is one of the largest industrial centers in the state. Iron, manganese, coal, and limestone are found nearby. Steel, rubber, fabricated metal, electrical equipment, and electronic devices are among its chief products. It is the seat of Etowah County, a diversified agricultural area.

Union troops sacked Gadsden in 1863 and rode on toward Rome, Georgia. Two heroes were born of this action. Fifteen-year-old Emma Sansom bravely guided General Nathan Bedford Forrest and his men across a ford on Black Creek after the bridge was destroyed. John Wisdom made a night ride of 67 miles to warn the defenders of Rome that the Yankees were coming, a ride the people of Alabama celebrate more than Paul Revere's.

In 1887, electricity came to Gadsden when William P. Lay built an electrical plant, the result of years of effort to interest investors in the industrial future of the region. In 1902, it was replaced with a hydro-electric plant on Big Wills Creek. Eventually, Lay's dream of developing the water resources of the Coosa-Alabama river system led to the organization of the Alabama Power Company in 1906.

What to See and Do

Center for Cultural Arts. Center features wide variety of cultural and artistic traveling exhibits from the US and Europe; children's museum with hands-on exhibits features a miniature "walk-through" city. (Daily; closed hols) 501 Broad St. Phone 205/543-2787. ¢¢

Gadsden Museum of Fine Arts. Features works by local, national, and intl artists. Antique china and crystal collection, historical memorabilia. (Sun-Fri; closed hols) 2829 W Meighan Blvd. Phone 205/546-7365. **FREE**

Horton Mill Covered Bridge. This 220-ft-long structure is the highest covered bridge in the US, 70 ft above the Black Warrior River. Trails. (Daily) 18 mi W on US 278, then 11 mi S on AL 75. **FREE**

Noccalula Falls Park. Black Creek drops 90 ft over a limestone ledge on Lookout Mt; according to legend, these falls were named for an Indian chief's daughter who leaped to her death after being disappointed in love. A 65-mi trail ending at DeSoto Falls in DeSoto State Park in Fort Payne (see) incl 4 waterfalls and many Native American sites. Also originating in the park is the Lookout Mt Parkway, a scenic drive extending 100 mi to Chattanooga, TN. Swimming pool, bathhouse; nature and hiking trails, miniature golf, picnic area, playground, camping, hookups (fee). Pioneer homestead and museum; train. Botanical gardens. (Daily) Noccalula Rd. Phone 205/549-4663 (office) or 205/543-7412 (campground). Fee for each activity. Admission ¢-¢¢

Weiss Dam and Lake. An Alabama Power Company project impounds a 30,200-acre lake. Swimming, fishing, boating (daily); picnicking. Tours of power plant (daily, by appt). 18 mi NE off US 411. Phone 205/526-8467.

Motel/Motor Lodge

★ **KEY WEST INN.** *10535 AL 168 (35957), 20 mi N on US 431. 256/593-0800; fax 256/593-9100; res 800/833-0555. www.keywestinn.net.* 41 rms, 2 story. Oct-Dec: S, D $46.50-$51.50; each addl $5; under 18 free; lower rates rest of yr. Crib free. Pet accepted, some restrictions; $5. TV; cable (premium). Complimentary continental bkfst. Restaurant opp 11 am-4 pm. Ck-out 11 am. Meeting rm. Some refrigerators. Cr cds: A, DS, MC, V.

Greenville

(F-3) *See also Montgomery*

Settled 1819 **Pop** 7,492 **Elev** 422 ft
Area code 334 **Zip** 36037

What to See and Do

Hank Williams, Sr. Boyhood Home & Museum. Restored house where Hank Williams, Sr. country music legend, lived as a young boy. Large collection of memorabilia incl recordings, posters, and sheet music. (Daily) Approx 20 mi S on US 31, at 127 Rose St in Georgiana. Phone 334/376-2396. ¢¢

Motel/Motor Lodge

★★ **RAMADA INN.** *941 Fort Dale Rd (36037), jct AL 185, I-65, E off Greenville Exit 130, on Fort Dale Rd.* 334/382-2651; fax 334/382-2651. 96 rms, 2 story. S, D $57; each addl $6; under 18 free. Crib free. Pet accepted; $5. TV; cable. Pool. Coffee in rms. Restaurant 6 am-2 pm, 5-9 pm. Bar 4:30-9 pm. Ck-out noon. Meeting rms. Business servs avail. In-rm modem link. Cr cds: A, C, D, DS, MC, V.

Gulf Shores

(H-2) *See also Mobile*

Pop 3,261 **Elev** 6 ft **Area code** 334
Zip 36542 **Web** www.gulfshores.com
Information Alabama Gulf Coast Convention & Visitors Bureau, 3150 Gulf Shores Pkwy, PO Box 457, 36547; 334/968-7511 or 800/745-SAND

Located on Pleasure Island, southeast of Mobile, Gulf Shores is separated from the mainland by the Intracoastal Waterway. Between Alabama Point on the east and Mobile Point on the west is a 32-mile stretch of white sand beach that includes Orange Beach. Swimming and fishing in the Gulf are excellent, and charter boats are available. The island also has a number of freshwater lakes. At the eastern end, a bridge across Perdido Bay connects Orange Beach with Pensacola, Florida.

What to See and Do

Bon Secour National Wildlife Refuge. Consists of 6,000 acres of coastal lands ranging from sand dunes to woodlands; native and migratory birds, small mammals, and reptiles incl the endangered loggerhead sea turtle. Swimming, fishing (fresh and salt water); foot trails, hiking. Visitor center (Daily; closed hols). AL 180 W. Phone 334/540-7720. **FREE**

Fort Morgan Park. This area on the western tip of Mobile Point was explored by the Spanish in 1519. Between that time and 1813, Spain, France, England and, finally, the United States held this strategic point. It was the site of 2 engagements during the War of 1812. Fishing pier. Picnicking, concessions. 22 mi W on AL 180 (Fort Morgan Pkwy). ¢ Park admission incl

   Fort Morgan. This star-shaped brick fort was begun in 1819 and replaced a sand and log fort that figured in 2 battles during the War of 1812. Fort Morgan's most famous moment occurred during the Battle of Mobile Bay (Aug 1864). The Confederates' use of mines, then known as torpedoes, was the source of Union Admiral Farragut's legendary command, "Damn the torpedoes, full speed ahead!" Following the battle, the fort withstood a 2-wk siege before surrendering to Union forces. The fort was in active use during the Spanish-American War, WWI, and WWII. (Daily; closed Jan 1, Thanksgiving, Dec 25) Phone 334/540-7125 or 334/540-7127. ¢

   Fort Morgan Museum. (1967) Patterned after the 10-sided citadel damaged in 1864, the museum displays military artifacts from the War of 1812 through WWII; local history. (Daily; closed Jan 1, Thanksgiving, Dec 25) **FREE**

Gulf State Park. The 6,000-acre park incl more than 2 mi of white sand beaches on the Gulf and freshwater lakes. Swimming, bathhouse, water-skiing, surfing, fishing in Gulf of Mexico (825-ft pier) and in lakes, marina, boathouse, rentals; hiking, bicycling, tennis, 18-hole golf (fee). Picnic area, pavilion, grills, restaurant, resort inn (see MOTELS). Cabins (for res contact Cabin Res, 20115 AL 135, phone 334/948-7275). Camping (14-day max in season; phone 334/948-6353 Mon-Fri for res). (Daily) Standard fees. 2 mi E on AL 182 from jct AL 59. Phone 334/948-7275.

Zooland Animal Park. A 15-acre park with native and exotic animals; petting zoo; concession. (Daily; closed Thanksgiving, Dec 25) AL 59 S to 12th Ave. Phone 334/968-5731. ¢¢

Annual Events

Mardi Gras Celebration. Late Feb.

Pleasure Island Festival of Art. Early Mar.

National Shrimp Festival. Second wkend Oct.

Motels/Motor Lodges

★★ **BEST WESTERN ON THE BEACH.** *337 E Beach Blvd; AL 182 (36547). 334/948-7047; fax 334/948-7339; res 800/788-4557. www.best western-onthebeach.com.* 111 units, 6 story, 50 kits. May-Sep: S, D $99-$225; under 12 free; wkly rates; lower rates rest of yr. Crib $5. TV; cable, VCR (movies). 2 pools; whirlpools. Restaurant 6 am-11 pm. Ck-out 11 am. Meeting rms. Business servs avail. Refrigerators. On Gulf beach. Cr cds: A, C, D, DS, MC, V.
D 🛌 ⌨ 🏖 🐾 SC

★★ **HAMPTON INN.** *22988 Perdido Beach Blvd (36561), AL 59 to AL 182 E/Beach Blvd. 334/974-1598; fax 334/974-1599; res 800/981-6242; toll-free 888/485-3726.* 65 rms, 3 story. May-Labor Day: S, D $99-$159; each addl $10; under 12 free; higher rates special events; lower rates rest of yr. Crib free. TV; cable (premium). Complimentary continental bkfst, coffee in rms. Restaurant nearby. Ck-out 11

am. Meeting rms. Business servs avail. In-rm modem link. Pool. Refrigerators, microwaves. Some balconies. On beach. Cr cds: A, C, D, DS, MC, V.
D 🛌 ⌨ 🐾 SC

★★★ **HILTON GARDEN INN BEACHFRONT.** *23092 Perdido Beach Blvd (36561), AL 59 to AL 182 E/Beach Blvd. 334/974-1600; fax 334/974-1012; toll-free 888/674-6866. www.hilton.com.* 137 rms, 6 story. May-Labor Day: S, D $129-$189; suites $265; hols (2-day min); lower rates rest of yr. Crib free. TV; cable (premium). Complimentary coffee in rms. Restaurant 6 am-9 pm. Rm serv 5-9 pm. Bar. Ck-out noon. Meeting rms. Business center. In-rm modem link. Coin lndry. Indoor/outdoor pool; whirlpool. Refrigerators, microwaves. Balconies. On beach. Cr cds: A, C, D, DS, JCB, MC, V.
D 🛌 ⌨ 🏖 🐾 🏃

★★★ **HOLIDAY INN WHITE SANDS RESORT.** *365 E Beach Blvd (36542), on AL 182. 334/948-6191; fax 334/948-8240; toll-free 800/662-4853. www.whitesandsresorts.com.* 149 rms, 4-6 story. May-Sep: S, D $143-$248; each addl $12; under 19 free; lower rates rest of yr. Crib free. TV; cable (premium). Pool; wading pool, whirlpool, poolside serv. Complimentary coffee in rms. Restaurant 6-11 am, 5-10 pm. Bar from 11 am (in season); entertainment. Ck-out 11 am. Coin lndry. Meeting rms. Business servs avail. In-rm modem link. Sundries. Exercise equipt. Patios, balconies. On beach. Cr cds: A, D, DS, JCB, MC, V.
D 🛌 ⌨ 🏖 ⚡ 🐾

★ **THE LIGHTHOUSE RESORT MOTEL.** *455 E Beach Blvd (36547). 334/948-6188; fax 334/948-6100.* 219 rms, 1-5 story, 136 kits. May-Labor Day: S, D $73-$120; kit. units $86-$160; wkly rates; lower rates rest of yr. Crib $3. TV; cable (premium). 3 pools, 2 heated, 1 indoor; whirlpool. Restaurants nearby. Ck-out 11 am. Business servs avail. Refrigerators. Private patios, balconies. On Gulf beach. Cr cds: A, D, DS, MC, V.
D 🛌 ⌨ 🐾

★ **THE REGAL INN & SUITES.** *1517 S McKenzie St (36535), 8 mi N* on AL 59. 334/943-3297; fax 334/943-7548; toll-free 888/282-3297. 90 rms, 2 story. May-Aug: S, D $69-79; suites $99-109; under 12 free; lower rates rest of yr. TV; cable (premium). Pool. Complimentary continental bkfst. Ck-out 11 am. Meeting rms. Business servs avail. Exercise equipt. Game rm. Cr cds: A, DS, MC, V.

⌫ 👤

Hotel

★★ HOLIDAY INN EXPRESS. 24700 Perdido Beach Blvd (36561), AL 59 to AL 182 E/Beach Blvd. 334/974-1634; fax 334/974-1185; toll-free 888/974-7444. 119 rms, 6 story. May-Labor Day: S, D $109-$159; each addl $10; under 21 free; lower rates rest of yr. Crib free. TV; cable (premium). Complimentary continental bkfst. Restaurant opp 10 am-10 pm. Ck-out noon. Meeting rms. Business servs avail. In-rm modem link. Pool. Some refrigerators, microwaves. Balconies. On beach. Cr cds: A, DS, MC, V.

D ⌫ ↘ 🔥 SC

Resorts

★★★ PERDIDO BEACH RESORT. 27200 Perdido Beach Blvd (36561), 8 mi E of AL 59, on AL 182. 334/981-9811; fax 334/981-5670; res 800/634-8001; toll-free 800/634-7263. Email webmaster@perdidobeachresort.com; www.perdidobeachresort.com. 333 rms, 9 story, 12 suites. June-Aug: D $175; each addl $10; suites $309; under 16 free; lower rates rest of yr. Crib avail. Valet parking avail. Indoor/outdoor pools, children's pool, whirlpool. TV; cable (DSS). Complimentary coffee in rms, toll-free calls. Restaurant 6 am-11 pm. Bar. Ck-out noon, ck-in 4 pm. Conference center, meeting rms. Business center. Bellhops. Concierge serv. Dry cleaning. Gift shop. Exercise equipt, sauna. Golf. Tennis, 4 courts. Beach access. Supervised children's activities. Picnic facilities. Video games. Cr cds: A, C, D, DS, MC, V.

D ↻ 🏌 🏄 ➤ 👤 ↘ 🔥 👤

★★ QUALITY INN. 931 W Beach Blvd (36547). 334/948-6874; fax 334/948-5232; res 800/228-5151; toll-free 800/844-6913. Email info@qibeach side.com; www.qibeachside.com. 158

units, 6 story, 72 kits. May-Labor Day: S, D $112-$152; each addl $6; suites, kits. $162-$265; under 18 free; wkly rates; lower rates rest of yr. Crib $6. TV; cable. 2 pools, 1 indoor; poolside serv. Playground. Restaurant 7-10 am, 5-10 pm. Bar 5-11 pm. Ck-out 11 am. Coin lndry. Meeting rms. Business servs avail. Sundries. Some refrigerators. Patios, balconies. On beach. Cr cds: A, DS, MC, V.

D ↻ ↘ 🔥 SC

Restaurants

★ BOUDANZ. 326 Gulf Shore Pkwy (36542). 334/948-4349. Specializes in gumbo, jambalaya, etouffe. Hrs: 4 pm-2:30 am. Closed Thanksgiving, Dec 24, 25. Bar. Lunch $4.99-$8.99; dinner $12.50-$17.25. Child's menu. Entertainment: wkends. Parking. Nautical decor. Cr cds: A, MC, V.

D ➤

★ GIFT HORSE. 209 W Laurel (32535), on US 98. 334/943-3663. Specializes in apple cheese casserole, fried biscuits, blueberry muffins. Own desserts. Hrs: 11 am-9 pm. Closed Dec 25. Lunch buffet: $8.50; dinner buffet: $11.50. Sun brunch $11.50. Child's menu. Restored building (1912); antique tables. Cr cds: MC, V.

D SC

★ HAZEL'S FAMILY RESTAURANT. 25311 Perdido Beach Blvd (36561), 6 mi E of AL 59, on AL 182. 334/981-4628. Hrs: 7 am-9:30 pm; Fri, Sat to 10 pm. Bkfst $2.99-$6.25; lunch $2.29-$5.99; dinner $5.95-$18.95. Sat, Sun brunch, $7.95. Child's menu. Parking. Cr cds: A, D, MC, V.

D SC ➤

★ KIRK KIRKLAND'S HITCHIN' POST. 3401 Gulf Shores Pkwy (36542), AL 59, N of Intracoastal Bridge. 334/968-5041. Email kirkland@gulftel.com. Specializes in baby-back ribs, steak, mesquite-grilled fish. Hrs: 11 am-9 pm; Fri, Sat to 9:30 pm. Closed hols. Lunch $3.95-$9.99; dinner $6.99-$16.99. Casual dining; open country-style kitchen for viewing. Cr cds: A, D, MC, V.

D SC ➤

★ MIKEE'S SEAFOOD. 1st St (36547), at 2nd Ave E. 334/948-6452. Hrs: 11 am-11 pm. Bar. Lunch $3-

$12; dinner $4-$15. Child's menu. Parking. Nautical decor. Cr cds: A, D, DS, MC, V.

D ⊒

★ **ORIGINAL OYSTER HOUSE.** *701 Hwy 51 (36542). 334/948-2445. www. theoysterhouse.com.* Specializes in seafood. Salad bar. Hrs: 11 am-10 pm; Fri, Sat to 11 pm. Closed Dec 24, 25. Bar. Lunch $5-$9.95; dinner $5-$19. Child's menu. Parking. Nautical decor. On Bayou. Cr cds: A, C, D, DS, MC, V.

D

★★ **PERDIDO PASS.** *27501 Perdido Beach Blvd (36561), 8 mi E of AL 59, on AL 182, at Alabama Point Bridge. 334/981-6312.* Specializes in seafood, grilled steak. Hrs: 11 am-9 pm. Bar. Lunch à la carte entrees: $4.99-$7.99; dinner à la carte entrees: $11.99-$19.99. Child's menu. Parking. Overlooks Gulf of Mexico. Cr cds: A, C, D, DS, MC, V.

D ⊒

★ **SEA-N-SUDS.** *405 E Beach Blvd (36542). 334/948-7894.* Specializes in fried seafood. Salad bar. Hrs: 11 am-9 pm. Closed Sun off-season; Thanksgiving; also Dec. Bar. Lunch $3.95-$11.95; dinner $3.95-$11.95. Parking. On pier, overlooking gulf. Cr cds: A, D, MC, V.

D

★★ **ZEKE'S LANDING.** *26619 Perdido Beach Blvd (36561), 7 mi E on AL 182. 334/981-4001. Email zekerest@ gulftel.com.* Specializes in seafood, prime rib. Hrs: 4-11 pm; Apr-Oct hrs vary. Bar. Dinner $12.95-$34.95. Child's menu. Parking. Overlooking harbor. Cr cds: A, D, DS, MC, V.

D ⊒

Guntersville

(B-4) *See also Gadsden, Huntsville*

Pop 7,038 **Elev** 800 ft **Area code** 256
Zip 35976
Web www.lakeguntersville.org

Information Chamber of Commerce, 200 Gunter Ave, PO Box 577; 205/582-3612 or 800/869-5253

A thriving port and power-producing center of the Tennessee Valley Authority, this town was once the site of a Cherokee village. In the 1820s, steamboats plying the river turned Guntersville into a boom-town; still the Cherokees and settlers continued to live alongside each other peacefully. "Boat Day," it was said, was a great occasion for the settlers and Cherokees alike.

The Cumberland River Trail, the route Andrew Jackson took on his way to the Creek War in 1813, passed through Guntersville, and Cherokees from this area joined and fought bravely with Jackson's troops against the Creeks. But in 1837, just 24 years later, General Winfield Scott, under the direction of Andrew Jackson, rounded up the area's Cherokees and moved them westward.

Today Guntersville receives and distributes river freight. South of town is the plateau of Sand Mountain, one of the great food-producing sections of the state. Part of the growing resort area of north Alabama's TVA lake country, Guntersville's municipal parks have numerous boat docks and launches.

What to See and Do

Buck's Pocket State Park. Natural pocket of the Appalachian mountain chain on 2,000 acres. Fishing; boat launch; hiking trails, picnic facilities, playground, concession, primitive and improved camping. Visitor center. 16 mi N & E via AL 227, County 50 to Groveoak. Phone 256/659-2000.

Guntersville Dam and Lake. (1939) Fifth of the 9 TVA dams on the Tennessee River, it impounds a 67,900-acre lake that is 76 mi long. It is a favorite recreation area for swimming, fishing, and boating. Lobby (daily). 12 mi W and N via AL 69 & County 240, 50. **FREE**

Lake Guntersville State Park. A 5,909-acre park with ridge tops and meadows. Swimming beach, water-skiing, fishing, boating; hiking, bicycling, golf (18 holes, fee), tennis. Nature programs. Picnicking, playground, concession, restaurant, chalets, lakeside cottages, resort inn on Taylor Mt (see RESORT). Camping (hookups). 6 mi NE off AL 227 on Guntersville Reservoir. Phone 256/571-5444 or 800/548-4553.

Motels/Motor Lodges

★★ **BEST WESTERN.** *751 US 431 (35957), jct AL 168.* 256/593-8410; *fax 256/593-8410.* 116 rms, 2 story. S $39-$46; D $48-$60; each addl $5; under 12 free. Crib free. Pet accepted. TV; cable. Pool; wading pool. Ck-out 11 am. Business servs avail. Cr cds: A, C, D, DS, MC, V.

★ **COVENANT COVE LODGE AND MARINA.** *7001 Val Monte Dr (35976).* 256/582-1000; *fax 256/582-1385.* 53 units, 2 story. Apr-Oct: S, D $47-$56; each addl $5; suites, kit. units $78-$93; under 19 free; lower rates rest of yr. Crib $5. Pet accepted. TV; cable (premium). Pool. Complimentary continental bkfst. Restaurant adj 11 am-10 pm. Bar 3:30 pm-1 am; Thurs-Sat noon-2 am. Ck-out 11 am. Coin lndry. Meeting rms. Business servs avail. Gift shop. Balconies. Picnic tables, grills. On lake; swimming. Cr cds: A, C, D, DS, MC, V.

★★ **HOLIDAY INN.** *2140 Gunter Ave (35976).* 256/582-2220; *fax 256/582-2059.* 100 rms, 2-3 story, 20 kits. S, D $55-$75; each addl $6; kits. $65-$75; under 19 free. Crib free. TV; cable (premium). Pool. Coffee in rms. Restaurant 6 am-9 pm; Fri, Sat to 10 pm; Sun to 8 pm. Bar; entertainment Mon-Sat. Ck-out 11 am. Meeting rms. Business servs avail. Health club privileges. Refrigerators. View of lake. Cr cds: A, C, D, DS, JCB, MC, V.

Resort

★★ **LAKE GUNTERSVILLE STATE PARK AND LODGE.** *1155 Lodge Dr (35976), 6 mi NE on AL 227.* 256/571-5440; *fax 256/571-5459; toll-free 800/548-4553.* 100 rms in lodge, 2 story, 15 cottages, 20 chalets. Mar-Oct: lodge: S $55-$59; D $57-$61; each addl $5; suites $98; kit. cottages for 4 (2-day min) $99; chalet for 1-6, $99; under 12 free; golf plans; lower rates rest of yr. Maid serv daily in lodge,

alternate days in cottages. Crib $5. TV. Pool; wading pool, sauna. Playground. Dining rm 7 am-10 pm; Sun from 11:30 am. Box lunches. Ck-out 11 am, ck-in 2 pm. Coin lndry. Meeting rms. Grocery 2 mi. Sports dir. Lighted tennis. 18-hole golf, greens fee $15, pro, putting green. Private beach, waterskiing, launch ramps. Seaplane docking. Rec rm. Hiking, fitness, nature trails. Some fireplaces. Private patios, balconies. Heliport. Native American artifact "gold mine." Cr cds: A, MC, V.

Hamilton

(B-2) *See also Russellville*

Pop 5,787 **Elev** 498 ft **Area code** 205 **Zip** 35570

What to See and Do

Natural Bridge of Alabama. Two spans of sandstone, longest is 148 ft, created by natural erosion of a tributary stream more than 200 million yrs ago. Picnicking. (Daily) 1 mi W of AL 5 on US 278. Phone 205/486-5330. ¢¢

Motel/Motor Lodge

★★ **BEST WESTERN OF HAMILTON.** *2031 Military St S (35806), 1 mi S on US 43 S, near US 78 E, 278 W.* 205/921-7831; *fax 205/921-5239; toll-free 800/240-3127.* 80 rms, 2 story. S $49-$54; D $53-$58; each addl $5; under 19 free. Crib free. TV; cable. Pool. Restaurant 6 am-2 pm, 5-10 pm. Ck-out noon. Coin lndry. Meeting rms. Business servs avail. In-rm modem link. Golf privileges. Cr cds: A, C, D, DS, JCB, MC, V.

Horseshoe Bend National Military Park

See also Alexander City

(12 mi N of Dadeville on AL 49)
Early Spanish explorations led by De-Soto found the Creeks in Alabama and Georgia living in a settled communal-agricultural society governed by complex rituals and customs. Following the American Revolution, a horde of settlers moved south and west of the Appalachians. Despite territorial guarantees in the Treaty of 1790, the United States repeatedly forced land and road concessions from the Creeks. The Creek Indian Agency was ordered to oversee trade and to reestablish the Native Americans' prehistoric agricultural economy.

The Lower Creeks of Georgia adjusted to life with the settlers. The Upper Creeks living in Alabama did not and vowed to defend their land and their customs after heeding the preachings of Tecumseh in 1811. When a few Upper Creeks, called Red Sticks, killed settlers near the Tennessee border, the Indian Agency ordered the Lower Creeks to execute the offending warriors. The order produced civil war within the Creek Nation by the spring of 1813. By summer settlers became involved in the fray, attacking an Upper Creek munitions convoy at Burnt Corn Creek, fearing the Creeks' intentions.

The Upper Creeks retaliated on August 30, 1813, attacking Fort Mims and killing an estimated 250 people. Soon after, the militias of Georgia, Tennessee, and the Mississippi Territory were brought in to combat the uprising of the "Red Sticks." Georgia troops defeated the Creeks in two battles at Autosee and Calabee Creek, but the Tennessee Militia, under Andrew Jackson, was the most effective force; battles were fought by Jackson's army at Talladega, Emuckfaw, and Enitachopco. In March of 1814 they struck and routed the Creeks at Horseshoe Bend of the Tallapoosa River, the bloodiest battle of the Creek War. The peace treaty that followed soon after cost the Creeks more than 20 million acres of land, opening a vast and rich domain to settlement, and eventually led to the statehood of Alabama in 1819.

For Jackson, Horseshoe Bend was the beginning; for the Creek Nation, the beginning of the end. In the 1830s, during Jackson's presidency, they were forced to leave Alabama and move to "Indian Territory" (Oklahoma).

A museum at the visitor center depicts the battle with a slide presentation and an electric map exhibit. The park contains 2,040 acres of forested hills and is situated on the banks of the Tallapoosa River. A three-mile loop road tour with interpretive markers traverses the battle area. There are nature trails, picnic areas, and a boat ramp. (Daily; closed Dec 25) Contact 11288 Horseshoe Bend Rd, Daviston 36256. Phone 256/234-7111. **FREE**

Huntsville

(A-4) *See also Athens, Decatur*

Settled 1805 **Pop** 159,789 **Elev** 641 ft
Area code 256
Web www.huntsville.org
Information Convention & Visitors Bureau, 700 Monroe St, 35801; 256/551-2230 or 800/772-2348

In Huntsville the old and the new in Alabama meet. Now the seat of Madison County, the constitutional convention of Alabama Territory met here in 1819 and set up the state legislature. Many stately houses of that era may be seen. Today Huntsville is deeply involved in space exploration. The NASA-Marshall Space Flight Center is NASA's rocketry headquarters and where the space station was built.

Situated in a curving valley, Huntsville was an early textile town processing cotton raised in the surrounding country. Six Alabama governors called it home; so did the Confederate Secretary of War. The University of Alabama-Huntsville is located here.

What to See and Do

Alabama Constitution Village. Re-created complex of bldgs commemorating Alabama's entry into the Union at the 1819 Constitutional Convention; period craft demonstrations and activities; guides in period dress. (Mon-Sat; closed Dec 24-Jan) 404 Madison St. Phone 256/564-8100. ¢¢¢

Big Spring International Park. The town's water supply, this natural spring produces 24 million gallons daily. The first homesteader was John Hunt, and it was this spring around which the town's nucleus grew. Spragins St, W of Courthouse Sq.

Burritt Museum & Park. Unusual 11-rm house built in shape of a cross. Exhibitions on gems and minerals, archaeology, antiques, historical items. On the grounds of this 167-acre park are 4 authentically furnished cabins, a blacksmith shop, a smokehouse, and a church. Nature trails, gardens, picnicking. Panoramic view of city. Museum (Mar-late Dec, Tues-Sun). Grounds (daily). 3101 Burritt Dr, just off Monte Sano Blvd. Phone 256/536-2882. ¢¢

Huntsville Depot Museum. Opened in 1860 as "passenger house" and eastern division headquarters for the Memphis & Charleston railroad Co, the Huntsville depot was captured by Union troops and used as a prison; Civil War graffiti survives. Streetcar trips (addl fee); transportation exhibits. (Mar-Dec, Mon-Sat; closed hols) 320 Church St. Phone 256/564-8100 or 800/678-1819. ¢¢¢

Huntsville Museum of Art. Five galleries featuring traditional and contemporary work by regional and national artists; permanent collection and changing exhibits. Tours, lectures, concerts, films. (Tues-Sun; closed hols) Downtown, 300 Church St. Phone 256/535-4350. **FREE**

Madison County Nature Trail. Original house on first homestead. Chapel; covered bridge; 16-acre lake, waterfall; wooded hiking trails. Braille trail. (Daily) 12 mi SE on S Shawdee Rd, Green Mt. Phone 256/883-9501.

Monte Sano State Park. A 2,140-acre scenic recreation area on top of 1,800-ft Monte Sano ("Mountain of Health"). Hiking trails. Picnicking (tables, shelters, barbecue pits, fire-places), playground, concession. Camping, cabins. Amphitheater. Park open all yr. Standard fees. 4 mi E, off US 431. Phone 256/534-3757 or 256/534-6589.

Twickenham Historic District. A living museum of antebellum architecture, the district contains Alabama's largest concentration of antebellum houses. Several of the houses are occupied by descendants of original builders/owners. Tours can be self-guided; guided tours avail for groups. Contact the Convention and Visitors Bureau. Downtown, S and E of Courthouse Sq. Phone 256/551-2230.

⭐ **US Space and Rocket Center.** Space exhibits incl Apollo capsule and space shuttle objects returned from orbit. Rocket Park displays development of Apollo-Saturn V moon rocket and life-size space shuttle model. Omnimax Theater with tilt dome screen seats 280 and shows 45-min space shuttle and science films photographed by astronauts. NASA bus tours are escorted 1- or 2-hr bus trips through Marshall Space Flight Center, featuring mission control, space station construction, and tank where astronauts simulate weightlessness. US Space Camp offers 1-wk programs for children grade 4 and up. Campground. (Daily; closed Thanksgiving, Dec 25) 5 mi W on AL 20 just off I-565 at Exit 15. Phone 256/837-3400 or 800/63-SPACE. ¢¢¢

Von Braun Center. Largest multi-purpose complex in northern Alabama, named for noted space pioneer, Dr. Wernher von Braun. Center has 9,000-seat arena, 2,171-seat concert hall, 502-seat theater-playhouse; 100,000-sq-ft exhibit space, 25,000-sq-ft meeting rms; the city Tourist Info Center (24-hr phone 256/533-5723). Downtown, 700 Monroe St. Phone 256/533-1953.

Annual Events

Panoply of the Arts Festival. Big Spring Intl Park. Last wkend Apr.

Big Spring Jam. Big Spring Intl Park. Music Festival. Late Sep.

Motels/Motor Lodges

★★ **BAYMONT INN.** 4890 University Dr NW (35816). 256/830-8999; fax 256/837-5720; res 800/301-0200; toll-free 800/428-3438. 102 rms, 3 story. S $41.95; D $49.95-$54.95; each addl $5; under 18 free. Crib free. Pet accepted. TV. Pool. Complimentary continental bkfst. Restaurant adj open 24 hrs. Ck-out noon. Meeting rm. Business servs avail. In-rm modem link. Cr cds: A, C, D, DS, MC, V.

★★ COMFORT INN UNIVERSITY.
3788 University Dr (35816). 256/533-3291; fax 256/536-7389; toll-free 800/638-7949. 67 rms, 2 story, 8 suites. S $44; D $48; suites $49; under 16 free. Crib $4. TV; cable (premium). Pool. Complimentary continental bkfst. Restaurant opp open 24 hrs. Ck-out 11 am. Meeting rms. Business servs avail. Health club privileges. Refrigerators. Cr cds: A, D, DS, MC, V.

★ ECONOMY INN.
3772 University Dr NW (35816). 256/534-7061; fax 256/534-7061. 82 rms, 2 story. S $27-$49; D $30-$49; suites $39-$59; under 18 free. Crib free. Pet accepted, some restrictions; $12.50. TV; cable (premium), VCR avail (movies). Pool. Complimentary coffee in lobby. Restaurant nearby. Ck-out 11 am. Refrigerator in suites. Cr cds: A, C, D, DS, JCB, MC, V.

★★ GUESTHOUSE SUITES.
4020 Independence Dr NW (35816). 256/837-8907; fax 256/837-5435; toll-free 800/331-3131. 112 kit. suites, 1-2 story. Suites $75-$105; some wkend rates. Crib free. Pet accepted, some restrictions; $50. TV; cable (premium), VCR avail. Pool; whirlpool. Complimentary continental bkfst. Ck-out noon. Business servs avail. Valet serv Mon-Fri. Airport transportation. Sports court. Health club privileges. Fireplaces. Private patios, balconies. Picnic tables. Cr cds: A, C, D, DS, MC, V.

★★ HAMPTON INN.
4815 University Dr; US 72 (35816). 256/830-9400; fax 256/830-0978; toll-free 800/426-7866. 164 rms, 3 story. S, D $50-$60; under 18 free. Crib free. TV; cable (premium). Heated pool; whirlpool. Complimentary continental bkfst. Ck-out noon. Business servs avail. In-

rm modem link. Health club privileges. Cr cds: A, C, D, DS, MC, V.

★★ HOLIDAY INN WEST I-565.
9035 Madison Blvd (35758), 3 mi S, near Intl Airport. 256/772-7170; fax 256/464-0762; res 800/465-4329; toll-free 800/826-9563. Email hiwhsvat@mindspring.com. 173 rms, 2 story. S, D $82; suites $125; under 18 free. Crib free. TV; cable (premium), VCR avail. Pool; whirlpool. Complimentary coffee in rms. Restaurant 6 am-10 pm. Bar 11 am-11 pm. Ck-out 11 am. Meeting rms. Business servs avail. In-rm modem link. Valet serv. Free airport transportation. Health club privileges. Cr cds: A, D, DS, JCB, MC, V.

Ripe cotton plant

★ LA QUINTA INN.
3141 University Dr NW (35816). 256/533-0756; fax 256/539-5414; toll-free 800/687-6667. 130 rms, 2 story. S $52; D $58; each addl $6; under 18 free. Crib free. Pet accepted, some restrictions. TV; cable. Pool. Complimentary continental bkfst. Restaurant adj open 24 hrs. Ck-out noon. Meeting rms. Business servs avail. In-rm modem link. Refrigerators avail. Health club privileges. Cr cds: A, C, D, DS, MC, V.

Hotels

★★★ **COURTYARD BY MAR-RIOTT.** *4804 University Dr (35816). 256/837-1400; fax 256/837-3582; toll-free 800/321-2211. www.courtyard. com.* 149 rms, 3 story. S $66; each addl (after 1st person) $10; suites $76; under 12 free; wkend rates. Crib free. TV; cable (premium). Pool; whirlpool. Restaurant 6-10:30 am. Bar 4-11 pm. Coin lndry. Meeting rms. In-rm modem link. Valet serv. Exercise equipt. Refrigerator in suites. Cr cds: A, DS, MC, V.

D ≃ ⫪ ⫰ ⫲ SC

★★★ **HILTON HUNTSVILLE.** *401 Williams Ave (35801), at Freedom Plaza. 256/533-1400; fax 256/534-4581; res 800/445-8667.* 279 rms, 4 story. S $95-$103; D $105-$113; each addl $10; suites $130-$295. Crib free. Pet accepted. TV; cable. Pool; whirl-pool, poolside serv. Restaurant 6 am-10 pm. Bars 11 am-midnight; entertainment Mon-Sat. Ck-out noon. Convention facilities. Business center. In-rm modem link. Free air-port transportation. Exercise equipt. Health club privileges. Wet bar in suites. Civic Center, city park opp. Luxury level. Cr cds: A, C, D, DS, ER, JCB, MC, V.

D ⬟ ≃ ⫪ ⫰ ⫲ ⫳ ⫴

★★★ **HOLIDAY INN RESEARCH PARK.** *5903 University Dr NW (35806), at Madison Square Mall. 256/830-0600; fax 256/830-9576; res 800/465-4329; toll-free 800/845-7275. Email hsvrp@aol.com.* 198 rms, 5 story, 2 suites. Mar-July, Oct: S, D $93; suites $125; under 16 free; lower rates rest of yr. Crib avail. Parking lot. Indoor/outdoor pools, whirlpool. TV; cable (premium), VCR avail. Complimentary coffee in rms, news-paper, toll-free calls. Restaurant. Bar. Meeting rms. Business center. Bell-hops. Dry cleaning, coin lndry. Free airport transportation. Exercise privi-leges, sauna. Golf. Video games. Cr cds: A, C, D, DS, ER, JCB, MC, V.

D ⫵ ≃ ⫪ ⫲ ⫳ SC ⫴

★★ **HOLIDAY INN SPACE CEN-TER.** *3810 University Dr (35816), W on US 72 at jct AL 53. 256/837-7171; fax 256/837-9257; res 800/465-4329; toll-free 800/345-7720. Email hispace@ worldnet.att.net; www.holiday-inn.com/ hsv-spacectr.* 112 rms, 2 story. S, D $69; under 12 free; some wkend rates. Crib free. Pet accepted, some restrictions; $50 refundable. TV; cable (premium). Pool. Coffee in rms. Restaurant 6:30 am-2 pm, 5:30-10 pm. Bar 4 pm-2 am. Ck-out noon. Coin lndry. Meeting rms. Business servs avail. In-rm modem link. Bell-hops. Valet serv. Sundries. Free air-port transportation. Health club privileges. Cr cds: A, DS, V.

⫶ ≃ ⫳ ⫲ SC

★★★ **MARRIOTT.** *5 Tranquility Base (35805), at Space Center. 256/830-2222; fax 256/895-0904; toll-free 800/ 228-9290. Email hmsales@hiwaay.net; www.marriott.com.* 290 rms, 7 story. S, D $69-$120; suites $275; under 18 free; wkend rates. Crib free. Pet accepted, some restrictions. TV; cable (premium). Indoor/outdoor pool; whirlpool, poolside serv. Restaurants 7 am-10 pm. Bar 5 pm-2 am. Ck-out noon. Convention facilities. Business center. In-rm modem link. Concierge serv. Airport transportation. Exercise equipt; sauna. Game rm. Space and Rocket Museum adj. Cr cds: A, DS, MC, V.

D ⫵ ≃ ⫪ ⫰ ⫳ ⫲ SC ⫴

★★★ **SHERATON INN AIRPORT.** *1000 Glenn Hearn Blvd (36619), at Huntsville Intl Airport. 256/772-9661; fax 256/464-9116.* 148 rms, 6 story. S, D $79-$89; suites $89-$109; under 18 free. Crib free. TV; cable (premium). Pool. Restaurant 6 am-10 pm. Rm serv from 7 am. Bar 11 am-10:30 pm. Ck-out noon. Meeting rms. Business cen-ter. Lighted tennis. 18-hole golf, pro. Exercise equipt; sauna. Bathrm phone in suites. In air terminal. Luxury level. Cr cds: A, C, D, DS, JCB, MC, V.

D ⫶ ⫰ ≃ ⫪ ⫴ ⫳ ⫲ SC ⫴

All Suite

★★★ **RADISSON SUITE HOTEL.** *6000 S Memorial Pkwy (35802), at Gate 1 NASA Space Flight Center. 256/ 882-9400; fax 256/882-9684; toll-free 800/333-3333. Email rhi_hvil@ radisson.com; www.radisson.com.* 153 suites, 3 story. May-Oct: S $68-$78; D $73-$83; each addl $5-$10; kit. units $78-$199; under 17 free; wkly rates; lower rates rest of yr. Crib free. TV; cable (premium). Pool; whirlpool. Complimentary coffee in rms. Restaurant 6 am-2 pm, 5-10 pm. Bar 11 am-midnight. Ck-out noon. Free lndry facilities. Meeting rms. Business center. In-rm modem link. Free airport, railroad station, bus depot transportation. Exercise equipt. Refrigerators, wet bars. Picnic tables. Cr cds: A, DS, MC, V.

Restaurants

★★ **FOGCUTTER.** *3805 University Dr NW (35816).* 256/539-2121. Specializes in steak, seafood. Hrs: 11 am-2 pm, 5-10:30 pm. Closed hols. Res accepted. Bar. Lunch $3.95-$7.95; dinner $9.95-$18.95. Nautical decor; antiques. Cr cds: A, C, D, MC, V.

★★ **OL' HEIDELBERG.** *6125 University Dr NW # E-14 (35806).* 256/922-0556. Specializes in Wienerschnitzel, sauerbraten. Hrs: 11 am-9 pm; Fri, Sat to 10 pm. Closed hols. Lunch $3.75-$6.75; dinner $5.50-$14.50. Bavarian decor. Family-owned. Cr cds: A, C, MC, V.

Jasper

(C-3) *See also Birmingham, Cullman*

Settled 1815 **Pop** 13,553 **Elev** 339 ft
Area code 205 **Zip** 35501

Motels/Motor Lodges

★ **DAYS INN MOTEL.** *101 6th Ave NW (35501).* 205/221-7800; fax 205/221-7800; toll-free 800/329-7466. 44 rms, 2 story. June-July: S $55; D $60; each addl $5; under 12 free; lower rates rest of yr. Crib free. TV; cable (premium). Pool. Complimentary continental bkfst. Restaurant adj 9 am-10 pm. Ck-out 11 am. Coin lndry. Business servs avail. Valet serv. Many refrigerators. Cr cds: A, C, D, DS, MC, V.

★ **JASPER INN.** *1301 US 78 W Bypass (35501).* 205/221-3050; fax 205/221-3050; toll-free 800/554-0238. 153 rms, 2-4 story. S $34; D $42; each addl $6; under 12 free. Crib

free. TV, VCR avail (movies $3). Pool; wading pool. Restaurant 6 am-2 pm, 5-9 pm. Ck-out noon. Meeting rms. Business servs avail. Valet serv. Cr cds: A, C, D, DS, MC, V.

★ **TRAVEL RITE INN.** *200 Mall Way (36602),* opp mall. 205/221-1161; fax 205/221-1161. 60 rms, 2 story. S $31-$34; D $40; each addl $3; under 12 free. Crib $4. Pet accepted. TV. Restaurant adj 6 am-11 pm. Ck-out 11 am. Meeting rm. Cr cds: A, C, D, DS, MC, V.

Mobile

(G-1) *See also Dauphin Island, Gulf Shores*

Founded 1702 **Pop** 196,278 **Elev** 7 ft
Area code 334 **Web** www.mobile.org

Information Convention & Visitors Corporation, PO Box 204, 36601; 334/208-2000 or 800/566-2453

Mobile, Alabama's largest port city, blends old Southern grace with new Southern enterprise. The city was begun in 1702 when Jean Baptiste le Moyne, Sieur de Bienville, moved his colony from Twenty-Seven Mile Bluff to the present site of Mobile.

Shipping, shipbuilding, and a variety of manufacturers make Mobile a great industrial center. Today many millions of tons of cargo annually clear this international port. Paper, petroleum products, textiles, food processing, and woodworking are among the principal industries.

While remaining very much the vibrant industrial seaport, Mobile has still managed to retain its air of antebellum graciousness and preserve its past in the Church Street, DeTonti Square, Oakleigh Garden, and Old Dauphinway historical districts. These areas are famous for azaleas, oak-lined streets, and an extraordinary variety of architectural styles.

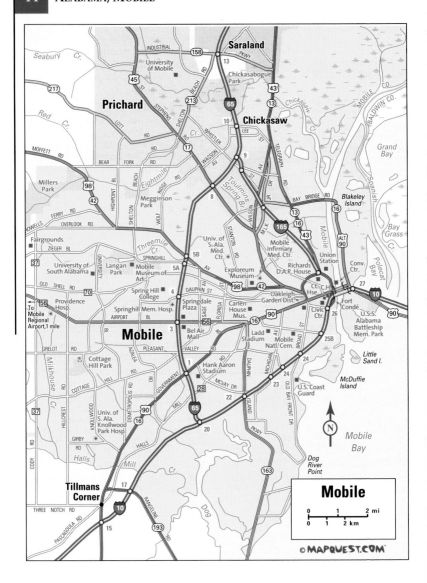

What to See and Do

Alabama State Docks. Berths for 35 ocean-going vessels of up to 45-ft draft; 1,000-ft-wide turning basin. (Mon-Fri; closed hols) Port of Mobile. Phone 334/441-7001.

Battleship Memorial Park, USS *Alabama*. Visitors may tour 35,000-ton USS *Alabama*, which serves as a memorial to the state's men and women who served in WWII, the Korean conflict, Vietnam, and Desert Storm. Also, submarine USS *Drum*, WWII aircraft, a B-52 bomber, and an A-12 Blackbird spy plane. (Daily; closed Dec 25) Parking fee. 1 mi E via Bankhead and Wallace Tunnels on Battleship Pkwy, US 90. Phone 334/433-2703. ¢¢¢

Bellingrath Gardens and Home. This 905-acre estate comprises natural woodland and some 65 acres of planted gardens on the Isle-aux-Oises (Fowl) River. It is also a bird sanctuary. Many varieties of native and other trees are background for the innumerable flowers and flowering plants that are in bloom all yr. Each season has its own special flowers but many bloom for more than 1 year. There are approximately 250,000 azalea plants of 200 varieties, camellias, roses, water lilies, dogwood, and hydrangeas. Travels to world-famed gardens abroad inspired the Bellingraths to create their gardens in the 1920s. Visitors receive a pictorial map showing gardens' walks and principal features. Incl in the gardens' admission is the world's largest public display of Boehm porcelain. There is a restaurant, a video display at the entrance, and a free "pet motel" near the Exit. The Bellingrath house, in the center of the gardens, is furnished with antiques, fine china, and rare porcelain; it is open to a few people at a time (daily tours). Since the home is located within the gardens, it is not possible to visit the house without visiting the gardens. The riverboat *Southern Belle* provides 45-min cruises along the Fowl River. House, gardens, and river cruise (daily). 20 mi SW via US 90 or I-10 and Bellingrath Hwy, near Theodore. Phone 334/973-2217 or 800/247-8420. Gardens ¢¢; house and gardens ¢¢¢¢; river cruise ¢¢¢¢; gardens, house, and river cruise ¢¢¢¢¢

Bragg-Mitchell Mansion. (1855) Greek Revival 20-rm mansion sits amidst 12 acres of landscaped grounds. Restored interior incl extensive faux-grained woodwork and stenciled moldings; period furnishings. (Sun-Fri; closed hols) 1906 Springhill Ave. Phone 334/471-6364. ¢¢

Exploreum Museum of Science. Hands-on investigative science and health museum. More than 80 life science, earth science, physical science, and "imagination" exhibits and displays. (Tues-Sat; closed hols) 1906 Springhill Ave. Phone 334/476-6873. ¢¢

Fort Condé Mobile Visitor Welcome Center. Reconstructed 1724-35 French fort features workable reproductions of 1740s naval cannon, muskets, and other arms. Staffed by soldiers dressed in period French uniforms. (Daily; closed Mardi Gras, Dec 25) 150 S Royal St at Church St. Phone 334/434-7304. **FREE**

Gray Line City tours. 210 S Washington Ave. Phone 334/432-2228.

Greyhound racing. Mobile Greyhound Park. Pari-mutuel betting; restaurant. Minimum age 18. (Nightly Mon, Wed-Sat, matinees Mon, Wed, Fri, Sat; closed mid-late Dec) W via I-10, Theodore-Dawes Exit (#13). Phone 334/653-5000.

Malbis Greek Orthodox Church. (1965) Impressive Byzantine church copied from a similar one in Athens, Greece. Pentelic marble is from same quarries that supplied the Parthenon; skilled artists from Greece created the authentic paintings; hand-carved figures and ornaments were brought from Greece. Stained-glass windows, dome with murals, icons, and many works of art depicting life of Christ. Guided tours by appt. (Daily exc Dec 25) 13 mi E off I-10 Exit 38 or US 90. Phone 334/626-3050. **FREE**

Mobile Museum of Art. Permanent collection incl furniture, decorative arts; American and European 19th-century paintings and prints; contemporary arts and crafts; changing exhibits. (Tues-Sun; closed hols) 4850 Museum Dr on S shore of lake in Langan Park. Phone 334/343-2667. **FREE**

Museum of Mobile. Paintings, documents, and artifacts of Mobile's French, British, Spanish, and Confederate periods; Mobile's maritime history, ship models, antique carriages, arms collection, Mardi Gras and other costumes. World's 2nd-largest collection of Edward Marshall Boehm porcelains. Guided tours by appt. (Tues-Sun; closed hols) 355 Government St in Bernstein-Bush House (1872), an Italianate town house. Phone 334/434-7569. **FREE**

Oakleigh. This 1833 antebellum house stands on the highest point of Simon Favre's old Spanish land grant, surrounded by azaleas and the live oaks for which it was named. Bricks for the first story were made on the site; the main upper portion is of hand-hewn timber. The Historic Mobile Preservation Society has furnished the house in the pre-1850 period; 1850s Cox-Deasy Creole cottage incl in tour. Museum collection of local items. (Daily; closed hols) 350 Oakleigh Place. Phone 334/432-1281. ¢¢

Phoenix Fire Museum. Fire fighting equipment; memorabilia dating from first Mobile volunteer company (1819); steam fire engines; collection of silver trumpets and helmets.

Housed in restored fire station (1859). Guided tours by appt. (Tues-Sun; closed hols) 203 S Claiborne St. Phone 334/434-7554. **FREE**

University of South Alabama. (1964) 12,000 students. Theater productions presented during school yr at USA/Wright Auditorium (phone 334/460-6305) and at Saenger Theatre (phone 334/438-5686). Of architectural interest on campus are Seaman's Bethel Theater (1860); the Plantation Creole House (1828), a reconstructed Creole cottage; and Mobile town house (1870), a Federal-style bldg showing Italianate and Greek Revival influences that also houses the USA campus art gallery. Tours of campus. 307 University Blvd. Phone 334/460-6141 or 334/460-6211.

Annual Events

Senior Bowl Football Game. Ladd Stadium. Third Sat Jan.

Historic Mobile Tours. Houses, buildings open to visitors. Second wkend Mar.

Blessing of the Fleet. Bayou la Batre, 25 mi SW. Phone 334/824-2415. Fourth Sun June.

Bay Fest. Various musical performers provide entertainment on 5 stages. Downtown, in the historic district. Phone 334/470-7730. First wkend Oct.

Greater Gulf State Fair. Commercial, industrial, military, and educational exhibits; entertainment. Phone 334/344-4573. Mid-Oct.

Seasonal Event

Azalea Trail Festival. During the period when the azaleas are usually at full bloom, many events are scheduled to entertain visitors in the city. A 35-mi-long driving tour winds through the floral streets in and around Mobile; printed guides available. Azaleas were first introduced to Mobile in the early 18th century and today they grow throughout the city. The Convention & Visitors Corporation has further details and maps for self-guided tours of Azalea Trail route and local historic sites. Phone 800/566-2453. Mar-early Apr.

Motels/Motor Lodges

★★ **HAMPTON INN.** *330 S Beltline Hwy (36609). 334/344-4942; fax 334/341-4520; res 800/426-7866. Email mobbl01@hihotel.com.* 118 units, 2 story. S $46; D $56; each addl $5; under 18 free. Crib free. TV; cable (premium). Pool. Complimentary continental bkfst. Ck-out 11 am. Business servs avail. In-rm modem link. Cr cds: A, C, D, DS, MC, V.

★ **LA QUINTA INN.** *816 S Beltline Hwy (36609). 334/343-4051; fax 334/343-2897; res 800/531-5900. Email lq0804gm@laquinta.com.* 122 units, 2 story. S, D $59-$79; each addl $8; under 18 free. Crib free. Pet accepted, some restrictions. TV; cable (premium). Pool. Complimentary continental bkfst, coffee in rms. Restaurant adj open 24 hrs. Ck-out noon. Business servs avail. In-rm modem link. Cr cds: A, C, D, DS, MC, V.

★★★ **RAMADA PLAZA HOTEL.** *600 S Beltline Hwy (36608), jct I-65 and Airport Blvd. 334/344-8030; fax 334/344-8055.* 236 rms, 4 story. S $79-$99; D $89-109; each addl $10; under 18 free. Crib $10. TV; cable (premium). 2 pools, 1 indoor; wading pool, whirlpool. Restaurant 6 am-1 pm, 5-10 pm. Bar; entertainment. Ck-out 1 pm. Meeting rms. Business servs avail. In-rm modem link. Bellhops. Sundries. Free airport transportation. Lighted tennis. Putting green. Exercise equipt. Cr cds: A, DS, MC, V.

★ **RED ROOF INN SOUTH.** *5450 Coca Cola Rd (36619). 334/666-1044; fax 334/666-1032; res 800/843-7663; toll-free 800/733-7633. www.redroof. com.* 108 rms, 2 story. S $36-$60; D $48.49-$56.99; each addl $8; under 18 free. Crib free. Pet accepted, some restrictions. TV; cable. Complimentary coffee in lobby. Restaurant nearby. Ck-out noon. Business servs avail. Cr cds: A, C, D, DS, MC, V.

Hotels

★★★ **ADAMS MARK HOTEL.** *64 S Water St (36602). 334/438-4000; fax 334/415-3060; res 800/444-2326. www.adamsmark.com.* 375 units, 28 story. S, D $150-$170; each addl $12; suites $215-$315; under 18 free; wkend rates. Crib free. Covered parking $6.50. TV; cable. Pool. Restaurant 6:30 am-2 pm, 5:30-11 pm. Rm serv 24 hrs. Bar 11 am-midnight; entertainment. Ck-out noon. Convention facilities. Business center. In-rm modem link. Concierge serv. Shopping arcade. Luxury level. Cr cds: A, C, D, DS, MC, V.

★★★ **CLARION HOTEL @ BEL AIR MALL.** *3101 Airport Blvd (36606), I-65 Airport Blvd Exit.* 334/476-6400; fax 334/476-9050; res 800/252-7466. 250 rms, 20 story. S, D $69-$89; each addl $10; suites $150-$200; under 18 free. Crib free. Pet accepted, some restrictions. TV; cable (premium), VCR avail. Pool; whirlpool. Restaurant 6:30-2 am. Bar. Ck-out noon. Convention facilities. Business servs avail. In-rm modem link. Some refrigerators. Some balconies. Cr cds: A, C, D, DS, JCB, MC, V.

★★ **DRURY INN-MOBILE.** *824 S Beltline Hwy (36609).* 334/344-7700; fax 334/344-7700; res 800/378-7946. 110 rms, 4 story. S $69; D $80; each addl $10; under 18 free. Crib avail. Pet accepted. Parking lot. Pool. TV; cable (premium), VCR avail. Complimentary continental bkfst, coffee in rms, toll-free calls. Restaurant nearby. Ck-out noon, ck-in 3 pm. Meeting rms. Business servs avail. Dry cleaning, coin lndry. Exercise equipt. Golf. Cr cds: A, C, D, DS, MC, V.

★★ **HOLIDAY INN I-10 BELGRATH.** *5465 Hwy 90 W (36619), I-10 Exit 15 B.* 334/666-5600; fax 334/666-2773. 124 rms, 5 story, 35 suites. June-Sep: S, D $71; each addl $10; suites $90; lower rates rest of yr. Crib avail. Pet accepted, some restrictions, fee. Parking lot. Pool, children's pool, whirlpool. TV; cable, VCR avail. Complimentary continental bkfst, coffee in rms, newspaper, toll-free calls. Restaurant 6 am-10 pm. Bar. Ck-out noon, ck-in 3 pm. Meeting rms. Business servs avail. Bellhops. Dry cleaning, coin lndry. Free airport transportation.

Exercise equipt. Golf. Tennis. Cr cds: A, C, D, DS, ER, JCB, MC, V.

★★★ **RADISSON ADMIRAL SEMMES HOTEL.** *251 Government St (36602).* 334/432-8000; fax 334/405-5942; res 800/333-3333. 170 rms, 12 story. S, D $94-$114; each addl $10; suites $138-$350; studios $105; under 17 free; wkend rates. Crib free. Parking $4. TV; cable (premium). Heated pool; whirlpool, poolside serv. Restaurant 5:45 am-10 pm. Rm serv 6-2 am. Bar; entertainment Fri, Sat. Ck-out 11 am. Meeting rms. Business center. In-rm modem link. Health club privileges. Some refrigerators. Restored landmark hotel in heart of historical district; antiques, artwork. Cr cds: A, C, D, DS, JCB, MC, V.

★ **SHONEY'S INN.** *5472-A Inn Rd (36619), at I-10 Exit 15 B.* 334/660-1520; fax 334/666-4240; res 800/222-2222. *www.shoneysinn.com.* 105 rms, 3 story, 13 suites. Pet accepted, some restrictions, fee. Parking lot. Pool. TV; cable (premium). Complimentary continental bkfst, coffee in rms, newspaper. Restaurant 6 am-midnight. Ck-out noon, ck-in 2 pm. Business servs avail. Dry cleaning. Golf. Tennis. Cr cds: A, D, DS, MC, V.

Resort

★★★ **MARRIOTT GRAND HOTEL.** *1 Grand Blvd (36564), 23 mi SE of Mobile on US 98 Scenic.* 334/928-9201; fax 334/928-1149; res 800/544-9933. *www.marriottgrand.com.* 281 rms, 3 story, 25 suites. Apr-July: S, D $199; suites $400; lower rates rest of yr. Crib avail. Valet parking avail. Pool, whirlpool. TV; cable. Complimentary coffee in rms, newspaper. Restaurant 7 am-11 pm. 24-hr rm serv. Bar. Ck-out noon, ck-in 4 pm. Conference center. Business center. Bellhops. Dry cleaning. Gift shop. Free airport transportation. Exercise equipt. Golf. Tennis, 8 courts. Beach access. Bike rentals. Supervised children's activities. Hiking trail. Picnic facilities. Cr cds: A, C, D, DS, ER, JCB, MC, V.

B&B/Small Inn

★ **MALAGA INN.** *359 Church St (36602). 334/438-4701; fax 334/438-4701; toll-free 800/235-1586.* 35 rms, 3 story, 3 suites. S $79; D $89; each addl $10; suites $100. Crib avail. Parking lot. Pool. TV; cable. Complimentary continental bkfst, coffee in rms, newspaper. Restaurant 7 am-10 pm. Bar. Ck-out 11 am, ck-in 2 pm. Meeting rm. Business servs avail. Dry cleaning. Exercise privileges. Golf. Tennis. Cr cds: A, C, DS, MC, V.

Restaurants

★★★ **THE GRAND DINING ROOM.** *1 Grand Blvd. 334/928-9201.* Seafood menu. Own baking. Hrs: 7-10:30 am, noon-2 pm, 6-9:30 pm. Res accepted. Bar. Bkfst $7.95-$10.95; lunch $10.95-$21.50; dinner $10.95-$21.50. Child's menu. Parking. Overlooks Mobile Bay. Cr cds: A, C, D, DS, MC, V.

★ **PIER 4.** *1420 Battleship Pkwy (36527). 334/626-6710.* Specializes in shrimp Dijon, snapper Ponchartrain. Own desserts. Hrs: 11 am-9 pm; Fri, Sat to 10 pm. Closed Thanksgiving, Dec 25. Lunch $4.50-$8.50; dinner $8.95-$19.25. Child's menu. Parking. View of bay. Cr cds: A, C, D, DS, V.

★★★ **THE PILLARS.** *1757 Government St (36604). 334/478-6341.* Specializes in fresh gulf seafood, veal, Angus beef. Own baking. Hrs: 5-10 pm. Closed Sun; hols. Res accepted. Wine cellar. Dinner $14.95-$19.50. Complete meals: $18-$24. Child's menu. Restored plantation house. Cr cds: A, D, DS, MC, V.

★ **ROUSSOS SEAFOOD.** *166 S Royal St (36602), I-10 Water St Exit to Fort Conde Welcome Center. 334/433-3322. www.roussosrestaurant.com.* Specializes in fresh seafood, steak, chicken. Hrs: 11 am-10 pm. Closed Sun; hols. Res accepted. Bar. Lunch $4.95-$21.95; dinner $4.95-$21.95. Child's menu. Parking. Nautical decor. Family-owned. Cr cds: A, D, DS, MC, V.

★★★ **RUTH'S CHRIS STEAK HOUSE.** *271 Glenwood St (36606). 334/476-0516.* Specializes in steak, seafood. Hrs: 5-10 pm; Sun to 9 pm. Closed Thanksgiving, Dec 25. Res accepted. Bar. Dinner á la carte entrees: $30-$50. Parking. Cr cds: A, D, DS, MC, V.

Montgomery (E-4)

See also Hamilton

Settled 1819 **Pop** 187,106 **Elev** 287 ft
Area code 334
Web www.montgomery.al.us

Information Montgomery Area Chamber of Commerce Visitors Center, 300 Water St, 36104; 334/262-0013

Between tall, stately columns on the portico of the state capitol, a bronze star marks the spot where Jefferson Davis was inaugurated president of the Confederate States of America on February 18, 1861. At that moment, Montgomery became the Confederacy's first capital. From this city went the telegram "Fire on Fort Sumter" that began the Civil War. Approximately 100 years later Montgomery became embroiled in another kind of "war," the battle for civil rights.

Today Montgomery is home to the nation's first Civil Rights Memorial. The memorial chronicles key events and lists the names of approximately 40 people who died in the struggle for racial equality from 1955-68.

Montgomery is a city of considerable distinction, with many historic houses and buildings. Although Montgomery's most important business is government, it is also a livestock market and a center of manufacturing. As an educational center it offers many cultural activities.

What to See and Do

Alabama Shakespeare Festival. Professional repertory company performs classic and contemporary comedy and drama. Musical performances as well. Two theaters: 750-seat Festival Stage and 225-seat Octagon. (Nov-

Sep, Wed-Sun; wkend matinees)
Hotel/play packages available. Inquire
about facilities for the disabled and
hearing impaired. #1 Festival Dr.
Phone 800/841-4273 (box office).

Alabama State University. (1874)
5,500 students. Authorized by the
legislature in 1873 as the Lincoln
Normal School, this university was
moved from Marion to Montgomery
in 1887. On campus are an art
gallery, African-American collection,
and Tullibody Fine Arts Center (daily
during academic yr; closed hols).
Tours. S Union & I-85. Phone
334/229-4100.

⭐ **Civil Rights Memorial.** Designed by
Vietnam Veterans Memorial artist
Maya Lin. Washington Ave & Hull St
at the Southern Poverty Law Center.

⭐ **Dexter Avenue King Memorial
Baptist Church.** (1877) The Rev Dr.
Martin Luther King, Jr. was a pastor
here from 1954-60; from the church
he directed the Montgomery bus
boycott, which sparked the modern
civil rights movement; mural and
original painting "The Beginning of
a Dream." (Mon-Sat, by appt; closed
hols) 454 Dexter Ave. Phone
334/263-3970.

F. Scott and Zelda Fitzgerald Museum.
The famous author and his wife lived
in this house from 1931-32. Museum
contains personal artifacts detailing
the couple's public and private lives.
Paintings by Zelda, letters and pho-

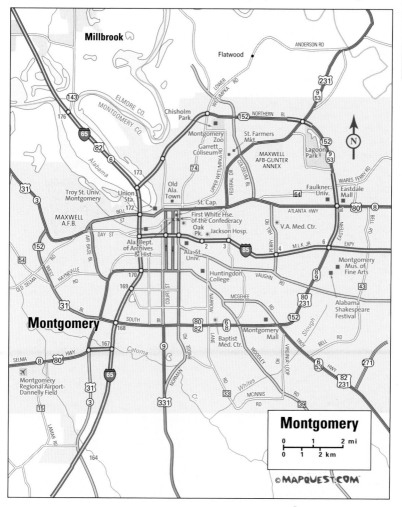

tographs; 25-min video presentation. (Wed-Sun; closed hols) 919 Felder Ave. Phone 334/264-4222. **FREE**

Greyhound racing. VictoryLand Track. Clubhouse, restaurant. Over 19 yrs only. (Nightly Mon-Sat; Mon, Wed, Fri, Sat afternoons; closed early Jan, Thanksgiving, late Dec) 20 mi E via I-85, Exit 22, in Shorter. Phone 334/269-6087. ¢

Jasmine Hill Gardens. Extensive 17-acre garden, flowering yr round. Designed as setting for statues, fountains, and other works of art, incl an exact copy of the ruins of the Temple of Hera in Olympia, Greece. Features a series of pools and avenues of flowering cherries, azaleas, and longleaf pine; 1830s cottage. Gardens (Tues-Sun). 8 mi N on US 231, then right on Jasmine Hill Rd, follow signs for 2 mi, near Wetumpka. Phone 334/567-6463. ¢¢

Lower Commerce Street Historic District. Wholesale and railroad district along the Alabama River. Bldgs, primarily Victorian in style, date from the 1880s to turn of the century. Riverfront tunnel to Riverfront Park dates to cotton days. 100 blk of Commerce St.

Montgomery Museum of Fine Arts. Collections of 19th- and 20th-century American art; European works on paper; regional and decorative arts. Hands-on children's exhibits. Lectures, concerts. (Tues-Sun; closed hols) 1 Museum Dr. Phone 334/244-5700. **FREE**

Montgomery Zoo. An 8-acre zoo housing 147 species; 600 mammals, birds, and reptiles in geographical groupings. (Daily; closed Jan 1, Dec 25) 2301 Colosseum Pkwy. Phone 334/240-4900. ¢¢

Old Alabama Town. Incl the Ordeman-Shaw House, an Italianate town house (ca 1850) with period furnishings; service bldgs with household items; reconstructed 1840 barn; carriage house; 1820s log cabin depicting pioneer life; shotgun cottage depicting black urban life; urban church (ca 1890); country doctor's office; drugstore museum and cotton gin museum; corner grocery from the late 1890s; 1-rm schoolhouse; exhibition (Grange) hall. Taped driving tour of historic Montgomery also avail. Films, tours, information center. (Daily; closed hols) 301 Columbus St. Phone 334/240-4500 or 334/240-4501. ¢¢¢

State Capitol. (1851) Seat of Alabama's government for more than 100 yrs. Bainbridge at Dexter Ave. Phone 334/242-3935. Opp the capitol are

First White House of the Confederacy. (1835) This 2-story, white frame house was the residence of Jefferson Davis and his family while Montgomery was the Confederate capital. Moved from its original location at Bibb and Lee streets in 1921, it is now a Confederate museum containing period furnishings, personal belongings, and paintings of the Davis family and Confederate mementos. (Mon-Fri; closed hols) 644 Washington Ave. Phone 334/242-1861. **FREE**

Alabama Department of Archives and History. Houses historical museum and genealogical research facilities. Artifact collections incl exhibits on the 19th century, the military, and early Alabama Native Americans. Also an interactive children's gallery. (Mon-Sat; closed hols) 624 Washington Ave. Phone 334/242-4363. **FREE**

Annual Events

Southern Livestock Exposition and World Championship Rodeo. Garrett Coliseum. NE on Federal Dr. Late Mar-early Apr.

Jubilee City Fest. Downtown. Memorial Day wkend.

Alabama National Fair. Garrett Coliseum. NE on Federal Dr. Early Oct.

Blue-Gray Football Classic. Cramton Bowl. Dec 25.

Motels/Motor Lodges

★ ★ **BAYMONT INN.** *5225 Carmichael Rd (36106). 334/277-6000; fax 334/279-8207; res 800/301-0200.* 102 rms, 3 story. S, D $42.95-$52.95; each addl $7; under 18 free. Crib free. TV; cable. Pool. Continental bkfst in rms. Ck-out noon. Meeting rm. Business center. In-rm modem link. Cr cds: A, C, D, DS, ER, JCB, MC, V.

D ✦ ➬ ➘ 🔥

★ ★ **BEST WESTERN STATE HOUSE INN.** *924 Madison Ave (36104). 334/265-0741; fax 334/834-*

6126; toll-free 800/552-7099. 162 rms, 6 story. S $44-$60; D $52-$58; each addl $6; suites $85; under 12 free. Crib free. TV; cable. Pool; wading pool. Restaurant 6 am-10 pm. Bar from 3 pm. Ck-out noon. Meeting rms. Business services avail. Cr cds: A, C, D, DS, MC, V.

D ⇌ 🔌 🐾 SC

★★ **COURTYARD BY MARRIOTT.** 5555 Carmichael Rd (36117). 334/272-5533; fax 334/279-0853; res 800/321-2211. 146 units, 3 story. S $89; D $99; each addl $10; suites $99-$109; under 18 free; wkend rates. Crib free. TV; cable. Pool; whirlpool. Bar 4-11 pm. Ck-out noon. Guest lndry. Meeting rms. Business servs avail. In-rm modem link. Exercise equipt. Health club privileges. Refrigerators avail. Some private patios, balconies. Cr cds: A, D, DS, JCB, MC, V.

D ⇌ 🏋 🔌 🐾

★★ **DAYS INN.** 2625 Zelda Rd (36107), I-85 Exit 3. 334/269-9611; fax 334/262-7393; res 800/325-2525; toll-free 800/329-7466. 120 rms, 2 story. S, D $55-$60; each addl $5; under 12 free. Crib free. Pet accepted; $5. TV; cable. Pool. Complimentary continental bkfst. Coin lndry. Ck-out noon. Business servs avail. In-rm modem link. Health club privileges. Cr cds: A, C, D, DS, MC, V.

🐾 ⇌ 🔌 🐾 SC

★ **ECONO LODGE.** 1040 W S Blvd (36105), near Montgomery Airport. 334/286-6100; fax 334/286-6100. 35 rms, 2 story. S $40-$50; D $45-$55; each addl $4; under 18 free. Crib free. TV; cable (premium). Complimentary continental bkfst. Restaurant adj open 24 hrs. Ck-out 11 am. Cr cds: A, C, D, DS, MC, V.

D 🔌 🐾 SC

★★ **FAIRFIELD INN BY MARRIOTT.** 5601 Carmichael Rd (36117), I-85 Exit 6 at E Blvd. 334/270-0007; fax 334/270-0007. 133 rms, 3 story. S $51.95; D $53-$59; each addl $6; under 18 free. Crib free. TV; cable. Pool. Complimentary continental bkfst. Restaurant adj 6 am-11 pm. Ck-out noon. In-rm modem link. Valet serv Mon-Fri. Cr cds: A, C, D, DS, MC, V.

D ⇌ 🔌 🐾 SC

★★ **HOLIDAY INN.** 1100 W South Blvd (36105), I-65 Exit 168. 334/281-1660; fax 334/281-1660. 150 rms, 4 story. S, D $51-$56; suites $67-$72; under 10 free. Crib free. Pet accepted, some restrictions. TV; cable (premium). Pool. Restaurant 6 am-10 pm. Bar 4-11 pm. Ck-out noon. Coin lndry. Meeting rms. Business servs avail. In-rm modem link. Bellhops. Free airport transportation. Cr cds: A, C, D, DS, ER, MC, V.

D 🐾 ⇌ 🔌 🐾 SC

★★★ **HOLIDAY INN EAST.** 1185 Eastern Bypass 231 (36117). 334/272-0370; fax 334/270-0339. 213 rms, 2 story. S, D $71.95-$79.95; each addl $10; suites $160; under 16 free; golf plan. Crib free. Pet accepted. TV. Indoor pool; whirlpool. Restaurant 6:30-9:30 am, 5:30-9:30 pm. Bar 4 pm-1 am. Ck-out noon. Meeting rms. Business servs avail. In-rm modem link. Bellhops. Valet serv. Sundries. Putting green. Exercise equipt; sauna. Game rm. Rec rm. Cr cds: A, C, D, DS, JCB, MC, V.

D 🐾 ⇌ 🏋 🔌 🐾 SC

★ **LA QUINTA INN.** 1280 Eastern Blvd (36117). 334/271-1620; fax 334/244-7919; toll-free 800/687-6667. 130 rms, 2 story. S $50.40; D $60; each addl $6; under 18 free. Crib free. Pet accepted. TV; cable (premium), VCR avail (movies). Pool. Complimentary continental bkfst. Restaurant adj 6 am-10 pm; Fri, Sat to 11 pm. Ck-out noon. Meeting rms. Business servs avail. In-rm modem link. Cr cds: A, C, D, DS, MC, V.

D 🐾 ⇌ 🔌 🐾 SC

★★ **RAMADA INN.** 1355 Eastern Blvd (36117). 334/277-2200; fax 334/270-3338. www.ramada.com. 152 rms, 2 story. S $54-$57; D $55-$57; each addl $8. Crib free. TV; cable. Pool. Complimentary continental bkfst. Bar from 4 pm; entertainment. Ck-out noon. Meeting rms. Business servs avail. In-rm modem link. Cr cds: A, C, D, DS, JCB, MC, V.

D ⇌ 🔌 🐾 SC

★ **WYNFIELD INN.** 1110 Eastern Blvd (36117), SE at jct I-85. 334/272-8880; fax 334/272-8880. 64 rms, 2 story. S $35-$42; D $45-$60; each addl $6; under 18 free. Crib free. TV; cable. Pool. Complimentary conti-

nental bkfst. Ck-out 11 am. Coin
lndry. Meeting rms. Business servs
avail. In-rm modem link. Private
patios, balconies. Cr cds: A, C, D, DS,
JCB, MC, V.

Hotels

★★ **HAMPTON INN.** *1401 Eastern
Byp Blvd (36117). 334/277-2400; fax
334/277-6546; res 800/426-7866.
Email mgmal01@hi-hotel.com.* 105
units, 2 story. S $61-$65; D $65-$69;
under 18 free. Crib free. TV; cable
(premium). Pool. Complimentary
continental bkfst, coffee in rms.
Restaurant adj. Ck-out noon. Business servs avail. In-rm modem link.
Cr cds: A, DS, MC, V.

★★ **HOLIDAY INN HOTEL AND
SUITES.** *120 Madison Ave (36104).
334/264-2231; fax 334/263-3179.* 172
rms, 6 story. S $69; D $75; suites $79-
$89. Crib free. TV. Pool. Restaurant 6
am-10 pm. Bar 11 am-midnight. Ck-
out noon. Meeting rms. Business center. In-rm modem link. Free covered
parking. Free airport transportation.
Cr cds: A, C, D, DS, ER, JCB, MC, V.

All Suite

★★ **COMFORT SUITES.** *5924
Monticello Dr (36117), I-85 Exit 6.
334/272-1013; fax 334/260-0425; res
800/228-5150. Email csmtg@aol.com;
www.hostmark.com.* 49 suites, 3 story.
Suites $69.95-$125; wkend rates. Crib
free. TV; cable (premium). Pool.
Complimentary continental bkfst.
Coffee in rms. Ck-out noon. Business
servs avail. In-rm modem link. Cr
cds: A, DS, MC, V.

Restaurants

★★ **SAHARA.** *511 E Edgemont Ave
(36111). 334/262-1215.* Mediterranean menu. Specializes in fresh
seafood, steak. Hrs: 11 am-10 pm.
Closed Sun; hols. Bar. Lunch $5.95-
$9.95; dinner $9.95-$18.95. Cr cds:
A, D, DS, MC, V.

★★★ **VINTAGE YEAR.** *405
Cloverdale Rd (36106). 334/264-8463.*

Specializes in chicken, seafood. Hrs:
6-10 pm. Closed Sun, Mon; hols. Bar.
Wine list. Dinner a la carte entrees:
$14-$19. Cr cds: A, DS, MC, V.

Natural Bridge

(see Hamilton)

Opelika

(D-5) *See also Auburn, Tuskegee; also see
Columbus, GA*

Settled 1836 **Pop** 22,122 **Elev** 822 ft
Area code 334 **Zip** 36801

Motels/Motor Lodges

★★ **BEST WESTERN MARINER
INN.** *1002 Columbus Pkwy (36801), jct
I-85 and US 280. 334/749-1461; fax
334/749-1468; toll-free 800/528-1234.*
95 rms, 2 story. S $29-$34; D $36-$46;
each addl $7; under 12 free; wkly
rates. Crib $7. Pet accepted. TV; cable.
Indoor pool; whirlpool. Complimentary coffee in lobby. Restaurant
nearby. Bar 3 pm-2 am, Sat to midnight. Business center. In-rm modem
link. Cr cds: A, C, D, DS, MC, V.

★ **DAYS INN.** *1014 Anand Ave
(36804). 334/749-5080; fax 334/749-
5080; toll-free 800/329-7466.* 43 rms,
2 story. S $38-$45; D $42-$50; each
addl $5; suites $65-$80; under 12
free; higher rates special events. Crib
free. Pet accepted; $5. TV; cable (pre-
mium). Indoor pool; wading pool,
whirlpool. Complimentary continental bkfst. Restaurant opp open 24 hrs.
Ck-out 11 am. Refrigerators. Cr cds:
A, C, D, DS, MC, V.

★★ **HOLIDAY INN.** *1102 Columbus
Pkwy (36830), 2 mi SE on US 280 at jct
I-85 Exit 62. 334/745-6331; fax
334/749-3933.* 120 rms, 2 story. S
$47-$80; D $52-$85; each addl $5;
under 18 free; football wkends (2-day
min). Crib free. TV; cable, VCR avail.

Pool. Restaurant 6 am-2 pm, 5-10 pm. Bar 3 pm-midnight. Ck-out noon. Meeting rms. Business center. In-rm modem link. Exercise equipt. Cr cds: A, C, D, DS, JCB, MC, V.

Restaurant

★ **PROVINO'S.** *3903-B Pepperell Pkwy (36801). 334/742-0340.* Hrs: 4:30-10 pm; Sun 11 am-9 pm; early-bird dinner Sun-Thurs 4:30-6:30 pm. Closed hols. Wine, beer. Lunch, dinner $7.95-$12.95. Italian atmosphere. Cr cds: A, MC, V.

Ozark

(F-5) *See also Dothan, Troy*

Pop 12,922 **Elev** 409 ft **Area code** 334
Zip 36360
Web www.snowhill.com/ozark
Information Ozark Area Chamber of Commerce, 308 Painter Ave; 334/774-9321 or 800/582-8497

What to See and Do

Blue Springs State Park. This 103-acre park features a spring-fed pool, swimming pool, bathhouse; tennis, picnic facilities, playground, softball field, primitive and improved campsites. Standard fees. 20 mi NE via AL 105, County 33, AL 10. Phone 334/397-4875.

Russell Cave National Monument

See also Scottsboro; also see Chattanooga, TN

(8 mi W of Bridgeport off US 72 via County 91, then County 98)

This cave shelter is located on the edge of the Tennessee River Valley.

Stone Age man made his home here in a giant rm 210 ft long, 107 ft wide and averaging 26 ft in height. Excavation of refuse and debris deposited in the cave has dated the site to approx 7000 BC. Archaeological exploration has revealed a record of almost continuous habitation to AD 1650. Paleo, Archaic, Woodland, and Mississippian cultures are represented. The 310-acre site, given to the US by the National Geographic Society, is administered by the National Park Service and is preserved in its natural state.

The visitor center has displays detailing the daily life of the cave's prehistoric occupants incl exhibitions of weapons, tools, and cooking processes. Audiovisual programs; slide programs. Area and visitor center (Daily; closed Jan. 1, Thanksgiving, Dec 25). Contact 3729 County Rd 98, Bridgeport 35740. Phone 256/495-2672. **FREE**

Russellville

(A-2) *See also Florence, Sheffield*

Pop 7,812 **Elev** 764 ft **Area code** 256
Zip 35653
Web www.getaway.net/fklcoc
Information Franklin County Area Chamber of Commerce, PO Box 44; 256/332-1760

Restaurant

★ **SPEEDY PIG BAR-B-Q.** *13670 US 43 SE (35653). 256/332-3380. Email stevej@speedypig.com; www.speedypig. com.* Specializes in barbecue ribs, sandwiches. Hrs: 11 am-9 pm. Closed Sun; Easter, Dec 25. Lunch, dinner $4-$7. Child's menu. Cr cds: A, C, D, DS, MC, V.

Scottsboro

(A-4) *See also Huntsville*

Pop 13,786 **Elev** 653 ft **Area code** 256
Zip 35768

Motels/Motor Lodges

★ **DAYS INN.** *23945 John T. Reid Pkwy (35768). 256/574-1212; fax 256/574-1212; toll-free 800/329-7466. www.daysinn.com.* 79 rms, 2 story. May-Aug: S $50; D $60; each addl $5; under 12 free; lower rates rest of yr. Crib avail. Parking lot. Pool. TV; cable (premium). Complimentary continental bkfst, newspaper, toll-free calls. Ck-out 11 am, ck-in 2 pm. Business center. Coin lndry. Golf. Cr cds: A, C, D, DS, JCB, MC, V.
🄳 ⬚ ⬚ ⬚ ⬚ ⬚ 🆂🄲 ⬚

★★ **HAMPTON INN.** *46 Micah Way (35769), jct US 72 and AL 35. 256/259-4300; fax 256/259-0919.* 50 rms, 2 story. S $46-$65; D $52-$75; each addl $6; under 19 free; higher rates 2nd wkend June. Crib free. TV; cable (premium). Heated pool. Complimentary continental bkfst. Restaurant adj 11 am-10 pm. Ck-out 11 am. Business servs avail. In-rm modem link. Refrigerators. Cr cds: A, C, D, DS, MC, V.
🄳 ⬚ ⬚ ⬚ 🆂🄲

Selma

(E-3) *See also Montgomery*

Settled 1815 **Pop** 23,755 **Elev** 139 ft
Area code 334 **Zip** 36701
Web www.olcg.com/selma

Information Chamber of Commerce, 513 Lauderdale St, PO Drawer D, 36702; 334/875-7241 or 800/457-3562

High on a bluff above the Alabama River, Selma is a marketing, agricultural, and manufacturing center. William Rufus King, vice president under Franklin Pierce, named the town after a poem by the Gaelic poet Ossian. The classic lines of Greek Revival and elegance of Georgian Colonial architecture blend with early American cottages, Victorian mansions, and modern houses to lend the city an air of the antebellum South. Once an arsenal of the Confederacy—second only to Richmond—Selma was a leading target for Union armies in 1865.

Selma fell on April 2, 1865, when 2,000 troops were captured, ending the city's role as the Confederacy's supply depot. The naval foundry (where the warships *Tennessee, Huntsville, Tuscaloosa,* and others were built), a rolling mill, powder works, and an arsenal were all destroyed. With defeat came an end to the era of wealthy plantation owners and a leisurely living where horse racing and cockfighting were gentlemanly diversions.

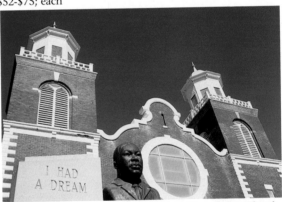

Bust of Martin Luther King, Jr. at Brown Chapel AME Church

Selma was also the scene of civil rights activity in the mid-1960s with a march on the Edmund Pettus bridge. Spiritual leadership was provided by Dr. Martin Luther King, Jr. and Andrew Young at the Brown Chapel AME Church.

County farmers raise cattle, pecan trees, cotton, soybeans, hay, corn, and grain. Selma is also the headquarters of a number of industries. The town became an inland port city in 1969 when a nine-ft-deep channel on the Alabama River was completed.

What to See and Do

Black Heritage Tour. Selma was a leading city in the march toward civil rights. Visit Brown Chapel AME Church (also a part of the Martin Luther King, Jr. self-guided Street Walking Tour), the Edmund Pettus Bridge, the National Voting Rights Museum, Selma University, the Dallas County Courthouse, and the Wilson Bldg. Contact Chamber of Commerce.

Cahawba. Alabama's first permanent capitol was a flourishing town in 1820. By 1822, 184 town lots were sold for $120,000. Nearly swept away by floods in 1825, the capital was moved to Tuscaloosa in 1826; Cahawba was close to being abandoned by 1828 but rose again. By 1830 it had become the most important shipping point on the Alabama River. Despite another flood in 1833 and subsequent rebuilding in 1836, the city reached a peak population of approximately 5,000 by 1850. However, the Civil War and a 3rd flood finally finished the town. Today only a few of the original bldgs remain intact. Ruins incl the brick columns of a mansion on the river, old cemeteries, and walls enclosing artesian wells. Site currently under development as an historical park; in-progress archeological projects may be viewed by visitors. Welcome center. (Daily; closed Thanksgiving, Dec 25) 9 mi W on AL 22, then 4 mi S on county road. Phone 334/872-8058. **FREE**

Annual Events

Historic Selma Pilgrimage. Guides conduct daylight and candlelight tours of historic houses; antique show. Contact Chamber of Commerce. Mid-Mar.

Reenactment of the Battle of Selma. Battlefield Park. Late Apr.

Cahawba Festival. Bluegrass and country music, arts and crafts show; flea market; greased pole climbing contests; games; regional food; walking tours of the old town. Phone 334/872-8058. Second Sat May.

Tale Telling Festival. Early Oct.

Motel/Motor Lodge

★★ **HOLIDAY INN.** *US 80 (36701), 3 mi W.* 334/872-0461; fax 334/872-0461. 165 rms, 2 story. S $50-$53; D $55-$60; each addl $5; under 19 free. Crib free. Pet accepted. TV; cable. Pool; wading pool. Restaurant 6 am-2 pm, 5-10 pm. Bar 5 pm-1 am. Ck-out noon. Meeting rms. Business servs avail. In-rm modem link. Valet serv. Cr cds: A, C, D, DS, JCB, MC, V.

[D] [🐾] [⚊] [⚊] [🔥] [SC]

B&B/Small Inn

★★★ **GRACE HALL BED & BREAKFAST.** *506 Lauderdale St (36701).* 334/875-5744; fax 334/875-9967. www.selmaalabama.com/gracehal.htm. 6 rms, 2 story. S $70-$90; D $77-$107; each addl $15; higher rates special events. Pet accepted. TV; cable (premium), VCR. Complimentary full bkfst. Ck-out 11 am, ck-in 4 pm. Business servs avail. Health club privileges. Antiques. Library/sitting rm. Restored antebellum mansion (1857); some original furnishings. Cr cds: A, DS, MC, V.

[⚊] [⚊] [⚊] [⚊] [⚊] [⚊] [⚊]

Restaurants

★★ **MAJOR GRUMBLES.** *1300 Water Ave (36703).* 334/872-2006. Specializes in char-broiled chicken and steak, seafood. Hrs: 11 am-10 pm. Closed Sun; hols. Res accepted Mon-Fri. Bar. Lunch $5.95-$13.95; dinner $7-$20. Located on river in former cotton warehouse (1850). Cr cds: A, DS, MC, V.

[D] [⚊]

★★ **TALLY-HO.** *507 Mangum Ave (36701).* 334/872-1390. Specializes in seafood, steak. Own baking. Hrs: 5-10 pm. Closed Sun; hols. Res accepted. Bar. Dinner $8-$15.50. Child's menu. Entrance and waiting area in old log cabin. Cr cds: A, C, D, DS, MC, V.

[D] [⚊]

Sheffield

(A-2) *See also Florence, Russellville*

Settled 1815 **Pop** 10,380 **Elev** 502 ft
Area code 256 **Zip** 35660
Information Colbert County Tourism and Convention Bureau, PO Box 440, Tuscumbia 35674; 256/383-0783

One of the Quad Cities, along with Florence (see), Tuscumbia, and Muscle Shoals, Sheffield was named for the industrial city in England. Andrew Jackson is said to be the first white man to foresee the potential of this stretch of the river. Deposits of iron ore spurred the building of five huge iron-making furnaces by 1888, giving Sheffield its start as a part of the major industrial center of the South.

What to See and Do

🌀 **Ivy Green.** (1820) Birthplace and early home of Helen Keller. Anne Sullivan, of Boston's Perkins Institute, was hired to come to Tuscumbia and help Helen Keller, who after an illness was left blind and deaf at the age of 19 months. Miss Sullivan and Helen lived together in a small cottage that had once been the plantation office. The cottage area incl the pump at which Helen learned her first word, "water"; the Whistle Path between the house and outdoor kitchen; and many personal items. (Daily; closed hols) (See ANNUAL EVENT and SEASONAL EVENT) 300 W North Commons in Tuscumbia. Phone 256/383-4066. ¢¢

Annual Event

Helen Keller Festival. Ivy Green (see). Late June.

Seasonal Event

The Miracle Worker. Ivy Green (see). Outdoor performance of William Gibson's prize-winning play based on Helen Keller's life. Limited number of tickets avail at gate; advance purchase recommended. Price incl tour of Ivy Green preceding play. Phone 256/383-4066. Mid-June-July, Fri, Sat.

Motels/Motor Lodges

★ **KEY WEST INN.** *1800 Hwy 72 (35674), 3 mi S. 256/383-0700; fax 256/383-3191; toll-free 800/833-0555.* 41 rms, 2 story. S $43-$60; D $48-$60; each addl $5; under 18 free. Crib free. Pet accepted, some restrictions; $5. TV; cable (premium). Complimentary continental bkfst. Restaurant nearby. Ck-out noon. Coin lndry. Meeting rm. Business servs avail. Some refrigerators. Cr cds: A, C, D, DS, MC, V.
D 🐾 🔌 🛏 SC

★★ **RAMADA SHOALS HOTEL AND CONFERENCE CENTER.** *4205 Hatch Blvd (35660). 256/381-3743; fax 256/381-2838.* 150 rms, 2 story. S $42-$57; D $42-$64; each addl $7; suites from $125; under 18 free. Crib free. Pet accepted; $10. TV; cable (premium). Pool; whirlpool, poolside serv. Coffee in rms. Restaurant 6 am-10 pm. Bar 4 pm-1 am; entertainment. Ck-out noon. Meeting rms. Business servs avail. Free airport transportation. Golf privileges. Some in-rm whirlpools, refrigerators. Cr cds: A, C, D, DS, JCB, MC, V.
D 🐾 ☕ 🏌 🔌 🔥 SC

Hotel

★★★ **HOLIDAY INN.** *4900 Hatch Blvd (35660). 256/381-4710; fax 256/381-7313. Email acshf@lodgian.com; www.basshotels.com/holiday-inn_franchisee=sheal.* 201 rms, 3 story, 3 suites. S, D $69; each addl $6; suites $150. Crib avail. Pool, whirlpool. TV; cable (DSS). Complimentary coffee in rms, toll-free calls. Restaurant 6:30 am-10 pm. Bar. Ck-out noon, ck-in 3 pm. Meeting rms. Fax servs avail. Bellhops. Dry cleaning, coin lndry. Free airport transportation. Exercise privileges. Golf, 18 holes. Tennis, 4 courts. Hiking trail. Video games. Cr cds: A, C, D, DS, MC, V.
D ⚡ 🏌 🏊 🎾 🏄 🔌 🏊

Restaurants

★★ **GEORGE'S STEAK PIT.** *1206 Jackson Hwy (35660). 256/381-1531. www.georgessteakpit.com.* Specializes in steak, fresh seafood. Hrs: 4:30-10:30 pm. Closed Sun, Mon; hols. Bar. Dinner $11-$25.50. Cr cds: A, D, MC, V.
D 🔌

★ **SOUTHLAND.** *1309 Jackson Hwy (35660). 256/383-8236.* Specializes in barbecued chicken and pork, catfish, homemade pies. Hrs: 10 am-8:30 pm; Sun 11 am-5 pm. Closed Mon. Lunch $4.50-$6.95; dinner $4.50-$11.95. Family-owned. Cr cds: A, MC, V.
Ⓓ

Sylacauga

(D-4) *See also Alexander City, Talladega*

Pop 12,520 **Elev** 600 ft **Area code** 256 **Zip** 35150
Information Sylacauga Chamber of Commerce, 17 W Fort Williams St, PO Box 185; 256/249-0308

The city's fortune is literally its foundation—a bed of prized translucent white marble estimated to be 32 miles long, 1½ miles wide and about 400 feet deep. The bed is, in many places, only 12 feet below ground level. Marble from Sylacauga (said to mean "meeting place of the Chalaka Indians") has been used in the United States Supreme Court Building and many other famous buildings in the US and abroad. Sylacauga stone is also crushed and ground for use in products such as paint, putty, plastics, asphalt tile, and rubber.

What to See and Do

DeSoto Caverns Park. Scenic 80-acre wooded park, famous for its historic mammoth, onyx caverns. Visited by Hernando DeSoto in 1540, the onyx caverns are the historic birthplace of the Creek Nation and one of the 1st officially recorded caves in the United States—reported to President Washington in 1796. On display in the caverns is a 2,000-yr-old "Copena" burial ground, Civil War gunpowder mining center, and a moonshine still from Prohibition when the caverns were known as "the bloody bucket." The main cavern, the Great Onyx Cathedral, is larger than a football field and higher than a 12-story bldg; a sound, laser, and water show is presented here. Featured at the park is DeSoto's

Lost Trail, a ¾-acre maze (fee). Visitors also may view a water-powered rock-cutting saw in operation, pan for gold and gemstones, or visit the Bow and Arrow Arcade. Other facilities incl picnic areas, shipboard playground, RV campground, and tepee island. Guided tours of the caverns. Park (daily). Fee for activities. 12 mi NW via AL 21 & County 36; on AL 76, 5 mi E of jct US 280. Phone 256/378-7252.

Talladega

(C-4) *See also Anniston, Birmingham, Sylacauga*

Founded 1834 **Pop** 18,175 **Elev** 555 ft **Area code** 256 **Zip** 35161
Web www.talladega.com
Information Chamber of Commerce, 210 East St S, PO Drawer A; 256/362-9075

Andrew Jackson defeated the Creeks in this area on November 9, 1813; it was the first of the battles in which he defeated the Creek Confederacy. Today Talladega is both a center of diverse manufacturing and a center of preservation, with many fine old buildings. It is the home of Talladega College, founded by two former slaves, and the Alabama Institute for the Deaf and Blind. Logan Martin Lake, to the northwest, offers excellent water and outdoor recreation activities, and a large section of the Talladega National Forest is to the east. A Ranger District office is located in Talladega as well.

What to See and Do

Cheaha State Park. This park includes Mt Cheaha (2,407 ft), the state's highest point with an observation tower on top, and 2,719 acres of rugged forest country in the surrounding foothills. The area is mentioned in Hernando DeSoto's journal of his 1540 expedition. (During the expedition, the Spanish introduced hogs and horses to local Native Americans.) Swimming in Lake Cheaha, sand beach, wading area, swimming pool, bathhouse, fishing, boating; hiking, picnicking, camping, cabins. Motel, restaurant. Park (daily). Standard fees. 7 mi NE on AL 21, then 15 mi E on County 398. Phone 256/488-5111.

Talladega National Forest. This 364,428-acre forest offers high ridges with spectacular views of valleys heavily wooded with Southern pine and hardwood. Divided into 2 sections, the park incl the Talladega and the beautiful Oakmulgee, SW of Birmingham. The Talladega division has lake swimming (fee), fishing, hiking trails, incl the 100-mi Pinhoti National Recreation Trail, a national byway extending from AL 78 to Cheaha State Park. Camping (no electric hookup; fee). Contact District Ranger. SE on AL 77. Phone 256/362-2909.

Talladega Superspeedway. Said to be one of the world's fastest speedways, with 33-degree banks in the turns. Stock car races incl the Winston "500" NASCAR Winston Cup Race, the Sears DieHard 500 NASCAR Winston Cup Race, the Birmingham Automobile Dealers 500K, and the NASCAR Busch Grand National Series Race. 10 mi N on AL 77, then 6 mi E on I-20. Also here is

> **International Motorsports Hall of Fame.** Official hall of fame of motor sports, with memorabilia and displays of over 100 vehicles. Race car simulator. Gift shop. (Daily) Annual hall of fame induction ceremony (late Apr). Speedway Blvd. Phone 256/362-5002. ¢¢¢

Talladega-Texaco Walk of Fame. An outdoor tribute to stock car racers incl a memorial for Davey Allison. Downtown.

Troy

(F-4) *See also Montgomery, Ozark*

Settled 1824 **Pop** 13,051 **Elev** 543 ft
Area code 334 **Zip** 36081
Web www.pikecounty.com
Information Pike County Chamber of Commerce, 246 US 231 North; 334/566-2294

What to See and Do

Troy State University. (1887) 4,700 students. Guided tours of campus. Home of the National Hall of Fame of Distinguished Band Conductors and the Malone Art Gallery. University Ave, 1½ mi SE. Phone 334/670-3000 or 334/670-3196.

Motel/Motor Lodge

★ **ECONO LODGE.** *1013 Hwy 231 (36081).* 334/566-4960; fax 334/566-5858. 69 rms, 2 story. S $38-$43; D $43-$51; each addl $5; under 18 free; higher rates football wkends. Crib free. Pet accepted. TV; cable (premium). Pool. Complimentary continental bkfst. Ck-out 11 am. Business servs avail. Cr cds: A, C, D, DS, MC, V.
D 🐾 ➳ ➷ 🔥 SC

Restaurant

★ **MOSSY GROVE SCHOOL-HOUSE.** *1902 Elba Hwy (36079).* 334/566-4921. Specializes in ribeye steak, char-broiled shrimp, seafood. Hrs: 5-9 pm. Closed Sun, Mon; hols. Res accepted. Dinner complete meals: $4.95-$14.95. Child's menu. Restored schoolhouse (1857); original fireplace, blackboard; antiques. Cr cds: MC, V.
D

Tuscaloosa

(C-2) *See also Bessemer*

Founded 1818 **Pop** 77,759 **Elev** 227 ft
Area code 205 **Web** www.tcvb.org
Information Convention & Visitors Bureau, PO Box 32167, 35403; 205/391-9200 or 800/538-8696

Located on the Black Warrior River, Tuscaloosa (Choctaw for "Black Warrior") was the capital of Alabama from 1826-46. It was an exciting capital; cotton was a highly profitable crop, and the planters gave extravagant parties. But an increase in cotton production toppled prices, and the capital was moved to Montgomery. Although the Civil War ravaged the university and most of the town, some antebellum houses do remain. After the war, industry and farm trading grew, making Tuscaloosa the busy, pleasant metropolis it is today. It is also the home of the University of Alabama.

What to See and Do

Children's Hands-on Museum. Participatory exhibits for children incl a Choctaw Indian Village, a bank, and general store, as well as a hospital and TV studio. Also avail is a computer and science lab resource center. (Tues-Sat) 2213 University Blvd. Phone 205/349-4235. ¢¢

Lake Lurleen State Park. This 1,625-acre park has a 250-acre lake. Swimming, bathhouses, fishing (piers), bait and tackle shop, boating (ramps, rentals); hiking, picnic shelters, playgrounds, concession, camping. Standard fees. 12 mi NW off US 82. Phone 205/339-1558.

Moundville Archaeological Park. Group of more than 20 Native American ceremonial mounds (AD 1000-1450); reconstructed village and temple with displays depicting Native American lifestyles and activities. The Archaeological Museum traces prehistory of southeastern Native Americans and exhibits products of this aboriginal culture. Nature trails along river. Picnic facilities. Tent and trailer sites (fee). (Daily; hols) 16 mi S on AL 69 in Moundville, part of the Alabama Museum of Natural History. Phone 205/371-2572. ¢¢

University of Alabama. (1831) 21,000 students. Tours of the 850-acre campus may be arranged in Rose Administration Bldg, Rm 151 (Mon-Sat). The information desk is located in Ferguson Student Union. On the campus is an art gallery in Garland Hall with changing exhibits, a museum of natural history, a 60-acre arboretum on Loop Rd, and the Paul W. Bryant Museum. The Frank Moody Music Bldg holds concerts and is home of the largest pipe organ in the Southeast. Four antebellum bldgs remain, the only ones on campus spared from burning by Union troops. University Blvd (US 11) between Thomas St and 5th Ave E. Phone 205/348-6010. Other bldgs on campus are

Gorgas House. (1829) A 3-story brick structure named for General Josiah Gorgas, former univ president. One of the school's original structures, Gorgas now houses a museum with historical exhibits; Spanish Colonial silver display. (Daily; closed all univ hols) 9th Ave & Capstone Dr. **FREE**

The Old Observatory. (1844) The only pre-Civil War classroom bldg still standing.

Little Round House. (Sentry Box ca 1860) Once used by students on guard duty, it was fired on but not destroyed by Union troops. Adj Gorgas Library.

Denny Chimes. A 115-ft-high tower erected in honor of former univ president Dr. George H. Denny. On the quarter-hr the Westminster Chimes are struck, and selections are played each afternoon on the campanile (carillon). University Blvd, opp President's Mansion.

Will T. Murphy African American Museum. (ca 1925) House features 2 rms with changing exhibits relating to culture and heritage of African Americans; antique doll collection; rare books; some period furnishings. (By appt only) 2601 Paul Bryant Dr. Phone 205/758-2861. ¢¢

Annual Event

Moundville Native American Festival. Moundville Archaeological Park (see). Celebrates the culture of the Southeastern Native Americans with craft demonstrations, songs, dances, and folktales. Final day (Sat) is Indian Market Day when artisans exhibit their wares. Phone 205/371-2572. Late Sep.

Motels/Motor Lodges

★★ **BEST WESTERN PARK PLAZA.** *3801 McFarland Blvd (35405), at jct US 82 Bypass, I-20, I-59. 205/556-9690; fax 205/556-9690; res 800/528-1234; toll-free 800/235-7282. www.bestwestern.com.* 120 rms, 2 story. S $56.95-$62.95; D $60.95-$66.95; each addl $5. Crib free. TV; cable (premium). Pool; whirlpool. Complimentary bkfst. Restaurant adj 11 am-10 pm. Ck-out noon. Business servs avail. In-rm modem link. Cr cds: A, C, D, DS, MC, V.

★★★ FOUR POINTS SHERATON HOTEL. *320 Paul Bryant Dr (35401). 205/752-3200; fax 205/343-1138; res 800/325-3535; toll-free 800/477-2262. Email cwynn4pts@compuserve.com.* 152 units, 3 story. S, D $93-$99; each addl $10; suites $189-$269; under 17 free. Crib free. TV; cable (premium), VCR avail (movies). Pool; poolside serv. Restaurant 6:30 am-11 pm. Bar 4-11 pm. Ck-out noon. Meeting rms. Business servs avail. In-rm modem link. Bellhops. Free airport, railroad station transportation. Tennis. Refrigerator in suites. Cr cds: A, D, DS, MC, V.

★★ HAMPTON INN UNIVERSITY. *600 Harper Lee Dr (35401). 205/553-9800; fax 205/553-0082; res 800/426-7866.* 102 rms, 3 story. S $66; D $72; under 18 free; higher rates special events. Crib free. TV; cable (premium). Pool. Complimentary continental bkfst, coffee in rms. Ck-out noon. Business servs avail. In-rm modem link. Valet serv. Gift shop. Health club privileges. Cr cds: A, D, DS, MC, V.

★★ RAMADA INN. *631 Skyland Blvd E (35405); res 800/272-6232.* 108 rms, 2 story. S $39-$63; D $47-$85; each addl $5; under 18 free. Crib free. Pet accepted. TV; cable. Pool. Restaurant 6 am-2 pm, 5-10 pm. Bar 5 pm-1 am; Fri, Sat to 2 am; entertainment Mon-Sat. Ck-out noon. Meeting rms. Business servs avail. Valet serv. Cr cds: A, C, D, DS, JCB, MC, V.

★ SLEEP INN. *4300 Skyland Blvd (35405), I-59/I-20 Exit 76. 205/556-5696; fax 205/556-5696; res 800/753-3746. Email www.sleepinnbay@aol.com.* 73 rms, shower only, 2 story, 20 suites. S, D $37-$42; suites $52; each addl $5; under 17 free. Crib free. TV; cable (premium), VCR (movies avail $3). Pool. Complimentary continental bkfst, coffee in rms. Restaurant adj open 24 hrs. Ck-out noon. Meeting rm. Business servs avail. In-rm modem link. Exercise equipt. Cr cds: A, C, D, DS, ER, JCB, MC, V.

★ SUPER 8 MOTEL. *4125 McFarland Blvd E (35405), I-20 Exit 73. 205/758-8878; fax 205/752-8331; res 800/800-8000.* 62 rms, 3 story. No elvtr. S $35.99; D $38.99; each addl $5; under 12 free. Crib free. TV; cable (premium). Complimentary coffee. Ck-out 11 am. Cr cds: A, DS, MC, V.

★ TRAVELODGE. *3920 E McFarland Blvd (35405), 3½ mi S at jct US 82, I-20, I-59. 205/553-1550; fax 205/553-1550; res 800/322-3489.* 166 rms, 2 story. S, D $50-$70; each addl $5; under 19 free. Crib free. TV; cable. Pool. Playground. Complimentary continental bkfst, coffee in rms. Bar 5-10 pm. Ck-out noon. Meeting rms. Business servs avail. Valet serv. Sundries. Cr cds: A, C, D, DS, JCB, MC, V.

Restaurants

★★ HENSON'S CYPRESS INN. *501 Rice Mine Rd N (35406). 205/345-6963.* Specializes in catfish, steak, chicken. Own desserts. Hrs: 11 am-2 pm, 5:30-9:30 pm; Fri, Sat 5-10 pm; Sun 5:30-9 pm. Closed hols. Bar. Lunch $5.95-$8.95; dinner $10.95-$16.95. Child's menu. Riverfront view. Cr cds: A, D, MC, V.

★★ O'CHARLEY'S. *3799 McFarland Blvd E (35405). 205/556-5143.* Specializes in seafood, prime rib. Hrs: 11 am-11 pm; Fri, Sat to midnight; Sun 10 am-10 pm. Closed Dec 25. Bar. Lunch $4.99-$6.99; dinner $6.19-$12.99. Sat, Sun brunch, $4.99-$12.99. Child's menu. Cr cds: A, D, DS, MC, V.

★ TREY YUEN. *4200 McFarland Blvd E (35405), in Delchamp Plaza S. 205/752-0088.* Specializes in Mongolian beef. Hrs: 11 am-2:30 pm, 4:30-10 pm. Closed hols. Bar. Lunch $4-$10; dinner $5-$12. Chinese decor. Cr cds: A, D, MC, V.

Tuskegee

(E-5) *See also Auburn, Montgomery*

Settled ca 1763 **Pop** 12,257
Elev 468 ft **Area code** 334 **Zip** 36083
Information Office of the Mayor, City Hall, 101 Fonville St; 334/727-2180

An important part of Tuskegee's history lies in the story of Tuskegee Institute and two well-known men in African Amerian history, Booker T. Washington and George Washington Carver. But it was Lewis Adams, a former slave, who was largely responsible for gathering financial support from northern and southern whites to launch Tuskegee Normal and Industrial Institute. It began on July 4, 1881 with 30 students housed in an old frame building; Booker T. Washington was its president. Tuskegee also has a number of antebellum houses and a Ranger District office of the Tuskegee National Forest.

What to See and Do

★ **Tuskegee Institute National Historic Site.** (1881) Booker T. Washington is generally given credit for having founded Tuskegee Institute. In 1965 the college was designated a National Historical Landmark in recognition of the outstanding role it has played in the educational, economic, and social advancement of African Americans in our nation's history. In 1974 Congress established Tuskegee Institute National Historic Site to incl "The Oaks," home of Booker T. Washington, the George Washington Carver Museum, and the Historic Campus District. The 5,000-acre campus consists of more than 160 bldgs. (Daily; closed Jan 1, Thanksgiving, Dec 25) Phone 334/727-6390 for site information. **FREE**

Tuskegee National Forest. An 11,077-acre forest with fishing; hunting, hiking on Bartram National Recreation Trail. Atasi and Taska picnic sites. Primitive camping. Tsinia Wildlife Viewing Area. Contact District Ranger, 125 National Forest Rd 949. E via US 80. Phone 334/727-2652.

Conference Center

★★★ **KELLOGG CONFERENCE CENTER.** *PO Box 1243 (36087), at Tuskegee University. 334/727-3000; fax 334/724-2746; res 800/949-6161. Email onkrouse@acd.tusk.edu; www.tusk.edu.* 98 rms, 4 story, 10 suites. Mar-Apr, Sep-Oct: S, D $85; each addl $10; suites $175; under 17 free; lower rates rest of yr. Parking garage. Indoor pool, lap pool, whirlpool. TV; cable, VCR avail. Restaurant. Bar. Ck-out noon, ck-in 3 pm. Meeting rms. Business center. Bellhops. Dry cleaning. Gift shop. Exercise privileges. Golf. Tennis. Supervised children's activities. Picnic facilities. Cr cds: A, C, D, DS, ER, JCB, MC, V.

ARKANSAS

Arkansas's areas of forested wilderness are much the same as those De Soto discovered in 1541. In the lovely Ozark and Ouachita mountain ranges, separated by the Arkansas River, there are splendid hardwood forests and streams. Pine and hardwood trees shade streams filled with enough black bass, bream, and trout to restore any angler's faith. There are deer, geese, ducks, and quail to hunt and feast on in season. Ducks fly over eastern Arkansas, and such towns as Stuttgart make a big event of hunting them. The White River National Wildlife Refuge east of here is a wilderness area. Caves, springs, meadows, valleys, bayous, rice and cotton fields, and magnificent lakes and rivers dot the state. For an enjoyable backwoods vacation the visitor can hardly do better, with a choice of either a quiet rustic resort or cosmopolitan Hot Springs National Park—the renowned spa dedicated to sophisticated pleasures as well as the therapeutic treatment of the visitor.

Population: 2,551,373
Area: 53,187 square miles
Elevation: 54-2,753 feet
Peak: Magazine Mountain (Logan County)
Entered Union: June 15, 1836 (25th state)
Capital: Little Rock
Motto: The people rule
Nickname: The Natural State
Flower: Apple Blossom
Bird: Mockingbird
Tree: Pine
Fair: Early-mid October, 2001, in Little Rock
Time Zone: Central
Website: www.arkansas.com

In contrast is the Arkansas that is one of the major producers of bromine brine in the United States. In addition, a large amount of crude oil and bauxite (aluminum ore) comes from Arkansas every year. Sixty useful tree varieties grow here, and timber is big business. In fact, practically every crop except citrus fruit is cultivated on its acres, including rice, strawberries, peaches, grapes, apples, cotton, soybeans, sorghum, and wheat. Arkansas is also a state plentiful in raw materials and has the only diamond field in North America open to the public. Preserved as Crater of Diamonds State Park (see MURFREESBORO), visitors may dig for diamonds on a "finders, keepers" basis.

Because Arkansas was remote, of rugged terrain, and slightly off-track of the western surge of frontier expansion, the area was slow to develop. After the Spaniards came the French—Marquette and Joliet visited the territory in 1673, and La Salle took possession for France in 1682. The first permanent settlement was made by Henri de Tonty in 1686 at Arkansas Post (see), which today is a national memorial (see). It was not until 1804, a year after Arkansas and the rest of the Louisiana Purchase had become US property, that the government paid any attention to the area. A United States headquarters was established at Arkansas Post; in 1819 the Arkansas Territory was organized and two years later the capital was moved to Little Rock.

When to Go/Climate

Arkansas enjoys a generally moderate climate, punctuated by hot, humid sum-

The Ozarks

mers and mild winters. Early spring can be rainy and damp. Mild winter temperatures (daytime in the 50s) make this a comfortable time as well.

AVERAGE HIGH/LOW TEMPERATURES (°F)

FORT SMITH

Jan 48/26	**May** 81/58	**Sep** 85/62
Feb 54/30	**June** 88/66	**Oct** 76/49
Mar 64/39	**July** 93/70	**Nov** 63/38
Apr 74/49	**Aug** 92/69	**Dec** 51/29

LITTLE ROCK

Jan 49/29	**May** 81/59	**Sep** 85/64
Feb 54/33	**June** 89/67	**Oct** 75/51
Mar 64/42	**July** 92/72	**Nov** 63/42
Apr 73/51	**Aug** 91/70	**Dec** 53/33

Parks and Recreation Finder

Directions to and information about the parks and recreation areas below are given under their respective town/city sections. Please refer to those sections for details.

NATIONAL PARK AND RECREATION AREAS

Key to abbreviations. I.H.S. = International Historic Site; I.P.M. = International Peace Memorial; N.B. = National Battlefield; N.B.P. = National Battlefield Park; N.B.C. = National Battlefield and Cemetery; N.C.A. = National Conservation Area; N.E.M. = National Expansion Memorial; N.F. = National Forest; N.G. = National Grassland; N.H.P. = National Historical Park; N.H.C. = National Heritage Corridor; N.H.S. = National Historic Site; N.L. = National Lakeshore; N.M. = National Monument; N.M.P. = National Military Park; N.Mem. = National Memorial; N.P. = National Park; N.Pres. = National Preserve; N.R.A. = National Recreational Area; N.R.R. = National Recreational River; N.Riv. = National River; N.S. = National Seashore; N.S.R. = National Scenic Riverway; N.S.T. = National Scenic Trail; N.Sc. = National Scientific Reserve; N.V.M. = National Volcanic Monument.

Place Name	Listed Under
Arkansas Post N.Mem.	same
Buffalo N.Riv.	same
Fort Smith N.H.S.	FORT SMITH
Hot Springs N.P.	same
Ouachita N.F.	HOT SPRINGS & HOT SPRINGS NATIONAL PARK
Ozark N.F.	RUSSELLVILLE
Pea Ridge N.M.P.	ROGERS
St. Francis N.F.	HELENA

STATE PARK AND RECREATION AREAS

Key to abbreviations. I.P. = Interstate Park; S.A.P. = State Archaeological Park; S.B. = State Beach; S.C.A. = State Conservation Area; S.C.P. = State Conservation Park; S.Cp. = State Campground; S.F. = State Forest; S.G. = State Garden; S.H.A. = State Historic Area; S.H.P. = State Historic Park; S.H.S. = State Historic Site; S.M.P. = State Marine Park; S.N.A. = State Natural Area; S.P. = State Park; S.P.C. = State Public Campground; S.R. = State Reserve; S.R.A. = State Recreation Area; S.Res. = State Reservoir; S.Res.P. = State Resort Park; S.R.P. = State Rustic Park.

Place Name	Listed Under
Bull Shoals S.P.	BULL SHOALS LAKE AREA
Crater of Diamonds S.P.	MURFREESBORO
Crowley's Ridge S.P.	JONESBORO
DeGray Lake Resort S.P.	ARKADELPHIA
Devil's Den S.P.	FAYETTEVILLE
Jacksonport S.P.	NEWPORT
Jenkins' Ferry State Historic Monument	MALVERN
Lake Catherine S.P.	MALVERN
Lake Charles S.P.	WALNUT RIDGE
Lake Chicot S.P.	DUMAS
Lake Dardanelle S.P.	RUSSELLVILLE
Lake Fierson S.P.	JONESBORO
Lake Fort Smith S.P.	ALMA
Lake Ouachita S.P.	HOT SPRINGS
Logoly S.P.	MAGNOLIA
Millwood S.P.	ASHDOWN
Moro Bay S.P.	EL DORADO
Mount Nebo S.P.	RUSSELLVILLE
Old Davidsonville S.P.	POCAHONTAS
Petit Jean S.P.	same
Pinnacle Mountain S.P.	LITTLE ROCK
Queen Wilhelmina S.P.	MENA
Village Creek S.P.	FORREST CITY
White Oak Lake S.P.	CAMDEN
Withrow Springs S.P.	EUREKA SPRINGS
Woolly Hollow S.P.	CONWAY

Water-related activities, hiking, various other sports, picnicking and visitor centers, camping, as well as cabins and lodges are available in many of these areas. Camping: $7.50-$18.50/day. Swimming: $2-$2.25; under 6 free. Pets on leash only. Campers must register at the park office before occupying a site; all sites assigned, reservations available. Parks open all year; some facilities closed December-February or March. Brochures on state parks may be obtained from the Dept of Parks and Tourism, Parks Div, One Capitol Mall, Little Rock 72201; 501/682-1191 or 888/ATPARKS.

FISHING AND HUNTING

Nonresident fishing license: annual, $30; 14-day, $20; 7-day, $15; 3-day, $10. Trout permit, $7.50. Largemouth bass can be found in all big lakes; trout in the White, Little Red, Spring, and Little Missouri rivers; bluegill and crappie in most Arkansas lakes and rivers. Annual nonresident hunting license: basic (for small game), $75; annual nonresident all game hunting license: $195. Nonresident short trip license (5 days for small game) for anything in season except deer, turkey, and bear, $50. Nonresident all game license 5 days, $125; 3 days, $95. State duck stamp: $7. Licenses may be ordered by phone, 800/364-GAME (credit card only). Arkansas fishing and hunting regulations are available from the Game and Fish Commission, #2 Natural Resources Dr, Little Rock 72205; 501/223-6300 or 800/364-GAME.

Driving Information

Safety belts are mandatory for all persons in front seat of vehicle. Every driver who regularly transports a child under the age of 5 years in a motor vehicle registered in this state, except one operated for hire, shall provide for the protection of such child by properly placing, maintaining, and securing such child in a child passenger safety seat meeting federal standards. With any child 3-5 years of age, a safety belt shall be sufficient. For further information phone 501/569-2000.

CALENDAR HIGHLIGHTS

APRIL

Arkansas Folk Festival (Mountain View). Arts and crafts, parade, rodeo, traditional music of the Ozarks, games, food. Phone 870/269-8098.

MAY

Riverfest (Little Rock). Visual and performing arts festival. Food, crafts, entertainment, fireworks. Phone 501/376-4781.

JUNE

Old Fort River Festival (Fort Smith). Arts and crafts festival, entertainment, sporting events. Phone 501/783-6118.

JULY

Rodeo of the Ozarks (Springdale). Parsons Arena. Phone 501/751-4694.

AUGUST

National Invitational Explorer Canoe Race (Batesville). Races on the White River. Phone 870/793-2378.

Watermelon Festival (Hope). Seed-spitting, melon-eating contests; arts and crafts, music. Phone 870/777-3640.

SEPTEMBER

Summerset (North Little Rock). Races, tournaments, food, entertainment, children's activities, fireworks. Labor Day wkend. Phone 501/758-1424 or 800/643-4690.

OCTOBER

Arkansas State Fair & Livestock Show (Little Rock). State Fairgrounds. Rodeo shows and more. Phone 501/372-8341.

Frontier Days (Hope). Old Washington Historic State Park. Period activities and demonstrations. Phone 870/983-2684.

INTERSTATE HIGHWAY SYSTEM

The following alphabetical listing of Arkansas towns in *Mobil Travel Guide* shows that these cities are within 10 miles of the indicated Interstate highways. A highway map, however, should be checked for the nearest exit.

Highway Number	Cities/Towns within 10 miles
Interstate 30	Arkadelphia, Benton, Hope, Little Rock, Malvern.
Interstate 40	Alma, Conway, Forrest City, Fort Smith, Little Rock, Morrilton, Russellville.
Interstate 55	Blytheville.

Additional Visitor Information

A variety of pamphlets and maps are distributed by the Arkansas Department of Parks and Tourism, One Capitol Mall, Little Rock 72201; 501/682-7777 or 800/NATURAL.

There are tourist information centers at several points of entry into Arkansas; travel consultants provide suggested tour routes, a state tour guide and literature on places of interest. The centers are open daily and located in the following cities: Bentonville, US 71S; Blytheville, I-55S; Corning, US 67S; Fort Smith/Van Buren (Dora), I-40E; El Dorado, US 167N; Harrison, US 65S; Helena, US 49E; Lake Village, jct US 65, 82 & AR 144; Mammoth Spring, US 63; Red River, US 71N; Siloam Springs, US 412E; Texarkana, I-30E; and West Memphis, I-40W. Inquire locally for exact locations.

From Little Rock, drive southwest via I-30 to Benton and travel Arkansas 5 west to Hot Springs. Inside the vintage town is Hot Springs National Park, encompassing restored 1920s bath houses, 30 miles of mountain hiking trails, a lovely, century-old resort hotel, and numerous spas for taking the thermal, healing waters. In town, too, are a prestigious thoroughbred racing track, wax museum, passion play, aquarium, and Bill Clinton's high school. Immediately south of town is Lake Hamilton, with resorts, a touring riverboat, and marinas. A short drive further south, via Arkansas 7, is DeGray Lake Resort State Park on beautiful DeGray Lake, with a lodge, golf course, horseback riding, and fishing. Heading north again on I-30 toward Little Rock, take Arkansas 171 west a couple of miles to Lake Catherine State Park, surrounded by forested hills, perfect for hiking, camping, and cabin stays. **(Approx 160 mi)**

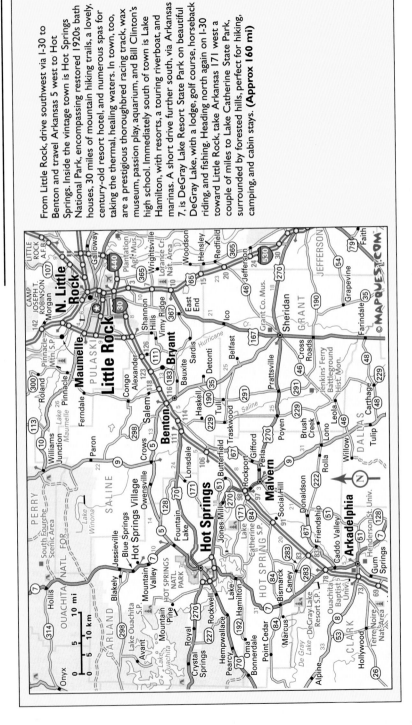

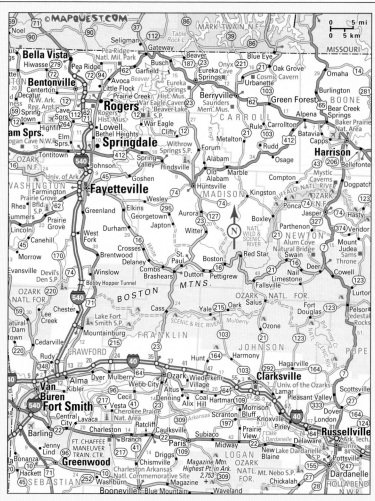

From Fort Smith, drive north on Highway 71, a designated scenic route, through the rugged, forested Boston Mountains, to Fayetteville, site of a home used as Union and Confederate headquarters during the Civil War, and the graceful, historic University of Arkansas; and to Rogers, jumping off point for War Eagle Caverns and the vintage War Eagle grist mill. Head east on Highway 62 to Pea Ridge National Military Park, site of the largest Civil War battle west of the Mississippi; and east again to Eureka Springs, a profusely Victorian town of breathtaking beauty, perched on cliffs and filled with restored buildings occupied by bed-and-breakfast inns, shops, museums, and cafes. Travel further east on Highway 62 to Harrison; then south on Scenic Arkansas 7 to Mystic Caverns, mountain cabin retreats and another access point to the Buffalo National River, at Ponca, with log cabins, canoeing, hot-air ballooning, camping, hiking, and horseback riding. Continue south on Scenic Arkansas 7 through the Ozark National Forest— spectacular in spring with blooming dogwood and in fall with changing leaves—to I-40, which leads west again to Fort Smith.
(Approx 275 mi)

Alma

(C-1) *See also Fort Smith*

Pop 2,959 **Elev** 430 ft **Area code** 501
Zip 72921

What to See and Do

Lake Fort Smith State Park. This
125-acre park is surrounded by the
Boston Mts, Fort Smith, and Shepherd Springs lakes. The western end
of the 140-mi Ozark Highlands Trail
begins here and, for a few miles, runs
in conjunction with the 7-mi Evan's
Point Loop Trail, offering excellent
views of waterfalls, box canyons, and
towering bluffs. Swimming pool,
bathhouse, lifeguard, fishing, boating
(rentals); hiking trails; tennis, picnicking, playground, limited camping (hookups), cabins. Visitor center,
interpretive programs (summer).
Standard fees. (Daily) 13 mi N on US
71. Contact Superintendent, PO Box
4, Mountainburg 72946. Phone 501/
369-2469. **FREE**

**White Rock Mountain Recreation
Area.** A 94-acre primitive area at the
summit of 2,287-ft White Rock peak
with panoramic views. Nature trails,
picnicking, camping. Six mi from the
summit on Forest Service Road 1505
is 82-acre Shores Lake with water
sports, boating (ramp), picnicking,
camping (fee). Fees charged at recreation sites. (Daily) 13 mi NE on AR
215, forest roads, in Boston Mts of
Ozark National Forests. Phone
501/369-4128 or 501/667-2191.

Wiederkehr Wine Cellars. Guided
wine-tasting tour (gourmet and nonalcoholic beverage tasting for persons
under 21); self-guided tour of vine-
yards; observation tower; restaurant;
gift shop. Tours. (Daily; closed hols)
4 mi S of I-40 Exit 41, near Altus.
Phone 501/468-WINE or 800/622-
WINE. **FREE**

Restaurant

★ ★ ★ **WIEDERKEHR WINE CEL-
LARS.** *3324 Swiss Family Dr (72821),
on AR 186, 4½ mi S of I-40 Exit 41.
501/468-3551. Email wiederke@ipa.net;
www.wiederkehrwinecellarsl.bizonthe.*

net. Specializes in beef and cheese
fondues, quiche Lorraine, Matterhorn
schnitzel. Own baking. Hrs: 11 am- 9
pm. Closed hols. Res accepted. Lunch
$4.50-$7.25; dinner $8.50-$23.75.
Child's menu. Winery tours. Family-
owned. Cr cds: A, D, DS, MC, V.
◨

Arkadelphia

(E-3) *See also Hot Springs, Malvern*

Settled 1809 **Pop** 10,014 **Elev** 245 ft
Area code 870 **Zip** 71923
Web www.arkadelphia.dina.org
Information Chamber of Commerce,
107 N 6th St, PO Box 38; 870/246-
5542 or 800/874-4289

On a bluff overlooking the Ouachita
River and once an important landing
for steamboats, this community is
now an agricultural and industrial
center producing boats, wood products, jeans, commercial roofing,
brake shoes, and fiberglass vaults. It
is the home of Henderson State University (1890) and Ouachita Baptist
University.

What to See and Do

DeGray Lake. DeGray Dam
impounds the waters of the Caddo
River to form this 13,000-acre lake
with 207 mi of shoreline. Waterskiing, fishing; boating, swimming
beach; picnicking, visitor center,
camping (fee). (Daily) 1 mi NW off
AR 7. Phone 870/246-5501. Per vehicle ¢¢ On the NE shore is

DeGray Lake Resort State Park. A
938-acre resort park. Swimming,
fishing, boating (houseboat and
sailboat rentals, marina, launch).
Nature trail; 18-hole golf and pro
shop, tennis. Picnicking, playground, store, laundry, restaurant,
lodge (see). Camping (many water,
electric hookups; dump station; res
avail Apr-Oct). Visitor center; interpretive programs. Guided hikes,
lake cruises, square dances, hay
rides, live animal demonstrations,
evening slides, and films. Standard
fees. 6 mi N of I-30, on AR 7. Contact Superintendent, Rte 3, PO Box

490, Bismarck 71929;. Phone 870/865-2801 (visitor center).

Henderson State University Museum. Victorian house (1893) of C.C. Henderson, with displays of Caddo artifacts and items of historic interest. (Mon, Wed, Fri afternoons) 10th & Henderson Sts. Phone 870/246-7311 or 870/246-5511. **FREE**

Hot Springs National Park. (see). 32 mi N via AR 7.

Ouachita Baptist University. (1886) 1,350 students. On the banks of the Ouachita River, surrounded by the foothills of the Ouachita Mts. McClellan Hall contains the official papers and memorabilia of US Senator John L. McClellan. Campus tours. Phone 870/245-5206.

Annual Events

Festival of the Two Rivers. Arts and crafts, juried art show, contests, games, food. Phone 870/246-5542. Mid-Apr.

Clark County Fair. Sep.

Motels/Motor Lodges

★★ **BEST WESTERN CONTINENTAL INN.** *136 Valley St (71923). 870/246-5592; fax 870/246-3583.* 59 rms, 2 story. S, D $52; each addl $5; family rates; higher rates hols. Crib free. Pet accepted. TV; cable (premium), VCR avail. Complimentary coffee in rms. Restaurant 6 am-10 pm. Ck-out 11 am. Coin lndry. Pool. Playground. Cr cds: A, C, D, DS, MC, V.
🄳 🐾 ⛱ 🛏 🐾 SC

★★ **QUALITY INN.** *Jct I-30 and AR 7 (71923). 870/246-5855; fax 870/246-8552; res 800/228-5151; toll-free 800/342-4876. www.qualityinns.com.* 59 rms, 2 story, 3 suites. May-Sep: S $59; D $66; each addl $5; suites $80; under 16 free; lower rates rest of yr. Crib avail. Pet accepted, some restrictions. Parking lot. Pool. TV; cable (premium). Complimentary full bkfst, coffee in rms, newspaper, toll-free calls. Restaurant. Business center. Dry cleaning, coin lndry. Free airport transportation. Golf, 18 holes. Tennis, 10 courts. Cr cds: A, C, D, DS, ER, JCB, MC, V.
🄳 🐾 🎿 🏊 🛏 🐾 SC 🏃

Restaurants

★ **BOWEN'S.** *I-30 and AR 7 (71923), AR 7 Exit 78. 870/246-8661.* Specializes in chicken, beef. Salad bar. Hrs: 6 am-9 pm; Fri, Sat to 9:30 pm. Closed Dec 25. Res accepted. Bkfst $1.75-$5.75. Buffet: $4.35; lunch $2-$10. Buffet: $4.85; dinner $2-$10. Buffet: $6.50. Child's menu. Cr cds: A, DS, MC, V.
🄳 🍽

★ **KREG'S CATFISH.** *2805 W Pine St (71923), I-30 Exit 73. 870/246-5327.* Seafood menu. Specializes in catfish, chicken. Hrs: 11 am-8:30 pm; Fri, Sat to 9 pm. Closed hols. Lunch, dinner $3.50-$8.50. Cr cds: DS, MC, V.
🄳

Arkansas Post National Memorial

See also Dumas, Pine Bluff

Arkansas Post was established at a Quapaw Indian village in 1686 as a trading post by Henri de Tonty, lieutenant to La Salle during the latter's pioneer explorations. Although the post was never a major French settlement, by 1759 it had grown to an impressive 40-man garrison. Ownership abruptly changed hands following the British victory in the French and Indian War. France ceded Louisiana, including the Arkansas territory, to Spain in 1762. Spanish interests, however, were not long served. The Spaniards joined the American patriots during the American Revolution, not out of sympathy but as a matter of self-interest. The resulting skirmishes between Spain and Britain over the territory came to an end less than two years after Yorktown. Unable to cope with raids and aggressive frontiersmen, Spain ceded the territory back to France.

The Post was bought by the United States as part of the Louisiana Purchase in 1803. In 1819 it became the capitol of the new Arkansas Territory and the home of Arkansas's first newspaper, the Arkansas *Gazette*. In

1821 the capital and the *Gazette* both moved to Little Rock. The Post continued as a river port until the Civil War, when battles and numerous floods finally destroyed the little town.

Arkansas Post was made a state park in 1929 and a national memorial in 1964. Fishing, hiking, and picnicking are enjoyed on the 389 acres of this wildlife sanctuary. Personnel and exhibits, including a partial replica of a 1783 Spanish fort, tell the story of the post. Visitor center (daily; closed Jan 1, Dec 25). Contact Superintendent, 1741 Old Post Rd, Gillett 72055; 501/548-2207.

What to See and Do

Arkansas Post Museum. Museum and five bldgs housing artifacts of Arkansas's first settlers; colonial kitchen; 1877 log house with period furnishings; Civil War memorabilia; child's 3-rm furnished playhouse. (Mar-mid-Dec, Wed-Sun; closed hols) 5 mi S of Gillett on US 165 (Great River Rd). Phone 870/548-2634. **FREE**

Ashdown

(F-1)

Founded 1892 **Pop** 5,150 **Elev** 327 ft **Area code** 870 **Zip** 71822

What to See and Do

Millwood Dam and Reservoir. This dam impounds a 29,500-acre lake. Swimming, fishing; playgrounds, camping (electric hookups; fee). (Daily) 9 mi E on AR 32. Phone 870/898-3343. Adj is

Millwood State Park. Approx 800 acres. Fishing, boating (rentals, marina); hiking trails, picnicking, playground, rest rms, store, camping (hookups, dump station). Standard fees. Visitor center. Contact Superintendent, 1564 AR 32E. Phone 870/898-2800.

Batesville

(B-5) *See also Greers Ferry Lake Area, Mountain View, Newport*

Pop 9,187 **Elev** 364 ft **Area code** 870 **Zip** 72501
Web www.batesville.dina.org
Information Batesville Area Chamber of Commerce, 409 Vine St; 870/793-2378

Annual Events

Ozark Scottish Festival. Lyon College. Pipe bands, Highland dancing, Scottish feast, Parade of Clans. Late Apr.
White River Water Carnival. Parade, arts and crafts, beauty pageant. Late July-early Aug.
National Invitational Explorer Canoe Race. White River, from Cotter to Batesville. Phone 870/793-2378. Last day of Water Carnival.

Motel/Motor Lodge

★★ **BEST WESTERN SCENIC MOTOR INN.** *773 Batesville Blvd (72501), 2 mi S at jct US 167, AR 25. 870/698-1855; fax 870/698-1855; res 800/528-1234. www.bestwestern.com.* 40 rms, 2 story. Mar-Oct: S $61; D $65; each addl $4; under 12 free; lower rates rest of yr. Parking lot. Pool. TV; cable (premium), VCR avail. Complimentary coffee in rms, toll-free calls. Restaurant 5 am-8 pm. Ck-out noon, ck-in 3 pm. Tennis, 2 courts. Cr cds: A, C, D, DS, MC, V.

Hotel

★★ **RAMADA INN.** *1325 N St. Louis St (71701), US 167 N. 870/698-1800; fax 870/698-1800; toll-free 800/272-6232. Email ramada@arkansas.net.* 124 units, 2 story. S $53; D $59; each addl $6; suites $105; under 18 free. Crib free. Pet accepted. TV; cable (premium). Pool; whirlpool. Coffee in rms. Restaurant 6 am-2 pm, 5-9:45 pm; Sun 6 am-2 pm. Private club 4 pm-midnight. Ck-out noon. Coin lndry. Meeting rms. Some refrigerators; microwaves avail. Cr cds: A, DS, MC, V.

Benton

(D-3) *See also Hot Springs, Little Rock, Malvern*

Founded 1836 **Pop** 18,177 **Elev** 416 ft
Area code 501 **Zip** 72015
Web www.bentonchamber.org
Information Chamber of Commerce, 607 N Market St; 501/315-8272 or 501/315-8290

Benton is the seat of Saline County. A large amount of bauxite mined in the United States comes from this area. The city also has important wood products factories.

What to See and Do

Gann Museum. This is the only known bldg made of bauxite; dug from a nearby farm, hand-sawed into blocks, and allowed to harden. It originally was a medical office built in 1893 by patients who could not afford to pay the doctor. Contains furniture and artifacts reflecting local pioneer, Native American, and church history; Niloak pottery. (Tues, Thurs, Sun; tours by appt; closed Jan 1, Thanksgiving, Dec 25) 218 S Market St. Phone 501/778-5513. **FREE**

Hot Springs National Park. (see). 27 mi W via US 70.

Unrated Dining Spot

BROWN'S. *18718 I-30 (72015), Exit 118.* 501/778-5033. Specializes in seafood, catfish, chicken. Salad bar. Hrs: 6:30 am-9 pm. Closed Thanksgiving, Dec 25. Bkfst buffet: $3.99; lunch buffet: $5.99; dinner buffet: $7.99. Child's menu. Country decor. Country store adj. Cr cds: DS, MC, V.
⎣D⎦

Bentonville

(A-1) *See also Fayetteville, Rogers, Springdale*

Founded 1837 **Pop** 11,257
Elev 1,305 ft **Area code** 501
Zip 72712 **Web** www.nwanews.com/bbvchamber
Information Bentonville-Bella Vista Chamber of Commerce, 412 S Main St; 501/273-2841

Bentonville was named for Thomas Hart Benton, the first senator from Missouri and a militant champion of pioneers. Benton was also the great-uncle of the painter by the same name. The town square maintains a turn-of-the-century character.

What to See and Do

Peel Mansion & Historic Gardens. Villa tower Italianate mansion (1875) built by Colonel Samuel West Peel, the first native-born Arkansan to serve in US Congress, has been restored and refurnished in Victorian style. The 180-acre site also has an outdoor museum of historic roses, perennials, and native plants. The pre-Civil War Andy Lynch log cabin serves as gatehouse and gift shop. (Tues-Sat) 400 S Walton Blvd. Phone 501/273-9664. ¢¢

Annual Event

Sugar Creek Arts & Crafts Fair. Mid-Oct.

Motels/Motor Lodges

★★ **BEST WESTERN BENTONVILLE INN.** *2800 SE Walton (72712), US 71 Exit 65.* 501/273-9727; res 800/528-1234. 54 rms, 2 story. S $43-$47; D $47; each addl $5; suite $85; under 12 free; higher rates special events. Crib $5. Pet accepted, some restrictions; $5. TV; cable (premium). Pool. Complimentary coffee in lobby. Restaurant adj 6 am-10 pm. Ck-out 11 am. Business servs avail. In-rm modem link. Many refrigerators; microwaves avail. Cr cds: A, DS, MC, V.

★★ **RAMADA INN.** *1209 N Walton Blvd (72712), US 71 Exit 72. 501/273-2451; fax 501/273-7611; toll-free 800/548-2772.* 152 rms, 2 story. S, D $56-$75; each addl $8; under 18 free; wkend rates; higher rates special events. Crib avail. TV; cable (premium). Indoor pool; poolside serv. Restaurant 6 am-2 pm, 5-10 pm. Business servs avail. Exercise equipt. Rec rm. Cr cds: A, C, D, DS, ER, JCB, MC, V.

★ **SUPER 8.** *2301 SE Walton Blvd (72712), US 71W, Exit 62. 501/273-1818; fax 501/273-5529.* 52 rms, 2 story. S $47.60; D $52.73; suite $77.70; higher rates special events. Crib avail. Pet accepted. TV; cable (premium). Pool. Complimentary continental bkfst. Restaurant adj 6 am-11:30 pm. Ck-out 11 am. Free airport transportation. Picnic tables. Cr cds: A, C, D, DS, MC, V.

Hotel

★★ **HOLIDAY INN EXPRESS HOTEL & SUITES.** *2205 SE Walton Blvd (72712). 501/271-2222; fax 501/271-2227; res 800/465-4329. Email hiebntvl@arkansas.net; www.hiexpress.com/bentonvillear.* 84 rms, 4 story, 20 suites. S, D $68; suites $95; under 18 free; wkend rates. Crib avail. TV; cable (premium). Complimentary continental bkfst. Restaurant opp 5:30 am-11 pm. Ck-out 11 am. Meeting rms. Business center. In-rm modem link. Coin lndry. Exercise equipt; sauna. Some microwaves; in-rm whirlpool, refrigerator in suites. Cr cds: A, DS, MC, V.

Restaurant

★★ **FRED'S HICKORY INN.** *1502 N Walton Blvd (72712), 1 mi S of US 71 Exit 72. 501/273-3303.* Specializes in barbecue, spaghetti, steak. Hrs: 11 am-10 pm; Sat from 5:30 pm. Closed hols. Res accepted. Bar. Lunch $4-$9; dinner $9-$20. Child's menu. Parking. Five dining rms. Family-owned. Cr cds: A, D, DS, MC, V.

Berryville

(A-2) *See also Eureka Springs, Harrison*

Founded 1850 **Pop** 3,212
Elev 1,200 ft **Area code** 870
Zip 72616
Web www.cswnet.com/~berryvil/

Information Chamber of Commerce, PO Box 402; 870/423-3704

This area is known for poultry raising and dairy farming. There is also good fishing. Berryville is the southern gateway to the Table Rock Lake Area in Missouri (see).

What to See and Do

Carroll County Heritage Center. Local historical exhibits and genealogical material housed in old courthouse (1880). (Mon-Fri; closed hols) 403 Public Sq. Phone 870/423-6312. ¢

Cosmic Cavern. Cavern below mountain features Ozark's largest underground lake; electrically lighted; constant 58°F. Visitor center, picnic area. 1-hr guided tours (daily). 7 mi N on AR 21. Phone 870/749-2298. ¢¢

Saunders Memorial Museum. Revolvers, pistols, and small arms, some originally owned by Pancho Villa, Jesse James, and Wild Bill Hickok; antiques; handcrafts; silver; china; rugs; and furniture. (Apr-Oct, Mon-Sat) 115 E Madison, on AR 21. Phone 870/423-2563. ¢¢

Annual Events

Ice Cream Social. Historic Sq. 2nd wkend June.

Carroll County Fair. Wk of Labor Day.

Saunders Memorial Muzzleloading and Frontier Gun Shoot & Handcrafters' Show. Costumed contestants; gun show. Last full wkend Sep.

Blytheville (B-7)

Settled 1880 **Pop** 22,906 **Elev** 255 ft
Area code 870 **Zip** 72315
Information Chamber of Commerce,
PO Box 485, 72316; 870/762-2012

Blytheville is one of two seats of Mississippi County. It is a leading industrial and retail trade center for northeast Arkansas and maintains its agricultural heritage. Duck hunting is good here, especially on the Mississippi Flyway. Mallard Lake, 12 miles west on AR 18, has good bass, bream, and crappie fishing. Big Lake Wildlife Refuge, 12 miles west on AR 18, is a winter nesting area for migratory waterfowl.

Motels/Motor Lodges

★★ **BEST WESTERN INN.** *3700 S Division St (72315). 870/762-5200; fax 870/763-2580.* 40 rms, 2 story. June-Sep: S $57; D $57-$84; each addl $5; under 12 free. Crib free. TV; cable (premium). Complimentary continental bkfst. Ck-out 11 am. Business servs avail. Coin lndry. Pool. Some in-rm whirlpools; microwaves avail. Cr cds: A, C, D, DS, MC, V.
⬜ 🏊 🚭 ♨ SC

★★ **COMFORT INN.** *1520 E Main St (72315), jct I-55 and AR 18. 870/763-7081; fax 870/763-7081; toll-free 800/228-5150.* 105 rms, 2 story. S $49; D $54; each addl $5; under 18 free. Crib free. TV; cable (premium). Pool. Complimentary continental bkfst. Restaurant 11 am-11 pm. Private club. Ck-out noon. Meeting rms. Business servs avail. Microwaves avail. Cr cds: A, C, D, DS, ER, MC, V.
⬜ 🏊 🚭 ♨ SC

★★ **HAMPTON INN.** *301 N Access Rd (72315), ½ mi NE of jct AR 18, I-55 Exit 67. 870/763-*
5220; fax 870/762-1397; res 800/426-7866. 87 rms, 2 story. S $41.50; D $45.50; each addl $4; under 12 free. Crib free. Pet accepted. TV; cable (premium). Pool. Complimentary continental bkfst. Restaurant 10 am-9 pm. Ck-out noon. Microwaves avail. Cr cds: A, C, D, DS, MC, V.
⬜ 🐾 🏊 🏋 🏌 🚭 ♨ 🏃 🐾

★★ **HOLIDAY INN.** *1121 E Main (72315). 870/763-5800; fax 870/763-1326; res 800/465-4329.* 153 rms, 2 story. Mar-mid-Sep: S, D $65; under 19 free; wkend rates; lower rates rest of yr. Crib free. Pet accepted. TV; cable (premium). 2 pools, 1 indoor; whirlpool, steam rm, poolside serv. Restaurant 5:30 am-11 pm. Bar 4 pm-1 am, closed Sun; entertainment. Ck-out noon. Coin lndry. Meeting rms. Cr cds: A, DS, MC, V.
⬜ 🏊 🏋 🚭 ♨ 🐾

Buffalo National River

(Buffalo Point Contact Station, 17 mi S of Yellville via AR 14, 268; Tyler Bend Visitor Center, 11 mi N of Marshall via US 65)

Buffalo National River, preserving 135 miles of the free-flowing river in the scenic Ozarks of northwestern Arkansas, is known for its diversity. In the spring, whitewater enthusiasts float the upper river from Ponca to

Stair-Step Falls, Buffalo National River

Pruitt, stopping at primitive campgrounds at Steel Creek, Kyles Landing, Erbie, and Ozark. These areas also provide river access. Springs, waterfalls, streams, and woods along the river attract hikers; Lost Valley features self-guided hikes. River levels fluctuate; contact park headquarters for information on floatable areas. Primitive campgrounds on lower and middle stretches include Hasty, Carver, Mt Hersey, Woolum, Maumee, and Rush.

Visitor information is available at Buffalo Point Contact Station, at Tyler Bend Visitor Center and at Pruitt Ranger Station. They offer swimming; fishing; canoe rentals. Self-guided trails and hikes. Picnicking. Camping (fee). Programs and demonstrations led by interpreters. Evening programs blend natural and historic interpretation. The interpreters also lead float trips for novices and for those desiring a guided trip.

Housekeeping cabins are available from April through November. For information concerning cabin reservations contact the Buffalo Point Concessioner, HCR #66, Box 388, Yellville 72687; 870/449-6206. For general information contact the Superintendent, Buffalo National River, Box 1173, Harrison 72602; 870/741-5443.

Bull Shoals Lake Area

(A-3) *See also Harrison, Mountain Home*

(11 mi W of Mountain Home via AR 5, 178)

Area code 870

Bull Shoals Lake, on the White River in the Ozarks, was created by the US Army Corps of Engineers as a flood control and hydroelectric project in 1952. The lake has a 1,000-mile shoreline with recreation areas and boat docks at many points. Fishing is excellent both in the lake and in the White River below the dam, and other recreational activities abound. Fees charged at most recreation areas. Phone 870/425-2700.

What to See and Do

Bull Shoals State Park. More than 680 acres at SE corner of lake below dam. Fishing for trout; boating (ramp, rentals, dock). Hiking trails. Picnicking, playground, store. Camping (hookups, dump station; daily). Visitor center; interpretive programs (Apr-Oct). Standard fees. Golden Age Passport (see MAKING THE MOST OF YOUR TRIP). 6 mi N of Mountain Home on AR 5, then 7 mi W on AR 178. For further info contact the Superintendent, PO Box 205, Bull Shoals 72619. Phone 870/431-5521.

Note. Since Bull Shoals Dam serves as a hydroelectric plant, the water level in the river may rise and fall suddenly. A horn sounds when water levels are changing; however, due to weather conditions, the horn may be difficult to hear.

Resorts

★★ **BEL'ARCO.** *2 Crestline Dr (71639), 1 mi S, off AR 178, 3 mi W of Dam.* 870/445-4242; fax 870/445-7123; toll-free 877/423-5253. 60 units, 23 kits. S, D $45-$160; each addl $8; kit. units $55-$95; under 16 free. Crib free. TV; cable, VCR avail. Pool. Playground. Coffee in rms. Dining rms 7 am-10 pm. Box lunches. Picnics. Private club. Ck-out 11 am. Coin lndry. Grocery ½ mi. Package store 3 mi. Meeting rms. Business servs avail. In-rm modem link. Free airport transportaion. Tennis. Lawn games. Rec rm. Exercise equipt; sauna. Fish storage. Some refrigerators; microwaves avail. Some private patios, balconies. Picnic tables, grills. Cr cds: A, DS, MC, V.

Ⓓ Ⓣ ☂ ≈ 🐂 🐾

★★★ **GASTON'S WHITE RIVER RESORT.** *1777 River Rd (72642), 3 mi SE of Dam, 2 mi off AR 178.* 870/431-5202; fax 870/431-5216. Email gastons@mtnhome.com; www.gastons.com. 74 cottages (1-10 bedrm), 1-2 story, 47 kits. (with boat). S, D $69-$83; each addl $14; suites $98-$146; cottages $83-$805; kits. $83.25; under 6 free; fishing rates. Crib free. Pet accepted. TV; cable. Pool. Playground. Dining rm 6:30 am-10 pm. Box lunches, shore lunches, picnics, cookouts. Bar. Ck-out 11 am. Grocery. Meeting rms. Business center. In-rm modem link. Gift shop. Airport, bus depot transportation. Tennis. Golf privileges, greens fee $9-$12.50. Boats, motors. Dock. Lawn games. Rec rm. Fishing guides; clean, store area. Hiking trail; riverside walk. 3,200-ft private landing strip. Refrigerators, fireplaces. Private patios, balconies. Picnic tables. On river. Cr cds: MC, V.

★★ **SUGARLOAF INN.** *1406 N Diamond Blvd (72630), 16 mi N, 2 mi SW of ME 27 on Sugarloaf Mt. 870/422-7144; toll-free 800/422-7144. Email info@sugarloaf.com.* 42 rms, 325 condos, 2-5 bedrm, 3-4 story. A/C in inn, some condos. EP, Dec 25-Mar: D $89-$185; studio $110-$208; 2-5 bedrm $158-$526; under 12 free; higher rates hols; lower rates rest of yr. Crib $11. TV; cable. 2 pools, 1 indoor; whirlpool. Dining rm 7-10 am, 6-9 pm; hrs vary summer. Bar. Ck-out 11 am, ck-in 4 pm. Meeting rms. Tennis. Golf. Downhill ski on site; x-country ski adj. Exercise rm; sauna, steam rm. Massage. Fishing, hiking, whitewater rafting. Mountain bike rentals, guides. Lawn games. Cr cds: A, DS, MC, V.

B&B/Small Inn

★★ **RED RAVEN INN.** *PO Box 1217 (72687). 870/449-5168; fax 870/449-5168. www.bbonline.com.* 6 units, 3 story. No rm phones. S, D $55-$65. Children over 7 yrs only. TV in game rm. Complimentary full bkfst. Restaurant nearby. Ck-out 11 am, ck-in 2 pm. Lawn games. Picnic tables. On river. Restored Queen Anne/Victorian mansion; high ceilings, antiques, oak woodwork. Library; art gallery. Totally nonsmoking. Cr cds: DS, MC, V.

Cottage Colonies

★ **SHADY OAKS RESORT.** *HC 62, Box 128 (72634), 5 mi S on AR 178, on Jimmie Creek Arm of Bull Shoals Lake. 870/453-8420; fax 870/453-7813; toll-free 800/466-7625. Email shdyoaks@southshore.com; www. southshore.com/~shdyoaks.* 11 kit. cottages (1, 2 and 4 bedrm). Cottages $60-$75. Crib free. Pet accepted. TV,

VCR avail. Pool. Playground. Ck-out 10 am, ck-in 3 pm. Coin lndry. Grocery 5 mi. Package store 7 mi. Airport transportation. Boats, motors; lighted dock. Game rm. Rec rm. Lawn games. Fishing guides; clean, store. Refrigerators, microwaves. Private patios. Picnic tables, grills. Lake swimming, waterskiing, scuba diving. Nature walks. Cr cds: DS, MC, V.

★ **SILVER RUN CABINS.** *14 Silver Run Ln (72687). 870/449-6355; fax 870/449-4774; res 800/741-2022. Email silver@southshore.com.* 6 kit. cottages, shower only. No rm phones. Mar-Nov: S, D $47-$75; each addl $5; under 7 free; lower rates rest of yr. TV. Whirlpool. Restaurant nearby. Ck-out 11 am, ck-in 2 pm. Refrigerators, microwaves, fireplaces. Balconies. Grills. Cr cds: MC, V.

Restaurants

★★ **178 CLUB.** *2109 Central Blvd (72619), ½ mi S on AR 178. 870/445-4949. Email dine@178club.com; www. 178club.com.* Specializes in seafood. Hrs: 11 am-10 pm; Sun 9:30 am-9 pm; Sun brunch to 1 pm; winter hrs vary. Closed Mon; Jan 1, Dec 25. Res accepted Fri, Sat. Bar. Lunch $1.95-$5; dinner $2.25-$17.95. Sun brunch $6.50. Child's menu. Cr cds: A, MC, V.

★ **VILLAGE WHEEL.** *AR 178 (72619), center of town. 870/445-4414.* Specializes in omelets, broasted chicken. Salad bar. Hrs: 6 am-9 pm; Fri, Sat to 10 pm. Closed Thanksgiving, Dec 25. Bkfst $1.65-$5.50; lunch $2.30-$5.45; dinner $4.50-$19.95. Child's menu. Cr cds: MC, V.

Camden

(F-3) *See also El Dorado, Magnolia*

Founded 1824 **Pop** 14,380 **Elev** 198 ft
Area code 870 **Zip** 71701
Web www.camden.dina.org

Information Camden Area Chamber of Commerce, 141 Jackson SW, PO Box 99; 870/836-6426

Camden, home to many large industries, is situated on the Ouachita River, which is navigable throughout the year.

What to See and Do

Confederate Cemetery. More than 200 veterans of the Civil War and many unknown soldiers are buried here. Adams Ave & Pearl St.

Fort Lookout. Rifle trenches and cannon pits are still evident on the site of the old fort overlooking Ouachita River. It was one of several forts constructed to guard the town. End of Monroe St.

McCollum-Chidester House. (1847) Once a stage coach headquarters, this historic house was used as headquarters at various times by Confederate General Sterling Price and Union General Frederick Steele. Contains original furnishings; mementos of the Civil War period. Setting for segments of the TV mini-series *North and South.* 926 Washington St NW. Phone 870/836-9243. Tour (Apr-Oct, Wed-Sat) ¢¢ Also incl

Leake-Ingham Building. (1850) Used as a law office before the Civil War and as a freedmen's bureau during Reconstruction; now houses books and other memorabilia of the antebellum South.

Poison Spring Battleground Historical Monument. Site of Union defeat during Steele's Red River Campaign into southwest Arkansas. Exhibits and diorama tracing troop movement; trail to small spring; picnic area. 7 mi NW on AR 24, then 2 mi W on AR 76. **FREE**

White Oak Lake State Park. Swimming; fishing for bass, crappie, and bream on 2,765-acre lake; boating (rentals). Hiking trails. Picnicking, store. Camping (hookups, dump station). Visitor center; interpretive programs. Standard fees. (Daily) 20 mi NW on AR 24, then 3 mi SE on AR 387. Contact the Superintendent, Rte 2, Box 28, Bluff City 71722. Phone 870/685-2748. **FREE**

Annual Event

County Fair and Livestock Show. Sep.

Motel/Motor Lodge

★★ **RAMADA INN.** *950 S California (71701), 2 mi S on US 79N Bypass.* 870/836-8822; fax 870/836-8822; toll-free 800/272-6232. 112 rms, 4 story. S $49.50; D $53.50; suite $85; each addl $5; under 18 free. Crib free. TV; cable (premium). Indoor pool; wading pool. Restaurant 6 am-2 pm, 5-10 pm; wkends from 7 am. Bar 5 pm-midnight; entertainment. Ck-out noon. Meeting rms. Sundries. Exercise equipt. Some refrigerators. Cr cds: A, C, D, DS, ER, JCB, MC, V.
D ⤆ 术 ⊠ 🔥 SC

Conway

(C-4) *See also Morrilton*

Founded 1871 **Pop** 26,481 **Elev** 316 ft
Area code 501 **Zip** 72033
Web www.conwayarkcc.org

Information Chamber of Commerce, PO Box 1492; 501/327-7788 or 501/327-7789

Among the many products manufactured here are school furniture and buses, automotive testing equipment, vending machines, agricultural machinery, shoes, folding cartons, bolts, and pianos. Conway also is home to the University of Central Arkansas, Central Baptist College, and Hendrix College.

What to See and Do

Cadron Settlement Park. Replica of blockhouse built by early settlers in the 1770s. Also within this day-use park is Tollantusky Trail, which contains much historical info and beautiful scenery. (Daily) About 5 mi W via US 64, then S on AR 319. Phone 501/329-2986. **FREE**

Hendrix College. (1876) 1,034 students. Mills Center houses Congressional office contents and some personal papers of former Congressman Wilbur D. Mills, chairman of House Ways and Means Committee and graduate of Hendrix College (Mon-Fri; closed hols and wk of Dec 25). Front & Washington Sts, N side of town on US 64, 65. Phone 501/450-1349 or 501/329-6811.

Petit Jean State Park. (see). W via AR 60, 113, 154.

Toad Suck Ferry Lock and Dam. Site of 1820 river crossing; public viewing platform; historical markers. Adj park offers fishing; boating; picnicking; camping (fee; electric and water avail). (All yr) 5 mi W on AR 60, on the Arkansas River. Phone 501/329-2986. **FREE**

Woolly Hollow State Park. Within this 400-acre wooded park surrounding 40-acre Lake Bennett is the Woolly Cabin, a restored one-rm log structure built 1882, and many historical markers. Swimming beach; fishing; boating (rentals). Hiking trails. Picnicking; playground, snack bar. Camping (hookups). Interpretive programs (Memorial Day-Labor Day, daily). Standard fees. 12 mi N on US 65, 6 mi E on AR 285. Contact the Superintendent, 82 Woolly Hollow Rd, Greenbrier 72058. Phone 501/679-2098.

Annual Events

Toad Suck Daze. Regional celebration featuring toad jumping; bluegrass, country and gospel music; carnival rides; arts and crafts. Phone 501/327-7788. First wkend May.

Faulkner County Fair. Mid-Sep.

Motels/Motor Lodges

★★ **BEST WESTERN.** *I-40 and US 64 (72032), jct I-40, US 64E at Exit 127. 501/329-9855; fax 501/327-6110; res 800/528-1234; toll-free 800/800-6298. Email bwest@cyberback.com; www.bestwestern.com.* 70 rms, 2 story. S $39-$59; D $46-$69; each addl $5; suites $66-$76; under 18 free. Crib $5. Pet accepted, some restrictions. TV; cable (premium). Pool. Restaurant 6 am-9 pm. Ck-out noon. In-rm modem link. Coin lndry. Valet serv. Health club privileges. Microwaves avail. Cr cds: A, DS, MC, V.

★★ **COMFORT INN.** *150 US 65 N (72033), I-40 and US 65N, Exit 125. 501/329-0300; fax 501/329-8367. www.conwayonline.com.* 60 rms, 2 story. May-Oct: S $45-$55; D $55-$70; each addl $5; suites $59; under 18 free; lower rates rest of yr. Crib $5. Pet accepted, some restrictions. TV; cable (premium). Pool; whirlpool. Complimentary continental bkfst. Restaurant opp 11 am-10 pm. Ck-out 11 am. Meeting rm. Business servs avail. Health club privileges. Microwaves avail. Cr cds: A, DS, MC, V.

★ **DAYS INN.** *1002 E Oak St (72032), US 64 and I-40, Exit 127. 501/450-7575; fax 501/450-7001; toll-free 800/329-7466.* 58 rms, 2 story. S $40-$58; D $52-$60; each addl $5; suites $89-$94; under 12 free. Crib free. TV; cable (premium). Pool. Complimentary continental bkfst. Restaurant nearby. Ck-out 11 am. Meeting rms. Business servs avail. In-rm modem link. Microwaves avail. Cr cds: A, C, D, DS, ER, JCB, MC, V.

★★ **RAMADA INN.** *815 E Oak St (72033), US 64 at I-40, Exit 127. 501/329-8392; fax 501/329-0430; toll-free 800/272-6232.* 78 rms, 2 story. S $46-$60; D $52-$66; each addl $6; under 18 free. Crib free. Pet accepted, some restrictions. TV; cable (premium). Heated pool. Restaurant open 24 hrs. Ck-out noon. Meeting rms. Business servs avail. In-rm modem link. Airport transportation. Sundries. Some refrigerators. Cr cds: A, C, D, DS, ER, JCB, MC, V.

Restaurant

★ **FU LIN.** *195 Farris Rd (72032), opp UCA campus. 501/329-1415.* Specializes in beef dishes. Hrs: 11 am-9 pm; Fri, Sat to 10 pm; Sun to 2:30 pm. Closed hols. Lunch $3.99-$5.75; dinner $5.25-$13.95. Sun brunch buffet: $3.99. Cr cds: DS, MC, V.

Dumas (E-5)

Pop 5,520 **Elev** 163 ft **Area code** 870 **Zip** 71639

Information Chamber of Commerce, 165 S Main, PO Box 431; 870/382-5447

What to See and Do

Arkansas Post National Memorial. (see) 17 mi NE via US 165, then E on AR 169.

Desha County Museum. Artifacts depicting history of area; agricultural display, arrowhead collection. Log house farmstead. (Tues, Thurs, Sun; closed hols) 1 mi on US 165E. Phone 870/382-4222. **FREE**

Lake Chicot State Park. Surrounding Arkansas's largest natural lake (formed centuries ago when the Mississippi changed its course); famous for its bream, crappie, catfish, and bass fishing. Swimming pool, lifeguard; boating (rentals, ramp, marina). Picnicking, playground. Camping (hookups, dump station), cabins, store, coin lndry. Visitor center; exhibits; interpretive programs. Archery lessons (summer). Phone 870/265-5480. ¢

Norrell and No 2 Locks & Dams. Major recreation areas: **Wild Goose Bayou,** N of Norrell Lock; **Merrisach Lake,** W of Lock No 2; **Pendleton Bend,** W of Dam No 2; **Moore Bayou,** S of Gillet on US 165; **Notrebes Bend,** E of Dam No 2. All areas offer fishing; boating; picnicking, playground. Camping only at Merrisach Lake, Notrebes Bend and Pendleton Bend (electric hookups, dump stations) and Moore Bayou. Fees charged at some areas. (Daily) About 11 mi E & N via US 165, 1; E on 44, then S on unnumbered roads before crossing river. Phone 870/548-2291. **FREE**

White River National Wildlife Refuge. 30 mi NE via US 165, AR 1 NE to St. Charles. (See STUTTGART).

Motel/Motor Lodge

★ **REGENCY INN.** *722 US 65 S (72033), 1 mi S on US 65.* 870/382-2707; fax 870/382-2836. 52 rms, 2 story. S $36; D $40; each addl $4. Crib $2. Pet accepted. TV; cable. Pool. Complimentary continental bkfst. Ck-out noon. Coin lndry. Some refrigerators; microwaves avail. Cr cds: A, C, D, DS, MC, V.
D 🐾 ➳ 🖼 🐾 SC

El Dorado (F-3)

See also Camden, Magnolia

Pop 23,146 **Elev** 286 ft **Area code** 870 **Zip** 71730
Web www.eldorado.dina.org
Information Chamber of Commerce, 201 N Jackson; 870/863-6113

Legend has it that when Matthew F. Rainey's wagon broke down one day in a forest of hardwood and pine, he was so discouraged he offered all his worldly goods for sale. The farmers in the area were such eager customers that Rainey decided to open a store on the spot and call the place El Dorado. The town led a quiet existence until oil was discovered in 1921. Soon it was inundated with drillers, speculators, engineers, and merchants. Before the year was out there were 460 oil-producing wells, and the name El Dorado had a significant ring. Today this flourishing community is the location of an oil refinery, chemical plants, and many other industries.

What to See and Do

Arkansas Museum of Natural Resources. Ten-acre outdoor exhibit depicts working examples of oil production from 1920s to present. Museum exhibits; research center. Gift shop. Picnic area. (Daily; closed hols) 15 mi N via AR 7, at 3853 Smackover Bypass. Phone 870/725-2877. **FREE**

Moro Bay State Park. Fishing; boating. Hiking. Picnicking, playground, store. Camping (hookups, dump station). Visitor center. Standard fees. (Daily) 25 mi NE via AR 15, at the confluence of Moro Bay, Raymond Lake, and the Ouachita River. Phone 870/463-8555. **FREE**

South Arkansas Arboretum. Seventeen-acre arboretum featuring indigenous trees and plants. Nature trails, wooden bridges. (Mon-Sat; closed hols) 501 Timberlane. Phone 870/862-8131. **FREE**

Annual Event

Union County Fair. Mid-Sep.

Motels/Motor Lodges

★★ **BEST WESTERN KINGS INN.**
*1920 Junction City Rd (71730), AR 167
Exit 82B. 870/862-5191; fax 870/863-
7511; res 800/528-1234.* 131 rms, 2
story. S $59-$65; D $65-$71; each
addl $7; wkend rates. Crib free. Pet
accepted. TV; cable (premium). 2
pools, 1 indoor; wading pool, whirlpool. Sauna. Playground. Restaurant
6 am-2 pm, 5-9 pm. Private club 4-11
pm. Ck-out noon. Coin lndry. Meeting rms. Business servs avail. Valet
serv. Sundries. Airport transportation.
Lighted tennis. Refrigerators; microwaves avail. Balconies. Picnic tables.
On 8 acres. Cr cds: A, C, D, DS,
MC, V.

🅳 🔧 ✈ 🏊 🎿 🖼 🔥

★★ **COMFORT INN.** *2303 Junction
City Rd (71730), AR 167 Exit 82. 870/
863-6677; fax 870/863-8611; toll-free
800/638-7949.* 70 units, 2 story. S, D
$57-$63; each addl $7; under 12 free.
Crib free. Pet accepted. TV; cable
(premium). Pool; whirlpool. Complimentary continental bkfst. Ck-out
noon. Coin lndry. In-rm modem
link. Free airport transportation. Balconies. Cr cds: A, C, D, DS, MC, V.

🅳 🔧 🏊 🖼 🔥 SC

Eureka Springs

(A-2) *See also Berryville, Harrison,
Rogers*

Founded 1879 **Pop** 1,900
Elev 1,329 ft **Area code** 501
Zip 72632
Web www.eurekaspring.org
Information Chamber of Commerce,
PO Box 551; 501/253-8737 or 800/6-
EUREKA

Eureka Springs is a lovely Victorian
city. In the 19th century this was a
well-known health spa; its springs,
which gushed from limestone
crevices, gained a reputation for having curative powers. Thousands of
people with every possible affliction
flocked to the city. Visitors continue
to come to this community, drawn
by the charm of the area, the
scenery, and the fishing.

What to See and Do

Eureka Springs Gardens. Specialty
gardens and natural garden settings
project changing panorama of color,
form, and shadow, from sunrise to
sunset. (Apr-wkend before Thanksgiving, daily) 5 mi W off US 62.
Phone 501/253-9256 or 501/253-
9244 (Color Hotline). ¢¢¢

Eureka Springs Historical Museum.
19th-century area artifacts incl
household items, tools, and photographs. (Apr-Oct, daily; rest of yr,
closed Mon) 95 S Main St. Phone
501/253-9417. ¢

Frog Fantasies. Museum display fea-
turing thousands of man-made frogs.
Gift shop. (Daily) 151 Spring St.
Phone 501/253-7227. ¢

Hammond Museum of Bells. More
than 30 lighted exhibits trace the
history and structure of bells from
800 B.C. to the present; more than
1,000 primitive, antique, and fine art
bells. Narrated audio tour. (Apr-early
Nov, daily). 2 Pine St. Phone
501/253-7411. ¢¢

Onyx Cave Park. Unusual onyx formations in 57°F cave; blind cave fish
display; museum of Gay 90s costumes, dolls; antique button collection; gift shop, picnicking.
Continuous tours (daily). 3 mi E on
US 62, 3½ mi N on Onyx Cave Rd.
Phone 501/253-9321. Cave tours ¢¢

Pivot Rock and Natural Bridge. The
top of Pivot Rock is 15 times as wide
as the bottom; yet it is perfectly balanced. A natural bridge and caves
believed to be hiding places of Jesse
James are nearby. (Apr-mid-Nov) ½
mi W on US 62, 2½ mi N on Pivot
Rock Rd. Phone 501/253-8982. ¢¢

Sacred Arts Center. More than 1,000
works of Christian art. (Tues-Sun)
Passion Play Rd off Hwy 62 E. Phone
501/253-9200. Pass for Sacred Arts
Center, Bible Museum, and Holy
Land ¢¢

> **Bible Museum.** Rare bibles, arti-
> facts, and more than 6,000 vol-
> umes in 625 languages, incl works
> on papyrus, parchment and clay
> cylinders and cones dating from
> 2000 B.C. (Tues-Sun) 935 Passion
> Play Rd. Phone 501/253-9200.

> **New Holy Land.** Re-creation of
> Holy Land as it was when Jesus
> was alive; Dead Sea; Jordan River;

Sea of Galilee; Nativity scene; Last Supper re-creation. (Tues-Sun)

Christ of the Ozarks. A seven-story-tall statue of Jesus, more than one million pounds in weight and with an arm spread of 65 ft.

Sightseeing.

Eureka Springs & North Arkansas Railway. Powered by restored 1906 steam engines; dining car. (Apr-Oct, Mon-Sat) 299 N Main St (AR 23). Phone 501/253-9623. ¢¢

Eureka Springs Trolley. Regularly scheduled trips through the city, historic district, and many points of interest. (Apr-Nov) ¢¢

Thorncrown Chapel. Sensational glass chapel structure tucked into the woods in the Ozarks, designed by Arkansas' noted architect E. Fay Jones. 12968 Hwy 62 W. Phone 501/253-7401.

Withrow Springs State Park. This 700-acre recreation area stretches across mountains and valleys along the bluffs of War Eagle River. The waters of a large spring gush from a shallow cave at the foot of a towering bluff. Heated swimming pool (Memorial Day-mid-Aug, Wed-Sun; also Labor Day wknd) lifeguard; canoeing (rentals). Hiking, tennis. Picnicking, snack bar, concession, playground. Camping (hookups; dump station). Visitor center. Standard fees. (Daily) 20 mi S on Eureka Spring Hwy 23. Phone 501/559-2593. ¢

Annual Events

Spring Tour of Historic Homes. Early Apr.

Ozark Folk Festival. Old-time music, square dancing, Gay 90s costume parade, other events. Early Oct.

Seasonal Events

Country Music Shows. Various productions with country music, comedy skits, and other family entertainment. For schedules contact Chamber of Commerce. Most shows Apr-Oct.

The Great Passion Play. Mt Oberammergau. Portrayal of life of Jesus from Palm Sunday through the Ascension; evening performances. Phone 501/253-9200 or 800/882-PLAY. Late Apr-late Oct, Tues-Wed and Fri-Sun.

Motels/Motor Lodges

★★ **1876 INN.** *2023 E Van Buren (72632), US 62E and AR 23S. 501/253-7183; fax 501/253-7183; toll-free 800/643-3030. Email inn1876@ipa.net; www.eureka-springs-usa.com/1876inn.* 69 rms, 4 story, 3 suites. Oct: S, D $79; each addl $7; suites $119; under 15 free; lower rates rest of yr. Crib avail. Parking garage. Pool, whirlpool. TV; cable. Complimentary continental bkfst, coffee in rms, toll-free calls. Restaurant nearby. Ck-out 11 am, ck-in 2 pm. Meeting rm. Business servs avail. Concierge. Gift shop. Golf. Hiking trail. Picnic facilities. Cr cds: DS, MC, V.

🄳 ⚡ 🛅 🛝 ⛵ 🔀 🐾

★★ **THE ALPEN DORF.** *6554 US 62 (72632). 501/253-9475; fax 501/253-2928; toll-free 800/771-9872.* 30 rms, 2 story. Mid-May-late Oct: S $38-$42; D $42-$59; each addl $5; suites $79-$99; kit. units $65-$75; under 18 free; lower rates rest of yr. Pet accepted. TV; cable. Pool. Playground. Restaurant nearby. Ck-out 11 am. Cr cds: A, DS, MC, V.

🐟 ⚡ 🛝 ⛵ 🔀 🔀 🐾

★★ **BEST WESTERN INN OF THE OZARKS.** *US 62W (72632), 1 mi W. 501/253-9768; fax 501/253-9768; toll-free 800/552-3785. Email bestinn@zipa.net.* 122 rms, 2 story. S $32-$69; D $38-$73; each addl $5; suites $85-$125; under 18 free; higher rates: some hol wknds, War Eagle festival. Crib free. Pet accepted. TV; cable (premium), VCR avail. Heated pool. Restaurant 6:30 am-9 pm. Serv bar. Ck-out 11 am. Coin lndry. Meeting rms. Business servs avail. In-rm modem link. Lighted tennis. Golf privileges, greens fee $25. Rec rm. Some bathrm phones; wet bar in suites. Some balconies. Picnic tables. Cr cds: A, C, D, DS, MC, V.

🄳 🐟 ⛵ 🔀 🐾 🆂🅲 🛝

★★ **COLONIAL MANSION INN.** *154 Huntsville Rd (72632). 501/253-7300; fax 501/253-7309; res 800/638-2622. www.eureka-springs-usa.com/colonial.* 30 rms, 2 story, 1 suite. May-Oct: S $58; D $68; each addl $5; suites $150; lower rates rest of yr. Crib avail, fee. Pet accepted, some restrictions. Valet parking avail. Pool. TV; cable. Complimentary continental bkfst, toll-free calls. Ck-out 11 am, ck-in 2 pm. Free airport transportation. Golf, 18 holes. Cr cds: A, DS, MC, V.

⬛🔲🔲🔲 **SC**

★ **DAYS INN.** *120 W Van Buren St (72632). 501/253-8863; fax 501/253-7885; toll-free 800/329-7466. Email daysinn@ipa.net; www.the.daysinn. com.* 24 rms, 2 story. May-Oct: S, D $79; each addl $8; suites $135; children $4; under 17 free; lower rates rest of yr. Crib avail. Pet accepted, some restrictions, fee. Parking lot. Pool. TV; cable, VCR avail. Complimentary continental bkfst, coffee in rms, toll-free calls. Restaurant. Business servs avail. Concierge. Golf, 18 holes. Supervised children's activities. Hiking trail. Picnic facilities. Video games. Cr cds: A, C, D, DS, MC, V.

⬛🔲🔲🔲🔲🔲

★ **DOGWOOD INN.** *170 Huntsville Rd (72632), ¼ mi S of US 62. 501/253-7200; toll-free 800/544-1884. Email abeaver@arkansas.net.* 33 rms, 2 story. June-Oct: S $42-$48; D $48-$56; each addl $5; higher rates special events; lower rates rest of yr. Crib $5. Pet accepted; $10. TV; cable (premium). Pool; whirlpool. Playground. Complimentary continental bkfst. Restaurant nearby. Ck-out 11 am. Business servs avail. In-rm modem link. Cr cds: A, DS, MC, V.

⬛🔲🔲🔲

★★ **EUREKA MATTERHORN TOWERS.** *130 W Van Buren (72632), on US 62. 501/253-9602; fax 501/253-2850; toll-free 800/426-0838. Email fmtowers@aol.com.* 35 units, 4 story. May-Oct: S, D $58-$74.50; each addl $10; suites $109.50-$114; under 16 free; higher rates: hol wknds, special events; lower rates rest of yr. Crib free. TV; cable (premium). Heated pool. Complimentary continental bkfst. Restaurant nearby. Ck-out 11 am. Sundries. In-rm whirlpools. Some refrigerators; microwaves avail. Cr cds: A, MC, V.

⬛🔲🔲🔲

★ **JOY MOTEL.** *US 62W (72632), 1 mi W. 501/253-9568; fax 501/253-5757; res 501/253-9568; toll-free 877/569-7667. www.joymotel.com.* 45 rms, 2 story, 3 suites. May-Oct: S, D $54; each addl $5; suites $73; children $5; under 12 free; lower rates rest of yr.

Crib avail. Pet accepted, some restrictions, fee. Parking lot. Pool. TV; cable (premium). Restaurant 7 am-9 pm. Ck-out noon, ck-in 1 pm. Fax servs avail. Golf. Tennis. Hiking trail. Picnic facilities. Cr cds: A, D, DS, MC, V.

⬛⬛🔲🔲🔲🔲🔲🔲 **SC**

★ **ROAD RUNNER INN.** *3034 Mundell Rd (72632), 10 mi W on AR 187. 501/253-8166; fax 501/253-0231; toll-free 888/253-8166. Email roadrun@ ipa.net; www.eureka-springs-usa.com/ roadrunner.* 12 rms, 2 story. June-Aug, Oct: S, D $47; each addl $6; under 11 free; lower rates rest of yr. Crib avail. Pet accepted, some restrictions. Parking lot. TV; cable (premium). Complimentary coffee in rms. Ck-out 11 am, ck-in 2 pm. Hiking trail. Picnic facilities. Cr cds: A, MC, V.

⬛🔲🔲🔲

★★ **SWISS VILLAGE INN.** *183 E Van Buren (72632), ½ mi SE on US 62. 501/253-9541; fax 501/253-4011; toll-free 800/447-6525.* 55 rms, 2 story. Mid-May-Aug, Oct: S, D $55-$72; suites $77-$150; lower rates Mar-mid-May, Sep, Nov. Closed rest of yr. Crib free. Pet accepted. TV; cable (premium). Heated pool; whirlpool. Complimentary continental bkfst. Restaurant nearby. Ck-out 11 am. Some in-rm whirlpools, refrigerators. Balconies. Sun decks. Picnic tables. Cr cds: A, D, DS, MC, V.

⬛⬛🔲🔲🔲🔲🔲🔲

★★ **TALL PINES MOTOR INN.** *3 Pivot Rock Rd (72632), W on US 62. 501/253-8096. Email talpines@ipa.net; www.eureka-spring-usa.com/tallpines.* 6 suites. May-Oct: S, D $65; each addl $6; suites $89; under 11 free; lower rates rest of yr. Crib avail, fee. Pool. TV; cable (premium). Complimentary coffee in rms. Restaurant nearby. Ck-out 11 am, ck-in 2 pm. Golf. Picnic facilities. Cr cds: A, DS, MC, V.

⬛🔲🔲🔲🔲

★ **TRADEWINDS MOTEL.** *143 W Van Buren (72632), on US 62. 501/253-9774.* 17 units, 1 kit. unit. Apr-Nov: S $24-$52; D $28-$56; each addl $5; suites $85-$125; higher rates special events. Crib $4. TV; cable. Pool. Complimentary continental bkfst. Restaurant nearby. Ck-out 11 am. Microwaves avail. Picnic tables. Cr cds: A, DS, MC, V.

★ **VICTORIA INN.** *4028 E Van Buren (72632), 2 mi E on US 62, opp entrance to Passion Play. 501/253-6000; fax 501/253-8654; toll-free 800/844-6835.* 90 rms, 3 story. S $42-$79; D $55-$70; each addl $5; suites $66-$93; under 15 free. Crib $5. TV; cable (premium), VCR avail (movies). Indoor pool; whirlpool. Restaurant 7 am-8 pm. Bar 5 pm-1 am. Ck-out 11 am. Meeting rms. Business servs avail. Sundries. Game rm. Rec rm. Balconies. Cr cds: A, DS, MC, V.

Flatiron Building, Eureka Springs

Hotels

★ **BASIN PARK.** *12 Spring St (72632). 501/253-7837; fax 501/253-6985; toll-free 800/643-4972. Email bphchres@ipa.net; www.basinpark.com.* 35 rms, 7 story, 24 suites. June-Oct: S, D $109; each addl $10; suites $169; lower rates rest of yr. Crib avail. Pet accepted, some restrictions. Parking lot. Pool, children's pool, whirlpool. TV; cable (premium), VCR avail. Complimentary continental bkfst, coffee in rms. Restaurant 11 am, closed Mon. Bar. Ck-out 11 am, ck-in 3 pm. Meeting rms. Business center. Bellhops. Concierge. Gift shop. Exercise rm, sauna, steam rm. Golf, 18 holes. Tennis, 4 courts. Bike

rentals. Supervised children's activities. Hiking trail. Picnic facilities. Cr cds: A, DS, MC, V.

★★ **NEW ORLEANS HOTEL.** *63 Spring St (72632). 501/253-8630; fax 501/253-5949; toll-free 800/243-8630.* 22 rms, 6 story, 19 suites. No elvtr. S, D $60-$125; each addl $10; higher rates: wkends, Oct. TV; cable. Restaurant 5-10 pm. Bar. Ck-out noon. Free valet parking. Golf privileges. In-rm whirlpools, refrigerators. Balconies. Restored hotel, built in 1892; antique furnishings, Victorian decor. Located in historic downtown district. Cr cds: A, C, D, DS, MC, V.

B&Bs/Small Inns

★★ **ARSENIC & OLD LACE B&B INN.** *60 Hillside Ave (72632). 501/253-5454; fax 501/253-2246; toll-free 800/243-5223. Email arseniclace@prodigy.net.* 5 rms, 3 story. No rm phones. Apr-Oct: S, D $125-$160; wkend rates; lower rates rest of yr. Children over 14 yrs only. TV; cable, VCR (movies). Complimentary full bkfst; afternoon refreshments. Restaurant nearby. Ck-out 11 am, ck-in 3-6 pm. Fireplaces, in-rm whirlpools. Balconies. Many antiques. Totally nonsmoking. Cr cds: A, DS, MC, V.

★★ **BRIDGEFORD HOUSE.** *263 Spring St (72632). 501/253-7853; fax 501/253-5497. Email bridgefordbb@earthlink.net; www.bridgefordhouse.com.* 4 rms, 2 story. No rm phones. S $85-$105; each addl $20; 2-day min wkends. Children over 10 yrs only. TV; cable, VCR avail. Complimentary full bkfst, coffee in rms. Ck-out 11 am, ck-in 3 pm. Refrigerators; microwaves avail. Some in-rm fireplaces, whirlpools. Built in 1884; antiques. Totally nonsmoking. Cr cds: A, DS, MC, V.

★★ **CRESCENT COTTAGE INN.** *211 Spring St (72632). 501/253-6022; fax 501/253-6234; toll-free 800/223-3246. Email raphael@ipa.net; www.1881crescentcottageinn.com.* 3 rms, 3 story, 1 suite. D $94-$132; suite $112. Children over 13 yrs only. TV; cable, VCR (movies). Complimentary full bkfst. Restaurant nearby. Ck-out 11 am, ck-in 2:30 pm. Business servs avail. Refrigerators, fireplace, in-rm whirlpools. Porches. Built in 1881; antiques. Totally nonsmoking. Cr cds: A, DS, MC, V.

★★★ **HEARTSTONE INN AND COTTAGES.** *35 Kings Hwy (72632). 501/253-8916; fax 501/253-5361; toll-free 800/494-4921. Email heartinn@ ipa.net; www.heartstoneinn.com.* 7 rms, 2 story, 3 suites. Apr-Dec: S, D $90; each addl $15; suites $110; lower rates rest of yr. Parking lot. TV; cable, VCR avail. Complimentary full bkfst, coffee in rms, newspaper. Restaurant nearby. Ck-out 11 am, ck-in 4 pm. Meeting rm. Fax servs avail. Concierge. Gift shop. Golf. Hiking trail. Picnic facilities. Cr cds: A, DS, MC, V.

★★ **INN AT ROSE HALL.** *56 Hillside Ave (72632). 501/253-5405; fax 501/253-5405; toll-free 800/828-4255. Email theangel@ipa.net; www.eureka springsangel.com.* 9 rms, 2 story, 1 suite. May-July, Sep-Oct: S, D $165; suites $150; under 16 free; lower rates rest of yr. Parking lot. TV; cable (premium), VCR avail. Complimentary full bkfst, coffee in rms, newspaper, toll-free calls. Ck-out 11 am, ck-in 2 pm. Meeting rm. Business servs avail. Whirlpool. Golf, 18 holes. Tennis, 2 courts. Hiking trail. Picnic facilities. Video games. Cr cds: A, DS, MC, V.

★★ **MORNINGSTAR RETREAT.** *370 Star Ln (72632), E on US 62, 7 mi S on Rock House Rd (County Rd 302). 501/253-5995; toll-free 800/298-5995. Email amstar7@aol.com; www. avey.com.* 5 units, 4 kit. suites, 1 kit. cottage. Apr-Oct: S, D $95-$120; each addl $10; wkly rates; wkends 2-day min; lower rates rest of yr. Crib free. Complimentary coffee in rms. Ck-out 3 pm, ck-in 11 am. Refrigerators, microwaves; some in-rm whirlpools, fireplaces. Balconies. Picnic tables, grills. Lawn games. On Kings River. Totally nonsmoking. Cr cds: DS, MC, V.

★★ **SCANDIA INN.** *227 W Van Buren (72632), 1 mi W on US 62. 501/253-8922; fax 501/253-9219; toll-free 800/523-8922. Email scandia@ipa.net; www.scandiainn.com.* 6 rms. No rm phones. S, D $59-$99; suite $99-$159. TV; cable (premium), VCR avail. Complimentary full bkfst. Restaurant nearby. Ck-out 11 am, ck-in 1 pm. Business servs avail. Golf privileges. Whirlpool. Cr cds: A, DS, MC, V.

Cottage Colony

★★ **RED BUD VALLEY RESORT.** *369 County Rd 340 (72632), 2 mi E on US 62, 1 mi S on Rockhouse Rd. 501/ 253-9028; fax 501/253-9373.* 17 kit. cottages, 1-2 story. No rm phones. Kit. cottages $79-$140 (2-day min); under 7 free; special package plans; 3-day min hols; lower rates rest of yr. TV; VCR avail (movies $3). Playground. Restaurant nearby. Ck-out 11 am, ck-in 3 pm. Maid serv twice wkly. Gift shop. Swimming. Hiking. Fishing guides, clean and store. Microwaves avail. Balconies. Picnic tables, grills. Located in 200-acre valley with private park, roaming wildlife and spring-fed, stocked lake. Cr cds: MC, V.

All Suite

★★★ **PALACE HOTEL & BATH HOUSE.** *135 Spring St (72632). 501/ 253-7474; fax 501/253-7494. Email phbh@lpa.net; www.palacehotelbath house.com.* 3 story, 8 suites. Oct: S, D $140-$160; lower rates rest of yr. Adults only. Parking lot. TV; cable. Complimentary continental bkfst, coffee in rms. Restaurant nearby. Ck-out noon, ck-in 3 pm. Business servs avail. Steam rm. Golf, 18 holes. Cr cds: A, DS, MC, V.

Restaurants

★ **BUBBA'S BARBECUE.** *166 W Van Buren (72632). 501/253-7706.* Specializes in barbecue meats. Hrs: 11 am-9 pm. Closed Sun; hols. Lunch, dinner $2.95-$18.95. Eclectic decor. No cr cds accepted.

★ **HYLANDER STEAK AND RIB.** *309 W Van Buren (72632). 501/253-*

7360. Email pgysuz@aol.com. Specializes in barbecue dishes, prime rib. Hrs: 4-10 pm; Fri, Sat to 11 pm. Closed Tues; Dec 25. Res accepted. Bar. Dinner $5.95-$15.95. Casual atmosphere. Antiques. Elvis memorabilia. Cr cds: A, DS, MC, V.

D ⬜

★ **OLD TOWN PUB.** *2 N Main (72632). 501/253-7147.* Specializes in sandwiches, hamburgers. Hrs: 11:30 am-3 pm. Closed Sun. Lunch $3.50-$5.95. Casual dining in sports pub. No cr cds accepted.

SC ⬜

★★ **PLAZA.** *55 S Main St (72632). 501/253-8866. www.esplaza.com.* Specializes in filet mignon, lobster tail. Hrs: 11:30 am-9:30 pm. Lunch $3.50-$6.50; dinner $7-$22.50. Art collection. Cr cds: A, DS, MC, V.

D ⬜

★★ **VICTORIAN SAMPLER.** *44 Prospect St (72632). 501/253-8374.* Specializes in chilled soup, desserts. Hrs: 11:30 am-3 pm. Closed Thanksgiving; also Dec-mid-Mar. Lunch $4.50-$6.95. Restored Victorian mansion; antiques. Gift shop on premises. Cr cds: DS, MC, V.

Fayetteville

(B-1) *See also Rogers, Springdale*

Pop 42,099 **Elev** 1,400 ft
Area code 501
Web www.fayettevillear.com
Information Chamber of Commerce, 123 W Mountain St, PO Box 4216, 72702; 501/521-1710 or 800/766-4626

This is a resort center in the Ozark Mountains. The countryside is famous for its scenery, spring and fall. There are many lakes and streams nearby for fishing. Fayetteville is the home of the University of Arkansas.

What to See and Do

Arkansas Air Museum. Exhibit spanning the history of manned flight; features collection of antique and WWII aircraft. (Daily; closed Jan 1, Thanks-

giving, Dec 25) 5 mi S on US 71, at Drake Field. Phone 501/521-4947. ¢

Devil's Den State Park. Situated in a scenic valley in the Boston Mts, this 2,000-acre park in the heart of rugged Ozark terrain incl unusual sandstone formations; Devil's Den Cave; and the Devil's Icebox, where the temperature never goes above 60°F. Swimming pool (summer; lifeguard); fishing; canoeing (rentals). Nature, hiking, bridle, mountain biking trails. Picnicking, playground, restaurant (summer), snack bar, store. Camping (electric hookups, dump station; standard fees); horse camp; cabins, coin lndry. Visitor center has exhibits, camping, and backpack equipment rentals. Interpretive programs. (Daily) 8 mi S on US 71, then 18 mi SW of West Fork on AR 170. For res contact Superintendent, Devil's Den State Park, 11333 AR 74W, West Fork 72774. Phone 501/761-3325.

Headquarters House. (1853) Greek Revival house, residence of wealthy Union sympathizer Judge Jonas Tebbetts, was used as headquarters for both Union and Confederate forces during the Civil War; period furnishings, local historical artifacts, Civil War relics. (By appt) 118 E Dickson St. Phone 501/521-2970. **Donation**

Prairie Grove Battlefield State Park. Park covers approx 130 acres of the 3.5-sq-mi site where more than 18,000 Union and Confederate forces fought on Dec 7, 1862; the armies suffered a combined loss of 2,500 dead, wounded, or missing. Hindman Hall Museum houses visitor center with exhibits, battle diorama, artifacts, audiovisual presentation. Historic structures in the park incl Battle Monument, a chimney from Rhea's Mill; Borden House, scene of the heaviest fighting of the battle; a spring house, smokehouse, detached kitchen, schoolhouse, church, blacksmith shop, and sorghum mill. Guided tours (summer, daily; rest of yr by appt). Picnicking, playground. 10 mi W on US 62 in Prairie Grove. Contact Superintendent, PO Box 306, Prairie Grove 72753;. Phone 501/846-2990. **FREE**

University of Arkansas. (1871) 14,700 students. 1125 W Maple St. Phone 501/575-2000. On campus are

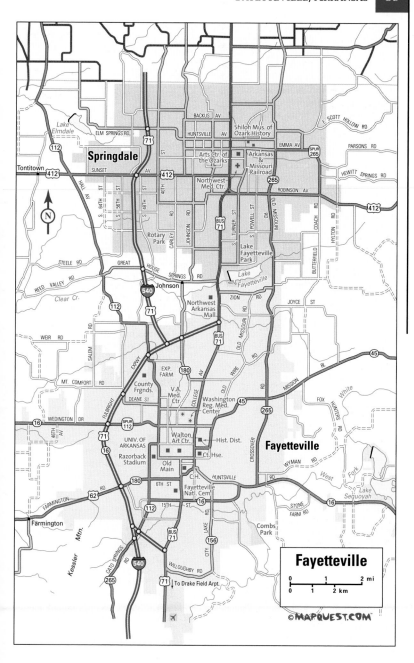

Fayetteville

Fine Arts Center. Incl a theater, concert hall, library, and exhibition gallery. (Daily; closed hols). Garland St. For concert and theater schedule. Phone 501/575-4752.

University Museum. Houses science, natural history, and ethnological exhibits; films. (Daily; closed hols, also Dec 24-Jan 1). Garland St. Phone 501/575-3466.

Walton Arts Center. Musicals, opera, plays, symphonies. Dickson & Springs Sts. For ticket info phone 501/443-5600.

Special Event

Battle Reenactment. Prairie Grove Battlefield State Park. Costumed volunteers reenact historic battle and demonstrate war tactics and life of a Civil War soldier. First full wkend Dec.

Motels/Motor Lodges

★★ **BEST WESTERN WINDSOR SUITES.** *1122 S Futrall (72701), at US 71 and 62. 501/587-1400; fax 501/587-1400; res 800/528-1234.* 68 rms, 2 story, 37 suites. S $55-$70; D $60-$75; each addl $5; suites $65-$105; under 18 free; higher rates special events. Crib free. Pet accepted, some restrictions. TV; cable (premium), VCR avail. Complimentary continental bkfst, coffee in rms. Restaurant nearby. Ck-out 11 am. Meeting rms. Business center. In-rm modem link. Coin lndry. Exercise equipt. Indoor pool; whirlpool. Bathrm phone, in-rm whirlpool in suites. Some refrigerators, wet bars; microwaves avail. Cr cds: A, D, DS, JCB, MC, V.

★★ **CLARION INN.** *1255 S Shiloh Dr (72701), jct US 71 and 62. 501/521-1166; fax 501/521-1204; res 800/252-7466; toll-free 800/223-7275.* 197 units, 2 story. S, D $62-$76; each addl $4; suites $110; higher rates: wkends, special events; under 17 free. Crib free. TV; cable (premium). Indoor pool; whirlpool. Coffee in rms. Restaurant 6 am-10 pm. Rm serv from 7 am. Private club 4:30 pm-1 am. Ck-out noon. Coin lndry. Business center. In-rm modem link. Bellhops. Valet serv. Airport, bus depot transportation. Exercise equipt; sauna. Game rm. Many

refrigerators; microwaves avail. Cr cds: A, C, D, DS, MC, V.

★ **DAYS INN.** *2402 N College Ave (72703). 501/443-4323; fax 501/443-4323; res 800/329-7466.* 150 rms, 2 story, 6 suites. S, D $45-$72; each addl $5; suites $80-$115. Crib free. Pet accepted, some restrictions; $50 deposit. TV; cable (premium), VCR avail. Pool. Complimentary continental bkfst. Ck-out noon. Coin lndry. Meeting rms. Business servs avail. Cr cds: A, C, D, DS, MC, V.

★★★ **INN AT THE MILL.** *3906 Greathouse Springs Rd (72741), 7 mi N on US 71, Exit 50. 501/443-1800; fax 501/443-3879; res 800/CLARION.* 48 rms, 8 suites, 2 story. S, D $92-$98; each addl $5; suites $130-$160; under 18 free. Crib free. TV; cable. Complimentary continental bkfst. Restaurant. Ck-out noon. Meeting rm. Health club privileges. Microwaves avail; whirlpool in suites. Some balconies. Historic water mill built 1835. Cr cds: A, DS, MC, V.

★★ **RAMADA INN.** *3901 N College Ave (72703). 501/443-3431; fax 501/443-1927; res 800/272-6232; toll-free 888/443-4866.* 120 rms, 2 story. S $49-$59; D $55-$65; each addl $6; under 18 free. Crib free. Pet accepted. TV; cable (premium). Pool. Complimentary coffee in lobby. Restaurant 6 am-10 pm; Sat, Sun from 7 am. Private club 5-11 pm. Ck-out noon. Meeting rms. Business servs avail. Valet serv. Tennis. Health club privileges. Cr cds: A, C, D, DS, MC, V.

★ **RED ROOF INN.** *1000 Futrall (72701). 501/442-3041; fax 501/442-0744; res 800/REDROOF; toll-free 800/THEROOF. Email 10584@ redroof.com.* 80 units, 2 story. S, D $43-$48; each addl $5; suites $69; under 16 free; wkly rates. Pet accepted; $10. TV; cable (premium). Pool. Ck-out noon. Coin lndry. Refrigerators; microwaves avail. Cr cds: A, D, DS, MC, V.

Hotel

★★★ **HILTON INN.** *70 N East Ave (72701). 501/442-5555; fax 501/442-*

2105; res 800/445-8667. 235 rms, 15 story. S $67-$92; D $69-$100; each addl $8; suites $150-$299. Crib free. Pet accepted, some restrictions. TV; cable (premium), VCR avail. Indoor/outdoor pool. Coffee in rms. Restaurant 6:30 am-9 pm; wkends from 6:30 am. Bar 3 pm-midnight. Meeting rm. Business servs avail. Gift shop. Free parking. Free airport, bus depot transportation. Microwaves in suites. Cr cds: A, C, D, DS, MC, V.

🄳 🐾 🏊 🔾 🔥

Restaurant

★★ **UNCLE GAYLORD'S.** *315 W Mountain (72701). 501/444-0605. Email hfbrandon@aol.com.* Specializes in San Francisco-style food. Hrs: 7 am-10 pm; Sun, Mon to 2 pm. Closed Thanksgiving, Dec 25. Res accepted. Bar. Bkfst $3.25-$7; lunch $5.50-$6.25; dinner $9-$18. Casual dining. Cr cds: A, MC, V.

🄳

Forrest City

(D-6) *See also Helena*

Founded 1866 **Pop** 13,364 **Elev** 276 ft
Area code 870 **Zip** 72335
Web www.forrestcity.dina.org
Information Chamber of Commerce, 203 N Izard; 870/633-1651

This town is named for Confederate General Nathan Bedford Forrest, who contracted to put a railroad across Crowley's Ridge, on which the city stands. The ridge, 100 feet high and composed of loess (windblown, fine, yellowish loam that generally stands in vertical cliffs), roughly parallels the Mississippi from Missouri to Helena, Arkansas.

What to See and Do

Village Creek State Park. Approx 7,000-acre park with two lakes situated entirely upon the unusual geologic formation of Crowley's Ridge. Swimming; fishing; boating (rentals). Hiking trails; tennis. Picnicking, playground, store. Camping (hookups, dump station); ten fully equipped cabins. Visitor center with history, geology, and botany exhibits; audio-visual presentations; interpretive programs (summer). (Daily) Standard fees. E on I-40 Exit 242, then 13 mi N on AR 284. Contact Superintendent, Rte 3, Box 49-B, Wynne 72396. Phone 870/238-9406. **FREE**

Annual Event

Harvest Festival. Hot air balloon races; 5K run. Late Sep-early Oct.

Motels/Motor Lodges

★★ **BEST WESTERN INN.** *1306 N Hwy 17 (72021), approx 20 mi W on I-40, Exit 216. 870/734-1650; fax 870/734-1657; res 800/528-1234.* 100 rms, 2 story. S $54.50; D $59.50; each addl $5; under 12 free; higher rates duck season. Crib $3. Pet accepted, some restrictions. TV; cable. Pool. Complimentary full bkfst. Restaurant 6 am-9 pm. Ck-out noon. Exercise equipt. Playground. Some in-rm whirlpools. Picnic tables, grills. Cr cds: A, C, D, DS, MC, V.

🄳 🐾 🛁 🏊 🎿 🔾 🔥

★ **DAYS INN AND SUITES.** *350 Barrow Hill Rd (72335). 870/633-0777; fax 870/633-0770; toll-free 800/329-7466.* 53 rms, 2 story, 52 suites. S, D $59.95; each addl $4; suites $59.95-$64.95; family rates. Crib avail. TV; cable (premium). Complimentary full bkfst. Restaurant 6 am-10 pm. Ck-out 11 am. Meeting rm. Business servs avail. Pool. Refrigerator, microwave in suites; some in-rm whirlpools. Cr cds: A, C, D, DS, ER, JCB, MC, V.

🄳 🏊 🔾 🔥 SC

Fort Smith

(C-1) *See also Alma*

Pop 72,798 **Elev** 450 ft **Area code** 501
Web www.fschamber.com
Information Chamber of Commerce, 612 Garrison Ave, PO Box 1668, 72902; 501/783-6118

The original fort was built on the Arkansas River in 1817 to stand between the Osages upstream and

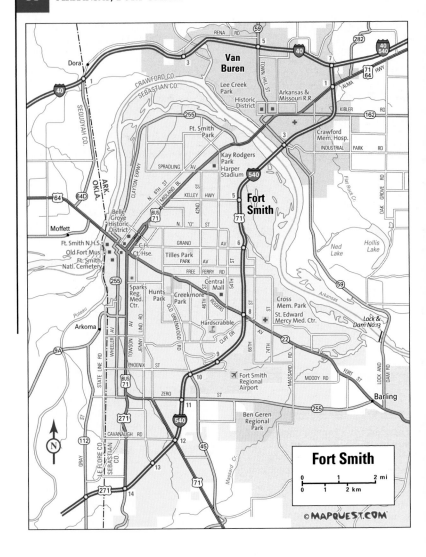

the Cherokees downstream. It also gave protection to traders, trappers, and explorers and encouraged settlement in the area. Captain John Rogers became the first settler in 1821; by 1842 the town had a population of nearly 500.

In 1848, when gold was discovered in California, Fort Smith immediately became a thriving supply center and starting point for gold rush wagons heading south across the plains. Bandits, robbers, gamblers, and cutthroats moved in. Without peace officers, the territory was wild and tough until 1875, when Judge Isaac C. Parker—known later as "the hang-ing judge"—was sent in to clean it up. He was judge of the Federal District Court at Fort Smith for 21 years; during his first 14 years there were no appeals of his decisions. Under Parker's rule, 151 men were sentenced to die and about 79 hanged, sometimes as many as six at a time. Parker was a strict judge with a reputation for knowing and respecting the rules of evidence.

Today Fort Smith is a leading manufacturing center in Arkansas, with more than 200 manufacturing plants and major corporations. Boston Mountain to the north is a good hunting area.

What to See and Do

Fort Smith Art Center. Built in 1879 as a residence. Changing exhibits monthly; guided tours. (Tues-Sat, also Sun afternoons; closed hols, Dec 24-Jan 1) 423 N 6th St. Phone 501/782-1156. **FREE**

Fort Smith National Historic Site. Park contains foundations of first Fort Smith; the original commissary from the second Fort Smith; the famous Judge Parker's courtrm, jail, and reconstructed gallows. (Daily; closed Jan 1, Dec 25) 301 Parker Ave. Phone 501/783-3961. ¢

Old Fort Museum. Regional history, period pharmacy with working soda fountain, transportation exhibit with 1899 steam fire pumper. Changing exhibits. (Tues-Sun; closed hols) 320 Rogers Ave. Phone 501/783-7841. ¢¢

Annual Events

Old Fort Days Rodeo. Memorial Day.

Old Fort River Festival. Arts and crafts, entertainment, sporting events. Mid-June.

Arkansas-Oklahoma State Fair. Late Sep.

Motels/Motor Lodges

★★ **BEST WESTERN TRADE-WINDS INN.** *101 N 11th St (72901), off Garrison Ave.* 501/785-4121; fax 501/785-0316; res 800/528-1234. 129 rms, 2 story. S $39-$49; D $50; each addl $5; suites $63-$100; under 12 free. Crib free. Pet accepted. TV; cable (premium). Pool. Complimentary continental bkfst. Private club Mon-Fri 3 pm-5 am; Sat, Sun from 7 pm; entertainment. Ck-out noon. Meeting rms. Business servs avail. Free airport, bus depot transportation. Health club privileges. Wet bar, microwave in suites. Cr cds: A, C, D, DS, MC, V.

★★★ **FOUR POINTS HOTEL.** *5711 Rogers Ave (72903), I-540 (AR 22) Exit 8.* 501/452-4110; fax 501/452-4891. 151 rms, 2 story. S, D $59.95; each addl $10; suites $59-$89.95. Crib $10. Pet accepted. TV; cable (premium). Pool; wading pool. Complimentary full bkfst, coffee in rms. Restaurant 6-9:30 am. Private club 5 pm-1 am. Ck-out noon. Meeting rms. Business servs avail. In-rm modem link. Airport transportation. Refrigerators. Cr cds: A, C, D, DS, MC, V.

★ **SUPER 8 MOTEL.** *3810 Towson Ave (72901).* 501/646-3411; fax 501/646-3411; res 800/800-8000. 50 rms, 2 story. May-Sep: S $34; D $45; each addl $5; under 16 free; lower rates rest of yr. Crib avail. Pet accepted, fee. Pool. TV; cable (premium). Complimentary continental bkfst, coffee in rms. Restaurant, closed Sun. Ck-out 11 am, ck-in 10 pm. Fax servs avail. Golf. Cr cds: A, C, D, DS, ER, JCB, MC, V.

Hotels

★★ **ASPEN HOTEL AND SUITES.** *2900 S 68th (72903).* 501/452-9000; fax 501/484-0551; toll-free 800/627-9417. Email aspenhotel@aol.com; www.aspenhotelandsuites.com. 49 rms, 2 story, 4 suites. S, D $59-$74.50; each addl $5; suites $115; under 12 free; family rates; package plans. Crib $5. TV; cable (premium). Complimentary continental bkfst, coffee in rms. Restaurant nearby. Ck-out 11 am. Meeting rms. Business servs avail. In-rm modem link. Free airport transportation. Tennis privileges. Golf privileges, greens fee $18, pro, driving range. Exercise equipt. Pool. In-rm whirlpool, refrigerator, microwave in suites. Cr cds: A, DS, MC, V.

★★ **HOLIDAY INN CITY CENTER.** *700 Rogers Ave (72901).* 501/783-1000; fax 501/783-0312; res 800/465-4329. Email hi426gm@sagehotel.com; www.holiday-inn.com/ftsmithar. 247 rms, 9 story, 8 suites. S, D $109; suites $129. Crib avail. Pet accepted, some restrictions, fee. Valet parking avail. Indoor pool, whirlpool. TV; cable (premium). Complimentary coffee in rms, newspaper, toll-free calls. Restaurant 6 am-10 pm. Bar. Ck-out 11 am, ck-in 3 pm. Meeting rms. Business servs avail. Bellhops. Dry cleaning. Gift shop. Free airport transportation. Exercise equipt, sauna. Golf. Cr cds: A, C, D, DS, ER, JCB, MC, V.

[icons]

★★ **RAMADA INN.** *5103 Towson Ave (72901). 501/646-2931; fax 501/ 648-9085; res 800/272-6232. Email ramadafsm@aol.com; www.the.ramada. com.* 155 rms, 2 story, 8 suites. May-Aug: S $51; D $57; each addl $6; suites $75; under 16 free; lower rates rest of yr. Crib avail. Parking lot. Pool, lap pool. TV; cable (DSS), VCR avail. Complimentary continental bkfst, newspaper, toll-free calls. Restaurant 6 am-8 pm. Rm serv 24 hrs. Bar. Meeting rms. Business center. Concierge. Dry cleaning. Exercise privileges, sauna. Golf. Tennis. Picnic facilities. Cr cds: A, C, D, DS, JCB, MC, V.

[icons]

All Suite

★ **THOMAS QUINN SUITES.** *815 N B St (72903). 501/782-0499.* 9 kit. suites, 2 story. S $59; D $79. Crib $3. TV; cable (premium). Complimentary coffee in rms. Restaurant nearby. Ck-out noon. Concierge. Whirlpool. Restored 1863 house; 2nd floor added 1916. Corinthian columns. New Orleans style patio. Near historic attractions. Cr cds: A, DS, MC, V.

[icons]

Restaurants

★ **CALICO COUNTY.** *2401 S 56th St (72903). 501/452-3299. Email maccalico@aol.com.* Specializes in chicken-fried steak, catfish. Hrs: 6:30 am-9 pm; Sun from 7 am. Closed Thanksgiving, Dec 25. Bkfst $4-$6; lunch, dinner $5-$9. Child's menu. Country atmosphere, antique kitchen tools. Cr cds: A, D, DS, MC, V.

[icons]

★ **THE LIGHTHOUSE INN.** *6000 Midland (72904). 501/783-9420.* Specializes in seafood, steak. Hrs: 11 am-9:30 pm; Fri to 10 pm; Sat 5-10 pm. Res accepted. Bar. Lunch $4.95-$6.75; dinner $9.95-$35.95. Child's menu. Old lighthouse on river. Cr cds: A, D, DS, MC, V.

[icon]

Greers Ferry Lake Area

(C-4) *See also Batesville, Mountain View*

(The dam is approx 64 mi N of Little Rock via US 67/167, AR 5, 25, near Heber Srings.)

Area code 501

This 50-mi-long lake, impounded by a dam built by the US Army Corps of Engineers, was dedicated by President John F. Kennedy shortly before his assassination in November 1963. Since then the area has developed rapidly, now offering 15 public recreation areas on more than 31,000 acres. Swimming, waterskiing, scuba diving; hunting; boating (rentals, marina, ramps). Nature trail up Sugar Loaf Mountain. Picnicking. Camping. Fee charged for some recreation areas. For further information contact Heber Springs Chamber of Commerce, 1001 W Main, Heber Springs 72543. Phone 501/362-2444 or 800/77-HEBER.

What to See and Do

Little Red River. One of the finest trout streams in the area is stocked wkly. Trout weighing more than 15 pounds have been caught. Five commercial docks.

William Carl Gardner Visitor Center. Provides tourist info and houses exhibits interpreting history and culture of the southern Ozark region; displays relate history of the Corps of Engineers and their projects in Arkansas; interpretive slide/tape programs; guided tours of Greers Ferry Dam and Powerhouse depart from visitor center (Memorial Day-Labor Day, Mon-Fri). Nature trail with access for the disabled (guided tours in summer by appt). Visitor center (Mar-Oct, daily; Feb, Nov, Dec, wkends; closed Jan, Thanksgiving, Dec 25). 3 mi NE of Heber Springs on AR 25. Phone 501/362-9067. **FREE**

Motels/Motor Lodges

★ **BUDGET INN.** *616 W Main St (72543), at jct AR 25B, 110. 501/362-8111; res 888/297-7955; toll-free 888/ 297-0955.* 25 rms. S $36; D $42; each addl $5; suites, studio rms $47. Crib $5. Pet accepted. TV; cable. Pool. Complimentary coffee. Restaurant nearby. Ck-out 11 am. Cr cds: A, D, DS, MC, V.

★ **LAKESHORE RESORT.** *801 Case Ford Rd; AR 210 W (72543), 1½ mi N off AR 25 on AR 210W. 501/362-2315.* 7 kit. units. May-Oct: S, D $53; each addl $6; apt $90; wkly, monthly rates; lower rates rest of yr. Crib free. TV; cable. Restaurant nearby. Ck-out 11 am. Airport transportation. Private dock; boat stall $5. Refrigerators. Microwaves avail. Picnic tables, grills. On lake; 4 acres of hilly, wooded grounds. Cr cds: A, DS, MC, V.

★★★ **RED APPLE INN.** *1000 Club Rd (72543), on Eden Isle. 501/362-3111; fax 501/362-8900; res 800/733-2775.* 59 rms, 2 story. Mar-Nov: S, D $95; suites $125; under 12 free; hols 2-day min; lower rates rest of yr. Crib free. TV; cable (premium). Complimentary coffee in rms. Restaurant (see RED APPLE DINING ROOM). Bar 5:30 pm-midnight. Ck-out noon. Meeting rms. Business servs avail. In-rm modem link. Bellhops. Shopping arcade. Coin lndry. Airport transportation. Lighted tennis. 18-hole golf, greens fee $15-$25, pro, driving range. Pool; wading pool, poolside serv. Playground. Lawn games. Some refrigerators, fireplaces. Many balconies. Cr cds: A, C, D, DS, MC, V.

Resort

★★ **FAIRFIELD BAY RESORT.** *Lost Creek Pkwy (72088), AR 16E. 501/884-3333; fax 501/884-3345.* 250 units, 1-3 story, 220 kits. S, D $59-$150; under 18 free; golf plan. Crib free. TV; cable (premium), VCR avail (movies). 4 pools; wading pool. Playground. Supervised children's activities (June-Sep). Five restaurants, hrs vary. Ck-out 10 am, ck-in 4 pm. Grocery. Coin lndry. Business servs avail. Sports dir. Tennis, 12 outdoor courts, 6 lighted, pro. 18-hole golf, pro, putting green, driving range. Miniature golf. Waterskiing. Marina; boat rentals. Horse stables. Bowling alley. Summer theater. Rec rm. Game rm.

Refrigerators, microwaves; some fireplaces. Some balconies. Picnic tables, grills. Occupies 14,000 wooded acres and borders lake. Cr cds: A, DS, MC, V.

Restaurants

★★ **CAFE KLASER.** *106 S 2nd (72543). 501/206-0688.* Specializes in stuffed steaks, sauteed shrimp. Own baking. Hrs: 11 am-1:30 pm; Thurs-Sat 11 am-9 pm. Closed Sun. Res accepted. Lunch $3.95-$5.95; dinner $5.95-$14.95. Child's menu. Parking. Intimate atmosphere. Cr cds: MC, V.

★★ **CAPTAIN'S HOUSE.** *603 W Quitman (72543). 501/362-3963. Email mermaid@arkansas.net.* Specializes in char-broiled steak, chicken, seafood. Salad bar. Hrs: 11 am-8 pm; Fri, Sat to 9 pm; Sun to 2 pm. Res accepted. Lunch $5-$7; dinner $7-$18. Child's menu. In old home (1914). Cr cds: A, D, DS, MC, V.

★ **CHINA DELIGHT.** *1632 Hwy 25 N (72543). 501/362-7054.* Specializes in Cantonese dishes. Hrs: 11 am-9 pm. Closed Thanksgiving, Dec 25. Lunch $3.25-$4.95. Buffet: $4.95; dinner $5.50-$9. Buffet: $7.25. Chinese decor. Cr cds: A, DS, MC, V.

★ **MR B'S CATFISH.** *1120 Hwy 25N (72543). 501/362-7692.* Seafood menu. Specializes in catfish, steak. Hrs: 11 am-9 pm; Fri, Sat to 10 pm; winter hrs vary. Closed Mon; Thanksgiving, Dec 25. Lunch $3.90-$7.95; dinner $5.20-$22.95. Child's menu. No cr cds accepted.

★★ **RED APPLE DINING ROOM.** *1000 Club Rd, 5 mi W on AR 110, on Eden Isle. 501/362-3111.* Specializes in souffles. Own baking. Hrs: 7 am-9 pm; Fri, Sat to 10 pm. Res accepted. Bkfst $5.95-$8.95; lunch $5.75-$8.95; dinner $10.50-$25. Sun brunch $12.95. Child's menu. Entertainment: combo Sat. Jacket. Mediterranean decor; fountains, Spanish gates, gardens. Cr cds: A, D, DS, MC, V.

Harrison

(B-3) *See also Berryville, Bull Shoals Lake Area, Eureka Springs*

Pop 9,922 **Elev** 1,182 ft
Area code 870 **Zip** 72601
Information Chamber of Commerce, PO Box 939; 870/741-2659 or 800/880-6265

Harrison, headquarters for a rustic resort area in the wild and beautiful Ozarks, is excellent for vacationing. The entire region is scenic, especially along AR 7.

What to See and Do

Boone County Heritage Museum. History and antiques from the Civil War and the Missouri & North Arkansas Railroad Co. Indian artifacts, old clocks, medical, and domestic tools from the 1800s. (Mar-Nov, Mon-Fri; Dec-Feb, Thurs only) 110 S Cherry. Phone 870/741-3312. ¢

Float trips. Excursions down the Buffalo River through the Ozark Mountains and the forested hill country. For info contact Buffalo National River (Float Trips), National Park Service, Dept of the Interior, PO Box 1173, 72602. Phone 870/741-5443.

Mystic Caverns. Two caves with large formations; 35-ft pipe organ, eight-story crystal dome. One-hr guided tours cover ⅜ mi of lighted walks (may be strenuous). (Mar-Nov; closed Thanksgiving) 8 mi S on AR 7. Phone 870/743-1739. ¢¢¢

Annual Events

Crooked Creek Crawdad Days. Spring festival. Arts, crafts, music. May.

Northwest Arkansas Bluegrass Music Festival. Aug.

Coca-Cola Airshow of the Ozarks. Sep.

Northwest Arkansas District Fair. 2 mi S off US 65. Livestock show, rodeo. Sep.

Harvest Homecoming. Music, food, crafts. Oct.

Motels/Motor Lodges

★★ **COMFORT INN.** *1210 US 62/65N (72601).* 870/741-7676; fax 870/741-0827; res 800/228-5150. 93 rms, 2 story. May-Oct: S $42-$52; D $49-$59; each addl $7; suites $65-$80; under 18 free; lower rates rest of yr. Crib free. TV; cable (premium). Complimentary continental bkfst. Meeting rms. In-rm modem link. Coin lndry. Health club privileges. Heated pool. Game rm. Refrigerators in suites. Cr cds: A, C, D, DS, JCB, MC, V.
🄳 ⇔ ✈ ⊠ 🔥

★ **DAYS INN.** *1425 US 62/65N (72601).* 870/391-3297; fax 870/365-7378; res 888/391-3297; toll-free 800/329-7466. 82 rms, 3 story, 7 suites. May-Oct: S $50-$63; D $52-$68; each addl $5; suites $95-$125; under 12 free; family rates; package plans; higher rates special events; lower rates rest of yr. Crib free. TV; cable (premium), VCR avail. Complimentary continental bkfst. Restaurant adj 6 am-10 pm. Private club from 4 pm; entertainment wkends. Ck-out 11 am. Meeting rms. Business servs avail. In-rm modem link. Free airport transportation. Pool; whirlpool. In-rm whirlpool in suites. Totally nonsmoking. Cr cds: A, C, D, DS, MC, V.
🄳 ⇔ ⊠ 🔥 SC

★★ **RAMADA INN.** *1222 N Main St (72601).* 870/741-7611; fax 870/741-7610; toll-free 800/741-4776. 100 rms, 2 story. June-Oct: S $49-$55; D $56-$58; each addl $7; under 18 free; higher rates: some hol wkends, War Eagle wkend; lower rates rest of yr. Crib free. Pet accepted, some restrictions. TV; cable (premium). Pool; wading pool. Playground. Ck-out noon. Meeting rms. Business servs avail. Sundries. Game rm. Cr cds: A, C, D, DS, MC, V.
🄳 🐾 ⇔ ⊠ 🔥 SC

★ **SUPER 8 MOTEL.** *1330 US 62/65N (72601).* 870/741-1741; fax 870/741-8858; res 800/800-8000. 50 units, 2 story. June-Oct: S $48; D $52; under 12 free; lower rates rest of yr. Crib free. Pet accepted, some restrictions. TV; cable (premium). Pool. Continental bkfst. Restaurant nearby. Ck-out 11 am. Business servs avail. Game rm. Some in-rm whirlpools. Cr cds: A, D, DS, MC, V.
🄳 🐾 ♨ 🏊 ⇔ 🎿 ⊠ 🔥

Restaurants

★ **J. H. MCCLINTOCK'S.** *1423 US 62/65N (72601).* 870/741-1943. Specializes in prime rib, jumbo shrimp. Hrs: 6 am-8:30 pm; Fri, Sat to 10 pm. Closed Jan 1, Dec 25. Bkfst a la carte entrees: $2.99-$6; lunch a la carte entrees: $2.95-$7; dinner a la carte entrees: $5-$35. Child's menu. Parking. Country decor. Cr cds: DS, MC, V.

D [♿]

★ ★ **OL' ROCKHOUSE.** *416 S Pine St (72601).* 870/741-8047. Specializes in smoked brisket, Louisiana-style catfish. Own soup. Hrs: 11 am-9 pm; Sun to 3 pm. Closed Thanksgiving, Dec 25. Res accepted. Lunch, dinner $4.95-$11.95. Child's menu. Casual dining. Cr cds: DS, MC, V.

D SC [♿]

Heber Springs

see Greers Ferry Lake Area

Helena

(D-6) *See also Forrest City*

Pop 7,491 **Elev** 195 ft **Area code** 870
Zip 72342
Information Phillips County Chamber of Commerce, PO Box 447; 870/338-8327

Helena, a river barge port of call since 1880, was once described by Samuel Clemens as occupying "one of the prettiest situations on the Mississippi." This broad, flat section of the Mississippi River Valley is part of the cotton country known as "the Delta" and is the southern end of Crowley's Ridge, a stretch of wind-deposited yellowish loess hills that runs north to the Missouri border.

What to See and Do

Delta Cultural Center. Housed in 1912 Missouri Pacific rail depot, center has exhibits on history of "the Delta." (Mon-Sat, also Sun and hol afternoons; closed Jan 1, Thanksgiving, Dec 25) 95 Missouri St. Phone 870/338-4350. **FREE**

Phillips County Museum. Native American artifacts, Civil War relics; local history collection; glass, china; paintings, costumes. (Tues-Sat; closed major hols) 623 Pecan St, adj to public library. Phone 870/338-7790 or - 870/338-3537. **FREE**

St. Francis National Forests. Almost 21,000 acres, incl 510-acre Storm Creek Lake, 520-acre Bear Creek Lake. Swimming; fishing, hunting for small game; boating. Picnicking. Camping. Fees may be charged at recreation sites. (Daily) 2 mi N on forest service road. Contact Supervisor, 605 W Main, Russellville 72801. Phone 870/968-2354. **FREE**

Victorian and Edwardian Houses. An assortment of restored historic houses. To arrange for guided tours contact Delta Heritage Tours, phone 870/338-9141 or 870/338-3690. Fees vary according to number in group.

Annual Event

King Biscuit Blues Festival. Phone 870/338-8798. 2nd wkend Oct.

Seasonal Event

Warfield Concert Series. Series of productions by internationally known artists. Tickets at Chamber of Commerce. Sep-May.

Motel/Motor Lodge

★ **DELTA INN.** *1207 US 49 W (72390), 3 mi N on US 49.* 870/572-7915; fax 870/572-3757. 100 rms. S $37; D $42; each addl $5; kit. units $48; under 16 free. Crib $5. Pet accepted. TV; cable (premium). Pool. Complimentary continental bkfst. Restaurant nearby. Ck-out 11 am. Business servs avail. Cr cds: A, D, DS, MC, V.

D [♿] [≈] [✦] [≈] [♨]

B&Bs/Small Inns

★ ★ **EDWARDIAN INN.** *317 Biscoe St (72342).* 870/338-9155; fax 870/338-4215; toll-free 800/598-4749. 12 rms, 3 story. S $50-$56; D $65-$75; each addl $15; under 12 free. Crib free. TV; cable. Complimentary full bkfst. Ck-out 11 am, ck-in 2 pm. Balconies. Grills. Near Mississippi River. Restored historic mansion; built 1904. Many antiques. Cr cds: A, C, D, MC, V.

★★ **MAGNOLIA HILL B&B.** *608 Perry St (72342). 870/338-6874; fax 870/338-7938.* 8 rms, 3 story, 1 suite. S $65; D $75; each addl $10; suites $95; under 5 free; higher rates Blues Festival. TV; cable (premium). Complimentary full bkfst, coffee in rms. Restaurant nearby. Ck-out noon, ck-in 1 pm. Whirlpool. Microwaves avail. Queen Anne Victorian house built 1895. Totally nonsmoking. Cr cds: A, DS, MC, V.

Hope

(F-2) *See also Murfreesboro*

Founded 1852 **Pop** 9,643 **Elev** 348 ft
Area code 870 **Zip** 71801
Web www.hope-arkansas.com
Information Chamber of Commerce, 108 W 3rd, PO Box 250, 71802-0250; 870/777-3640

Hope is the birthplace of the 42nd President of the United States, William Jefferson Clinton, who lived here until age eight. The annual Watermelon Festival regularly has winners in the 150-200 pound range. The all-time winner weighed in at 260 pounds.

What to See and Do

Clinton Birthplace Home. First home of President Bill Clinton; he lived here from the time of his birth in 1946 until his mother married Roger Clinton in 1950. A National Register Historic Site. Visitor center; gift shop. (Tues-Sat; spring and summer, also Sun afternoons) 117 S Hervey. Phone 870/777-4455. ¢¢

Old Washington Historic State Park. During the early 19th century Washington was a convenient stop on the Southwest Trail, visited by such men as Stephen Austin, Sam Houston, and Davy Crockett. Washington became the Confederate capital for the state after Little Rock was captured in 1863. The park preserves and interprets the town's past from 1824-75. 9 mi NW on AR 4. Many historic structures remain, incl

Old Tavern. (ca 1840) with detached kitchen, taproom; blacksmith shop where, between 1826-31, James Black designed the bowie knife for James Bowie; **1874 Courthouse** now serving as park info center; **Confederate state capitol** from 1863-65; **Royston House**, restored residence of Arkansas Militia General Grandison D. Royston, president of Arkansas Constitutional Convention of 1874; **Sanders House** (1845), restored Greek Revival house; **Purdom House**, which served as medical offices of Dr James Purdom; **gun museum** with more than 600 antique weapons; and **Goodlett cotton gin.**

Guided tours of park incl historical bldgs (daily; closed hols). Contact Park Superintentent, PO Box 98, Washington 71862. Phone 870/983-2733 or 870/983-2684. ¢¢¢

Annual Events

Jonquil Festival. Old Washington Historic State Park. Coincides with blooming of jonquils planted by early settlers. Craft demonstrations, bluegrass music. Mid-Mar.

Watermelon Festival. Ice-cold Hope watermelon, entertainment, games, contests, arts and crafts. Phone 870/777-3640. 3rd wkend Aug.

Frontier Days. Old Washington Historic State Park. Pioneer activity demonstrations: knife-making and throwing, lye soap-making, lard rendering, turkey shoot. 3rd wkend Oct.

Motels/Motor Lodges

★★ **BEST WESTERN OF HOPE.** *I-30 and Hwy 278 (71801), Exit 30. 870/777-9222; fax 870/777-9077; res 800/528-1234; toll-free 800/429-4494.* 75 rms, 2 story. S $49-$54; D $59-$64; under 12 free. Crib $10. Pet accepted. TV; cable (premium). Pool. Coffee in rms. Restaurant adj 6 am-10 pm. Ck-out noon. Coin lndry. Bathrm phones, refrigerators. Some microwaves. Cr cds: A, C, D, DS, ER, JCB, MC, V.

★ **SUPER 8.** *2000 Holiday Dr (71801), jct I-30, AR 4. 870/777-8601; fax 870/777-3142; res 800/800-8000.* 100 rms, 2 story. S $26.88; D $35.88; each addl $7; under 12 free. Crib free. Pet accepted. TV; cable (premium). Pool. Playground. Complimentary continental bkfst. Coffee in rms. Ck-out noon. Coin lndry. Meeting rms. Business servs avail. Tennis. Lawn games. Some refrigerators; microwaves avail. Landscaped grounds; bridges. Cr cds: A, C, D, DS, MC, V.

Hot Springs and Hot Springs National Park

(D-3)

Settled Town of Hot Springs: 1807 **Pop** 32,462 **Elev** 632 ft **Area code** 501 **Web** www.hotsprings.org

Information Convention & Visitors Bureau, 134 Convention Blvd, PO Box K, 71902; 501/321-2277 or 800/772-2489

One of the most popular spas and resorts in the United States, the colorful city of Hot Springs surrounds portions of the nearly 4,700-acre Hot Springs National Park. Approximately one million gallons of thermal water flow daily from the 47 springs within the park. The springs have been administered by the federal government since 1832.

At an average temperature of 143°F, the water flows to a reservoir under the headquarters building; here it is distributed to bathhouses through insulated pipes. Some of it is cooled to 90°F without being exposed to air or mixed with other water. Bathhouses mix cooled and hot thermal water to regulate bath temperatures. The only differences among bathhouses are in the appointments and service.

The Libbey Memorial Physical Medicine Center specializes in hydrotherapy treatments given under the supervision of a registered physical therapist. Patients may be referred to this center by registered physicians or may get a standard bath without a referral.

Hot Springs, however, is more than a spa. It is a cosmopolitan city visited by travelers from all over the world; it is also a delightful vacation spot in the midst of beautiful wooded hills, valleys, and lakes of the Ouachita region. Swimming, boating, and water sports are available at nearby Catherine, Hamilton, and Ouachita lakes. All three offer good year-round fishing for bream, crappie, bass, and rainbow trout. The 42nd President of the United States, William Jefferson Clinton, grew up here. A Ranger District office of the Ouachita National Forests is located in Hot Springs.

What to See and Do

Arkansas Alligator Farm & Petting Zoo. Houses alligators, rhesus monkeys, mountain lions, bobcats, llamas, pygmy goats, ducks, and other animals. (Daily) 847 Whittington Ave. Phone 501/623-6172. ¢¢

Auto tours. Just N of Bathhouse Row, drive from the end of Fountain St up Hot Springs Mountain Dr to scenic overlooks at Hot Springs Mountain Tower and a picnic area on the mountaintop. West Mountain Dr, starting from either Prospect Ave (on the south) or from Whittington Ave (on the north) also provides excellent vistas of the city and surrounding countryside.

Bath House Show. Two-hr show of music and comedy acts derivative of 1930s-present; musical anthologies, reenactments of radio shows. (Feb-Dec, schedule varies; closed Jan) 701 Central Ave. For res phone 501/623-1415. ¢¢¢

Coleman's Crystal Mine. Visitors may dig for quartz crystals; tools supplied. Shop. (Daily; closed Dec 25) 16 mi N on AR 7N. Phone 501/984-5328. ¢¢

Dryden Potteries. Pottery-making demonstrations. (Mon-Fri; closed Jan 1, Thanksgiving, Dec 25) 341 Whittington Ave. Phone 501/623-4201. **FREE**

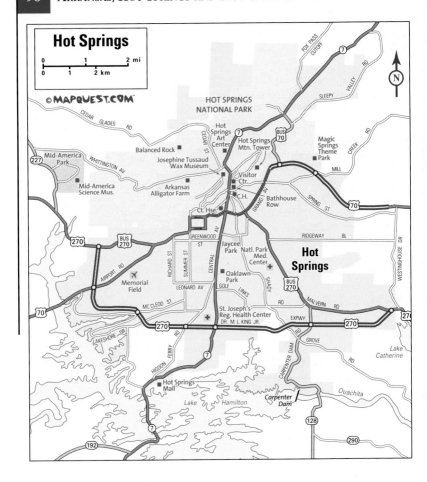

Hot Springs Mountain Tower. Tower rises 216 ft above Hot Springs National Park; glass-enclosed elevator rides 1,256 ft above sea level for spectacular view of Ouachita Mts; fully enclosed viewing area and, higher up, open-air deck. (Daily; closed Jan 1, Thanksgiving, Dec 25) Fountain St & Hot Springs Mountain Dr, atop Hot Springs Mountain. Phone 501/623-6035. ¢¢

Josephine Tussaud Wax Museum. Over 100 figures displayed. (Daily; closed Jan 1, Thanksgiving, Dec 25) 250 Central Ave. Phone 501/623-5836. ¢¢

Lake Catherine State Park. S & E via AR 128, 171. (See MALVERN).

Mid-America Science Museum. Exhibits focus on life, energy, matter, perception, state of Arkansas.

Museum features 35,000-gallon fresh-water aquarium; erosion table; laser theater; ham radio station. Restaurant, gift shop. (Memorial Day-Labor Day, daily; rest of yr, daily Tues-Sun; closed hols) 500 Mid-America Blvd. Phone 501/767-3461. ¢¢

Ouachita National Forests. The Ouachita (WASH-i-taw), located in 15 counties in west-central Arkansas and southeast Oklahoma, covers approx 1.7 million acres and incls seven wilderness areas, 35 developed recreation areas, 7 equestrian trails, 9 navigable rivers, and 8 lakes suitable for boating. Some recreation areas charge fees. (Daily) 12 mi W on US 270 or 20 mi N on AR 7. For info contact Forest Supervisor, PO Box 1270, 71902. Phone 501/321-5202. On Lake Ouachita is

Lake Ouachita State Park. Approx 400 acres. Swimming; fishing; boating (rentals, marina). Hiking trails. Picnicking. Camping (hookups, dump station), cabins. Interpretive programs, exhibits. Standard fees. (Daily) 3 mi W on US 270, 12 mi N on AR 227. For res phone 501/767-9366.

Sightseeing tours.

Belle of Hot Springs. Sightseeing, lunch, and dinner cruises along Lake Hamilton on 400-passenger vessel (Feb-Nov, daily). Charter cruises avail. 5200 Central Ave (AR 7S). Phone 501/525-4438. ¢¢¢

White and Yellow Duck Tours. The "Amphibious Duck" travels on land and water. Board in the heart of Hot Springs and proceed on to Lake Hamilton around St. John's Island. (Daily) 406 Central Ave. Phone 501/623-1111. ¢¢¢

Tiny Town. Indoor mechanical village; handmade miniatures. (Apr-Nov, daily) 374 Whittington Ave. Phone 501/624-4742. ¢¢

☒ **Walking tour.** Start at

Park Headquarters and Visitor Center. Exhibit on workings and origin of the hot springs. Outside fountains bubble hot spring water. A self-guided nature trail starts here and follows the Grand Promenade. Visitor center is located in the Hill Wheatley Plaza at the park entrance (daily; closed Jan 1, Dec 25). Gulpha Gorge Campground is avail for stays limited to 14 days Apr-Oct, and to 30 days in a calendar yr (fee). Naturalist gives evening campfire programs in summer. Inquire at National Park Fordyce Visitor Center on Bathhouse Row. Reserve & Central Aves. Walk a few yards E to the

Grand Promenade. Leads through a landscaped park above and behind Bathhouse Row, offering pleasant vistas of the city. Follow the Grand Promenade to Fountain St, where it ends. Turn left down the hill to Central Ave and find

Bathhouse Row. Tours of the Fordyce Bathhouse are offered in summer months; inquire at visitor center. (Daily; closed July 4, Thanksgiving, Dec 25) Behind Maurice Bathhouse are the

Two Open Hot Springs. At the S end of Bathhouse Row return to starting point.

Seasonal Event

Thoroughbred racing. Oaklawn Jockey Club, 2705 Central Ave. Daily. Under 10 yrs not admitted. Phone 623-4411 or 800/OAKLAWN. Jan-Apr.

Motels/Motor Lodges

★★ **AVANELLE MOTOR LODGE.** *1204 Central Ave (71901). 501/321-1332; fax 501/321-1332; toll-free 800/225-1360.* 88 rms, 2 story, 16 kits. S $44-$50; D $49-$56; each addl $5; suites from $62; kit. units $54-$58; under 17 free. Crib $2. Pet accepted. TV; cable (premium). Heated pool. Restaurant 7 am-1 pm; 5-10 pm. Ck-out 11 am. Meeting rms. Cr cds: A, DS, MC, V.

⬛🔧🏊🏋🏃🛶🔥

★ **BRADY MOUNTAIN RESORT.** *4120 Brady Mountain Rd (71968), 11 mi W on US 270, then 6 mi N. 501/767-3422; fax 501/767-6506.* 32 units, 17 kits. Sep: S, D $45-$49; each addl $3; kit. units $49-$190; apt $58; wknds (2-day min); lower rates rest of yr. TV. Pool. Restaurant 7 am-8 pm. Ck-out 11 am. Fishing boats, equipt, guide; ski boat, skis; boat dock, ramps. Rec rm. Game rm. Refrigerators. Microwaves avail. Private patios. Picnic tables, grills. On Lake Ouachita, surrounded by forest. Cr cds: A, D, DS, MC, V.

⬛⚓🏋🏊🏃🛶🔥

★ **DAYS INN HAMILTON RESORT.** *106 Lookout Point (71913), 6 mi S on US 7. 501/525-5666; fax 501/525-5666; res 800/329-7464; toll-free 800/995-9559.* 58 rms, 2 story. Feb-Aug: S, D $45-$60; each addl $5; under 12 free; wkly rates; wknds (2-day min); lower rates rest of yr. TV; cable (premium), VCR (movies). Pool; whirlpool. Playground. Complimentary coffee in lobby. Restaurant nearby. Ck-out 11 am. Meeting rms. Game rm. Lawn games. Massage. Some refrigerators; microwaves avail. Balconies. Picnic tables. Cr cds: A, C, D, DS, MC, V.

⬛⚓🏊🛶🔥

★★ **HAMPTON INN.** *151 Temperance Hill Rd (71913). 501/525-7000; fax 501/525-7626.* 82 rms, 4 story, 17 suites. Feb-Apr, June-Oct: S $84; D $91; suites $114-$124; under 18 free; lower rates rest of yr. Crib free. TV; cable (premium). Complimentary continental bkfst. Restaurant nearby. Ck-out 11 am. In-rm modem link. Sundries. Pool. Some bathrm phones, in-rm whirlpools. Refrigerator, microwave, wet bar in suites. Cr cds: A, D, DS, MC, V.

D ≈ ⊠ 🔥 SC

★★ **QUALITY INN.** *1125 E Grand Ave (71901). 501/624-3321; fax 501/624-5814; res 800/228-5151.* 138 rms, 2 story. S, D $54-$64; each addl $5; under 18 free. Crib $4. Pet accepted; $5. TV; cable (premium). Pool; whirlpool. Playground. Ck-out 11 am. Meeting rm. In-rm modem link. Coin lndry. Game rm. Refrigerators, microwaves avail. Cr cds: A, C, D, DS, MC, V.

D 🐾 🖎 🏂 ≈ 🏌 ⊠ 🔥

★ **SUPER 8 MOTEL.** *4726 Central Ave (71913). 501/525-0188; fax 501/525-7449; res 888/526-0188; toll-free 800/800-8000.* 63 rms, 3 story. S $47; D $55; suites $67; under 12 free. Crib free. TV; cable. Complimentary coffee in lobby. Ck-out 11 am. Business servs avail. Cr cds: A, C, D, DS, MC, V.

D ⊠ 🔥 SC

Hotels

★★★ **ARLINGTON RESORT HOTEL AND SPA.** *239 Central Ave (71901). 501/623-7771; fax 501/623-2243; toll-free 800/643-1502. Email arl@arkansas.net; www.arlingtonhotel.com.* 481 rms, 11 story, 42 suites. S $98; D $112; each addl $20; suites $172; under 17 free. Crib avail. Valet parking avail. Pool. TV; cable. Complimentary coffee in rms, newspaper. Restaurant. Bar. Ck-out 11 am. Conference center, meeting rms. Business center. Bellhops. Concierge. Dry cleaning, coin lndry. Gift shop. Salon/barber. Exercise privileges, sauna, steam rm. Golf. Tennis, 11 courts. Bike rentals. Hiking trail. Cr cds: A, D, DS, MC, V.

D 🖎 🏂 🏌 🏇 ≈ 🏃 🏂 ⊠ 🔥 🏃

★★★ **THE AUSTIN HOTEL & CONVENTION CENTER.** *305 Malvern Ave (71901). 501/623-6600; fax 501/624-7160; res 877/623-6697; toll-free 800/445-8667. www.theaustinhotel.com.* 200 rms, 14 story. S, D $69-$239; each addl $5; suites $169-$349; under 18 free. Crib free. Valet parking $5. TV; cable (premium). Indoor/outdoor pool; whirlpool. Restaurant 7 am-2 pm, 5-9 pm. Bar 3 pm-2 am; entertainment. Ck-out 11 am. Convention facilities. Business servs avail. Concierge. Golf privileges. Health club privileges. Full service spa with mineral water. Cr cds: A, DS, MC, V.

D 🖎 ≈ 🏂 🏌

★★ **RAMADA INN.** *218 Park Ave (71901). 501/623-3311; fax 501/623-8871; toll-free 888/624-3311.* 191 rms, 11 story, 1 suite. Feb-Aug, Oct: S $72; D $82; each addl $10; suites $250; under 18 free; lower rates rest of yr. Pet accepted, some restrictions. Pool, children's pool. TV; cable. Complimentary continental bkfst, coffee in rms, newspaper, toll-free calls. Restaurant 6 am-10 pm. Bar. Ck-out noon, ck-in 3 pm. Meeting rms. Concierge. Dry cleaning. Golf, 18 holes. Cr cds: A, C, D, DS, MC, V.

🐾 🏌 ≈ ⊠ 🔥

Resorts

★★ **CLARION ON THE LAKE.** *4813 Central Ave (71913). 501/525-1391; fax 501/525-0813; res 800/252-7466; toll-free 800/432-5145. Email 735fom_hotsprings@sunbursthospitality.com; www.clariononthelake.com.* 149 rms, 7 story. May-Sep: S $89.95-$155.95; D $99.95-$165.95; each addl $10; under 12 free; lower rates rest of yr. Crib avail. Pet accepted. TV; cable (premium). Pool. Continental bkfst. Restaurant 11 am-10 pm. Ck-out 11 am. Coin lndry. Meeting rms. Business servs avail. Tennis. Golf privileges. Health club privileges. Boat rentals, waterskiing. Playground. Some refrigerators; microwaves avail. Balconies. Cr cds: A, DS, MC, V.

🐾 ≈ 🏌 🏂 🏇 ⊠ 🔥 SC

★★ **LAKE HAMILTON RESORT.** *2803 Albert Pike Rd (71913), 3 mi W on US 270. 501/767-5511; fax*

501/767-8576; toll-free 800/426-3184. Email lhresort@direclynx.net; www.lake hamiltonresort.com. 104 suites, 3 story. Jan-Oct: suites $79-$94; under 18 free; lower rates rest of yr. Closed Dec. Crib free. Pet accepted. TV; cable. 2 pools, 1 indoor; whirlpool. Playground. Restaurant 7 am-9 pm. Box lunches. Picnics. Bar 4 pm-1 am. Ck-out noon, ck-in 2 pm. Coin lndry. Convention facilities. Business servs avail. In-rm modem link. Valet. Grocery, package store ½ mi. Airport transportation. Lighted tennis. Private swimming beach. Boat dock, launching ramp, rentals; motorboats; waterskiing. Entertainment. Exercise equipt; sauna. Game rm. Fishing guides. Refrigerators; microwaves avail. Balconies. Picnic tables, grills. Scenic view from all rms. 10 acres on Lake Hamilton; elaborate landscaping. Fountain; duck pond; lakeside gazebo. Cr cds: A, DS, MC, V.

⬛ 🐾 🛋 🛎 ⩰ ✈ 🏄 🛶 🔥 ✈ 🆂🅲

B&B/Small Inn

★★ **VINTAGE COMFORT BED AND BREAKFAST.** *303 Quapaw Ave (71901). 501/623-3258; fax 501/620-4302; toll-free 800/608-4682. Email info@vintagecomfort.com; www.vintage comfort.com.* 4 rms. S, D $60-$90; each addl $15; child $10. Children over 6 yrs only. TV in lobby; cable. Complimentary full bkfst. Restaurant nearby. Ck-out 11 am, ck-in 3 pm. Airport transportation. Balconies. Antiques; sitting rm. Cr cds: A, DS, MC, V.

🛶 🔥

Cottage Colonies

★★ **BUENA VISTA RESORT.** *201 Aberina St (71913), 4 mi S on AR 7, then ½ mi SE on Buena Vista. 501/525-1321; fax 501/525-8293; res 800/ 255-9030.* 50 kit. units, 1-2 story. June-Aug: S, D $74-$106; each addl $5; suites $125; under 5 free; lower rates rest of yr. Crib $5. Pet accepted, some restrictions. TV; cable. Pool. Playground. Ck-out 11 am, ck-in 3 pm. Coin lndry. Package store 1½ mi. Conference center. Business servs avail. Lighted tennis. Miniature golf. Lawn games. Rec rm. Game rm. Fishing; clean, store area. Refrigerators. Balconies. Picnic tables, grills. 10 acres on Lake Hamilton. Cr cds: MC, V.

🐾 🛋 🏄 🛶 🔥

★ **SHORECREST RESORT.** *360 Lakeland Dr (71913). 501/525-8113.* 25 kit. cottages. Feb-early Sep: S $45; D $51-$60; each addl $4; lower rates rest of yr. Crib free. Pet accepted. TV; cable. Pool. Ck-out 11 am, ck-in 2 pm. Grocery 1½ blks; package store ¼ mi. Private beach. Complete marina nearby. Lawn games. Fishing guides; clean, store area. Refrigerators. Private patios. Picnic tables; grills. Scenic, wooded location on Lake Hamilton. Cr cds: DS, MC, V.

⬛ 🐾 🛋 🛶 🔥 🆂🅲

Restaurants

★★ **BOHEMIA.** *417 Park Ave (71901). 501/623-9661.* Specializes in roast duck, Wienerschnitzel. Hrs: 11 am-9 pm; Mon, Wed from 4 pm; Fri, Sat 4-9:30 pm. Closed Sun; hols; also part of Dec, Jan. Res accepted. Lunch $3.50-$4.95; dinner $4.95-$13.25. Child's menu. Original paintings; extensive plate collection. Cr cds: A, DS, MC, V.

⬛ 🍴

Bathhouse Row

★ **CAJUN BOILERS.** *2806 Albert Pike Hwy (71913). 501/767-5695.* Cajun menu. Specializes in seafood, steak, chicken. Hrs: 4-10 pm. Closed Sun; Thanksgiving, Dec 25. Wine, beer. Dinner $4.50-$22.95. Child's menu. Parking. Dock for boat dining. Cr cds: A, D, MC, V.
D ⬚

★★ **COY'S STEAK HOUSE.** *300 Coy St (71901), off Hwy 70 E. 501/321-1414.* Specializes in steak, seafood. Hrs: 5-9:30 pm; Fri, Sat to 10 pm. Closed Thanksgiving, Dec 24, 25, 31. Bar. Dinner $9.95-$29.95. Child's menu. Valet parking. Old English atmosphere; antiques, paintings. Family-owned. Cr cds: A, D, DS, MC, V.
D ⬚

★ **DON JUAN.** *1311 Albert Pike Rd A (71913). 501/321-0766.* Specializes in vegetarian dishes. Hrs: 11 am-10 pm. Closed hols. Res accepted. Lunch a la carte entrees: $2.99-$5.69; dinner a la carte entrees: $3.99-$10.59. Child's menu. casual dining. Cr cds: DS, MC, V.
D ⬚

★ **FADED ROSE.** *210 Faded Rose (71901). 501/624-3200.* Specializes in steak, seafood. Hrs: 11 am-10 pm. Closed Thanksgiving, Dec 25. Lunch, dinner $2-$17.95. In former hotel (1889). Cr cds: A, D, DS, MC, V.
D ⬚

★★★ **HAMILTON HOUSE.** *130 Van Lyell Tr (71913), 6 mi S on AR 7. 501/525-2727. www.gourmetdining. com.* Specializes in fresh seafood, beef. Own baking. Hrs: 5:30-10 pm. Closed Sun; Jan 1, Easter, Thanksgiving, Dec 25. Res accepted. Bar. Wine list. Dinner $10-$36.90. Child's menu. Entertainment: pianist. Valet parking. 1929 mansion with elaborate decor, many antiques; underground tunnel connects house to Lake Hamilton. Cr cds: A, DS, MC, V.
D ⬚

★★ **HOT SPRINGS BRAU-HOUSE.** *801 Central Ave (71901). 501/624-7866.* Specializes in jaegerschnitzel, sauerbraten, Alpine chicken. Hrs: 3-10 pm. Closed Mon; hols. Res accepted. Bar. Dinner $7.95-$9.95. Complete meal: $12.95-$14.95. Child's menu. Entertainment:

wkends, hols. In cellar of 110-yr-old bldg. Cr cds: A, DS, MC, V.
D ⬚

★ **MCCLARD'S BAR-B-Q.** *505 Albert Pike (71913), 2 mi W on US 270. 501/624-9586.* Specializes in barbecue ribs, hot tamale spread. Hrs: 11 am-8 pm. Closed Sun, Mon; Thanksgiving, Dec 25. Lunch, dinner $4-$8. Child's menu. Parking. Casual, 1940s atmosphere. Family-owned. No cr cds accepted.
D ⬚

★★ **MILLER'S CHICKEN AND STEAK HOUSE.** *4723 Central Ave (71913), 5 mi S on AR 7. 501/525-8861. Email maecorp@hotsprings.net.* Specializes in fried chicken, catfish. Hrs: 5-10 pm. Closed Mon; also Dec-mid-Jan. Res accepted. Bar. Dinner $8.25-$25.95. Child's menu. Parking. Family-owned. Cr cds: DS, MC, V.
D ⬚

★ **MOLLIE'S.** *538 W Grand Ave (71901). 501/623-6582.* Specializes in kosher-style foods. Hrs: 11 am-9 pm. Closed Sun; Jan 1, Thanksgiving, Dec 25. Bar. Lunch $4-$5; dinner $5.95-$17.95. Child's menu. Parking. Family-owned. Cr cds: A, D, DS, MC, V.
D ⬚

★★★ **THREE MONKEYS.** *707 Central Ave (71901). 501/609-0003. www. three-monkeys.com.* Menu changes daily. Hrs: 6-10 pm. Closed Sun; Dec 25. Res accepted. Bar. Wine list. Dinner a la carte entrees: $7.50-$24.95. Street parking. Eclectic atmosphere. Cr cds: A, D, DS, MC, V.
D ⬚

Jonesboro

(B-6) *See also Walnut Ridge*

Founded 1859 **Pop** 46,535 **Elev** 320 ft **Area code** 870 **Zip** 72401

Information Greater Jonesboro Chamber of Commerce, 1709 E Nettleton, PO Box 789, 72403; 870/932-6691

Largest city in northeast Arkansas, Jonesboro is on Crowley's Ridge, the long, narrow ridge of loess (fine, windblown, yellowish loam) that stretches 150 miles from the Missouri line to Helena more or less parallel to the Mississippi River. Rice, cotton, soybean, wheat, and livestock processing, manufacturing, and shipping are the principal businesses of this community; education and medicine are also important. Hunting and fishing are popular in this area.

What to See and Do

Arkansas State University. (1909) 10,155 students. Eight colleges and a graduate school on 800-acre campus. Tours of campus. NE edge of town on US 49. Phone 870/972-2100. Also here is

> **Ellis Library, Convocation Center, and Museum.** Houses natural and state history displays. (Daily) **FREE**

Craighead Forest Park. Approx 600 acres with swimming; fishing; paddleboats. Picnicking, playground. Camping (hookups, showers, dump station). Fee for most activities. (Daily exc Jan 1, Thanksgiving, Dec 25) 2 mi S on AR 141. Phone 870/933-4604. **FREE**

Crowley's Ridge State Park. This 271-acre rolling area, once a campground for the Quapaw, has two lakes, miles of wooded hills, and is colorful with dogwood in season. The ridge is named for Benjamin Crowley, whose homestead and burial place are here. Swimming (lifeguard); fishing; boating (paddleboat rentals). Hiking trails. Picnicking, playground, restaurant, store, coin lndry nearby. Camping (many hookups, dump station), cabins. Interpretive programs (summer). Standard fees. (Daily) 15 mi N on AR 141. Phone 870/573-6751.

Lake Frierson State Park. Famous for its brilliant array of dogwood blossoms in spring, this 135-acre park is located on the eastern shore of 350-acre Lake Frierson, which fronts the western edge of Crowley's Ridge. Fishing; boating (rentals, ramp). Hiking trails. Picnicking, playground. Camping. (Daily) 10 mi N on AR 141. Phone 870/932-2615.

Motels/Motor Lodges

★ **DAYS INN.** *2406 Phillips Dr (72401), E off Caraway at AR 63. 870/932-9339; fax 870/931-5289; res* 800/329-7466. 46 rms. S, D $31.95; each addl $5; suites $37.95-$40.95; under 12 free. Crib free. Pet accepted. TV; cable (premium). Complimentary continental bkfst. Restaurant opp 6 am-10 pm. Ck-out 11 am. Sundries. Cr cds: A, DS, MC, V.

D ⊠ ⊕ ⊷ ⚓ ⊠ ⊨

★★ **JONESBORO HOLIDAY INN.** *3006 S Caraway (72401), N off US 63 Bypass. 870/935-2030; fax 870/935-3440; res 800/465-4329. Email hinn@insolwwb.net.* 179 rms, 2 story. S, D $65; each addl $7; suites $65-$100. Crib free. Pet accepted. TV; cable (premium). Indoor pool; whirlpool. Restaurant 6 am-10 pm. Bar 4 pm-midnight, Sat from 5 pm; entertainment Mon-Sat. Ck-out noon. Coin lndry. Meeting rms. Business servs avail. Airport transportation. Exercise equipt. Game rm. Rec rm. Cr cds: A, C, D, DS, JCB, MC, V.

D ⊠ ⊕ ⊷ ☇ ≈ ⚓ ⊠ ⊨

★★ **PARK PLACE INN.** *1421 S Caraway Rd (72401), off US 63 Bypass, near Municipal Airport. 870/935-8400; fax 870/935-7644.* 135 rms, 2 story. S $42.50; D $49.50; suites $65; under 18 free. Crib free. TV; cable (premium). Pool. Restaurant 11 am-10 pm. Private club 4:30 pm-2 am. Ck-out noon. Coin lndry. Sundries. Free airport transportation. Microwaves avail. Cr cds: A, C, D, DS, MC, V.

≈ ⊠ ⊨

★★ **WILSON INN.** *2911 Gilmore Dr (72401), off US 63. 870/972-9000; fax 870/972-9000; toll-free 800/945-7667.* 108 rms, 5 story, 31 suites, 59 kits. S, D $39.95-$44.95; each addl $5; suites $54.95; under 19 free. Crib free. Pet accepted. TV; cable (premium), VCR avail. Complimentary continental bkfst. Restaurant adj 11 am-10 pm. Ck-out noon. Meeting rms. Business servs avail. Health club privileges. Refrigerators; microwaves avail. Wet bar in suites. Cr cds: A, C, D, DS, JCB, MC, V.

D ⊠ ⊠ ⊨ SC

Hotel

★★ **HOLIDAY INN EXPRESS.** *2407 Phillips Dr (72401). 870/932-5554; fax 870/932-2586; toll-free 800/465-4329. Email jbrexp@insolwwb.net; www.hi express.com.* 103 rms, 4 story. S, D

$59; each addl $7; suites $70; under 18 free. Pet accepted, some restrictions. TV; cable (premium). Complimentary continental bkfst, coffee in rms. Restaurant nearby. Ck-out noon. Meeting rms. In-rm modem link. Coin lndry. Health club privileges. Microwave in suites. Cr cds: A, DS, MC, V.

D �’ 🖅 🖅 🔥 SC

Restaurant

★ **FRONT PAGE CAFE.** *1101 S Caraway Rd (72401), Caraway Plaza area. 870/932-6343.* Specializes in country foods, flying rolls. Hrs: 7 am-8:30 pm; Fri-Sun to 9:30 pm. Closed July 4, Thanksgiving, Dec 25. Bkfst $2-$5; lunch, dinner $4-$10. Casual country dining. Cr cds: MC, V.

D ⤴

Little Rock and North Little Rock (D-4)

Settled Little Rock: 1812 **Pop** Little Rock: 175,795; North Little Rock: 61,741 **Elev** 286 ft **Area code** 501 **Web** www.littlerock.com

Information Little Rock Convention & Visitors Bureau, PO Box 3232, Little Rock 72203; 501/376-4781 or 800/844-4781

These two separate cities on opposite sides of the Arkansas River are closely allied in every way and, from the standpoint of the tourist, are one community. Little Rock, the state capital, is a regional center for transportation, entertainment, culture, medicine, education, commerce, and industry. More than a "city of roses," it is known for its warm hospitality and recreational facilities. Little Rock is a modern, forward-looking capital.

Little Rock apparently got its name from French explorers who called this site on the Arkansas River "La Petite Roche" to distinguish it from larger rock outcroppings up the river. The first shack probably was built on the site in 1812, and by 1819 a town site had been staked. The community became the territorial capital in 1821

when the seat of government was moved here from Arkansas Post (see). The first steamboat, the *Eagle,* came up the Arkansas River in 1822.

What to See and Do

Arkansas Arts Center. Exhibits incl paintings, drawings, prints, sculpture, and ceramics; public classes in visual and performing arts; library, restaurant, theater. Performances by the Arkansas Arts Center Children's Theater; community events. (Daily; closed Dec 25) MacArthur Park. Phone 501/372-4000. **FREE**

Arkansas Repertory Theatre. Professional theatrical productions. 6th & Main Sts. Phone 501/378-0405.

Arkansas Symphony Orchestra. (Sep-May) Robinson Center Music Hall. For schedule contact Arkansas Symphony Orchestra Society, PO Box 7328, Little Rock 72217. Phone 501/666-1761.

Burns Park. More than 1,500 acres with fishing; boating. Wildlife trail; 27-hole golf, miniature golf, tennis. Camping (10-day max). Amusement rides, water slide (spring-fall); nine-hole Frisbee golf course. Fee for some activities. (Daily) Off I-40 at exit 150 in North Little Rock. Phone 501/791-8537. **FREE**

Decorative Arts Museum. Restored Greek Revival mansion (1839) houses decorative art objects ranging from Greek and Roman period to contemporary American; ceramics, glass, textiles, crafts, Oriental works of art. (Daily) 7th & Rock Sts. Phone 501/372-4000. **FREE**

Museum of Discovery. Exhibits on the sciences, social sciences, and technology. (Daily; closed hols) 500 E Markham, in River Market Entertainment District. Phone 501/396-7050 or 800/880-6475. ¢¢

The Old Mill. (1828) Old waterwheel gristmill. Two stones on the road to the mill are original milestones laid out by Jefferson Davis. This scenic city park is famous for its appearance in the opening scene of *Gone with the Wind.* (Daily) Fairway at Lakeshore in North Little Rock. Phone 501/791-8537. **FREE**

Pinnacle Mountain State Park. A cone-shaped mountain juts 1,000 ft above this heavily forested, 1,800-acre park; bordered on the west by

9,000-acre Lake Maumelle. Fishing; boating (ramps). Hiking, backpacking. Picnicking, playground. Visitor center with natural history exhibits; interpretive programs. Standard fees. (Daily; closed Thanksgiving, Dec 25) 7 mi W via AR 10, 2 mi N via AR 300. Contact Superintendent, 11901 Pinnacle Valley Rd, Roland 72135. Phone 501/868-5806.

★ **Quapaw Quarter Historic Neighborhoods.** Encompassing the original town of Little Rock and its early additions through the turn of the century, this area contains three National Register historic districts and well over 150 bldgs listed on the National Register of Historic Places. Named for Arkansas's native Quapaw, the area incl sites and structures associated with the history of Arkansas's capital city from the 1820s to the present. A tour of historic houses in the area is held the first wkend of May. Contact the Quapaw Quarter Assn, PO Box 165023, 72216. Phone 501/371-0075.

Restored sites in the area incl

Arkansas Territorial Restoration. Built in the 1820s-50s, the restoration incl four houses, outbldgs, and a log house arranged to give a realistic picture of pre-Civil War Arkansas. Reception center houses exhibits, crafts shop. Guided tours. (Daily; closed hols) 3rd & Scott Sts. Phone 501/324-9351. ¢

The Old State House. Originally designed by Kentucky architect Gideon Shryock, this beautiful Greek Revival bldg was the capitol from 1836 to 1911; it now houses a museum of Arkansas history. Features incl: restored governor's office and legislative chambers; Granny's Attic, a hands-on exhibit; President William J. Clinton exhibit; interpretive display of Arkansas' First Ladies' gowns. Self-guided tours.(Daily) 300 W Markham St. Phone 501/324-9685. **FREE**

Villa Marre. (1881) Restored Italianate mansion reflects exuberance of period with ornate parquet floors, walnut woodwork, and highly decorated stenciled ceilings; antique furnishings are mainly Victorian with some American empire and Edwardian pieces. House featured in opening credits of TV series *Designing Women.* Tours (Mon-Fri mornings, also Sun afternoons). 1321 Scott St. Phone 501/371-0075. ¢¢

River Cruises. Dinner, moonlight, and charter cruises. (June-Sep, Mon, Wed, Fri) Riverfront Park in North Little Rock. Phone 501/376-4150. ¢¢¢¢

State Capitol. A reduced-scale replica of the nation's capitol, the bldg is constructed of Batesville (AR) limestone. On south lawn is 1,600-bush rose garden comprising 150 varieties. The legislature meets the second Mon in Jan of odd-numbered yrs for 60 days. Self-guided and guided tours (Mon-Fri). W end of Capitol Ave. Phone 501/682-5080. **FREE**

Toltec Mounds Archeological State Park. This 182-acre park is the site of one of the largest and most complex prehistoric Native American settlements in the Lower Mississippi Valley; several mounds and a remnant of the embankment are visible. Guided on-site tours (by appt; fee); paved trail is accessible to the disabled. Tours depart from the visitor center, which has exhibits explaining how archaeologists work and the history of the site; audiovisual programs; archaeological laboratory. (Tues-Sat, also Sun afternoons; closed hols) 15 mi SE of North Little Rock, off US 165 on AR 386. Phone 501/961-9442. ¢

War Memorial Park. On approx 200 acres are rides and amusements. Golf, tennis, fitness center. Picnicking. (Daily) W Markham & Fair Park Blvd. Phone 501/791-8537. Also here is

Little Rock Zoo. More than 500 animals on 40 acres. (Daily; closed Jan 1, Thanksgiving, Dec 25) Phone 501/666-2406 or 501/663-4733. ¢¢

Wild River Country. A 23-acre water theme park with nine different water attractions. (June-Labor Day, daily; May, wkends) Jct I-40 and I-430, Crystal Hill Rd. Phone 501/753-8600. ¢¢¢

Annual Events

Arkansas All-Arabian Horse Show. Barton Coliseum. 2nd full wkend Apr.

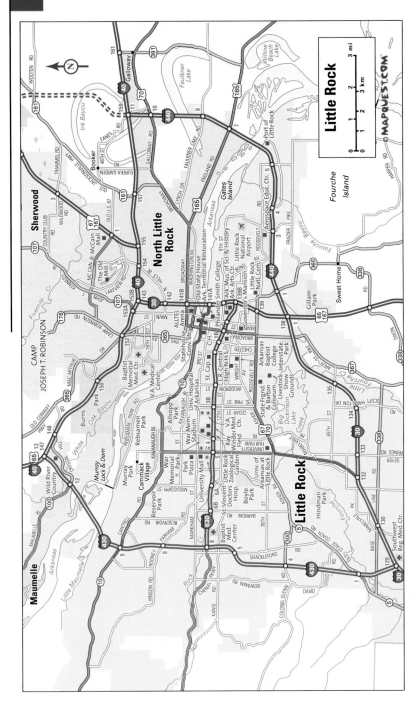

Riverfest. Little Rock area. Visual and performing arts festival incl exhibits by 60 artists; ballet, symphony, opera, theater, jazz, bluegrass, and rock groups; children's area; bike race, 5-mi run; concessions. Phone 501/376-4781. Memorial Day wkend.

Wildwood Festival. 20919 Denny Rd. Series of musical programs, exhibits, lectures, and events centered on the performing arts. Phone 501/821-7275 or 888/278-7727. June.

Summerset. North Little Rock area. Farewell to summer festival; visual and performing arts, concessions, 5-km run, sporting tournaments, entertainers, child's activities, fireworks. Labor Day wkend.

Arkansas State Fair and Livestock Show. 2300 W Roosevelt Rd. Rodeo and other events. Phone 501/372-8341. Early-mid Oct.

Additional Visitor Information

Travelers may stop at the Visitor Information Centers (daily) at the Statehouse Convention Center, and Little Rock National Airport to get more information. Telefun, 501/372-3399, is a 24-hour pre-recorded entertainment hotline with a bi-weekly update on events in the Little Rock area. For any additional information contact the Little Rock Convention & Visitors Bureau, Statehouse Plaza, PO Box 3232, Little Rock 72203; 501/376-4781 or 800/844-4781.

Motels/Motor Lodges

★★ **AMERISUITES.** *10920 Financial Center Pkwy (72211). 501/225-1075; fax 501/225-2209; res 800/833-1516.* 130 kit. suites, 4 story. S, D $83-$125; under 18 free; wkly rates. Crib free. TV; cable (premium), VCR (movies). Heated pool. Complimentary continental bkfst, coffee in rms. Restaurant nearby. Ck-out noon. Coin lndry. Meeting rms. Business servs avail. In-rm modem link. Free airport transportation. Health club privileges. Refrigerators, microwaves. Cr cds: A, C, D, DS, JCB, MC, V.

D ⛱ 🏋 ⊠ 🔥

★★ **COURTYARD BY MARRIOTT.** *10900 Financial Center Pkwy (72211). 501/227-6000; fax 501/227-6912; toll-free 800/321-2211.* 149 rms, 3 story. S, D $79-$89; suites $105; wkly rates. Crib free. TV; cable (premium). Heated pool; whirlpool. Complimentary coffee in rms. Restaurant 6:30-10 am; wkends 7-11 am. Bar Mon-Thurs 4-11 pm. Ck-out noon. Coin lndry. Meeting rms. Business servs avail. In-rm modem link. Valet serv. Sundries. Exercise equipt; sauna. Some refrigerators. Microwave in suites. Balconies. Cr cds: A, C, D, DS, MC, V.

D ⛱ 🏋 ⊠ 🔥 SC

★ **DAYS INN.** *3200 Bankhead Dr (72206), 8 mi E on I-440, near airport. 501/490-2010; fax 501/490-2229; res 800/329-7466.* 115 rms, 2 story, 12 kits. S, D $48-$53; each addl $5; kits. $58-$63; under 18 free. Crib free. Pet accepted. TV; cable (premium). Pool. Complimentary continental bkfst, coffee in rms. Restaurant adj open 24 hrs. Ck-out noon. Coin lndry. Business servs avail. In-rm modem link. Sundries. Free airport transportation. Some refrigerators. Cr cds: A, C, D, DS, MC, V.

D 🐾 ⛱ 🏋 ⊠ 🔥

★★ **HAWTHORN SUITES.** *4301 E Roosevelt Rd (72206), I-440 Exit 3, at airport. 501/376-2466; fax 501/376-0253.* 110 units, 5 story, 13 suites, 18 kit. units. S, D $47.95-$69.95; suites $64.95-$69.95; kit. units $45.95-$55.95; under 18 free. Crib free. Pet accepted, some restrictions. TV; cable (premium), VCR. Whirlpool. Complimentary continental bkfst. Ck-out noon. Meeting rm. Business servs avail. In-rm modem link. Bellhops. Parking. Free airport transportation. Refrigerators. Cr cds: A, C, D, DS, MC, V.

D 🏋 ✈ ⊠ 🔥 🏃 🖐

★★ **LA QUINTA INN.** *2401 W 65th St (72209), I-30 Exit 135. 501/568-1030; fax 501/568-5713; res 800/687-6667.* 113 rms, 2 story. S $59-$64; D $66-$75; each addl $7; suites $89; under 18 free. Crib free. Pet accepted, some restrictions. TV; cable (premium). Pool. Complimentary continental bkfst. Restaurant adj open 24 hrs. Ck-out noon. Business servs avail. In-rm modem link. Cr cds: A, C, D, DS, MC, V.

D 🐾 ⛱ ⊠ 🔥 🏃

★★ **LA QUINTA INN AT OTTER CREEK.** *11701 I-30 (72209). 501/455-2300; fax 501/455-5876; res 800/531-5900.* 145 rms, 3 story. S, D $64-$79; each addl $7; suites $139-$147; under 18 free. Crib free. Pet accepted, some restrictions. TV; cable (premium), VCR avail. Pool; whirlpool. Complimentary continental bkfst. Restaurant 11 am-2 pm, 5-10 pm; Sat from 5 pm; Sun to 2 pm. Bar 4 pm-midnight. Ck-out noon. Coin lndry. Meeting rms. Business servs avail. In-rm modem link. Health club privileges. Cr cds: A, C, D, DS, MC, V.

🄳 🏃 ⌦ 🏋 🛷 🔌 ♨ 🚶

★ **MASTERS ECONOMY INN.** *707 I-30 (72202), 9th St Exit. 501/372-4392; fax 501/372-1732; res 800/633-3434.* 170 rms, 8 story. S $34; D $38; each addl $4; studio rms $50; under 18 free. Crib $6. TV; cable (premium). Pool. Restaurant 6 am-10 pm. Ck-out noon. Coin lndry. Meeting rms. Business servs avail. Free garage parking. Exercise equipt. Game rm. Cr cds: A, C, D, DS, MC, V.

🄳 ⌦ 🏋 🔌 ♨

★ **MOTEL 6.** *7501 I-30 (72209), Exit 134. 501/568-8888; fax 501/568-8355; toll-free 800/466-8356.* 130 units, 3 story. S $31.99, D $37.99; each addl $3; suites $48.44; under 17 free. Crib free. Pet accepted, some restrictions. TV; cable (premium). Pool. Coffee in lobby. Restaurant adj open 24 hrs. Ck-out noon. Coin lndry. In-rm modem link. Patios. Cr cds: A, C, D, DS, MC, V.

🄳 🏃 ⌦ 🔌 ♨ SC

★★ **RAMADA INN.** *200 US 67 N (72076), 13 mi NE, James St Exit (10A). 501/982-2183; fax 501/928-7331.* 97 rms, 2 story. S, D $50-$55; each addl $6; under 18 free. Crib free. TV; cable. Pool. Restaurant 6:30-10 am, 11 am-1:30 pm, 5-8 pm. Ck-out noon. Coin lndry. Meeting rms. Business servs avail. Sundries. Cr cds: A, C, D, DS, MC, V.

🄳 ⌦ 🔌 ♨ SC

★ **RED ROOF INN.** *7900 Scott Hamilton Dr (72209), I-30 Exit 134. 501/562-2694; fax 501/562-1723; res 800/733-7663. Email idd47@redroof. com.* 108 rms, 2 story. S $30-$35; D $36-$46; under 18 free. Crib free. Pet accepted. TV; cable (premium). Restaurant adj open 24 hrs. Ck-out

noon. Business servs avail. In-rm modem link. Cr cds: A, C, D, DS, MC, V.

🄳 🏃 ⌦ 🔌 ♨

Hotels

★★★ **ARKANSAS' EXCELSIOR.** *3 Statehouse Plaza (72201). 501/375-5000; fax 501/375-4721; toll-free 800/527-1745.* 417 units, 19 story, 22 suites. S $115, D $125; each addl $10; suites $200-$580; under 18 free; wkend rates. Crib free. TV; cable (premium). Restaurant 6:30 am-11 pm; 3 dining rms. Bar 11 am-midnight, Sun to 10 pm. Ck-out 11 am. Convention facilities. Business center. In-rm modem link. Concierge. Shopping arcade. Valet parking. Free airport transportation. Exercise equipt. Health club privileges. 18-story glass atrium in lobby. Luxury level. Cr cds: A, C, D, DS, MC, V.

🄳 ⚓ 🏋 🔌 ♨ 🚶

★★ **BEST WESTERN INN-TOWN HOTEL.** *600 I-30 (72202). 501/375-2100; fax 501/374-9045; res 800/528-1234.* 134 units, 8 story, 25 kit. suites. S, D $55-$62; each addl $7; suites $65-$92; under 18 free. TV; cable (premium), VCR in suites (free movies). Heated pool; whirlpool. Coffee in rms. Restaurant 6 am-2 pm, 5-10 pm. Bar 4 pm-midnight. Ck-out noon. Coin lndry. Meeting rms. Business servs avail. Free airport transportation. Exercise equipt. Coin lndry. Parking. Refrigerator, microwave in suites. Cr cds: A, DS, MC, V.

🄳 ⌦ 🏋 🔌 ♨ SC

★★★ **CAPITAL HOTEL.** *111 W Markham St (72201). 501/374-7474; fax 501/370-7091; toll-free 800/766-7666. Email hospitality@capitalhotel-lb. com.* 125 rms, 4 story. S $127-$147; D $148-$168; each addl $20; suites $290-$385; under 12 free; wkend rates; package plans. Valet parking $9. TV; cable (premium), VCR avail. Restaurant 6:30 am-2 pm, 6-11 pm. Rm serv 24 hrs. Bar 11 am-midnight, closed Sun. Ck-out 1 pm. Meeting rms. Business servs avail. In-rm modem link. Gift shop. Health club privileges. Historic bldg (1877); turn-of-the-century ambience. Cr cds: A, C, D, DS, MC, V.

🄳 ♨

★★ **HAMPTON INN.** *6100 Mitchell Dr (72209), I-30, Exit 133. 501/562-6667; fax 501/568-6832; res 800/426-7866. Email litml01@hihotel.com.* 120 rms, 4 story. S $58; D $68; under 18 free. Crib avail. Pet accepted, fee. Parking lot. Pool. TV; cable (DSS). Complimentary continental bkfst, coffee in rms, newspaper, toll-free calls. Restaurant nearby. Ck-out noon, ck-in 3 pm. Meeting rm. Business servs avail. Dry cleaning. Exercise equipt. Golf. Video games. Cr cds: A, C, D, DS, MC, V.

★★★ **HILTON.** *925 S University Ave (72204). 501/664-5020; fax 501/664-3104; res 800/445-8667; toll-free 800/932-3322. Email lrhdos@aol.com; www.hilton.littlerock.com.* 256 rms, 3 story, 10 suites. Mar-June, Sep-Nov: S, D $101; each addl $10; suites $225; lower rates rest of yr. Crib avail. Valet parking avail. Pool, children's pool. TV; cable (premium). Complimentary coffee in rms, newspaper, toll-free calls. Restaurant. Bar. Conference center, meeting rms. Bellhops. Dry cleaning, coin lndry. Free airport transportation. Exercise privileges. Golf, 18 holes. Tennis, 5 courts. Picnic facilities. Cr cds: A, C, D, DS, JCB, MC, V.

★★★ **HILTON INN NORTH RIVERFRONT.** *2 Riverfront Pl (72114). 501/371-9000; fax 501/907-4800; toll-free 800/445-8667. Email donn-blecher@hilton.com.* 207 rms, 2 story, 12 suites. Mar, Oct: S $99; D $109; each addl $10; suites $139; under 18 free; lower rates rest of yr. Crib avail. Parking lot. Pool. TV; cable (premium). Complimentary coffee in rms, newspaper, toll-free calls. Restaurant 6-11 pm. Bar. Ck-out noon, ck-in 3 pm. Meeting rms. Business center. Dry cleaning. Free airport transportation. Exercise equipt. Cr cds: A, C, D, DS, MC, V.

★★ **HOLIDAY INN SELECT-WEST.** *201 S Shackleford Rd (72211), jct I-430 and I-630. 501/223-3000; fax 501/223-2833; toll-free 800/465-4329. Email beth.boyd@lrar.com; www.holiday-inn.com/lit-west.* 261 rms, 5 story. S, D $88-$99; each addl $8; suites $135-$299; under 18 free; wkly, wkend rates. Crib avail. Pet accepted.

TV; cable (premium). Indoor/outdoor pool; whirlpool, poolside serv. Complimentary coffee in rms. Restaurant 6 am-10 pm. Rm serv 5 pm-midnight. Bar 5 pm-midnight; entertainment. Ck-out noon. Meeting rms. Business servs avail. In-rm modem link. Bellhops. Valet serv. Concierge. Coin lndry. Free airport, railroad station transportation. Exercise equipt; sauna. Game rm. Cr cds: A, DS, MC, V.

B&B/Small Inn

★★★ **EMPRESS OF LITTLE ROCK.** *2120 S Louisiana (72206). 501/374-7966; fax 501/375-4537; toll-free 877/374-7966. Email hostess@theempress.com; www.theempress.com.* 5 rms, 3 story. Mar-May, Oct-Dec: S $130; D $150; each addl $50; suites $180; lower rates rest of yr. Parking lot. TV; cable. Complimentary full bkfst, coffee in rms, newspaper, toll-free calls. Restaurant. Ck-out 11 am, ck-in 4 pm. Meeting rm. Business center. Concierge. Dry cleaning. Gift shop. Exercise privileges. Golf. Tennis. Picnic facilities. Cr cds: A, MC, V.

All Suite

★★ **BEST WESTERN GOVERNORS INN SUITES.** *1501 Merrill Dr (72211). 501/224-8051; fax 501/224-8051; res 800/528-1234; toll-free 800/422-8051. www.bestwestern.com/governorsinnsuites.* 49 suites, 3 story. S, D $74-$105; under 12 free; wkend rates. Crib free. TV; cable (premium), VCR avail. Pool; whirlpool. Complimentary full bkfst, coffee in rms. Ck-out noon. Meeting rms. Business servs avail. In-rm modem link. Bellhops. Sundries. Health club privileges. Refrigerators, some wet bars. Cr cds: A, DS, MC, V.

Restaurants

★★ **1620.** *1620 Market St (72211). 501/221-1620.* Specializes in grilled talapia, pan sauteed steak, grilled salmon/sea bass. Hrs: 5:30-9 pm; Fri, Sat to 9:30 pm. Closed Sun; hols. Res accepted. Bar. Dinner $8.90-$27.50. Parking. Cr cds: A, D, DS, MC, V.

The Old Mill

★★★ **ALOUETTE'S.** *11401 N Rodney Parham (72212). 501/225-4152. www.alouettes.com.* Specializes in smoked duck salad, Dover sole, lobster bisque. Hrs: 5:30-9 pm; Fri, Sat to 9:30 pm. Closed Sun, Mon; hols. Bar. Wine cellar. Dinner $8-$28. Parking. Romantic atmosphere. Cr cds: A, D, DS, MC, V.

★★ **ANDRE'S HILLCREST.** *605 N Beechwood (72205). 501/666-9191.* Specializes in heart-healthy dishes. Own pastries. Hrs: 11 am-9:30 pm; Sun brunch 10 am-2 pm. Closed Mon; Jan 1, Thanksgiving, Dec 25. Res accepted. Bar. Lunch $5.25-$10.50; dinner $6.50-$21.50. Brunch $4.25-$9.50. Parking. Converted old house decorated with artwork. Cr cds: A, D, DS, MC, V.

★ **BROWNING'S.** *5805 Kavanaugh Blvd (72207), in Pulaski Heights shopping center. 501/663-9956.* Specializes in Mexican cuisine. Hrs: 11 am-9 pm. Closed Sun, Mon; hols. Wine, beer. Lunch $3.15-$5.50; dinner $4.75-$9.25. Child's menu. Parking. Mexican decor; murals. Cr cds: A, DS, MC, V.

★ **BRUNO'S LITTLE ITALY.** *315 N Bowman Rd #15 (72211). 501/224-4700.* Specializes in saltimbocca, Neapolitan pizza. Own pasta. Hrs: 5-10 pm. Closed Sun; hols. Dinner $6.95-$14.95. Child's menu. Parking. Family-owned since 1949. Cr cds: A, D, DS, MC, V.

★★★ **CAFE ST. MORITZ.** *225 E Markham (72201). 501/372-0411.* Specializes in souffle, seafood, lamb. Hrs: 11 am-9 pm; Sat from 6 pm; Sun brunch 11 am-2 pm. Closed Mon; hols. Res accepted. Bar. Lunch $6-$11; dinner $7-$22. Sun brunch $6-$11. Child's menu. Parking. French country decor. Cr cds: A, D, DS, MC, V.

★★★ **CASSINELLI 1700.** *1700 N Main St (72114). 501/753-9399.* Specializes in Neptune salad, homemade sausage, rack of lamb. Hrs: 11 am-10:30 pm; Fri to 11 pm; Sat 5-11 pm. Closed Sun; hols. Res accepted. Bar. Wine list. Lunch $4.25-$11.50; dinner $24-$42. Entertainment: pianist. Cr cds: A, D, DS, MC, V.

★ **CHIP'S BARBECUE.** *9801 W Markham St (72205), in Markham Plaza. 501/225-4346.* Specializes in barbecued ribs, chicken. Own pies. Hrs: 10 am-8 pm. Closed Sun, Mon. Lunch á la carte entrees: $3.95-$7.60; dinner á la carte entrees: $6.75-$8.50. Child's menu. Parking. Family-owned since 1961. Cr cds: A, DS, MC, V.
D

★ **FADED ROSE.** *1615 Rebsamen Park Rd (72207), 2 mi W on Cantrell Rd. 501/663-9734.* Cajun/Creole menu. Specializes in seafood, steak. Hrs: 11 am-11 pm; Sun noon-9:30 pm. Closed Thanksgiving, Dec 25. Bar. Lunch $3.50-$7; dinner $4-$17. Child's menu. Parking. Rustic atmosphere. Cr cds: A, D, DS, MC, V.
D

★★ **GRAFFITI'S.** *7811 Cantrell Rd (72207). 501/224-9079. www.menu menumenu.com.* Specializes in fettuccine seafood, chicken Mediterranean, fettuccine wild and creamy. Hrs: 5-9:30 pm. Closed Sun; hols. Bar. Dinner $4.95-$13.75. Local artwork; exposed wine racks. Cr cds: A, C, D, DS, MC, V.
D

★★ **LA SCALA.** *2721 Kavanaugh Rd (72205). 501/663-1196.* Specializes in fresh seafood, pasta. Hrs: 11 am-10 pm; Sat from 5:30 pm. Closed Sun; hols. Res accepted. Bar. Lunch $6-$10; dinner $10-$25. Parking. Secluded restaurant in historic district. Cr cds: A, D, DS, MC, V.
D

★★ **SIR LOIN'S INN.** *801 W 29th St (72115), 3 blks N on I-30, Exit 107. 501/753-1361.* Specializes in prime rib, teriyaki chicken. Salad bar. Hrs: 5:30-9:30 pm; Fri, Sat from 5 pm. Closed Sun; hols. Bar. Dinner $13.95-$29.95. Family-owned. Cr cds: A, D, DS, MC, V.
D

★★★ **SPAULE.** *5713 Kavanaugh (72207). 501/664-3663. www.spaule. com.* Specializes in nouveau cuisine. Menu changes monthly. Hrs: 5:30-10 pm. Closed Sun; hols. Bar. Dinner $3.50-$14.50. Bistro-style decor. Cr cds: A, MC, V.
D

Unrated Dining Spots

BUFFALO GRILL. *1611 Rebsamen Park Rd (72202), 2 mi W on Cantrell Rd. 501/663-2158.* Specializes in hamburgers. Hrs: 11 am-10 pm; Sun 11:30 am-9 pm. Closed Thanksgiving, Dec 25. Lunch $3-$3.50; dinner $5.25-$11.95. Child's menu. Parking. Cr cds: A, DS, MC, V.
D

DELICIOUS TEMPTATIONS. *11220 N Rodney Parham Rd (72212), in Pleasant Valley Plaza. 501/225-6893.* Specializes in pita sandwiches, homemade desserts. Hrs: 8 am-8 pm; Sat, Sun to 2 pm. Wine, beer. Bkfst $2.50-$7.50; lunch, dinner $2.50-$7.50. Sun brunch $2.50-$7.50. Child's menu. Parking. Cr cds: A, D, DS, MC, V.
D

Magnolia

(F-3) *See also Camden, El Dorado*

Founded 1852 **Pop** 11,151 **Elev** 325 ft **Area code** 870

Information Magnolia-Columbia County Chamber of Commerce, 202 N Pine, PO Box 866; 870/234-4352

Created to serve as the seat of Columbia County, Magnolia was largely dependent on cotton for many years. The town boomed with the discovery of oil in 1937. Today there are many wells in the vicinity, as well as chemical, aluminum, plastic, steel, lumber, and structural wood plants.

What to See and Do

Logoly State Park. Situated on 368 acres of forested coastal plain, this park is the first in Arkansas's system to be set aside for environmental education. Formerly a Boy Scout camp, Logoly represents southern Arkansas before commercial logging operations began. Most of the park has been designated a Natural Area because of its unique plant life and 11 natural springs. Well-marked hiking trails, observation stands, and photo blinds.

Picnicking. Tent camping. Visitor center displays flora, fauna, and history of the area; interpretive programs, exhibits. Standard fees. (Daily; closed Jan 1, Dec 25) 6 mi N on US 79, on County 47 (Logoly Rd). Phone 870/695-3561. **FREE**

Southern Arkansas University. (1909) 2,700 students. On 781-acre campus is Greek theater and model farm; Ozmer House, an original dog-trot style farmhouse; Carl White Caddo Native American Collection is on permanent display in the Magale Library, phone 870/235-4170. Campus tours. N on N Jackson St, off US 79. Phone 870/235-4000.

Motel/Motor Lodge

★★ **BEST WESTERN COACHMAN'S INN.** *420 E Main St (71753). 870/234-6122; fax 870/234-1254; res 800/528-1234.* 84 rms, 2 story. S $49-$59; D $59-$69. Crib free. Pet accepted, some restrictions. TV; cable (premium). Pool. Complimentary continental bkfst, coffee in rms. Restaurant 11 am-9 pm. Ck-out noon. Meeting rms. Business servs avail. In-rm modem link. Refrigerators. Balconies. Cr cds: A, C, D, DS, ER, MC, V.

B&B/Small Inn

★★ **MAGNOLIA PLACE.** *510 E Main St (71753). 870/234-6122; fax 870/234-1254.* 5 rms, 4 with shower only, 2 story, 1 suite. S, D $89-$99; suite $149. Children over 14 yrs only. TV; cable. Pool privileges. Complimentary full bkfst. Restaurant adj 11 am-9 pm, closed Sun. Ck-out noon. Built 1910 and furnished with many antiques; wrap-around porch with rocking chairs. Gardens, bird sanctuary. Totally nonsmoking. Cr cds: A, C, D, DS, ER, MC, V.

Malvern

(E-3) See also Arkadelphia, Benton, Hot Springs

Pop 9,256 **Elev** 312 ft **Area code** 501 **Zip** 72104

Information Chamber of Commerce, 213 W 3rd St, PO Box 266; 501/332-2721

Although dubbed "the brick capital of the world," Malvern also manufactures lumber and aluminum. The city also has small mining operations, mostly in barium and rare minerals.

What to See and Do

Hot Springs National Park. (see) 20 mi NW via US 270.

Jenkins' Ferry State Historic Monument. Civil War battleground site. Swimming; fishing. Picnicking. Exhibits. 16 mi E on US 270, 6 mi S on AR 291, 2 mi SW on AR 46.

Lake Catherine State Park. Approx 2,200 acres with swimming, water sports, fishing, boating (rentals, ramp, dock). Hiking. Picnicking in pine groves. Camping (hookups, dump station; standard fees), cabins, coin lndry, store. Visitor center; nature programs (summer). SW on I-30 Exit 97, 12 mi N on AR 171. Contact Superintendent, 1200 Catherine Park Rd, Hot Springs 71913. Phone 501/844-4176.

Annual Events

Brickfest. Courthouse grounds. Town festival with bands, singing groups, arts and crafts, contests, concession stands. Last wkend June.

County Fair and Livestock Show. Wkend after Labor Day.

Motel/Motor Lodge

★ **SUPER 8 MOTEL.** *US 270 W; RR 8 Box 719-6 (72104), I-30 and US 270 Overpass, Exit 98B. 501/332-5755; fax 501/332-3401; toll-free 800/800-8000.* 74 rms, 2 story. S $38.88; D $40.88; under 12 free. Crib free. TV. Complimentary continental bkfst. Ck-out 11 am. Cr cds: A, C, D, DS, MC, V.

Mena (D-1)

Founded 1896 **Pop** 5,475
Elev 1,150 ft **Area code** 501
Zip 71953
Information Mena/Polk County
Chamber of Commerce, 524 Sherwood St; 501/394-2912

This town was named after the wife
of a Dutch coffee broker who provided financial assistance for the
construction of the Kansas City,
Pittsburg, and Gulf Railroad (now
Kansas City Southern Railroad). A
Ranger District office of the Ouachita
National Forests (see HOT SPRINGS
AND HOT SPRINGS NATIONAL
PARK) is located here.

What to See and Do

Janssen Park. Historic park contains
a log cabin built in 1851; two small
lakes, spring, and picnic areas. Opp
post office.

Queen Wilhelmina State Park. This
640-acre park atop Rich Mt boasts
magnificent scenery and more than
100 species of flowers, mosses, and
ferns. A miniature railroad takes visitors on a 1½-mi circuit of the mountaintop in the summer (fee). The
original inn (1898) was built by the
Kansas City Railroad as a luxury
retreat; financed by Dutch investors,
the inn was named for the reigning
queen of the Netherlands. The current bldg is a reconstruction of the
original. The park also offers hiking
trails, miniature golf; picnicking,
playground; store, restaurant; coin
lndry. Camping (electric and water
hookups), shower facilities. Interpretive programs, exhibits (summer).
Animal park. Standard fees. (Daily)
13 mi NW on AR 88. Contact the
Superintendent, 3877 AR 88W, PO
Box 53A. Phone 501/394-2863 or
800/264-2477. Also here is

> **Talimena Scenic Drive.** This 55-mi
> "roller-coaster" drive through the
> Ouachita National Forests to Talihina, OK, passes through the park
> and other areas rich in botanical
> and geological interest. In addition
> to campgrounds in the park, there

are other camping locations along
the drive (fees may be charged).
Drive may be difficult in winter.
Follow AR 88 N & W, OK 1.

Annual Event

Lum & Abner Days. Downtown. Festival in honor of famed radio personalities features arts and crafts,
fiddlers' contest, entertainment. 1st
wkend June.

B&B/Small Inn

★★ **QUEEN WILHELMINA
LODGE.** *3877 AR 88 (71953), 13 mi
NW on AR 88, in Queen Wilhelmina
State Park.* 501/394-2863; fax 501/
394-0061. 38 units, 2 story. No rm
phones. Mar-Nov: D $65-$85; each
addl $5; suites $100; under 12 free;
lower rates rest of yr. Crib free.
Supervised children's activities
(Memorial Day-Labor Day) ages 7-14.
Dining rm 7 am-9 pm. Ck-out 11
am. Meeting rms. Gift shop. Airport
transportation. Miniature golf. Hiking trails. Picnic tables, grills. Modern design; native stone; windmill
garden. Cr cds: A, DS, MC, V.
D ⛷ ⛶ ⚞

Morrilton

(C-3) *See also Conway, Russellville*

Founded 1870 **Pop** 6,551 **Elev** 389 ft
Area code 501 **Zip** 72110
Web www.mev.net
Information Chamber of Commerce,
120 N Division; 501/354-2393

What to See and Do

Museum of Automobiles. Founded by
former Arkansas governor Winthrop
Rockefeller, the museum features an
attractive display of antique and classic cars. There are autos from Rockefeller's personal collection as well as
changing exhibits of privately-owned
cars. (Daily; closed Dec 25) 15 mi SW
of Morrilton. 8 Jones Ln, Petit Jean
Mt. Phone 501/727-5427. ¢¢

Petit Jean State Park. (see). 9 mi S
on AR 9, 12 mi W on AR 154.

Annual Event

Great Arkansas PigOut Festival.
Food, family fun. Softball, volleyball, tennis, 3-on-3 basketball tournaments. Children's activities; hog calling, pig chase. Local and nationally known entertainment. Phone 501/354-2393. First full wkend Aug.

Motel/Motor Lodge

★★ **BEST WESTERN INN.** *356 Hwy 95 (22902), Exit 107. 501/354-0181; fax 501/354-1458; toll-free 800/251-1962.* 55 rms, 2 story. S, D $38-$52; each addl $4; under 12 free; higher rates special events. Crib free. Pet accepted, some restrictions. TV; cable (premium). Pool. Complimentary coffee in lobby. Restaurant adj 6 am-9 pm. Ck-out noon. Meeting rms. Business servs avail. Some refrigerators, microwaves. Cr cds: A, D, DS, MC, V.
🐾 ➳ 🔌 🔥 SC

Mountain Home

(B-4) *See also Bull Shoals Lake Area*

Pop 9,027 **Elev** 820 ft **Area code** 870 **Zip** 72653
Web www.mtnhomechamber.com
Information Chamber of Commerce, PO Box 488; 870/425-5111 or 800/822-3536

This is a vacation town situated midway between Arkansas's two big Ozark lakes: Bull Shoals (see) and Norfork. Fishing in lakes and rivers is good; all varieties of water sports are available on both lakes. There are many resorts and marinas in this popular area.

What to See and Do

Norfork Lake. This 40-mi lake, impounded by a dam on the North Fork of the White River, is one of Arkansas's most attractive water vacation areas. Water sports; fishing for largemouth, striped, and white bass, walleye, crappie, bream, bluegill, and catfish; rainbow and brown trout are found in the North Fork River below the dam; hunting; boating (ramps, rentals, ten marinas). Picnicking, lodges. Camping (seasonal, some electric hookups; fee). Toll-free state bridges cross the lake. Fees charged at some areas. (Daily) 9 mi NE on US 62. Phone 870/425-2700.

Annual Event

Baxter County Fair. Fairgrounds. Arts and crafts. Mid-Sep.

Motels/Motor Lodges

★★ **BEST WESTERN CARRIAGE INN.** *963 Hwy 62E (72653). 870/425-6001; fax 870/425-6001; res 800/528-1234.* 82 rms, 2 story. S $43-$57; D $50-$62; each addl $6; under 12 free. Pet accepted. TV; cable (premium). Pool. Restaurant (see CHELSEA'S). Private club from 4:30 pm, closed Sun. Ck-out noon. Meeting rms. Cr cds: A, C, D, DS, MC, V.
🐾 🍽 🔌 ➳ 🐟 ➳ 🔥 🏃

★★ **HOLIDAY INN.** *1350 SW US 62 (72653), 1 mi SW. 870/425-5101; fax 870/425-5101; res 800/465-4329.* 100 rms, 2 story. S $49; D $52; each addl $7; under 18 free. Crib free. Pet accepted. TV; cable (premium), VCR avail. Pool. Restaurant 6 am-10 pm. Private club 5 pm-1 am, closed Sun; entertainment. Ck-out noon. Coin lndry. Meeting rms. Business servs avail. In-rm modem link. Airport transportation. Health club privileges. Cr cds: A, C, D, DS, MC, V.
D 🐾 🍽 🔌 ➳ 🐟 🏃 ✈ ➳ 🔥

★★ **RAMADA INN.** *1127 NE US 62 (72653). 870/425-9191; fax 870/424-5192; res 800/214-8378.* 80 rms, 2 story. S $44-$48; D $51-$55; each addl $7; under 18 free. Crib free. TV; cable (premium), VCR avail. Indoor pool. Coffee in rms. Restaurant 6 am-9 pm. Ck-out noon. Meeting rms. Business servs avail. In-rm modem link. Sundries. Beauty shop. Health club privileges. Cr cds: A, C, D, DS, MC, V.
D 🍽 ➳ 🐟 🏃 ➳ 🔥

Resort

★ **TEAL POINT RESORT.** *715 Teal Point Rd (72653), 6 mi E on US 62, then ½ mi N on AR 406. 870/492-5145; fax 870/492-5215; res 870/492-5145; toll-free 888/789-1023. Email tealpt@mtnhome.com; www.norfolk.com/tealpoint.* June-Aug: S, D $65; each addl $5; suites $220; children

$5; lower rates rest of yr. Crib avail. Pet accepted, some restrictions, fee. Parking lot. Pool, whirlpool. TV; cable. Restaurant nearby. Ck-out 9 am, ck-in 3 pm. Meeting rm. Fax servs avail. Coin lndry. Gift shop. Golf, 18 holes. Tennis, 8 courts. Beach access. Hiking trail. Picnic facilities. Cr cds: A, DS, MC, V.

Mountain View

(B-4) *See also Batesville, Greers Ferry Lake Area*

Pop 2,439 **Elev** 768 ft **Area code** 870 **Zip** 72560 **Web** www.mtnviewcc.org
Information Mountain View Area Chamber of Commerce, PO Box 133; 870/269-8098

The folk music heritage brought to these mountains by the early settlers is still an important part of the community today. Each Saturday night, if the weather is nice, folks head for the courthouse square with chairs and instruments to hear and play music. A Ranger District office of the Ozark National Forest (see RUSSELLVILLE) also is here.

Cottage Colony

★ **BLUE PARADISE RESORT.** *1034 CR 989 (72653), Tealpoint Rd, 6 mi E on US 62, then ½ mi N. 870/492-5113.* 17 (1-3 bedrm) kit. cottages (boat incl). Mar-Nov: kit. cottages $38-$96; each addl $5; wkly & monthly rates; lower rates rest of yr. TV; cable. Pool. Playground. Ck-out 9 am, ck-in 3 pm. Grocery. Coin lndry. Gift shop. Boats, motors, rowboats, pontoon boats. Float trips, guides. Lawn games. Rec rm. Lighted dock. Fish clean station. Microwaves avail. Picnic tables, grills. On Norfork Lake. Cr cds: A, DS, MC, V.

Restaurants

★★ **CHELSEA'S.** *965 US 62E. 870/425-6001. Email bestwest24@ aol.com; www.chelseasfinedining.com.* Specializes in seafood, steak. Hrs: 4:30-9:30 pm; Sun brunch 6:30-10 am. Closed hols. Bar. Dinner $5.95-$34.95. Sun brunch $19.95. Child's menu. Casual elegance; Queen Anne chairs. Cr cds: A, D, DS, MC, V.

★ **FRED'S FISH HOUSE.** *US 62E (72653), 6 mi E. 870/492-5958.* Specializes in seafood, chicken, steaks. Hrs: 11 am-9 pm. Closed Sun; Thanksgiving, Dec 25. Wine, beer. Lunch $3.95-$10.95; dinner $6.95-$14.95. Child's menu. Overlooks Lake Norfork. Cr cds: A, DS, MC, V.

Annual Events

Arkansas Folk Festival. Citywide. 3rd wkend Apr.

Merle Travis Tribute. Ozark Folk Center. Late May.

Arkansas State Fiddlers' Contest. Ozark Folk Center. Late Sep.

Herb Harvest Fall Festival. Ozark Folk Center. Concerts, crafts demonstrations, races, fiddlers' jamboree, contests. Early Oct.

Bean Fest and Great Arkansas Championship Outhouse Race. Homemade "outhouses" race around courthouse square. Music, tall-tale contest, games. Last Sat Oct.

Motels/Motor Lodges

★ **DOGWOOD MOTEL.** *HC 71 Box 86 AR 14 E (72560), 1 mi E of Downtown. 870/269-3847; fax 870/269-2997; toll-free 888/686-9275. Email dogwoodmotel@mvtel.net; www. dogwoodmotel.com.* 30 rms, 1 story. May-Oct: S $54; D $52; each addl $5; under 10 free; lower rates rest of yr. Parking lot. Pool. TV; cable. Complimentary toll-free calls. Restaurant nearby. Ck-out 11 am, ck-in 1 pm. Business servs avail. Free airport transportation. Golf, 9 holes. Tennis, 3 courts. Cr cds: DS, MC, V.

★ **OZARK FOLK CENTER.** *AR 382 Spur (72650), 1 mi N on AR 14, 1 mi*

W on AR 382. 870/269-3871; fax 870/269-2909; res 800/264-3665. 60 rms. Apr-Nov: S, D $50-$55; each addl $5; under 13 free; lower rates rest of yr. Crib free. TV; cable. Pool. Restaurant 7 am-8 pm. Ck-out 11 am. Meeting rms. Rec rm. Private patios. Overlooks Ozark woods. In Ozark Folk Center State Park; operated by AR Dept of Parks and Tourism. Cr cds: A, DS, MC, V.

Hotel

★★ **BEST WESTERN FIDDLERS' INN.** *HC 72 Box 45 (72560), ½ mi N on AR 14, at jct AR 9. 870/269-2828; res 800/528-1234. www.bestwestern fiddlersinn.com.* 46 rms, 2 story, 2 suites. Apr-Oct: S, D $75; each addl $8; suites $95; under 12 free; lower rates rest of yr. Crib avail. Parking lot. Pool. TV; cable. Complimentary toll-free calls. Restaurant 6 am-8 pm. Ck-out 11 am, ck-in 2 pm. Fax servs avail. Cr cds: A, C, D, DS, MC, V.

B&B/Small Inn

★★ **INN AT MOUNTAIN VIEW.** *307 W Washington St (72560), 1 blk W of Court Sq. 870/269-4200; fax 870/269-2956.* 10 rms, 2 story. No rm phones. Mar-Jan 1: S $52; D $62; each addl $18; kit unit $97. Adults only. Complimentary 7-course bkfst. Restaurant nearby. Ck-out 11 am, ck-in 2 pm. Business servs avail. Built in 1886; antiques. Totally nonsmoking. Cr cds: A, DS, MC, V.

Restaurant

★ **BAR NONE BAR-B-Q.** *803 W Main St (72560). 870/269-2200. www. barnonebar-b-q.com.* Specializes in dry-rubbed ribs, hickory barbecue, steak. Hrs: 11 am-8 pm; Fri, Sat to 9 pm; Sun to 3 pm. Closed Mon, Tues; hols. Res accepted. Lunch, dinner $3.95-$15.95. Child's menu. Family dining. Cr cds: A, DS, MC, V.

Murfreesboro

(E-2) *See also Hope*

Pop 1,542 **Elev** 340 ft **Area code** 870 **Zip** 71958

Information Chamber of Commerce, PO Box 166; 870/285-3131

What to See and Do

Crater of Diamonds State Park. This 888-acre pine-covered area along the banks of the Little Missouri River contains the only North American diamond mine open to the public (fee; assessment and certification free). Worked commercially from 1906-49, this rare 36½-acre field is open to amateur diamond hunters. More than 70,000 diamonds have been found here, incl such notables as Uncle Sam (40.23 carats), Amarillo Starlight (16.37 carats), and Star of Arkansas (15.33 carats). Other stones found here incl amethyst, agate, jasper, quartz. Hiking trail. Picnicking, playground, coin lndry, restaurant (seasonal). Camping (hookups, dump station; standard fees). Visitor center; exhibits; interpretive programs. (Daily; closed Jan 1, Thanksgiving, Dec 25) 2 mi SE on AR 301. Contact the Superintendent, Rte 1, Box 364. Phone 870/285-3113. ¢¢

The Ka-Do-Ha Indian Village. Excavated ancient Native American ceremonial site; prehistoric mound builder village; trading post; museum; arrowhead hunting; tours of excavations. (Daily; closed Thanksgiving, Dec 25) Off AR 27, follow signs. Phone 870/285-3736. ¢¢ Opp is

Arkansas Horse Park. Features the Peruvian Paso, "the world's smoothest-riding horse." Video history of breed. Riding demonstrations. Self-guided stable tours. (Daily) Phone 870/285-3736. ¢¢

Newport

(C-5) *See also Batesville*

Founded 1875 **Pop** 7,459 **Elev** 224 ft
Area code 870 **Zip** 72112
Information Newport Area Chamber of Commerce, 210 Elm, PO Box 518; 870/523-3618

The town was named Newport because in 1873 it was a new port on the White River. The seat of Jackson County, it is in an agricultural area with farming as the basic industry. Hunting, boating, and fishing are major recreational activities. The White River, Black River, and 35 lakes are nearby.

What to See and Do

Jacksonport State Park. Swimming, fishing. Picnicking; coin lndry. Camping (hookups, dump station). Standard fees. (Daily) 3 mi NW on AR 69 in Jacksonport. Contact Park Superintendent, PO Box 8, Jacksonport 72075. Phone 870/523-2143. Also here are

> **Carriage House.** Houses a buckboard, buggy, surrey, and a sulky used in racing thoroughbred horses from the surrounding plantations. **FREE**

> **Courthouse Museum.** Restored courthouse (1869); furniture represents various periods of Delta life. Indian Room; War Memorial Room with uniforms and relics; original papers. (Tues-Sun; closed hols) ¢

> **Mary Woods II.** Refurbished White River steamboat, berthed at Jacksonport Landing, houses maritime museum. (May-early Sep, Tues-Sun; Sep and Oct, wkends) ¢

Annual Event

Portfest & State Catfish Cooking Contest. In Jacksonport State Park (see). Catfish dinners, arts and crafts show, footraces, concerts, stage entertainment, waterski show. First wkend June.

Motel/Motor Lodge

★★ **PARK INN INTERNATIONAL.** *901 Hwy 367N. (72112). 870/523-5851; fax 870/523-9890; res 800/670-7273; toll-free 800/633-2275.* 58 rms, 2 story. S $52; D $62; each addl $3; under 16 free. Crib avail. Pet accepted, some restrictions. Parking lot. Pool. TV; cable (premium), VCR avail. Complimentary coffee in rms, newspaper, toll-free calls. Restaurant 6 am-9 pm. Bar. Ck-out noon, ck-in noon. Meeting rms. Fax servs avail. Dry cleaning, coin lndry. Exercise privileges. Golf, 18 holes. Cr cds: A, C, D, DS, JCB, MC, V.

North Little Rock

see Little Rock

Paris

(C-2) *See also Fort Smith, Russellville*

Pop 3,674 **Elev** 432 ft
Area code 501 **Zip** 72855
Web www.paris-ar.com
Information Paris Area Chamber of Commerce, 301 W Walnut; 501/963-2244 or 800/980-8660

Petit Jean State Park

See also Morrilton, Russellville

(I-40 Exit 108 at Morrilton, 9 mi S on AR 9, 12 mi W on AR 154)

This nearly 3,000-acre rugged area is the oldest and one of the most beautiful of the Arkansas parks. Both the park and forested Petit Jean Mountain, 1,100 feet high, are named for a French girl who is said to have disguised herself as a boy to accompany her sailor sweetheart to

America. While in the New World the girl contracted an unknown disease and died, never having returned to France. Legend has it that she was buried on the mountain by friendly Native Americans.

Adjoining the park is the Museum of Automobiles (see MORRILTON) and Winrock Farm, former governor Winthrop Rockefeller's experimental demonstration farm, where he raised Santa Gertrudis cattle. The park also offers a swimming pool (lifeguard); boating (paddleboat, fishing boat rentals). Hiking trails, tennis. Picnicking, playgrounds, restaurant, snack bar (Memorial Day-Labor Day). Camping (hookups, rent-a-camp, dump station), trailer sites, cabins, lodge. Interpretive programs. Visitor center (phone 501/727-5441). Standard fees. Contact the Superintendent, 1285 Petit Jean Mountain Rd, Morrilton 72110; phone 501/727-5431 or 800/264-2462 (cabins and lodge res).

Motels/Motor Lodges

★★ **PETIT JEAN MOUNTAIN STATE PARK MATHER LODGE.** *1069 Petit Jean Mountain Rd (72110), 20 mi SW of Morrilton on AR 154, in Park.* 501/727-5431; fax 501/727-5479; toll-free 800/264-2462. 56 units, 1-2 story, 20 kits. S $45; D $50; each addl $5; kit. units $75; cabins $55; under 12 free. Pool. Playground. Restaurant 7 am-8 pm. Ck-out 11 am. Meeting rm. Gift shop. Tennis. Paddleboats. State-owned. Naturalist programs daily Memorial Day-Labor Day. Scenic view overlooking valley and Arkansas River. Cr cds: A, DS, MC, V.

Cottage Colony

★★★ **TANYARD SPRINGS.** *144 Tanyard Spring Rd (72110), AR 154, on Petit Jean Mt.* 501/727-5200; fax 501/727-5228; toll-free 888/826-9273. 13 kit. cabins. No rm phones. S, D $125-$150; each addl $15; under 16 free; Crib free. Ck-out 11 am, ck-in 4 pm. Meeting rms. Business servs avail. Tennis privileges. Miniature golf. Lawn games. Fireplaces. Private picnic tables, grills. Individually themed, hand-crafted cabins; each named for historic personality; many

antiques. On 187 wooded acres with lake. Cr cds: A, DS, MC, V.

Pine Bluff (E-4)

Founded 1819 **Pop** 57,140 **Elev** 230 ft
Area code 870
Web www.pinebluff.com
Information Convention Center & Visitors Bureau, 1 Convention Center Plaza, 71601; 870/536-7600 or 800/536-7660

What to See and Do

Arkansas Entertainers Hall of Fame. Programs and displays trace the careers of featured Arkansas entertainers. Incl are Johnny Cash, Glen Campbell, Billy Bob Thornton, and Mary Steenburgen. Personal memorabilia belonging to the stars is also on display. (Mon-Fri; Sat-Sun, seasonal) One Convention Center Plaza. Phone 870/536-7600 or 800/536-7600. **FREE**

Arkansas Post National Memorial. (see) 40 mi SE on US 65, then 17 mi N on US 165, then 2 mi E on AR 169.

Jefferson County Historical Museum. Features exhibits on history of Pine Bluff and Jefferson County, development of area transportation, incl river, roads, and rail; displays of Victorian artifacts and clothing used by early settlers. (Mon-Sat; closed hols) 201 E 4th St. Phone 870/541-5402. **FREE**

Navigation Pool (Lock) No 4. Ste. Marie and Sheppard Island have fishing, boat launching facilities, picnicking. Ste. Marie also has a fishing dock designed for use by the disabled. Some facilities closed during winter months. 5 mi E on AR 81 at jct AR 425, US 65. Phone 870/534-0451. **FREE**

Pioneer Village. Re-created pioneer village with several historic structures, incl a log cabin, mercantile store, blacksmith shop, barn, physician's Victorian home, and a church. Tours. (Mid-June-mid-Aug, Mon-Fri, wkends by appt) 25 mi SE via US 79 in Rison. Phone 870/325-7289. **FREE**

Motel/Motor Lodge

★ **INN OF PINE BLUFF.** *210 N Blake St (71601), jct US 65, US 79.* 870/534-7222; fax 870/534-5705; toll-free 800/890-7222. 90 units, 2 story. S, D $45; each addl $5; suites $53-$60; under 12 free. Pet accepted. TV; cable (premium). Pool. Complimentary continental bkfst. Restaurant adj 6 am-midnight. Ck-out noon. Meeting rms. Business servs avail. Exercise equipt. Microwaves avail. Picnic tables, grills. Cr cds: A, C, D, DS, MC, V.

Hotel

★★ **RAMADA INN.** *2 Convention Center Dr (71601), S off Main St, behind Convention Center.* 870/535-3111; fax 870/534-5083; res 800/272-6232. 200 units, 5 story, 84 suites. S, D $69; each addl $5; suites $79-$89; under 18 free. Crib free. Pet accepted, some restrictions. TV: cable. Indoor pool; whirlpool. Restaurant 6:30 am-10 pm. Bar 4-10 pm. Ck-out 11 am. Business servs avail. In-rm modem link. Meeting rm. Indoor putting green. Exercise equipt; sauna. Beauty shop. Gift shop. Game rm. Refrigerators; microwave, wet bar in suites. Atrium, balconies. Cr cds: A, C, D, DS, MC, V.

B&B/Small Inn

★★ **MARGLAND BED AND BREAKFAST.** *703 W 2nd St (71601), off US 65.* 870/536-6000; fax 870/536-7941; toll-free 800/545-5383. Email lethompson@prodigy.net. 22 rms, 2 story. S, D $85-$105; under 12 free. Crib free. TV: cable (premium), VCR avail (free movies). Pool. Complimentary continental bkfst. Ck-out, ck-in noon. Business servs avail. Exercise equipt. Picnic tables; grills. Four turn-of-the-century houses, porches, leaded glass; Victorian decor, antiques, old wicker. Totally nonsmoking. Cr cds: A, DS, MC, V.

Restaurant

★★ **JONES CAFE.** *3910 AR 65S (71601), 2 mi S.* 870/534-6678. Spe-cializes in pies, fresh vegetables. Hrs: 6 am-9 pm; Sun 11 am-2 pm. Closed hols. Res accepted. Bkfst $3-$5; lunch, dinner $2.50-$12. Gift shop. Casual dining. Cr cds: A, D, DS, MC, V.

Pocahontas

(B-6) *See also Jonesboro, Walnut Ridge*

Pop 6,151 **Elev** 310 ft **Area code** 870 **Zip** 72455

Information Randolph County Chamber of Commerce, 121 E Everett St, PO Box 466; 870/892-3956

What to See and Do

Old Davidsonville State Park. This 163-acre park on the Black River was the site of historic Davidsonville, a small town established by French settlers in 1815; the first post office and courthouse in the state were located here. Fishing; canoeing and boating (no motors; rentals). Hiking trails. Picnicking, playground; snack bar, coin lndry nearby. Camping (tent sites, hookups, dump station; fee). Visitor center (exhibits of local artifacts). Standard fees. (Daily) 2 mi W on US 62, 9 mi S on AR 166. Phone 870/892-4708.

Annual Event

Randolph County Fair. Fairgrounds. Late Aug-early Sep.

Motel/Motor Lodge

★ **COTTONWOOD INN MOTEL.** *2203 Hwy 67S (72455).* 870/892-2581; fax 870/892-7529. 50 rms, 1-2 story. S $36; D $44; each addl $2; suites $49-$55; kit. units $62-$66; under 12 free wkdays; higher rates hol wkends. Crib free. TV; cable (premium), VCR avail (movies). Complimentary coffee in lobby. Restaurant nearby. Ck-out 11 am. Meeting rm. Cr cds: A, C, D, DS, ER, JCB, MC, V.

Rogers

(B-2) *See also Bentonville, Eureka Springs, Fayetteville, Springdale*

Founded 1881 **Pop** 24,692
Elev 1,371 ft **Area code** 501
Web www.rogers.dina.org
Information Chamber of Commerce, 317 W Walnut, 72756; 501/636-1240 or 800/364-1240

This pleasant town in the Ozark area has diversified industries including the manufacture of air rifles, electric motors, pumps, tools, stereo speakers, and office furniture and the processing of poultry.

What to See and Do

Beaver Lake. Variety of water sports on 30,000-acre reservoir with 483-mile shoreline. Swimming, waterskiing; fishing, hunting; boating (ramp, marine station, rental boats, motors). Picnicking, playground. Camping (hookups, dump station). Fee for some activities. (Daily) 4 mi E on AR 12. Phone 501/636-1210. ¢¢¢

Pea Ridge National Military Park. A decisive battle was fought here March 7-8, 1862, saving Missouri for the Union and resulting in the deaths of three Confederate generals: McCulloch, McIntosh, and Slack. Auto tour through historic area; the Elkhorn Tavern has been restored. Visitor center (daily; closed Jan 1, Thanksgiving, Dec 25). 10 mi NE on US 62. Phone 501/451-8122. Per vehicle ¢¢

Motel/Motor Lodge

★ **BEAVER LAKE LODGE - THE OZARKS.** *14733 Dutchmans Dr (72756), 4 mi E on AR 12 (RR 7), then ¼ mi N. 501/925-2313; res 501/925-2313. www. beaverlake.com/beaver-lakelodge.* 25 rms, 1 story, 2 suites. July: S, D $59; suites $115; lower rates rest of yr. Parking lot. Pool. TV; cable. Complimentary toll-free calls. Restaurant nearby. Ck-out 11 am, ck-in 2 pm. Golf. Tennis. Beach access. Hiking trail. Picnic facilities. Cr cds: A, MC, V.

Hotel

★★ **RAMADA INN.** *1919 Hwy 71 Business, S 8th (72758), jct 94E. 501/636-5850; fax 501/636-5202; res 800/433-8558.* 126 rms, 2 story, 1 suite. Oct: S, D $85; suites $125; lower rates rest of yr. Crib avail. Pet accepted. Parking lot. Pool. TV; cable (premium), VCR avail. Complimentary coffee in rms. Restaurant 6 am-9 pm. Bar. Ck-out noon, ck-in 1 pm. Meeting rms. Business servs avail. Bellhops. Dry cleaning, coin lndry. Exercise privileges. Golf, 18 holes. Tennis, 6 courts. Beach access. Hiking trail. Picnic facilities. Cr cds: A, D, DS, MC, V.

Restaurant

★★ **TALE OF THE TROUT.** *4611 W New Hope Rd (72758). 501/636-0508.* Specializes in steaks, trout, quail. Hrs: 5-9:30 pm. Closed Sun; hols. Dinner $16-$22.40. Private club. Overlooks trout stream. Cr cds: A, D, DS, MC, V.

Unrated Dining Spot

WAR EAGLE MILL. *11045 War Eagle Rd (72756), 12 mi E on AR 12, then 1½ mi on War Eagle Rd, 501/789-5343. Email zoe@ipa.net; www.wareaglemill.com.* Specializes in biscuits and gravy, buckwheat waffles, beans and cornbread. Hrs: 8:30 am-5 pm. Closed Thanksgiving, Dec 25; Jan; also wkdays in Feb. Bkfst $1.50-$4.25; lunch $1.75-$4.50. Child's menu. Reproduction of 1873 mill. Mill products and gift shop. Cr cds: DS, MC, V.

Russellville (C-3)

See also Morrilton, Paris

Founded 1842 **Pop** 21,260 **Elev** 354 ft
Area code 501 **Zip** 72801
Web www.russellville.dina.org
Information Chamber of Commerce, 708 W Main St; 501/968-2530

What to See and Do

Holla Bend National Wildlife Refuge. Late Nov-Feb is best time for viewing ducks and geese; other species incl golden and bald eagles, herons, egrets, sandpipers, and scissor-tailed flycatchers. Fishing (Mar-Oct). Self-guided auto tour. (Daily) 14 mi SE via AR 7, 155. Phone 501/229-4300. Per vehicle ¢¢

Lake Dardanelle. More than 300 mi shoreline on lake formed by Dard-anelle Dam, the largest in Arkansas River Navigation System. NW edge of town on AR 326. On lake is

Lake Dardanelle State Park. Swim-ming, fishing, boating (rentals, marina), bicycling, hiking and nature trails, miniature golf. Pic-nicking. Camping (hookups, dump station). Seasonal interpretive pro-grams. Standard fees. (Daily) Phone 501/967-5516.

Petit Jean State Park. (see). 12 mi S on AR 7, then 14 mi E on AR 154.

Potts Tavern/Museum. (1850) Former stagecoach stop on the Butterfield Overland mail route between Mem-phis and Fort Smith. Restored; museum, ladies' hats display. (Sat and Sun) 6 mi SE via I-40, Exit 88. ¢

Annual Events

Valley Fest. 300 E Third St. Barbecue cook-offs, 3-on-3 basketball, volley-ball, fishing derby, rides, and games. Phone 501/968-7819. Late Aug.

Pope County Fair. Mid-Sep.

Motel/Motor Lodge

★★ **HOLIDAY INN.** *Hwy 7 (72476), at jct I-40. 501/968-4300; fax 501/968-4300; toll-free 800/465-4329.* 149 units, 2 story. S $58; D $68; each addl $10; under 18 free. Crib free. Pet accepted, some restrictions. TV; cable (premium). Pool. Complimentary continental bkfst, coffee in rms. Restaurant 6 am-2 pm, 4-10 pm; Sun from 7 am. Private club 4:30 pm-midnight; closed Sun. Ck-out noon. Meeting rms. Business servs avail. In-rm modem link. Airport transporta-tion. Microwaves avail. Cr cds: A, C, D, DS, ER, JCB, MC, V.

Searcy

(C-4) *See also Greers Ferry Lake Area, Little Rock*

Founded 1860 **Pop** 15,180 **Elev** 264 ft
Area code 501 **Zip** 72143

Motel/Motor Lodge

★★ **COMFORT INN.** *107 S Rand St (72143), 1 blk off US 67/167, Exit 46. 501/279-9100; fax 501/268-1884; toll-free 800/228-5150.* 60 rms, 2 story. S $50; D $60; under 14 free. Crib $5. Pet accepted. TV; cable (premium). Pool. Complimentary continental bkfst. Restaurant nearby. Ck-out 11 am. Cr cds: A, C, D, DS, ER, JCB, MC, V.

Hotel

★★ **HAMPTON INN.** *3204 E Race St (72143), 1 blk W off US 67/167, Exit 46. 501/268-0654; fax 501/278-5546; res 800/426-7866; toll-free 800/737-0654. Email searhamp@csw.com.* 103 rms, 2 story, 3 suites. May-Aug: S $61; D $65; suites $76; under 16 free; lower rates rest of yr. Crib avail. Pet accepted, some restrictions, fee. Park-ing lot. Indoor/outdoor pools, chil-dren's pool, whirlpool. TV; cable (premium). Complimentary continen-tal bkfst, coffee in rms, newspaper, toll-free calls. Restaurant 6 am-11 pm. Bar. Ck-out noon, ck-in 3 pm. Meeting rm. Business center. Dry cleaning, coin lndry. Free airport transportation. Exercise equipt, sauna. Golf, 18 holes. Tennis, 4 courts. Hiking trail. Video games. Cr cds: A, C, D, DS, JCB, MC, V.

Springdale

(B-2) *See also Bentonville, Fayetteville, Rogers*

Pop 29,941 **Elev** 1,329 ft
Area code 501
Web www.springdale.com
Information Chamber of Commerce, 202 W Emma Ave, PO Box 166, 72765; 501/872-2222 or 800/972-7261

What to See and Do

Arts Center of the Ozarks. Visual and performing arts center. Art gallery (Mon-Sat; closed 2 wks around Dec 25); concerts; theater productions (fee). 214 S Main. Phone 501/751-5441.

Annual Event

Rodeo of the Ozarks. Held in the Arena at Emma Ave & Old Missouri Rd. Early July.

Motels/Motor Lodges

★ **DAYS INN.** *4677 W Sunset Ave (72762). 501/751-7200; fax 501/756-2900; toll-free 800/329-7466.* 84 rms, 4 story, 25 suites. S $65; D $71; suites $95-$130; under 12 free; wkend rates; higher rates special events. Crib free. TV; cable (premium). Complimentary continental bkfst, coffee in rms. Restaurant nearby. Ck-out 11 am. Meeting rms. Business center. In-rm modem link. Coin lndry. Exercise equipt. Some refrigerators, microwaves. Cr cds: A, D, DS, MC, V.

★★ **EXECUTIVE INN.** *2005 S Thompson St (72764), jct 412E, Downtown. 501/756-6101; fax 501/756-6101; toll-free 800/544-6086.* 101 rms, 2 story. S, D $44-$50; each addl $6; under 18 free; higher rates football wkends. Crib free. Pet accepted. TV; cable. Pool. Complimentary coffee in rms. Restaurant 6:30 am-2 pm, 5-9 pm; Sat, Sun 7 am-9 pm. Bar 5 pm-2 am; Sat, Sun from 6 pm. Ck-out noon. Coin lndry. Meeting rms. Some refrigerators, microwaves. Cr cds: A, C, D, DS, JCB, MC, V.

★★ **HAMPTON INN.** *1700 S 48th St (72762). 501/756-3500; fax 501/927-3500; toll-free 800/426-7866.* 102 rms, 3 story, 35 kit. suites. S $79; D $86; each addl $7; kit. suites $99-$116; under 18 free; wkend rates; higher rates special events. Crib free. Pet accepted, some restrictions. TV; cable (premium), VCR avail (movies). Complimentary continental bkfst. Restaurant opp 6 am-11 pm. Ck-out noon. Meeting rms. Business servs avail. In-rm modem link. Coin lndry. Free airport transportation. Golf privileges. Exercise equipt. Pool privileges. Some fireplaces. Cr cds: A, D, DS, MC, V.

Conference Center

★★ **HOLIDAY INN.** *1500 S 48th St (72762). 501/751-8300; fax 501/751-4640; toll-free 800/465-4329.* 206 units, 8 story, 22 suites. S, D $119; suites $135-$160; under 18 free. Crib free. Pet accepted. TV; cable (premium), VCR avail (movies). Indoor pool; whirlpool. Complimentary coffee. Restaurant 6 am-2 pm, 5-10 pm. Bar 4-11 pm. Ck-out noon. Coin lndry. Business center. In-rm modem link. Gift shop. Free airport transportation. Exercise equipt. Microwaves avail. Cr cds: A, DS, MC, V.

Restaurants

★ **A. Q. CHICKEN HOUSE.** *1207 N Thompson (72765), 1 mi N. 501/751-4633.* Specializes in Southern pan-fried chicken, hickory-smoked steak and ribs. Hrs: 11 am-9 pm; Sun to 8:30 pm. Closed Dec 25. Wine, beer. Lunch, dinner $3-$7.95. Child's menu. Fireplaces. Cr cds: A, D, DS, MC, V.

★★ **MARY MAESTRI'S.** *956 E Henri de Tonti Blvd (72762), 2 mi W on AR 412. 501/361-2536.* Own baking, pasta, spumoni. Hrs: 5:30-9:30 pm. Closed hols. Res accepted. Wine, beer. Dinner $8.95-$20.95. Child's menu. Antique furniture, oil paintings. Family-owned since 1923. Cr cds: A, D, DS, MC, V.

Stuttgart

(D-5) *See also Pine Bluff*

Settled 1878 **Pop** 10,420 **Elev** 217 ft
Area code 870 **Zip** 72160
Web www.stuttgart.ar.us
Information Chamber of Commerce, 507 S Main, PO Box 932; 870/673-1602

White River National Wildlife Refuge. More than 113,000-acre bottomland with 165 small lakes. Fishing, hunting for duck, deer, turkey, squirrel, raccoon; boat access. Picnicking. Primitive camping. (Mar-Oct, daily) 25 mi SE on US 165 to De Witt, then 16 mi NE on AR 1 to St. Charles. Inquire locally for road conditions. Contact Refuge Manager, PO Box 308, De Witt 72042. Phone 870/946-1468. **FREE**

Annual Event

Wings Over The Prairie Festival. Incl championship duck calling contest, midway, exhibits, other contests. Thanksgiving wk.

Motel/Motor Lodge

★★ **BEST WESTERN.** *704 W Michigan St (72160). 870/673-2575; fax 870/673-2575. 72 rms, 2 story. Mid-Nov-mid-Jan: S $55-$75; D $60-$85; each addl $5; suites $85; family rates; lower rates rest of yr. Crib free. Pet accepted, some restrictions. TV; cable (premium), VCR. Complimentary coffee in rms. Restaurant adj 6 am-10 pm. Ck-out noon. Meeting rm. Indoor pool. Some refrigerators. Cr cds: A, D, MC, V.*
D 🐾 ⊠ ⊠ 🔥 SC

Walnut Ridge

(B-6) *See also Jonesboro, Pocahontas*

Pop 4,388 **Elev** 270 ft **Area code** 870
Zip 72476

Information Walnut Ridge Area Chamber of Commerce, PO Box 842; 870/886-3232

What to See and Do

Lake Charles State Park. In the northeastern foothills of the Arkansas Ozarks, this 645-acre lake offers swimming beach; bass, crappie, catfish, and bream fishing. Nature trail. Camping (hookups, bathhouse, dump station). Visitor center; interpretive programs (Memorial Day-Labor Day, daily). Standard fees. Two mi S on US 67, 8 mi W on US 63, 4 mi SW on AR 25. Phone 870/878-6595.

GEORGIA

Georgia, beloved for its antebellum gentility and then devastated by General William Tecumseh Sherman's march to the sea, is now a vibrant, busy state typifying the economic growth of the New South. Founded with philanthropic and military aims, the only colony where rum and slavery were forbidden, the state nevertheless had the dubious honor of accepting the last shipment of slaves to this country. It boasts Savannah, one of the oldest planned cities in the country, and Atlanta, one of the newest of the South's great cities, rebuilt atop Civil War ashes.

The Georgia Colony was founded by James Oglethorpe on behalf of a private group of English trustees and was named for King George II of England. Georgia's barrier islands not only sheltered the fledgling colony, they provided a bulwark on the Spanish Main for English forts to oppose Spanish Florida and helped end the centuries-old struggle for domination among Spanish, French, and English along the South Atlantic Coast.

Population: 7,788,240
Area: 58,876 square miles
Elevation: 0–4,784 feet
Peak: Brasstown Bald Mountain (Between Towns, Union counties)
Entered Union: Fourth of original 13 states (January 1, 1788)
Capital: Atlanta
Motto: Wisdom, Justice, and Moderation
Flower: Cherokee Rose
Bird: Brown Thrasher
Tree: Live Oak
Fair: October 15-21st, 2001, in Macon
Time Zone: Eastern
Website: www.georgia.org

Today a year-round vacation mecca, the Golden Isles were at times Native American hunting lands, vast sea island plantations, fishing communities isolated after the Civil War, and rich men's private preserves. The Colony trustees brought English artisans to found strong colonies at Savannah, Brunswick, and Darien, where Scottish Highlanders introduced golf to the New World. The Cherokee made early peace with Oglethorpe and remained within the state to set up the Republic of the Cherokee Nation a century later. Gradually, however, all Native American lands of both Creek and Cherokee were ceded; the Cherokees were banished and their lands, including the capital, distributed by lottery.

From their settlements at Savannah, Brunswick, and the coastal islands, Georgia colonists followed the rivers (many of them flowing north) to found inland ports such as Augusta. Colonial boundaries were extended to the Mississippi River by the State of Georgia, but the unfortunate manipulations of land speculators in the legislature deeded all of Mississippi, Alabama, Tennessee, and more, for sale as the Yazoo Tract for one-and-one-half cents an acre. Though repudiated by a subsequent legislature and declared unconstitutional by the Supreme Court, the lands were gone forever, and Georgia no longer extended from the Mississippi to the sea. It is, however, still the largest state east of the Mississippi.

Georgia's lot in the Civil War was a harsh one from the time Sherman opened his campaign in Georgia on May 4, 1864, until he achieved the Union objective of splitting the South from the Mississippi to the sea. Reconstruction ushered in the reign of carpetbaggers and a long, slow recovery.

Georgia boasts many firsts: the *Savannah*, the first steamship to cross the ocean (1819); America's first nuclear-powered merchant ship, the *Savannah* (1959); the first big American gold strike (1828); the cotton gin, invented by Eli Whitney (1793); and the first use of ether as an anesthetic (1842), by Georgia doctor Crawford W. Long.

Georgia produces peanuts, pecans, cotton, peaches, wood pulp, and paper products. Near Atlanta a number of national manufacturing and commercial concerns contribute to a diversified economy. Georgia marble is prized the world over.

Georgia boasts many wonders, from its Blue Ridge vacationlands in the north—where Brasstown Bald Mountain rises 4,784 feet—to the deep "trembling earth" of the ancient and mysterious Okefenokee Swamp bordering Florida. Stone Mountain, a giant hunk of rock that rises from the plain near Atlanta, is the world's largest granite exposure. The coastal Golden Isles, set off by the mysterious Marshes of Glynn, support moss-festooned oaks that grow down to the white sand beaches. Visitors still pan for gold in the country's oldest gold mining town, Dahlonega, and find semiprecious stones in the Blue Ridge.

Historical attractions are everywhere, from the world's largest brick fort near Savannah to the late President Franklin D. Roosevelt's "Little White House" at Warm Springs. There is the infamous Confederate prison at Andersonville and the still-lavish splendor of the cottage colony of 60 millionaires of the Jekyll Island Club, now a state-owned resort. The battlefield marking Sherman's campaign before Atlanta and the giant ceremonial mounds of indigenous Native Americans are equally important national shrines.

Tourism is one of Georgia's primary industries. The state's Visitor Information Centers, which are staffed year-round, offer brochures and computerized information to travelers on major highways.

When to Go/Climate

Short winters and mild temperatures are the rule in Georgia. Summers are hot and humid in the southern part of the state; winters can be cold and incl snowfall in the northern regions.

AVERAGE HIGH/LOW TEMPERATURES (°F)

ATLANTA

Jan 50/32	**May** 80/59	**Sep** 82/64
Feb 55/35	**June** 86/66	**Oct** 73/52
Mar 64/43	**July** 88/70	**Nov** 63/43
Apr 73/50	**Aug** 87/69	**Dec** 54/35

SAVANNAH

Jan 60/38	**May** 84/63	**Sep** 85/68
Feb 62/41	**June** 89/69	**Oct** 78/57
Mar 70/48	**July** 91/72	**Nov** 70/48
Apr 78/55	**Aug** 90/72	**Dec** 62/41

Parks and Recreation Finder

Directions to and information about the parks and recreation areas below are given under their respective town/city sections. Please refer to those sections for details.

NATIONAL PARK AND RECREATION AREAS

Key to abbreviations. I.H.S. = International Historic Site; I.P.M. = International Peace Memorial; N.B. = National Battlefield; N.B.P. = National Battlefield Park; N.B.C. = National Battlefield and Cemetery; N.C.A. = National Conservation Area; N.E.M. = National Expansion Memorial; N.F. = National Forest; N.G. = National Grassland; N.H.P. = National Historical Park; N.H.C. = National Heritage Corridor; N.H.S. = National Historic Site; N.L. = National Lakeshore; N.M. = National Monument; N.M.P. = National Military Park; N.Mem. = National Memorial; N.P. = National Park; N.Pres. = National Preserve; N.R.A. = National Recreational Area; N.R.R. = National Recreational River; N.Riv. = National River; N.S. = National Seashore; N.S.R. = National Scenic Riverway; N.S.T. = National Scenic Trail; N.Sc. = National Scientific Reserve; N.V.M. = National Volcanic Monument.

CALENDAR HIGHLIGHTS

JANUARY

Georgia Heritage Festival (Savannah). Walking tours, open house at historic sites, crafts show, waterfront festival, parade, concerts, Georgia Day. Phone Historic Savannah Foundation 912/233-7787.

MARCH

Auto racing (Atlanta). Atlanta Motor Speedway. NASCAR Winston Cup, Busch Grand National, IMSA, and ARCA events. Phone 770/946-4211.

Cherry Blossom Festival (Macon). Historic tours, concerts, fireworks, hot-air balloons, sporting events, parade. Phone 912/751-7429.

Augusta Invitational Rowing Regatta (Augusta). At Augusta Riverfront Marina.

APRIL

Masters Golf Tournament (Augusta). Augusta National Golf Course. Phone 706/667-6000.

Seafood Festival (Savannah). Waterfront. Restaurants offer samples; entertainment, arts and crafts. Contact Savannah Waterfront Association 912/234-0295.

Spring Tour of Homes (Athens). Held by Athens-Clarke Heritage Foundation. Contact Fire Hall #2; phone 706/353-1801 or -1820.

SEPTEMBER

US 10 K Classic and Family Sports Festival (Marietta). Phone 770/432-0100.

OCTOBER

Georgia State Fair (Macon). Central City Park. Grandstand shows, midway, exhibit bldgs. Phone 912/746-7184.

DECEMBER

Christmas in Savannah (Savannah). Month-long celebration incl tours of houses, historical presentations, parades, music, caroling, and cultural events. Phone 800/444-CHARM.

Place Name	Listed Under
Andersonville N.H.S.	ANDERSONVILLE
Appalachian N.S.T.	DAHLONEGA
Chattahoochee N.F.	DAHLONEGA
Chickamauga and Chattanooga N.M.P.	same
Cumberland Island N.S.	same
Fort Frederica N.M.	same
Fort Pulaski N.M.	same
Jimmy Carter N.H.S.	AMERICUS
Kennesaw Mountain N.B.P.	same
Martin Luther King, Jr, N.H.S.	ATLANTA
Ocmulgee N.M.	same

STATE PARK AND RECREATION AREAS

Key to abbreviations. I.P. = Interstate Park; S.A.P. = State Archaeological Park; S.B. = State Beach; S.C.A. = State Conservation Area; S.C.P. = State Conservation Park; S.Cp. = State Campground; S.F. = State Forest; S.G. = State Garden; S.H.A. = State Historic Area; S.H.P. = State Historic Park; S.H.S. = State Historic Site; S.M.P. = State Marine Park; S.N.A. = State Natural Area; S.P. = State Park; S.P.C. = State Public Campground; S.R. = State Reserve; S.R.A. = State Recreation Area; S.Res. = State Reservoir; S.Res.P. = State Resort Park; S.R.P. = State Rustic Park.

Place Name	Listed Under
Alexander H. Stephens S.P.	WASHINGTON
Amicalola Falls S.P.	DAHLONEGA
Crooked River S.P.	CUMBERLAND ISLAND N.S.
Dahlonega Courthouse Gold Museum S.H.S.	DAHLONEGA
Elijah Clark S.P.	WASHINGTON
Florence Marina S.P.	LUMPKIN
Fort King George S.H.S.	DARIEN
Fort McAllister S.P.	FORT McALLISTER HISTORIC PARK
Fort Mountain S.P.	CHATSWORTH
Fort Yargo S.P.	WINDER
Franklin D. Roosevelt S.P.	PINE MOUNTAIN
General Coffee S.P.	DOUGLAS
Georgia Veterans Memorial S.P.	CORDELE
Hofwyl-Broadfield Plantation S.H.S.	DARIEN
Indian Springs S.P.	same
Jarrell Plantation S.H.S.	FORSYTH
John Tanner S.P.	CARROLLTON
Kolomoki Mounds S.P.	BLAKELY
Lapham-Patterson House S.H.S.	THOMASVILLE
Laura S. Walker S.P.	WAYCROSS
New Echota S.H.S.	CALHOUN
Providence Canyon S.C.P.	LUMPKIN
Red Top Mountain S.P.	CARTERSVILLE
Reed Bingham S.P.	ADEL
Robert Toombs House S.H.S.	WASHINGTON
Seminole S.P.	BAINBRIDGE
Stephen C. Foster S.P.	OKEFENOKEE SWAMP
Traveler's Rest S.H.S.	TOCCOA
Unicoi S.P.	HELEN
Vann House S.H.S.	CHATSWORTH
Vogel S.P.	DAHLONEGA
Wormsloe S.H.S.	SAVANNAH

Water-related activities, hiking, riding, various other sports, picnicking and visitor centers, as well as camping and rental cottages, are avail in many of these areas. Most state parks welcome campers, and there are many comfort stations with hot showers, electric outlets, and lndry. All parks listed have trailer dump stations, with the exception of Providence Canyon. Camping is limited to 2 wks at any one park. Res may be made up to 11 months in advance. Parks are open yr-round, 7 am-10 pm.

Georgia park vacationers may enjoy cottages at several state parks. These provide complete housekeeping facilities—kitchens with electric ranges and refrigerators, living rms, bedrms (linens provided), porches, outdoor grills, and picnic tables. They are air-conditioned for summer and heated for winter.

Cottages are avail at Amicalola Falls, Black Rock Mt, Cloudland Canyon, Crooked River, Elijah Clark, Florence Marina, Fort Mt, Franklin D. Roosevelt, Georgia Veterans Memorial, Hard Labor Creek, Hart, Indian Springs, John Tanner, Little Ocmulgee, Magnolia Springs, Mistletoe, Red Top Mt, Seminole, Stephen C. Foster, Tugaloo, Unicoi, Vogel, and Will-A-Way (in Fort Yargo) parks. Phone 800/864-7275. Cottage res can be made up to 11 months in advance; there is a 2-day minimum stay at cottages.

Domestic pets allowed in state parks only if kept on leash not longer than 6 ft and accompanied by owner at all times. No pets allowed in any cottages, site bldgs, or swimming areas. Fees are subject to change.

Detailed information on state parks may be obtained from the Dept of Natural Resources, State Parks & Historic Sites, 205 Butler St SE, Suite 1352, Atlanta 30334; phone 404/656-2770.

FISHING AND HUNTING

Georgia's range of fresh and saltwater fishing rivals any other state in variety. There are 26 major reservoirs totaling more than 400,000 acres, and 10 major river systems traverse the state, with thousands of mi of clear, cold-water trout streams and smaller, warm-water streams. Approximately 60,000 small lakes and ponds add to the freshwater total. Some 200 species of freshwater fish are found, 40 of which are considered desirable by game anglers, incl largemouth, shoal, and striped bass, and crappie and channel catfish. Mountain streams in northern Georgia are a natural source of trout. Fishing in black-water swamp areas in southern Georgia is just as famous for lunker bass and big bream. Coastal waters are good for mackerel, redfish, speckled trout, and giant tarpon; no license required.

A state fishing license is required for all freshwater fishing; nonresident: season $24; 7-day permit $7; 1-day permit $3.50; trout stamp (required to fish in trout waters or to keep trout caught): season $13. Fees subject to change. For further information on saltwater fishing contact Dept of Natural Resources, Coastal Resources Division, 1 Conservation Way, Brunswick 31520-8600; 912/264-7218. For further information on freshwater fishing contact Dept of Natural Resources, Wildlife Resources Division, 2123 US 278SE, Social Circle 30279; 770/918-6418.

There is hunting from the Blue Ridge in northern Georgia to the piney woods of the south. Nonresident: season, $59; 7-day, $25; 1-day, $5.50; big game (deer, wild turkey), $118. Preserve license, $12; bow hunting permit, $25. Wildlife Management Area stamp, $73. Waterfowl stamp, $5.50 (federal stamp also required). Fees subject to change. For seasons, bag limits, other details write Dept of Natural Resources, Wildlife Resources Division, 2111 US 278SE, Social Circle 30279; 770/918-6416.

Driving Information

Safety belts are mandatory for all persons in front seat of vehicle and all minors anywhere in vehicle; ages 3 and 4 may use a regulation safety belt; age 2 and under must use an approved safety seat. For further information phone 404/657-9300.

INTERSTATE HIGHWAY SYSTEM

The following alphabetical listing of Georgia towns in *Mobil Travel Guide* shows that these cities are within 10 miles of the indicated Interstate highways. A highway map, however, should be checked for the nearest exit.

Highway Number	Cities/Towns within 10 miles
Interstate 16	Dublin, Macon, Savannah.
Interstate 20	Atlanta, Augusta, Carrollton, Madison.
Interstate 75	Adel, Atlanta, Calhoun, Cartersville, Cordele, Dalton, Forsyth, Macon, Marietta, Perry, Tifton, Valdosta.
Interstate 85	Atlanta, Buford, Commerce, La Grange, Norcross.
Interstate 95	Brunswick, Darien, Jekyll Island, St. Simons Island, Savannah.

Additional Visitor Information

For visitor information, incl brochures and other materials, contact Dept of Industry, Trade, and Tourism, PO Box 1776, Atlanta 30301-1776; phone 404/656-3590 or 800/VISIT-GA. Visitor centers are located in Augusta, Columbus, Kingsland, Lavonia, Plains, Ringgold, Savannah, Sylvania, Tallapoosa, Valdosta, and West Point. Information avail 8:30 am-5:30 pm.

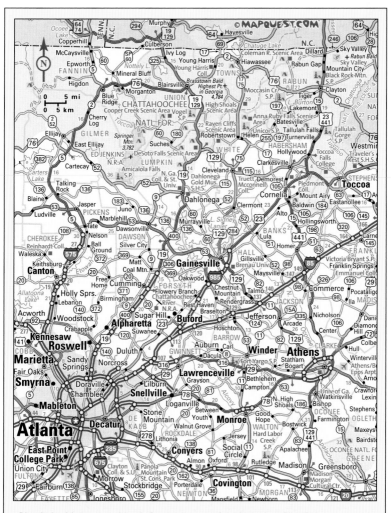

Blue Ridge Mountains—North Georgia is part of the legendary Blue Ridge Mountain range. Easily reached from Atlanta via Highway 400, it's a popular destination for scenic driving and mountain recreation, particularly in fall foliage season and also in summer, when the mountain region stays cooler than the plateau or plain. One of the most developed destinations here is Helen, a mock Bavarian village with many tourist attractions, including Babyland General Hospital, Anna Ruby Falls, Nacoochee Indian Mound, and Unicoi State Park. Dahlonega is a gold-rush town that offers close proximity to many natural and recreational resources at Amicalola State Park, including the highest waterfall (729 feet) in the eastern United States. Nearby is the southern terminus of the historic 2,000-mile Appalachian Trail. **(Approx 190 mi)**

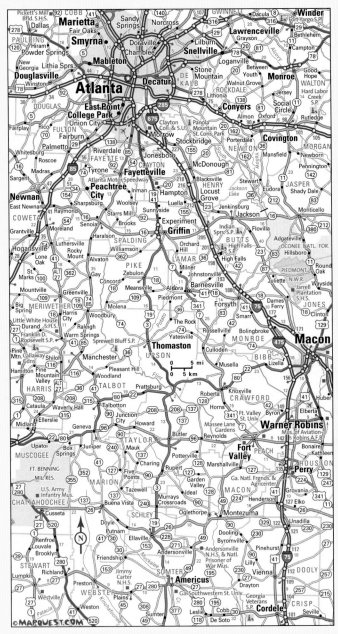

Many visitors make the pilgrimage to the small, sleepy town of Plains to see the tiny depot out of which Jimmy Carter ran his presidential campaign. The Carters still live in Plains—you can join his Sunday School if he's in town. The Jimmy Carter National Historic Site in his old high school tells the complete all-American story. The route from Atlanta runs along US 41 through Jonesboro (where Margaret Mitchell set the fictional Tara in *Gone With the Wind*) to US 19 through the lovely little town of Americus (near the new National Prisoner of War Museum at the notorious Civil War POW camp of Andersonville) toward Plains. **(Approx 320 mi)**

Adel

(G-4) *See also Tifton, Valdosta*

Pop 5,093 **Elev** 240 ft **Area code** 912 **Zip** 31620

Information Adel-Cook County Chamber of Commerce, 100 S Hutchinson Ave, PO Box 461; 912/896-2281

What to See and Do

Reed Bingham State Park. Park incl 400-acre lake. Waterskiing, fishing, boating (ramp); nature trails, picnicking, arboretum, camping. Standard hrs, fees. Contact Superintendent, Rte 2, Box 394B-1. 6 mi W off GA 37. Phone 912/896-3551.

Motels/Motor Lodges

★ **DAYS INN.** *1200 W 4th St (30121). 912/896-4574; fax 912/896-4575; toll-free 800/329-7466.* 78 rms, 2 story. S, D $34.99-$39.99; each addl $5; under 12 free. Crib $5. Pet accepted; $5. TV; cable (premium), VCR avail (movies). Pool. Restaurant open 24 hrs. Ck-out 11 am. Meeting rm. Business servs avail. Cr cds: A, C, D, DS, MC, V.

★ **HOWARD JOHNSON.** *1103 W 4th St; I-75 Exit 10 (31620). 912/896-2244; fax 912/896-2245; toll-free 800/446-4656.* 70 rms, 2 story. S $32.99-$34.99; D $35.99-$37.99; each addl $5; suite $59.99; under 17 free; wkly rates. Crib $5. Pet accepted; $5. TV; cable. Pool. Complimentary coffee in lobby. Restaurant nearby. Ck-out noon. Cr cds: A, C, D, DS, MC, V.

★ **SUPER 8 MOTEL.** *1102 W 4th St (31620). 912/896-4523; fax 912/896-4524; toll-free 800/800-8000.* 50 rms, 2 story. S $32.99-$34.99; D $35.99-$37.99; each addl $5; under 12 free; wkly rates. Crib $5. Pet accepted; $5. TV; cable. Pool. Complimentary coffee in lobby. Restaurant nearby. Ck-out 11 am. Cr cds: A, C, D, DS, MC, V.

Albany

(F-3) *See also Americus, Cordele*

Founded 1836 **Pop** 78,122 **Elev** 208 ft **Area code** 912 **Web** www.albanyga.com

Information Convention & Visitors Bureau, 225 W Broad Ave, 31701; 912/434-8700 or 800/475-8700

Albany lies in a semitropical setting of oaks and pines located in the Plantation Trace region of the state. Colonel Nelson Tift, a Connecticut Yankee, led a party up the Flint River from Apalachicola, Florida, and constructed the first log buildings in Albany. Settlers followed when the Native Americans were moved to western lands. Paper-shell pecans grown in surrounding Dougherty County have made this the "pecan capital of the world." Surrounded by numerous plantations, the area is also well-known for quail hunting.

What to See and Do

Albany Museum of Art. Permanent and changing exhibits of works by national and regional artists. (Tues-Sun; closed hols) 311 Meadowlark Dr. Phone 912/439-8400. **FREE**

Chehaw Park. On 775 acres. Boating, nature trails, picnicking, camping (dump station). 2½ mi NE on GA 91. Per vehicle ¢ Also here is

> **Chehaw Wild Animal Park.** Wildlife preserve (100 acres) where elephant, giraffe, deer, buffalo, llama, and other animals roam in natural habitats. Protective trails, elevated walkways. (Daily; closed Jan 1, Thanksgiving, Dec 25) Phone 912/430-5275. ¢

Lake Chehaw. At the confluence of the Kinchafoonee and Muckalee creeks and the Flint River. Waterskiing, fishing, boating. 2 mi NE off GA 91.

Thronateeska Heritage Center. Sponsors Museum of History and Science. Complex of former railroad bldgs houses exhibits on local and natural history and model trains; Discovery Rm for children. Also here is Wetherbee Planetarium. (Thurs-Sat 12-4; also Tues eves, June-Dec; closed hols) 100 Roosevelt Ave. Phone 912/432-6955. ¢¢

Annual Event

Fall on the Flint Festival. Entertainment, parade, exhibits, athletic contests. Last wkend Sep.

Motels/Motor Lodges

★★ **COMFORT SUITES MERRY ACRES.** *1400 Dawson Rd (31707). 912/888-3939; fax 912/435-4431; res 888/726-3939. www.merryacres.com.* 62 suites, 2 story. S $89-$104; D $95-$150; each addl $7; under 18 free. Crib $5. TV; cable (premium). Pool privileges. Playground. Complimentary continental bkfst, coffee in rms. Restaurant 11 am-2 pm, 5-10 pm. Bar 4 pm-midnight. Ck-out noon. Meeting rms. Business servs avail. In-rm modem link. Valet serv. Airport transportation. Refrigerators. Cr cds: A, C, D, DS, ER, JCB, MC, V.

★★ **HAMPTON INN.** *806 N Westover Blvd (31707), at Albany Mall. 912/883-3300; fax 912/435-4092; toll-free 800/426-7866.* 82 rms, 2 story. S $57-$61; D $61-$64; under 18 free; wkend rates. Crib free. TV; cable. Pool. Complimentary continental bkfst. Coffee in rms. Restaurant adj 6 am-midnight. Ck-out noon. Meeting rm. In-rm modem link. Valet serv. Health club privileges. Cr cds: A, D, DS, MC, V.

★★ **HOLIDAY INN EXPRESS.** *911 E Oglethorpe Expy (31705). 912/883-1650; fax 912/883-1163.* 151 rms, 4 story. S, D $56; each addl $5; under 19 free. Crib free. TV; cable (premium). Pool. Complimentary bkfst, coffee in rms. Ck-out noon. Meeting rms. Business servs avail. In-rm modem link. Free airport transportation. Refrigerators, microwaves. Tennis privileges. Golf privileges. Cr cds: A, C, D, DS, MC, V.

★★ **QUALITY INN MERRY ACRES.** *1500 Dawson Rd (31706). 912/435-7721; fax 912/439-9386; res 800/221-2222; toll-free 888/462-7721. www.merryacres.com.* 108 rms. S $58-$168; D $65-$175; each addl $5; suites $156-$163; under 18 free. Crib $5. TV; cable. Pool; wading pool. Playground. Restaurant 11 am-2 pm, 5-10 pm. Complimentary continental bkfst. Coffee in rms. Bar 4 pm-midnight. Ck-out noon. Meeting rms. Business servs avail. In-rm modem link. Valet serv. Sundries. Exercise equipt. Some refrigerators, wet bars. Cr cds: A, D, DS, MC, V.

★★ **RAMADA INN.** *2505 N Slappey Blvd (31701). 912/883-3211; fax 912/439-2806; res 800/2RAMADA. www.ramada-albany.com.* 158 rms, 2 story. S $54; D $60; each addl $7; suites $75; under 18 free; wkend rates. Crib free. Pet accepted. TV; cable (premium), VCR avail. Pool; wading pool. Coffee in rms. Restaurant 6:30 am-2 pm, 5-10 pm; Sun 7 am-2 pm. Rm serv 7 am-9 pm. Bar 5-10 pm. Ck-out noon. Meeting rms. Business servs avail. In-rm modem link. Bellhops. Valet serv. Free airport transportation. Sundries. Cr cds: A, C, D, DS, MC, V.

Americus

(E-3) *See also Albany, Andersonville, Cordele*

Founded 1832 **Pop** 16,512 **Elev** 355 ft
Area code 912 **Zip** 31709
Web www.gomm.com/americus

Information Americus-Sumter County Chamber of Commerce, Tourism Division, 400 W Lamar St, Box 724; 912/924-2646 or 888/278-6837

Americus is at the center of an area once known as the "granary of the Creek nations," so called because Native Americans favored this area for the cultivation of maize. The town was named, it is said, either for Americus Vespucius or for the settlers themselves, who were referred to as "merry cusses" because of their happy-go-lucky ways. The town flourished in the 1890s. Many Victorian/Gothic Revival buildings remain from that period.

Today, peanuts, corn, cotton, small grain, and pecans are grown, and bauxite and kaolin are mined in the area. Americus is also a manufacturing center, producing lumber commodities, metal lighting equipment, heating products, and textiles. The town's livestock sales are second in volume in the state. Plains, nine miles west via US 280, is the hometown of the 39th president, Jimmy Carter.

Jimmy Carter enjoying retirement.

What to See and Do

Americus Historic Driving Tour. Tour features 38 houses of various architectural styles, incl Victorian, Greek Revival, and Classical Revival. Contact the Chamber of Commerce.

Andersonville National Historic Site. (See ANDERSONVILLE) 11 mi NE on GA 49.

Georgia Southwestern College. (1906) 2,600 students. One-hundred-eighty-seven-acre campus with lake. Wheatly & Glessner Sts, 2 mi E of jct US 19, 280. Also here is

> **Carter Display.** focusing on former President Jimmy Carter and First Lady Rosalynn Carter; photographs, memorabilia; located in James Earl Carter Library. (Daily exc during school breaks, hols) **FREE**

■ Jimmy Carter National Historic Site. Visitor center is located in Plains High School, where Jimmy and Rosalynn Carter attended grammar and high school. Campaign memorabilia; cassette auto driving tour of Plains

avail. (Daily; closed Jan 1, Dec 25) 8 mi W on US 280 in Plains. Plains High School is located at 300 N Bond St. Phone 912/824-3413. **FREE**

Motels/Motor Lodges

★★★ **WINDSOR HOTEL.** *125 W Lamar St (31709). 912/924-1555; fax 912/924-1555; res 888/297-9567. Email windsor@sowega.net.* 53 units, 3 story. S, D $70; under 15 free. TV; cable (premium). Coffee in rms. Restaurant (see GRAND DINING ROOM). Bar 4 pm-midnight, closed Sun. Ck-out noon. Meeting rms. Business servs avail. In-rm modem link. Bellhops. Valet serv. 3-story atrium lobby. Period-style rms with 12-ft ceilings and ceiling fans. Cr cds: A, D, DS, MC, V.

🄳 ⛴ 🔥

B&B/Small Inn

★★★ **1906 PATHWAY INN BED & BREAKFAST.** *501 S Lee St (31709). 912/928-2078; fax 912/928-2078; toll-free 800/889-1466. Email info@1906 pathwayinn.com; www.1906pathway inn.com.* 5 rms, 2 story. Feb-May, Sep-Nov: S $85; D $125; each addl $20; children $10; under 12 free; lower rates rest of yr. Pet accepted, fee. Parking lot. TV; cable, VCR avail. Complimentary full bkfst. Restaurant nearby. Ck-out 11 am, ck-in 4 pm. Meeting rm. Business servs avail. Concierge. Gift shop. Whirlpool. Golf. Tennis. Hiking trail. Picnic facilities. Video games. Cr cds: A, DS, MC, V.

🄳 ⛴ 🔥 ⛴ ⛴ 🔥

Restaurant

★★★ **GRAND DINING ROOM.** *125 W Lamar St. 912/924-1555. www. windsor-americus.com.* Specializes in seafood, desserts. Hrs: 6:30-9:30 am, 11:30 am-2 pm, 6-9 pm; Fri to 9:30 pm; Sat 6-9:30 pm; Sun 11:30 am-2 pm. Closed Sun. Res accepted. Wine list. Bkfst a la carte entrees: $3.15-$6.95; lunch buffet $7.95; dinner a la carte entrees: $13.95-$26. Elegant decor; antique chandeliers, fireplace. Cr cds: D, DS, MC, V.

🄳 ⛴

Andersonville

See also Americus, Cordele, Perry

Pop 277 **Elev** 390 ft **Area code** 912 **Zip** 31711

What to See and Do

Andersonville National Historic Site. The Confederate Military Prison, Camp Sumter, was built on a 26-acre tract in early 1864 by soldiers and slaves requisitioned from nearby plantations. The lofty pines that grew in the local sandy soil were cut and used to form a stockade. Built to accommodate 10,000 men, the prison at one time held as many as 33,000. Overcrowding, inadequate food, insufficient medicines, and a breakdown of the prisoner exchange system resulted in a high death rate. The site is now a memorial to all prisoners of war throughout history. Incl on grounds are escape tunnels and wells dug by prisoners, Confederate earthworks, 3 reconstructed sections of stockade wall, and state monuments. Park (daily). On GA 49. Phone 912/924-0343. **FREE** Also here are

National Prisoner of War Museum. Exhibits, interpretive programs, and interactive videos depict the role of military prisoners in the history of the nation (Daily; closed Jan 1, Dec 25). Visitor Center.

Providence Spring. The spring, which bubbled up from the ground after a heavy rain, was said to be in answer to the prisoners' prayers during the summer of 1864.

Andersonville National Cemetery. Graves of more than 17,000 Union soldiers and veterans of US military are in striking contrast to the landscaped grounds. The initial interments were Union soldiers who died in the prison camp. Dedicated as a national cemetery on Aug 17, 1865. ½ mi N of prison site.

Civil War Village of Andersonville. Restored village from the days of the Civil War. Welcome center, pioneer farm, museum (fee), antique shops. (Daily; closed Dec 25) Church St. Phone 912/924-2558. **FREE**

Annual Event

Andersonville Historic Fair. Center of town. Civil War reenactments, old time craftspeople, antique dealers; RV campsites. Contact Andersonville Historic Fair, PO Box 6; 912/924-2558. Memorial Day wkend and 1st wkend Oct.

Athens

(B-4) *See also Commerce, Madison, Winder*

Founded 1801 **Pop** 45,734 **Elev** 775 ft **Area code** 706 **Web** www.visitathensga.com **Information** Convention & Visitors Bureau, 300 N Thomas St, 30601; 800/653-0603; or Athens Welcome Center, 280 E Dougherty St, 30601; 706/353-1820

Georgia's "Classic City" is the site of the University of Georgia, chartered in 1785. Diversified industry produces nonwoven fabrics, textiles, clocks, electronic components, precision parts, chemicals, and animal feed. Lyman Hall, a signer of the Declaration of Independence, proposed the University, and Abraham Baldwin, the acknowledged founding father, wrote the charter. Although allotted 10,000 acres by the legislature in 1784, it was another 17 years before Josiah Meigs, Baldwin's successor and first official president, erected a few log buildings, called it Franklin College, and held classes under the tolerant eyes of curious Cherokees.

Athens was incorporated in 1806. Its setting on a hill beside the Oconee River is enhanced by towering oaks and elms, white-blossomed magnolias, old-fashioned boxwood gardens, and many well-preserved and still-occupied antebellum houses.

What to See and Do

Double-barreled cannon. (1863) A unique Civil War weapon cast at Athens' foundry. Believed to be the only double-barreled cannon in the world. City Hall lawn, College & Hancock Aves.

Historic Houses. For tour information, contact Athens Welcome Center in Church-Waddel-Brumby House (see) or contact Athens Convention & Visitors Bureau.

Taylor-Grady House. (1839) Restored Greek Revival mansion surrounded by 13 columns said to symbolize 13 original states; period furniture. (Mon-Fri; closed hols) 634 Prince Ave. Phone 706/549-8688. ¢¢

Church-Waddel-Brumby House. (ca 1820) Restored Federal-style house thought to be oldest residence in Athens. Houses **Athens Welcome Center,** which has information on self-guided tours of other historic houses and bldgs (Mon-Sat, Sun afternoons) 280 E Dougherty St. Phone 706/353-1820. **FREE**

University President's House. (ca 1855) Greek Revival mansion surrounded on 3 sides by massive Corinthian columns. Extensive gardens and picket fences complement classic design. Private residence. 570 Prince Ave.

Founders Memorial Garden. Memorial to founders of Ladies' Garden Club of Athens, the first garden club in the US. 325 S Lumpkin St, on Univ of Georgia campus. Phone 706/542-3631.

Other historic houses. in Athens incl Ross Crane House (Sigma Alpha Epsilon Fraternity) (1842), 247 Pulaski St; Lucy Cobb Institute (1858), 200 N Milledge Ave; Joseph Henry Lumpkin House (1841), 248 Prince Ave; Old Franklin Hotel (1845), 480 E Broad St; Governor Wilson Lumpkin House (1842), S campus, Univ of Georgia. Univ of Georgia, N campus, also has numerous pre-1860 bldgs.

Sandy Creek Nature Center. Approximately 200 acres of woods, fields, and marshland; incl a live animal exhibit, a 180-yr-old cabin, nature trails. (Mar-late Nov, Tues-Sat; rest of yr, Mon-Fri; closed hols) ½ mi N of Athens bypass, off US 441. Phone 706/613-3615. **FREE**

Sandy Creek Park. Swimming (beach), fishing, boating; hiking, tennis, basketball, picnicking, playgrounds, primitive camping. Walkways. (Tues-Sun) N on US 441. Phone 706/613-3631. ¢ Also located in park is

ENSAT Center. Model of sustainable "green" architecture with ecological exhibits. (Tues-Sat) Phone 706/613-3615. **FREE**

Tree That Owns Itself. White oak, descendant of original tree, stands on plot deeded to it. Dearing & Finley Sts.

University of Georgia. (1785) 30,000 students. Consisting of 13 schools and colleges, the main campus extends more than 2 mi S from the Arch (1858), College Ave & Broad St. Nearby are farms managed by the College of Agriculture, a forestry preserve, and Univ Research Park. Historic buildings incl Demosthenian Hall (1824); chapel (1832), housing an oil painting (17 x 23½ ft) of the interior of St. Peter's Basilica; Old College (1806), oldest bldg, designed after Connecticut Hall at Yale; Waddel Hall (1821); and Phi Kappa Hall (1834). Phone 706/542-1472. Also on campus are

Butts-Mehre Heritage Museum. Exhibits, video displays, and trophy cases display Georgia sports memorabilia. Third and 4th floors of Butts-Mehre Heritage Hall, Lumpkin St & Pinecrest Dr. (Mon-Fri). Phone 706/542-9094. **FREE**

Georgia Museum of Art. Contains more than 8,000 pieces, incl Eva Underhill Holbrook Collection; traveling and special exhibits. (Tues-Sun; closed hols, wk of Dec 25) Phone 706/542-4662. **FREE**

State Botanical Garden. Approx 300 acres with natural trails, wildlife, and special collections. Gardens (daily); conservatory/visitor center (Tues-Sun); Callaway Bldg (Mon-Fri). 2450 S Milledge Ave. Phone 706/542-1244. **FREE**

Annual Events

Spring Tour of Homes. A bicentenial celebration of Athens architecture, 33rd annual. Held by Athens-Clarke Heritage Foundation. Contact Fire Hall #2, 489 Prince Ave, 30601; 706/353-1801 or 706/353-1820. Last wkend Apr.

Marigold Festival. GA 78 to Cherokee Rd, in Winterville. Arts, crafts, antiques, parades, and other events. Phone 706/742-8600. Late June.

Crackerland Tennis Tournament. Dan Magill Tennis Complex, Univ of Georgia. Juniors, late July-early Aug. Seniors, mid-Aug.

North Georgia Folk Festival. Sandy Creek Park. Phone 706/613-3620. Late Sep or early Oct.

Motels/Motor Lodges

★★ **COURTYARD BY MARRIOTT.** *166 Finley St (30601). 706/369-7000; fax 706/548-4224. www.courtyard.com.* 105 rms, 2-3 story. S, D $74; suites $95-$105; higher rates: univ football games, graduation. Crib free. TV; cable (premium), VCR avail. Pool; whirlpool. Restaurant adj 6:30-10:30 am. Bar. Ck-out noon. Coin lndry. Meeting rms. Business servs avail. In-rm modem link. Free airport transportation. Exercise equipt. Refrigerators; microwaves avail. Cr cds: A, D, DS, ER, MC, V.

⊡ 🛏 🕅 📑 🔥 SC

★★ **HOLIDAY INN ATHENS.** *197 E Broad St (30603), at Lumpkin St. 706/549-4433; fax 706/548-3031; res 800/465-4329; toll-free 800/862-8436.* 308 rms, 2-6 story. S, D $84-$104; suites $134; under 19 free; wkend rates; higher rates football wkends. Crib free. TV; cable (premium). Indoor pool; whirlpool. Coffee in rms. Restaurant 7 am-2 pm, 5:30-10 pm. Bar 4 pm-1 am; closed Sun. Ck-out noon. Coin lndry. Convention facilities. Business center. In-rm modem link. Free airport transportation. Exercise equipt. Some balconies. Adj to Univ of Georgia. Luxury level. Cr cds: A, D, DS, JCB, MC, V.

⊡ 🛏 🕅 📑 🔥 🕅

★★ **HOLIDAY INN EXPRESS.** *513 W Broad St (30601), US 29, 78, 129, 441. 706/546-8122; fax 706/546-1722; res 800/HOLIDAY.* 160 rms, 5 story. S $61-$67, D $67-$73; suites $110; under 18 free; wkend rates; higher rates: graduation, football wkends. Crib free. Pet accepted, some restrictions. TV; cable (premium), VCR avail. Pool. Complimentary coffee in rms. Restaurant 6:30 am-9:30 pm. Bar 4:30 pm-1 am; entertainment, dancing Tues-Sat. Ck-out noon. Bellhops. Valet serv. Meeting rms. Business servs avail.

In-rm modem link. Sundries. Cr cds: A, D, DS, MC, V.

⊡ 🛏 🛏 🕅 📑 🔥

Hotel

★★ **BEST WESTERN COLONIAL INN.** *170 N Milledge Ave (30601). 706/546-7311; fax 706/546-7959; toll-free 800/592-9401. Email emoore@email.msn.com; www.bestwestern.com/colonialinnathens.* 70 rms, 2 story. Apr-Aug, Oct: S $79; D $89; each addl $7; under 12 free; lower rates rest of yr. Crib avail. Pet accepted, fee. Parking lot. Pool. TV; cable (DSS). Complimentary continental bkfst, coffee in rms, newspaper, toll-free calls. Restaurant nearby. Ck-out 11 am, ck-in 2 pm. Dry cleaning, coin lndry. Golf. Tennis. Cr cds: A, C, D, DS, MC, V.

⊡ 🛏 🕅 📑 🛏 📑 🔥 SC

B&Bs/Small Inns

★★★ **NICHOLSON HOUSE.** *6295 Jefferson Rd (30607). 706/353-2200; fax 706/353-7799; res 706/353-2200. Email chneely@aol.com; www.bbonline.com/ga/nicholson.* 7 rms, 1 story, 2 suites. Apr-June, Sep-Dec: S, D $105; each addl $15; suites $115; lower rates rest of yr. TV; cable (premium). Complimentary full bkfst. Ck-out 11 am, ck-in 4 pm. Meeting rm. Fax servs avail. Golf. Hiking trail. Cr cds: A, DS, MC, V.

⊡ 🕅 📑 🔥

★★★ **RIVENDELL BED AND BREAKFAST.** *3581 S Barnett Shoals Rd (30677), approx 8 mi S on US 441, then 5 mi W on Barnett Shoals Rd. 706/769-4522; fax 706/769-4393. Email rivendel@negia.net; www.negia.net/~rivendel/.* 5 rms, 2 share bath, 2 story. Some rm phones. S, D $65-$80; football wkends (2-night min). Children over 10 yrs only. Complimentary full bkfst. Ck-out 11 am, ck-in 5-8 pm. Concierge serv. English country home set upon 11 woodland acres; on Oconee River. Totally non-smoking. Cr cds: MC, V.

📑 🔥

Restaurants

★★ **HARRY BISSETTS.** *279 E Broad St (30601), on GA 78. 706/353-7065. www.harrybissetts.com.* Specializes in barbecue shrimp, veal, Angus steaks. Hrs: 11:30 am-3 pm, 5:30-10 pm; Mon from 5:30 pm; Fri, Sat to 11 pm; Sat, Sun brunch to 3:30 pm. Closed Dec 25. Bar. Lunch $5.50-$9.50; dinner $12-$24. Sat, Sun brunch, $7.95. Storefront bldg; bar area was once a bank. Cr cds: A, D, DS, MC, V.

★ **LAST RESORT GRILL.** *184 W Clayton St (30601). 706/549-0810. www.lastresortgrill.com.* Specializes in praline chicken, salmon and grits, shiitake roma pasta. Hrs: 11 am-3 pm, 5-10 pm; Fri, Sat to 11 pm. Closed hols. Bar. Lunch $3.95-$6.95; dinner $6.95-$16.95. Child's menu. Eclectic decor. Cr cds: A, D, MC, V.

Unrated Dining Spot

VARSITY. *1000 W Broad St (30601). 706/548-6325.* Specializes in hot dogs, hamburgers. Hrs: 10 am-10 pm; Fri, Sat to midnight. Lunch $1-$1.50; dinner $1-$1.50. Brunch $1-$1.50. School cafeteria atmosphere; pennant flag display. No cr cds accepted.

Atlanta (C-2)

Founded 1837 **Pop** 394,017
Elev 1,050 ft **Area code** 404
Web www.atlanta.com
Information Convention & Visitors Bureau, 233 Peachtree St NE, Suite 2000, 30303; 404/222-6688

Suburbs Marietta, Norcross. (See individual alphabetical listings.)

When Atlanta was just 27 years old, 90 percent of its houses and buildings were razed by Union armies after a 117-day siege. Rebuilt by railroads in the 20th century, the city gives an overall impression of 20th-century modernism.

Standing Peachtree, a Creek settlement, occupied Atlanta's site until 1813. Lieutenant George R. Gilmer led 22 recruits to build a fort here because of difficulties among the Creek and Cherokee. This became the first white settlement and grew into an important trading post.

After Georgia's secession from the Union on January 19, 1861, the city became a manufacturing, storage, supply, and transportation center for the Confederate forces. This made Atlanta the target and last real barrier on General William Tecumseh Sherman's march to the sea. Although Atlanta had quartered 60,000 Confederate wounded, it was untouched by actual battle until Sherman began the fierce fighting of the Atlanta Campaign on May 7, 1864, with the engagement at Tunnel Hill, just over the Tennessee line. Despairing of capturing the city by battle, Sherman undertook a siege.

Guns were brought in, and Atlanta civilians got a foretaste of 20th-century warfare as the population and defenders alike were subjected to continuous bombardment by the Union's heaviest artillery. People took refuge in cellars, trenches, and dugouts. Those who could escaped southward by wagon, foot, or train until Union forces seized the railroad 20 miles south at Jonesboro on September 1. General Hood evacuated Atlanta that same night, and the mayor surrendered the city the next day, September 2. Although the terms of surrender promised protection of life and property, Sherman ordered the city evacuated. All but 400 of the 3,600 houses and commercial buildings were destroyed in the subsequent burning.

Many citizens had returned to the city by January of 1865. By June, steps had been taken to reorganize business and repair wrecked railroad facilities. In 1866, Atlanta was made federal headquarters for area reconstruction. During the Reconstruction Convention of 1867-68 called by General John Pope in Atlanta, the city offered facilities for the state government if it should be chosen the capital. The convention accepted this proposition, and Atlanta became the capital on April 20, 1868.

Atlanta's recovery and expansion as a rail center was begun by 1872, when two more railroads met here. Today

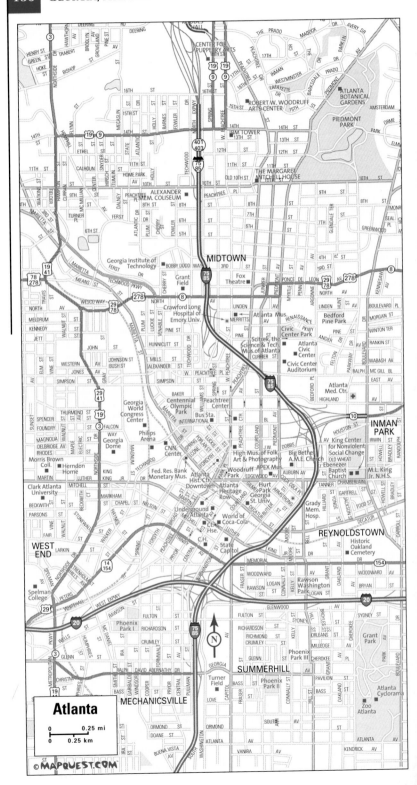

Atlanta

0   0.25 mi
0   0.25 km

©MAPQUEST.COM

hundreds of manufacturers produce a wide variety of commodities.

Metropolitan Atlanta's population of 2.8 million is as devoted to cultural activities (such as its famed Alliance Theatre) as it is to its many golf courses and its major sports teams. Peachtree Street today considers itself the South's main street and is more Fifth Avenue than Scarlett O'Hara's beloved lane. Skyscrapers, museums, luxury shops, and hotels rub shoulders along this concourse where Coca-Cola was first served; there are few peach blossoms left.

There are 29 colleges and universities in Atlanta. Georgia Institute of Technology, home of "a rambling wreck from Georgia Tech and a hell of an engineer," is one of the nation's top technological institutes. Other schools include Georgia State, Emory, and Oglethorpe universities. Atlanta University Center is an affiliation of six institutions of higher learning: Atlanta University, Spelman, Morehouse, Clark, and Morris Brown colleges, and the Interdenominational Theological Center.

Transportation

Airport. See ATLANTA HARTSFIELD AIRPORT AREA.

Car Rental Agencies. See IMPORTANT TOLL-FREE NUMBERS.

Public Transportation. Buses & subway trains (MARTA), phone 404/848-4711.

Rail Passenger Service. Amtrak 800/872-7245.

What to See and Do

A.G. Rhodes Memorial Hall. (1903) Outstanding example of Victorian Romanesque architecture. Open to the public during restoration process (Mon-Fri, Sun; closed hols). 1516 Peachtree St NW. Phone 404/885-7800. ¢¢

Atlanta Botanical Garden. Features 15 acres of outdoor gardens: Japanese, rose, perennial, and others. Fuqua Conservatory with tropical, desert, and rare plants from around the world; and special exhibit area for carnivorous plants. (Tues-Sun; closed Jan 1, Thanksgiving, Dec 25)

1345 Piedmont Ave. Phone 404/876-5859. ¢¢¢

Atlanta Cyclorama. Tells the story of the 1864 Battle for Atlanta as the studio revolves around a massive painting and diorama completed in 1885. (Daily) At Georgia & Cherokee Aves in Grant Park. Phone 404/658-7625. ¢¢

Atlanta History Center. Center consists of 5 major structures and 33 acres of woodlands and gardens. 130 W Paces Ferry Rd. Phone 404/814-4000. Admission to entire complex ¢¢¢ On site are

> **Atlanta History Museum.** Historical exhibits relating to Atlanta, the Civil War, Southern folk life, and African Americans. (Daily; closed hols)

> **McElreath Hall.** Research library, archives, and Cherokee Garden Library with gardening and horticulture research collection (Mon-Fri; closed hols). Special events.

> **Swan House.** (1928) A classically styled mansion preserved as an example of early 20th-century architecture and decorative arts. Mansion is part of spacious landscaped grounds that incl terraces with cascading fountains, formal boxwood garden, and Victorian playhouse. On premises is the Philip Trammell Shutze Collection of Decorative Arts. (Daily; closed hols) Guided tours.

> **Tullie Smith Farm.** Guided tours of 1840 plantation-style farmhouse, herb gardens, pioneer log cabin, and other outbldgs; craft demonstrations.

Atlanta State Farmers' Market. Owned and operated by the state and covering 146 acres, this is one of the largest farmers' markets of its kind in the Southeast. (Daily; closed Dec 25) 10 mi S on I-75 Exit 237 in Forest Park. Phone 404/366-6910. **FREE**

Cable News Network studio tour. View technicians, writers, editors, producers, and on-air journalists in the studio headquarters of a 24-hr all-news cable television network (45-min tour; res recomended). Children under 6 not allowed. (Daily; closed Easter, Thanksgiving, Dec 25) At 1 CNN Center, Techwood Dr & Marietta St. Phone 404/827-2300. ¢¢¢

Fernbank Natural History Museum. Monumental 4-story modern museum which houses an IMAX theater, exhibits on geography and local habitats; play areas; cafe. 767 Clifton Rd NE. Phone 404/370-0960. ¢¢ Incl

Fernbank Science Center. Center incl exhibit hall, observatory, planetarium (fee), science library; also forest area (65 acres) with marked trails. (Hrs for facilities vary; closed hols) 156 Heaton Park Dr NE. Phone 404/378-4311. **FREE**

Fort McPherson. Military reservation since May 4, 1889. Historical tours (Mon-Fri, by appt). Lee St, US 29, approx 3 mi SW via I-75 & Lakewood Freeway to fort. Phone 404/464-3556 or 404/464-2204. **FREE**

Fox Theatre. (1929) The "Fabulous Fox," one of the most lavish movie theaters in the world, was conceived as a Shriners' temple with a 4,678-seat auditorium, world's largest Moller organ console, and 3 elaborate ballrms; restored theater's ornate architecture combines exotic Moorish and Egyptian details. Hosts ballet, Broadway shows, summer film series, full spectrum of musical concerts, theatrical events, trade shows, and conventions. Tours (Mon, Wed, Thurs, Sat). 660 Peachtree St NE. Phone 404/881-2100 for details. Tours. ¢¢

Gray Line bus tours. Contact 705 Lively Ave, Norcoss 30071. Phone 404/767-0594.

Kennesaw Mountain National Battlefield Park. (see) 25 mi NW off US 41.

Margaret Mitchell House. Home of the famous Atlanta native, author of *Gone With the Wind,* written here in a cramped basement apartment. The museum displays the typewriter on which the manuscript was written, Mitchell's Pulitzer Prize, and a great collection of movie posters. Hr-long guided tours (daily). 990 Peachtree St at 10th St. Phone 404/249-7012. ¢¢-¢¢

☒ **Martin Luther King, Jr, National Historic Site.** A 2-blk area in memory of the famed leader of the civil rights movement and winner of the Nobel Peace Prize. Features incl the Freedom Hall Complex, Chapel of All Faiths, the King Library and Archives, and the reflecting pool; films and slides on Dr. King's life and work may be viewed in the screening rm (fee). The National Park Service operates an information center; phone 404/331-6922 (daily; closed hols). (Daily; closed Jan 1, Dec 25) 450 Auburn Ave. Phone 404/331-5190. **FREE**

King Birthplace. 450 Auburn Ave. Phone 404/331-3920 for tour information. **FREE** Nearby is

Ebenezer Baptist Church. Dr. King was co-pastor at Ebenezer from 1960-68. Next door to the church is the gravesite with an eternal flame. (Mon-Sat, donation) 407 Auburn Ave.

Museum of the Jimmy Carter Library. Museum with exhibits on life in White House, major events during the Carter administration, and the life of President Carter. Incl full-scale replica of the Oval Office. (Daily; closed Jan 1, Thanksgiving, Dec 25) 1 Copenhill Ave. Phone 404/331-0296. ¢¢

Parks. Atlanta parks offer dogwood blooms in spring and varied recreational facilities, incl golf, swimming, and picnic areas.

Grant Park. Many mi of walks and roads; visible traces of breastworks built for defense of Atlanta; cyclorama depicting the Battle of Atlanta; Atlanta Zoo with a variety of species. Swimming, tennis, picnicking, park (daily). Zoo (daily; closed Jan 1, Thanksgiving, Dec

Ebenezer Baptist Church

25). Cherokee Ave SE. Phone 404/624-5600. Zoo ¢¢¢-¢¢¢¢.

Chastain Memorial Park. Swimming; tennis, golf, picnicking, amphitheater. Fees for various activities. Between Powers Ferry Rd & Lake Forrest Dr.

Piedmont Park. Home of the Arts Festival of Atlanta. Swimming (fee); lake; tennis (fee), picnicking. Off of Monroe Dr on Park Dr. Phone 404/875-7275.

Centennial Olympic Park. Twenty-one-acre park constructed for the 1996 Summer Olympics serves as Atlanta's downtown centerpiece; features the Fountain of Rings (where water shoots up in the shape of Olympic rings), an amphitheater and Great Lawn for festivals and concerts, a visitor center, and a memorial to the 2 people killed in the bombing here during the Games. Bounded by Marietta Ave, Techwood Dr, and Baker St.

Professional sports.

National League baseball (Atlanta Braves). Turner Field. Capitol Ave. Phone 404/522-7630.

NBA (Atlanta Hawks). Georgia Dome. 1 Georgia Dome Dr. Phone 404/827-3800.

NFL (Atlanta Falcons). Georgia Dome. 1 Georgia Dome Dr. Phone 770/945-1111.

Robert W. Woodruff Arts Center. 1280 Peachtree St NE. Largest arts complex in the Southeast; headquarters of Atlanta College of Art and

High Museum of Art. European art from the early Renaissance-present; Samuel H. Kress, J. J. Haverty, Ralph K. Uhry print collection and Richman collection of African art; photographs; decorative arts; traveling exhibitions. (Tues-Sun; closed hols) Also tours, lectures, films; for schedule phone 404/733-4444. Phone 404/733-4400 for general information. ¢-¢¢¢.

Symphony Hall. Largest auditorium in Arts Center. Permanent home of Atlanta Symphony Orchestra and Chorus; performances (Sep-May and mid-June-mid-Aug). Phone 404/733-5000 for schedule, ticket information.

Alliance Theatre Company. Six mainstage productions, 2 studio theater productions, and 2 children's theater productions are presented annually. (Sep-May) Phone 404/733-5000 for schedule, ticket information.

SciTrek-The Science and Technology Museum of Atlanta. The worlds of science and high technology are examined through self-guided tour of more than 100 "hands-on" exhibits. Traveling exhibits, demonstrations, films, lectures, and workshops are frequently offered. (Daily; closed hols) 395 Piedmont Ave at Pine St. Phone 404/522-5500. ¢¢

Six Flags Over Georgia. A family theme park featuring Georgia's history under the flags of England, France, Spain, the Confederacy, Georgia, and the US. More than 100 rides, shows, and attractions, incl the Georgia Cyclone roller coaster, modeled after Coney Island's famous Cyclone; the Ninja roller coaster with 5 upside down turns; water rides; children's activities; live shows. Restaurants. (Mid-May-early Sep, daily; early Mar-mid-May and early Sep-Oct, wkends only) 12 mi W via I-20, Exit 13C Six Flags Pkwy, just beyond Atlanta city limits. Phone 770/948-9290. ¢¢¢¢

State Capitol. (1884-89) The dome, topped with native gold, is 237 ft high. Inside are historical flags, statues, and portraits. Tours 9:30 am, 10:30 am, 1 pm, and 2 pm (Mon-Fri). 1 Capitol Sq. Phone 404/656-2844. **FREE** On the 4th floor is

Georgia Capitol Museum. Exhibits of wildlife, snakes, fish, rocks, minerals, and fossils. Dioramas of Georgia industry. (Call capitol bldg for days open; may change due to extensive restoration) **FREE**

★ **Stone Mountain Park.** This 3,200-acre park surrounds the world's largest granite monolith, which rises 825 ft from the plain. A monument to the Confederacy, the deep relief carving on the mountain's face depicts 3 figures: Gen Robert E. Lee, Gen "Stonewall" Jackson, and Confederate President Jefferson Davis. It was first undertaken by Gutzon Borglum after WWI, continued by Augustus Lukeman, and completed by Walker Hancock. The top of the mountain is accessible by foot or by cable car (fee). Surrounding the sculpture are: **Memorial Hall**, a Civil War museum with commentary in 7 languages about the mountain and its carving; an **antebellum plantation** featuring 19 bldgs restored and furnished with 18th- and 19th-century heirlooms, formal and kitchen gardens, cookhouse, slave quarters, country store, and other outbldgs; **Antique Auto and Music Museum** housing cars dating from 1899 and antique mechanical music collection; riverboat *Scarlett O'Hara*, providing scenic trips around 363-acre lake; **scenic railroad** with full-size replicas of Civil War trains that make 5-mi trip around base of mountain. Also, a laser show is projected onto the N face of the mountain in 50-min productions (Apr, Sat 8:30); and a 732-bell carillon plays concerts (Wed-Sun). In addition, the park has 10 mi of nature trails where wild and domestic animals live on 20 wooded acres; beach with bathhouse, fishing, boat rentals; tennis courts, 36-hole golf course, miniature golf, ice-skating; picnicking, snack bars, and 3 restaurants; inn; and campground with tent and trailer sites (hookups, dump station). Most attractions are open daily (addl fees; closed Dec 25). For further information contact PO Box 778, Stone Mountain 30086. 19 mi E on US 78. Phone 770/498-5600. Per vehicle ¢¢¢

⊡ **Underground Atlanta.** A "festival marketplace" featuring shops, push-cart peddlers, restaurants and night-clubs, street entertainers, and various attractions. The 6-blk area was created in the 1920s when several viaducts were built over existing streets at 2nd-story level to move traffic above multiple rail crossings. Merchants moved their shops to 2nd floors, relegating 1st floors to oblivion for nearly half a century. Today's visitor descends onto the cobblestone streets of a Victorian city in perpetual night. On lower Alabama St the shops are housed in the original, once-forgotten storefronts. Underground Atlanta was first "discovered" in the late 1960s and flourished as a center of nightlife before being closed down in 1981 due to a combination of crime and subway construction. The "rediscovered" Underground combines the original

belowground streets with above-ground plazas, promenades, fountains, more shops and restaurants, and a 138-ft light tower. (Daily; closed Dec 25) Bounded by Wall, Central, Peachtree Sts & Martin Luther King Jr Dr. Phone 404/523-2311. Highlighted here is

The World of Coca-Cola. A square blk of interactive displays and exhibits trace history of Coca-Cola from its introduction in 1886 at Jacob's Pharmacy Soda Fountain on Atlanta's Peachtree St to present; world's largest collection of Coca-Cola memorabilia; movies; old-fashioned soda fountain. (Daily; closed hols and 3-4 days during yr for maintenance) 55 Martin Luther King Jr Dr, between Central Ave & Washington St, S of the New Georgia Railroad Depot. Phone 404/676-5151. ¢¢- ¢¢¢

William Breman Jewish Heritage Museum. Largest Jewish heritage museum in the Southeast. Houses a Holocaust gallery and heritage gallery, which tells the story of Atlanta's Jewish community from the first German immigrants in 1845. (Sun-Fri) 1440 Spring St NW. Phone 404/873-1661. ¢¢

Wren's Nest. Eccentric, Victorian house of Joel Chandler Harris, journalist and transcriber of "Uncle Remus" stories. Original family furnishings, books, photographs. Ongoing restoration. (Tues-Sun; closed hols) Group tours (25+) Tues-Sat (res required); Individual tours Tues, Thurs, Sat. 1050 Ralph D. Abernathy Blvd SW. Phone 404/753-7735. ¢¢¢

Yellow River Game Ranch. A 24-acre animal preserve on the Yellow River where more than 600 animals roam free in a natural wooded area. Visitors can pet, feed, and photograph the animals. Some of the animals at the park incl deer, bears, cougars, and buffalo. (Daily; closed hols) 4525 US 78 in Lilburn, approx 17 mi E. Phone 770/972-6643. ¢¢-¢¢¢.

Zoo Atlanta. Features natural habitat settings and is known for its primate center, aviary, and representative Southeastern habitats exhibits. (Daily) 800 Cherokee Ave SE, in Grant Park. Phone 404/624-5600. ¢¢¢

Annual Events

Auto Racing. Atlanta Motor Speedway. S on I-75, exit 77, then approx 15 mi S on US 19/41. NASCAR Winston Cup, Busch Grand National, IMSA, and ARCA events. Phone 770/946-4211 for racing schedule.

Atlanta Steeplechase. At Seven Branches Farm in Cumming. Phone 404/237-7436. First Sat Apr.

Atlanta Dogwood Festival. Phone 404/329-0501. Early Apr in Piedmont Park

BellSouth Golf Classic. (see MARIETTA) Early May.

Seasonal Events

Georgia Renaissance Festival. Approx 20 mi S on I-85, exit 12. Hundreds of costumed characters, authentic crafts, games, and food in a re-created 16th-century English village. Phone 770/964-8575. Seven wkends, Apr 21-early June. ¢¢¢-¢¢¢¢

Theater of the Stars. Fox Theatre. Six Broadway musicals with professional casts. For ticket information phone 404/252-8960. Late June-early Nov.

Additional Visitor Information

For information, contact the Convention and Visitors Bureau, 233 Peachtree St NE, Suite 2000, 30303; 404/222-6688. Welcome centers are located at Underground Atlanta, at Peachtree Center Mall, at Lenox Square Mall, and at the Atlanta Hartsfield Airport.

Atlanta Hartsfield Airport Area

For additional accommodations, see ATLANTA HARTSFIELD AIRPORT AREA, which follows ATLANTA.

City Neighborhoods

Many of the restaurants, unrated dining establishments, and some lodgings listed under Atlanta incl neighborhoods as well as exact street addresses. Geographic descriptions of these areas are given.

Buckhead. S of the northern city limits, W of Lenox and Peachtree Rds, N of Wesley Rd, and E of Northside Dr.

Downtown. S of North Ave, W of I-75/I-85, N of I-20, and E of Northside Dr. **N of Downtown:** N of North Ave. **E of Downtown:** E of I-75/I-85.

Midtown/Piedmont Park. S of I-85, W of Piedmont Ave, N of North Ave, and E of I-75/85.

Motels/Motor Lodges

★ **ATLANTA DOWNTOWN TRAVELODGE.** *311 Courtland St NE (30303), Downtown. 404/659-4545; fax 404/659-5934. Email sleepybear@ mindspring.com; www.travelodge.com/ atlanta.* 71 rms, 3 story. Jan-Nov: S $90; D $115; each addl $10; under 18 free; lower rates rest of yr. Crib avail. Parking garage. Pool. TV; cable (premium). Complimentary continental bkfst, coffee in rms, newspaper, toll-free calls. Restaurant nearby. Ck-out noon, ck-in 3 pm. Business center. Concierge. Dry cleaning. Exercise privileges. Golf, 18 holes. Tennis, 5 courts. Cr cds: A, C, D, DS, ER, JCB, MC, V.

D ⚹ 🏌 ≋ 🛉 🔌 🔥 SC 🛉

★★ **ATLANTA NORTHLAKE COURTYARD.** *4083 Lavista Rd (30084), I-285 Exit 28, adj to Northlake Festival Mall. 770/938-1200; fax 770/934-6497; res 800/321-2211.* 128 units, 2 story, 20 suites. S $94; D $104; suites $110-$120; under 18 free; wkly, wkend rates. Crib free. TV; cable (premium). Pool; whirlpool. Complimentary coffee in rms. Restaurant 6:30-10 am, 5-10 pm; Sat, Sun 7 am-noon, 5-10 pm. Bar 4-11 pm. Ck-out noon. Coin lndry. Meeting rms. Business servs avail. In-rm modem link. Valet serv. Exercise equipt. Some refrigerators. Private patios, balconies. Cr cds: A, C, D, DS, MC, V.

D ≋ 🛉 🔌 🔥

★★ **COMFORT INN BUCKHEAD.** *2115 Piedmont Rd NE (30324), in Buckhead. 404/876-4444; fax 404/ 873-1007; res 800/228-5150. Email comfort_inn@mindspring.com.* 186 rms, 3 story. Jan-Sep: S, D $59-$95; each addl $6; suites $99-$149; under 18 free; higher rates special events; lower rates rest of yr. Crib free. TV; cable (premium). Pool. Complimentary continental bkfst. Ck-out noon. Coin lndry. Meeting rms. Business servs avail. Some refrigerators. Cr cds: A, DS, MC, V.

⊡ ⌖ ⊿ ⊿ SC

★★ **COURTYARD BY MARRIOTT.**
3000 Cumberland Blvd (30339), I-285 Cobb Pkwy Exit 13, N of Downtown. 770/952-2555; fax 770/952-2409; res 800/321-2211. 182 rms, 8 story. S $89; D $109; under 12 free. Crib free. TV; cable (premium). Indoor pool; whirlpool. Complimentary coffee in rms. Restaurant 6:30-10 am, 5-10:30 pm; wkends 7-11 am. Bar 5-11 pm. Ck-out noon. Meeting rms. Business servs avail. In-rm modem link. Valet serv. Sundries. Exercise rm; sauna. Health club privileges. Some refrigerators. Balconies. Cr cds: A, D, DS, MC, V.

⊡ ⌖ ⌖ ⌖ ⊿ ⌖ ⊿

★ **DAYS INN.** *6840 Shannon Pkwy (30291), 15 mi SW on I-85, Exit 13 in Union City.* 770/964-3777; fax 770/964-6631; res 800/329-7466. 100 rms, 2 story. S $49-$59; D $57-$63; each addl $5; under 18 free; higher rates Race Wkend. Crib free. TV; cable (premium), VCR avail. Complimentary continental bkfst, coffee in rms. Restaurant opp 6 am-10 pm. Ck-out noon. Meeting rms. Coin lndry. Pool. Some refrigerators, microwaves. Cr cds: A, D, DS, MC, V.

⊡ ⌖ ⌖ ⊿ ⌖

★★★ **EMORY INN.** *1641 Clifton Rd (30329), N of Downtown.* 404/712-6700; fax 404/712-6701; toll-free 800/933-6679. 107 rms, 2 story. S, D $84-$125; under 18 free. Crib free. TV; cable (premium). Pool; whirlpool. Coffee in rms. Restaurant 7 am-2 pm, 5-10 pm; Sat 7-10 am, 5-10 pm. Ck-out noon. Coin lndry. Convention facilities. Business center. In-rm modem link. Bellhops. Valet serv. Tennis privileges. Health club privileges. Microwaves avail. Antiques. Library/sitting rm. Cr cds: A, D, DS, MC, V.

⊡ ⌖ ⌖ ⌖ ⌖ ⊿ ⌖ ⌖

★★ **FAIRFIELD INN.** *1470 Spring St NW (30309), in Midtown/Piedmont Park.* 404/872-5821; fax 404/874-3602; toll-free 800/818-9745. Email fairfieldmidtown@mindspring.com. 182 rms, 4 story. S $64; D $69; each addl $10; under 18 free; higher rates conventions. Crib free. TV; cable (premium). Pool. Complimentary continental bkfst. Ck-out noon.

Meeting rms. Business servs avail. Exercise equipt. Some refrigerators. Cr cds: A, C, D, DS, MC, V.

⊡ ⌖ ⌖ ⊿ ⌖ SC

★★ **HAMPTON INN BUCKHEAD.**
3398 Piedmont Rd NE (30305), in Buckhead. 404/233-5656; fax 404/237-4688; toll-free 800/426-7866. 154 rms, 6 story. S $85-$92; D $90-$102; higher rates: wkends, special events; under 18 free. Crib free. TV; cable (premium). Pool. Complimentary continental bkfst. Coffee in rms. Restaurant adj 11 am-11 pm. Ck-out noon. Meeting rms. Business servs avail. In-rm modem link. Valet serv. Health club privileges. Cr cds: A, D, DS, MC, V.

⊡ ⌖ ⊿ ⌖ SC

★★ **LENOX INN.** *3387 Lenox Rd (30326), in Buckhead.* 404/261-5500; fax 404/261-6140; res 800/821-0900. 180 rms, 3 story, 5 suites. May-Oct: S, D $99; suites $124; lower rates rest of yr. Crib avail. Parking lot. Indoor/outdoor pools, children's pool, whirlpool. TV; cable. Complimentary continental bkfst, coffee in rms, newspaper. Restaurant 7 am-10 pm. 24-hr rm serv. Bar. Ck-out noon, ck-in 3 pm. Meeting rms. Business center. Bellhops. Concierge. Dry cleaning. Gift shop. Exercise privileges. Supervised children's activities. Cr cds: A, D, DS, JCB, MC, V.

⊡ ⌖ ⌖ ⌖ ⊿ ⌖ SC ⌖

★★ **QUALITY INN NORTHEAST.**
2960 NE Expy (I-85) (30341), I-85 Exit 33, at Shallowford Rd, N of Downtown. 770/451-5231; fax 770/454-8704; res 800/221-2222. Email qualityinnne@aol.com. 153 rms, 2 story. S, D $42-$51; family rates. Crib free. TV; cable (premium). Pool. Complimentary continental bkfst. Coffee in rms. Ck-out noon. Coin lndry. Meeting rms. Business servs avail. In-rm modem link. Bellhops. Microwaves avail. Cr cds: A, C, D, DS, MC, V.

⊡ ⌖ ⊿ ⌖

★★ **RAMADA INN - SIX FLAGS.**
4225 Fulton Industrial Blvd (30336), I-20W Exit 14, W of Downtown. 404/691-4100; fax 404/691-2117; toll-free 800/272-6232. 229 rms, 4-5 story. Apr-mid-Sep: S, D $58-$78; each addl $10; lower rates rest of yr. Crib $10. TV; cable (premium). Pool. Bar 3 pm-2:30 am; entertainment. Ck-out 11

am. Coin lndry. Meeting rms. Business servs avail. Game rm. Some refrigerators. Grill. Cr cds: A, D, DS, MC, V.

D ☒ ☒ ♨ SC

★ **RED ROOF INN DRUID HILLS.**
1960 N Druid Hills Rd (30329), I-85 Exit 31, N of Downtown. 404/321-1653; fax 404/248-9774; toll-free 800/843-7663. 115 rms, 3 story. S, D $48-$65; under 18 free. Crib free. Pet accepted, some restrictions. TV; cable (premium). Complimentary coffee in lobby. Restaurant nearby. Ck-out noon. In-rm modem link. Health club privileges. Cr cds: A, C, D, DS, MC, V.

D ☜ ☒ ♨ SC

★★ **RESIDENCE INN ATLANTA MARRIOTT DUNWOODY.** *1901 Savoy Dr (30341), I-285 at Chamblee-Dunwoody Exit 22, N of Downtown.* 770/455-4446; fax 770/451-5183; toll-free 800/331-3131. 144 kit. suites, 2 story. S, D $99-$119; wkend rates. Crib free. Pet accepted, some restrictions. TV; cable (premium), VCR avail. Heated pool; whirlpools. Complimentary continental bkfst. Ck-out noon. Coin lndry. Meeting rm. Business servs avail. In-rm modem link. Valet serv. Health club privileges. Many fireplaces; microwaves avail. Private patios, balconies. Picnic tables, grills. Cr cds: A, D, DS, MC, V.

D ☜ ☒ ☒ ♨ SC

★★★ **SUMMERFIELD SUITES BY WYNDHAM.** *505 Pharr Rd (30305), in Buckhead.* 404/262-7880; fax 404/262-3734; toll-free 800/833-4353. www.summerfieldsuites.com. 88 suites, 3 story. No elvtr. S, D $199-$239; wkend rates. Crib free. Pet accepted, some restrictions. TV; cable (premium), VCR. Heated pool; whirlpool. Complimentary continental bkfst, coffee in rms. Restaurant opp 11 am-midnight. Ck-out 11 am. Coin lndry. Meeting rms. In-rm modem link. Valet serv. Sundries. Exercise equipt. Refrigerators, microwaves. Balconies. Picnic tables, grills. Cr cds: A, DS, MC, V.

D ☜ ☒ ⻏ ☒ ☒ SC

★★★ **SUMMERFIELD SUITES HOTEL.** *760 Mt Vernon Hwy (30328), N of Downtown.* 404/250-0110; fax 404/943-0358; toll-free 800/833-4353.

122 kit. suites, 2-3 story. 1-bedrm $159; 2-bedrm $199; wkend rates. Crib free. Pet accepted, some restrictions. TV; cable (premium), VCR (movies $6). Heated pool; whirlpool. Complimentary continental bkfst, coffee in rms. Ck-out 11 am. Coin lndry. Meeting rms. Business servs avail. In-rm modem link. Exercise equipt. Microwaves avail. Picnic tables, grills. Cr cds: A, D, DS, JCB, MC, V.

D ☒ ☜ ⻏ ☒ ☒ ♨ ⻏

★ **SUPER 8.** *3701 Jonesboro Rd SE (30354), S of Downtown.* 404/361-1111; fax 404/366-0294; toll-free 800/800-8000. 73 rms, 2 story. S $45-$150; D $50-$150; each addl $5; suites $75-$90; under 18 free. Crib $5. TV; cable (premium). Pool. Complimentary continental bkfst. Restaurant nearby. Ck-out 11 am. Coin lndry. Meeting rms. Business servs avail. In-rm modem link. Sundries. Some refrigerators, microwaves. Cr cds: A, C, D, DS, MC, V.

D ☒ ☒ ♨ ☒ SC

★★ **WYNDHAM VININGS HOTEL.** *2857 Paces Ferry Rd (30339), I-285 Exit 12, N of Downtown.* 770/432-5555; res 800/996-3426. www.wyndham.com. 159 rms, 4 story. S, D $125-$135; suites $149-$150; under 17 free; wkend rates. Crib free. TV; cable (premium). Heated pool; whirlpool, poolside serv. Restaurant 6:30 am-2 pm, 5-10 pm. Rm serv 4-10 pm. Bar 4 pm-midnight. Ck-out noon. Meeting rms. Business servs avail. In-rm modem link. Valet serv. Tennis privileges. Health club privileges. Private patios, balconies. Cr cds: A, D, DS, MC, V.

D ⻏ ☒ ⻏ ☒ ♨

Hotels

★★ **BEST WESTERN INN.** *330 W Peachtree St NW (30308), Downtown.* 404/577-6970; fax 404/659-3244; toll-free 800/528-1234. Email innatpeachtrees@aol.com. 110 rms, 4 story. S $145; D $165; each addl $10; under 18 free. TV; cable (premium). Complimentary full bkfst. Ck-out noon. Meeting rm. Business center. Coin lndry. Covered parking. Airport transportation. Exercise equipt. Health club privileges. Some refrigerators, microwaves. Near Merchandise Mart & Apparel Mart. Cr cds: A, DS, MC, V.

🄳 🕅 🛏 🐾 🏃 SC

★★ **COUNTRY HEARTH INN ATLANTA.** *5793 Roswell Rd (30342), in Sandy Springs, N of Downtown. 404/252-6400; fax 404/851-9306; res 888/294-6497. Email sheral@ mindspring.com; www.countryhearth. com.* 81 rms, 5 story, 1 suite. June-Sep: S, D $89; each addl $6; suites $147; lower rates rest of yr. Crib avail, fee. Parking lot. Pool. TV; cable (DSS). Complimentary continental bkfst, coffee in rms, newspaper, toll-free calls. Restaurant nearby. Ck-out noon, ck-in 3 pm. Meeting rm. Business center. Dry cleaning. Salon/barber. Exercise privileges. Golf. Tennis. Picnic facilities. Cr cds: A, C, D, DS, MC, V.

🄳 🕅 🐾 🛏 🕅 🛏 🐾 SC 🕅

★★★ **CROWNE PLAZA RAVINIA.** *4355 Ashford Dunwoody Rd (30346), 1 blk N I-285 Exit 21, adj Perimeter Mall, N of Downtown. 770/395-7700; fax 770/392-9503; res 800/554-0055.* 495 rms, 15 story. S $149-$189; D $159-$199; each addl $10; suites $350-$1,150; under 18 free; wkend rates. Crib free. Valet parking $9. TV; cable (premium), VCR avail. Indoor pool; whirlpool. Restaurants 6 am-11 pm (see also LA GROTTA RAVINIA). Rm serv to 1 am. Bar noon-2 am; entertainment Mon-Sat. Ck-out noon. Convention facilities. Business center. In-rm modem link. Concierge. Gift shop. Lighted tennis. Exercise equipt; sauna. Microwaves, refrigerator avail. Luxury level. Cr cds: A, DS, MC, V.

🄳 🛏 🕅 🏃 🛏 🐾 🕅

★ **DAYS INN ATLANTA DOWN-TOWN.** *300 Spring St (30308), Downtown. 404/523-1144; fax 404/522-1694; res 800/329-7466. Email daysinn2@mindspring.com.* 263 rms, 10 story. Crib avail, fee. Parking lot. Pool. TV; cable (premium). Complimentary coffee in rms, newspaper. Restaurant 6 am-10 pm. Bar. Ck-out 11 am, ck-in 3 pm. Conference center, meeting rm. Bellhops. Dry cleaning. Gift shop. Exercise equipt. Golf. Video games. Cr cds: A, C, D, DS, ER, JCB, MC, V.

🄳 🕅 🛏 🕅 🛏 🐾

★★★ **DOUBLETREE.** *3342 Peachtree Rd NE (30326), in Buckhead. 404/231-1234; fax 404/231-5236; toll-free 800/222TREE.* 221 rms, 6 story. S, D $124-$134; each addl $10; suites from $159; under 18 free; wkend rates. Crib $10. TV; cable (premium). Complimentary coffee in rms. Restaurant 6:30 am-10 pm; Sat, Sun from 7 am. Bar 4 pm-midnight; Sun from noon. Ck-out noon. Meeting rms. Business servs avail. In-rm modem link. Sundries. Health club privileges. Cr cds: A, C, D, DS, ER, JCB, MC, V.

🄳 🕅 🕅 🛏 🐾

★★★ **DOUBLETREE GUEST SUITES.** *2780 Windy Ridge Pkwy (30339), I-285 Cobb Pkwy Exit 13, N of Downtown. 770/980-1900; fax 770/980-1528; toll-free 800/843-5858.* 155 suites, 8 story. Suites $169-$189; under 18 free; wkly, wkend rates. Crib free. TV; cable (premium). Pool. Complimentary full bkfst, coffee in rms. Restaurant 11 am-2 pm, 5-10 pm. Bar 11-1 am; Sun to 12:30 am; entertainment Tues-Sat. Ck-out noon. Meeting rms. Business servs avail. In-rm modem link. Bathrm phones, in-rm whirlpools, refrigerators. Some private patios, balconies. Cr cds: A, C, D, DS, MC, V.

🄳 🛏 🛏 🐾 SC

★★★ **DOUBLETREE GUEST SUITES.** *6120 Peachtree-Dunwoody Rd (30328), N of Downtown. 770/668-0808; fax 770/668-0008; toll-free 800/222-8733. www.doubletreehotels.com.* 224 suites, 6 story. Suites $69-$159; under 18 free; wkend rates. Crib free. TV; cable (premium), VCR avail. Indoor/outdoor pool; whirlpool. Coffee in rms. Restaurant 6 am-11 pm. Bar 4:30 pm-2 am. Ck-out noon. Coin lndry. Meeting rms. Business center. In-rm modem link. Exercise equipt; sauna. Health club privileges. Refrigerators; microwaves avail. Cr cds: A, C, D, DS, ER, JCB, MC, V.

🄳 🛏 🕅 🛏 🐾 SC 🕅

★★★ **EMBASSY SUITES.** *2815 Akers Mill Rd SE (30339), I-285 Exit 13, N of Downtown. 770/984-9300; fax 770/955-4183; res 800/EMBASSY.* 261 suites, 9 story. S $159-$199; D $189-$219; each addl $20; under 18 free; wkend rates. Crib free. TV; cable (premium). Indoor pool; whirlpool. Sauna. Complimentary full bkfst.

Restaurant 11 am-10 pm. Bar to midnight. Ck-out noon. Meeting rms. Business servs avail. In-rm modem link. Gift shop. Refrigerators; microwaves avail. Garden atrium, glass elvtrs. Cr cds: A, D, DS, MC, V.

★★★ **EMBASSY SUITES HOTEL ATLANTA.** *3285 Peachtree Rd NE (30305), GA 400, in Buckhead. 404/261-7733; fax 404/261-6857; res 800/EMBASSY.* 317 suites, 16 story. Suites $159-$225; under 18 free; wkend rates; higher rates special events. Crib free. TV; cable (premium). 2 pools, 1 indoor; whirlpool. Complimentary full bkfst, coffee in rms. Restaurant 11 am-2 pm, 5-10 pm. Bar 11-1 am. Ck-out noon. Coin lndry. Meeting rms. Business servs avail. In-rm modem link. Gift shop. Airport transportation. Exercise equipt; sauna. Health club privileges. Refrigerators, wet bars. Cr cds: A, C, D, DS, MC, V.

★★★★★ **FOUR SEASONS HOTEL.** *75 14th St (30309), Grand Bldg, in Midtown/Piedmont Park. 404/881-9898; fax 404/873-4692; res 800/332-3442. Email judith.dumrauf@ fourseasons.com; www.fourseasons. com/atl.* Set amidst the residential-calm of the midtown cultural district, this neo-classical, marble and granite tower has a breathtaking three-story atrium, lobby, and a luxurious interior. There are 244 elegant guest rooms, including 18 suites, and 15,500 square feet of meeting space boasting a skyline-view ballroom, a 5th-floor outdoor terrace, and a fifth-floor private dining room. The Woodruff Arts Center is just steps away. 244 rms, 19 story. S, D $240-$335; each addl $30; suites $550-$2,000; under 18 free; wkend rates. Crib free. Pet accepted. Garage parking, valet $18. TV; cable (premium), VCR avail. Indoor pool; whirlpool, poolside serv. Restaurant 6:30 am-11 pm (see also PARK 75 AT THE FOUR SEASONS). Rm serv 24 hrs. Bar 11:30-1 am; entertainment. Ck-out 1 pm. Meeting rms. Business center. In-rm modem link. Concierge. Gift shop. Barber, beauty shop. Exercise

rm; sauna, steam rm. Spa. Refrigerators, minibars. Cr cds: A, DS, MC, V.

★★★ **GEORGIAN TERRACE.** *659 Peachtree St NE (30308), in Midtown/ Piedmont Park. 404/897-1991; fax 404/724-9116; res 800/651-2316. www.grandheritage.com.* 320 kit. suites, 19 story. S $175-$650; D $195-$670; each addl $20; under 18 free; package plans. Crib free. Pet accepted, some restrictions. Valet parking $12; garage $12. TV; cable (premium), VCR avail. Complimentary coffee in rms. Restaurant 11 am-9 pm. Rm serv 24 hrs. Bar 11 am-11 pm. Ck-out noon. Convention facilities. Business center. In-rm modem link. Concierge. Gift shop. Exercise equipt. Heated pool; poolside serv. Bathrm phones, refrigerators, microwaves, minibars. Some balconies. Luxury level. Cr cds: A, C, D, DS, ER, MC, V.

★★★ **GRAND HYATT ATLANTA.** *3300 Peachtree Rd NE (30305), in Buckhead. 404/365-8100; fax 404/233-5686; res 800/233-1234. Email cdorazio@ atlghpo.hyatt.com; www.atlanta.hyatt. com.* 416 rms, 25 story, 22 suites. S $265; D $290; each addl $25; suites $475; under 18 free. Crib avail. TV; cable (DSS), VCR avail. Restaurant. Bar. Meeting rms. Video games. Cr cds: A, C, D, DS, JCB, MC, V.

★★★ **HILTON ATLANTA.** *255 Courtland St NE (30303), at Harris St, Downtown. 404/659-2000; fax 404/ 222-2967; toll-free 800/445-8667. www.atlanta.hilton.com.* 1,224 rms, 30 story. S $139-$295; D $145-$295; each addl $25; suites from $350; family, wkend rates. Crib free. Valet parking $12, garage avail. TV; cable (premium), VCR avail. Pool; whirlpool, poolside serv. Restaurant open 24 hrs; dining rm (see NIKOLAI'S ROOF). Bars 11:30-2 am; Sun 12:30 pm-midnight; entertainment. Ck-out 11 am. Convention facilities. Business center. In-rm modem link. Shopping arcade. Lighted tennis, pro. Exercise rm; sauna. Health club privileges. Some bathrm phones. Balconies. Luxury level. Cr cds: A, C, D, DS, ER, JCB, MC, V.

★★ HOLIDAY INN ATLANTA
DOWNTOWN. *101 International Blvd (30202), Downtown. 404/524-5555; fax 404/524-0218; res 800/465-4329; toll-free 800/535-0707. Email atlantaadmin@crownam.com; www. holiday-inn.com.* 257 rms, 11 story, 3 suites. S $159; D $169; each addl $10; suites $350; under 18 free. Crib avail. Parking garage. Pool, whirlpool. TV; cable (DSS). Complimentary coffee in rms, newspaper. Restaurant 6:30 am-12:30 pm. Bar. Ck-out noon, ck-in 3 pm. Conference center, meeting rms. Business center. Bellhops. Concierge. Dry cleaning. Gift shop. Exercise privileges. Tennis. Video games. Cr cds: A, C, D, DS, JCB, MC, V.

★★ HOLIDAY INN BUCKHEAD.
3377 Peachtree Rd (30326), GA 400, in Buckhead. 404/264-1111; fax 404/233-7061; toll-free 800/465-4329. Email acct.hi.lenox@internetmci.com. 297 rms, 11 story. S, D $119-$149; each addl $10; suites $150-$250; under 18 free; wkend, hol rates; higher rates special events. Crib free. TV; cable (premium), VCR avail. Pool. Complimentary coffee in rms. Restaurant 6 am-2 pm, 5-11 pm. Bar from 5 pm. Ck-out 11 am. Coin lndry. Meeting rms. Business servs avail. In-rm modem link. Concierge. Health club privileges. Many refrigerators. Cr cds: A, C, D, DS, JCB, MC, V.

★★ HOLIDAY INN SELECT. *4386
Chamblee Dunwoody Rd (30341), I-285, Exit 22, N of Downtown. 770/457-6363; fax 770/458-5282; res 800/465-4329. Email gpullin@bristol hotels.com; www.basshotels.com.* 248 rms, 5 story, 2 suites. Jan-Mar, May-June, Sep-Oct: S, D $144; each addl $10; under 18 free; lower rates rest of yr. Crib avail. Pet accepted, some restrictions, fee. Parking lot. Pool. TV; cable (premium). Complimentary continental bkfst, coffee in rms, newspaper, toll-free calls. Restaurant 6 am-10 pm. Bar. Ck-out noon, ck-in 3 pm. Meeting rms. Business center. Bellhops. Dry cleaning, coin lndry. Gift shop. Free airport transportation. Exercise privileges. Golf. Hiking trail. Video games. Cr cds: A, C, D, DS, ER, JCB, MC, V.

★★★ HYATT REGENCY. *265
Peachtree St NE (30303), in Peachtree Center, Downtown. 404/577-1234; fax 404/588-4137; toll-free 800/233-1234.* 1,264 rms, 23 story. S, D $185-$240; each addl $25; suites from $450; under 18 free; wkend rates. Crib free. Garage $17-$20. TV; cable (premium). Pool; poolside serv. Restaurant 6:30-1 am. Bar noon-2 am. Ck-out noon. Convention facilities. Business center. In-rm modem link. Concierge. Gift shop. Exercise equipt. Health club privileges. Minibars; many refrigerators in suites. Many balconies. Luxury level. Cr cds: A, C, D, DS, ER, JCB, MC, V.

★★★ JW MARRIOTT HOTEL
LENOX. *3300 Lenox Rd NE (30326), at Peachtree Rd, in Buckhead. 404/262-3344; fax 404/262-8689; res 800/228-9290; toll-free 800/321-2211. www. marriotthotels.com.* 367 rms, 24 story, 40 suites. Feb-June, Sep-Dec: S, D $229; suites $750; lower rates rest of yr. Crib avail. Valet parking avail. Indoor pool, lap pool, whirlpool. TV; cable. Complimentary coffee in rms, newspaper, toll-free calls. Restaurant 24-hr rm serv. Bar. Conference center, meeting rms. Business center. Bellhops. Concierge. Dry cleaning. Gift shop. Exercise equipt, sauna, steam rm. Golf. Tennis. Cr cds: A, C, D, DS, MC, V.

★★★ MARRIOTT MARQUIS. *265
NE Peachtree Center Ave (30303), Downtown. 404/521-0000; fax 404/586-6299; res 800/228-9290.* 1,671 rms, 47 story. S, D $240-$260; each addl $20; suites $350-$1,500; under 18 free; wkend rates. Crib free. Garage $17. TV; cable (premium), VCR avail. Indoor/outdoor pool; whirlpool, poolside serv. Restaurants 6 am-midnight. Rm serv 24 hrs. Bar 11-2 am, Sun from 12:30 pm. Ck-out noon. Convention facilities. Business center. In-rm modem link. Shopping arcade. Barber, beauty shop. Exercise equipt; sauna. Health club privileges. Refrigerators. Bathrm phone in suites. Luxury level. Cr cds: A, D, DS, MC, V.

★★★ MARRIOTT NORTH CEN-
TRAL. *2000 Century Blvd NE (30345), I-85 Exit 32; in Century Center Park, N of Downtown. 404/325-*

0000; fax 404/325-4920; res 800/228-9290. 287 rms, 15 story. S, D $175; suites from $275; wkend rates. Crib free. TV; cable (premium). Heated pool; poolside serv. Complimentary coffee in lobby. Restaurant 6:30 am-2 pm, 5-11 pm. Bar 2 pm-midnight. Ck-out noon. Convention facilities. Business servs avail. In-rm modem link. Gift shop. Barber. Lighted tennis. Exercise equipt. Some refrigerators. Luxury level. Cr cds: A, DS, MC, V.

⬛ 🏷 ⛱ 🚶 🔥

★★★ **OMNI HOTEL.** *100 CNN Center (30335), Downtown.* 404/659-0000; fax 404/525-5050; toll-free 800/843-6664. www.omnihotel.com. 458 rms, 15 story. S $250; D $275; each addl from $25; suites $775-$2,200; under 18 free; wkend rates. Crib free. Garage in/out $15-$18. TV; cable (premium), VCR avail. Restaurant 7 am-11 pm. Rm serv 6:30-2 am. Bars 11-1 am. Ck-out noon. Convention facilities. Business center. In-rm modem link. Concierge. Shopping arcade. Barber, beauty shop. Valet parking. Airport transportation. Health club privileges. Bathrm phones, minibars, wet bars. Balconies. Omni Sports Coliseum, Georgia Dome, Centennial Olympic Park, Georgia World Congress Center adj. Cr cds: A, C, D, DS, MC, V.

⬛ 🚶 ⛱ 🔥 🚶

★★★ **RADISSON INN.** *2061 N Druid Hills Rd NE (30329), at I-85 Exit 31, in Buckhead.* 404/321-4174; fax 404/636-7264; res 800/333-3333. 208 rms, 9 story. S, D $109-$119; under 18 free; wkend rates. Crib free. TV; cable (premium), VCR avail. Pool. Complimentary coffee in rms. Ck-out noon. Meeting rms. Business servs avail. In-rm modem link. Exercise equipt. Near Lenox Sq. Luxury level. Cr cds: A, D, DS, MC, V.

⬛ ⛱ 🚶 ⛱ 🔥

★★★ **RENAISSANCE ATLANTA HOTEL DOWNTOWN.** *590 W Peachtree St NW (30308), at North Ave, in Midtown/Piedmont Park.* 404/881-6000; fax 404/815-5010; toll-free 800/228-9898. Email rhi.atlbr.dom@renaissancehotels.com; www.renaissancehotels.com. 504 rms, 25 story. S $165-$215; D $180-$240; suites $370-$750; under 18 free; wkend rates. Crib free.

Self park $7, valet $12. TV; cable (premium). Pool; poolside serv. Coffee in rms. Restaurant 6:30 am-midnight. Bar from 11 am. Ck-out noon. Meeting rms. Business center. Concierge. Gift shop. Exercise equipt. Health club privileges. Bathrm phones, minibars; some refrigerators, wet bars. Balconies. Luxurious rms; European-style personal service. Luxury level. Cr cds: A, DS, MC, V.

⬛ ⛱ 🚶 🔥 🚶

★★★ **RENAISSANCE WAVERLY.** *2450 Galleria Pkwy (30339), I-285 Exit 13, N of Downtown.* 770/953-4500; fax 770/953-0740; res 770/953-4500; toll-free 800/468-3571. www.renaissancehotels.com/atlrb. 521 rms, 14 story. S $169-$234; D $189-$254; each addl $20; suites $700-$1,400; under 18 free; wkend rates. Crib free. TV; cable (premium), VCR avail. 2 pools, 1 indoor; whirlpool. Complimentary coffee in rms. Restaurant 6 am-10 pm. Rm serv 24 hrs. 3 bars 11:30-1 am. Ck-out noon. Convention facilities. Business center. In-rm modem link. Concierge. Shopping arcade. Exercise equipt; sauna, steam rm. Massage. Racquetball. Bathrm phones; refrigerator in suites. Luxury level. Cr cds: A, D, DS, ER, JCB, MC, V.

⬛ ⛱ 🚶 🏸 ⛱ 🔥 🚶

★★★★ **THE RITZ-CARLTON.** *181 Peachtree St NE (30303), Downtown.* 404/659-0400; fax 404/688-0400; res 800/241-3333. This 25-story, 441-room hotel is in the center of the financial and legal district and a luxurious alternative to downtown's convention-hotel offerings. For high-level business executives, there are four floors of 76 "club" rooms that incl an exclusive lounge, five daily food-presentations, and a personal concierge staff. The property's Atlanta Grill features southern-regional cuisine and steaks, chops, and grilled seafood. 447 rms, 25 story. S, D $186-$265; suites $450-$1,165; under 12 free; wkend, hol rates. Crib free. Valet parking $17, in/out $10. TV; cable (premium), VCR avail. Restaurant. Rm serv 24 hrs. Bar 11:30-2 am; entertainment. Ck-out noon. Convention facilities. Business center. In-rm modem link. Concierge. Gift shop. Exercise equipt; steam rm. Massage. Health club privileges. Refrigerators, minibars.

Luxury level. Cr cds: A, D, DS, JCB, MC, V.

★ ★ ★ ★ **THE RITZ-CARLTON BUCKHEAD.** *3434 Peachtree Rd NE (30326), in Buckhead. 404/237-2700; fax 404/239-0078; toll-free 800/241-3333.* With its rich, clublike decor of overstuffed sofas, chandeliers, fresh flowers, and polished-wood paneling, this 553-room, uptown hotel feels like a palatial home. Located 15 minutes from downtown, the property sits in a fashionable neighborhood across from fine shopping at Lenox Square and Phipps Plaza. Chef Joel Antunes' French-Mediterranean cuisine at The Dining Room is only one of the impressive culinary options. 553 rms, 22 story. S, D $195-$215; suites $365-$1,200; under 12 free; wkend rates. Crib free. Valet parking $18; self-park in/out $8. TV; cable (premium), VCR avail. Indoor pool; whirlpool, poolside serv. Restaurants 6:30 am-midnight (see also THE CAFE and THE DINING ROOM). Rm serv 24 hrs. Bar 11-2 am; entertainment. Ck-out noon. Convention facilities. Business center. In-rm modem link. Concierge. Shopping arcade. Airport transportation. Tennis privileges, pro. Golf privileges, greens fee $85-$95. Exercise equipt; sauna, steam rm. Massage. Bathrm phones, minibars. Luxury level. Cr cds: A, C, D, DS, ER, JCB, MC, V.

★ ★ ★ **SHERATON BUCKHEAD ATLANTA.** *3405 Lenox Rd NE (30326), in Buckhead. 404/261-9250; fax 404/848-7391; toll-free 800/325-3535. Email alombardi@starlodge.com; www.sheraton.com.* 361 rms, 10 story. S $135-$195; D $150-$210; suites $275-$495; under 14 free; wkend rates. Crib free. Covered parking $8. Pet accepted, some restrictions. TV; cable (premium). Pool; poolside serv. Restaurant 6:30 am-2 pm, 5-10 pm. Bars noon-2 am. Ck-out noon. Convention facilities. Business center. In-rm modem link. Concierge. Gift shop. Exercise equipt. Some refrigerators, wet bars; bathrm phone in suites. Some balconies. Luxury level. Cr cds: A, DS, MC, V.

★ ★ ★ **SHERATON COLONY SQUARE.** *188 14th St NE (30361), at Peachtree St, in Midtown/Piedmont Park. 404/892-6000; fax 404/872-9192; res 800/325-3535; toll-free 800/422-7895. www.sheraton.com/colony square.* 437 rms, 27 story, 30 suites. Apr-June, Sep-Nov: S, D $205; each addl $2; suites $375; under 18 free; lower rates rest of yr. Crib avail. Valet parking avail. Pool. TV; cable, VCR avail. Complimentary coffee in rms, newspaper, toll-free calls. Restaurant. Bar. Ck-out 3 pm, ck-in 3 pm. Conference center, meeting rms. Business center. Bellhops. Concierge. Dry cleaning. Gift shop. Exercise equipt. Golf, 18 holes. Tennis, 2 courts. Cr cds: A, C, D, DS, JCB, MC, V.

★ ★ **SIERRA SUITES HOTELS.** *2010 Powers Ferry Rd NW (30339), NW on I-285 to I-75 Exit 110, N of Downtown. 770/933-8010; fax 770/933-8181; res 800/474-3772; toll-free 800/4SIERRA.www.sierrasuites.com.* 89 kit. suites, 3 story. S $49.95-$89.95; D $59.95-$99.95; wkly, wkend rates; higher rates hols. Crib free. TV; cable (premium). Pool. Complimentary coffee in rms. Restaurant nearby. Business servs avail. In-rm modem link. Coin lndry. Exercise equipt. Health club privileges. Refrigerators, microwaves. Grills. Cr cds: A, C, D, DS, JCB, MC, V.

★ ★ ★ **SUITE HOTEL AT UNDERGROUND.** *54 Peachtree St (30303), at Underground Atlanta, Downtown. 404/223-5555; fax 404/223-5049; toll-free 877/477-5549. Email thesuite@mindspring.com; www.suitehotel.com.* 156 suites, 16 story. S $145-$220; D $155-$230; each addl $10; under 16 free; wkend rates. Crib free. Valet parking $12. TV; cable (premium). Coffee in rms. Restaurant 7-10 am, 5-11 pm. Ck-out noon. Meeting rms. Business servs avail. In-rm modem link. Health club privileges. Bathrm phones. Cr cds: A, DS, MC, V.

★ ★ ★ **SWISSHOTEL ATLANTA.** *3391 Peachtree Rd NE (30326), in Buckhead. 404/365-0065; fax 404/233-8786; toll-free 800/253-1397. www.swissotel.com.* 365 rms, 22 story. S $295-$365; D $315-$385; suites $380-$1,500; under 16 free; wkend rates. Crib free. Garage parking $11, valet $15. TV; cable (premium), VCR avail. Indoor pool; poolside serv. Restaurant 6:30 am-11 pm. Rm serv 24 hrs. Bar 11 am-midnight; Fri, Sat to 1 am. Ck-out noon. Convention facilities. Business center. In-rm modem link. Concierge. Gift shop. Beauty shop. Exercise equipt; steam rm. Bathrm phones, minibars. Art and photo collection. Luxury level. Cr cds: A, DS, MC, V.

⊡ ⊠ 🛆 ⊠ 🐾 SC 🏃

★★★ **W ATLANTA.** *111 W Perimeter Center (30346), I-285 Exit 21, N of Downtown.* 770/396-6800; fax 770/399-5514; toll-free 800/683-6100. 274 rms, 12 story, 154 kit. suites. S $99-$165; D $109-$179; each addl $15; kit. suites $99-$165; wkend rates. Crib free. TV; cable (premium). Pool; poolside serv. Complimentary coffee in lobby. Restaurant 6-10 am, noon-2 pm, 6-10 pm. Rm serv 6 am-11 pm. Bar 5:30 pm-midnight. Ck-out noon. Coin lndry. Meeting rms. Business servs avail. Exercise equipt; sauna. Microwaves avail. Balconies. Situated in parklike setting. Cr cds: A, C, D, DS, JCB, MC, V.

⊡ ⊠ 🛆 ⊠ 🐾 SC

★★★ **THE WESTIN ATLANTA NORTH AT PERIMETER.** *7 Concourse Pkwy NE (30328), N of Downtown.* 770/395-3900; fax 770/395-3935; toll-free 888/733-7666. www.westin.com. 370 rms, 20 story. S $129-$169; D $139-$179; each addl $20; suites $275-$850; under 18 free; wkend rates. Crib free. TV; cable (premium). Heated pool; whirlpool, sauna, poolside serv. Restaurant 6:30 am-11 pm. Rm serv 24 hrs. Bar 4:30 pm-1 am, Sun to 12:30 am; entertainment Mon-Wed. Ck-out noon. Convention facilities. Business servs avail. In-rm modem link. Free parking. Tennis privileges. 18-hole golf privileges, pro. Health club privileges. Some refrigerators. Luxury level. Cr cds: A, DS, MC, V.

⊡ 🎿 ⊱ ⊠ 🛆 ⊠ 🐾 SC

★★★ **WESTIN PEACHTREE PLAZA.** *210 Peachtree St NW (30303), at International Blvd, Downtown.* 404/659-1400; fax 404/589-7424; res

800/228-3000. www.westin.com. 1,068 rms, 73 story. S $185-$205; D $235-$255; each addl $25; suites $385-$1,450; under 18 free; wkend rates. Crib free. Pet accepted, some restrictions. Garage $17; valet, in/out $14. TV; cable (premium), VCR avail. Indoor pool; poolside serv. Restaurants 6 am-11 pm. Rm serv 24 hrs. Bars (1 revolving rooftop) 11-2 am; entertainment. Ck-out 1 pm. Convention facilities. Business center. In-rm modem link. Concierge. Shopping arcade. Exercise equipt; sauna. Massage. Health club privileges. Many bathrm phones; refrigerators avail. 73-story circular tower built around 8-story atrium. Luxury level. Cr cds: A, C, D, DS, ER, JCB, MC, V.

⊡ 🐾 ⊠ 🛆 ⊠ 🐾 🏃

Olympic Stadium and Turner Field

★★ **WYNDHAM MIDTOWN ATLANTA.** *125 Tenth St NW (30309), at Peachtree St, in Midtown/Piedmont Park.* 404/873-4800; fax 404/872-7377; res 800/996-3426. Email wyndhammidtown@wyndham.com. 191 rms, 11 story. S $258; D $278; each addl $10; suites $250-$500; under 18 free; wkly, wkend rates. Crib free. Covered in/out parking $5; valet parking $12. TV; cable (premium), VCR avail. Indoor pool; whirlpool. Complimentary coffee in rms. Restaurant 6:30 am-10 pm; Sat, Sun from 7 am. Bar 4:30 pm-11 pm, Fri, Sat to 1 am. Ck-out noon. Meeting rms. Business servs avail. In-rm modem link. Exercise equipt; sauna, steam rm. Massage. Many refrigerators. Cr cds: A, D, DS, JCB, MC, V.

B&Bs/Small Inns

★★ **ANSLEY INN.** *253 15th St NE (30309), N of Downtown. 404/872-9000; fax 404/892-2318; toll-free 800/446-5416. Email ansleyinn@mindspring.com; www.ansleyinn.com.* 22 rms, 3 story. S, D $100-$150; wkly, monthly rates. TV; cable (premium). Complimentary full bkfst. Restaurant nearby. Ck-out noon, ck-in 3 pm. Business servs avail. In-rm modem link. Valet serv. Concierge serv. In-rm whirlpools. Turn-of-the-century English Tudor house; art gallery. Cr cds: A, C, D, DS, JCB, MC, V.

★★ **BENTLEY'S BED AND BREAK-FAST.** *6860 Peachtree Dunwoody Rd (30328), N of Downtown. 770/396-1742; fax 770/396-1742.* 4 rms. S, D $135. Premium cable TV in common rm. Complimentary full bkfst. Restaurant nearby. Ck-out varies, ck-in 4 pm. Business servs avail. Concierge serv. Built in 1930s as a summer home. Totally nonsmoking. Cr cds: A, DS, MC, V.

★★ **BEVERLY HILLS INN.** *65 Sheridan Dr (30305), in Buckhead. 404/233-8520; fax 404/233-8659; toll-free 800/331-8520. Email info@beverlyhillsinn.com; www.beverlyhillsinn.com.* 18 kit. suites, 3 story. S, D $90-$120; each addl $10-$15; wkly, monthly rates. Crib avail. Pet accepted, some restrictions. TV; cable. Pool privileges. Complimentary continental bkfst. Restaurant nearby. Ck-out noon, ck-in 2 pm. Valet serv. Business servs avail. In-rm modem link. Health club privileges. Microwaves avail. Balconies. European-style hotel restored to 1929 ambience. Cr cds: A, DS, MC, V.

★★★ **GASLIGHT INN BED & BREAKFAST.** *1001 St. Charles Ave NE (30306), 3 mi NE on I-75 to I-85 Exit 96; in Midtown/Piedmont Park. 404/875-1001; fax 404/876-1001. Email innkeeper@gaslightinn.com; www.gaslightinn.com.* 6 rms, 2 story, 3 suites. S, D $85-$125; each addl $12;

suites $149-$195; wkly rates; wkend rates (2-day min). TV; cable (premium), VCR avail. Complimentary continental bkfst. Restaurant nearby. Ck-out noon, ck-in 3 pm. Business servs avail. In-rm modem link. Street parking. Many refrigerators; some in-rm whirlpools, microwaves, mini-bars, wet bars, fireplaces. Balconies. Grills. Built in 1903. Totally non-smoking. Cr cds: A, DS, MC, V.

★★ **KING-KEITH HOUSE B&B.** *889 Edgewood Ave NE (30307), Downtown. 404/688-7330; fax 404/584-0730; res 404/688-7330; toll-free 800/728-2879. Email kingneith@mindspring.com.* 5 rms, 2 share bath, 3 story. S, D $75-$125; each addl $15. TV; cable. Complimentary full bkfst. Restaurant nearby. Ck-out noon, ck-in 2 pm. Valet serv. Concierge serv. Guest lndry. Street parking. Some refrigerators. Picnic tables, grills. Antiques. Totally non-smoking. Cr cds: A, DS, MC, V.

★★★ **SERENBE BED & BREAK-FAST.** *10950 Hutcheson Ferry Rd (30268), 45 mi SW on I-85, Exit 16, follow signs to Spur 14 (S Fulton Pkwy), 13 mi to Rivertown Rd, 2.2 mi then left on Cochran Mill Rd, 4.2 mi to Hutcheson Ferry Rd, right 3 mi. 770/463-2610; fax 770/463-4472. Email steve@serenbe.com; www.serenbe.com.* 7 rms, 1 story. S $125; D $140; each addl $25. Crib avail. Pool, whirlpool. TV; cable (DSS), VCR avail, CD avail. Complimentary full bkfst, coffee in rms, newspaper. Meeting rm. Business servs avail. Supervised children's activities. Hiking trail. Picnic facilities. No cr cds accepted.

★★★ **SHELLMONT INN.** *821 Piedmont Ave NE (30303), in Midtown/Piedmont Park. 404/872-9290; fax 404/872-5379. Email innkeeper@shelmont.com; www.shelmont.com.* 5 rms, 2 story, 2 suites. S $160; D $260; each addl $25; suites $260; children $25. Crib avail. Parking garage. TV; cable (DSS), VCR avail, CD avail. Complimentary full bkfst, coffee in rms, newspaper, toll-free calls. Restaurant nearby. Ck-out 11 am, ck-in 3 pm. Business servs avail. Concierge. Gift shop. Exercise privileges. Golf. Tennis. Cr cds: A, C, D, DS, JCB, MC, V.

★★★ **SUGAR MAGNOLIA.** *804 Edgewood Ave NE (30307), E of Downtown. 404/222-0226; fax 404/681-1067. Email sugmag@aol.com.* 4 rms, 2 story. S, D 75-$120. Crib free. TV. Complimentary continental bkfst; coffee in library. Ck-out 11 am, ck-in 2 pm. Concierge serv. Business center. Street parking. Refrigerators; some fireplaces. Balcony. Victorian house (1892) in historic Inman Park district; period furnishings. Totally nonsmoking. Cr cds: MC, V.

All Suites

★★ **REGENCY SUITES.** *975 W Peachtree St NE (30309), at 10th St, in Midtown/Piedmont Park. 404/876-5003; fax 404/817-7511; toll-free 800/642-3629. Email sales@regency suites.com; www.regencysuites.com.* 96 rms, 9 story, 96 suites. S $159; D $179; each addl $20. Crib avail. Parking garage. TV; cable (premium). Complimentary continental bkfst, coffee in rms, newspaper, toll-free calls. Restaurant nearby. Ck-out noon, ck-in 3 pm. Meeting rms. Business center. Dry cleaning, coin lndry. Gift shop. Exercise equipt. Golf, 18 holes. Tennis, 6 courts. Cr cds: A, C, D, DS, ER, JCB, MC, V.

★★★ **SHERATON SUITES GALLERIA ATLANTA.** *2844 Cobb Pkwy SE (30339), I-285 Exit 13, N of Downtown. 770/955-3900; fax 770/916-3165; res 800/325-3535; toll-free 800/689-6671. Email sales@sheraton galleria.com; www.sheratongalleria. com.,* 17 story, 278 suites. June, Sep-Oct: S, D $159; each addl $10; suites $159; under 18 free; lower rates rest of yr. Crib avail. Parking garage. Indoor/outdoor pools, lap pool, whirlpool. TV; cable (premium), VCR avail. Complimentary coffee in rms, newspaper, toll-free calls. Restaurant 6:30 am-10:30 pm. Bar. Ck-out noon, ck-in 3 pm. Meeting rms. Business center. Concierge. Dry cleaning. Gift shop. Exercise equipt. Golf. Video games. Cr cds: A, C, D, DS, ER, JCB, MC, V.

Conference Centers

★★★ **MARRIOTT EVERGREEN CONFERENCE RESORT.** *1 Lakeview Dr (30083), E on US 78, in Stone Mt State Park. 770/879-9900; fax 770/465-3264; res 800/228-9290. www.evergreenresort.com.* 247 rms, 5 story, 21 suites. Apr-Oct: S, D $169; suites $189; children $99; lower rates rest of yr. Crib avail. Valet parking avail. Indoor/outdoor pools, whirlpool. TV; cable, VCR avail. Complimentary coffee in rms, newspaper. Restaurant. 24-hr rm serv. Bar. Meeting rms. Business center. Bellhops. Concierge. Dry cleaning. Gift shop. Exercise equipt. Golf, 18 holes. Tennis, 20 courts. Beach access. Bike rentals. Supervised children's activities. Hiking trail. Picnic facilities. Video games. Cr cds: A, D, DS, MC, V.

★★ **RAMADA INN - CENTRAL ATLANTA.** *418 Armour Dr NE (30324), in Midtown/Piedmont Park. 404/873-4661; fax 404/872-1292; res 800/2RAMADA; toll-free 800/272-6232. Email riccatl@aol.com; www.yp. bellsouth.com/ramada.* 350 rms, 5 story, 15 suites. Jan, Mar, June-Sep: S $149; D $159; each addl $10; suites $250; under 18 free; lower rates rest of yr. Crib avail. Pet accepted, fee. Parking lot. Pool. TV; cable (premium), VCR avail. Complimentary continental bkfst, coffee in rms, newspaper, toll-free calls. Restaurant noon-midnight. 24-hr rm serv. Bar. Ck-out noon, ck-in 3 pm. Conference center, meeting rms. Business center. Bellhops. Concierge. Dry cleaning, coin lndry. Gift shop. Salon/barber. Free airport transportation. Exercise privileges. Golf. Tennis. Cr cds: A, C, D, DS, ER, JCB, MC, V.

★★★ **SHERATON HOTEL.** *165 Courtland St (30303), Downtown. 404/659-6500; fax 404/524-1259.* 747 rms, 12 story. S $170; D $180; each addl $10; suites $275-$675; under 18 free; wkend rates. Crib free. Covered parking $12. TV; cable (premium). Indoor/outdoor pool; whirlpool, poolside serv. Restaurant 6:30 am-11 pm. Bar 11-2 am; Sun to 12:30 am. Ck-out noon. Convention facilities.

Business center. In-rm modem link. Concierge. Barber, beauty shop. Exercise equipt; sauna. Health club privileges. Game rm. Some bathrm phones. Some private patios, balconies. Cr cds: A, DS, MC, V.

Restaurants

★★★ **103 WEST.** *103 W Paces Ferry Rd (30305), in Buckhead.* 404/233-5993. *www.buckheadrestaurants.com.* Specializes in peppered yellowfin tuna, grilled ostrich loin, baby rack of lamb. Own baking. Hrs: 5:30-11 pm. Closed Sun; hols. Res accepted. Bar. Wine cellar. Dinner a la carte entrees: $17-$34.50. Entertainment: pianist. Valet parking. Chef-owned. Cr cds: A, D, DS, MC, V.

D

★★★ **THE ABBEY.** *163 Ponce de Leon Ave NE (30308), at Piedmont Rd and North Ave, in Midtown/Piedmont Park.* 404/876-8831. *www.theabbey restaurant.com.* Specializes in seafood, game, veal. Own baking. Hrs: 6-10 pm. Closed hols. Res accepted. Bar. Wine cellar. Dinner a la carte entrees: $18-$28. Entertainment: harpist. Valet parking. Former church; 50-ft arched and vaulted ceiling. Costumed servers. Cr cds: A, D, DS, MC, V.

★★★ **ABRUZZI RISTORANTE.** *2355 Peachtree Rd NE (30305), at Peachtree Battle Shopping Center, in Buckhead.* 404/261-8186. Specializes in Capellini alla Nico, homemade spinach ravioli, osso buco. Hrs: 11:30 am-2 pm, 5:30-10 pm. Closed Sun; hols. Res required. Bar. Lunch $20; dinner $45. Parking. Jacket. Understated Florentine decor. Cr cds: A, D, DS, MC, V.

D

★ **AGNES & MURIEL'S.** *1514 Monroe Dr (30324), in Midtown/Piedmont Park.* 404/885-1000. Specializes in turkey meatloaf, grilled salmon pot pie. Hrs: 10 am-11 pm; Fri, Sat to midnight; Sat, Sun brunch to 3 pm. Closed Dec 25. Bar. Lunch a la carte entrees: $3.95-$10.95; dinner a la carte entrees: $3.95-$14.95. Sat, Sun brunch, $3.95-$10.95. 1950s decor. Cr cds: A, D, DS, MC, V.

D

★★ **ANIS.** *2974 Grandview Ave (30305), in Buckhead.* 404/233-9889. Specializes in grilled tuna with aioli, bouillabaise. Hrs: 11:30 am-2:30 pm, 6-10 pm; Fri, Sat to 10:30 pm. Closed Sun; hols. Bar. Lunch, dinner $7-$15. Entertainment: Mon, Thurs. Parking. European decor. Cr cds: A, C, D, MC, V.

D

★★★ **ANTHONY'S.** *3109 Piedmont Rd NE (30305), in Buckhead.* 404/262-7379. *www.anthonysfinedining.com.* Specializes in wild game, seafood, steak. Own baking. Hrs: 6-10 pm. Closed hols. Res accepted. Bar. Wine cellar. Dinner a la carte entrees: $18.95-$29.95. Valet parking. Plantation house (1797); antiques, fireplaces. Cr cds: A, D, DS, MC, V.

D

★★★ **ARIA.** *490 E Paces Ferry Rd (30305), in Buckhead.* 404/233-7673. Specializes in pan-roasted duck breast with dark plums in a sweet corn crepe, tenderloin of Jameson's farm veal with leeks and fennel sauce, pan-roasted halibut with Manilla clams and turnip mostrarda. Hrs: 6-10 pm; Fri, Sat to 11 pm. Closed Sun; hols. Res accepted. Bar. Wine cellar. Dinner a la carte entrees: $20-$30. Valet parking. Built in 1930; interior was salvaged from the library of the J. Carroll Payne House. Converted to restaurant in 1976; elegant dining. Cr cds: A, D, DS, MC, V.

D

★★ **ARUGULA.** *3639 Piedmont Rd NE (30305), in Buckhead.* 404/814-0959. *www.arugula.net.* Specializes in Mahi Mahi, tropical mango gazapacho, upside down apple Gabby. Hrs: 11:30 am-2:30 pm, 5-10 pm; Sat from 5 pm. Closed Sun; hols. Res accepted. Bar. Lunch $7-$10.50; dinner $10.50-$19.50. Valet parking. Modern decor. Cr cds: A, MC, V.

D

★★ **ATLANTA FISH MARKET.** *265 Pharr Rd (30305), in Buckhead.* 404/262-3165. *www.buckheadrestaurant.com.* Specializes in seafood. Hrs: 11 am-2:30 pm, 5:30-11 pm; Fri to midnight; Sat 11:30 am-midnight; Sun 4-

10 pm. Closed Thanksgiving, Dec 25. Bar. Lunch $7.50-$25; dinner $12.50-$26.50. Child's menu. Parking. Cr cds: A, D, DS, MC, V.

[D]

★★ **BABETTE'S CAFE.** *471 N Highland Ave NE (30307), 3½ mi E on Freedom Pkwy, Exit 96, S on N Highland Ave, E of Downtown. 404/523-9121. www.babettescafe.com.* Specializes in cassoulet, artichoke ravioli, steamed mussels with strawberries and serrano peppers. Hrs: 6-10 pm; Fri, Sat to 11 pm; Sun 5-9 pm; Sun brunch 10:30 am-2 pm. Closed Mon; hols. Bar. Dinner $10.25-$18.50. Sun brunch $5.25-$8.50. Child's menu. Romantic dining. Cr cds: A, D, DS, MC, V.

[D]

★★★★ **BACCHANALIA.** *1198 Howell Mill Rd, Suite 100 (30318), in Buckhead. 404/365-0410.* Formerly housed in a Buckhead cottage, this restaurant is now an unexpected gem tucked into a 1920s meatpacking plant in West Midtown. The change in location has added an air of exciting adventure to Clifford Harrison and Anne Quatrano's New-American dining room. From the scents of the cook's-market-entrance, to the soaring, industrial-chic decor with Midtown-skyline views, everything is stunning. Specializes in seafood, game. Own baking. Hrs: 11:30 am-1:30 pm, 6-10 pm. Closed Sun, Mon; hols. Res accepted. Wine list. Lunch prix fixe: $35; dinner prix fixe: $50. Parking. Cr cds: A, DS, MC, V.

[D] [SC]

★★ **BASIL'S MEDITERRANNEAN CAFE.** *2985 Grandview Ave (30305), in Buckhead. 404/233-9755. www.basilsmediterranneancafe.com.* Kosher menu. Hrs: noon-3 pm, 6-10 pm; Sun, Mon from 6 pm; Fri to 11 pm; Sat 6-11 pm. Closed hols. Res accepted. Bar. Lunch a la carte entrees: $4.50-$8.25; dinner a la carte entrees: $8.25-$13.95. Entertainment: piano bar. Valet parking. Cr cds: A, D, DS, MC, V.

[D]

★★ **BLUE RIDGE GRILL.** *1261 W Paces Ferry Rd (30327), in Buckhead. 404/233-5030.* Specializes in fresh seafood, duck, grilled vegetables.

Own baking. Hrs: 11:30 am-2:30 pm, 5:30-10 pm; Fri to 11 pm; Sat 5:30-11 pm; Sun brunch to 2:30 pm. Closed hols. Res accepted. Bar. Lunch $9.95-$16.95; dinner $16-$29. Sun brunch $9-$16. Adirondack mountain lodge. Cr cds: A, D, DS, MC, V.

[D] [≡]

★★★★ **BONE'S.** *3130 Piedmont Rd NE (30305), in Buckhead. 404/237-2663.* Specializes in aged prime beef, seafood, live Maine lobster. Own desserts. Hrs: 11:30 am-2:30 pm, 5:30-10:30 pm; Fri to 11 pm; Sat, Sun 5:30-11 pm. Closed hols. Res accepted. Bar. Wine cellar. Lunch $8.95-$16.95; dinner $21.95-$36. Valet parking. Atlanta's premier steakhouse. Club atmosphere; wood paneling, fireplace. Cr cds: A, D, DS, MC, V.

[D] [≡]

★★★ **BRASSERIE LE COZE.** *3393 Peachtree Rd (30326), in Lenox Sq Mall, in Buckhead. 404/266-1440. Email blca@aol.com.* Specializes in mussels, coq au vin, desserts. Hrs: 11:30 am-2:30 pm, 5:30-11 pm; Sat 11:30 am-3:30 pm, 5:30-11 pm. Closed Sun; Thanksgiving, Dec 25. Res accepted. Bar. Wine list. Lunch $7.50-$16; dinner $13-$22. Stylish decor. Cr cds: A, DS, MC, V.

[D] [≡]

★★ **BUCKHEAD DINER.** *3073 Piedmont Rd (30305), in Buckhead. 404/262-3336. www.buckheadrestaurants.com.* Specializes in sauteed grouper, veal and wild mushroom meat loaf, white chocolate banana cream pie. Hrs: 11 am-midnight; Sun 10 am-10 pm. Closed Thanksgiving, Dec 25. Bar. Lunch $5.95-$14.95; dinner $5.95-$15.95. Valet parking. Update of classic, stainless steel-wrapped diner. Cr cds: A, D, DS, MC, V.

[D] [≡]

★★ **THE CABIN.** *2678 Buford Hwy NE (30324), in Buckhead. 404/315-7676.* Specializes in steak, seafood. Hrs: 11:30 am-2:30 pm, 5:30-10 pm; Fri to 11 pm; Sat 5:30-11 pm. Closed Sun; hols. Res accepted. Bar. Lunch $4.95-$9.95; dinner $16.95-$28.95. Child's menu. Valet parking (dinner). Log cabin built in 1931. Cr cds: A, D, DS, MC, V.

[D] [≡]

★★★ **THE CAFE.** *3434 Peachtree Rd NE.* 404/237-2700. Specializes in French bistro cuisine. Own pastries. Hrs: 6:30 am-11:30 pm; Sun brunch to 2:30 pm. Bar. Bkfst a la carte entrees: $7-$15; lunch a la carte entrees: $10-$22; dinner a la carte entrees: $20-$30. Sun brunch $38. Child's menu. Entertainment: pianist. Valet parking. Antiques, original art. Cr cds: A, D, DS, MC, V.
D

★★ **CAFE TU TU TANGO.** *220 Pharr Rd (30305), in Buckhead.* 404/841-6222. *www.cafetututango.com.* Specializes in Cajun chicken egg rolls, Barcelona stir-fry, Hurricane shrimp. Hrs: 11:30 am-11 pm; Wed to midnight; Thurs to 1 am; Fri, Sat to 2 am. Bar. Lunch, dinner a la carte entrees: $3.95-$7.95. Valet parking. Artist's studio decor; painters at work. Cr cds: A, DS, MC, V.
D

★★ **CAMEAUX LOUISIANA.** *9925 Haynes Bridge Rd (30022), 25 mi N on GA 400, Exit 9.* 770/442-2524. Specializes in boiled crawfish, crab cakes, crawfish etouffee. Hrs: 11:30 am-10 pm; Fri, Sat to 11 pm. Closed Jan 1, Dec 25. Res accepted. Bar. Lunch $3.95-$9.95; dinner $8.95-$21.95. Child's menu. Entertainment: jazz, blues Tues, Thurs-Sat. Cajun ambience. Cr cds: A, D, DS, MC, V.
D

★ **CAMILLE'S.** *1186 N Highland Ave (30306), in Midtown/Piedmont Park.* 404/872-7203. *www.sangennaro.com.* Specializes in calamari, linguini with clams, rice balls. Hrs: 5:30-10:30 pm. Bar. Dinner $10.25-$14.95. Parking. Cr cds: A, MC, V.
D

★★★★ **CANOE.** *4199 Paces Ferry Rd NW (30339), N of Downtown.* 770/432-2663. *Email canoe@bellsouth.net; www.canoe/atl.com.* Specializes in slow-roasted Carolina rabbit with Swiss chard-country bacon ravioli and balsamic glaze, grilled tuna steak and potatoes with roasted pearl onions and sherry vinegar, oak-roasted venison with spiced pumpkin puree and apple chestnut compote. Menu changes seasonally. Hrs: 11:30 am-2:30 pm, 5:30-10 pm; Fri to 11 pm; Sat 5:30-11:30 pm; Sun 5:30-9 pm; Sun brunch 10:30 am-2:30 pm. Closed Jan 1, Thanksgiving, Dec 25. Res accepted. Bar. Wine list. Lunch $7.95-$13.95; dinner $12.95-$19.95. Sun brunch $7.95-$13.50. Valet parking. Situated on Chattahoochee River. Landscaped grounds enhance outdoor dining experience. Cr cds: A, D, DS, MC, V.
D

★★★ **CARBO'S CAFE.** *3717 Roswell Rd (30342), in Buckhead.* 404/231-4433. *www.carbos-cafe.com.* Specializes in seafood, veal, steak. Own baking. Hrs: 5:30-10 pm. Closed Sun; hols. Res accepted. Bar. Wine cellar. Dinner complete meals: $18.95-$29.95. Entertainment: piano bar. Valet parking. European decor; antiques, fireplaces, fountain. Cr cds: A, DS, MC, V.
D

★★★ **CASSIS.** *3300 Peachtree Rd.* 404/365-8100. Specializes in grilled meats, fish, bistro items. Hrs: 6:30 am-2:30 pm. Res accepted. Bar. Wine list. Bkfst a la carte entrees: $8.25-$16. Buffet: $13; lunch a la carte entrees: $8.50-$19. Sun brunch $24.95. Child's menu. Valet parking. View of waterfall, gardens. Cr cds: A, D, DS, MC, V.
D

★★★ **CHOPS.** *70 W Paces Ferry Rd (30305), in Buckhead.* 404/262-2675. *www.buckheadrestaurants.com.* Specializes in steak, lobster, fresh seafood. Own pastries. Hrs: 11:30 am-2:30 pm, 5:30-11 pm; Fri to midnight; Sat 5:30 pm-midnight; Sun 5:30-10 pm. Closed hols. Res accepted. Bar. Lunch a la carte entrees: $7.95-$15.95; dinner a la carte entrees: $14.75-$34.50. Valet parking. Art Deco motif. Cr cds: A, D, DS, MC, V.
D

★★ **CIRCLE SUSHI.** *8725 Roswell Rd (30350), N of Downtown.* 770/998-7880. Specializes in teriyaki, sushi. Hrs: noon-2:30 pm, 5:30-10 pm; Sat, Sun from 5:30 pm. Closed Memorial Day, Thanksgiving, Dec 25. Res accepted. Wine, beer. Lunch $5.50-$20; dinner $15-$30. Parking. Cr cds: A, D, DS, MC, V.
D

★★★ **CITY GRILL.** *50 Hurt Plz (30303), in the Hurt Bldg, Ste 200,*

Downtown. 404/524-2489. Specializes in blue crab cakes with lemon linguine, mustard-crusted aged New York strip, chocolate pecan souffle. Own pastries. Hrs: 11:30 am-2 pm, 6-10 pm; Sat from 6 pm. Closed Sun; hols. Res accepted. Bar. Wine cellar. Lunch a la carte entrees: $7-$15; dinner a la carte entrees: $17-$29. Valet parking (dinner). Rotunda entrance; bronze chandeliers, marble columns, wall murals. Cr cds: A, D, DS, MC, V.

★ **THE COLONNADE.** *1879 Cheshire Bridge Rd (30324), in Buckhead. 404/874-5642.* Specializes in fried chicken, turkey, seafood. Hrs: 11 am-2:30 pm, 5-9 pm; Fri, Sat to 10 pm; Sun 11 am-9 pm. Closed Dec 24-25. Bar. Lunch $4.50-$14; dinner $5.95-$16. Parking. Casual dining. Family-owned. No cr cds accepted.

★★★ **COOHILL'S.** *1100 Peachtree St NE (30309), in Midtown/Piedmont Park. 404/724-0901. www.coohill.com.* Specializes in chops, prime beef, seafood. Hrs: 11:30 am-2 pm, 5:30-10 pm; Sat 5:30-11 pm. Closed Sun; hols. Res accepted. Bar. Wine list. Lunch $8.95-$15.95; dinner $17.95-$28.95. Entertainment: pianist Thurs-Sat. Parking. Southern steak house. Modern decor. Cr cds: A, D, DS, MC, V.

★★★ **COUNTRY PLACE.** *1197 Peachtree St NE (30361), Colony Square Complex, in Midtown/Piedmont Park. 404/881-0144. www.peasantsrestarants. com.* Hrs: 11 am-2:30 pm, 5:30-10 pm; Sat from 5:30 pm; Sun 5:30-9 pm. Closed Thanksgiving, Dec 25. Res accepted. Bar. Lunch $8.49-$16.49; dinner $14.99-$23.99. Entertainment: pianist Thurs-Sat. Parking. Cr cds: A, D, DS, MC, V.

★★ **DAILEY'S.** *17 International Blvd (30303), Downtown. 404/681-3303.* Specializes in pepper-crusted swordfish, desserts. Hrs: 11 am-2:30 pm, 5:30-11 pm; Fri to midnight; Sat 5:30-midnight; Sun from 5:30 pm. Closed hols. Res accepted. Bar. Lunch $4.95-$12.95; dinner $17-$29. Entertainment: jazz trio; pianist. Con-

verted warehouse; vaulted ceiling. Cr cds: A, D, DS, MC, V.

★★ **DANTE'S DOWN THE HATCH.** *3380 Peachtree Rd NE (30326), across from Lenox Sq, in Buckhead. 404/266-1600. www.dantes downthehatch.com.* Specializes in mixed fondue dinners. Own desserts. Hrs: 4-11:30 pm; Fri, Sat to 12:30 am; Sun 5-11 pm. Closed Jan 1, Dec 25. Res accepted. Bar. Dinner $13-$27. Entertainment: classical guitarist; jazz trio. Parking. Nautical decor. Antique English, Polish ship figureheads. Shipboard dining within multilevel vessel. Family-owned. Menu translated in 51 languages. Cr cds: A, D, DS, MC, V.

★★★★★ **THE DINING ROOM.** *3434 Peachtree Rd NE. 404/237-2700. www.ritzcarlton.com.* French chef Joel Antunes, who succeeded chef Guenter Seeger's 11-year tenure, has brought a fresh, younger feel to this stoic, Ritz-Carlton dining room with his daily changing, market-driven menu and a kitchen redesign allowing chefs a view of the dining room. The menu, offered as a five-course tasting paired with wines or a la carte, is modern-French-Mediterranean cuisine with slight Asian accents. Specializes in rice paper Napoleon of raspberries, peach tart with lemon verbena ice cream. Hrs: 6 pm-midnight. Closed Sun; hols. Res accepted. Bar. Wine cellar. Dinner prix fixe: $65-$112. Valet parking. Jacket. Cr cds: A, D, DS, MC, V.

★★ **DISH.** *870 N Highland Ave NE (30306), E of Downtown. 404/897-3463.* Specializes in grilled prosciutto-wrapped pork filet with carmelized onion relish and potato fluff, creamy wild mushroom risotto. Hrs: 5:30-10 pm; Fri, Sat to 11 pm. Closed hols. Res accepted. Bar. Dinner $11-$19. Former filling station (1939). Cr cds: A, DS, MC, V.

★ **DUSTY'S BARBECUE.** *1815 Briarcliff Rd NE (30329), E of Downtown. 404/320-6264. www.dustys.com.* Specializes in chicken, beef, baby back ribs. Hrs: 11 am-9:30 pm; Fri, Sat to 10:30 pm. Closed Jan 1, Thanksgiving, Dec 25. Lunch, dinner $3.70-$12.25. Child's menu. Parking. Casual dining. Cr cds: A, D, DS, MC, V.

[D] [symbol]

★★ **ECLIPSE DI LUNA.** *764 Miami Cir (30324), 5 mi NW of Piedmont, in Buckhead.* 404/846-0449. Specializes in tapas. Hrs: 11:30 am-2:30 pm, 5-10 pm; Fri, Sat to 11 pm; Sun from 6 pm. Closed hols. Res accepted. Bar. Lunch, dinner $6-$8. Entertainment: band Fri, Sat. Parking. Eclectic decor. Cr cds: A, D, DS, MC, V.

[D]

★★ **EMBERS SEAFOOD GRILLE.** *234 Hilderbrand Dr (30328), N on GA 9.* 404/256-0977. Specializes in seafood, steak. Hrs: 6-10 pm; Fri, Sat to 10:30 pm. Closed Sun. Res accepted. Bar. Dinner $11.95-$19.95. Child's menu. Parking. Modern wall hangings. Cr cds: A, D, DS, MC, V.

[D] [symbol]

★★ **ENCORE AT THE FOX.** *654 Peachtree St (30308), in Fox Bldg, in Midtown/Piedmont Park.* 404/881-0223. Specializes in grilled filet of beef, crispy sweet-and-sour calamari, roasted Chilean sea bass. Hrs: 11:15 am-2 pm. Closed Sat, Sun; Jan 1, Dec 25. Res accepted. Bar. Lunch $6-$10. Cr cds: A, D, DS, MC, V.

[D] [symbol]

★ **FIESTA GRILL.** *240 Peachtree St (30303), lobby level of Merchandise Mart, Downtown.* 404/524-9224. Specializes in camarones diablo, fajitas. Hrs: 11 am-11 pm; Sat from noon; Sun 5-10 pm. Closed Thanksgiving, Dec 25. Bar. Lunch $5.95-$7.95; dinner $6.49-$14.99. Child's menu. Southwestern decor. Cr cds: A, D, DS, MC, V.

[D] [symbol]

★★ **FOOD STUDIO.** *887 W Marietta St, Studio K 102 (30318), N of Downtown.* 404/815-6677. *www.the foodstudio.com.* Specializes in ahi tuna tartare, apricot-honey glazed duck, pecan-encrusted halibut. Hrs: 11:30 am-2:30 pm, 5:30-11 pm; Fri to midnight; Sat 5:30 pm-midnight. Closed hols. Res accepted. Bar. Lunch $7.95-$12.95; dinner $15.95-$25.95. Valet parking. Contemporary decor in

refurbished 1904 plow factory bldg. Cr cds: A, DS, MC, V.

[D]

★★ **FRATELLI DI NAPOLI.** *2101-B Bennett St (30309), in Buckhead.* 404/351-1533. *www.fratelli.net.* Specializes in pasta, veal. Hrs: 5-11 pm; Fri, Sat to midnight. Closed Thanksgiving, Dec 25. Bar. Dinner $12-$18. Valet parking. Italian decor. Cr cds: A, D, DS, MC, V.

[D] [symbol]

★ **GEORGIA GRILLE.** *2290 Peachtree Rd (30309), in Buckhead.* 404/352-3517. *www.menus.atlanta. com.* Specializes in pork, chicken, seafood. Hrs: 6-10 pm; Fri, Sat to 11 pm; Sun to 9 pm. Closed Dec 25, Thanksgiving. Bar. Dinner $5.95-$19.95. Parking. Southwestern decor. Cr cds: A, MC, V.

[D] [symbol]

★★★ **HARVEST RESTAURANT.** *853 N Highland Ave NE (30306), 5 mi NE on Ponce De Leon to N Highland Ave, E of Downtown.* 404/876-8244. Specializes in seared Chilean sea bass, chicken with honey pecan sauce, chili-rubbed pork tenderloin. Hrs: 11:30 am-2:30 pm, 5:30-10 pm; Fri to 11 pm; Sat 5:30-11 pm; Sun brunch 11 am-2:30 pm. Closed Labor Day, Thanksgiving, Dec 25. Bar. Lunch, dinner $10.95-$17.95. Sun brunch $6.95-$10.95. Valet parking. Paintings, antiques; 3 fireplaces. Cr cds: A, MC, V.

[D]

★★ **HAVELI.** *225 Spring St (30303), in Gift Mart, Downtown.* 404/522-4545. Specializes in chicken tikka, daal maharani, baingan bharta. Hrs: 11:30 am-2:30 pm, 5:30-10 pm; Sun from 5:30 pm. Closed Dec 25. Res accepted. Bar. Lunch buffet: $6.95; dinner a la carte entrees: $11.95-$15.95. Parking. Indian decor. Cr cds: A, D, DS, MC, V.

[D] [symbol]

★★ **HORSERADISH GRILL.** *4320 Powers Ferry Rd (30342), N of Downtown.* 404/255-7277. *www.horseradish grill.com.* Specializes in skillet-fried chicken, grilled prime veal chops, lemon chess pie. Hrs: 11:30 am-2:30 pm, 5:30-10 pm; Fri to 11 pm; Sat 5-11 pm; Sun to 9 pm. Closed Jan 1, Thanksgiving, Dec 25. Bar. Lunch

$6.95-$15.95; dinner $15.95-$24.95. Child's menu. Parking. Modern art, stone fireplace; herb garden area with stone walk. Cr cds: A, D, DS, MC, V.

D

★★★ **HSU'S GOURMET CHINESE.** *192 Peachtree Center Ave (30303), Downtown. 404/659-2788. www. hsus.com.* Specializes in Peking Duck, asparagus shrimp in black bean sauce, steamed salmon with ginger sauce. Hrs: 11:30 am-10:30 pm; Sun from 5 pm. Closed July 4, Thanksgiving, Dec 25. Res accepted. Bar. Wine list. Lunch a la carte entrees: $5.95-$13.95; dinner a la carte entrees: $10.95-$18.95. Validated parking (dinner). Chinese decor. Cr cds: A, D, DS, MC, V.

D ⊷

★★★ **IMPERIAL FEZ.** *2285 Peachtree Rd NE (30309), in Buckhead. 404/351-0870. www.imperialfez.com.* Specializes in lamb couscous, shish kebab, fish tagine. Hrs: 6-11:30 pm. Res accepted. Dinner a la carte entrees: $14-$25. Complete meals: $35-$50. Child's menu. Entertainment: Moroccan dancers. Valet parking. Tented ceilings; low tables with silk cushioned seating. Cr cds: A, D, DS, MC, V.

D ⊷

★ **INDIGO COASTAL GRILL.** *1397 N Highland Ave (30306), in Midtown/ Piedmont Park. 404/876-0676. www. indigocoastalgrill.com.* Specializes in seafood, organically grown vegetables, Key lime pie. Hrs: 5:30-10 pm; Fri, Sat to 11 pm; Sun brunch 11 am-2:30 pm. Closed July 4, Thanksgiving, Dec 25. Res accepted. Bar. Dinner $12.75-$18.95. Sun brunch $6.95-$10.95. Nautical decor; aquarium. Vintage 1950s jukebox. Cr cds: A, D, MC, V.

D ⊷

★★ **JIM WHITE'S HALF SHELL.** *2349 Peachtree Rd NE (30305), in Peachtree Battle Shopping Center, in Buckhead. 404/237-9924. www.jim whiteshalfshell.citysearch.com.* Specializes in seafood. Hrs: 5-10 pm; Fri, Sat to 11 pm. Closed Sun; hols. Bar. Dinner $15.95-$29. Child's menu. Parking. Nautical decor. Family-owned. Cr cds: A, D, DS, MC, V.

★★★ **LA GROTTA.** *2637 Peachtree Rd NE (30305), in Buckhead. 404/231-1368. www.la-grotta.com.* Specializes in veal, seafood, steak. Own pasta, sauces, desserts. Hrs: 6-10:30 pm. Closed Sun; hols; last wk June-1st wk July. Res accepted. Bar. Wine list. Dinner $15-$25.50. Valet parking. Jacket. Cr cds: A, D, DS, MC, V.

D

★★★ **LA GROTTA RAVINIA.** *4355 Ashford Dunwoody Rd. 770/395-9925. www.menus.atlanta.com/home/lagrotta. html.* Specializes in grilled veal chops, portabello mushrooms, fettucine with shrimp and scallops. Hrs: 11:30 am-2 pm, 5:45-10 pm; Sat from 5:45 pm. Closed Sun; hols. Res accepted. Wine list. Lunch a la carte entrees: $7.95-$13.95; dinner a la carte entrees: $12.95-$22.95. Valet parking. Windows overlook gardens, patio. Cr cds: A, D, DS, MC, V.

D

★★ **LA PAZ RESTAURANTE-CANTINA.** *6410 Roswell Rd (30328), in Sandy Springs, N of Downtown. 404/256-3555. www.lapaz.com.* Specializes in Mexican cuisine. Hrs: 11:30 am-2:30 pm, 5-10 pm; Fri to 11 pm; Sat 5-11 pm, Sun 5-10 pm. Bar. Dinner a la carte entrees: $3.99-$13.99. Child's menu. Parking. Cr cds: A, D, DS, MC, V.

D ⊷

★★★ **LE ST. AMOUR.** *1620 Piedmont Ave NE (30324), in Midtown/Piedmont Park. 404/881-0300.* Specializes in duck confit with truffles and sauteed potatoes, boneless rabbit stuffed with baked garlic and figs, trilogie de poisson. Hrs: 11 am-2:30 pm, 6-10:30 pm; Sat from 6 pm. Closed Sun. Res accepted; required Fri, Sat. Bar. Wine cellar. Lunch a la carte entrees: $6-$17; dinner a la carte entrees: $19-$22. Sun brunch $7-$17. Valet parking. In antique home. French countryside motif; contemporary French atmosphere. Cr cds: A, DS, MC, V.

D ⊷

★★ **LOMBARDI'S.** *94 Upper Pryor St (30303), Downtown. 404/522-6568.* Specializes in pasta, pizza, veal. Hrs: 11 am-9 pm; Sat 5-11 pm. Closed

Sun; hols. Res accepted. Bar. Lunch a la carte entrees: $8.50-$12.95; dinner a la carte entrees: $9.95-$16.95. Parking. Cr cds: A, DS, MC, V.

D ▭

★★ **LUNA SI.** *1931 Peachtree Rd (30309), in Brookwood Village Shopping Center, in Buckhead.* 404/355-5993. Specializes in beef, seafood, game. Menu changes monthly. Hrs: 5:30-10 pm; Fri, Sat to 11 pm. Closed Sun; July 4, Thanksgiving, Dec 25. Res required. Bar. Dinner $12-$21. Cr cds: A, D, DS, MC, V.

D

★★★ **MACARTHUR'S.** *2171 Peachtree Rd (30309), in Buckhead.* 404/352-3400. *www.macarthurs.com.* Specializes in prime rib MacArthur's style, pecan-crusted grouper, boneless rainbow trout. Hrs: 4-11 pm; Sun to 10 pm; Sun brunch 11 am-3 pm. Closed Thanksgiving, Dec 25. Res accepted. Bar. Wine list. Dinner a la carte entrees: $8.95-$19.95. Sun brunch $4.95-$18.95. Valet parking. Cr cds: A, D, DS, MC, V.

D ▭

★★ **MAGGIANO'S LITTLE ITALY.** *3368 Peachtree Rd NE (30326), 8 mi N on Peachtree Rd, in Buckhead.* 404/816-9650. *www.maggianos.net.* Specializes in calamari fritte, mostaccioli eggplant marinara, New York steak Contadina-style. Hrs: 11:30 am-10 pm; Fri, Sat to 11 pm. Closed Thanksgiving, Dec 25. Res accepted. Bar. Lunch a la carte entrees: $3.95-$16.95; dinner a la carte entrees: $5.95-$29.95. Valet parking. Cr cds: A, C, D, DS, MC, V.

D

★★★ **THE MANSION.** *179 Ponce De Leon Ave (30308), in Midtown/Piedmont Park.* 404/876-0727. Specializes in fresh seafood, aged beef, lamb. Own baking. Hrs: 11 am-2 pm, 6-11 pm. Closed Sun; Dec 25. Res accepted. Bar. Wine list. Lunch $7-$16; dinner $18-$26. Parking. Shingle-style Victorian mansion (1885); garden, gazebo. Cr cds: A, D, DS, MC, V.

D

★ **MARY MAC'S TEAROOM.** *224 Ponce De Leon Ave (30308), in Midtown/Piedmont Park.* 404/876-1800. *www.marymacs.com.* Specializes in baked and fried chicken, fresh vegetables. Own desserts. Hrs: 11 am-8:30 pm; Sun to 3 pm. Closed hols. Lunch, dinner complete meals: $6-$10. Child's menu. Entertainment: pianist. Parking. Informal neighborhood cafe. Family-owned. Cr cds: A.

★★★ **MCKENDRICK'S.** *4505 Ashford Dunwoody Ave (30346), 10 mi NE on I-285, Exit 21, N of Downtown.* 770/512-8888. *www.mckendricks.com.* Specializes in cold water lobster tail, porterhouse steak, prime-aged beef. Hrs: 11:30 am-2:30 pm, 5:30-10 pm; Fri to 11 pm; Sat 5:30-11 pm; Sun from 5:30 pm. Closed hols. Res accepted. Bar. Lunch $6.95-$14.95; dinner $15.95-$49. Valet parking. Globe lighting. Cr cds: A, D, DS, MC, V.

D ▭

★★ **MCKINNON'S LOUISIANE.** *3209 Maple Dr (30305), in Buckhead.* 404/237-1313. *www.mckinnons.com.* Specializes in fresh seafood. Hrs: 6-10 pm. Closed Sun; hols. Res accepted. Bar. Dinner $13.95-$18.95. Entertainment: pianist (wkends). Parking. Country French decor. Family-owned. Cr cds: D, DS, MC, V.

D

★ **MICK'S UNDERGROUND.** *75 Upper Alabama St (30303), Downtown.* 404/525-2825. Specializes in hamburgers, chicken, pasta. Own desserts. Hrs: 11 am-10 pm; Fri, Sat to 11 pm; Sun noon-7 pm. Bar. Lunch, dinner $3.50-$13.95. Child's menu. Cr cds: A, D, DS, MC, V.

D ▭

★★★ **MI SPIA.** *4505 Ashford Dunwoody Rd (30346), in Park Place Shopping Center, N of Downtown.* 770/393-1333. *www.mispia.com.* Specializes in honey-glazed salmon, grain mustard marinated pork chops, saffron fettuccine. Hrs: 11:30 am-2:30 pm, 5-10 pm; Fri to 11 pm; Sat 5-11 pm; Sun from 5 pm. Closed hols. Res accepted. Bar. Lunch $7.95-$10.95; dinner $11.95-$21.95. Contemporary decor. Cr cds: A, D, DS, MC, V.

D

★★ **MUMBO JUMBO.** *89 Park Pl NE (30303), Downtown.* 404/523-0330. *www.mumbojumbo-atl.com.* Specializes in mumbo jumbo gumbo, beef tenderloin. Hrs: 11:30 am-2:30 pm,

5:30-11 pm; Sat, Sun from 5:30 pm.
Closed hols. Res accepted. Bar. Lunch
$6.95-$14.95; dinner $7.95-$28.50.
Valet parking (dinner). Spanish
decor. Cr cds: A, D, DS, MC, V.
D

★★★ **NAKATO JAPANESE.** *1776
Chershire Bridge Rd NE (30324), in
Buckhead.* 404/873-6582. Specializes
in sushi, teppan. Hrs: 5:30-10 pm;
Fri, Sat to 11 pm; Sun 5-10 pm. Res
accepted. Bar. Dinner $11-$35.
Child's menu. Valet parking. Japan-
ese garden. Cr cds: A, D, DS, MC, V.
D ⊠

★★★ **NAVA.** *3060 Peachtree Rd
(30305), in Buckhead.* 404/240-1984.
www.buckheadrestaurants.com. Specializes in red chile-seared giant scallops,
wood-roasted pork tenderloin, sun
corn-crusted snapper. Hrs: 11:30 am-
2:30 pm, 5:30-11 pm; Fri to midnight; Sat 5 pm-midnight; Sun
5:30-10 pm. Closed hols. Res
accepted. Bar. Wine cellar. Lunch
$7.25-$15.50; dinner $14.50-$28.95.
Valet parking. Genuine New Mexican
plaster, sculpture, and artwork. Cr
cds: A, D, DS, MC, V.
D

★★ **NICKIEMOTO'S.** *990 Piedmont
Ave (30309), in Midtown/Piedmont
Park.* 404/253-2010. Specializes in
sushi, fish, noodle dishes. Hrs: 11:30
am-11 pm; Sat noon-midnight; Sun
from noon. Closed Dec 25. Bar. Wine
list. Lunch, dinner $4-$16.95. Parking. Cr cds: A, D, DS, MC, V.
D ⊠

★★★ **NIKOLAI'S ROOF.** *255
Courtland St NE.* 404/221-6362. *www.
hilton.com.* Specializes in turbot á la
vapeur sur un lit de chanterelles, la
coupe royale de gibier aux airelles et
poivres, piroshkis. Own baking. Menu
recited. Hrs: Sittings: 6 pm, 9 pm. Res
accepted. Wine list. Dinner prix fixe:
6-course $67.50. Valet parking. Jacket.
Elegant decor; views from 30th floor.
Cr cds: A, C, D, DS, MC, V.
D

★ **NINO'S ITALIAN RESTAURANT.**
*1931 Cheshire Bridge Rd (30324), in
Buckhead.* 404/874-6505. Specializes
in veal, pasta. Hrs: 5:30-11 pm.
Closed Jan 1, July 4, Dec 25. Res
accepted. Bar. Dinner $8.95-$20.95.

Parking. Oil paintings, Italian sculpture. Cr cds: A, D, DS, MC, V.
⊠

★ **OK CAFE.** *1284 W Paces Ferry Rd
(30327), in Buckhead.* 404/233-2888.
Hrs: 6 am-midnight; Fri to 3 am; Sat
7-3 am; Sun from 7 am. Closed hols.
Wine, beer. Bkfst $5-$8; lunch $4-
$10; dinner $4.95-$12. Parking.
Diner atmosphere. Cr cds: A, D, DS,
MC, V.
D

★★★ **PANO'S & PAUL'S.** *1232 W
Paces Ferry Rd (30327), in Buckhead.*
404/261-3662. *www.buckhead
restaurants.com.* Specializes in cold
water lobster tail, broiled prime veal
sirloin steak, flourless chocolate
melt cake in chocolate soup. Own
baking. Hrs: 6-10 pm; Fri to 11 pm;
Sat 5:30-11 pm. Closed Sun; hols.
Res accepted. Bar. Wine cellar. Dinner a la carte entrees: $17.50-
$37.50. Entertainment: pianist Fri,
Sat. Parking. Chef-owned. Cr cds: A,
C, D, DS, MC, V.
D

★★★★ **PARK 75 AT THE FOUR
SEASONS.** *75 14th St.* 404/881-
9898. This lovely, flower-filled
restaurant is proof of this luxury
hotel chain's commitment to excellent dining. Chef Brooke Vosika's
rich, New-American cuisine highlighted with southern flavors is presented with consistent and attentive
service. The gardenlike dining room
terrace, with its canopy of ficus trees,
overlooks a breathtaking, three-story
atrium-lobby, and the adjacent
lounge is a perfect place for lighter
fare and cocktails. Specializes in rack
of lamb, foie gras and smoked duck
fricasse, spicy carrots consomme.
Hrs: 6:30 am-10:30 pm; Sun brunch
11 am-2 pm. Res accepted. Bar. Wine
list. Bkfst a la carte entrees: $5-$9;
lunch a la carte entrees: $15-$23;
dinner a la carte entrees: $17-$27.
Entertainment: pianist. Cr cds: D,
DS, MC, V.
D

★★★ **PETITE AUBERGE.** *2935 N
Druid Hill Rd (30329), Toco Hills Center, E of Downtown.* 404/634-6268.
Specializes in beef Wellington, rack
of lamb, bouillabaisse maison. Hrs:
11:30 am-2:30 pm, 6-10 pm; Sat

from 6 pm. Closed Sun; hols. Res accepted. Bar. Wine list. Lunch $5.95-$11.95; dinner $12.50-$19.95. European decor. Family-owned. Cr cds: D, DS, MC, V.

★★ **PITTYPAT'S PORCH.** *25 International Blvd (30303), Downtown.* *404/525-8228.* Specializes in fresh coastal fish, Savannah crab cakes, coastal venison pie. Salad bar. Own desserts. Hrs: 5-9 pm. Closed Labor Day, Dec 25; July 4 wk; also 1 wk in Dec. Res accepted. Bar. Dinner $17.95-$23.95. Child's menu. Entertainment: pianist. Parking. Collection of rocking chairs in lounge. Cr cds: A, D, DS, MC, V.

World of Coca-Cola Pavillion

★★ **PLEASANT PEASANT.** *555 Peachtree St (30308), in Midtown/Piedmont Park. 404/874-3223.* Specializes in lobster sliders, pecan-crusted salmon, seasonal herb chicken. Hrs: 11:30 am-2:30 pm, 5:30-9:30 pm; Sat, Sun 5:30 pm-10:30 pm. Closed Thanksgiving, Dec 25. Res accepted. Bar. Lunch $6.95-$10.95; dinner $11.95-$20.95. Parking. New York-style bistro. Cr cds: A, D, DS, MC, V.

★★★ **PRICCI.** *500 Pharr Rd (30305), in Buckhead. 404/237-2941. www.buckheadrestaurants.com.* Own breads. Hrs: 11 am-11 pm; Fri to midnight; Sat 5 pm-midnight; Sun from 5 pm. Closed hols. Res accepted. Bar. Lunch $7.50-$12.95;

dinner $14-$23. Valet parking. Cr cds: A, D, DS, MC, V.

★★★ **PRIME.** *3393 Peachtree Rd NE (30326), in Buckhead. 404/812-0555. www.prime-restaurants.com.* Specializes in steak, seafood, sushi. Hrs: 11:30 am-2:30 pm, 5-10 pm; Fri, Sat to 11 pm; Sun from 4 pm. Closed hols. Res accepted. Bar. Lunch a la carte entrees: $8.95-$14; dinner a la carte entrees: $14.95-$32.50. Entertainment: pianist, saxophonist Fri, Sat. Valet parking. Japanese-American atmosphere. Cr cds: A, D, DS, MC, V.

★★ **RAY'S ON THE RIVER.** *6700 Powers Ferry Rd (30339), I-285, Exit 15; N of Downtown. 770/955-1187. www.raysontheriver.com.* Specializes in hickory-grilled seafood, steaks. Hrs: 11:30 am-2:30 pm, 5-10 pm; Fri to 12:30 am; Sat 5 pm-12:30 am; Sun 9:30 am-3 pm, 5-10 pm. Closed Dec 25. Bar. Lunch $3.95-$11.95; dinner $14.95-$21.95. Sun brunch $17.95. Child's menu. Entertainment: jazz Tues-Sat. Valet parking wkends. View of Chattahoochee River. Cr cds: A, D, DS, MC, V.

★★ **ROCK BOTTOM.** *3242 Peachtree Rd (30305), in Buckhead. 404/264-0253. www.brewfood.com.* Specializes in wood-fired pizza, honey chicken sandwich. Hrs: 11:30 am-11 pm; Fri, Sat to midnight. Closed Thanksgiving, Dec 25. Bar. Lunch, dinner $4.95-$16.95. Child's menu. Valet parking. Brewery; pool tables. Cr cds: A, D, DS, MC, V.

★★★ **RUTH'S CHRIS STEAK HOUSE.** *5788 Roswell Rd (30328), in Sandy Springs, N of Downtown. 404/255-0035. www.ruthschrisandysprings.com.* Specializes in prime beef, fresh seafood. Hrs: 5-11 pm; Sun to 10 pm. Closed July 4, Dec 25. Res accepted. Bar. Wine list. Dinner a la carte entrees: $16.95-$29.95. Valet parking. Cr cds: A, D, DS, MC, V.

D

★★★★ **SEEGER'S.** *111 W Paces Ferry Rd (30305), in Buckhead. 404/846-9779. www.seegers.com.* Chef/owner Guenter Seeger, formerly of The Ritz-Carlton Buckhead, uses 36 years of culinary training to create cutting-edge, flawlessly prepared cuisine with bright flavors and impeccable ingredients. The dining room, reminiscent of Seeger's German heritage, mirrors his crisp, culinary philosophy. It is an expansive yet simple space with warm touches. Choose the five-course, prix fixe menu or the eight-course chef's tasting. Hrs: 6-10 pm. Closed Sun. Cr cds: DS, MC, V.

D 🖼

★ **SEOUL GARDEN.** *5938 Buford Hwy (30340), 8 mi NE on Buford Hwy. 770/452-0123.* Specializes in sushi, Korean and Japanese dishes. Hrs: 10:30 am-midnight. Res accepted. Lunch, dinner $5.95-$49.95. Parking. Cr cds: A, DS, MC, V.

D 🖼

★★ **SOHO CAFE.** *4200 Paces Ferry Rd, Ste 107 (30339), in Vinings Jubilee Shopping Center, N of Downtown. 770/801-0069. www.sohoatlanta. com.* Specializes in salmon wrapped in rice paper, shrimp relleno. Hrs: 11:30 am-2:30 pm, 5:30-10:30 pm; Fri to 11 pm; Sat 5:30-11 pm; Sun 5:30-9:30 pm. Closed hols. Bar. Wine list. Lunch $5-$15; dinner $10-$20. Entertainment: jazz Mon. Parking. Contemporary atmosphere. Cr cds: A, D, MC, V.

D

★★ **SOTO JAPANESE RESTAURANT.** *3330 Piedmont Rd (30305), in Buckhead. 404/233-2005.* Specializes in sushi. Hrs: 6-11:30 pm; Fri, Sat to 12:30 am. Closed Sun; hols. Res accepted. Dinner $25-$35. Parking. Cr cds: A, D, DS, MC, V.

D

★★ **SOUTH CITY KITCHEN.** *1144 Crescent Ave (30309), in Midtown/Piedmont Park. 404/873-7358. www.bold american.com.* Specializes in grilled barbecue swordfish, sauteed shrimp and scallops, old Charleston she-crab soup. Hrs: 11 am-3:30 pm, 5-11 pm;

Fri, Sat to midnight; Sun to 10 pm. Closed Memorial Day, Thanksgiving, Dec 25. Res accepted. Bar. Lunch $6.75-$13.50; dinner $10.75-$23.50. Sun brunch $7.75-$13.95. Parking. Contemporary decor. Cr cds: A, DS, MC, V.

★★ **SOUTH OF FRANCE.** *2345 Cheshire Bridge Rd (30324), in Buckhead. 404/325-6963. Email southof france@aol.com.* Specializes in bouillabaise a la Marseillaise, rack of lamb, duck with orange sauce. Hrs: 11 am-2 pm, 6-10 pm; Fri 11 am-2 pm, 5:30-11 pm; Sat 5:30-11 pm. Closed Sun; hols. Res accepted. Bar. Lunch a la carte entrees: $7.95-$12.95; dinner a la carte entrees: $12.95-$24.95. Entertainment: Wed-Sat. Parking. Country French decor. Cr cds: A, DS, MC, V.

D 🖼

★ **SUBURB-A-NIGHT PIZZA.** *1090 Alpharetta St (30075), approx 5 mi NW on Holcomb Bridge Rd (US 140). 770/594-8765.* Specializes in pizza, sandwiches, fresh pasta. Hrs: 5 pm-2 am; Sun to 10 pm. Closed Tues; hols. Bar. Dinner $4.95-$15.95. Parking. Converted house. Cr cds: MC, V.

🖼

★ **SUNDOWN CAFE.** *2165 Cheshire Bridge Rd (30324), in Buckhead. 404/321-1118.* Specializes in burritos, enchiladas, fajitas. Hrs: 11 am-2 pm, 5:30-10 pm; Fri to 11 pm; Sat 5:30-11 pm. Closed Sun; hols. Bar. Lunch $5.95-$9.95; dinner $8.95-$17.95. Parking. Southwestern decor. Cr cds: C, DS, MC, V.

D 🖼

★★ **THAD AND JOE'S.** *889 W Peachtree (30309), in Midtown/Piedmont Park. 404/874-5535.* Specializes in osso buco, monkfish stew, roasted duck with lychee fruit. Hrs: 5 pm-2 am; Wed-Fri from 11 am. Closed Sun; Jan 1, Dec 25. Res accepted. Bar. Lunch $3.15-$8; dinner $11.50-$17.50. Child's menu. Valet parking wkends. French island bistro decor. Cr cds: A, DS, MC, V.

🖼

★★ **THAI CHILI.** *2169 Briarcliff Rd NE (30329), in Briar Vista Shopping Center, E of Downtown. 404/315-6750. www.thaichilicuisine.com.* Specializes in salmon curry, veggie and tofu

delight, spicy pork. Hrs: 11 am-2:30 pm, 5-10 pm; Sat, Sun from 5 pm. Closed Dec 25. Res accepted. Wine, beer. Lunch $5.25-$8.95; dinner $6.95-$19.95. Elegant decor. Cr cds: A, D, MC, V.
D

★★ **TOMTOM.** 3393 Peachtree Rd (30326), in Lenox Sq Mall, in Buckhead. 404/264-1163. www.menus. atlanta.com/home/tomtom.html. Specializes in fresh fish, pasta, chicken. Hrs: 11:30 am-10 pm; Sun to 9 pm. Closed Easter, Thanksgiving, Dec 25. Res accepted. Bar. Lunch $7-$11; dinner $8-$16. Entertainment: pianist. Valet parking. Cr cds: A, C, D, DS, MC, V.
D

★★ **TOULOUSE.** 2293-B Peachtree Rd NE (30309), in Buckhead. 404/351-9533. www.toulouserestaurant.com. Specializes in fish, oven-roasted cuisine. Own baking. Hrs: 5:30-10 pm; Sun brunch 11:30 am-2 pm. Closed Jan 1, Dec 25. Res accepted. Bar. Dinner $10-$19.95. Sun brunch $17.95. Paintings by local artists. Cr cds: A, DS, MC, V.
D

★★★ **VENI VIDI VICI.** 41 14th St (30309), at W Peachtree, in Midtown/Piedmont Park. 404/875-8424. www. buckheadrestaurants.com. Specializes in homemade pasta, antipasto, wood-burning rotisserie meats. Hrs: 11 am-11 pm; Sat 5 pm-midnight; Sun 5-10 pm. Closed hols. Res accepted. Bar. Lunch a la carte entrees: $8.95-$12.95; dinner a la carte entrees: $12.95-$24.50. Entertainment: jazz Wed, Sun. Valet parking. Open kitchen. Vaulted ceilings. Cr cds: A, D, DS, MC, V.
D

★★ **VILLA CHRISTINA.** 4000 Perimeter Blvd (30319), I-285, Exit 21, N of Downtown. 404/303-0133. www. villachristina.com. Specializes in steak, fresh seafood, desserts. Hrs: 11:30 am-2:30 pm, 6-10 pm; Sat from 6 pm. Closed Sun; hols. Res accepted. Windows overlook 8 acres of gardens, walks, and waterfalls. Bar. Wine list. Lunch $9-$14; dinner $19-$29. Valet parking. Contemporary decor. Cr cds: A, D, DS, MC, V.
D

★★★ **THE VININGS INN.** 3011 Paces Mill Rd (30339), N of Downtown. 770/438-2282. www.viningsinn.com. Specializes in crab cakes, lamb, pasta. Hrs: 11:30 am-2:30 pm, 5:30-10 pm. Closed Sun. Bar. Lunch $6.50-$9.95; dinner $14.95-$27. Free valet parking. An 1840s house. Original fireplace; oil paintings. Cr cds: A, D, DS, MC, V.
D

★★ **VINNY'S ON WINDWARD.** 5355 Windward Pkwy (30004). 770/772-4644. Specializes in rack of lamb with raspberry demi-glaze, shrimp and scallops with pumpkinseed pesto, spinach and ricotta-stuffed veal chop. Hrs: 11 am-11 pm; Sun from 5 pm. Closed July 4, Thanksgiving, Dec 25. Res accepted. Bar. Lunch $3.75-$13.25; dinner $9.75-$25.95. Valet parking. Cr cds: A, D, DS, MC, V.
D

★★★ **WAVERLY GRILL.** 2450 Galleria Pkwy. 770/953-4500. Specializes in crab and shrimp strudel, whole-fried catfish, Mississippi mud pie. Hrs: 5:30-10 pm. Res accepted. Bar. Wine list. Dinner a la carte entrees: $4-$23. Child's menu. Valet parking. Cr cds: A, D, DS, MC, V.
D

★ **YEN JING CHINESE RESTAURANT.** 5302 Buford Hwy A-6 (30340), 8 mi NE on Buford Hwy, in Koreatown Plz. 770/454-6688. www.yenjing. homepage.com. Specializes in soup, salad, dumplings. Hrs: 11 am-11 pm. Res accepted. Lunch $4.95-$6.95; dinner $2.95-$19.95. Parking. Cr cds: MC, V.
D

★ **ZOCALO.** 187 10th St (30309), in Midtown/Piedmont Park. 404/249-7576. www.menusonline.com. Specializes in chiles rellenos, carnos asada, taco bar. Hrs: 11:30 am-2:30 pm, 5:30-11 pm; Sat 11:30 am-midnight; Sun 10:30 am-10 pm. Closed hols. Lunch $4.25-$7.75; dinner $7.75-$22.95. Parking. Mexican decor. Cr cds: A, D, DS, MC, V.
D

Unrated Dining Spots

FAT MATT'S. 1811 Piedmont (30324), in Midtown/Piedmont Park. 404/607-

1622. Email fatmatts@mindspring.com.
Specializes in fried fish and chicken,
barbecue pork. Hrs: 11:30 am-11:30
pm; Fri, Sat to 12:30 am; Sun from 2
pm. Closed Easter, Dec 25. Lunch,
dinner $3.50-$15. Child's menu. Parking. Casual dining; colorful decor. No
cr cds accepted.

[D]

KAMOGAWA. *3300 Peachtree Rd
(30305). 404/841-0314.* Japanese
menu. Specializes in Japanese dishes.
Sushi bar. Hrs: 11:30 am-2 pm, 6-11
pm; Sat, Sun from 6 pm. Res
accepted. Lunch $11.95-$17.95; dinner $18.95-$32. Entertainment.
Japanese gardens. Cr cds: DS, MC, V.

[D]

THE VARSITY. *61 N Ave (30308), in
Midtown/Piedmont Park. 404/881-
1706. www.thevarsity.com.* Specializes
in hot dogs, hamburgers, fried
peach pie. Hrs: 9 am-11:30 pm; Fri,
Sat to 1:30 am. Bkfst $2-$4.50;
lunch $2-$4.50; dinner $4-$4.50.
Parking. One of world's largest
drive-ins. Graffitiesque decor; tiered
seating. Adj Georgia Tech campus.
No cr cds accepted.

[D]

THE VARSITY JR. *1085 Lindbergh Dr
NE (30324), in Buckhead. 404/261-
8843.* Specializes in hot dogs. Hrs: 10
am-11 pm; Sun from 11 am. Closed
Thanksgiving, Dec 25. Lunch, dinner
$1-$3. Parking. 1950s drive-in. Family-
owned. No cr cds accepted.

[D]

Atlanta Hartsfield Airport Area

(C-2) *See also Atlanta*

Services and Information
Information. 404/530-6600.
Lost and Found. 404/530-2100.
Weather. 770/486-8834.
Cash Machines. Concourse A.

Airlines. Aeromexico, Air Canada,
Air Jamaica, Air Tran, ALM-Antillean,
American, American West, ASA, Aus-
trian, British Airways, Continental,
Delta, JAL, Kiwi Intl, KLM Royal
Dutch, Korean Air, Lufthansa, Malev
Hungarian, Mexicana, Midway, Mid-
west Express, Northwest, Reno,
Sabena, Swissair, TWA, United, USAir,
Vanguard, Varig, Western Pacific.

Motels/Motor Lodges

★ **DAYS INN COLLEGE PARK.**
*4601 Best Rd (30337), S on I-85, Exit
Riverdale Rd W, then N on Best Rd.
404/761-6500; fax 404/763-3267; toll-
free 800/329-7466.* 161 rms, 6 story.
S, D $70-$89; each addl (after 4th
person) $10; higher rates special
events. Crib free. TV; cable (premium). Pool. Playground. Coffee in
rms. Restaurant 6 am-10 pm. Bar 5
pm-midnight. Ck-out noon. Meeting
rms. Business center. Valet serv. Free
airport transportation. Exercise
equipt. Many refrigerators. Cr cds: A,
C, D, DS, MC, V.
[D] [icons]

★★ **HAMPTON INN AIRPORT.**
*1888 Sullivan Rd (30337), S via I-85
Exit 18, E on Riverdale Rd, S on Airport
Rd. 770/996-2220; fax 770/996-2488;
toll-free 800/426-7866.* 130 units, 4
story. S, D $65-$85; under 18 free.
Crib free. TV; cable (premium). Pool.
Complimentary continental bkfst.
Restaurant adj 11-2 am. Ck-out noon.
Meeting rm. Business servs avail. In-
rm modem link. Free airport trans-
portation. Exercise equipt. Public
park adj. Cr cds: A, C, D, DS, MC, V.
[D] [icons]

★★ **RAMADA PLAZA.** *1419 Virginia Ave (30337), N on I-85, Exit 19
Virginia Ave W. 404/768-7800; fax
404/767-5451; toll-free 800/272-6232.*
247 rms, 6 story. S, D $69-$89; each
addl $10; suites $99-$139; under 12
free. Crib free. TV; cable (premium).
Pool. Restaurants 6 am-11 pm. Rm
serv. Bar 4 pm-midnight. Ck-out
noon. Coin lndry. Meeting rms. Business center. In-rm modem link. Bellhops. Valet serv. Gift shop. Free
airport transportation. Exercise
equipt. Some in-rm whirlpools. Cr
cds: A, C, D, DS, MC, V.
[D] [icons]

Hotels

★★ **COURTYARD BY MARRIOTT SOUTH.** *2050 Sullivan Rd (30337), S on I-85 to Riverdale Rd, E to Best Rd, S to Sullivan Rd.* 770/997-2220; *fax 770/994-9743; res 800/321-2221.* 144 rms, 3 story. S $99; D $109; suites $125-$135; under 12 free; wkly, wkend rates. Crib free. TV; cable (premium). Indoor pool; whirlpool. Coffee in rms. Restaurant 6:30-10 am; wkends to 11 am. Bar 5-11 pm. Ck-out noon. Coin lndry. Meeting rms. Business servs avail. In-rm modem link. Valet serv. Sundries. Exercise equipt. Some private patios, balconies. Cr cds: A, C, D, DS, ER, JCB, MC, V.

🄳 🏊 🏋 🏃 ✈ 🛶 🔥

★★★ **HILTON ATLANTA AIRPORT.** *1031 Virginia Ave (30354), N on I-85, Exit 19 Virginia Ave E.* 404/767-9000; *fax 404/768-0185; res 800/HILTONS. Email atlaasalesadm@hilton.com.* 503 rms, 17 story. S $99-$224; D $129-$244; each addl $15; suites $400-$500; family, wkend rates. Crib free. TV; cable (premium), VCR avail. 2 pools, 1 indoor; whirlpool, poolside serv. Coffee in rms. Restaurant 6 am-midnight. Rm serv 24 hrs. Bar 11:30-2 am. Ck-out noon. Convention facilities. Business center. In-rm modem link. Concierge. Gift shop. Barber, beauty shop. Valet parking. Free airport transportation. Lighted tennis. Exercise rm; sauna. Massage. Minibars; some bathrm phones, wet bars; refrigerators avail. Luxury level. Cr cds: A, C, D, DS, ER, JCB, MC, V.

🄳 🏌 🏊 🏋 ✈ 🛶 🔥 🏃

★ **HOWARD JOHNSON HOTEL.** *1377 Virginia Ave (30344).* 404/762-5111; *fax 404/762-1277; res 800/446-4656. www.hojo.com.* 191 rms, 6 story. S $129; D $159; each addl $10; under 17 free. Crib avail. Parking lot. Pool. TV; cable (premium). Complimentary coffee in rms, newspaper, toll-free calls. Restaurant. Bar. Meeting rms. Business servs avail. Dry cleaning, coin lndry. Free airport transportation. Exercise equipt. Golf. Video games. Cr cds: A, C, D, DS, MC, V.

🄳 🏋 🏊 🏋 ✈ 🛶 🔥

★★★ **MARRIOTT ATLANTA AIRPORT.** *4711 Best Rd (30337), S on I-85, Exit Riverdale Rd W.* 404/766-7900; *fax 404/209-6808; toll-free 800/228-9290. Email bstewart@marriott.com; www.marriott.com.* 638 rms, 15 story. S $139-$165; suites $200-$650; under 18 free; package plans. Crib free. TV; cable (premium), VCR avail. Indoor/outdoor pool; whirlpool, poolside serv. Restaurant 6:30 am-midnight. Bar 5 pm-2 am; Sun 12:30 pm-midnight; entertainment. Ck-out noon. Convention facilities. Business center. In-rm modem link. Concierge. Gift shop. Barber, beauty shop. Valet parking. Free airport transportation. Lighted tennis. Exercise equipt; sauna. Game rm. Refrigerators avail. Some balconies. Luxury level. Cr cds: A, C, D, DS, JCB, MC, V.

🄳 🏌 🏊 🏋 ✈ 🛶 🔥 SC 🏃

★★★ **RENAISSANCE CONCOURSE HOTEL.** *1 Hartsfield Centre Pkwy (30354), I-85 Exit 20, at Hartsfield Centre.* 404/209-9999; *fax 404/209-7031; res 800/468-3571.* 387 rms, 11 story. S $165-$205; D $185-$225; suites $225-$1,450; wkend rates. Crib free. Valet parking $6. TV; cable (premium). 2 pools, 1 indoor; whirlpool, poolside serv. Complimentary coffee in rms. Restaurant 6 am-11 pm. Rm serv 24 hrs. Bar 11-1 am; entertainment Mon-Sat. Ck-out 1 pm. Convention facilities. Business center. In-rm modem link. Concierge. Gift shop. Exercise equipt; sauna. Massage. Refrigerators, minibars; microwaves avail. Balconies. Luxury level. Cr cds: A, D, DS, MC, V.

🄳 🏊 🏋 ✈ 🛶 🔥 🏃

★★★ **SHERATON GATEWAY HOTEL.** *1900 Sullivan Rd (30337), S on I-85, Exit 18.* 770/997-1100; *fax 770/991-5906; res 800/325-3535; toll-free 800/784-9400. www.sheraton.com.* 384 rms, 12 story, 11 suites. May-June, Oct: S $189; D $199; each addl $10; suites $350; under 16 free; lower rates rest of yr. Crib avail. Parking garage. Indoor/outdoor pools, whirlpool. TV; cable (premium). Complimentary coffee in rms, newspaper. Restaurant 6 am-10:50 pm. 24-hr rm serv. Bar. Ck-out noon, ck-in 3 pm. Conference center, meeting rms. Business center. Bellhops. Concierge. Gift shop. Free airport transportation. Exercise equipt. Video games. Cr cds: A, D, DS, MC, V.

🄳 🏊 🏋 ✈ 🛶 🔥 SC 🏃

★ ★ ★ **WESTIN HOTEL.** *4736 Best Rd (30337), S on I-85, Exit Riverdale Rd W. 404/762-7676; fax 404/559-7388; toll-free 800/228-3000.* 495 units, 10 story. S, D $170-$199; suites $175-$600; wkend plans. Crib free. Pet accepted, some restrictions. TV; cable (premium), VCR avail. Indoor/outdoor pool; whirlpool, poolside serv. Complimentary coffee in rms. Restaurant 6:30 am-11 pm; Sun from 12:30 pm. Rm serv 24 hrs. Bar 11-2 am. Ck-out noon. Convention facilities. Business center. In-rm modem link. Gift shop. Free airport transportation. Exercise equipt; sauna. Minibars; some bathrm phones; microwave in suites. Luxury level. Cr cds: A, C, D, DS, ER, JCB, MC, V.

Augusta (C-6)

Founded 1736 **Pop** 44,639 **Elev** 414 ft
Area code 706
Web www.augustaga.org
Information Metropolitan Convention & Visitors Bureau, 1450 Greene St, Suite 110, 30901; 706/823-6600 or 800/726-0243.

Augusta was the second town marked off for settlement by General James E. Oglethorpe. Today it is as famed for golf as for its red Georgia clay bricks. The city has been a military outpost and upriver trading town, the leading 18th-century tobacco center, a river shipping point for cotton, the powder works for the Confederacy, an industrial center for the New South, and a winter resort.

During the Revolution, the town changed hands several times, but Fort Augusta, renamed Fort Cornwallis by its British captors, was finally surrendered to "Lighthorse Harry" Lee's Continentals on June 5, 1781.

The Civil War played havoc with many of the wealthy families who had contributed to the Confederate cause. To help revive their depleted bank accounts, some Summerville residents opened their houses to paying guests. Attracted by Augusta's mild winter climate, northern visitors began an annual migration in increasing numbers, and by the turn of the 20th century Augusta had become a popular winter resort. Many wealthy northerners built winter residences here in the 1920s. Golf courses and country clubs added to the lure. The Masters Tournament attracts the interest of golfers worldwide.

Augusta's many firsts include the state's first medical academy (chartered 1828); the first and oldest newspaper in the South to be published continuously, the *Augusta Chronicle* (1785); the first steamboat to be launched in southern waters (1790), invented and built by William Longstreet; and the experimental site for one of Eli Whitney's early cotton gins.

Augusta lies at the head of navigation on the Savannah River. Its importance as a cotton market, a producer of cotton textiles, kaolin tiles, and brick has been enhanced by diversified manufacturing, processing of cottonseed, farm products, and fertilizers. Fort Gordon, an army base southwest of the city, also contributes to the area's economy. With the Medical College of Georgia, Augusta is a leading medical center in the Southeast.

What to See and Do

Augusta Museum of History. (1802) Historic and natural science collections. (Tues-Sun; closed hols) 560 Reynolds St. Phone 706/722-8454. ¢¢

Augusta State University. (1925) 5,600 students. Site of Augusta Arsenal (1826-1955), of which portions are preserved. 2500 Walton Way, between Katharine St & Arsenal Ave. Phone 706/737-1444.

Confederate Powder Works Chimney. A memorial honoring war dead, this brick chimney is all that remains of what was once the second-largest powder factory in the world. 1717 Goodrich St.

Cotton Exchange. Handsome brick bldg, built in 1886, now houses historical exhibits and serves as a visitor center. (Daily) 32 8th St. Phone 706/823-6600. **FREE**

Gertrude Herbert Institute of Art. Old Ware's Folly Mansion (1818)

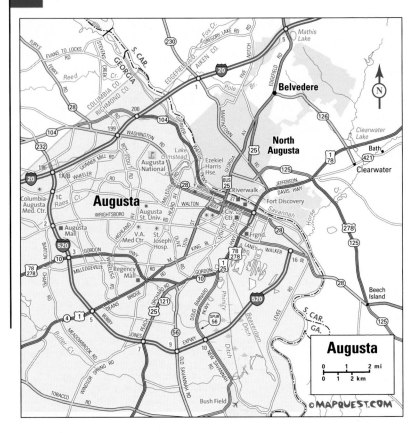

Augusta

0   1   2 mi
0   1   2 km

© MAPQUEST.COM

houses changing exhibits, works by local artists. (Tues-Sat; closed hols) 506 Telfair St. Phone 706/722-5495. **Donation**

Harris House. (ca 1795) House of Ezekiel Harris, tobacco merchant. Period furnishings. Tours (Tues-Fri; also Sat afternoons by appt.) 1822 Broad St. Phone 706/724-0436. ¢

Meadow Garden. House (1791-1804) of George Walton, signer of the Declaration of Independence. Period furnishings. Guided tours (Mon-Fri; also Sat and Sun by appt) 1320 Independence Dr. Phone 706/724-4174. ¢¢

Morris Museum of Art. Houses collection of paintings by Southern artists depicting landscapes, portraits, and Civil War scenes; also has small folk-art collection. (Tues-Sun) Free admission Sun. 1 10th St. Phone 706/724-7501. ¢¢

National Science Center's Fort Discovery. An innovative hands-on science, communications, and technology center with 250 interactive exhibits; high-tech theater, Com-

puter World, KidScape for children ages 3-7. Also here is a Teacher Resource Center, traveling exhibits, and a science store. (Daily; closed hols) 1 7th St. Phone 706/821-0200. ¢¢¢

Riverwalk. Augusta's high Savannah River levee has been lavishly restored as a promenade for strollers, skaters, and cyclists, linking the city's major attractions.

St. Paul's Episcopal Church. (1750) Granite Celtic cross in churchyard marks site of fort and the spot where Augusta began, established by Oglethorpe in 1736 in honor of Princess Augusta. Oglethorpe Park, a recreational area on the Savannah River, is located behind the church; picnicking. 605 Reynolds St. Phone 706/724-2485.

Annual Events

Augusta Invitational Rowing Regatta. At Augusta Riverfront Marina. Late Mar or early Apr.

Masters Golf Tournament. Augusta National Golf Course. First full wk Apr. Phone 706/667-6000.

Seasonal Events

Augusta Symphony Orchestra. Phone 706/826-4705. Fall-spring.

Augusta Opera Association. Phone 706/826-4710. Fall-spring.

Motels/Motor Lodges

★★ **AMERISUITES.** *1062 Claussen Rd (30907), I-20, Exit 66 off Clausen Rd. 706/733-4656; fax 706/736-1133; res 800/833-1516. www.amerisuites. com.* 111 suites, 6 story. S $59; D $64; each addl $5; under 12 free; wkend rates. Pet accepted. TV; cable (premium), VCR avail. Pool; whirlpool. Complimentary bkfst, coffee in rms. Restaurant nearby. Ck-out noon. Coin lndry. Meeting rms. Business center. Health club privileges. Exercise equipt. Refrigerators, microwaves. Picnic table. Business suites avail. Cr cds: A, D, DS, MC, V.

★★ **COURTYARD BY MARRIOTT.** *1045 Stevens Creek Rd (30901), I-20 at Washington Rd. 706/737-3737; fax 706/738-7851; toll-free 800/321-2211.* 130 rms, 2 story. S, D $69; each addl $10; suites $84-$94; wkend rates. TV; cable (premium). Pool; whirlpool. Restaurant 6-9:30 am; Sat 7 am-noon; Sun 7 am-1 pm. Bar; closed Sat, Sun. Ck-out noon. Coin lndry. Meeting rms. Business servs avail. Valet serv. Exercise equipt. Health club privileges. Refrigerators avail. Private patios, balconies. Cr cds: A, C, D, DS, MC, V.

★ **DAYS INN.** *3026 Washington Rd (30907), I-20, Exit 65. 706/738-0131; fax 706/738-0131; res 800/DAYSINN.* 124 rms, 2 story. S, D $45-$65; each addl $5; under 12 free; Crib free. TV; cable (premium). Pool. Complimentary full bkfst, coffee in rms. Restaurant 6 am-10 pm. Ck-out 11 am. Refrigerators, microwaves; some in-rm whirlpools. Cr cds: A, D, DS, MC, V.

★★ **HOLIDAY INN.** *1103 15th St (30901). 706/724-5560; fax 706/774-6821; res 800/HOLIDAY.* 42 rms, 2 story, 4 suites. S, D $54; each addl $5; suites $58; under 19 free. Crib $5. TV; cable (premium). Complimentary continental bkfst. Restaurant nearby. Ck-out noon. Business servs avail. In-rm modem link. Refrigerators, microwaves. Cr cds: A, D, DS, MC, V.

★ **KNIGHTS INN AUGUSTA.** *210 Boy Scout Rd (30909), I-20, Exit 65. 706/737-3166; fax 206/731-9204; res 800/843-5644.* 109 rms, 10 kits. S $21.95, D $26.95; kits. $32.95-$50.95; wkly rates. Pet accepted. TV; cable. Pool. Complimentary coffee. Restaurant nearby. Ck-out 11 am. Coin lndry. Cr cds: A, DS, MC, V.

★★★ **RADISSON SUITES INN.** *3038 Washington Rd (30907), at I-20. 706/868-1800; fax 706/868-7300; res 800/333-3333.* 176 units, 4 story, 152 suites. S $59-$99; D $69-$109; each addl $10; under 18 free. Crib free. Pet accepted; $25. TV; cable (premium). Pool. Complimentary bkfst. Coffee in rms. Restaurant 6:30-9:30 am, 5 pm-9 pm; Sat & Sun from 7 am. Bar 5-7 pm. Ck-out noon. Coin lndry. Meeting rms. Business center. In-rm modem link. Health club privileges. Some wet bars. Bathrm phone, refrigerator, microwave in suites. Cr cds: A, C, D, DS, MC, V.

★ **VALU-LODGE.** *1365 Gordon Hwy (30901). 706/722-4344; fax 706/724-4437.* 146 rms, 2 story. S $36.95-$42.95; D $39.95-$45.95; each addl $3; under 17 free; wkend, wkly rates. Crib free. Pet accepted. TV; cable (premium). Pool. Restaurant 6 am-10 pm. Rm serv. Bar 4 pm-1 am. Ck-out 11 am. Some refrigerators; microwaves avail. Cr cds: A, C, D, DS, MC, V.

Hotels

★★★ **RADISSON RIVERFRONT HOTEL AUGUSTA.** *2 10th St (33870). 706/722-8900; fax 706/823-6513; res 800/333-3333. Email irene. peterson@hotelmail.cc; www.radisson. com/augustaga_riverfront.* 237 rms, 11 story. S, D $119; suites $135-$475. Crib free. Pet accepted, some restrictions. TV; cable (premium). Pool. Complimentary coffee in rms.

Restaurant 6:30 am-2 pm, 5:30-11 pm. Bar 11-1 am; Sun 12:30 pm-midnight. Ck-out noon. Meeting rms. Business servs avail. In-rm modem link. Golf privileges, greens fee $40-$60, putting green, driving range. Exercise equipt; saunas. Health club privileges. Some refrigerators. On Savannah River. Cr cds: A, DS, MC, V.

D ⬛ 🏋 ⬛ 🏃 ⬛ 🐾 SC

★★★ **SHERATON HOTEL.** *2651 Perimeter Pkwy (30909), I-520 Wheeler Rd Exit. 706/855-8100; fax 706/860-1720; toll-free 800/325-3535.* 179 rms, 30 suites. S, D $104; each addl $10; suites $159; under 17 free. Crib free. Pet accepted, some restrictions. TV; cable (premium), VCR in suites. 2 pools, 1 indoor. Complimentary coffee in rms. Restaurant 6:30 am-10:30 pm. Bars. Ck-out noon. Coin lndry. Convention facilities. Business center. In-rm modem link. Concierge. Gift shop. Free airport transportation. Exercise equipt; sauna. Refrigerator, microwave in suites. Cr cds: A, C, D, DS, JCB, MC, V.

D ⬛ 🏊 ⬛ 🏃 ⬛ 🐾 SC 🏃

B&Bs/Small Inns

★★ **1810 WEST INN.** *254 N Seymour Dr (30824), 30 mi W on I-20 Exit 59. 706/595-3156; fax 706/595-3155; toll-free 800/515-1810.* 11 rms, 2 story, 2 suites. S $55-$65, D $65-$75; each addl $10; suites $69-$75; guest house $325; wkly rates; higher rates special events. Children over 12 yrs only. TV; cable (premium), VCR (avail) in common rm. Complimentary continental bkfst. Restaurant nearby. Ck-out noon, ck-in 3 pm. In-rm modem link. Concierge serv. Golf privileges, pro, putting green, driving range. Some fireplaces, balconies. Picnic tables, grills. Restored farmhouse (1810); antiques. Totally nonsmoking. Cr cds: A, DS, MC, V.

🏃 ⬛ 🐾

★★★ **AZALEA INN BED & BREAKFAST.** *316 Greene St (30901). 706/724-3454; fax 706/724-1033. Email azalea@theazaleainn.com; www.theazaleainn.com.* 15 rms, 3 story, 5 suites. Apr: S, D $350; suites $420; lower rates rest of yr. Parking lot. TV; cable (premium), VCR avail. Complimentary continental bkfst, coffee in rms, newspaper, toll-free calls. Restaurant nearby. Ck-out 11 am, ck-in 3

pm. Business center. Concierge. Dry cleaning. Free airport transportation. Golf. Tennis, 4 courts. Hiking trail. Picnic facilities. Cr cds: A, MC, V.

D 🛄 🏋 ⬛ 🐾 🏊

★★★ **ROSEMARY HALL & LOOK-AWAY HALL.** *804 Carolina Ave (29841), 2 mi N on GA 25. 803/278-6222; fax 803/278-4877; toll-free 800/531-5578.* 23 rms in 2 bldgs, 2 story. S, D $75-$195. Children over 12 yrs only. TV; cable. Complimentary full bkfst; refreshments. Restaurant nearby. Ck-out 11 am, ck-in 3 pm. Concierge serv. Business servs avail. Golf privileges, pro, putting green, driving range. Health club privileges. Two inns (1898 and 1902) restored and furnished with period pieces. Landscaped grounds. Totally non-smoking. Cr cds: A, D, DS, MC, V.

D 🐾 🌿 🏋 🏃 🏃 ⬛ 🐾

Restaurants

★★★ **CALVERTS.** *475 Highland Ave (30909), in Surrey Center. 706/738-4514.* Specializes in roast rack of lamb, seafood, prime rib. Hrs: 5-10 pm. Closed Sun; hols. Res accepted. Bar. Wine list. Dinner $11.95-$25.95. Family-owned. Cr cds: A, D, DS, MC, V.

D ⬛

★★★ **LA MAISON.** *404 Telfair St (30901). 706/722-4805. www.zip2.com.* Specializes in rack of lamb, fresh game, smoked salmon in potato crust with herb sauce. Hrs: 6-10 pm. Closed Sun; hols. Res accepted. Bar. Wine cellar. Dinner $14.50-$35. In restored Victorian home (ca 1800). Cr cds: A, D, DS, MC, V.

D SC ⬛

Bainbridge

(G-2) *See also Thomasville*

Founded 1829 **Pop** 10,712 **Elev** 135 ft
Area code 912 **Zip** 31717
Web www.bainbridgega.com/chamber

Information Bainbridge-Decatur County Chamber of Commerce, PO Box 736, 31718; 912/246-4774 or 800/243-4774

On the banks of 37,500-acre Lake Seminole, Bainbridge is Georgia's first inland port. It is a town of giant water oaks and live oaks on the Flint River. Andrew Jackson's troops built an earthworks defense (Fort Hughes) near the present town during the Indian Wars (1817-21). The town was later named in honor of William Bainbridge, commander of the frigate *Constitution*. The forests were so rich in this area that Bainbridge was known as the wealthiest town in the state when fortunes were made in lumbering in the early 20th century.

What to See and Do

Earl May Boat Basin and Park. This 600-acre park on Lake Seminole has exhibit of turn-of-the-century steam engines and locomotives. Beach swimming, boating (ramps); volleyball court, playing fields, camping (hookups). Visitor center (Mon-Sat; closed hols). W Shotwell St at bypass.

Seminole State Park. Lake Seminole, shallow by Georgia standards, holds a greater number of fish species than any other lake in the state. Swimming beach, waterskiing, fishing, boating; miniature golf, picnicking, concession, camping, cottages. Standard hrs, fees. Contact Superintendent, Rte 2, Donalsonville 31745. 23 mi W on GA 253. Phone 912/861-3137.

Annual Events

Riverside Arts Festival. Arts festival featuring a different state each year. First wk May.

Decatur County Fall Festival and Fair. Carnival rides, exhibits, livestock show. Mid-Oct.

Motel/Motor Lodge

★ **SUPER 8.** *751 W Shotwell St (31717). 912/246-0015; fax 912/246-0015; toll-free 800/800-8000.* 53 rms, 2 story. S $39-$45; D $44-$45; each addl $5; suites $66; under 19 free; wkly rates; higher rates Bass Fishing Tournament. Crib free. TV; cable. Pool; whirlpool. Complimentary continental bkfst. Restaurant nearby. Ck-out 11 am. Meeting rms. Business

servs avail. Refrigerator, wet bar in suites. Cr cds: A, C, D, DS, JCB, MC, V.
[D] [≈] [≈] [&] [SC]

Hotel

★★ **CHARTER HOUSE INN.** *1401 Tallahassee Hwy (31717), at jct US 27S, 84 Bypass. 912/246-8550; fax 912/246-0260; toll-free 800/768-8550. Email leslie@thecharterhouseinn.com; www.thecharterhouseinn.com.* 124 rms, 2 story. S $45-$50; D $50-$55; each addl $5; suites $95-$135; under 18 free. Crib free. TV; cable (premium). Pool. Restaurant 6 am-2 pm, 5-10 pm. Bar 4 pm-midnight; closed Sun. Ck-out noon. Valet serv. Meeting rms. Business servs avail. Cr cds: A, DS, MC, V.
[✈] [≈] [&] [⚲]

Blakely

(F-2) *See also Dothan, AL*

Founded 1826 **Pop** 5,595 **Elev** 275 ft
Area code 912 **Zip** 31723
Web www.blakelyearlychamber.com
Information Chamber of Commerce, 52 Court Square, PO Box 189; 912/723-3741

Named for US Navy Captain Johnston Blakeley, a hero of the War of 1812, this is an important peanut producing area.

What to See and Do

Coheelee Creek Covered Bridge. Southernmost standing covered bridge in US, built in 1891. Old River Rd, 9 mi SW via GA 62.

Courthouse Square. On the grounds stands what may be the world's only monument honoring the peanut and a

  Confederate Flag Pole. The South's last remaining wooden Confederate flag pole, erected in 1861.

Kolomoki Mounds State Park. Native American mounds, temple mound, and some excavation indicate a settlement here between AD 800-1200. Swimming pool, fishing, boating (ramps, dock) on Kolomoki Lake; trails, picnicking, camping. Standard hrs, fees. 6 mi N off US 27. Contact Superintendent, Rte 1, Box 114. Phone 912/723-5296. In park is

Indian Museum. Exhibits explain artifacts and civilization of Kolomoki, Weeden Island, and Swift Creek cultures. Entry into excavated burial mound. (Tues-Sun; closed Jan 1, Thanksgiving, Dec 25) ¢

B&B/Small Inn

★ ★ ★ **TARRER INN.** *155 S Cuthbert St (31737), 15 mi S on GA 27. 912/ 758-2888; fax 912/758-2825; toll-free 888/282-7737. Email tarrerinn@ surfsouth; www.tarrerinn.com.* 12 rms, 1 suite. S $89; suites $105. Crib avail. Street parking. TV; cable, VCR avail. Complimentary full bkfst, coffee in rms, newspaper. Restaurant, closed Tues. Bar. Ck-out 11 am, ck-in 3 pm. Meeting rms. Business center. Dry cleaning. Golf, 18 holes. Tennis, 4 courts. Bike rentals. Hiking trail. Picnic facilities. Cr cds: A, D, DS, MC, V.

Restaurant

★ **OUR PLACE.** *310 S Main St (31723), in Sawyer Shopping Center. 912/723-8880.* Specializes in fried chicken, hamburgers, steak. Hrs: 5:30 am-9:30 pm; Sun to 2 pm. Closed hols. Bkfst $2-$5; lunch buffet: $5.80; dinner $2.50-$10.75. Child's menu. Cr cds: MC, V.

Brunswick

(G-6) *See also Golden Isles, St. Simons Island*

Settled 1771 **Pop** 16,433 **Elev** 10 ft
Area code 912
Web www.bgislesvisitorsb.com
Information Brunswick-Golden Isles Visitors Bureau, 4 Glynn Ave, 31520; 912/265-0620 or 800/933-2627

Brunswick, on the southern third of Georgia's seacoast, separated from the "Golden Isles" by the Marshes of Glynn and the Intracoastal Water-

way, was laid out in 1771 by the Colonial Council of the Royal Province of Georgia. Named to honor George II of the House of Brunswick (Hanover), it later became the seat of Glynn County, named in honor of John Glynn, member of the British Parliament and sympathizer with the colonists' struggle for independence.

Gateway to St. Simons Island, Jekyll Island, and Sea Island (see all), Brunswick is also a manufacturing and seafood processing town. Among its principal products are pulp, paper, lumber machinery, lumber products, and processed seafood. Its harbor is a full oceangoing seaport, as well as a home port to coastal fishing and shrimping fleets. Brunswick is known as one of the shrimp capitals of the world. Natural beauty is enhanced by plantings of palms and flowering shrubs along main avenues, contrasting with moss-covered ancient oaks in spacious parks.

What to See and Do

Cumberland Island National Seashore. (see) S, off the coast.

Fort Frederica National Monument. (see) 12 mi NE via St. Simons/Sea Island Causeway (toll).

James Oglethorpe Monument. Honors founder of Georgia. Queens Square, E side of Newcastle St.

Lover's Oak. Giant oak said to be more than 900 yrs old; the trunk, at a point 3 ft above ground, measures 13 ft in diameter. Albany & Prince Sts.

Marshes of Glynn. Marshes separate Brunswick from St. Simons Island, Sea Island, Little St. Simons Island, and Jekyll Island. Traversed by causeways connecting with US 17, the vast saltwater marshes are bisected by several rivers and the Intracoastal Waterway. Of them Sidney Lanier wrote "Oh, like to the greatness of God is the greatness within the range of the marshes, the liberal marshes of Glynn." Marshes of Glynn Overlook Park has picnic facilities, view of marshes.

Mary Miller Doll Museum. Collection of 4,000 dolls, dollhouses, miniatures, boats, and toys; exhibit subjects incl antique dolls, foreign dolls, and modern doll artists. (Mon-Fri; closed hols) 1523 Glynn Ave.

Phone/Fax 912/267-7569. Tours of 10 or more ¢¢

Motels/Motor Lodges

★★ **BEST WESTERN BRUNSWICK INN.** *5323 New Jesup Hwy Exit 36B (31523). 912/264-0144; fax 912/262-0992; res 800/528-1234.* 143 rms, 2 story. S $45-$55; D $49-$59; each addl $4; under 12 free. Crib free. Pet accepted. TV; cable. Pool; wading pool. Complimentary continental bkfst. Restaurant nearby. Ck-out 11 am. Coin lndry. Picnic tables. Cr cds: A, C, D, DS, ER, MC, V.

D ⚿ 🏊 📶 🔥

★★ **COMFORT INN.** *5308 New Jesup Hwy (31523), at I-95 Jesup Exit 7B. 912/264-6540; fax 912/264-9296; res 800/228-5150; toll-free 800/551-7591.* 118 rms, 5 story. S $49-$79; D $59-$99; each addl $6; under 18 free. Crib $6. Pet accepted. TV; cable (premium). Pool. Complimentary continental bkfst. Restaurant adj open 24 hrs. Ck-out noon. Meeting rms. Business servs avail. In-rm modem link. Cr cds: A, D, DS, MC, V.

D ⚿ 🏊 📶 🔥

★★ **HAMPTON INN BRUNSWICK.** *112 Tourist Dr (31520), I-95, Exit 7A. 912/261-0002; fax 912/265-5599; res 800/426-7866. Email brunswick_hampton_inn@meristar.com.* 128 rms, 3 story. S $60; D $68; under 18 free. Crib avail. TV; cable (premium). Pool. Coffee in rms. Complimentary continental bkfst. Restaurant adj 6 am-10 pm. Ck-out noon. Meeting rms. Business servs avail. Some refrigerators. Cr cds: A, C, D, DS, JCB, MC, V.

D 🏊 📶 🔥

★★ **JAMESON INN.** *661 Scranton Rd (31520), 2 mi E of I-95, Exit 8. 912/267-0800; fax 912/265-1922; res 800/JAMESON; toll-free 800/526-3766. Email brunswick.ga@jamesoninns.com; www.jamesoninns.com.* 60 rms, 2 story. S $58; D $63; each addl $5; suites $115-145; under 16 free. Crib free. TV; cable (premium), VCR avail (movies). Pool. Complimentary continental bkfst. Restaurant nearby. Ck-out 11 am. Business servs avail. In-rm modem link. Exercise equipt.

Some refrigerators; microwaves avail. Cr cds: A, DS, MC, V.

D 🏊 🏋 📶 🔥 SC

★★ **QUALITY INN.** *125 Venture Dr (31525), I-95 Exit 8. 912/265-4600; fax 912/265-8268; res 800/228-5151; toll-free 888/394-8495.* 83 rms, 2 story. S $55-$75; D $59-$89; each addl $6; under 17 free. Crib free. TV; cable (premium). Pool. Complimentary continental bkfst, coffee in rms. Ck-out 11 am. Meeting rm. In-rm modem link. Some refrigerators; microwaves avail. Cr cds: A, D, DS, MC, V.

D 🏊 📶 🔥

★ **SLEEP INN.** *5272 New Jesup Hwy (31525), I-95, Exit 7B. 912/261-0670; fax 912/264-0441; toll-free 800/638-7949.* 93 rms, 90 with shower only, 2 story. S $49-$79; D $59-$89; under 18 free. Crib $2. Pet accepted. TV; cable. Pool. Complimentary continental bkfst. Restaurant adj open 24 hrs. Ck-out noon. Business center. In-rm modem link. Valet serv. Cr cds: A, DS, MC, V.

⚿ 🏊 🏋 🔥 🏋

B&B/Small Inn

★★ **BRUNSWICK MANOR.** *825 Egmont St (31520). 912/265-6889; fax 912/265-7879.* 4 rms, 2 story. No rm phones. S, D $75-$100; 2-night package. Children over 12 yrs only. Some TVs. Whirlpool. Complimentary full bkfst; afternoon refreshments. Ck-out noon, ck-in 3 pm. Some street parking. Antique furnishings, reproductions. Restored Victorian residence (1886) in Old Town section, opp Halifax Sq. Totally nonsmoking. Cr cds: MC, V.

📶 🔥

All Suite

★★★ **EMBASSY SUITES.** *500 Mall Blvd (31525), I-95 Exit 8, near Glynco Jet Port Airport. 912/264-6100; fax 912/267-1615; res 800/362-2779; toll-free 800/432-3229. Email embassy@darientel.net; www.embassysuites.com.* 130 suites, 5 story. S, D $149; each addl $10; under 16 free. Crib free. Pet accepted. TV; cable (premium). Pool. Complimentary full bkfst, coffee in rms. Ck-out noon. Meeting rms.

Business servs avail. In-rm modem link. Free airport transportation. Exercise equipt. Health club privileges. Refrigerators, microwaves, wet bars; some in-rm whirlpools. Skylit atrium lobby. Cr cds: A, DS, MC, V.

✈ 🐾 🏊 🏋 🔥

Restaurants

★ **CAPTAIN JOE'S.** *5296 New Jesup Hwy (US 341) (31523).* 912/264-8771. Specializes in seafood, steak. Salad bar. Hrs: 11 am-10 pm. Closed Dec 25. Res accepted. Lunch $4-$12.75; dinner $7-$14.75. Child's menu. Parking. Nautical decor. Cr cds: D, DS, MC, V.

D 🏊

★ **MATTEO'S ITALIAN RESTAU-RANT.** *5448 New Jesup Hwy (US 341) (31523),* I-95 Exit 7B. 912/267-0248. Specializes in pizza, spaghetti, cannoli. Hrs: 11 am-9:30 pm; Sat from 4 pm. Closed Sun; hols. Wine, beer. Lunch, dinner $3.25-$10.50. Parking. Italian cafe atmosphere; wrought-iron booths. Cr cds: A, D, MC, V.

D

★★ **NEW CHINA.** *3202 Glynn Ave (US 17) (31520).* 912/265-6722. Specializes in Oriental bird nest, kung bo ding. Hrs: 11 am-10:30 pm; Fri, Sat to 11 pm. Wine, beer. Lunch $3.50-$5.75; dinner $5.50-$9.50. Child's menu. Parking. Chinese decor. Family owned. Cr cds: A, MC, V.

D 🏊

★★ **WILSONS SEAFOOD.** *3848 Darien Hwy (31521).* 912/267-0801. www.glenncounty.com/wilsons. Specializes in seafood, steak. Hrs: 11:30-2 am; Sun to 11 pm. Bar. Dinner $8.95-$21. Child's menu. Parking. Cr cds: MC, V.

D SC 🏊

Buford

(B-3) *See also Atlanta, Gainesville*

Pop 8,771 **Elev** 1,187 ft
Area code 770 **Zip** 30518
Web www.gcvb.org

Information Gwinnett Convention & Visitors Bureau, 1505 Lakes Pkwy, Suite 110, Lawrenceville 30043; 770/277-6212 or 888/494-6638

What to See and Do

Lake Lanier Islands. A 1,200-acre, yr-round resort. Swimming, water-skiing, beach and water park with wave pool, 10 waterslides, and other attractions, fishing, boating (ramps, rentals); horseback riding, two 18-hole golf courses, tennis, picnicking, hotel, resort (see), cottages. Tent and trailer camping (hookups). Special events are held May-Oct. Fees for some activities. For further information contact 6950 Holiday Rd, Lake Lanier Islands 30518. N of town, on Lake Lanier. Phone 770/932-7200.

Winery tours. Chateau Elan Winery and Resort. Tours, tastings; restaurants; 18-hole golf course (fee); special events (fee). (See RESORTS) (Daily; closed Thanksgiving, Dec 25) 1½ mi NW on I-85, Exit 48, Braselton. Phone 800/233-WINE. **FREE**

Motels/Motor Lodges

★ **AMERICAN INN.** *4267 Buford Dr (30180).* 770/932-0111; fax 770/932-0111. 40 rms, 2 story. S $43.55; D $49.95. Crib free. TV; cable (premium). Restaurant adj 7 am-10 pm. Ck-out 11 am. In-rm modem link. Cr cds: A, D, DS, MC, V.

D 🏊 🔥

★★ **HOLIDAY INN SUWANEE.** *2955 GA 317 (30024),* I-85 Exit 44. 770/945-4921; fax 770/945-0440; res 800/465-4329. Email swlga@ix.net-com.com. 120 rms, 2 story. S $71-$75; D $81-$85; each addl $6; under 18 free. Crib $6. TV; cable (premium). Pool; wading pool. Restaurant 6:30 am-2 pm, 5-10 pm. Bar 3:30 pm-1 am; Fri, Sat to 1 am. Ck-out 11 am. Coin lndry. Meeting rms. Business servs avail. Valet serv. Sundries. Putting green. Microwaves avail. Cr cds: A, DS, MC, V.

D 🏊 🔥 SC

Resorts

★★★ **HILTON LAKE LANIER ISLANDS RESORT.** *7000 Holiday Rd (30518),* I-85 N to I-985 N, Exit 1. 770/945-8787; fax 770/932-5471; toll-free 800/768-5253. 224 rms, 4 story. Apr-Oct: S, D $139-$159. Crib free. TV; cable (premium). Heated pool; wading pool, whirlpool, poolside serv. Playground. Supervised children's activities (Memorial Day-Labor Day). Coffee in rms. Dining rm 6:30 am-10 pm. Box lunch, snack bar, picnics. Bar 11-1 am. Ck-out noon, ck-in 3 pm. Grocery 1 mi. Package store 5 mi. Convention facilities. Business center. In-rm modem link. Bellhops. Valet serv. Concierge. Gift shop. Lighted tennis. 18-hole golf, greens fee $55 (incl cart), pro, putting green, driving range. Beach, boats, water skiing, swimming. Hiking. Bicycles (rentals). Lawn games. Exercise equipt; sauna. Some refrigerators. Balconies. Picnic tables, grills. Water park nearby. On lake. Cr cds: A, C, D, DS, ER, MC, V.

[icons]

★ ★ ★ **INN AT CHATEAU ELAN.**
100 Rue Charlemagne (30517), N on I-85, Exit 48. 770/932-0900; fax 770/271-6000; toll-free 800/233-9463. www.chateauelan.com. 310 rms, 5 story. Mar-mid-June, mid-Sep-mid-Nov: S, D $190-$250; suites $200-$300; wkend, hol rates; golf plan; lower rates rest of yr. Crib free. TV; cable (premium), VCR avail. 4 pools, 2 indoor; whirlpools, poolside serv. Playground. Supervised children's activities. Complimentary coffee in rms. Minibars. Restaurant (see CHATEAU ELAN'S LE CLOS). Rm serv 24 hrs. Bar 11 am-11:45 pm; entertainment weekends. Ck-out noon, ck-in 3 pm. Gift shop. Convention center. Business center. In-rm modem link. Bellhops. Valet serv. Concierge. Airport transportation. Lighted tennis, pro. 63-hole golf, 9-hole par-3 golf, greens fee $65-$125, pro, putting green, driving range. Exercise rm; sauna. Massage. Bicycle rentals. Hiking trails. Rec rm. Game rm. Picnic tables. Art gallery; 2 ballrms. 200 acre winery with tours. Cr cds: A, C, D, DS, JCB, MC, V.

[icons]

★ ★ ★ **RENAISSANCE PINEISLE RESORT.** *9000 Holiday Rd (30518), 3 mi N on GA 13, then 3 mi W on GA 347. 770/945-8921; fax 770/945-1024; res 800/468-3571. www.renaissance hotels.com.* 250 rms, 5 story. S $79-$119; D $89-$149; each addl $20; 1-, 2-bedrm suites $175-$548; under 18 free; MAP, golf, tennis, other plans avail. Crib free. TV; cable (premium), VCR avail. Indoor/outdoor pool; whirlpool, poolside serv. Supervised children's activities (late Mar-late Nov); ages 4-18. Complimentary coffee. Dining rm 6:30-10 pm (see also BREEZES). Box lunches; snack bar. Rm serv 24 hrs. Bar 11-2 am; Sat to midnight; Sun 12:30 pm-midnight. Afternoon tea. Ck-out noon, ck-in 3 pm. Concierge. Lndry avail. Valet parking. Convention facilities. Business center. In-rm modem link. Gift shop. Tennis, pro. 18-hole golf, greens fee $49-$59 (incl cart), pro, driving range, putting green. Swimming, private beach, waterskiing; water park adj. Boats, motors, sailboats, canoes, pontoon boats, houseboats, docks; instruction avail. Complimentary sunset cruises. Bicycles. Horseback riding lessons. Lawn games. Soc dir; entertainment. Game rm. Exercise equipt; weight machine, bicycles, sauna. Massage. Picnic tables. Private patios, balconies. Many decks. Cr cds: A, DS, MC, V.

[icons]

B&B/Small Inn

★ ★ ★ **WHITWORTH INN.** *6593 McEver Rd (30542), NE on I-985 Exit 2, N on 347, then N on McEver Rd. 770/967-2386; fax 770/967-2649. Email visit@whitworthinn.com; www. whitworth.com.* 10 rms, 2 story. S $59; D $69; each addl $10; under 12 free. Crib avail. Parking lot. TV; cable (DSS), VCR avail. Complimentary full bkfst, newspaper. Restaurant nearby. Ck-out 11 am, ck-in 3 pm. Business center. Golf. Tennis. Cr cds: A, MC, V.

[icons]

Restaurants

★ ★ ★ **BREEZES.** *9000 Holiday Rd. 770/945-8921. www.pineisle.com.* Specializes in grilled steak, seafood. Own baking. Hrs: 6:30 am-10 pm. Res accepted. Bar. Bkfst a la carte entrees: $6.95-$10.95; lunch a la carte entrees: $7.95-$14; dinner a la carte entrees: $15-$26.95. Sun brunch $24.95. 15% serv chg. Entertainment: two-piece band Tues-Sat (Mar-

Oct). Valet parking. View of Lake Lanier. Cr cds: A, D, DS, MC, V.

★★ **CHATEAU ELAN'S LE CLOS.** *100 Tour De France. 770/932-0900. www.chateauelan.com.* Specializes in classical French cuisine. Hrs: 6:30-9:30 pm. Closed Sun-Tues. Res required. Dinner complete meals: 8-course $88. Festive atmosphere of an authentic French chateau. Located in a winery complex with gift shop, museum, and wine tasting. Cr cds: A, D, DS, MC, V.

Calhoun

(A-1) *See also Dalton, Rome*

Pop 7,135 **Elev** 715 ft **Area code** 706
Zip 30701
Web www.gordonchamber.org
Information Gordon County Chamber of Commerce, 300 S Wall St; 706/625-3200 or 800/887-3811

Once called Oothcaloga, "place of the beaver dams," the name was changed in 1850 to honor John Caldwell Calhoun, Secretary of State to President John Tyler. Although the town was directly in the path of General Sherman's 1864 march to the sea, Calhoun was not destroyed. Now Calhoun is the seat of Gordon County and center of a dairy, beef cattle, and poultry raising area. The town has a major carpet industry and several major manufacturing companies that provide a wide range of products.

What to See and Do

New Echota State Historic Site. (Restoration of final Eastern Cherokee capital) (1825-38) Incl the Worcester house (1828), the Council House, the print shop, courthouse, the Vann Tavern (1805), an 1830s log store, and a museum orientation center. Citizens of Calhoun bought the 200-acre site in the early 1950s and donated it to the state. After establishing a government in 1817, the legislature of the Cherokee Indian Nation established a capital surrounding the site of their Council House in 1825. The written form of the Cherokee language, created by the brilliant Sequoyah, had been developed by 1821, and the print shop was built in 1827. The first issue of the Cherokee newspaper, the *Cherokee Phoenix,* was printed in this shop in 1828 in both Cherokee and English; the paper continued publication until 1834. Samuel A. Worcester, a most able missionary, arrived from Boston in 1827 and built a house, which is the only original bldg still standing. The Vann Tavern, built by Cherokees at another location, was moved to the park as part of the restoration. The Cherokee Nation had a legislative hall, a supreme court house, a mission, and several other bldgs at New Echota. At the height of Cherokee prosperity, gold was found in Cherokee territory, then incl parts of Georgia, North Carolina, Alabama, and Tennessee. In 1835, after a long legal battle, the Cherokees were forced to agree to sell their territory and move to Oklahoma. In the winter of 1838-39 the Cherokees were driven to their new location over the "Trail of Tears," ¼ of them dying en route. Many hid out in the Great Smoky Mts; their descendants now form the Eastern Cherokees. The bldgs of the restored New Echota are furnished authentically and are a dramatic reconstruction of a remarkable episode in Native American history. (Tues-Sat, also Sun afternoons; closed Jan 1, Thanksgiving, Dec 25) Tours. Contact Site Superintendent, 1211 Chatsworth Hwy NE. ½ mi E of I-75, Exit 131 on GA 225. Phone 706/624-1321. ¢

Resaca Confederate Cemetery. Site of the Civil War battle that opened the way to Atlanta for General Sherman. Civil War markers and cemetery on the Civil War Discovery Trail. (Daily) 5 mi N on I-75, Resaca exit (133). **FREE**

Motels/Motor Lodges

★ **DAYS INN.** *742 Hwy 53 SE (30120), at I-75 Exit 129. 706/629-8271; fax 706/629-8271.* 120 rms, 2 story. S $30-$42; D $35-$49; each addl $5; suites $65; under 12 free; lower rates May & Sep. Crib free. Pet accepted; $4. TV; cable. Pool. Playground. Ck-out noon. Coin lndry. Business servs avail. Some refrigerators. Cr cds: A, C, D, DS, ER, MC, V.

★ **HOWARD JOHNSON.** *1220 Red Bud Rd (30701), I-75 Exit 130. 706/629-9191; fax 706/629-0873; res 800/446-4656; toll-free 800/846-3271.* 99 rms, 2 story. S $49; D $54; each addl $5; under 18 free. Crib free. Pet accepted. TV; cable (premium). Pool. Restaurant 6:30 am-2 pm, 5-9 pm. Ck-out noon. Meeting rms. Business servs avail. In-rm modem link. Bellhops. Valet serv. Cr cds: A, C, D, DS, JCB, MC, V.

★★★ **JAMESON INN.** *189 Jameson St SE (30701). 706/629-8133; fax 706/629-7985; res 800/526-3766. Email calhoun.ca@jamesoninns. com.* 59 rms, 2 story. S $52; D $56; each addl $4; suite $70; under 12 free. Crib free. TV; cable (premium), VCR avail. Pool. Complimentary continental bkfst. Restaurant adj open 24 hrs. Ck-out 11 am. Business servs avail. In-rm modem link. Exercise equipt. Some refrigerators, microwaves. Cr cds: A, C, D, DS, MC, V.

★★ **QUALITY INN - CALHOUN.** *915 Hwy 53 E SE (30701), E off I-75 Exit 129. 706/629-9501; fax 706/629-9501; res 800/228-5151; toll-free 800/225-4686. www.qualityinn.com/hotel/GA 246.* 100 rms, 2 story. Mar-Apr, June-Aug: S $56; D $60; each addl $5; under 18 free; lower rates rest of yr. Crib avail. Pet accepted, some restrictions, fee. Parking lot. Pool. TV; cable, VCR avail. Complimentary continental bkfst, coffee in rms, newspaper, toll-free calls. Restaurant. Ck-out 11 am, ck-in 1 pm. Meeting rm. Fax servs avail. Coin lndry. Golf, 18 holes. Tennis, 3 courts. Picnic facilities. Cr cds: A, C, D, DS, MC, V.

Restaurant

★ **PENGS PAVILLION.** *1120 S Wall St (30701), I-75 Exit 129. 706/629-1453.* Specializes in Mongolian beef. Hrs: 11 am-9 pm. Closed Sun; hols. Res accepted. Lunch $4.25-$4.75; dinner $6.50-$9.25. Parking. Chinese

decor; murals, lanterns. Cr cds: A, D, DS, MC, V.

Carrollton (C-2)

Pop 16,029 **Elev** 1,116 ft
Area code 770 **Zip** 30117
Web www.carroll-ga.org
Information Carroll County Chamber of Commerce, 200 Northside Dr; 770/832-2446

Carrollton was named in honor of Charles Carroll, one of the signers of the Declaration of Independence. The town serves as a regional retail, service, manufacturing, and health care center for several counties in western Georgia and eastern Alabama. Carrollton is home to Southwire, one of the nation's largest privately owned rod and cable manufacturing companies. The world's largest tape and record manufacturing plant, owned by Sony, is located here as well.

What to See and Do

John Tanner State Park. Two lakes offer the longest beach in the state park system. Swimming, fishing, boating (rentals); picnicking, camping, motel. Standard hrs, fees. Contact Superintendent, 354 Tanner's Beach Rd. 6 mi W off GA 16. Phone 770/830-2222.

State University of West Georgia. (1933) 7,500 students. A unit of the state univ system. On campus are John F. Kennedy Memorial Chapel and

    Thomas Bonner House. (ca 1840) Restored plantation house, campus information center. (Mon-Fri; closed hols, school breaks) Maple St. Phone 770/836-6464.

Motel/Motor Lodge

★★ **COMFORT INN.** *128 Hwy 61 Connector (30180), N on GA 61, at jct I-20. 770/459-8000; fax 770/459-8413; res 800/228-5150.* 64 rms, 2 story. Memorial Day-mid-Sep: S $49-

$69; D $59-$79; each addl $6; under 18 free; higher rates auto races; lower rates rest of yr. Crib $6. TV; cable (premium), VCR avail. Pool. Complimentary continental bkfst. Restaurant opp 6 am-11 pm. Ck-out 11 am. Business servs avail. In-rm modem link. Some in-rm whirlpools, refrigerators. Cr cds: A, C, D, DS, ER, JCB, MC, V.

Restaurant

★★ **MAPLE STREET MANSION.** *401 Maple St (30117). 770/834-2657.* Specializes in prime rib, Maple Hill pie. Hrs: 11 am-10 pm; Sat 4-11 pm. Closed Sun, Mon; Jan 1, Dec 24, 25. Res accepted. Bar. Lunch $3.95-$6.95; dinner $5.95-$21.95. Parking. In restored house (1894) built by Georgian industrialist Leroy Mandeville. Cr cds: A, D, DS, MC, V.

Cartersville

(B-2) *See also Atlanta, Marietta, Rome*

Founded 1832 **Pop** 12,035 **Elev** 787 ft
Area code 770 **Zip** 30120
Web www.notatlanta.org
Information Cartersville/Bartow County Convention & Visitors Bureau, PO Box 200397; 770/387-1357 or 800/733-2280

Cartersville is in the center of an area rich in minerals. Its economy is based on textile manufacturing, plastics, the quarrying of limestone, and the mining of ocher, barite, and manganese. An Anheuser-Busch brewery also contributes to the economy.

What to See and Do

Allatoona Lake. (US Army Corps of Engineers) Swimming, waterskiing, fishing, boating (ramps); hiking trails, overlook, picnicking, camping (fee). Contact Park Ranger, PO Box 487. Headquarters is 3 mi N on I-75, exit 125, then E on GA 20, then 4 mi S on Spur 20. Phone 770/382-4700.

Etowah Indian Mounds Historic Site and Archaeological Area. The most impressive of more than 100 settlements in the Etowah Valley, this village was occupied from AD 1000-1500. It was the home of several thousand people of a relatively advanced culture. Six earthen pyramids grouped around 2 public squares, the largest of which occupies several acres, served as funeral mounds, bases for temples, and the residences of the chiefs. Museum displays artifacts from the excavations; crafts, foods, way of life of the Etowah; painted white marble mortuary. (Tues-Sun; closed Jan 1, Thanksgiving, Dec 25) 3 mi S, off GA 113, 61. Phone 770/387-3747. ¢

Kennesaw Mountain National Battlefield Park. (see) Approx 20 mi SE off US 41.

Red Top Mountain State Lodge Park. Swimming, waterskiing, boating (ramps, dock, marina); trails, miniature golf, picnicking, concession. Restaurant, lodge. Camping, cottages. Standard hrs, fees. 2 mi E of I-75, Exit 123. Phone 770/975-0055.

William Weinman Mineral Museum. Displays of cut gemstones, minerals, and rocks from Georgia and around the world; simulated limestone cave with waterfall. (Tues-Sun; closed hols) I-75 Exit 126, 51 Mineral Museum Dr. Phone 770/386-0576. ¢¢

Motels/Motor Lodges

★★ **BUDGET HOST.** *851 Cass White Rd NW (30121), I-75N Exit 127. 770/386-0350; fax 770/387-0591; toll-free 800/283-4678.* 92 rms, 3 story. S $21.95-$49.95; D $26.95-$89.95; each addl $5. Crib $2. Pet accepted; $2. TV; cable. Pool. Restaurant 6 am-2 pm, 5-9 pm. Ck-out 11 am. Coin lndry. Cr cds: A, DS, MC, V.

★★ **COMFORT INN.** *28 SR 20 Spur SE (30121). 770/387-1800; fax 770/387-1800; res 800/228-5150.* 60 rms, 2 story. S $32-$48; D $39-$60; each addl $5; under 18 free; higher rates special events. TV; cable. Pool. Complimentary continental bkfst. Restaurant nearby. Ck-out 11 am. Some refrigerators, microwaves. Cr cds: A, C, D, DS, JCB, MC, V.

★ **DAYS INN.** *5618 Hwy 20 SE (30121), at jct I-75 Exit 125. 770/382-1824; fax 770/606-9312; res 800/ DAYSINN.* 52 rms, 2 story. Mar-Aug, Dec: S $55; D $60; each addl $5; under 12 free; higher rates: baseball, football games; lower rates rest of yr. Crib free. TV; cable (premium). Pool. Complimentary continental bkfst. Restaurant adj 6 am-11 pm; wkends to 2 am. Ck-out noon. Some refrigerators. Cr cds: A, D, DS, MC, V.

★★ **HOLIDAY INN CARTERSVILLE.** *2336 Hwy 411 NE (30120), jct I-75 Exit 126. 770/386-0830; fax 770/386-0867; res 800/465-4329.* 144 rms, 2 story. S, D $67; each addl $6; under 19 free. Crib free. Pet accepted. TV; cable (premium). Pool. Coffee in lobby. Restaurant 6 am-10 pm. Bar 5 pm-midnight. Ck-out noon. Meeting rms. Business servs avail. In-rm modem link. Valet serv. Sundries. Exercise equipt. Health club privileges. Lawn games. Whirlpool in suites. Cr cds: A, C, D, DS, MC, V.

★★ **RAMADA LIMITED.** *45 SR 20 Spur SE (30121), at jct I-75 Exit 125. 770/382-1515; fax 770/382-1515; toll-free 800/272-6232.* 50 rms, 2 story. S $42-$75, D $45-$105; each addl $8; under 12 free. Crib free. TV; cable (premium). Pool. Complimentary continental breakfast. Restaurant nearby. Ck-out 11 am. Meeting rm. Business servs avail. In-rm modem link. Cr cds: A, C, D, DS, ER, JCB, MC, V.

Restaurant

★ **MORRELL'S.** *I-75 & Hwy 20 (30120), I-75 Exit 125. 770/382-1222.* Specializes in prime rib, barbecued pork and chicken. Hrs: 6 am-10 pm. Closed Thanksgiving, Dec 25. Bkfst $1.50-$4.50; lunch $4.25-$5.95; dinner $5.95-$15.95. Child's menu. Parking. Cr cds: A, D, MC, V.

Chatsworth

(A-2) *See also Calhoun, Dalton; also see Chattanooga, TN*

Pop 2,865 **Elev** 750 ft **Area code** 706 **Zip** 30705

Information Chatsworth-Murray County Chamber of Commerce, 126 N Third Ave; 706/695-6060

Murray County has a strong carpet industry. Almost a third of the land is forest and mountains. Opportunities for fishing, hunting, camping, backpacking, and mountain biking abound in the surrounding Cohutta Wilderness and woodlands. A Ranger District office of the Chattahoochee National Forest is located in Chatsworth. Talcum, a mineral that most people know only as a comfort to the skin, was once mined here in large quantities.

What to See and Do

Carters Lake. Swimming, fishing, boating (ramps); hiking trails, overlooks, camping (mid-Apr-late Oct; fee). For

Covered bridge over the Broad River

more information visit Resource
Manager's office at dam site. 15 mi S,
off US 411. Phone 706/334-2248.

Chattahoochee National Forest. (See
DAHLONEGA)

Fort Mountain State Park. A mountain park with ruins of a prehistoric
stone wall; observation tower. Swimming, fishing, paddleboats (rentals);
self-guided nature trail, picnicking,
cabins, camping. Standard hrs, fees.
7 mi E via GA 52. Contact Superintendent, 181 Fort Mountain Park Rd.
Phone 706/695-2621.

Vann House State Historic Site.
(1804) This brick house was the
showplace of the Cherokee Nation.
James Vann was half Scottish, half
Cherokee. His chief contribution to
the tribe was his help in establishing
the nearby Moravian Mission for the
education of the young Cherokees.
The 3-story house, with ft-thick brick
walls, is modified Georgian in style;
partly furnished. (Tues-Sun; closed
Jan 1, Thanksgiving, Dec 25) Contact
Manager, 82 GA 225 N. 3 mi W on
GA 52-A at jct GA 225 in Spring
Place. Phone 706/695-2598. ¢

Annual Event

Appalachian Wagon Train. 1 mi E via
US 76. Horse and mule shows, trail
rides, square dancing, parade. Phone
706/695-7122. Late June-early July.

Hotel

**★★ COHUTTA LODGE & CONFER-
ENCE CENTER.** *500 Cochise Tr*
(30705), 10 mi E on GA 52. 706/695-
9601; fax 706/695-0913. Email
info@cohuttalodge.com; www.cohuta
lodge.com. 61 rms, 2-3 story. May-Dec:
S, D $69-$99; each addl $8; suites $99;
kit. units $105-$125; cottage $165;
under 12 free; Oct wkends (2-day
min); lower rates rest of yr. Crib free.
TV. Indoor pool. Complimentary coffee in rms. Restaurant (see COHUTTA
DINING ROOM). Ck-out 11 am. Coin
lndry. Meeting rms. Business servs
avail. Gift shop. Lighted tennis. Game
rm. Lawn games. Many refrigerators.
Balconies. Picnic tables. Cr cds: A, DS,
MC, V.
✕ ⛷ ☀ 🐾

Restaurant

★★ COHUTTA DINING ROOM.
500 Cochise Tr. 706/695-9601.
www.cohuttalodge.com. Specializes in
prime rib, seafood. Salad bar. Hrs:
8:30-10:30 am, 11:30 am-3 pm, 5-
8:30 pm; Fri, Sat 8-10:30 am, 5-9:30
pm; Sun 8-10:30 am, 11:30 am-8 pm.
Closed Dec 24, 25. Bkfst 4.95-$6.95.
Buffet: $5.95; lunch $1.50-$6.25; din-
ner $5.75-$15.75. Entertainment:
pianist Fri, Sat. Parking. Cr cds: A, D,
DS, MC, V.
[D]

Chickamauga and Chattanooga National Military Park

See also Dalton; also see Chattanooga,
TN

(9 mi S of Chattanooga, TN on US 27)
Web www.nps.gov/chch/

Established in 1890, this is the oldest
and largest national military park in
the United States. The two-day battle
fought at Chickamauga was one of
the Civil War's fiercest, with 36,000
casualties, and was the greatest success of Confederate armies in the
West. However, the inability of General Braxton Bragg to follow up the
success of September 19-20, 1863,
and his defeat two months later on
Missionary Ridge at Chattanooga,
Tennessee, meant the loss of a strategic railway center and opened the
gateway to a Union advance into the
deep South.

General Bragg had evacuated Chattanooga on September 9 to maintain
rail communications southward after
Union Commander Rosecrans had
abruptly crossed the Tennessee River
southwest of the city. However, with
the arrival of reinforcements from
Lee's army in the east giving him a
numerical advantage, Bragg turned
back north to surprise Rosecrans'
scattered forces. On September 18,
the two armies stumbled into each

other on the west bank of Chickamauga Creek.

By the morning of September 19, Union troops attacked and were driven back in heavy fighting. Confederate troops broke the Union line the morning of the 20th, sweeping the entire right wing and part of the center from the field. Union troops on the left, with the aid of reserve corps and all under the command of General George H. Thomas, took up new positions on Snodgrass Hill, holding up under terrific assaults by Confederates until the Union army was able to retreat in good order to Chattanooga. Thomas earned the nickname "Rock of Chickamauga."

US 27 extends more than three miles through the 5,400-acre Chickamauga Battlefield, where the battle has been commemorated by markers, monuments, tablets, and artillery pieces. Woods and fields are kept as close as possible to the way they were in wartime, and some old buildings lend added atmosphere.

Chickamauga Battlefield is but one of 17 areas forming the National Military Park. Other major areas (all in Tennessee) are Point Park on Lookout Mountain, the Reservations on Missionary Ridge, Signal Point on Signal Mountain, and Orchard Knob in Chattanooga—totaling nearly 3,000 acres.

The Chickamauga visitor center, on US 27 at the north entrance to the battlefield, is the logical starting point for auto tours. The center has the Fuller Collection of American Military Shoulder Arms, consisting of 355 weapons, as well as a 26-minute multimedia program (fee) describing the Battle of Chickamauga. Visitor center (daily; closed Dec 25). Park (daily). The National Park Service also offers guided tours, walks, evening programs, and musket/cannon firing demonstrations (June-Aug). For further information, contact PO Box 2128, Fort Oglethorpe 30742; 706/866-9241. **FREE**

Motel/Motor Lodge

★ **CHANTICLEER LODGE.** *1300 Mockingbird Ln (30750), 8 mi S on GA 157, 3 mi from foot of mountain. 706/* 820-2015; fax 706/820-1060. 16 rms. S $35-$48; D $40-$86; each addl $6. TV; cable. Pool. Complimentary continental bkfst. Restaurant nearby. Ckout 11 am. Picnic tables, grill. Cr cds: A, MC, V.

Clayton

(A-4) *See also Hiawassee, Toccoa*

Pop 1,613 **Elev** 1,925 ft
Area code 706 **Zip** 30525
Web www.gamountains.com/rabun
Information Rabun County Chamber of Commerce, Box 750; 706/782-4812; a Rabun County Welcome Center is located on US 441 N; 706/782-5113 or 706/782-4812

Located in the mountainous and forested northeast corner of Georgia, Clayton offers visitors a wide variety of activities, including hiking, mountain climbing, camping, boating, fishing, hunting, skiing, and whitewater rafting. A Ranger District office of the Chattahoochee National Forest (see DAHLONEGA) is located in Clayton.

What to See and Do

Chattooga Wild and Scenic River. Originating in the mountains of North Carolina, the Chattooga tumbles southward 57 mi to its terminus, Lake Tugaloo, between Georgia and South Carolina. Designated a Wild and Scenic River by Congress in 1974, the Chattooga is one of the few remaining free-flowing streams in the Southeast. Scenery along the river is spectacular, with gorges, waterfalls, and unusual rock formations. 8 mi SE via US 76.

Foxfire Museum and Center. Located in replica of log cabin, the museum contains artifacts and crafts of early Appalachian life, incl the inner workings of an old gristmill. (Mon-Sat; closed hols) 2 mi N on US 441, in Mountain City. Phone 706/746-5828. Museum **FREE** Center ¢¢

Raft trips. Southeastern Expeditions. Whitewater raft trips on the Chattooga River in NE Georgia ranging in length from ½-day to 3 days. (Mar-

Oct) Contact 50 Executive Park South, Suite 5016, Atlanta 30329. Phone 404/329-0433 or 800/868-7238. ¢¢¢¢

Annual Event

Homemakers' Harvest Festival. 6 mi N on US 23, 441 in Dillard. Mountain arts and crafts. Three wkends Oct.

Columbus

(E-2) *See also Pine Mountain (Harris County)*

Founded 1827 **Pop** 178,681
Elev 250 ft **Area code** 706
Web www.columbusga.com/ccvb
Information Tourist Division, Convention and Visitors Bureau, 1000 Bay Ave, PO Box 2768, 31901; 706/322-1613 or 800/999-1613; or the Georgia Welcome Center, 1751 Williams Rd; 24-hr visitors information hotline 706/322-3181

Power from the falls of the Chattahoochee River feeds the industries of this dynamic city. With a nine-foot-deep navigable channel to the Gulf of Mexico, it is at the head of navigation on the Chattahoochee. Originally a settlement of the Creek Indians, the site was chosen as a border stronghold by Governor Forsyth in 1828. The city reached a peak of frenzied manufacturing and commerce between 1861-64, when it supplied the Confederate Army with shoes, caps, swords, and pistols.

The Columbus Iron Works (1853) supplied Columbus and the surrounding area with cast iron products, farming equipment, steam engines, and industrial and bldg supplies. It was a major supplier of cannons for the Confederate States during the Civil War. Reconstruction created havoc for a time, but by 1874 Columbus' industries were more numerous and varied than before the war: from 1880-1920 a commercial ice-making machine was produced in the town, and by the beginning of World War II Columbus was a great iron-working center and the second largest producer of cotton in the South.

Much of the original city plan of 1827 is still evident, with streets 99 to 164 feet wide flanked by magnificent trees. Dogwood and wisteria add color in the spring. The atmosphere is exemplified by the brick-lined streets and gaslights in the 28-block historic district and by the Victorian gardens, gazebos, and open-air amphitheaters on the Chattahoochee Promenade along the banks of the river.

What to See and Do

Columbus Convention and Trade Center. Converted from the historic Columbus Iron Works. Exhibit space, banquet facilities, outdoor amphitheater. 801 Front Ave. Phone 706/327-4522.

The Columbus Museum. Features Chattahoochee Legacy, a regional history gallery with re-created period settings; fine and decorative arts galleries; and Transformations, a youth-oriented participatory gallery. (Tues-Sun; closed hols) 1251 Wynnton Rd. Phone 706/649-0713. **FREE**

Fort Benning. Largest infantry post in the US, established during WWI, the fort was named for Confederate General Henry L. Benning of Columbus. Infantry School; demonstrations of Airborne 5000 at Jump Tower (Mon mornings). 5 mi S on US 27. Phone 706/545-2958 for information. **FREE** Here is

National Infantry Museum. Exhibits of US infantry weapons, uniforms, equipment from the Revolutionary War to the War in the Gulf; experimental and developmental weapons; collection of foreign weapons and equipment. (Daily; closed hols) Phone 706/545-2958. **FREE**

Springer Opera House. (1871) Restored Victorian theater in which many famous performers have appeared, incl Shakespearean actor Edwin Booth; museum. Guided tours. 103 10th St at 1st Ave. Phone 706/327-3688 (box office) for performance schedule, fee information.

Woodruff Museum of Civil War Naval History. Salvaged remains of Confederate gunboats *Jackson* and *Chattahoochee;* relics, ship models, uniforms, paintings, and other exhibits on Confederate naval operations. (Tues-Sun; closed Thanksgiving, Dec 25) 202 4th St. Phone 706/327-9798. **Donation**

Annual Event

Riverfest Weekend. At riverfront. Last wkend Apr.

Motels/Motor Lodges

★★ BAYMONT INN AND SUITES.
2919 Warm Springs Rd (31909). 706/ 323-4344; fax 706/596-9622; toll-free 800/301-0200. 102 rms, 3 story. S $43.95-$48.95; D $51.95-$56.95; suites $58.95-$63.95; under 18 free. Crib free. Pet accepted, some restrictions. TV; cable. Pool. Complimentary continental bkfst, coffee in rms. Restaurant opp 11 am-10 pm. Ck-out noon. Meeting rm. Business servs avail. In-rm modem link. Valet serv. Refrigerator, microwave in suites. Cr cds: A, C, D, DS, MC, V.

★★ BEST WESTERN COLUMBUS.
3443 B Macon Rd (31907), I-185 Exit 4. 706/568-3300; fax 706/563-2388; res 800/528-1234. www.bestwestern. com/columbus. 78 rms, 4 story, 4 suites. Mar-Sep: S, D $80; each addl $6; suites $115; under 18 free; lower rates rest of yr. Crib avail. Parking lot. Pool. TV; cable (premium). Complimentary continental bkfst, coffee in rms, newspaper, toll-free calls. Restaurant nearby. Ck-out noon, ck-in 2 pm. Business center. Dry cleaning. Exercise equipt. Golf. Cr cds: A, C, D, DS, JCB, MC, V.

★★ COURTYARD BY MARRIOTT.
3501 Courtyard Way (31904), adj to Peachtree Mall. 706/323-2323; fax 706/327-6030; toll-free 800/321-2211. 139 rms, 2 story. S $72-$82; D, suites $99.95; under 18 free; wkend rates. Crib free. TV; cable, VCR. Pool. Restaurant 6:30-10 am, 5-10 pm; Sat, Sun 7 am-noon. Bar 5-10 pm. Ck-out noon. Coin lndry. Meeting rms. In-rm modem link. Valet serv. Exercise equipt. Some refrigerators. Private patios, balconies. Cr cds: A, D, DS, MC, V.

★ LA QUINTA INN.
3201 Macon Rd (31906), I-185 Exit 4. 706/568-1740; fax 706/569-7434; toll-free 800/687- 6667. 122 rms, 2 story. S, D $59; suites $85; under 18 free. Crib free. Pet accepted. TV; cable (premium). Pool. Complimentary continental bkfst. Restaurant adj open 24 hrs. Ck-out noon. Coin lndry. Business servs avail. In-rm modem link. Valet serv. Some refrigerators. Grills. Cr cds: A, C, D, DS, MC, V.

Hotels

★★ HAMPTON INN-COLUMBUS AIRPORT.
5585 Whitesville Rd (31904), I-185 Exit 6, near Metropolitan Airport. 706/576-5303; fax 706/ 596-8076; toll-free 800/426-7866. 119 rms, 2 story. S $64; D $69; under 18 free. Crib $5. TV; cable (premium), VCR. Pool. Complimentary continental bkfst. Restaurant nearby. Ck-out noon. Meeting rm. Business servs avail. In-rm modem link. Sundries. Free airport transportation. Health club privileges. Cr cds: A, DS, MC, V.

★★★ HILTON HOTEL.
800 Front Ave (31901). 706/324-1800; fax 706/576-4413; toll-free 800/524-4020. 177 rms, 6 story. S $84-$126; D $94-$136; each addl $10; suites $125-$375; family, wkend rates. Crib free. TV; cable (premium). Pool. Restaurant 6:30 am-2 pm, 5-10:30 pm. Bar noon-midnight. Ck-out noon. Meeting rms. Business servs avail. In-rm modem link. Free airport, bus depot transportation. Incorporates 100-yr-old grist mill into design. Convention Center (former Columbus Iron Works facility) opp. Cr cds: A, C, D, DS, MC, V.

★★ SHERATON INN.
5351 Sidney Simons Blvd (31904), I-185 Exit 6, near Metropolitan Airport. 706/327-6868; fax 706/327-0041; res 800/325-3535. 178 rms, 5 story. S, D $80-$84; each addl $5; under 18 free. Crib free. TV; cable. Heated pool; whirlpool. Restaurant 6:30 am-2 pm, 5-9:30 pm; Sat, Sun from 7 am. Bar 4 pm-1 am. Ck-out noon. Meeting rms. Business servs avail. In-rm modem link. Free airport, bus depot transportation. Health club privileges. Game rm.

Some refrigerators. Cr cds: A, C, D, DS, MC, V.

Restaurants

★★★ BLUDAU'S GOETCHIUS HOUSE. *405 Broadway (31901).* 706/324-4863. Specializes in fresh seafood, veal. Hrs: 5-9:45 pm; Fri, Sat to 10:45 pm. Closed Sun. Res accepted. Bar. Dinner $13.95-$39.95. Parking. In restored antebellum mansion (1839). Cr cds: A, D, DS, MC, V.

★★ MALONE'S. *2955 Warm Springs Rd (31909).* 706/324-3250. Specializes in fajitas, fresh seafood, steak. Hrs: 11 am-10 pm. Closed Thanksgiving, Dec 25. Bar. Lunch $5.95-$8.95; dinner $8.95-$15.95. Child's menu. Parking. Cr cds: A, D, DS, MC, V.

Unrated Dining Spot

COUNTRY'S NORTH. *6298 Veterans Pkwy (31909), at Main St Village.* 706/660-1415. Specializes in barbecued chicken, ribs, and beef. Hrs: 11 am-10 pm; Fri, Sat to 11 pm. Closed hols. Res accepted. Lunch, dinner $6-$8. Child's menu. Western decor. Cr cds: MC, V.

Commerce

(B-4) *See also Athens, Gainesville*

Pop 4,108 **Elev** 931 ft **Area code** 706 **Zip** 30529

What to See and Do

Crawford W. Long Medical Museum.
Museum contains diorama of Dr. Long's first use of ether as an anesthetic in surgery, an enormous breakthrough in medicine. Also here are documents, artifacts, and history of anesthesia exhibit. Entrance is in Jackson County Historical Society bldg, which has other exhibits on local history. A 3rd bldg has an 1840s doctor's office, an apothecary shop, a 19th-century general store exhibit, and an herb garden. (Tues-Sat; closed hols) 10 mi SW via GA

15, on College St in Jefferson or 5 mi S on I-85, Exit 50. Phone 706/367-5307. **Donation**

Motels/Motor Lodges

★★ HOLIDAY INN EXPRESS.
30747 Hwy 441 S (30529), S at I-85, Exit 53. 706/335-5183; fax 706/335-6588; toll-free 800/465-4329. 96 rms, 2 story. S, D $52-$85; under 18 free; higher rates special events. Crib free. Pet accepted, some restrictions. TV; cable (premium). Pool. Complimentary continental bkfst. Ck-out noon. Coin lndry. Meeting rm. Business servs avail. In-rm modem link. Exercise equipt. Microwaves avail. Cr cds: A, D, DS, MC, V.

★ HOWARD JOHNSON INNS & SUITES.
148 Eisenhower Dr (30529), 3 mi N at I-85. 706/335-5581; fax 706/335-7889; res 800/446-4656. Email 1578@hotel.cendant.com. 120 rms, 2 story. S $40-$55; D $45-$74; each addl $5; under 18 free. Crib free. Pet accepted. TV; cable (premium), VCR avail (movies). Pool; wading pool. Complimentary continental bkfst. Restaurant 6 am-10 pm. Ck-out noon. Microwaves avail. Cr cds: A, D, DS, MC, V.

Cordele

(E-3) *See also Albany, Perry*

Founded 1888 **Pop** 10,321 **Elev** 319 ft **Area code** 912 **Zip** 31015

Information Cordele-Crisp Tourism Commission, 302 E 16th Ave, PO Box 158; 912/273-3526

Watermelons, sweet potatoes, soybeans, pecans, cotton, peanuts, corn, and cantaloupes are produced in Crisp County, of which Cordele is the seat. The local state farmers market sells more watermelons than any other market in the state; Cordele residents thus refer to their city as the "Watermelon Capital of the World." Garment making and the manufacture of enormous baling presses for scrap metals, agricultural implements, air conditioners, foundry products, mobile homes, livestock feed, fiberglass items, steel fittings, and several other industries are locally important.

What to See and Do

Georgia Veterans Memorial State Park. Swimming pool, waterskiing, fishing, boating; golf, picnicking, concession, camping, cabins. Museum; model airplane field with historic aircraft. Standard hrs, fees. Contact Park Manager, 2459-A Hwy 280 W. 9 mi W via US 280. Phone 912/276-2371.

Annual Event

Watermelon Festival. Parade; watermelon-eating, seed-spitting, and largest watermelon contests; fishing rodeo; Miss Heart of Georgia contest; arts and crafts; entertainment. Early-mid-July.

Motels/Motor Lodges

★★ CORDELE CONFERENCE CENTER. *1711 E 16th Ave (31010), at jct US 280, I-75 Exit 33. 912/273-4117; fax 912/273-1344; res 800/228-5151.* 187 rms, 2 story. S, D $50; golf plans. Crib free. Pet accepted. TV; cable (premium). Pool. Restaurant 6 am-10 pm. Ck-out noon. Meeting rms. Business servs avail. In-rm modem link. Valet serv. Sundries. Cr cds: A, D, DS, MC, V.

★ SUPER 8 MOTEL. *566 Farmers Market Rd (31015), I-75 Exit 35. 912/276-1008; fax 912/276-0222; toll-free 800/800-8000.* 120 rms, 2 story. S $32.95; D $36.95-$39.95; under 10 free. TV; cable (premium). Pool. Complimentary continental bkfst. Ck-out 11 am. Cr cds: A, C, D, DS, MC, V.

Hotel

★★ COMFORT INN. *1601 16th Ave. E (31015), I-75 Exit 33. 912/273-2371; fax 912/273-8351; res 800/228-5150.* 59 rms, 2 story. Mar, June-July, Oct, Dec: S $50; D $65; each addl $5; lower rates rest of yr. Crib avail, fee. Parking lot. Pool. TV; cable (pre-mium), VCR avail. Complimentary continental bkfst, coffee in rms, newspaper, toll-free calls. Restaurant. Ck-out 11 am, ck-in 3 pm. Meeting rm. Fax servs avail. Dry cleaning. Golf, 18 holes. Cr cds: A, C, D, DS, MC, V.

Restaurants

★★ DAPHNE LODGE. *US 280 W (31015). 912/273-2596.* Specializes in sauteed scallops, bacon-baked oysters. Hrs: 5:30-10 pm. Closed Sun, Mon; hols. Res accepted. Dinner $7.95-$18.95. Plantation manor house surrounded by pines. Cr cds: A, D, DS, MC, V.

★ OLDE INN. *2536 US 280 W (31015). 912/273-1229.* Specializes in seafood, steak. Hrs: 6-10 pm. Closed Sun, Mon; July 4, Thanksgiving, Dec 25. Res accepted. Wine, beer. Dinner $9-$21.75. Child's menu. Late 1800s bldg; original fireplace. Cr cds: A, MC, V.

Cumberland Island National Seashore

See also Brunswick, Jekyll Island, St. Simons Island

(Off the coast, NE of St. Marys)
Cumberland Island National Seashore, off the coast of Georgia, is an island 16 miles long and one and a half to three miles wide. It is accessible by passenger tour boat, which operates year-round. Mainland departures are from St. Marys (fee); reservations by phone are necessary.

A visit to the island is a walking experience, and there are no restaurants or shops. The island's western side is fringed with salt marsh, and white sand beaches face the Atlantic Ocean. The interior is forested primarily by live oak; interspersed are freshwater marshes and sloughs. Activities include viewing the scenery and wildlife, swimming, and exploring historical areas led by a ranger. Native Americans, Spanish, and English have all lived on the island; most structures date from the pre-Civil War plantation era, though there are turn-of-the-century buildings built by the Thomas Carnegie family. Camping (daily); reservations by phone necessary. Ferry (Mid-Mar-Sep, daily; winter, Thurs-Mon; closed Dec 25) For further information contact the Superintendent, PO Box 806, St. Marys 31558; 912/882-4335.

Crooked River State Park. Swimming pool, water sports, fishing in coastal tidewaters, boating; hiking, picnicking, camping, cottages. Three mi W of St. Marys on GA 40, then 8 mi N on GA 40 Spur. Contact Superintendent, 3092 Spur 40, St. Marys 31558; 912/882-4335.

Dahlonega

(A-3) *See also Gainesville*

Settled 1833 **Pop** 3,086 **Elev** 1,454 ft
Area code 706 **Zip** 30533
Web www.dahlonega.org
Information Dahlonega-Lumpkin County Chamber of Commerce, 13 Park St S; 706/864-3711

Gold fever struck this area in 1828, 20 years before the Sutter's Mill discovery in California. Dahlonega, derived from the Cherokee for the color yellow, yielded so much ore that the federal government established a local mint which produced $6,115,569 in gold coins from 1838-61. Dahlonega is the seat of Lumpkin County, where tourism, manufacturing, higher education, and agribusiness are the major sources of employment. A US Forest Service Visitor Center is located in Dahlonega.

What to See and Do

Amicalola Falls State Park. Highest waterfall in the eastern US (729 ft). Trout fishing. Hiking trails. Picnicking, concession, restaurant. Camping, cabins, lodge. For fee information, contact Superintendent, Star Rte, Box 215, Dawsonville 30534. 20 mi W off GA 52. Phone 706/265-8888.

Chattahoochee National Forest. This vast forest (748,608 acres) incl Georgia's Blue Ridge Mts toward the N, which have elevations ranging from 1,000 to nearly 5,000 ft. Because the forest ranges from the Piedmont to mountainous areas, the Chattahoochee has a diversity of trees and wildlife. There are 25 developed camping areas, 24 picnicking areas, 10 wilderness areas, and 6 swimming beaches. For the Chattahoochee-Oconee National Forest Recreation Area directory, contact the US Forest Service, 508 Oak St NW, Gainesville 30501. Phone 770/536-0541. In the forest are

Anna Ruby Falls. Approx 1,570 acres surrounding a double waterfall, with drops of 50 and 153 ft. This scenic area is enhanced by laurel, wild azaleas, dogwood, and rhododendron. Visitor center. Off GA 356, 6 mi N of Helen. Parking fee ¢

Appalachian National Scenic Trail. Eleven lean-tos are maintained along the 79 mi marked southern portion of the trail. Following the crest of the Blue Ridge divide, the trail begins outside Dahlonega and continues for 2,000 mi to Mt Katahdin, Maine.

Track Rock Gap. Well-preserved rock carvings of ancient Indian origin; figures resemble animal and bird tracks, crosses, circles, and human footprints. Off US 76, 8 mi SW of Young Harris.

Dahlonega Courthouse Gold Museum State Historic Site. Exhibits on first major gold rush; display of gold coins minted in Dahlonega. Film shown every ½-hr. (Daily; closed Jan 1, Thanksgiving, Dec 25) Contact Manager, Public Sq, Box 1. On the Sq, in old Lumpkin County Courthouse (1836). Phone 706/864-2257. ¢¢

Gold panning.

Consolidated Gold Mines. Underground mine tour (40-45 min) through tunnel network; displays of original equipment used. Instructors avail for gold panning. (Daily; closed Dec 25) 125 Consolidated Gold Mine Rd, at jct GA 52, US 19 & GA 9. Phone 706/864-8473. ¢¢

Crisson's Gold Mine. Gold and gem panning; indoor panning (winter). Demonstration of working stamp mill, more than 100 yrs old. Gift shop. (Daily; closed Dec 25) 2½ mi N via US 19 to end of Wimpy Mill Rd, then 1 mi E. Phone 706/864-6363 or 706/864-7998. ¢¢

Gold Miners' Camp. Gold panning near the Chestatee River in an authentic mining setting. (May-Oct, daily) 2½ mi S via GA 60. Phone 706/864-6373. ¢¢

Lake Winfield Scott. A US Forest Service Recreation Area with an 18-acre lake in the Blue Ridge Mts. Swimming, bathhouse, fishing; picnicking, campsites (fee). (May-Oct) Contact the Ranger District Office, Box 9, Blairsville 30512. 15 mi N on US 19, 129, then 4 mi SW on GA 180. Phone 706/745-6928. Parking ¢

North Georgia College and State University. (1873) 3,500 students. Part of the state univ system, North Georgia College's administration bldg, Price Memorial, was built on the foundation of the old US Branch Mint; unique gold steeple. Liberal arts and military college. College Ave. Phone 706/864-1800.

Vogel State Park. Rugged area in the heart of N Georgia's mountains. At the foot of Blood and Slaughter mountains, 22-acre Lake Trahlyta has swimming, bathhouse, fishing, boating; picnicking, grills, playground, camping, 36 furnished cabins. Standard hrs, fees. Contact Superintendent, 7485 Vogel State Park Rd, Blairsville 30512. 25 mi N off US 19/129, S of Blairsville. Phone 706/745-2628. Parking ¢

Annual Events

Gold Panning Competition. Consolidated Gold Mine. Third wkend Apr.

Gold Rush Days. Third wkend Oct.

Motel/Motor Lodge

★ **SUPER 8 MOTEL.** *20 Mountain Dr SW; Hwy 60 S (38305). 706/864-4343; fax 706/864-4343; toll-free 800/800-8000.* 60 rms, 2 story. S $37-$125; D $45-$125; each addl $5; under 18 free. TV; cable (premium). Pool. Complimentary coffee in lobby. Restaurant adj 6 am-midnight. Ck-out noon. Some refrigerators. Cr cds: A, C, D, DS, MC, V.

D ⇔ ⊠ 🐾 SC

Resort

★★ **FORREST HILLS MOUNTAIN RESORT.** *135 Forest Hill Rd (30533), 12 mi W on GA 52, then right on Wesley Chapel Rd. 706/864-6456; fax 706/864-0757; toll-free 800/654-6313. Email foresths@alltell.net.* 27 kit. cottages (1-4 bedrm). June, Aug, Oct, Nov MAP: S, D $89-$185; wkly rates; higher rates special events; lower rates rest of yr. TV; VCR (movies $3.50). Pool. Complimentary coffee in rms. Dining rm 8:30-10:30 am, 6-8 pm. Ck-out 11 am, ck-in 3 pm. Grocery 4 mi. Meeting rms. Business center. Maid serv bi-wkly. Gift shop. Tennis. Hiking. Microwaves; many in-rm whirlpools, fireplaces. Porches. Picnic tables. Grills. Surrounded by north Georgia mountain forest. Cr cds: A, DS, MC, V.

D 🐾 🏊 ⇝ ⇔ ⚁ ⊠ 🐾

B&B/Small Inn

★★ **THE SMITH HOUSE.** *84 S Chestatee St (30533). 706/867-7000; fax 706/864-7564; toll-free 800/852-9577. Email info@smithhouse.com; www.smithhouse.com.* 16 rms, 2 story. June-Aug, Oct-Nov: S $129; lower rates rest of yr. Parking lot. Pool. TV; cable (premium), VCR avail. Complimentary continental bkfst, coffee in rms. Restaurant (see SMITH HOUSE). Ck-out 11 am, ck-in 2 pm. Meeting rms. Concierge. Gift shop. Golf. Tennis, 10 courts. Picnic facilities. Cr cds: A, MC, V.

D 🏋 ⚁ ⇔ ⊠ 🐾

Restaurant

★ **SMITH HOUSE.** *84 S Chestatee St. 706/867-7000. www.smithhouse.com.* Specializes in country cooking. Hrs: 11 am-3 pm, 4-7:30 pm; Sun 11 am-7 pm; winter hrs vary. Closed Mon. Lunch complete meals: $10.25-$13.95; dinner complete meals: $11.50-$14.50. Family-style dining in Blue Ridge Mt tradition. Family-owned. Cr cds: A, MC, V.

D

Dalton

(A-2) *See also Calhoun; also see Chattanooga, TN*

Founded 1837 **Pop** 21,761 **Elev** 759 ft
Area code 706 **Web** www.nwgeorgia.
com/daltoncvb/

Information Convention and Visitors Bureau, 2211 Dug Gap Battle Rd, PO Box 2046, 30722-2046; 706/272-7676 or 800/331-3258

Once a part of the Cherokee Nation, Dalton was involved in fierce battles and skirmishes in the Civil War as Union forces advanced on Atlanta. Today, Dalton has more than 100 carpet outlets and manufactures a large portion of the world's carpets. Dalton also produces other tufted textiles, chemicals, latex, thread, and yarn.

What to See and Do

Chickamauga and Chattanooga National Military Park. (see) 23 mi N via I-75, GA 2, then 2 mi S via US 27.

Crown Garden and Archives. Headquarters of the Whitfield-Murray Historical Society. Genealogical library; changing exhibits incl Civil War items; permanent exhibit on the history of bedspread tufting in the area. (Tues-Fri; closed Jan 1, wk of July 4, Thanksgiving, wk of Dec 25) 715 Chattanooga Ave, 2 mi N via I-75 and US 41, Walnut Ave Exit. Phone 706/278-0217. **Donation**

Annual Event

Prater's Mill Country Fair. 10 mi NE on GA 2. Arts and crafts show, food, late 1800s entertainment, canoeing on Coahulla Creek, pony rides, exhibits; 3-story gristmill in operation. Phone 706/275-6455. Mother's Day wkend and Columbus Day wkend.

Motels/Motor Lodges

★★ **BEST WESTERN INN.** *2106 Chattanooga Rd (30720), at I-75 Rocky Face Exit 137. 706/226-5022; fax 706/226-5022; res 800/528-1234.* 99 rms, 2 story. S $40; D $45; each addl $5; under 12 free. Crib $6. Pet accepted. TV; cable. Heated pool. Playground. Restaurant 6-10 am, 5-9:30 pm. Bar 4 pm-midnight; entertainment Fri, Sat. Ck-out noon. Beauty shop. Coin lndry. Meeting rms. Business servs avail. In-rm modem link. Sundries. Cr cds: A, C, D, DS, MC, V.

★★ **HERITAGE QUALITY MOTEL.** *2107 Chattanooga Rd (30720), at I-75 Exit 137. 706/278-1448; fax 706/226-9716; res 800/446-4656; toll-free 800/843-5644.* 106 rms, 2 story. S $33.95-$39.95; D $45.95-$49.95; under 18 free. Crib free. Pet accepted, some restrictions. TV; cable. Pool; wading pool. Restaurant 6 am-2 pm, 5:30-9:30 pm. Bar 5 pm-midnight. Ck-out 11 am. Health club privileges. Picnic tables. Cr cds: A, C, DS, MC, V.

★★ **HOLIDAY INN.** *515 Holiday Dr (30720), I-75 Exit 136. 706/278-0500; fax 706/226-0279; toll-free 800/465-4329.* 199 rms, 2 story. S $59-$69; D $64-$72; under 19 free; wkend rates. Crib free. Pet accepted. TV; cable (premium). Pool; wading pool. Coffee in rms. Restaurant 6:30 am-1:30 pm, 5:30-10 pm. Bar 5-10 pm, closed Sun. Ck-out noon. Coin lndry. Meeting rms. Business servs avail. In-rm modem link. Valet serv. Exercise equipt. Cr cds: A, C, D, DS, JCB, MC, V.

Restaurant

★★ **DALTON DEPOT.** *110 Depot St (30720). 706/226-3160.* Specializes in baby back ribs, prime rib, fresh fish. Hrs: 11 am-10 pm; Fri, Sat to 11 pm. Closed Sun; hols. Res accepted. Bar. Lunch $6-$12; dinner $8-$15. Child's menu. Entertainment: band Fri, Sat. Parking. Train depot atmosphere and decor. Cr cds: A, D, DS, MC, V.

Darien

(F-6) *See also Brunswick, Jekyll Island, St. Simons Island, Sea Island*

Founded 1736 **Pop** 1,783 **Elev** 20 ft
Area code 912 **Zip** 31305
Web www.mcintoshcounty.com
Information McIntosh Chamber of Commerce, PO Box 1497; 912/437-4192

James Oglethorpe recruited Scots Highlanders to protect Georgia's frontier on the Altamaha River in 1736. Calling their town Darien, the Scots guarded Savannah from Spanish and native attack and carved out large plantations from the south Georgia wilderness. After 1800 Darien thrived as a great timber port until the early 20th century. Today, shrimp boats dock in the river over which Darien Scots once kept watch.

What to See and Do

Fort King George State Historic Site. (1721) South Carolina scouts built this fort near an abandoned Native American village and Spanish mission to block Spanish and French expansion into Georgia, thereby establishing the foundation for the later English Colony of Georgia. The fort and its blockhouse have been entirely reconstructed to original form. Museum interprets the periods of Native American, Spanish, and British occupations, the settlement of Darien, and Georgia's timber industry. (Tues-Sun; closed Jan 1, Thanksgiving, Dec 25) 1½ mi E of US 17 on Fort King George Dr. Contact Superintendent, PO Box 711. Phone 912/437-4770. ¢

Golden Isles. (see) SE off US 17.

Hofwyl-Broadfield Plantation State Historic Site. (1807) The evolution of this working rice plantation (1807-1973) is depicted through tours of the 1851 plantation house, museum, and trails. Tours (Tues-Sun; closed Jan 1, Thanksgiving, Dec 25). Contact Manager, 5556 US 17N, Brunswick 31525. 6 mi S on US 17. Phone 912/264-7333. ¢

Annual Event

Blessing of the Shrimp Fleet. At Darien Bridge. Apr or May.

Douglas (F-5)

Founded 1858 **Pop** 10,464 **Elev** 259 ft
Area code 912 **Zip** 31533
Web www.douglasga.org
Information Chamber of Commerce, 46 John Coffee Rd, PO Box 2470, 31534; 912/384-1873

The town's central location between I-75 and I-95 has helped Douglas develop into a leading trade and distribution center for the southeast. A number of *Fortune* 500 companies operate within Coffee County.

What to See and Do

General Coffee State Park. A 1,510-acre park on the 17-Mile River in Coffee County. Swimming pool, fishing; nature trails, picnicking, playgrounds, camping, lodging. Standard hrs, fees. Contact Manager, Rte 2, Box 83, Nicholls 31554. 6 mi E on GA 32. Phone 912/384-7082.

Motels/Motor Lodges

★ **DAYS INN.** *907 N Peterson Ave (31533).* 912/384-5190; fax 912/384-5190; toll-free 800/329-7466. 70 rms, 2 story. S, D $36-$45; each addl $5; under 12 free. Crib free. Pet accepted. TV; cable (premium), VCR (movies). Pool. Complimentary continental bkfst. Restaurant adj 6 am-midnight. Ck-out noon. Health club privileges. Microwaves avail. Cr cds: A, C, D, DS, MC, V.

🐕 🏊 🚫 🐾 SC

★ ★ **HOLIDAY INN.** *1750 S Peterson Ave; US 441S (31533).* 912/384-9100; fax 912/384-9100; toll-free 800/465-4329. 100 rms, 2 story. S $54; D $59; each addl $5; under 18 free. Crib free. Pet accepted, some restrictions. TV; cable (premium). Pool. Restaurant 6-10 am, 11 am-2 pm, 5-10 pm. Bar 4 pm-midnight. Ck-out noon. Meeting rms. Business servs avail. In-rm modem link. Free airport transportation. Some refrigerators; microwaves avail. Picnic tables. Cr cds: A, C, D, DS, MC, V.

★★ **THE INN AT DOUGLAS.** *1007 N Peterson Ave (31533). 912/384-2621; fax 912/384-2621; toll-free 877/843-4667.* 100 rms, 2 story. June-Aug: S $42-$49; D $47-$54; each addl $5; lower rates rest of yr. Crib free. Pet accepted. TV; cable (premium). Pool. Restaurant 6 am-midnight. Bar 4 pm-2 am; entertainment. Ck-out noon. Meeting rms. Grills, picnic tables. Cr cds: A, C, D, DS, MC, V.

Dublin (D-4)

Pop 16,312 **Elev** 228 ft **Area code** 912
Information Dublin-Laurens County Chamber of Commerce, PO Box 818, 31040; 912/272-5546

The seat of Laurens County, Dublin sits on land once occupied by Creek Indians. Area industries manufacture a wide range of goods, incl textiles, carpeting, missile control systems, and computer components. The first aluminum extrusion plant in the US is located here. Agricultural products include soybeans, wheat, grain, peanuts, corn, cotton, and tobacco.

What to See and Do

Dublin-Laurens Museum. Local history museum featuring Native American artifacts, art, textiles, and relics from early settlers. (Tues-Fri; closed Jan 1, Thanksgiving, Dec 25) Bellevue & Academy at Church. Phone 912/272-9242. **FREE**

Fish Trap Cut. Believed to have been built between 1000 BC and AD 1500, this large rectangular mound, smaller round mound, and canal may have been used as an aboriginal fish trap. Oconee River, GA 19.

Historic buildings. Greek Revival and Victorian houses can be found along Bellevue Ave.

Annual Event

St. Patrick's Festival. Incl parade, ball, contests, golf tournaments, arts and crafts show, square dancing, and entertainment. Mar.

Motels/Motor Lodges

★★ **HOLIDAY INN.** *US 441 S (31040), 3 mi S on US 319/441 at jct I-16. 912/272-7862; fax 912/272-1077; res 800/HOLIDAY.* 124 rms, 2 story. S $54; D $59; each addl $5; suites $79; under 18 free; wkly rates. Crib free. Pet accepted. TV; cable (premium). Pool. Complimentary bkfst. Restaurant 6:30-9:30 am, 11:30 am-2 pm, 6-9 pm. Bar 5 pm-1 am; entertainment. Ck-out noon. Meeting rms. Business servs avail. In-rm modem link. Valet serv. Airport transportation. Exercise equipt. Health club privileges. Cr cds: A, D, DS, MC, V.

Eatonton

(C-4) *See also Madison, Milledgeville*

Pop 4,737 **Elev** 575 ft **Area code** 706
Zip 31024
Web www.oconee.com/epchamber
Information Eatonton-Putnam Chamber of Commerce, 105 Sumter St, PO Box 4088; 706/485-7701 or 706/485-4875

In the early 19th century, large tracts of land in this area were acquired and put under cultivation; by the mid-1800s the town of Eatonton had become a center of planter culture, that archetypal romantic concept of cotton fields, mansions, wealth, and southern grace. Joel Chandler Harris was born in Eatonton in 1848. He successfully immortalized the traditional ways of the Old South by creating the character "Uncle Remus" to retell the "Br'er Rabbit" and "Br'er Fox" folk tales heard on the plantation.

Eatonton is also the hometown of Alice Walker, author of *The Color Purple,* an acclaimed depiction of the South of a different time. Eatonton, the seat of Putnam County, is known as the largest dairy producer in the state.

What to See and Do

Alice Walker: A Driving Tour. Driving tour past the author's birthplace, church, and house where she grew up. Contact the Chamber of Commerce for brochure and information. Phone 706/485-7701.

Indian Springs State Park. (see) 35 mi W via GA 16 to Jackson, then 5 mi SE on GA 42.

Lake Oconee. Lawrence Shoals Recreation Area. E on GA 16 & N on GA 44 (see MADISON). **Lake Sinclair.** S on US 441 (see MILLEDGEVILLE). Both Georgia Power Co projects created by the impoundment of the Oconee River.

Rock Eagle Effigy

Rock Eagle Effigy. This 8-ft-high mound of milky white quartz is shaped like a great prone bird, wings spread, head turned eastward, 102 ft from head to tail and 120 ft wingtip to wingtip. Archaeologists estimate the monument is more than 5,000 yrs old and was probably used by Native Americans for religious ceremonies. It may be viewed from an observation tower. 7 mi N on US 441, located in Rock Eagle 4-H Center. Phone 706/485-2831. **FREE**

Uncle Remus Museum. Log cabin made from 2 original slave cabins. Reconstruction of cabin fireplace; shadow boxes with illustrations of 12 tales; mementos of era, first editions; diorama of old plantation; other relics. (June-Aug, daily; rest of yr, Wed-Mon) 3 blks S of courthouse on

US 441 in Turner Park. Phone 706/485-6856. ¢

Annual Event

Putnam County Dairy Festival. Parade, dairy and farming-related contests, arts and crafts fair, entertainment. First Sat June.

Forsyth

(D-3) *See also Macon*

Pop 4,268 **Elev** 705 ft **Area code** 912 **Zip** 31029
Web www.hom.net/monroe

Information Forsyth-Monroe County Chamber of Commerce, 267 Tift College Dr, PO Box 811; 912/994-9239

What to See and Do

Indian Springs State Park. (see) 17 mi N on GA 42.

Jarrell Plantation State Historic Site. Authentic plantation with 20 historic bldgs dating from 1847-1940. Plain-style plantation house, sawmill, grist mill, blacksmith shop, farm animals. Seasonal demonstrations. (Tues-Sun; closed Jan 1, Thanksgiving, Dec 25) 18 mi E of I-75 exit 60 on GA 18E, then N on Jarrell Plantation Rd. Phone 912/986-5172. ¢

The Whistle Stop Cafe. Town of Juliette, GA was where the movie *Fried Green Tomatoes* was filmed. Cafe and other stores along McCrackin St Cafe (Mon-Sat and Sun afternoons). I-75, exit 61, then 8 mi E to Juliette. Phone 912/994-3670.

Motels/Motor Lodges

★★ **BEST WESTERN HILL TOP INN.** *951 Hwy 42 N (31029), jct I-75, Exit 63. 912/994-9260; fax 912/994-9260; toll-free 800/528-1234.* 120 rms,

2 story. S, D $40-$75; each addl $6; under 12 free. Crib $6. TV; cable. Pool; wading pool. Ck-out noon. Business servs avail. In-rm modem link. Cr cds: A, C, D, DS, MC, V.

★★ **HAMPTON INN.** *520 Holiday Circle (31029), at I-75 Exit 61. 912/994-9697; fax 912/994-3594; toll-free 800/426-7866.* 124 rms, 4 story. S $49; D $52-$56; under 18 free. Crib free. Pet accepted. TV; cable (premium). Pool privileges. Complimentary continental bkfst. Ck-out noon. Meeting rm. In-rm modem link. Health club privileges. Cr cds: A, C, D, DS, MC, V.

★★ **HOLIDAY INN.** *480 Holiday Circle (31029), at I-75 Exit 61, Tift College Dr and Juliette Rd. 912/994-5691; fax 912/994-3254; res 800/HOLIDAY.* 120 rms, 2 story. S, D $59-$69; each addl $5. Crib free. Pet accepted, some restrictions. TV; cable (premium). Pool; wading pool. Coffee in rms. Restaurant 6 am-10 pm. Bar 4 pm-midnight; closed Sun. Ck-out noon. Coin lndry. Meeting rms. Business center. In-rm modem link. Exercise equipt. Golf privileges. Game rm. Chapel on premises. Cr cds: A, C, D, DS, JCB, MC, V.

Unrated Dining Spot

WHISTLE STOP CAFE. *471 McCrackin St (31046), 3 mi E. 912/994-3670.* Specializes in barbecued ribs, country cooking. Hrs: 9 am-2:30 pm; Sat 8:30 am-3 pm; Sun noon-4 pm. Closed hols. Bkfst $2-$3.75; lunch $1.95-$6.95. Film site of *Fried Green Tomatoes*. Cr cds: MC, V.

Fort Frederica National Monument

See also Brunswick, Jekyll Island, St. Simons Island, Sea Island

(12 mi NE of Brunswick via St. Simons/Sea Island Causeway-toll)

Fort Frederica marked the southern boundary of British Colonial North America. It was carefully planned by the Trustees in London in 1736 and included the town of Frederica, named after Frederick, Prince of Wales.

Having picked the site of the fort on a bluff commanding the Frederica River, General James Oglethorpe returned to England and helped select families to build and settle it. Forty-four men and 72 women and children landed at St. Simons Island on March 16, 1736. In 1738, a regiment of 650 British soldiers arrived. The fort was then strengthened with "tabby" (a kind of cement made of lime, oyster shells, sand, and water), and the whole town was enclosed with earth and timber works from 10 to 13 feet high that included towers and a moat.

Oglethorpe used Fort Frederica as a command post for his invasion of Florida. He built other forts on St. Simons and other islands and attacked Spanish outposts to the south. In July 1742, Spaniards launched an attack on Fort Frederica, but Oglethorpe repulsed this with an ambush at Bloody Marsh, ending Spanish attempts to gain control of Georgia.

Frederica flourished as a military town until after the peace of 1748. With the withdrawal of the regiment the following year, the shopkeepers and tradesmen at Frederica had to move elsewhere. The town did not long survive these losses. Archaeological excavations have exposed some of it, and stabilization work has been done by the National Park Service. Outdoor exhibits make it easy to visualize the town as it was, and the visitor center has exhibits, touch computers, and a film dealing with its life and history. Self-guided audio tour (fee). (Daily; closed Dec 25) Contact the Superintendent, Rte 9, Box 286-C, St. Simons Island 31522; 912/638-3639. Golden Age Passport (see MAKING THE MOST OF YOUR TRIP). Entrance per vehicle ¢¢

Fort McAllister Historic Park

See also Savannah

(25 mi S of Savannah, via GA 144 from I-95 or US 17; 10 mi E of Richmond Hill off US 17)

This Confederate fort built for the defense of Savannah stands on the left bank of the Great Ogeechee River, commanding the river's mouth. Fort McAllister's fall on December 13, 1864, marked the end of Sherman's march to the sea, opening communications between the Union Army and the fleet and rendering further defense of Savannah hopeless.

Prior to this, McAllister had proved that its type of massive earthwork fortifications could stand up against the heaviest naval ordnance. It protected the blockade-running ship *Nashville* from pursuit by Union gunboats in July and November 1862. It successfully resisted the attacks of *Monitor*-type ironclads of the Union Navy in 1863. The USS *Montauk* shelled the fort with the heaviest shells ever fired by a naval vessel against a shore work up to that time. The fort sustained only one casualty. There were huge holes in its parapets, but the damage was minor. Its gun emplacements were separated by large "traverses," several used to house powder magazines. The fort that seemed to be "carved out of solid earth" was termed "a truly formidable work" by a Union naval officer in 1864. General Sherman called the capture of the fort and overpowering its garrison "the handsomest thing I have seen in this war." Union losses were 24 killed, 110 wounded (mostly by mines outside the fort); the Confederate garrison of 230 men had 70 casualties—16 killed and 54 wounded—in the 15-minute battle.

The earthworks have been restored to approximate conditions of 1863-64. A museum containing mementos of the *Nashville* and the fort was completed in 1963 and opened on the centennial of the great bombardment. (Tues-Sat, also Sun afternoon; closed Thanksgiving, Dec 25; fee)

Fort McAllister has a campground and day-use facilities (fee); boating (ramps, dock). For further information, contact the Superintendent, 3894 Fort McAllister Rd, Richmond Hill 31324; 912/727-2339. ¢

Fort Pulaski National Monument

See also Savannah

(15 mi E of Savannah off US 80)

A unit of the Department of the Interior's National Park Service, Fort Pulaski National Monument was established by President Coolidge in 1924. The site, named in honor of Revolutionary war hero Casimir Pulaski, commemorates an international turning point in the history of fortification and artillery. It was here on April 11, 1862, that newly developed rifled cannons easily overtook a masonry fortification. After centuries of use throughout the world, both masonry forts and smooth-bore cannons were obsolete.

Most visitors begin the tour at the visitor center, which contains a small museum, an information desk, and a bookstore featuring more than 300 items on the Civil War and other site-related and regional subjects.

Restored to its mid-19th-century appearance, the fort contains several rooms, or casemates, depicting garrison life during its Confederate (1861-62) and Union (1862-75) occupations. This exhibit includes an officer's quarters and mess, medical dispensary, chapel, quartermaster's office, supply room, and enlisted men's quarters. Other displays include several examples of smooth-bore and rifled artillery and carriages. While self-guided tours are available year-round, ranger conducted programs and demonstrations are presented daily in the summer.

There are three major trails in the monument. The nature trail is a quarter-mile paved loop through several historic sites. The picnic trail is a half-mile paved trail from the visitor center to the picnic and recreation area, which borders the vast salt marshes and forested hammocks of the Savannah River estuary. The third trail follows the historic dike originally surveyed by Robert E. Lee. A walk on any segment of the trail provides excellent opportunities to see a wide variety of plants and wildlife, as well as scenic views of the fort.

Fishing, boating, and other water-related activities are offered at the park. The north channel shoreline and the bridge approaches at the south channel are the best fishing locations. A boat ramp and fishing dock just off US 80 at Lazaretto Creek provide more opportunities for fishing.

All facilities are open daily except Dec 25. Contact Superintendent, PO Box 30757, Savannah 31410; 912/786-5787. Entrance fee per person ¢

Gainesville

(B-3) *See also Buford, Dahlonega*

Pop 17,885 **Elev** 1,249 ft
Area code 770
Information Gainesville/Hall County Convention & Visitors Bureau, 830 Green St, 30501; 770/536-5209

What to See and Do

Green Street Historical District. A broad street with Victorian and Classical Revival houses dating from the late 19th and early 20th centuries. Here is

    Green Street Station. Home of Georgia Mts Historical and Cultural Trust. Houses historical and arts and crafts exhibits of NE Georgia as well as the Mark Trail Memorial Exhibit. (Tues-Fri; closed hols) Phone 770/536-0889. ¢

Lake Lanier Islands. W edge of town (see BUFORD).

Seasonal Event

Road Atlanta. 8 mi S via GA 53. Sports car and motorcycle racing.

Also street-driving and road-racing training programs. Phone 770/967-6143. Mar-Nov.

Motel/Motor Lodge

★★ **HOLIDAY INN.** *726 Jesse Jewell Pkwy (30504). 770/536-4451; fax 770/538-2880; res 800/HOLIDAY. Email holidayinn1@mindspring.com.* 132 rms, 2-3 story. S $63-$100; D $68-$105; each addl $5; under 19 free. Crib free. Pet accepted. TV; cable (premium). Pool. Restaurant 6:30 am-9 pm. Bar. Ck-out noon. Coin lndry. Meeting rms. In-rm modem link. Bellhops. Valet serv. Free railroad station, bus depot transportation. Cr cds: A, C, D, DS, MC, V.
D 🐾 🐕 🌊 🏊 ♨ 🛶

Hotel

★★ **BEST WESTERN-LANIER CENTRE HOTEL.** *400 E.E. Butler Pkwy (30501). 770/531-0907; fax 770/531-0788; res 800/WESTERN; toll-free 800/782-8966. Email bw005@bellsouth.net; www.guests-inc.com.* 122 rms, 4 story, 1 suite. S $85; D $92; each addl $7; suites $340; under 18 free. Crib avail. Parking lot. Pool. TV; cable (premium), VCR avail. Complimentary coffee in rms, newspaper, toll-free calls. Restaurant. Bar. Ck-out noon, ck-in 3 pm. Meeting rms. Business servs avail. Dry cleaning. Exercise rm. Golf, 18 holes. Tennis, 5 courts. Cr cds: A, C, D, DS, ER, JCB, MC, V.
D 🏋 🏌 🏊 🎾 🎿 🌊 🛶

B&B/Small Inn

★★★ **DUNLAP HOUSE BED & BREAKFAST.** *635 Green St NE (30501). 770/536-0200; fax 770/503-7857; toll-free 800/276-2935. Email dunlaphouse@mindspring.com; www.dunlaphouse.com.* 10 rms, 2 story. S $95-$150; D $105-$155. TV; cable. Complimentary full bkfst, coffee in rms. Restaurant opp 5:30-10 pm. Ck-out 11 am, ck-in 3 pm. Business servs avail. In-rm modem link. Built 1910. Totally nonsmoking. Cr cds: A, DS, MC, V.
D 🌊 🛶 SC

Restaurants

★★ **POOR RICHARD'S.** *1702 Park Hill Dr (30501). 770/532-0499.* Scandinavian menu. Specializes in prime rib, steaks, seafood. Hrs: 5-10 pm; Fri, Sat to 11 pm. Closed Sun; hols. Res accepted Mon-Thurs. Bar. Dinner $5.95-$36.95. Complete meals: $9.95-$16.95. Child's menu. Cr cds: A, MC, V.

★★★ **RUDOLPH'S.** *700 Green St (30501). 770/534-2226.* Specializes in steak Rudolph. Own baking. Hrs: 11:30 am-2 pm, 5:30-10 pm; Mon, Sat from 5:30 pm. Closed Sun; hols. Res accepted. Bar. Wine list. Dinner $12.95-$17.95. Child's menu. In restored historic residence (1915). Cr cds: A, D, DS, MC, V.

Golden Isles

See also Brunswick, Jekyll Island, St. Simons Island, Sea Island

Four barrier subtropical islands off Georgia's coast at Brunswick. Best known of the group are Sea Island (see), St. Simons Island (see), and Jekyll Island (see), all of which may be reached by road. Others are Cumberland, Little St. Simons Island, Ossabaw, St. Catherine's, and Sapelo, reachable only by water.

Native Americans hunted on these islands for giant turtles, waterfowl, deer, and other animals. Spaniards established a chain of missions, which existed for about a century, the largest on St. Simons. The French made halfhearted efforts to settle on the islands. James Oglethorpe built Fort Frederica (see) on St. Simons in 1736 and later defeated Spanish forces attempting to recapture the island.

Now the Golden Isles are resort areas, offering beautiful scenery, swimming, a wide variety of sports facilities, and accomodations.

Helen

See also Toccoa

Pop 300 **Elev** 1,446 ft **Area code** 706
Zip 30545
Web www.WhiteCounty.com/Helen
Information Helen/White County Convention & Visitors Bureau, 726 Brucken St, PO Box 730; 706/878-2181 or 800/858-8027

The natural setting of the mountains and the Chattahoochee River helped create the atmosphere for this logging town, transformed into a charming alpine village. Helen was reborn in 1969 when the citizens, with the help of a local artist, decided to improve the town's appearance.

The result is the relaxed atmosphere of a small Bavarian town. Quaint cobblestone streets, gift shops with an international flavor, crafters, restaurants, and festivals—a bit of the Old World in the heart of the mountains of northeast Georgia.

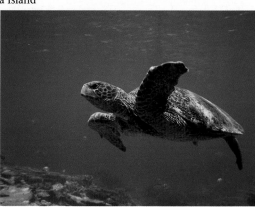
Caption

What to See and Do

Anna Ruby Falls. In Chattahoochee National Forest (see DAHLONEGA).

Stovall Covered Bridge over Chickamauga Creek. The smallest covered bridge in Georgia. 7 mi E on GA 255.

Unicoi State Park. A 1,081-acre park adj to Anna Ruby Falls. Swimming beach, fishing, paddleboat (rentals), canoeing (rentals); nature and hiking trails, picnicking, camping, cottages, lodge/conference center (see MOTELS), restaurant, craft shop. Programs on natural resources, folk culture. Standard hrs, fees. Contact Director of Sales, PO Box 849. 2 mi NE on GA 356. Phone 878-2201.

Annual Events

Volksmarch. Bavarian walk in the forest. Third wkend Apr.

Hot Air Balloon Race & Festival. First wkend June.

Seasonal Events

Fasching Karnival. German Mardi Gras. Jan-Feb.

Oktoberfest. German music and beer festival; one of the longest running Oktoberfests in the country. Sep-Oct.

Motels/Motor Lodges

★★ **CASTLE INN.** *8590 Main St (30545). 706/878-3140; fax 706/878-2470; toll-free 877/878-3140. www.castleinn/helen.com.* 12 rms, 2 story. Sep-Oct (2-day min wkends): S, D $108; each addl $10; under 16 free; golf, package plans; lower rates rest of yr. Crib $3. TV; cable (premium). Coffee in rms. Restaurant 11:30 am-midnight. Ck-out 11 am. Cr cds: A, DS, MC, V.
🄳 🐾 🔥

★★ **COMFORT INN.** *101 Edelweiss Strasse (30545). 706/878-8000; fax 706/878-1234; res 800/228-5150; toll-free 800/443-6488.* 60 rms, 2 story. June-Oct: S $140; D $150; each addl $5; under 18 free; lower rates rest of yr. Parking lot. Pool. TV; cable (premium). Complimentary continental bkfst, newspaper. Restaurant nearby. Ck-out 11 am, ck-in 4 pm. Fax servs avail. Golf, 18 holes. Tennis, 3 courts. Cr cds: A, C, D, DS, MC, V.
🐾 📡 📶 🔥

★★ **HEIDI MOTEL.** *8820 N Main St (30545), 4 blks W of town center. 706/878-2689; fax 706/878-1238. Email windmill@stc.net.* 14 rms, 2 story. Sep-Oct (2-day min wkends): S, D $45-$259; each addl $5; under 10 free; higher rates hols; lower rates rest of yr. TV; cable (premium), VCR avail. Heated pool. Restaurant nearby. Ck-out 11 am. Cr cds: A, DS, MC, V.
🄳 📶 🔥 📶 SC

★★ **UNICOI LODGE AND CONFERANCE CENTER.** *Hwy 356 (30545), 1 mi N on GA 75, 2 mi E on GA 356. 706/878-2201; fax 706/878-1897.* 100 rms, 2-3 story; 30 kit. units. Apr-Nov: S, D $69-$110; each addl $6; under 12 free; kit. units $65-$85 (2-day min; 1-wk min June-Aug); lower rates rest of yr. Parking $2. TV; cable, VCR avail (movies). Coffee in rms. Restaurant 7 am-8 pm. Ck-out 11 am. Meeting rms. Sundries. Lighted tennis. Access to all facilities of state park. Game rm. Cr cds: A, D, DS, MC, V.
🄳 🐾 📶 📶 🔥

B&B/Small Inn

★★ **BURNS-SUTTON HOUSE INN.** *855 Washington St (30523), 15 mi E lon TN 17 to TN 75. 706/754-5565; fax 706/754-9698; toll-free 800/789-0883. www.georgiamagazine.com/burns-sutton.* 7 rms, 2 share bath, 3 story, 3 suites. May-Oct: S, D $65-$95; each addl $20; suites $75-$150; under 8 free; wkly plans; lower rates rest of yr. Cable TV in common rm; VCR avail (movies). Complimentary full bkfst. Restaurant 11 am-2:30 pm, 5:30-10 pm. Business servs avail. Some fireplaces. Picnic tables, grills. Built in 1901; Victorian style and decor. Totally nonsmoking. Cr cds: MC, V.
📶 📶 SC

Restaurant

★★ **HOFBRAUHAUS.** *1 Main St (30545). 706/878-2248.* Specializes in prime rib, veal, seafood. Hrs: 5-9:30 pm; Fri, Sat to 10 pm; Sun 3-9 pm. Closed Dec 25. Res accepted. Bar. Dinner $10.75-$19.95. Child's menu. German decor. Cr cds: A, D, DS, MC, V.
🄳 📶

Hiawassee

(A-3) *See also Clayton*

Pop 547 **Elev** 1,980 ft **Area code** 706 **Zip** 30546

A picturesque mountain town in the heart of Georgia's "Little Switzerland," Hiawassee is on Lake Chatuge, surrounded by Chattahoochee National Forest (see DAHLONEGA). Its backdrop is a range of the Blue Ridge Mountains topped by Brasstown Bald Mountain, Georgia's highest peak. Rock hunting, incl hunting for the highly prized amethyst crystal, is a favorite activity in surrounding Towns County. Mountaineers of North Georgia gather from 26 surrounding counties to participate in a fair, the rule of which is "everybody can bring something."

Annual Events

Georgia Mountain Fair. Individual accomplishment and "friendlier living" is theme of gathering of mountain farm people; arts and crafts, farm produce, flowers, minerals, Native American relics; board splitting, soap and hominy making, quilting; general store, still, farm museum, midway, music hall; entertainment, parade. Camping, beach, and tennis courts at Georgia Mountain Fairgrounds and Towns County Recreation Park. Phone 706/896-4191. Twelve days early Aug.

Fall Celebration. At the fairgrounds. Phone 706/896-4191. Ten days mid-Oct.

Resorts

★ ★ ★ **BRASSTOWN VALLEY RESORT.** *6321 US 76 (30582), approx 5 mi W. 706/379-9900; fax 706/379-4615; toll-free 800/201-3205. Email info@brasstownvalley.com; www.brasstownvalley.com.* 97 rms, 5 story, 5 suites. May-Nov: S, D $179; each addl $25; suites $300; under 12 free; lower rates rest of yr. Valet parking avail. Indoor/outdoor pools, whirlpool. TV; cable (premium). Complimentary coffee in rms, newspaper, toll-free calls. Restaurant 7 am-10 pm. Bar. Ck-out noon, ck-in 4 pm. Meeting rms. Business center. Bellhops. Concierge. Dry cleaning, coin lndry. Gift shop. Exercise equipt, sauna, steam rm. Golf. Tennis, 4 courts. Downhill skiing. Supervised children's activities. Hiking trail. Picnic facilities. Cr cds: A, D, DS, MC, V.

🅳 ♿ ⚒ ⌖ 🌅 🎿 🏊 🛎 🆂🅲 🎣

★ ★ ★ **FIELDSTONE RESORT & MARINA.** *3499 US 76 W (30546), 3 mi W. 706/896-2262; fax 706/896-*

4128; toll-free 800/545-3408. Email fld1@alltel.net; www.fieldstoneinn.com. 66 rms, 2 story. Apr-Nov: S, D $89-$115; each addl $7; under 14 free; lower rates rest of yr. Crib free. TV; cable (premium), VCR avail. Pool. Playground. Complimentary coffee in lobby. Restaurant adj 7 am-3 pm, 5-9 pm; Fri, Sat to 10 pm. Ck-out 11 am. Meeting rm. Business servs avail. Street parking. Lighted tennis. Exercise equipt; weights, bicycles. Lawn games. Microwaves avail. Patios, balconies. Picnic tables. On Lake Chatuge. Cr cds: A, DS, MC, V.

🅳 ♿ 🎿 🌅 🛎 🆂🅲

★ **SALALE LODGE.** *1340 76 E (30546), 1½ mi S. 706/896-3943; fax 706/896-4773.* 4 rms, 2 story. July-Oct: S $29-$69; D $34-$74; each addl $5; under 12 free; higher rates: country music season, fall foliage; lower rates rest of yr. Pet accepted, some restrictions. TV; cable (premium). Restaurant nearby. Ck-out 11 am. Refrigerators, microwaves. On lake; swimming. Cr cds: DS, MC, V.

🅳 🚤 ⚒ ⌖ 🛎 🎣 🌅 ♿ 🏊

Indian Springs State Park

(5 mi SE of Jackson on GA 42)

Called "the oldest state park in the United States," this was originally a gathering place for Creek Native Americans, who valued sulphur springs for curative powers. General William McIntosh, a Creek, headed the encampment in this area in 1800. In 1821, McIntosh signed a treaty ceding most of the Creek lands between the Flint and Ocmulgee rivers and north to the Chattahoochee. In 1825, he relinquished the rest of the Creek land in Georgia.

The state disposed of all Native American lands except 10 acres called Indian Springs Reserve. Butts County citizens bought an adjoining 513 acres, donating it to the state for a park with a mineral spring, a 105-acre lake, and a museum (summer only). Swimming beach, fishing, boating (rentals); nature trails, picnicking, camping, cottages. Standard hrs, fees. Contact Superintendent, 678 Lake Clark Rd, Flovilla 30216; 770/504-2277.

Jekyll Island

See also Brunswick, Golden Isles, St. Simons Island, Sea Island

Pop 1500 (est) **Elev** 5 ft
Area code 912
Web www.jekyllisland.com
Information Jekyll Island Convention & Visitors Bureau, PO Box 13186, 31527; 912/635-3636 or 800/841-6586

Connected to the mainland by a causeway, Jekyll Island, the smallest of Georgia's coastal islands (see GOLDEN ISLES) with 5,600 acres of highlands and 10,000 acres of marshland, was favored by Native Americans for hunting and fishing. Spanish missionaries arrived in the late 16th and early 17th centuries and established a mission. In 1734, during an expedition southward, General James Oglethorpe passed by the island and named it for his friend and financial supporter, Sir Joseph Jekyll. Later, William Horton, one of Oglethorpe's officers, established a plantation on the island.

Horton's land grant passed to several owners before the island was sold to Christophe du Bignon, a Frenchman who was escaping the French Revolution. It remained in the du Bignon family as a plantation for almost a century. In 1858, the slave ship *Wanderer* arrived at the island and unloaded the last major cargo of slaves ever to land in the United States. In 1886, John Eugene du Bignon sold the island to a group of wealthy businessmen from the northeast, who formed the Jekyll Island Club.

Club members who wintered at Jekyll in exclusive privacy from early January to early April included J.P. Morgan, William Rockefeller, Edwin Gould, Joseph Pulitzer, and R.T. Crane, Jr. Some built fabulous "cottages," many of which are still standing. But by World War II, the club had been abandoned for economic and social reasons, and in 1947 the island was sold to the state. The Jekyll Island Authority was created to conserve beaches and manage the island while maintaining it as a year-round resort.

What to See and Do

Cumberland Island National Seashore. (see) S, off the coast.

Jekyll Island Club Historic District. Once one of the nation's most exclusive resorts, this restored district is a memorable example of turn-of-the-century wealth. Exhibition bldgs and shops are open daily (closed Jan 1, Dec 25). Tours are avail (daily, fee; tickets, information at the Visitor Center, the former Jekyll Island Club stables) for Mistletoe Cottage (1900), Indian Mound (or Rockefeller) Cottage (1892), du Bignon Cottage (1884), and the Faith Chapel (1904). Period rms and changing exhibits can be viewed in several houses.

Summer Waves. Eleven-acre water park featuring wave pool, enclosed speed slide, serpentine slides, tubing river, children's pool; picnicking, concessions. (Late May-early Sep, daily) 210 S Riverview Dr. Phone 912/635-2074. ¢¢¢¢

Annual Events

Country by the Sea Music Festival. Top country music stars perform on Jekyll's Beach. Early June.

Beach Music Festival. Famous beach music groups perform all afternoon. Late Aug.

Motels/Motor Lodges

★ ★ **CLARION RESORT BUCCANEER.** *85 S Beachview Dr (31527), I-95 Exit 6. 912/635-2261; fax 912/635-4732; toll-free 800/253-5955. www.motelproperties.com.* 206 rms, 2-4 story, 120 kits. Early May-mid-Aug: S, D $119-$179; each addl $10; under 19 free; wkly rates; lower rates rest of yr. Crib $4. TV; cable. Pool; wading pool, poolside serv (in season). Playground. Supervised children's activities (June-Aug); ages 4-12. Restaurant 7 am-10 pm. Ck-out 11 am. Coin lndry. Meeting rms. Business servs avail. In-rm modem link. Bellhops. Sundries. Airport transportation. Tennis. 18-hole golf privileges, pro, putting green. Game rm. Lawn games. Microwaves avail. Private patios, balconies. Beachfront. Cr cds: A, C, D, DS, MC, V.

★★ COMFORT INN AND SUITES.
711 Beachview Dr (31527). 912/635-2211; fax 912/635-2381; toll-free 800/228-5150. www.motelproperties.com. 180 suites, 2 story, 78 kits. Mid-May-mid-Aug: S, D $99-$179; each addl $10; kits. $149-$189; under 18 free; wkly rates; lower rates rest of yr. Crib $4. Pet accepted; $10. TV; cable. Pool; wading pool, whirlpools. Playground. Complimentary continental bkfst. Restaurant 6 am-11 pm. Ck-out 11 am. Coin lndry. Meeting rms. Sundries. Airport transportation. Tennis privileges. Golf privileges, pro, putting green, driving range. Refrigerators, microwaves; some in-rm whirlpools. Private patios, balconies. On ocean. Cr cds: A, C, D, DS, MC, V.

★★ HOLIDAY INN BEACH RESORT.
200 S Beachview Dr (31527). 912/635-3311; fax 912/635-2901; res 800/HOLIDAY; toll-free 800/753-5955. 205 units, 2-4 story. May-mid-Sep: S, D $119-129; each addl $10; lower rates rest of yr; under 18 free. Crib free. Pet accepted; $7.50. TV; cable (premium). Pool; wading pool, poolside serv (in season). Playground. Restaurant 7 am-2 pm, 5:30-10 pm. Bar 5 pm-2 am; entertainment. Ck-out 11 am. Lndry facilities. Meeting rms. Business servs avail. In-rm modem link. Bellhops. Sundries. Gift shop. Tennis. Bicycles. Private patios, balconies. On beach. Cr cds: A, D, DS, MC, V.

Resort

★★★ VILLAS BY THE SEA.
1175 N Beachview Dr (31527). 912/635-2521; fax 912/635-2569; toll-free 800/841-6262. Email villas@darientel.com. 166 kit. villas, 1-2 story. Late Mar-early Sep: 1-bedrm $99-$154, 2-bedrm $174-$189, 3-bedrm $224-$239; wkly: 1-bedrm $594-$924, 2-bedrm $1,044-$1,134; 3-bedrm $1,344-$1,434; package plans; lower rates rest of yr. Crib $7. Pet accepted; fee. TV; cable, VCR avail. Pool; wading pool, whirlpool. Playground. Dining rm 7 am-2 pm, 5-10 pm. Bar. Ck-out

11 am, ck-in 4 pm. Grocery 3 mi. Coin lndry. Package store 3 mi. Convention facilities. Business servs avail. Gift shop. Lighted tennis privileges, pro. Golf privileges, pro. Bicycle rentals. Private beach. Microwaves. Private patios, balconies. Picnic tables, grills. On 17 acres. Cr cds: A, C, D, DS, MC, V.

Villa/Condo

★★★ JEKYLL ISLAND CLUB MOTEL.
371 Riverview Dr (31527). 912/635-2600; fax 912/635-2818; toll-free 800/535-9547. Email jiclub@technonot.com; www.jekyllclub.com. 134 units, 4 story, 20 suites. Mar-Aug: S, D $129-$189; each addl $20; suites $189-$259; under 17 free; MAP, AP, golf plans; lower rates rest of yr. Crib free. TV; cable, VCR (movies avail). Heated pool; poolside serv. Supervised children's activities (June-Aug); ages 5-12. Dining rm 7 am-2 pm, 6-10 pm (see also GRAND DINING ROOM). Bar 3 pm-midnight; closed Sun. Ck-out noon, ck-in 4 pm. Meeting rms. Business servs avail. In-rm modem link. Concierge. Shopping arcade. Valet parking. Airport transportation. 9 tennis courts; 1 indoor; 5 lighted. Three 18-hole golf courses and one 9-hole course, greens fee $29, cart $26, pro, putting green, driving range. Marina; deep sea and sportfishing. Swimming beach. Bicycle rentals; croquet. Originally founded as an exclusive retreat for members of high society; historic club house (1887) has been restored. Cr cds: A, DS, MC, V.

Restaurants

★★ BLACKBEARD'S.
200 N Beachview Dr (31527). 912/635-3522. Specializes in coastal seafood, steak. Hrs: 11 am-9 pm. Bar. Lunch $3.50-$7.50; dinner $4.95-$18.50. Child's menu. Parking. Nautical decor. View of ocean, dunes, and beach. Cr cds: A, D, MC, V.

★★★ GRAND DINING ROOM.
371 Riverview Dr. 912/635-2600. www.jekyllclub.com. Specializes in fresh seafood, beef, pork. Own bak-

ing. Hrs: 7 am-2 pm, 6-9 pm. Res accepted. Bar. Wine list. Bkfst $7.95-$9.95; lunch $5.95-$12.95; dinner $18.75-$29.95. Sun brunch $15.95. Child's menu. Entertainment: pianist. Valet parking. Jacket (dinner). White columned dining rm; fireplaces, crystal wall lamps. Cr cds: A, D, DS, MC, V.

☐ D

★ **LATITUDE 31.** *1 Pier Rd (31527), in Historic District.* 912/635-3800. Specializes in stuffed flounder, romano-crusted chicken, desert fire fettucine. Hrs: 5:30-9 pm. Closed Mon; hols. Res accepted. Bar. Dinner $8.95-$17.95. Child's menu. On pier overlooking Jekyll River. Cr cds: D, DS, MC, V.

☐ D ☐

★ **ZACHRY'S SEAFOOD.** *44 Beachview Dr (31527).* 912/635-3128. Mediterranean menu. Specializes in fresh seafood, chicken, steak. Salad bar. Hrs: 11 am-9 pm; Fri, Sat to 10 pm; winter to 8 pm. Closed Mother's Day, Thanksgiving, Dec 25. Wine, beer. Lunch $2.50-$14.95; dinner $2.50-$14.95. Child's menu. Cr cds: D, MC, V.

☐ D ☐

Kennesaw Mountain National Battlefield Park

(B-2)

(Approx 3 mi NW of Marietta off US 41 or I-75 Exit 116)

At Kennesaw Mountain in June of 1864, General William Tecumseh Sherman executed the last of a series of flanking maneuvers that were started 100 miles to the north on May 7. The Battle of Kennesaw Mountain stalled but did not halt General Sherman's invasion of Georgia. Kennesaw Mountain National Battlefield Park commemorates the 1864 Atlanta campaign.

In a series of flanking maneuvers and minor battles in May and June,

Sherman's 100,000-man Union army forced the 65,000-man Confederate army, under the command of General Joseph E. Johnston, back from Dalton to the vicinity of Kennesaw Mountain 20 miles north of Atlanta. On June 19, Johnston took position and dug in, anchoring his right flank on the steep mountain slopes and extending his left flank several miles to the south. He trusted that strong fortifications and rugged terrain would make up for the disparity in numbers.

The Confederates abandoned their positions after a heavy day's fighting and occupied strong points between Kennesaw and Lost mountains. Sherman first tried to march around to an area just south of the Confederate position, but Johnston shifted 11,000 troops to counter the maneuver. In fierce fighting at Kolb's Farm on June 22 Confederate attacks were repulsed, but Sherman was temporarily stymied.

Although the Confederate entrenchments seemed strong, Sherman suspected that they were weakly held. A sharp frontal attack, he decided, might break through and destroy Johnston's entire army. On the morning of June 27, after a heavy artillery bombardment, Sherman struck the Confederate line at two places simultaneously. At Pigeon Hill, 5,500 attackers were quickly driven under cover by sheets of Southern bullets. Two miles to the south, 8,000 Union infantrymen stormed up Cheatham Hill and for a few minutes engaged the Confederates in hand-to-hand combat on top of their earthworks. Casualties were so severe that the location was nicknamed "Dead Angle." By noon both attacks had failed. Sherman had lost 3,000 men, Johnston only 500.

Sherman reverted to his flanking strategy, and on July 2, the Confederates withdrew, eventually to Atlanta. The siege and fall of Atlanta soon followed. Sherman then began his devastating "March to the Sea."

The Visitor Center, on Old US 41 and Stilesboro Road, north of Kennesaw Mountain, has exhibits, an audiovisual program, and information (daily; closed Dec 25). A road leads to the top of Kennesaw Mountain (daily: Mon-Fri, drive or walk;

Sat and Sun, bus leaves every ½ hr between the months of Feb and Nov, or walk—no driving). (The Cheatham Hill area, in the south-central section of the park, has the same hours as the Kennesaw Mountain road; closed Dec 25).

Park (daily; closed Dec 25). Self-guided tours. For additional information contact Park Ranger, 900 Kennesaw Mountain Dr, Kennesaw 30152-4854; 770/427-4686. **FREE**

La Grange

(D-2) *See also Pine Mountain (Harris County)*

Settled 1828 **Pop** 25,597 **Elev** 772 ft **Area code** 706 **Zip** 30240
Web www.lagrange-ga.org
Information La Grange-Troup County Chamber of Commerce, 111 Bull St, Box 636, 30241-0636; 706/884-8671

Motels/Motor Lodges

★★ **BEST WESTERN.** *1601 Lafayette Pkwy (30241), I-85 Exit 4.* 706/882-9540; fax 706/882-3929; res 800/528-1234. 101 rms, 2 story. S $40-$45; D $45-$50; each addl $5; under 12 free. Crib free. TV; cable. Pool. Complimentary continental bkfst. Restaurant nearby. Ck-out 11 am. Meeting rms. Business servs avail. Health club privileges. Cr cds: A, C, D, DS, MC, V.
🄳 ⇌ 🏋 ⊠ 🐾

★★ **RAMADA INN.** *1513 Lafayette Pkwy (30241), GA 109 at I-85.* 706/884-6175; fax 706/884-1106; res 800/2RAMADA. 146 rms, 2 story. S, D $55-$65; each addl $8; suites $140. Crib free. TV; cable. Pool. Complimentary coffee in rms. Restaurant 6:30 am-2 pm, 5:30-10 pm. Bar 4:30 pm-2 am. Ck-out noon. Meeting rms. Business servs avail. In-rm modem link. Valet serv. Exercise equipt. Some refrigerators. Cr cds: A, D, DS, MC, V.
🄳 ⇌ 🏋 ⊠ 🐾 🏋

Lumpkin

(E-2) *See also Americus, Columbus; also see Eufaula, AL*

Pop 1,250 **Elev** 593 ft **Area code** 912 **Zip** 31815

Annual Event

Westville events. Westville has many different events throughout the yr. Of special interest are the Spring Festival (early Apr), the May Day celebration (early May), Independence Day (July 4), "Fair of 1850" (late Oct-early Nov), and a variety of Christmas activities (Dec). Phone 912/838-6310.

Macon (D-3)

Founded 1823 **Pop** 106,612 **Elev** 325 ft **Area code** 912
Web www.maconga.org
Information Macon-Bibb County Convention & Visitors Bureau, Terminal Station, 200 Cherry St, PO Box 6354, 31208; 912/743-3401 or 800/768-3401

What to See and Do

Georgia Music Hall of Fame. Georgia's musical heritage is explored through different exhibits such as the Soda Fountain playing songs of the 50s, the Jazz Club, Gospel Chapel, and Rythm and Blues Revue. Videos can be selected for viewing in the Georgia Theater. (Daily; closed Jan 1, Thanksgiving, Dec 25, 26) 200 Martin Luther King, Jr, Blvd. Phone 912/738-0017. ¢¢¢

Georgia Sports Hall of Fame. Built to resemble a classic ballpark, the new Hall houses exhibits on Georgia's famous athletes, pro teams, and college teams. (Mon-Sat) Call for admission pricing. 301 Cherry St. Phone 912/752-1585.

Annual Events

Cherry Blossom Festival. Historic tours, concerts, fireworks, hot air bal-

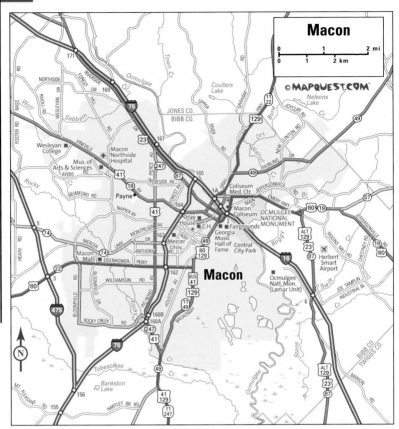

loons, sporting events, parade. Phone 912/751-7429. Mar 16-25.

Georgia State Fair. Central City Park. Grandstand shows, midway, exhibit bldgs. Phone 912/746-7184. Oct 15-21.

Motels/Motor Lodges

★★ **BEST WESTERN RIVERSIDE.** *2400 Riverside Dr (31204), I-75 Exit 54. 912/743-6311; fax 912/743-9420; toll-free 888/454-4565.* 122 rms, 2 story. S, D $54; under 18 free. Crib free. TV; cable (premium). Pool. Complimentary coffee in rms. Restaurant 6:30 am-9 pm. Bar 5 pm-midnight. Ck-out noon. Coin lndry. Meeting rms. Business servs avail. In-rm modem link. Valet serv. Health club privileges. Refrigerators; microwaves avail. Cr cds: A, C, D, DS, MC, V.

D ⊷ ⊁ ⚒ SC

★★ **COMFORT INN.** *2690 Riverside Dr (31204), I-75 Exit 54. 912/746-8855; fax 912/746-8881; toll-free 800/228-5150.* 120 rms, 3 story. June-Dec: S $59; D $64; under 18 free; higher rates Cherry Blossom Festival; lower rates rest of yr. Crib free. TV; cable (premium). Pool. Complimentary continental bkfst, coffee in rms. Bar 4-10 pm; closed Sun. Ck-out noon. Meeting rms. Business servs avail. In-rm modem link. Some refrigerators; microwaves avail. Cr cds: A, C, D, DS, JCB, MC, V.

D ⊷ ⊁ ⚒ SC

★★ **COURTYARD BY MARRIOTT.** *3990 Sheraton Dr (31210), I-75 Exit 55A. 912/477-8899; fax 912/477-4684; res 800/321-2211.* 108 rms, 3 story. S $84; D $94; suites $119; wkend rates. Crib free. TV; cable (premium). Pool; whirlpool. Complimentary coffee in rms. Bar 5-10 pm. Ck-out noon. Guest lndry. Meeting rm. Business servs avail. In-rm modem link. Valet serv. Exercise equipt. Health club privileges. Some refrigerators; microwaves avail. Balconies. Cr cds: A, D, DS, MC, V.

D ⊷ ⊁ ⊁ ⚒ ⊁

★★ **HAMPTON INN.** *3680 Riverside Dr (31210), I-75 Exit 55A. 912/471-0660; fax 912/471-2528; toll-free 800/426-7866.* 151 rms, 2 story. S $59-$69; D $65-$69; under 18 free. Crib free. Pet accepted; $10. TV; cable. Pool. Complimentary continental bkfst. Coffee in rms. Ck-out noon. Business servs avail. In-rm modem link. Valet serv. Health club privileges. Cr cds: A, D, DS, MC, V.

D �ä9 ⚊ ⊠ 🦅 **SC**

★★ **HOLIDAY INN EXPRESS.** *2720 Riverside Dr (31204), I-75 Exit 54. 912/743-1482; fax 912/745-3967; res 800/HOLIDAY.* 93 rms, 6 story. S, D $51-$69; each addl $6; suites $69; under 18 free. Crib free. Pet accepted. TV; cable (premium). Pool. Complimentary continental bkfst. Ck-out noon. Meeting rm. Business servs avail. In-rm modem link. Valet serv. Health club privileges. Cr cds: A, D, DS, MC, V.

D �ä9 ⚊ 🕅 ⊠ 🦅

★ **RODEWAY INN.** *4999 Eisenhower Pkwy (31206), I-475 Exit 1. 912/781-4343; fax 912/784-8140; res 800/228-2000. www.rodeway.com.* 55 rms, 2 story. S $38-$42; D $48-$54; each addl $4; under 18 free; higher rates Cherry Blossom Festival. Crib $4. Pet accepted. TV; cable (premium), VCR avail (movies). Pool. Complimentary continental bkfst. Restaurant nearby. Ck-out 11 am. Coin lndry. Business servs avail. Refrigerators, microwaves. Cr cds: A, DS, MC, V.

D �ä9 ⚊

Hotel

★★★ **CROWNE PLAZA.** *108 1st St (31201). 912/746-1461; fax 912/738-2460; toll-free 800/227-6963. www.impachotels.com.* 298 units, 16 story. S, D $79-$109; each addl $10; suites $175-$279; under 18 free. Crib free. Valet parking $6; self-park $5. TV; cable (premium). Pool. Restaurants 7 am-10 pm. Bar 4 pm-2 am; entertainment. Ck-out noon. Convention facilities. In-rm modem link. Gift shop. Airport transportation. Exercise equipt; sauna. Luxury level. Cr cds: A, C, D, DS, JCB, MC, V.

D ⚊ 🕅 ⊠ 🦅 **SC**

B&B/Small Inn

★★★★ **1842 INN.** *353 College St (31201). 912/741-1842; fax 912/741-1842; toll-free 800/336-1842. Email the1842inn@worldnet.att.net; www.the1842inn.com.* A stately, white-pillared facade welcome visitors at this Greek Revival, antebellum mansion with an adjoining, Victorian cottage. The bed and breakfast offers 21 elegant rooms, some with whirlpools and fireplaces and all with period antiques, Oriental rugs, and paintings. The garden courtyard is a pleasant place for breakfast before exploring the unending array of nearby National Register historic landmarks. 21 rms, 2 story. S $165; D $255; each addl $50; under 12 free. Crib avail. Pet accepted, some restrictions, fee. Valet parking avail. TV; cable, CD avail. Complimentary continental bkfst, coffee in rms, newspaper, toll-free calls. Restaurant. Bar. Meeting rm. Business servs avail. Concierge. Dry cleaning. Gift shop. Exercise privileges. Golf. Tennis, 36 courts. Cr cds: A, C, D, MC, V.

D �ä9 🌣 🕅 🏊 🕅 🏊 🦅

Restaurant

★★★ **NATALIA'S.** *2720 Riverside Dr (31204). 912/741-1380.* Specializes in lamb chops, fish in parchment. Hrs: 6-11 pm. Closed Sun; hols; July 4 wk. Res accepted. Bar. Dinner $12.50-$25. Antiques, paintings, photographs on display. Cr cds: A, MC, V.

D

Madison

(C-4) *See also Athens, Eatonton*

Pop 3,483 **Elev** 667 ft **Area code** 706 **Zip** 30650

Information Welcome Center, 115 E Jefferson, PO Box 826; 706/342-4454 or 800/709-7406

General Sherman spared Madison on his Civil War march to the sea. The result is a contemporary city with a wealth of well-preserved antebellum and Victorian residences. Several movies have been filmed in the town to take advantage of the 19th-century atmosphere.

What to See and Do

Lake Oconee. Approx 19,000-acre lake with 374 mi of shoreline was created by the impoundment of the Oconee River. Beach swimming, fishing, boating, marinas; picnicking, camping. Some fees at recreation areas. E on I-20. Phone 706/485-8704. Parking ¢

Madison-Morgan Cultural Center. Romanesque Revival school bldg (1895) with art galleries, restored schoolrm, museum of local history, original auditorium, and ongoing schedule of performances. (Tues-Sun; closed hols) 434 S Main St. Phone 706/342-4743. ¢¢

Annual Events

Spring Tour of Homes. Historic houses, scenic gardens, period furnishings, and antiques. Third wkend Apr.

Holiday Tour of Homes. Historic private homes. First wkend Dec.

Motels/Motor Lodges

★ **DAYS INN.** *2001 Eatonton Hwy (30650), 2 mi S at jct US 129/441, I-20 Exit 51. 706/342-1839; fax 706/342-1839; toll-free 800/329-7466.* 77 rms, 2 story. S, D $49.95; each addl $5; under 18 free; higher rates special events. Crib free. Pet accepted; $10. TV; cable (premium). Pool; wading pool. Restaurant 6:30-9:30 am, 11 am-3 pm, 5-8:30 pm. Ck-out noon. Cr cds: A, C, D, DS, MC, V.
D ✦ ≈ ⊠ 🔥 SC

★★ **HOLIDAY INN EXPRESS.** *10111 Alcovy Rd (30014), 27 mi on I-20 Exit 45A. 770/787-4900; fax 770/385-9805; toll-free 800/788-1390.* 29 rms, 2 story, 21 suites. Apr-Aug: S, D $70; each addl $5; suites $75; under 18 free; lower rates rest of yr. Crib avail. Pet accepted, some restrictions, fee. Parking lot. Pool. TV; cable (premium). Complimentary continental bkfst, coffee in rms, newspaper, toll-free calls. Restaurant. Ck-out noon, ck-in 3 pm. Meeting rm. Business servs avail. Dry cleaning, coin

lndry. Exercise equipt. Golf, 18 holes. Cr cds: A, C, D, DS, JCB, MC, V.
D ✦ 🛎 ≈ 🧍 ⊠ 🔥 ⊠

B&Bs/Small Inns

★★ **BRADY INN BED AND BREAK-FAST.** *250 N 2nd St (30650). 706/342-4400; res 706/342-9287.* 7 rms. No rm phones. S $65; D $75; suite $150. TV in sitting rm; cable, VCR avail (movies). Complimentary full bkfst. Restaurant nearby. Ck-out noon, ck-in 6 pm. Health club privileges. Restored Victorian cottage in historic downtown. Cr cds: A, DS, JCB, MC, V.
🔥

★★ **BURNETT PLACE CIRCLE 1830.** *317 Old Post Rd (30650). 706/342-4034.* 3 rms, 2 story. S $75; D $85; each addl $10. TV; cable (premium), VCR avail (movies). Complimentary full bkfst; afternoon refreshments. Restaurant nearby. Ck-out 11 am, ck-in 3 pm. Picnic tables, grills. Federal-style house (ca 1830) typical of the Piedmont region. Cr cds: MC, V.
🔥

Marietta

(B-2) *See also Atlanta, Norcross*

Founded 1834 **Pop** 44,129
Elev 1,128 ft **Area code** 770
Web www.cobbcvb.com

Information Cobb County Convention & Visitors Bureau, 1100 Circle 75 Pkwy, Suite 125, PO Box 672827, 30006-0048; 770/933-7228 or 800/451-3480. A welcome center is located at 4 Depot St; 770/429-1115

What to See and Do

Kennesaw Civil War Museum. The L & N steam locomotive *General,* permanently housed here, was taken from this spot in 1862 by Union raiders in an attempt to cut Confederate supply lines. The raiders were chased and captured by the train crew. Incl exhibits and video about the raid. (Daily; closed hols) 6 mi N via US 41 or I-75 to Exit 118, at

2829 Cherokee St in Kennesaw. Phone 770/427-2117 or 800/742-6897. ¢¢

Kennesaw Mountain National Battlefield Park. (see) Approx 3 mi NW off US 41 or I-75, follow signs.

White Water. Water theme park with 40 rides; body flumes, rapids ride, wave pool, float. (Memorial Day-Labor Day, daily; May, wkends) Marietta Pkwy, I-75 Exit 113. Phone 770/424-WAVE. ¢¢¢¢ Adj is

> **American Adventures.** Children's amusement park with over a dozen rides. (Daily; closed hols) Fee for various activities. Phone 770/424-6683. Parking ¢

Annual Event

US 10K Classic and Family Sports Festival. Phone 770/432-0100. Labor Day wkend.

Motels/Motor Lodges

★ **BEST INN.** *1255 Franklin Rd SE (30067), I-75 Exit 111.* 770/955-0004; *fax* 770/955-0004; *res* 800/BESTINN. 116 rms, 3 story. S $43.88-$59.88; D $50.88-$69.88; under 18 free. Crib free. TV; cable (premium). Pool. Complimentary coffee in lobby. Restaurant nearby. Ck-out 1 pm. In-rm modem link. Microwaves avail. Cr cds: A, D, DS, MC, V.
D ⚉ ⇌ ⊠ ⚑

★★ **BEST WESTERN BRADBURY SUITES.** *4500 Circle 75 Pkwy (30339), I-75 Exit 110, N of Downtown.* 770/956-9919; *fax* 770/955-3270; *toll-free* 800/528-3270. 247 rms in 2 bldgs, 3-5 story. S, D $55-$89; each addl $5; suites $75; under 6 free. Crib free. TV; cable (premium). Pool; whirlpool. Complimentary full bkfst buffet. Coffee in rms. Restaurant nearby. Ck-out noon. Coin lndry. Meeting rms. Business servs avail. In-rm modem link. Health club privileges. Some refrigerators; microwaves avail. Cr cds: A, D, DS, MC, V.
D ⇌ ⊠ ⚑ SC

★ **ECONO LODGE NORTHWEST.** *1940 Leland Dr (30067), I-75 Exit 110.* 770/952-0052; *fax* 770/952-0501; *res* 800/55ECONO. 108 rms, 3 story. S $50; D $55; each addl $5; under 16 free; wkly rates; higher rates special

events. TV; cable (premium). Restaurant adj 6 am-4 pm. Ck-out 11 am. Coin lndry. Meeting rms. Sundries. Cr cds: A, C, D, DS, ER, JCB, MC, V.
D ⚉ ⚔ ⚑ ⇌ ⚑

★★ **HAMPTON INN.** *455 Franklin Rd SE (30067), I-75 Exit 112.* 770/425-9977; *fax* 770/427-2545; *toll-free* 800/426-7866. 140 rms, 4 story. S, D $69-$79; under 18 free. Crib free. TV; cable (premium). Pool; wading pool. Complimentary continental bkfst. Restaurant nearby. Ck-out noon. Meeting rm. Business servs avail. In-rm modem link. Valet serv. Health club privileges. Microwaves avail. Cr cds: A, C, D, DS, ER, MC, V.
D ⇌ ⊠ ⚑ SC

★★ **HAWTHORN SUITES.** *1500 Parkwood Circle NW (30339), I-75 Exit 110, N of Downtown.* 770/952-9595; *fax* 770/984-2335; *res* 800/338-7812. 280 rms, 2-3 story. S, D $99; suites $135-$195; wkend, monthly rates. Crib free. Pet accepted; $100. TV; cable (premium). Heated pool; whirlpool. Complimentary full bkfst. Restaurant nearby. Ck-out noon. Coin lndry. Meeting rms. In-rm modem link. Valet serv. Lighted tennis. Exercise equipt. Health club privileges. Refrigerators, microwaves. Private patios, balconies. Picnic tables, grills. Elaborate landscaping, flowers. Cr cds: A, C, D, DS, MC, V.
D ⚉ ⇌ ⚔ ⚑ ⚑ ⇌ ⚑

★ **LA QUINTA INN.** *2170 Delk Rd SE (30067), I-75 N Delk Rd Exit 111.* 770/951-0026; *fax* 770/952-5372; *toll-free* 800/531-5900. 130 rms, 3 story. S $60-$70; D $65-$75; each addl $6; under 18 free. Crib free. Pet accepted, some restrictions. TV; cable (premium). Pool. Complimentary continental bkfst. Restaurant adj 6 am-10 pm; wkends to 11 pm. Ck-out noon. Meeting rm. In-rm modem link. Valet serv. Some refrigerators, microwaves. Cr cds: A, C, D, DS, MC, V.
D ⚉ ⇌ ⊠ ⚑ SC

★★ **WINDSOR INN.** *2655 Cobb Pkwy (30152), approx 5 mi N on US 41.* 770/424-6330; *fax* 770/419-8837; *toll-free* 800/494-3767. *Email* salba@bellsouth.net. 31 rms. Mar-Sep: S $40-$45; D $40-$55; each addl $5; suite $70; under 5 free; higher rates special events; lower rates rest of yr. TV;

cable (premium). Pool; wading pool. Continental bkfst, coffee in rms. Ck-out 11 am. Refrigerators; microwaves avail. Picnic tables. Cr cds: A, DS, MC, V.

★★ **WYNDHAM GARDEN MARIETTA.** *1775 Parkway Pl NW (30067), I-75 Exit 112.* 770/428-4400; *fax 770/428-9782; toll-free 800/544-5064.* 218 rms, 10 story. S, D $99-$109; under 12 free; wkend rates. Crib free. TV; cable (premium). Pool. Coffee in rms. Restaurant 6:30 am-10 pm. Bar 4 pm-midnight; Sun 4 pm-midnight. Ck-out noon. Meeting rms. Business servs avail. In-rm modem link. Bell-hops. Valet serv. Exercise equipt. Some refrigerators. Some balconies. Cr cds: A, C, D, DS, JCB, MC, V.

Hotels

★★ **HOLIDAY INN.** *2265 Kingston Ct SE (30067), I-75 Exit 111.* 770/952-7581; *fax 770/984-9518; res 800/holiday.* 196 rms, 5-7 story, 55 suites. S, D $109; each addl $10; suites $99-$109; under 18 free; higher rates special events. Crib free. TV; cable (premium). Pool. Complimentary coffee in rms. Restaurant 6:30 am-2 pm, 5-10 pm; wkends from 7 am. Bar 5 pm-midnight. Ck-out noon. Meeting rms. Business servs avail. In-rm modem link. Exercise equipt. Cr cds: A, D, DS, MC, V.

★★★ **HYATT REGENCY SUITES ATLANTA.** *2999 Windy Hill Rd (30067), I-75N to Windy Hill Exit 110, N of Downtown.* 770/956-1234; *res 800/223-1234. www.atlanta.suites. hyatt.com.* 200 suites, 7 story. S $89-$165; D $89-$190; under 18 free; wkend rates. Crib free. TV; cable (premium). Heated pool; whirlpool. Complimentary coffee in rms. Restaurant 6:30 am-11 pm. Bar 11:30 am-midnight. Ck-out noon. Meeting rms. Business center. In-rm modem link. Tennis privileges. Golf privileges. Exercise equipt; sauna. Health club privileges. Refrigerators; some microwaves. Cr cds: A, C, D, DS, ER, JCB, MC, V.

★★★ **MARIETTA CONFERENCE CENTER & RESORT.** *500 Powder Springs St (30064).* 770/427-2500; *fax 770/218-9097; toll-free 888/685-2500. Email info@mariettaresort.com; www. mariettaresort.com.* 199 rms, 6 story. S $159-$204; D $169-$219; each addl $15; suites $250-$1,250; under 18 free; wkend, hol rates; golf plans. Crib free. Valet parking $3-$10. TV; cable (premium), VCR avail. Complimentary coffee in rms. Restaurant 6:30 am-10 pm. Rm serv 24 hrs. Bar noon-1 am; entertainment. Ck-out 11 am. Meeting rms. Business center. In-rm modem link. Concierge. Gift shop. Lighted tennis. 18-hole golf, greens fee $37.50-$55, pro, putting green, driving range. Exercise equipt; sauna. Massage. Pool; whirlpool, poolside serv. Lawn games. Refrigerators, minibars. Cr cds: A, DS, MC, V.

B&B/Small Inn

★★★ **THE WHITLOCK.** *57 Whitlock Ave (30064), 1 blk W of town square; in National Register Historic District.* 770/428-1495; *fax 770/919-9620. Email alexis@whitlockinn.com; www.whitlockinn.com.* 5 rms, 2 story. S, D $100-$125. Children over 12 yrs only. TV; cable (premium). Complimentary continental bkfst. Restaurant nearby. Ck-out 11 am, ck-in 3 pm. Business servs avail. In-rm modem link. Concierge serv. Gift shop. Lawn games. Victorian mansion built in 1900. Totally nonsmoking. Cr cds: A, DS, MC, V.

Restaurants

★★★ **1848 HOUSE.** *780 S Cobb Dr (30060), entrance on Pearl St at Cobb Pkwy.* 770/428-1848. *www.1848house. com.* Specializes in Charleston she-crab soup, house-smoked center-cut pork chop, Savannah rock shrimp cake. Own baking. Hrs: 6-9:30 pm; Sun 5:30-8 pm; Sun brunch 10:30 am-2:30 pm. Closed Mon; Jan 1, Dec 25. Res accepted. Bar. Wine cellar. Dinner a la carte entrees: $13.95-$25.95. Sun brunch $19.95. Child's menu. Valet parking. Ten dining rms in Greek-revival plantation house completed in 1848; 13 landscaped acres. Cr cds: A, D, DS, MC, V.

★★ **FOOD MERCHANT.** *2143-C Roswell Rd (30062). 770/579-5515.* Specializes in seafood stew, bayou Angus sirloin, vegetarian farfalle pasta. Hrs: 11:30 am-2 pm, 5-9:30 pm; Fri to 10 pm; Sat 5-10 pm. Closed Sun; Thanksgiving, Dec 25. Wine, beer. Lunch $3.50-$13.95; dinner $3.50-$13.95. Child's menu. Contemporary murals. Cr cds: A, D, DS, MC, V.

D

★★ **GRAZIE A BISTRO.** *1000 Whitlock Ave NW (30064). 770/499-8585. www.grazie.home.mindspring.com.* Specializes in fresh fish, steak, pasta. Hrs: 11 am-2 pm, 5 pm-midnight; Sun brunch to 2 pm. Closed hols. Res accepted. Bar. Lunch $3-$7; dinner $8-$18. Sun brunch $5-$7. Entertainment: pianist; vocalists Fri, Sat. Cr cds: A, C, D, DS, MC, V.

D

★★ **LA STRADA.** *2930 Johnson Ferry Rd NE (30067). 770/640-7008.* Specializes in stuffed shrimp Fra Diavolo, soft shell crab, tiramisu. Hrs: 5-10 pm; Fri, Sat to 11 pm. Closed hols. Bar. Dinner $7.95-$14.95. Child's menu. Cr cds: A, D, DS, MC, V.

★ **OLD SOUTH BAR-B-Q.** *601 Burbank Circle (30080), approx 5 mi S off Cobb Pkwy (US 41) on Windy Hill Rd. 770/435-4215.* Specializes in beef, chicken, pork. Hrs: 11 am-9:30 pm. Closed Mon; hols. Lunch, dinner $2.50-$7.50. Child's menu. Parking. Casual dining. Family-owned. Cr cds: MC, V.

D

★★ **SHILLING'S ON THE SQUARE.** *19 N Park Square NE (30060). 770/428-9520.* Specializes in steak, fresh seafood. Hrs: 10:30 am-midnight; Sun brunch 10:30 am-2 pm. Closed Jan 1, Dec 25. Res accepted. Bar. Lunch $5.95-$7.95; dinner $8.95-$19.95. Sun brunch $4.50-$6.95. Tavern decor; century-old wood bar, stained-glass panels, tin ceiling. Cr cds: A, D, DS, MC, V.

D

Milledgeville

(D-4) *See also Eatonton, Macon*

Founded 1803 **Pop** 17,727 **Elev** 335 ft
Area code 912 **Zip** 31061
Web www.milledgevillega.com/cvb.htm

Information Convention & Visitors Bureau, 200 W Hancock St, Box 219; 912/452-4687 or 800/653-1804

Annual Event

Browns Crossing Craftsmen Fair. 9 mi W via GA 22. Features original works, incl paintings, weavings, pottery, woodcarvings, graphics. Third wkend Oct.

Motels/Motor Lodges

★ **DAYS INN.** *2551 N Columbia St (31061). 912/453-8471; fax 912/453-8482; toll-free 800/329-7466.* 100 rms, 2 story, 2 kit. units. S $51; D $56; each addl $4; suites $95-$147; under 14 free; wkly rates avail. Crib $5. TV; cable (premium). Pool; wading pool, whirlpool. Complimentary continental bkfst. Ck-out 11 am. Meeting rms. Business servs avail. Lighted tennis. Exercise equipt; sauna. Cr cds: A, D, DS, MC, V.

D ⚬ ⚬ ⚬ ⚬ ⚬ SC

★★ **HOLIDAY INN.** *2627 N Columbia St (31061), approx 4 mi N. 912/452-3502; fax 912/453-3591; res 800/465-4329. Email mlgga98@aol.com.* 170 rms, 2 story. S $64, D $69; each addl $5; suites $125; under 18 free. Crib free. TV; cable (premium). Pool; wading pool. Restaurant 6 am-2 pm, 5:30-9 pm. Bar. Ck-out noon. Meeting rms. Business servs avail. In-rm modem link. Valet serv. Wet bar, whirlpool in some suites. Cr cds: A, C, D, DS, JCB, MC, V.

D ⚬ ⚬ ⚬ ⚬

Norcross

See also Atlanta, Buford, Winder

Pop 5,947 **Elev** 1,057 ft
Area code 770
Web www.norcrossgeorgia-gvt.com
Information City of Norcross, 65 Lawrenceville St, 30071; 770/448-2122

Norcross, a suburb of Atlanta, is located approximately 20 miles northeast of the city. Citizens have preserved many old residences; there is a 112-acre Historic District here with a restored downtown square.

Motels/Motor Lodges

★★ **BEST WESTERN BRADBURY INN.** *5985 Oakbrook Pkwy (30093), I-85 Exit 37. 770/662-8175; fax 770/840-1183; toll-free 800/230-1542.* 121 rms, 1-3 story. S, D $59-$89; suites $89-$119; under 18 free; wkend rates. Crib free. TV; cable (premium). Pool. Complimentary full bkfst, coffee in rms. Ck-out noon. Coin lndry. Meeting rms. Business servs avail. In-rm modem link. Valet serv. Exercise equipt. Health club privileges. Some refrigerators; microwaves avail. Cr cds: A, C, D, DS, MC, V.
D SC

★★ **CLUBHOUSE INN.** *5945 Oakbrook Pkwy (30093), I-85 Exit 37. 770/368-9400; fax 770/416-7370.* 147 rms, 2-3 story, 25 kit. suites. S, D $79-$89; each addl $10; kit. suites $94; under 18 free. Crib free. TV; cable (premium). Pool; whirlpool. Complimentary full bkfst. Restaurant adj 11 am-11 pm. Ck-out noon. Coin lndry. Meeting rms. Business servs avail. Valet serv. Microwave, wet bar in suites. Balconies. Picnic tables, grills. Cr cds: A, D, DS, MC, V.
D

★★ **COURTYARD BY MARRIOTT.** *6235 McDonough Dr (30093), I-85 Exit 37. 770/242-7172; fax 770/840-8768; toll-free 800/321-2211.* 122 rms, 2 story. S, D $82; suites $102; under 18 free; wkend rates. Crib free. TV; cable (premium), VCR avail. Pool; whirlpool. Restaurant 6:30-10 am; Sat, Sun 7-11 am. Bar Mon-Fri 5-11 pm. Ck-out noon. Coin lndry. Meeting rms. Business servs avail. In-rm modem link. Valet serv. Sundries. Exercise equipt. Health club privileges. Bathrm phone in suites. Private patios, balconies. Cr cds: A, C, D, DS, MC, V.
D SC

★★ **FAIRFIELD INN.** *6650 Bay Circle Dr (30071), I-285 Exit 23B. 770/441-1999; fax 770/441-1999; res 800/228-2800.* 135 rms, 3 story. S, D $42-$49; under 18 free. Crib free. TV; cable (premium). Pool. Complimentary continental bkfst. Restaurant nearby. Ck-out noon. Business servs avail. In-rm modem link. Valet serv. Sundries. Cr cds: A, D, DS, MC, V.
D

★ **LA QUINTA INN.** *5375 Peachtree Industrial Blvd (30092). 770/449-5144; fax 770/840-8576; toll-free 800/687-6667. www.laquinta.com.* 130 rms, 3 story. S, D $59-$66; each addl $7; suites $100; under 18 free. Crib free. TV; cable (premium). Pool. Complimentary continental bkfst. Restaurant nearby. Ck-out noon. Meeting rms. Business servs avail. In-rm modem link. Sundries. Some refrigerators. Cr cds: A, C, D, DS, MC, V.
D SC

★★ **QUALITY INN.** *6045 Oakbrook Pkwy (30093), I-85 Exit 37. 770/449-7322; fax 770/368-1868; res 800/228-5151.* 108 rms, 2 story. S, D $49-$89; each addl $10; wkly rates; higher rates special events. Crib free. TV; cable. Pool. Complimentary continental bkfst, coffee in rms. Restaurant adj open 24 hrs. Ck-out 11 am. Guest lndry. Business servs avail. In-rm modem link. Sundries. Refrigerators, microwaves avail. Cr cds: A, C, D, DS, MC, V.
D

★ **RED ROOF INN.** *5171 Brook Hollow Pkwy (30071), I-85 Exit 38. 770/448-8944; fax 770/448-8955.* 115 rms, 3 story. S $40.99; D $55.99-$59.99; each addl $7; under 18 free. Crib free. Pet accepted, some restrictions. TV; cable (premium). Complimentary coffee in lobby. Restaurant nearby. Ck-out noon. Sundries. Cr cds: A, DS, MC, V.
D

Hotels

★ ★ ★ **ATLANTA MARRIOTT NOR-CROSS.** *475 Technology Pkwy (30092), in Technology Park. 770/263-8558; fax 770/263-0766; toll-free 800/228-9290.* 222 rms, 6 story. S $124; suites $200-$250; under 12 free. Crib free. TV; cable (premium). Indoor pool. Restaurant 6:30-9 am, 11 am-2 pm, 5-10 pm. Bar 4 pm-midnight. Ck-out noon. Meeting rms. Business servs avail. In-rm modem link. Concierge. Gift shop. Exercise equipt; sauna. Refrigerators avail. Cr cds: A, C, D, DS, JCB, MC, V.

D ⛊ ≋ ✝ ⬆ 🔥 SC

★ ★ ★ **HILTON ATLANTA NORTH-EAST.** *5993 Peachtree Industrial Blvd (30092). 770/447-4747; fax 770/447-5528; res 800/HILTONS; toll-free 800/445-8667. www.hilton.com.* 272 rms, 10 story. S, D $94-$144; each addl $10; suites $185-$295; family, wkend rates. TV; cable (premium). Indoor/outdoor pool; whirlpool, poolside serv. Restaurant 6:30 am-10 pm. Bar 11-12:30 am. Ck-out noon. Convention facilities. Business center. In-rm modem link. Gift shop. Golf privileges. Exercise equipt; sauna. Cr cds: A, DS, MC, V.

D ⛊ ⛊ ≋ ✝ ⬆ 🔥 SC ✝

★ ★ **HOLIDAY INN ATLANTA/ROSWELL.** *1075 Holcomb Bridge Rd (30076), NW on Holcomb Bridge Rd. 770/992-9600; fax 770/993-6539; res 800/465-4329. Email hiroswellsales@excelonline.com; www.holiday-inn.com/atl-roswell.* 173 rms, 7 story. S, D $119-$139; each addl $10; suites $139-$250; under 18 free; wkend rates. Crib free. TV; cable (premium). Pool. Complimentary coffee in lobby. Restaurant 6:30 am-10:30 pm. Bar noon-midnight. Ck-out noon. Meeting rms. Business servs avail. In-rm modem link. Exercise equipt. Health club privileges. Refrigerators avail. Cr cds: A, DS, MC, V.

D ≋ ✝ ⬆ 🔥 SC

★ ★ **HOLIDAY INN SELECT.** *6050 Peachtree Industrial Blvd (30071). 770/448-4400; fax 770/840-8008; res 800/465-4329. Email atlptexecsec@cooperhotels.com; www.basshotels.com/holiday-inn?_franchisee=atlpt.* 240 rms, 9 story, 7 suites. S $159; D $169; each addl $10; suites $189; under 17 free. Crib avail. Parking lot. Indoor/outdoor pools, whirlpool. TV; cable (premium). Complimentary coffee in rms, newspaper, toll-free calls. Restaurant 6 am-11 pm. Bar. Ck-out noon, ck-in 3 pm. Meeting rms. Business center. Bellhops. Concierge. Dry cleaning, coin lndry. Exercise privileges. Golf. Tennis. Picnic facilities. Cr cds: A, C, D, DS, JCB, MC, V.

D ⛊ ⛊ ≋ ✝ ⬆ ⬆ 🔥 SC ✝

★ ★ **HOMEWOOD SUITES BY HILTON.** *10775 Davis Dr (30004), 8 mi NW on 400 Exit 8. 770/998-1622; fax 770/998-7834; res 800/225-5466. Email atlap01@hws-hotel.com.* 112 kit. suites, 6 story. S $79-$109; D $89-$119; each addl $10; suites $79-$119; under 18 free; family rates; package plans. Crib free. Pet accepted; $50. TV; cable (premium), VCR avail. Complimentary continental bkfst, coffee in rms. Restaurant nearby. Ck-out noon. Meeting rms. Business center. In-rm modem link. Gift shop. Coin lndry. Exercise equipt. Pool. Refrigerators, microwaves. Some balconies. Grills. Cr cds: A, DS, MC, V.

D 🐾 ≋ ✝ ⬆ 🔥 SC ✝

★ ★ ★ **MARRIOTT.** *1775 Pleasant Hill Rd (30096), approx 6 mi NE via I-85 Exit 40, then NW on Pleasant Hill Rd, adj to Gwinnett Mall. 770/923-1775; fax 770/923-0017; toll-free 800/228-9290.* 426 rms, 8-17 story. S, D $149-$189; suites $225-$325; wkend rates. Crib free. TV; cable (premium). Indoor/outdoor pool; whirlpool, poolside serv. Restaurant 6:30 am-10 pm. Bar 5 pm-2 am; Sun to midnight; entertainment. Ck-out noon. Convention facilities. Business center. In-rm modem link. Lndry facilities. Gift shop. Covered parking. Exercise equipt; sauna. Some balconies. On 11 landscaped acres. Luxury level. Cr cds: A, D, DS, ER, JCB, MC, V.

D ≋ ✝ ⬆ 🔥 SC ✝

All Suites

★ ★ ★ **AMBERLEY SUITE HOTEL.** *5885 Oakbrook Pkwy (30093), I-85 Exit 37. 770/263-0515; fax 770/263-0185; toll-free 800/365-0659.* 177

suites, 3 story. S, D $59-$139; under 18 free; wkend, wkly rates. Crib free. TV; cable (premium). Pool; whirlpool. Complimentary full bkfst. Restaurant 6:30 am-1:30 pm, 5-9 pm, Sat, Sun 7:30-10:30 am. Bar 5-11 pm, closed Fri, Sat. Ck-out noon. Coin lndry. Meeting rms. Business center. In-rm modem link. Valet serv. Sundries. Exercise equipt; sauna. Health club privileges. Refrigerators. Cr cds: A, D, DS, MC, V.

★★ AMERISUITES GWINNETT MALL. *3390 Venture Pkwy NW (30096), 2 mi N on I-85, Exit 40. 770/623-6800; fax 770/623-0911; toll-free 800/833-1516.* 114 suites, 6 story. S $99-$129; D $109-$139; higher rates special events. Crib avail. Pet accepted. TV; cable (premium), VCR (movies $6). Pool. Complimentary continental bkfst, coffee in rms. Restaurant opp 11 am-10 pm. Ck-out noon. Meeting rms. Business center. In-rm modem link. Exercise equipt. Health club privileges. Refrigerators, microwaves. Cr cds: A, C, D, DS, JCB, MC, V.

★★ HAWTHORN SUITES. *2060 Crescent Center Blvd. (30084), 5 mi S to I-285 Exit 28. 770/496-1070; fax 770/939-9947; res 800/537-1133.* 113 suites, 6 story. Apr-Nov: S $76.95-$124.95; D $81.95-$135.95; under 15 free; higher rates special events; lower rates rest of yr. Crib free. TV; cable (premium). Pool; whirlpool. Complimentary full bkfst, coffee in rms. Restaurant nearby. Ck-out noon. Coin lndry. Meeting rms. Business servs avail. In-rm modem link. Valet serv. Sundries. Refrigerators. Cr cds: A, C, D, DS, JCB, MC, V.

★★ HOMEWOOD SUITES. *450 Technology Pkwy (30092). 770/448-4663; fax 770/242-6979; res 800/225-5466.* 92 suites, 2-3 story. Suites $110-$195; wkend rates. Crib free. Pet accepted, some restrictions; $50. TV; cable. Pool; whirlpool. Complimentary continental bkfst, coffee in rms. Restaurant nearby. Ck-out noon. Coin lndry. Meeting rms. Business center. In-rm modem link. Valet serv. Sundries. Exercise equipt. Health club privileges. Refrigerators, microwaves.

Picnic tables, grills. Cr cds: A, DS, MC, V.

Restaurants

★★ DICK & HARRY'S. *1570 Holcomb Bridge Rd (30076), in Holcomb Woods Village Shopping Center. 770/641-8757. www.dickandharrys. com.* Specializes in crab cakes, barbecued salmon, emu. Hrs: 11:30 am-2:30 pm, 5:30-10 pm; Fri to 11 pm; Sat 5:30-11 pm. Closed Sun; hols. Res accepted. Bar. Lunch $6-$12; dinner $12-$20. Child's menu. Valet parking Fri, Sat. Casual dining. Cr cds: A, C, D, DS, MC, V.

★★ DOMINICK'S. *95 S Peachtree St (30071). 770/449-1611.* Specializes in Dominick's chicken, spedini bread, Dominick's ravioli. Hrs: 11 am-2:30 pm, 5-10 pm; Sat from 5 pm; Sun 5-9 pm. Closed Dec 25. Res accepted. Bar. Lunch $5.50-$21.50; dinner $11-$21.50. Child's menu. Parking. Originally a hardware store; original brick, original tin tiled ceiling; 175 yrs old. Cr cds: A, D, DS, MC, V.

★★★ HI LIFE. *3380 Holcomb Bridge Rd (30092), in Corners Court Shopping Center. 770/409-0101.* Email hilife@mindspring.com; www.hilifekitchencocktails.com. Specializes in Maine lobster, lemon grass and shellfish stew, tuna poke. Hrs: 11 am-10 pm; Thurs-Sat to 11 pm. Closed Jan 1, Thanksgiving, Dec 25. Res accepted. Bar. Wine list. Lunch $4-$15; dinner $4-$22. Child's menu. Parking. Contemporary American decor. Cr cds: A, DS, MC, V.

★★ KILLER CREEK CHOP HOUSE. *1700 Mansell Rd (30004), 8 mi NW on GA 400 Exit 8. 770/649-0064.* Specializes in steak, chops, seafood. Hrs: 5-11 pm; Fri to midnight; Sat 4 pm-midnight; Sun 3-10 pm. Closed hols. Bar. Dinner $12.95-$24.95. Child's menu. Valet parking. Open kitchen. Cr cds: A, D, DS, MC, V.

★★★ LICKSKILLET FARM. *1380 Old Roswell Rd (30077), approx 5 mi NW on Holcomb Bridge Rd (US 140). 770/475-6484.* Specializes in Australian rack of lamb, penne salmon, steak. Hrs: 11:30 am-2 pm, 6-10 pm; Mon from 6 pm; Sat from 5:30 pm; Sun 5:30-9 pm; Sun brunch 10:30 am-2 pm. Closed July 4, Dec 25. Res accepted. Bar. Lunch $7.95-$9.95; dinner $14.95-$22.95. Sun brunch $19.95. Entertainment: pianist Sun brunch. Parking. 1846 farmhouse furnished with many antiques; original fireplaces. Family-owned. Cr cds: A, D, DS, MC, V.

D

★★★ **VAN GOGH'S.** *70 W Crossville Rd (30075), approx 5 mi NW on Holcomb Bridge Rd (US 140). 770/993-1156. www.knowwheretogo.com.* Specializes in seafood, grilled portobello mushrooms, crab cakes. Own desserts. Hrs: 11:30 am-2:30 pm, 5-10:30 pm; Fri, Sat to 11:30 pm; Sun 5-10 pm. Closed hols. Res accepted. Bar. Wine list. Lunch $4.95-$13.95; dinner $13.95-$25.95. Child's menu. Valet parking. European ambiance. Cr cds: A, D, DS, MC, V.

D

Unrated Dining Spot

SIA'S. *1035 Medlock Bridge Rd (30097). 770/497-9727. www.siasrestaurant.com.* Specializes in seafood, chicken, beef. Hrs: 11:30 am-2 pm, 5:30-10 pm; Sat 5-10 pm. Res accepted. Bar. Wine list. Lunch $9.50-$12.50; dinner $18.95-$28. Entertainment. Cr cds: D, DS, MC, V.

D

Ocmulgee National Monument

(2 mi E of Macon on US 80, Alt 129)

Ocmulgee, the most scientifically excavated of the South's major Native American sites, shows evidence of 12,000 years of settlement, incl six successive occupations from at least 10,000 BC to 1825. The major remains consist of nine ceremonial mounds, a funeral mound, and a restored ceremonial earth lodge of the early Mississippian Period (AD 900-1100).

Exhibits and dioramas in the museum depict this sequence: Paleo-Indian Period, from more than 12,000 years ago, when Ice Age hunters trailing mammoth and other now-extinct game arrived using stone-tipped spears. During the Archaic Period, after the Ice Age ended, hunter-gathering people hunted small game and supplemented their diet with mussels, fish, seeds, berries, and nuts. They made polished stone tools and camped along the streams. By 2000 BC, crude pottery was fashioned. During the Woodland Period (beginning 1000 BC), some plants were cultivated, villages were larger, and mounds were being built. Pottery was stamped with elaborate designs carved into wooden paddles. The Early Mississippian Period began about AD 900, when invaders brought cultivated corn, beans, squash, and tobacco to the Macon Plateau. They built a large town with burial and temple mounds and circular, earth-covered council chambers. This ceremonial center declined around AD 1100. Late Mississippian Period villagers of the Lamar Culture combined elements of the Mississippian and older Woodland ways of life. They may have been direct ancestors of the historic Creek who lived here when Europeans first settled Georgia. The Creek soon became involved in the struggle between France, Spain, and England for possession of the New World.

Exhibits and dioramas in the museum show the Native American from earliest origins to his removal to Oklahoma in the early 1800s. Great Temple Mound, more than 40 feet high, is the largest in the park. An audio program is conducted in the restored earthlodge, which was the Mississippian council chamber. (Daily; closed Jan 1, Dec 25) For information, contact the Superintendent, 1207 Emery Hwy, Macon 31217; 912/752-8257.

Okefenokee Swamp

See also Waycross

(In SE corner of state, S of Waycross, E of Valdosta)
Web www.fws.gov
Information Refuge Manager, Rte 2, Box 3330, Folkston 31537; 912/496-7836

One of the largest preserved freshwater wetlands in the United States, the Okefenokee Swamp encompasses more than 700 square miles, stretching an average of 25 miles in width and 35 miles in length. The swamp's southern border is beyond the Florida line. Called "land of trembling earth" by Native Americans, its lakes of dark brown water, lush with moss-draped cypress, are headwaters for the Suwannee and St. Marys rivers. The swamp embraces vast marshes, termed "prairies," which comprise 60,000 acres.

What to See and Do

Okefenokee National Wildife Refuge. Occupies more than 90 percent of the swamp region and harbors bears, deer, bobcats, alligators, and aquatic birds. Naturalists have discovered many rare plants on the swamp floor, which has been described as "the most beautiful and fantastic landscape in the world." The cypress stand mi after mi, their dense formations broken by watery "prairies" or covered by deposits of peat ranging to 15 ft in thickness. It is possible to cause small trees and shrubs to shake by stamping on the "trembling earth"; these trees take root in the crust of peat beds and never reach the solid bottom. Such forests are interspersed with varied swamp vegetation. The bay, one of the swamp's most distinctive trees, blooms from May-Oct, producing a white flower in contrast to its rich evergreen foliage. Aquatic flowers, such as yellow spatterdock and white water lily, blend with pickerel-weed and golden-club and swamp iris in the spring. The swamp is also the home of the sandhill crane and round-tailed muskrat. (Hrs vary with season) Phone 912/496-7836. Per vehicle ¢¢

Okefenokee Swamp Park. This park located on Cowhouse Island has a serpentarium and reptile shows. Guided boat tours (fee); canoe rentals. Cypress boardwalk into swamp to 90-ft-high observation tower. Picnicking. Interpretive centers, video. (Daily) No overnight facilities. Camping available at nearby Laura S. Walker State Park (see WAYCROSS). Phone 912/283-0583. Admission fee ¢¢¢

Stephen C. Foster State Park. Park offers access to Billy's Lake, Minnie's Lake, and Big Water (daily during daylight hrs without a guide). Fishing, boating (rentals, basin, dock, ramp), canoeing (rentals), sightseeing boat tours; nature trails, picnicking, concession, camping, cabins. Museum. Standard hrs, fees. Phone 912/637-5274.

Suwannee Canal Recreation Area. Area provides entry to the Chesser, Grand, Mizell, and Chase prairies, where small lakes and "gator holes" offer some of the nation's finest bird-watching. Area also has restored swamp homestead and guided swamp tours. Boating (ramp, boat, and motor rentals), canoeing, guided boat tours; nature trails, boardwalk (¾ mi) with observation tower. Picnicking. Visitor center. (Daily; closed Dec 25) Fees for some activities. Phone 912/496-7836. Per vehicle ¢¢

Wilderness canoeing. There are 7 overnight stops and trips avail from 2 to 5 days (3-day limit Mar and Apr); wooden platforms for campsites. Mar to May and Oct through early Nov are most popular times. By advance res (2 months) and special permit from Refuge Manager. Phone 912/496-3331. Fee per person per night ¢¢¢

Perry

(E-3) *See also Andersonville, Cordele, Macon*

Pop 9,452 **Elev** 337 ft **Area code** 912
Zip 31069 **Web** www.perryga.com
Information Perry Area Convention & Visitors Bureau, 101 General

Courtney Hodges Blvd, PO Box 1619;
912/988-8000

The early-blooming wildflowers and
trees of March and April have made
Perry a favorite stopover place for
spring motorists. The town is full of
stately houses and historical
churches. Perry is known as the
"Crossroads of Georgia" because of
its location near the geographic center of the state.

What to See and Do

Massee Lane Gardens. Ten-acre
camellia garden reaches height of
bloom between Nov and Mar; large
greenhouse, Japanese garden, rose
garden. Colonial-style headquarters
contains more than 300 sculptures of
Boehm and other porcelains. Headquarters incl the Annabelle Lundy
Fetterman Educational Museum,
exhibition hall (rare books, porcelain), auditorium with presentation
on history of gardens, gift shop.
Bldgs (Nov-Mar, daily; rest of yr,
Mon-Fri); grounds (daily). 14 mi W
on GA 127 to Marshallville, then 3
mi N on GA 49. Phone 912/967-2722
or 912/967-2358. ¢¢

The Andersonville Trail. Along drive
are American Camellia Society gardens, 2 state parks, antebellum
houses, and Andersonville National
Historic Site. For information contact
the Chamber of Commerce. A 75-mi
loop drive from Perry to Cordele (see).

Annual Events

Mossy Creek Barnyard Festival. Deep
Piney Woods, N on I-75, exit 43A, 3
mi E. Semiannual event with crafters,
artists, entertainment, and demonstrations. Phone 912/922-8265. Two
days late Apr and 2 days late Oct.

**Old Fashioned Christmas at the
Crossroads.** Community Christmas
tree, parade, candlelight service. Dec.

Motels/Motor Lodges

★★ **COMFORT INN.** *1602 Sam
Nunn Blvd (31069). 912/987-7710; fax
912/988-2624; res 800/228-5150; toll-
free 800/642-7710.* 102 rms, 2 story,
12 suites. S, D $45-$80; each addl $5;
suites $69-$90; under 18 free. Crib
free. TV; cable (premium). Indoor
pool; whirlpool. Complimentary

continental bkfst. Restaurant nearby.
Ck-out 11 am. Coin lndry. Meeting
rm. Business servs avail. In-rm
modem link. Valet serv. Sundries.
Exercise equipt; sauna. Refrigerators;
some wet bars. Cr cds: A, C, D, DS,
ER, JCB, MC, V.

★★ **DAYLIGHT INN.** *102 Valley Dr
(31069), US 341 at I-75 Exit 43.
912/987-2142; fax 912/987-0468.* 80
rms, 2 story. S, D $41-$52; each addl
$5; under 18 free. Crib free. TV;
cable. Pool; wading pool. Complimentary coffee, continental bkfst.
Restaurant nearby. Ck-out noon.
Business servs avail. Private patios,
balconies. Cr cds: A, DS, MC, V.

★★ **HOLIDAY INN PERRY.** *200 Valley Dr (31069), US 341 I-75 Exit 43.
912/987-3313; fax 912/988-8269; res
800/HOLIDAY; toll-free 800/808-8804.*
203 rms, 2 story. S, D $54; under 18
free. Crib free. TV; cable (premium).
Pool. Complimentary coffee in lobby.
Restaurant 6-10 am, 11 am-2 pm, 5-
10 pm. Bar 4:30 pm-12:30 am. Coin
lndry. Meeting rms. Business servs
avail. Valet serv. Sundries. Exercise
equipt. Some refrigerators. Cr cds: A,
D, DS, MC, V.

★★ **NEW PERRY HOTEL-MOTEL.**
*800 Main St (31069). 912/987-1000;
fax 912/987-5779; toll-free 800/877-
3779.* 39 hotel rms, 3 story, 17 motel
rms. S $28-$45; D $39-$49; each addl
$2. Crib $2. Pet accepted; $5/day. TV;
cable. Pool. Restaurant (see NEW
PERRY). Ck-out noon. Meeting rms.
Built in 1925; landscaped grounds.
Cr cds: A, MC, V.

★★ **QUALITY INN.** *1504 Sam Nunn
Blvd (31069), US 341 at I-75, Exit 43.
912/987-1345; fax 912/987-5875; res
800/228-5151.* 66 rms, 1 story, 3
suites. S $49.95; D $54.95; each addl
$5; suites $75; under 18 free. Crib
avail. Pet accepted, some restrictions,
fee. Parking lot. Pool, children's pool.
TV; cable. Complimentary continental bkfst, coffee in rms, newspaper,
toll-free calls. Restaurant 11:30 am-
9:30 pm, closed Sun. Bar. Ck-out 11
am, ck-in 1 pm. Meeting rm. Business servs avail. Dry cleaning. Exer-

cise privileges. Golf. Tennis, 4 courts. Picnic facilities. Cr cds: A, C, D, DS, ER, JCB, MC, V.

D ◄ 𝕏 �🛏 🏊 ⁂ ▨ 🔥

★★ **RAMADA LIMITED.** *100 Market Pl Dr (31069), I-75 Exit 43. 912/987-8400; fax 912/987-3133; toll-free 888/987-8400.* 60 rms, 2 story. S $44; D $48; each addl $4; under 18 free; higher rates special events. Crib avail. Pet accepted, some restrictions; $5. TV; cable (premium). Complimentary continental bkfst. Restaurant adj 6 am-10 pm. Ck-out 11 am. Meeting rm. In-rm modem link. Valet serv. Golf privileges. Indoor pool; whirlpool. Bathrm phones; many refrigerators, microwaves. Cr cds: A, D, DS, JCB, MC, V.

D ◄ 𝕏 🛏 ▨ 🔥

★ **TRAVELODGE.** *100 Westview Ln (31069), I-75 Exit 42. 912/987-7355; fax 912/987-7250; res 800/578-7878. www.thetravelodge.com/perry0.* 59 rms, 2 story, 2 suites. Feb-Nov: S $59; D $65; each addl $5; under 12 free; lower rates rest of yr. Crib avail, fee. Parking lot. Pool. TV; cable (premium), VCR avail. Complimentary continental bkfst, coffee in rms, newspaper, toll-free calls. Restaurant. Ck-out 11 am, ck-in 1 pm. Meeting rm. Fax servs avail. Coin lndry. Tennis. Cr cds: A, D, DS, MC, V.

D ⁂ 🛏 ▨ 🔥 SC

B&B/Small Inn

★★ **THE EVANS-CANTRELL HOUSE B&B.** *300 College St (31030), 12 mi NW on US 341. 912/825-0611; fax 912/822-9925; res 912/825-0611; toll-free 888/923-0611.www.bbonline. com/ga.* 3 rms, 2 story, 1 suite. S $75; D $85; each addl $15; suites $105; children $15; under 12 free. Street parking. TV; cable (premium), VCR avail. Complimentary full bkfst, toll-free calls. Restaurant. Ck-out 11 am, ck-in 3 pm. Meeting rm. Fax servs avail. Exercise equipt. Golf, 9 holes. Tennis, 2 courts. Cr cds: A, DS, MC, V.

𝕏 ⁂ 𝕏 ▨ 🔥

Restaurant

★★ **NEW PERRY.** *800 Main St. 912/987-1000.* Specializes in fried chicken, country ham. Hrs: 7 am-2:30 pm, 5-8:30 pm. Res accepted.

Bkfst $3.75-$5.50; lunch $6.60-$7.25; dinner $9.85-$12.85. Overlooks pool, gardens. Cr cds: A, MC, V.

D

Pine Mountain (Harris County)

(D-2) *See also Columbus, La Grange*

Pop 875 **Elev** 860 ft **Area code** 706 **Zip** 31822

What to See and Do

◼ **Callaway Gardens.** This distinctive public garden and resort, consisting of 14,000 acres of gardens, woodlands, lakes, recreation areas, and wildlife, was conceived by prominent textile industrialist Cason J. Callaway to be "the finest garden on earth since Adam was a boy." Originally the family's wkend vacation spot in the 1930s, Callaway and his wife Virginia expanded the area and opened it to the public in 1952. Today Callaway Gardens is home to more than 50 varieties of butterflies, 230 varieties of birds, and more than 100 species of plantlife, incl the rare plunifolia azalea, indigenous to the area. The complex allows swimming, boating, and other water recreation around 13 lakes, incl 175-acre Mountain Creek Lake and the white sand beach of Robin Lake; 23 mi of roads and paths for hiking or jogging, 63 holes of golf (a 9-hole and three 18-hole courses), 17 lighted tennis courts, and 2 indoor racquetball courts, skeet and trapshooting ranges, hunting for deer or quail on 1,000-acre preserve, picnicking, country store; cottages, villas, and resort (see), dining pavilion; and 5,000-ft paved and lighted runway and terminal. On US 27. Also on garden grounds are

Cecil B. Day Butterfly Center. An 8,000-sq-ft, glass-enclosed conservatory housing up to 1,000 free-flying butterflies, as well as ground pheasants; exotic plants and waterfalls.

Ida Cason Callaway Memorial Chapel. A woodland chapel patterned after rural wayside chapels of the 16th and 17th centuries; organ concerts yr-round. **Pioneer Log Cabin** is an authentic 18th-century structure in which life of early Georgia settlers is demonstrated. Phone 706/663-2281 or 800/225-5292. ¢¢¢

John S. Sibley Horticultural Center. Five acres displaying unique collections of exotic and native plants, seasonal flowerbeds, and lush green lawns; also sculpture garden and 22-ft waterfall.

Mr. Cason's Vegetable Garden. Vegetable garden (7½ acres) that produces hundreds of varieties of fruits, vegetables, and herbs; setting for "Victory Garden South" television show.

Franklin D. Roosevelt State Park. One of the largest parks in the state system has many historic bldgs and King's Gap Indian trail. Swimming pool, fishing; hiking, bridle, and nature trails, picnicking, camping, cottages. Standard hrs, fees. Contact Superintendent, 2970 Hwy 190E. 5 mi SE off jct US 27, GA 190. Phone 706/663-4858.

★ **Little White House Historic Site.** Cottage in which President Franklin D. Roosevelt died on Apr 12, 1945, is preserved as it was on the day he died. On display is original furniture, memorabilia, and the portrait on which Elizabeth Shoumatoff was working when the president was stricken with a massive cerebral hemorrhage. A film about Roosevelt's life at Warm Springs and in Georgia is shown at the F. D. Roosevelt Museum and Theater. Picnic area, snack bar. (Daily; closed Jan 1, Thanksgiving, Dec 25) Approx 15 mi E on GA 18 & GA 194, then ½ mi S on GA 85W in Warm Springs. Phone 706/655-5870. ¢¢

Motels/Motor Lodges

★★ **DAVIS INN.** *5585 State Park Rd, Hwy 354 (31822), jct US 27S. 706/663-2522; fax 706/663-7571; toll-free 888/346-2668.* 23 rms, 1-2 story, 10 kit. units, 15 condos (1-2 bedrm). S, D $70-$80; each addl $10; kit. units, condos $90-$185; under 12 free; wkends (2-day min). TV; cable (premium). Swimming privileges. Complimentary coffee in lobby. Restaurant

nearby. Ck-out noon. Meeting rms. Lighted tennis privileges. Golf privileges, pro, putting green, driving range. Health club privileges. Picnic tables, grills. Adj Callaway Gardens. No cr cds accepted.

★ **VALLEY INN RESORT.** *14420 US Hwy 27 E (31811), 6 mi S on US 27. 706/628-4454; fax 706/628-7165; toll-free 800/944-9393. Email valleyinnresort@juno.com.* 20 rms, 4 kits. Mar-Dec; S, D $55-$72; each addl $12; kit. cottages $105-$120; under 6 free; wkly rates; lower rates rest of yr. Crib $4. TV; cable. Pool. Playground. Coffee in rms. Ck-out noon. Sundries. Tennis privileges. 63-hole golf privileges. Health club privileges. Picnic tables, grills. On 22-acre lake with flat-bottom boats. Cr cds: A, MC, V.

Resort

★★★ **CALLAWAY GARDENS.** *US Hwy 27 (31822), S on US 27, 1 mi S of GA 18. 706/663-2281; fax 706/663-5068; toll-free 800/225-5292. Email info@callawaygardens.com; www.callawaygardens.com.* 349 rms, 1-3 story, 155 cottages (2-bedrm), 49 villas. Mid-Mar-mid-Apr & mid-Nov-late Dec: S, D $111-$121; each addl $15; suites $154-$200; luxury villas (1-4 bedrm) $136-$350; cottages $111-$184; under 18 free; MAP rates, golf, tennis plans; lower rates rest of yr. Crib free. TV; cable. 3 pools; wading pool, lifeguard in summer. Playground. Supervised children's activities (June-mid-Aug); ages 6 months-18 yrs. 8 dining rms 6:30 am-10 pm (see also GEORGIA ROOM). Box lunches, snack bar. Bar 5 pm-1 am, closed Sun. Ck-out noon, ck-in 4 pm. Grocery 1 mi. Coin lndry. Package store nearby. Convention facilities. Business center. Bellhops. Valet serv. Concierge. Local airport transportation. Lighted tennis, pro. Three 18-hole, one 9-hole golf, greens fee $75-$110 (incl cart), pros. Swimming, private beach, waterskiing. Paddle boats, sailboats. Bicycles avail; 7-mi bicycle trail. Horseback riding nearby. Skeet & trap shooting. Soc dir; entertainment, movies. Rec rm. Exercise equipt. Refrigerators avail. Private patios, balconies. Picnic tables, grills. On 14,000 acres; butterfly conservatory on site. Cr cds: A, DS, MC, V.

Restaurants

★★ **BULLOCH HOUSE.** *Hwy 41S (31830), 15 mi E on GA 18, then S on GA 85.* 706/655-9068. Specializes in Southern cooking. Salad bar. Hrs: 11 am-2:30 pm; Fri, Sat 11 am-2:30 pm, 5-8:30 pm. Closed hols. Res accepted. Lunch $4.50. Buffet: $5.95; dinner $6.95-$8.95. Buffet: $7.95. Child's menu. Parking. House built 1892; original floors, fireplaces. Cr cds: A, D, DS, MC, V.

★★★ **GEORGIA ROOM.** *US 27.* 706/663-2281. *www.callawaygardens. com.* Specializes in sauteed veal chop, breast of duck confit. Own baking. Hrs: 6-9 pm. Closed Sun, Mon. Res accepted. Wine list. Dinner a la carte entrees: $18-$28. Cr cds: A, D, DS, MC, V.

★★★ **OAK TREE VICTORIAN RESTAURANT.** *US 27 (31811), 5 mi S of Callaway Gardens.* 706/628-4218. Specializes in veal pirozhki, onion soup, prime rib. Hrs: 6-9:30 pm. Closed Sun; hols. Res accepted. Wine cellar. Dinner $7.95-$23.95. Victorian house (1871). Cr cds: A, D, DS, MC, V.

★ **VICTORIAN TEA ROOM.** *70 Broad St (31830), 15 mi E on GA 18, then S on GA 85.* 706/655-2319. Specializes in grilled chicken sandwiches, salads, desserts. Salad bar. Hrs: 11:30 am-3 pm; Fri, Sat to 8 pm. Closed Jan 1, Thanksgiving, Dec 25. Lunch $2.95-$5.95. Buffet: $5.95-$6.95; dinner buffet: $5.95-$6.95. Child's menu. In 1906 bldg; many antiques. Cr cds: MC, V.

Plains

(see Americus)

Pop 875 **Elev** 860 ft **Area code** 706 **Zip** 31822

Rome

(B-1) *See also Calhoun, Cartersville*

Founded 1834 **Pop** 30,326 **Elev** 605 ft **Area code** 706 **Zip** 30161 **Web** www.romegeorgia.com

Information Greater Rome Convention & Visitors Bureau, 402 Civic Center Hill, PO Box 5823, 30162-5823; 706/295-5576; or 800/444-1834

Annual Event

Heritage Holidays. River rides, parade, tours, wagon train, arts and crafts fair, music. Mid-Oct.

Motels/Motor Lodges

★★ **DAYS INN.** *840 Turner McCall Blvd (30161), at Broad St (US 27/GA 20).* 706/295-0400; fax 706/295-0400; res 800/329-7466. www.daysinn.com. 103 rms, 5 story, 2 suites. S $50; D $55; each addl $5; suites $75; children $5; under 12 free. Crib avail. Parking lot. Pool. TV; cable (premium). Complimentary continental bkfst, coffee in rms, newspaper, toll-free calls. Restaurant. Ck-out 11 am, ck-in 2:30 pm. Meeting rms. Business servs avail. Dry cleaning, coin lndry. Golf. Tennis, 5 courts. Cr cds: A, C, D, DS, MC, V.

★★ **RAMADA INN ON THE RIVER.** *707 Turner McCall Blvd (30165).* 706/232-0444; fax 706/232-3872; res 800/272-6232. 155 rms, 2 story. S $60; D $65; each addl $5; under 18 free. Crib free. TV; cable (premium). Pool. Restaurant open 24 hrs. Ck-out noon. Free lndry facilities. Meeting rms. Business servs avail. Valet serv. Exercise equipt. Cr cds: A, C, D, DS, MC, V.

Conference Center

★★ **HOLIDAY INN SKYTOP.** *20 Hwy 411 E (30161), 2 mi E of town center.* 706/295-1100; fax 706/291-7128; toll-free 800/465-4329. Email hiskytop@prodigy.net. 197 rms, 2 story, 10 suites. Apr-June, Sep-Oct:

S $66; D $72; each addl $6; suites $90; under 16 free; lower rates rest of yr. Crib avail, fee. Pet accepted, fee. Parking lot. Indoor/outdoor pools. TV; cable (premium). Complimentary coffee in rms, newspaper. Restaurant. Bar. Ck-out noon, ck-in 3 pm. Meeting rms. Business center. Dry cleaning, coin lndry. Exercise equipt, sauna. Golf, 18 holes. Tennis, 10 courts. Cr cds: A, C, D, DS, JCB, MC, V.

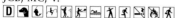

Savannah (E-7)

Founded 1733 **Pop** 137,560 **Elev** 42 ft
Area code 912 **Web** www.savcvb.com

Information Savannah Area Convention & Visitors Bureau, 101 E Bay St, 31401; PO Box 1628, 31402; 912/944-0456 or 800/444-2427

Savannah has a wealth of history and architecture that few American cities can match. Even fewer have managed to preserve the same air of colonial grace and charm. The city's many rich, green parks are blooming legacies of the brilliance of its founder, General James E. Oglethorpe, who landed at Yamacraw Bluff with 120 settlers on February 12, 1733. His plan for the colony was to make the "inner city" spacious, beautiful, and all that a city should be. Bull Street, named for Colonel William Bull, one of Oglethorpe's aides, stretches south from the high bluffs overlooking the Savannah River and is punctuated by five handsome squares and Forsyth Park.

Savannah then changed its outer garb of wood palisades to a gray "Savannah brick" fort surmounting the bluff. By Revolutionary times wharves served ocean trade, and sailors caroused in seamen's inns. The town had its liberty pole and a patriots' battalion when news of Lexington came. The Declaration of Independence led to Savannah's designation as capital of the new state. By December, however, the British had retaken the city with 2,000 troops, and the Royal Governor, who

had fled earlier, returned. An attempt to recapture Savannah by American troops failed, and more than 1,000 Americans and 700 Frenchmen were killed. General "Mad Anthony" Wayne's forces finally drove the British from Savannah in 1782.

In 1795, tobacco culture and Eli Whitney's cotton gin brought prosperity back to Savannah. Meanwhile, the city's growth followed the orderly pattern laid out by Colonel Bull. By the first decade of the new century, Classical Revival or Regency architecture had superseded Georgian Colonial. Savannah, with new forts protecting the estuary and strengthening Fort Wayne on the bluff, fared better during the War of 1812. Afterward, architect William Jay and master builder Isaiah Davenport added splendid mansions that fronted palm-lined squares. The steamboat *Enterprise* plied upriver from here to Augusta in 1816; three years later, on May 22, 1819, the SS *Savannah* set sail from Savannah for Liverpool to be the first steamer to cross the Atlantic. Savannah had become the leading market and shipping point for cotton, naval stores, and tobacco, and prosperity increased until the Civil War.

Throughout the war, Savannah tried to hold its own. Fort Pulaski (see), which the Confederates took control of even before Secession, was retaken by a Union artillery assault on April 11, 1862, and became a Union military prison. Despite repeated Union naval battering, the Confederates held Fort McAllister (see) until Sherman marched to the sea and captured it on December 13, 1864. Although Confederate troops resisted for three days after Sherman demanded Savannah's surrender, Union forces eventually occupied the city, and Confederates were forced to escape to Hutchison Island.

Reconstruction was painful but 20 years later cotton was king again. Surrounding pine forests produced lumber and resins; the Cotton and Naval Stores Exchange was launched in 1882 while financiers and brokers strode the streets with confidence. By the 20th century Savannah turned to manufacturing. With more than 200 industries by World War II, the city's

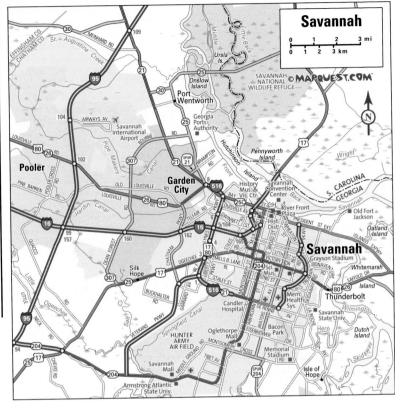

prosperity has been measured by the activity of its port, which included shipbuilding booms during both world wars. Extensive developments by the Georgia Port Authority in the past decade have contributed to the city's commercial, industrial, and shipping growth.

Today more than 1,400 historically and architecturally significant buildings have been restored in Savannah's historic district, making it one of the largest urban historic landmark districts in the country. Another area, the Victorian district south of the historic district, offers some of the best examples of post-Civil War Victorian architecture in the country. The city that launched the Girl Scouts of America also plays host to modern Girl Scouts who visit the shrine of founder Juliette Gordon Low.

What to See and Do

City Hall. (1905) A gold dome tops the 4-story neoclassic facade of this bldg, which replaced the original 1799 structure. A tablet outside com-

memorates sailing of the SS *Savannah;* a model is displayed in the Council Chamber. Another tablet is dedicated to the *John Randolph,* the first iron-sided vessel launched in American waters (1834). (Mon-Fri) Bull & Bay Sts. **FREE**

Fort McAllister Historic Park. (see) 25 mi S via GA 144.

Fort Pulaski National Monument. (see) 15 mi E off US 80.

Historic Savannah Waterfront Area. Restoration of the riverfront bluff to preserve and stabilize the historic waterfront incl a 9-blk brick concourse of parks, studios, museums, shops, restaurants, and pubs. John P. Rousakis Riverfront Plaza.

Savannah History Museum. This 19th-century railroad shed was renovated to house historical orientation center. Mural in lobby chronicles major events in Savannah's 250-yr history. (Daily; closed Jan 1, Thanksgiving, Dec 25). 303 Martin Luther King Jr Blvd, adj Savannah Visitor Center. Phone 912/238-1779. ¢¢ Here are

Auxiliary Theater. Special audio-visual presentations.

Exhibit Hall. Artifacts, antiques, and memorabilia from Savannah's past; pre-colonial Native American artifacts, Revolutionary and Civil war uniforms and weapons; 1890 Baldwin locomotive; replica of the SS *Savannah,* first steamboat to cross the Atlantic.

Main Theater. Orientation film provides an overview of the history of Savannah from 1733-present as seen through the eyes of Gen James E. Oglethorpe.

Savannah National Wildlife Refuge. N via US 17 or US 17A, across the Savannah River in South Carolina.

Savannah Science Museum. Exhibits of live reptiles and amphibians; exhibits on the natural, physical, medical, and technological sciences. Planetarium shows (Sat and Sun afternoons). (Tues-Sat, also Sun afternoons; closed hols) 4405 Paulsen St. Phone 912/447-8655. ¢¢

Ships of the Sea Museum. Ship models, figureheads; scrimshaw, sea artifacts; ship's carpenter shop. (Tues-Sun; closed hols) 41 Martin Luther King Blvd. Phone 912/232-1511. ¢¢

Sightseeing tours.

Touring Savannah. Various guided bus tours of Historic Landmark district and other areas. Tours depart from Visitor Center (see ADDITIONAL VISITOR INFORMATION) and downtown hotels and inns. (Daily; closed St. Patrick's Day, Thanksgiving, Dec 25) 250 Martin Luther King Blvd. Phone 912/234-8128. ¢¢¢-¢¢¢¢

Gray Line bus tours. Contact 215 W Boundary St, 31401. Phone 912/234-8687.

Telfair Museum of Art. Site of Royal Governor's residence from 1760 to end of American Revolution. Regency mansion (1818) is one of 3 surviving bldgs in Savannah by William Jay, English architect. Period rms with family furnishings, silverware, porcelains; Octagon Rm. Telfair is the oldest public art museum in the SE, with a permanent collection of 18th-, 19th-, and 20th-century American and European paintings and sculpture; prints, silver, decorative arts. Concerts, lectures, tours. (Tues-Sun; closed hols) 121 Barnard St. Phone 912/232-1177. ¢¢

Trustees' Garden Site. Original site of 10-acre experimental garden modeled in 1733 after the Chelsea Gardens in London by colonists who hoped to produce silk, wine, and drugs. Peach trees planted in garden were responsible for Georgia's peach industry. Fort Wayne occupied the site in 1762. Not of military importance until the Revolution, the fort was named for General "Mad Anthony" Wayne. Strengthened by the British (1779), the Americans rebuilt it during the War of 1812. The massive buttressed brick walls later served as the foundation for a municipal gas company bldg. The **Pirates' House** (1734), former inn for visiting seamen, has been restored and is a restaurant; Robert Louis Stevenson referred to the inn in *Treasure Island.* E Broad St.

US Customs House. (1850) Erected on site of colony's first public bldg. The granite columns' carved capitals were modeled from tobacco leaves. Tablet on Bull St marks site where John Wesley preached his first Savannah sermon; tablet on Bay St marks site of Oglethorpe's headquarters. Bull & E Bay Sts.

Wormsloe State Historic Site. Remains of early fortified 18th-century tabby house. (Tabby is a kind of cement made from lime, oyster shells, sand, and water.) Visitor center exhibits outline history of site and of Noble Jones family, owners for more than 200 yrs. (Tues-Sun) Contact Manager, 7601 Skidaway Rd, 31406. 8 mi SE on Skidaway Rd. Phone 912/353-3023. ¢

Annual Events

Georgia Heritage Festival. Walking tours, open house at historic sites, crafts show, waterfront festival, parade, concerts, Georgia Day. Late Jan-mid-Feb.

St. Patrick's Day Parade. Rivals New York City's in size. Mar.

Savannah Tour of Homes & Gardens. Sponsored by Christ Episcopal Church with Historic Savannah Foundation. Day and candlelight tours of more than 30 private homes and gardens. Contact 18 Abercorn St, 31401. Phone 912/234-8054. Mar.

Walking Tour of Old Savannah Gardens. Incl 8 private walled gardens in historic Savannah, tea at antebellum Green-Meldrim House. Phone 912/238-0248. Early Apr.

Night In Old Savannah. At the Savannah Visitor Center. Foods of more than 25 countries; entertainment incl jazz, country, and rhythm and blues. Mid-Apr.

Seafood Festival. Waterfront. Restaurants offer samples; entertainment, arts and crafts. Contact Savannah Waterfront Association. Phone 912/234-0295. First wkend in May.

Savannah Scottish Games & Highland Gathering. Old Fort Jackson, 2 mi E via President St extension. The clans gather for a wkend of Highland games, piping, drumming, dancing, and the traditional "Kirkin' o' th' Tartans." Second Sat May.

Christmas in Savannah. Month-long celebration incl tours of houses, historical presentations, parades, music, caroling, and cultural events. Dec.

Additional Visitor Information

The Savannah Visitors Center, 301 Martin Luther King, Jr Blvd, is open daily, providing information on area attractions (incl a free visitors guide with translations in French, German, Spanish, and Japanese). All guided bus tours depart from the center on a regular basis.

Visitor information is also avail from the Savannah Area Convention & Visitors Bureau, PO Box 1628, 31402-1628; 912/644-6401 or 800/444-2427.

Motels/Motor Lodges

★ ★ **BAYMONT INN & SUITES.** 8484 Abercorn St (31416). 912/927-7660; fax 912/927-6392; res 800/301-0200. 103 rms, 3 story. S $45.95; D $51.95; under 18 free. Crib free. Pet accepted, some restrictions. TV; cable (premium). Pool. Complimentary continental bkfst, coffee in rms. Restaurant nearby. Ck-out noon. Coin lndry. Meeting rm. In-rm modem link. Valet serv. Some refrigerators. Cr cds: A, DS, MC, V.
⎅ 🐾 ⚏ 🗶 🔥 SC

★ ★ **COURTYARD BY MARRIOTT.** 6703 Abercorn St (31405). 912/354-7878; fax 912/354-1432; toll-free 800/321-2211. 144 rms, 3 story, 12 suites. Feb-Nov: S $88; D $98; suites $102-$112; wkend rates; lower rates rest of yr. Crib free. TV; cable. Pool; whirlpool. Restaurant 6:30-10 am, 5-10 pm; Sat 7-11 am, 5-10 pm; Sun 7 am-noon. Bar 5-10 pm; closed Sun. Ck-out noon. Coin lndry. Meeting rms. Business servs avail. In-rm modem link. Valet serv. Guest lndry. Sundries. Exercise equipt. Private patios, balconies. Cr cds: A, C, D, DS, MC, V.
⎅ ⚏ 🗶 ⚏ 🔥 SC

★ **DAYS INN ABERCORN/SOUTH-SIDE.** 11750 Abercorn St (31419), at Mercy Blvd. 912/927-7720; fax 912/925-8424; toll-free 800/329-7466. Email 6945@hotel.cendant.com; www.daysinn.com. 114 rms, 2 story. S $55; D $60; each addl $5; under 12 free. Crib free. TV; cable (premium). Complimentary continental bkfst. Restaurant nearby. Ck-out 11 am. Whirlpool. St Joseph's hospital adj. Cr cds: A, DS, MC, V.
⎅ ⚏ 🔥 SC

★ ★ **FAIRFIELD INN.** 2 Lee Blvd (31405), at Abercorn Rd. 912/353-7100; fax 912/353-7100; toll-free 800/228-2800. 135 rms, 3 story. Mar-Aug: S, D $59-$70; each addl $5; under 18 free; higher rates: wkends, special events; lower rates rest of yr. Crib free. TV; cable (premium). Pool. Complimentary continental bkfst. Ck-out noon. Business servs avail. In-rm modem link. Health club privileges. Cr cds: A, D, DS, MC, V.
⎅ ⚏ ⚏ 🔥 SC

★ **GUESTHOUSE INN I95 EXIT 94.** 390 Canbrake Rd (31419), I-95 Exit 16. 912/927-2999; fax 912/927-9830; res 800/214-8378. i95guesthouseinn.com. 56 rms, 2 story. S $45-$50; D $55-$60; each addl $5; under 17 free. Crib free. Pet accepted, some restrictions; $5. TV; cable (premium). Pool. Complimentary continental bkfst, coffee in rms. Restaurant opp 6 am-midnight. Ck-out 11 am. Cr cds: A, DS, MC, V.
⎅ 🐾 🔥

★ ★ **HAMPTON INN.** 17007 Abercorn St (31419), I-95 Exit 16. 912/925-1212; fax 912/925-1227; res 800/

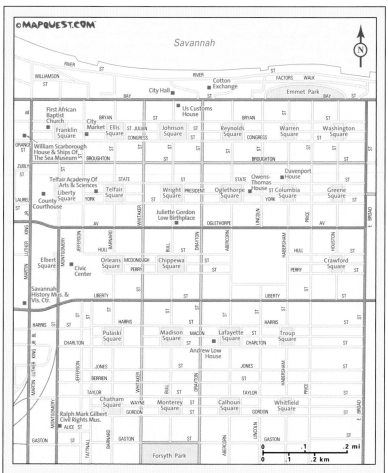

HISTORIC DISTRICT

Start, as the city of Savannah did when it was founded by the British, at the bank of the Savannah River. Here the old warehouses built with ballast stones now house hotels, restaurants, and shops, and ships continue up the channel to port. From River Street's cobblestone paths, climb upstairs to Factor's Walk, the more refined promenade at the top of the bluff, where cotton merchants ("factors") once plied their trade at the Cotton Exchange. At stately City Hall, turn down Bull Street towards Johnson Square, one of the score of pocket parks that make Savannah so charming. Continuing down Bull Street, you can sample four more city squares before landing at Forsyth Park, with its moss-shrouded oaks and dramatic fountain. Or for a shorter walk, turn upriver from Johnson Square and walk west on Congress Street to City Market, where many cafes and clubs occupy historic buildings, and the brick sidewalks are dotted with cafe tables.

426-7866. 62 rms, 2 story. S $58-$74; D $61-$84. Crib free. TV; cable (premium). Pool. Complimentary continental bkfst, coffee in lobby. Restaurant adj 7 am-10 pm. Ck-out 11 am. Business servs avail. Cr cds: A, D, DS, MC, V.

★★ **HAMPTON INN HOTEL.** *201 Stephenson Ave (31405).* 912/355-4100; fax 912/356-5385; res 800/426-7866. 129 rms, 2 story. S $59; D $69; under 18 free; higher rates special events. Crib free. TV; cable (premium). Pool. Complimentary continental bkfst. Restaurant adj 11 am-10 pm. Ck-out noon. Meeting rms. Business servs avail. In-rm modem link. Health club privileges. Cr cds: A, DS, MC, V.

★★ **HOMEWOOD SUITES.** *5820 White Bluff Rd (31405).* 912/353-8500; fax 912/354-3821; res 800/ALL-HOME. 106 kit. suites, 2-3 story. S, D $109-$159; under 18 free; wkend rates. Crib free. TV; cable, VCR. Pool; whirlpool. Complimentary continental bkfst, coffee in rms. Restaurant adj 11 am-11 pm. Ck-out 11 am. Coin lndry. Meeting rms. Business center. In-rm modem link. Valet serv. Sundries. Exercise equipt. Sports court. Microwaves. Cr cds: A, C, D, DS, MC, V.

★ **QUAIL RUN LODGE.** *1130 Bob Harmon Rd (31408), E via I-16, Exit Dean Forest Rd, 3 mi N, adj Savannah Intl Airport.* 912/964-1421; fax 912/966-5646; toll-free 800/062-7035. 171 rms, 2 story. S $60; D $65; each addl $8; suites $80-$90; under 16 free. Crib free. TV; cable (premium). Pool. Restaurant 6-10 am, 11 am-2 pm, 5:30-8:30 pm. Bar 2 pm-midnight. Ck-out noon. Meeting rms. Business servs avail. Bellhops. Valet serv. Free airport transportation. Microwaves avail. Private patios, balconies. Cr cds: A, MC, V.

★ **SUPER 8 MOTEL.** *15 Fort Argyle Rd (31419), I-95 at GA 204 (Exit 16).* 912/927-8550; fax 912/921-0135; res 800/800-8000. www.innworks.com. 61 rms, 2 story. May-Sep: S $48; D $53; each addl $5; under 13 free; lower rates rest of yr. Crib avail. Pet accepted, some restrictions, fee. Parking lot. Pool. TV; cable (premium). Complimentary continental bkfst, coffee in rms, toll-free calls. Restaurant nearby. Ck-out 11 am, ck-in 1 pm. Business servs avail. Golf. Cr cds: A, D, DS, MC, V.

Hotels

★★ **CLUBHOUSE INN.** *6800 Abercorn St (31405).* 912/356-1234; fax 912/352-2828; toll-free 800/258-2466. 122 rms, 2 story, 16 suites. S, D $74-$84; each addl $10; suites $89-$99; under 16 free; wkend rates; higher rates special events. Crib free. TV; cable (premium). Pool; whirlpool. Complimentary full bkfst. Restaurant opp 11 am-10 pm. Ck-out noon. Coin lndry. Meeting rms. Business servs avail. In-rm modem link. Health club privileges. Refrigerator, wet bar in suites. Balconies. Grills. Cr cds: A, DS, MC, V.

★ **DAYS INN SUITES.** *201 W Bay St (31401).* 912/236-4440; fax 912/232-2725; toll-free 877/542-7666. 196 rms, 7 story, 57 suites. Mar-Nov: S $126; D $136; each addl $10; suites $155; under 11 free; lower rates rest of yr. Crib avail. Parking garage. Pool. TV; cable (premium). Complimentary coffee in rms. Restaurant 5 am-2:30 pm. Ck-out 11 am, ck-in 3 pm. Meeting rms. Business center. Concierge. Dry cleaning. Exercise privileges. Golf. Tennis. Video games. Cr cds: A, D, DS, MC, V.

★★★ **HYATT REGENCY SAVANNAH.** *2 W Bay St (31401), on riverfront.* 912/238-1234; fax 912/238-3678; res 800/233-1234. Email sales3401@aol.com; www.hyatt.com. 347 rms, 7 story. Mar-June, Sep-Nov: S $155-$200; D $180-$225; each addl $25; suites $234-$900; under 18 free; wkend rates; lower rates rest of yr. TV; cable (premium). Indoor pool. Restaurant 6:30 am-10 pm; Fri, Sat to midnight; Sun 9 am-3 pm. Bar noon-1 am, Sun noon-midnight; entertainment Tues-Sat. Ck-out noon. Convention facilities. Business center. In-rm modem link. Concierge. Shopping arcade. Garage parking; valet $12. Lighted tennis privileges, pro. 18-hole golf privileges, pro, putting green. Exercise equipt. Some refrigerators. Heliports. Cr cds: A, DS, MC, V.

⊡ 🏋 ⛷ ≋ 🏃 🖏 🔥 SC 🏃

★★★ **THE MULBERRY INN.** *601 E Bay St (31401). 912/238-1200; fax 912/236-2184. www.savannahhotel. com.* 122 rms, 3 story, 26 suites. Mid-Feb-Oct: S $135-$179; D $145-$189; suites $165-$225; under 18 free; package plans; higher rates special events; lower rates rest of yr. Crib free. TV; cable (premium). Pool. Complimentary coffee. Restaurant 7 am-2 pm, 6-9:30 pm. Bar. Ck-out noon. Meeting rms. Business servs avail. In-rm modem link. Health club privileges. Refrigerator in suites. Early 1800s Victorian structure, in the Historic District. Elegant Old Savannah decor; many objets d'art, antiques, paintings. Cr cds: A, D, DS, MC, V.

⊡ 🛁 ≋ 🏃 🖏 🔥 🏃

★★★ **SAVANNAH MARRIOTT RIVERFRONT.** *100 General McIntosh Blvd (31401). 912/233-7722; fax 912/233-4885; res 800/228-9290. Email bsmith@savmarriott.com.* 383 rms, 8 story, 46 suites. S, D $145-$190; each addl $20; suites $219-$519; under 18 free. Crib free. Garage (fee). TV; cable (premium). 2 pools, 1 indoor; whirlpool, poolside serv. Restaurant 6:30 am-midnight. Bar 3-10 pm. Ck-out 11 am. Convention facilities. Business servs avail. In-rm modem link. Concierge. Shopping arcade. Exercise equipt. Wet bar in suites. Balconies. On river. Cr cds: A, C, D, DS, ER, JCB, MC, V.

⊡ 🛁 ≋ 🏃 🖏 🔥 🏃

B&Bs/Small Inns

★★★ **BALLASTONE INN & TOWNHOUSE.** *14 E Oglethorpe Ave (31401). 912/236-1484; fax 912/236-4626; toll-free 800/822-4553. Email inn@ballastone.com.* 17 rms, 4 story. S, D $195-$255; each addl $20; suites $315. Children over 16 yrs only. TV; cable, VCR (free movies). Complimentary full bkfst. Restaurant nearby. Bar. Ck-out 11 am, ck-in 3 pm. Concierge. Health club privileges. Some in-rm whirlpools, fireplaces. Victorian mansion (1838)

with period antiques. Courtyard garden with fountain. Cr cds: A, MC, V.

🖏 🔥

★★ **BED & BREAKFAST INN.** *117 W Gordon St (31401). 912/233-9481; fax 912/233-2537. Email bnbinn@ msn.com.* 14 rms, 4 story. No elvtr. S $80-$105; D $85-$110; each addl $12. Crib $8. TV; cable. Complimentary full bkfst. Restaurant nearby. Ck-out 11 am, ck-in 2 pm. Some refrigerators. Restored 1853 Federal townhouse in the Historic District. Totally nonsmoking. Cr cds: A, DS, MC, V.

🔥

★★★ **EAST BAY INN.** *225 E Bay St (31401). 912/238-1225; fax 912/232-2709; toll-free 800/500-1225. Email innkeeper@eastbayinn.com.* 28 rms, 3 story. S, D $109-$129; each addl $10; under 12 free. Pet accepted, some restrictions; $25. TV; cable. Complimentary continental bkfst. Dining rm 11 am-3 pm; dinner hrs vary; closed Sun. Ck-out 11 am, ck-in 3 pm. Business servs avail. In-rm modem link. Built in 1853; formerly a cotton warehouse. Antiques. Opp historic waterfront of Savannah River. Cr cds: A, C, D, DS, MC, V.

⊡ 🐾 🖏 🔥

★★★ **ELIZA THOMPSON HOUSE.** *5 W Jones St (31401). 912/236-3620; fax 912/238-1920; toll-free 800/348-9378. Email elizath@aol.com; www. elizathompsonhouse.com.* 25 rms, 3 story, 1 suite. Mar-May, Sep-Dec: S, D $99; each addl $20; suites $250; children $12; lower rates rest of yr. Street parking. TV; cable. Complimentary full bkfst, newspaper. Restaurant. Bar. Meeting rm. Business servs avail. Concierge. Gift shop. Golf. Tennis, 4 courts. Beach access. Bike rentals. Hiking trail. Cr cds: A, MC, V.

⊡ 🛁 🏋 ⛷ 🖏 🔥

★★★ **FOLEY HOUSE.** *14 W Hull St (31401). 912/232-6622; fax 912/231-1218; toll-free 800/647-3708.* 19 rms, 3-4 story. No elvtr. S, D $135-$250; each addl $15; under 12 free. TV; VCR avail (free movies). Complimentary continental bkfst. Ck-out noon, ck-in 3 pm. In-rm modem link. Fireplaces, some in-rm whirlpools. Some private patios, balconies. Restored

1896 home and carriage house in heart of Historic District. Individually decorated rms; antiques, artwork. Totally nonsmoking. Cr cds: A, D, MC, V.

★★★ **GASTONIAN INN.** *220 E Gaston St (31401). 912/232-2869; fax 912/232-0710; toll-free 800/322-6603. Email gastoniann@aol.com; www. gastonian.com.* 14 rms, 4 story, 3 suites. Feb-June, Sep-Nov: S $225; D $295; each addl $75; suites $375; lower rates rest of yr. Valet parking avail. TV; cable, VCR avail. Complimentary full bkfst, coffee in rms, newspaper, toll-free calls. Restaurant, closed Sun. 24-hr rm serv. Business center. Concierge. Dry cleaning. Gift shop. Bike rentals. Cr cds: DS, MC, V.

Ripe peaches for sale

★★★★ **THE KEHOE HOUSE.** *123 Habersham St (31401), on Columbia Sq. 912/232-1020; fax 912/231-1587; toll-free 800/820-1020.* This towering, Renaissance-Revival mansion situated on a historic park was built in 1892 for William Kehoe, an Irish immigrant and founder of Kehoe Iron Works. The interiors recreate the glory of antebellum Georgia with paintings, period antiques and reproductions, and original carpets. Rates for the 13 guestrooms and two townhouse-suites including evening hors d'oeuvres and a full breakfast. 15 rms, 2 and 5 story, 2 suites. S, D $195-$250; each addl $35. Crib free. TV; cable. Complimentary full bkfst, afternoon tea and wine. Restaurant noon-10 pm. Ck-out 11 am, ck-in 3 pm. 24-hr concierge. Bar serv. Meeting rm. Business servs avail. Health club privileges. Totally nonsmoking. Cr cds: A, D, DS, MC, V.

★★★ **MAGNOLIA PLACE INN.** *503 Whitaker St (31401). 912/236-7674; fax 912/236-1145; toll-free 800/ 238-7674. Email info@magnoliaplace inn.com; www.magnoliaplaceinn.com.* 13 rms, 3 story. S, D $135-$250; each addl $25. Children over 11 yrs only. TV; cable, VCR (movies). Complimentary continental bkfst. Ck-out 11 am, ck-in 2:30 pm. Concierge serv. Fireplaces; some in-rm whirlpools. Private patios, balconies. Built in 1878; many antiques. Cr cds: A, DS, MC, V.

★★★ **MANOR HOUSE.** *201 W Liberty St (31401), 9 blks S on W Liberty St. 912/233-9597; fax 912/236-9419; toll-free 800/462-3595. Email histinnso@ aol.com; www.manorhouse-savannah. com.* 3 story, 5 suites. Mar-May, Oct, Dec: S, D $200; each addl $25; suites $200; lower rates rest of yr. Pet accepted, some restrictions. Parking lot. TV; cable (premium), VCR avail, CD avail. Complimentary continental bkfst, newspaper. Restaurant nearby. Business servs avail. Concierge. Golf. Tennis, 10 courts. Beach access. Bike rentals. Cr cds: A, MC, V.

★★ **OLDE HARBOUR INN.** *508 E Factors Walk (31401). 912/234-4100; fax 912/233-5979; toll-free 800/553-6533. www.oldeharbourinn.com.* 24 kit. suites, 3 story. S, D $175-$215; each addl $10; under 12 free; wkly, monthly rates; package plans. Crib free. Pet accepted, some restrictions; $35. TV; cable (premium). Complimentary continental bkfst; refreshments. Business servs avail. Balconies. Antiques. Built in 1892, originally housed offices and warehouse of an oil company. Cr cds: A, D, DS, MC, V.

★★★ **THE PRESIDENT'S QUARTERS INN.** *225 E President St (31401). 912/233-1600; fax 912/238-0849; toll-free 800/233-1776. Email pqinn@aol.com; www.presidents quarters.com.* 11 rms, 4 story, 8 suites. Mar-June, Sep-Oct: S, D $160; each addl $20; suites $200; children $20; under 10 free; lower rates rest of yr. Crib avail. TV; cable (premium), VCR avail. Restaurant. Ck-out 11 am, ck-in 2 pm. Meeting rms. Golf. Tennis, 10 courts. Cr cds: C, D, DS, MC, V.

★★ **RIVER STREET INN.** *115 E River St (31401). 912/234-6400; fax 912/234-1478; res 800/678-8946; toll-free 800/253-4229. Email info@river streetinn.com; www.riverstreetinn.com.* 86 rms, 3 story, 1 suite. Mar-May, Sep-Nov: S $189; D $199; each addl $10; suites $250; under 12 free; lower rates rest of yr. Crib avail. Parking garage. TV; cable (premium). Complimentary coffee in rms, newspaper, toll-free calls. Restaurant 11 am-11 pm. Bar. Ck-out noon, ck-in 4 pm. Meeting rms. Fax servs avail. Dry cleaning. Gift shop. Exercise privileges, whirlpool. Golf. Cr cds: A, D, MC, V.

★★ **SEVENTEEN HUNDRED NINETY INN & RESTAURANT.** *307 E President St (31401). 912/236-7122; fax 912/236-7123; toll-free 800/ 487-1790. Email 1790inn@msn.com; www.17hundred90.com.* 14 units, 3 story. S, D $119-$189. Crib free. TV; cable (premium). Complimentary continental bkfst. Dining rm 11:30 am-2 pm, 6-10 pm; Sat, Sun from 6 pm. Bar noon-1 am. Ck-out 11 am, ck-in 3 pm. Refrigerators; some fireplaces. Antiques. Cr cds: A, DS, MC, V.

Restaurants

★★★ **45 SOUTH.** *20 E Broad St (31401), on grounds of Pirates' House Restaurant. 912/233-1881. www.the pirateshouse.com.* Specializes in grilled Ahi tuna with foie gras, seared breast of duck with ginger beets, sliced breast of pheasant with wild mushrooms. Own baking. Hrs: 6-9 pm. Closed Sun; hols. Res accepted. Bar. Wine list. Dinner a la carte entrees: $18.50-$29.50. Valet parking. Jacket. In 1852 bldg. Cr cds: A, D, DS, MC, V.

★★ **BISTRO SAVANNAH.** *309 W Congress St (31401). 912/233-6266. www.restaurantanson.com.* Mediterranean menu. Hrs: 5:30-10:30 pm; Fri, Sat to 11 pm. Res accepted. Bar. Dinner a la carte entrees: $12.95-$21.95. Bistro atmosphere. Local art on display. Cr cds: A, MC, V.

★★ **CHART HOUSE.** *202 W Bay St (31401). 912/234-6686. Email siero@aol.com; www.charthouse.com.* Mediterranean menu. Specializes in steak, seafood, prime rib. Hrs: 5-10 pm; Sat to 10:30 pm; Sun to 9 pm. Res accepted. Bar. Dinner a la carte entrees: $14.95-$19.95. Child's menu. Nautical decor; on historic waterfront; covered balcony over Savannah River. 3 flrs; beamed ceilings; artwork. Cr cds: A, D, DS, MC, V.

★★★★ **ELIZABETH ON 37TH.** *105 E 37th St (31401). 912/236-5547. www.savannah-online.com/elizabeth.* Opened in 1981 by chef Elizabeth Terry and her husband Michael, this charming restaurant is a birthplace of New-Southern cuisine. The interior of the 1900, Greek-Revival-style mansion feels like home with brightly painted walls, antique chairs, and warm service. The fresh tastes and authenticity of the cuisine (Terry extensively researched 18th and 19th-century Savannah cooking) draws admiration from across the country. Specializes in regional Southern cuisine. Hrs: 6-10 pm. Closed hols. Res accepted. Dinner $22.50-$29.50. Parking. Cr cds: A, D, DS, MC, V.

★★ **GARIBALDI'S CAFE.** *315 W Congress (31401). 912/232-7118. www.anson.net.* Specializes in fresh fish, veal, pasta. Own desserts. Hrs: 5:30-10:30 pm; Fri, Sat to midnight. Res accepted. Bar. Dinner a la carte entrees: $8.95-$24.95. Former 1871 Germania firehouse in historic dis-

trict. Italian cafe decor; 1842 antique mirror, paintings. Cr cds: A, MC, V.
D

★★ **JOHNNY HARRIS.** *1651 E Victory Dr (31404). 912/354-7810.* Specializes in barbecue, prime rib, seafood. Hrs: 11:30 am-10:30 pm; Fri, Sat to midnight. Closed Sun; Jan 1, Dec 25. Res accepted. Bar. Lunch $4.95-$7.95; dinner $7.95-$18.95. Child's menu. Entertainment: Fri, Sat. Jacket (Sat night in main dining rm). 1930s night club atmosphere. Savannah's oldest continuously operating restaurant. Cr cds: A, D, DS, MC, V.
D ⬚

★★ **MRS WILKES' DINING ROOM.** *107 W Jones St (31401). 912/232-5997.* Specializes in barbecued pork chops, fried chicken, banana pudding. Own desserts. Hrs: 8-9 am, 11 am-3 pm. Closed Sat, Sun; hols. Bkfst complete meals: $5; lunch complete meals: $8. Boarding house-style seating and service. 1870 brick house; original wallpaper. Article clippings about boarding house, famous guests. No cr cds accepted.
D

★★★ **OLDE PINK HOUSE.** *23 Abercorn St (31412). 912/232-4286.* Specializes in seafood, beef, veal. Hrs: 5:30-10:30 pm; Fri, Sat to 11 pm. Res accepted. Bar. Dinner a la carte entrees: $14.95-$22.95. Entertainment: jazz pianist Tues-Sun. Restored 18th-century mansion. Cr cds: A, D, DS, MC, V.
⬚

★ **PEARL'S ELEGANT PELICAN.** *7000 La Rochie (31406). 912/352-8221.* Specializes in seafood. Hrs: 5-10 pm; Fri, Sat to 10:30 pm. Closed Jan 1, Thanksgiving, Dec 25. Bar. Dinner $9.95-$17.95. Child's menu. Parking. Multilevel dining rm provides view of the Herb River and marshlands. Family-owned. Cr cds: A, D, DS, MC, V.
D ⬚

★★ **RIVER'S END.** *3122 River Dr (31404). 912/354-2973. www.riversend.com.* Specializes in seafood, steak, pasta. Own baking. Hrs: 5-10 pm; Fri, Sat to 11 pm. Closed Sun; Thanksgiving, Dec 24, 25. Res accepted. Bar. Wine list. Dinner a la carte entrees: $10.95-$19.95. Child's menu. Entertainment: pianist. Parking. Overlooks Intracoastal Waterway; dockage. Cr cds: A, D, DS, MC, V.
D ⬚

★★ **RIVER HOUSE.** *125 W River St (31401). 912/234-1900. www.riverhouseseafood.com.* Specializes in seafood, poultry, steak. Hrs: 11 am-10 pm; Fri, Sat noon-11 pm. Closed Thanksgiving, Dec 25. Res accepted. Bar. Lunch $6-$13; dinner $13.95-$23.95. Child's menu. In an old cotton warehouse. Cr cds: A, D, DS, MC, V.
D ⬚

★★ **SEASONS OF SAVANNAH.** *315 W St. Julian St (31401), City Market. 912/233-2626.* Specializes in steak, seafood, pasta. Hrs: 11:30 am-2:30 pm, 6-9 pm; Fri, Sat to 10 pm. Res accepted. Bar. Lunch $5.95-$9.95; dinner $14.95-$22.95. Local artwork. Cr cds: A, D, DS, MC, V.

★★ **SHRIMP FACTORY.** *313 E River St (31401). 912/236-4229. www.theshrimpfactory.com.* Specializes in pine bark stew, fresh fish and shrimp with special sauces, lobster. Hrs: 11 am-10 pm; Fri, Sat to 11 pm; Sun from noon. Closed Thanksgiving, Dec 25. Bar. Lunch $5.50-$13.90; dinner $14.90-$23.90. Child's menu. Located on river. Cr cds: A, D, DS, MC, V.
⬚

★ **WILLIAMS SEAFOOD.** *8010 Tybee Rd (31410). 912/897-2219.* Specializes in seafood, chicken, beef. Hrs: 11:30 am-9:30 pm; Sun 11 am-9 pm. Closed Thanksgiving, Dec 25. Bar. Lunch, dinner $5.25-$17.95. Child's menu. Casual atmosphere. Nautical prints. Family-owned. Cr cds: A, D, DS, MC, V.
D

Sea Island

See also Brunswick, Golden Isles, Jekyll Island, St. Simons Island

Pop 750 (est) **Elev** 11 ft
Area code 912 **Zip** 31561

Resort

★ ★ ★ ★ THE CLOISTER. *100 1st St (31561), 9 mi E of US 17. 912/638-3611; fax 912/638-5823; toll-free 800/732-4752. www.seaisland.com.* This all-inclusive resort sits off the coast of Georgia; a five-mile-long island that remained relatively uninhabited until auto magnate Howard Coffin began development in 1924. Today, visitors of all ages to the 286-room property enjoy a plethora of recreations including 17 clay tennis courts, 54 holes of golf, a beach club, a spa, a shooting school, horseback riding, and various water sports. 286 rms, 1-3 story, private patios, balconies. 200 rental homes available. AP, mid-Mar-May: S $310-$670; D $370-$730; each addl $75; 6-12 yrs $31; 3-5 yrs $23; under 2 free; spa, golf, tennis, shooting school plans; lower rates rest of yr. Serv charge 15%/day. Garage avail; free parking. TV; cable, VCR avail (movies $5). 2 pools, 1 heated; wading pool, whirlpool, poolside serv; lifeguard. Free supervised children's activities (late May-early Sep); ages 3-11. Dining rm 7:30-9:30 am, noon-2 pm, 7-9:30 pm (see also CLOISTER MAIN DINING ROOM). Box lunches, snack bar, outdoor buffets. Rm serv 6:30 am-midnight. Bar 1 pm-12:30 am. Ck-out noon, ck-in 4 pm. Executive conference facilities. Business center. In-rm modem link. Valet serv. Package store. Grocery 1 mi. Airport, railroad station, bus depot transportation. Sports dir. 18 tennis courts, pros, pro shop. 54-hole golf, greens fee $125-$195 (incl cart, range, storage), no greens fees under 18, 9-hole rate avail, shop, putting greens, driving range, pro shop, learning center. 5 mi. private beach. Vintage yachts, fishing charter boats; dock. Nature walks. Bicycles. Lawn games. Trap and skeet shooting; instruction. Soc dir; entertainment, dancing (resident instructor), movies on Sun. Rec rm. Exercise rm; sauna, steam rm. Spa. Beach club; lockers avail; steam bath. Cr cds: A, DS, MC, V.

D ⬚ 🏌 🎿 🏊 🎣 🏃

Restaurant

★ ★ CLOISTER MAIN DINING ROOM. *100 Hudson Pl. 912/638-3611. www.seaisland.com.* Specializes in seafood, prime rib, steak. Own baking. Menu changes daily. Hrs: 7 am-midnight. Res required. Bar. Wine cellar. Bkfst complete meals: $16; lunch complete meals: $21; dinner complete meals: $52. Child's menu. Entertainment: orchestra Mon-Sat. Valet parking. Jacket. Colonial decor. Family-owned. Cr cds: MC, V.

D

St. Simons Island

(G-7) *See also Brunswick, Golden Isles, Jekyll Island, Sea Island*

Pop 12,026 **Elev** 0-30 ft
Area code 912 **Zip** 31522
Web www.bgislesvisitorsb.com
Information St. Simons Visitor Center, 530 B Beachview Dr, Neptune Park; 800/933-2627

What to See and Do

Coastal Alliance for the Arts. Exhibitions of works by regional artists, traveling exhibits, lectures. (Mon-Sat; closed hols) 319 Mallory St. Phone 912/638-8770. **FREE**

Cumberland Island National Seashore. (see) S, off the coast.

Fort Frederica National Monument. (see) N end of island.

Museum of Coastal History. Housed in restored 1872 lightkeeper's house; exhibits on history of St. Simons lighthouse and Golden Isles. (Daily; closed hols) 101 12th St. Phone 912/638-4666. ¢¢ Incl

> **St. Simons Lighthouse.** The original lighthouse (1810), which was 75 ft high, was destroyed by Confederate troops in 1861 to prevent it from guiding Union invaders onto the island. The present lighthouse, 104 ft high, has been in continuous operation, except during wartime, since 1872. Visitors may climb to the top. S end of island.

Annual Events

Homes & Gardens Tour. Tour of houses and gardens on St. Simons Island and Sea Island. Varies each yr. Phone 912/638-3166. Mid-Mar.

Sunshine Festival. Neptune Park. Juried arts and crafts exhibits, food, fireworks on July 4. Wkend closest to July 4.

Georgia Sea Island Festival. Neptune Park. Traditional crafts and music. Phone 912/638-9014. Third wkend Aug.

Golden Isles Art Festival. Neptune Park. Juried arts and crafts exhibits, demonstrations, entertainment, food. Mid-Oct.

Motels/Motor Lodges

★ **DAYS INN.** *1701 Frederica Rd (31522). 912/634-0660; fax 912/638-7115; toll-free 800/870-3736.* 101 rms, 2 story. Mar-Sep: S, D $89; each addl $10; under 12 free; lower rates rest of yr. Crib free. TV; cable (premium). Pool. Complimentary continental bkfst, coffee in rms. Restaurant adj open 24 hrs. Ck-out noon. Meeting rms. Business servs avail. Bicycle rentals. Refrigerators, microwaves. Cr cds: A, DS, MC, V.

⬛ 🏊 📶 🐾

★★ **ISLAND INN.** *301 Main St (31522), in Plantation Village. 912/638-7805; fax 912/638-7805; toll-free 800/673-6323. www.stsimons destinations.com.* 74 units, 2 story, 12 kits. May-Sep: S, D $76-$96; each addl $10; kit. units $86-$96; under 18 free; golf packages; lower rates rest of yr. Crib free. TV; cable. Pool; whirlpool. Playground. Complimentary continental bkfst. Ck-out 11 am. Business servs avail. Health club privileges. Cr cds: A, DS, MC, V.

⬛ 🏊 📶 🐾 SC

★ **QUEENS COURT.** *437 Kings Way (31522). 912/638-8459; fax 912/638-0054.* 23 rms, 2 story. S $50; D $56; each addl $3-$4; suites $64; kit. units $72. TV; cable. Pool. Restaurant nearby. Ck-out 11 am. Some refrigerators. Cr cds: MC, V.

🏊 🐾

★ **SEA GATE INN.** *1014 Ocean Blvd (31522). 912/638-8661; fax 912/638-4932; toll-free 800/562-8812.* 48 units, 2-4 story, 16 kits. Early Mar-Sep: S, D $60-$130; each addl $7; suites $80-$320; kit. units $70-$320; under 10 free; lower rates rest of yr. Crib free. TV; cable. Pool; wading pool. Complimentary continental bkfst. Ck-out noon. Lawn games. Some refrigerators; microwaves avail. Balconies. On beach. Cr cds: A, DS, MC, V.

🏊 📶 🐾

Hotel

★★★ **KING & PRINCE BEACH RESORT.** *201 Arnold Rd (31522). 912/638-3631; fax 912/634-1720; toll-free 800/342-0212. www.kingand prince.com.* 184 units, 4 story. Mar-early Nov: S, D $120-$160; kit. villas $275-$380; higher rates wkends; lower rates rest of yr. Crib free. TV; cable (premium), VCR avail. 5 pools, 1 indoor; whirlpool, poolside dining (May-Sep). Coffee in rms. Restaurant 7-10:30 am, 11:30 am-10 pm. Bar 11 am-midnight; Sun 1-9 pm. Ck-out 11 am. Meeting rms. Business servs avail. Airport transportation. 4 tennis courts. 18-hole golf, greens fee $55, pro. Exercise equipt. Some refrigerators. Some private patios, balconies. Resort-type hotel (1935); on ocean. Cr cds: A, D, DS, MC, V.

⬛ 🏌 🏊 🎾 📶 🐾

Resort

★★★ **SEA PALMS GOLF AND TENNIS RESORT.** *5445 Frederica Rd (31522). 912/638-3351; fax 912/634-8029; toll-free 800/841-6268. www. gacoast.seapalms.* 155 units, 1-3 story, 77 kit. villas. Mar-Oct: S $129; D $139; 1-bedrm $169; 2-bedrm $268; under 14 free; golf, tennis plans; lower rates rest of yr. Crib $10. TV; cable, VCR avail (movies). 3 pools; poolside serv. Playground. Dining rm 7 am-10:30 pm. Box lunches, snack bar, outdoor buffets. Bar 11 am-midnight. Ck-out 11 am, ck-in 4 pm. Convention facilities. Business servs avail. In-rm modem link. 12 clay tennis courts, 3 lighted, pro, clinics. 27-hole golf, greens fee $40, golf cart $17, pro, putting greens, driving range. Private beach. Skeet shooting nearby. Exercise equipt; sauna. Private patios, balconies. Cr cds: A, C, D, MC, V.

⬛ 🏌 🎾 🏊 🎾 ⛷ 📶 🐾

B&B/Small Inn

★★ **ST. SIMONS INN BY THE LIGHTHOUSE.** *609 Beachview Dr (31522), near lighthouse.* 912/638-1101; fax 912/638-0943. Email st.simonsinn@mindspring.com. 34 rms, 3 story. Mid-Mar-Oct: S, D $79-$105; each addl $7.50; under 12 free; 2-day min summer; lower rates rest of yr. Crib $5. TV. Pool. Complimentary continental bkfst. Restaurant nearby. Ck-out 11 am, ck-in 3 pm. Business servs avail. Refrigerators, microwaves. Within walking distance from attractions, beach. Cr cds: A, D, DS, MC, V.

Restaurants

★ **BENNIE'S RED BARN.** *5514 Frederica Rd (31522).* 912/638-2844. Specializes in steak, lamb & pork chops, seafood, chicken. Hrs: 5:30-10:30 pm. Closed hols. Res accepted. Bar. Dinner $9.95-$19.75. Child's menu. Entertainment: Wed-Sat. Parking. Family-owned. Rustic country ambience. Cr cds: DS, MC, V.

★★ **BLANCHE'S COURTYARD.** *440 Kings Way (31522).* 912/638-3030. Specializes in broiled and grilled fresh seafood, steak. Own desserts. Hrs: 5:30-9:15 pm; winter to 9 pm. Closed Mon; Thanksgiving, Dec 24-25. Res accepted. Bar. Dinner $11.50-$20. Entertainment: Sat. Parking. Cr cds: A, D, DS, MC, V.

★ **BROGEN'S.** *200 Pier Alley (31522), in Pier Village.* 912/638-1660. Specializes in hamburgers, chicken Swiss sandwiches. Hrs: 11:30-2 am. Closed Jan 1, Easter, Dec 25; Sun Oct-Apr. Bar. Lunch, dinner a la carte entrees: $2.95-$6.95. View of pier. Cr cds: A, D, DS, MC, V.

★★ **CHELSEA.** *1226 Ocean Blvd (31522).* 912/638-2047. Specializes in seafood, pasta, prime rib. Hrs: 5:30-10 pm; early bird dinner to 6:30 pm. Res accepted. Bar. Dinner $8.95-$21.95. Child's menu. Parking. Cr cds: D, MC, V.

★★ **J. MAC'S.** *407 Mallery St (31522).* 912/634-0403. Specializes in seafood, crab cakes, rack of lamb. Hrs: 5:30-10 pm. Closed Sun; hols. Res accepted. Bar. Dinner a la carte entrees: $12.95-$27.95. Bistro atmosphere. Cr cds: A, MC, V.

★ **MIYABI SEAFOOD & STEAK.** *202 Retreat Village Center (31522), Frederica Rd.* 912/638-0885. Specializes in seafood, steak, chicken. Sushi bar. Hrs: 5:30-10 pm; Fri to 10:30 pm; Sat 5-10:30 pm; Sun 4:30-9:30 pm. Closed Thanksgiving, Dec 25; also Super Bowl Sun. Res accepted. Bar. Dinner $9.95-$25.50. Child's menu. Parking. Tableside preparation. Traditional Japanese decor. Cr cds: A, D, DS, MC, V.

★★★ **ROONEY'S.** *2465 Demere Rd (31522).* 912/638-7097. Specializes in Angus beef, seafood, pasta. Hrs: 5:30-10 pm. Closed Mon; hols; 1st wk Jan. Res accepted. Bar. Wine list. Dinner a la carte entrees: $12.95-$22.95. Parking. Modern art on display. Cr cds: A, MC, V.

Statesboro (E-6)

Settled 1796 **Pop** 15,854 **Elev** 258 ft
Area code 912 **Zip** 30458
Information Convention and Visitors Bureau, 322 S Main St, PO Box 1516; 912/489-1869

Annual Event

Regional Ogeechee Fair. Fairgrounds, GA 67. Second wk Oct.

Motels/Motor Lodges

★★ **COMFORT INN.** *316 S Main St (30458).* 912/489-2626; fax 912/489-2626; toll-free 800/228-5150. 65 rms, 2 story, 8 kits. S, D $45-$60; each addl $5; kits. $60; under 18 free; higher rates special events. Crib free. TV; cable (premium), VCR (movies avail). Pool. Complimentary bkfst buffet, coffee in rms. Ck-out 11 am. Business servs avail. In-rm modem link. Coin lndry. Health club privileges. Refrigerators, microwaves. Cr cds: A, C, D, DS, MC, V.

★ **DAYS INN.** *461 S Main St (30458). 912/764-5666; fax 912/489-8193; toll-free 800/329-7466.* 44 rms, 1-2 story. S $36-$52; D $38-$64; each addl $5; under 17 free. Crib free. Pet accepted. TV; cable (premium), VCR avail (movies). Pool. Complimentary continental bkfst. Restaurant adj 11 am-10 pm. Ck-out 11 am. Cr cds: A, C, D, DS, JCB, MC, V.

★★ **JAMESON INN.** *1 Jameson Ave (30458). 912/681-7900; fax 912/681-7905; toll-free 800/541-3268.* 39 rms, 2 story. S $51; D $56; each addl $5; suites $97-$137; under 12 free. Crib free. TV; cable (premium). Pool. Complimentary continental bkfst. Restaurant nearby. Ck-out 11 am. Business servs avail. In-rm modem link. Exercise equipt. Opp Georgia Southern College. Cr cds: A, D, DS, MC, V.

Hotel

★★ **RAMADA INN.** *230 S Main St (30458). 912/764-6121; fax 912/764-6121; res 800/2RAMADA; toll-free 800/272-6232.* 129 rms, 2 story. S, D $50; each addl $3; under 18 free. Crib free. Pet accepted, some restrictions. TV; cable (premium). Pool; wading pool. Complimentary bkfst buffet. Restaurant 6:30 am-2 pm, 5-10 pm. Bar 5 pm-midnight. Ck-out noon. Coin lndry. Meeting rms. Business servs avail. In-rm modem link. Valet serv. Cr cds: A, DS, MC, V.

B&B/Small Inn

★★★ **HISTORIC STATESBORO INN.** *106 S Main St (30458). 912/489-8628; fax 912/489-4785; toll-free 800/846-9466. Email frontdesk@ statesboroinn; www.statesboroinn.com.* 18 rms, 2 story. S, D $75-$120; each addl $10. Crib free. TV; cable (premium), VCR avail. Complimentary full bkfst. Dining rm (public by res). Ck-out 11 am, ck-in 2 pm. Business servs avail. In-rm modem link.

Health club privileges. Some in-rm whirlpools, fireplaces. Private patios. Built 1904. Many antiques. Cr cds: A, DS, MC, V.

Thomasville

(G-3) *See also Bainbridge*

Pop 17,457 **Elev** 285 ft **Area code** 912
Zip 31792
Information Welcome Center, 135 N Broad St, PO Box 1540, 31799; 912/225-3919

Annual Event

Rose Festival. Parade, rose show, arts and crafts. Late Apr.

Motels/Motor Lodges

★ **DAYS INN.** *3538 US Hwy 84 E (31728), 13 mi W on US 84. 912/377-4400; fax 912/377-4400; toll-free 800/329-7466.* 34 rms, 2 story. S $40; D $45; each addl $5; suites $55-$65; under 12 free; higher rates: Rose Parade, Rattlesnake Roundup, Mule Day. Crib free. TV; cable. Pool. Complimentary coffee in lobby. Restaurant opp 6 am-11 pm. Ck-out 11 am. Business servs avail. Cr cds: A, D, DS, JCB, MC, V.

★★ **GUEST HOUSE INN.** *15138 Hwy 19 S (31792). 912/226-7111; fax 912/226-7257; toll-free 800/805-2526.* 147 rms, 2 story. S $64; D $69; each addl $5; suite $130; under 19 free; wkend rates; higher rates: Rose Festival, Sun Belt Expo (Oct). Crib free. TV; cable. Pool; whirlpool. Restaurant 6:30 am-2 pm, 5:30-10 pm. Bar 4:30 pm-midnight; closed Sun; entertainment. Ck-out noon. Coin lndry. Meeting rms. Business servs avail. In-rm modem link. Valet serv. Cr cds: A, C, D, DS, JCB, MC, V.

Resort

★★★ **MELHANA THE GRAND PLANTATION.** *301 Showboat Ln (31792). 912/226-2290; fax 912/226-*

4585; res 888/920-3030. Email info@ melhana.com; www.melhana.com. 24 rms, 2 story, 4 suites. Oct-May: S, D $650; each addl $75; lower rates rest of yr. Crib avail, fee. Pet accepted, some restrictions. Valet parking avail. Indoor pool, lap pool. TV; cable (DSS), VCR avail. Complimentary full bkfst, newspaper, toll-free calls. Restaurant 6-10 pm. 24-hr rm serv. Ck-out 11 am, ck-in 3 pm. Meeting rms. Business servs avail. Bellhops. Concierge. Dry cleaning. Gift shop. Exercise equipt. Golf, 18 holes. Tennis, 5 courts. Bike rentals. Picnic facilities. Cr cds: A, C, D, DS, MC, V.

B&Bs/Small Inns

★★★ 1884 PATON HOUSE INN.

445 Remington Ave (31792). 912/226-5197; fax 912/226-9903. Email 1884@ rose.net; www.1884paxtonhouseinn. com. 8 rms, 2 story, 1 suite, 1 kit. unit. S $85-$95; D $90-$110; suite $125-$185; kit. unit $185; wkend (2-day min). Children over 12 yrs only. TV; cable (premium), VCR avail. Complimentary full bkfst. Restaurant nearby. Ck-out 11 am, ck-in 3-6 pm. Gift shop. Indoor pool. Built in 1884. Extensive porcelain collection. Totally nonsmoking. Cr cds: A, DS, MC, V.

★★ GRAND MANOR BED AND BREAKFAST INN. 817 S Hansell St

(31792). 912/228-0023. 4 rms, 1 with shower only, 2 story. No rm phones. S $65-$85; D $70-$90; each addl $10; under 3 free; special event wkends (2-day min). Cable TV in library, VCR avail (movies). Complimentary full bkfst. Restaurant nearby. Ck-out 11 am, ck-in 3 pm. Lighted tennis privileges. 18-hole golf privileges, pro, putting green, driving range. Victorian house built in 1893 with wrap-around porch. Totally nonsmoking. Cr cds: A, DS, MC, V.

★★ SERENDIPITY COTTAGE. 339

E Jefferson St (31792), NE of Broad, in Dawson St Historic Area. 912/226-8111; fax 912/226-2656; toll-free 800/383-7377. Email goodnite@rose.net; www.serendipitycottage.com. 4 rms, 2 story. S $85; D $90; each addl $20;

under 12 free. Street parking. TV; cable (premium), VCR avail, CD avail. Complimentary full bkfst, coffee in rms. Restaurant. Ck-out 11 am, ck-in 4 pm. Fax servs avail. Exercise privileges. Golf, 18 holes. Tennis, 10 courts. Bike rentals. Cr cds: A, DS, MC, V.

★★ SUSINA PLANTATION INN.

1420 Meridian Rd (31792), 12 mi SW via US 319, then 1 mi N via GA 93, then W on GA 156, follow signs. 912/377-9644. 8 rms, 2 story. No rm phones. MAP: S $125; D $150. Pool. Ck-out noon, ck-in 2 pm. Lighted tennis. Picnic tables, grills. 1841 plantation house set amid 115 acres of lawns, oaks, and magnolias. Cr cds: A, DS, MC, V.

Restaurants

★★ HARRISON'S. 119 N Broad St

(31792). 912/226-0074. Specializes in fettucini Mileo, pollo e salsiccia con melanzane, vitello al popi. Own baking. Hrs: 11 am-2 pm, 5-9 pm; Fri, Sat to 10 pm. Closed Sun; Jan 1, Thanksgiving, Dec 25. Res accepted. Bar. Lunch, dinner a la carte entrees: $9.50-$16.95. Entertainment: Thurs, Fri. Dining in mid-1800s hotel bldg. Cr cds: A, DS, MC, V.

★★ PLAZA RESTAURANT. 217 S

Broad St (31792). 912/226-5153. Specializes in fresh seafood, Greek salad, Western steak. Salad bar. Own soups, sauces. Hrs: 7 am-9:30 pm; Sun 7 am-2 pm. Closed hols. Bar. Bkfst $2.50-$7; lunch $4-$6. Buffet: $4.50; dinner $6.50-$16.95. Child's menu. Entertainment: Fri. Parking. Family-owned. Cr cds: A, D, DS, MC, V.

Tifton

(F-4) See also Adel

Pop 14,215 **Elev** 357 ft **Area code** 912
Zip 31794

Web www.surfsouth.com/business/tiftchamber

Information Tifton-Tift County Chamber of Commerce, 100 Central Ave, PO Box 165, 31793; 912/382-6200

Motels/Motor Lodges

★★ **COMFORT INN.** *1104 King Rd (31794), I-75 Exit 19. 912/382-4410; fax 912/382-3967; res 800/228-5150; toll-free 800/223-5234. Email comfort inn148@aol.com; www.comfortinn. com/hotel/ga148.* 86 rms, 2 story, 4 suites. Mar, July, Nov: S $80; D $85; each addl $5; suites $130; lower rates rest of yr. Crib avail. Street parking. Indoor pool, whirlpool. TV; cable (premium). Complimentary full bkfst, coffee in rms, newspaper, toll-free calls. Restaurant. Ck-out 11 am, ck-in 3 pm. Business center. Exercise equipt. Golf. Cr cds: A, D, DS, JCB, MC, V.

★ **DAYS INN.** *1008 8th St W (31794), I-75 Exit 20. 912/382-7210; fax 912/386-8146.* 72 rms, 2 story. S $40; D $45; each addl $5; under 12 free; higher rates special events. TV; cable. Pool. Complimentary continental bkfst. Ck-out noon. Cr cds: A, D, DS, MC, V.

★★ **RAMADA INN.** *1211 US Hwy 82 W (31793), 2 mi W on US 82 at jct I-75 Exit 18. 912/382-8500; fax 912/386-5913; toll-free 800/2RAMADA.* 100 units, 2 story. S, D $50-$65; each addl $5; under 12 free. Crib free. TV; cable (premium). Pool. Complimentary bkfst. Bar 4 pm-2 am; closed Sun; entertainment. Ck-out noon. Meeting rms. Business center. Cr cds: A, C, D, DS, JCB, MC, V.

Restaurants

★ **CHARLES SEAFOOD RESTAURANT.** *701 W 7th St (US 82) (31794). 912/382-9696.* Specializes in seafood, BBQ sandwiches. Hrs: 11 am-2 pm, 5-10 pm. Closed Sun; July 4, Dec 25. Lunch, dinner $2.29-$9.95. Cr cds: D, MC, V.

★ **CHINA GARDEN.** *1020 W 2nd St (31794), I-75 Exit 19. 912/382-1010.* Specializes in beef, chicken. Hrs: 11 am-2 pm, 5-9 pm; Sat from 11:30 am. Closed Sun; Chinese New Year, July 4, Thanksgiving, Dec 25. Lunch a la carte entrees: $4.50-$12.99. Buffet: $4.99; dinner a la carte entrees: $4.50-$12.99. Buffet: $10.95. Cr cds: A, MC, V.

Toccoa

(A-4) See also Clayton, Commerce, Gainesville

Pop 8,266 **Elev** 1,017 ft
Area code 706 **Zip** 30577
Information Toccoa-Stephens County Chamber of Commerce, 901 E Currahee St, PO Box 577; 706/886-2132

Motels/Motor Lodges

★ **DAYS INN TOCCOA.** *1101 S Big A Rd (30577). 706/886-9461; fax 706/282-0907; res 800/329-7466.* 78 rms, 2 story. Early Apr-Nov: S $36; D $45; each addl $5; under 15 free; lower rates rest of yr. Crib $5. TV; cable (premium). Pool. Complimentary continental bkfst. Ck-out 11 am. Meeting rms. Cr cds: A, C, D, DS, MC, V.

★★ **SHONEY'S INN.** *14227 Jones St (30553), 20 mi SE on GA 17 Exit 58. 706/356-8848; fax 706/356-2951; toll-free 800/222-2222.* 60 rms, 2 story. S $40-$53; D $45-$64; each addl $5; under 18 free; higher rates special events. Crib free. Pet accepted; $10. TV; cable (premium). Pool. Coffee in lobby. Restaurant adj 6 am-midnight. Ck-out noon. Meeting rms. Business servs avail. In-rm modem link. Some refrigerators; microwave in suites. Cr cds: A, D, DS, MC, V.

Tybee Island

(E-7) *See also Savannah*

Pop 2,842 **Elev** 17 ft **Area code** 912
Zip 31328 **Web** www.savcvb.com

Information Savannah Area Convention & Visitors Bureau, 222 W Oglethorpe Ave, PO Box 1628, Savannah 31402-1628; 912/944-0456 or 800/444-2427

What to See and Do

Fort Pulaski National Monument. (see) 3 mi W on US 80.

Tybee Museum and Lighthouse. Museum is housed in a coastal artillery battery built 1898. Battery Garland is one of 6 gun emplacements that made up Fort Screven. Museum traces history of Tybee from colonial times to 1945; exhibits on Martello Tower, Civil War, Fort Screven; doll and gun collections. The lighthouse is one of the oldest active lighthouses in the US; visitors may climb to the top for a scenic view of Tybee and historic Fort Screven. Exhibits and gift shop in 1880s lighthouse keeper's cottage. (Mon, Wed-Sun; closed Jan 1, Thanksgiving, Dec 25). N end of island. Phone 912/786-5801. ¢¢

Resort

★★ **BEST WESTERN DUNES INN.** *1409 Butler Ave (31328). 912/786-4591; fax 912/786-4593; toll-free 888/678-0763. bestwestern.com/dunesinn.* 32 rms, 2 story, 14 kit. units. Apr-Sep: S, D $79-$125; kit. units $89-$135; under 12 free; wkly rates; higher rates: special events, hols (3-day min); lower rates rest of yr. Crib $5. TV; cable, VCR avail (movies). Pool. Complimentary coffee in lobby. Restaurant adj 5 am-10 pm. Ck-out 11 am. Business servs avail. In-rm modem link. Refrigerators avail. Balconies. Opp beach. Cr cds: A, DS, MC, V.
D ⛱ ⛱ 🐾 SC

B&B/Small Inn

★ **HUNTER HOUSE BED & BREAKFAST.** *1701 Butler Blvd (33952). 912/786-7515. www.tybeeisland.com.* 4 rms, 1 story, 2 suites. Apr-Sep: S, D $100; suites $140; lower rates rest of yr. TV; cable (DSS). Restaurant 6-9:30 pm, closed Sun. Bar. Ck-out noon, ck-in 3 pm. Golf. Beach access. Cr cds: A, MC, V.
🐾 🧍 🔥

Restaurants

★ **BREAKFAST CLUB.** *1500 Butler Ave (31328). 912/786-5984.* Specializes in eggs Florentine, the Grill Cleaner's Special. Hrs: 6 am-12:30 pm. Closed Dec 25. Bkfst $2.35-$8.95; lunch $2.35-$8.95. Child's menu. Old-time diner atmosphere. Family-owned. Cr cds: D, DS, MC, V.
D ⊟

★★ **HUNTER HOUSE.** *1701 Butler Ave. 912/786-7515.* Mediterranean menu. Specializes in seafood, steak. Hrs: 6-9:30 pm. Closed Sun; hols. Res required. Bar. Dinner $10-$18. Cr cds: A, MC, V.

★ **MACELWEE'S SEAFOOD HOUSE.** *101 Lovell Ave (US 80) (31328). 912/786-4259. www.tybeeisland.com.* Specializes in grilled, fried and steamed seafood & steak. Hrs: 4-9:30 pm; Fri to 10 pm; Sat, Sun 12:30-10 pm. Closed Easter, Thanksgiving, Dec 25. Bar. Lunch, dinner $6.99-$19.95. Child's menu. View of ocean. Cr cds: A, D, MC, V.
D ⊟

Valdosta

(G-4) *See also Adel*

Settled 1860 **Pop** 39,806 **Elev** 229 ft
Area code 912
Web www.datasys.net/valdtourism

Information Valdosta-Lowndes County Convention & Visitors Bureau, 1703 Norman Dr, Suite F, PO Box 1964, 31603-1964; 912/245-0513 or 800/569-8687

When local citizens discovered that surveyors had left the town off the railroad right-of-way, they lost no time moving the town four miles east of the original community (then called Troupville). Named for Val de

Aosta (Vale of Beauty), the governor's estate, Valdosta later became a rail center with seven branch lines of three systems. One of the state's most prosperous small cities, Valdosta's products include timber, tobacco, and cattle. Agriculture, tourism, Valdosta State University, and Moody Air Force Base, 12 miles to the north, also contribute to the economy. Valdosta is in the center of a large wooded area with many lakes nearby.

What to See and Do

The Crescent (Valdosta Garden Center). (1898) Neo-Classical house named for the dramatic 2-story, crescent-shaped porch supported by 13 columns. House incl grand staircase, 2nd-floor bathrm with gold-leaf tiles and fireplace, and ballrm on 3rd floor. In garden are chapel and octagonal school house. (Mon-Fri; also by appt) 904 N Patterson St. Phone 912/244-6747. ¢

Lowndes County Historical Society Museum. Originally a Carnegie library, now contains collection of artifacts from Civil War to present; genealogical library. (Mon-Fri; closed hols) 305 W Central Ave. Phone 912/247-4780. ¢

Motels/Motor Lodges

★★ **BEST WESTERN KING OF THE ROAD.** *1403 N St. Augustine Rd (31602), 1 blk W of jct GA 133, I-75 Exit 5. 912/244-7600; fax 912/245-1734; res 800/528-1234. www.best westerm.com.* 131 rms, 3 story, 6 suites. Mar-Apr, July-Aug, Oct: S $54; D $60; each addl $4; suites $109; under 17 free; lower rates rest of yr. Crib avail, fee. Pet accepted, some restrictions. Parking lot. Pool. TV; cable (premium). Complimentary continental bkfst, coffee in rms, newspaper, toll-free calls. Restaurant 5:30-8:30 pm, closed Sun. Bar. Ck-out 11 am, ck-in 1 pm. Meeting rms. Business center. Bellhops. Dry cleaning. Golf. Cr cds: A, C, D, DS, MC, V.
D ▨ ⌘ ⊠ ⊠ ☒ SC ⚑

★★ **BEST WESTERN LAKE PARK INN.** *6972 Bellville Rd (31636), S on I-75 Exit 1. 912/559-4939; fax 912/559-4944; toll-free 800/528-1234.* 60 rms, 2 story. S, D $39-$42; under 18 free; family rates. Crib free. TV; cable (premium), VCR avail (movies). Compli-

mentary continental bkfst, coffee in rms. Restaurant adj open 24 hrs. Ck-out 11 am. In-rm modem link. Pool. Cr cds: A, D, DS, MC, V.
D ▨ ⊠ ☒ SC

★★ **CLUBHOUSE INN AND SUITES VALDOSTA.** *1800 Club House Dr (31601), I-75 at GA 94, Exit 5. 912/247-7755; fax 912/245-1359; toll-free 800/258-2466.* 121 rms, 2 story, 17 suites. S, D $58-$68; suites $76-$86; each addl $5; under 16 free; wkly rates; golf plans. Crib free. TV; cable (premium). Pool; whirlpool. Complimentary bkfst buffet; evening refreshments. Ck-out noon. Meeting rms. Business center. In-rm modem link. Refrigerator in suites. Some private patios, balconies. Cr cds: A, C, D, DS, MC, V.
D ▨ ⊠ ☒ SC ⚑

★★ **COMFORT INN CONFERENCE CENTER.** *2101 W Hill Ave (31601), at jct US 84, I-75 Exit 4. 912/242-1212; fax 912/242-2639; res 800/228-5150.* 138 rms, 2 story. S $46-$50; D $50-$57; each addl $5; suites $90; under 18 free. TV; cable (premium). Pool. Coffee in rms. Complimentary continental bkfst. Bar 11 am-11 pm. Ck-out noon. Business center. Valet serv. Guest lndry. Airport transportation. Lawn games. Cr cds: A, C, D, DS, MC, V.
D ⚑ ⌘ ⊠ ☒ ☒ ⚑

★★ **HAMPTON INN.** *1705 Gornto Rd (31601), I-75, Exit 5, adj Valdosta Mall. 912/244-8800; fax 912/244-6602; res 800/HAMPTON.* 102 rms, 2 story. S $56; D $61; under 18 free. Crib free. TV; cable (premium). Pool. Complimentary continental bkfst. Coffee in rms. Restaurant adj 6 am-11 pm. Ck-out noon. Business servs avail. In-rm modem link. Valet serv. Health club privileges. Cr cds: A, C, D, DS, MC, V.
D ⊠ ⚑ ⊠ ⚑

★★ **QUALITY INN SOUTH.** *1902 W Hill Ave (31601), I-75 at US 84, Exit 4. 912/244-4520; fax 912/247-2404; res 800/228-5151.* 48 rms, 2 story. S $34.95-$49.95; D $37.95-$54.95; each addl $4; under 17 free. Crib $4. Pet accepted. TV; cable. Pool. Playground. Complimentary continental bkfst. Restaurant 11 am-2 pm, 5-10 pm. Bar 2-11 pm; Sat to midnight; closed Sun. Ck-out noon. Business servs avail. Cr cds: A, C, D, DS, ER, MC, V.

★★ **RAMADA LIMITED.** *2008 W. Hill Ave (31601), jct US 84, I-75 Exit 4. 912/242-1225; fax 912/247-2755; res 800/2ramada. Email ramada@surf south.com.* 102 rms, 2 story. S $44; D $49; under 18 free; golf plans. Crib free. Pet accepted; $5. TV; cable. Complimentary continental bkfst. Pool. Ck-out noon. Business servs avail. Health club privileges. Valet serv. Cr cds: A, C, D, DS, MC, V.

★ **SHONEY'S INN.** *1828 W Hill Ave (31601), I-75 Exit 4. 912/244-7711; fax 912/244-0361; res 800/222-2222.* 96 rms, 2 story. S $38-$46; D $42-$50; each addl $5; suite $65-$75; under 18 free. Crib free. TV; cable. Pool. Restaurant adj 6 am-midnight. Ck-out noon. Meeting rm. Business servs avail. Cr cds: A, DS, MC, V.

★ **TRAVELODGE.** *1330 N St. Augustine Rd (31601), I-75 Exit 5. 912/242-3464; fax 912/242-3464; toll-free 800/578-7878.* 88 rms, 2 story. S $34-$41; D $38-$51; each addl $4; under 18 free. Crib free. Pet accepted. TV; cable (premium). Pool. Complimentary full bkfst. Coffee in rms. Restaurant. Bar. Ck-out noon. Business servs avail. Valet serv. Some refrigerators. Balconies. Cr cds: A, C, D, DS, JCB, MC, V.

Restaurants

★★ **CHARLIE TRIPPER'S.** *4479 N Valdosta Rd (31602). 912/247-0366.* Specializes in Angus beef, seafood, steak. Hrs: 6-10 pm. Closed Sun, Mon; hols. Res accepted. Bar. Dinner $12.95-$16.95. Parking. Cr cds: A, D, DS, MC, V.

★★ **JP MULLDOONS.** *1405 Gornto Rd (31602). 912/247-6677.* Specializes in chicken, steak, fresh seafood. Hrs: 11 am-10 pm. Closed Sun, Mon; hols. Res accepted. Bar. Lunch $7.95-$16.95; dinner $7.95-$16.95. Enter-

tainment: pianist. Parking. Cr cds: A, MC, V.

★★ **MOM & DAD'S.** *4143 N Valdosta Rd (31602). 912/333-0848.* Specializes in fish, veal, beef. Hrs: 5-10 pm. Closed Sun, Mon; hols. Bar. Dinner $6.95-$14. Child's menu. Parking. Cr cds: A, D, DS, MC, V.

Warm Springs

(see Pine Mountain (Harris County))

Washington

(C-5) *See also Athens*

Settled 1769 **Pop** 4,279 **Elev** 618 ft
Area code 706 **Zip** 30673
Web www.washingtonga.org

Information Washington-Wilkes Chamber of Commerce, 104 Liberty St, Box 661; 706/678-2013

What to See and Do

Callaway Plantation. Complete working plantation complex incl red brick Greek Revival mansion (1869); gray frame "Federal plainstyle" house (ca 1790) with period furnishings; hewn log kitchen (ca 1785) with utensils, agricultural equipment. RV parking (hookups). (Tues-Sun; closed hols) For further information contact the Chamber of Commerce. 5 mi W on US 78. ¢¢

Washington-Wilkes Historical Museum. Located in white frame, antebellum house (ca 1836), the museum incl period furnishings, US Civil War mementos, Native American items, earthenware. (Tues-Sat, also Sun afternoons; closed Jan 1, Thanksgiving, Dec 25) 308 E Robert Toombs Ave. Phone 706/678-2105. ¢

Motel/Motor Lodge

★★ **JAMESON INN.** *115 Ann Denard Dr (30673). 706/678-7925; fax 706/678-7925.* 41 rms, 2 story. S $52; D $56; each addl $4; suites $111-

$147; under 12 free; higher rates Masters Tournament. Crib $4. TV; cable. Complimentary continental bkfst. Restaurant adj open 24 hrs. Ck-out 11 am. Some refrigerators. Cr cds: A, D, DS, MC, V.

Waycross (F-5)

Settled 1818 **Pop** 16,410 **Elev** 135 ft
Area code 912 **Zip** 31501
Web www.okefenokeeswamp.com

Information Tourism & Conference Bureau, 200 Lee Ave, PO Box 137, 31502; 912/283-3742

The name Waycross reflects the town's strategic location at the intersection of nine railroads and five highways. Situated at the edge of the Okefenokee Swamp, the town's early settlers put up blockhouses to protect themselves from local Native Americans. The production of naval stores and the marketing of furs were of prime importance before Okefenokee became a national wildlife refuge. Today the economy of Waycross is based on a diversity of industries, incl timber, railroad, mobile homes, and tourism.

What to See and Do

Southern Forest World. Exhibits, with audiovisual displays, detail development and history of forestry in the South; logging locomotive, fire tower, 38-ft model of a loblolly pine, giant cypress tree. Nature trails. (Daily; closed hols) 2 mi W between US 1 & US 82 on N Augusta Ave. Phone 912/285-4056. ¢

Annual Events

Okefenokee Spring Fling. Okefenokee Swamp Park (see OKEFENOKEE SWAMP). Fish fry, theater, crafts. Every Sat in Mar, Apr, May.

Pogofest. Parade, exhibits, barbecue. Oct.

Motels/Motor Lodges

★★ **HOLIDAY INN.** *1725 Memorial Dr (31501), at jct US 84. 912/283-*
4490; fax 912/283-4490; toll-free 800/465-4329. www.okeswamp.com. 148 rms, 2 story. S $45-$50; D $51-$55; each addl $5; under 19 free. Crib free. Pet accepted. TV; cable (premium). Pool. Complimentary full bkfst. Coffee in rms. Restaurant 6 am-2 pm, 5-9:30 pm. Bar 3 pm-midnight, Sat from 5 pm; closed Sun. Ck-out noon. Coin lndry. Meeting rms. In-rm modem link. Bellhops. Valet serv. Sundries. Airport, bus depot transportation. Exercise equipt. Health club privileges. Putting green. Game rm. Microwaves avail. Some private patios, balconies. Cr cds: A, C, D, DS, JCB, MC, V.

★ **PINECREST MOTEL.** *1761 Memorial Dr (31501). 912/283-3580; fax 912/283-4490.* 30 rms. S $28; D $33; each addl $3; under 18 free. Crib $3. TV; cable (premium). Pool. Restaurant adj 6 am-10 pm. Ck-out noon. Health club privileges. Cr cds: A, D, MC, V.

Winder

(B-3) *See also Athens, Atlanta*

Pop 7,373 **Elev** 984 ft **Area code** 770
Zip 30680

Information Barrow County Chamber of Commerce, 6 Porter St, PO Box 456; 770/867-9444

Motels/Motor Lodges

★ **DAYS INN.** *802 N Broad St (30656), US 11 N at US 78. 770/267-3666; fax 770/267-7189; toll-free 800/329-7466.* 45 rms, 2 story. S, D $45-$55; each addl $5; under 17 free; wkly rates. Crib free. Pet accepted, some restrictions; $5. TV; cable (premium). Complimentary continental bkfst. Restaurant nearby. Meeting rms. Business servs avail. In-rm modem link. Pool. Some refrigerators, microwaves. Cr cds: A, DS, MC, V.

KENTUCKY

The spirits of native sons Abraham Lincoln, Daniel Boone, and Henry Clay are still present in many aspects of modern-day Kentucky. Known for such traditions as mountain music, mint juleps, and the Derby, Kentucky's rich heritage has not faded over time. Although the bluegrass is blue only for a short time in the spring, and although few self-respecting Kentuckians will dilute a good bourbon with sugar and mint leaves, Kentucky has not sought to distance itself from its history. To many, this is still the land where Lincoln was born, where Zachary Taylor spent his youth, and where Harriet Beecher Stowe witnessed the auctioning of slaves and found the inspiration to write *Uncle Tom's Cabin*. Such pioneers and visionaries continue to be revered today perhaps more so in Kentucky than anywhere else. The state itself has been assured immortality through the words of Stephen Foster's song, "My Old Kentucky Home."

Population: 3,960,825
Area: 40,409 square miles
Elevation: 257-4,145 feet
Peak: Black Mountain (Harlan County)
Entered Union: June 1, 1792 (15th state)
Capital: Frankfort
Motto: United We Stand, Divided We Fall
Nickname: Bluegrass State
Flower: Goldenrod
Bird: Kentucky Cardinal
Fair: August 17-27, 2001, in Louisville
Time Zone: Eastern and Central
Website: www.kentuckytourism.com

Kentucky stretches from Virginia to Missouri, a geographic and historic bridge in the westward flow of American settlement. The state can be divided into four sections: the Bluegrass, the south central cave country, the eastern mountains, and western lakes. Each differs drastically in geography, culture, and economics. A circular area in the north central portion of the state, the Lexington plain, is bluegrass country, home of great horses and gentlemen-farmers. A predominantly rural nature has remained even though a patina of industry has been imposed, thanks to generous tax laws that have added industrial muscle to almost every major community. The great dams of the Tennessee Valley Authority have harnessed floods, generated cheap power, lured chemical plants, and created new vacation resources.

More than 450 million pounds of burley and dark tobacco are typically grown in Kentucky each year. The principal crop is followed by corn, soybeans, and wheat. Cattle, hogs, sheep, and poultry round out the farm family. Not all of Kentucky's corn is served on the cob; much of it winds up as bourbon whiskey, respected and treasured in much of the world. Kentucky is a major mining state as well, with rich deposits of bituminous coal, petroleum, natural gas, fluorspar, natural cement, and clay. Tobacco and food products, electronic equipment, transportation equipment, chemicals, and machinery are the principal factory products.

Horse farm in Kentucky Bluegrass country

The Cumberland Gap, a natural passageway through the mountains that sealed the Kentucky wilderness off from Virginia, was the gateway of the pioneers. Dr. Thomas Walker, the first recorded explorer to make a thorough land expedition into the state, arrived in 1750. Daniel Boone and a company of axmen hacked the Wilderness Road through the Cumberland Gap and far into the wilds. The first permanent settlement was at Harrodsburg in 1774, followed quickly by Boonesborough in 1775. Richard Henderson, founder of the Transylvania company, asked Congress to recognize Transylvania as the 14th state; instead Virginia claimed Kentucky as one of its counties, and Transylvania passed into history. Finally, in 1792 Congress admitted Kentucky as a state. The Civil War found Kentucky for the Union but against abolition. It remained officially with the North, but fought on both sides.

When to Go/Climate

Kentucky enjoys a temperate climate with 4 distinct seasons. Winter snowfall ranges from 5 to 10 inches in the southwestern part of the state to as much as 40 inches in the highest elevations. Thunderstorms are common in the Ohio River valley in spring and summer.

AVERAGE HIGH/LOW TEMPERATURES (°F)

LOUISVILLE

Jan 40/32	**May** 76/55	**Sep** 80/59
Feb 45/27	**June** 84/63	**Oct** 69/46
Mar 56/36	**July** 87/67	**Nov** 57/37
Apr 67/45	**Aug** 86/66	**Dec** 45/29

Parks and Recreation Finder

Directions to and information about the parks and recreation areas below are given under their respective town/city sections. Please refer to those sections for details.

NATIONAL PARK AND RECREATION AREAS

Key to abbreviations. I.H.S. = International Historic Site; I.P.M. = International Peace Memorial; N.B. = National Battlefield; N.B.P. = National Battlefield Park; N.B.C. = National Battlefield and Cemetery; N.C.A. = National Conservation Area; N.E.M. = National Expansion Memorial; N.F. = National Forest; N.G. = National Grassland; N.H.P. = National Historical Park; N.H.C. = National Heritage Corridor; N.H.S. = National Historic Site; N.L. = National Lakeshore; N.M. = National Monument; N.M.P. = National Military Park; N.Mem. = National Memorial; N.P. = National Park; N.Pres. = National Preserve; N.R.A. = National Recreational Area; N.R.R. = National Recreational River; N.Riv. = National River; N.S. = National Seashore; N.S.R. = National Scenic Riverway; N.S.T. = National Scenic Trail; N.Sc. = National Scientific Reserve; N.V.M. = National Volcanic Monument.

Place Name	Listed Under
Abraham Lincoln Birthplace N.H.S.	same
Big South Fork N.R.A.	CUMBERLAND FALLS STATE RESORT PARK
Cumberland Gap N.H.	same
Daniel Boone N.F.	same
Land Between the Lakes	same
Mammoth Cave N.P.	same

CALENDAR HIGHLIGHTS

MARCH

Spiral Stakes. (Covington). Turfway Park Race Track in Florence. One of the largest pursed Thoroughbred races for 3-yr-olds. Race culminates wk-long festival. Phone 606/371-0200.

APRIL

Rolex-Kentucky Event and Trade Fair. (Lexington). Three-day endurance test for horse and rider in dressage, cross-country, and stadium jumping. Fair features boutiques. Phone 606/233-2362.

APRIL

Kentucky Derby Festival. (Louisville). Two-wk celebration with Pegasus Parade, Great Steamboat Race, Great Balloon Race, mini-marathon, concerts, and sports tournaments. Contact Kentucky Derby Festival; phone 502/584-6383 or 800/928-FEST.

MAY

Governor's Derby Breakfast. (Frankfort). Breakfast, entertainment, and Kentucky crafts. Phone 502/564-2611.

JUNE

Capital Expo Festival (Frankfort). Capital Plaza Complex. Traditional music, country music, fiddling; workshops, demonstrations, arts and crafts; balloon race, dancing, games, contests, puppets, museum exhibitions, ethnic and regional foods, entertainment.

Festival of the Bluegrass (Lexington). Kentucky Horse Park. Top names in Bluegrass music, with more than 20 bands appearing. Incl special shows for children; crafts; workshops with the musicians. The 600-acre park has more than 750 electric hookups for campers. Phone 606/846-4995.

AUGUST

Kentucky Heartland Festival (Elizabethtown). Freeman Lake Park. Antique auto show, arts and crafts, races, hot air balloon, bluegrass music, games and food. Phone 270/765-4334 or 270/769-2391.

Kentucky State Fair (Louisville). Livestock shows; championship horse show; home and fine arts exhibits; midway, entertainment. Contact VP of Expositions; phone 502/367-5180.

SEPTEMBER

Riverfest (Covington). One of the largest fireworks displays in the country; shot from barges moored on the Ohio River. Phone 513/749-3764.

OCTOBER

Big River Arts & Crafts Festival (Henderson). Audubon State Park. More than 250 exhibitors. Phone 270/926-4433.

Daniel Boone Festival (Barbourville). Celebrates Boone's search for a route through Kentucky. Square dancing, musket shooting, reenactment of Native American treaty signing, horse show, parade, old time fiddling, long rifle shoot between neighboring states, exhibits, antique displays, arts and crafts, parade, entertainment, homemade candies and cakes. The Cherokee make annual pilgrimage to city. Phone 606/546-4300.

STATE PARK AND RECREATION AREAS

Key to abbreviations. I.P. = Interstate Park; S.A.P. = State Archaeological Park; S.B. = State Beach; S.C.A. = State Conservation Area; S.C.P. = State Conservation Park; S.Cp. = State Campground; S.F. = State Forest; S.G. = State Garden; S.H.A. = State Historic Area; S.H.P. = State Historic Park; S.H.S. = State Historic Site; S.M.P. = State Marine Park; S.N.A. = State Natural Area; S.P. = State Park; S.P.C. = State Public Campground; S.R. = State Reserve; S.R.A. = State Recreation Area; S.Res. = State Reservoir; S.Res.P. = State Resort Park; S.R.P. = State Rustic Park.

Place Name	Listed Under
Barren River Lake S.Res.P.	GLASGOW
Ben Hawes S.P.	OWENSBORO
Big Bone Lick S.P.	WALTON
Blue Licks Battlefield S.P.	MAYSVILLE
Breaks I.P.	same
Buckhorn Lake S.Res.P.	HAZARD
Carter Caves S.R.P.	OLIVE HILL
Cumberland Falls S.Res.P.	same
Dale Hollow Lake S.Res.P.	MONTICELLO
Dr. Thomas Walker S.H.S.	BARBOURVILLE
E.P. "Tom" Sawyer S.P.	LOUISVILLE
Fort Boonesborough S.P.	WINCHESTER
General Burnside S.P.	SOMERSET
General Butler S.Res.P.	CARROLLTON
Grayson Lake S.P.	OLIVE HILL
Green River Lake S.P.	CAMPBELLSVILLE
Greenbo Lake S.Res.P.	ASHLAND
Jenny Wiley S.Res.P.	PRESTONSBURG
John James Audubon S.P.	HENDERSON
Kenlake S.Res.P.	same
Kentucky Dam Village S.Res.P.	GILBERTSVILLE
Kincaid Lake S.P.	WILLIAMSTOWN
Lake Barkley S.Res.P.	CADIZ
Lake Cumberland S.Res.P.	JAMESTOWN
Lake Malone S.P.	GREENVILLE
Levi Jackson Wilderness Road S.P.	LONDON
Lincoln Homestead S.P.	BARDSTOWN
My Old Kentucky Home S.P.	BARDSTOWN
Natural Bridge S.Res.P.	same
Old Fort Harrod S.P..	HARRODSBURG
Pennyrile Forest S.Res.P.	MADISONVILLE
Perryville Battlefield S.H.S.	DANVILLE
Pine Mountain S.Res.P.	PINEVILLE
Rough River Dam S.Res.P.	same
Waveland S.H.S.	LEXINGTON

Water-related activities; hiking, riding and various other sports; picnicking and camping are avail in many of these areas. Eighteen areas have lodges and/or cottages (rates vary; phone 800/255-PARK for information); 30 have tent and trailer sites (Apr-Oct: $12 for two persons; $1 each addl person over 16 years; sr citizens rate; electricity and water included; primitive camping $8.50; rates subject to change). Thirteen state parks have campgrounds open yr-round. Campsites are rented on a first-come, first-served basis; pets on leash only. No entrance fee is charged at state parks. For further information on state parks or camping, contact the Kentucky Department of Parks, 500 Mero St, Frankfort 40601; 502/564-2172 or 800/255-PARK incl the Canadian provinces of Ontario and Quebec.

FISHING AND HUNTING

Mountain streams, giant lakes, and major rivers all invite the angler and are productive throughout the yr. Both largemouth bass and crappie can be found throughout the state. Lake Cumberland (see SOMERSET) has walleye; Laurel River Lake (see CORBIN), Lake Cumberland tailwaters, and Paintsville Lake have trout; Buckhorn, Cave Run (see MOREHEAD), and Green River lakes have muskie; Lake Barkley, Kentucky Lake (see GILBERTSVILLE), and tailwaters have sauger; and Lake Cumberland has striped bass. Statewide nonresident fishing license: $30; trout stamp $5; nonresident 3-day fishing license $12.50; 15-day license $20; no fishing license required for children under age 16. Annual nonresident hunting license: $95; deer permit with 2 tags, gun or archery $21; turkey permit $17.50; 5-day small game license $27.50. For open season dates and other details contact the Dept of Fish and Wildlife Resources, #1 Game Farm Rd, Frankfort 40601. Phone 502/564-4336 or 800/858-1549.

Tennessee Valley Authority Recreation Sites

Many of Kentucky's major recreation areas have developed around projects of the Tennessee Valley Authority. The flood-control and power projects in the west have created Kentucky Lake (see GILBERTSVILLE, KENLAKE STATE RESORT PARK), with a scenic shoreline of 2,380 miles, big Lake Barkley (see CADIZ), and Land Between the Lakes (see). The TVA (Land Between the Lakes, 100 Van Morgan Dr, Golden Pond, KY 42211. Phone 502/924-2000) will furnish material on the authority and its lakes, incl recreation maps. Navigation charts are available at nominal cost from Map Sales, TVA, 101 Haney Bldg, Chattanooga, TN 37402-2801.

Driving Information

Children under 40 inches in height must be in an approved safety seat anywhere in vehicle. In addition, all persons anywhere in vehicle are required to use safety belts. For further information phone 502/695-6356.

Highway Number	Cities/Towns within 10 miles
Interstate 24	Cadiz, Gilbertsville, Hopkinsville, Paducah.
Interstate 64	Ashland, Frankfort, Georgetown, Lexington, Louisville, Morehead, Olive Hill, Winchester.
Interstate 65	Bowling Green, Cave City, Elizabethtown, Glasgow, Hodgenville, Horse Cave, Louisville, Mammoth Cave Natl Park, Park City, Shepherdsville.
Interstate 71	Carrollton, Covington, Louisville, Walton.
Interstate 75	Berea, Corbin, Covington, Georgetown, Lexington, London, Mount Vernon, Richmond, Walton, Williamsburg, Williamstown.

Additional Visitor Information

The Department of Travel, Dept MR, PO Box 2011, Frankfort 40602, phone 800/225-8747, distributes literature and information, incl a list of the state's many interesting festivals and fairs. The *Kentucky Official Vacation Guide* is informative, comprehensive, and is revised annually.

There are 8 welcome centers in Kentucky; visitors who stop by will find information and brochures most helpful in planning stops at points of interest. Their locations are as follows: Florence Welcome Center, I-75 southbound Exit 180, Walton; Franklin Welcome Center, I-65 northbound Exit 2, Franklin; Hopkinsville Welcome Center, I-24 westbound Exit 89, Hopkinsville; Grayson Welcome Center, I-64 westbound Exit 181, Grayson; Shelby County Welcome Center, I-64 eastbound Exit 28, Shelbyville; Bullitt County Welcome Center, I-65 southbound Exit 116, Shepherdsville; Whitehaven Welcome Center, I-24 eastbound and US 45, Paducah; and Williamsburg Welcome Center, I-75 northbound Exit 11, Williamsburg.

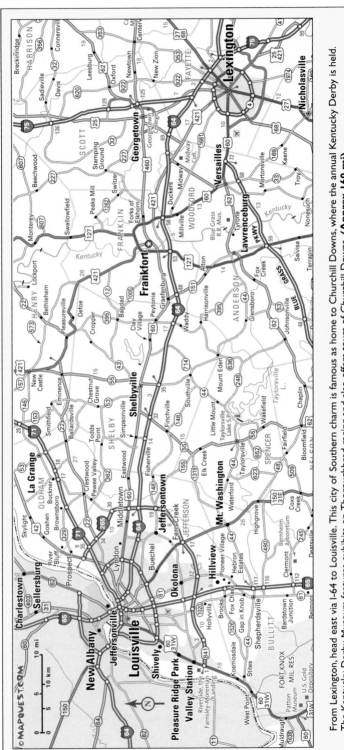

From Lexington, head east via I-64 to Louisville. This city of Southern charm is famous as home to Churchill Downs, where the annual Kentucky Derby is held. The Kentucky Derby Museum features exhibits on Thoroughbred racing and also offers tours of Churchill Downs. **(Approx 160 mi)**

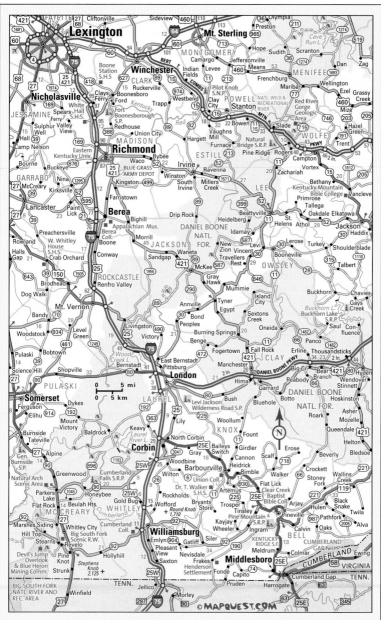

From Lexington, take I-75 and Highway 25E to the Cumberland Mountains—the rugged landscapes, winding hollers, and mountain towns of eastern Kentucky draw city folk for scenic drives (particularly in fall), camping, and river and trail recreation (hiking and mountain biking in summer, cross-country skiing in winter). Once a busy thoroughfare for westward-bound pioneers, the Cumberland Gap National Historic Park is now isolated in a remote corner where Kentucky, Virginia, and Tennessee come together. **(Approx 260 mi)**

Abraham Lincoln Birthplace National Historic Site

See also Elizabethtown, Hodgenville

(3 mi S of Hodgenville on US 31E/ KY 61)
Web www.nps.gov/ablilincomj.htm

On February 12, 1809, the Sinking Spring Farm, named after a small limestone spring, became the birthplace of Abraham Lincoln, the 16th President of the United States. Less than three years later, in 1811, Thomas Lincoln, the President's father, moved the family to Knob Creek Farm, located about ten miles northeast. Later moves eventually took the Lincoln family to Indiana and Illinois.

The Lincoln Farm Association purchased the farm in 1905. In 1916 the Lincoln Farm Association deeded the farm to the War Department and was later transferred to the National Park Service in 1933. Today 110 acres of the original Lincoln Farm are contained within the 116-acre park.

★ Visitor Center Audiovisual program (18 min) and exhibits explore Lincoln's background and environment. Thomas Lincoln's Bible is on display.

More than 100,000 citizens contributed funds to construct the granite and marble Memorial Building in 1911. Inside is the log cabin originally believed to be the Lincoln birthplace; research has revealed that this is most likely not the case. The cabin was disassembled, moved, exhibited, and stored many times before being reconstructed permanently inside the Memorial Building. (Daily; closed Thanksgiving, Dec 25) For specific and possible holiday closures contact Superintendent, 2995 Lincoln Farm Rd, Hogdenville 42748; 270/358-3137. **FREE**

Annual Events

Martin Luther King's Birthday. Sun, mid-Jan.

Lincoln's Birthday. Wreath-laying ceremony. Afternoon of Feb 12.

Founders Day. Festivities commemorating the park's founding (July 17,1916). Wkend nearest July 17.

Ashland

(B-8) *See also Olive Hill*

Settled 1815 **Pop** 23,622 **Elev** 548 ft
Area code 606
Information Ashland Area Convention & Visitors Bureau, 728 Greenup Ave, PO Box 987, 41105; 606/329-1007 or 800/377-6249

Set in the highlands of northeastern Kentucky, on the Ohio River, Ashland is an industrial city that produces oil, steel, and chemicals.

What to See and Do

Central Park. A 47-acre park with prehistoric Native American mounds. Sport facilities; playgrounds, picnicking. Phone 606/327-2046.

Boyhood home of Abraham Lincoln

Covered bridges.

Bennett's Mill Bridge. Built in 1855 to service mill customers, bridge spans Tygarts Creek. At 195 ft, this is one of Kentucky's longest single-span covered bridges; original footings and frame intact. Closed to traffic. 8 mi W on KY 125 off KY 7.

Oldtown Bridge. Built 1880 to Burr's design; 194-ft, dual-span bridge crosses Little Sandy River. Closed to traffic. 14 mi W via US 23, then 9 mi S on KY 1.

Greenbo Lake State Resort Park. A 3,330-acre park, with 225-acre lake, has early buffalo (pig-iron) furnace. Swimming pool (Memorial Day-Labor Day), fishing, boating (marina); hiking, bicycle rentals, tennis, picnicking, playground, lodge, tent and trailer sites (Apr-Oct). Recreation program for children. 18 mi W via US 23 to KY 1. Phone 606/473-7324.

Kentucky Highlands Museum. Displays trace history and cultural heritage of the region. Period clothing; Native American artifacts; WWII memorabilia; industrial exhibits. Gift shop. (Tues-Sat; closed hols) 1624 Winchester. Phone 606/329-8888. **FREE**

Paramount Arts Center. Historical 1930's Art Deco theatre. Hosts children, events, concerts. Tours. (Daily) 1300 Winchester Ave. Phone 606/324-3175.

Annual Event

Poage Landing Days Festival. Central Park. Fiddle festival, national, and local entertainers, arts and crafts, children's activities. Third wkend Sep.

Motels/Motor Lodges

★ **DAYS INN.** 12700 SR 180 (41102). 606/928-3600; fax 606/928-6515. 63 rms, 2 story. S $46-$59; D $52-$64; each addl $5; under 18 free. Crib free. Pet accepted; $5. TV; cable (premium), VCR avail (movies). Pool. Complimentary continental bkfst, coffee in rms. Restaurant nearby. Ck-out noon. Coin lndry. Meeting rms. Business center. In-rm modem link. Exercise equipt. Some refrigerators,

microwaves. Picnic tables. Cr cds: A, D, DS, MC, V.

★★ **FAIRFIELD INN BY MARRIOTT.** 10945 Rte 60 (70112), I-64 Exit 185. 606/928-1222; fax 606/928-1222; toll-free 800/228-2800. 63 rms, 3 story, 8 suites. S $55-$60; D $60-$65; each addl $6; suites $65-$75; under 18 free. Crib avail. TV; cable (premium). Complimentary continental bkfst. Restaurant adj 6 am-11 pm. Ck-out noon. Meeting rms. Business servs avail. Sundries. Indoor pool; whirlpool. Game rm. Refrigerators, microwaves in suites. Cr cds: A, C, D, DS, ER, JCB, MC, V.

★ **KNIGHTS INN.** 7216 US 60 (41102). 606/928-9501; fax 606/928-4436; res 800/843-5644; toll-free 800/497-7560. 124 rms. S $38; D $43; kit. units $42-$47; each addl $5; under 18 free. Crib free. Pet accepted; $5. TV; cable (premium). Pool. Complimentary continental bkfst. Restaurant nearby. Ck-out noon. Meeting rms. Business servs avail. Refrigerators. Cr cds: A, C, D, DS, MC, V.

Hotel

★★ **ASHLAND PLAZA HOTEL.** One Ashland Plaza (41101), I-64 Exit 185. 606/329-0055; fax 606/325-4513; res 800/346-6133. 157 rms, 10 story. S $78-$80; D $84-$88; each addl $6; under 18 free; wknd, hol plans; higher rate special events. Crib $6. TV; cable (premium), VCR avail. Complimentary coffee in lobby. Restaurant 6 am-2 pm, 5-10 pm; Sun to 9 pm. Bar 4 pm-1:30 am; closed Sun. Ck-out noon. Meeting rms. Business servs avail. Free airport, railroad station transportation. Health club privileges. Cr cds: A, D, DS, MC, V.

Resort

★★ **GREENBO LAKE STATE RESORT.** HC 60, Box 562 (41144). 606/473-7324; fax 606/473-7741; toll-free 800/325-0083. www.kystateparks.com/greenbo. 36 rms, 3 story. Mid-May-Aug: S $53-$58; D $63-$68; each addl $5; under 16 free; golf plan;

lower rates rest of yr. TV; cable. Complimentary coffee in lobby. Restaurant 7 am-9 pm. Box lunches. Grocery 2 mi. Coin lndry 2 mi. Meeting rms. Business servs avail. Shopping arcade. Tennis privileges. 18-hole golf privileges, greens fee $13, pro. Boats. Hiking. Bicycle rentals. Lawn games. Social dir. Rec rm. Game rm. Pool; wading pool, lifeguard. Playground. Supervised children's activities. Many balconies. On lake. Cr cds: A, C, D, DS, MC, V.

Restaurant

★★ **DRAGON PALACE.** *807 Carter Ave (41101).* 606/329-8081. Specializes in orange chicken, seafood Imperial, sizzling combo. Hrs: 11 am-9 pm; Fri, Sat noon-10 pm; Sun noon-9 pm. Closed Mon. Bar. Lunch a la carte entrees: $2.55-$5.25; dinner a la carte entrees: $6.50-$14.95. Cr cds: A, C, D, DS, MC, V.

Barbourville

(D-7) *See also Corbin, Pineville*

Founded 1800 **Pop** 3,658 **Elev** 986 ft
Area code 606 **Zip** 40906
Information Knox County Chamber of Commerce, 196 Daniel Boone Dr, Suite 205; 606/546-4300

In the valley of the scenic Cumberland River, Barbourville is protected by a $2.5-million flood wall built around the city. Tobacco, coal mining, and timber are the area's major industries. The city has also produced two Kentucky governors, a lieutenant governor, three US congressmen, and many other statesmen who served outside Kentucky.

What to See and Do

Daniel Boone National Forest. (see) 24 mi NW on US 25.

Dr. Thomas Walker State Historic Site. Replica of original log cabin built in 1750 by Dr. Thomas Walker; surrounded by 12 acres of parkland. Miniature golf (fee). Picnic area, shelter, playground. Grounds (daily). 5

mi SW on KY 459. Phone 606/546-4400. **FREE**

Annual Event

Daniel Boone Festival. Celebrates Boone's search for a route through Kentucky. Square dancing, musket shooting, reenactment of Native American treaty signing, horse show, parade, old time fiddling, long rifle shoot between neighboring states, exhibits, antique displays, arts and crafts, parade, entertainment, homemade candies and cakes. The Cherokee make annual pilgrimage to city. Seven days early Oct.

Bardstown

(C-5) *See also Elizabethtown*

Settled 1775 **Pop** 6,801 **Elev** 647 ft
Area code 502 **Zip** 40004
Web www.win.net/bardstown

Information Bardstown-Nelson County Tourist & Convention Commission, PO Box 867; 502/348-4877 or 800/638-4877

One of Kentucky's oldest settlements, Bardstown includes many historic sites. It is the seat of Nelson County, home of four bourbon distilleries. Today, the chief agricultural product is tobacco.

What to See and Do

Bernheim Forest. (see) 14 mi NW on KY 245 in Shepherdsville.

Jim Beam American Outpost. Visitors can tour the historic Beam family home and stroll the grounds. Craft shop. (Daily; closed hols) 15 mi NW on KY 245 in Clermont. Phone 502/543-9877. **FREE**

Lincoln Homestead State Park. In a compound framed by split rail fences is a replica of the cabin built on this land, which was originally settled in 1782 by Abraham Lincoln, Sr, grandfather of the President. This was the home of Thomas Lincoln until he was 25. Furnished in pioneer style, incl several pieces made by Thomas Lincoln. Also, the Berry House, home of Nancy Hanks during her courtship by Thomas Lincoln; pioneer relics, photostatic copies of the Thomas and Nancy Lincoln marriage bonds. A replica of the blacksmith and carpenter shop where Thomas Lincoln worked is also in the compound. Houses (May-Sep, daily; Oct, wkends). The 150-acre park offers 18-hole golf (daily, fee). Picnic facilities, playground. 20 mi SE on US 150 to KY 528. Phone 606/336-7461. Museum ¢

The Mansion. House of Ben Johnson, a powerful political figure of Kentucky's past, was site of raising of first Confederate flag in 1861. Tours. Overnight stays avail. (Daily; closed Dec 25) 1003 N 3rd St. Phone 502/348-2586. ¢¢

My Old Kentucky Dinner Train. Scenic dining excursions aboard elegant, restored dining cars from the 1940s. Round trip through countryside incl 4-course meal; 5-course meal Fri and Sat eves. (Feb-Dec, Tues-Sun) Departs from 602 N 3rd St. Phone 502/348-7300. ¢¢¢¢

My Old Kentucky Home State Park. The composer Stephen Foster occasionally visited his cousin, Judge John Rowan, at the stately house, Federal Hill (1795). These visits may have inspired him to write "My Old Kentucky Home," a melody that is a lasting favorite. The house and its 290 acres of grounds are now a state park. Attendants wear period costumes; period furnishings. Golf course. Picnic area, playground. Tent and trailer sites (standard fees). Guided tour (fee). Gardens; amphitheater (see SEASONAL EVENT). (Daily; closed Jan 1, Thanksgiving, wk of Dec 25) For information contact Superintendent, PO Box 323. 1 mi E on US 150. Phone 502/348-3502. Grounds **FREE**

Spalding Hall. (ca 1825) Once part of St. Joseph College; used as hospital in Civil War. Former dormitory; now houses art and pottery shop. (May-Oct, daily; rest of yr, Tues-Sun) Just off N 5th St. Phone 502/348-2999. **FREE** Also here are

> **Bardstown Historical Museum.** Features items covering 200 yrs of local history. Exhibits incl Native American artifacts, Lincoln papers concerning Lincoln-Reed suit, John Fitch papers, and replica of first steamboat, Stephen Foster memorabilia, tools and utensils of Trappist Monks, Civil War artifacts, gifts of King Louis Phillipe and King Charles X of France, pioneer items, period costumes (1850s-90s), natural science display. (May-Oct, daily; rest of yr, Tues-Sun) Phone 502/348-2999. **FREE**

Oscar Getz Museum of Whiskey History. Copper stills, manuscripts, documents, bottles, and advertising art chronicle the history of whiskey from pre-colonial days to Prohibition era. (May-Oct, daily; rest of yr, Tues-Sun) 114 N 5th St. Phone 502/348-2999. **FREE**

St. Joseph Proto-Cathedral. (1816) First Catholic cathedral W of the Allegheny Mts. Paintings donated by Pope Leo XII. (Daily) 310 W Stephen Foster, at jct US 31E, 62. Phone 502/348-3126.

Wickland. (1813-17). Stately Georgian mansion, residence of 2 Kentucky governors, Charles A. Wickliffe and J.W. Beckham, and former Louisiana governor R.C. Wickliffe (all of one family). Handsomely furnished with many original antiques. (Appt only; closed hols) E on US 62. Phone 502/348-5428. ¢¢

Seasonal Event

Stephen Foster, The Musical. J. Dan Talbott Amphitheater, in My Old Kentucky Home State Park. Musical with 50 Foster melodies, tracing composer's triumphs and romance. Nightly Tues-Sun; Sat also matinee. In the event of rain, indoor theater is used. Phone 502/348-5971 or 800/626-1563 for prices, res. Early June-early Sep.

Motels/Motor Lodges

★★ **BARDSTOWN PARKVIEW MOTEL.** *418 E Stephen Foster Ave (40004), at jct US 150. 502/348-5983; fax 502/349-6973; toll-free 800/732-2384.* 38 rms, 1-2 story, 10 kit. units. June-Labor Day: S $50; D $55; each addl $5; suites, kit. units $65-$85; lower rates rest of yr. Crib free. Pet accepted. TV; cable. Pool. Complimentary continental bkfst. Restaurant 11 am-9 pm. Bar. Ck-out 11 am. Coin lndry. Refrigerators, wet bars.

My Old Kentucky Home State Park opp. Cr cds: A, DS, MC, V.

[icons] SC

★★ **BEST WESTERN GENERAL NELSON.** *411 W Stephen Foster (40004).* 502/348-3977; fax 502/348-3977; res 800/258-1234; toll-free 800/225-3977. www.generalnelson.com. 52 rms. S, D $69; each addl $10; under 12 free. Crib avail. Pet accepted, some restrictions, fee. Parking lot. Pool, whirlpool. TV; cable (premium), VCR avail. Complimentary continental bkfst, coffee in rms, toll-free calls. Restaurant nearby. Ck-out 11 am, ck-in 2 pm. Meeting rms. Internet dock/port avail. Dry cleaning, coin lndry. Gift shop. Golf. Tennis. Picnic facilities. Cr cds: A, C, D, DS, MC, V.

[icons]

★★ **HOLIDAY INN.** *1875 New Haven Rd (40004), 2 mi S on US 31E Exit 21, at Bluegrass Pkwy.* 502/348-9253; fax 502/348-5478. Email hibard@bardstown.com. 102 rms, 2 story. May-Sep: S, D $59-$89; each addl $5; under 19 free; lower rates rest of yr. Crib free. Pet accepted, some restrictions. TV; cable (premium), VCR avail (movies). Pool. Playground. Restaurant 6 am-2 pm, 5-9 pm; Fri, Sat to 10 pm. Bar. Ck-out 11 am. Meeting rms. Business servs avail. In-rm modem link. 9-hole par 3 golf, driving range. Exercise equipt. Some refrigerators, microwaves Cr cds: A, D, DS, JCB, MC, V.

[icons]

★ **OLD BARDSTOWN INN.** *510 E Stephen Foster Ave (40004), off US 150E.* 502/349-0776; fax 502/349-0776; toll-free 800/894-1601. 32 rms, 2 story, 1 suite. June-Nov: S $52; D $58; lower rates rest of yr. Crib avail. Pet accepted, fee. Parking lot. Pool. TV; cable. Complimentary continental bkfst. Restaurant nearby. Ck-out 11 am, ck-in 2 pm. Fax servs avail. Bellhops. Golf, 18 holes. Cr cds: A, DS, MC, V.

[icons]

Hotel

★★ **HAMPTON INN.** *985 Chambers Blvd (40004), I-65 Exit 112.* 502/349-0100; fax 502/349-1191; res 800/HAMPTON. Email bdstw01@hi-hotel.com; www.hampton.com/hi/bardstown. 103 rms, 2 story, 3 suites. Apr-Nov: S $70; D $75; suites $125; under 18 free; lower rates rest of yr. Crib avail, fee. Pet accepted, fee. Parking lot. Indoor pool. TV; cable (premium). Complimentary continental bkfst, coffee in rms, newspaper, toll-free calls. Restaurant nearby. Ck-out noon, ck-in 3 pm. Meeting rms. Business servs avail. Dry cleaning. Exercise privileges. Golf. Tennis, 4 courts. Picnic facilities. Cr cds: A, D, DS, MC, V.

[icons] SC

B&Bs/Small Inns

★★ **JAILER'S INN BED AND BREAKFAST.** *111 W Stephen Foster Ave (40004).* 502/348-5551; fax 502/349-1837; toll-free 800/948-5551. Email cpaul@jailersinn.com; www.jailersinn.com. 6 rms. No rm phones. S, D $65-$105; each addl $5-$10. Closed Jan. Crib free. TV; cable, VCR avail. Complimentary full bkfst; afternoon refreshments. Restaurant adj 11 am-9 pm. Ck-out 11 am, ck-in 2 pm. Some in-rm whirlpools. Built 1819 as jail, then converted to jailer's residence. Antiques, Oriental rugs. Cr cds: A, DS, MC, V.

[icons]

★ **THE OLD TALBOTT TAVERN.** *107 W Stephen Foster Ave (40004).* 502/348-3494; fax 502/348-3404; toll-free 800/4TAVERN. Email talbott@bardstown.com. 7 rms, 2 story. S, D $80-$125. TV; cable. Complimentary continental bkfst. Ck-out 11 am, ck-in 2 pm. Colonial furnishings; antiques. In original post office bldg built 1812. Cr cds: A, MC, V.

[icons]

Restaurant

★★ **KURTZ.** *418 E Stephen Foster Ave (40004).* 502/348-8964. Specializes in country ham, fried chicken, biscuit pudding with bourbon sauce. Hrs: 11 am-9 pm; Sun noon-8 pm. Closed Mon; Dec 25. Res accepted. Bar. Lunch $5.95-$8.95; dinner $9.95-$15.95. Parking. State park adj. Cr cds: C, D, DS, MC, V.

[icon]

Berea

(C-6) *See also Mount Vernon, Richmond*

Settled 1855 **Pop** 9,126 **Elev** 1,034 ft
Area code 606 **Zip** 40403
Web www.4berea.com

Information Tourist and Convention Commission, 201 N Broadway; 606/986-2540 or 800/598-5263

Berea College and diverse industry provide the income for this community in the foothills of the Cumberland Mountains and the Daniel Boone National Forest. Designated the "Folk Arts and Crafts Capital of Kentucky" by the state legislature, Berea boasts more than 155 antique shops, 40 craft shops, and working studios. Indian Fort Mountain nearby is the site of prehistoric fortifications. A Ranger District office of the Daniel Boone National Forest (see) is located here.

What to See and Do

Churchill Weavers. Established 1922, Churchill is one of the nation's oldest producers of handwoven goods. Self-guided tours through loomhouse (Mon-Fri; closed Dec 25). Gift shop and outlet shop (daily; closed Dec 25). Lorraine Ct, exit I-75 to US 25N. Phone 606/986-3127. **FREE**

The Studio Craftspeople of Berea. An organization of craftspeople working in various media invite visitors to visit their studios. The Tourist and Convention Commission has a list of studios open to the public.

Annual Events

Kentucky Guild of Artists & Craftsmen's Fair. Indian Fort Theater. Crafts, art, folk dances, singing. Phone 606/986-3192. Third wkend May and 2nd wkend Oct.

Berea Craft Festival. Indian Fort Theater, at Berea College. Entertainment, regional food, crafts demonstrations. Phone 606/986-2258. Three days mid-July.

Celebration of Traditional Music Festival. Features traditional music, dancers, concerts. Last wkend Oct.

Motels/Motor Lodges

★ **DAYS INN.** *KY 595 and I-75 (40403), Exit 77.* 606/986-7373; fax 606/986-3144. 60 rms, 2 story. S $43-$45; D $49-$51; each addl $5; family rates. Crib free. Pet accepted; $5. TV. Pool. Complimentary coffee in lobby. Restaurant adj. Ck-out 11 am. Meeting rm. Business servs avail. Miniature golf. Cr cds: A, D, DS, MC, V.

★★ **HOLIDAY MOTEL INC.** *100 Jane St (40403), ½ mi E of I-75 Exit 76 on KY 21.* 859/986-9311; fax 859/986-9311. Email holmotel@aol.com. 62 rms. S, D $45; each addl $5; suites $56. Crib $5. TV; cable. Pool. Restaurant adj 7 am-10 pm. Ck-out 11 am. Cr cds: A, MC, V.

Hotel

★★★ **BOONE TAVERN HOTEL.** *Main St & Prospect St (40403), 1 mi E of I-75 Exit 76, on KY 21.* 606/986-9358; fax 606/986-7711; toll-free 800/366-9358. www.4berea.com/tavern. 58 rms. S $55-$80; D $65-$90; each addl $10; under 12 free. Crib $10. TV. Restaurant 7-9:30 am, 11:30 am-2 pm, 6-8 pm. Ck-out 11 am. Meeting rms. Gift shop. Health club privileges. Established 1909. Operated by Berea College; most furniture handmade by students. Cr cds: A, C, D, DS, MC, V.

Restaurants

★ **DINNER BELL.** *I-75 (40403), Exit 76.* 606/986-2777. Specializes in country cooking. Hrs: 7 am-9 pm; Fri, Sat to 10 pm; winter hrs vary. Bkfst $1.65-$5.95; lunch $1.99-$4.95; dinner $4.50-$11.95. Child's menu. Parking. Country and antique shop. Cr cds: DS, MC, V.

★ **PAPALENO'S.** *108 Center St (40403), adj Berea College.* 606/986-4497. Specializes in soups, salads, pizza. Hrs: 11 am-10 pm; Fri, Sat to 11 pm. Closed Thanksgiving, Dec 25. Lunch, dinner $1.65-$12.50. Child's menu. Cr cds: A, C, D, DS, MC, V.

Bowling Green

(D-4)

Founded 1780 **Pop** 40,641 **Elev** 496 ft
Area code 270
Web www.bowlinggreen.chamber.ky.
net

Information Bowling Green Area
Chamber of Commerce, 812 State St,
PO Box 51, 42102; 270/781-3200

In the early days of the community,
county court was held in the house
of Robert Moore, a founder of the
town, and visiting lawyers would idle
away their time bowling on the
lawn—hence the name. A cultural
center for southern Kentucky with a
variety of industries, Bowling Green
is also sustained by Warren County's
dairy cattle, livestock, and tobacco
farms. For a short time, it was the
Confederate capital of Kentucky.

What to See and Do

Beech Bend Park. Water park incl
swimming pool, waterslide, paddleboats; 8 rides, miniature golf; picnic
area, camping. Separate fee for each
activity. (Late May-early Sep, daily)
798 Beech Bend Rd. Phone 270/781-
7634. ¢

Capitol Arts Center. Restored Art
Deco bldg; national and local live
presentations, gallery exhibits. (Mon-
Fri; closed hols) Admission varies
with event. 416 E Main. Phone
270/782-2787.

Historic Riverview at Hobson Grove.
(1857) House in Italianate style, furnished with collection of Victorian
furniture from 1860-90. (Feb-mid-
Dec, Tues-Sun; closed hols) 1100 W
Main Ave, in Hobson Grove Park.
Phone 270/843-5565. ¢¢

★ **National Corvette Museum.**
Hands-on educational exhibits and
displays on history of this classic
American car. More than 50 vintage
cars. (Daily; closed Jan 1, Thanksgiving, Dec 25) I-65 exit 28. Phone
270/781-7973. ¢¢¢

Western Kentucky University. (1906)
15,800 students. High on a hill,
Western Kentucky Univ was built
around the site of a Civil War fort.
College St & 15th St. Phone 270/745-
0111. On campus are

Kentucky Museum. Collections incl
costumes, implements, art works,
and textiles relating to the cultural
history of Kentucky and the
region. Exhibits, tours, special programs. Gift shop. (Tues-Sun; closed
univ hols) Kentucky Bldg, Kentucky St. Phone 270/745-2592. ¢ In
same bldg is

Kentucky Library. Contains 30,000
books, manuscripts, maps, broad-
sides, photographs, sheet music,
scrapbooks, materials relating to
Kentucky and to genealogical
research of Kentucky families.
(Mon-Sat; closed univ hols) 1 Big
Red Way. Phone 270/745-2592.
FREE

Hardin Planetarium. Varying programs yr-round. 1 Big Red Way.
Phone 270/745-4044 for schedule
and fees.

Motels/Motor Lodges

★★ **BEST WESTERN CONTINEN-
TAL INN.** *700 Interstate Dr (42101),
I-65N Exit 28, at US 31W.* 502/781-
5200; fax 502/782-0314; toll-free
800/528-1234. 100 rms, 2 story. S
$40-$50; D $50-$70; each addl $3;
higher rates special events. Complimentary continental bkfst. Crib $3.
TV; cable. Heated pool; wading pool.
Restaurant open 24 hrs. Ck-out
noon. Business servs avail. Cr cds: A,
D, DS, MC, V.
⛱ 🐾 ♿ SC

★★ **BEST WESTERN INN.** *166
Cumberland Trace Rd (42102), 1 blk E
of I-65 Exit 22.* 270/782-3800; fax
502/782-2384. 179 rms, 2-3 story. S,
D $62-$69; suites $99-$110. Crib
free. TV; cable. 2 pools, 1 indoor;
wading pool, whirlpool. Playground.
Restaurant open 24 hrs. Ck-out
noon. Coin lndry. Meeting rms. Sundries. Gift shop. Tennis. Exercise
equipt; sauna. Game rm. Lawn
games. Some refrigerators. Enclosed
courtyard. Cr cds: A, DS, MC, V.
D 🦌 ⛱ 🏃 🐾 ♿

★★ **FAIRFIELD INN.** *1940 Mel
Browning St (42104), I-65 Exit 22.*
502/782-6933; fax 502/782-6967; toll-
free 800/228-2800. 105 rms, 3 story. S
$52; D $59; under 18 free. Crib free.
TV; cable (premium). Heated pool.
Complimentary continental bkfst.
Restaurant adj 6 am-10 pm. Ck-out

noon. Meeting rms. Business servs avail. In-rm modem link. Refrigerator avail. Cr cds: A, D, DS, MC, V.

D ⊠ ⊠ 🔥 SC

★ **GREENWOOD EXECUTIVE INN.** *1000 Executive Way (42102), 2¾ mi SE, off US 231; 1 blk W of I-65 Exit 22. 502/781-6610; fax 502/781-7985; toll-free 800/354-4394.* 150 rms, 4 story. S $45-$55; D $55-$65; each addl $5; suites $95-$130; higher rates special events. Crib $5. TV; cable (premium), VCR avail (movies). Pool. Restaurant 6 am-2 pm, 5-10 pm. Bar noon-1 am; Fri, Sat to 2 am; entertainment. Ck-out noon. Meeting rms. Business servs avail. Airport, bus depot transportation. Cr cds: A, C, D, DS, MC, V.

D ⊠ ⊠ 🔥 SC

★★ **HAMPTON INN.** *233 Three Springs Rd (42104), I-65 Exit 22, W on KY 231. 502/842-4100; fax 502/782-*

3377; toll-free 800/426-7866. 131 rms, 4 story. S $64; D $74; under 18 free; higher rates special events. Crib avail. TV. Pool. Complimentary continental bkfst. Coffee in rms. Restaurant nearby. Meeting rms. Ck-out noon. Business servs avail. In-rm modem link. Health club privileges. Cr cds: A, C, D, DS, MC, V.

D ⊠ ⊠ 🔥 SC

★★ **HOLIDAY INN.** *3240 Scottsville Rd (42104), 2¾ mi SE on US 231, 1 blk W of I-65 Exit 22. 270/781-1500; fax 270/842-0030; res 800/465-4329. Email bghotel@aol.com; www.hionline. com.* 107 rms, 2 story. S $49-$80; D $90; each addl $10; under 19 free. Crib free. Pet accepted. TV; cable (premium). Pool; wading pool. Restaurant 6:30-10 am, 5-9 pm. Bar 5-10 pm. Ck-out noon. Business servs avail. In-rm modem link. Sun-

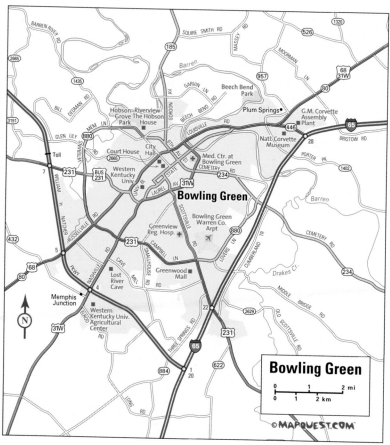

Bowling Green

0   1   2 mi
0   2 km

© MAPQUEST.COM

dries. Exercise equipt. Cr cds: A, DS, MC, V.

★★ **NEW FRIENDSHIP INN.** *3160 Scottsville Rd (42104), 2½ mi E on US 231; 1 blk W of I-65 Exit 22. 270/781-3460; fax 502/781-3463.* 52 rms. S $41; D $45-$59; each addl $3; under 16 free; higher rates special events. Crib free. Pet accepted, some restrictions. TV; cable (premium). Pool. Playground. Complimentary continental bkfst. Restaurant adj 6 am-11 pm. Ck-out 11 am. Business servs avail. Free airport transportation. Refrigerators. Picnic tables, grills. Cr cds: A, DS, MC, V.

Restaurants

★★ **ANDREW'S.** *1423 US 31 Bypass (42104). 270/781-7680.* Specializes in seafood, beef, flambe cooking. Hrs: 11 am-10 pm; Fri, Sat to 11 pm; Sun from 11:30 am. Bar. Lunch, dinner $4.95-$19.95. Child's menu. Red oak paneling with stained and beveled glass. Cr cds: A, DS, MC, V.

★★ **MARIAH'S.** *801 State St (42102). 270/842-6878.* Specializes in steak, seafood, salad. Hrs: 11 am-10 pm; Fri, Sat to 11 pm; Sun to 9 pm. Closed Memorial Day, Labor Day, Dec 25. Bar. Lunch $6.95-$10; dinner $9.95-$15.95. Child's menu. Parking. Historic home from 1800s; large mural of downtown early 1940s. Cr cds: A, D, DS, MC, V.

Breaks Interstate Park

See also Pikeville

(7 mi SE of Elkhorn City, KY and 8 mi N of Haysi, VA on KY-VA 80)

Where the Russell Fork of the Big Sandy River plunges through the mountains is called the "Grand Canyon of the South," the major focus of this 4,600-acre park on the Kentucky-Virginia border. From the entrance, a paved road winds through an evergreen forest and then skirts the canyon rim. Overlooks provide a spectacular view of the "Towers," a huge pyramid of rocks. Within the park are extraordinary rock formations, caves, springs, a profusion of rhododendron and, of course, the five-mile-long, 1,600-foot-deep gorge.

The visitor center houses historical and natural exhibits, including a coal exhibit (Apr-Oct, daily). Laurel Lake is stocked with bass and bluegill. Swimming pool, pedal boats; hiking and bridle trails, mountain bike trails; picnicking, playground, camping (Apr-Oct, fee); motor lodge, cottages (year-round), restaurant, gift shop. Park (daily); facilities (Apr-late Dec, daily). For further information contact Breaks Interstate Park, PO Box 100, Breaks, VA 24607; 540/865-4413 or 800/982-5122. Memorial Day-Labor Day, per car ¢

Cadiz

(D-3) *See also Gilbertsville, Land Between The Lakes*

Pop 2,148 **Elev** 423 ft **Area code** 270 **Zip** 42211
Information Cadiz-Trigg County Tourist Commission, PO Box 735; 270/522-3892; or visit Tourist Information Center, US 68E at I-24 interchange

With the development of "Land Between The Lakes," a 170,000-acre wooded peninsula between the Tennessee Valley Authority's Kentucky Lake and the Army Corps of Engineers' Lake Barkley on the Cumberland River, Cadiz became a staging area for the major recreation project. The area covers much of Trigg County, of which Cadiz is the seat.

What to See and Do

Barkley Dam, Lock, and Lake. (see) 35 mi NW in Gilbertsville. On lakeshore is

  Lake Barkley State Resort Park. A 3,700-acre park on a 57,920-acre lake. Swimming beach, pool, bathhouse (seasonal), fishing, boating, canoeing (ramps, rentals, marina); hiking, backpacking, horseback riding (seasonal); 18-hole golf course (yr-round), tennis, trap-shooting, shuffleboard, basketball. Picnicking, restaurant, cottages, lodge (see RESORT). Camping (fee). Children's programs. Lighted airstrip. Standard fees. 7 mi W on KY 80 to KY 1489. Phone 270/924-1131 or 800/325-1708.

Kenlake State Resort Park. (see) 16 mi SW on US 68, KY 80.

Original Log Cabin. Four-rm log cabin, furnished with 18th- and 19th-century artifacts, was occupied by a single family for more than a century. (Mon-Fri; closed hols) 22 Main St. Phone 270/522-3892. **FREE**

Recreation areas.

Cadiz Public Use Area. Fishing; launching ramp; playground, picnic area. On US 68 on W side of town. **FREE**

Hurricane Creek Public Use Area. Swimming; launching ramp; playground, improved campsites (fee). (Apr-mid-Oct, daily) Golden Age Passport accepted (see MAKING THE MOST OF YOUR TRIP). 12 mi NW via KY 274. Phone 270/522-8821.

Motel/Motor Lodge

★ ★ **COUNTRY INN AND SUITES.** *153 Broadbent Blvd (42211), I-24 Exit 65. 270/522-7007; fax 270/522-3893; toll-free 800/456-4000.* 48 rms, 2 story. S $52; D $57; each addl $5; under 18 free. Crib free. Pet accepted. TV; cable (premium). Pool. Complimentary continental bkfst. Coffee in rms. Restaurant adj. Ck-out noon. Business servs avail. Cr cds: A, C, D, DS, MC, V.

Resort

★ ★ ★ **LAKE BARKLEY STATE RESORT PARK.** *3500 State Park Rd (42211), 10 mi NW on KY 1489, 3½ mi N of US 68 in Lake Barkley State Resort Park. 270/924-1131; fax 270/924-0013; toll-free 800/325-1708. www.state.ky.us.* 124 rms, 2 story, 13 kit. cottages. Apr-Oct: S $59-$74; D $69-$84; each addl $5; suites $160; kit. cottages $150; under 16 free; some lower rates rest of yr. Crib free. TV. Pool; wading pool, whirlpool,

lifeguard in summer. Children's program; playground. Dining rm 7-10:30 am, 11:30 am-2:30 pm, 5-9 pm. Ck-out noon (cottages 11 am), ck-in 4 pm. Coin lndry. Meeting rms. Business servs avail. Maid serv in lodge. Free transportation to lodge from park airport. Lighted tennis. 18-hole golf, greens fee $20. Beach; waterskiing; boats. Lawn games. Trap shooting. Soc dir; entertainment. Rec rm. Exercise rm; sauna, steam rm. Some private patios, balconies. Picnic tables. State-owned; facilities of park avail. Cr cds: A, C, D, DS, MC, V.

Campbellsville

See also Jamestown

Pop 9,577 **Elev** 813 ft **Area code** 270 **Zip** 42718
Web www.campbellsvilleky.com
Information Taylor County Tourist Commision, Court St & Broadway, PO Box 4021, 42719; 270/465-3786 or 800/738-4719

Located geographically in the heart of Kentucky, Campbellsville is near the junction of the Pennyrile, Bluegrass, and Knobs regions of the state. Nearby, at Tebbs Bend, the Battle of Green River was fought on July 4, 1863. Also in the vicinity is the town of Greensburg, with its interesting historic district dating to the 18th century.

What to See and Do

Green River Lake State Park. Beach, fishing, marina (rentals); picnicking, camping. (Daily) Standard fees. 6 mi S on KY 55. Phone 270/465-8255.

Motels/Motor Lodges

★ ★ **CAMPBELLSVILLE LODGE.** *1400 E Broadway (42718). 270/465-7001; fax 270/465-7001; res 800/528-1234; toll-free 800/770-0430. Email bwestern@kyol.net; www.bestwestern lodge.com.* 60 rms. S $52; each addl $5; suites $55-$89; under 18 free. Crib free. TV; cable (premium). Pool;

whirlpool. Playground. Complimentary continental bkfst. Restaurant nearby. Ck-out 11 am. Meeting rms. Business servs avail. In-rm modem link. Some refrigerators, microwaves. Cr cds: A, DS, MC, V.

★ **LAKEVIEW MOTEL.** *1291 Old Lebanon Rd (42718), 1 mi N on KY 289, across from lake.* 270/465-8139; toll-free 800/242-2874. 16 rms, 1 story. Crib avail. TV; cable. Ck-out 11 am, ck-in 11 pm. Business servs avail. Cr cds: A, D, MC, V.

Restaurant

★ **CREEKSIDE.** *350 W Broadway (42718).* 270/465-7777. Specializes in beef, seafood, regional dishes. Salad bar. Hrs: 11 am-9 pm; Fri, Sat to 10 pm. Res accepted. Lunch $1.95-$7.95. Buffet Sun: $7.95; dinner $2.50-$15.95. Buffet Sat: $11.95. Child's menu. Cr cds: MC, V.

Carrollton (B-5)

Founded 1794 **Pop** 3,715 **Elev** 469 ft
Area code 502 **Zip** 41008
Information Carroll County Tourism Commission, PO Box 293; 502/732-7036 or 800/325-4290

At the confluence of the Ohio and Kentucky rivers, this tree-shaded residential town is named in honor of Charles Carroll. Originally from Carrollton, Maryland, Carroll was one of the signers of the Declaration of Independence.

What to See and Do

General Butler State Resort Park. A 791-acre memorial to William O. Butler, native of Carrollton and hero of Battle of New Orleans. Within the park is a 30-acre lake. Swimming, fishing, boating (rentals); nature trails, 9-hole golf (fee), tennis, ski area (fee). Picnic sites, playground, grocery adj; cottages, lodge, and dining room (see RESORT). Tent and trailer camping (daily, standard fees). Recreation program. 2 mi S on KY

227. Phone 502/732-4384 for fees or information.

Historic District. Self-guided auto tour of historic sites and houses. Tour begins at Old Stone Jail, corner of Highland & Court Sts. Tourist center on 2nd floor houses small museum on local history. **FREE**

Annual Events

Kentucky Scottish Weekend. Celebration of Scottish heritage incl pipe bands, bagpipers; Scottish athletic competition, Celtic music; British auto show. Phone 502/239-2665. Second wkend May.

Blues to the Point—Two Rivers Blues Festival. Point Park. Two-day event with regional and national blues music performances. Early Sep.

Motels/Motor Lodges

★ **DAYS INN.** *61 Inn Rd (41008), I-71 Exit 44.* 502/732-9301; fax 502/732-5596; toll-free 800/329-7466. 84 rms. S, D $55; each addl $6; under 19 free; higher rates special events. Crib free. TV; cable (premium). Pool. Complimentary bkfst buffet. Ck-out noon. Meeting rms. Business servs avail. In-rm modem link. Downhill ski 2 mi. Microwaves avail. Cr cds: A, C, D, DS, MC, V.

★★ **HOLIDAY INN EXPRESS.** *141 Inn Rd (41008), at I-71 Exit 44.* 502/732-6661; fax 502/732-6661; toll-free 800/465-4329. 62 rms, 2 story. S, D $59; each addl $6; under 19 free; some wkend rates; higher rates special events. Crib free. Pet accepted, some restrictions. TV; cable (premium). Complimentary continental bkfst. Restaurant nearby. Ck-out noon. Meeting rm. Business servs avail. In-rm modem link. Downhill ski 2 mi. Microwaves avail. Cr cds: A, C, D, DS, JCB, MC, V.

Resort

★★★ **GENERAL BUTLER STATE RESORT PARK.** *US Hwy 227 (41008), 2 mi N of I-71 Exit 44, in General Butler State Resort Park.* 502/732-4384; fax 502/732-4270; toll-free 800/325-0078. 56 rms in 2-3 story lodge, 23 kit. cottages. No elvtr in lodge. S $55;

D $65; each addl $5; kit. cottages $73-$140; under 17 free. Crib free. TV; cable (premium), VCR avail. Pool; wading pool, lifeguard in summer. Playground. Free supervised children's activities (late May-early Sep). Dining rm 7 am-9 pm. Ck-out noon; cottages 11 am. Meeting rm. Business center. Gift shop. Lighted tennis. 9-hole golf, greens fee $10, miniature golf. Swimming in lake; boats, paddleboats. Downhill ski on site. Private patios, balconies. Picnic tables, grills. State-owned; all facilities of state park. Cr cds: A, C, D, DS, MC, V.

B&B/Small Inn

★ **CARROLLTON INN.** *218 Main St (41008). 502/732-6905; fax 502/732-0318.* 11 rms. S $39.95; D $49.95; each addl $5; under 16 free; higher rates special events. Crib free. TV; cable. Restaurant (see also CARROLLTON INN). Bar. Ck-out 11 am, ck-in noon. Business servs avail. Cr cds: A, MC, V.

Restaurant

★★ **CARROLLTON INN.** *3rd and Main Sts. 502/732-6905.* Specializes in beef, seafood, bbq ribs. Hrs: 11 am-9:30 pm; Fri, Sat to 10 pm; Sun to 8 pm. Closed Dec 25. Res accepted. Bar. Lunch $3-$6; dinner $5.95-$14.95. Child's menu. Cr cds: A, MC, V.

Cave City

See also Glasgow, Horse Cave, Park City

Pop 1,953 **Elev** 636 ft **Area code** 270 **Zip** 42127 **Web** www.cavecity.com

Information Cave City Convention Center, PO Box 518; 270/773-3131 or 800/346-8908

Located in the heart of Cave Country, this village primarily serves tourists passing through the region en route to Mammoth Cave and other commercially operated caves nearby.

What to See and Do

Crystal Onyx Cave. Helectites, stalagmites, stalactites, onyx columns, rare crystal onyx rimstone formations; Native American burial site dating from 680 BC. Temperature in cave 54°F. Guided tours every 45 min. Improved and primitive camping adj (fee). (Feb-Dec, daily; closed Thanksgiving, Dec 25) 2 mi SE on KY 90, off I-65. 8709 Happy Valley Rd. Phone 270/773-2359. Guided tours ¢¢

Kentucky Action Park. Chairlift to top of mountain, slide downhill in individual alpine sleds with braking system. Go-carts, bumper boats, bumper cars (fees); horseback riding (fee). (Memorial Day-Labor Day, daily; Easter-Memorial Day, Labor Day-Oct, wkends) 1½ mi W on KY 70. Phone 270/773-2636. ¢¢

Mammoth Cave Chair Lift and Guntown Mountain. Lift ascends 1,350 ft to Guntown Mt. On grounds is authentic reproduction of 1880s frontier town; museums, saloon, entertainment. Train ride (fee). Water slide. Onyx Cave tours (Apr-Nov, daily). (Memorial Day-Labor Day, daily; May-Memorial Day and Labor Day-mid-Oct, Sat, Sun only) Admission incl chair lift. At jct KY 70, I-65. Phone 270/773-3530. ¢¢

Mammoth Cave National Park. (see) 10 mi W via I-65, KY 70.

Motels/Motor Lodges

★ **DAYS INN.** *822 Mammoth Cave St (42127), ¾ mi W on KY 70; 2 blks NE of I-65 Exit 53. 270/773-2151; fax 502/773-2151.* 110 rms, 2 story. Late May-early Sep: S $56; D $66; each addl $5; under 12 free; lower rates rest of yr. Crib free. Pet accepted. TV; cable (premium); VCR avail (movies). Heated pool; wading pool. Restaurant 6 am-10 pm (seasonal). Ck-out noon. Coin lndry. Meeting rms. Business servs avail. Game rm. Some in-rm whirlpools. Private patios, balconies. Cr cds: A, C, D, DS, JCB, MC, V.

★★ **HOLIDAY INN.** *Hwy 90 & I-65; 102 Happy Valley Rd (88401), I-65 Exit 53. 502/773-3101; fax 615/773-6082; toll-free 800/465-4329. Email cav@ musselmanhotels.com; www.mussel*

manhotels.com. 105 rms, 2 story. Memorial Day-Labor Day: S, D $62-$67; each addl $5; under 18 free; higher rates Highland Games; lower rates rest of yr. Crib free. Pet accepted; $7. TV; cable (premium). Complimentary continental bkfst, coffee in rms. Restaurant nearby. Ck-out 11 am. Meeting rms. Business servs avail. In-rm modem link. Coin lndry. Heated pool. Game rm. Some refrigerators, microwaves. Picnic tables, grills. Cr cds: A, C, D, DS, JCB, MC, V.

★ **KUNTICKY INN.** *1009 Doyle Ave (42127), I-65 Exit 53.* 502/773-3161; fax 502/773-5494; toll-free 800/528-1234. 50 rms. Mid-May-early Sep: S $59-$69; D $64-$69; each addl $5; under 12 free; higher rates special events; lower rates rest of yr. Crib $5. TV; cable. Pool; wading pool. Complimentary coffee in lobby. Restaurant opp 5 am-11 pm. Ck-out 11 am. Coin lndry. Cr cds: A, C, D, DS, MC, V.

★★ **QUALITY INN.** *Mammoth Cave Rd (42127), W on KY 70, 90.* 502/773-2181; fax 502/773-3200; toll-free 800/321-4245. 100 rms, 2 story. Memorial Day-Labor Day: S $42-$62; D $48-$68; each addl $6; under 12 free; higher rates special events; lower rates rest of yr. Crib $6. Pet accepted. TV; cable (premium). Pool. Playground. Restaurant to 11 pm. Ck-out 11 am. Business servs avail. Game rm. Picnic tables. Cr cds: A, C, D, DS, MC, V.

★ **SUPER 8 MOTEL.** *88 Stockpen Rd (42765), I-65 Exit 65.* 502/524-4888; fax 502/524-5888; toll-free 800/800-8000. 50 rms, 2 story. May-mid-Sep: S $47; D $51; each addl $4; under 12 free; higher rates special events; lower rates rest of yr. Crib free. Pet accepted; $6. TV; cable (premium). Complimentary continental bkfst. Restaurant nearby. Ck-out 11 am. Business servs avail. Some in-rm whirlpools. Cr cds: A, C, D, DS, MC, V.

Restaurant

★ **SAHARA STEAK HOUSE.** *413 E Happy Valley St (42127).* 270/773-3450. Specializes in steak, seafood. Salad bar. Hrs: 11 am-9 pm; Sat from 3 pm. Closed Thanksgiving, Dec 25. Lunch $2.95-$6.95; dinner $4.95-$23.95. Child's menu. Cr cds: A, C, D, DS, MC, V.

Corbin

(D-6) *See also Barbourville, London, Williamsburg*

Settled 1883 **Pop** 7,419 **Elev** 1,080 ft
Area code 606 **Zip** 40701
Information Tourist & Convention Commission, 101 N Depot St; 606/528-6390 or 800/528-7123

What to See and Do

Colonel Harland Sanders' Original Restaurant. (1940) Authentic restoration of the first Kentucky Fried Chicken restaurant. Displays incl original kitchen, artifacts, motel rm. Original dining area is still in use. (Daily; closed Dec 25) 2 mi N on US 25. **FREE**

Cumberland Falls State Resort Park. (see) 19 mi SW via US 18W, KY 90.

Laurel River Lake. A 5,600-acre lake with fishing; boating (launch, rentals); hiking, recreation areas, picnicking, camping (fee). (See ANNUAL EVENT) Contact the US Army Corps of Engineers, Resource Manager, 1433 Laurel Lake Rd, London 40741. For camping information, contact London District Ranger, US Forest Service, PO Box 907, London 40741; 606/864-4163. Approx 10 mi W, in Daniel Boone National Forest (see); access from I-75, US 25W, KY 312 & KY 192. Phone 606/864-6412. **FREE**

Annual Event

Nibroc Festival. Costumes, mountain arts and crafts, parade, horse shows, square dancing, beauty pageant, midway, entertainment, food booths. Boat races on Laurel River Lake. Early Aug.

Motels/Motor Lodges

★★ **BEST WESTERN INN.** *2630 Cumberland Falls Rd (40701), I-75 Exit 25.* 606/528-2100; fax 606/523-1704; res 888/528-2100; toll-free 800/528-

1234. Email bestwest@2geton.net; www.2geton.net/bestwest. 63 rms, 2 story. S, D $49.99; under 12 free. Crib free. TV; cable (premium). Pool. Complimentary continental bkfst, coffee in rms. Ck-out 11 am. Business servs avail. Some refrigerators; microwaves avail. Cr cds: A, C, D, DS, MC, V.

D ⊠ ⊠ 🐾 SC

★ **KNIGHTS INN.** *37 Hwy 770 (40701), I-75 Exit 29. 606/523-1500; fax 606/523-5818; toll-free 800/843-5644.* 109 rms, 10 kits. S $37.75; D $44.95; each addl $6; kit. units $49; under 18 free; wkly rates. Crib $2. TV; cable (premium). Pool. Restaurant nearby. Ck-out noon. Cr cds: A, C, D, DS, MC, V.

D ⊠ ⊠ 🔥 🐾 SC

Covington (Cincinnati Airport Area)

(B-6) *See also Walton*

Founded 1815 **Pop** 43,264 **Elev** 531 ft
Area code 606
Web www.nkycvb.com/
Information Northern Kentucky Convention and Visitors Bureau, 50 E River Center Blvd, Suite 40, 41011; 606/261-4677 or 800/782-9659

This town is linked to Cincinnati, Ohio, by five broad bridges spanning the Ohio River. Named for a hero of the War of 1812, Covington in its early days had many German settlers who left their mark on the city. East of the city, the Licking River meets the Ohio. The suspension bridge (1867) that crosses from Third and Greenup streets to Cincinnati is the prototype of the Brooklyn Bridge in New York City. The adjacent riverfront area includes Covington Landing, a floating restaurant-entertainment complex.

What to See and Do

Cathedral Basilica of the Assumption. (1901) Patterned after the Abbey of St. Denis and the Cathedral of Notre Dame, France, the basilica has massive doors, classic stained-glass windows (incl one of the largest in the world), murals, and mosaics by local and foreign artists. (Daily exc hols) Guided tours (Sun, after 10 am mass; also by appt). Madison Ave & 12th St. Phone 606/431-2060. Tour ¢

Devou Park. A 550-acre park with lake overlooking the Ohio River. Golf (fee), tennis. Picnic grounds. Lookout point, outdoor concerts (mid-June-mid-Aug). (Daily) Western Ave. Phone 606/292-2151. **FREE** In park is

Behringer-Crawford Museum. Exhibits on local archaeology, paleontology, history, fine art, and wildlife. (Tues-Sun) 1600 Montague Rd. Phone 606/491-4003. ¢

MainStrasse Village. Approx 5 sq blks in Covington's old German area. Historic district of residences, shops, and restaurants in more than 20 restored bldgs dating from mid-late 1800s. (See ANNUAL EVENTS) Phone 606/491-0458. Also featured in the

Carroll Chimes Bell Tower. Completed in 1979, this 100-ft tower has a 43-bell carillon and mechanical figures that portray the legend of the Pied Piper of Hamelin. Philadelphia St, W end of Village.

Oldenberg Brewery/Museum. Functioning microbrewery with guided tours; large brewing memorabilia collection; replica 1930s beer truck; beer garden (seasonal); pub; gift shop. (Daily) 400 Buttermilk Pike, Fort Mitchell 41017. Phone 606/341-2802. Museum tour ¢¢

Riverboat cruises. Sightseeing cruises on the Ohio River; also lunch, dinner, and moonlight cruises. Full-day and ½-day cruises by appt. Contact BB Riverboats, 1 Madison Ave, 41011; or Queen City Riverboats, 303 O'Fallon St, PO Box 131, Dayton 41074. Phone 606/261-8500 (BB Riverboats) or 606/292-8687 (Queen City Riverboats). ¢¢

Annual Events

Jim Beam Stakes Race. Turfway Park Race Track in Florence. One of the largest pursed Thoroughbred races for 3-yr-olds. Race culminates wk-long festival. Phone 606/371-0200. Last Sat in Mar.

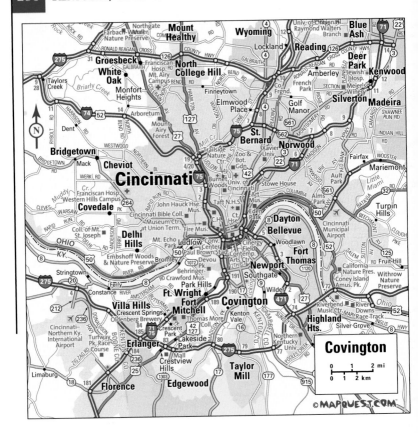

Covington

0   1   2 mi
0 1 2 km

©MAPQUEST.COM

Maifest. MainStrasse Village. Traditional German spring festival with entertainment, arts and crafts, food, games, and rides. Phone 606/491-0458. Third wkend May.

Riverfest. Banks of Ohio River. One of the largest fireworks displays in the country; shot from barges moored on river. Labor Day wkend.

Oktoberfest. MainStrasse Village. Entertainment, arts and crafts, food. Early Sep.

Seasonal Event

Horse racing. Turfway Park Race Course. 3 mi SW at 7500 Turfway in Florence. Thoroughbred racing Wed-Sun. Phone 606/371-0200 or 800/733-0200. Early Sep-early Oct and late Nov-early Apr.

Motels/Motor Lodges

★★ **BEST WESTERN INN.** *7821 Commerce Dr (41042), I-75/71 Exit 181, 1 blk E to Commerce Dr. 606/525-0090; fax 606/525-6743; toll-free 800/*

528-1234. 51 rms, 3 story. June-Sep: S, D $59-$69; each addl $5; under 12 free; higher rates special events; lower rates rest of yr. Crib free. TV; cable (premium). Complimentary continental bkfst. Restaurant nearby. Ck-out 11 am. Business servs avail. Pool. Some bathrm phones, in-rm whirlpools, refrigerators, wet bars. Cr cds: A, C, D, DS, MC, V.

D ⊷ ⊠ ⊠ ⊠ SC

★★ **COURTYARD BY MARRIOTT.** *46 Cavalier Blvd (41042), I-71/75 Exit 182. 606/371-6464; fax 606/371-3443.* 78 rms, 3 story. S, D $99-$149; suites $165-$200; under 18 free; higher rates Jazzfest (3-day min). Crib free. TV; cable (premium). Complimentary coffee in rms. Restaurant adj 7 am-11 pm. Ck-out noon. Meeting rms. Business servs avail. In-rm modem link. Valet serv. Guest lndry. Exercise equipt. Indoor pool; whirlpool. Bathrm phones; some in-rm whirlpools, refrigerators, microwaves. Cr cds: A, D, DS, MC, V.

D ⊷ ⊠ ✕ ⊠ ⊠

★★ **CROSS COUNTRY INN-GREATER CINCINNATI.** *7810 Commerce Dr (41042), I-75 Exit 181. 606/283-2030; fax 606/283-0171; res 800/521-1429. www.crosscountryinns.com.* 112 rms, 2 story. S $39.99; D $46.99; each addl $7; under 17 free. Crib avail. Parking lot. Pool. TV; cable (premium). Complimentary toll-free calls. Restaurant nearby. Ck-out noon, ck-in 1 pm. Business servs avail. Video games. Cr cds: A, C, D, DS, MC, V.

⬛ 🏊 ➡️ 🔥

★★ **FAIRFIELD INN.** *50 Cavalier Blvd (41042), I-75 Exit 182. 859/371-4800; fax 859/371-4800. Email kalahar@aol.com.* 135 rms, 3 story. S, D $52-$68; under 18 free; higher rates special events. Crib free. TV; cable (premium). Heated pool. Complimentary continental bkfst. Restaurant adj 11 am-10 pm. Ck-out noon. Meeting rm. Business servs avail. In-rm modem link. Valet serv. Health club privileges. Cr cds: A, D, DS, MC, V.

⬛ 🏊 🏋️ 🎿 ➡️ 🔥

★★ **HAMPTON INN.** *7393 Turfway Rd (41042), I-75 Exit 182. 606/283-1600; fax 606/283-0680; toll-free 800/426-7866. Email cvgsfol@hi-hotel.com.* 117 rms, 4 story. S, D $76-$79; under 18 free; higher rates: special events, Dec 31. Crib free. TV; cable (premium). Pool. Complimentary continental bkfst. Coffee in rms. Restaurant adj 7-2 am. Ck-out noon. Meeting rms. Business servs avail. Sundries. Free airport transportation. Cr cds: A, C, D, DS, JCB, MC, V.

⬛ 🏊 🏋️ ➡️ 🔥

★★★ **HOLIDAY INN.** *2100 Dixie Hwy (41011), 8 mi SW on I-75/71, Exit 188B. 606/331-1500; fax 606/331-2259.* 214 rms, 2 story. S, D $109-$129; under 18 free; family, wkend rates; higher rates: special events, Jazz Festival. Crib free. TV; cable. Indoor pool; whirlpool. Playground. Complimentary coffee in rms. Restaurant 6 am-2 pm, 5-11 pm. Ck-out 11 am. Meeting rms. Business servs avail. In-rm modem link. Bellhops. Valet serv. Sundries. Free airport transportation. Exercise equipt.

Health club privileges. Game rm. Cr cds: A, DS, MC, V.

⬛ 🏊 🏋️ ➡️ 🔥

★ **KNIGHTS INN.** *8049 Dream St (41042), jct I-75/71 and US 42/127, Exit 180. 606/371-9711; fax 606/371-4325; toll-free 800/843-5644.* 116 rms, 10 kits. S, D $37-$62; each addl $6; kit. units $48-$58; under 18 free. Crib free. Pet accepted, some restrictions. TV; cable (premium). Pool. Restaurant nearby. Ck-out noon. Meeting rm. Business servs avail. Some microwaves. Cr cds: A, C, D, DS, MC, V.

⬛ 🐾 🏊 ➡️ 🔥 SC

★★★ **RESIDENCE INN.** *2811 Circleport Dr (41018), W on I-275 Exit 2. 606/282-7400; fax 606/282-1790; res 800/331-3131.* 96 suites, 3 story. No elvtr. Suites $79-$179; higher rates special events. Crib free. Pet accepted; $100. TV; cable (premium), VCR avail. Heated pool; whirlpool. Complimentary continental bkfst, coffee in rms. Ck-out noon. Meeting rms. Business servs avail. In-rm modem link. Valet serv. Sundries. Coin lndry. Free airport transportation. Exercise equipt. Refrigerators, microwaves; some fireplaces. Picnic tables, grills. Cr cds: A, C, D, DS, MC, V.

⬛ 🐾 🏊 🏋️ ✈️ ➡️ 🔥 SC

★★ **SIGNATURE INN TURFWAY.** *30 Cavalier Ct (41042), I-75/71, Exit 182 (Turfway Rd). 606/371-0081; fax 606/371-0081.* 125 rms, 2 story. S, D $65-$75; each addl $7; under 18 free; wkend rates; higher rates special events. Crib free. TV; cable (premium); VCR avail. Pool. Complimentary continental bkfst. Restaurant adj 5:30 am-10:30 pm. Ck-out noon. Meeting rms. Business center. In-rm modem link. Valet serv. Free airport transportation. Health club privileges. Cr cds: A, DS, MC, V.

⬛ 🏊 🏋️ ➡️ 🔥 🚶

Hotels

★★★ **CLARION HOTEL RIVERVIEW.** *668 W 5th St (41011), at I-71/75 Exit 192. 606/491-1200; fax 606/491-0326; res 800/292-2079. www.choicehotels.com.* 236 rms, 18 story. S, D $74-$104; suites $199; under 18 free. Crib free. TV; cable (premium). Indoor/outdoor pool; whirlpool, poolside serv. Coffee in rms. Restaurants 7-1 am (see also RIVERVIEW). Rm serv to 11 pm. Bars from 11 am. Ck-out 11 am. Meeting rms. Business servs avail. In-rm modem link. Gift shop. Barber. Free airport transportation. Exercise equipt. Rec rm. Cr cds: A, C, D, DS, MC, V.

★★ DRAWBRIDGE INN AND CONVENTION CENTER. 2477 Royal Dr (41017), at I-75/71 Exit 186. 859/341-2800; fax 859/341-5644; toll-free 800/354-9793. Email info@ drawbridgeinn.com; www.drawbridge inn.com. 477 rms, 8 suites. Apr-Oct: S, D $119; each addl $10; suites $250; under 17 free; lower rates rest of yr. Crib avail. Parking lot. Indoor/outdoor pools, lifeguard, whirlpool. TV; cable (premium), VCR avail. Complimentary coffee in rms, newspaper. Restaurant noon-midnight. Bar. Ck-out noon, ck-in 3 pm. Conference center, meeting rms. Business center. Bellhops. Concierge. Dry cleaning, coin lndry. Gift shop. Salon/barber. Free airport transportation. Exercise privileges, sauna. Golf. Tennis, 2 courts. Downhill skiing. Picnic facilities. Video games. Cr cds: A, C, D, DS, JCB, MC, V.

★★ HAMPTON INN RIVERFRONT (DOWNTOWN AREA). 200 Crescent Ave (41011), on I-75/71 Exit 192. 859/581-7800; fax 859/581-8282; res 800/426-7866. Email cvgky01@hi-hotel.com; www.hampton-inn.com. 151 rms, 6 story. S $79-$84; D $84-$91; under 18 free; wkend rates (summer); higher rates special events. Crib free. TV; cable (premium). Complimentary continental bkfst. Coffee in rms. Restaurant nearby. Ck-out noon. Meeting rms. Business servs avail. In-rm modem link. Valet serv (Mon-Fri). Exercise equipt. Indoor pool. Cr cds: A, DS, MC, V.

★★★ HILTON INN. 7373 Turfway Rd (41042), I-75 Exit 182. 606/371-4400; fax 606/371-3361; toll-free 800/ 932-3322. www.hilton.com. 206 units, 5 story. S $99-$129; D $109-139; each addl $10; suites $159-$399; family, wkend rates. Crib free. TV; cable (premium). Pool; poolside serv. Coffee in rms. Restaurant 6:30 am-11 pm. Bar; entertainment. Ck-out noon. Meeting rms. Business servs avail. In-rm modem link. Bellhops. Concierge. Gift shop. Free airport transportation. Tennis. Exercise equipt; sauna. Some refrigerators; microwaves avail. Elaborate landscaping. Original artwork. Luxury level. Cr cds: A, C, D, DS, JCB, MC, V.

★★★ HOLIDAY INN. 1717 Airport Exchange Blvd (41018), I-275 Exit Mineola Pike. 606/371-2233; fax 606/371-5002. 306 rms, 6 story. S, D $95-$119; suites $149-$175; under 18 free; higher rates special events. Crib free. TV; cable (premium). Indoor pool; whirlpool. Complimentary coffee in rms. Restaurant 6 am-11 pm. Bar. Ck-out noon. Coin lndry. Convention facilities. Business center. In-rm modem link. Gift shop. Free airport transportation. Exercise equipt; sauna. Microwaves avail. Minibar in suites. Cr cds: A, D, DS, JCB, MC, V.

All Suite

★★★ EMBASSY SUITES. 10 E River Center Blvd (41011). 859/261-8400; fax 859/261-8486; toll-free 800/362-2779. Email escr@fuse.net; www. embassy-suites.com. 226 rms, 8 story. 226 suites. June-Sep: S $149; D $159; each addl $10; under 17 free; lower rates rest of yr. Crib avail. Pet accepted, some restrictions. Valet parking avail. Indoor pool, whirlpool. TV; cable. Complimentary full bkfst, coffee in rms, newspaper, toll-free calls. Restaurant 7 am-10 pm. Bar. Ck-out noon, ck-in 3 pm. Meeting rms. Business center. Bellhops. Dry cleaning, coin lndry. Gift shop. Exercise privileges, sauna. Golf. Cr cds: A, C, D, DS, MC, V.

Restaurants

★★ DEE FELICE CAFE. 529 Main St (41011). 606/261-2365. Specializes in Creole and Cajun dishes. Own pasta. Hrs: 11 am-2:30 pm, 5-11 pm. Closed hols. Res accepted. Bar. Lunch $5.95-$9.95; dinner $12.95-$18.95. Entertainment: jazz nightly. Street parking. Bistro cafe atmosphere. Cr cds: A, C, D, DS, MC, V.

★★ **MIKE FINK.** *Foot of Greenup St (41011), near Covington Landing.* 606/261-4212. Specializes in fresh seafood, raw bar. Hrs: 11 am-10 pm; Sat to 11 pm; Sun 10 am-9 pm. Res accepted. Bar. Lunch $5-$9; dinner $11-$29. Parking. Old paddlewheel steamer, permanently moored. Scenic view of Cincinnati. Cr cds: A, C, D, DS, MC, V.

D ⬛

★ **ORIENTAL WOK.** *317 Buttermilk Pike (41017), SW via I-75 Exit 186, 3 blks E on Buttermilk Pike.* 606/331-3000. Specializes in Cantonese and Szechwan dishes. Hrs: 11 am-9:30 pm; Fri to 10:30 pm; Sat 4-10:30 pm; Sun from 11:30 am. Closed Thanksgiving, Dec 25. Res accepted. Bar. Lunch $4.95-$7.50; dinner $7.50-$16.95. Child's menu. Entertainment: Fri, Sat. Parking. Fountain with goldfish. Cr cds: A, D, DS, MC, V.

D ⬛

★★ **RIVERVIEW.** *668 W 5th St, I-75/71 Exit 192.* 606/491-5300. Specializes in steak, seafood. Own desserts. Hrs: 11:30 am-2 pm, 5-10 pm; Fri, Sat 5-11 pm; Sun 5-9 pm. Closed Dec 25. Res accepted. Bar. Wine list. Lunch $4.95-$9.95; dinner $16.95-$24.95. Sun brunch $13.95. Child's menu. Entertainment: harpist. Parking. On 18th floor. Revolving restaurant overlooking river, Cincinnati skyline. Cr cds: A, C, D, DS, MC, V.

D ⬛

★★★ **SOUTH BEACH GALLERY AT THE WATER.** *14 Pete Rose Pier (41011), on River.* 606/581-1414. www.waterfrontinc.com. Specializes in seafood, steak, chops. Raw bar. Sushi bar. Hrs: 5:30-10 pm; Sat from 5 pm; Sun 5-9 pm. Res accepted. Bar. Dinner $16.95-$31.50. Entertainment: pianist Tues-Sat. Valet parking. Elegant, 2-story floating restaurant with panoramic view of Cincinnati skyline. Art Deco decor with tropical accents. Cr cds: A, C, D, MC, V.

D ⬛

Unrated Dining Spot

BB RIVERBOATS. *1 Madison Ave (41011), Covington Landing, on Riverfront.* 606/261-8500. Email bbriver@

one.net; www.bbriverboats.com. Specializes in beef, chicken. Hrs: 9 am-10 pm. Res required. Bar. Lunch complete meals: $19.50-$20.50; dinner complete meals: $27.95-$34.95. Child's menu. Parking. Cruises on Ohio River, at the Port of Cincinnati. Limited cruises Nov-Apr. Cr cds: A, C, D, DS, MC, V.

D **SC**

Cumberland Falls State Resort Park

See also Corbin, Williamsburg

(19 mi SW of Corbin via US 25W, KY 90)

In this 1,657-acre park on the Cumberland River is a magnificent waterfall, 65 feet high and 125 feet wide, amid beautiful scenery. Surrounded by Daniel Boone National Forest (see), this awesome waterfall is the second largest east of the Rockies. By night, when the moon is full and the sky clear, a mysterious moonbow appears in the mist. This is the only place in the Western Hemisphere where this phenomenon can be seen. Swimming pool (seasonal); fishing; nature trails, nature center, riding (seasonal), tennis. Picnicking, playground, lodge (see RESORT), cottages. Tent and trailer campsites (standard fees). For information phone 800/325-0063.

What to See and Do

Big South Fork National River/Recreation Area. (See JAMESTOWN, TN) Approx 12 mi W on KY 90, then approx 25 mi S on US 27 to Oneida, TN, then 20 mi W on TN 297.

Blue Heron Mining Community. Recreated mid-20th Century mining town where 300 miners were once employed. Depot has exhibits on history of town with scale models, photographs. Town features giant coal tipple built in 1937 and metal frame representations of miners' houses, church, school, company store. Snack bar and gift shop (Apr-Oct). A scenic railway line connects Blue Heron with the town of Stearns (see SOMERSET). In Big South Fork National River/Recreation Area (KY side); S via US 27 and KY 92 to Stearns, then 9 mi W on KY 742 (Mine 18 Rd). Phone 606/376-3787 (KY) or 931/879-3625 (TN). **FREE**

Sheltowee Trace Outfitters. River rafting, canoeing, and "funyak" trips in the scenic Cumberland River Gorge below the falls; Big South Fork Gorge, Rockcastle River. Five- to 7-hr trips, appointments necessary. (Memorial Day-Sep; daily; Apr-mid-May and Sep-Oct, Sat and Sun). For information contact Sheltowee Trace Outfitters, PO Box 1060, Whitley City 42653. Phone 606/376-5567 or 800/541-7238. ¢¢¢¢

Resort

★★ CUMBERLAND FALLS STATE PARK. *7351 Hwy 90 (40701), in Cumberland Falls State Resort Park. 606/528-4121; fax 606/528-0704; toll-free 800/325-0063.* 52 rms in 3-story lodge, 26 kit. cottages. Apr-Oct: S $55; D $65; each addl $5; kit. cottages for 1-4, $67-$81; cottages for 6-8, $130; under 17 free; lower lodge rates Nov-Mar. Closed 5 days late Dec. Crib free. TV. Pool; wading pool, lifeguard. Dining rm 7-10:30 am, 11:30 am-4 pm, 5-8 pm. Ck-out noon, cottages 11 am; ck-in 4 pm. Meeting rms. Business servs avail. Gift shop. Tennis. Lawn games. Rec dir. Rec rm. Hiking trails. Fireplace in most cottages. On river. State-operated. Cr cds: A, C, D, DS, MC, V.

D ⬤ ♨ 🏃 ⛱ 🎿 🔥

Cumberland Gap National Historical Park

See also Pineville; also see Harrogate, TN

Web www.nps.gov/cuga/index.htm

Information Park Superintendent, US 25E, Box 1848, Middlesboro 40965; 606/248-2817.

Cumberland Gap, a natural passage through the mountain barrier that effectively sealed off the infant American coastal colonies, was the open door to western development. Through this pass first came Dr. Thomas Walker in 1750, followed by Daniel Boone in 1769. In 1775, Boone and 30 axmen cut a 208-mile swath through the forests from Kingsport, Tennessee, to the Kentucky River, passing through the Cumberland Gap. Settlers poured through the pass and along Boone's "Wilderness Road," and in 1777 Kentucky became Virginia's westernmost county. Although pioneers were harassed by Native Americans during the Revolution, travel over the Wilderness Road continued to increase and became heavier than ever. After the Revolution, the main stream of western settlement poured through Cumberland Gap and slowed only when more direct northerly routes were opened. During the Civil War, the gap was a strategic point, changing hands several times.

Nearly 22,300 acres of this historic and dramatically beautiful countryside in Kentucky, Tennessee, and Virginia have been set aside as a national historical park. More than 50 miles of hiking trails provide a variety of walks, long and short. Park (daily; closed Jan 1, Dec 25).

What to See and Do

Camping. Tables, fireplaces, water, and bathhouse. Fourteen-day limit. Off US 58. ¢¢¢

Civil War fortifications. Throughout the Gap area.

Hensley Settlement. An isolated mountain community, now a restored historic site, that is accessible by hiking 3.5 mi up the Chadwell Gap trail or by driving up a jeep road.

Pinnacle Overlook. Broad vistas of mountains and forests viewed from a high peak jutting above the Cumberland valley. Vehicles over 20 ft in length and all trailers are prohibited.

Tri-State Peak. View of meeting point of Kentucky, Virginia, and Tennessee.

Visitor Center. Historical exhibits, audiovisual program. (Closed hols) At W end of park (near Middlesboro).

Daniel Boone National Forest

See also Hazard, London, Morehead, Williamsburg

(Stretches roughly north-south from Morehead on US 60 to Whitley City on US 27)

Within these 692,164 acres is some of the most spectacular scenery in Kentucky, from the Cave Run and Laurel River lakes to the Natural Arch Scenic Area. The forest includes the Red River Gorge Geological Area, known for its natural arches. The gorge has colorful rock formations and cliffs that average 100 to 300 feet high. A scenic loop drive of the gorge begins north of Natural Bridge State Resort Park (see) on KY 77. The nearest camping facilities (fee) are located at Koomer Ridge, on KY 15 between the Slade (33) and Beattyville (40) exits of Mount Parkway.

The Sheltowee Trace National Recreation Trail runs generally north to south, beginning near Morehead (see) and continuing to Pickett State Rustic Park, TN (see JAMESTOWN, TN), a total distance of more than 260 miles. Forest Development Road 918, the main road into the Zilpo Recreation Area, has been designated a National Scenic Byway. The 11.2-mile road features a pleasant, winding trip through Kentucky hardwood forest, with interpretive signs and pull-overs with views of Cave Run Lake.

Cave Run Lake (see MOREHEAD) has swimming beaches, boat ramps, and camping at Twin Knobs and Zilpo recreation areas. Laurel River Lake (see CORBIN) has boat ramps and camping areas at Holly Bay and Grove (vehicle access). Clay Lick (Cave Run Lake), Grove, White Oak (Laurel River Lake) have boat-in camping. Hunting and fishing permitted in most parts of the forest under Kentucky regulations; back-packing is permitted on forest trails. For further information contact the Forest Supervisor, 1700 Bypass Rd, Winchester 40391; 606/745-3100 or 800/255-7275.

Danville

(C-6) *See also Harrodsburg*

Founded 1775 **Pop** 12,420
Elev 989 ft **Area code** 606
Zip 40422
Web www.danville-ky.com
Information Danville-Boyle County Convention & Visitors Bureau, 304 S 4th St; 606/236-7794 or 800/755-0076

Birthplace of Kentucky government, Danville is near the geographical center of the state. Ten yrs after the city was founded, it became the first capital of the Kentucky district of Virginia. Later, nine conventions were held leading to admission of the state to the Union. From 1775-92, Danville was the most important center in Kentucky, the major settlement on the Wilderness Road. "Firsts" seem to come naturally to Danville, which

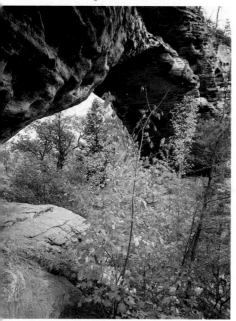

Daniel Boone National Forest

claims the state's first college, first log courthouse, first post office, first brick courthouse, first school for the deaf, and first law school.

One of the largest tobacco markets in the state, Danville has also attracted several industrial plants.

What to See and Do

Constitution Square State Shrine. Authentic reproduction of Kentucky's first courthouse square stands at exact site where first state constitution was framed and adopted in 1792. Original post office; replicas of jail, courthouse, meetinghouse; restored row house, Dr. Goldsmith House, and Grayson Tavern. Governor's Circle has a bronze plaque of each Kentucky governor. Museum store, art gallery. (Daily) On US 127 in center of town, 134 S 2nd. Phone 606/239-7089. **FREE**

Herrington Lake. Formed by Dix Dam, one of the world's largest rock-filled dams, Herrington has 333 mi of shoreline. Balanced fish population maintained through conservation program. Fishing (fee), boat launch (fee; rentals); camping (hookups), cabins. 3 mi N off KY 33. Phone 606/236-4286. **FREE**

Kids Farm Education Center. A working farm open to the public to experience wildlife management techniques, exotic animals, and wild game in a natural setting. (Daily) 636 Quirks Run Rd. Phone 606/236-1414. ¢¢

McDowell House and Apothecary Shop. Residence and shop of Dr Ephraim McDowell, noted surgeon of the early 19th century. Restored and refurbished with period pieces. Large apothecary ware collection. Gardens incl trees, wildflowers, and herbs of the period. (Mar-Oct, daily; rest of yr, Tues-Sun; closed hols) 125 S 2nd St. Phone 606/236-2804. ¢¢

Perryville Battlefield State Historic Site. A 100-acre park, once a field, appears much as it did Oct 8, 1862, when Confederate forces under Gen Braxton Bragg and Union troops under Gen Don Carlos Buell clashed. A total of 4,241 Union soldiers and 1,822 Confederate troops were killed, wounded, or missing. Still standing are the Crawford House, used by Bragg as headquarters, and Bottom House, center of some of the heaviest fighting. Mock

battle is staged each yr (wkend nearest Oct 8). A 30-acre area at the N end of what was the battle line incl a memorial erected in 1902 to the Confederate dead and one raised in 1931 to the Union dead. Museum with artifacts from battle, 9-by-9-ft, detailed battle map, battle dioramas (fee). Hiking. Picnicking, playground. Self-guided tours. (Apr-Oct, daily; rest of yr by appt) 10 mi W on US 150, 4 mi N on US 68. Phone 606/332-8631. **FREE**

Pioneer Playhouse Village-of-the-Arts. Reproduction of an 18th-century Kentucky village on a 200-acre site; drama school, museum. Camping (fee). (See SEASONAL EVENT) (May-mid-Oct, daily) 1 mi S on Stanford Ave, US 150. Phone 606/236-2747. **FREE**

Seasonal Event

Pioneer Playhouse. Pioneer Playhouse Village-of-the-Arts. Summer stock; Broadway comedies, musicals. Tues-Sat eves. Phone 606/236-2747. Mid-June-late Aug.

Motels/Motor Lodges

★ **COUNTRY HEARTH INN.** *US 127 (40422), at jct 127 Bypass, 150 Bypass.* 606/236-8601; fax 606/236-0314. 81 rms, 2 story. S, D $55-$65; each addl $6; under 19 free. Crib free. Pet accepted. TV; cable (premium). Pool. Coffee in rms. Restaurant open 24 hrs. Ck-out noon. Meeting rms. Business servs avail. In-rm modem link. Refrigerators, microwaves avail. Cr cds: A, D, DS, MC, V.

[D] [icons]

★ **DAYS INN.** *96 Daniel Dr (40422).* 606/236-8600; fax 606/236-4299; toll-free 800/329-7466. 63 rms. S, D $55-$69; under 19 free. Crib free. TV; cable (premium). Pool; whirlpool. Sauna. Complimentary continental bkfst. Ck-out noon. Meeting rm. Business servs avail. Coin lndry. Microwaves avail. Cr cds: A, D, DS, JCB, MC, V.

[D] [icons] SC

★ **SUPER 8 MOTEL.** *3663 Hwy 150-127 Bypass (40422), at US 127 Bypass.* 606/236-8881; fax 606/236-8881; toll-free 800/800-8000. 49 units, 2 story. S $41.88; D $51.88-$56.88; each addl

$5; under 12 free. Crib free. Pet accepted, some restrictions. TV; cable (premium). Complimentary coffee. Restaurant nearby. Ck-out 11 am. Meeting rms. Business servs avail. Valet serv. Guest lndry. Some refrigerators; microwaves avail. Cr cds: A, C, D, DS, MC, V.

Elizabethtown

(C-5) *See also Bardstown, Fort Knox, Hodgenville*

(see Covington (Cincinnati Airport Area))

Founded 1797 **Pop** 18,167 **Elev** 731 ft
Area code 270 **Zip** 42701
Web www.ltadd.org/etowntourism

Information Elizabethtown Tourism & Convention Bureau, 1030 N Mulberry St; 270/765-2175 or 800/437-0092

The Lincoln story has deep roots in this town. Thomas Lincoln, the President's father, owned property and worked in Elizabethtown; it is the town to which Thomas Lincoln brought his bride, Nancy Hanks, immediately after their marriage. Abe's older sister Sarah was born in Elizabethtown. After his first wife's death, Thomas Lincoln returned to marry Sarah Bush Johnston.

What to See and Do

Abraham Lincoln Birthplace National Historic Site. (see) 13 mi SE via US 31 or KY 61.

Brown-Pusey Community House. (1825) This former stagecoach inn is an excellent example of Georgian Colonial architecture; General George Custer lived here from 1871-73. Restored as a historical genealogy library (fee) and community house; garden. (Mon-Sat; closed hols) 128 N Main St, at Poplar St. **FREE**

Lincoln Heritage House. Double log cabin (1789, 1805) was home of Hardin Thomas. Unusual trim work done by Thomas Lincoln. Pioneer implements, early surveying equipment, period furniture. Park facilities incl pavilions, paddle and row boats, canoes. (June-Sep, Tues-Sun) For information contact the Tourism & Convention Bureau. 1 mi N on US 31W in Freeman Lake Park. **FREE**

Schmidt's Coca-Cola Museum. Very large private collection of Coca-Cola memorabilia incl several thousand items. Complete 1890s marble ice cream parlor; complete tray collection; stained glass chandelier; 3-ft, Tiffany-style bottle. Lobby contains magnificent collection of *koi* (carp) in Japanese garden. (Mon-Fri; closed hols) 2½ mi W on US 31. ¢

Annual Events

Hardin County Fair. Hardin County Fairgrounds. Mid-July.

Kentucky Heartland Festival. Freeman Lake Park. Antique auto show, arts and crafts, canoe race, running event, hot air balloon, bluegrass music, games, food. Last full wkend Aug.

Motel/Motor Lodge

★★ **BEST WESTERN CARDINAL INN.** 642 E Dixie Ave (42701). 502/765-6139; fax 502/737-9944; toll-free 800/528-1234. 54 rms, 2 story. S, D $44-$49; each addl $4; under 18 free; higher rates Kentucky Derby. Crib avail. Pet accepted, some restrictions; $25 deposit. TV; cable (premium). Complimentary continental bkfst. Coffee in rms. Pool. Playground. Ck-out 11:30 am. Coin lndry. Cr cds: A, C, D, DS, MC, V.

★★ **COMFORT INN ATRIUM GARDENS.** 1043 Executive Dr (42701), I-65 Exit 94. 270/769-3030; fax 502/769-2516. 133 rms, 2 story. S, D $63.95-$79.95; each addl $6; under 18 free; higher rates Kentucky Derby. Crib free. Pet accepted. TV; cable (premium). Indoor pool. Complimentary continental bkfst. Restaurant adj 6 am-11 pm. Ck-out 11:30 am. Coin lndry. Meeting rms. Business servs avail. Indoor putting green. Game rm. Many refrigerators; some wet bars. Cr cds: A, C, D, DS, ER, JCB, MC, V.

★ **DAYS INN.** *2010 N Mulberry St (42701), at jct I-65, KY 62 (Exit 94).* 270/769-5522; fax 502/769-3211. 121 rms, 2 story. S $38-$43; D $43-$50; each addl $5; higher rates Derby wkend. Crib free. Pet accepted; $5. TV; cable (premium). Pool. Playground. Restaurant open 24 hrs. Ck-out 11 am. Coin lndry. Sundries. Gift shop. Game rm. Cr cds: A, D, DS, MC, V.

★★ **HAMPTON INN.** *1035 Executive Dr (40209).* 502/765-6663; fax 502/769-3151. 60 rms. S, D $59-$69; under 18 free; higher rates Kentucky Derby. Crib free. TV; cable (premium). Indoor pool; whirlpool. Complimentary continental bkfst, coffee in rms. Restaurant nearby. Ck-out 11 am. Meeting rms. Business center. Some refrigerators, microwaves. Cr cds: A, C, D, DS, MC, V.

Restaurants

★★ **GREEN BAMBOO.** *902 N Dixie (42701), in Governor's Shopping Center.* 270/769-3457. Specializes in Mongolian beef, Mandarin chicken, lobster. Hrs: 11 am-2:30 pm, 4:30-9:30 pm. Closed Thanksgiving, Dec 25. Lunch $4.25-$4.50; dinner $7.25-$18. Child's menu. Asian decor. Cr cds: A, DS, MC, V.

★ **JERRY'S.** *612 E Dixie Ave (42701).* 270/769-2336. Specializes in J-Boy, Husky, strawberry pie. Hrs: open 24 hrs. Closed Dec 25. Bkfst $2.50-$5.65; lunch $3.65-$5.65; dinner $4.65-$8.50. Child's menu. Parking. Cr cds: A, DS, MC, V.

★★ **STONE HEARTH.** *1001 N Mulberry (42701).* 270/765-4898. Specializes in beef, seafood. Salad bar. Hrs: 11 am-2 pm, 5-9 pm. Closed Sun; Jan 1, Dec 25. Lunch $5.75-$6.75; dinner $11.95-$18.95. Old English decor. Cr cds: A, D, DS, MC, V.

Florence

(see Covington (Cincinnati Airport Area))

Fort Knox

See also Elizabethtown, Louisville, Shepherdsville

Elev 740 ft **Area code** 502 **Zip** 40121 **Web** www.knox.army.mil

Information Public Affairs Office, US Army Armor Center & Fort Knox, PO Box 995; 502/624-4788 or -3051

This military post, established in 1918, is home for the US Army Armor Center and School and the Army's home of Mounted Warfare. Named for Major General Henry Knox, first Secretary of War, the post has been a major installation since 1932, when mechanization of the Army began.

What to See and Do

Patton Museum of Cavalry and Armor. The Armor Branch Museum was named in honor of General George S. Patton, Jr. Collection incl US and foreign armored equipment, weapons, art, and uniforms; mementos of General Patton's military career, incl the sedan in which he was riding when he was fatally injured in 1945. Also on display are a 10-by-12-ft section of the Berlin Wall and foreign armored equipment from Operation Desert Storm. (Daily; closed hols) Bldg 4554, Fayette Ave. Phone 502/624-3812. **FREE**

United States Bullion Depository. Two-story granite, steel, and concrete bldg. Opened in 1937, the bldg houses part of the nation's gold reserves. The depository and the surrounding grounds are not open to the public. Gold Vault Rd.

Annual Event

Armored Vehicle Presentation. Patton Museum. Operational armored vehicle demonstration features restored WWII tanks and authentically uniformed troops. July 4.

Hotel

★★ **RADCLIFF INN.** *438 S Dixie Blvd (40160), 2½ mi S on US 31E. 270/351-8211; fax 270/351-3227; toll-free 800/421-2030. Email qinn286867@aol.com; www.radcliffinn.com.* 83 rms, 3 story, 2 suites. S $55; D $60; each addl $5; suites $80; under 17 free. Crib avail. Parking lot. Pool. TV; cable (premium), VCR avail. Complimentary continental bkfst, coffee in rms, newspaper, toll-free calls. Restaurant 11 am-9 pm. Ck-out noon, ck-in 3 pm. Dry cleaning, coin lndry. Gift shop. Golf, 18 holes. Tennis, 5 courts. Cr cds: A, C, D, DS, JCB, MC, V.

D 🛂 🏌 ✈ 🏊 🦮 🔥

Frankfort

(C-6) *See also Lexington*

Founded 1786 **Pop** 25,968 **Elev** 510 ft **Area code** 502 **Zip** 40601
Information Frankfort/Franklin County Tourist and Convention Commisssion, 100 Capital Ave; 502/875-8687

Frankfort is split by the Kentucky River, which meanders through the city. Although rich farmlands funnel burley tobacco and corn through Frankfort, the chief crop is politics, especially when the legislature is in session. Frankfort was chosen as the state capital in 1792 as a compromise to settle the rival claims of Lexington and Louisville. Frankfort was briefly held by the Confederates during the Civil War. Later, the "corn liquor" industry blossomed in this area, utilizing water from flowing limestone springs. Bourbon distilleries carry on this tradition.

What to See and Do

Daniel Boone's Grave. Monument to Boone and his wife. Boone died in Missouri but his remains were brought here in 1845. In Frankfort Cemetery, 215 E Main St.

Kentucky Military History Museum. Exhibits trace Kentucky's involvement in military conflicts through 2 centuries. Weapons, flags, uniforms. (Daily; closed hols) Old State Arsenal, E Main St. Phone 502/564-3265. **FREE**

Kentucky State University. (1886) 2,550 students. Liberal studies institution. Jackson Hall (1887) has art and photo gallery exhibits (Sep-mid-May); King Farouk butterfly collection in Carver Hall. Jackson Hall and Hume Hall (1909) on historic register. E Main St. Phone 502/227-6000.

Kentucky Vietnam Veterans Memorial. Unique memorial is a 14-ft sundial that casts a shadow across veterans' names on the anniversary of their death. Memorial contains more than 1,000 names. Adj to State Library & Archives, 300 Coffee Tree Rd.

Liberty Hall. (ca 1796) Fine example of Georgian architecture, built by the first US senator from Kentucky, John Brown, is completely restored to its original state and furnished with family heirlooms. Period gardens. (Mar-Dec, Tues-Sun; closed hols) 218 Wilkinson St, at W Main St. Phone 502/227-2560. **¢¢** On the same blk is

Orlando Brown House. (1835) Early Greek-revival house built for Orlando Brown, son of Senator John Brown; original furnishings and artifacts. (Mar-Dec, Tues-Sun; closed hols) 202 Wilkinson St. Phone 502/227-2560. **¢¢** Combination ticket avail for both houses.

Old Governor's Mansion. (1798) Georgian-style residence of 33 governors until 1914, when the new mansion was built. Restored to the style of the 1800s. Tours (Tues and Thurs afternoons; closed hols). 420 High St. Phone 502/564-3449. **FREE**

Old State Capitol Building. Kentucky's 3rd capitol bldg, erected in 1827-29, was used as the capitol from 1829-1909 and was the first Greek Revival statehouse west of the Alleghenies. Completely restored and furnished in period style, the bldg features an unusual self-balanced double stairway. (Mon-Sat, also Sun afternoons) Broadway & Lewis Sts. **FREE** In the Old Capitol Annex are

Kentucky History Museum. Exhibits pertaining to the history and development of the state and the culture of its people. (Mon-Sat, also Sun afternoons; closed hols) Phone 502/564-3016. **FREE**

Library. Manuscripts, maps, photographs, and special collections cover Kentucky's history; genealogy section. (Mon-Sat; closed hols) Phone 502/564-3016. **FREE**

State Capitol. (1910) Bldg noted for Ionic columns and the high central dome on an Ionic peristyle, topped with a lantern cupola. In the rotunda are statues of Abraham Lincoln, Jefferson Davis, Henry Clay, Dr. Ephraim McDowell, and Alben Barkley, vice president under Harry S Truman. Guided tours. (Mon-Sat and Sun afternoons; closed hols) Capitol Ave, on an elevation overlooking the Kentucky River. Phone 502/564-3449. **FREE** On grounds are

Floral Clock. Functioning outdoor timepiece is adorned with thousands of plants and elevated above reflecting pool. Mechanism moves a 530-pound minute hand and a 420-pound hr hand. Visitors toss thousands of dollars in coins into the pool, all of which are turned over to state child-care agencies.

Governor's Mansion. (1914) Official residence of the Governor is styled after the Petit Trianon, Marie Antoinette's villa at Versailles. Guided tours (Tues and Thurs mornings). Phone 502/564-3449. **FREE**

Annual Events

Governor's Derby Breakfast. State Capitol. Breakfast, entertainment, and Kentucky crafts. Phone 502/564-2611. First Sat May.

Capital Expo Festival. Capital Plaza Complex. Traditional music, country music, fiddling; workshops, demonstrations, arts and crafts; balloon race, dancing, games, contests, puppets, museum exhibitions, ethnic and regional foods, entertainment. First full wkend June.

Motels/Motor Lodges

★★ **BEST WESTERN PARKSIDE INN.** 80 Chenault Rd (40601), I-64 Exit 58. 502/695-6111; fax 502/695-6111; res 800/528-1234. 98 rms, 2 story. S, D $48-$65; each addl $5; suites $75-$85; under 12 free; higher rates Kentucky Derby. Crib free. TV; cable (premium). Indoor/outdoor pool; whirlpool. Complimentary continental bkfst. Ck-out noon.

Lndry facilities. Meeting rms. Business servs avail. Airport transportation. Exercise equipt. Game rm. Refrigerator avail. Cr cds: A, C, D, DS, ER, JCB, MC, V.

[icons]

★ **BLUEGRASS INN.** 635 Versailles Rd (40601). 502/695-1800; fax 502/695-1800; toll-free 800/322-1802. 62 rms, 2 story. S $36-$42; D $42-$48; each addl $6; under 14 free; higher rates Kentucky Derby. Crib free. Pet accepted. TV; cable. Pool. Complimentary coffee in lobby. Restaurant adj; 9 am-10 pm. Ck-out noon. Business servs avail. Some refrigerators. Cr cds: A, C, D, DS, ER, MC, V.

[icons]

★ **DAYS INN.** I-64 And US Hwy 127 Exit 53 (40601), I-64 Exit 53B. 502/875-2200; fax 502/875-3574; toll-free 800/329-7466. 122 rms, 2 story. S $38; D $44; each addl $6; age 13-17, $1; under 12 free. Crib free. TV; cable. Pool. Continental bkfst. Ck-out 11 am. Sundries. Cr cds: A, C, D, DS, MC, V.

[icons]

Hotel

★★★ **HOLIDAY INN.** 405 Wilkinson Blvd (40601). 502/227-5100; fax 502/875-7147. 189 rms, 8 story. S, D $85; each addl $10; suites $100-$175; higher rates Kentucky Derby. Crib free. TV; cable (premium). Heated pool; whirlpool. Coffee in rms. Restaurants 6 am-1:30 pm, 5-9:30 pm. Bar 5-11:30 pm, Sun to 11 pm. Ck-out noon. Meeting rms. Business servs avail. In-rm modem link. Shopping arcade. Covered parking. Exercise equipt; sauna. Game rm. Some refrigerators. Cr cds: A, D, DS, MC, V.

[icons]

Restaurant

★ **JIM'S SEAFOOD.** 950 Wilkinson Blvd (40601). 502/223-7448. Specializes in surf and turf. Hrs: 11 am-2 pm, 4-10 pm; Sat from 4 pm. Closed Sun; hols. Res accepted. Wine, beer. Lunch $3.95-$6.95; dinner $7.95-$13.95. Child's menu. View of river. Family-owned. Cr cds: A, DS, MC, V.

[icons]

Georgetown

(C-6) *See also Frankfort, Lexington, Paris*

Settled 1776 **Pop** 11,414 **Elev** 871 ft
Area code 502 **Zip** 40324
Information Georgetown/Scott
County Tourism Commission, 401
Outlet Center Dr, Suite 240; 502/863-
2547 or 888/863-8600

Royal Spring's crystal-clear water
flows in the center of this city. This
spring attracted pioneer settlers who
established an outpost at Georgetown and rebuffed frequent Native
American attacks. The town was
named for George Washington and
was incorporated in 1790 by the Virginia legislature. Today it remains a
quiet college town, with a large portion of the business area designated
as a historic district.

What to See and Do

Cardome Centre. Former house of
Civil War Governor J. F. Robinson
and later home of the Academy of
the Sisters of the Visitation. Now
houses **Georgetown and Scott
County Museum** (daily; closed hols)
and serves as community center.
(Mon-Fri, also by appt; closed hols)
800 Cincinnati Pike, I-75 exit
125/126, on US 25N. Phone 502/863-
1575. **FREE**

Royal Spring Park. Location of Royal
Spring, largest in Kentucky and
source of city water since 1775. Former site of McClelland's Fort (1776),
first paper mill in the west, pioneer
classical music school, and state's
first ropewalk. Reputed site of first
bourbon distillation in 1789. Cabin
of former slave relocated and
restored here for use as an information center (mid-May-mid-Oct, Tues-
Sun). Picnicking. (Daily) Water St.
Phone 502/863-2547.

Scott County Courthouse. (1877)
Designed in second Empire style by
Thomas Boyd of Pittsburgh. Part of
the historic business district. (Mon-Fri;
closed hols) 101 E Main St, at Broadway. Phone 502/863-7850. **FREE**

**Toyota Motor Manufacturing, Ken-
tucky, Inc.** About 400,000 cars and
350,000 engines are made here annually. The Visitor Center has interac-

tive exhibits. One-hr tours of the
plant (ages 8 and up) incl video presentation and tram ride through different levels of production. Visitor
Center (Mon-Fri). Tours (res are
required; Tues and Thurs). 1001
Cherry Blossom Way. Phone 502/868-
3027 or 800/TMM-4485. **FREE**

Motel/Motor Lodge

★ **SHONEY'S INN.** *200 Shoney Dr
(40324), jct I-75 and US 62.* 502/868-
9800; fax 502/868-9800; res 800/222-
2222. 104 rms, 3 story, 15 suites. S
$55.95; D $60.95; under 18 free. TV;
cable. Pool. Complimentary coffee in
lobby. Restaurant adj 6 am-11 pm.
Ck-out noon. Meeting rms. Business
servs avail. In-rm modem link. Cr
cds: A, D, DS, MC, V.

D 🏊 🈲 🐾

Gilbertsville

*See also Cadiz, Land Between The
Lakes, Paducah*

Pop 500 (est) **Elev** 343 ft
Area code 270 **Zip** 42044
Web www.kentuckylake.com/mccc/
index.htm
Information Marshall County Cham-
ber of Commerce, Inc, 17 US 68 W,
Benton 42025; 270/527-7665

Fishing parties heading for Kentucky
Lake stop in Gilbertsville for last-
minute provisions. The area also
caters to tourists bound for the resorts
and state parks. Chemical plants have
been built nearby, utilizing Kentucky
Dam's hydroelectric power.

What to See and Do

Barkley Lock and Dam. A 1,004-mi
shoreline created by damming of the
Cumberland River; navigation lock,
canal, hydroelectric generating plant,
flood control and recreation areas;
information and visitor center. Contact the Resource Manager, PO Box
218, Grand Rivers 42045. 5 mi E.
Phone 270/362-4236. **FREE**

Kenlake State Resort Park. (see) SE
on Purchase Pkwy, US 68.

Kentucky Dam. Longest dam in the TVA system, 22 mi upstream from Paducah; 206 ft high, 8,422 ft long, built at cost of $118 million, created lake 184 mi long with 2,380 mi of shoreline. Regulates flow of water from Tennessee River into the Ohio River. Carries US 62/641 across northern end of Kentucky Lake. Viewing balcony (daily); tours of powerhouse (by appt). Phone 270/362-4221. **FREE**

Kentucky Dam Village State Resort Park. A 1,352-acre park on a 160,300-acre lake. Fishing, swimming beach, pool, bathhouse (seasonal), waterskiing, boating (rentals, launching ramps, docks); hiking, 18-hole and miniature golf (seasonal fee), tennis, picnicking, playground, shops, grocery, camping, lodge (see RESORT), cottages. Supervised recreation. Lighted 4,000-ft airstrip. Just S of town off US 62/641 on Kentucky Lake. Phone 270/362-4271 for fees and information.

Resort

★★ KENTUCKY DAM MOTEL. *Highway 641 (42029), ¾ mi W of Kentucky Dam on US 62/641; 2 mi E of I-24 Exit 27.* 270/362-4271; fax 270/362-8747; toll-free 800/325-0146. 86 lodge rms, 2 story; 70 kit. cottages. Apr-Oct: S $58; D $68; each addl $5; kit. cottages for 2-8, $77-$154; under 16 free; lower rates rest of yr. Crib free. TV. Pool; wading pool, lifeguard in season. Dining rm 7 am-9 pm. Ck-out noon (cottages 11 am), ck-in 4 pm. Convention facilities. Airport transportation. Lighted tennis. 18-hole golf, greens fee $15. Miniature golf. Lawn games. Game rm. Many microwaves. Private patios, balconies. Picnic tables. On lake; beach, marina. State-owned; all state park facilities avail. Cr cds: A, C, D, DS, MC, V.
🐾 ⚡ 🏌 ≈ 🔥 **SC**

Restaurant

★ PATTI'S. *J. H. O'Bryan Ave (42045), I-24 Exit 31, on US 453.* 270/362-8844. *Email pattis@apex.net; www.pattis-settlement.com.* Hrs: 10:30 am-9 pm. Closed wk of Dec 25. Res accepted. Lunch $5.50-$10.99; dinner $10.99-$18.99. Gift shops.

Stained glass, antiques. Family-owned. Cr cds: DS, MC, V.
D

Glasgow

(D-5) *See also Cave City, Horse Cave, Mammoth Cave National Park, Park City*

Settled 1799 **Pop** 12,351 **Elev** 790 ft
Area code 270 **Zip** 42141
Web www.glasgow-ky.com
Information Glasgow-Barren County Chamber of Commerce, 118 E Public Square; 270/651-3161

Glasgow was one of the first towns to be settled in the "barrens," then an almost treeless plateau west of the bluegrass section of Kentucky. Today, lumber products are important in Glasgow although tobacco is the leading money crop, followed by dairy products.

What to See and Do

Barren River Dam and Lake. Impounds waters of Barren River and its tributaries. There is good bass fishing, boating (ramps), water sports; picnic areas, camping, lodge, cabins (most have fee). 12 mi SW on US 31E. Contact 11088 Finney Rd. Phone 270/646-2055. Other recreation areas and campsites incl **Baileys Point, Beaver Creek, Browns Ford** (no campsites), **the Narrows, Peninsula** (no campsites), **the Tailwater, Walnut Creek,** and

Barren River Lake State Resort Park. Approx 2,100 acres with a 10,000-acre lake. Swimming beach, pool, fishing, boating (rentals); hiking, horseback riding, bicycle trails, 18-hole golf course, tennis, picnicking, playground, tent and trailer sites (Apr-Oct, standard fees), cottages, lodge (see RESORT). Some fees. 1149 State Park Rd in Lucas, 42156. Phone 270/646-2151.

Annual Event

Highland Games and Gathering of Scottish Clans. 14 mi S via US 31E in Barren River Lake State Resort Park (see). Six-day festival. Wkend following Memorial Day.

Motels/Motor Lodges

★ **DAYS INN.** *105 Days Inn Blvd (42141). 270/651-1757; fax 270/651-1755; res 800/DAYSINN.* 59 rms, 2 story. S, D $49-$61; each addl $6; suites $55-$65; under 18 free; higher rates Highland Games. Crib free. TV; cable (premium). Complimentary coffee in rms. Restaurant adj 6 am-10 pm. Ck-out noon. Meeting rms. Business servs avail. In-rm modem link. Valet serv. Indoor pool; whirlpool. Some in-rm whirlpools, refrigerators, microwaves. Cr cds: A, D, DS, MC, V.

🅳 🐾 🈁 ➳ 🏃 🏂 🖼 🔥

★ **HOUSTON INN.** *US 68 (42141), ½ mi W on US 68; ½ blk W of US 31E Bypass. 270/651-5191; fax 270/651-9233; toll-free 800/452-7469.* 80 rms, 2 story. S $34-$50; D $40-$55; each addl $5; under 13 free. Pet accepted; $5. TV; cable. Heated pool. Restaurant. Ck-out 11 am. Coin lndry. Meeting rms. Business servs avail. In-rm modem link. Cr cds: A, DS, MC, V.

🐾 ➳ 🖼 🔥 **SC**

Resort

★★★ **BARREN RIVER LAKE STATE RESORT PARK.** *1149 State Park Rd (42156), 12 mi SW on US 31E, in State Park. 270/646-2151; fax 270/646-3645.* 51 rms, 1-3 story, 22 kit. cottages. S $62; D $72; each addl $5; 2-bedrm kit. cottages (up to 6) $140-$170; under 17 free. Closed 5 days wk of Dec 25. Crib free. TV. Pool; wading pool, lifeguard. Free supervised children's activities. Dining rm 7 am-9 pm. Ck-out noon (cottages 11 am), ck-in 4 pm. Meeting rms. Business servs avail. Lighted tennis. 18-hole golf, greens fee $19. Gift shop. Rec rm. Private patios, balconies. Picnic tables. On lake. State-owned; all facilities of state park avail. Cr cds: A, C, D, DS, MC, V.

🅳 🐾 🈁 🏃 🏂 ➳ 🏂 🖼 🔥

B&B/Small Inn

★★★ **FOUR SEASONS COUNTRY INN.** *4107 Scottsville Rd (42141). 270/678-1000; fax 270/678-1017.* 21 rms, 3 story, 5 suites. S, D $70-$78; each addl $5; suites $125; wkly rates. Crib $5. TV; cable (premium). Heated pool. Complimentary continental bkfst. Restaurant nearby. Ck-out noon, ck-in 2 pm. Business servs avail. Refrigerators; some in-rm whirlpools. Antique reproductions. Cr cds: A, D, DS, MC, V.

🅳 🐾 🈁 ➳ 🏃 🖼 🔥

Restaurant

★★ **BOLTON'S LANDING.** *2433 Scottsville Rd (42141), 1½ mi S on US 31E. 270/651-8008.* Specializes in chicken, catfish, pasta. Hrs: 11 am-2 pm, 4:30-8:30 pm; Sat 4:30-9 pm. Closed Sun; hols. Lunch $5.75-$7.29; dinner $6.50-$14.95. Child's menu. Original art work. Cr cds: A, DS, MC, V.

🅳 🔙

Greenville

See also Hopkinsville, Madisonville

Settled 1799 **Pop** 4,689 **Elev** 538 ft
Area code 270 **Zip** 42345
Information Chamber of Commerce, PO Box 313; 270/338-5422

Located in the heart of the western Kentucky coal, oil, and natural gas fields, Greenville is the seat of Muhlenberg County. There is good hunting and fishing in the area.

What to See and Do

Lake Malone State Park. A 325-acre park on 788-acre Lake Malone; located in a hardwood tree forest, with tall pines on scenic cliffs. A natural rock bridge, steep sandstone bluffs, and a wooded shoreline can be seen from a ride on the lake. Swimming beach, fishing for bass, bluegill, crappie, boating (ramp, rentals, motors); hiking trail, picnicking, playground, tent and trailer camping (Apr-mid-Nov). (Daily) Standard fees. For information contact the Park Superintendent, Dunmor 42339. 8 mi S on KY 973, between US 431 and KY 181. Phone 270/657-2111.

Harrodsburg

(C-6) See also Danville

Founded 1774 **Pop** 7,335 **Elev** 886 ft
Area code 606 **Zip** 40330
Web www.harrodsburgky.com
Information Harrodsburg/Mercer
County Tourist Commission, 103 S
Main St, PO Box 283; 606/734-2364
or 800/355-9192

When James Harrod and a troop of
surveyors came here early in 1774
and established a township, they
were creating Kentucky's first permanent white settlement. Here, the first
corn in Kentucky was grown, the
first English school was established,
and the first gristmill in the area was
operated. Today the state's oldest
city, its sulphur springs and historical
sites make it a busy tourist town.
Tobacco, cattle, and horse-breeding
are important to the economy.

What to See and Do

Harrodsburg Pottery and Craft Shop.
Demonstrations of candle-dipping,
herbal and wreath arrangements;
other crafts. Herbal garden; greenhouse. (Mar-Dec, daily; rest of yr,
wkends; closed Easter, Thanksgiving,
Dec 25) 1026 Lexington Rd. Phone
606/734-9991. **FREE**

Morgan Row. (1807-45) Probably the
oldest standing row house W of the
Alleghenies; once a stagecoach stop
and tavern. Houses Harrodsburg Historical Society Museum (Tues-Sat).
220-222 S Chiles St, behind courthouse. Phone 606/734-5985. **FREE**

Old Fort Harrod State Park. This 28-
acre park incl a reproduction of Old
Fort Harrod in an area known as Old
Fort Hill, site of the original fort
(1774). The stockade shelters Ann
McGinty Block House, George Rogers
Clark Block House, James Harrod
Block House, and the first school,
complete with hand-hewn benches.
Authentic cooking utensils, tools,
and furniture are displayed in the
cabins. Mansion Museum incl Lincoln Rm, Confederate Rm, gun collection, Native American artifacts.
Lincoln Marriage Temple shelters the
log cabin in which Abraham Lincoln's parents were married on June
12, 1806 (moved from its original
site in Beech Fork). Pioneer Cemetery. Picnic facilities, playground, gift
shop. Living history crafts program
in fort (mid-Apr-late Oct). Museum
(mid-Mar-Nov, daily); fort (daily;
closed Thanksgiving, wk of Dec 25;
also Mon in Jan). On US 68/127 in
town. Phone 606/734-3314. ¢¢

Old Mud Meeting House. (1800) First
Dutch Reformed Church west of the
Alleghenies. The original mud-thatch
walls have been restored. (By appt
only) 4 mi S off US 68. Phone
606/734-5985. **FREE**

Shaker Village of Pleasant Hill. (1805-
1910). Thirty-three bldgs (1805-59)
incl frame, brick, and stone houses.
Center Family House has exhibits;
Trustees' House (see RESTAURANT)
has twin spiral staircases. Craft shops
with reproductions of Shaker furniture, Kentucky craft items; craft
demonstrations; lodging in 15
restored bldgs. Yr-round calendar of
special events incl music, dance, and
Sep wkend big events. (Daily; closed
Dec 24, 25) Sternwheeler offers 1-hr
excursions on Kentucky River (Late
Apr-Oct; fee). 7 mi NE on US 68.
Phone 606/734-5411. ¢¢

Annual Event

Pioneer Days Festival. Third wkend
Aug.

Seasonal Event

The Legend of Daniel Boone. James
Harrod Amphitheater, in Old Fort
Harrod State Park (see). Outdoor
drama traces the story of Boone.
Tues-Sun. For information contact
PO Box 365; 606/734-3346 or
800/852-6663. Mid-June-Aug.

Motel/Motor Lodge

★ ★ **BEST WESTERN.** *1680 Danville
Road (40330), 3 mi S on US 127.
606/734-9431; fax 606/734-5559; res
800/528-1234.* 69 rms, 3 story. S $53-
$57; D $58-$62; each addl $5; under
12 free. Crib free. TV; cable (premium). Pool. Complimentary continental bkfst. Restaurant adj 6:30
am-10 pm. Ck-out 11 am. Business
servs avail. Valet serv. Many refrigerators; microwaves avail. Balconies.

Miniature golf course adj. Cr cds: A, C, D, DS, MC, V.

B&Bs/Small Inns

★★★ **BEAUMONT INN.** *638 Beaumont Inn Dr (40330), off US 127. 606/734-3381; fax 606/734-6897; toll-free 800/352-3992.* 33 rms. S $65-$85; D $85-$110; each addl $25; under 12, $15. Closed late Dec-Feb. TV; cable. Pool; wading pool, lifeguard. Dining rm (public by res). Ck-out noon. Meeting rms. Business servs avail. Gift shop. Golf privileges. Lawn games. Rms are in 4 bldgs; main bldg furnished with antiques. Cr cds: A, D, DS, MC, V.

★★ **SHAKER VILLAGE OF PLEASANT HILL.** *3501 Lexington Rd (40330), Shaker Village of Pleasant Hill. 859/734-5411; fax 859/734-7278; res 800/734-5611. www.shakervillageky.org.* 76 rms, 4 story, 3 suites. Apr-Oct: S $60; D $70; each addl $10; suites $125; under 17 free; lower rates rest of yr. Crib avail. Parking lot. TV; cable (premium), VCR avail. Complimentary full bkfst. Restaurant 7:30 am-8:30 pm. Ck-out 11 am, ck-in 3 pm. Meeting rms. Business center. Gift shop. Exercise privileges. Hiking trail. Cr cds: MC, V.

Restaurant

★★ **TRUSTEES' HOUSE AT PLEASANT HILL.** *3501 Lexington Rd. 606/734-5411. www.tourky.com.shakervillage/.* Specializes in traditional Kentucky and Shaker dishes. Hrs: 7-9:30 am, 11:30 am-2:30 pm, 5:30-8:30 pm. Closed Dec 24, 25. Res accepted. Bkfst complete meals: $6.50-$8.75; lunch complete meals: $6.50-$8.75; dinner complete meals: $11.50-$18. Child's menu. Restored Shaker village; Shaker decor. Cr cds: MC, V.

Hazard (D-7)

Pop 5,416 **Elev** 867 ft **Area code** 606 **Zip** 41701

Information Hazard-Perry County Chamber of Commerce & Tourism Commission, 601 Main St, Suite 3; 606/439-2659

In rugged mountain country, Hazard is a coal mining town, a trading center and the seat of Perry County. Both town and county were named for Commodore Oliver Hazard Perry, naval hero of the War of 1812.

What to See and Do

Bobby Davis Memorial Park. Picnic area, reflecting pool, WWII Memorial, 400 varieties of shrubs and plants. (Daily) Walnut St. In the park is

> **Bobby Davis Park Museum.** Community museum housing local historical artifacts and photographs relating to life on Kentucky River waterways. (Mon-Fri; closed hols) Phone 606/439-4325. **FREE**

Buckhorn Lake State Resort Park. This 856-acre park encompasses a 1,200-acre lake. Swimming beach, pool, bathhouse (seasonal), fishing, boating (ramp, motors, rentals); hiking, bicycle rentals, miniature golf, tennis, picnicking, playground. Lodge (see RESORT), cottages. 25 mi NW via KY 15/28. Phone 606/398-7510 for fees and information.

Carr Fork Lake. A 710-acre lake. Beach, fishing, boating (ramps, marina); picnic shelters, camping (hookups, dump station; fee). Observation points. Some facilities seasonal. 15 mi SE. Phone 606/642-3308.

Daniel Boone National Forest. (see) 15 mi W on KY 80.

Annual Event

Black Gold Festival. On Main St. Celebrates local coal resources. Food and craft booths, games, entertainment, carnival, parade. Phone 606/436-0161. Third full wkend Sep.

Motels/Motor Lodges

★★ **HOLIDAY INN.** *200 Dawahare Dr (41701), off Daniel Boone Pkwy. 606/436-4428; fax 606/436-4428.* 81 rms, 2 story. S, D $54-$70; each addl $6; suites $125-$186; under 16 free. Crib avail. TV; cable. 2 pools, 1 indoor; whirlpool. Restaurant 5:30

am-11 pm. Bar 3 pm-midnight. Ck-out 11 am. Meeting rms. Business servs avail. In-rm modem link. Sundries. Cr cds: A, C, D, DS, JCB, MC, V.

[D] [icons] SC

★ **SUPER 8 MOTEL.** *125 Village Ln (41701), off Daniel Boone Pkwy. 606/436-8888; fax 606/439-0768; toll-free 800/800-8000.* 86 rms, 2 story, 11 suites. S $43.88-$48.88; D $46.88-54.88; each addl $3; suites $49.88-$78.88; under 12 free. Crib free. TV; cable (premium). Coffee in rms. Complimentary continental bkfst. Restaurant nearby. Ck-out 11 am. Business servs avail. Cr cds: A, C, D, DS, MC, V.

[D] [icons] SC

Resort

★★ **BUCKHORN LAKE STATE RESORT PARK.** *4441 KY Hwy 1833 (41721), 25 mi W on KY 28, in Buckhorn Lake State Resort Park. 606/398-7510; fax 606/398-7077; toll-free 800/325-0058.* 36 rms, 2 story. Memorial Day-Labor Day: S $53; D $63; each addl $5; cottages $104-$146; under 16 free; lower rates rest of yr. Crib free. TV; cable (premium). Pool; wading pool, lifeguard. Supervised children's activities (Memorial Day-Labor Day). Dining rm 7 am-9 pm. Ck-out noon. Meeting rms. Business servs avail. Gift shop. Tennis. Miniature golf. Game rm. Rec rm. Lawn games. Balconies. Picnic tables, grills. On lake; beach facilities, boat rental. State-owned; all facilities of state park avail. Cr cds: A, DS, MC, V.

[icons]

Henderson

(C-3) *See also Owensboro*

Founded 1797 **Pop** 25,945 **Elev** 409 ft
Area code 270 **Zip** 42420
Web www.go-henderson.com
Information Tourist Commission, 2961 US 41N; 270/826-3128 or 800/648-3128

Henderson was developed by the Transylvania Company and named for its chief executive, Colonel Richard Henderson. This town along the banks of the Ohio River has long attracted residents, most notably naturalist John James Audubon, W.C. Handy, well-known "father of the Blues," and A.B. "Happy" Chandler, former governor and commissioner of baseball.

What to See and Do

John James Audubon State Park. Here stand 692 acres of massive hardwood trees, woodland plants, nature preserve, densely forested tracts, and 2 lakes favored by migratory birds and described in Audubon's writings. Swimming beach, bathhouse (seasonal), fishing, paddleboat rentals (seasonal); 9-hole golf (yr-round; fee), picnicking, playground, tent and trailer camping (standard fees), cottages (yr-round). Supervised recreation; guided nature walks. (Daily) Some fees. 2 mi N on US 41. Phone 270/826-2247. **FREE**

Annual Events

W.C. Handy Blues & Barbecue Festival. Mid-June.

Bluegrass in the Park. Audubon Mill Park. First wkend Aug.

Big River Arts & Crafts Festival. Audubon State Park (see). More than 250 exhibitors. Early Oct.

Seasonal Event

Horse Racing. Ellis Park. 5 mi N on US 41. Thoroughbred racing. Tues-Sun. Phone 812/425-1456. Early July-Labor Day.

Motels/Motor Lodges

★ **DAYS INN.** *2044 US 41 N (42420). 270/826-6600; fax 270/826-3055; toll-free 800/329-7466.* 117 rms, 2 story. S, D $50-$80; each addl $6; suites $70-$100; under 12 free. Crib free. Pet accepted; $5. TV; cable (premium). Pool. Coffee in rms. Restaurant 6 am-2 pm, 5-9 pm; Sun to 3 pm. Bar 11-2 am; entertainment. Ck-out 11 am. Coin lndry. Meeting rms. Business center. Valet serv. Some refrigerators. Cr cds: A, C, D, DS, MC, V.

[D] [icons] SC

★ **SCOTTISH INN.** *2820 US 41 N (42420). 270/827-1806; fax 270/827-*

1806; res 800/251-1962; toll-free 877/ 417-3251. 60 rms, 2 story, 2 suites. June-Sep: S $35; D $40; each addl $5; suites $55; children $5; under 10 free; lower rates rest of yr. Crib avail, fee. Pet accepted, some restrictions, fee. Parking lot. Pool. TV; cable (DSS), VCR avail. Complimentary continental bkfst, toll-free calls. Restaurant, closed Sun. Ck-out 11 am, ck-in 2 pm. Dry cleaning, coin lndry. Exercise privileges. Golf, 11 holes. Tennis, 2 courts. Picnic facilities. Cr cds: A, C, D, DS, MC, V.

Hodgenville

(C-5) *See also Elizabethtown*

Founded 1789 **Pop** 2,721 **Elev** 730 ft
Area code 270 **Zip** 42748
Information LaRue County Chamber of Commerce, 72 Lincoln Square, PO Box 176; 270/358-3411

Robert Hodgen built a mill and tavern here and entertained many prominent people. Young Abraham Lincoln often came to the mill with corn to be ground from his father's farm seven miles away. Soon after Hodgen's death in 1810, the settlement surrounding his tavern adopted his name and was known thereafter as Hodgenville. In 1909 a bronze statue of Lincoln was erected on the town square.

What to See and Do

Abraham Lincoln Birthplace National Historic Site. (see) 3 mi S on US 31E (KY 61).

Lincoln Jamboree. Family entertainment featuring traditional and modern country music. (Sat eves; res recommended in summer) 2 mi S on US 31E. Phone 270/358-3545. ¢¢

Lincoln Museum. Dioramas depicting events in Lincoln's life; memorabilia; special exhibits. (Daily; closed Jan 1, Thanksgiving, Dec 25) 66 Lincoln Sq. Phone 270/358-3163. ¢¢

✪ **Lincoln's Boyhood Home.** Replica of the log cabin where Lincoln lived for 5 yrs (1811-16) during his childhood; contains historic items and antiques. (Apr-Oct, daily) 7 mi NE on US 31E, on Knob Creek Farm. Phone 270/549-3741. ¢

Annual Events

Founder's Day. Lincoln Birthplace NHS. Arts, crafts, music. Wkend nearest July 17.

Lincoln Days Celebration. Railsplitting competition; pioneer games; classic car show; arts and crafts exhibits; parade. Second wkend Oct.

Hopkinsville

(D-3) *See also Cadiz; also see Clarksville, TN*

Founded 1797 **Pop** 29,809 **Elev** 548 ft
Area code 270 **Zip** 42240
Web www.ci.hopkinsville.ky.us
Information Hopkinsville-Christian County Chamber of Commerce, 1209 S Virginia St, PO Box 1382; 502/885-9096 or800/842-9959

The tobacco auctioneers' chant has long been the theme song of Hopkinsville. Industry has moved in, and Hopkinsville now manufactures precision springs, magnetic wire, lighting fixtures, bowling balls, hardwood, plastic and cement products, non-woven textiles, wearing apparel, and hydraulic motors. Tobacco redrying and flour and cornmeal milling are also done here. Fort Campbell military post has played an important role in the city's growth.

Hopkinsville was the site of the Night Rider War, brought on by farmers' discontent at the low prices they received for their dark tobacco. They raided the town in December 1907, burning several warehouses. In 1911, the culprits were tried and their group disbanded. Hopkinsville was a stop on the "Trail of Tears." The site of the Cherokee encampment is now a park with a museum and memorial dedicated to those who lost thier lives. Famous sons of the town include Adlai Stevenson, Vice President of the United States 1892-97; Edgar Cayce, famous clairvoyant, who is buried here; Colonel Wil Starling, Chief of the White House Secret Service 1914-44; and

Ned Breathitt, Governor of Kentucky 1963-67.

What to See and Do

Fort Campbell. One of the nation's largest military installations (105,000 acres); home of 101st Airborne Div (Air Assault). Wickham Hall houses Don F. Pratt Museum, which displays historic military items (daily; closed Jan 1, Dec 25). 16 mi S on US 41A, in both KY and TN. Phone 270/798-2151. **FREE**

Jefferson Davis Monument State Shrine. (see) 11 mi E on US 68 in Fairview.

Pennyrile Forest State Resort Park. (see MADISONVILLE) Approx 17 mi NW on KY 109.

Pennyroyal Area Museum. Exhibits feature area's agriculture and industries, Native American artifacts, miniature circus, old railroad items. Civil War items; 1898 law office furniture; Edgar Cayce exhibit, books. (Mon-Sat; closed hols) 217 E 9th St. Phone 270/887-4270. ¢

Annual Events

Dogwood Festival. Features bike tours along the Dogwood Trail, band concerts and historical walking tours. Phone 270/885-9096. Last 2 wks Apr.

Little River Days. Downtown. Festival consists of road races, canoe races; arts and crafts; entertainment; square dance; children's events. Early May.

Western Kentucky State Fair. Midway, rides, concerts, local exhibits and events. First wk Aug.

Motel/Motor Lodge

★★ **BEST WESTERN.** *4101 Fort Campbell Blvd (42240). 270/886-9000; fax 270/886-9000.* 111 rms, 3 story. S, D $50; each addl $5; under 12 free. Crib free. Pet accepted, some restrictions. TV; cable (premium). Pool. Continental bkfst. Restaurant nearby. Bar 5-10 pm. Ck-out noon. Meeting rms. Business servs avail. Health club privileges. Cr cds: A, D, DS, MC, V.
🄳 🔧 🐾 ⚒ 🏊 🏋 🛏 🔥 🔥

★★ **HOLIDAY INN.** *2910 Fort Campbell Blvd (42240). 270/886-4413; fax 270/886-4413.* 101 rms, 5 story. S, D $49-$79; each addl $6; under 19 free. Crib free. Pet accepted. TV; cable (premium). Indoor pool. Restaurant 6 am-1:30 pm, 5-9:30 pm. Bar 4 pm-midnight. Ck-out noon. Meeting rms. Business servs avail. In-rm modem link. Valet serv. Sundries. Exercise equipt; sauna. Cr cds: A, C, D, DS, JCB, MC, V.
🄳 🔧 🏊 🏋 🛏 🔥

Restaurant

★ **WOODSHED PIT BAR-B-QUE.** *1821 W 7th St (42240). 270/885-8144.* Specializes in barbecue, ham, corn bread. Hrs: 11 am-8 pm. Closed Sun; hols. Bkfst $3-$4.50; lunch $3.50-$9.95; dinner $3.50-$9.95. No cr cds accepted.
🄳 🍽

Horse Cave

(D-5) *See also Cave City, Glasgow*

Pop 2,284 **Elev** 132 ft **Area code** 270 **Zip** 42749

Tobacco, livestock, and caves are important sources of local income. The town took its name from a nearby cave, which provided water for the area's first settlers ("horse" meant large).

What to See and Do

Horse Cave Theatre. Southern Kentucky's resident professional festival theatre. Six of the season's plays run in rotating repertory in summer. Art gallery; concessions. (June-Nov, nightly Tues-Sun; matinees Sat, Sun) Phone 800/342-2177 for schedule, res. ¢¢¢¢

☒ **Kentucky Down Under/Mammoth Onyx Cave.** Exotic bird garden; wallabies, emus, sheep, and other animals in Australian outback setting. Petting zoo; bison and elk overlook. (Apr-Oct, daily) Guided cave tour (45 min) incl Mammoth Onyx Column (45 ft high); colorful stalactites, stalagmites, flowstone, and hanging bridges; cave temperature approximately 60°F. Tours (daily; closed Jan 1, Dec 25) 2 mi NW on KY 218, just E of I-65, exit 58. Phone 270/786-2634 or 800/762-2869. ¢¢¢

Jamestown

(E-6) *See also Somerset*

Pop 1,641 **Elev** 1,024 ft
Area code 270 **Zip** 42629
Web www.lakecumberlandvacation.
com
Information Russell County Tourist
Commission, 650 S KY 127, PO Box
64, Russell Springs 42642; 270/866-
4333

What to See and Do

Wolf Creek Dam. US Army Corps of
Engineers dam; 258 ft high, 5,736 ft
long, draining a 5,789-sq-mi area,
and creating 101-mi-long Lake Cumberland (see SOMERSET). Camping
(mid-Mar-Nov; fee). Visitor center. 12
mi S via US 127. Phone 606/679-
6337. On N shore of lake is

> **Lake Cumberland State Resort
> Park.** More than 3,000 acres on a
> 50,250-acre lake. Swimming pools,
> fishing, boating (ramps, rentals,
> dock); hiking, riding (seasonal), 9-
> hole par-3 and miniature golf (sea-
> sonal), tennis, shuffleboard,
> bicycling (rentals), picnicking, play-
> ground, lodge (see RESORTS), rental
> houseboats, cottages, tent and
> trailer camping (Apr-Nov; standard
> fees). Nature center, supervised
> recreation. 14 mi S on US 127.
> Phone 270/343-3111 or 800/325-
> 1709 for rates and information.

Motel/Motor Lodge

★ **CUMBERLAND LODGE.** *US Hwy
127 S (42642), N on US 127. 270/866-
4208; fax 270/866-4206.* 53 rms, 2
story. S $40; D $50; each addl $5;
under 12 free; higher rates wkends,
special events. Crib free. TV; cable
(premium), VCR avail (movies). Pool.
Complimentary continental bkfst,
coffee in rms. Restaurant adj 5 am-11
pm. Ck-out 11 am. Meeting rm. Exercise equipt. Some refrigerators. Cr
cds: A, DS, MC, V.
🅳 ⛱ 🏋 ⛷ 🐾

Resorts

★★ **JAMESTOWN RESORT AND
MARINA.** *3677 S KY 92 (42629),
4 mi S on KY 92E. 270/343-5253; fax
270/343-5252.* 40 rms in main bldg,

2 story, 4 kit. units, 18 kit. cottages
(1-3 bedrm). Memorial Day-Labor
Day, EP: S, D $129.95-$139.95; each
addl $10; kit. units $149.95-
$169.95; kit. cottages $69.95-
$109.95; under 16 free; lower rates
rest of yr. Crib free. TV; cable, VCR.
Pool. Playground. Complimentary
coffee in rms. Restaurant adj (seasonal) 7 am-10 pm. Ck-out 10 am,
ck-in 2 pm. Grocery. Coin lndry.
Meeting rms. Gift shop. Tennis.
Boats. Waterskiing. Lake swimming.
Hiking. Lawn games. Miniature golf.
Fishing guides. Refrigerators; some
minibars. Balconies. Grills. A 300-
acre lakeside development; more
than 800 boat slips. Cr cds: A, DS,
MC, V.
🅳 ⛱ 🏋 ⛷ 🏊 🐾 ⛹

★★★ **LAKE CUMBERLAND STATE
RESORT PARK.** *5465 State Park Rd
(42629), 10 mi S, in Lake Cumberland
State Park. 270/343-3111; fax
270/343-5510; toll-free 800/325-1709.
www.lakecumberlandpark.com.* 63 rms
in lodge, 13 in annex, 30 kit. cottages (1-2 bedrm). Apr-Oct: S $54-
$72; D $64-$82; each addl $5;
cottages for 2-4, $81-$130; under 16
free; lower lodge rates rest of yr.
Crib free. TV; cable. 2 pools, 1
indoor; 2 wading pools. Supervised
children's activities (Memorial Day-
Labor Day). Dining rm 7-10:30 am,
11:30 am-2:30 pm, 5-9 pm. Ck-out
noon, cottages 11 am, ck-in 4 pm.
Coin lndry. Convention facilities.
Business servs avail. Gift shop. Tennis. 9-hole golf, greens fee $8;
putting green. Exercise equipt.
Miniature golf $2.50. Waterskiing.
Marina; boat, houseboat rental.
Lawn games. Soc dir. Entertainment.
Rec rm. Balconies overlook lake.
State-owned; all facilities of state
park avail. Cr cds: A, C, DS, MC, V.
🅳 ⛱ 🏋 ⛷ 🐾 🏊 ⛹ ⛹

Jefferson Davis Monument State Shrine

See also Hopkinsville

*(10 mi E of Hopkinsville on US 68 in
Fairview)*

The monument, a cast-concrete obelisk 351 feet tall, ranks as the fourth tallest obelisk in the country and the tallest of such material. It marks the birthplace of Jefferson Davis, the only President of the Confederate States of America. Overlooking a 19-acre park, the monument was built at a cost of $200,000 raised by public subscription and was dedicated in 1924. Visitors may take an elevator to the top (fee).

The son of a Revolutionary War officer, Jefferson Davis was born here in 1808, less than 100 miles from Abraham Lincoln's birthplace. Davis graduated from West Point, became a successful cotton planter in Mississippi, was elected to the US Senate, and was Secretary of War in President Franklin Pierce's Cabinet. Elected President of the Confederacy, he served for the duration of the war, was captured in Georgia, and imprisoned for two yrs. Picnic area; playground. (May-Oct, daily) Phone 270/886-1765.

Kenlake State Resort Park

See also Cadiz, Land Between The Lakes

(16 mi NE of Murray on KY 94)

Located 16 miles northeast of Murray (see), Kenlake State Resort Park lies on 1,800 acres with a four-mile shoreline on 160,300-acre Kentucky Lake. Pool, bathhouse (seasonal), waterskiing; fishing, boating (ramps, rentals, marina); hiking trail; nine-hole golf (rentals), shuffleboard, tennis (indoor, outdoor, shop), picnicking, playgrounds, cottages, dining room, lodge (see RESORT), tent and trailer sites (Apr-Oct, standard fees). For rates and information phone 270/474-2211 or 800/325-0143.

Motel/Motor Lodge

★ **EARLY AMERICAN MOTEL.** *16749 US Hwy 68 E (42048), jct US 68 and KY 80. 270/474-2241.* 18 rms, 7 kits. Late May-early Sep: S $37.95; D $41.95-$63.95; each addl $5; kit. units $48.95-$68.95; under 12 free; wkly rates; lower rates rest of yr. Crib free. Pet accepted. TV; cable. Pool. Playground. Complimentary coffee in rms. Restaurant adj 6 am-9 pm. Ck-out 10 am. Rec rm. Lawn games. Picnic tables, grills. Cr cds: A, DS, MC, V.

Resort

★★ **KENLAKE STATE RESORT PARK.** *542 Kenlake Rd (42048), KY 94 at jct US 68. 270/474-2211; fax 270/474-2018; toll-free 800/425-0143. www.kenlake.com.* 48 rms in lodge, 1 story, 34 cottages. S $57; D $67; each addl $5.45; 1-3 bedrm cottages $81-$119; lower rates rest of yr. Closed Christmas wk. Crib free. TV. Pool; wading pool. Playground. Dining rm 7 am-9 pm. Ck-out noon (lodge rms), 11 am (cottages); ck-in 4 pm (lodge rms and cottages). Meeting rms. Lighted tennis, some indoor. 9-hole golf, greens fee $10, putting green. Lawn games. Rec rm. Picnic tables, grills. State-owned; all state park facilities avail. Cr cds: A, D, DS, MC, V.

Restaurant

★★ **BRASS LANTERN.** *16593 US 68E (42048), jct KY 80. 270/474-2773. Email lantern1@1dd.net; www. brasslantern.com.* Specializes in prime rib, filet mignon. Salad bar. Hrs: 5-8:30 pm. Closed Mon, Tues exc mid-June-mid-Aug; also late Dec-late Mar. Res accepted. Dinner $9.50-$24.95. Child's menu. Cr cds: A, C, D, DS, MC, V.

Land Between the Lakes

See also Cadiz, Gilbertsville; also see Paris, TN

Information Land Between the Lakes, 100 Van Morgan Dr, Golden Pond 42211; 800/LBL-7077

This 170,000-acre wooded peninsula, running 40 miles from north to south and located between Kentucky Lake and Lake Barkley in western Kentucky and Tennessee, is one of the largest outdoor recreation areas in the country.

There are four major family campgrounds: **Hillman Ferry, Piney, Energy Lake** (year-round; electric hookups; fee), and **Wranglers campground,** which is equipped for horseback riders. Eleven other lake access areas offer more primitive camping (fee). All areas offer swimming, fishing, boating, ramps; picnic facilities. Family campgrounds have planned recreation programs (summer).

There is a 5,000-acre wooded Environmental Education Area that includes the Nature Station, which presents interpretive displays of native plant and animal life. Within this area are several nature trails. Elk and Bison Prairie is a drive-through wildlife viewing area featuring native plants and wildlife (daily; fee). Nature center (Mar-Nov, daily; fee).

What to See and Do

Golden Pond Visitor Center. Main orientation center for Land Between the Lakes visitors. Planetarium presentation (Mar-Dec, fee). Seasonal programs. Visitor center (daily).

The Homeplace-1850. Living history farm. (Apr-Nov, daily) 17 mi SE of Aurora via US 68, Land Between the Lakes exit. ¢¢

The Nature Station. Interpretive displays of native animals and plants. (Mar-Nov, daily) 14 mi NE of Aurora via US 68, Land Between the Lakes exit. ¢¢

Lexington

(C-6) See also Frankfort, Paris, Richmond, Winchester

Founded 1779 **Pop** 225,366
Elev 983 ft **Area code** 859

Information Lexington Convention & Visitors Bureau, 301 E Vine St, 40507; 859/233-1221 or 800/845-3959

A midland metropolis rooted in the production of tobacco and thoroughbreds, Lexington is a gracious city decorated with rich bluegrass and dotted with aristocratic old houses. The legendary steel-blue tint of the bluegrass is perceptible only in May's early morning sunshine, but throughout spring, summer, and fall it is unrivaled for turf and pasture.

An exploring party camping here in 1775 got news of the Battle of Lexington and so named the spot. The city was established four yrs later, rapidly becoming a center for barter and a major producer of hemp (used by New England's clipper ships). Lexington cashed in on its tobacco crop when smoking became popular during the Civil War. Pioneers who settled here brought their best horses with them from Maryland and Virginia; as they grew wealthy, they imported bloodlines from abroad to improve the breed. The first races were held in Lexington in 1780, and the first jockey club was organized in 1797.

Lexington is the world's largest burley tobacco market, with well over 100 million pounds sold each year. Precious bluegrass seed, beef cattle, and sheep are also merchandised in Lexington. More than 50 major industries, manufacturing everything from peanut butter and bourbon to air brakes and ink jet printers, are located here.

What to See and Do

★ **Ashland.** (1806) Estate on 20 acres of woodland was the home of Henry Clay, statesman, orator, senator, and would-be president. Occupied by the Clay family for 5 generations, Ashland is furnished with family possessions and furniture. The estate was named for the ash trees that surround it. A number of outbldgs still stand. (Daily; closed Mon from Nov-Mar; closed hols, also Jan) Richmond Rd (E Main St), at Sycamore Rd. Phone 859/266-8581. ¢¢¢

Headley-Whitney Museum. Unusual bldgs house display of bibelots (small decorative objects) executed in precious metals and jewels; Asian porcelains, paintings, decorative arts, shell grotto, special exhibits; library. (Tues-Sun; closed hols) 4435 Old Frankfort Pike, 4½ mi NW of New Circle Rd. Phone 859/255-6653. ¢¢

Horse farms. More than 400 in area, most concentrated in Lexington-Fayette County. Although the majority are thoroughbred farms, other varieties such as standardbreds, American saddle horses, Arabians, Morgans, and quarter horses are bred and raised here as well. Farms may be seen by taking one of the many tours offered by tour companies in Lexington.

Hunt-Morgan House. (ca 1812-1814) In Gratz Park area, a historic district with antebellum residences. Federal-period mansion with a cantilevered elliptical staircase and fanlight doorway. Built for John Wesley Hunt, Kentucky's first millionaire. Later occupied by his grandson, General John Hunt Morgan, known as the "Thunderbolt of the Confederacy." Nobel Prize-winning geneticist Thomas Hunt Morgan was also born in this house. Family furniture, portraits, and porcelain. Walled courtyard garden. Gift shop. (Tues-Sun; closed hols, late Dec-Feb) 201 N Mill St, at W 2nd St. Phone 859/233-3290. ¢¢

★ **Kentucky Horse Park.** More than 1,000 acres of beautiful bluegrass fill the park; features Man O' War grave and memorial, visitor center with wide-screen film presentation *Thou Shalt Fly Without Wings*. Also located within park are the **Intl Museum of the Horse, Parade of Breeds**

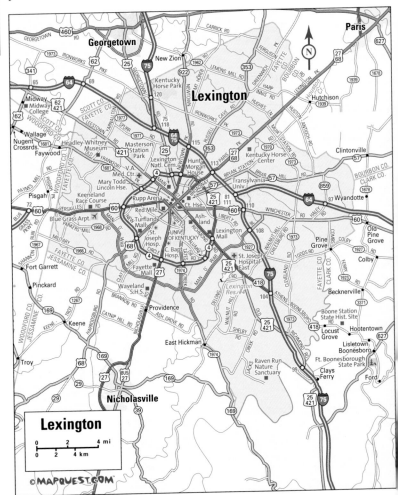

(seasonal), **Calumet Trophy Collection, Sears Collection** of hand-carved miniatures; **Hall of Champions** stable that houses famous thoroughbreds and standardbreds; walking farm tour, antique carriage display. Swimming; tennis, ball courts, picnic area, playgrounds, campground (fee). Special events (see ANNUAL EVENTS); horsedrawn rides (fee). (Mid-Mar-Oct, daily; rest of yr, Wed-Sun; closed Jan 1, Thanksgiving, late Dec) Parking fee (seasonal). Contact Director, 4089 Iron Works Rd, 40511. 6 mi N via I-75, Kentucky Horse Park exit 120, on Iron Works Pike. Phone 859/233-4303 or 800/568-8813. General admission ¢¢¢ Also on grounds is

American Saddle Horse Museum. Museum dedicated to the American Saddlebred horse, Kentucky's only native breed. Contemporary exhibits on the development and current uses of the American Saddlebred. Multimedia presentation. Gift shop. (May-Sep, daily; rest of yr, Wed-Sun; closed hols) 4093 Iron Works Pkwy. Phone 859/259-2746. ¢¢

Lexington Cemetery. Buried on these 170 acres are Henry Clay, John C. Breckinridge, General John Hunt Morgan, the Todds (Mrs Abraham Lincoln's family), coach Adolph Rupp, and many other notable persons. Also interred are 500 Confederate and 1,110 Union veterans. Sunken gardens, lily pools, 4-acre flower garden, extensive plantings of spring-flowering trees and shrubs. (Daily) 833 W Main St, on US 421. Phone 859/255-5522.

Mary Todd Lincoln House. Childhood residence of Mary Todd Lincoln is authentically restored; period furnishings, personal items. (Mid-Mar-Nov, Mon-Sat; closed hols) 578 W Main St. Phone 859/233-9999. ¢¢

Opera House. (1886) Restored and reconstructed opera house is a regional performing arts center; performances incl Broadway shows and special events. (Sep-June) Contact Lexington Center Corp, Performing Arts, 430 W Vine St, 40507. 401 W Short St. Phone 859/233-4567.

Sightseeing tours. There are many tour companies that offer tours of working horse farms in the Lexington area. Many of these companies also offer historic sightseeing tours. For more information contact the Convention & Visitors Bureau.

Transylvania University. (1780) 926 students. The oldest institution of higher learning west of the Allegheny Mts, it has educated 2 US vice presidents, 36 state and territorial governors, 34 ambassadors, 50 senators, 112 members of the US House of Representatives, and Confederate President Jefferson Davis. Thomas Jefferson was one of Transylvania's early supporters. Henry Clay taught law courses and was a member of the university's governing board. Administration Bldg, "Old Morrison" (1833), Greek Revival architecture, was used as hospital during Civil War. Tours of campus (by appt). N Broadway & 3rd St. Phone 859/233-8120.

University of Kentucky. (1865) 24,000 students. Area of S Limestone St & Euclid Ave. Phone 859/257-9000 for information on bus and walking tours. **FREE** On campus are

William S. Webb Museum of Anthropology. Exhibits incl cultural history of Kentucky and evolution of man. (Mon-Fri; closed hols) Lafferty Hall. Phone 859/257-8208. **FREE**

Art Museum. Permanent collections; special exhibitions. (Tues-Sun; closed hols and Dec 26-Jan 2) Singletary Center for the Arts, Euclid Ave & Rose St. Phone 859/257-5716. **FREE**

Victorian Square. Shopping area located in downtown restoration project. Specialty stores; restaurants; Children's Museum (phone 859/258-3253); parking in 400-car garage with covered walkway into mall. Vine St, across from Triangle Park, the Convention Center, and Rupp Arena. Phone 859/252-7575.

Waveland State Historic Site. Greek Revival mansion (1847) with 3 original outbldgs. Exhibits depict plantation life of 1840s. Playground. (Mar-Dec, Mon-Sat and Sun afternoons) 225 Waveland Museum Ln. Phone 859/272-3611. ¢¢

Annual Events

Blue Grass Stakes. Keeneland Race Course (see SEASONAL EVENTS).

Three-yr-olds; one of last major prep races before Kentucky Derby. Mid-Apr.

Rolex-Kentucky Event & Trade Fair. Kentucky Horse Park. Three-day endurance test for horse and rider in dressage, cross-country and stadium jumping. Fair features boutiques. Phone 859/233-2362. Late Apr.

High Hope Steeplechase. Kentucky Horse Park. Mid-May.

Egyptian Event. Kentucky Horse Park. Activities highlighting rare Egyptian Arabian horses. Show classes, Walk of Stallions, Breeder's Sale, native costumes, seminars, art auction, and Egyptian Bazaar. Early June.

Festival of the Bluegrass. Kentucky Horse Park. Campground. Top names in Bluegrass music, with more than 20 bands appearing. Incl special shows for children; crafts; workshops with the musicians. The 600-acre park has more than 750 electric hookups for campers. For information, tickets, contact PO Box 644, Georgetown 40324; 859/846-4995. Second full wkend June.

Junior League Horse Show. The Red Mile Harness Track. Outdoor Saddlebred horse show. Contact PO Box 1092, 40589; 859/252-1893. Six days early-mid-July.

Grand Circuit Meet. The Red Mile Track (see SEASONAL EVENTS). Features Kentucky Futurity race, the final leg of trotting's Triple Crown. Mon-Sat. Phone 859/255-0752. Two wks, late Sep-early Oct.

Seasonal Events

Thoroughbred racing. Keeneland Race Course, 6 mi W on US 60. Phone 859/288-4333. Three wks Apr and 3 wks Oct.

Harness racing. The Red Mile Harness Track, 1200 Red Mile Rd, 1½ mi S on US 68. Also site of Grand Circuit racing (see ANNUAL EVENTS). Phone 859/255-0752. Night racing (May and late Sep-early Oct, Wed-Sat).

Motels/Motor Lodges

★★ **BEST WESTERN REGENCY.** *2241 Elkhorn Rd (40505), I-75 Exit 110.* 859/293-2202; fax 859/293-1821. 112 rms, 2 story. S $54-$74; D $59-$79; suite $139; under 18 free. Crib free. Pet accepted; $10. TV; cable (premium). Pool; whirlpool.

Sauna. Complimentary continental bkfst. Restaurant nearby. Ck-out 11 am. Coin lndry. Meeting rms. Business servs avail. Cr cds: A, C, DS, MC, V.

★★ **CAMPBELL HOUSE INN.** *1375 Harrodsburg Rd (40504).* 859/255-4281; fax 859/254-4368. 370 rms, 3 story. S $59-$89; D $69-$99; each addl $10; suites $89-$189; under 12 free. Crib free. TV; cable. Heated pool; poolside serv. Restaurants 6 am-10 pm. Bar 9-1 am; entertainment. Ck-out noon. Coin lndry. Convention facilities. Business servs avail. In-rm modem link. Bellhops. Valet serv. Sundries. Gift shop. Barber, beauty shop. Free airport transportation. Tennis. 18-hole golf, pro. Exercise equipt. Game rm. Bathrm phones, refrigerators. Cr cds: A, D, DS, MC, V.

★★ **COMFORT INN.** *2381 Buena Vista Dr (40505), I-75 Exit 110.* 859/299-0302; fax 859/299-2306. 124 rms, 3 story. S $59-$69; D $69-$89; each addl $7; under 18 free. Crib free. TV; cable (premium). Indoor pool; whirlpool. Complimentary continental bkfst. Restaurant nearby. Ck-out noon. Meeting rms. Business servs avail. Exercise equipt. Refrigerators, microwaves avail. Cr cds: A, D, DS, JCB, MC, V.

★ **DAYS INN.** *5575 Athens Boonesboro Rd (40509), I-75 Exit 104.* 859/263-3100; fax 859/263-3120; toll-free 800/329-7466. www.daysinn.com. 56 rms, 2 story. S $40-$60; D $45-$65; each addl $5; family rates; higher rates special events. Crib free. Pet accepted. TV. Complimentary continental bkfst. Restaurant nearby. Ck-out 11 am. Business servs avail. In-rm modem link. Some microwaves. Cr cds: A, C, D, DS, MC, V.

★★ **HOLIDAY INN LEXINGTON NORTH.** *1950 Newton Pike (40511), ½ blk S of I-75 Exit 115.* 859/233-0512; fax 859/231-9285; res 800/465-4329. 303 rms, 2 story. S $109.95; D $114.95; suites $250; under 18 free. Crib free. Pet accepted, some restrictions. TV; cable (premium). Indoor pool; whirlpool. Supervised children's activities (Memorial Day-Labor Day). Coffee in rms. Restaurant 6 am-2 pm, 5-10 pm. Bar 2 pm-1 am. Ck-out noon. Coin lndry. Convention facilities. Business center. In-rm modem link. Bellhops. Sundries. Gift shop. Putting green. Exercise equipt; sauna. Game rm. Some refrigerators, microwaves. Cr cds: A, C, D, DS, MC, V.

★ **LA QUINTA INN.** *1919 Stanton Way (40511), I-64/75 Exit 115. 859/231-7551; fax 859/281-6002.* 129 rms, 2 story. S $64; D $68; each addl $8; under 18 free; higher rates some wkends. Crib free. Pet accepted, some restrictions. TV; cable. Pool. Complimentary continental bkfst. Coffee in rms. Restaurant adj 6 am-10 pm; wkends to 11 pm. Ck-out noon. Business servs avail. In-rm modem link. Valet serv. Guest lndry. Cr cds: A, C, D, DS, MC, V.

★ **MICROTEL.** *2240 Buena Vista Dr (40505), I-75 Exit 110. 859/299-9600; fax 859/299-8719; toll-free 800/456-7610. www.microtelinn.com.* 99 rms, 2 story. Apr-Oct: S $37.95; D $42.95; under 16 free; lower rates rest of yr. Crib free. TV; cable. Coffee in lobby. Restaurant adj open 24 hrs. Ck-out noon. In-rm modem link. Cr cds: A, C, D, DS, MC, V.

★★ **QUALITY INN NORTHWEST.** *1050 Newtown Pike (40511), I-75/I-64 Exit 115. 859/233-0561; fax 859/231-6125; res 800/228-5151; toll-free 800/638-7949. Email vm649@aol.com; www.qualityinn.bizland.com.* 109 rms, 2 story. Mar-Oct: S, D $89.95; each addl $5; under 18 free; lower rates rest of yr. Crib avail. Pet accepted, some restrictions. Parking lot. Pool. TV; cable. Complimentary continental bkfst, coffee in rms, newspaper, toll-free calls. Ck-out noon, ck-in 1 pm. Meeting rms. Business servs avail. Dry cleaning, coin lndry. Gift shop. Exercise equipt. Golf, 18 holes. Picnic facilities. Cr cds: A, C, D, DS, ER, JCB, MC, V.

★★ **RAMADA INN & CONFERENCE CENTER.** *2143 N Broadway (40505), I-75 Exit 113. 859/299-1261;* fax 859/293-0048; res 800/2RAMADA. Email ramadainnlexky@aol.com. 146 rms, 2-3 story. S, D $100-$110; each addl $10; under 18 free; wkend rates. Crib free. TV; cable (premium). Indoor/outdoor pools; whirlpool. Restaurant 6:30 am-2 pm, 5-10 pm; Fri, Sat to 11 pm. Bar 4:30 pm-midnight; entertainment Fri, Sat. Ck-out 11 am. Meeting rms. In-rm modem link. Bellhops. Valet serv. Free airport transportation. Lighted tennis. Putting green. Exercise equipt; sauna. Rec rm. Balconies. Cr cds: A, C, D, DS, MC, V.

★ **RED ROOF INN.** *1980 Haggard Ct (40505), US 27, 68 at jct I-64, I-75 Exit 113. 859/293-2626; fax 859/299-8353; toll-free 800/843-7663.* 108 rms, 2 story. S $35.99-$45.99; D $41.99-$61.99; each addl $7; under 18 free. Crib free. Pet accepted, some restrictions. TV; cable (premium). Complimentary coffee in lobby. Restaurant nearby. Ck-out noon. Business servs avail. Cr cds: A, DS, MC, V.

★ **SHONEY'S INN.** *2753 Richmond Rd (40509), jct US 25 and KY 4. 859/269-4999; fax 859/268-2346; toll-free 800/222-2222.* 102 rms, 2 story. S $57-$67; D $62-$72; each addl $5; under 18 free. Crib free. TV; cable. Pool. Complimentary coffee in lobby. Restaurant adj 6 am-midnight; wkends to 2 am. Ck-out noon. Meeting rms. Business servs avail. Valet serv. Sundries. Cr cds: A, C, D, DS, MC, V.

★★ **SPRINGS INN.** *2020 Harrodsburg Rd (40503). 859/277-5751; fax 859/277-3142; toll-free 800/354-9503. Email reservations@springsinn.com.* 196 rms, 2 story. S $58; D $68; suites $88-$160. Crib free. TV; cable. Pool; wading pool. Restaurant 6:30 am-10 pm; Sun 7 am-8:30 pm. Bar 11 am-midnight; entertainment Wed-Sat. Ck-out noon. Meeting rms. Business servs avail. Valet serv. Gift shop. Free airport transportation. Cr cds: A, DS, MC, V.

★ **SUPER 8 MOTEL.** *2351 Buena Vista Rd (40505), I-75 Exit 110. 859/299-6241; fax 859/299-6241; toll-free*

800/800-8000. www.super8.com. 62 rms, 2 story. Apr-Oct: S $41.99; D $50.99-$60.99; each addl $5; under 12 free; wkly rates; higher rates horse racing; lower rates rest of yr. Crib free. Pet accepted. TV; cable (premium). Complimentary coffee in lobby. Restaurant adj open 24 hrs. Ck-out 11 am. Cr cds: A, C, D, DS, MC, V.

Hotels

★★ **COURTYARD BY MARRIOTT.** *775 Newtown Ct (40511). 859/253-4646; fax 859/253-9118; toll-free 800/321-2211. Email cy.lexno.gm@ marriott.com; www.courtyard.com/ lexno.* 146 rms, 3 story, 12 suites. Mar-June, Sep-Oct: S, D $94; each addl $5; suites $114; under 17 free; lower rates rest of yr. Crib avail. Parking lot. Indoor pool, whirlpool. TV; cable (premium). Complimentary coffee in rms, newspaper, toll-free calls. Restaurant nearby. Bar. Ck-out noon, ck-in 3 pm. Meeting rms. Business servs avail. Dry cleaning, coin lndry. Exercise privileges, sauna. Golf, 18 holes. Tennis, 2 courts. Picnic facilities. Cr cds: A, C, D, DS, MC, V.

★★ **HAMPTON INN.** *2251 Elkhorn Rd (40505), I-75 Exit 110. 859/299-2613; fax 859/299-9664; res 800/426-7866. Email lexeh01@hi-hotel.com.* 125 rms, 5 story. Apr-Aug, Oct: S $79; D $89; under 18 free; lower rates rest of yr. Crib avail. Pet accepted. Parking lot. Indoor pool. TV; cable (premium), VCR avail. Complimentary continental bkfst, coffee in rms, newspaper, toll-free calls. Restaurant. Ck-out noon. Meeting rms. Business servs avail. Dry cleaning. Exercise equipt. Golf. Cr cds: A, D, DS, MC, V.

★★★ **HILTON SUITES.** *245 Lexington Green Cr (40503). 859/271-4000; fax 859/273-2975.* 174 suites, 6 story. S $115-$165; D $125-$180; each addl $10; family rates; wkend package plans; higher rates: Kentucky Derby, race season. Crib free. TV; cable (premium). Pool; poolside serv. Coffee in rms. Restaurant 6:30 am-2 pm, 5-10 pm. Bar 2 pm-1 am. Ck-out noon. Meeting rms. Business center. In-rm modem link. Free airport, bus depot transportation. Exercise equipt; sauna. Refrigerators. Cr cds: A, C, D, DS, ER, JCB, MC, V.

★★ **HOLIDAY INN.** *5532 Athens Boonesboro Rd (40509), I-75 Exit 104. 859/263-5241; fax 859/563-4333; toll-free 800/394-8407. Email hol.innso@ worldnet.att.com.* 144 rms, 2 story, 5 suites. Mar-Oct: S, D $80; suites $115; under 18 free; lower rates rest of yr. Crib avail. Pet accepted, some restrictions. Parking lot. Indoor/outdoor pools, whirlpool. TV; cable. Complimentary coffee in rms, newspaper, toll-free calls. Restaurant. Bar. Ck-out noon, ck-in 3 pm. Meeting rms. Business servs avail. Dry cleaning, coin lndry. Exercise equipt, sauna. Golf. Cr cds: A, C, D, DS, JCB, MC, V.

★★★ **HYATT REGENCY LEXINGTON.** *401 W High St (40507). 859/253-1234; fax 859/254-7430; res 800/233-1234.* 365 rms, 16 story. S $140; D $183; suites $275-$650; under 18 free; wkend plans. Crib free. TV; cable (premium), VCR avail. Indoor pool. Restaurants 6 am-10:30 pm. Bar 11-1 am. Ck-out noon. Convention facilities. Business center. In-rm modem link. Concierge. Shopping arcade. Free airport transportation. Exercise equipt. Sun deck. Luxury level. Cr cds: A, C, D, DS, ER, JCB, MC, V.

★★★ **RADISSON PLAZA HOTEL.** *369 W Vine St (40507). 859/231-9000; fax 859/281-3737; toll-free 800/333-3333. www.radisson.com.* 367 rms, 22 story. S $155; D $165; each addl $10; suites $190-$390; under 18 free; wkend rates. Crib free. Pet accepted. Valet parking $8. TV; cable (premium), VCR avail (movies). Indoor pool; whirlpool, poolside serv. Coffee in rms. Restaurant 6 am-11 pm. Rm serv to 1 am; wkends to 2 am. Bar 11:30-1 am; entertainment. Ck-out noon. Convention facilities. Business center. Concierge. Gift shop. Free airport transportation. Lighted tennis privileges. Exercise equipt; sauna. Health club privileges. Rec rm. Some refrigerators. Wet bar in suites. Atrium with fountains.

Luxury level. Cr cds: A, C, D, DS, ER, JCB, MC, V.

Resort

★★★★ **MARRIOTT'S GRIFFIN GATE RESORT.** *1800 Newtown Pike (40511), I-64 and I-75 Exit 115.* 859/231-5100; *fax* 859/255-9944. This 409-room, 21-suite resort sits in the heart of Kentucky Bluegrass Country. Although outdoor recreations, including a championship golf course, tennis courts, and an indoor and outdoor pool, would please any leisure guest, dataport and voice mail-equipped rooms, a business center, and corporate-team-challenge programs attract business clientele. Four restaurants include The Mansion, serving fine, American-continental cuisine in a beautiful, southern-antebellum mansion. 409 rms, 7 story. S $110-$154; D $129-$169; suite $295-$850; under 18 free; golf plans. Crib free. Pet accepted, some restrictions; $40. TV; cable (premium). 2 pools, 1 indoor; whirlpool, poolside serv. Playground. Supervised children's activities (summer). Dining rm 6 am-11 pm (see also MANSION AT GRIFFIN GATE). Bar 11-1 am. Ck-out noon. Coin lndry. Convention facilities. Business center. In-rm modem link. Valet serv. Gift shop. Barber, beauty shop. Package store 1 mi. Airport transportation. Sports dir. Lighted tennis, pro. 18-hole golf, greens fee $28-$62, pro, putting green. Seasonal activities incl walking tours, pool activities. Game rm. Exercise rm; sauna. Refrigerator in suites. Private patios, balconies. Picnic tables. Luxury level. Cr cds: A, C, D, DS, ER, JCB, MC, V.

B&Bs/Small Inns

★★ **1823 HISTORIC ROSE HILL INN.** *233 Rose Hill Ave (40383), 15 mi W on US 60, left on Main St, right on Rose Hill.* 859/873-5957; *fax* 859/873-1813; *toll-free* 800/307-0460. *Email innkeepers@rosehillinn.com; www.rosehillinn.com.* 4 rms, 2 story, 2 suites. S $85; D $99; each addl $15; suites $139; children $10. Crib avail. Pet accepted, some restrictions. Parking lot. TV; cable (DSS), VCR avail, CD avail. Complimentary full

bkfst, newspaper, toll-free calls. Restaurant noon-10 pm. Ck-out noon, ck-in 4 pm. Business servs avail. Golf, 18 holes. Tennis, 4 courts. Hiking trail. Picnic facilities. Cr cds: A, DS, MC, V.

★★★ **BED AND BREAKFAST AT SILLS INN.** *270 Montgomery Ave (40383), approx 15 mi W on US 60 to Versailles; 2 blks S of Courthouse on Main St, left on Montgomery Ave.* 859/873-4478; *fax* 859/873-7099; *toll-free* 800/526-9801. *Email sillsinn@aol.com; www.sillsinn.com.* 12 rms, 3 story. S, D $79-$159; each addl $25; wkly rates; higher rates Kentucky Derby. TV; cable, VCR. Complimentary full bkfst. Complimentary coffee in rms. Ck-out 11 am. Meeting rms. Business center. In-rm modem link. Valet serv. Concierge serv. Free airport transportation. Health club privileges. Some refrigerators, minibars; microwaves avail. Balconies. Restored Victorian-style house. Totally nonsmoking. Cr cds: A, DS, MC, V.

★★★ **GRATZ PARK INN.** *120 W 2nd St (40507).* 606/231-1777; *fax* 606/233-7593; *toll-free* 800/528-1234. *Email gratzinn@aol.com; www.gratz park.com.* 44 rms, 3 story, 6 suites. S, D $130; each addl $10; suites $250-$325; under 12 free. Crib free. TV; cable (premium). Complimentary continental bkfst. Restaurant 7-9:30 am, 5-10 pm; Fri to 11 pm; Sat 7-11 am, 5-11 pm; Sun 7-11 am. Ck-out noon. Meeting rms. Business servs avail. In-rm modem link. Free airport transportation. Health club privileges. Elegantly restored bldg (1916). Cr cds: A, DS, MC, V.

All Suite

★★★★ **SHERATON SUITES LEXINGTON.** *2601 Richmond Rd (40509), near jct New Circle Rd (KY 4).* 859/268-0060; *fax* 859/268-6209; *res* 800/325-3535; *toll-free* 800/262-3774. *www.sheraton.com.* 5 story, 155 suites. Apr, Oct: S $165; D $175; each addl $10; under 17 free; lower rates rest of yr. Crib avail. Valet parking avail. Pool. TV; cable (DSS). Complimentary coffee in rms, newspaper, toll-free calls. Restaurant 6:30 am-10 pm. Bar. Ck-out noon, ck-in 3 pm. Meeting rms. Business center. Bellhops. Concierge. Dry cleaning. Salon/barber. Free airport transportation. Exercise privileges. Golf, 18 holes. Tennis, 2 courts. Cr cds: A, D, DS, JCB, MC, V.

Restaurants

★★ **A-LA LUCIE.** *159 N Limestone St (40507), at Church St.* 606/252-5277. Specializes in fresh seafood, ethnic foods. Hrs: 6-9 pm. Closed Sun; hols. Res accepted. Bar. Dinner $13.95-$22. Intimate cafe. Cr cds: A, D, DS, MC, V.

★★★ **COACH HOUSE.** *855 S Broadway (40504), US 68.* 606/252-7777. Specializes in tuna, rack of lamb. Hrs: 11 am-2 pm, 5-10 pm; Sat from 5 pm. Closed Sun; Thanksgiving, Dec 25. Res accepted. Bar. Wine cellar. Lunch $5.50-$8.95; dinner $13.50-$25. Entertainment: jazz band Fri, Sat. Family-owned. Cr cds: A, C, D, DS, MC, V.

★★ **DARRYL'S 1891 RESTAURANT AND TAVERN.** *3292 Nicholasville Rd (40503), US 27, 1 blk S of New Circle Rd.* 859/272-1891. Specializes in prime rib, pork ribs. Hrs: 11 am-11 pm; Fri, Sat to midnight; Sun to 10 pm. Closed Dec 25. Res accepted. Bar. Lunch $3.99-$9.99; dinner $6.79-$15.99. Child's menu. Parking. Old English bldg. Braille menu. Cr cds: A, C, D, DS, MC, V.

★★ **DE SHA'S GRILLE AND BAR.** *101 N Broadway (40507).* 606/259-3771. *Email DeShas1@hlc.com; www.deshas.com.* Specializes in regional dishes. Hrs: 11 am-11 pm; Fri, Sat to midnight; Sun to 10 pm. Closed Thanksgiving, Dec 25. Bar. Lunch $3.95-$8.95; dinner $13.95-$19.95. Child's menu. Validated parking. In Victorian Sq. Antique bar; oak staircase to upper level. View of park. Cr cds: A, C, D, DS, MC, V.

★★ **DUDLEY'S.** *380 S Mill St (40508), in Dudley Sq.* 606/252-1010.

www.dudleysrestaurant.com. Specializes in seafood, beef, pasta. Hrs: 11:30 am-2:30 pm, 5:30-10 pm; Fri, Sat to 11 pm. Closed hols. Res accepted. Bar. Lunch $5.50-$9.50; dinner $13-$23. Parking. Restored school (1851); paintings. Cr cds: A, D, MC, V.

★★ **MALONE'S.** *3347 Tataes Creek Rd (40502), in shopping center.* 606/335-6500. *www.malones.com.* Specializes in steak, seafood. Hrs: 11:30 am-10 pm; Sat to 11 pm; Sun 11 am-9 pm; Sun brunch 11 am-2 pm. Closed hols. Res accepted. Dinner $6.95-$25.95. Sun brunch $5.95. Child's menu. Parking. Cr cds: A, DS, MC, V.

★★★ **MANSION AT GRIFFIN GATE.** *1800 Newtown Pike.* 606/288-6142. Specializes in beef, game, fresh seafood. Hrs: 6-10 pm; Fri, Sat to 10:30 pm. Res accepted. Bar. Wine list. Dinner $23.95-$38.95. Valet parking. Greek Revival mansion built 1873; antiques; crystal chandeliers. Cr cds: A, C, D, DS, MC, V.

★★ **RAFFERTY'S.** *2420 Nicholasville Rd (40503), US 27.* 606/278-9427. *www.raffertys.com.* Specializes in Danish baby-back pork ribs, prime rib. Hrs: 11 am-10:30 pm; Fri, Sat to 11 pm. Closed Thanksgiving, Dec 25. Bar. Lunch $4.95-$14.99; dinner $4.95-$14.99. Child's menu. Cr cds: A, D, DS, MC, V.

★★ **REGATTA SEAFOOD GRILLE.** *161 Lexington Green Circle (40503), in Lexington Green Mall.* 859/273-7875. *www.regattaseafood.com.* Specializes in fresh seafood, pasta. Hrs: 11:30 am-10 pm; Fri, Sat to 11 pm. Closed Dec 25. Res accepted. Bar. Lunch $5.95-$8.95; dinner $8.95-$16.95. Child's menu. Cr cds: A, D, DS, MC, V.

★★ **TONY ROMA'S.** *161 Lexington Green Circle (40503).* 606/272-7526. Specializes in ribs, chicken. Hrs: 11 am-10 pm; Fri, Sat to 11 pm. Closed Thanksgiving, Dec 25. Bar. Lunch

$4.99-$8.99; dinner $6.99-$15.99. Child's menu. Cr cds: A, D, DS, MC, V.

London

See also Corbin

Founded 1825 **Pop** 5,757
Elev 1,255 ft **Area code** 859
Zip 40741
Web www.tourky.com/london
Information London-Laurel County Tourist Commission, 140 W Daniel Boone Parkway; 859/878-6900 or800/348-0095

Motels/Motor Lodges

★★ **BEST WESTERN.** *207 W Hwy 80 (40741), ¼ mi E of I-75 Exit 41.* 606/864-2222; fax 606/878-2825; toll-free 800/528-1234. 100 rms, 2 story. June-Oct: S $51; D $60; each addl $5; lower rates rest of yr. Crib $3. TV; cable (premium). Indoor pool; whirlpool. Complimentary continental bkfst. Restaurant 7 am-9 pm. Ck-out noon. Meeting rms. Cr cds: A, C, D, DS, MC, V.

★★ **BUDGET HOST WESTGATE INN.** *254 W Daniel Boone Pkwy (40741), Exit 41 on KY 80.* 606/878-7330; fax 606/878-7330; res 800/283-4678. www.budgethost.com. 46 rms, 2 story. Aug: S $43; D $46; each addl $3; suites $67; under 12 free; lower rates rest of yr. Crib avail. Pet accepted, some restrictions. Parking lot. Pool. TV; cable (DSS). Complimentary continental bkfst, toll-free calls. Restaurant noon-midnight. Ck-out 11 am, ck-in 8 pm. Meeting rm. Business servs avail. Free airport transportation. Golf, 18 holes. Tennis. Picnic facilities. Cr cds: A, C, D, DS, MC, V.

★★ **HAMPTON INN.** *125 Adams Rd (40701), I-75 Exit 38.* 606/877-1000; fax 606/523-1130; res 800/426-7866. Email cbmky01@hi-hotel.com. 82 rms, 2 story. S $51.95-$59.95; D $61.95-$71.95; under 18 free. Crib free. TV; cable (premium). Heated pool. Complimentary continental bkfst. Coffee in rms. Restaurant opp 6 am-10 pm. Ck-out noon. Meeting rms. Business servs avail. In-rm modem link. Health club privileges. Some refrigerators, whirlpools. Cr cds: A, C, D, DS, ER, JCB, MC, V.

Hotels

★★ **COMFORT SUITES.** *1918 W Hwy 192 (40741), I-75 Exit 38.* 606/877-7848; fax 606/877-7907; res 800/228-5150., 3 story. 62 suites. Apr-Sep: S $71; D $77; each addl $8; under 18 free; lower rates rest of yr. Crib avail. Indoor pool. TV; cable (premium), VCR avail. Complimentary continental bkfst, coffee in rms, newspaper, toll-free calls. Restaurant. Ck-out noon, ck-in 3 pm. Meeting rm. Business servs avail. Dry cleaning, coin lndry. Exercise privileges. Golf. Tennis. Cr cds: A, C, D, DS, JCB, MC, V.

★★ **HOLIDAY INN EXPRESS.** *400 GOP St (40741), jct I-75 and KY 80.* 606/878-7678; fax 606/878-7654; res 800/465-4329; toll-free 800/831-3958. Email holidayinnex@kih.net; www.londonky.com/holidayinnexpress. 60 rms, 2 story. Mar, May-July, Sep-Oct: S, D $85; each addl $7; lower rates rest of yr. Crib avail. Pet accepted, some restrictions. Parking lot. Indoor/outdoor pools, whirlpool. TV; cable (premium). Complimentary continental bkfst, coffee in rms, newspaper, toll-free calls. Restaurant 11 am-10 pm. Ck-out 11 am, ck-in 4 pm. Dry cleaning. Hiking trail. Cr cds: A, C, D, DS, JCB, MC, V.

Louisville

(C-5) *See also Fort Knox, Shepherdsville*

Founded 1778 **Pop** 269,063
Elev 462 ft **Area code** 502
Web www.louisville-visitors.com

Information Convention and Visitors Bureau, 400 S first St, 40202; 502/584-2121 or 800/792-5595

Louisville is a unique city. It has southern graces and a determined dedication to music and the arts, but to the world Louisville is "Derby City" for at least two weeks of every year. Since its first running on May 17, 1875, the Kentucky Derby has generated tremendous excitement. Modeled after England's Epsom Derby, it is the oldest race in continuous existence in the US. The first Saturday in May each year world attention focuses on Churchill Downs as the classic "run for the roses" is played out against its backdrop of Edwardian towers and antique grandstands.

The social highlight of a very social city, Derby festivities are a glamorous mélange of carnival, fashion show, spectacle, and celebration of the horse. From the opening strains of "My Old Kentucky Home," played before the big race, until the final toast of bourbon is made, Louisville takes on a uniquely festive character. Afterward, the center of thoroughbred racing quickly returns to normalcy—a city southern in manner, midwestern in pace.

Situated at the falls of the Ohio River, Louisville is a city long nurtured by river traffic. The Spanish, French, English, Scottish, Irish, and Germans all had roles in its exploration, settlement, and development. George Rogers Clark established the first real settlement, a base for military operations against the British, on a spit of land above the falls, now entirely erased by the river. Named after Louis XVI of France, the settlement became an important portage point around the falls; later a canal bypassed them. Today the McAlpine Locks and Dam provide modern navigation around the falls of the Ohio.

Louisville is a top producer of bourbon and a leader in synthetic rubber, paint and varnish, cigarettes, home appliances, and aluminum for home use.

This is a community that takes its culture seriously, with a public subscription Fund for the Arts subsidizing the Tony Award-Winning Actors Theater. The city also boasts the Kentucky Center for the Arts, home of ballet, opera, art and music groups, and other cultural organizations.

Transportation

Car Rental Agencies. See IMPORTANT TOLL-FREE NUMBERS.

Public Transportation. Buses (Transit Authority of River City), phone 502/585-1234.

Airport Information

Louisville International Airport. Information 502/367-4636; lost and found 502/368-6524; weather 502/968-6025.

What to See and Do

American Printing House for the Blind. The largest and oldest (1858) publishing house for the blind. In addition to books and music in Braille, it issues talking books, magazines, large type textbooks, and educational aids. Tours (Mon-Thurs; closed hols). 1839 Frankfort Ave, 3 mi E. Phone 502/895-2405. **FREE**

Bellarmine College. (1950) 2,300 students. A 115-acre campus. Liberal arts and sciences. The campus houses the Thomas Merton Studies Center, with his manuscripts, drawings, tapes, and published works (Tues-Fri, by appt; closed hols); phone 502/452-8187. Guided campus tours (by appt). Newburg Rd, 5 mi SE. Phone 502/452-8000.

Cave Hill Cemetery. Burial ground of George Rogers Clark. Colonel Harland Sanders, of fried chicken fame, is also buried here. Rare trees, shrubs, and plants; swans, geese, ducks. (Daily) 701 Baxter Ave, at E end of Broadway. Phone 502/451-5630.

✪ **Churchill Downs.** Founded in 1875, this historic and world-famous thoroughbred race track is the home of the Kentucky Derby, "the most exciting 2 minutes in sports." (See ANNUAL EVENTS) Spring race meet, late Apr-June; fall race meet, late Oct-late Nov; Kentucky Derby, first Sat May. 700 Central Ave. Phone 502/636-4400. ¢-¢¢ Adj is

✪ **Kentucky Derby Museum.** Features exhibits on thoroughbred racing and the Kentucky Derby. Multi-image show, hands-on exhibits, artifacts, educational

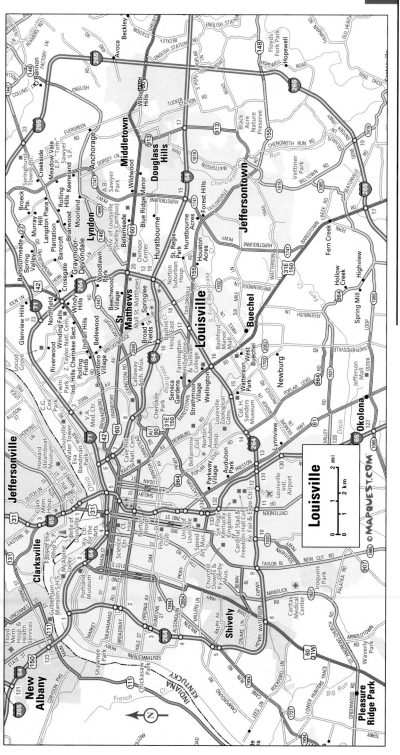

programs, tours, and special events. Outdoor paddock area with thoroughbreds. Tours of Churchill downs (weather permitting). Gift shop; cafe serving lunch (wkdays). (Daily; closed Thanksgiving, Oaks & Derby Days, Dec 25) Phone 502/637-1111 or 502/637-7097. ¢¢

Colonel Harland Sanders Museum. Artifacts and memorabilia relating to Colonel Harland Sanders and Kentucky Fried Chicken. Audiovisual displays, 28-min film "Portrait of a Legend." (Mon-Thurs, limited hrs Fri; closed hols and first Fri in May) 1441 Gardiner Lane. Phone 502/874-8300. **FREE**

E.P. "Tom" Sawyer State Park. Approx 370 acres with swimming pool. Tennis; archery range; BMX track; ballfields; gymnasium, games area. Picnicking. Some fees. 3000 Freys Hill Rd. Phone 502/426-8950.

Farmington. (1810) Federal-style house built from plans drawn by Thomas Jefferson. Abraham Lincoln visited here in 1841. Furnished with pre-1820 antiques; hidden stairway, octagonal rms; museum room; blacksmith shop, stone barn, 19th-century garden. Guided tour (Tues-Sun; closed hols) Grounds and gardens (Tues-Sun; free). 3033 Bardstown Rd N, at jct Watterson Expwy (I-264), 6 mi SE on US 31E. Phone 502/452-9920. ¢¢

The Filson Club. Historical library (fee); manuscript collection, photographs, and prints collection. (Mon-Sat; closed hols) 1310 S 3rd St. Phone 502/635-5083. Mansion tour **FREE**

Historic districts. Features renovated Victorian housing; W Main St Historic District is a concentration of cast iron bldgs being renovated on Main St between first and 8th Sts; Butchertown is a renovated 19th-century German community between Market St & Story Ave; Cherokee Triangle is a well-preserved Victorian neighborhood with diverse architectural details; and Portland is an early settlement and commercial port with Irish and French heritage. Old Louisville, between Breckinridge and 9th Sts, near Central Park.

Jefferson County Courthouse. (1835-60) Designed by Gideon Shryock in Greek Revival style. Cast-iron floor in rotunda supports statue of Henry Clay. Magnificent cast-iron monumental stair and balustrade in 68-ft rotunda. Statues of Thomas Jefferson and Louis XVI, as well as war memorial on grounds. Guided tours (by appt). (Mon-Fri; closed hols) Jefferson St between 5th & 6th Sts. Phone 502/574-5761. **FREE**

Kentucky Center for the Arts. Three stages present national and intl performers showcasing a wide range of music, dance, and drama. Distinctive glass-arched lobby features a collection of 20th-century sculpture and provides a panoramic view of Ohio River and Falls Fountain. Restaurant, gift shop, parking garage. 5 Riverfront Plaza. Phone 502/584-7777 or 800/775-7777 for schedule and ticket information.

Kentucky Fair and Exposition Center. More than 1 million sq ft complex incl coliseum, exposition halls, stadium, amusement park. More than 1,500 events take place throughout the yr, incl Univ of Louisville football, basketball, Louisville Riverfrogs, and Milwaukee Brewers minor league affiliate, the Louisville Redbirds. I-65S at I-264W. Phone 502/367-5000.

Kentucky Kingdom—The Thrill Park. Amusement and water park with more than 110 rides and attractions, incl 5 roller coasters. (Memorial Day-Labor Day, daily; early Apr-Memorial Day, Fri eves, Sat and Sun; Labor Day-late Sep, Sat and Sun) Adj to Kentucky Fair and Exposition Center, 937 Phillips Ln. Phone 502/366-7508. ¢¢¢¢

Locust Grove. (ca 1790) Home of General George Rogers Clark from 1809-18. Handsome Georgian mansion on 55 acres; original paneling, staircase; authentic furnishings; garden; 8 restored outbldgs. Visitor center features audiovisual program. (Daily; closed hols, Derby Day) 6 mi NE on River Rd, then 1 mi SW at 561 Blankenbaker Ln. Phone 502/897-9845. ¢¢

Louisville Falls Fountain. World's largest floating fountain sprays water 375 ft high. Light shows, with more than 100 colored lights, offered nightly. (May-Nov) On the Ohio River, between Clark Memorial Bridge and Conrail Bridge.

Louisville Presbyterian Theological Seminary. (1853) 250 students. On 52-acre campus is Gardencourt, a renovated turn-of-the-century mansion, and the Archaeological Museum, with collection of Palestinian pottery (daily; closed hols). 1044 Alta Vista Rd, ½ mi off US 60 Business, adj to Cherokee Park. Phone 502/895-3411. **FREE**

Louisville Science Center. Hands-on scientific exhibits; aerospace hall; IMAX 4-story screen film theater (fee); Egyptian mummy's tomb; World We Create interactive exhibit. (Daily; closed Thanksgiving, Dec 24-25) 727 W Main St. Phone 502/561-6111. ¢¢

Louisville Slugger Museum & Bat Factory. Manufacturers of Louisville Slugger baseball bats and Power-bilt golf clubs. No cameras. Children over 8 yrs only; must be accompanied by adult. Tours (Mon-Sat; closed hols). 800 W Main St. Phone 502/588-7228. ¢¢

Louisville Zoo. Modern zoo exhibits more than 1,600 animals in naturalistic settings. In HerpAquarium are simulated water, desert, and rain forest ecosystems. Islands exhibit highlights endangered species and habitats. Camel and elephant rides (summer). (Daily; closed Jan 1, Thanksgiving, Dec 25). 1100 Trevilian Way, 7 mi SE via I-65, I-264 to Poplar Level Road N. Phone 502/459-2181. ¢¢¢

Otter Creek Park. A 3,000-acre park located on the site of Rock Haven, a town destroyed by 1937 flood. Much of the park that fronts the Ohio River consists of steep cliffs or very wooded banks. Otter Creek is a small, deeply entrenched stream with steep banks. Artifacts found here indicate that many Native American tribes used the Otter Creek area as hunting and fishing grounds. Swimming pools; fishing; boating (ramp); miniature golf, tennis, basketball, picnic facilities, tent and trailer sites, cabins, lodge, and restaurant. Nature center (Mar-Nov; Tues-Sun), wildlife area. Park (daily). For fees, information contact Park Manager, 850 Otter Creek Park Rd, Vine Grove 40175. 30 mi SW via US 31W and KY 1638, near Fort Knox. Phone 502/583-3577. **FREE**

Sightseeing.

Riverboat excursion. Two-hr afternoon trips on sternwheeler *Belle of Louisville.* (Memorial Day-Labor Day, Tues-Sun); sunset cruise (Tues and Thurs); dance cruise (Sat). Riverfront Plaza, wharf, 4th St and River Rd. Phone 502/574-BELL for rates and schedules.

Spalding University. (1814) 1,400 students. Liberal arts college. On campus is Whitestone Mansion (1871), a Renaissance Revival house with period furniture (Mon-Fri; closed hols), art gallery. 851 S 4th St. Phone 502/585-9911. **FREE**

Thomas Edison House. Restored 1850 cottage where Edison lived while working for Western Union after the Civil War. Bedrm furnished in the period; 4 display rms with Edison memorabilia and inventions: phonographs, records, and cylinders, early bulb collection. (Limited hrs; call for appt) 729-31 E Washington. Phone 502/585-5247. ¢

University of Louisville. (1798) 23,000 students. On Belknap Campus is the Ekstrom Library with the John Patterson rare book collection, original town charter signed by Thomas Jefferson and the Photo Archives, one of largest collections of photographs in the country. Also here is an enlarged cast of Rodin's sculpture *The Thinker;* a Foucault pendulum more than 73 ft high, demonstrating the Earth's rotation; and the largest concert organ in the Midwest. Two art galleries feature works by students and locals as well as national and intl artists (Sun-Fri). The grave of Supreme Court Justice Louis D. Brandeis is located under the School of Law portico. Contact information centers at 3rd St entrance or at corner first & Brandeis Sts. 3 mi S at 3rd St & Eastern Pkwy. Phone 502/852-6565. Also on campus are

J.B. Speed Art Museum. Oldest and largest in state. Traditional and modern art, English Renaissance Rm, sculpture collection, Kentucky artists; special exhibits. Cafe, shop, and bookstore; tours on request. (Tues-Sun; closed hols) 2035 S 3rd St. Phone 502/634-2700. **FREE**

Rauch Memorial Planetarium. Planetarium shows (Sat afternoons). Phone 502/852-6665. ¢¢

Water Tower. Restored tower and pumping station built in the classic style in 1860. Tower houses Louisville Visual Art Association, Center for Contemporary Art. Exhibits vary. (Daily; closed hols) Zorn Ave & River Road. Phone 502/896-2146. **FREE**

Zachary Taylor National Cemetery. The 12th President of the US is buried here, near the site where he lived from infancy to adulthood. The Taylor family plot is surrounded by this national cemetery, established 1928. (Daily) 4701 Brownsboro Rd, 7 mi E on US 42. Phone 502/893-3852.

Annual Events

Kentucky Derby Festival. Two-week celebration with Pegasus Parade, Great Steamboat Race (between *Belle of Louisville* and *Delta Queen*), Great Balloon Race, mini-marathon, concerts, sports tournaments. For information on tickets for festival events contact Kentucky Derby Festival, 1001 S 3rd St, 40203; phone 502/584-6383 or 800/928-FEST. Early May.

Kentucky Derby. Churchill Downs. The first jewel in the Triple Crown. Contact Churchill Downs, 700 Central Ave, 40208; 502/636-4400. First Sat May.

Kentucky State Fair. Kentucky Fair & Exposition Center. Livestock shows; championship horse show; home and fine arts exhibits; midway, entertainment. Contact VP of Expositions, PO Box 37130, 40233; 502/367-5000. Aug.

Corn Island Storytelling Festival. Recaptures bygone days of yarn spinning. Events held at various sites in city. Programs incl ghost stories at night in Long Run Park. For information contact Festival Director, 12019 Donohue Ave, 40243. Sep.

Seasonal Events

Performing arts. Louisville Orchestra (502/587-8681), Kentucky Opera (502/584-4500), Broadway Series (502/584-7469), Louisville Ballet (502/583-3150); all at Kentucky Center for the Arts; 502/584-7777. Actors Theatre, 316 W Main St, phone

Churchill Downs

502/584-1265. Kentucky Shakespeare Festival, free plays in Central Park, Mon-Sat, mid-June-early Aug; phone 502/583-8738.

Horse racing. Churchill Downs (see).

Additional Visitor Information

The Louisville Convention & Visitors Bureau, 400 S First St, 40202, phone 502/582-3732 or 800/792-5595, provides literature and information. Also avail is information about several unique areas of special interest, such as **Old Louisville, Butchertown, Phoenix Hill, Cherokee Triangle,** and the **Main St Preservation District.**

The Convention & Visitors Bureau also operates 3 visitor information centers that can be found on westbound I-64, in the central lobby of Louisville Intl Airport, and downtown at first & Liberty Sts.

For information on parks and course in the area, phone the Metropolitan Park and Recreation Board, 502/222-2154.

City Neighborhoods

Many of the restaurants, unrated dining establishments, and some lodgings listed under Louisville incl neighborhoods as well as exact street addresses. Geographic descriptions of these areas are given.

Downtown. S of the Ohio River, W of Shelby St, N of Oak St, and E of 9th St. **S of Downtown:** S of Oak St. **E of Downtown:** E of Shelby St.

Old Louisville. S of Breckenridge St, W of I-65, N of Eastern Pkwy, and E of 9th St.

Motels/Motor Lodges

★ ★ **BEST WESTERN.** *4805 Brownsboro Rd (40207), N of Downtown.* 502/893-2551; fax 502/895-2417; toll-free 800/528-1234. Email bestwestern 18076@aol.com; www.bestwestern.com/ brownsboroinn. 144 rms, 2 story, 14 suites. May: S, D $95; each addl $8; suites $125; under 17 free; lower rates rest of yr. Crib avail. Parking lot. Indoor/outdoor pools, lifeguard, whirlpool. TV; cable (premium), VCR avail. Complimentary continental bkfst, coffee in rms, toll-free calls. Restaurant nearby. Bar. Ck-out noon, ck-in 3 pm. Meeting rms. Business servs avail. Dry cleaning, coin lndry. Free airport transportation. Exercise equipt. Golf. Cr cds: A, C, D, DS, JCB, MC, V.

D 🛏 ➰ 🛅 🏃 ➰ 🔥 SC

★ ★ **BRECKINRIDGE INN.** *2800 Breckinridge Ln (40220), I-264 Exit 18A, S of Downtown.* 502/456-5050; fax 502/456-1577. www.travelbase. com. 123 rms, 2 story. S, D $65-$95; each addl $7; under 12 free. Crib $7. Pet accepted; $50. TV; cable. 2 pools, 1 indoor; lifeguard. Restaurant 7 am-1:30 pm, 5-9 pm. Bar. Ck-out noon. Meeting rms. Business servs avail. Valet serv. Coin lndry. Sundries. Gift shop. Barber shop. Free airport transportation. Lighted tennis. Exercise equipt, sauna. Cr cds: A, D, DS, MC, V.

D ➰ ➰ ➰ 🛅 🏃 ➰ 🔥

★ ★ **COMFORT SUITES.** *1850 Resource Way (40299), E of Downtown.* 502/266-6509; fax 502/266-9014. 70 suites. S, D $79-$159. Crib free. TV; cable (premium). Indoor pool; whirlpool. Complimentary continental bkfst, coffee in rms. Restaurant nearby. Ck-out 11 am. Business center. Free airport transportation. Refrigerators, microwaves. Cr cds: A, D, DS, MC, V.

D ➰ 🛅 🔥 🏃

★ ★ **COURTYARD BY MARRIOTT.** *9608 Blairwood Rd (40222), I-64 Hurstbourne Ln Exit 15, E of Downtown.* 502/429-0006; fax 502/429-5926. 151 rms, 4 story. S, D $109; suites $125; under 18 free; wkend rates. Crib free. TV; cable (premium). Pool; whirlpool. Complimentary coffee in rms. Bar 5:30-10 pm. Ck-out noon. Coin lndry. Meeting rms. Business servs avail. In-rm modem link. Valet serv. Exercise equipt. Health club privileges. Refrigerators; microwaves avail. Cr cds: A, D, DS, MC, V.

D 🛏 ➰ 🏃 ➰ 🔥 🏃

★ ★ ★ **EXECUTIVE INN MOTOR HOTEL.** *978 Phillips Ln (40209), I-65 and I-264 Exit Fair/Expo Center, S of Downtown.* 502/367-6161; fax 502/363-1880; toll-free 800/626-2706. Email toetken@execinn.win.net; www. win.net/~execinn/. 465 rms, 2-6 story. S $85; D $95; each addl $10; suites $109-$282; under 18 free. Crib free. Pet accepted. TV; cable, VCR avail. 2 pools, 1 indoor; wading pool, poolside serv, lifeguard. Restaurants 6:30 am-midnight. Bar 11 am-midnight, closed Sun. Ck-out 1 pm. Convention facilities. Business servs avail. Bellhops. Sundries. Gift shop. Barber, beauty shop. Free airport transportation. Exercise rm; sauna. Lawn games. Some private patios, balconies. Tudor-inspired architecture. Cr cds: A, C, D, DS, MC, V.

D ➰ ➰ 🛅 🏃 ➰ 🔥 SC

★ ★ **FAIRFIELD INN BY MARRIOTT.** *9400 Blairwood Rd (40222), I-64 Exit 15, E of Downtown.* 502/339-1900; fax 502/339-2494; res 800/228-2800. Email fi377gm@sage-hospitality.com. 105 rms, 3 story. S, D $60-$85; each addl $10; under 18 free. Crib free. TV; cable (premium). Pool. Continental bkfst. Restaurant adj 6 am-11 pm. Ck-out noon. Meeting rms. In-rm modem link. Lndry facilities. Cr cds: A, DS, MC, V.

D ➰ ➰ 🔥 SC

★ ★ ★ **FOUR POINTS HOTEL AND SUITES.** *9802 Bunsen Way (40299), I-64 Exit 15, E of Downtown.* 502/499-0000; fax 502/493-2905; res 800/325-3535. Email fpadmin@earthlink.com. 108 rms, 5 story, 30 suites, 38 kit. units. S, D $44.95; each addl $5; suites $54.95; kit. units $44.95; under 19 free. Crib free. Pet accepted, some restrictions. TV; cable (premium). Complimentary continental bkfst 6-10 am. Restaurant nearby. Ck-out noon. Meeting rms. Business servs avail. In-rm modem link. Free airport transportation. Refrigerators; microwaves avail. Cr cds: A, D, DS, MC, V.

★★ **HAMPTON INN.** *1902 Embassy Square Blvd (40299), I-64 Hurstbourne Pkwy Exit 15, E of Downtown.* 502/4 91-2577; fax 502/491-1325; toll-free 800/426-7866. 119 rms, 2 story. S $65; D $77; under 18 free. Crib free. TV; cable (premium). Pool. Continental bkfst. Coffee in rms. Restaurant nearby. Ck-out noon. Meeting rm. Business servs avail. In-rm modem link. Microwaves avail. Cr cds: A, C, D, DS, MC, V.

★★ **HAMPTON INN AIRPORT FAIREXPO.** *800 Phillips Ln (40209), near Louisville Intl Airport, S of Downtown.* 502/366-8100; fax 502/366-0700; res 800/426-7866. 130 rms, 4 story. S $79-$89; D $84-$94; under 18 free; wkend rates; higher rates: summer, special events. Crib free. TV; cable (premium). Coffee in rms. Pool; lifeguard. Complimentary continental bkfst. Restaurant nearby. Ck-out noon. Meeting rm. Business servs avail. Free airport transportation. Exercise equipt. Cr cds: A, C, D, DS, MC, V.

★★ **HOLIDAY INN.** *1465 Gardiner Ln (40213), E of Downtown.* 502/452-6361; fax 502/451-1541; toll-free 800/465-4329. 200 rms, 3 story. S, D $98; each addl $7; under 18 free; wkend rates. Crib free. Pet accepted. TV; cable (premium). Pool; poolside serv, lifeguard. Complimentary coffee in rms. Restaurant 11 am-11 pm. Bar to midnight. Ck-out noon. Coin lndry. Meeting rms. Business servs avail. In-rm modem link. Bellhops. Valet serv. Free airport transportation. Tennis. Exercise equipt. Game rm. Cr cds: A, C, D, DS, JCB, MC, V.

★ **RED ROOF INN.** *9330 Blairwood Rd (40222), 1 blk N of I-64 Exit 15, E of Downtown.* 502/426-7621; fax 502/426-7933. 108 rms, 2 story. S $35.99-$69.99; D $43.99-$79.99;

each addl $7-$9; under 18 free. Crib free. Pet accepted. TV; cable. Complimentary coffee. Restaurant nearby. Ck-out noon. Business servs avail. In-rm modem link. Cr cds: A, C, D, DS, ER, JCB, MC, V.

★★ **RESIDENCE INN.** *120 N Hurstbourne Pkwy (40222), E of Downtown.* 502/425-1821; fax 502/425-1672. 96 kit. suites, 2 story. 1-bedrm $106-$120; 2-bedrm $119-$149; family rates; wkend rates. Crib free. Pet accepted. TV; cable (premium). Heated pool; whirlpool, lifeguard. Complimentary continental bkfst. Ck-out noon. Coin lndry. Business servs avail. In-rm modem link. Valet serv. Sport court. Health club privileges. Refrigerators, microwaves, fireplaces. Grills. Cr cds: A, D, DS, MC, V.

★★ **SIGNATURE INN.** *1301 Kentucky Mills Dr (40299), I-64 Exit 17, E of Downtown.* 502/267-8100; fax 502/267-8100. 119 rms, 3 story. S $66-$72; D $73-$80; under 18 free. Crib free. TV; cable (premium). Coffee in rms. Indoor pool; whirlpool. Complimentary continental bkfst. Restaurant adj 6:30 am-10 pm. Ck-out noon. Coin lndry. Meeting rms. Business center. In-rm modem link. Valet serv. Exercise equipt; sauna. Golf privileges. Some refrigerators; microwaves avail. Cr cds: A, D, DS, MC, V.

★★ **SIGNATURE INN.** *6515 Signature Dr (40213), I-65 Exit 128, S of Downtown.* 502/968-4100; fax 502/968-4100; toll-free 800/822-5252. 123 rms, 2 story. S $67-$70; D $74-$77; under 18 free; wkend rates Dec-Feb. Crib free. TV; cable (premium). Pool. Complimentary continental bkfst. Restaurant adj 6 am-11 pm. Ck-out noon. Meeting rms. Business center. In-rm modem link. Valet serv. Sundries. Free airport transportation. Health club privileges. Refrigerators, microwaves. Cr cds: A, D, DS, JCB, MC, V.

★ **SUPER 8 MOTEL.** *4800 Preston Hwy (40213), off I-65 Exit 130, S of Downtown.* 502/968-0088; fax 502/968-0088; res 800/800-8000. 100 rms, 3 story. S $43.88; D $53.88; each addl $5; under 12 free. Crib free. Pet accepted, some restrictions. TV; cable (premium). Complimentary coffee in lobby. Restaurant opp open 24 hrs. Ck-out 11 am. Business servs avail. In-rm modem link. Free airport transportation. Cr cds: A, C, D, DS, MC, V.

★ **TRAVELODGE.** *9340 Blairwood Rd (40222), E of Downtown. 502/425-8010; fax 502/425-2689; toll-free 800/ 578-7878.* 108 rms, 3 story. S, D $47-$75; each addl $6; under 18 free; higher rates Kentucky Derby. Crib free. Pet accepted; $25 deposit. TV; cable (premium). Complimentary continental bkfst, coffee in rms. Restaurant nearby. Ck-out noon. Meeting rms. Business servs avail. Valet serv. Heated pool; whirlpool. Some refrigerators. Cr cds: A, C, D, DS, ER, JCB, MC, V.

Hotels

★★★★ **CAMBERLEY BROWN HOTEL.** *335 W Broadway (40202), Downtown. 502/583-1234; fax 502/ 587-7006; res 888/555-8000. Email brownhotel@win.net; www.camberley hotels.com.* The sparklingly restored lobby of this hotel exudes Southern elegance with intricate plaster moldings, polished woodwork, stained glass, and crystal chandeliers. Built by philanthropist J. Graham Brown in 1923, the property's Georgian Revival-style bldg remains a cornerstone of Louisville social life. The elegance of the public spaces continues through 292 rooms and suites and the magnificent, mirrored Crystal Ballroom. 287 rms, 16 story, 6 suites. S, D $219; suites $435; under 18 free. Crib avail. Valet parking avail. TV; cable (premium), VCR avail. Complimentary newspaper. Restaurant 6 am-3 pm. 24-hr rm serv. Bar. Ck-out 11 am, ck-in 3 pm. Conference center, meeting rms. Business center. Bellhops. Concierge. Dry cleaning. Gift shop. Salon/barber. Free airport transportation. Exercise privileges. Golf. Cr cds: A, C, D, DS, MC, V.

★★★ **EXECUTIVE WEST.** *830 Phillips Ln (40209), S of Downtown.*

502/367-2251; fax 502/363-2087; toll-free 800/626-2708. www.executive west.com. 576 rms, 8 story, 35 suites. S, D $125; suites $165; under 18 free. Crib avail. Pet accepted, fee. Parking lot. Indoor/outdoor pools, lap pool, lifeguard. TV; cable (premium), VCR avail. Complimentary coffee in rms, newspaper, toll-free calls. Restaurant 6:30 am-11 pm. Bar. Ck-out noon, ck-in 3 pm. Conference center, meeting rms. Business servs avail. Bellhops. Concierge. Dry cleaning. Gift shop. Salon/barber. Free airport transportation. Exercise rm, sauna. Golf, 18 holes. Tennis, 6 courts. Downhill skiing. Cr cds: A, C, D, DS, JCB, MC, V.

★★★ **GALT HOUSE.** *140 N 4th Ave (40202), Downtown. 502/589-5200; fax 502/589-3444; toll-free 800/626-1814. Email info@galthouse.com.* 600 suites, 18 story. S $145; D $160; each addl $10; 2-bedrm suites $475; under 16 free. Crib free. TV; cable. Pool privileges adj. Restaurant adj 6:30 am-midnight. Bar from 11 am. Ck-out noon. Garage parking. Refrigerators, wet bars. Some private patios, balconies. Overlooks Ohio River. 18-story atrium. Cr cds: A, C, D, DS, MC, V.

★★ **THE GALT HOUSE HOTEL.** *140 N Fourth Ave (40202), at River Rd, Downtown. 502/589-5200; fax502/ 589-3444; res 800/626-1814. Email info@galthouse.com.* 656 rms, 25 story. S $110; D $120; each addl $10; suites $275; under 16 free. Crib free. TV; cable. Pool; lifeguard. Restaurants 6:30 am-midnight; dining rm 5:30-10:30 pm. Bar 11:30-1 am. Ck-out noon. Convention facilities. Shopping arcade. Garage parking. Refrigerator in suites. Overlooks Ohio River. Cr cds: A, C, D, DS, JCB, MC, V.

★★ **HOLIDAY INN.** *1325 S Hurstbourne Pkwy (40222), at I-64 Exit 15, E of Downtown. 502/426-2600; fax 502/423-1605; toll-free 800/465-4329. www.holidayinnhurstbourne.com.* 267 rms, 7 story. S, D $99-$125; suites $125-$275; under 18 free. Crib free. Pet accepted, some restrictions. TV; cable (premium). Indoor pool; lifeguard. Coffee in rms. Restaurant 6:30

am-10 pm. Bar noon-midnight. Ck-out noon. Meeting rms. Business servs avail. In-rm modem link. Bellhops. Valet serv. Free airport transportation. Exercise equipt, sauna. Refrigerator in suites. Cr cds: A, DS, MC, V.

[🅳 🐾 ⚓ 🏋 🏊 🔥 SC]

★★ HOLIDAY INN LOUISVILE DWTN. *120 W Broadway (40202), Downtown.* 502/582-2241; fax 502/584-8591; res 800/HOLIDAY; toll-free 800/626-1558. 287 rms, 12 story. S $95-$115; D $103-$125; each addl $10; suites $350; under 18 free. Crib free. Pet accepted. TV; cable, VCR avail. Indoor pool; lifeguard. Coffee in rms. Restaurant 6 am-11 pm. Bar 11-2 am. Ck-out noon. Convention facilities. Business servs avail. In-rm modem link. Gift shop. Barber. Free airport transportation. Exercise equipt. Health club privileges. Some refrigerators. Some balconies. Luxury level. Cr cds: A, C, D, JCB, MC, V.

[🅳 🐾 ⚓ 🏋 🏊 🔥]

★★★ HYATT REGENCY LOUISVILLE. *320 W Jefferson (40202), Downtown.* 502/587-3434; fax 502/540-3128; toll-free 800/233-1234. 388 rms, 18 story. S, D $89-$180; each addl $25; suites $250-$650; under 18 free. Crib free. TV; cable (premium), VCR avail. Indoor pool; whirlpool. Restaurants 6:30 am-midnight. Bars 11-2 am; Sun to midnight. Ck-out noon. Convention facilities. Business center. In-rm modem link. Concierge. Gift shop. Tennis. Exercise equipt. Garage. Access to shopping center via enclosed walkway. Modern design. Luxury level. Cr cds: A, C, D, DS, MC, V.

[🅳 🏂 🏋 ⚓ 🏊 🛐 🏃]

★★★ MARRIOTT EAST. *1903 Embassy Square Blvd (40299), E of I-264 at jct I-64, Hurstbourne Pkwy (Exit 15), E of Downtown.* 502/499-6220; fax 502/499-2480. 254 rms, 10 story. S, D $109-$139; under 18 free. Crib free. TV; cable (premium). Indoor pool, whirlpool; poolside serv, lifeguard. Restaurant 6:30 am-2 pm, 5-10 pm. Bar 2 pm-2 am. Ck-out 11 am. Convention facilities. Business servs avail. In-rm modem link. Concierge. Exercise equipt. Balconies. Cr cds: A, C, D, DS, ER, JCB, MC, V.

[🅳 ⚓ 🏋 🏊 🔥]

★★★★ THE SEELBACH HILTON LOUISVILLE. *500 4th Ave (40202), Downtown.* 502/585-3200; fax 502/585-9240; res 800/HILTONS; toll-free 800/333-3399. Email larry_hollingsworth@merisatar.com; www.hilton.com. Built in 1905 by brothers Otto and Louis Seelbach, this 321-room property is on the National Register of Historic Places. From presidents to movie stars to authors (F. Scott Fitzgerald wrote about the hotel in *The Great Gatsby*), everyone seems drawn here. The entrance alone is dramatic with its muraled ceilings, marble columns, and regal staircase leading to the impeccable Oakroom restaurant. 285 rms, 12 story, 36 suites. Mar-May, Oct: S $199; D $214; each addl $15; suites $650; under 18 free; lower rates rest of yr. Crib avail. Pet accepted. Valet parking avail. TV; cable (DSS), VCR avail. Complimentary coffee in rms, newspaper. Restaurant 7 am-11 pm. 24-hr rm serv. Bar. Ck-out 1 pm, ck-in 3 pm. Conference center, meeting rms. Business center. Bellhops. Concierge. Dry cleaning. Gift shop. Free airport transportation. Exercise privileges. Golf. Tennis. Video games. Cr cds: A, C, D, DS, ER, JCB, MC, V.

[🅳 🐾 🏋 🏌 🏋 🏃 🏊 🔥 SC 🏇]

B&Bs/Small Inns

★★ COLUMBINE BED AND BREAKFAST. *1707 S Third St (40208), in Old Louisville.* 502/635-5000; res 800/635-5010. Email bbcolumbine@aol.com. 5 rms, 1 with shower only, 3 story, 1 suite. S $65-$80; D $70-$95; suite $70-$115; wkly, wkend rates. Children over 12 yrs only. TV; cable, VCR (movies). Complimentary full bkfst. Ck-out 11 am, ck-in 3 pm. Business servs avail. In-rm modem link. House built in 1900 with full-length porch. English garden. Cr cds: A, MC, V.

[🏋 🏇 ✈ 🏊 🔥 🛐]

★★ OLD LOUISVILLE INN. *1359 S 3rd St (40208), in Old Louisville.* 502/635-1574; fax 502/637-5892. Email info@oldlouinn.com; www.oldlouinn.com. 10 rms, 3 story. No rm phones. D $75-$95; suites $110-$195; under 12 free. Crib free. TV in sitting rm; VCR avail (movies). Complimentary full bkfst. Restaurant nearby. Ck-out noon, ck-in 3 pm. Business servs

avail. Exercise equipt. Some in-rm whirlpools. Individually decorated rms in Victorian house (1901); antique furnishings. Ceiling murals. Cr cds: A, DS, MC, V.

★★ **WOODHAVEN BED AND BREAKFAST.** *401 S Hubbards Ln (40207), E of Downtown.* 502/895-1011; fax 502/895-1011; res 888/895-1011. *www.bbonline.com/ky/woodhaven.* 7 rms, 2 story. S, D $70-$150. Crib free. Pet accepted. TV; cable (premium). Complimentary full bkfst, coffee in rms. Ck-out 11:30 am, ck-in 3 pm. Gothic Revival house built in 1853. Totally nonsmoking. Cr cds: A, MC, V.

All Suite

★★ **AMERISUITES.** *701 S Hurstbourne Pkwy (40222), E of Downtown.* 502/426-0119; fax 502/426-3013; res 800/833-1516. Email loclo@prime hospitality.com; www.amerisuites.com. 123 kit. units, 5 story. June-Aug: S, D $84-$128; each addl $10; higher rates special events; lower rates rest of yr. Crib free. TV; cable (premium), VCR (movies). Heated pool. Complimentary continental bkfst, coffee in suites. Restaurant nearby. Ck-out noon. Meeting rms. Business center. Coin lndry. Free airport transportation. Exercise equipt. Refrigerators, microwaves. Cr cds: A, DS, MC, V.

Restaurants

★★ **ASIATIQUE.** *106 Sears Ave (40207), E of Downtown.* 502/899-3578. Email asiatique@mail.com; www.asiatique.bigstep.com. Specializes in wok-seared Pacific salmon, roasted Mandarin quail, ginger-dusted softshell crab. Hrs: 5-10:30 pm; Fri, Sat to 11:30 pm; Sun to 10 pm. Closed hols. Res accepted. Bar. Dinner $15-$18. Child's menu. Parking. Elegant atmosphere; modern art decor. Cr cds: A, D, MC, V.

★★★ **CAFE METRO.** *1700 Bardstown Rd (40205), in Highland area, E of Downtown.* 502/458-4830. Email uptown.cafe@gte.net. Specializes in grilled swordfish, salmon with cucumber caper dill sauce, jaegerschnitzel. Hrs: 6-10 pm; Fri, Sat to 11 pm. Closed Sun; hols. Res accepted. Bar. Dinner a la carte entrees: $18.95. Parking. Collection of pre-WWI German posters. Cr cds: A, D, DS, MC, V.

★ **CAFE MIMOSA.** *1216 Bardstown Rd (40204), E of Downtown.* 502/458-2233. Specializes in chicken, pork, shrimp. Sushi bar. Hrs: 11 am-10 pm; Fri, Sat to 11 pm; Sun from 10 pm; Sun brunch to 2 pm. Lunch, dinner $4.50-$10.95. Sun brunch $6.95. Child's menu. Parking. Vietnamese artwork. Cr cds: A, D, DS, MC, V.

★ **DARRYL'S 1815.** *3110 Bardstown Rd (40205), I-264 Exit 16, E of Downtown.* 502/458-1815. Specializes in steak, chicken, ribs. Hrs: 11 am-11 pm; Fri, Sat to midnight. Bar. Lunch $4.99-$9.99; dinner $4.99-$18.99. Child's menu. Cr cds: A, C, D, DS, MC, V.

★★★ **THE ENGLISH GRILL.** *335 W Broadway.* 502/583-1234. www.camberleyhotels.com. Specializes in fresh seafood, rack of lamb, steak. Hrs: 5-11 pm. Closed Sun. Res accepted. Bar. Dinner $17.25-$24.95. English motif; leaded and stained-glass windows; artwork featuring English scenes and thoroughbred horses. Cr cds: A, D, MC, V.

★★★ **FERD GRISANTI.** *10212 Taylorsville Rd (40299), E of Downtown.* 502/267-0050. Email reservations@ ferdgrisanti.com; www.ferdgrisanti.com. Specializes in veal, pasta. Own baking. Hrs: 5-10 pm; Fri, Sat to 11 pm. Closed Sun. Res accepted. Bar. Wine list. Dinner $8.50-$18.95. Child's menu. Parking. Contemporary Italian decor; artwork. In historic Jeffersontown. Cr cds: A, C, D, DS, MC, V.

★★ **FIFTH QUARTER STEAK-HOUSE.** *1241 Durrett Ln (40213), S of Downtown.* 502/361-2363. Specializes in prime rib. Salad bar. Hrs: 11 am-10 pm; Fri to 11 pm; Sat 4-11 pm. Closed Dec 25. Bar. Lunch

$4.59-$7.99; dinner $8.99-$19.99. Entertainment: guitarist, Mon-Sat. Parking. Rustic decor. Cr cds: A, C, D, DS, MC, V.

D SC ⌐

★ **JESSIE'S FAMILY RESTAURANT.** *9609 Dixie Hwy (40272), S of Downtown.* 502/937-6332. Hrs: 5 am-10 pm; Sun 5:30 am-2:45 pm. Closed July 4 wkend, Thanksgiving, Dec 24-26. Bkfst a la carte entrees: $1.95-$4.95; lunch a la carte entrees: $1.75-$5.95; dinner a la carte entrees: $1.75-$5.95. Family-owned. Cr cds: D, DS, MC, V.

D SC ⌐

★ **KOREANA II.** *5009 Preston Hwy (40213), S of Downtown.* 502/968-9686. Specializes in beef, pork, chicken. Hrs: 11 am-10 pm. Closed Easter, Thanksgiving, Dec 25. Res accepted. Lunch $4.99-$8.99; dinner $7.25-$13.95. Child's menu. Parking. Cr cds: A, D, DS, MC, V.

SC ⌐

★★★ **KUNZ'S FOURTH AND MARKET.** *115 S 4th St (40202), at Market St, Downtown.* 502/585-5555. Specializes in seafood, steak. Raw bar. Salad bar (lunch). Own breads. Hrs: 11 am-10:30 pm; Fri, Sat to 11:30 pm; Sun 4-10 pm. Closed Dec 25. Res accepted. Bar. Lunch $5.95-$8.95; dinner $10.95-$24.95. Child's menu. Family-owned since 1892. Cr cds: A, D, DS, MC, V.

D ⌐

★★★ **LE RELAIS.** *2817 Taylorsville Rd (40205), at Bowman Field, I-264 Exit 17, Taylorsville Rd, E of Downtown.* 502/451-9020. Specializes in fish, crab cakes, lamb chops. Hrs: 11:30 am-2 pm, 5:30-10 pm; Sat, Sun from 5:30 pm. Closed Mon; hols. Res accepted. Bar. Lunch a la carte entrees: $4.25-$10.25; dinner a la carte entrees: $14-$22.50. Parking. Formerly room in airport administration bldg; view of landing strip. Cr cds: A, D, MC, V.

D

★★★★ **LILLY'S.** *1147 Bardstown Rd (40204), E of Downtown.* 502/451-0447. Email lillslp@aol.com. A brightly colored, neon sign marks the window of chef Kathy Cary's innovative dining room, a hint to the art-deco-style interior that lies beyond the red-brick entrance. Her seasonally changing menu, which in its early days showed more of a Kentucky accent, has an eclectic, urban edge (noisy dining room and all) with dishes such as seared scallops in mango-tarragon beurre blanc. Specializes in pork tenderloin marinated and grilled in seasonal sauces, rack of lamb with demi-glaze. Hrs: 11 am-3 pm, 5:30-10 pm; Fri, Sat to 11 pm. Closed Sun, Mon; hols; also 2 wks in Aug. Res accepted. Lunch $10-$15; dinner $25-$36. Cr cds: A, DS, MC, V.

D ⌐

★★ **LYNN'S PARADISE CAFE.** *984 Barret Ave (40204), Downtown.* 502/583-3447. www.lynnsparadisecafe.com. Specializes in breakfast burrito, portobella wrap, walnut-crusted chicken. Hrs: 7 am-10 pm. Closed Mon; also Thanksgiving, Dec 25. Res accepted. Bar. Lunch $4.50-$9; dinner $8-$15. Child's menu. Parking. Colorful decor; casual atmosphere. Cr cds: MC, V.

D ⌐

★★ **MAMA GRISANTI.** *3938 DuPont Circle (40207), E of Downtown.* 502/893-0141. Specializes in lasagne, fettucini Alfredo, veal parmesan. Own pasta. Hrs: 5-10:30 pm; Fri, Sat to 11:30 pm; Sun to 10 pm. Res accepted. Bar. Lunch $4.95-$8.50. Buffet: $6.25; dinner $6-$16. Child's menu. Family-owned. Cr cds: A, C, D, DS, MC, V.

D ⌐

★★ **MASTERSON'S.** *1830 S 3rd St (40208), S of Downtown.* 502/636-2511. Email sales@mastersons.com; www.mastersons.com. Specializes in regional cooking, Greek dishes. Hrs: 11 am-10 pm; Sun 11:30 am-4 pm. Closed hols. Res accepted. Bar. Lunch $3.25-$9.75. Buffet: $7; dinner $9.25-$19.75. Sun brunch $9. Child's menu. Parking. Near Univ of Louisville. Family-owned and operated for 60 yrs. Cr cds: A, D, DS, MC, V.

D SC ⌐

★ **OLD SPAGHETTI FACTORY.** *235 W Market St (40202), Downtown.* 502/581-1070. Specializes in spaghetti. Hrs: 11:30 am-2 pm, 5-10 pm; Fri 5-11 pm; Sat 11:30-11 pm; Sun 11:30 am-10 pm. Closed Thanksgiving, Dec 24, 25. Bar. Lunch complete meals:

$3.25-$5.45; dinner complete meals: $4.75-$9.25. Child's menu. Cr cds: A, D, DS, MC, V.

[D] [≛]

★★ **SICHUAN GARDEN.** *9850 Linn Station Rd (40223), in Plainview Shopping Center, E of Downtown.* 502/426-6767. Specializes in Sichuan orange beef, Mandarin seafood-in-a-net, beef tenders. Hrs: 11:30 am-9:30 pm; Fri, Sat to 10:30 pm; Sun brunch noon-2 pm. Closed Thanksgiving. Res accepted. Bar. Lunch $4.75-$5.95; dinner $5.95-$12.95. Sun brunch $6.95. Entertainment: pianist Fri, Sat. Frosted glass rm dividers. Cr cds: A, D, DS, MC, V.

[D] [≛]

★ **THAI SIAM.** *3002½ Bardstown Rd (40205), in Shopping Center, E of Downtown.* 502/458-6871. Specializes in traditional Thai dishes. Hrs: 11 am-2 pm, 5-9 pm; Fri, Sat 5-10 pm; Sun 5-9 pm. Closed Mon; hols. Res accepted. Wine, beer. Lunch $6.50-$7; dinner $8.50-$16. Parking. Casual dining. Cr cds: DS, MC, V.

[D] [≛]

★★ **TIMOTHY'S.** *826 E Broadway (40204), Downtown.* 502/561-0880. Specializes in pasta, fresh seafood, white chili. Hrs: 11:30 am-2 pm, 5:30-11 pm; Sat from 5:30 pm. Closed Sun, Mon; Easter, Thanksgiving, Dec 25. Res accepted. Bar. Lunch $5.95-$10.95; dinner $7.95-$24.95. Parking. Contemporary decor; vintage bar. Cr cds: A, C, D, DS, MC, V.

[D] [≛]

★★ **UPTOWN CAFE.** *1624 Bardstown Rd (40205), S of Downtown.* 502/458-4212. Email uptown.cafe@ gte.net. Specializes in duck ravioli, salmon croquettes, veal pockets. Hrs: 11:30 am-11 pm; Fri, Sat to midnight. Closed Sun; hols. Bar. Lunch $6.25-$9.75; dinner $6.25-$17.95. Parking. Converted storefront. Cr cds: A, D, DS, MC, V.

[D] [≛]

★★★ **VINCENZO'S.** *150 S 5th St (40202), Downtown.* 502/580-1350. Email vgabriele@aol.com; www.onguide. com/net/vincenzo.htm. Specializes in crepes Agostino, veal Gabriele. Own baking. Hrs: 11:30 am-2:30 pm, 5:30-10 pm; Fri, Sat 5:30-11 pm. Closed

Sun; hols. Res accepted. Wine list. Lunch a la carte entrees: $7.95-$12.95; dinner a la carte entrees: $17.95-$26.95. Entertainment: pianist Fri, Sat. Valet parking. Cr cds: A, D, DS, MC, V.

[D] [≛]

★★ **WINSTON'S.** *3101 Bardstown Rd (40205), in Sullivan College, E of Downtown.* 502/456-0980. Specializes in local and regional dishes. Hrs: 11 am-2:30 pm, 5:30-9:30 pm; Sun brunch 9:30 am-2 pm. Closed Mon-Thurs; hols. Res accepted. Bar. Lunch $8-$14; dinner $10-$30. Sun brunch $10. Child's menu. Parking. Operated by senior culinary students. Cr cds: A, DS, MC, V.

[D]

Madisonville (D-3)

Founded 1807 **Pop** 16,200 **Elev** 470 ft
Area code 270 **Zip** 42431
Web www.madisonvillenet.com
Information Madisonville-Hopkins County Chamber of Commerce, 15 E Center St; 270/821-3435

Annual Event

Hopkins County Fair. Last wk July-first wk Aug.

Motels/Motor Lodges

★★ **BEST WESTERN.** *Pennyrile Pkwy (42440), 6 mi S on Pennyrile Pkwy, Exit 37.* 270/258-5201; fax 270/258-9072. 60 rms, 2 story. S $35; D $40-$49; each addl $3; under 12 free. Crib free. Pet accepted. TV; cable (premium), VCR avail (movies). Pool. Complimentary bkfst buffet. Coffee in rms. Restaurant open 24 hrs. Ck-out noon. Meeting rm. Business servs avail. Refrigerators avail. Cr cds: A, D, DS, MC, V.

[D] [🐾] [≊] [🐟] [🖼] [🔥]

★ **DAYS INN.** *1900 Lantaff Blvd (42431), US 41 Bypass Exit 44.* 270/821-8620; fax 270/825-9282; res 800/DAYSINN. 143 rms, 2 story. S $52-$57; D $57-$62; each addl $5; suites $90-$120. Crib free. Pet accepted. TV; cable (premium). Indoor pool. Sauna. Complimentary continental bkfst. Restaurant 6-10 am, 11 am-2 pm, 5-10 pm; Sat 6-10 am, 5-10 pm; Sun to 2 pm. Ck-out noon. Meeting rms. Business servs avail. Sundries. Health club privileges. Cr cds: A, C, D, DS, MC, V.

Resort

★★ **PENNYRILE FOREST STATE RESORT PARK.** *20781 Pennyrile Lodge Rd (42408), 9 mi S of Dawson Springs on County Rd 398 in Pennyrile State Forest, 2 mi S of KY 109.* 270/797-3421; fax 270/797-3413; toll-free 800/325-1711. 24 lodge rms, 2 story, 13 kit. cottages. Memorial Day-Labor Day: S $56; D $66; each addl $5; kit. cottages $87-$100; under 16 free; higher rates hol wkends; lower rates rest of yr. Crib free. TV. Pool; lifeguard. Dining rm 7-10:30 am, 11:30 am-2:30 pm, 5-9 pm. Ck-out noon, cottages 11 am, ck-in 4 pm. Meeting rms. Tennis. 9-hole golf, greens fee $6. Mountain biking. Miniature golf. Lawn games. Private patios, balconies. Picnic tables, grills. State-owned property; all state park facilities avail. Cr cds: A, DS, MC, V.

Mammoth Cave National Park

See also Cave City, Horse Cave, Park City

(on KY 70, 10 mi W of Cave City or 8 mi NW of Park City on KY 255)
Web www.nps.gov/maca

This enormous underground complex of intertwining passages totaling more than 350 miles in length was carved by mildly acidic water trickling for thousands of yrs through limestone. Species of colorless, eyeless fish, crayfish, and other creatures make their home within. Visible are the remains of a crude system used to mine 400,000 pounds of nitrate to make gunpowder for use in the War of 1812. The cave was the scene of an experiment aimed at the cure of tuberculosis. Mushroom growing was also attempted within the cave.

Above ground the park consists of 52,830 acres with sinkholes, rivers, 70 miles of hiking trails. Picnicking; lodging (see MOTEL). Camping (Mar-Dec, daily; some fees). An orientation movie is offered at the visitor center (daily exc Dec 25), phone 270/758-2328. Evening programs are conducted by park interpreters (summer, daily; spring and fall, wkends).

Ranger-led trips of Mammoth Cave vary greatly in distance and length. Trails are solid, fairly smooth, and require stooping or bending in places. Most tours involve steps and extensive walking; many are considered strenuous; proper footwear is recommended (no sandals); a sweater or wrap is also advised, even though it may be a hot August day above ground. Tours are conducted by experienced National Park Service interpreters. Contact Superintendent, Mammoth Cave 42259.

What to See and Do

Miss Green **Riverboat Trip.** Round-trip cruise (60 min) through scenic and wildlife areas of the park. (Apr-Oct, daily) Advance tickets may be purchased at visitor center. Phone 270/758-2243. ¢¢

✪ **Cave tours.** Depart from the visitor center (schedules vary with season; no tours Dec 25), phone 270/758-2328. Advance res are highly recommended. Tickets may be purchased in advance through Destinet Outlets; phone 800/967-2283. (The following is a partial list of available cave tours.)

Frozen Niagara. This moderately strenuous tour (2 hrs) explores huges pits and domes and decorative dripstone formations. ¢¢¢

Historic. A 2-mi guided tour highlighting the cave's rich human history; artifacts of Native Americans, early explorers; ruins of mining operations. ¢¢¢

Travertine. Quarter-mile Travertine (1 hr) is considered an easy tour through Drapery Rm, Frozen Niagara, and Crystal Lake. Designed for those unable to take many steps. ¢¢¢

Violet City. A 3-mi lantern-light tour (3 hrs) of historic features, incl tuberclosis hospital huts and some of the cave's largest rms and passageways. Inquire for schedule. ¢¢¢

Motel/Motor Lodge

★ **MAMMOTH CAVE HOTEL.** *KY 70 (42259), I-65 Exit 53 on KY 70 to park entrance, or Exit 48 on KY 255 to entrance, then 3 mi inside park.* 270/758-2225; fax 270/258-2301. 42 rms, 2 story. 20-rm motor lodge. S, D $62-$72; each addl $7; cottages: S, D $46-$52; family rates. Crib $5. TV. Restaurants 7 am-7:30 pm. Ck-out noon. Coin lndry (summer). Meeting rms (winter). Business servs avail. Gift shop. Tennis. Lawn games. Private patios, balconies. Cr cds: A, DS, MC, V.

Mayfield

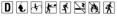

(D-2) See also Murray

Settled 1823 **Pop** 9,935 **Elev** 492 ft
Area code 270 **Zip** 42066
Web www.ldd.net/commerce/mayfield
Information Mayfield-Graves County Chamber of Commerce, 201 E College; 270/247-6101

Rich clay fields in the area provide clay for all parts of the country. Tobacco is an important crop in this area.

Hotel

★ **DAYS INN.** *1101 W Housman St (42066), 2 mi W on US 45 Bypass, at jct KY 121.* 270/247-3700; fax 270/247-3135; res 800/329-7466; toll-free 800/606-6025. 80 rms, 2 story. May-Oct: S $48; D $55; each addl $7; under 18 free; lower rates rest of yr. Crib free. TV; cable. Pool. Restaurant 6 am-2 pm, 5-10 pm. Ck-out noon. Meeting rms. In-rm modem link. Valet serv. Lawn games. Cr cds: A, DS, MC, V.

Maysville

(B-7) See also Covington, Lexington

Founded 1787 **Pop** 7,169 **Elev** 514 ft
Area code 859 **Zip** 41056
Information Tourism Commission, 216 Bridge St; 859/564-9411

This Ohio River town first known as Limestone was established by the Virginia Legislature. By 1792 it had become a leading port of entry for Kentucky settlers. Daniel Boone and his wife maintained a tavern in the town for several yrs. Maysville is now an important burley tobacco market. Many bldgs and sites in the eight-block historic district are included on the National Historic Register.

Annual Events

Sternwheeler Annual Regatta. 16 mi NE in Augusta. Mid-June.

Simon Kenton Festival. Historic Washington. Third wkend Sep.

Monticello *(D-6)*

Pop 5,357 **Elev** 923 ft **Area code** 859
Zip 42633
Information Monticello-Wayne County Chamber of Commerce, PO Box 566; 859/348-3064 or 888/326-8689

Motel/Motor Lodge

★★ **GRIDER HILL DOCK AND INDIAN CREEK LODGE.** *Hwy 1266 (42602), 20 mi W on KY 90, then 5 mi N on KY 734, 1266, on Lake Cumberland.* 606/387-5501; fax 606/387-7023. 22 rms, 2 story, 12 kit. cottages, 20 houseboats. S $34-$48; D $42-$62; each addl $6; kit. cottages for 2-10, $50-$136; houseboats for 6-12, $475-$2,000 (3-day wkends; deposit required). Closed Nov-Mar. TV; cable. Restaurant 6 am-9 pm. Ck-out noon. On lake; swimming, boats, motors, dockage. Cr cds: A, DS, MC, V.

Morehead

(C-7) *See also Olive Hill*

Pop 8,357 **Elev** 748 ft **Area code** 859 **Zip** 40351

Information Tourism Commission, 150 E first St; 859/784-6221

Annual Events

Appalachian Celebration. Week devoted to history and heritage of Appalachia in Kentucky; dances, concerts, arts and crafts, exhibitions. Late June.

Kentucky Hardwood Festival. Appalachian arts and crafts, pageant, parade, contests, antiques, logging contests. Second wkend Sep.

Motels/Motor Lodges

★ **DAYS INN.** *170 Toms Dr (40351), I-64 Exit 137. 606/783-1484; fax 606/ 783-1484; toll-free 800/329-7466.* 50 rms, 2 story. S $44; D $55; under 12 free; higher rates univ graduation. Crib free. TV; cable (premium). Complimentary continental bkfst. Restaurant adj 6 am-11 pm. Ck-out 11 am. Coin lndry. Some refrigerators. Cr cds: A, C, D, DS, MC, V.

★★ **HOLIDAY INN.** *1698 Flemingsburg Rd (40351), jct I-64, KY 32. 606/ 784-7591; fax 606/783-1859; toll-free 800/272-6232.* 141 rms, 2 story. S, D $55-$65; each addl $6; under 19 free; higher rates special events. Crib free. TV; cable (premium). Pool. Restaurant 6:30 am-2 pm, 5-9 pm. Ck-out noon. Meeting rms. Business servs avail. In-rm modem link. Cr cds: A, C, D, DS, JCB, MC, V.

★ **SUPER 8 MOTEL.** *602 Fraley Dr (40351), I-64 Exit 137. 606/784-8882; fax 606/784-9882; toll-free 800/800-8000.* 56 rms, 3 story. S $37.88-$43.88; D $46.88-$54.88; under 12 free; higher rates special events. Crib

free. TV; cable (premium). Complimentary coffee in lobby. Restaurant opp 7 am-10 pm. Ck-out noon. Coin lndry. Cr cds: A, C, D, DS, MC, V.

Mount Vernon

(D-6) *See also Berea*

Pop 2,654 **Elev** 1,156 ft **Area code** 859 **Zip** 40456

Motels/Motor Lodges

★ **ECONO LODGE.** *1375 Richmond Rd (40456), US 25 and I-75 Exit 62. 606/256-4621; fax 606/256-4622; toll-free 800/638-7949.* 35 rms, 2-3 story. S $29.50-$32, D $36-$40.50; family rates; higher rates: hol wkends, special events. Crib $5. Pet accepted, some restrictions. TV; cable. Pool. Complimentary coffee in lobby. Restaurant nearby. Ck-out 11 am. Cr cds: A, C, D, DS, ER, JCB, MC, V.

★★ **KASTLE INN MOTEL.** *I-75 & US 25 Exit 59 (40456), E of I-75 Exit 59. 606/256-5156; fax 606/256-5156; toll-free 800/965-4366.* 50 rms, 2 story. Mar-Nov: S $48; D $56; each addl $6; lower rates rest of yr. Crib avail. Pet accepted. Parking lot. Pool. TV; cable. Complimentary toll-free calls. Restaurant 6 am-10 pm. Ck-out 11 am, ck-in 2 pm. Meeting rm. Fax servs avail. Golf, 9 holes. Tennis, 2 courts. Cr cds: A, C, D, DS, ER, JCB, MC, V.

Murray

(E-3) *See also Mayfield*

Pop 14,439 **Elev** 515 ft **Area code** 270 **Zip** 42071

Information Murray Tourism Commission, PO Box 190; 270/759-2199 or 800/651-1603

Annual Events

Calloway County Fair. June.
Freedom Fest. July 4th.

Motels/Motor Lodges

★ **DAYS INN.** 517 S 12th St (42071), US 641S. 270/753-6706; fax 270/753-6708. S $47.50-$60; D $52.50-$65; each addl $5; under 13 free; higher rates special events. Crib free. Pet accepted; $5. TV; cable (premium). Complimentary continental bkfst. Coffee in rms. Restaurant nearby. Ck-out 11 am. Business servs avail. Pool. Health club privileges. Some in-rm whirlpool, refrigerators, microwaves. Cr cds: A, DS, MC, V.

★ **MURRAY PLAZA COURT.** 502 S 12th St (42071), US 641S. 270/753-2682. 40 rms, 2 story. S $33; D $36.30; each addl $5; wkly plans; higher rates special events. Crib $6. Pet accepted, some restrictions. TV; cable (premium). Complimentary coffee in lobby. Restaurant opp 6-2 am. Ck-out noon. Cr cds: A, DS, MC, V.

★ **SHONEY'S INN.** 1503 N 12th St (42071). 270/753-5353; fax 270/753-5353. 67 rms, 2 story. S $44-$48; D $49-$53; each addl $5; higher rates special events; crib free. Pet accepted; $5; TV; cable (premium). Complimentary coffee in lobby. Restaurant adj 6 am-10 pm. Ck-out noon. Meeting rms. Business servs avail. In-rm modem link. Pool. Cr cds: A, DS, MC, V.

Natural Bridge State Resort Park

See also Winchester

(On KY 11 near Slade)

Surrounded by 1,899 acres and a 54-acre lake in Daniel Boone National Forest (see), the natural bridge is 78 feet long and 65 feet high. The park has balanced rock and native hemlocks. Swimming pool (seasonal), fishing, boating; nature trails and center (no pets are allowed on the trails), picnicking, playground; dining room, cottages, lodge (see

RESORT). Tent and trailer sites (Apr-Oct; standard fees), central service bldgs. Skylift (mid-Apr-Oct, daily; fee); square dance pavilion; festivals. For prices, information phone 859/663-2214 or 800/325-1710.

Resort

★★ **NATURAL BRIDGE STATE PARK.** 2135 Natural Bridge Rd (40376), 2 mi S of Mountain Pkwy on KY 11, in Natural Bridge State Resort Park. 606/663-2214; fax 606/663-5037; toll-free 800/325-1710. www.state.ky.us/agencies. 35 rms, 2 story, 10 kit. cottages. Memorial Day-Labor Day: S $57; D $67; each addl $5; kit. cottages $75-$105; under 16 free; lower rates rest of yr. Closed Christmas hols. Crib free. TV; cable. Pool; wading pool, lifeguard. Playground. Supervised children's activities (Memorial Day- Labor Day). Dining rm 7-10:30 am, 11:30 am-4 pm, 5-9 pm. Ck-out noon, cottages 11 am, ck-in 4 pm. Meeting rms. Business servs avail. Miniature golf. Balconies. Picnic tables, grills. State-owned property; all park facilities avail. Cr cds: A, C, D, DS, MC, V.

Olive Hill

(C-7) See also Morehead

Pop 1,809 **Elev** 160 ft **Area code** 859 **Zip** 41164

Resort

★★ **CARTER CAVES STATE RESORT PARK.** 344 Caveland Dr (41164), 3 mi N on KY 182, 5 mi NE of I-64 Exit 161, in Carter Caves State Resort Park. 606/286-4411; fax 606/286-6185. www.kystateparks.com. 28 rms in lodge, 2 story, 15 kit. cottages. Memorial Day-Labor Day and special events: S $57; D $67; each addl $5; kit. cottages $75-$95; under 16 free; lower rates rest of yr. Crib free. TV. 2 pools; wading pool, lifeguard. Playground. Ck-out noon, cottages 11 am, ck-in 4 pm. Meeting rms. Business servs avail. Gift shop. Tennis. 9-hole golf, greens fee $11, putting green, miniature golf. Refrigerator in cottages. Private patios, balconies. Picnic tables, grills. State-owned property; all facilities of park avail. Cr cds: A, C, D, DS, MC, V.

🅳 ⚡ 🏊 👥 🏃 🌊 ⛵ 🔥 SC

Owensboro (C-4)

Settled 1800 **Pop** 53,549 **Elev** 401 ft
Area code 270 **Zip** 42303
Web www.visitowensboro.com

Information Owensboro-Daviess County Tourist Commission, 215 E 2nd St; 270/926-1100 or 800/489-1131

Third largest city in Kentucky, Owensboro serves as the major industrial, commercial, and agricultural hub of western Kentucky. A progressive arts program has provided Owensboro with a symphony orchestra, fine art museum, dance theatre, science museum, and theater workshop. In spring the many historic houses along tree-arched Griffith Avenue are brightened by dogwood and azalea blossoms.

Once known as Yellow Banks from the color of the clay on the Ohio River's high banks, the town saw clashes between Union and Confederate troops during the Civil War. An earlier clash between the values of the North and South occured when Harriet Beecher Stowe found inspiration for her novel *Uncle Tom's Cabin* after a visit to a local plantation.

What to See and Do

Ben Hawes State Park. Approx 300 acres with hiking; 9-hole, 18-hole golf (fee, rentals), picnicking, playground. 4 mi W off US 60. Phone 270/684-9808 or 270/685-2011 (golf).

Owensboro Area Museum of Science & History. Live reptiles, insects; archaeological, geological, and ornithological displays; historic items. Gift shop. (Tues-Sun; closed hols) 220 Daviess St. Phone 270/687-2732. **Donation**

Owensboro Museum of Fine Art. Permanent collection incl 16th-20th-century American, French, and English paintings, drawings, sculpture, and graphic and decorative arts. Special collection of 19th- and 20th-century regional art; Appalachian folk art. (Tues-Sun; closed hols) 901 Frederica St. Phone 270/685-3181. ¢

Windy Hollow Recreation Area. Area of 214 acres offers swimming, 240-ft water slide (Memorial Day-Labor Day, fee), fishing; miniature golf (fee). Grocery. Tent and trailer camping (fee). Park (Apr-Oct, daily). 10 mi SW off KY 81. Phone 270/785-4150.

Annual Events

International Bar-B-Q Festival. Cooks compete with recipes for mutton, chicken, burgoo. Also tobacco spitting, pie-eating, fiddling contests. Arts and crafts, music, dancing. Early May.

Daviess County Fair. Four days late July-early Aug.

Seasonal Event

Owensboro Symphony Orchestra. 122 E 18th St. RiverPark Center. Incl guest appearances by renowned artists, ballet companies. Phone 270/684-0661. Oct-Apr.

Motels/Motor Lodges

★ **DAYS INN.** *3720 New Hartford Rd (42301), jct US 60 Bypass and US 231. 270/684-9621; fax 270/684-9626; toll-free 800/329-7466.* 122 rms, 2 story. S $44; D $48; each addl $4; under 18 free. Crib free. TV; cable (premium). Pool. Complimentary coffee in rms. Restaurant 6 am-9 pm. Rm serv 5-9 pm. Ck-out noon. Business servs avail. In-rm modem link. Cr cds: A, D, DS, MC, V.

🅳 🌊 ⛵ 🔥 SC

★★★ **EXECUTIVE INN RIVERMONT.** *1 Executive Blvd (42301). 270/926-8000; fax 270/926-8000; toll-free 800/626-1936.* 550 rms, 2-7 story S, D $39-$65; suites $85-$135; under 18 free. Crib free. TV; cable (premium). 2 pools, 1 indoor. Restaurants 6 am-10 pm. Bar 4 pm-2 am; closed Sun; entertainment. Ck-out 11 am. Convention facilities. Business center. Bellhops. Shopping arcade. Free airport transportation. Indoor tennis. Exercise equipt; sauna, steam rm. Game rm. Refrigerators. Patios, balconies. On river. Cr cds: A, D, DS, MC, V.

🅳 🏊 🌊 👥 ✈ ⛵ 🔥 SC 🏃

★★ **HOLIDAY INN.** *3136 W 2nd St (42304). 270/685-3941; fax 270/926-2917; toll-free 800/465-4329.* 145 rms, 2 story. S, D $59-$69; suites $95; under 19 free. Crib free. Pet accepted. TV; cable (premium). Indoor pool; whirlpool. Playground. Coffee in rms. Restaurant 6 am-2 pm, 5-9 pm; Sun 6 am-2 pm. Bar 3 pm-2 am; closed Sun. Ck-out noon. Meeting rms. Business center. In-rm modem link. Exercise equipt; sauna. Cr cds: A, C, D, DS, JCB, MC, V.

⊡ 🐾 ⤴ 🕇 🖂 🔥 SC 🚶

Restaurants

★★ **COLBY'S.** *202 W 3rd St (42303). 270/685-4239.* Specializes in fresh seafood, Angus beef. Hrs: 11 am-10 pm; Fri, Sat to 11 pm. Closed Sun; hols. Bar. Lunch $6-$10; dinner $9-$18. Child's menu. Historic house (1895); restored; antiques. Cr cds: A, D, DS, MC, V.

SC 🖃

★ **MOONLITE BAR-B-Q.** *2840 W Parish Ave (42301). 270/684-8143. www.moonlite.com.* Specializes in mutton, ribs, chicken. Hrs: 9 am-9 pm; Fri, Sat to 9:30 pm; Sun brunch 10 am-3 pm. Closed hols. Wine, beer. Bkfst $3.10-$10.95; lunch, dinner $3.10-$10.95. Sun brunch $8.95. Child's menu. Parking. Family-owned. Cr cds: A, D, DS, MC, V.

⊡ 🖃

★ **RUBY TUESDAY.** *5000 Frederica St (42301), US 431, in Towne Square Mall. 270/926-8324.* Specializes in steak, fajitas, chicken. Salad bar. Hrs: 10 am-10 pm; Fri, Sat to 11 pm; Sun to 8:30 pm. Res accepted. Lunch $4-$8; dinner $10-$18. Child's menu. Cr cds: A, D, DS, MC, V.

⊡ 🖃

Paducah

(D-2) *See also Gilbertsville*

Founded 1827 **Pop** 27,256 **Elev** 339 ft
Area code 270 **Web** www.Paducah-tourism.org
Information Paducah-McCracken County Convention and Visitors Bureau, 128 Broadway, PO Box 90, 42002; 270/443-8783 or 800/723-8224

What to See and Do

Market House. (1905) S 2nd St & Broadway. Now a cultural center housing

> **Market House Museum.** Early Americana, incl complete interior of drugstore more than 100 yrs old. River lore, Alben Barkley and Irvin S. Cobb memorabilia, Native American artifacts, old tools. (Mar-Dec, Tues-Sun; closed hols) PO Box 12. Phone 270/443-7759. ¢

> **Yeiser Arts Center.** Monthly changing exhibits; collection ranges from European masters to regional artists. Gift shop. Tours. (Tues-Sun; closed hols). 200 Broadway. Phone 270/442-2453. ¢

> **Market House Theatre.** A 250-seat professionally directed community playhouse. (All yr) 132 Market House Sq. Phone 270/444-6828. ¢¢¢

Memorials.

> **Irvin S. Cobb Memorial.** Oak Grove Cemetery.

> **Alben W. Barkley Monument.** The senator and vice president was one of Paducah's most famous citizens. 28th & Jefferson Sts.

> **Chief Paduke Statue.** Memorial to the Chickasaw chief by Lorado Taft. 19th & Jefferson Sts.

Museum of the American Quilter's Society. More than 200 quilts exhibited. Special exhibits scheduled regularly. Gift shop. (Apr-Oct, Tues-Sun; rest of yr, Tues-Sat; closed Jan 1, Thanksgiving, Dec 25) 215 Jefferson St. Phone 270/442-8856. ¢¢

Red Line Scenic Tour. Self-guided driving tour (with map) of city points of interest, incl Market House and City Hall, designed by Edward Durell Stone. Obtain tour folders at the Visitors Bureau, 128 Broadway, 42001. 128 Broadway. Phone 270/443-8783.

Whitehaven. Antebellum mansion remodeled in Classical Revival style in 1903; elaborate plasterwork, stained glass, 1860s furnishings. State uses a portion of the house as a tourist welcome center and rest area. Tours (afternoons). (Daily; closed Jan

1, Thanksgiving, Dec 24, 25) I-24, exit 7. Phone 270/554-2077. **FREE**

Annual Events

Dogwood Trail Celebration. Blossoming of dogwood and azalea is celebrated with a 12-mi trail, spotlighted at night. Driving tours begin at Paducah City Hall. Mid-Apr.

Kiwanis West Kentucky-McCracken County Fair. Carson Park, 301 Joe Clifton Dr. Society and Western horse shows; harness racing; motorcycle racing; gospel singing. Last full wk June.

Summer Festival. Hot-air balloons, symphony, fireworks, free entertainment nightly. Events along riverfront and throughout city. Last wk July.

Seasonal Event

Players Bluegrass Downs. 150 Downs Dr. 2 mi W at 32nd & Park Ave. Pari-mutuel horse racing. Thurs-Sun. Phone 270/444-7117. Oct.

Motels/Motor Lodges

★★ **COURTYARD BY MARRIOTT.** 3835 Technology Dr (42001), 1 mi E at I-24, Exit 4. 270/442-3600; fax 270/442-3619. 100 rms, 3 story. S $69; D $79; under 18 free; higher rates special events. Crib free. TV; cable (premium). Complimentary coffee in rms. Restaurant nearby. Bar 5-10 pm; entertainment Mon-Sat. Ck-out noon. Valet serv. Guest lndry. Exercise equipt. Indoor pool; whirlpool. Some in-rm whirlpools, refrigerators, microwaves. Cr cds: A, C, D, DS, MC, V.
🄳 ⛼ ⛼ ⛼ ⛼ SC

★ **DAYS INN.** 3901 Hinkleville Rd (42001), 3½ mi E on US 60, at I-24. 270/442-7501; fax 270/442-7500; toll-free 800/329-7466. 122 rms, 2 story. S $45-$50; D $50-$55; each addl $5; under 18 free. Crib free. TV; cable (premium). Pool. Complimentary continental bkfst. Restaurant adj 11 am-10 pm. Ck-out noon. Business servs avail. Refrigerators avail. Cr cds: A, D, DS, MC, V.
⛼ ⛼ ⛼ SC

★ **DENTON MOTEL AND SUITES.** 2550 Lone Oak Rd (42003), 1 mi S of I-24 Exit 7. 270/554-1626; fax 270/554-1626. 34 rms, 2 story. S $47-$52; D $52-$59; each addl $7; under 13

free; package plans; higher rates special events. Crib avail. TV; cable (premium). Complimentary coffee in lobby. Restaurant nearby. Business servs avail. Health club privileges. Refrigerators avail. Cr cds: A, C, D, DS, MC, V.
🄳 ⛼ ⛼ ⛼

★★ **DRURY INN.** 3975 Hinkleville Rd (42001). 270/443-3313; fax 270/443-3313. 118 rms, 5 story. S $59-$70; D $65-$80 each addl $8; suites $70-$80; under 18 free. Crib free. Pet accepted. TV; cable. Indoor pool; whirlpool. Complimentary full bkfst. Ck-out noon. Health club privileges. Cr cds: A, C, D, DS, MC, V.
🄳 ⛼ ⛼ ⛼ ⛼ ⛼ ⛼ ⛼

★★ **HOLIDAY INN EXPRESS.** 3994 Hinkleville Rd (42001), I-24 and US 60, Exit 4. 270/442-8874; fax 270/443-3367. Email pahex@apex.net; www.midamcorp.com/holidayinnexpress. 76 rms, 3 story. S $80.50; D $90.50; each addl $10; under 18 free; higher rates special events. Crib avail. Pet accepted, some restrictions. TV; cable (premium), VCR avail. Complimentary continental bkfst. Ck-out 11 am. Meeting rm. Business servs avail. Coin lndry. Health club privileges. Indoor pool; whirlpool. Game rm. Bathrm phones, refrigerators, microwaves, minibars; some in-rm whirlpools. Cr cds: A, C, D, DS, JCB, MC, V.
🄳 ⛼ ⛼ ⛼ ⛼ SC

★★ **J. R.'S EXECUTIVE INN.** 1 Executive Blvd (42001), 10 mi W of I-24 Exit 16. 270/443-8000; fax 270/444-5317; res 800/866-3636. Email bige@apex.net; www.jrsexecutiveinn.com. 399 rms, 4 story, 34 suites. S $59-$64; D $69-$74; each addl $5; suites $125; under 12 free; wknd plans; higher rates special events. Crib avail. TV; cable (premium). Restaurant 6 am-10 pm. Bar 11 am-10 pm; Fri, Sat to 2 am; closed Sun; entertainment Sat. Ck-out noon. Convention facilities. Business servs avail. Bellhops. Sundries. Shopping arcade. Gift shop. Grocery store. Barber, beauty shop. Coin lndry. Free airport transportation. Exercise equipt. Indoor pool. Game rm. Refrigerators; minibars, wet bars in suites. Balconies. On river. Cr cds: A, C, D, MC, V.
🄳 ⛼ ⛼ ⛼ SC

Bluegrass musicians

alwork, many antiques. Cr cds: A, DS, MC, V.

★ **JEREMIAH'S.** *225 Broadway (42001).* 270/443-3991. Specializes in charcoal-grilled steak, frog legs. Hrs: 4-11 pm. Closed Sun; Dec 25. Res accepted. Bar. Dinner $11.99-$20.99. Former bank (1800s); rustic decor. Cr cds: A, C, D, DS, MC, V.

★★ **QUALITY INN.** *1380 Irvin Cobb Dr (42003), W on I-24, Exit 7.* 270/443-8751; fax 270/442-0133. 101 rms, 2 story. Mar-Nov: S $39.99-$48.99; D $48.99-$58.99; each addl $7; family, wkly rates; higher rates special events; lower rates rest of yr. Crib avail. Pet accepted, some restrictions. TV; cable (premium). Complimentary continental bkfst. Restaurant nearby. Ck-out 11 am. Meeting rms. Business servs avail. Coin lndry. Pool. Cr cds: A, C, D, DS, ER, JCB, MC, V.

★ **SUPER 8.** *5125 Old Cairo Rd (42001), E on I-24, Exit 3.* 270/575-9605; fax 270/575-9605. 42 rms, 2 story. S $45-$50; D $50-$60; each addl $5; under 12 free; higher rates special events. Crib $7. TV; cable (premium). Complimentary continental bkfst. Restaurant opp 6 am-10 pm. Ck-out 11 am. Business servs avail. Refrigerators, microwaves. Cr cds: A, D, DS, MC, V.

Restaurants

★ **C.C. COHEN.** *103 S 2nd St (42001).* 270/442-6391. Email alan_raidt@prodigy.com. Specializes in beef, seafood, steaks. Hrs: 11 am-9 pm; Fri, Sat to 10 pm. Closed Sun; hols. Res accepted. Bar. Lunch $3.50-$6.50; dinner $9.50-$20. Child's menu. Entertainment: Fri, Sat. In Cohen Bldg (ca 1870); early decorative met-

★★ **WHALER'S CATCH.** *123 N 2nd St (42001).* 270/444-7701. Specializes in Southern-style seafood. Hrs: 11 am-2 pm, 5-9 pm. Closed Sun; hols. Res accepted. Bar. Lunch $4.99-$6.99; dinner $11.95-$32.95. Child's menu. New Orleans atmosphere. Cr cds: A, DS, MC, V.

Paris

(C-6) *See also Georgetown, Lexington*

Founded 1789 **Pop** 8,730 **Elev** 845 ft
Area code 859 **Zip** 40361
Information Paris-Bourbon County Chamber of Commerce, 525 High St, #114; 859/987-3205

Annual Events

Central Kentucky Steam and Gas Engine Show. Bourbon County Park. Old operating farm machinery; steam traction engines; old gasoline tractors; threshing grain; flea market; country music. July.

Bourbon County Fair. Carnival; farm and craft exhibits. Late July.

Motel/Motor Lodge

★ **HOWARD JOHNSON INN.** *2011 Alverson Dr (40361).* 606/987-0779; fax 606/987-0779; toll-free 800/654-2000. www.hojo.com. 49 rms, 2 story. S $47-$55; D $52-$60; each addl $5;

under 18 free. Crib avail. TV; cable. Pool. Complimentary continental bkfst. Coffee in rms. Restaurant opp 6 am-10 pm. Ck-out noon. Meeting rm. Business servs avail. Cr cds: A, C, D, DS, JCB, MC, V.

D ⇌ ⇌ ⇌ SC

B&Bs/Small Inns

★★ **AMELIA'S FIELD COUNTRY INN.** *617 Cynthiana Rd (40361). 606/987-5778; fax 606/987-9075.* 4 rms, 2 story. S, D $75-$100. Closed Jan-mid-Feb. TV in common rm. Complimentary full bkfst. Restaurant Thurs-Sun noon-2 pm, 6-9:30 pm. Ck-out 12:30 pm, ck-in 3 pm. Lawn games. Built in 1936, Colonial Revival. Cr cds: A, D, MC, V.

D ⇌

★★ **ROSEDALE BED & BREAKFAST.** *1917 Cypress St (40361). 606/987-1845; res 800/644-1862. www.cre8iv.com/rosedale.html.* 4 rms, 2 share baths, 2 story. S $65; D $65-$90; each addl $15; family, wkly rates. Children over 12 yrs only. TV in common rm; TV, VCR avail (movies). Complimentary full bkfst. Restaurant nearby. Ck-out noon, ck-in 3 pm. Gift shop. Guest lndry. Lawn games. Built in 1862, previously home of Civil War general. Cr cds: MC, V.

⇌ ⇌

Park City

See also Bowling Green

Pop 549 **Elev** 650 ft **Area code** 270 **Zip** 42160

Resort

★★ **PARK MAMMOTH RESORT.** *US 31W and I-65 (42160), 1½ mi S off US 31W; 1½ mi SE of I-65 Park City Exit 48. 270/749-4101; fax 270/749-2524.* 92 rms, 2 story. June-Oct: S $45; D $58; each addl $5; under 18 free; golf plan; lower rates rest of yr. Crib free. TV; cable, VCR avail (movies). Indoor pool; wading pool. Sauna. Playground. Dining rm 7-10 am, 11:30 am-1 pm, 5-8:30 pm. Ck-out noon. Meeting rms. Business servs avail. Gift shop. Lighted tennis. 36-hole

golf, greens fee $10. Miniature golf. Lawn games. Rec rm. Miniature train ride. On 2,000 acres. Cr cds: A, C, D, DS, ER, JCB, MC, V.

⇌ ⇌ ⇌ ⇌ ⇌ ⇌

Pikeville

(C-8) *See also Prestonsburg*

Founded 1824 **Pop** 6,324 **Elev** 685 ft **Area code** 859 **Zip** 41501
Web www.kymtnnet.org/PikeB.html
Information Pike County Chamber of Commerce, 225 College St, Suite 2; 859/432-5504

Location of the notorious Hatfield-McCoy feud, Pikeville sits astride the Levisa Fork of the Big Sandy River and is the seat of Pike County, a leading producer of deep-mined coal. The town was named for Zebulon M. Pike, the explorer.

Annual Event

Hillbilly Days Spring Festival. Antique car show, music, arts and crafts. Third wkend Apr.

Motel/Motor Lodge

★★ **LANDMARK INN.** *146 S Mayo Tr (41502). 606/432-2545; fax 606/432-2545; toll-free 800/831-1469.* 103 rms, 4 story. S $55; D $65; each addl $10; under 12 free. Crib free. Pet accepted, some restrictions. TV; cable (premium), VCR avail (movies). Pool. Rooftop restaurant 6 am-10 pm; Sun to 3 pm. Bar; entertainment. Ck-out noon. Coin lndry. Sundries. Meeting rms. Valet serv. Some balconies. Cr cds: A, C, D, DS, MC, V.

D ⇌ ⇌ ⇌ ⇌ SC

Pineville

(D-7) *See also Barbourville*

Settled 1799 **Pop** 2,198 **Elev** 1,015 ft **Area code** 859 **Zip** 40977

Annual Event

Mountain Laurel Festival. Pine Mountain State Resort Park. College women from entire state compete for Festival Queen title. Parade, art exhibits, contests, sporting events, concerts. Memorial Day wkend.

Resort

★★ **PINE MOUNTAIN STATE RESORT PARK.** *1050 State Park Rd (40977), 1 mi S on US 25E. 606/337-3066; fax 606/337-7250; toll-free 800/325-1712.* 30 rms, 2 story, 19 1-2 bedrm kit. cottages. Memorial Day-Labor Day: S $59; D $69; each addl $5.46; kit. cottages $85-$99; under 16 free; lower lodge rates rest of yr. Crib free. TV; cable. Pool; lifeguard. Supervised children's activities (June-Aug). Meeting rm. Business servs avail. Dining rm 7 am-9 pm; Sun 7-10:30 am, noon-3 pm, 5-9 pm. Ck-out noon, cottages 11 am, ck-in 4 pm. 9-hole golf, greens fee $11, carts $10, miniature golf. Lawn games. Rec rm. Balconies, patios. Picnic tables. State-owned; all park facilities avail. Cr cds: A, C, D, DS, MC, V.

Prestonsburg

(C-8) *See also Pikeville*

Settled 1791 **Pop** 3,558 **Elev** 642 ft
Area code 859 **Zip** 41653
Information Floyd County Chamber of Commerce, 245 North Lake Dr; 859/886-0364

Annual Event

Kentucky Apple Festival. In Paintsville, 11 mi N via US 23/460. Parade, amusement rides, antique car show, arts and crafts, flea market, 5K run, postage cancellation, square dancing, music, and entertainment. Phone 859/789-4355. First Sat Oct.

Seasonal Event

Jenny Wiley Theatre. Jenny Wiley State Resort Park (see). Broadway musicals. For schedule contact General Mgr, PO Box 22; 859/886-9274. Mid-June-late Aug.

Motels/Motor Lodges

★ **DAYS INN.** *512 S Mayo Tr (41240), 12 mi N on US 23/460. 606/789-3551; fax 606/789-9299; toll-free 800/329-7466.* 72 rms, 2 story. S $45-$70; D $55-$70; each addl $5; under 12 free; higher rates Apple Festival. Crib free. Pet accepted. TV; cable (premium). Pool. Complimentary continental bkfst. Restaurant opp 6 am-9:30 pm. Ck-out 11 am. Business servs avail. Exercise equipt. Cr cds: A, C, D, DS, MC, V.

★★ **HOLIDAY INN.** *1887 US 23 N (41653). 606/886-0001; fax 606/886-9850.* 117 rms, 3 story. S, D $66; each addl $6; under 19 free. Crib free. Pet accepted, some restrictions. TV; cable. Heated pool; whirlpool, poolside serv. Restaurant 6 am-10 pm. Rm serv from 7 am. Bar; entertainment Thurs, Fri. Ck-out noon. Coin lndry. Meeting rms. Business servs avail. In-rm modem link. Exercise equipt. Refrigerators avail. Cr cds: A, D, DS, MC, V.

Resort

★★ **JENNY WILEY STATE RESORT PARK.** *75 Theater Ct (41653), 2 mi S on US 23, then 1½ mi N on KY 3, in Jenny Wiley State Resort Park. 606/886-2711; fax 606/889-0462.* 49 rms, 2 story, 18 kit. cottages (1-2 bedrm). Memorial Day-Labor Day: S $57; D $67; each addl $5; kit. cottages $85-$95; under 16 free; rates vary rest of yr. Crib free. TV; cable (premium). 2 pools; wading pool. Playground. Supervised children's activities (Memorial Day- Labor Day). Dining rm 7 am-9 pm. Ck-out noon, cottages 11 am, ck-in 4 pm. Meeting rms. Business servs avail. Gift shop. Social dir. 9-hole golf, greens fee $10. Lawn games. Private patios, balconies. Picnic tables, grills, hiking trails. On lake. State-owned; all park facilities avail. Cr cds: A, D, DS, MC, V.

Conference Center

★★ **RAMADA INN.** *624 James Trimble Blvd (41240), off US 23. 606/789-4242; fax 606/789-6788; res 800/272-6232; toll-free 800/951-4242. Email ramada@webjammer.net; www.ramadapaintsville.com.* 123 rms, 3 story, 5 suites. July-Oct: S $9000; D $9500; each addl $5; suites $160; under 12 free; lower rates rest of yr. Crib avail. Parking lot. Indoor/outdoor pools, whirlpool. TV; cable (DSS), VCR avail, CD avail. Complimentary toll-free calls. Restaurant 8 am-9 pm. Ck-out noon, ck-in 3 pm. Meeting rms. Business servs avail. Bellhops. Dry cleaning, coin lndry. Gift shop. Exercise equipt. Golf, 18 holes. Tennis, 2 courts. Hiking trail. Picnic facilities. Cr cds: A, C, D, DS, ER, JCB, MC, V.

Richmond

(C-6) *See also Berea, Lexington, Winchester*

Founded 1798 **Pop** 21,155 **Elev** 975 ft
Area code 859 **Zip** 40475
Web www.richmond-ky.com
Information Tourism & Visitor Center, 345 Lancaster Ave; 859/626-8474 or 800/866-3705.

Annual Event

Madison County Fair & Horse Show. Last wk July.

Motels/Motor Lodges

★★ **BEST WESTERN ROAD STAR INN.** *1751 Lexington Rd (40475), near I-75 Exit 90/90A. 859/623-9121; fax 859/623-3160; res 800/528-1234; toll-free 800/575-5339. Email road starinn@pcystems.net.* 95 rms, 2 story. S, D $59; under 17 free. Crib free. Pet accepted. TV; cable (premium). Heated pool. Continental bkfst. Coffee in rms. Restaurant nearby. Ck-out noon. Meeting rm. Business servs avail. In-rm modem link. Some refrigerators. Cr cds: A, C, D, DS, MC, V.

★ **DAYS INN.** *2109 Belmont Dr (40475), I-75 Exit 90b. 859/624-5769; fax 859/624-1406; toll-free 800/329-7466.* 70 rms, 2 story. S $42; D $47; each addl $5; under 18 free. Pet accepted, some restrictions; $5. TV; cable (premium). Pool. Restaurant adj open 24 hrs. Ck-out 11 am. Meeting rm. Business servs avail. Cr cds: A, C, D, DS, JCB, MC, V.

★★ **HOLIDAY INN.** *100 Eastern Bypass (40475), I-75 Exit 87. 859/623-9220; fax 859/624-1458; toll-free 800/465-4329.* 141 rms, 2 story. S, D $59; each addl $5; under 19 free. Crib free. TV; cable. Pool. Coffee in rms. Restaurant 6:30-10:30 am, 5-9 pm. Ck-out 11 am. Meeting rms. Business servs avail. In-rm modem link. Bellhops. Some refrigerators. Picnic tables. Near Eastern Kentucky Univ. Cr cds: A, C, D, DS, JCB, MC, V.

★ **SUPER 8.** *107 N Keeneland Dr (47547), I-75, Exit 90B. 859/624-1550; fax 859/624-1553.* 63 rms, 2 story. S $39.88; D $49.88; each addl $5; under 18 free; weekly rates; higher rates college events, races. Crib free. Pet accepted; $5. TV; cable (premium). Complimentary continental bkfst. Restaurant adj open 24 hrs. Ck-out 11 am. Cr cds: A, D, DS, MC, V.

Rough River Dam State Resort Park

(On KY 79 at NE end of Rough River Lake)

This 637-acre park is at the northeast end of 4,860-acre Rough River Lake, on KY 79. Beach with bathhouse, pool (seasonal); fishing; boat dock (ramps, rentals); hiking and fitness trail, 9-hole golf, pro shop, driving range, miniature golf, tennis, shuffleboard, picnicking, playgrounds, lodge (see RESORT), dining room, cottages. Tent and trailer camping (Apr-Oct, standard fees); central service bldg. Planned recreation. For fees and information phone 270/257-2311.

Resort

★★ **ROUGH RIVER DAM STATE PARK RESORT.** *450 Lodge Rd (40119), off KY 79 in park.* 270/257-2311; fax 270/257-8682; toll-free 800/325-1713. www.kystateparks.com. 40 rms, 2 story, 17 kit. cottages. Memorial Day-Labor Day: S $59; D $69; each addl $5; kit. cottages $97-$110; under 16 free; lower rates rest of yr. Closed Christmas wk. Crib free. TV; cable. Pool; lifeguard. Playground. Dining rm 7-10:30 am, 11:30 am-4 pm, 5-9 pm; Sun noon-9 pm; winter to 8 pm. Ck-out noon, cottages 11 am, ck-in 4 pm. Coin lndry. Meeting rms. Business servs avail. Lighted tennis. 9-hole golf, greens fee $9, driving range. Miniature golf. Airstrip. Private patios, balconies. Picnic tables, grills (cottages). On lake; marina and boat rental. State-owned property; all facilities of park avail. Cr cds: A, C, D, DS, MC, V.
D ⟨icons⟩ SC

Shepherdsville

(C-5) *See also Elizabethtown, Fort Knox, Louisville*

Pop 4,805 **Elev** 449 ft **Area code** 502 **Zip** 40165

Motel/Motor Lodge

★★ **BEST WESTERN SOUTH.** *211 S Lakeview Dr (40165), I-65 Exit 117.* 270/543-7097; fax 270/543-2407; toll-free 800/528-1234; toll-free 877/543-5080. www.bestwestern.com. 85 rms, 2 story. S $53; D $58; each addl $4; suites $66-$70; under 12 free; higher rates Kentucky Derby. Crib free. TV; cable (premium). Pool; wading pool. Restaurant 6:30 am-2 pm, 5-10 pm; Sun 6:30 am-2 pm, 5-9 pm. Bar 4 pm-midnight; entertainment Thurs-Sat. Ck-out noon. Meeting rm. Business servs avail. Cr cds: A, DS, MC, V.
D ⟨icons⟩ SC

Somerset

(D-6) *See also Jamestown, London*

Founded 1801 **Pop** 10,733 **Elev** 975 ft **Area code** 859 **Zip** 42501

Information Somerset/Pulaski Convention & Visitors Bureau, 522 Ogden St; 859/679-6394 or 800/642-6287

Motels/Motor Lodges

★ **DAYS INN OF SOMERSET.** *125 N US Hwy 27 (42503).* 606/678-2052; fax 606/678-8477; res 800/DAYSINN. 54 rms, 2 story. May: S $50; D $55; each addl $6; under 12 free; lower rates rest of yr., fee. TV; cable (premium). Ck-out 11 am. Cr cds: C, D, DS, MC, V.
⟨icon⟩

★★ **LANDMARK INN.** *1201 S US 27 (42501), 1 mi S of KY 80.* 606/678-8115; fax 606/679-4904; toll-free 800/585-3503. 157 rms, 2 story. S $48, D $54; each addl $6; suites $75; under 12 free. Crib free. TV; cable (premium). Pool. Playground. Restaurant 11 am-10 pm. Ck-out 11 am. Coin lndry. Business servs avail. In-rm modem link. Free local airport transportation. Cr cds: A, D, DS, MC, V.
D ⟨icons⟩

★ **SOMERSET LODGE.** *725 S Hwy 27 (42501).* 606/678-4195; fax 606/679-3299; toll-free 800/256-3446. 100 rms, 1-2 story. S $42; D $50; each addl $5; under 12 free. Pet accepted; $85. TV; cable (premium). Pool; wading pool. Playground. Restaurant 6 am-9 pm. Ck-out noon. Meeting rms. Business servs avail. Lawn games. Cr cds: A, C, D, DS, MC, V.
D ⟨icons⟩ SC

South Union

See also Bowling Green

Founded 1807 **Elev** 608 ft **Area code** 270 **Zip** 42283

Information Logan County Chamber of Commerce, 116 S Main St, Russellville 42276; 270/726-2206

Annual Events

Shaker Festival. Tour of historic bldgs; Shaker foods, music; craft demonstrations. June.

Tobacco Festival. 12 mi SW on US 68 in Russellville. Parade; reenactment of the Jesse James bank robbery; house tours in historic district; tobacco displays; antiques; arts and crafts exhibits; bicycle rides; run (5 mi), fun run (1 mi); entertainment. One wk mid-Oct.

B&B/Small Inn

★ **SHAKER TAVERN.** *KY 73 (42283). 270/542-6801.* 6 rms, 5 share bath, 2 story. No rm phones. S, D $65-$75; wkly rates. TV in common rm. Complimentary full bkfst. Ck-out 9 am, ck-in 5 pm. Built 1869. Totally non-smoking. Cr cds: MC, V.

Walton

(B-6) *See also Covington (Cincinnati Airport Area)*

Pop 2,034 **Elev** 930 ft **Area code** 859
Zip 41094

Motels/Motor Lodges

★ **DAYS INN.** *11177 Frontage Rd (41094), jct I-75, KY 338 Exit 175. 859/485-4151; fax 859/485-1239; res 800/325-2525.* 137 rms, 2 story. S, D $39-$55; each addl $7. Crib free. Pet accepted. TV; cable. Pool. Playground. Restaurant adj open 24 hrs. Ck-out 11 am. Sundries. Cr cds: A, C, D, DS, ER, JCB, MC, V.

★ **ECONO LODGE.** *11165 Frontage Rd (41094), jct I-75, KY 338 Exit 175. 859/485-4123; fax 859/485-9366; toll-free 800/553-2666.* 60 rms, 2 story. S $38-$65; D $44-$95; each addl $5; under 18 free; higher rates special events. Crib free. TV; cable (premium). Pool. Playground. Complimentary continental bkfst. Restaurant open 24 hrs. Ck-out 11

am. Business servs avail. Cr cds: A, C, D, DS, MC, V.

Wickliffe

See also Paducah

Pop 851 **Elev** 330 ft **Area code** 270
Zip 42087

What to See and Do

Wickliffe Mounds. Remnants of a Mississippian culture of 1,000 yrs ago. Museum exhibits, pottery, ongoing excavations. (Mar-Nov, daily; closed Thanksgiving) On US 51/60/62 in NW area of city. Phone 270/335-3681. ¢¢

Williamsburg

(D-6) *See also Corbin*

Founded 1817 **Pop** 5,493 **Elev** 951 ft **Area code** 859 **Zip** 40769
Information Tourist & Convention Commission, PO Box 2; 859/549-0530

Motels/Motor Lodges

★ **DAYS INN.** *510 Hwy 92 W (40769), 1½ blks W of I-75 Exit 11. 606/549-1500; fax 606/549-8312; res 800/329-7466; toll-free 800/215-2995.* 86 rms, 2 story. S $36; D $45; each addl $4; under 12 free. Crib free. TV; cable (premium). Pool. Continental bkfst. Restaurant opp open 24 hrs. Ck-out 11 am. Business servs avail. Cr cds: A, D, DS, MC, V.

★ **SUPER 8 MOTEL.** *30 W Hwy 92 (40769), I-75 Exit 11. 606/549-3450; fax 606/549-8161; res 800/800-8000.* 100 rms, 2-3 story. No elvtr. S, D $65; under 18 free. Crib free. Pet accepted. TV; cable (premium). Pool. Complimentary continental bkfst. Ck-out noon. Meeting rms. Business servs avail. In-rm modem link. Cr cds: A, D, DS, MC, V.

Williamstown

(B-6) *See also Covington (Cincinnati Airport Area)*

Settled 1820 **Pop** 3,023 **Elev** 974 ft
Area code 859 **Zip** 41097
Information Grant County Chamber of Commerce, 149 N Main St, PO Box 365; 859/824-3322

Motel/Motor Lodge

★ **DAYS INN.** *211 Hwy 36 W (41097), I-75 Exit 154. 606/824-5025; fax 606/824-5028; toll-free 800/329-7466.* 50 rms, 1-2 story. S $36-$40; D $45-$51; each addl $5; under 12 free. Crib free. Pet accepted, some restrictions. TV; cable. Pool. Coffee in lobby. Restaurant adj. Ck-out 11 am. Cr cds: A, C, D, DS, MC, V.

Restaurant

★ **COUNTRY GRILL.** *21 Taft Hwy (41035), 2 mi N on I-75, Exit 159. 606/824-6000.* Specializes in chicken, pasta, homemade soup. Hrs: 7 am-9 pm; Fri to 10 pm; Sat 8 am-10 pm; Sun from 8 am. Closed hols. Res accepted. Bkfst $2.85-$7.75; lunch $4.50-$6.95; dinner $6.50-$13.95. Child's menu. Cr cds: A, DS, MC, V.

Winchester

(C-7) *See also Lexington*

Pop 15,799 **Elev** 972 ft **Area code** 859 **Zip** 40391
Information Winchester-Clark County Tourism Commission, 2 S Maple; 859/744-0556

What to See and Do

◩ **Fort Boonesborough State Park.** Site of settlement where Daniel Boone defended his fort against Native American sieges. The fort houses craft shops where costumed "pioneers" produce wares; a museum with Boone memorabilia and other historical items; and an audiovisual program (Apr-Labor Day, daily; after Labor Day-Oct, Wed-Sun). Exhibits in cabins and blockhouses re-create life at the fort. Sand beach, swimming pool, bathhouse, fishing, boating (ramp, dock); miniature golf, picnicking, playground, snack bar. Tent and trailer sites (standard fees). Rec dir; special events all yr. 9 mi SW via KY 627, located on the Kentucky River. Phone 859/527-3131. Museum ¢¢

Annual Event

Daniel Boone Pioneer Festival. College and Lykins Parks. Juried arts and crafts, antiques, street dance, 5K run, 2-mi walk, bicycle race, concerts, music, food, fireworks. Phone 859/744-0556. Labor Day wkend.

Motels/Motor Lodges

★★ **HAMPTON INN.** *1025 Early Dr (40391). 606/745-2000; fax 606/745-2001.* 60 rms, 2 story. S $56-$66; D $59-$69; under 18 free; higher rates special events. Crib avail. TV; cable (premium). Pool. Complimentary continental bkfst. Coffee in rms. Restaurant adj 6 am-10 pm. Ck-out 11 am. Coin lndry. Meeting rms. Business servs avail. Valet serv. Sundries. Exercise equipt. Cr cds: A, D, DS, MC, V.

★★ **HOLIDAY INN.** *1100 Interstate Dr (40391), I-64 E, Exit 96. 606/744-9111; fax 606/745-1369.* 64 rms, 2 story. S, D $59; under 19 free; higher rates special events. Crib free. Pet accepted. TV; cable (premium). Pool. Complimentary coffee in rms. Restaurant 6:30 am-1 pm, 6-8:30 pm; Sat 7-10:30 am; Sun 7 am-2 pm. Ck-out 11 am. Coin lndry. Meeting rms. Business servs avail. Some refrigerators. Cr cds: A, C, D, DS, MC, V.

LOUISIANA

The soil of Louisiana was carried down from the central valley of the United States by the Ouachita, Mississippi, Red, Sabine, and Pearl rivers. Much of the state is a flat, moist, rich-soiled delta with a distinct historic and ethnic atmosphere.

The area was discovered by Spaniards, named by the French (for Louis XIV), and settled by both. People with the blood of those French Canadians driven from Acadia (Nova Scotia) by the British in 1755 are called Acadians ("Cajuns"). Americans of English, Irish, and German origin also helped settle Louisiana.

The land is semitropical, beautifully unusual, full of legend and tradition; a land of bayous with cypress and live oak overhung with Spanish moss. Some of its people live in isolation on the bayous and riverbanks, where they still fish, trap, and do a little farming. Southern and southwestern Louisiana are predominantly Roman Catholic; the northern section is largely Protestant. It is the only state whose divisions are called parishes rather than counties.

Population: 4,372,035
Area: 44,520 square miles
Elevation: 0-535 feet
Peak: Driskill Mountain
  (Bienville Parish)
Entered Union: April 30, 1812
  (18th state)
Capital: Baton Rouge
Motto: Union, Justice,
  Confidence
Nicknames: Bayou State,
  Sportsman's Paradise, Pelican
  State
Flower: Magnolia
Bird: Eastern Brown Pelican
Tree: Bald Cypress
Fair: Late October-Early
  November, 2001, in
  Shreveport
Time Zone: Central
Website:
  www.louisianatravel.com

The northern and southern parts of the state are quite different topographically. In the southern area are fine old mansions and sugar cane plantation estates, many of which are open to the public. (See BATON ROUGE for a plantation tour.) The north is more rural, with beautiful rivers, hills, forests, and cotton plantation mansions. This is the area from which the colorful Huey Long came; he was born in Winnfield.

Petroleum and natural gas taken from far underground, shipped abroad, or processed in large plants, contribute to Louisiana's thriving industrial and manufacturing economy. As these businesses expand, the service sector continually grows to meet demands.

Hernando de Soto discovered the Mississippi in 1541. La Salle claimed Louisiana for France in 1682. Pierre le Moyne, Sieur d'Iberville, first came to the state in 1699. His brother Jean Baptiste le Moyne, Sieur de Bienville, founded New Orleans in 1718, three years after the founding of Natchitoches by Cavalier St. Denis.

To prevent Louisiana from falling into the hands of the English, Louis XV of France gave it to his cousin, Charles III of Spain. In 1801 Napoleon regained it for France, though no one in Louisiana knew of this until 1803, only 20 days before the Louisiana Purchase made it US territory.

This colorful history established it as the state it is—individual, different, exciting. It remains the old Deep South at its best—gracious, cultured, and hospitable.

When to Go/Climate

Temperatures in Louisiana rarely dip below freezing—even in winter. Summers are hot, with oppressive humidity. Hurricane season runs from June 1 through Nov 1, and Gulf coast towns are prime targets during this time of year. Annual rainfall can exceed 65 inches in the coastal areas.

AVERAGE HIGH/LOW TEMPERATURES (°F)

NEW ORLEANS

Jan 61/42	May 84/65	Sep 87/70
Feb 64/44	June 89/71	Oct 79/59
Mar 72/52	July 91/73	Nov 71/51
Apr 79/58	Aug 90/73	Dec 64/45

SHREVEPORT

Jan 55/35	May 83/62	Sep 87/66
Feb 61/38	June 90/69	Oct 79/54
Mar 69/46	July 93/72	Nov 68/45
Apr 77/54	Aug 93/71	Dec 59/37

Parks and Recreation Finder

Directions to and information about the parks and recreation areas below are given under their respective town/city sections. Please refer to those sections for details.

NATIONAL PARK AND RECREATION AREAS

Key to abbreviations. I.H.S. = International Historic Site; I.P.M. = International Peace Memorial; N.B. = National Battlefield; N.B.P. = National Battlefield Park; N.B.C. = National Battlefield and Cemetery; N.C.A. = National Conservation Area; N.E.M. = National Expansion Memorial; N.F. = National Forest; N.G. = National Grassland; N.H.P. = National Historical Park; N.H.C. = National Heritage Corridor; N.H.S. = National Historic Site; N.L. = National Lakeshore; N.M. = National Monument; N.M.P. = National Military Park; N.Mem. = National Memorial; N.P. = National Park; N.Pres. = National Preserve; N.R.A. = National Recreational Area; N.R.R. = National Recreational River; N.Riv. = National River; N.S. = National Seashore; N.S.R. = National Scenic Riverway; N.S.T. = National Scenic Trail; N.Sc. = National Scientific Reserve; N.V.M. = National Volcanic Monument.

Place Name	Listed Under
Jean Lafitte N.H.P. and Preserve	NEW ORLEANS
Kisatchie N.F.	ALEXANDRIA

STATE PARK AND RECREATION AREAS

Key to abbreviations. I.P. = Interstate Park; S.A.P. = State Archaeological Park; S.B. = State Beach; S.C.A. = State Conservation Area; S.C.P. = State Conservation Park; S.Cp. = State Campground; S.F. = State Forest; S.G. = State Garden; S.H.A. = State Historic Area; S.H.P. = State Historic Park; S.H.S. = State Historic Site; S.M.P. = State Marine Park; S.N.A. = State Natural Area; S.P. = State Park; S.P.C. = State Public Campground; S.R. = State Reserve; S.R.A. = State Recreation Area; S.Res. = State Reservoir; S.Res.P. = State Resort Park; S.R.P. = State Rustic Park.

Place Name	Listed Under
Chemin-a-Haut S.P.	BASTROP
Chicot S.P.	OPELOUSAS
Cypremort Point S.P.	FRANKLIN
Fontainebleau S.P.	COVINGTON
Lake Bistineau S.P.	MINDEN
Sam Houston Jones S.P.	LAKE CHARLES
St. Bernard S.P.	NEW ORLEANS

CALENDAR HIGHLIGHTS

JANUARY

Sugar Bowl College Football Classic (New Orleans). Superdome. Phone 504/525-8573.

FEBRUARY

Mardi Gras (New Orleans). Perhaps the most famous celebration in the United States. Officially opens 2 wks before Shrove Tuesday; incl torchlight parades, street dancing, costume balls, and masquerades. Phone 504/566-5005.

APRIL

Festival International de Louisiane (Lafayette). Artists from Africa, Canada, Caribbean, Europe, and the US celebrate Louisiana culture. Phone 337/232-8086.

MAY

New Orleans Jazz & Heritage Festival (New Orleans). Eleven stages offer everything from rock 'n roll to jazz, blues, and Afro-Caribbean. Evening concerts in various concert halls and clubs. Phone 504/522-4786.

JULY

Natchitoches-Northwestern Folk Festival (Natchitoches). N.S.U. Prather Coliseum. Festival spotlights a different industry or occupation each year and works to preserve Louisiana folk art forms; music, dance, crafts, storytelling, foods. Phone 318/357-4332.

SEPTEMBER

Louisiana Shrimp and Petroleum Festival and Fair (Morgan City). Amusement rides, hands-on children's village, coronation and ball, blessing of the shrimp and petroleum fleets on Berwick Bay, parade, fireworks, and food. Phone 504/385-0703.

OCTOBER

Blues Festival (Baton Rouge). Three-day event featuring blues, Cajun, zydeco, and gospel music. Traditional Louisiana cuisine.

Louisiana State Fair (Shreveport). Fairgrounds. One of the largest fairs in the country; annually draws more than 300,000 people. Entertainment; agriculture and livestock competition. Phone 318/635-1361.

DECEMBER

Christmas Festival of Lights (Natchitoches). More than 140,000 lights are turned on after a full day of celebration to welcome the Christmas season. Phone 318/352-8072 or 800/259-1714.

Water-related activities, hiking, various other sports, picnicking and visitor centers, as well as camping, are avail in many of these areas. An admission fee ($2/vehicle for up to 4 people, 50 cents;/each additional) is charged at most Louisiana state parks. Many parks have swimming, fishing, boating (rentals), camping (unimproved sites, $10/site/night; improved, $12/site/night; 2-wk max). Swimming pools are operated Memorial Day-Labor Day. Some parks have cabins (2-wk max res made at each park). Reservations for Oct-Mar are placed between July 1-3 by phone only on "first come" basis annually. After July 3, res will be accepted by phoning or writing the particular park. Res for Apr-Sep are placed between Jan 2-4 by phone only on "first come" basis annually. After Jan 4, res will be accepted by phoning or writing the particular park. **Note:** Res may only be made between 8 am-5 pm, Mon-Fri. In the event that the above dates fall on a wkend or holiday, res may be made the following business day. Golden Age Passport accepted. Pets on leash only; not permitted within any state park bldg. For further information contact the Office of State Parks, PO Box 44426, Baton Rouge 70804-4426; 225/342-8111 or 888/677-1400.

FISHING AND HUNTING

Nonresident fishing license: $31; 3-day, $20. Nonresident saltwater fishing license: $36; 3-day, $20. Marine conservation stamp (required for saltwater fishing): $3. Fishing licenses are valid from the date of purchase until June 30. Nonresident basic season hunting license: $86; 5-day, $51. Nonresident All Game Season: $160.50; 5-day, $95.50. Nonresident migratory game bird license (3-day) $45.50; nonresident waterfowl (duck) stamp: $13.50. Nonresident archery license: $25.50. For details on hunting and fishing regulations contact Louisiana Department of Wildlife and Fisheries, PO Box 98000, Baton Rouge 70898; 225/765-2887 or 888/765-2602.

Driving Information

Safety belts are mandatory for all persons in front seat of vehicle. Children under 13 yrs must be in an age- or size-appropriate restraint system anywhere in vehicle. For further information phone 225/925-6991.

INTERSTATE HIGHWAY SYSTEM

The following alphabetical listing of Louisiana towns in the *Mobil Travel Guide* shows that these cities are within 10 miles of the indicated Interstate highways. A highway map should be checked, however, for the nearest exit.

Highway Number	Cities/Towns within 10 miles
Interstate 10	Baton Rouge, Jennings, Kenner, Lafayette, Lake Charles, Metairie, New Orleans, Slidell.
Interstate 12	Baton Rouge, Covington, Hammond, Slidell.
Interstate 20	Bossier City, Minden, Monroe, Ruston, Shreveport, West Monroe.
Interstate 49	Alexandria, Lafayette, Natchitoches, Opelousas, Shreveport.
Interstate 55	Hammond, Kenner.
Interstate 59	Slidell.

Additional Visitor Information

For detailed information on Louisiana, contact the Office of Tourism, Inquiry Section, PO Box 94291, Baton Rouge 70804-9291; 225/342-8119 or 800/33-GUMBO.

There are several tourist information centers in Louisiana; visitors will find information and brochures helpful in planning stops at points of interest. Some of the locations are as follows: in the northern part of the state on westbound I-20 at Tallulah and on eastbound I-20 at Greenwood; in the central part of the state on the eastern border on US 84 at Vidalia; in the southern part of the state at Baton Rouge in Memorial Hall of the State Capitol, on St. Ann St in the French Quarter in New Orleans, southbound on I-59 near Pearl River, westbound on I-10 near Slidell, southbound on I-55 at Kentwood, eastbound on I-10 near Sabine River and S of the Louisiana-Mississippi state line on US 61 in St. Francisville. (Daily; hrs may vary)

Hordes of New Orleans visitors head straight for Plantation Alley, a 100-mile-or-so stretch of levee roads, and the Great River Road (Highway 1), where a dozen or more historic plantation homes are open to public tours, despite guidebook warnings about petrochemical plants overshadowing the antebellum homes. **(Approx 225 mi)**

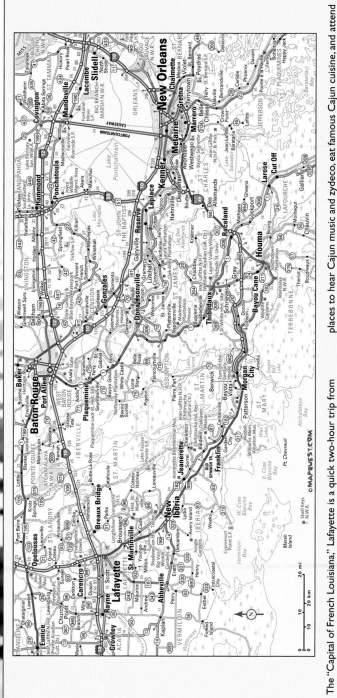

The "Capital of French Louisiana," Lafayette is a quick two-hour trip from New Orleans via I-10, or a sticky, more adventurous day-long trip through the Cajun wetlands via the Old Spanish Trail national highway US 90. It's a good-time college town (University of Southwestern Louisiana) with wonderful places to hear Cajun music and zydeco, eat famous Cajun cuisine, and attend colorful local festivals. Outside Lafayette itself, many towns, such as Breaux Bridge, Eunice, and Abbeville, make appealing rural destinations for the same great Cajun culture, food, and music. **(Approx 300 mi)**

Alexandria (D-3)

Founded 1806 **Pop** 49,188 **Elev** 82 ft
Area code 318 **Web** www.apacvv.org
Information Alexandria/Pineville
Area Visitors & Convention Bureau,
707 Main St, 71301; 318/443-7049

In the heart of Louisiana, Alexandria
became the center of the 1864 Red
River Campaign of the Civil War,
which resulted in the burning of the
town. During World War II camps
Beauregard, Livingston, Claiborne,
Polk, and Alexandria Air Force Base,
all nearby, feverishly trained young
Americans to fight. The largest
maneuvers in US history, involving
472,000 troops, took place in this
area.

Both Alexandria and Pineville,
located on the Red River where it is
joined by the Bayou Rapides, are centers for farming and livestock production, lumbering, and light
manufacturing. Water sports are popular at Fort Buhlow Lake and other
nearby lakes.

What to See and Do

Alexandria Museum of Art. National
and regional changing exhibits.
(Tues-Sat; closed hols) 933 Main St.
Phone 318/443-3458. ¢¢

Bringhurst Park. Alexandria Zoo (fee).
Tennis; 9-hole golf. Picnicking, play-
ground. (Daily) 3016 Masonic Dr.
Phone 318/473-1385. **FREE**

Cotile Recreation Area. Swimming,
bathhouse, waterskiing; fishing; boating (ramp). Picnicking. Tent and
trailer camping (fee). (Daily) Addl fee
for boat, ski rig. 75 Cotile Lake Rd.
Phone 318/793-8995. Per vehicle ¢¢

Kent House. (ca 1800) Restored
French Colonial plantation house
furnished with period pieces; outbldg
incl milkhouse, barn, cabins,
detached kitchen, carriage house,
sugar mill, spinning and weaving
cottage. Herb and formal gardens;
open-hearth cooking demonstration
(Oct-Apr, Wed). Guided tours. (Daily;
closed Jan 1, Thanksgiving, Dec 25) 1
blk W on Bayou Rapides Rd off US
165/71. Phone 318/487-5998. ¢¢

Kisatchie National Forest. Louisiana's
only national forest covers 600,000
acres. Dogwood and wild azalea
bloom in the shadows of longleaf,
loblolly, and slash pine. Wild Azalea
National Recreation Trail, the state's
longest hiking trail (31 mi), is in the
Evangeline District. Swimming, waterskiing; fishing, hunting. Hiking; off-
road vehicles. Picnicking. Camping
(tent and trailer sites). Fees are
charged at some recreation sites. N,
W, and S of town. Contact Forest
Supervisor, 2500 Shreveport Hwy,
Pineville 71360. Phone 318/473-7160.

National Cemetery. (1867) Shamrock St in Pineville. Also in Pineville
is **Rapides Cemetery** (1772), at
David St

Motels/Motor Lodges

**★★ BEST WESTERN INN &
SUITES.** *2720 W MacArthur Dr
(71303). 318/445-5530; fax 318/445-
8996; res 800/528-1234; toll-free 888/
338-2008.* 198 rms, 2 story. S $52; D
$58; each addl $6; suites $81-$125;
under 18 free. Crib free. Pet accepted.
TV; cable (premium). Indoor pool;
wading pool, whirlpool. Complimentary continental bkfst. Restaurant adj
5-10 pm. Bar 4-10 pm. Ck-out noon.
Meeting rms. Business servs avail.
Bellhops. Valet serv. Airport transportation. Health club privileges.
Microwaves avail. Picnic tables. Cr
cds: A, D, DS, MC, V.

🐕 🏊 🕴 🛐 🔥

★ DAYS INN. *1146 MacArthur Dr
(71303). 318/443-1841; fax 318/448-
4845; res 800/329-7466.* 66 rms, 2
story. S, D $42; each addl $5; under
16 free. Crib avail. Pet accepted, fee.
Parking lot. Pool. TV; cable. Complimentary continental bkfst. coffee in
rms. Restaurant nearby. Ck-out 11
am, ck-in 1 pm. Cr cds: A, DS, MC, V.

🐕 🏊 🛐 🔥

**★ HOWARD JOHNSON EXPRESS
INN.** *6014 Old Boyce Rd (71301).
318/442-5190; fax 318/442-5190; res
800/446-4656.* 44 rms, 2 story. S
$51.98-$57.75; D $56.70-$63; under
12 free; higher rates special events.
TV; cable (premium). Complimentary
coffee in rms. Restaurant nearby. Ck-
out 11 am. Cr cds: A, C, DS, MC, V.

🄳 ⓛ 🕴 🔆 ✈ 🛐 🔥

★ **RODEWAY INN.** *742 MacArthur Dr (71301). 318/448-1611; fax 318/473-2984; toll-free 800/638-7949.* 121 rms, 2 story. S $36-$40; D $40-$50; each addl $10; suites $57-$62; studio rms $38-$50; under 17 free. Crib free. Pet accepted; $25 deposit. TV; cable (premium), VCR avail. Pool; wading pool. Ck-out noon. Business servs avail. Airport transportation. Microwaves avail. Cr cds: A, C, D, DS, MC, V.

Hotels

★★ **HOLIDAY INN MACARTHUR DRIVE.** *2716 N MacArthur Dr (71303). 318/487-4261; fax 318/445-0891; res 800/465-4329; toll-free 800/787-8336.* 127 rms, 2 story. S, D $69; each addl $10. Crib avail. TV; cable. Restaurant 6:30 am-9:30 pm. Bar. Ck-out noon, ck-in 2 pm. Meeting rms. Cr cds: A, C, D, DS, MC, V.

★★★ **RADISSON HOTEL BENTLEY.** *200 DeSoto St (71301), adj to Jackson St Bridge. 318/448-9600; fax 318/561-6134; res 800/333-3333.* 178 rms, 8 story. S $72; D $82; each addl $10; suites $100-$220; package plans; wkend rates. Crib free. TV; cable (premium), VCR avail. Pool; whirlpool, poolside serv. Restaurant (see BENTLEY ROOM). Bar 2:30 pm-2 am; entertainment, Mon-Sat. Ck-out noon. Meeting rms. Business center. Free valet parking; garage. Golf privileges. Exercise equipt. Some refrigerators. Opp river. Restored hotel, built 1908; on National Register of Historic Places. 18th-century period furnishings in all rms. Cr cds: A, C, D, DS, MC, V.

Conference Center

★★ **HOLIDAY INN.** *701 4th St (71301). 318/442-9000; fax 318/442-9007. Email generalmgr@alexccholiday inn.com.* 173 rms, 7 story, 10 suites. S $79; D $89; each addl $10; suites $175; under 19 free. Crib avail. Parking garage. Pool, whirlpool. TV; cable (premium), VCR avail. Complimentary coffee in rms, newspaper, toll-free calls. Restaurant 6:30 am-10 pm. Bar. Ck-out 11 am, ck-in 2 pm. Meet-

ing rms. Business center. Bellhops. Dry cleaning, coin lndry. Free airport transportation. Exercise privileges. Golf, 9 holes. Tennis, 4 courts. Video games. Cr cds: A, C, D, DS, JCB, MC, V.

Restaurants

★★★ **BENTLEY ROOM.** *100 DeSoto St. 318/448-9600.* Specializes in fresh Gulf fish, steak, Louisiana-style pastas. Hrs: 6:30 am-10 pm; Sun brunch 11 am-2 pm. Res accepted. Bar. Bkfst $3.95-$6; lunch $5.50-$12.95; dinner $10.95-$26.95. Sun brunch $7.50-$14.95. Child's menu. Entertainment: pianist Tues-Sat. Valet parking. Formal, elegant atmosphere. Cr cds: A, D, DS, MC, V.

★★ **CUCOS.** *2303 MacArthur Dr (71301), S on I-71. 318/442-8644.* Specializes in chimichangas, grilled fajitas. Hrs: 11 am-10 pm; Fri, Sat to 11:30 pm. Closed Thanksgiving, Dec 25. Bar. Lunch $4-$6; dinner $6.95-$18. Child's menu. Cr cds: A, D, DS, MC, V.

Bastrop

(A-4) *See also Monroe and West Monroe*

Founded 1846 **Pop** 13,916 **Elev** 126 ft
Area code 318 **Zip** 71220

Information Bastrop-Morehouse Chamber of Commerce, 512 E Jefferson, PO Box 1175, 71221; 318/281-3794

Bastrop is one of the few industrial cities in northern Louisiana. Wood pulp and wood products are the principal output. This is a center of the Monroe Gas Field, with its more than 1,700 producing wells. Bastrop is also a cattle and agricultural area with cotton, rice, and soybeans the staple crops. Seasonal hunting for dove, quail, duck, squirrel, and deer is popular.

What to See and Do

Bussey Brake Reservoir. On 2,200 acres. Fishing; boating (fee). Camping (fee). (Daily; closed Dec 25) 7 mi N on LA 599. Phone 318/281-4507. **FREE**

Chemin-a-Haut State Park. More than 500 wooded acres at the intersection of bayous Chemin-a-Haut and Bartholomew. A portion of the "high road to the South" was originally a Native American trail. Swimming, bathhouse; fishing; boating (rentals). Hiking. Picnicking. Tent and trailer sites (hookups, dump station). All-yr overnight cabins capacity of 4, max of 6. Standard fees. (Daily) 10 mi N on US 425. Phone 318/283-0812 or 888/677-2436. Per vehicle ¢

Snyder Memorial Museum. Museum covers 150 yrs of Morehouse Parish history; antique furniture, kitchen utensils, farm equipment, clothing and Native American artifacts. Gallery features changing art and photographic exhibits. (Daily) 1620 E Madison Ave. Phone 318/281-8760. **FREE**

Annual Event

North Louisiana Cotton Festival and Fair. Sep.

Motels/Motor Lodges

★ **BASTROP INN.** *1053 E Madison (71220), 1 mi E on US 165, LA 2. 318/281-3621; fax 318/283-1501; res 800/227-8767. Email bastrop.inn@bayou.com.* 109 rms, 1-2 story. S $30-$48; D $32-$52; suites $44-$65; studio rms $46-$63; under 12 free. Crib free. TV; cable (premium). Pool. Complimentary coffee in rms. Complimentary continental bkfst. Restaurant 5 am-11 pm. Private club 3 pm-midnight. Ck-out noon. Coin lndry. Meeting rms. Business center. Sundries. Free airport transportation. Golf privileges. Refrigerators. Cr cds: A, D, DS, MC, V.
➤ ➤ ➤

★ **COUNTRY INN.** *1815 E Madison (71220). 318/281-8100; fax 318/281-5895.* 30 rms, 2 story. S $33-$38; D $38-$43; each addl $5; under 12 free. Crib free. TV; cable (premium). Complimentary coffee in rms. Restaurant adj 11 am-midnight. Ck-out noon.

Business servs avail. Refrigerators. Cr cds: A, C, D, DS, MC, V.
➤ ➤ ➤

Baton Rouge

(E-5) *See also Jackson, St. Francisville*

Founded 1719 **Pop** 219,531 **Elev** 58 ft
Area code 225 **Web** www.bracvb.com
Information Baton Rouge Area Convention & Visitors Bureau, 730 North Blvd, PO Box 4149, 70821; 225/383-1825 or 800/LAROUGE

Named by its French founders for a red post that marked the boundary between the lands of two Native American tribes, Baton Rouge, the busy capital of Louisiana, is also a major Mississippi River port. Clinging to its gracious past, the area has restored antebellum mansions, gardens, tree-shaded campuses, splendid Cajun and Creole cuisine, and historic attractions that reflect the culture and struggle of living under ten flags over a period of three centuries. Institutions of higher education in Baton Rouge include Louisiana State University, Southern University, and Agricultural and Mechanical College.

What to See and Do

🟥 **Downtown Riverfront.** Along the banks of the Mississippi in downtown Baton Rouge is the

Louisiana Arts and Science Center Riverside. Originally a railroad station, this bldg houses fine art, sculpture; cultural and historical exhibits; Egyptian exhibition; Discovery Depot, hands-on galleries and science exhibits for children. Outside are a sculpture garden and restored 5-car train. (Tues-Sun; closed hols) 100 S River Rd. Phone 225/344-5272. ¢¢ Along riverfront is

Old State Capitol. Completed in 1849, Louisiana's old state capitol may be the country's most extravagant example of the Gothic Revival style popularized by the British Houses of Parliament. The richly-ornamented bldg was enlarged in 1881 and abandoned as the capitol in 1932. Self-guided tours. (Tues-

Sun; closed hols) Adj to the Old State Capitol are the river observation deck and the

USS *Kidd*. WWII *Fletcher*-class destroyer. Visitors may roam decks and explore interior compartments. Unique dock allows ship to be exhibited completely out of water when Mississippi River is in its low stages. Adjacent museum houses ship model collection, maritime artifacts, restored P-40 Flying Tiger fighter plane. Visitor center, observation tower overlooks river; Memorial Wall dedicated to service personnel. (Daily; closed Thanksgiving, Dec 25) 305 S River Rd. Phone 225/342-1942. ¢¢

Greater Baton Rouge Zoo. Walkways overlook 140 acres of enclosed habitats for more than 900 animals and birds. Sidewalk trams and miniature train tour zoo (fee). (Daily; closed Jan 1, Dec 25) 6 mi N off I-10, Exit 8 then right on Thomas Rd. Phone 225/775-3877. ¢¢

Heritage Museum and Village. Turn-of-the-century Victorian house with period rms, exhibits. Also rural village replicas incl church, school, store, and town hall. (Mon-Sat; closed hols) 1606 Main St, 11 mi N on LA 19 in Baker. Phone 225/774-1776. **FREE**

Houmas House. (1840) Large restored sugar plantation features Greek Revival mansion with early Louisiana-crafted furnishings, spiral staircase, belvedere, hexagonal *garconnieres* in gardens. Used in filming of *Hush, Hush, Sweet Charlotte*. (Daily; closed Jan 1, Thanksgiving, Dec 25) 22 mi SE on I-10 to Gonzales, then right 4 mi S on LA 44 to River Rd in Burnside. Phone 225/473-7841 or 225/522-2262. ¢¢¢

Laurens Henry Cohn, Sr. Memorial Plant Arboretum. This unusual 16-acre tract of rolling terrain contains more than 120 species of native and adaptable trees and shrubs; several major plant collections; herb/fragrance garden; tropical collection in greenhouse. Tours by appt. (Daily; closed Jan 1, Dec 25) 12056 Foster Rd. Phone 225/775-1006. **FREE**

Louisiana State University and Agricultural and Mechanical College. (1860) 26,607 students. Highland Rd, SW edge of city. Phone 225/388-3202. On campus are

Indian Mounds. These mounds are believed to have served socio-religious purposes and date from 3,300-2,500 B.C. At corner of Field House Dr & Dalrymple Drs. **FREE**

Memorial Tower. Built in 1923 as a monument to Louisianians who died in WWI. Houses LSU Museum of Art that features original 17th- through mid-19th-century rms from England and America. Self-guided tours. (Daily; closed hols) Phone 225/388-4003. **FREE**

Museum of Geoscience. Exhibits pertaining to archaeology, geology, and geography. (Mon-Fri) In Howe/Russell Geoscience Complex. Phone 225/388-3202. **FREE**

Museum of Natural Science. Features extensive collection of birds from around the world; wildlife scenes incl Louisiana marshlands and swamps, Arizona desert, alpine regions, and Honduran jungles. (Mon-Sat) Foster Hall. Phone 225/388-2855. **FREE**

Outdoor Greek Theater. Natural amphitheater seats 3,500.

Rural Life Museum. Museum complex is divided into plantation, folk architecture and exhibits bldg. Plantation incl blacksmith shop, open-kettle sugar mill, commissary, church. (Mar-Oct, daily; rest of yr, Mon-Fri) Under 12 only with adult. Entrance at jct I-10 & Essen Lane, at Burden Research Plantation. Phone 225/765-2437. ¢¢

Tiger Cage. Home of Mike VI, LSU Bengal Tiger mascot. (Daily feeding).

Union Art Gallery. (Daily) Union Bldg. Phone 225/388-5141. **FREE**

Magnolia Mound Plantation. Early 19th-century, Creole-style bldg restored to emphasize lifestyle of colonial Louisiana; period rms; detached kitchen with garden; wkly demonstrations of open-hearth Creole cooking. Costumed docents. Visitor center; gift shop. (Tues-Sun; closed hols) 2161 Nicholson Dr. Phone 225/343-4955. ¢¢

Nottoway Plantation. (ca 1860) One of the South's most imposing houses, Nottoway contains more than 50,000 sq ft, incl 64 rms, 200 windows, and 165 doors. In a near-perfect state of "originality," the house is famous for its all-white ballroom. Restaurant; overnight accommodations avail. Tours (daily; closed Dec 25). 18 mi S via LA 1. Phone 225/545-2730. ¢¢

Old Governor's Mansion. Mansion restored to period of 1930s, when it was built for Governor Huey P. Long. Original furnishings, memorabilia of former governors. (Sat and Sun; closed hols) 502 North Blvd. Phone 225/387-2464. ¢

Parlange Plantation. (1750) Owned by relatives of the builder, this working plantation is a National Historic Landmark. It incl a French Colonial home with a rare example of "bousillage" construction. Doorways and ceiling moldings are of hand-carved cypress; two octagonal, brick dovecotes flank the driveway. (Daily; closed hols) 19 mi W on US 190, then 8 mi N on LA 1. Phone 225/638-8410. ¢¢¢

The bayou

⭐ **Plantations and St. Francisville.** Driving tour (approx 100 mi). Drive N from Baton Rouge on US 61 approx 23 mi, then turn E on LA 965 to

Oakley. (1806) While living at Oakley and working as a tutor, John James Audubon painted 32 of his *Birds of America*. Spanish Colonial Oakley is part of **Audubon State Commemorative Area**, a 100-acre tract set aside as a wildlife sanctuary. House and park (daily; closed Jan 1, Thanksgiving, Dec 25). Phone 225/635-3739. ¢ Return to US 61, drive N approx 4 mi to St. Francisville (see). Just E of town on LA 10 & US 61 is

Rosedown. (1835) Magnificently restored antebellum mansion with many original furnishings; 28 acres of formal gardens incl century-old camellias and azaleas, fountains, gazebos, and an *allee* of century-old, moss-draped live oaks. (Daily; closed Dec 25) For schedule info phone 225/635-3332. ¢¢ Continue W to US 61, then drive N approx 2 mi to

The Myrtles. (1796) Known as one of "America's most haunted mansions," this carefully restored house of French influence boasts outstanding examples of wrought iron and ornamental plasterwork; period furniture. (Daily; closed hols) 7747 Hwy 61. Phone 225/635-6277. ¢¢ Drive N on US 61 approx 1 mi to LA 66, then W on Highland Rd to

Greenwood. (1830) Original Greek Revival plantation house survived the Civil War and post-war economic recession only to burn in 1960. A working plantation producing cattle, hay, and pecans, Greenwood has been rebuilt and furnished with period antiques. (Daily; closed hols) 6838 Highland Rd. Phone 225/655-4475. ¢¢ Return to US 61 and proceed N to

Cottage Plantation. (1795-1850). The oldest part of the main house was begun during Spanish control of area. Outbldgs incl smokehouse, school, slave cabins. Accommodations and breakfast avail. Tours (daily; closed hols). Phone 225/635-3674. ¢¢ Return to Baton Rouge via US 61.

Plaquemine Locks. The locks were built (1895-1909) to control the water level between the Bayou Plaquemine and the Mississippi. Larger locks built at Port Allen in 1961 caused the closing of these historic locks designed by George Goethals, who later designed the Panama Canal. When built, the

Plaquemine Locks had the highest freshwater lift (51 ft) in the world. Area features original lockhouse and locks; interpretive center with displays; observation tower with view of Mississippi. (Tue-Sun; closed hols) 15 mi S on LA 1, across from Old City Hall. Phone 225/383-1825. **FREE**

Port Hudson State Commemorative Area. This 650-acre area encompasses part of a Civil War battlefield, site of the longest siege in American military history. It features viewing towers (40 ft), Civil War guns, trenches, and hiking trails. Interpretive programs tell the story of how in 1863, 6,800 Confederates held off a Union force of 30,000 to 40,000 men. (Daily; closed Jan 1, Thanksgiving, Dec 25) 15 mi N via US 61. Phone 225/654-3775 or 888/677-3400. Per vehicle ¢

State Capitol. (1932) Built during Huey P. Long's administration, the 34-story, 450-ft *moderne* skyscraper capitol is decorated with 27 different varieties of marble. Memorial Hall floor is laid with polished lava from Mt Vesuvius; the ceiling is leafed in gold. Observation tower offers view of city; Loredo Taft sculpture groups on either side of entrance symbolize the pioneer and patriotic spirit. Tour of first floor on request at information desk; observation tower (daily; closed hols). 3rd St & Spanishtown Rd. Phone 225/342-7317 or 800/LAROUGE. **FREE** The Capitol complex incl the

Capitol Grounds. On the S side are formal gardens that focus on a sunken garden with a monumental statue erected over the grave of Huey P. Long, who was buried here in 1935 after being assassinated in the Capitol. To the E more gardens surround the

Old Spanish Arsenal museum. One-time military garrison that dates from the Spanish Colonial period. Beyond, across Capitol Lake, is the

Governor's Mansion. Greek Revival/Louisiana plantation in style, the mansion was built in 1963 to replace an earlier official residence. Tours (Mon-Fri, by appt). 1001 Capitol Access Rd. Phone 225/342-5855. **FREE** To the SW are the

Pentagon Barracks. Built in 1822 as part of a US military post, the columned, galleried bldgs later became the first permanent home of Louisiana State University. Also on grounds is the

Louisiana State Library. Collection of some 350,000 books, incl extensive section of Louisiana historical books, maps and photographs. (Mon-Fri; closed hols) 760 N 3rd St. Phone 225/342-4913. **FREE**

West Baton Rouge Museum. Exhibits incl large-scale 1904 model sugar mill; bedroom featuring American Empire furniture; sugar plantation slave cabin (ca 1850) and French Creole house (ca 1830); changing exhibits. (Tues-Sat, also Sun afternoons; closed hols) 2 mi W on I-10, at 845 N Jefferson in Port Allen. Phone 225/336-2422. **FREE**

Annual Events

Bonne Fete. Downtown area, particularly North Blvd. Juried shows and exhibits featuring up to 120 artisans and craftspeople and 1,200 performers. Performing arts, incl drama, music, dance, children's theater, and street entertainment. Special events incl RunForAll, gallery show, Children's Village, and art demonstrations. Traditional Louisiana and intl cuisine. Phone 225/383-1825. Late March.

Blues Festival. Downtown area, particularly North Blvd. Three-day event featuring blues, Cajun, zydeco, and gospel music. Traditional Louisiana cuisine. Phone 225/383-1825. Oct.

Christmas on the River. Dec.

Motels/Motor Lodges

★★ **BEST WESTERN.** *5668 Hilton Ave (70808). 225/924-6500; fax 225/924-3074; toll-free 800/528-1234.* 121 rms, 2 story, 55 suites, 55 kit. units. S, D, kit. units $99-$119; under 18 free. Crib free. TV; cable (premium). Pool; whirlpool. Complimentary full bkfst. Complimentary coffee in rms. Restaurant nearby. Ck-out noon. Meeting rms. Business center. In-rm modem link. Tennis. Exercise equipt. Refrigerators; micro-

waves avail. Some balconies. Cr cds:
A, C, D, DS, MC, V.

D ⊠ ⊠ ⊠ ⊠ ⊠ SC ⊠

★ **LA QUINTA INN.** *2333 S Acadian Thruway (70808), off I-10 Exit 157B. 225/924-9600; fax 225/924-2609; res 800/531-5900.* 142 rms, 2 story. S, D $71-$81; suites $125; under 18 free; higher rates special events. Crib free. Pet accepted, some restrictions. TV; cable (premium). Pool. Complimentary continental bkfst. Coffee in rms. Restaurant adj open 24 hrs. Ck-out noon. Coin lndry. Business servs avail. In-rm modem link. Valet serv. Airport transportation. Health club privileges. Cr cds: A, C, D, DS, MC, V.

D ⊠ ⊠ ⊠ ⊠ ⊠ ⊠

★★ **QUALITY SUITES.** *9138 Bluebonnet Centre Blvd (70809), off I-10 Bluebonnet Exit. 225/293-1199; fax 225/296-5014; res 800/555-1212. Email qsuites@eatel.net.* 120 rms, 3 story. S, D $89-$99; suites $150; under 18 free; wkend, monthly rates. Crib free. TV; cable (premium). Pool. Complimentary bkfst. Coffee in rms. Restaurant 6 am-9:30 pm; Sat, Sun 7 am-10:30 pm. Bar 5-10 pm. Ck-out 11 am. Coin lndry. Meeting rms. Business servs avail. In-rm modem link. Health club privileges. Refrigerators, microwaves. Balconies. Picnic tables, grills. Cr cds: A, C, D, DS, ER, JCB, MC, V.

D ⊠ ⊠ ⊠ ⊠ ⊠ ⊠

★★ **SHONEY'S INN.** *9919 Gwen Adelle Dr (70816), at Jct I-12, US 61; Airline Hwy Exit 2B. 225/925-8399; fax 225/927-1731; toll-free 800/222-2222.* 195 rms, 2 story. S, D $55; suites $70; under 18 free; wkend rates. Crib free. Pet accepted, some restrictions. TV; cable (premium). Pool. Complimentary continental bkfst. Restaurant 6 am-midnight; Fri, Sat to 3 am. Ck-out noon. Meeting rms. Business servs avail. In-rm modem link. Microwaves avail. Cr cds: A, C, D, DS, ER, MC, V.

D ⊠ ⊠ ⊠ ⊠ SC

Hotels

★★ **HAMPTON INN.** *4646 Constitution Ave (70808), off I-10 Exit 158. 225/926-9990; fax 225/923-3007; res 800/426-7866. www.hampton-inn.com.* 140 rms, 8 story, 1 suite. Mar-May, Sep: S $74; D $81; suites $140; under 18 free; lower rates rest of yr.,

fee. Parking lot. Pool. TV; cable (premium), VCR avail. Complimentary continental bkfst, coffee in rms, newspaper, toll-free calls. Restaurant. Ck-out noon, ck-in 9 pm. Meeting rms. Business center. Dry cleaning. Exercise privileges. Golf. Tennis. Cr cds: D, MC.

D ⊠ ⊠ ⊠ ⊠ ⊠ SC ⊠

★★★ **HILTON BATON ROUGE.** *5500 Hilton Ave (70808), I-10 Exit 158 at College Dr. 225/924-5000; fax 225/925-1330. Email batonrougehilton@ excelonline.com.* 300 rms, 21 story. S, D $109-$149; each addl $10; suites $150-$495. Crib free. TV; cable (premium), VCR avail. Heated pool. Restaurant 6:30 am-2 pm, 5-10 pm; Sun brunch 10 am-2 pm. Bar 2 pm-midnight. Ck-out noon. Convention facilities. Business center. In-rm modem link. Sundries. Free airport transportation. Exercise equipt; sauna. Luxury level. Cr cds: A, C, D, DS, ER, MC, V.

D ⊠ ⊠ ⊠ ⊠ ⊠ ⊠

★★ **HOLIDAY INN SOUTH.** *9940 Airline Hwy (70816), at jct I-12, US 61. 225/924-7021; fax 225/924-9816; res 800/465-4329; toll-free 888/814-9602.* 330 rms, 3 suites. S, D $89; under 18 free. Crib avail. Parking lot. Indoor/outdoor pools, children's pool, whirlpool. TV; cable (premium). Complimentary coffee in rms, newspaper, toll-free calls. Restaurant 6:30 am-10 pm. Bar. Ck-out noon, ck-in 3 pm. Conference center, meeting rms. Business servs avail. Dry cleaning, coin lndry. Exercise equipt. Golf, 18 holes. Cr cds: A, C, D, DS, JCB, MC, V.

D ⊠ ⊠ ⊠ ⊠ ⊠

★★★ **RADISSON HOTEL AND CONFERENCE CENTER.** *4728 Constitution Ave (70808). 225/925-2244; fax 225/930-0140. www.radissonbtr. com.* 294 rms, 5 story. S, D $94-$129; each addl $10; suites $125-$350; family rates; wkend rates. Crib free. TV; cable (premium). Pool; poolside serv. Complimentary coffee in rms. Restaurant 6 am-2 pm, 5-10 pm; wkends to 11 pm. Rm serv 24 hrs. Bar. Ck-out noon. Meeting rms. Business center. In-rm modem link. Concierge. Gift shop. Sundries. Free airport transportation. Tennis privileges. Health club privileges. Some balconies. Cr cds: A, D, DS, MC, V.

D ⊠ ⊠ ⊠ ⊠ SC ⊠

B&B/Small Inn

★★★ **NOTTOWAY PLANTATION RESTAURANT & INN.** *30970 Great River Rd (Hwy 405) (70788), 20 mi S, on LA 1.* 225/545-2730; *fax 225/545-8632. Email nottoway@att.net; www. nottoway.com.* 13 rms, 3 story, 3 suites. S $95-$250; D $125-$250; each addl $30; suites $200-$250. Crib free. TV. Pool. Complimentary full bkfst. Complimentary coffee in rms. Restaurant (see also RANDOLPH HALL). Ck-out 11 am, ck-in 2:30 pm. Business servs avail. Bellhops. Balconies. Antiques. Library/sitting rm. Antebellum mansion; Corinthian columns, hand-carved marble mantels, 65-ft long Grand White ballroom. Tours avail. On Mississippi River. Cr cds: A, DS, MC, V.

All Suite

★★ **CHASE SUITE HOTEL BY WOODFIN.** *5522 Corporate Blvd (70808), N of I-10 Exit 158.* 225/927-5630; *fax 225/926-2317; toll-free 800/ 966-3346. www.woodfinsuitehotels. com.* 80 kit. suites, 2 story. Suites $129-$169; wkend rates. Crib free. TV; cable (premium), VCR avail. Pool; whirlpool. Complimentary bkfst buffet. Restaurant nearby. Rm serv. Ck-out noon. Coin lndry. Meeting rms. Business servs avail. In-rm modem link. Valet serv. Tennis. Health club privileges. Fireplaces; microwaves avail. Grills. Cr cds: A, C, D, DS, JCB, MC, V.

★★★ **EMBASSY SUITES.** *4914 Constitution Ave (70808), off I-10 Exit 158.* 225/924-6566; *fax 225/923-3712; res 800/EMBASSY; toll-free 800/ 433-4600. Email gm@btrcs.embassy suites.com; www.embassybatonrouge. com.* 223 suites, 8 story. S $139; D $149; each addl $10; suites $139; under 17 free. Crib avail. Parking lot. Indoor pool, whirlpool. TV; cable (premium). Complimentary full bkfst, coffee in rms, newspaper. Restaurant 11 am-11 pm. Bar. Ck-out noon, ck-in 3 pm. Meeting rms. Business center. Bellhops. Dry cleaning, coin lndry. Gift shop. Free airport transportation. Exercise equipt,

sauna, steam rm. Golf. Tennis. Video games. Cr cds: A, C, D, DS, MC, V.

Restaurants

★ **CABIN.** *General Delivery MSC 85 (70738), I-10 S to LA 44 S, Jct LA 44 and 22, Exit 182.* 225/473-3007. Specializes in gumbo, red beans & rice, buttermilk pie. Hrs: 11 am-9 pm; Mon to 3 pm; Fri, Sat to 10 pm; Sun to 6 pm. Closed Jan 1, Thanksgiving, Dec 25. Res accepted. Bar. Lunch, dinner $4.95-$15.95. Child's menu. Parking. Former Monroe Plantation slave cabins (ca 1840); old farm tools, household antiques. Cr cds: A, DS, MC, V.

★★★ **CHALET BRANDT.** *7655 Old Hammond Hwy (70809).* 225/927-6040. Specializes in fresh seafood, veal, duck. Own pastries. Hrs: 11:30 am-2 pm, 5:30-10 pm; Mon, Tues to 2 pm. Closed Sun; hols; wk of July 4. Res accepted. Lunch $9.95-$16.95; dinner $10.95-$28.95. Child's menu. Parking. Jacket. Chef-owned. Cr cds: A, D, MC, V.

★★ **DAJONEL'S.** *7327 Jefferson Hwy (70806).* 225/924-7537. *www.sjbcorp. com.* Specializes in steak, veal, seafood. Hrs: 11:30 am-2:30 pm, 5-10 pm; Sun brunch 11 am-2 pm. Closed Jan 1, Dec 25. Bar. Lunch $7.95-$16.95; dinner $13.95-$24.95. Sun brunch $18.95. Parking. European country inn atmosphere. Cr cds: A, D, DS, MC, V.

★★ **DON'S SEAFOOD & STEAK HOUSE.** *6823 Airline Hwy (70805).* 225/357-0601. *www.sjbcorp.com.* Specializes in seafood, steak. Oyster bar. Hrs: 11 am-10 pm; Fri, Sat to 11 pm. Closed Thanksgiving, Dec 25. Res accepted. Bar. Lunch, dinner $6.95-$16.99. Child's menu. Cr cds: A, D, DS, MC, V.

★★★ **JUBAN'S.** *3739 Perkins Rd (70808), in Shopping Center.* 225/346-8422. *Email jubanrest@aol.com; www. lagumbo.com.* Specializes in stuffed soft-shell crab, crawfish-stuffed shrimp, veal. Hrs: 11:30 am-2 pm, 5:30-10 pm; Sat from 5:30 pm. Closed

Sun; hols. Res accepted. Bar. Wine list. Lunch $6.50-$19; dinner $13-$27. Child's menu. Cr cds: A, C, D, DS, MC, V.

D 🍴

★★★★ **LAFITTE'S LANDING.** *404 Claiborne Ave (70346), 30 mi S on I-10, Exit 182 to Donaldsonville, under Sunshine Bridge. 225/473-1232. www. jfolse.com.* Chef John Folse, who touts this restaurant's Plantation Corridor location as the Napa Valley of New Orleans, has helped revitalize downtown after moving from his original Viala Plantation location to Bittersweet Plantation. The menu, attracting diners since 1978, is still true Louisiana cuisine with a strong emphasis on local ingredients and several historical preparations. Two upstairs suites provide bed and breakfast. Specializes in soft-shell crawfish, rack of lamb, breast of mallard. Hrs: 6-10 pm; Sun 11 am-3 pm. Closed Mon; Jan 1, July 4, Dec 25. Res required. Bar. Wine list. Lunch $16-$28; dinner $19-$28. Valet parking. Cr cds: A, D, DS, MC, V.

D 🍴

★ **MIKE ANDERSON'S.** *1031 W Lee Dr (70820), 4 mi S of I-10 Exit 158. 225/766-7823.www.mikeandersonbr. com.* Specializes in seafood. Oyster bar. Hrs: 11 am-2 pm, 5-9:30 pm; Sun 11 am-9 pm. Closed hols. Res accepted Mon-Fri (lunch only). Bar. Lunch $6.25-$7.95; dinner $8.95-$17.95. Child's menu. Parking. Cr cds: A, DS, MC, V.

D SC 🍴

★★ **PLACE.** *5255 Florida Blvd (70806), 3 mi W of Airline Hwy. 225/ 924-5069. Email klmplace@aol.com.* Specializes in steak, fresh seafood, veal. Hrs: 11 am-2:30 pm, 5-10 pm; Sun, Mon to 2:30 pm. Closed Dec 25. Res accepted. Bar. Lunch $8.95-$16; dinner $14.95-$24.95. Parking. Patio with fountain. Cr cds: A, D, DS, MC, V.

D 🍴

★★ **RANDOLPH HALL.** *30970 Hwy 405. 225/545-2730. Email nottoway@ worldnet.att.net; www.nottoway.com.* Specializes in gumbo, jambalaya. Hrs: 11 am-3 pm, 6-9 pm. Closed Dec 25. Res accepted. Bar. Lunch a la carte entrees: $8.95-$16.95; dinner a la carte entrees: $15-$22. Child's menu.

Entertainment: pianist wkends. Parking. Plantation atmosphere. Cr cds: A, DS, MC, V.

D 🍴

★★★ **RUTH'S CHRIS STEAK HOUSE.** *4836 Constitution (70808). 225/925-0163.* Steak menu. Specializes in steak, live Maine lobster. Hrs: 11:30 am-11:30 pm; Sat 4 pm-midnight. Closed Sun; hols. Bar. Lunch a la carte entrees: $10.95-$29.95; dinner a la carte entrees: $10.95-$29.95. Parking. Cr cds: A, D, DS, MC, V.

D 🍴

Bossier City

(B-2) *See also Shreveport*

Pop 52,721 **Elev** 174 ft **Area code** 318 **Web** www.shreveport-bossier.org

Information Shreveport-Bossier Convention & Tourist Bureau, 629 Spring St, PO Box 1761, Shreveport 71166; 318/222-9391 or 800/551-8682

Barksdale Air Force Base, home of the 8th Air Force and the 2nd Bombardment Wing, is located near Bossier City.

What to See and Do

Eighth Air Force Museum. Aircraft displayed incl B-52D Stratofortress, P-51 Mustang, and F-84F Thunderstreak. Desert Storm memorabilia. Gift shop. (Daily) Barksdale Air Force Base, N gate. Phone 318/456-3067. **FREE**

Isle of Capri Casino. 77 Isle of Capri Blvd. Phone 318/678-7777 or 800/THE-ISLE.

Touchstone Wildlife & Art Museum. Various dioramas depict animals and birds in their natural habitats. (Tues-Sun; closed hols) 5 mi E on US 80. Phone 318/949-2323. ¢

Seasonal Event

Thoroughbred racing. Louisiana Downs. 3 mi E on US 80 at I-220. Wed-Sun; also Memorial Day, July 4, Labor Day. Phone 800/551-RACE. Late June-mid-Nov.

Motels/Motor Lodges

★★ **HOLIDAY INN.** *2015 Old Minden Rd (71111), at I-20, Old Minden Rd Exit 21.* 318/742-9700; fax 318/747-4641; toll-free 800/465-4329. 212 rms, 2 story. S $71-$78, D $81-$88; each addl $10; suites $150-$160; under 18 free. Crib free. TV; cable (premium). Pool; whirlpool, steam rm, poolside serv. Restaurant 6:30 am-2 pm, 5-10 pm; Sat 7-11:30 am, 5-10 pm; Sun 7-11:30 am. Bar 4 pm-2 am; entertainment Mon-Sat. Ck-out noon. Meeting rms. Business servs avail. Bellhops. Sundries. Free airport, bus depot transportation. Lawn games. Cr cds: A, C, D, DS, MC, V.

⬚ ⬚ ⬚ ⬚ SC

★ **LA QUINTA INN.** *309 Preston Blvd (71111), at I-20 Old Minden Rd Exit.* 318/747-4400; fax 318/747-1516; toll-free 800/NUROOMS. 130 rms, 2 story. Apr-Nov: S $71; D $81; suites $99; under 18 free; lower rates rest of yr. Crib free. TV; cable (premium). Pool. Complimentary continental bkfst. Restaurant adj open 24 hrs. Ck-out noon. Business servs avail. In-rm modem link. Airport transportation. Cr cds: A, C, D, DS, MC, V.

⬚ ⬚ ⬚ ⬚ SC

All Suite

★★ **RESIDENCE INN BY MAR-RIOTT.** *1001 Gould Dr (71111), at I-20 Old Minden Rd Exit.* 318/747-6220; fax 318/747-3424; toll-free 800/331-3131. Email ri.shvbb.gm@marriott.com; www.residenceinn.com/shvbb. 2 story, 72 suites. S $135; D $165; suites $165. Crib avail. Pet accepted, fee. Parking lot. Pool, whirlpool. TV; cable (premium), VCR avail. Complimentary continental bkfst, coffee in rms, newspaper, toll-free calls. Ck-out noon, ck-in 3 pm. Meeting rm. Business center. Dry cleaning, coin lndry. Exercise privileges. Golf. Tennis. Picnic facilities. Cr cds: A, C, D, DS, JCB, MC, V.

⬚ ⬚ ⬚ ⬚ ⬚ ⬚ ⬚ ⬚ SC ⬚

Casino

★ **ISLE OF CAPRI CASINO & HOTEL.** *711 Isle of Capri Blvd (71111), on I-20 at Airline Dr Exit.* 318/678-7777; fax 318/425-4617; res 800/THEISLE. Email ala_zikra@ islecorp.com; www.isleofcapricasino. com. 310 rms, 12 story, 20 suites. Apr-Sep: S, D $125; suites $250; lower rates rest of yr. Valet parking avail. Pool, whirlpool. TV; cable (premium). Complimentary coffee in rms, newspaper, toll-free calls. Restaurant 5-11 pm. 24-hr rm serv. Bar. Ck-out noon, ck-in 3 pm. Conference center, meeting rms. Bellhops. Concierge. Dry cleaning. Gift shop. Exercise equipt. Golf. Supervised children's activities. Video games. Cr cds: A, D, DS, MC, V.

⬚ ⬚ ⬚ ⬚ ⬚ ⬚

Restaurant

★★ **RALPH & KACOO'S.** *1700 Old Minden Rd (71111), located in Bossier Cross Roads Shopping Center.* 318/747-6660. Email rkbosr@lsouth.net. Specializes in fresh seafood, broiled fish. Own desserts. Hrs: 11 am-10 pm; Fri, Sat to 10:30 pm; Sun 3-9 pm; Sun brunch 11 am-3 pm. Closed wkdays. Bar. Lunch, dinner $5.95-$18.95. Sun brunch $15.95. Entertainment: jazz band Sun brunch. Cr cds: A, C, D, DS, MC, V.

⬚ ⬚

Covington

(E-6) *See also Hammond, Kenner, Metairie, New Orleans, Slidell*

Founded 1813 **Pop** 7,691 **Elev** 25 ft
Area code 504 **Zip** 70433
Web www.neworleansnorthshore. com

Information St. Tammany Parish Tourist & Convention Commission, 68099 LA 59, Mandeville 70471; 504/892-0520 or 800/634-9443

Covington is situated in a wooded area north of Lake Pontchartrain, which is crossed via the 24-mile Lake Pontchartrain Causeway from New Orleans. With mild winters and semitropical summers, Covington is a town of pecan, pine, and oak woods, vacation houses, and recreational opportunities. A number of thoroughbred horse farms are also in the area.

What to See and Do

Fontainebleau State Park. A live oak *allee* forms the entrance to this 2,700-acre park on the N shore of Lake Pontchartrain; on grounds are the ruins of a plantation brickyard and sugar mill. Swimming, fishing, boating, picnicking, tent and trailer sites (hookups, dump station). Standard fees. (Daily) 12 mi SE on US 190. Phone 504/624-4443 or 888/677-3668. Per vehicle ¢

St. Tammany Art Association. Gallery. (Tues-Sat, also Sun afternoons) 129 N New Hampshire St. Phone 504/892-8650.

Tammany Trace. Follows old Illinois Central Railroad corridor for 31 mi, ending in Slidell, LA. ten-ft-wide, paved hiking/biking trail; unpaved equestrian trail. (Daily; closed Dec 25) LA 59, Exit Koop Dr. Phone 800/43-TRACE. **FREE**

Motel/Motor Lodge

★★ **HOLIDAY INN.** *501 N Hwy 190 (70433), at Jct I-12.* 504/893-3580; fax 504/893-4807; toll-free 800/465-4329. 156 rms, 2 story. S $79-$89; D $89-$99; each addl $6; under 18 free. Crib free. TV; cable (premium), VCR avail in suites. Indoor/outdoor pool; whirlpool. Coffee in rms. Restaurant 6:30 am-2 pm, 5:30-10 pm; Sun to 9 pm. Bar from 5:30 pm. Ck-out noon. Coin lndry. Meeting rms. Business servs avail. Cr cds: A, C, D, DS, ER, JCB, MC, V.
[D] 🏊 ➲ 🖐 SC

Restaurants

★ **ABITA BREW PUB.** *72011 Holly St (70420), N on LA 21 to LA 435E.* 504/892-5837. www.abita.com. Hrs: 11 am-10 pm. Closed hols. Bar. Lunch, dinner $5.75-$17. Microbrewery; brewery tours Sat, Sun. Cr cds: A, D, DS, MC, V.
[D] ➲

★★★★ **ARTESIA.** *21516 Hwy 36 (70420).* 504/892-1662. Often referred to as the country sibling of owner Vicky Bayley's Mike's on the Avenue in New Orleans, this quaint restaurant is housed in a two-story,

1885 Creole mansion listed on the National Register of Historic Places. The young chef, John Besh, creates a frequently changing, country-French menu focusing on vibrant, local ingredients with dishes such as spicy crab soup with garlic croutons. Specializes in Alain Assaud soup de poissons (saffron-based crab soup), terrine of smoked fois gras over tapenade and fig compound, slow-roasted duckling. Hrs: 11:30 am-2 pm, 5:30-10 pm; Sat 5:30-10 pm; Sun brunch 11 am-3 pm. Closed Mon, Tues. Res accepted. Wine, beer. Lunch à la carte entrées: $6-$12; dinner à la carte entrées: $16-$25. Sun brunch $19.95. Cr cds: D, MC, V.
[D]

★★★ **DAKOTA.** *629 N Hwy 190 (70433).* 504/892-3712. Email dakota@fastband.com. Specializes in steak, lamb, fresh seafood. Hrs: 11 am-2:30 pm, 5-10 pm; Fri to 11 pm; Sat 5-11 pm. Closed Sun; hols. Res accepted. Bar. Lunch $9-$11.75; dinner $15-$24. Child's menu. Contemporary southern Louisiana cuisine. Local artwork on display. Cr cds: A, D, MC, V.
[D]

★★ **FUSION BISTRO.** *321 N Columbia St (70433).* 504/875-7620. Mediterranean menu. Specializes in pepper-seared filet mignon. Hrs: 11:30 am-2:30 pm, 5:30-9 pm; Fri, Sat to 10 pm. Closed Sun; Thanksgiving, Dec 25. Res accepted. Bar. Lunch $6.95-$9.25; dinner $8.95-$21. Child's menu. Parking. Contemporary decor; casual atmosphere. Cr cds: A, D, DS, MC, V.
[D]

★★★★ **LA PROVENCE.** *US 190E (70445), 7 mi from Causeway on US 190E.* 504/626-7662. www.laprovence.com. Don't think for a minute that the 45-minute drive from New Orleans isn't worth it to dine at this charming, Lake Pontchartrain restaurant. Chef Chris Kerageorgiou's fabulous sauces alone attract diners from miles around and his classic, French menu features splendid, Provencal preparations of game, veal, seafood and duck. The wooded, French-country-inn atmosphere only adds to the romance. Own baking. Hrs: 4-11 pm; Sun 1-9 pm. Closed Mon, Tues; Dec 25, July 4. Res accepted.

Wine list. Dinner $18-$32. Prix fixe: $24.95-$29.95. Cr cds: A, D, MC, V.

★ ★ ★ **TREY YUEN.** *600 N Causeway (70448), ½ mi S of N end of Causeway. 504/626-4476.* Specializes in crawfish in lobster sauce, Szechwan alligator, soft-shell crab. Hrs: 11:30 am-2 pm, 5-10 pm; Mon, Tues from 5 pm; Fri to 11 pm; Sat 5-11 pm. Closed Sun; hols; Mardi Gras. Bar. Lunch $4.95-$7.50; dinner $9.50-$20. Overlooks rock garden. Family-owned. Cr cds: A, D, DS, MC, V.

Franklin

(F-4) *See also Morgan City, New Iberia*

Founded 1808 **Pop** 9,004 **Elev** 15 ft
Area code 337 **Zip** 70538
Information Tourism Department, City of Franklin, 300 Iberia St, PO Box 567; 337/828-2555, 337/828-6326, or 800/962-6889

Said to be named by founder Guinea Lewis for Benjamin Franklin, this town on the Bayou Teche is a center of salt mining, sugar refining, sugarcane growing, and the manufacturing of carbon black, which is used in the production of rubber and ink.

What to See and Do

Chitimacha Cultural Center. Museum exhibits, crafts, and 10-min video focus on history and culture of Chitimacha tribe of Louisiana. Walking tours. A unit of Jean Lafitte National Historical Park (see NEW ORLEANS). (Daily; closed Jan 1, Dec 25) Approx 15 mi N on LA 87 in Charenton. Phone 504/589-3882 or 337/923-4830. **FREE**

Cypremort Point State Park. This 185-acre site offers access to the Gulf of Mexico. Man-made beach in the heart of a natural marsh affords fresh and saltwater fishing and other seashore recreation opportunities. (Daily) Standard fees. 5 mi N via US 90, 16 mi W via LA 83, then 7 mi

SW on LA 319. Phone 337/867-4510. Per vehicle ¢

Grevemberg House. (ca 1850) Greek Revival house with fine collection of antique furnishings dating from the 1850s; children's toys; paintings and Civil War relics. (Daily; closed hols) St. Mary Parish Museum. City Park on Sterling Rd. Phone 337/828-2092. ¢¢

Oaklawn Manor Plantation. (1837) Restored in 1927, the massive Greek Revival house has walls 20 inches thick, is furnished with European antiques, and is surrounded by one of the largest groves of live oaks in the US. Home of Louisiana Governor Mike Foster. (Daily; closed hols) 5 mi NW off US 90, LA 182. Phone 337/828-0434. ¢¢¢

Motel/Motor Lodge

★ ★ **BEST WESTERN FOREST MOTOR.** *1909 Main St (70538). 337/828-1810; fax 337/828-1810; res 800/528-1234; toll-free 800/828-1812.* 75 rms, 2 story, 13 suites. S $74; D $85; each addl $5; children $5; under 12 free. Pool. TV; cable (premium), VCR avail. Restaurant 5:30 am-9:30 pm. Bar. Ck-out noon, ck-in 4 pm. Meeting rms. Business servs avail. Dry cleaning. Golf, 9 holes. Cr cds: A, C, D, DS, MC, V.

Hammond

(E-6) *See also Baton Rouge, Covington, Kenner*

Pop 15,871 **Elev** 47 ft **Area code** 504

Motel/Motor Lodge

★ ★ **QUALITY INN.** *14175 US 190 W (70401). 504/542-8555; fax 504/542-8555.* 62 rms, 2 story. S $43; D $48; each addl $5; under 12 free; higher rates special events. Pet accepted, some restrictions. TV; cable (premium). Pool. Restaurant 6 am-10 pm. Bar. Ck-out 11 am. Meeting rm. Valet serv. Cr cds: A, DS, MC, V.

Restaurant

★★★ **TREY YUEN.** *2100 N Morrison Blvd (70401). 504/345-6789. www. treyyuen.com.* Specializes in alligator, soft-shelled crabs & crawfish. Hrs: 11 am-2 pm, 5-10 pm; Fri to 11 pm; Sat 5-11 pm; Sun 11:30 am-9:30 pm. Closed hols. Bar. Lunch a la carte entrees: $4.75-$7.50; dinner a la carte entrees: $4.50-$15. Complete meals: $11.50 & $15. Exotic dining rms overlook rock garden with pagoda and bridge over pool stocked with Chinese carp. Cr cds: A, D, DS, MC, V.

Houma

(F-6) See also Morgan City, Thibodaux

Founded 1832 **Pop** 30,495 **Elev** 0-12 ft **Area code** 504

Information Houma-Terrebonne Tourist Commission, 1702 S St, Charles St, PO Box 2792, 70361; 504/868-2732 or 800/688-2732

Situated on Bayou Terrebonne and the Intracoastal Waterway, Houma has for many years been a center for fishing, shrimping, and fur trapping. Known as the "Venice of America," Houma is famous for Cajun food and hospitality.

What to See and Do

Annie Miller's Swamp & Marsh Tours. Boat trips (2-3 hr) through winding waterways in swamps and wild marshlands. See birds, alligators, wild game, tropical plants, and flowers. (Mar-Oct, 2 departures daily) Phone 504/879-3934. ¢¢¢¢

Fishing. Excellent fresh and saltwater angling in nearby bays and bayous. Fishing best May-Nov. Charter boats avail.

Southdown Plantation House/Terrebonne Museum. (1893) The first floor, Greek Revival in style, was built in 1859; the second floor, late Victorian/Queen Anne in style, was added in 1893; 21-rm house incl stained glass, Boehm and Doughty porcelain bird collection, Terreboone

Parish history rm, re-creation of Allen Ellender's senate office, antique furniture, Mardi Gras costumes. (Tues-Sat; closed hols) LA 311 & St. Charles St. Phone 504/851-0154. ¢¢

Annual Events

Grand Bois Inter Tribal. Mar and Sep.

Blessing of the Shrimp Fleet. Apr.

Jackson

(D-5) See also Baton Rouge, St. Francisville

Pop 3,891 **Elev** 180 ft **Area code** 225 **Zip** 70748 **Web** www.feliciana.com

Information Feliciana Chamber of Commerce, PO Box 667; 504/634-7155

What to See and Do

Jackson Historic District. District incl 123 structures covering approximately 65 percent of town; structures range from storefronts and warehouses to cottages and mansions; architectural styles range from Renaissance and Greek Revival to Queen Anne and California stick-style bungalow.

Milbank Historic House. (1836) Greek Revival townhouse, originally built as a banking house for the Clinton-Port Hudson Railroad, features 1st- and 2nd-floor galleries supported by twelve 30-ft columns. Overnight stays avail. Tours (daily; closed hols). 3045 Bank St. Phone 225/634-5901. ¢¢

B&Bs/Small Inns

★★ **MILBANK HISTORIC HOUSE.** *3053 Bank St (70748). 225/634-5901; fax 225/634-5901.* 4 units, 3 share bath, 2 story. No rm phones. S, D $75; suite $100-$125. TV in some rms. Complimentary full bkfst, coffee. Restaurant nearby. Ck-out 11 am, ck-in 2 pm. Golf privileges. Balconies. Antiques. Library/sitting rm. Former bank and newspaper office (1836). Cr cds: DS, MC, V.

★★ **VILLAGE INN.** *Hwy 68. (70748). 225/654-6868.* 18 units, 2 story, 7 suites. No rm phones. S, D, suites $55-$150. Closed Dec 24-26; 1 wk in Jan. Pool. Complimentary full bkfst. Dining rm 8-9:30 am, 11:30 am-3 pm; Thurs-Sat 5:30-9 pm. Ck-out noon, ck-in 3 pm. Lawn games. Antiques. Library/sitting rm; fireplace in some rms. Antebellum house (1830); veranda. Cr cds: MC, V.

Jennings

(E-3) *See also Lake Charles*

Founded 1888 **Pop** 11,305 **Elev** 22 ft
Area code 337 **Zip** 70546
Web www.fp1.centuryinter.net/jenningschamber
Information Greater Jennings Chamber of Commerce, 414 N Cary Ave, PO Box 1209; 337/824-0933

The Southern Pacific Railroad urged Midwesterners to settle in Jennings soon after its line was built in 1880. The town was chartered in 1884. Louisiana's first oil well, five miles northeast, came in on September 21, 1901, bringing pioneer oil developers to the area. Today Jennings remains a center of beef, soybean, and rice production, while oil continues to contribute to the local economy.

What to See and Do

W.H. Tupper General Merchandise Museum. Over 10,000 items on display recreating the atmosphere of early 20th-century life in rural Louisiana. Toy collection; period clothing; drugs and toiletries; Native Amercan basketry. Gift shop. (Mon-Sat; closed hols) 311 N Main St. Phone 337/821-5532 or 800/264-5521. ¢¢

Zigler Museum. Museum contains galleries of wildlife and natural history, European, and American art; antique handguns. (Mon-Sat; closed hols) 411 Clara St. Phone 337/824-0114. ¢

Motel/Motor Lodge

★★ **HOLIDAY INN OF JENNINGS.** *603 Holiday Dr (70546), I-10 and LA 26. 337/824-5280; fax 337/824-7941; res 800/465-4329.* 131 rms, 2 story. S, D $54; each addl $5. Crib free. TV. Pool. Restaurant 6 am-2 pm, 5-8 pm. Rm serv. Bar 4 pm-2 am; Sat to midnight; closed Sun. Ck-out noon. Meeting rms. Business servs avail. Bellhops. Cr cds: A, D, DS, MC, V.

Restaurant

★ **GOLDEN DRAGON.** *3014 N Frontage Rd (70546), I-10 and LA 26. 337/824-4280. Email dragonshot@usa.net.* Specializes in Cantonese, Cajun cuisine. Hrs: 10 am-9:30 pm; Fri to 10 pm; Sat 5-10 pm. Closed Sun; Dec 25. Lunch buffet: $2.99-$5.99; dinner $2.99-$22.99. Child's menu. Aquarium. Cr cds: A, D, DS, MC, V.

Kenner

See also Metairie, New Orleans

Pop 72,033 **Elev** 5 ft **Area code** 504

Motel/Motor Lodge

★ **LA QUINTA INN.** *2610 Williams Blvd (70062), near New Orleans Intl Airport. 504/466-1401; fax 504/466-0319; toll-free 800/687-6667.* 194 rms, 5 story. S, D $85-$95; under 18 free. Crib free. TV. Pool. Complimentary continental bkfst. Restaurant nearby. Ck-out noon. Coin lndry. Meeting rms. Business servs avail. In-rm modem link. Valet serv. Free airport transportation. Cr cds: A, D, DS, MC, V.

Hotels

★★★ **HILTON NEW ORLEANS AIRPORT.** *901 Airline Dr (70062), near New Orleans Intl Airport. 504/469-5000; fax 504/466-5473; res 800/HILTONS; toll-free 800/872-5914.*

317 units, 6 story. S $115-$177; D $127-$189; each addl $12; suites $325-$450; family rates; wkend rates. Crib free. TV; cable (premium), VCR avail. Pool; whirlpool, poolside serv. Coffee in rms. Restaurant 6 am-10:30 pm. Bar 11-1 am. Ck-out 1 pm. Convention facilities. Business center. In-rm modem link. Gift shop. Free airport transportation. Lighted tennis. Golf privileges, putting green. Exercise equipt. Minibars. Cr cds: A, C, D, DS, ER, JCB, MC, V.

★★ HOLIDAY INN. *2929 Williams Blvd (70062), near New Orleans Intl Airport. 504/467-5611; fax 504/469-4915; toll-free 800/887-7371.* 302 rms, 5 story, 1 suite. Feb-May, July, Oct-Nov: S, D $139; lower rates rest of yr. Crib avail. Parking lot. Indoor pool, whirlpool. TV; cable (premium), VCR avail. Complimentary coffee in rms, newspaper, toll-free calls. Restaurant 6 am-midnight. Bar. Ck-out noon, ck-in 3 pm. Conference center, meeting rms. Business center. Bellhops. Concierge. Dry cleaning, coin lndry. Gift shop. Free airport transportation. Exercise equipt. Golf. Tennis. Picnic facilities. Video games. Cr cds: A, C, D, DS, JCB, MC, V.

★★★ RADISSON NEW ORLEANS AIRPORT. *2150 Veterans Memorial Blvd (70062), near New Orleans Intl Airport. 504/467-3111; fax 504/461-0572; res 800/333-3333. Email lanewair@usa.net; www.radisson.com/neworleansla_airport.* 241 rms, 8 story, 3 suites. Mar-Apr, Oct-Nov: S, D $129; suites $275; under 18 free; lower rates rest of yr. Parking lot. Pool. TV; cable (premium), VCR avail. Complimentary coffee in rms, newspaper. Restaurant 6 am-10 pm. Bar. Meeting rms. Business servs avail. Bellhops. Dry cleaning. Gift shop. Free airport transportation. Exercise privileges. Golf, 18 holes. Tennis, 15 courts. Cr cds: A, C, D, DS, ER, JCB, MC, V.

Lafayette

(E-4) *See also New Iberia, Opelousas, St. Martinville*

Founded 1823 **Pop** 94,440 **Elev** 41 ft
Area code 337
Information Lafayette Convention & Visitors Commission, 1400 NW Evangeline Thrwy, PO Box 52066, 70505; 800/346-1958

Acadians from Nova Scotia came to the Lafayette area to escape British persecution. A significant percentage of today's residents continues to speak French or a patois and to maintain a strong feeling of kinship with Nova Scotia and France. These descendants of the French Acadians form the nucleus of the Louisiana Cajuns, who have contributed greatly to the state's rich culture.

Today Lafayette is a commercial city built around retail trade, light industry, agriculture, and oil. Area farmers produce soybeans, rice, and sugarcane as well as beef and dairy products. Many oil companies drilling for and pumping offshore oil have regional offices in the area, with headquarters in Lafayette's Heymann Oil Center.

Despite its industrial image Lafayette has retained its "small-town" charm. Live oaks and azaleas abound around the town, as do clumps of native iris, the city's official flower. Tours of the navigable Bayou Vermilion are now available to visitors.

What to See and Do

Acadian Village: A Museum of Acadian Heritage and Culture. This restored 19th-century Acadian village features fine examples of unique Acadian architecture with houses, a general store, and a chapel. Crafts displays and sales. (Daily; closed Mardi Gras, hols) 5 mi S via US 167, Johnston St S, Ridge Rd W. Phone 337/981-2364 or 800/962-9133. ¢¢

Chretien Point Plantation. (1831) Restored Greek Revival mansion, site of a Civil War battle; stairway copied for Tara in the 1939 movie *Gone with* *the Wind.* (Daily; closed hols) 5 mi W on I-10 to LA 93, 11 mi N to LA 356, W 1 blk to Parish Rd 2-151, then 1 mi N. Phone 337/662-5876 or 337/233-7050. ¢¢¢

Lafayette Museum. (1800-49) Once residence of Alexandre Mouton, first Democratic governor of the state, the house is now a museum with antique furnishings, Civil War relics, and carnival costumes. (Tues-Sun; closed Mardi Gras, hols) 1122 Lafayette St. Phone 337/234-2208. ¢¢

Lafayette Natural History Museum, Planetarium, and Nature Station. Planetarium programs; environmental trails and nature station; changing exhibits. (Daily; closed Mardi Gras, hols) 637 Girard Park Dr. Phone 337/291-5544. Museum **FREE**

University Art Museum. There are 2 locations: the permanent collection is at 101 Girard Park Dr (Mon-Fri; closed hols); changing exhibits are staged at Fletcher Hall, East Lewis, and Girard Park Circle (Mon-Fri, also Sun afternoons; closed hols). Phone 337/482-5326. **FREE**

University of Southwestern Louisiana. (1900) 16,200 students. The tree-shaded campus serves as an arboretum with many Southern plant species. Cypress Lake, a minia-

Cajun cooking

ture Louisiana cypress swamp, has fish, alligators, and native irises. E University Ave. Phone 337/482-1000.

Annual Events

Azalea Trail. Mid-Mar.

Festival International de Louisiane. International and Louisiana performing and visual arts and cuisine. Phone 337/232-8086. Mid-Apr.

Festivals Acadiens. Cajun music and food festival. Third wkend Sep.

Seasonal Event

Thoroughbred racing. Evangeline Downs. 3 mi N on US 167. Parimutuel betting. Proper attire required in clubhouse. Phone 337/896-7223. Early Apr-Labor Day.

Motels/Motor Lodges

★★ **BEST WESTERN HOTEL ACADIANA.** *1801 W Pinhook Rd (70508), 5 mi SW of I-10 Exit 103A, via Evangeline Thrwy. 337/233-8120; fax 337/234-9667; toll-free 800/826-8386. Email bwhotelacadiana@yahoo.com; www.bestwestern.com/hotelacadiana.* 290 rms, 6 story. S, D $78; each addl $10; suites $210-$275; under 18 free. TV; cable (premium), VCR avail. Pool. Coffee in rms. Restaurant 6 am-10 pm. Bars 5 pm-2 am; entertainment Tues-Sat. Ck-out noon. Coin lndry. Convention facilities. Business center. In-rm modem link. Free airport transportation. Refrigerators, wet bars. Luxury level. Cr cds: A, DS, MC, V.

⊡ ✈ ⊠ ▨ SC ⅍

★★ **HOLIDAY INN EXPRESS.** *2503 SE Evangeline Thrwy (70508), near Municipal Airport. 337/234-2000; fax 337/234-6373; toll-free 888/366-8661. Email hielft@aol.com.* 102 rms, 2 story. S, D $64-$69; each addl $5; under 18 free; higher rates Crawfish Festival. Crib free. TV; cable (premium), VCR avail. Complimentary bkfst. Restaurant adj 6:30 am-1 pm, 5-9 pm. Ck-out noon. Coin lndry. Meeting rms. Business servs avail. Free airport transportation. Health club privileges. Some refrigerators, wet bars; microwaves avail. Cr cds: A, DS, MC, V.

⊡ ✈ ⊠ ▨ SC

★ **LA QUINTA MOTOR INN.** *2100 NE Evangeline Thrwy (70507), I-10 Exit 103A.* 337/233-5610; fax 337/235-2104; toll-free 800/531-5900. 140 rms, 2 story. S, D $65-$72; each addl $7; under 18 free. Crib free. Pet accepted, some restrictions. TV; cable (premium). Pool. Complimentary continental bkfst. Restaurant adj open 24 hrs. Ck-out noon. Business servs avail. In-rm modem link. Health club privileges. Microwaves avail. Cr cds: A, C, D, DS, MC, V.
⊡ 🦃 ⊠ 🔥 SC

★★ **RAMADA INN NORTH.** *2716 NE Evangeline Thrwy (70507), at I-10.* 337/233-0003; fax 337/233-0360; res 800/2RAMADA; toll-free 800/473-0360. www.ramadainnlafayette.com. 225 rms, 2 story. S, D $65-$77; each addl $4; under 18 free. Crib free. Pet accepted, some restrictions. TV; cable (premium). Pool; wading pool. Complimentary full bkfst. Complimentary coffee in rms. Restaurant 6:30 am-1 pm, 6-10 pm. Bar 4:30 pm-2 am. Ck-out noon. Coin lndry. Meeting rms. In-rm modem link. Bellhops. Valet serv. Free airport transportation. Health club privileges. Game rm. Cr cds: A, DS, MC, V
⊡ 🦃 ⊠ ⊠ 🔥 SC

★ **RED ROOF INN.** *1718 N University Ave (70507), I-10 Exit 101.* 337/233-3339; fax 337/233-7206; toll-free 800/843-7663. 108 rms, 2 story. S $36; D $41-$49; each addl $8; under 18 free; higher rates special events. Crib free. Pet accepted, some restrictions. TV. Complimentary coffee in lobby. Restaurant nearby. Ck-out noon. Business servs avail. Cr cds: A, C, D, DS, MC, V.
⊡ 🦃 ⊠ 🔥 SC

★ **TRAVELODGE LAFAYETTE CENTER.** *1101 W Pinhook Rd (70503).* 337/234-7402; fax 372/234-7404; res 800/578-7878. 61 rms, 2 story. S $55; D $60; under 18 free; higher rates special events. Crib free. TV; cable (premium). Pool. Complimentary continental bkfst, coffee in rms. Restaurant adj 11 am-10 pm. Ck-out noon. In-rm modem link. Valet serv. Health club privileges. Refrigerators avail. Cr cds: A, D, DS, MC, V.
⊠ 🧍 🔥 ✈ ⊠ 🔥

Hotels

★★ **COMFORT INN LAFAYETTE.** *1421 SE Evangeline Thrwy (70501), near Municipal Airport.* 337/232-9000; fax 337/233-8629; res 800/228-5150; toll-free 800/800-8752. Email cbreaux@eatel.net; www.comfortinnlafayette.com. 196 rms, 2 story, 4 suites. S $79; D $84; each addl $1; suites $110; under 18 free. Crib avail. Pet accepted, some restrictions. Pool. Parking lot. TV; cable (premium). Complimentary continental bkfst, coffee in rms. Restaurant 6 am-10 pm. Bar. Ck-out noon, ck-in 2 pm. Meeting rms. Business servs avail. Bellhops. Dry cleaning, coin lndry. Free airport transportation. Exercise equipt, sauna. Golf. Tennis. Cr cds: A, C, D, DS, ER, JCB, MC, V.
⊡ 🦃 🧍 ✈ ⊠ 🧍 ✈ ⊠ 🔥 SC

★★★ **HILTON LAFAYETTE & TOWERS.** *1521 W Pinhook Rd (70503).* 337/235-6111; fax 337/261-0311; res 800/445-8667; toll-free 800/332-2586. Email jeff_patton@hilton.com; www.hilton.com. 327 rms, 15 story. S, D $105-$145; each addl $15; suites $180-$260. TV; cable (premium), VCR avail. Pool; poolside serv. Restaurant 6 am-10 pm. Bar 11:30-2 am. Ck-out noon. Business servs avail. In-rm modem link. Airport transportation. Exercise equipt. Game rm. Some bathrm phones. Private patios. Boat dock. River walk. Luxury level. Cr cds: A, DS, MC, V.
⊡ ⊠ 🧍 ⊠ 🔥 SC

B&B/Small Inn

★★ **LA MAISON DE CAMPAGNE.** *825 Kidder Rd (70520), N on I-49, Exit 7, E on LA 182.* 337/896-6529; fax 337/896-1494; toll-free 800/895-0235. Email fmclemore@afo.net. 4 rms, 2 story. S, D $95-$135; each addl $25; higher rates special events. TV in common rm; cable (premium). Complimentary full bkfst. Meeting rms. Business servs avail. Free airport transportation. Pool. Restored Victorian home built 1871. Cr cds: A, DS, MC, V.
⊠ ⊠ 🔥

Restaurants

★★ **BLAIR HOUSE.** *1316 Surrey (70501).* 337/234-0357. www.blairhouse@aol.com. Cajun/Creole menu.

Specializes in steak, fresh seafood, Cajun dishes. Own baking. Hrs: 11 am-10 pm; Fri to 10:30 pm; Sat 5-10:30 pm. Closed Sun; hols. Res accepted. Bar. Lunch $7-$13; dinner $8.95-$24.95. Child's menu. Parking. Family-owned. Cr cds: A, DS, MC, V.

★★★ CAFE VERMILIONVILLE. *1304 W Pinhook Rd (70503). 337/237-0100. Email poncho@globalreach.net; www.cafev.com.* Specializes in fresh seafood, grilled steaks, Acadian crawfish dishes. Own baking. Hrs: 11 am-2 pm, 5:30-10 pm; Sat 5:30-10 pm. Closed Sun; hols. Res accepted. Bar. Lunch $8-$15.95; dinner $16.95-$25. Parking. Cr cds: A, C, D, DS, ER, MC, V.

★★ CHARLEY G'S SEAFOOD GRILL. *3809 Ambassador Caffery Pkwy (70503). 337/988-4745. www.charleygs.com.* Specializes in Creole, Cajun cuisine. Hrs: 11 am-2 pm, 5-10 pm; Fri to 11 pm; Sat 5-11 pm; Sun brunch 11 am-2 pm. Closed hols. Res accepted. Bar. Lunch, dinner à la carte entrées: $7.50-$22. Sun brunch $6.50-$18.50. Entertainment: Fri-Sun. Parking. Cr cds: A, D, DS, MC, V.

★★ DON'S SEAFOOD & STEAK HOUSE. *301 E Vermilion St (70501). 337/235-3551.* Cajun/Creole menu. Specializes in stuffed red snapper, crabmeat au gratin, oyster en brochette. Hrs: 11 am-9:30 pm; Fri, Sat to 10:30 pm. Closed Dec 25, Mardi Gras. Res accepted. Bar. Lunch $6.95-$10.95; dinner $9.50-$17.50. Child's menu. Parking. Rustic decor. Cr cds: A, DS, MC, V.

★★ I MONELLI. *4017 Johnston St (70503). 337/989-9291. Email bjbi-monelli@aol.com.* Specializes in cannelloni, spaghetti al pesto, shrimp scampi. Hrs: 11 am-2 pm, 5:30-10 pm; Sat from 5:30 pm. Closed Sun, Mon; hols; Mardi Gras, Ash Wednesday. Res accepted. Lunch a la carte entrees: $3.95-$9.95; dinner a la carte entrees: $7.95-$18.95. Parking. Intimate dining. Cr cds: A, DS, MC, V.

★★ LA FONDA. *3809 Johnston St (70503). 337/984-5630.* Specializes in steak, chicken. Own tortillas. Hrs: 11 am-10 pm. Closed Sun, Mon; wk of July 4, Thanksgiving following Tues. Bar. Lunch $5-$16; dinner $5-$16. Parking. Cr cds: A, C, D, DS, MC, V.

★ POOR BOY'S RIVERSIDE INN. *240 Tubing Rd (70518), S on US 90E, Rte on Southpark Rd, E on Frontage to Tubing Rd. 337/235-8559.* Seafood menu. Specializes in flounder, shrimp, crabmeat dishes. Hrs: 11 am-10 pm; Fri, Sat to 11 pm; Sun 5-11 pm. Closed hols. Res accepted. Lunch complete meals: $6.75; dinner complete meals: $9.50-$21.95. Parking. In rural setting overlooking pond. Family-owned. Cr cds: A, D, DS, MC, V.

★ PREJEANS. *3480 Hwy 167N (70507). 337/896-3247. www.prejeans.com.* Specializes in alligator, steak, fresh seafood. Hrs: 11 am-10 pm; Fri, Sat to 11 pm. Closed hols. Bar. Lunch a la carte entrees: $6.95-$9.95; dinner a la carte entrees: $14.95-$22.95. Child's menu. Entertainment: Cajun band. Parking. Cajun artifacts; mounted & stuffed wildlife on display, including a 14-ft alligator believed to have been 65 yrs old when captured. Cr cds: A, D, DS, MC, V.

★★ ROBIN'S. *1409 Henderson Hwy (70517), I-10, Exit 115, 2 mi E on LA 352. 337/228-7594.* Specializes in crawfish, crabmeat au gratin, frogs' legs étouffées. Hrs: 10 am-10 pm; Sun to 4 pm. Closed Mon; Thanksgiving, Dec 24-26. Res accepted. Lunch, dinner $7-$17. Child's menu. Parking. Cr cds: A, C, D, DS, MC, V.

★★★ RUTH'S CHRIS STEAK HOUSE. *620 W Pinhook Rd (70503). 337/237-6123.* Steak menu. Specializes in prime beef, Maine lobster. Hrs: 11:30 am-10:30 pm; Sat from 4 pm; Sun 5-10 pm. Closed hols. Res accepted. Bar. Lunch $14-$26; dinner $25-$40. Parking. Cr cds: A, D, DS, MC, V.

Unrated Dining Spot

RANDOL'S. *2320 Kaliste Saloom Rd (70508). 337/981-7080. www.randols. com.* Specializes in steamed crabs, crawfish. Hrs: 5-10 pm. Closed hols. Bar. Dinner $5.95-$14.95. Child's menu. Entertainment: Cajun music. Cr cds: MC, V.

D

Lake Charles (E-2)

Founded ca 1781 **Pop** 70,580
Elev 20 ft **Area code** 337
Web www.visitlakecharles.org
Information Southwest Louisiana Convention & Visitors Bureau, located off I-10 on North Beach, 1211 N Lakeshore Dr, PO Box 1912, 70602; 337/436-9588 or 800/456-SWLA

Around 1781, a Frenchman named Charles Sallier settled on the shore of a pleasant lake, married, and built a house. His property became known to travelers as "Charlie's Lake," and his hospitality became famous. However, the town grew slowly until the Southern Pacific Railroad's link between Houston and New Orleans was finished. Stimulated by railroad transportation and under the more sedate name of "Lake Charles," the town began its real growth, mainly via timber and rice culture. Captain J.B. Watkins began a tremendous penny-postcard publicity campaign in 1887. It was effective, but not so effective as the discovery of oil and sulphur early in the 20th century. In 1926, when a deepwater port was opened, the city's future was assured.

A massive reforestation project centered around Lake Charles and begun in the 1950s revitalized the area's lumber industry. Now oil, rubber, and chemicals have joined cattle and rice to make this a vital industrial center. McNeese State University is located in Lake Charles.

What to See and Do

Brimstone Historical Society Museum. Commemorates turn-of-the-century birth of the local sulphur industry with exhibits explaining the development of the Frasch mining process; other exhibits deal with southwest Louisiana; also traveling exhibits. (Mon-Fri; closed hols) 800 Picard Rd in Frasch Park, 11 mi W via I-10, Exit N onto Ruth St, then W on Logan St in Sulphur. Phone 337/527-7142. **FREE**

Creole Nature Trail National Scenic Byway. Follows LA 27 in a circular route ending back at Lake Charles. Unique composite of wildflowers, animals, shrimp, crab, and many varieties of fish, plus one of the largest alligator populations in the world; winter habitat of thousands of ducks and geese; views of several bayous, Intracoastal Waterway, oil platforms, beaches, four wildlife refuges, and a bird sanctuary. Automobile nature trail (180 mi); walking nature trail (1½ mi). (Daily) For map contact the Convention & Visitors Bureau. Begins 15 mi SW off I-10 via LA 27. **FREE**

Fishing, hunting. On and around Lake Calcasieu. Fishing in Calcasieu River; deep sea, jetty fishing at Cameron, Gulf of Mexico.

★ **Historic "Charpentier."** District incl 20 sq blks of downtown area; architectural styles range from Queen Anne, Eastlake and "Carpenter's Gothic" (known locally as "Lake Charles style") to Western stick-style bungalows. Tours (fee) and brochures describing self-guided tours may be obtained at the Convention & Visitors Bureau.

Imperial Calcasieu Museum. Items of local historical interest. Complete rms and shops; toy collection, rare Audubon prints. Gibson-Barham Gallery houses art exhibits. On premises is the 300-yr-old Sallier Oak tree. (Tues-Sat; closed hols) 204 W Sallier St. Phone 337/439-3797. ¢

Port of Lake Charles. Docks and turning basin. Ships pass down the Calcasieu ship channel and through Lake Calcasieu. W end of Shell Beach Dr.

Sam Houston Jones State Park. The approx 1,000 acres incl lagoons in a densely wooded area at the confluence of the W fork of the Caslcasieu and Houston Rivers and Indian Bayou. Fishing; boating (rentals, launch). Nature trails, hiking. Picnicking. Tent and trailer sites (hookups, dump station), cabins. Standard fees. (Daily) 12 mi N, off US 171 on LA 378. Phone 337/855-2665 or 888/677-7264. Per vehicle ¢

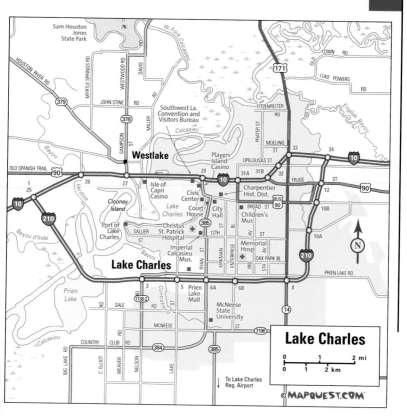

Lake Charles

© MAPQUEST.COM

Annual Events

Contraband Days. Lake Charles Civic Center. Honors "gentleman pirate" Jean Lafitte. Boat races, midway, concerts, arts and crafts display. Phone 800/456-7952 or 337/436-5508. Two wks early May. 1205 N Lake Shore Dr. 337/436-5508.

CFMA Cajun Music and Food Festival. Burton Coliseum. Entertainment, contests, arts and crafts. Phone 800/456-7952. Late July. 1205 N Lake Shore Dr.

Seasonal Event

Horse racing. Delta Downs. 30 mi W via I-10 in Vinton. Minimum age 18. Jacket required in Clubhouse, Skyline. Thoroughbreds Sep-Mar, Thurs-Sat eves; Sun matinee; no racing hols. Also quarterhorse racing Apr-Labor Day. 2717 Hwy 3063 in Vinton. Phone 337/589-7441, 337/433-3206 or 800-737-3358.

Motels/Motor Lodges

★★ **BEST WESTERN RICHMOND SUITES.** 2600 Moeling St (70615). 337/433-5213; fax 337/439-4243; res 800/528-1234; toll-free 800/643-2582. www.bestwestern.com/richmond. 146 rms, 2 story, 30 kit. suites. S, D $84; each addl $10; kit. suites $99-$119; under 18 free. Crib free. TV; cable (premium). Pool; whirlpool. Playground. Complimentary full bkfst. Ck-out noon. Coin lndry. Meeting rms. Business servs avail. In-rm modem link. Airport transportation. Exercise equipt. Microwaves avail. Private patios, balconies. Grills. Cr cds: A, C, D, DS, MC, V.

★★ **PLAYERS ISLAND RIVERBOAT HOTEL AND CASINO.** 505 N Lakeshore Dr (70602), I-10 Exits 29 and 30A. 337/437-1500; fax 337/437-6010; toll-free 800/977-7529. 269 rms, 4 story. S $79-$109; D $88-$129; suites $200-$300; wkend rates. Crib free. TV; cable (premium). Pool; poolside serv.

Coffee in rms. Restaurant 7 am-11 pm; Fri-Sat to 2 am. Bar 11 am-11:30 pm. Ck-out noon. Convention facilities. Business servs avail. In-rm modem link. Bellhops. Valet serv. Some refrigerators, wet bars. On lake. Cr cds: A, C, D, DS, MC, V.

Restaurants

★★ **ALADDIN LEBANESE RESTAURANT.** *2009 Enterprise Blvd (70601). 337/494-0062.* Specializes in veal perigordine, chicken shwarma, kibbie dinner. Own desserts. Hrs: 11 am-2 pm, 5:30-11 pm. Closed Sun, Mon; Good Friday, Thanksgiving, Dec 25. Res accepted. Lunch $3.75-$7.50; dinner $7.50-$21.50. Child's menu. Intimate atmosphere. Cr cds: DS, MC, V.

★★★ **CAFE MARGAUX.** *765 Bayou Pines E (70601). 337/433-2902. Email dcflyntmw@aol.net.* Specializes in seafood, veal. Own pastries. Hrs: 11 am-2 pm, 6-10 pm; Sat from 6 pm. Closed Sun; Dec 25. Res accepted. Bar. Wine cellar. Lunch $6.50-$12.75. Buffet: $8.75; dinner $18.50-$24.50. Parking. Cr cds: A, D, DS, MC, V.

★★ **HARLEQUIN STEAKS & SEAFOOD.** *1717 Hwy 14 (70601), at Legion St. 337/439-2780.* Specializes in steak, crab dishes, tuna steak. Hrs: 4-11 pm. Closed Sun; hols. Res accepted. Bar. Dinner $10.50-$20.75. Child's menu. Parking. Several dining rms provide intimate atmosphere; attractive landscaping. Family-owned. Cr cds: A, MC, V.

★ **JEAN LAFITTE INN.** *501 W College St (70605). 337/474-2730.* Specializes in fresh seafood, steak, crawfish. Hrs: 11 am-10 pm. Closed Sun; hols. Bar. Lunch $6.25; dinner $8-$19.50. Child's menu. Parking. Acadian atmosphere; scenes and maps of Louisiana on walls, bookshelves with old books. Cr cds: A, MC, V.

★ **PAT'S OF HENDERSON.** *1500 Siebarth Dr (70615). 337/439-6618.* Specializes in rib-eye steak, stuffed snapper, seafood. Hrs: 11 am-10 pm.

Closed Thanksgiving, Dec 25. Res accepted. Bar. Lunch $6.95; dinner $10.95-$22.95. Child's menu. Parking. Colonial design with walnut paneling and framed portraits. Cr cds: A, D, MC, V.

★★ **PEKING GARDEN.** *2433 E Broad St (70601). 337/436-3597.* Specializes in Hunan cuisine, steak, seafood. Hrs: 11 am-2 pm, 5-9:30 pm; Fri, Sat to 10 pm; Sun 5-9 pm. Closed Thanksgiving, Dec 25. Bar. Lunch $4.75-$5.25; dinner $6.95-$10.75. Child's menu. Parking. Chinese artifacts in dining rm. Cr cds: A, MC, V.

★ **TONY'S PIZZA.** *335 E Prien Lake Rd (70601). 337/477-1611.* Specializes in pizza, deli sandwiches, salads. Own pasta. Hrs: 11:30-12:30 am. Closed Sun; Thanksgiving, Dec 25. Lunch, dinner a la carte entrees: $4.50-$7.50. Parking. Friendly, family-oriented atmosphere. Family-owned. Cr cds: A, DS, MC, V.

Many

(C-2) *See also Natchitoches*

Settled 1837 **Pop** 3,112 **Elev** 321 ft **Area code** 318 **Zip** 71449

Information Sabine Parish Tourist Commission, 920 Fisher Rd, phone 318/256-5880; or contact the Louisiana Tourist Center, LA 6W, phone 318/256-4114

What to See and Do

Fort Jesup State Commemorative Area. Fort established in 1822 by Zachary Taylor features restored 1830s army kitchen; reconstructed officers' quarters and museum (Daily; closed Jan 1, Thanksgiving, Dec 25); on 21 acres. Picnic facilities. 6 mi E on LA 6 to LA 3118. Phone 318/256-4117 or 888/677-5378. Per vehicle ¢

Hodges Gardens. Has 4,700 acres of gardens, greenhouses; 225-acre lake. Wild and cultivated flowers and plants all yr. Terrazzo map commemorating Louisiana Purchase. Wildlife, fishing boat rentals, picnic facilities. Special events incl Easter service, July 4 festival, and Christmas lights festival. (Daily; closed Jan 1, Dec 24-25) 12 mi S on US 171. Phone 318/586-3523. ¢¢¢

Toledo Bend Dam and Reservoir. W on LA 6. (See JASPER, TX).

Annual Events

Battle of Pleasant Hill Re-Enactment. 18 mi N on LA 175, N of Pleasant Hill. Three-day event incl beauty pageant, Confederate ball, parade, and battle reenactment. Early Apr.

Sawmill Days. 8 mi S via US 171 in Fisher. 3rd wkend May.

Sabine Free State Festival. 10 mi S in Florien. Beauty pageant; syrup-making, basket-weaving, and quilting demonstrations; arts and crafts exhibits; flea market. Phone 318/586-7286. First wkend Nov.

Metairie

(F-6) *See also Kenner, New Orleans*

Pop 149,428 **Elev** 5 ft **Area code** 504

Motels/Motor Lodges

★★ **HOLIDAY INN METAIRIE.** *3400 I-10 Service Rd (70001). 504/833-8201; fax 504/838-6829; res 800/465-4329.* 193 rms, 4 story. S, D $89-$149; each addl $15; under 18 free. Crib free. TV; cable (premium). Pool. Complimentary coffee in rms. Restaurant 6 am-2:30 pm, 5-10 pm; Sat, Sun from 7 am. Bar 5-10 pm. Ck-out noon. Coin lndry. Meeting rms. Business servs avail. In-rm modem link. Bellhops. Valet serv. Free airport transportation. Exercise equipt. Balconies. Cr cds: A, C, D, DS, ER, JCB, MC, V.

★ **LA QUINTA.** *5900 Veterans Memorial Blvd (70003). 504/456-0003; fax 504/885-0863; res 800/531-5900.* 153 rms, 3 story. S, D $82; suites $150; under 18 free. Pet accepted; some restrictions. TV; cable (premium). Pool. Complimentary conti-

nental bkfst. Restaurant adj open 24 hrs. Ck-out noon. Meeting rms. Business servs avail. In-rm modem link. Valet serv. Free airport transportation. Health club privileges. Cr cds: A, C, D, DS, ER, JCB, MC, V.

★★ **QUALITY HOTEL & CONFERENCE CENTER.** *2261 N Causeway Blvd (70001), I-10 and Causeway, Exit 228. 504/833-8211; fax 504/833-8213; toll-free 800/638-7949.* 204 rms, 10 story. S, D $69-$119; under 18 free; wkend rates; higher rates special events. Crib free. Pet accepted; $25 deposit. TV; cable (premium), VCR avail. Complimentary coffee in rms. Restaurant 6:30 am- 2 pm, 5-10 pm. Ck-out noon. Coin lndry. Meeting rms. Business servs avail. In-rm modem link. Bellhops. Valet serv. Gift shop. Free airport transportation. Exercise equipt; sauna. Microwaves avail. Cr cds: A, D, DS, MC, V.

Hotels

★★ **BEST WESTERN LANDMARK HOTEL.** *2601 Severn Ave (70002), I-10 at Causeway. 504/888-9500; fax 504/889-5793; toll-free 800/528-1234. www.bestwestern.com.* 342 rms, 17 story. S $69-$149; D $79-$189; each addl $10; suites $159-$375; higher rates special events. Crib free. TV; cable (premium). Pool. Restaurant 6:30 am-10 pm. Bar to 1 am. Ck-out 11 am. Coin lndry. Convention facilities. Business servs avail. Gift shop. Free airport transportation. Exercise equipt. Health club privileges. Balconies. Cr cds: A, C, D, DS, MC, V.

★★★ **DOUBLETREE HOTEL LAKESIDE NEW ORLEANS.** *3838 N Causeway Blvd (70002). 504/836-5253; fax 504/846-4562; toll-free 800/222-8733. Email rmitchell@doubletree lakeside.com; www.doubletreelakeside. com.* 198 rms, 16 story, 12 suites. Feb-May, Oct-Nov: S, D $169; each addl $10; suites $239; under 17 free; lower rates rest of yr. Crib avail. Valet parking avail. Indoor pool, whirlpool. TV; cable (premium). Complimentary coffee in rms, newspaper, toll-free calls. Restaurant 6:30 am-10 pm. Bar. Ck-out noon, ck-in 3 pm. Meeting rms. Business servs avail. Bellhops. Concierge. Dry cleaning, coin lndry. Gift shop. Salon/barber. Free airport transportation. Exercise rm, sauna, steam rm. Golf. Tennis, 2 courts. Hiking trail. Cr cds: A, C, D, DS, MC, V.

★★ **HOLIDAY INN NEW ORLEANS VETERANS.** *6401 Veterans Memorial Blvd at I-10 (70003), I-10 Exit 225. 504/885-5700; fax 504/454-8294. www.holiday-inn.com/msy-metairie.* 222 rms, 7 story. Jan-Apr, Oct-Nov: S, D $79-$150; each addl $10; under 18 free; lower rates rest of yr. Crib free. Pet accepted, some restrictions. TV; cable (premium). Pool; whirlpool. Restaurant 6 am-2 pm, 5-10 pm. Bar 4 pm-midnight. Ck-out 11 am. Meeting rms. Business center. In-rm modem link. Bellhops. Exercise equipt. Health club privileges. Valet serv. Free airport transportation. Balconies. Cr cds: A, DS, MC, V.

Restaurants

★★★ **ANDREA'S.** *3100 19th St (70002). 504/834-8583. Email nolandreas@aol.com.* Specializes in pasta dishes, seafood, veal. Own baking. Hrs: 11 am-10:30 pm; Sun to 9 pm; Sun brunch to 3 pm. Closed July 4, Labor Day. Res accepted. Bar. Wine list. Lunch, dinner $8.95-$26.50. Complete meals: $29.95. Brunch $19.95. Child's menu. Cr cds: A, D, DS, MC, V.

★★★ **CROZIER'S RESTAURANT FRANCAIS.** *3216 W Esplanade (70002). 504/833-8108. www.croziers.com.* Specializes in liver and onions with sauteed vegetables. Own baking. Hrs: 5:30-10 pm. Closed Sun, Mon; hols. Res accepted. Bar. Wine list. Dinner $20-$20.75. Child's menu. Parking. French country decor. Cr cds: A, D, DS, MC, V.

★★ **IMPASTATO'S.** *3400 16th St (70002). 504/455-1545.* Specializes in fresh Maine lobster, fresh grilled salmon, pecan-smoked filet mignon. Own pasta. Hrs: 5 pm-midnight; early-bird dinner 5-6 pm. Closed Sun, Mon; also Mardi Gras. Res accepted.

Bar. Dinner $20-$38. Entertainment: vocalist. Cr cds: A, D, MC, V.

★★ **INDIA PALACE.** *3322 N Turnball Dr (70002). 504/889-2436.* Specializes in vegetarian dishes. Hrs: 11 am-2:30 pm, 5:30-10 pm. Closed Thanksgiving, Dec 25. Res accepted. Bar. Lunch buffet: $7.95; dinner $9-$20. Cr cds: A, C, D, DS, MC, V.

★★ **LA RIVIERA.** *4506 Shores Dr (70006), off N Clearview Pkwy, 1 blk W on Belle Dr to Shores Dr. 504/888-6238. www.lariviera.com.* Specializes in pasta, veal dishes, seafood. Own baking. Hrs: 11:30 am-2 pm, 5:30-10 pm; Mon from 5:30; Sat 5:30-11 pm. Closed Sun; Thanksgiving, Dec 25; June 28-July 6. Res accepted. Bar. Lunch a la carte entrees: $10.95-$18; dinner a la carte entrees: $10.95-$18. Child's menu. Parking. Family-owned. Cr cds: A, D, DS, MC, V.

★★ **RALPH & KACOO'S.** *601 Veterans Memorial Blvd (70002). 504/831-3177.* Specializes in trout Ruby. Hrs: 11 am-10 pm; Fri, Sat to 11 pm; Sun to 9 pm. Closed Mardi Gras, Thanksgiving, Dec 25. Bar. Lunch $5.95-$17.95; dinner $5.95-$17.95. Valet parking. Cr cds: A, C, D, MC, V.

Unrated Dining Spot

MORNING CALL. *3325 Severn Ave (70002), at 17th St. 504/885-4068.* Specializes in beignets, New Orleans chicory coffee (cafe au lait). Hrs: Open 24 hrs. Closed Jan 1, Mardi Gras, Dec 25. Bkfst $1-$3; lunch, dinner $1-$3. No cr cds accepted.

Minden

(A-2) *See also Bossier City, Shreveport*

Founded 1836 **Pop** 13,661 **Elev** 259 ft
Area code 318 **Zip** 71055
Web www.minden.com

Information Chamber of Commerce, 110 Sibley Rd, PO Box 819, 71058; 318/377-4240 or 800/2-MINDEN

What to See and Do

Germantown Museum. Museum incl 3 bldgs completed in 1835 by Germans seeking freedom from persecution; replicas of commune smokehouse and blacksmith shop; records and artifacts used by settlers. (Wed-Sun) 8 mi NE via I-20 and Parish Rd 114. Phone 318/377-6061. ¢¢

Lake Bistineau State Park. This 750-acre park in heart of pine forest incl a large lake. Swimming, waterskiing; fishing; boating (rentals, launch). Tent and trailer sites, cabins. Standard fees. (Daily) 9 mi SW on US 79, 80, then 13 mi S on LA 163. Phone 318/745-3503 or 888/677-2478. Per vehicle ¢

Monroe and West Monroe

(B-4) *See also Bastrop*

Settled 1785 **Pop** Monroe: 54,909; West Monroe: 14,096 **Elev** 74 ft **Area code** 318 **Zip** West Monroe: 71291 **Web** www.bayou.com/visitors **Information** Monroe-West Monroe Convention & Visitors Bureau, 1333 State Farm Dr, Monroe 71202; 318/387-5691 or 800/843-1872

In March 1783 a swashbuckling young French adventurer named Jean Baptiste Filhiol, then in the service of the King of Spain, married the beautiful daughter of a wealthy Opelousas family. Shortly thereafter he took her in a keelboat up the Mississippi, Red, Black, and Ouachita rivers into the wilderness to establish a great personal estate. Flooded out, Filhiol and his bride moved downstream to the site of Monroe, where he settled, calling his post Fort Miro in honor of the Spanish governor.

Filhiol was an excellent administrator and the post prospered. In 1819 the first steamboat, the *James Monroe*, traveled up the Ouachita.

After some shipboard conviviality, residents decided to rename their town for the boat.

The Monroe natural gas field, one of the world's largest, affords the city a great industrial advantage; nearby forests provide raw materials for the paper products, furniture, and chemicals produced in Monroe.

What to See and Do

★ **Emy-Lou Biedenharn Foundation.** (Tues-Sun; closed hols) 2006 Riverside Dr. Phone 318/387-5281. **FREE** Includes

Bible Museum. Museum-library contains early and rare Bibles, archaeological artifacts, coins, antique musical instruments, and furnishings.

Biedenharn Family House. (1914) Built by Joseph Biedenharn, first bottler of Coca-Cola; contains antiques, fine furnishings, silver dating from 18th century, and Coca-Cola memorabilia.

Elsong Gardens & Conservatory. These formal gardens enclosed within brick walls were originally designed to accommodate musical events. Today background music is triggered by lasers as visitors stroll through separate gardens linked by winding paths. There are 4 fountains, incl a porcelain fountain from the garden of Russian Empress Catherine the Great.

Fishing, water sports. Ouachita River in city; Chenière Lake (3,600 acres) 4 mi W; D'Arbonne Lake (15,000 acres) 35 mi N; Bayou DeSiard (1,200 acres) 3 mi NE; Black Bayou (2,600 acres) 6 mi N.

Louisiana Purchase Gardens and Zoo. Formal gardens, moss-laden live oaks, waterways, and winding paths surround naturalistic habitats for more than 850 exotic animals in this 80-acre zoo; boat and miniature train rides. Picnicking, concessions. (Daily; closed Thanksgiving, Dec 25; rides, concessions, Apr-Oct only). Special trail for disabled. 1405 Berstien Park Dr. Phone 318/329-2400. ¢¢

Masur Museum of Art. Permanent and changing exhibits. (Tues-Thurs, also Fri-Sun afternoons; closed hols) 1400 S Grand St. Phone 318/329-2237. **FREE**

Northeast Louisiana University.
(1931) 11,000 students. 700 University Ave. Phone 318/342-1000. On campus are

Bry Hall Art Gallery. Art exhibits, photographs by American and foreign artists, students, faculty. (Mon-Fri; closed Easter, July 4, Thanksgiving, also mid-Aug-early Sep, mid-Dec-early Jan) Phone 318/342-1375. **FREE**

Museum of Natural History. Geological exhibits incl Native American, Latin American and African artifacts. (Mon-Fri; closed Easter, July 4, Thanksgiving, also mid-Aug-early Sep, mid-Dec-early Jan) 3rd floor of Hanna Hall. Phone 318/342-1878. **FREE**

Museum of Zoology. Fish collection is one of the largest and most complete in the nation. (Mon-Fri; closed Easter, July 4, Thanksgiving, also mid-Aug-early Sep, mid-Dec-early Jan) 1st floor of Garret Hall. Phone 318/342-1799. **FREE**

Rebecca's Doll House. Approx 2,000 antique artist dolls; French, German, Parian, china, cloth, metal, wax, composition, primitive, peddler, pin-cushion dolls. Hand-carved wooden dolls portray the Last Supper. (By appt only) 4500 Bon Aire Dr. ¢

Motels/Motor Lodges

★ **CIVIC CENTER INN.** *610 Lea Joyner Memorial Expy (71201), I-20 Exit Civic Center.* 318/323-4451; fax 318/323-1728. 92 rms, 2 story. S $42-$47; D $42-$57; each addl $5; under 12 free. Crib free. TV. Pool. Complimentary continental bkfst. Restaurant 6 am-10 pm. Bar 4 pm-midnight. Ck-out noon. Business servs avail. Privat patios, balconies. Cr cds: A, C, D, DS, ER, MC, V.

★ **DAYS INN.** *5650 Frontage Rd (71202).* 318/345-2220; fax 318/343-4098. 58 rms, 2 story. S $36-$39; D $39-$44; under 16 free. Crib free. TV; cable (premium). Pool. Complimentary continental bkfst. Business servs avail. In-rm modem link. Cr cds: A, C, D, DS, MC, V.

★★ **HOLIDAY INN.** *1051 US Hwy 165 Bypass (71203), ½ blk N of I-20 Exit N Bastrop.* 318/387-5100; fax

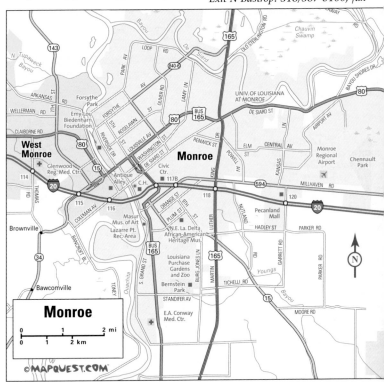

318/329-9126; res 800/465-4329. 260 rms, 2 story. S, D $66; each addl $6; suites $89-$250; under 18 free; some wkend rates. Crib free. TV; cable. 2 pools, 1 indoor; wading pool, whirl-pool, poolside serv. Restaurant 6 am-2 pm, 5-10 pm. Bars 4 pm-2 am. Ck-out noon. Coin lndry. Meeting rms. Business servs avail. In-rm modem link. Bellhops. Valet serv. Sundries. Free airport, bus depot, transportation. Putting green. Exercise equipt; sauna, steam rm. Game rm. Cr cds: A, D, DS, MC, V.

★ **LA QUINTA INN AIRPORT.** *1035 US 165 Byp S (71203). 318/322-3900; fax 318/323-5537; res 800/531-5900.* 130 units, 2 story. S $55; D $61; each addl $5; suites $75; under 18 free. Crib free. Pet accepted. TV; cable. Pool. Complimentary continental bkfst. Restaurant nearby. Meeting rms. Business servs avail. In-rm modem link. Free airport, bus depot transportation. Cr cds: A, D, DS, MC, V.

★ **RED ROOF INN.** *102 Constitution (71292). 318/388-2420; fax 318/388-2499; res 800/874-9000.* 97 rms, 3 story. S $36.99-$47.99; D $41.99-$52.99; each addl $6; under 18 free. Crib free. Pet accepted. TV; cable (premium). Complimentary coffee in lobby. Restaurant adj open 24 hrs. Ck-out noon. Business servs avail. Cr cds: A, DS, MC, V.

★ **STRATFORD HOUSE INN.** *927 Hwy 165 Bypass S (71202). 318/388-8868; fax 318/322-9893; toll-free 800/338-9893.* 40 rms, 2 story. S $39.95; D $43.95. Crib free. TV; cable. Complimentary continental bkfst. Restaurant opp open 24 hrs. Ck-out 11 am. Business servs avail. Cr cds: A, DS, MC, V.

★ **TRAVELODGE.** *2102 Louisville Ave (71201). 318/325-5851; fax 318/323-3808; res 800/057-8787.* 130 rms. S $37; D $43; suites $51-$53. Pet accepted. TV; cable. Pool. Playground. Complimentary continental bkfst. Restaurant 6:30-10:30 am. Bar 4 pm-2 am. Ck-out noon. Coin lndry. Meeting rms. Business servs avail. Valet serv. Cr cds: A, C, D, DS, MC, V.

Restaurants

★★ **CHATEAU.** *2007 Louisville Ave (71201). 318/325-0384.* Specializes in fresh seafood, steak. Hrs: 11 am-10 pm; Fri, Sat to 11 pm. Closed Sun; hols. Res accepted. Bar. Lunch $6.50-$8.50; dinner $8.50-$15. Entertainment: Fri, Sat. Cr cds: A, D, DS, MC, V.

★★ **WAREHOUSE NO. I.** *1 Olive St (71201), 2 blks S of US 80 and the Louisville Ave Bridge at the River. 318/322-1340.* Specializes in catfish, chicken, seafood. Hrs: 5-9 pm; Fri, Sat to 9:30 pm. Closed Sun; hols; also Mon after Easter. Bar. Dinner $8.95-$29.95. Child's menu. Valet parking. Located in old corrugated tin cotton warehouse on levee overlooking Ouachita River. Cr cds: A, D, DS, MC, V.

Morgan City

(F-5) *See also Franklin, Houma, Thibo-daux*

Founded ca 1850 **Pop** 14,531 **Elev** 5 ft **Area code** 504

Information St. Mary Parish Tourist Commission, PO Box 2332, 70381; 504/395-4905 or 800/256-2931

Originally named Brashear City for the Brashear family, upon whose plantation the town was laid out, the name was later changed to Morgan City in honor of Charles Morgan, president of the New Orleans, Opelousas, and Great Western Railroad, which established its western terminus in the town. Morgan, a shipping and railroad magnate, was responsible for dredging Morgan City's first port as well as operating the first steamboat on the Gulf of Mexico (1835).

Morgan City was a strategic point during the Civil War. Today it is an important inland port and commercial fishing center. In addition to its large shrimp industry, Morgan City has become a headquarters for offshore oil drilling.

What to See and Do

Brownell Memorial Park & Carillon Tower. Park preserves swamp in its natural state; on property is a 106-ft carillon tower with 61 bronze bells. (Daily) N off LA 70 on Lake Palourde. Phone 504/384-2283. **FREE**

Fishing and hunting. A vast interlocking network of bayous, rivers, and lakes with cypress, tupelo, gumwood forests, and sugarcane fields makes the whole area excellent for the hunting of small game and duck and for fishing.

Kemper Williams Park. This 290-acre park offers nature and jogging trails; tennis courts, golf driving range, baseball diamonds. Picnicking. Camping (hookups; addl fee). (Daily; closed hols) 8 mi W via US 90, Cotton Rd Exit in Patterson. Phone 504/395-2298. ¢

Lake End Park. Swimming beach; fishing in lake and bayous; boating (launch, marina). Picnicking (shelter). Tent and trailer sites (hookups; fee). (Daily) On Lake Palourde along LA 70. Phone 504/380-4623. Per vehicle ¢

Swamp Gardens and Wildlife Zoo. Outdoor exhibits depict both the history of the human settlement of the great Atchafalaya Basin and the natural flora and fauna of the swamp. Guided walking tours only. (Daily; closed Jan 1, Dec 25) 725 Myrtle St in Heritage Park. Phone 504/384-3343. ¢¢

Swamp tours.

Atchafalaya Basin Airboat tours. View wildlife and scenic bayous of Atchafalaya Basin in 1½- to 2-hr tours. (Apr-Aug, daily) Phone 504/384-4258. ¢¢¢¢

Cajun Jack's. Explore the area where the first Tarzan movie was filmed while learning about Cajun culture. Two scheduled tours daily (three in summer). US 90 to Patterson. Phone 504/395-7420. ¢¢¢¢

Scully's. See local wildlife while enjoying authentic Cajun seafood on 2-hr tours. (Mon-Sat; closed hols) 3141 LA 70. Phone 504/385-2388. ¢¢¢¢

Turn-of-the-Century House. Restored 1906 house with period furnishings and artifacts relating to local history; also elaborate Mardi Gras costumes. Guided tours. (Mon-Fri; closed hols) 715 Second St. Phone 504/380-4651. ¢¢

Annual Event

Louisiana Shrimp and Petroleum Festival and Fair. Saturday: Children's Day activities, amusement rides, parade, hands-on children's village, storytelling; coronation of adult court, coronation ball. Sunday: blessing of shrimp and petroleum fleets on Berwick Bay, parade, fireworks. Also arts and crafts fair; entertainment, gospel tent, music in park; food fest. Phone 504/385-0703. Labor Day wkend.

Motel/Motor Lodge

★★ **HOLIDAY INN MORGAN CITY.** *520 Roderick St (70380). 504/385-2200; fax 504/384-3813. Email lhmsharon@ aol.com.* 219 rms, 2 story. S, D $69-$79; each addl $10; suites $89-$99; under 18 free. Crib free. TV; cable (premium). Pool. Restaurant 5 am-10 pm. Bar 5-11 pm. Ck-out noon. Meeting rms. Business servs avail. In-rm modem link. Health club privileges. Cr cds: A, C, D, DS, JCB, MC, V.

Natchitoches

(C-3) *See also Many*

Founded 1714 **Pop** 16,609 **Elev** 125 ft
Area code 318 **Zip** 71457
Web www.natchitoches.net
Information Natchitoches Parish Tourist Commission, 781 Front St, 71458; 318/352-8072 or 800/259-1714

Natchitoches (NACK-a-tish) is the oldest permanent settlement in the Louisiana Purchase Territory. In 1714 a French expedition led by Louis Juchereau de St. Denis established a post on the site of the present city to open trade with the Native Americans and Spaniards in Texas. The following year Fort St. Jean Baptiste was constructed to provide protection against the Native Americans and to prevent the Spaniards from extending the frontier of Texas any farther eastward. The name Natchitoches is derived from the name of a Native American tribe. The town is on the Cane River a few miles from the Red River. A Ranger District office of the Kisatchie National Forests (see ALEXANDRIA) is in Natchitoches.

What to See and Do

Bayou Folk Museum. Displays depict history of Cane River country in restored house of writer Kate Chopin; period furniture. Also reconditioned blacksmith shop, doctor's office. (Daily; closed hols) 20 mi S, off LA 1 in Cloutierville. Phone 318/379-2233. ¢¢

Beau Fort Plantation. (1790) Restored Creole cottage (1½ story) at the head of an *allee* of live oaks boasts an 84-ft front gallery, enclosed courtyard, and landscaped gardens. (Daily; closed hols) 10 mi S via LA 1, 119 in Bermuda. Hwy 494. Phone 318/352-5340. ¢¢

Fort St. Jean Baptiste State Commemorative Area. On this 5-acre site is a replica of the fort as it was when first built to halt Spanish movement into Louisiana; restoration incl barracks, warehouse, chapel, mess hall, and Native American huts. (Daily; closed Jan 1, Thanksgiving, Dec 25) Standard fees. Downtown on Cane River. Phone 318/357-3101. Per vehicle ¢

Melrose Plantation. Complex of plantation bldgs incl Yucca House (ca 1795), the original cabin, the Big House, and the African House. Originally the residence of Marie Therese Coincoin, a former slave whose son developed the Spanish land grant into a thriving antebellum plantation. Melrose was restored at the turn of the 20th century by "Miss Cammie" Garrett Henry, who turned it into a repository of local arts and crafts. (Daily; closed hols) 16 mi S on LA 119. Phone 318/379-0055. ¢¢

National Fish Hatchery & Aquarium. Twenty tanks of indigenous fish, turtles, and alligators. (Daily; closed Jan 1, Dec 25) 615 Hwy 1 S. Phone 318/352-5324. **FREE**

Northwestern State University. (1884) 8,412 students. The 916-acre campus is on Chaplin's Lake. On campus are the Louisiana Sports Writers Hall of Fame in Prather Coliseum, the Archives Room of Watson Memorial Library, the Folklife Center, and the Williamson Archaeological Museum in Kyser Hall and the Normal Hill Historic District. College Ave at end of 2nd St. Phone 318/357-6361.

Annual Events

Melrose Plantation Arts & Crafts Festival. Juried works of more than 100 artists and craftspeople. Second wkend June.

Natchitoches-Northwestern Folk Festival. NSU Prather Coliseum. Festival spotlights a different industry or occupation each yr and works to preserve Louisiana folk art forms; music, dance, crafts, storytelling, foods. Phone. Third wkend July.

Natchitoches Pilgrimage. 781 Front St. City and Cane River tours of houses and plantations; also candlelight tour Sat. Phone 318/352-8072. Second full wkend Oct.

Christmas Festival of Lights. 550 2nd St. More than 140,000 lights are turned on after a full day of celebration to welcome the Christmas season. Phone 318/352-8072. First Sat Dec.

Motel/Motor Lodge

★★ **COMFORT INN.** *5362 Hwy 6 (71457), I-49 Exit 138. 318/352-7500; fax 318/352-7500; toll-free 800/228-5150.* 59 rms, 2 story. Dec: S $59; D $67; under 18 free; family rates; lower rates rest of yr. Crib avail. TV. Complimentary continental bkfst. Ck-out noon. In-rm modem link. Pool. Refrigerators, microwaves. Cr cds: A, D, DS, MC, V.
D 🛬 🐾 SC

★★ **RYDER INN.** *Hwy 1 S Bypass (71457), 3 mi S on LA 1 S Bypass. 318/357-8281; fax 318/352-9907; toll-free 888/252-8281.* 144 rms, 2 story. S $55; D $60; suites $125; under 18 free. Crib free. TV; cable (premium). Pool. Restaurant 6 am-2 pm, 5-10 pm; Sun from 7 am. Bar 5 pm-midnight. Ck-out 11 am. Coin lndry. Meeting rms. Business servs avail. In-rm modem link. Sundries. Free air-port, bus depot transportation. Health club privileges. Cr cds: A, D, DS, MC, V.

B&B/Small Inn

★★ **FLEUR DE LIS BED & BREAK-FAST.** *336 Second St (71457). 318/352-6621; toll-free 800/489-6621. www.virtualcites.com.* 5 rms, 2 story. Dec: S, D $100; each addl $10; suites $120; under 6 free; lower rates rest of yr. Parking lot. TV; cable (premium), VCR avail, CD avail. Complimentary full bkfst, newspaper, toll-free calls. Restaurant nearby. Ck-out 10:30 am, ck-in 3 pm. Meeting rm. Internet access avail. Exercise privileges. Golf, 18 holes. Tennis, 2 courts. Cr cds: A, DS, MC, V.

Restaurants

★★ **LANDING.** *530 Front St (71457). 318/352-1579. www.landing. com.* Cajun/Creole menu. Specializes in eggplant lafourche, red dirt shrimp, chicken Louisiane. Hrs: 11 am-2 pm, 5-10 pm; Sun to 9 pm; Sun brunch to 2 pm. Closed Mon; Thanksgiving, Dec 25. Res accepted. Bar. Lunch, dinner $5.95-$19.95. Sun brunch $15.95. Child's menu. Over-looks waterfront. Cr cds: A, MC, V.

★ **LASYONE MEAT PIE KITCHEN.** *622 2nd St (71457). 318/352-3353. Email lasyone@hotmail.com.* Specializes in meat pies, red beans and sausage, Cane River creme pie. Hrs: 7 am-7 pm. Closed Sun; hols. Res accepted. Bkfst $2.25-$5; lunch, dinner $4.95-$8.95. Built in 1859. Family-owned. No cr cds accepted.

★★ **MARINERS SEAFOOD & STEAK HOUSE.** *Hwy 1S Bypass (71457), off LA 1S Bypass, at Sibley Lake. 318/357-1220.* Specializes in steak, seafood. Salad bar. Hrs: 4:30-10 pm; Sun 11 am-9 pm; Sun brunch to 2 pm. Closed hols exc Easter. Res accepted. Bar. Dinner $10-15. Sun brunch $11.95. Child's menu. Patio dining. Nautical decor; view of lake. Cr cds: A, DS, MC, V.

New Iberia

(F-4) *See also Franklin, Lafayette, St. Martinville*

Founded 1779 **Pop** 31,828 **Elev** 20 ft
Area code 337 **Zip** 70560
Information Iberia Parish Tourist Com-mission, 2704 Hwy 14; 337/365-1540

New Iberia was settled by French and Acadians but named by the first Spanish settlers. Many families of original settlers still reside in and around New Iberia.

This area is known for its swamps, bayous, alligators, antebellum homes, factories, and cuisine. Sugarcane grows in the surrounding country and raw sugar is processed in and around New Iberia. The parish is com-prised not only of New Iberia, the parish seat, but Jeanerette, Delcambre, and the Village of Loreauville as well. Each city contributes to the unique culture of Iberia Parish, located in the heart of Cajun Country.

What to See and Do

Avery Island. An enormous mass of rock salt underlies the area. The salt was first mined in 1862, when a Union blockade left the Confeder-ate army and entire South in dire need of salt. Toll road onto island (fee); no bicycles or motorcycles permitted. 7 mi SW via LA 14, 329. On island are

> **McIlhenny Company.** Tabasco brand pepper sauce is made on the island. Guided tours of factory and Tabasco Country Store. (Mon-Sat; closed hols). Phone 337/365-8173. **FREE**

> **Jungle Gardens.** Avery Island's most spectacular feature was devel-oped by the late Edward Avery McIlhenny. Camellias, azaleas, irises, and tropical plants, in sea-son, form a beautiful display. Enor-mous flocks of egrets, cranes, and herons, among other species, are protected here and may be seen in early spring and summer; ducks and other wild fowl in winter. Chi-nese Garden contains a fine Bud-dha dating from AD 1000. (Daily) PO Box 126 on Avery Island. Phone 337/369-6243. ¢¢

Bouligny Plaza. In park are depic-tions of history of the area; gazebo, historic landmarks, beautiful view along the bayou. On Main St in center of town.

Konriko Rice Mill and Company Store. Tours of the oldest rice mill in US; next door is replica of the original company store, with antique fixtures and merchandise typical of Acadiana and Louisiana. Tours; film (Mon-Sat; closed hols). 309 Ann St. Phone 337/367-6163 or 800/551-3245. ¢¢

Rip van Winkle Gardens. Twenty acres of landscaped gardens and nature preserve. Also on premises is Victorian residence of 19th-century actor Joseph Jefferson (tours). Restaurant. Gift shop. (Daily; closed Jan 1, Thanksgiving, Dec 24-25) On Jefferson Island, 8 mi W off LA 14. Phone 337/365-3332. ¢¢¢

⊞ **Shadows-on-the-Teche.** (1834) Red brick and white-pillared Greek Revival house was built on the banks of the Bayou Teche by sugar planter David Weeks. Home to 4 generations of his family, it served as center of antebellum plantation system. The house was restored and its celebrated gardens created in the 1920s by the builder's great-grandson, Weeks Hall, who used the estate to entertain such celebrities as D.W. Griffith, Anais Nin, and Walt Disney. House is surrounded by three acres of azaleas, camellias, and massive oaks draped in Spanish moss. A National Trust for Historic Preservation property. (Daily; closed Jan 1, Thanksgiving, Dec 25) 317 E Main St. Phone 337/369-6446. ¢¢¢

Annual Events

Andalusia Mardi Gras Parade. Fri before Mardi Gras.

Sugar Cane Festival and Fair. Last wkend Sep.

Hotels

★★ **BEST WESTERN INN & SUITES.** 2714 Hwy 14 (70560). 337/364-3030; fax 337/367-5311. Email bwiberia@bellsouth.net. 100 rms, 2 story, 50 suites. S $52; D $57; each addl $6; suites $78; under 18 free. Parking lot. Pool, children's pool. TV; cable (premium). Complimentary continental bkfst, coffee in rms, newspaper, toll-free calls. Restaurant 10 am-9 pm, closed Sun. Bar. Ck-out noon, ck-in 2 pm. Meeting rms. Dry cleaning, coin lndry. Golf. Tennis. Cr cds: A, C, D, DS, MC, V.

🄳 🛍 🖅 ≈ 🏊 🕭 SC

★★ **HOLIDAY INN.** 2915 Hwy 14 (70560), 1 mi W at Jct US 90, LA 14. 337/367-1201; fax 337/367-7877. Email hiaveryisland@atel.net. 175 rms, 2 story, 2 suites. Apr-Sep: S, D $62; each addl $6; suites $125; under 18 free; lower rates rest of yr. Crib avail. Pet accepted, some restrictions. Parking lot. Pool. TV; cable (premium). Complimentary continental bkfst, coffee in rms, newspaper, toll-free calls. Restaurant 6 am-10 pm. Bar. Ck-out 11 am, ck-in 2 pm. Meeting rms. Business center. Dry cleaning, coin lndry. Exercise privileges. Golf, 18 holes. Picnic facilities. Video games. Cr cds: A, C, D, DS, JCB, MC, V.

🄳 🐾 🛍 ≈ 🕇 🏊 🕭 SC 🏌

B&B/Small Inn

★★★ **LE ROSIER.** 314 E Main St (70560). 337/367-5306; fax 337/367-1009; toll-free 888/804-ROSE. Email lerosier@msis.net. 6 rms, 2 story. S, D $95-$115. Children over 12 yrs only. Complimentary full bkfst. Restaurant (see LE ROSIER). Ck-out 11 am, ck-in 3 pm. Business servs avail. Built in 1870s; country inn atmosphere. Opp bayou. Totally nonsmoking. Cr cds: A, MC, V.

🄳 🛍 🖅 🕇 🕇 ≈ 🕭

Restaurants

★★★ **LE ROSIER.** 314 E Main St. 337/367-5306. www.lerosier.com. Cajun/Creole menu. Specializes in duck, rack of lamb, crabcakes. Own baking. Hrs: 11:30 am-2 pm, 6:30-10 pm; Sat from 6:30 pm. Closed hols. Res accepted. Wine. Lunch $16.95-$27.95; dinner $16.95-$27.95. Intimate dining rm overlooks garden; windows provide natural lighting. Cr cds: A, MC.

🄳

★ **LITTLE RIVER INN.** 1000 Parkview Dr (70563), Suite 16, in Bayou Landing Shopping Center. 337/367-7466. Cajun/Creole menu. Specializes in seafood and steaks. Hrs: 11 am-10 pm; Fri to 11 pm; Sat 5-11 pm.

Closed Sun; hols. Res accepted. Bar. Lunch, dinner $6-$16. Child's menu. Parking. Family-owned. Cr cds: A, C, D, DS, MC, V.

[D] [─⊰]

New Orleans (F-6)

Founded 1718 **Pop** 496,938 **Elev** 5 ft
Area code 504
Web www.neworleanscvb.com
Information New Orleans Metropolitan Convention & Visitors Bureau, 1520 Sugar Bowl Dr, 70112; 504/566-5011 or 800/672-6124

Suburbs Covington, Kenner, Metairie, Slidell. (See individual alphabetical listings.)

New Orleans is a beguiling combination of old and new. Named for the Duc d'Orléans, Regent of France, it was founded by Jean Baptiste Le Moyne, Sieur de Bienville. From 1763-1801 the territory of Louisiana was under Spanish rule. In 1801 Napoleon regained it for France, though no one in Louisiana knew of this until 1803, only 20 days before the Louisiana Purchase made it US territory. The first institution of higher learning in Louisiana, the College of Orleans, opened in New Orleans in 1811. The following year the first steamboat went into service between New Orleans and Natchez. Louisiana was admitted to the Union on April 30, 1812, with New Orleans as capital. The War of 1812 was over on January 8, 1815, when General Sir Edward Pakenham attacked New Orleans with a British force and was decisively defeated by General Andrew Jackson at Chalmette Plantation (now a National Historical Park). During the Civil War New Orleans was captured by Union forces and held under tight military rule for the duration.

The population is extremely cosmopolitan with its Creoles (descendants of the original French and Spanish colonists), Cajuns (descendants of the Acadians who were driven from Nova Scotia by the British in 1755), and other groups whose ancestors came from Italy, Africa, and the islands of the Caribbean.

Among tourists New Orleans is famous for the old-world charm of its French Quarter. Visitors come from all over the country to dine in its superb restaurants, listen to its incomparable jazz, and browse in Royal Street's fine antique shops. In the world of trade New Orleans is known as one of the busiest and most efficient international ports in the country. Over one hundred steamship lines dock here. As many as 52 vessels can be berthed at one time.

Transportation

Car Rental Agencies. See IMPORTANT TOLL-FREE NUMBERS.

Public Transportation. Streetcars & buses (Regional Transit Authority), phone 504/248-3900.

Rail Passenger Service. Amtrak 800/872-7245.

Airport Information

New Orleans International Airport. Information 504/464-0831; lost and found 504/464-2672; weather 504/828-4000.

What to See and Do

Auto or streetcar tour of universities and Audubon Park. Go SW on St. Charles Ave from Canal St; the St. Charles Ave streetcar can be picked at this same point. ¢ The first point of interest is

Lafayette Square. With statues of Franklin, Clay, and McDonough. A few blks beyond is

Lee Circle. Howard Ave, with a statue of Robert E. Lee by Alexander Doyle.

The Garden District. Bounded roughly by Magazine St, St. Charles, Jackson, and Washington Aves, was once the social center of New Orleans American (as opposed to Creole) aristocracy. There are still beautiful Greek Revival and Victorian houses with palms, magnolias, and enormous live oaks on the spacious grounds in this area. A walking tour of the Garden District, conducted by a national park ranger, departs from the corner of 1st & St. Charles (by appt; closed Mardi Gras, Dec 25). Next, continue on St. Charles about 3 mi to

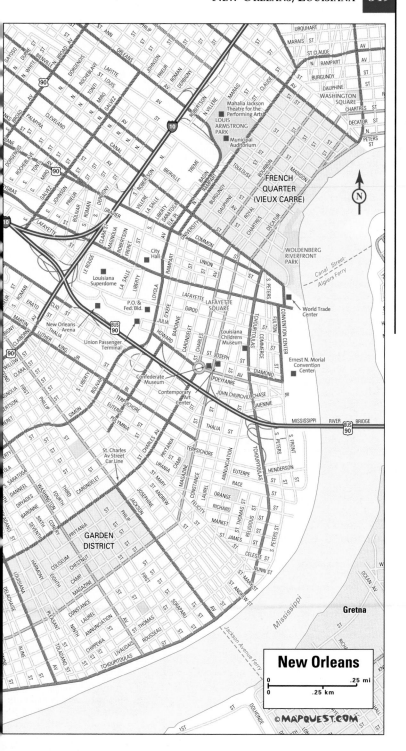

New Orleans

0   .25 mi
0   .25 km

© MAPQUEST.COM

Loyola University. (1912) 3,500 students. Bldgs on the 21-acre campus are Tudor Gothic in style. Tours are arranged through the Office of Admissions (Mon-Fri, twice daily). 6363 St. Charles Ave. Phone 504/865-3240 or 800/465-9652. Just beyond Loyola is

Tulane University. (1834) 11,500 students. The 110-acre main campus, located uptown, offers art galleries and other exhibits. The Tulane University Medical Center, located downtown, incl the School of Medicine, the School of Public Health and Tropical Medicine, and a 300-bed private hospital. 6823 St. Charles Ave. Phone 504/865-5000 (main campus), 504/588-5263 (Med Center). Directly across St. Charles Ave is

Audubon Park and Zoological Garden. This 400-acre park designed by the Olmstead brothers is nestled between St. Charles Ave and the Mississippi River and is surrounded by century-old live oak trees. The park features an 18-hole golf course, bicycle and jogging paths, and tennis courts. The zoo displays more than 1,800 animals in naturalistic settings. Among its attractions are the Louisiana swamp exhibit, the reptile "encounter," and the tropical bird house. (Daily; closed hols, Mardi Gras, and 1st Fri in May) 6500 Magazine St. Phone 504/861-2537. Zoo Cruise. Zoo admission ¢¢¢ Return to Canal Street via St. Charles Ave, either by automobile or streetcar.

Auto tour to City Park and Lake Pontchartrain. (allow 2-4 hrs) Drive NW on Esplanade or NE on North Carrollton Ave to the Esplanade entrance. Proceed along Lelong Dr to the

New Orleans Museum of Art. Incl among the special collections are the Peter Carl Fabergé jeweled *objets d'art;* early 19th-century Louisiana furnishings; Italian paintings from the 13th-18th centuries; 19th-century French art; ancient, European, and American glass; 18th-century portrait miniatures. Also incl is the art of Western Civilization from the pre-Christian era-present; the arts of Africa, the Far East, and pre-Columbian America; and an extensive photography collection. Special exhibits from various cultures and periods. (Tues-Sat; closed Mardi Gras and hols) 1 Collins Biebol City Park. Phone 504/488-2631. ¢¢¢ SW of the museum are the

Dueling Oaks. Where many an affair of honor was settled in the early 18th century. Just beyond are the

Bandstand and Peristyle. The latter an attractive classical structure. N of the Peristyle is a

Rose garden. Which also has azaleas, camellias, and gardenias. On the middle W edge of the park are the

Recreation areas. Four 18-hole golf courses, a driving range, lighted tennis courts, and lagoons for boating (fee). The N side of City Park is only a few blks from

Lake Pontchartrain. Take Wisner Blvd or Marconi Dr and stop off at Robert E. Lee Blvd near Wisner Blvd to see the

Southern Regional Research Center. Of the US Dept of Agriculture, 1100 Robert E. Lee Blvd, which finds and develops new and improved uses for southern farm crops. Guided tours by appt. (Mon-Fri; closed hols) 1150 Robert E. Lee Blvd. Phone 504/286-4200. **FREE** From the Research Center, the lake is 1½ mi away via Beauregard Ave. Follow Lakeshore Dr E to the

Patriotic Mardi Gras float

University of New Orleans. (1958) 16,084 students. On shores of Lake Pontchartrain, the 345-acre campus is the center of a residential area. Fine Arts Gallery (Mon-Fri; closed hols). 2000 Lake Shore Dr. Phone 504/280-6000. W along Lakeshore Dr are the

City Yacht Harbor, New Orleans Yacht Club, Southern Yacht Club. and a marina. About 2 mi W is the

Lake Pontchartrain Causeway. 24 mi long (toll). To return to the downtown area from the causeway, follow I-10.

Cemetery & Voodoo History Tour. Tour (approx 2 hrs) features St. Louis Cemetery #1, the oldest and most significant burial ground in New Orleans; visits to a practicing Voodoo priestess at her temple; Congo Square, the site of early slave gatherings and the home of legendary Voodoo Queen Marie Laveau. (Daily) At 334-B Royal St, in the courtyard of Cafe Beignet. Phone 504/947-2120. ¢¢¢

Confederate Museum. Collection of Civil War artifacts incl uniforms, weapons, medical instruments, battle flags; main hall contains section devoted to memorabilia of Jefferson Davis. (Mon-Sat; closed hols, Mardi Gras) 929 Camp St. Phone 504/523-4522. ¢¢

Destrehan Plantation. Built in 1787, this is the oldest plantation house left intact in the lower Mississippi Valley; ancient live oaks. Gift shop. Guided tours. (Daily; closed hols) Approx 11 mi W via LA 48 in Destrehan. ¢¢

Gray Line bus tours. Contact 1300 World Trade Center, 70130. 2 Canal St, Suite 13. Phone 504/569-1401 or 800/535-7786.

Historic New Orleans Custom House. Begun in 1848, interrupted by the Civil War, and completed in 1881, the Greek Revival bldg with neo-Egyptian details was used in part as an office by Major Gen Benjamin "Spoons" Butler during Union occupation, and in part as a prison for Confederate soldiers. A great dome was planned but the great weight of the existing bldg caused the foundation to settle and the dome was never completed. (In 1940 the bldg had sunk 30 inches, while the street level had been raised 3 ft.) Of particular interest is the famed Marble Hall, an architectural wonder. Self-guided tour. (Mon-Fri) Decatur & Canal Sts. **FREE**

Jean Lafitte National Historical Park and Preserve. Consists of 4 units: the New Orleans, Chalmette, Barataria, and Acadian. The Isleño, Chitimacha, and Tunica-Biloxi cultural centers operate through cooperative agreements with the park. (Daily) 365 Canal St, Suite 2400. Phone 504/589-3882. **FREE**

Acadian Unit. Consists of 3 Acadian cultural centers: Acadian Cultural Center (Lafayette), Wetlands Acadian Cultural Center (Thibodaux), and Prairie Acadian Cultural Center (Eunice). 501 Fisher Rd. For further info phone 318/232-0789. **FREE**

Barataria Preserve Unit. Visitor center has information desk, exhibits, movies. Trails through bottomland hardwood forest, swamp, and marsh. Guided and self-guided walks. Canoeing and fishing. (Daily; closed Dec 25) On W bank of the Mississippi, 15 mi S on LA 45 (Barataria Blvd). Phone 504/589-2330. **FREE**

Chalmette Unit. Scene of the 1815 Battle of New Orleans. Visitor center has audiovisual presentation of battle; museum; National Cemetery; two self-guided auto tour roads; field interpretation. (Daily; closed Mardi Gras, Dec 25) 6 mi E on St. Bernard Hwy (LA 46) in Chalmette (from Canal St take Rampart St, which merges into St. Claude Ave). Phone 504/589-4428. **FREE**

Chitimacha Cultural Center. (See FRANKLIN)

Isleño Center. Interprets history and contemporary culture of Canary Islanders who were settled here by the Spanish government in the late 1700s. Interpretive exhibits, info about self-guided auto tours to Isleño communities. (Wed-Sun; closed Mardi Gras, Dec 25) Approx 14 mi SE on LA 46. Phone 504/682-0862. **FREE**

New Orleans Unit. Walking tours which leave from the center incl the "Tour du Jour," which has a different theme each day; "History of New Orleans," an exploration of the French Quarter; "Faubourg Promenade," a tour of the Garden District (by appt) that departs from the corner of 1st & St. Charles Ave (on the St. Charles streetcar line). The Folklife/Visitor Center also offers exhibits and audiovisual programs; performances and demonstrations by traditional musicians, artists, and craftspeople; information about the ethnic population of the delta. Unit and tours (daily; closed Mardi Gras, Dec 25). Folklife/Visitor Center, 916 N Peters at Decatur St in French Quarter. Phone 504/589-2636. **FREE**

Longue Vue House & Gardens. A grand city estate furnished with original English and American antiques is located on eight acres of formal and picturesque gardens; changing exhibits in galleries and seasonal horticultural displays in gardens. (Daily; closed hols) 7 Bamboo Rd, I-10 Metairie Rd Exit. Phone 504/488-5488. ¢¢

Musée Conti—Wax Museum of Louisiana Legends. Costumed figures, incl Jean Lafitte, Andrew Jackson, and Marie Laveau with her voodoo dancers, depict the history and legends of New Orleans and the Louisiana Territory. Programs in French, German, Italian, Spanish, and Japanese. (Daily; closed Mardi Gras, Dec 25) 917 Conti St, in French Quarter. Phone 504/525-2605. ¢¢¢

National D-Day Museum. Opened June 6, 2000, this 70,500-sq-ft museum is devoted to D-Day and WWII memorabilia, oral histories, video, and animation. (Daily) 923 Magazine St. Phone 504/527-6012. ¢¢

❌ **New Orleans Historic Voodoo Museum.** Exhibits incl collection of photographs, masks, musical instruments, altars, and other items associated with the practice of voodoo. Gift shop. Guided tours; also walking tours (fee). (Daily) 724 Rue Dumaine, in French Quarter. Phone 504/523-7685. ¢¢

New Orleans Pharmacy Museum (*La Pharmacie Française*). (1823) Louis Dufilho, the first licensed pharmacist in the US, operated an apothecary shop here until 1867. Ground floor contains pharmaceutical memorabilia of 1800s incl apothecary jars filled with medicinal herbs and

voodoo powders, surgical instruments, pharmacy fixtures, and a black-and-rose Italian marble soda fountain (ca 1855). (Tues-Sun; closed hols) 514 Chartres St, in French Quarter. Phone 504/565-8027. ¢

Oak Alley Plantation. (1839) Quintessential antebellum, Greek Revival plantation house: *allee* of 300-yr-old live oaks lead to mansion surrounded by 1st- and 2nd-floor galleries supported by massive columns; interior remodeled in 1930s with antiques and modern furnishings of day. Featured in many films. Extensive grounds with many old trees. Picnicking, restaurant. Cottages. (Daily; closed Jan 1, Thanksgiving, Dec 25) W on I-10, Gramercy Exit 194, S on LA 641, W on LA 18. Phone 225/265-2151 or 800/44-ALLEY. ¢¢

Pitot House. (1799) One of the last remaining French Colonial/West Indies-style plantation houses along Bayou St. John. Residence of James Pitot, first elected mayor of incorporated New Orleans. Restored; furnished with antiques. (Wed-Sat; closed hols) 1440 Moss St. Phone 504/482-0312. ¢¢

Preservation Hall. Traditional New Orleans jazz concerts most eves. 726 St. Peter St. For schedule, fee info phone 504/522-2841.

Professional sports.

    NFL (New Orleans Saints). Louisiana Superdome, 5800 Airline Dr. Phone 504/733-0255.

River cruises. Daily excursions depart from the riverfront.

    Sternwheeler steamboat *Natchez* makes two-hr harbor cruises and evening dinner cruise. Jazz is featured on all cruises. New Orleans Steamboat Co, 1300 World Trade Center, 70130. Toulouse St. Wharf in the French Quarter behind Jackson Brewery. Phone 504/586-8777 or 800/233-2628. ¢¢¢¢-¢¢¢¢¢

    The river boat *John James Audubon* provides river transportation between the Aquarium of the Americas and the Audubon Zoo 7 mi upriver; round-trip or one-way, return may be made via St. Charles Avenue Streetcar (addl fee). Round-trip ticket price incl admission to both Audubon Zoo and Aquarium of the Americas. Phone 504/586-8777 or 800/233-2628. ¢¢¢¢

The sternwheelers **Delta Queen** and **Mississippi Queen** offer 3- to 12-night cruises on the Mississippi, Ohio, Cumberland, and Tennessee rivers yr-round. For details contact Delta Queen Steamboat Co, 30 Robin St Wharf, 70130-1890. Phone 504/586-0631 or 800/543-1949.

Paddlewheeler **Creole Queen** offers sightseeing cruises to Chalmette National Historical Park, site of the Battle of New Orleans; dinner and jazz cruises. The **Cajun Queen** offers harbor cruises from Aquarium of the Americas (1½-hr tour with narration and on-board alligators). For res contact New Orleans Paddlewheels, Inc, New Orleans International Cruise Ship Terminal, Poydras St Wharf, 70130. 610 S Peters. Phone 504/524-0814 or 504/529-4567. ¢¢¢-¢¢¢¢¢

Riverfront Area.

Riverfront Streetcar Line. Vintage streetcars follow a 1½ mi route along the Mississippi riverfront from Esplanade past the French Quarter to the World Trade Center, Riverwalk, Convention Center, and back. Exact change fare ¢ Between the streetcar line and the river, opp Jackson Square, is the

Moonwalk. This promenade atop the levee affords scenic views of the French Quarter, downtown and river. S of the Moonwalk is

Toulouse Street Wharf. Foot of Toulouse St and the river. Sales office and departure point for riverboat cruises and bus tours of city and countryside. S of the wharf is

Woldenberg Riverfront Park. Covering 17 acres on the riverfront, Woldenberg Park offers the city its first direct access to the river in 150 yrs; ships and paddlewheelers dock along the park. Between Toulouse & Canal Sts. In Woldenberg Park is

Aquarium of the Americas. A branch of the Audubon Institute, which also supervises the Audubon Zoo, the Aquarium of the Americas houses some 10,000 specimens representing more than 400 species; arranged around four ecosystems—Mississippi delta, Gulf of Mexico, Caribbean reef, and Amazon rain forest—the collections incl such exotic creatures as lemon sharks. River cruises are avail from the aquarium to Audubon Zoo. (Daily; closed Dec 25, also Mardi Gras) Along the river between Canal & Bienville Sts. Phone 504/861-2537. ¢¢¢ Across Canal St to the S is the

World Trade Center of New Orleans. Center houses offices of many maritime companies and foreign consulates involved in international trade. Revolving cocktail lounge on 33rd floor offers fine views of the city and river. Viewpoint observation deck on the 31st floor is accessed through an outside glass elevator located in lobby. (Daily; closed hols) 2 Canal St at river. Phone 504/525-2185. ¢ S of the World Trade Center are

Levee and docks. From the foot of Canal St turn right and walk along the busy docks to the coffee and general cargo wharves, which are most interesting. Smoking is forbidden in the dock area. Rides on the Canal Street Ferry are free. Along the docks are paddlewheel and other excursion boats. Continue S along riverfront to the

Riverwalk. This 1/2-mi-long festival marketplace has more than 140 national and local shops, restaurants and cafes. The Riverwalk structure was converted from world's fair pavilions. (Daily; closed Thanksgiving, Dec 25) 1 Poydras St. Phone 504/522-1555.

San Francisco Plantation. (1853-56) While a remarkable example of the "Steamboat Gothic" style in detail, the structure is typical of a Creole bldg: galleried with main living quarters on the second floor, dining rm, and various service rms on ground floor. Authentically restored, the interior features five decorated ceilings (two are original). Used as the setting of Frances Parkinson Keyes' novel *Steamboat Gothic*. (Daily; closed hols, Mardi Gras) Approx 35 mi W via US 61 or I-10 and LA 44 in Garyville. Phone 504/535-2341. ¢¢¢

St. Bernard State Park. Approx 350 acres near the Mississippi River with many viewing points of the river; network of man-made lagoons. Swimming. Picnicking. Playground. Trails. Camping. Standard fees.

(Daily) 501 St. Bernard Parkway. Phone 504/682-2101 or 888/677-7824. Per vehicle ¢

⭐ **St. Charles Avenue Streetcar.** The 13-mi line was begun in 1835; it is the oldest continuously operating street railway in the world. The line runs on St. Charles Ave from downtown through the Garden District, near the Audubon Zoo, and turns onto Carrollton Ave, the main thoroughfare of the uptown district, an area with many shops. Phone 504/248-3900. Exact change, one-way fare ¢

The Superdome. Dominating the skyline of downtown is the world's largest enclosed stadium arena; accommodates up to 87,500 people. Site of conventions, trade shows, concerts, the home games of the Saints football team, Tulane University football, and the annual Sugar Bowl Classic. 45-min tours (daily exc during some events; closed hols). 1500 Poydras. Phone 504/587-3808. ¢¢¢

⭐ **Walking tour in the Vieux Carré.** (Literally, "old square"), bounded by Iberville, North Rampart, and Esplanade Sts and the Mississippi River, usually called the **French Quarter.** Note that all street names change when they cross Canal and run into this old area of New Orleans. Entering the Quarter is to enter another world, one that seems to exist in a different time and move to a different rhythm. Begin the tour at

Jackson Square. Bordered by Chartres, St. Peter, Decatur, and St. Ann Sts. The area was established as a drill field in 1721 and was called the Place d'Armes until 1848, when it was renamed for Andrew Jackson, hero of the Battle of New Orleans. The statue of Jackson was the world's first equestrian statue with more than one hoof unsupported; the American sculptor, Clark Mills, had never seen an equestrian statue and therefore did not know the pose was thought impossible. The square and surrounding plaza is one of the best places in the Quarter for watching people and listening to sidewalk jazz musicians. S of the square, at St. Peter & Decatur, is

Jackson Brewery. This historic brewery was converted into a large retail, food, and entertainment complex with 75 shops and restaurants, outdoor dining, and a riverfront promenade. (Daily; closed Dec 25) Phone 504/566-7245. Facing across Jackson Square is the

Pontalba Building. Completed in 1850-51 by the Baroness Pontalba, to beautify the square. Still occupied and used as intended (duplex apartments above ground-floor offices and shops), the bldgs are now owned by the city and the Louisiana State Museum. **The 1850 House,** 523 St. Ann Street, is furnished in the manner of the period (Tues-Sun; closed hols). 523 St. Anne. Phone 504/524-9118. ¢¢ Across the square on Chartres St are the Cabildo and

St. Louis Cathedral. (1794) A minor basilica; this is the third church on this site and the oldest cathedral in the US (begun 1789, dedicated 1794). (Daily; closed Mardi Gras). For tour info phone 504/861-9521. **Donation** Behind the cathedral via Pirate's Alley (between the cathedral and the Cabildo) is the

Cathedral Garden. The monument in the center was erected in honor of French marines who died while nursing New Orleans' citizens during a yellow fever outbreak. Picturesque, narrow Pirate's Alley bordering the garden is a favorite spot for painters. On the Alley is the house in which William Faulkner lived when he wrote his first novel. The garden is also called St. Anthony's Square in memory of a beloved priest known as Pére Antoine. Return to the front of the cathedral via Pére Antoine's Alley, the little street opposite Pirate's Alley. Next to the cathedral is

The Presbytère. (1791) Architecturally similar to the Cabildo, the bldg was intended to house clergy serving the parish church. A series of fires kept the Presbytère incomplete until 1813, when it was finished by the US government. It is now a museum with changing and permanent exhibitions on Louisiana culture and history. The Presbytère, like the Cabildo, is part of the Louisiana State Museum complex. (Tue-Sun; closed hols) 751 Chartres St. Phone 504/568-

6968. ¢¢ E of the square, at the corner of St. Ann & Decatur, is the **French Market.** Which has been a farmers' market for nearly two centuries. The market's "Café du Monde" (see UNRATED DINING) is a popular and famous coffee stand specializing in café au lait (half coffee with chicory, half-hot milk) and beignets (square-shaped doughnuts sprinkled with powdered sugar). The cafe never closes (exc Dec 25), and café au lait and beignets are inexpensive. The downriver end of the French Market houses booths in which produce is sold. Just E of the market across Barracks St is

The Old US Mint. Designed by William Strickland in 1835, the mint produced coins for both the US and for the Confederate States. Today the Mint houses permanent exhibitions of jazz, Mardi Gras memorabilia, and the Louisiana State Museum's Historical Center, a research facility. (Tues-Sun; historical center also Mon, Tues by appt; closed hols) Esplanade and Decatur Sts. Phone 504/568-6968. ¢¢ From the Mint stroll up Esplanade past some unusual old houses to Chartres, then turn left and walk to the corner of Chartres & Ursulines. On the left side of the street is the Ursulines Convent, which dates back to 1749; on the right is

Beauregard-Keyes House and Garden. (ca 1826) Greek Revival, Louisiana raised cottage restored by its former owner, the novelist Frances Parkinson Keyes. Confederate Army Gen Pierre G.T. Beauregard lived here for more than a year following the Civil War. Exhibits incl the main house and servant quarters, which together form a handsome shaded courtyard. (Keyes actually lived informally in the servant quarters, which are filled with her books, antiques, and family heirlooms.) To the side of the main house is a formal garden (visible from both Chartres and Ursulines Sts) that is part of the guided tour conducted by costumed docents. (Mon-Sat; closed hols) 1113 Chartres St. Phone 504/523-7257. ¢¢ At Ursulines turn right, away from the river, and walk 1 blk to

Royal; turn right again. Midway down the blk is

Gallier House Museum. This elegant, Victorian town house by architect James Gallier, Jr has been restored to the period of his residency, 1860-68. (Daily; closed hols) 1118-32 Royal St. Phone 504/525-5661. ¢¢ Next walk 1½ blks up Royal (facing the business district's high-rise bldgs) to St. Philip, turn right and walk to Bourbon; on the corner is

"Lafitte's Blacksmith Shop." The origin of this structure has been lost in time, but it probably dates from 1772. By legend, it was once a blacksmith shop operated by the brothers Lafitte, infamous pirates. It is now a bar. 941 Bourbon St. Next, walk up Bourbon 1 blk to Dumaine, turn left and go 1 blk to

Madame John's Legacy. This is one of the oldest domestic bldgs in the Mississippi Valley, built about 1727, rebuilt 1788, restored 1981, and part of Louisiana State Museum (private). 632 Dumaine St. Return to Royal St, noticing throughout the French Quarter the beautiful cast-iron grillwork balconies, each with a distinctive theme in its pattern. Turn right on Royal and walk to

Maison Le Monnier. Built in 1811 and sometimes called the "skyscraper," this was the first bldg in the Vieux Carré more than 2 stories high. This house was used as the setting for George W. Cable's novel *Sieur George*. Notice the YLR, for Yves LeMonnier, worked into the grillwork. 640 Royal St (private). Across the street is

Adelina Patti's House and Courtyard. Former residence of the famous 19th-century opera prima donna. 631 Royal St.

Court of Two Sisters. This restaurant, with its beautiful, spacious patio, is a delightful place to drop in for a drink or a cup of tea. 613 Royal St.

Mid-19th-Century Townhouse. Headquarters of New Orleans Spring Fiesta Association (see ANNUAL EVENTS). Early 19th-century antiques, Victorian pieces; *objets d'art*. Guided tours (Mon-Fri afternoons). 826 St. Ann St. Phone 504/581-1367. ¢¢

Historic New Orleans Collection. (Museum and Research Center). Comprised of several historic bldgs housing a museum and comprehensive research center for state and local history. Main exhibition gallery presents changing displays on Louisiana's history and culture. The 1792 Merieult House features a pictorial history of New Orleans and Louisiana; the Williams Residence shows the elegant lifestyle of the collection's founders. There is also a touch tour for the visually impaired. (Tues-Sat; closed hols) No children under 12 in Williams Residence. 533 Royal St. Phone 504/523-4662. Gallery **FREE**. Guided tours of Merieult and Williams houses ¢

Brulatour Courtyard. 520 Royal St, is lined with interesting shops. Turn right at St. Louis Street and walk ½ blk to

Antoine's. In existence since 1840, Antoine's has been featured in novels and films and is where oysters Rockefeller was invented—"a dish so rich it was named Rockefeller." 713 St. Louis St. Continue on St. Louis 1½ blks, crossing Bourbon St, to the

Hermann-Grima Historic House. (1831) The Georgian design reflects the post-Louisiana Purchase American influence on traditional French and Spanish styles in the Quarter; the furnishings typify a well-to-do lifestyle during the period 1831-60. The restored house has elegant interiors, 2 landscaped courtyards, slave quarters, a stable, and a working, period kitchen; Creole cooking demonstrations on open hearth (Oct-May, Thurs). Tours. (Mon-Sat; closed hols) 820 St. Louis St. Phone 504/525-5661. ¢¢ Next, return to Royal and turn right to

Casa Faurie (Brennan's). The mansion (ca 1795) was built by an ancestor of French artist Edgar Degas. It later became headquarters of the Banque de la Louisiane; note the monogram, BL, worked into the grillwork. In 1819 the house was sold to Martin Gordon and became one of the social centers of the city; in 1828 Gen Andrew Jackson was

honored with a banquet in the house. Today the Casa Faurie is Brennan's, a distinctive restaurant, especially famous for its breakfasts; drinks are served on the patio (see RESTAURANTS). Across the street, the white marble bldg is the old US Circuit Court of Appeals. 417 Royal St. The next corner, Royal & Conti, was the city's original

Center of Banking. The old Louisiana State Bank, 403 Royal, was designed in 1821 by Benjamin Latrobe, one of the architects of the Capitol in Washington. The 343 Royal bldg was completed in the early 1800s for the old Bank of the United States. The old Bank of Louisiana, 334 Royal, was built in 1826; it is now the French Quarter Police Station. At the corner of Royal & Bienville turn right, away from the river, 4 blks to North Rampart, turn right and walk 5 blks to

Louis Armstrong Park. To the left of the entrance—built to resemble a Mardi Gras float—is a stand of very old live oak trees. This area was originally known as Congo Square, where slaves were permitted to congregate on Sunday afternoons; it was also the scene of voodoo rites. After the Civil War the square was named for Gen P.G.T. Beauregard. Louis Armstrong Park, which incl an extensive water garden that focuses upon a larger-than-life-size statue of Armstrong, was expanded from the original square and contains the municipal auditorium and the Theatre of the Performing Arts. To return to Jackson Square, walk back toward the river on St. Peter St.

For a more thorough tour of the many interesting points in the Vieux Carré and surrounding area see the *New Orleans Walking and Driving Tour* brochure, avail at the Visitor Information Center. 1520 Sugar Bowl. Phone 504/566-5011.

Annual Events

Sugar Bowl College Football Classic. Superdome. Jan 1. Phone: 504/525-8573.

Mardi Gras. (Literally "Fat Tuesday," the day before Lent begins) The New Orleans Carnival, perhaps the most famous celebration in the

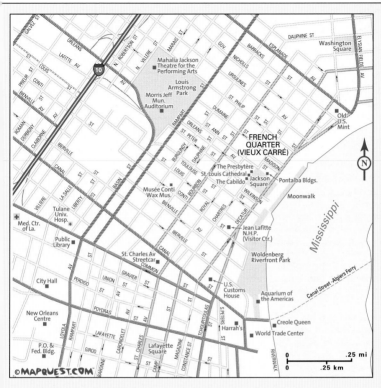

FRENCH QUARTER

Any French Quarter walking tour should start in Jackson Square, the beautiful city park that is the heart of the Vieux Carre, or Old Square. The square, peopled with street performers, brass bands, and fortune-tellers, is surrounded by the stately St. Louis Cathedral and the symmetrical Pontalba Buildings, some of which house the Louisiana State Museum. From behind the cathedral, a stroll down Royal Street would take in more of the Quarter's historic European architecture and wonderful window-shopping. A turn down Ursulines Avenue towards the river takes you through the residential section of the district and past the 1745 Ursuline Convent, the oldest building in the Quarter. Stop at the French Market, with sidewalk cafes, live bands, stands of exotic foodstuffs, and flea-market souvenirs; and the National Park Service Jean Lafitte Visitor Center (put your name in for their next guided tour). The Old US Mint is a must-see for the jazz exhibit alone, which illuminates the city's famous musical history. From here you can catch the Riverfront Streetcar, which rides along the levee and provides a view of the dramatic bend in the Mississippi River that gave the city the nickname "Crescent City," or walk along the levee's Moonwalk promenade to return to Jackson Square. Celebrate your introduction to New Orleans with coffee and beignets at Cafe du Monde across from the square.

United States, officially opens 2 wks before Shrove Tuesday and incl torchlight parades, street dancing, costume balls, masquerades. It is handled by 60 secret societies called "Krewes," of which the oldest is that of Comus, organized in 1857. Mardi Gras Day, Feb.

Spring Fiesta. Opening night parade; crowning of Queen and court. Tours of various New Orleans private houses and plantations. Blooming gardens; costumed hosts and hostesses. Contact 826 St. Ann St, 70116; 504/581-1367. Mid-Mar.

Louisiana Crawfish Festival. Rides, games, live entertainment, and an array of dishes featuring crawfish. Late Mar. Phone 504/271-3836.

French Quarter Festival. Features free musical entertainment; numerous stages throughout Quarter; jazz brunch; race (5 km); children's activities. Phone 504/522-5730. Apr. 100 Conti.

New Orleans Jazz and Heritage Festival. Outdoor wkend activities at Fair Grounds Race Track with Louisiana specialty foods, crafts and 11 stages of simultaneous music, incl traditional and contemporary jazz, rock, Gospel, rhythm and blues, ragtime, country and western, Cajun, folk, Latin, and Afro-Caribbean. Evening concerts in various concert halls and clubs. Contact PO Box 53407, 70153; 504/522-4786. Late Apr-early May. 1205 Northram Park.

Seasonal Event

Horse racing. Fair Grounds Racetrack. (1872) 1751 Gentilly Blvd, 5 mi N from French Quarter. America's third-oldest racetrack. Pari-mutuel betting. Jackets required in clubhouse. Phone 504/944-5515; for clubhouse res phone 504/943-2200. Wed-Sun late Nov-Mar.

City Neighborhoods

Many of the restaurants, unrated dining establishments, and some lodgings listed under New Orleans incl neighborhoods as well as exact street addresses. Geographic descriptions of these areas are given.

Central Business District. Fronting on the Mississippi River and bounded by Canal St, I-10 and US 90. **North of Central Business Dis-**

trict: N of I-10. **West of Central Business District:** W of I-10/US 90 Business.

Faubourg Marigny. Adj to the French Quarter across Esplanade Ave; S of McShane Place, W of Elysian Fields, and NE of Esplanade Ave.

French Quarter (Vieux Carré). Fronting on the Mississippi River and bounded by Esplanade Ave, N Rampart, Canal, and Decatur Sts.

Garden District. S of St. Charles Ave, W of Jackson Ave, N of Magazine St, and E of Washington Ave.

Motels/Motor Lodges

★★ **AMBASSADOR HOTEL.** 535 Tchoupitoulas St (70130), in Central Business District. 504/527-5271; fax 504/527-5270; toll-free 888/527-5271. Email pkastanek@ahno.com. 111 rms, 4 story. S, D $59-$179; under 18 free; higher rates special events (3, 4-day min). Crib free. Pet accepted; $50 deposit. Valet parking $12. TV; cable Complimentary coffee in rms. Restaurant 7 am-10 pm. Rm serv 6 am-9 pm. Bar. Ck-out noon. Busines servs avail. In-rm modem link. Bellhops. Concierge. Airport transportation. Cr cds: A, C, D, DS, MC, V.

🅳 🐾 ⬜ ⬜ 🔥

★★ **BIENVILLE HOUSE HOTEL.** 320 Decatur St (70130), in French Quarter. 504/529-2345; fax 504/525-6079; toll-free 800/535-7836. Email rtrahant@bienvillehouse.com. 83 rms, story. Sep-May: S, D $120-$210; each addl $20; suites $275-$650; under 18 free; lower rates rest of yr. Crib free. Valet parking $11-$15. TV; cable, VCR avail. Pool. Complimentary continental bkfst. Coffee in rms. Restaurant 11:30 am-2 pm, 5 pm-midnight. Ck-out noon. Meeting rms. Business servs avail. Bellhops. Valet serv. Health club privileges. Ba conies. Courtyard surrounds pool. Late 18th century bldg. Cr cds: A, C, D, DS, MC, V.

🅳 ⬜ 🏋 ⬜ 🔥

★★★ **CHATEAU LEMOYNE FRENCH QUARTER.** 301 Rue Dauphine St (70112), in French Quarter. 504/581-1303; fax 504/525-8531, res 800/747-3279; toll-free 800/447-2830. Email dhenrickle@bristolhotels. com. 171 rms, 5 story. S $89-$195; D $99-$225; each addl $15; suites

$205-$450; under 18 free; higher rates special events. Crib free. Valet parking $17. TV; cable (premium). Heated pool; poolside serv. Restaurant 6:30 am-2 pm, 6-10 pm. Bar 7 am-10 pm. Ck-out 11 am. Meeting rms. Business servs avail. In-rm modem link. Bellhops. Valet serv. Concierge. Health club privileges. Some bathrm phones in suites. Balconies. Tropical courtyards. Cr cds: A, C, D, DS, JCB, MC, V.

D ⌇ ⬒ 🔥

★ **FRENCH QUARTER COURT-YARD HOTEL.** *1101 N Rampart St (70116), in French Quarter.* 504/522-7333; fax 504/522-3908; toll-free 800/290-4233. Email fqch@neworleans.com. 51 rms, 2-3 story. S, D $69-$259; under 17 free; higher rates special events. Pet accepted. Valet parking $10. TV; cable. Pool; poolside serv. Complimentary continental bkfst. Restaurant nearby. Bar open 24 hrs. Ck-out noon. Business servs avail. Bellhops. Valet serv. Some balconies. Cr cds: A, C, D, DS, MC, V.

D 🐕 ⌇ ⬒ 🔥

★ ★ **HISTORIC FRENCH MARKET INN.** *501 Rue Decatur (70130), in French Quarter.* 504/561-5621; fax 504/569-0619; toll-free 888/211-3447. 92 units, 4 story. S, D $79-$299; each addl $10; suites $149-$399; higher rates special events. TV; cable (premium). Whirlpool. Complimentary continental bkfst. Restaurant nearby. Bar. Ck-out 11 am. Business servs avail. In-rm modem link. Bellhops. Concierge. Microwave avail. Built in 1753 for the Baron de Pontalba; served as residence for French governor. Cr cds: A, C, D, DS, MC, V.

D ⌇ 👤 ⬒ 🔥

★ ★ **HOLIDAY INN EXPRESS.** *10020 I-10 Service Rd (70127), I-10 Exit 244, N of Central Business District.* 504/244-9115; fax 504/244-9150; res 800/821-4009; toll-free 800/465-4329. 142 rms, 2 story. S, D $79-$129; each addl $10; suites $150; family rates; higher rates special events. Crib free. TV; cable (premium). Pool. Complimentary continental bkfst. Coffee in rms. Ck-out noon. Coin lndry. Business servs avail. In-rm modem link. Exercise equipt. Refrigerators, microwaves. Cr cds: A, C, D, DS, JCB, MC, V.

D ⌇ 👤 ⬒ 🔥 SC

★ ★ **HOTEL DE LA MONNAIE.** *405 Esplanade Ave (70116), in Faubourg Marigny.* 504/947-0009; fax 504/945-6841. 53 rms, 4 story. S $140; D $190; higher rates special events. Crib free. Pet accepted, some restrictions; $50. Garage parking $5.75. TV; cable (premium). Complimentary coffee in rms. Restaurant nearby. Ck-out noon. Business servs avail. Bellhops. Exercise equipt. Wading pool. Refrigerators, microwaves. Cr cds: A, C, MC, V.

🐕 👤 ⬒ 🔥

★ ★ ★ **LA QUINTA INN & SUITES.** *301 Camp St (70130).* 504/598-9977; fax 504/598-9978; toll-free 800/531-5900. Email lq0983gm@laquinta.com. 166 rms, 14 story, 16 suites. Jan-May, Sep-Nov: S, D $269; each addl $30; suites $399; under 17 free; lower rates rest of yr. Pet accepted, some restrictions. Valet parking avail. Pool, whirlpool. TV; cable (premium). Complimentary continental bkfst, coffee in rms, newspaper, toll-free calls. Restaurant 7:30 am-10:30 pm. Bar. Ck-out noon, ck-in 3 pm. Meeting rm. Bellhops. Dry cleaning, coin lndry. Exercise equipt. Golf. Tennis, 2 courts. Bike rentals. Video games. Cr cds: A, C, D, DS, MC, V.

D 🐕 🛇 👤 ⌇ ⬒ 👤 ⬒ 🔥

★ ★ ★ **LE RICHELIEU IN THE FRENCH QUARTER.** *1234 Chartres St (70116), in French Quarter.* 504/529-2492; fax 504/524-8179; toll-free 800/535-9653. www.lerichelieuhotel.com. 86 rms, 4 story. S $85-$140; D $95-$150; each addl $15; suites $170-$475; higher rates special events. Crib free. TV, VCR avail. Pool; poolside serv. Restaurant 7 am-9 pm. Bar to 1 am. Ck-out 1 pm. Business servs avail. Bellhops. Valet serv. Concierge. Health club privileges. Refrigerators. Balconies. Landscaped courtyard. Cr cds: A, DS, MC, V.

D ⌇ 🔥

★ **TRAVELODGE HOTEL WEST.** *2200 Westbank Expy (70058).* 504/366-5311; fax 504/368-2774; res 800/578-7878; toll-free 800/365-8669. Email tlneworlns@aol.com. 212 rms, 2 story. S $64; D $70; under 17 free;

wkly rates; higher rates special events (2-,4-day min). Crib free. TV; cable (premium). Complimentary coffee in rms. Restaurant 6 am-10 pm. Bar from 4 pm. Ck-out noon. Meeting rm. Business servs avail. In-rm modem link. Bellhops. Coin lndry. 3 pools. Many refrigerators, microwaves. Cr cds: A, C, D, DS, MC, V.

Hotels

★★ BOURBON ORLEANS - A WYNDHAM HISTORIC HOTEL.

717 Orleans St (70116), I-10 Exit 235 A, in French Quarter. 504/523-2222; fax 504/525-8166; res 800/996-3426. Email dmollov@wyndham.com; www. bourbonorleans.com. 168 rms, 6 story, 48 suites. Jan-May, Sep-Nov: S $219; D $239; each addl $20; suites $269; under 18 free; lower rates rest of yr. Valet parking avail. Pool. TV; cable (premium). Complimentary coffee in rms, newspaper. Restaurant 7 am-10 pm. Bar. Ck-out noon, ck-in 4 pm. Meeting rms. Bellhops. Concierge. Dry cleaning. Exercise privileges. Golf. Tennis. Cr cds: A, D, DS, JCB, MC, V.

★ CHATEAU MOTOR HOTEL.

1001 Rue Chartres (70116), in French Quarter. 504/524-9636; fax 504/525-2989. Email cmhnola@aol.com; www. chateauhotel.com. 45 rms, 2 story, 5 suites. S $79-$99; D $99-$119; each addl $10; suites $149-$165; under 18 free; higher rates special events. Crib free. TV; cable (premium). Pool. Restaurant 7 am-3 pm. Bar. Ck-out 1 pm. Business servs avail. Bellhops. Valet serv. Valet parking. Made up of 18th-century bldgs around courtyard. Cr cds: A, DS, MC, V.

★★★ CHATEAU SONESTA.

800 Iberville St (70112), in French Quarter. 504/586-0800; fax 504/586-1987; toll-free 800/SONESTA. Email reserv@ chateausonesta.com; www.chateau sonesta.com. 239 rms, 4 story, 12 suites. Jan-May, Oct-Nov: S, D $270; each addl $40; suites $650; under 17 free; lower rates rest of yr. Crib avail. Valet parking avail. Pool. TV; cable (premium), VCR avail. Complimentary coffee in rms, newspaper. Restaurant 11 am-midnight. Bar. Ck-out noon, ck-in 3 pm. Meeting rms.

Business center. Bellhops. Concierge. Dry cleaning. Gift shop. Salon/barber. Exercise privileges. Golf. Tennis. Picnic facilities. Video games. Cr cds: A, C, DS, JCB, V.

★★★ DAUPHINE ORLEANS HOTEL.

415 Dauphine St (70112), in French Quarter. 504/586-1800; fax 504/586-1409; toll-free 800/521-7111. Email fohfq@aol.com; www.dauphine orleans.com. 104 rms, 4 story, 7 suites. Jan-May, Sep-Nov: S, D $179; each addl $15; suites $359; under 17 free; lower rates rest of yr. Crib avail, fee. Valet parking avail. Pool. TV; cable (premium). Complimentary continental bkfst, newspaper. Restaurant nearby. Bar. Ck-out noon, ck-in 3 pm. Meeting rms. Bellhops. Concierge. Dry cleaning. Exercise equipt. Golf, 18 holes. Video games. Cr cds: A, D, DS, JCB, MC, V.

★★★ DOUBLETREE HOTEL.

300 Canal St (70140), in Central Business District. 504/581-1300; fax 504/522-4100; toll-free 800/222-8733. www. dtree.com. 363 rms, 17 story. S, D $99-$225; each addl $20; suites $250-$1,500; under 18 free. Crib free. Valet parking $16. TV; cable (premium). Pool; poolside serv. Coffee in rms. Restaurant 6:30 am-10 pm; Fri, Sat to 11 pm. Bar from 11 am. Ck-out noon. Convention facilities. Business center. Exercise equipt. Adj to French Quarter, convention center, and Aquarium of the Americas. Cr cds: A, C, D, DS, ER, MC, V.

★★★ EMBASSY SUITES HOTEL NEW ORLEANS.

315 Julia St (70130), in Central Business District. 504/525-1993; fax 504/522-3044; toll-free 800/362-2779. Email sales@ embassyneworleans.com; www.embassy neworleans.com. 282 suites, 16 story. S, D $200-$255; under 18 free. Crib free. Valet parking $15. TV; cable (premium), VCR avail. Heated pool; whirlpool, poolside serv. Complimentary full bkfst, coffee in rms. Restaurant 11:30 am-2 pm, 5-10 pm. Bar noon-midnight. Ck-out noon. Meeting rms. Business servs avail. In-rm modem link. Concierge. Gift shop. Exercise equipt. Game rm.

Refrigerators, microwaves. Balconies. Cr cds: A, DS, MC, V.

⬛ 🏊 🏃 ⬛ 🔥 SC

★★★ **FAIRMONT.** *123 Baronne St (70112), ½ blk off Canal St between University Place and Baronne, in Central Business District.* 504/529-7111; fax 504/522-2303; res 800/866-5577. www.fairmont.com. 615 rms, 12 story, 85 suites. Feb-May, Sep-Nov: S, D $249; each addl $30; suites $450; under 18 free; lower rates rest of yr. Crib avail. Pet accepted, some restrictions. Valet parking avail. Pool. TV; cable (premium). Complimentary newspaper. Restaurant 6 am-10 pm. Rm serv 24 hrs. Bar. Conference center, meeting rms. Business center. Bellhops. Concierge. Dry cleaning. Gift shop. Salon/barber. Exercise equipt. Golf. Tennis, 2 courts. Supervised children's activities. Video games. Cr cds: A, D, DS, MC, V.

⬛ 🏊 🏃 🍴 🏊 🏃 🎾 ⬛ 🔥

★★ **HAMPTON INN & SUITES-CONVENTION CENTER LOCATION.** *1201 Convention Center Blvd (70130).* 504/566-9990; fax 504/566-9997; res 800/292-0653. www.new orleans.com/hampton. 212 rms, 8 story, 76 suites. Jan-May, Oct-Nov: S $200; D $225; each addl $15; suites $425; under 18 free; lower rates rest of yr. Crib avail, fee. Valet parking avail. Pool. TV; cable (premium), VCR avail, CD avail. Complimentary continental bkfst, coffee in rms, newspaper, toll-free calls. Restaurant nearby. Bar. Ck-out 11 am, ck-in 3 pm. Meeting rms. Business center. Bellhops. Concierge. Dry cleaning, coin lndry. Free airport transportation. Exercise equipt. Picnic facilities. Cr cds: A, C, D, DS, MC, V.

⬛ 🏊 🏃 ⬛ 🔥 🏃

★★★ **HILTON NEW ORLEANS RIVERSIDE.** *2 Poydras St (70140), at the Mississippi River, in Central Business District.* 504/561-0500; fax 504/568-1721; res 800/HILTONS. Email valerie. miller@hilton.com. 1,600 rms, 29 story. S $170-$270; D $195-$295; each addl $25; suites from $490; wkend packages. Crib free. Valet parking $16. TV; cable (premium). 2 heated pools; whirlpool, poolside serv. Restaurant 6-2 am. Rm serv 24 hrs. Ck-out noon. Convention facilities. Business center. In-rm modem link. Concierge. Gift shop. Barber, beauty shop. Indoor, outdoor tennis, pro. Exercise rm; sauna. Minibars. Connected to riverwalk. Luxury level. Cr cds: A, C, D, DS, ER, JCB, MC, V.

⬛ 🏄 🐾 🏊 🍴 🏃 🏊 ⬛ 🔥 🏃

★★ **HOLIDAY INN DOWNTOWN-SUPERDOME.** *330 Loyola Ave (70112), in Central Business District.* 504/581-1600; fax 504/586-0833; res 800/465-4329; toll-free 800/535-7830. Email superdom@sprynet.com. 297 rms, 18 story. S $75-$150; D $90-$165; each addl $15; under 19 free. Crib free. Garage parking $11. TV; cable (premium). Heated pool. Restaurant 6 am-10 pm. Bar. Ck-out noon. Meeting rms. Business servs avail. In-rm modem link. Gift shop. Balconies. Luxury level. Cr cds: A, C, D, DS, JCB, MC, V.

⬛ 🏊 🏃 🏃 ⬛ 🔥 🏃

★★ **HOTEL CHATEAU DUPRE.** *131 Rue Decatur (70130), in French Quarter.* 504/569-0600; fax 504/569-0606. www.decaturhotels.com. 54 rms, 4 story, 11 suites. Sep-May: S, D $79-$249; suites $249-$399; under 12 free; higher rates special events; lower rates rest of yr. Crib free. Valet parking $13.95. TV; cable, VCR avail. Complimentary continental bkfst. Restaurant 7-2 am. Ck-out 11 am. Business servs avail. In-rm modem link. Refrigerator, microwave in suites. Cr cds: A, C, D, DS, JCB, MC, V.

⬛ 🏃 🏃 ⬛ 🔥

★★★ **HOTEL INTER-CONTINENTAL NEW ORLEANS.** *444 St. Charles Ave (70130), in Central Business District.* 504/525-5566; fax 504/523-7310; res 800/327-0200; toll-free 800/445-6563. Email neworleans@ interconti.com; www.new-orleans. interconti.com. 482 units, 15 story. S $225-$265; D $245-$285; each addl $20; suites $400-$2,000; under 17 free; wkend rates. Valet parking $17. TV; cable (premium). Heated pool; poolside serv. Restaurant 6 am-10 pm (see also VERANDA). Rm serv 24 hrs. Bars 11-1 am; entertainment. Convention facilities. Business center. In-rm modem link. Concierge. Gift shop. Beauty shop. Airport transportation. Exercise equipt. Massage. Bathrm phones; some refrigerators, minibars. Some balconies. Luxury level. Cr cds: A, DS, MC, V.

★★★ **HOTEL MAISON DE VILLE.** *727 Rue Toulouse (70130), in French Quarter.* 504/561-5858; fax 504/528-9939; toll-free 800/634-1600. Email maisondeville@travelbase.com; www.maisondeville.com. 16 rms, 3 story, 2 suites. Oct-May: S, D $225; suites $375; lower rates rest of yr. Valet parking avail. Pool. TV; cable, VCR avail. Complimentary continental bkfst, newspaper. Restaurant 6-10 pm. Ck-out noon, ck-in 3 pm. Fax servs avail. Bellhops. Concierge. Dry cleaning. Exercise privileges. Golf, 18 holes. Tennis, 20 courts. Cr cds: A, D, DS, MC, V.

★★★ **HOTEL MONTELEONE.** *214 Royal St (70130), in French Quarter.* 504/523-3341; fax 504/528-1019; toll-free 800/535-9595. Email reservations@hotelmonteleone.com; www.hotelmonteleone.com. 570 rms, 17 story, 27 suites. Sep-May: S $175; D $225; each addl $25; suites $1200; under 17 free; lower rates rest of yr. Crib avail. Valet parking avail. Pool, children's pool. TV; cable (DSS). Complimentary coffee in rms, newspaper. Restaurant 6:30 am-11 pm. Bar. Ck-out noon, ck-in 3 pm. Conference center, meeting rms. Business servs avail. Bellhops. Concierge. Dry cleaning. Gift shop. Salon/barber. Exercise privileges. Golf, 18 holes. Tennis, 4 courts. Bike rentals. Video games. Cr cds: A, C, D, DS, MC, V.

★★★ **HYATT REGENCY.** *500 Poydras Plz (70113), at Loyola, adj to Superdome, in Central Business District.* 504/561-1234; fax 504/587-4141; res 800/233-1234. www.hyatt.com. 1,184 rms, 32 story. S, D $119-$245; each addl $25; suites $350-$850; under 18 free; wkend rates. Crib free. Valet parking $15. TV; cable (premium), VCR avail. Heated pool; whirlpool, poolside serv. Restaurant 6 am-midnight. Bars 11-2 am. Ck-out noon. Convention facilities. Business center. In-rm modem link. Concierge. Barber, beauty shop. Airport transportation. Exercise equipt. Connected to Superdome and shopping complex. Luxury level. Cr cds: A, D, DS, MC, V.

★ **INTERNATIONAL HOUSE.** *221 Camp St (70130).* 504/553-9550; fax 504/200-6532; toll-free 800/633-5770. Email resagent@ihhotel.com; www.ih hotel.com. 116 rms, 12 story, 3 suites. Jan-Apr, Oct-Nov: S, D $249; each addl $30; suites $399; under 17 free; lower rates rest of yr. Crib avail, fee. Valet parking avail. TV; cable (premium), VCR avail, CD avail. Complimentary newspaper. Restaurant. Bar. Meeting rms. Business servs avail. Bellhops. Concierge. Dry cleaning. Gift shop. Exercise equipt. Golf. Cr cds: A, C, D, DS, ER, JCB, MC, V.

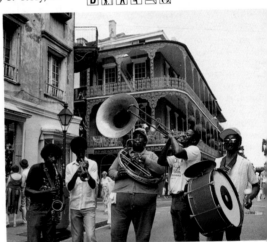

New Orleans jazz

★★★ **THE LAFAYETTE HOTEL.** *600 St. Charles Ave (70130), in Central Business District.* 504/524-4441; fax 504/523-7327; res 800/211-3447; toll-free 888/524-4441. ER. 44 rms, 5 story, 24 suites. S, D $155-$195; suites $275-$490; higher rates special events, wkends (2-day min), and Jazz Fest. Crib free. Valet parking $13. TV; cable (premium), VCR avail. Coffee in rms. Restaurant 7 am-11 pm. Bar. Ck-out 11 am. Business servs avail.

In-rm modem link. Concierge. Health club privileges. Minibars. Balconies. Renovated hotel first opened 1916. Cr cds: A, D, DS, JCB, MC, V.

★ **LANDMARK FRENCH QUARTER.** *920 N Rampart St (70116), in French Quarter. 504/524-3333; fax 504/522-8044; res 800/535-7862. Email info@nolahotels.com; www.nolahotels.com.* 100 rms, 3 story. S, D $99-$179; under 18 free; higher rates special events. Crib free. Garage $7. TV; cable. Pool; poolside serv. Restaurant 7-11 am, noon-midnight. Bar. Ck-out noon. Coin lndry. Business servs avail. Microwaves avail. Cr cds: A, DS, MC, V.

★★★ **LE MERIDIEN.** *614 Canal St (70130), in Central Business District. 504/525-6500; fax 504/525-8068; res 800/543-4300. www.lemeridien.com.* 494 rms, 30 story. S $185-$275; D $215-$295; each addl $30; suites $700-$1,700; under 16 free. Crib free. Garage $15; valet. TV; cable (premium), VCR avail. Heated pool; whirlpool, poolside serv. Coffee in rms. Restaurant (see LA GAULOISE BISTRO). Rm serv 24 hrs. Bar 4 pm-1 am; entertainment. Ck-out noon. Convention facilities. Business center. In-rm modem link. Concierge. Shopping arcade. Exercise rm; sauna. Bathrm phones, minibars. Adj to French Quarter. Cr cds: A, D, DS, JCB, MC, V.

★★★ **LE PAVILLON.** *833 Poydras St (70112), in Central Business District. 504/581-3111; fax 504/529-4415; res 800/535-9095. Email dclark@lepavillon.com; www.lepavillon.com.* 2190 rms, 10 story, 7 suites. Feb-May, Oct-Nov: S $350; D $370; each addl $20; suites $1495; under 17 free; lower rates rest of yr. Crib avail. Valet parking avail. Pool, whirlpool. TV; cable (DSS). Complimentary newspaper. Restaurant 6:30 am-10 pm. 24-hr rm serv. Bar. Conference center, meeting rms. Business servs avail. Bellhops. Concierge. Dry cleaning. Exercise privileges. Golf. Tennis, 16 courts. Cr cds: A, C, D, DS, MC, V.

★★★ **MAISON DUPUY.** *1001 Toulouse St (70112), at Burgundy, in French Quarter. 504/586-8000; fax 504/525-5334; res 800/535-9177. Email reservations@maisondupuy.com.* 200 rms, 5 story. S, D $205-$289; each addl $25; suites $240-$1500; under 17 free. Crib free. Valet parking $16. TV; cable (premium), VCR avail. Heated pool; poolside serv. Restaurant (see DOMINIQUE'S). Bar from 11 am. Ck-out 11 am. Valet serv. Meeting rms. Business servs avail. In-rm modem link. Exercise equipt. Balconies. Cr cds: A, C, D, DS, MC, V.

★★★ **NEW ORLEANS MARRIOTT.** *555 Canal St (70130), at Chartres St, in Central Business District. 504/581-1000. www.marriotthotels.com/msyla.* 1,290 units, 41 story. S, D $199-$219; each addl $20; suites $600-$1,200; under 17 free; wknd rates. Crib free. Valet parking $16. TV; cable (premium), VCR avail. Heated pool; wading pool, poolside serv. Restaurant 6:30 am-11 pm. Rm serv 24 hrs. Bar 10-2 am; entertainment. Ck-out noon. Coin lndry. Convention facilities. Business center. In-rm modem link. Concierge. Gift shop. Exercise equipt; sauna. Refrigerators avail. Adj to French Quarter. Luxury level. Cr cds: A, D, DS, MC, V.

★★★ **OMNI ROYAL CRESCENT.** *535 Gravier St (70130), in Central Business District. 504/527-0006; fax 504/523-0806; res 800/578-3200.* 98 rms, 8 story. S, D $229; suites $235-$335; under 18 free; higher rates special events. Valet parking $16. TV; cable (premium), VCR avail (movies). Restaurant. Rm serv 24 hrs. Ck-out noon. Meeting rms. Business servs avail. In-rm modem link. Concierge. Exercise equipt; sauna. Health club privileges. Pool; whirlpool, poolside serv. Cr cds: A, D, DS, MC, V.

★★★ **OMNI ROYAL ORLEANS.** *621 St. Louis St (70140), in French Quarter. 504/529-5333; fax 504/529-7089; res 800/843-6664. Email csanders@omnihotels.com; www.omnihotels.com.* 321 rms, 7 story, 25 suites. Sep-May: S, D $319; each addl $25; suites $459; under 17 free; lower rates rest of yr. Crib avail. Valet parking avail. Pool. TV; cable (premium), VCR avail. Complimentary coffee in rms, newspaper. Restaurant. Rm serv 24 hrs. Bar. Conference center, meeting rms. Business center. Bellhops. Concierge. Dry cleaning. Gift shop. Salon/barber. Exercise equipt. Golf. Video games. Cr cds: A, C, D, DS, MC, V.

★★★ **PELHAM HOTEL.** *444 Common St (70130), in Central Business District. 504/522-4444; fax 504/539-9010; res 888/211-3447. Email pelhamhotel@decaturhotel.com.* 60 air-cooled rms, 4 story. S, D $79-$325; each addl $10; suites $399-$499; under 17 free; higher rates special events. Crib $25. Valet parking $14. TV; cable (premium), VCR avail. Restaurant 7 am-10 pm. Bar. Ck-out 11 am. Meeting rms. Business servs avail. In-rm modem link. Concierge. Tennis privileges. Individually decorated rms; antiques, marble baths. Cr cds: A, DS, MC, V.

★★★ **PONTCHARTRAIN HOTEL.** *2031 St. Charles Ave (70140), in Garden District. 504/524-0581; fax 225/524-7828; toll-free 800/777-6193. www.pontchartrainhotel.com.* 104 rms, 12 story. S, D $130-$185; each addl $25; 1-2 bedrm suites $275-$600; under 12 free. Crib free. Valet parking $13. TV; cable, VCR avail. Restaurants 7 am-2:30 pm, 5:30-10 pm. Rm serv 24 hrs. Bar 11-1 am; entertainment Thurs-Sat. Ck-out 1 pm. Meeting rms. In-rm modem link. Airport transportation. Health club privileges. Many refrigerators; some wet bars. Landmark of historic neighborhood; rms are individually decorated with an antique motif. Cr cds: A, D, DS, MC, V.

★★ **PROVINCIAL HOTEL.** *1024 Rue Chartres (70116), in French Quarter. 504/581-4995; fax 504/581-1018; toll-free 800/535-7922. Email info@hotelprovincial.com; www.hotelprovincial.com.* 105 rms, 2-4 story. S, D $160-$185; each addl $20; suites from $225; under 17 free; higher rates special events. Crib free. Parking $10. TV; cable (premium), VCR avail. 2 pools; poolside serv. Complimentary coffee in lobby. Restaurant 7 am-10 pm. Bar. Ck-out noon. Meeting rm. Business servs avail. In-rm modem link. Valet serv. Microwaves avail. Balconies. Carriageway entrance; antique furnishings. Cr cds: A, DS, MC, V.

★★ **PRYTANIA PARK HOTEL.** *1525 Prytania St (70130), in Garden District. 504/524-0427; fax 504/522-2977; toll-free 800/862-1984. Email prytaniapk@aol.com; www.prytania parkhotel.com.* 62 units, 2 story, 49 kits. S $99-$109; D $109-$139; suites $119-$169; each addl $10; under 12 free; summer packages. Crib free. TV; cable. Complimentary continental bkfst. Restaurant nearby. Ck-out noon. Business servs avail. Health club privileges. Free parking. Refrigerators; some microwaves. Some balconies. Cr cds: A, DS, MC, V.

★★ **QUALITY INN MIDTOWN.** *3900 Tulane Ave (70119), W of Central Business District. 504/486-5541; fax 504/488-7440; toll-free 800/486-5541. Email jamiek@i-10.net; www.bigeasy hotels.com.* 102 rms, 4 story. S, D $99-$138; under 18 free; higher rates special events (2-,4-day min). TV; cable (premium). Complimentary coffee in rms. Restaurant 7 am-2 pm, 5-10:30 pm. Bar 11 am-midnight; Sat, Sun from 4 pm. Ck-out 11 am. Meeting rms. Business servs avail. In-rm modem link. Coin lndry. Free parking. Whirlpool. Some refrigerators, microwaves. Cr cds: A, DS, MC, V.

★★ **THE QUEEN AND CRESCENT HOTEL.** *344 Camp St (70130), in Central Business District. 504/587-9700; fax 504/587-9701; toll-free 800/975-6652. Email gboulmay@visitnola.com; www.queenandcrescenthotel.com.* 196 rms, 12 story, 1 suite. Jan-May, Sep-Nov: S $139; D $159; each addl $15; suites $179; under 12 free; lower rates rest of yr. Crib avail. Valet parking avail. TV; cable. Complimentary continental bkfst, newspaper. Restaurant nearby. Bar. Ck-out noon, ck-in 4 pm. Meeting rms. Business center. Bellhops. Concierge. Dry cleaning. Exercise equipt. Golf. Tennis, 12 courts. Video games. Cr cds: A, C, D, DS, MC, V.

★★★ **RADISSON.** *1500 Canal St (70112), in Central Business District.* 504/522-4500; fax 504/522-3627; res 800/333-3333. www.radissonnew orleans.com. 759 rms, 18 story. S, D $109-$189; each addl $15; suites $150-$350; under 18 free; higher rates special events. Valet parking (fee). TV; cable (premium). Pool; whirlpool, poolside serv. Complimentary coffee in lobby. Restaurant 6 am-2 pm, 5-10 pm. Bar. Ck-out 11 am. Coin lndry. Meeting rms. Business center. Concierge. Gift shop. Exercise equipt. Refrigerators in suites. Cr cds: A, C, D, DS, MC, V.

★★ **RAMADA.** *2203 St. Charles Ave (70140), in Garden District.* 504/566-1200; fax 504/581-1352; toll-free 800/265-1856. 133 units, 9 story. S, D $89-$189; each addl $10; suites $150-$250; under 18 free; higher rates special events. Crib free. TV; cable (premium). Complimentary coffee in lobby. Restaurant 6:30 am-2 pm, 5-10 pm. Bar 4-11 pm. Ck-out noon. Meeting rms. Business servs avail. In-rm modem link. Valet parking $10. Health club privileges. Some refrigerators; microwaves avail. Cr cds: A, C, D, DS, MC, V.

★★ **RAMADA ON CANAL.** *1732 Canal St (70112), in Central Business District.* 504/412-4000; fax 504/529-1609; res 800/236-6119. 1,036 rms, 17 story, 140 suites. S, D $190-$210; each addl $10; suites $250-$500; under 18 free; higher rates special events. Crib free. Valet parking $11. TV; cable (premium). Bar. Ck-out noon. Meeting rms. Business servs avail. Refrigerators, microwaves avail. Cr cds: A, D, DS, MC, V.

★★★ **ROYAL SONESTA.** *300 Bourbon St (70130), in French Quarter.* 504/586-0300; fax 504/586-0335; res 800/766-3782. Email reserv@royal sonestano.com; www.royalsonestano.com. 500 rms, 35 suites. Sep-May: each addl $40; lower rates rest of yr. Crib avail. Pet accepted, some restrictions, fee. Parking garage. Pool. TV; cable (premium). Complimentary newspaper. Restaurant 7 am-11 pm. Bar. Ck-out noon, ck-in 3 pm. Conference center, meeting rms. Business center. Bellhops. Concierge. Dry cleaning. Gift shop. Exercise equipt. Golf. Cr cds: A, C, D, DS, MC, V.

★★★ **SHERATON NEW ORLEANS HOTEL.** *500 Canal St (70130), adj to French Quarter, in Central Business District.* 504/525-2500; fax 504/595-5552; res 800/325-3535; toll-free 800/253-6156. Email sheraton_new_orleans@sheraton.com; www.sheraton.com/neworleans. 1,102 rms, 49 story. S $130-$215; D $155-$239; each addl $25; suites from $250; under 18 free. Crib free. Valet parking $16. TV; cable (premium), VCR avail (movies). Pool; poolside serv. Complimentary coffee in rms. Restaurants 6:30-11 pm. Rm serv 24 hrs. Bar from 11 am; entertainment. Ck-out noon. Convention facilities. Business center. In-rm modem link. Concierge. Shopping arcade. Exercise equipt. Microwaves avail. Cr cds: A, DS, MC, V.

★★★ **ST. LOUIS HOTEL.** *730 Bienville St (70130), in French Quarter.* 504/581-7300; fax 504/524-8925; toll-free 800/535-9111. Email reservations@stlouishotel.com; www.stlouishotel.com. 81 rms, 5 story, 4 suites. Jan-May, Sep-Nov: S, D $199; each addl $20; suites $269; under 16 free; lower rates rest of yr. Valet parking avail. TV; cable (premium). Complimentary newspaper. Restaurant. Bar. Meeting rms. Business servs avail. Bellhops. Concierge. Dry cleaning. Exercise privileges. Cr cds: A, C, D, MC, V.

★★ **W FRENCH QUARTER HOTEL.** *316 Rue Chartres (70130), in French Quarter.* 504/581-1200; fax 504/523-2910; res 877/946-8357. 100 rms, 5 story. S $125-$140; D $150-$160; each addl $25; suites $165-$200; under 16 free; higher rates special events. Crib free. Valet parking $15. TV; cable (premium). Pool; poolside serv. Coffee in lobby. Restaurant 7:30 am-10 pm (see also BACCO). Bar. Ck-out noon. Meeting rm. Business servs avail. In-rm modem link. Built around landscaped courtyard. Cr cds: A, D, DS, JCB, MC, V.

★★★ **THE W HOTEL NEW ORLEANS.** *333 Poydras St (70130), in Central Business District.* 504/525-9444; fax 504/581-7179; toll-free 800/522-6963. *www.whotels.com.* 439 units, 23 story. S, D $115-$295; each addl $15; suites $325-$900; under 12 free; higher rates special events. Crib free. Valet $14. TV; cable (premium). Pool. Restaurant 6 am-2 pm, 5:30-10 pm. Coffee in rms. Bar 4 pm-midnight. Ck-out noon. Convention facilities. Business servs avail. In-rm modem link. Concierge. Exercise equipt. Refrigerators avail. Luxury level. Cr cds: A, C, D, DS, MC, V.

★★★★ **WINDSOR COURT HOTEL.** *300 Gravier St (70130), in Central Business District.* 504/523-6000; fax 504/596-4513; res 800/262-2662. *Email resv@windsorcourthotel.com; www.windsorcourthotel.com.* It is hard to believe that this property only opened in 1984 given its art-and-antique-filled decor reminiscent of Windsor Castle and Royal Family life. Located just one block from the French Quarter in the center of the business district, each of the property's 264 suites and 58 rooms feature private balconies or bay windows, some with city or Mississippi River views. 324 units, 23 story, 275 suites. S, D $235-$320; suites $310-$990, each addl $25; under 18 free. Crib free. Valet parking $17. TV; cable (premium), VCR in all rooms. Heated pool; whirlpool, poolside serv. Restaurant (see also GRILL ROOM). Afternoon tea 2-6 pm. Rm serv 24 hrs. 2 bars from 9 am; entertainment. Ck-out noon. Convention facilities. Business servs avail, large suites have in-rm fax. In-rm modem link. Concierge. Gift shop. Airport transportation avail. Indoor tennis privileges adj, pro. 18-hole golf privileges. Exercise equipt; sauna, steam rm. Massage. Health club privileges. Bathrm phones, refrigerators, minibars; microwaves avail; wet bar in suites. Balconies. Cr cds: A, DS, MC, V.

★★ **WYNDHAM NEW ORLEANS.** *100 Rue Iberville (70130), in Canal Place Shopping Center, in French Quarter.* 504/566-7006; fax 504/553-5120; res 800/WYNDHAM. 438 rms, 18 story. S, D $160-$289; each addl $25; suites $329-$3,000; under 19 free; wkend packages. Crib free. Garage $15; valet. TV; cable (premium), VCR avail. Rooftop heated pool; poolside serv. Restaurant 6:30 am-10 pm. Rm serv 24 hrs. Bar 11-2 am; entertainment. Ck-out noon. Convention facilities. Business center. In-rm modem link. Concierge. Shopping arcade. Barber, beauty shop. 18-hole golf privileges, pro, putting green, driving range. Exercise equipt. Bathrm phones, minibars. Views of Mississippi River. Cr cds: A, C, D, DS, MC.

★★ **WYNDHAM RIVERFRONT.** *701 Convention Center Blvd (70130), in Central Business District.* 504/524-8200; fax 504/524-0600. *Email bpouwels@wyndham.com; www.wyndham.com.* 200 rms, 6 story, 2 suites. Feb-Apr, Sep-Nov: S, D $243; each addl $20; suites $700; under 18 free; lower rates rest of yr. Crib avail, fee. Valet parking avail. TV; cable (DSS), VCR avail. Complimentary coffee in rms, newspaper. Restaurant. Bar. Meeting rms. Bellhops. Concierge. Dry cleaning. Exercise equipt. Golf. Tennis. Video games. Cr cds: A, C, D, DS, MC, V.

B&Bs/Small Inns

★★ **CHIMES BED & BREAKFAST.** *1146 Constantinople St (70115), W of Central Business District.* 504/899-2621; fax 504/488-4639; res 800/749-4640; toll-free 800/729-4640. *Email bedbreak@gnofn.org; www.historiclodging/chimes.com.* 2 rms, 3 story, 2 suites. S, D $107; each addl $10; suites $135; children $10; under 6 free. Pet accepted, some restrictions, fee. Parking lot. TV; cable. Complimentary continental bkfst, coffee in rms, newspaper, toll-free calls. Restaurant. Meeting rm. Business center. Coin lndry. Exercise privileges. Tennis. Cr cds: A, MC, V.

★ **FRENCHMAN HOTEL.** *417 Frenchmen St (70116), in Faubourg Marigny.* 504/948-2166; fax 504/948-2258. 27 rms, 2 story. S, D $84-$135; each addl $20; summer rates. TV; cable (premium). Pool; whirlpool. Complimentary continental bkfst. Serv bar 24 hrs. Ck-out 11 am, ck-in 3 pm. Business servs avail. Concierge serv. Balconies. Two town houses built 1860; individually decorated rms; antiques. Rms overlook courtyard, pool and patio. Cr cds: A, D, DS, MC, V.

⚑ 🏊 🔥

★ **FRENCH QUARTER GUEST HOUSE.** *623 Ursulines Ave (70116), in French Quarter.* 504/529-5489; fax 504/524-1902; toll-free 800/529-5489. Email convento@aol.com. 19 rms, 2 story. Jan-May, Oct: S $125; D $145; each addl $10; lower rates rest of yr. Parking garage. TV; cable. Complimentary continental bkfst, toll-free calls. Restaurant nearby. Ck-out noon, ck-in 2 pm. Business center. Concierge. Golf. Cr cds: A, C, D, DS, MC, V.

🎿 🔥 **SC** 🏃

★★ **GIROD HOUSE.** *835 Esplanade Ave (70116), in French Quarter.* 504/944-2255; fax 504/945-1794. 6 suites, 2 story, 5 kit. suites. 1 rm phone. Sept-June: S, D $100-$225; wkends (3-day min); higher rates: special events, Mardi Gras, jazz fest; lower rates rest of yr. Children over 12 yrs only. TV. Complimentary continental bkfst, coffee in rms. Restaurant nearby. Ck-out 1 pm, ck-in varies. Business servs avail. In-rm modem link. Concierge serv. Street parking avail. Refrigerators; some fireplaces. Some balconies. Built in 1833 by first mayor of New Orleans. Creole decor; exotic flowers. Cr cds: A, MC, V.

D 🔥

★★★ **HOUSE ON BAYOU ROAD.** *2275 Bayou Rd (70119), in Faubourg Marigny.* 504/945-0992; fax 504/945-0993; res 800/882-2968. www.house onbayouroad.com. 9 rms, 1 with shower only, 2 story. Oct-May: S, D $165-$250; lower rates rest of yr. Children over 12 yrs only. TV; cable, VCR avail. Pool; whirlpool. Complimentary full bkfst; afternoon refreshments. Ck-out noon, ck-in 3 pm. Meeting rm. Business servs avail. Luggage handling. Concierge serv. Health club privileges. Indigo plantation house built in 1798, antiques. Dining rm overlooks tropical courtyard. Cr cds: A, MC, V.

🏊 🔥 🔥

★★★ **LAFITTE GUEST HOUSE.** *1003 Bourbon St (70116), in French Quarter.* 504/581-2678; fax 504/581-

2677; toll-free 800/331-7971. Email lafitteguesthouse@travelbase.com. 14 rms, 4 story. S, D $99-$189; each addl $25; under 5 free; higher rates special events. TV in common rm. Complimentary continental bkfst. Restaurant nearby. Concierge serv. Business servs avail. Parking $8.50. Some refrigerators, minibars. Balconies. Located in French manor building (1849). Many antiques. Totally nonsmoking. Cr cds: A, C, D, DS, JCB, MC, V.

🏃 🏃 🔥 🔥

★★ **LAMOTHE HOUSE.** *621 Esplanade Ave (70116), in Faubourg Marigny.* 504/947-1161; fax 504/943-6536; toll-free 800/367-5858. Email lam5675842@aol.com. 20 rms, 3 story. S, D $99-$195; suites $150-$250. Crib free. TV; cable (premium). Complimentary continental bkfst. Restaurant nearby. Ck-out 11 am, ck-in 2 pm. Business servs avail. Restored townhouse built around patio; antique furnishings. Adj to French Quarter. Cr cds: A, DS, MC, V.

🏊 🔥

★★★ **MELROSE MANSION.** *937 Esplanade Ave (70116), in Faubourg Marigny.* 504/944-2255; fax 504/945-1794; toll-free 800/650-3323. Email melrosemansion@worldnet.att.net. 8 rms, 2 story, 4 suites. D $225-$250; suites $325-$425. TV; cable, VCR avail. Heated pool. Complimentary continental bkfst. Restaurant nearby. Ck-out noon, ck-in 1 pm. Business servs avail. Exercise equipt. Some in-rm whirlpools in suites. Many refrigerators. Balconies. Antiques. Library. Historic Victorian-Gothic mansion (1884); pillared verandas, tropical patio. Overlooks French Quarter. Cr cds: A, D, DS, MC, V.

D 🏊 🏃 🏃 🔥 🔥

★ **RUE ROYAL INN.** *1006 Royal St (70116), in French Quarter.* 504/524-3900; fax 504/588-0566; res 800/776-3901. www.rueroyalinn.com. 17 rms, 4 story. Sep-May: S, D $85-$165; each addl $15; suites $165; under 12 free; hols, special events (3-4-day min); higher rates jazz fest. Pet accepted, some restrictions. TV; cable. Complimentary continental bkfst, coffee in rms. Ck-out noon, ck-in varies. Parking $10. Airport, railroad station transportation. Refrigerators; some microwaves. Built in 1830 as Creole townhouse. Cr cds: A, C, D, DS, JCB, MC, V.

⊡ ➤ 🔥 SC

★★★ **SONIAT HOUSE HOTEL.**
1133 Chartres St (70116), in French Quarter. 504/522-0570; fax 504/522-7208; toll-free 800/544-8808. Email info@soniathouse; www.soniathouse. com. 24 rms, 3 story, 7 suites. Mar-May, Oct-Nov: D $215; suites $475; lower rates rest of yr. Valet parking avail. TV; cable, VCR avail. Complimentary newspaper. Restaurant nearby. Bar. Ck-out 1 pm, ck-in 3 pm. Meeting rm. Business center. Concierge. Dry cleaning. Exercise privileges. Golf. Tennis. Cr cds: A, MC, V.

⊡ 🍴 🎿 🎾 🏌 🏊 🔥 🏃

★ **ST. PETER GUEST HOUSE.** *1005 St. Peter (70116), in French Quarter. 504/524-9232; fax 504/523-5198; toll-free 800/535-7815. Email sph5678@ aol.com.* 29 rms, 6 suites. S $59-$79; D $79-$179; higher rates special events. TV; cable. Complimentary continental bkfst. Restaurant nearby. Ck-out 11 am, ck-in 3 pm. Balconies. Built in pre-1900's as private residence; antiques. Cr cds: A, DS, MC, V.

🔥

Restaurants

★★★ **ALEX PATOUT.** *221 Royal St (70130), in French Quarter. 504/525-7788. Email info@patout.com; www. patout.com.* Specializes in Cajun smothered roast duck, smoked salmon. Hrs: 5:30-10 pm. Closed Dec 25. Res accepted. Bar. Dinner $15-$26. Child's menu. Cr cds: A, D, DS, MC, V.

⊡

★★ **ALLEGRO BISTRO.** *1100 Poydras (70163), in Central Business District. 504/582-2350.* Specializes in fettucini allegro, crispy duck with andouille rice. Hrs: 11 am-2:30 pm, 4-7 pm. Closed Sat, Sun; hols. Res accepted. Bar. Lunch, dinner $7-$15.95. Art deco atmosphere. Cr cds: A, D, DS, MC, V.

⊡ ▱

★★ **ANDREW JAEGER'S HOUSE OF SEAFOOD.** *622 Rue Conti (70130), in French Quarter. 504/522-4964. Email info@andrewjaegers.com; www.andrewjaegers.com.* Specializes in fresh seafood, veal, pasta. Own baking. Hrs: 6-11 pm. Closed Thanksgiving, Dec 25. Res accepted. Bar. Dinner $9.95-$25.95. Entertainment: New Orleans piano & blues. Three distinct levels of dining in 1832 French Quarter Creole cottage. Cr cds: A, D, MC, V.

⊡ ▱

★★★ **ANTOINE'S.** *713 St. Louis St (70130), in French Quarter. 504/581-4422. www.antoines.com.* Specializes in oysters Rockefeller, pompano en papillote, souffled potatoes. Hrs: 11:30 am-2 pm, 5:30-9:30 pm. Closed Sun; Mardi Gras, hols. Res required. Wine cellar. Lunch á la carte entrées: $12-$24; dinner á la carte entrées: $20-$50. Jacket (dinner). Many world-famous dishes have been created and served by Antoine's. Established 1840. Family-owned. Cr cds: A, D, MC, V.

⊡ ▱

★★★ **ARNAUD'S.** *813 Rue Bienville (70112), in French Quarter. 504/523-5433. www.arnauds.com.* French menu. Specializes in shrimp Arnaud, pompano en croute, filet Charlemond. Own desserts. Hrs: 11:30 am-2:30 pm, 6-10 pm; Fri to 10:30 pm; Sat 6-10:30 pm; Sun from 6 pm; Sun brunch 10 am-2:30 pm. Closed hols. Res accepted. Bar. Wine cellar. Lunch a la carte entrees: $10.25-$15.25. Complete meals: $10.25-$15.25; dinner $17.50-$40. Sun brunch $18.50-$26. Entertainment: Sun jazz brunch. Jacket (dinner). Built in 1790; opened in 1918 and restored to original design. Cr cds: A, D, DS, MC, V.

⊡ ▱

★★★ **BACCO.** *310 Chartres St, in French Quarter. 504/522-2426. Email jburger@bacco.com; www.bacco.com.* Specializes in wood-fired pizza, homemade pasta, fresh regional seafood. Hrs: 11:30 am-2 pm, 6:30-9:30 pm. Closed Mardi Gras, Dec 24-25. Res accepted. Bar. Bkfst $5-$10; lunch $7.75-$12; dinner $10.50-$27. Sun brunch $7-$15. Parking. Cr cds: A, MC, V.

⊡ ▱

★ **BANGKOK CUISINE.** *4137 S Carrollton Ave (70119), W of Central Business District. 504/482-3606.* Specializes in seafood. Hrs: 11 am-3 pm, 5-10 pm; Sat, Sun from 5 pm. Closed

July 4, Thanksgiving, Dec 25. Res accepted. Lunch $4.95-$6.95; dinner $7.95-$16.95. Parking. Candlelight dining. Cr cds: A, D, DS, MC, V.

D ▭⃗

★★★★ **BAYONA.** *430 Rue Dauphine (70112), in French Quarter. 504/525-4455. Email info@bayona. com; www.bayona.com.* Famed chef Susan Spicer turns out worldly, Mediterranean cuisine in this cozy, 200-year-old cottage. The surroundings are refined yet comfortable with two dining rooms, a wine room, and a tropical-feeling courtyard in the heart of the French Quarter. The menu follows in the same vein with vibrant, skilled flavors unpretentiously presented as in grilled mustard-crusted baby chicken with thyme honey. Specializes in grilled duck breast, fresh seafood. Hrs: 11:30 am-2 pm, 6-10 pm; Fri to 11 pm; Sat 6-11 pm. Closed Sun; Mardi Gras, Easter, Dec 25; also 1 wk Aug. Res required. Lunch $9-$16.75; dinner $11-$23. Cr cds: A, C, D, DS, MC, V.

D

★★★ **BEGUE'S.** *300 Bourbon St, in French Quarter. 504/553-2220.* Cajun/Creole menu. Specializes in seafood buffet. Hrs: 6:30 am-2 pm, 6-11 pm; Sun brunch 10:30 am-2:30 pm. Res accepted. Bar. Bkfst $3.50-$12.50; lunch $7-$16; dinner $15-$29. Sun brunch $22.50. Entertainment: pianist Thurs, Fri, Sun brunch. Overlooks courtyard. Cr cds: A, C, D, DS, MC, V.

D

★★★ **BELLA LUNA.** *914 N Peter (70116), Decatur at Dumaine, in French Quarter. 504/529-1583. www.bellaluna. com.* Specializes in house-cured pork chop in pecan crust, Maine lobster with spinach fettuccine. Hrs: 6-10:30 pm; Sun to 9:30 pm. Closed Mardi Gras, Dec 25. Res accepted. Bar. Dinner a la carte entrees: $15-$25. Valet parking. Located in French Market; view of Mississippi River. Cr cds: A, D, DS, MC, V.

D

★★★ **BISTRO AT MAISON DE VILLE.** *733 Toulouse St. 504/528-9206. www.maisondeville.com.* Specializes in local seafood. Own desserts. Hrs: 11:30 am-2 pm, 6-10 pm. Res accepted. Wine list. Lunch $10-$13;

dinner $17-$25. Bistro setting in 18th-century house. Cr cds: A, D, DS, MC, V.

D

★★ **BON TON CAFE.** *401 Magazine St (70130), in Central Business District. 504/524-3386.* Specializes in redfish Bon Ton, crawfish dishes. Hrs: 11 am-2 pm, 5-9:30 pm. Closed Sat, Sun; hols. Lunch a la carte entrees: $8.50-$19.50; dinner a la carte entrees: $17.50-$24.25. Child's menu. Wrought iron chandelier, shuttered windows, wildlife prints on exposed brick walls. Cr cds: A, DS, MC, V.

D ▭⃗

★★★ **BRENNAN'S.** *417 Royal St (70130), in French Quarter. 504/525-9711. www.brennanneworleans.com.* Specializes in bananas Foster. Own desserts. Hrs: 8 am-2:30 pm, 6-10 pm. Closed Dec 24 (evening), 25. Res required. Bar. Wine cellar. Bkfst a la carte entrees: $11.50-$35. Complete meals: $35; dinner a la carte entrees: $28.50-$35. Complete meals: $35. Located in 1795 bank where the Louisiana Purchase was handled. Family-owned. Cr cds: A, D, DS, MC, V.

D

★★★ **BRIGSTEN'S.** *723 Dante St (70118), W of Central Business District. 504/861-7610.* Specializes in rabbit, duck, seafood. Menu changes daily. Hrs: 5:30-10 pm. Closed Sun, Mon; hols, Dec 24. Res required. Dinner a la carte entrees: $14-$24. Parking. In restored 1900s house built from river barge timbers; French-country decor. Cr cds: A, D, DS, MC, V.

D

★★★ **BROUSSARD'S.** *819 Rue Conti (70112), in French Quarter. 504/581-3866. www.broussards.com.* Specializes in veal Broussard, Pompano Napoleon, bananas Foster. Hrs: 5:30-10 pm. Closed Dec 25. Res required. Bar. Dinner a la carte entrees: $19.75-$32.50. Entertainment: pianist Fri, Sat. Courtyard patio. Cr cds: A, MC, V.

D

★★ **CAFE GIOVANNI.** *117 Rue Decatur (70130), in French Quarter. 504/529-2154. www.cafegiovanni.com.*

Specializes in pasta gambino, spicy seared pork filet. Own desserts. Hrs: 5:30-10 pm; Fri, Sat to 11 pm. Closed hols; Mardi Gras; Sun in July & Aug. Res accepted. Dinner a la carte entrees: $12.95-$23.95. Valet parking. Arched brick doorway leads to dining area with mirrored column in center; French doors open to face Quarter. Cr cds: A, D, DS, MC, V.
⊡ ⊟

★ **CAFE PONTALBA.** *546 St. Peter St (70116), in French Quarter.* 504/522-1180. Specializes in gumbo, jambalaya, etouffe. Hrs: 10:30 am-10 pm. Closed Dec 25. Bar. Lunch, dinner $5.95-$16.95. Open restaurant overlooking Jackson Sq. Family-owned. Cr cds: D, DS, MC, V.
⊟

★ ★ **CAFE VOLAGE.** *720 Dublin St (70118), N of Central Business District.* 504/861-4227. Specializes in veal, duck, salmon. Hrs: 11 am-10 pm; Sun to 3 pm. Closed hols; Mardi Gras. Res accepted. Wine. Lunch a la carte entrees: $6.25-$8.95; dinner a la carte entrees: $14.95-$18.95. Sun brunch $13.95. Child's menu. Two intimate dining areas in 1800s Victorian cottage. Cr cds: D, MC, V.
⊡ ⊟

★ ★ ★ **CHRISTIAN'S.** *3835 Iberville St (70119), N of Central Business District.* 504/482-4924. Email christian srest73@aol.com. Specializes in oysters Roland, baby veal Christian, bouillabaisse. Own ices, ice cream. Hrs: 11:30 am-2 pm, 5:30-9:30 pm; Sat from 5:30 pm. Closed Sun, Mon; Dec 25. Res accepted. Bar. Wine cellar. Lunch complete meals: $9.75-$18.25; dinner a la carte entrees: $14.25-$24.95. Parking. Jacket (dinner). In renovated former church (1914). Cr cds: A, DS, MC, V.
⊡ ⊟

★ ★ ★ ★ **COMMANDER'S PALACE.** *1403 Washington Ave (70130), in Garden District.* 504/899-8221. www. commanderspalace.com. In the center of the Garden District stands this turquoise and white Victorian monument to Creole cuisine. The famed Brennan family has presided over the dining room since 1974, but Emile Commander originally founded it in 1880 as a fine restaurant for distinguished neighborhood families. The lush, garden setting hosts live Dix-

ieland music for the lively Saturday and Sunday jazz brunches. Specializes in turtle soup, fresh gulf fish, bread pudding souffle. Hrs: 11:30 am-1:30 pm, 6-9:30 pm; Sat brunch 11:30 am-12:30 pm; Sun brunch 10:30 am-1:30 pm. Closed Mardi Gras, Dec 24, 25. Res required. Bar. Wine cellar. Lunch $15-$18. Complete meals: $15-$20; dinner $25-$40. Complete meals: $36-$40. Sun brunch, $25-$30. Entertainment: Dixieland band at brunch. Valet parking. Cr cds: A, D, DS, MC, V.
⊡ ⊟

★ ★ **COURT OF TWO SISTERS.** *613 Royal St (70130), in French Quarter.* 504/522-7261. Email court2si@ communique.net; www.courtoftwosisters. com. Specializes in shrimp Toulouse, lobster etouffe. Hrs: 9 am-3 pm, 5:30-10 pm. Closed Dec 25. Res accepted. Bar. Dinner a la carte entrees: $15-$30. Complete meals: $37. Sun brunch $21. Child's menu. Entertainment: jazz trio at brunch. Built in 1832; spacious patio; courtyard. Family-owned. Cr cds: A, D, DS, MC, V.
⊡ ⊟

★ ★ **CRESCENT CITY BREW-HOUSE.** *527 Decatur St (70130), in French Quarter.* 504/522-0571. Specializes in Louisiana bouillabaisse, grilled tuna Orleans. Hrs: 11 am-10 pm; Fri, Sat to midnight. Closed Thanksgiving, Dec 25. Res accepted. Bar. Lunch, dinner $6.95-$18.95. Child's menu. Entertainment: jazz eves. 1795 bldg is active brewery; balcony dining area offers views of Mississippi River and Natchez Steamboat. Cr cds: A, D, DS, MC, V.
⊡ ⊟

★ ★ ★ ★ **DELMONICO.** *1300 St. Charles Ave (70130), in Garden District.* 504/525-4937. www.emerils.com. Another recent jewel in the crown of TV-personality and superstar-chef Emeril Lagasse, this historic icon-of-a-restaurant has operated since 1895. With elements of both Victorian and Edwardian architecture, the building's first floor was once a dairy creamery, and the second floor, a boxing gym. Now, with a brandname chef at the reins, the classic Creole menu has a new, inventive touch. Specializes in grand Creole cuisine. Hrs: 11:30 am-2 pm, 6-10 pm; Fri to 11 pm; Sat 6-11 pm; Sun

A steamboat on the mighty Mississippi

from 10:30 am. Res recommended. Bar. Lunch $12.50-$22; dinner $18-$30. Cr cds: D, DS, MC, V.

D

★★ **DESIRE OYSTER BAR.** *300 Bourbon St, in French Quarter. 504/586-0300.* Seafood menu. Specializes in Creole cuisine. Own baking. Hrs: 11 am-10:30 pm. Bar. Lunch, dinner $7-$15.25. Child's menu. Parking. Bistro doors and windows offer view of French Quarter streets. Cr cds: A, D, DS, MC, V.

D ⊟

★★★ **DOMINQUE'S.** *1001 Toulouse St, in French Quarter. 504/586-8000. Email chefdomini@aol.com; www. maisondupuy.com.* Specializes in grilled chimayo-crusted swordfish, fire-roasted Louisiana shrimp. Hrs: 11:30 am-2 pm, 6-10 pm. Res accepted. Bar. Wine list. Lunch $20-$28; dinner $20-$28. Valet parking. View of courtyard. Cr cds: A, D, DS, MC, V.

D

★★ **DOOKY CHASE.** *2301 Orleans Ave (70119), N of Central Business District. 504/821-0600.* Specializes in seafood, gumbo. Hrs: 11:30 am-10 pm. Closed Dec 25. Res accepted. Bar. Lunch $10.95; dinner $15-$25. Complete meal: $25. Parking. Collection of African-American artwork. Antique parlor rm for waiting. Family-owned for 50 yrs. Cr cds: A, D, DS, MC, V.

D ⊟

★★★★ **EMERIL'S RESTAURANT.** *800 Tchoupitoulas St (70130), in Central Business District. 504/528-9393.www.emerils.com.* There aren't many people today who wouldn't recognize this namesake establishment of TV personality and true celebrity-chef, Emeril Lagasse. Regardless of the hype, this Warehouse District restaurant where it all began continues to win praise for southern-inspired creations such as grilled salmon over lump crab and corn maque choux with mirliton slaw and cayenne-tomato syrup. If that's not enough, choose the daily-changing, degustation menu. Hrs: 11:30 am-2 pm, 6-10 pm; Fri, Sat to 11 pm. Closed Sun; Mardi Gras, hols; also 1st 3 wks July. Res required (dinner). 1,400-selection wine list. Lunch a la carte entrees: $15-$20; dinner a la carte entrees: $19-$30. Complimentary valet parking. Jacket (dinner). Cr cds: A, D, DS, MC, V.

D ⊟

★★ **FEELINGS CAFE.** *2600 Chartres St (70117), in Faubourg Marigny. 504/945-2222. www.feelingscafe.com.* Specializes in seafood, veal, duck. Own desserts. Hrs: 6-10 pm; Fri, Sat to 11 pm; Sun 11 am-2 pm, 6-10 pm. Closed Mardi Gras, Thanksgiving, Dec 25. Bar. Lunch $7-$14.75; dinner $11.75-$21.75. Sun brunch $14-$18.50. Entertainment: pianist Fri, Sat. Patio dining wkdays. Located in outbldg of 18th-century plantation; antiques, original artwork. Cr cds: A, D, DS, MC, V.

D ⊟

★★ **FIVE HAPPINESS.** *3605 S Carrollton Ave (70118), W of Central Business District. 504/482-3935. www. fivehappiness.com.* Specializes in Mandarin & Szechwan dishes. Hrs: 11:30 am-10:30 pm; Fri, Sat to 11:30 pm; Sun noon-10:30 pm. Closed Thanksgiving. Bar. Lunch $5.75; dinner $7.50. Cr cds: A, D, DS, MC, V.

D ⊟

★ **FRENCH MARKET.** *1001 Decatur St (70116), in French Quarter. 504/525-7879.* Specializes in fresh seafood. Oyster bar. Hrs: 11 am-11 pm. Closed Thanksgiving, Dec 25. Bar. Lunch, dinner $6.95-$20. Child's menu. Balcony dining. Beamed ceiling, gaslight sconces, brick bar. Cr cds: A, D, DS, MC, V.

★ ★ ★ **GABRIELLE.** *3201 Esplanade Ave (70119), N of Central Business District. 504/948-6233.* Specializes in contemporary Creole cuisine. Own sausage, desserts. Hrs: 5:30-10 pm. Closed Sun, Mon; hols, Mardi Gras. Res accepted. Bar. Dinner $15.50-$21. Parking. Casual bistro atmosphere. Cr cds: A, D, DS, MC, V.

D

★ ★ ★ **GALATOIRE'S.** *209 Bourbon St (70130), in French Quarter. 504/525-2021. www.galatoires.com.* Specializes in red snapper with sauteed crabmeat, oysters en bronchette. Hrs: 11:30 am-10 pm; Sun from noon. Closed Mon; hols, Mardi Gras. Lunch, dinner a la carte entrees: $13-$24. Jacket. Family-owned. Cr cds: A, D, DS, MC, V.

D

★ ★ ★ **GAUTREAU'S.** *1728 Soniat St (70115), W of Central Business District. 504/899-7397.* Specializes in seafood, contemporary Louisiana cooking. Hrs: 6-10 pm. Closed Sun; hols. Res accepted. Wine. Dinner a la carte entrees: $14-$28. Valet parking. Former drugstore from early 1900s; original medicine cabinets, pressed-tin ceiling. Cr cds: A, D, DS, MC, V.

★ ★ **GERARD'S DOWNTOWN.** *500 St. Charles Ave. 504/592-0200. Email tjmar58@aol.com; www.gerardsdowntown.com.* Menu changes seasonally. Hrs: 11:30 am-2:30 pm, 5:30-10 pm. Closed hols. Res accepted. Wine, beer. Lunch $8.50-$14; dinner $19-$27. Entertainment. Cr cds: A, C, D, DS, JCB, MC, V.

D

★ ★ ★ ★ ★ **GRILL ROOM.** *300 Gravier St. 504/522-1992. www.windsorcourthotel.com.* Housed in the Windsor Court Hotel, this elegant dining room dazzles with its magnificent glass and crystal center-table and lavish floral arrangements. Stunning presentations of regional-continental cuisine with an international flair, such as seared Maine lobster with truffle ravioli, caramelized leeks, and truffle fume, make this restaurant one of the best in a highly competitive town. Specializes in mushroom-crusted halibut, Chinese-style smoked lobster, grilled veal chop. Own baking. Hrs: 7-10:30 am, 11:30 am-2 pm, 6-10 pm; Fri, Sat to 10:30 pm; Sun brunch 9:30 am-2 pm. Res accepted. Bar. Wine cellar. Bkfst à la carte entrées: $8-$13; lunch à la carte entrées: $9.75-$19.75; dinner à la carte entrées: $31-$39. Sun brunch $27.50-$32.50. Entertainment: jazz Sun. Free valet parking. Jacket. Cr cds: A, D, DS, MC, V.

D

★ ★ **K-PAUL'S LOUISIANA KITCHEN.** *416 Chartres St (70130), in French Quarter. 504/524-7394. www.chefpaul.com.* Specializes in blackened fish and steak. Hrs: 11:30 am-2:30 pm, 5:30-10 pm; Mon from 5:30 pm; Fri, Sat to 10:30 pm. Closed Sun; Jan 1, Mardi Gras, Dec 24, 25. Res accepted; required upper level. Bar. Lunch $9.95-$12.95; dinner $15-$30. Cr cds: A, D, DS, MC, V.

D

★ ★ ★ **KELSEY'S.** *3923 Magazine St (70115), in Garden District. 504/897-6722. www.citysearch.com.* Specializes in seafood. Hrs: 11:30 am-2 pm, 5:30-9:30 pm; Fri to 10 pm; Sat 5:30-10 pm; Sun 5:30-9 pm. Closed Sun, Mon; hols. Res accepted. Bar. Lunch $6.95-$12.95; dinner $12.95-$24.95. Cr cds: A, D, DS, MC, V.

D

★ ★ **LA GAULOISE BISTRO.** *614 Canal St. 504/527-6712. Email meridien@gnofn.org; www.midirestaurant.com.* Specializes in rack of lamb, shrimp à la Provencal. Hrs: 11:30 am-2 pm, 6-10 pm; Sun brunch 10:30 am-2 pm. Res accepted. Wine. Bkfst $4.50-$12; lunch $4.95-$19.50; dinner $5.95-$24.50. Sun brunch $27.50. Valet parking. French bistro atmosphere with private balcony; bi-level dining area. Cr cds: A, D, DS, ER, MC, V.

D

★ ★ ★ **LEMON GRASS.** *217 Camp St. 504/523-1200. www.lemongrassrest.com.* Specializes in grilled shrimp, wok-smoked salmon steak, chicken roti. Hrs: 7:30 am-10:30 pm; Sat, Sun 7:30 am-noon, 6-11 pm. Res accepted. Wine, beer. Lunch $16-$30; dinner $15-$30. Child's menu. Entertainment. Cr cds: A, C, D, DS, JCB, MC, V.

★ ★ ★ **LOUIS XVI.** *730 Rue Bienville. 504/581-7000. www.louisXVI.com.* Specializes in lamb chop, seafood. Hrs: 7-11 am, 6-10 pm. Closed Mardi Gras, July 4. Res accepted. Bar. Bkfst a la carte entrees: $7-$12; dinner a la carte entrees: $18-$34. Child's menu. Entertainment: pianist, strolling guitarist. Valet parking. Jacket. Elegant decor, formal dining. Family-owned. Cr cds: A, MC, V.
D ⊟

★ ★ **MARISOL.** *437 Esplanade Ave (70116). 504/943-1912. Email food4 fuel@aol.com; www.marisolrestaurant. com.* Menu changes monthly. Hrs: 6-10 pm; Fri, Sat to 11 pm; Sun brunch 11 am-2 pm. Closed Mon; hols. Res accepted. Wine, beer. Dinner $18-$27. Brunch $8.95-$16. Entertainment. Cr cds: A, D, MC, V.
D

★ ★ ★ **MARTINIQUE.** *5908 Magazine St (70115), W of Central Business District. 504/891-8495.* Specializes in filet of beef with sauteed wild mushrooms, truffle bread pudding. Hrs: 6-10 pm; Fri, Sat to 10:30 pm. Closed Jan 1, Dec 25. Wine cellar. Dinner $9-$18. View of patio with fountain, greenery. Cr cds: A, MC, V.
D

★ ★ **MAXIMO'S ITALIAN GRILL.** *1117 Decatur (70116), in French Quarter. 504/586-8883.* Specializes in pasta, veal, seafood. Own desserts, ice cream. Hrs: 6-11 pm. Bar. Dinner $8.95-$28.95. Contemporary decor with antique light fixtures, jazz art. Cr cds: A, D, DS, MC, V.
⊟

★ ★ ★ **METRO BISTRO.** *200 Magazine St. 504/529-1900. www.metro bistro.net.* Specializes in cassoulet, bouillabaisse crab cakes. Hrs: 11 am-2 pm, 5:30-10 pm; Fri, Sat to 11 pm. Closed hols. Res accepted. Wine, beer. Lunch $8.50-$16; dinner $19-$26. Brunch $7.50-$16. Entertainment. Open kitchen viewing. Cr cds: A, D, DS, MC, V.
D ⊟

★ ★ **MICHAUL'S.** *840 St. Charles Ave (70130), in Central Business District. 504/522-5517.* Specializes in alligator sauce picante, blackened shrimp. Hrs: 5-10 pm; Fri to 11 pm; Sat 6 pm-mid-

night. Closed Sun; Easter, Thanksgiving, Dec 25; last 2 wks in Aug. Res accepted. Bar. Dinner $12.25-$18.95. Child's menu. Entertainment: Cajun, zydeco music; Cajun dance lessons. Offers complete Cajun cultural experience. Cr cds: A, D, DS, MC, V.
D ⊟

★ ★ **MIDI SOUTH OF FRANCE.** *614 Canal St (70130). 504/527-6712. www.miridienneworleans.com.* Menu changes seasonally. Hrs: 11:30 am-2 pm, 6-10 pm; Sun from 10:30 am . Res accepted. Wine, beer. Lunch $16-$24; dinner $18-$26. Entertainment. Cr cds: A, C, D, DS, ER, JCB, MC, V.
D

★ **MIKE ANDERSON'S SEAFOOD.** *215 Bourbon St (70130), in French Quarter. 504/524-3884. www.mike andersons.com.* Seafood menu. Specializes in broiled seafood, po-boys, guitreau. Oyster bar. Hrs: 11:30 am-10 pm; Fri, Sat to 11 pm. Closed Easter, Thanksgiving, Dec 25. Bar. Lunch, dinner $7.95-$15.95. Nautical decor. Balcony overlooks Bourbon St. Cr cds: A, D, DS, MC, V.
D ⊟

★ ★ **MOSCA'S.** *4137 US 90W (70094), 4½ mi W of Huey Long Bridge, W of Central Business District. 504/436-9942.* Specializes in shrimp, chicken, oysters. Own pasta. Hrs: 5:30-9:30 pm. Closed Sun, Mon; Dec 25; also Aug. Res accepted Sun-Fri. Bar. Dinner a la carte entrees: $25-$28. Parking. Family-owned. No cr cds accepted.
⊟

★ ★ ★ **MR B'S BISTRO.** *201 Royal St (70130), in French Quarter. 504/523-2078. www.mrbsbistro.com.* Specializes in hickory-grilled seafood. Hrs: 11:30 am-3 pm, 5-10 pm; Sun brunch 10:30 am-3 pm. Closed Mardi Gras, Dec 24, 25. Res accepted. Bar. Wine list. Lunch $9-$11. Complete meals: $10-$15; dinner $16-$23. Complete meals: $29-$38. Sun brunch $7.50-$17. Entertainment: Sun jazz brunch. Bistro decor with mahogany bar, etched-glass walls, white marble-topped tables. Cr cds: A, D, DS, MC, V.
D ⊟

★ ★ **NAPOLEAN HOUSE.** *500 Charles St (70130), in French Quarter.*

504/524-9752. www.napoleanhouse. com. Specializes in muffaletta, grilled breast of duck. Own breads. Hrs: 11 am-midnight; Fri, Sat to 1 am; Sun to 7 pm. Closed hols; Mardi Gras, Dec 24. Bar. Lunch a la carte entrees: $4.50-$10; dinner a la carte entrees: $13-$19. Historic 1797 bldg offers dining in central courtyard. Family-owned. Cr cds: A, D, DS, MC, V.
D ⊟

★★★ **NOLA.** *534 St. Louis St (70130), in French Quarter. 504/522-6652. www.emerils.com.* Specializes in roasted filet mignon, cedar plank roasted Gulf fish. Hrs: 11:30 am-2 pm, 6-10 pm; Fri, Sat to midnight; Sun from 6 pm. Closed Mardi Gras, Thanksgiving, Dec 24, 25. Res accepted. Bar. Lunch $12-$19; dinner $16-$22. In renovated warehouse. Original artwork. Cr cds: A, C, D, DS, MC, V.
D ⊟

★★★ **PALACE CAFE.** *605 Canal St (70130), in French Quarter. 504/523-1661. www.palacecafe.com.* Specializes in Andoville crusted fish, grilled veal chop, white chocolate bread pudding. Hrs: 11:30 am-2:30 pm, 5:30-10 pm; Sat, Sun brunch 10:30 am-2:30 pm. Closed Mardi Gras, Dec 24, 25. Res accepted. Bar. Lunch $10-$15; dinner $16-$30. Sat, Sun brunch, $12-15. Contemporary bistro decor. Cr cds: A, D, DS, MC, V.
D ⊟

★★★ **PELICAN CLUB.** *312 Exchange Pl (70130), in French Quarter. 504/523-1504.* Specializes in pecan-crusted fish with baked Louisiana oysters, Louisiana ciopinno with linguine. Hrs: 5-9:30 pm; Fri, Sat to 10 pm. Closed hols; Mardi Gras. Res accepted. Bar. Wine cellar. Dinner $5.50-$21.50. Prix fixe: $17.95. Entertainment: piano bar. Three dining rms in a converted townhouse. Casual elegance. Cr cds: A, D, DS, MC, V.
D

★★★ **PERISTYLE.** *1041 Dumaine St (70116), in French Quarter. 504/593-9535.* Specializes in pan-seared foie gras, crab salad, pan-roasted lamb loin chops. Hrs: 6-10 pm, Fri 11:30 am-1:30 pm, 6-11 pm. Closed Sun, Mon; hols. Res required wkends. Bar. Lunch complete meals: $18; dinner

complete meals: $18-$24. Free valet parking. Cr cds: A, DS, MC, V.
D

★ **PRALINE CONNECTION.** *542 Frenchmen St (70116), in Faubourg Marigny. 504/943-3934. www.praline connection.com.* Specializes in fried chicken, pork chops, bread pudding with praline sauce. Hrs: 11 am-10:30 pm; Fri, Sat to midnight. Closed Dec 25. Bar. Lunch $4-$7.95; dinner $4.50-$13.95. Child's menu. Candy rm features praline confections. Cr cds: A, D, DS, MC, V.
D ⊟

★★ **RED FISH GRILL.** *115 Bourbon St (70130), in French Quarter. 504/598-1200. www.redfishgrill.com.* Specializes in sweet potato catfish, barbecue shrimp po' boy, bananas Foster. Hrs: 11 am-3 pm, 5-11 pm; Sun brunch 10 am-3 pm. Closed Mardi Gras; Dec 24, 25. Res accepted. Bar. Lunch a la carte entrees: $4.50-$11.25; dinner a la carte entrees: $12.50-$21.95. Sun brunch $12.75-$16.75. Child's menu. Street parking. In converted department store. Casual dining. Cr cds: A, DS, MC, V.
D **SC**

★★★ **RIB ROOM.** *621 St. Louis St. 504/529-7045.* Specializes in rotisserie prime rib, seafood, traditional dishes with Creole flair. Own pastries. Hrs: 6:30-10 am, 11:30 am-2:30 pm, 6-10:30 pm. Res accepted. Bar. Wine cellar. Lunch $12-$17; dinner $20-$32. Sat, Sun brunch, $8.50-$15.50. Parking. Cr cds: A, D, DS, MC, V.
D ⊟

★★ **RUE BOURBON.** *241 Rue Bourbon (70130), in French Quarter. 504/524-0114. www.ruebourbon.com.* Specializes in gulf shrimp combo, shrimp and tasso pasta. Own desserts. Hrs: 5:30 pm-midnight. Res accepted. Bar. Dinner $12.95-$19.95. 1831 bldg. Cr cds: A, DS, MC, V.
⊟

★★ **SHALIMAR INDIAN CUISINE.** *535 Wilkinson St (70130), in French Quarter. 504/523-0099.* Specializes in vindaloo curry, shahi murgh, nargishi ghosht. Hrs: 11:30 am-2 pm, 5:30-10 pm. Closed Sun. Res accepted. Bar. Lunch buffet: $6.95;

dinner $6.95-$18.95. Indian decor.
Cr cds: A, D, DS, MC, V.

D

★ **SNUG HARBOR JAZZ BISTRO.**
*626 Frenchmen St (70116), in Faubourg
Marigny.* 504/949-0696. *www.snugjazz.
com.* Specializes in seafood, steak.
Hrs: 5-11 pm; Fri, Sat to midnight.
Closed Dec 25. Bar. Dinner $7-$22.
Entertainment: modern jazz. Casual
dining. Cr cds: A, MC, V.

D

★★ **TONY MORAN'S PASTA E
VINO.** *240 Bourbon St (70130), at Old
Absinthe House, in French Quarter.* 504/
523-3181. *www.oldepsonhouse.com.*
Specializes in Northern Italian cuisine,
fresh pasta. Hrs: 6 pm-midnight.
Closed Sun; Dec 25. Res accepted.
Bar. Dinner a la carte entrees: $7-$16.
1806 French Quarter bldg overlooks
small courtyard. Family-owned. Cr
cds: A, D, DS, MC, V.

D

★★ **TUJAGUE'S.** *823 Decatur St
(70116), in French Quarter.* 504/525-
8676. Specializes in shrimp Creole,
crawfish, crab and spinach bisque.
Hrs: 11 am-3 pm, 5-10 pm. Res
accepted. Bar. Lunch complete meals:
$6.95-$13.95; dinner complete
meals: $24.95-$28.95. Child's menu.
Established in 1856 in old Spanish
armory (1750); original tile, authentic beams. Oldest standing bar in
city. Cr cds: A, D, DS, MC, V.

D

★★★ **UPPERLINE.** *1413 Upperline
St (70115), W of Central Business District.* 504/891-9822. *www.upperline.
com.* Specializes in roast duck with
garlic port, braised lamb shank, fried
green tomatoes with shrimp
remoulade sauce. Hrs: 5:30-9:30 pm.
Closed Mon, Tues; Mardi Gras, July
4, Thanksgiving, Dec 25. Res
accepted. Bar. Wine cellar. Dinner a
la carte entrees: $13.50-$24. Complete meals: $28.50. Child's menu.
Parking. Famous for the local folk art
displayed. French windows offer
view of garden. Cr cds: A, DS, MC, V.

★★★ **VERANDA.** *444 St. Charles
Ave.* 504/525-5566. Specializes in
regional dishes, seafood. Hrs: 6:30
am-2 pm; Sun brunch 6:30 am-2:30

pm. Res accepted. Bkfst a la carte
entrees: $8.95-$13. Buffet: $12.95;
lunch a la carte entrees: $7-$14. Buffet: $11.95. Sun brunch $26. Complimentary valet parking. Gardenlike
setting. Cr cds: A, MC, V.

D

★★★ **ZOE BISTROT.** *333 Poydras
St.* 504/525-9444. Menu changes seasonally. Hrs: 6:30-10:30 am, 11:30
am-2:30 pm, 6-11 pm; Thurs, Fri, Sat
6 pm-midnight. Res accepted. Wine,
beer. Lunch $10-$19; dinner $18-
$28. Entertainment. Old movies in
bar. Cr cds: A, C, D, DS, JCB, MC, V.

D

Unrated Dining Spots

BIZOU RESTAURANT. *701 St.
Charles Ave (70130).* 504/524-4114.
*Email bizou@.net; www.bizounew
orleans.com.* Specializes in souffle,
mussels, oysters, filet mignon. Hrs: 11
am-3 pm, 5-10 pm. Closed Sun; hols.
Res required. Wine, beer. Lunch $8.50-
$18.50; dinner $14.50-$22.50. Enter-
tainment. Cr cds: A, D, DS, MC, V.

D

CAFE DU MONDE. *800 Decatur St
(70116), at St. Ann St in French Quarter.* 504/525-4544. *www.cafedumonde.
com.* Specializes in beignets, New
Orleans chicory coffee, cafe au lait.
Open 24 hrs. Closed Dec 25. Bkfst
$2-$5; lunch, dinner $2-$5. In
French Market. No cr cds accepted.

D

CAMELLIA GRILL. *626 S Carrollton
Ave (70118), W of Central Business
District.* 504/866-9573. Specializes in
omelettes, gourmet sandwiches,
pecan pie. Hrs: 9-1 am; Fri-Sat 8-3
am. Closed hols. Bkfst, lunch, dinner
$1.50-$7. Popular night spot; unique
place. Family-owned. No cr cds
accepted.

CENTRAL GROCERY. *923 Decatur St
(70116), in French Quarter.* 504/523-
1620. Specializes in muffuletta sandwich. Hrs: 8 am-5:30 pm; Sun from 9
am. Bkfst a la carte entrees: $3.75-
$6.95; lunch a la carte entrees: $3.75-
$6.95; dinner a la carte entrees:
$3.75-$6.95. Sandwich bar in Italian
grocery. Near Jackson Sq. Family-
owned. No cr cds accepted.

CHEZ NOUS CHARCUTERIE. *5701 Magazine St (70115), W of Central Business District. 504/899-7303.* Specializes in grillades, jambalaya. Hrs: 11 am-6:30 pm; Sat to 5 pm. Closed Sun; hols. Lunch a la carte entrees: $1.65-$6.50. Gourmet delicatessen in grocery store. Cr cds: MC, V.

CHRISTINO'S. *228 Camp St. 504/571-7500.* Specializes in Brunswick-braised monkfish. Own baking. Hrs: 6:30-10 am, 11:30 am-2 pm, 5:30-10 pm; Sat, Sun 6:30 pm-midnight. Res accepted. Bkfst $8-$13; lunch à la carte entrées: $8-$16; dinner à la carte entrées: $16-$29. Child's menu. Valet parking. Jacket (dinner). Etched-glass windows face street; chandeliers. Cr cds: A, D, DS, MC, V.
[D]

CLOVER GRILL. *900 Bourbon St (70116), in French Quarter. 504/598-1010. Email corgi909@aol.com; www.clovergrill.com.* Specializes in hamburgers, club sandwiches. Hrs: open 24 hrs. Bkfst à la carte entrées: $2-$5; lunch, dinner à la carte entrées: $3-$7. Open kitchen. Cr cds: A, MC, V.

LA MADELEINE. *547 St. Ann St (70116), in French Quarter. 504/568-0073.* Specializes in croissants, quiche, pastries. Own baking. Hrs: 7 am-9 pm. Closed Dec 25. Wine, beer. Bkfst $5; lunch dinner $7.50. Located in one of the famous Pontalba Bldgs (1851) on Jackson Sq. Cr cds: A, DS, MC, V.

MOTHER'S. *401 Poydras St (70130), in Central Business District. 504/523-9656.* Specializes in New Orleans plate lunches, po' boy sandwiches, Mother's Ferdi special. Hrs: 5 am-10 pm; Sun from 8 am. Bkfst à la carte entrées: $4.75-$7.50; lunch, dinner à la carte entrées: $3.75-$8. Former residence (1830); extensive collection of US Marine memorabilia, cafeteria-style service. Cr cds: MC, V.

Opelousas

(E-4) *See also Lafayette*

Founded ca 1720 **Pop** 18,151 **Elev** 70 ft **Area code** 337 **Zip** 70570

Information Tourist Information Center, 941 E Vine St, 337/948-6263 or 800/424-5442; or contact the Tourism & Activities Committee, 441 E Grolee, PO Box 712; 337/948-4731

Annual Events

Original Southwest Louisiana Zydeco Music Festival. Celebrates spicy culture of Creoles. Concerts, interpretive stage, 5-km run. Phone 337/942-2392. Sat before Labor Day.

Louisiana Yambilee. Yambilee Fairgrounds, US 190W. Held in honor of the yam; although often confused, the yam and the sweet potato are, technically, two distinct species. Last full wkend Oct.

Motel/Motor Lodge

★★ **QUALITY INN.** *4165 I-49 Service Rd (70570), I-49 Exit 15. 318/948-9500; fax 318/942-5035.* 67 rms, 2 story. S, D $60-$68; each addl $6; suites $98; under 18 free; higher rates special events. TV; cable (premium). Pool; whirlpool. Sauna. Restaurant 6:30-9:30 am, 11 am-1:30 pm, 6-10 pm; Sat, Sun 7-11 am. Bar from 4 pm, closed Sun. Ck-out noon. Meeting rms. Business servs avail. In-rm modem link. Balconies. Cr cds: A, C, D, DS, MC, V.
[D] [icons] [SC]

Restaurant

★★ **STEAMBOAT WAREHOUSE.** *525 N Main St (70589), 6 mi N via I-49, Exit 25. 337/826-7227.* Specializes in steamboat gangplank, eggplant pirogue, catfish Lizzy. Hrs: 5-10:30 pm; Sun 11 am-10 pm. Closed Mon; Dec 25. Bar. Lunch, dinner $9.95-$22.95. Restored 1830s steamboat warehouse. Cr cds: A, D, MC, V.
[D] [icon]

Ruston (B-3)

Founded 1884 **Pop** 20,027 **Elev** 319 ft **Area code** 318 **Zip** 71270

Information Ruston/Lincoln Convention and Visitors Bureau, 900 N Trenton; 318/255-2031 or 800/392-9032

Annual Event

Louisiana Peach Festival. Second wkend June.

Seasonal Event

Louisiana Passion Play. For res phone 318/255-6277 or 800/204-2101. June-Sep.

Motels/Motor Lodges

★★ **BEST WESTERN.** *1105 N Trenton St (71270), I-20 at US 167 Exit 85.* 318/251-0000; fax 318/251-1453; toll-free 800/528-1234. 52 rms, 2 story. S $40-$48; D $50-$60; each addl $3; higher rates special events. Crib $2. TV; cable (premium). Pool. Complimentary continental bkfst. Restaurant adj 11 am-midnight. Ck-out noon. Coin lndry. Business servs avail. In-rm modem link. Some refrigerators. Cr cds: A, C, D, DS, MC, V.

★★ **COMFORT INN.** *1801 N Service Rd (71270), I-20 Exit 86.* 318/251-2360; fax 318/251-2360; res 800/228-5150. 60 rms, 2 story. S, D $55-$60; each addl $5; under 18 free. Crib $5. TV; cable. Pool. Complimentary continental bkfst 6:30-9:30 am. Ck-out noon. Business servs avail. In-rm modem link. Cr cds: A, C, D, DS, MC, V.

Hotel

★★ **MAXWELL'S INN & CONFERENCE CENTER.** *401 N Service Rd (71270), ¾ mi E at Jct US 167, I-20.* 318/255-5901; fax 318/255-3729; toll-free 800/799-4559. Email jcbass1@aol.com. 140 rms, 1 story, 3 suites. Jun-Aug, Oct: S, D $79; each addl $5; suites $119; under 16 free; lower rates rest of yr. Crib avail. Pet accepted, some restrictions. Parking lot. Pool, lap pool, children's pool. TV; cable (premium), VCR avail, CD avail. Complimentary continental bkfst, coffee in rms, newspaper, toll-free calls. Restaurant 6 am-10 pm. Ck-out noon, ck-in 4 pm. Meeting rms. Bellhops. Dry cleaning, coin lndry. Exercise privileges. Golf. Tennis, 12 courts. Hiking trail. Picnic facilities. Cr cds: A, D, DS, ER, JCB, MC, V.

Shreveport

(B-2) *See also Bossier City*

Founded 1839 **Pop** 198,525
Elev 204 ft **Area code** 318
Web www.shreveport-bossier.org

Information Shreveport-Bossier Convention & Tourist Bureau, 629 Spring St, PO Box 1761, 71166; 318/222-9391 or 800/551-8682

What to See and Do

American Rose Center. Center consists of 60 individually designed rose gardens donated by rose societies from across the US; 20,000 rose-bushes. (Mid-Apr-Oct, daily) 14 mi W via I-20 to Exit 5, then N to 8877 Jefferson-Paige Rd. Phone 318/938-5402. ¢¢

Hamel's Amusement Park. 30-acre park with a variety of rides and games. (Summer, Wed-Sun; spring and fall, Sat and Sun) 3232 E 70th St. Phone 318/869-3566.

Water Town USA. Twenty-acre water activity theme park features speed slides, adventure slides, wave pool, plus 2 other pools; restaurant and concessions. (June-late Aug, daily; May, Sat and Sun; also Labor Day wknd) I-20 W, Industrial Loop Exit. Phone 318/938-5473. ¢¢¢-¢¢¢¢¢

Annual Events

Red River Revel Arts Festival. Riverfront area. National festival featuring fine arts, crafts, pottery, jewelery; music and performing arts; creative writing, poetry; ethnic foods. Phone 318/424-4000. Late Sep-early Oct.

Louisiana State Fair. Fairgrounds. One of the largest fairs in the country, annually draws more than 300,000 people. Entertainment; agriculture and livestock competition. Phone 318/635-1361. Late Oct-early Nov.

Motels/Motor Lodges

★★ **BEST WESTERN RICHMOND SUITES OF SHREVEPORT.** *5101 Monkhouse Dr (71109), I-20 Airport Exit (13), near Regional Airport.*

318/635-6431; fax 318/635-6040; res 800/528-1234; toll-free 800/447-2582. 121 rms, 56 suites, 2 story. S, D $69-$129; under 18 free. Crib free. TV; cable (premium). Pool; wading pool, whirlpool. Complimentary bkfst buffet, coffee in rms. Restaurant adj open 24 hrs. Ck-out noon. Coin lndry. Business servs avail. In-rm modem link. Free airport transportation. Exercise equipt; sauna. Cr cds: A, D, DS, MC, V.

🅳 🏌 🛬 🏋 ✈ 🏊 🔥

★ **DAYS INN.** *4935 W Monkhouse Dr (71109). 318/636-0080; fax 318/635-4517; toll-free 800/329-7466.* 148 rms, 3 story. Apr-Nov: S $35-$45; D $47-$52; each addl $6; family rates; higher rates racing season; lower rates rest of yr. Crib free. TV; cable. Pool. Complimentary continental bkfst. Ck-out 11 am. Sundries. Business servs avail. Cr cds: A, C, D, DS, MC, V.

🅳 🛬 🏊 🔥 SC

★★ **FAIRFIELD INN BY MAR-RIOTT.** *6245 Westport Ave (71129). 318/686-0102; fax 318/688-8791; res 800/228-2800.* 105 rms, 2 with shower only, 3 story. S $59-$66; D $69-$76; each addl $7; under 12 free. Crib free. TV; cable (premium). Pool. Complimentary continental bkfst. Ck-out noon. Meeting rms. Business servs avail. In-rm modem link. Valet serv. Sundries. Exercise equipt. Cr cds: A, D, DS, MC, V.

🅳 🏌 🛬 🏋 🏊 🔥

★★ **HOLIDAY INN FINANCIAL PLAZA.** *5555 Financial Plaza (71129), I-20 at Buncomb or Pines Rd Exit. 318/688-3000; fax 318/687-4462; res 800/465-4329. Email lseuser@shreve holidayinn.com.* 230 rms, 6 story. S, D $69-$79; each addl $10; suites $135-$165; under 18 free. Crib free. TV; cable (premium), VCR avail. Indoor/outdoor pool; wading pool, whirlpool, poolside serv. Restaurant 6 am-10 pm. Bar 11-1 am; entertainment. Ck-out noon. Business center. Coin lndry. Bellhops. Valet serv. Free airport transportation. Exercise equipt; saunas. Holidome. Private patios, balconies. Cr cds: A, C, D, DS, MC, V.

🅳 🛬 🏋 🏊 🔥 🏃

★★ **RAMADA INN.** *5116 Monkhouse Dr (71109). 318/635-7531; fax 318/635-1600; res 800/228-2828; toll-free 800/284-0224. Email sales@* ramada-shreveport.com. 255 rms, 2-4 story. S $59-$69; D $64-$74; each addl $10; suites $125-$150; under 18 free. Crib avail. Pet accepted. TV; cable (premium). Pool; whirlpool. Restaurant 6 am-10 pm. Bar 11-2 am; entertainment. Ck-out noon. Convention facilities. Business servs avail. Bellhops. Gift shop. Free airport, bus depot transportation. Exercise equipt. Game rm. Cr cds: A, C, D, DS, MC, V.

🅳 🏌 🛬 🏋 ✈ 🏊 🔥

Hotels

★★ **BEST WESTERN CHATEAU SUITE HOTEL.** *201 Lake St (71101), I-20 Exit 19A (Spring St). 318/222-7620; fax 318/424-2014; res 800/845-9334. Email gmcsh@worldnet.att.net; www.bestwestern.com.* 103 rms, 5 story, 50 suites. S, D $89; each addl $18; suites $129; under 17 free. Crib avail. Parking lot. Pool, whirlpool. TV; cable (premium). Complimentary full bkfst, coffee in rms, newspaper, toll-free calls. Restaurant nearby. Bar. Ck-out noon, ck-in 3 pm. Meeting rms. Business center. Bellhops. Dry cleaning, coin lndry. Gift shop. Free airport transportation. Exercise equipt. Golf. Video games. Cr cds: A, C, D, DS, ER, JCB, MC, V.

🅳 🏌 🛬 🏋 🏊 🔥 🏃

★★★ **SHERATON PIERREMONT.** *1419 E 70th St (71105). 318/797-9900; fax 318/798-2923; res 800/325-3535.* 267 rms, 6 story. S, D $109; each addl $10; suites $250-$450; under 18 free. Crib free. TV; cable (premium). Pool. Coffee in rms. Restaurant 6:30 am-10:30 pm. Bar. Ck-out noon. Convention facilities. Business center. In-rm modem link. Concierge. Gift shop. Free airport transportation. Exercise equipt. Refrigerators. Luxury level. Cr cds: A, C, D, DS, MC, V.

🅳 🏌 🛬 🏋 🏊 🔥 🏃

B&Bs/Small Inns

★★ **FAIRFIELD PLACE BED & BREAKFAST.** *2221 Fairfield Ave (71104). 318/222-0048; fax 318/226-0631. Email fairfldpl@aol.com; www.fairfieldbandb.com.* 6 rms, 2 story. S $98-$112; D $98-$145; each addl $14; suites $145. TV; cable (premium), VCR avail. Complimentary full bkfst. Restaurant nearby. Ck-out 11 am, ck-in 2 pm. Business servs avail. In-rm modem link. Private parking. Built in 1880 for a Louisiana Supreme Court Justice. Totally nonsmoking. Cr cds: A, DS, MC, V.

★★★ TWENTY-FOUR THIRTY-NINE FAIRFIELD. *2439 Fairfield Ave (71104). 318/424-2424; fax 318/459-1839. Email 2439fair@bellsouth.com; www.bbonline.com/la/fairfield.* 4 rms, 3 story. S, D $95-$165. TV; cable (premium). Complimentary full bkfst. Ck-out 11 am, ck-in by appt. Business servs avail. In-rm modem link. Antiques. Library/sitting rm. Victorian mansion (ca 1905); landscaped gardens, carved oak staircase, crystal chandeliers. Totally nonsmoking. Cr cds: A, C, D, DS, MC, V.

Restaurants

★★ DON'S SEAFOOD. *3100 Highland (71104). 318/865-4291.* Specializes in seafood, steak, crawfish in season. Hrs: 11 am-10 pm; Fri, Sat to 11 pm. Closed Thanksgiving, Dec 25. Res accepted. Bar. Lunch, dinner $6-$17.95. Child's menu. Family-owned. Cr cds: A, D, DS, MC, V.

★★★ MONSIEUR PATOU. *855 Pierremont Rd #135 (71106). 318/868-9822. www.sofdisk.com/comp/patou.* Specializes in filet mignon with wild mushroom sauce, lobster bisque, grilled fish with champagne sauce. Hrs: 11:30 am-2 pm, 6-11 pm. Closed Sun; hols. Res accepted. Bar. Wine cellar. Lunch complete meals: $32.95; dinner à la carte entrées: $50-$60. Formal dining, Louis XV decor; antiques. Cr cds: A, D, DS, MC, V.

★ SUPERIOR GRILL. *6123 Line Ave (71106). 318/869-3243. www.superior. com.* Specializes in mesquite-grilled fajitas, margaritas. Hrs: 11 am-10 pm; Fri, Sat to 11 pm. Closed Dec 25. Bar. Lunch $5-$9; dinner $7.50-$14.95. Mexican cantina-style decor. Cr cds: A, MC, V.

Slidell

(E-7) *See also Covington, New Orleans*

Pop 24,124 **Elev** 9 ft **Area code** 504
Web www.neworleansnorthshore.com

Information St. Tammany Parish Tourist & Convention Commission, 68099 LA 59, Mandeville 70471; 504/892-0520 or 800/634-9443

What to See and Do

Fort Pike State Commemorative Area. Fort was constructed in the 1820s to defend navigational channels leading to New Orleans. Visitors can stroll through authentic brick archways and stand overlooking the Rigolets as sentries once did. Picnicking. (Daily; closed Jan 1, Thanksgiving, Dec 25) 8 mi E via US 190, then 6 mi SW on US 90. Phone 504/662-5703 or 888/662-5703. Per vehicle ¢

🗷 **John C. Stennis Space Center.** Visitor center has indoor and outdoor exhibits, displays, demonstrations, and movies built around "Space-Oceans-Earth" theme. Space Shuttle Test Complex is on site. 45-min bus tour. (Daily; closed Easter, Thanksgiving, Dec 25) 12 mi NE via I-10 Exit 2, in Mississippi. Phone 601/688-2370. **FREE**

Slidell Cultural Center. Art gallery. (Mon-Fri, also Sun afternoons) 444 Erlanger St. Phone 504/646-4375. **FREE**

Motel/Motor Lodge

★ LA QUINTA INN. *794 E I-10 Service Rd (70461), Exit 266. 504/643-9770; fax 504/641-4476; res 800/531-5900. www.laquinta.com.* 177 rms, 2 story. S, D $69.99-$86.99; each addl $6; under 18 free; higher rates special events. Crib free. Pet accepted. TV; cable (premium), VCR avail. Pool. Complimentary continental bkfst. Restaurant adj. Bar. Ck-out noon. Coin lndry. Meeting rms. Business servs avail. In-rm modem link. Health club privileges. Game rm. Microwaves avail. Cr cds: A, D, DS, MC, V.

Hotel

★★ **RAMADA INN.** *798 E I-10 Service Rd (70461), I-10 Exit 266.* 504/643-9960; fax 504/643-3508; toll-free 800/272-6232. Email ramadads@bell south.net; www.ramada.com. 149 rms, 2 story, 2 suites. Feb, Apr: S $74; D $79; each addl $8; suites $140; under 18 free; lower rates rest of yr. Crib avail. Pet accepted, some restrictions. Parking lot. Pool, children's pool. TV; cable (premium). Complimentary coffee in rms, newspaper, toll-free calls. Restaurant 6 am-9 pm. Bar. Ck-out noon, ck-in 2 pm. Meeting rms. Business servs avail. Dry cleaning, coin lndry. Exercise privileges. Golf, 18 holes. Tennis, 15 courts. Video games. Cr cds: A, C, D, DS, MC, V.

Rosedown Plantation, St. Francisville

Restaurant

★★ **SAL & JUDY'S.** *US 190 W (70460), 16 mi on LA 190.* 504/882-9443. www.salandjudy.com. Specializes in crab claws, shrimp scampi. Hrs: 5-10 pm; Sun noon-7:30 pm. Closed Mon, Tues; hols; 1st 2 wks in Aug. Res required. Bar. Dinner $9.50-$15.50. Family-owned. Cr cds: A, D, DS, MC, V.

St. Francisville

(D-5) *See also Baton Rouge, Jackson*

Pop 1,700 **Elev** 115 ft
Area code 225 **Zip** 70775
Web www.saint-francisville.la.us
Information West Feliciana Historical Society, 11757 Ferdinand St, PO Box 338; 225/635-6330

What to See and Do

■ **Plantations and historic buildings.** (For details see What to See and Do under BATON ROUGE; the following directions are from St. Francisville.) **Catalpa,** 4 mi N on US 61; **Oakley,** 1 mi S via US 61, then 3 mi E on LA 965; **Cottage,** 5 mi N on US 61; **But-** ler **Greenwood,** 3 mi N on US 61; **Greenwood,** 3 mi N on US 61, then 4½ mi W on LA 66 to Highland Rd; **Rosedown,** E of town on LA 10. Also of interest are **Grace Episcopal Church** (1858), in town on LA 10; **Afton Villa Gardens,** 4 mi N on US 61; and the **Myrtles Plantation,** 1 mi N on US 61.

Annual Events

Audubon Pilgrimage. Tour of historic plantation houses, two gardens, and rural homestead. Third wkend Mar.

Angola Prison Rodeo. L.S.P. Rodeo Arena. Phone 504/655-4411. Every Sun Oct.

Southern Garden Symposium. Tribute to Southern gardening. Workshops, field trips. Phone 504/635-6330. Mid-Oct.

B&Bs/Small Inns

★★ **BARROW HOUSE INN.** *9779 Royal St (70775).* 225/635-4791; fax 225/635-1863. Email staff@topteninn. com; www.topteninn.com. 5 rms, 3 suites. 2 rm phones. S $75; D $85-$120; each addl $30; suites $135-$150. Closed Dec 22-25. TV, VCR. Complimentary afternoon refreshments. Dinner by advance res. Ck-out 11 am, ck-in 3-7 pm. Library/sitting rm. Built in 1809; antiques. Cr cds: A, DS, MC, V.

★ **ST. FRANCISVILLE INN.** *5720 Commerce St (70775).* 225/635-6502; fax 225/635-6421; res 225/635-6502; toll-free 800/488-6502. Email wolf sinn@aol.com; www.wolfsinn.com. 9 rms, 1-2 story. S $55-$65; D $65-$75; each addl $8; under 6 free. Crib free.

TV; cable. Pool. Complimentary full bkfst. Restaurant (see ST. FRANCISVILLE INN). Ck-out 11 am, ck-in noon. Business servs avail. Library/sitting rm. Built in 1880; Victorian architecture. Ceiling medallion decorated with Mardi Gras masks. Cr cds: A, DS, MC, V.

Restaurant

★★ **ST. FRANCISVILLE INN.** *5720 N Commerce St. 225/635-6502. Email wolfsinn@aol.com; www.wolfsinn.com.* Specializes in seafood, steak. Own desserts. Hrs: 6:30 am-8:30 pm. Closed hols. Bar. Lunch $3.95-$8.45; dinner $5.95-$16.95. Restored Victorian mansion (1880); New Orleans-style courtyard; large oak trees with Spanish moss. Cr cds: A, DS, MC, V.

St. Martinville

(F-4) *See also Lafayette, New Iberia*

Settled ca 1760 **Pop** 7,137 **Elev** 19 ft **Area code** 337 **Zip** 70582
Information Chamber of Commerce, Box 436; 337/394-7578

B&B/Small Inn

★★ **LA PLACE D'EVANGELINE.** *220 Evangeline Blvd (70582), I-10 Exit 109S. 337/394-4010; fax 337/394-7983; toll-free 800/621-3017. www.1sttravelerschoice.com.* 5 rms, 2 story. No rm phones. S, D $50-$80. Complimentary full bkfst. Restaurant (see LA PLACE D'EVANGELINE). Ck-out, ck-in 1 pm (flexible). Street parking. Library/sitting rm. Historic hotel, built early 1800s. Located on the banks of Bayou Teche, beneath the Evangeline Oak; near Evangeline Oak Park. Cr cds: A, DS, MC, V.

Restaurant

★ **LA PLACE D'EVANGELINE.** *220 Evangeline Blvd. 337/394-4010. Email phulin@worldnet.att.net; www.virtualcities.com.* Specializes in seafood. Hrs: 8 am-9 pm; Mon, Tues to 5 pm; Sun

to 2 pm. Closed Jan 1, Thanksgiving, Dec 25. Res accepted Fri, Sat. Bar. Bkfst $1.50-$5; lunch, dinner $4.95-$22. Child's menu. Casual dining; overlooks Bayou Teche. Cr cds: A, D, MC, V.

Thibodaux

(F-5) *See also Houma, Morgan City*

Pop 14,035 **Elev** 15 ft **Area code** 504 **Zip** 70301
Web www.thibodaux-chamber.com
Information Chamber of Commerce, 1048 Canal Blvd, PO Box 467, 70302; 504/446-1187

Motel/Motor Lodge

★ **HOWARD JOHNSON.** *201 N Canal Blvd (70301). 504/447-9071; fax 504/447-5752; res 800/952-2968. www.hojo.com.* 118 rms, 2 story. S $50-$150; D $55-$150; each addl $5; suites $80-$150; under 18 free; higher rates special events. Crib free. Pet accepted, some restrictions; $10. TV; cable (premium), VCR avail (movies). Coffee in rms. Complimentary full bkfst. Restaurant 6 am-10 pm; Sun, Mon to 9 pm. Rm serv 6 am-8 pm. Bar noon-2 am. Ck-out noon. Meeting rms. Business servs avail. In-rm modem link. Valet serv. Lighted tennis, pro. Exercise equipt; sauna. Pool; poolside serv. Game rm. Rec rm. Refrigerators, microwaves avail. Cr cds: A, C, D, DS, JCB, MC, V.

B&B/Small Inn

★★★ **MADEWOOD PLANTATION HOUSE.** *4250 LA 308 (70390), 20 mi NW on LA 308. 504/369-7151; fax 504/369-9848; res 504/369-7151.* 6 rms, 2 story, 2 suites. Mar-Apr: S $212; D $245; each addl $60; suites $245; lower rates rest of yr. Crib avail. TV; cable (premium), CD avail. Closed Thurs. Bar. Ck-out 10 am, ck-in 4 pm. Gift shop. Golf. Cr cds: A, DS, MC, V.

MISSISSIPPI

Bearded Spaniards in rusted armor followed De Soto across Mississippi in search of gold 80 years before the *Mayflower* landed in Massachusetts. De Soto died in the fruitless search. Pierre Le Moyne, Sieur d'Iberville, established Mississippi's first permanent settlement near Biloxi in 1699. There was no gold to be found, but the mighty Mississippi River had created something of infinitely greater value—an immense valley of rich, productive land on which cotton could be grown. It was cotton that established the great plantations, but while cotton still ranks first in agricultural production, the state also produces forestry, poultry, soybeans, and catfish. However, manufacturing is the number one industry in the state.

Population: 2,573,216
Area: 47,234 square miles
Elevation: 0-806 feet
Peak: Woodall Mountain (Tishomingo County)
Entered Union: December 10, 1817 (20th state)
Capital: Jackson
Motto: By valor and arms
Nickname: Magnolia State
Flower: Magnolia
Bird: Mockingbird
Tree: Magnolia
Fair: October 3-14, 2001, in Jackson
Time Zone: Central
Website: www.mississippi.org

Andrew Jackson became a hero in Mississippi after he defeated the Creek Indian nation and was again honored during a triumphal return through the state after winning the Battle of New Orleans in 1815. Mississippians enthusiastically named their capital after "Old Hickory" and they entertained him royally when he returned as an elder statesman in 1840.

For two years, northern Mississippi was the scene of some of the fiercest fighting in the Civil War. Following the Union defeat of Confederate forces at the Battle of Shiloh (Tennessee) in April 1862, General Ulysses S. Grant moved southwest into Mississippi. The following year, Grant besieged Vicksburg for 47

Mississippi River at sunset, Natchez

days. When the city finally fell, the fate of the Confederacy, according to some historians, was sealed. Yet battles still seesawed across and up and down the beleaguered state as railroads and telegraph lines were sliced by Northern raiders. Mississippi was left in shambles. It was after General William Tecumseh Sherman burned Jackson that he said, "War is Hell!" For Mississippi, the war was indeed hell, and the Reconstruction period was nearly as chaotic.

Today Mississippi's subtropical Gulf Coast provides vast quantities of shrimp and oysters; it is also a tremendously popular resort and vacation area. Fishing is good in many streams; hunting for waterfowl along the Mississippi River and for deer in other areas is also excellent. The state has beautiful forests, the antebellum traditions and pageantry of Natchez, the beautiful Natchez Trace Parkway, and many other attractions.

When to Go/Climate

Mild winters and hot summers are the norm in Mississippi. Rain is common, but snow is unusual. Hurricane season runs from June through Oct along the Gulf Coast.

AVERAGE HIGH/LOW TEMPERATURES (°F)

JACKSON

Jan 56/33	**May** 84/60	**Sep** 88/64
Feb 60/36	**June** 91/67	**Oct** 79/50
Mar 69/44	**July** 92/71	**Nov** 69/42
Apr 77/52	**Aug** 92/70	**Dec** 60/36

TUPELO

Jan 49/31	**May** 81/60	**Sep** 85/63
Feb 55/34	**June** 88/67	**Oct** 75/50
Mar 64/43	**July** 91/71	**Nov** 64/42
Apr 74/51	**Aug** 90/69	**Dec** 53/34

Parks and Recreation Finder

Directions to and information about the parks and recreation areas below are given under their respective town/city sections. Please refer to those sections for details.

NATIONAL PARK AND RECREATION AREAS

Key to abbreviations. I.H.S. = International Historic Site; I.P.M. = International Peace Memorial; N.B. = National Battlefield; N.B.P. = National Battlefield Park; N.B.C. = National Battlefield and Cemetery; N.C.A. = National Conservation Area; N.E.M. = National Expansion Memorial; N.F. = National Forest; N.G. = National Grassland; N.H.P. = National Historical Park; N.H.C. = National Heritage Corridor; N.H.S. = National Historic Site; N.L. = National Lakeshore; N.M. = National Monument; N.M.P. = National Military Park; N.Mem. = National Memorial; N.P. = National Park; N.Pres. = National Preserve; N.R.A. = National Recreational Area; N.R.R. = National Recreational River; N.Riv. = National River; N.S. = National Seashore; N.S.R. = National Scenic Riverway; N.S.T. = National Scenic Trail; N.Sc. = National Scientific Reserve; N.V.M. = National Volcanic Monument.

Place Name	Listed Under
Bienville N.F.	MENDENHALL
Brices Cross Roads N.B.C.	TUPELO
De Soto N.F.	HATTIESBURG
Delta N.F.	YAZOO CITY

Gulf Islands N.S.	same
Holly Springs N.F.	HOLLY SPRINGS
Homochitto N.F.	NATCHEZ
Natchez Trace Parkway	same
Tombigbee N.F.	LOUISVILLE
Tupelo N.B.	TUPELO
Vicksburg N.M.P. & Cemetery	VICKSBURG

STATE PARK AND RECREATION AREAS

Key to abbreviations. I.P. = Interstate Park; S.A.P. = State Archaeological Park; S.B. = State Beach; S.C.A. = State Conservation Area; S.C.P. = State Conservation Park; S.Cp. = State Campground; S.F. = State Forest; S.G. = State Garden; S.H.A. = State Historic Area; S.H.P. = State Historic Park; S.H.S. = State Historic Site; S.M.P. = State Marine Park; S.N.A. = State Natural Area; S.P. = State Park; S.P.C. = State Public Campground; S.R. = State Reserve; S.R.A. = State Recreation Area; S.Res. = State Reservoir; S.Res.P. = State Resort Park; S.R.P. = State Rustic Park.

Place Name	Listed Under
Buccaneer S.P.	PASS CHRISTIAN
Clarkco S.P.	MERIDIAN
George Payne Cossar and John W. Kyle S.P	SARDIS
Golden Memorial S.P.	PHILADELPHIA
Great River Road S.P.	CLEVELAND
Holmes County S.P.	KOSCIUSKO
Hugh White S.P.	GRENADA
Lake Lowndes S.P.	COLUMBUS
Legion S.P.	LOUISVILLE
Leroy Percy S.P.	GREENVILLE
Nanih Waiya S.P.	LOUISVILLE
Natchez S.P.	NATCHEZ
Paul B. Johnson S.P.	HATTIESBURG
Percy Quin S.P.	MCCOMB
Tombigbee and Trace S.P.	TUPELO
Wall Doxey S.P.	HOLLY SPRINGS
Winterville Mounds S.P.	GREENVILLE

Water-related activities, hiking, various other sports, picnicking, and visitor centers, as well as camping, are available in many of these areas. State parks provide fishing (free); boating, rentals ($6/day), launching ($5); swimming ($2; children $1); picnicking; tent and trailer facilities ($11-$14/night; 14-day max); primitive tent camping ($6-$8) and cabins ($30-$70/night; 14-day max). Pets on leash only; not allowed in cabin or on property. Scattered throughout the state are 89 roadside parks with picnic facilities. For further information, contact Information Services and Marketing, Dept of Wildlife, Fisheries and Parks, PO Box 451, Jackson 39205-0451. Phone 800/467-2757.

FISHING AND HUNTING

Anglers find limitless possibilities in Mississippi. There are no closed seasons, and size limits are imposed on game fish in only some areas (except sea-run striped bass and black bass on a few state waters). The Chickasawhay, Pearl, Homochitto, and Pascagoula rivers are endless sources for largemouth bass, crappie, bluegill, bream, and catfish, as are 6 large reservoirs and more than 170,000 acres of lakes. There are fishing camps at many lakes and reservoirs and on the Gulf Coast, where boats, bait, and tackle are available. Complete charter services for deep-sea fishing and fishing piers are featured along US 90 as well as at Gulf Coast resorts. Nonresident fishing license, 16 yrs and over: annual, $25; 3-day, $6.

CALENDAR HIGHLIGHTS

MARCH

Spring Pilgrimage (Vicksburg). Twelve antebellum houses are open to the public at this time. Three tours daily. Contact Convention and Visitors Bureau. Phone 601/636-9421 or 800/221-3536.

National Cutting Horse Association Show (Jackson). Entries from across the US participate in amateur to professional rider competitions. Phone 800/354-7695.

MAY

Blessing of the Fleet (Biloxi). Hundreds of vessels manned by descendants of settlers participate in this ritual of European origin.

Siege Reenactment (Vicksburg). Five hundred persons reenact the siege of Vicksburg. Contact Convention and Visitors Bureau. Phone 601/636-9421 or 800/221-3536.

JUNE

Delta Jubilee (Clarksdale). Statewide arts and crafts festival; Mississippi championship pork barbecue cooking contest; 5K run; antique car show. Contact Convention and Visitors Bureau. Phone 662/627-7337 or 800/626-3764.

JULY

Mississippi Deep-Sea Fishing Rodeo (Gulfport). Anglers from US, Canada, and Latin America compete in various types of sportfishing. Phone 228/863-2713 or 228/832-0079.

SEPTEMBER

Delta Blues and Heritage Festival (Greenville). Showcase of Blues greats. Phone 662/335-3523.

OCTOBER

Mississippi State Fair (Jackson). Agricultural and industrial exhibits and contests; entertainment. Phone 601/961-4000.

Great Mississippi River Balloon Race Weekend (Natchez). Food, music, entertainment. Contact Convention and Visitors Bureau. Phone 601/446-6345 or 800/647-6724.

Mississippi-Alabama State Fair (Meridian). Mississippi-Alabama Fairgrounds. Agricultural exhibits, carnival. Phone 228/482-8001 or 888/868-7720.

Hunting on some 1 million acres of the more than 30 state-managed public hunting areas is seasonal: quail, late Nov-late Feb; wild turkey (gobblers only), late Feb-late Apr; squirrel, mid-Oct-mid-Jan; deer, usually Oct-Jan; duck, reservoir areas, and major river lowlands, usually Dec-Jan; dove, Sep-Oct and winter. Public waterfowl management areas are located on some reservoirs and river lowlands. Licenses for nonresidents: all game (annual $225, 5-day $105); small game (annual $75, 5-day $30); archery and primitive firearms (must also purchase annual all-game permit) $30; waterfowl, state waterfowl stamp required $5. For detailed information contact the Dept of Wildlife, Fisheries and Parks, PO Box 451, Jackson 39205-0451. Phone 601/362-9212.

Driving Information

Safety belts are mandatory for front seat passengers. Children under 4 yrs must be in an approved safety seat anywhere in vehicle. In addition, safety belts are mandatory for all persons anywhere in vehicle when traveling on the Natchez Trace Parkway. Phone 601/987-1336.

INTERSTATE HIGHWAY SYSTEM

The following alphabetical listing of Mississippi towns in *Mobil Travel Guide* shows that these cities are within 10 miles of the indicated Interstate highways. A highway map should, however, be checked for the nearest exit.

Highway Number	Cities/Towns within 10 miles
Interstate 10	Biloxi, Gulfport, Ocean Springs, Pascagoula, Pass Christian.
Interstate 20	Jackson, Meridian, Vicksburg.
Interstate 55	Grenada, Jackson, McComb, Sardis.
Interstate 59	Hattiesburg, Laurel, Meridian.

Additional Visitor Information

Information booklets are avail from the Division of Tourism, PO Box 1705, Ocean Springs 39566; 800/WARMEST.

There are 11 welcome centers in Mississippi; visitors who stop by will receive information, brochures, and personal assistance in planning stops at points of interest. Their locations are as follows: at the northern end of the state, on I-55 S of Hernando; along the southern border, on I-55 S of Chatawa, on I-59 N of Nicholson, on I-10 at Waveland, and on I-10 at Pascagoula; by the eastern border, on I-20 E of Toomsuba; in the western section, on US 82 & Reed Rd in Greenville, on I-20 near Vicksburg, on US 61 Bypass & Seargent S. Prentiss Dr N of Natchez, and on I-78 W of border. Centers are open 8 am-5 pm, daily. For information on road conditions phone the Mississippi Highway Patrol, 601/987-1212.

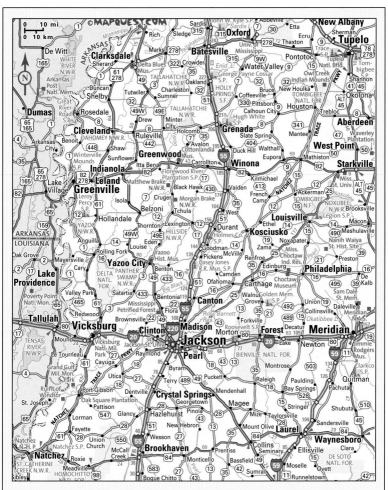

Natchez Trace—This old buffalo path, turned Indian trail, turned trade route is now the Natchez Trace National Parkway, rivaling the pastoral beauty of the Blue Ridge Parkway. The best times to drive the route from Jackson are spring and fall, and it also makes a lovely bike route from its northern terminus outside Nashville, TN, to its southern terminus near Natchez, MS. This charming city, once a busy Mississippi River port, draws visitors from around the country to its historic districts and antebellum homes, especially at "Pilgrimage" time in spring and fall when many private homes are open to public tours. A riverboat casino and many reasonably priced historic bed-and-breakfasts add to the city's appeal. The Natchez Trace National Parkway also passes Indian mounds, pioneer sites, and rolling farmland, and heads through Tupelo for a quick detour to Elvis Presley's birthplace. **(Approx 230 mi)**

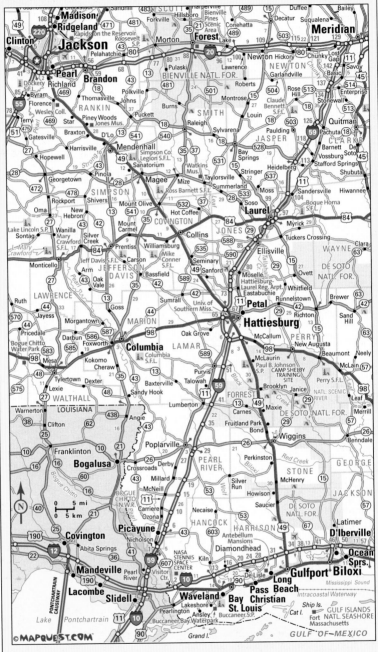

Mississippi Coast—A long back-roads drive along Highway 49 from Jackson leads to Mississippi's gulf coast, centered around the towns of Biloxi and Gulfport, both of which offer wide sandy beaches, modern casinos, and ferry rides to the Gulf Islands National Seashore. Visitors also enjoy visiting the Jefferson Davis Home and Presidential Library in Biloxi and the John C. Stennis Space Center in Gulfport.
(Approx 480 mi)

© MAPQUEST.COM

Biloxi

(H-5) *See also Gulfport, Ocean Springs, Pascagoula, Pass Christian*

Settled 1699 **Pop** 46,319 **Elev** 25 ft
Area code 228
Web www.biloxi.ms.us
Information Visitor Center, 710 Beach Blvd, 39530; 228/374-3105 or 800/BILOXI-3

The oldest town in the Mississippi Valley, Biloxi has been a popular resort since the 1840s. It has, since the 1870s, been a leading oyster and shrimp fishing headquarters; shrimp were first canned here in 1883.

The Sieur d'Iberville's first French fort was established at Ocean Springs, just east of Biloxi. In 1721, the third shipment of "Cassette girls" (so called after the boxes or "cassettes" in which they carried their possessions) landed at Ship Island, 12 miles south in the Gulf of Mexico. These 89 girls, carefully selected by a French bishop, were sent to become wives to the settlers. The area continues to reflect a strong ethnic heritage representing the eight flags that have flown over Biloxi during the past 300 years.

Magnolia trees, camellias, azaleas, roses, and crepe myrtle bloom along Biloxi's streets among the oaks draped with Spanish moss. There is freshwater, saltwater, and deep-sea fishing all year; crabbing, floundering, and mullet net casting. Biloxi is the home of Keesler AFB, the electronics and computer training center of the United States Air Force. In recent years, casinos have become a popular attraction in Biloxi, and many have been built along the Gulf of Mexico beach.

What to See and Do

⭐ **"Beauvoir"—Jefferson Davis Home and Presidential Library.** Estate where the Confederate president spent the last 12 yrs of his life. From

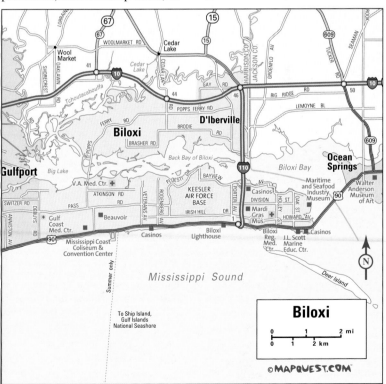

1903-57, "Beauvoir" also served as the Mississippi soldiers' home for Confederate veterans and their widows. Adj museums have Davis and Confederate artifacts. The Library Pavilion, where Davis wrote *The Rise and Fall of the Confederate Government* and *A Short History of the Confederate States of America*, contains his desk and books. Landscaped grounds covering 57 acres contain house, museums, 2 pavilions, Confederate cemetery with Tomb of the Unknown Soldier of the Confederate States of America, and Presidential Library. (Daily; closed Dec 25) 2244 Beach Blvd (US 90). Phone 228/388-1313. ¢¢¢

Casinos. From Gulfport to Biloxi, Mississippi's Gulf Coast is dotted with casinos. Many have adj hotels, and several host big-name entertainment. Some of the casinos incl the Grand Casino Biloxi, Isle of Capri, Palace, Boomtown, and Treasure Bay casinos. For more information contact the Mississippi Gulf Coast Convention and Visitors Bureau. Phone 888/467-4853.

Annual Events

Mardi Gras. Carnival and parade. Shrove Tuesday. Feb.

Garden Club Pilgrimage. Guided tour of historic houses, sites, and gardens. Mar or Apr.

Blessing of the Fleet. Gulf of Mexico. Hundreds of vessels manned by descendants of settlers participate in this ritual of European origin. First wkend May.

Seafood Festival. Point Cadet Plaza, E on US 90. Arts and crafts show, entertainment, seafood booths, contests. Last wkend Sep.

Motels/Motor Lodges

★ **BREAKERS INN.** *2506 Beach Blvd (39531). 228/388-6320; fax 228/388-7185; toll-free 800/624-5031.* 28 kit suites, 1-2 story. May-Sep: S, D $121-$171; higher rates: Memorial Day wkend, July 4, Labor Day; lower rates rest of yr. Pet accepted. TV; cable. Pool; wading pool. Playground. Restaurant nearby. Ck-out 11 am. Lndry facilities in rms. Business servs avail. In-rm modem link. Tennis. Lawn games. Opp gulf. Cr cds: A, DS, MC, V.

★★ **COMFORT INN.** *1648 Beach Blvd (39531), on US 90. 228/432-1993; fax 228/432-2297; res 800/228-5150. Email comfortinnbiloxi@aol.com.* 68 rms, 2 story. June-Aug: S, D $65-$145; each addl $8-$12; kits. $70-$150; under 18 free; higher rates hols (3-day min); lower rates rest of yr. Crib free. TV; cable (premium). Pool; whirlpool. Complimentary continental bkfst. Restaurant nearby. Ck-out 11 am. Balconies. Opp beach. Cr cds: A, C, D, DS, MC, V.

★ **DAYS INN.** *2046 Beach Blvd (39531). 228/385-1155; fax 228/385-2532; toll-free 800/329-7466.* 166 rms, 3 story, 83 kit Suites. S, D $64-$139; each addl $5; kit suites $89-$159; under 18 free; golf plans. Crib free. TV; cable (premium). Pool. Complimentary continental bkfst. Ck-out noon. Coin lndry. Business servs avail. Tennis. Balconies. Opp beach and gulf. Cr cds: A, D, DS, MC, V.

★★ **EDGEWATER INN.** *1936 Beach Blvd (39531). 228/388-1100; fax 228/385-2406; toll-free 800/323-9676. Email edgeinn@aol.com; www.gcww. com/edgewaterinn/.* 65 rms, 3 story. Mar-Sep: S, D $69-$159; each addl $6; suites $129-$199; under 13 free; wkly rates; package plans; higher rates hols; lower rates rest of yr. Crib $6. TV; cable. Indoor/outdoor pool. Restaurant open 24 hrs. Ck-out noon. Exercise equipt; sauna. Refrigerators. On Gulf; opp beach. Cr cds: A, C, D, DS, MC, V.

★★ **HOLIDAY INN.** *2400 Beach Blvd (39531). 228/388-3551; fax 228/385-2032; res 877/248-1500; toll-free 800/441-0882.* 268 rms, 4 story. S $59-$64; D $93-$98; each addl $10; golf plan; higher rates hols (3-day min). Crib avail. TV; cable. Pool; poolside serv. Playground. Restaurant. Bar 4:30 pm-midnight; entertainment. Coin lndry. Meeting rms. Business servs avail. In-rm modem link. Bellhops. Valet serv. Free airport transportation. Game rm. Refrigerators avail. Balconies. Opp ocean. Cr cds: A, C, D, DS, JCB, MC, V.

★★ **QUALITY INN.** *1865 Beach Blvd (39531). 228/388-3212; fax*

228/388-6541; toll-free 800/342-7519. 62 rms, 2 story. Apr-early Sep: S, D $60-$80; each addl $10; lower rates rest of yr. Crib $10. TV; cable (premium). Heated pool; poolside serv. Restaurant 7 am-2 pm, 5-9 pm. Bar from 5 pm. Ck-out noon. Meeting rms. Business servs avail. In-rm modem link. Bellhops. Sundries. On Gulf; private sand beach. Cr cds: A, C, D, DS, ER, JCB, MC, V.

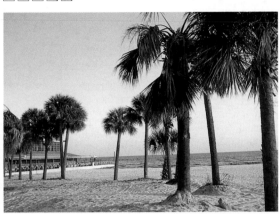

Mississippi Gulf Coast beach

Hotel

★ ★ ★ **GRAND CASINO HOTEL BILOXI.** *265 Beach Blvd (39530). 228/432-2500; fax 228/435-8966; toll-free 800/946-2946.* 491 rms, 12 story. S $59-$129; D $69-$139; each addl $10; suites $160-$220; under 16 free; wkday rates. Crib free. TV; cable. Pool; whirlpool, lifeguard. Supervised children's activities; ages 6 wks-12 yrs. Complimentary coffee in lobby. Restaurant 7 am-10 pm. Bar. Ck-out 11 am. Convention facilities. Business servs avail. Concierge. Shopping arcade. Beauty shop. Free airport transportation. Exercise equipt; sauna. Game rm. Rec rm. Refrigerator in suites. Balconies. On ocean. Cr cds: A, C, D, DS, MC, V.

Resort

★ ★ ★ **BEAU RIVAGE BY MIRAGE RESORTS.** *875 Beach Blvd (39530). 228/386-7111; res 888/567-6667. Email guestservices@beaurivage.com;* *www.beaurivage.com.* 32 floors; 1780 rooms. Prices change according to availability. Range from $79-$189. Children free under 17. Valet parking. TV. Movies to rent. Crib free. Handicap. Bar. Nightly entertainment. 12 Restaurants. 4 Bars. Spa. Exercise rm. Salon. Pool. Jacuzzi. Rm serv 24 hr. Ck-in 3 pm, ck-out 11 am. Golf privileges. Cr cds: A, DS, MC, V.

Restaurants

★ **CUCO'S.** *1851 Beach Rd (39531). 228/388-1982.* Specializes in chimichangas, fajitas, fried ice cream. Hrs: 11 am-11 pm; Fri, Sat to midnight; Sun to 10 pm. Closed Thanksgiving, Dec 25. Res accepted. Bar. Lunch $4.50-$6; dinner $5.95-$9.95. Mexican artwork on walls. Cr cds: A, C, D, DS, MC, V.

★ ★ **FRENCH CONNECTION.** *1891 Pass Christian Rd (39531). 228/388-6367.* Specializes in Tar Babies, smoked oysters, shrimp Robert. Own baking. Hrs: 5:30-9:30. Closed Sun, Mon; hols. Bar. Dinner $13.95-$28.95. Child's menu. Parking. Open-hearth cooking. Antiques. On grounds that were once part of Beauvoir, estate of Jefferson Davis. Cr cds: A, D, DS, MC, V.

★ **HOOK, LINE & SINKER SEAFOOD.** *2030 Beach Blvd (US 90) (39531). 228/388-3757.* Specializes in seafood. Oyster bar. Hrs: 11 am-10 pm; Fri, Sat 2-11 pm. Closed Mon; also 1 wk in Dec. Bar. Lunch $5-$20; dinner $10-$22. Child's menu. Parking. Nautical decor; view of gulf. Family-owned. Cr cds: A, C, D, DS, MC, V.

★ ★ ★ **MARY MAHONEY'S OLD FRENCH HOUSE.** *Rue Magnolia & US 90 (39530). 228/374-0163.* Specializes in half lobster Georgo, stuffed red snapper, seafood gumbo. Own bread pudding. Hrs: 11 am-10 pm. Closed Sun; Dec 24, 25. Bar. Wine cellar. Lunch complete meals: $7.95-$10.95; dinner complete meals: $14.95-$28.95. Child's menu. Parking. Colonial house and slave quarters built 1737. Antiques, fireplaces. Family-owned. Cr cds: A, D, DS, MC, V.

[D] [⊠]

★★ **O'CHARLEY'S.** *2590 Beach Blvd (US 90) (39531), at Edgewater Mall. 228/388-7883.* Specializes in beef, seafood. Hrs: 11 am-midnight. Bar. Lunch $3.99-$9.99; dinner $7.99-$16.95. Sun brunch $3.99-$12.99. Child's menu. Cr cds: A, C, D, DS, MC, V.

[D] [⊠]

Brices Cross Roads National Battlefield Site

(see Tupelo)

Clarksdale

(B-2) *See also Cleveland*

Founded 1869 **Pop** 19,717 **Elev** 175 ft
Area code 662 **Zip** 38614
Web www.clarksdale.com/tourism
Information Coahoma County Tourism Commission, 1540 Desoto, PO Box 160; 662/627-7337 or 800/626-3764

Named for John Clark, an Englishman who laid out the town in 1869, Clarksdale shared dual status with Friars Point as Coahoma County seat from 1892 until 1930. Sunflower Landing near Clarksdale is said to be the site where De Soto discovered the Mississippi River.

Clarksdale is located in the heart of the rich delta farmland, one of the state's top-ranking areas in cotton, soybean, and grain production.

Three lakes in the area make this a water sports center.

Annual Events

Delta Jubilee. Statewide arts and crafts festival; Mississippi championship pork barbecue cooking contest; 5K run; antique car show. First wkend June.

Sunflower River Blues and Gospel Festival. Wkend of outdoor concerts—blues on Saturday, gospel on Sunday—with local barbecue and other Southern specialties. First wkend Aug.

Motels/Motor Lodges

★★ **HAMPTON INN.** *710 S State St (38614), ½ mi S on US 61. 662/627-9292; fax 662/624-4763; toll-free 800/426-7866.* 93 rms, 2 story. S $56-$62; D $62-$68; each addl $6; under 18 free. Crib free. TV; cable. Indoor/outdoor pool; whirlpool. Complimentary continental bkfst. Restaurant 6 am-11 pm. Ck-out noon. Coin lndry. Meeting rms. Business servs avail. In-rm modem link. Exercise equipt. Some refrigerators. Some balconies. Cr cds: A, C, D, DS, JCB, MC, V.

[D] [≈] [🛉] [⊠] [🐾] [SC]

Casino

★★ **LADY LUCK CASINO & ENTERTAINMENT RESORT.** *777 Lady Luck Pkwy (38644), approx 20 mi N on US 61, W on US 49. 662/363-2250; fax 662/337-4590; res 800/576-5825; toll-free 800/789-5825.* 172 rms, 2 story. S, D $39-$69; each addl $10; suites $49-$79; under 18 free; higher rates blues fest. Crib free. TV; cable (premium). Pool. Complimentary coffee in lobby. Restaurant 11 am-11 pm. Bar open 24 hrs; entertainment. Ck-out noon. Coin lndry. Meeting rms. Business center. Bellhops. Valet serv. Concierge. Sundries. Gift shop. Golf privileges. Exercise equipt. Game rm. Refrigerators. On river. Cr cds: A, DS, MC, V.

[D] [🏌] [≈] [🛉] [⊠] [🐾] [🏌]

Cleveland

(C-2) *See also Clarksdale*

Pop 15,384 **Elev** 142 ft **Area code** 662 **Zip** 38732

Information Chamber of Commerce, Third St, PO Box 490; 662/843-2712 or 800/295-7473

Motels/Motor Lodges

★★ **HOLIDAY INN.** *US 61 S (38732), 1 mi S on US 61.* 601/846-1411; fax 601/843-1713; toll-free 800/533-8466. 119 rms, 2 story. S $41-$50; D $46-$55; each addl $5; under 18 free. Crib free. TV; cable. Pool. Restaurant 6 am-2 pm, 6-9 pm; closed wkends. Bar 5-11 pm; closed wkends. Ck-out noon. Business servs avail. In-rm modem link. Cr cds: A, C, D, DS, MC, V.

Columbus

(C-5) *See also Starkville*

Settled 1817 **Pop** 23,799 **Elev** 200 ft **Area code** 662
Web www.friendship.columbus.msus
Information Columbus Convention & Visitors Bureau, PO Box 789, 39703; 662/329-1191 or 800/327-2686 (exc MS)

Annual Event

Pilgrimage. Costumed guides conduct tours through 15 historic houses. Special events. First 2 wks of Apr.

Motels/Motor Lodges

★★ **COMFORT INN.** *1210 Hwy 45 N (39705).* 662/329-2422; fax 662/327-0311; res 800/228-5150. 64 rms, 2 story. S, D $53-57; each addl $4; under 12 free. Crib free. TV; cable. Complimentary continental bkfst. Restaurant opp 11 am-9 pm. Ck-out 11 am. Meeting rms. Business

servs avail. In-rm modem links. Cr cds: A, C, D, DS, JCB, MC, V.

★★ **HOLIDAY INN.** *506 Hwy 45 N (39701), ¼ mi S off US 82 Bypass.* 662/328-5202; fax 662/241-4979; toll-free 800/465-4329. 153 rms, 2 story. S, D $62-68; each addl $5. Crib free. TV; cable (premium). Pool. Restaurant 6 am-2 pm, 5:30-10 pm. Bar 4 pm-midnight. Ck-out noon. Meeting rms. Business servs avail. Valet serv. Cr cds: A, D, DS, MC, V.

Restaurant

★★ **HARVEY'S.** *200 Main St (39703).* 662/327-1639. www.eatwithus.com. Specializes in beef, seafood, salads. Hrs: 11 am-9:30 pm; Fri, Sat to 10 pm. Closed Sun; hols. Res accepted. Bar. Lunch $4.95-$9.95; dinner $6.95-$14.95. Child's menu. Restored tannery; antiques. Cr cds: A, DS, MC, V.

Corinth (A-5)

Founded 1854 **Pop** 11,820 **Elev** 455 ft
Area code 662 **Zip** 38834
Web www.corinth.net
Information Corinth Area Tourism Promotion Council, 810 Tate St, PO Box 1089, 38835-1089; 662/287-5269

Motel/Motor Lodge

★★ **EXECUTIVE INN.** *Hwy 72; 45 W (38834), jct US 45 Bypass.* 662/286-6071; fax 662/286-9608; res 800/354-3932. 70 rms, 2-3 story, 6 kits. S $42; D $47; kits $60; each addl $5; under 12 free. Crib free. TV; cable (premium). Pool. Restaurant 11 am-2 pm, 5-9 pm. Rm serv. Ck-out 11 am. Meeting rms. Cr cds: A, C, D, DS, MC, V.

Greenville (C-2)

Settled 1828 **Pop** 45,226 **Elev** 125 ft
Area code 662
Web www.techinfo.com/wccgb

Information Greenville Area Chamber of Commerce, PO Box 933, 38702-0933; 662/378-3141; or the Washington County Convention & Visitors Bureau, 410 Washington Ave, 38702; 662/334-2711

Greenville, which is not even on the Mississippi, is the state's largest river port. The Mississippi River was, in 1935, finally broken of its habit of stealing whole areas of the town, block by block. Levees forced the channel six miles westward and left a lake for a harbor. Before this, in 1927, the whole town was under water for 70 days. The first Greenville settlement was on the Blantonia Plantation (1828), which was purchased for the site of the third county seat. The first was flooded out; the second burned during shelling by Union gunboats in 1863.

What to See and Do

Birthplace of the Frog Exhibit. Muppet memorabilia from collectors and the family of the late Jim Henson, creator of the Muppets. (Memorial Day-Labor Day, daily; rest of yr, Mon-Fri) SE Deercreek Dr in Leland. Phone 662/686-2687. **Donation**

Annual Event

Delta Blues and Heritage Festival. Showcase of Blues greats. Phone 601/335-3523. Third wkend Sep. 119 S Theobold St.

Motels/Motor Lodges

★★ **HAMPTON INN.** *2701 Hwy 82 E (38703). 662/334-1818; fax 662/332-1761; res 800/426-7866.* 120 units, 2 story. S, D $52-$58; each addl $7; studio rms $59-$66; under 12 free. Crib free. TV; cable. Pool. Complimentary continental bkfst. Ck-out noon. Meeting rm. Business center. In-rm modem link. Cr cds: A, C, D, DS, MC, V.

★★ **HOLIDAY INN.** *2428 Hwy 82 E (38703). 662/334-6900; fax 662/332-5863; res 800/465-4329.* 119 rms, 2 story, 13 suites. S, D $47-$59; each addl $6; suites $67-$74; under 17 free. Crib $5. TV; cable. Heated indoor/outdoor pool; wading pool, whirlpool. Complimentary continental bkfst, coffee in rms. Ck-out noon. Coin lndry. Meeting rms. Business servs avail. In-rm modem link. Exercise equipt. Health club privileges. Refrigerators. Cr cds: A, C, D, DS, MC, V.

★★ **RAMADA INN.** *2700 US 82 E (38701). 662/332-4411; fax 662/332-4411; res 800/272-6232.* 121 rms, 2 story. Apr-Sep: S $50; D $55; each addl $5; suites $110; under 18 free; lower rates rest of yr. Crib avail. Pet accepted, some restrictions. Parking lot. Pool. TV; cable (premium), VCR avail. Complimentary full bkfst, coffee in rms, newspaper, toll-free calls. Restaurant 6 am-10 pm. Bar. Ck-out noon, ck-in 2 pm. Meeting rms. Business servs avail. Dry cleaning. Free airport transportation. Golf, 18 holes. Tennis, 4 courts. Supervised children's activities. Cr cds: A, C, D, DS, MC, V.

Restaurant

★ **SHERMAN'S.** *1400 S Main St (38701). 662/332-6924.* Specializes in steak, seafood. Hrs: 11 am-2 pm, 5-9 pm; Fri to 10 pm; Sat 5-10 pm. Closed hols. Bar. Lunch $5-$8; dinner $11-$18. Child's menu. Informal atmosphere. Wildlife prints. Family-owned. Cr cds: A, D, DS, MC, V.

Greenwood

(C-3) *See also Grenada*

Settled 1834 **Pop** 18,906 **Elev** 140 ft
Area code 662 **Zip** 38930
Web www.netdoor.com/com/gcvb

Information Convention & Visitors Bureau, PO Drawer 739; 662/453-9198 or 800/748-9064

Motels/Motor Lodges

★★ **COMFORT INN.** *401 W Hwy 82 (38930).* 662/453-5974; fax 662/455-6401; res 800/228-5150. 60 rms, 2 story. S $47-$49; D $49-$53; each addl $5; under 18 free; wkly rates. Crib $3. TV; cable. Pool. Complimentary continental bkfst. Restaurant opp 6 am-10 pm. Ck-out noon. Business servs avail. In-rm modem link. Park, picnic grounds opp. Cr cds: A, C, D, DS, MC, V.

★★★ **HAMPTON INN.** *635 Hwy 82 W (38930).* 662/455-5777; fax 662/455-4237; res 888/455-5770. 100 rms, 2 story. S $50-$52; D $56-$58; under 18 free. Crib free. TV; cable. Indoor/outdoor pool; wading pool. Complimentary continental bkfst. Restaurant 6 am-11 pm. Ck-out noon. Coin lndry. Meeting rms. Business servs avail. In-rm modem link. Valet serv. Tennis. Exercise equipt. Refrigerators. Some balconies. Cr cds: A, C, D, DS, MC, V.

Restaurant

★★ **CRYSTAL GRILL.** *423 Carrollton Ave (38930).* 662/453-6530. Specializes in seafood, steak. Hrs: 11 am-10 pm. Closed Mon; hols; Dec 24. Res accepted. Bar. Lunch $4.55-$7.45; dinner $4.75-$18.50. Child's menu. Family-owned. Cr cds: A, DS, MC, V.

Grenada

(C-4) *See also Greenwood*

Pop 10,864 **Elev** 195 ft **Area code** 662 **Zip** 38901

Information Grenada Tourism Commission, 1321 Sunset Plaza, Suite JJ, PO Box 1824; 662/226-2571 or 800/373-2571

Annual Event

Thunder on Water Festival. Grenada Lake. Parade, children's fishing rodeo, antique car show, boat light parade, and several speed boat races. Second wkend June.

Motels/Motor Lodges

★★ **BEST WESTERN GRENADA.** *1750 Sunset Dr (38901), I-55 Exit 206.* 662/226-7816; fax 662/226-5623; toll-free 800/880-8866. 61 rms, 2 story. S $42-$49; D $54-$66. Crib $5. Pet accepted, some restrictions. TV; cable. Pool. Complimentary full bkfst. Restaurant 6 am-10 pm. Ck-out noon. Meeting rms. Business servs avail. In-rm modem link. Lawn games. Cr cds: A, C, D, DS, MC, V.

★★ **COMFORT INN.** *1552 Sunset Dr (38901).* 662/226-1683; fax 662/226-9484; res 800/228-5150. 66 rms, 2 story. S $52-$90; D $55-$90; each addl $5; under 18 free; lower rates rest of yr. Crib $5. TV; cable. Pool; whirlpool. Complimentary continental bkfst. Restaurant nearby. Ck-out noon. Business servs avail. Refrigerators. Cr cds: A, C, D, DS, ER, JCB, MC, V.

★ **DAYS INN.** *1632 Sunset Dr (38901).* 662/226-8888; fax 662/227-9592; res 800/325-2525. 53 rms, 2 story. S $45-$69; D $55-$79; each addl $7; under 18 free. Crib free. TV; cable. Pool; whirlpool. Restaurants nearby. Ck-out noon. Refrigerators, microwaves avail. Cr cds: A, C, D, DS, MC, V.

★★ **HOLIDAY INN.** *1796 Sunset Dr (38901), ⅛ mi E of I-55 Exit 206.* 662/226-2851; fax 662/226-5058; res 800/456-4829; toll-free 800/800-5314. 130 rms, 2 story. S, D $50-$75; each addl $7; suites $165; under 18 free. Crib free. TV; cable (premium), VCR avail. Indoor pool; wading pool. Restaurant 6 am-2 pm, 5-10 pm. Bar. Ck-out noon. Coin lndry. Meeting rms. Business servs avail. In-rm modem link. Airport transportation. Cr cds: A, C, D, DS, MC, V.

Gulf Islands National Seashore

See also Biloxi, Gulfport, Ocean Springs

Information Park Office, 3500 Park Rd, Ocean Springs 39564; 228/875-0821

Headquarters and campground for the Mississippi district of this beautiful area are in Ocean Springs. Sparkling beaches, coastal marshes, and wildlife sanctuaries may be found on the four offshore islands (Petit Bois, Horn, East and West Ship) and the mainland area (Davis Bayou). The mainland areas are open year-round and are accessible from US 90.

In 1969, Hurricane Camille split Ship Island in two, leaving East Ship and West Ship Islands. Ship Island was once a base for French exploration and settlement (1699-1753) of the Gulf Coast from Mobile, Alabama, to the mouth of the Mississippi River. What is now East Ship Island once served as the staging area for a 50-ship British armada and an unsuccessful attempt to capture New Orleans in 1815 at the end of the War of 1812.

On West Ship Island is Fort Massachusetts. Construction of this brick coastal defense began in 1859, prior to the outbreak of the Civil War. Two years later the Mississippi militia took control of the fort from the United States Army Corps of Engineers after the state seceded from the Union. The Confederates later fortified it, naming it Fort Twiggs in honor of the New Orleans Confederate general. Repeated threats by Northern forces caused the Confederates to withdraw in September 1861. The fort was then reoccupied by Union soldiers, who called it Fort Massachusetts. For a time, the area east of the fort served as a prisoner-of-war camp, confining some 4,300 Confederate prisoners at one point. Completed in 1866, the fort was never fully armed. Free tours of the fort are offered daily (Mar-Nov). Concession boats run to Fort Massachusetts and West Ship Island from Gulfport (Mar-Oct), depending on weather conditions.

All four offshore islands are accessible year-round by boat only and are open to wilderness camping (except on West Ship Island), surf fishing, surf swimming (Memorial Day-Labor Day), boating, picnicking, and hiking. No motor vehicles or glass are allowed on the islands. Horn and Petit Bois are designated as wilderness areas, and special restrictions apply.

The mainland campground has water and electric hookups (fee) at 51 sites, a public boat dock, and picnic areas. The visitor center offers audiovisual programs, exhibits, boardwalks, and nature trails. Pets are allowed on leash only. **FREE**

Gulfport

(H-5) *See also Biloxi, Ocean Springs, Pass Christian*

Founded 1880 **Pop** 40,775 **Elev** 20 ft
Area code 228 **Web** www.biloxi.org
Information Chamber of Commerce, 1401 20th Ave, PO Drawer FF, 39502; 228/863-2933

Although chosen as an ideal site for a port and a railroad terminus in 1887, it was 1902 before the Gulf & Ship Island Railroad's New York owner fulfilled the plan. As a planned city, Gulfport has broad streets laid out in a regular rectangular pattern paralleling the seawall. This was in marked contrast to the narrow-streeted antebellum towns along the rest of the coast. When completed, the railroad, which ran through sparsely settled sections rich in timber, transformed southern Mississippi.

Gulfport turned to the resort business in the 1920s and had a real estate boom in 1925 when the Illinois Central Railroad bought the Gulf & Ship Island line. The boom collapsed a year later after having produced Gulfport's tower apartments and many hotels. After World War II, luxury motels took over. With the Mississippi Sound and a great number of lakes, rivers, bays, and bayous within a few minutes

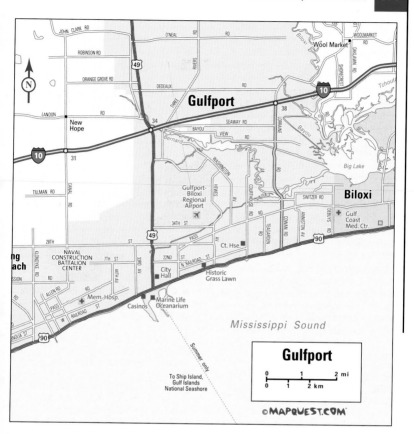

Gulfport

Mississippi Sound

To Ship Island,
Gulf Islands
National Seashore

© MAPQUEST.COM

drive from downtown, and with excellent facilities for deep-sea fishing, Gulfport is an angler's paradise.

Mississippi City, which has been incorporated into Gulfport, was the scene of the bare-knuckles fight for the heavyweight championship of the world on February 7, 1882, when John L. Sullivan beat Paddy Ryan under the live oaks now at the corner of US 90 and Texas Street.

What to See and Do

Boat trips. Passenger ferry leaves from Gulfport Yacht Harbor for trips to Ship Island. (Mar-Oct) Schedule varies; for information contact Ship Island Excursions, PO Box 1467, 39502. Phone 228/864-1014 (recording), or 228/864-3797 (office). Round-trip ¢¢¢¢

Gulf Islands National Seashore. (see)

⭐ **John C. Stennis Space Center.** Second-largest NASA field installation. Testing site of Saturn V, first and sec-

ond stages for the Apollo manned lunar program, including those for Apollo 11, which landed first men on moon in 1969. Original test stands were later modified to develop and test space shuttle main engines. The Stennis Space Center hosts NASA and 18 federal and state agencies involved in oceanographic, environmental, and national defense programs. Visitor Center with 90-ft Space Tower; films, demonstrations; indoor, outdoor exhibits; guided tours (daily; closed Easter, Thanksgiving, Dec 25). 38 mi W via I-10. Phone 228/688-2370. **FREE**

Port of Gulfport. Extends seaward from jct US 49, 90, located equidistant between New Orleans and Mobile, AL. One of the largest banana import facilities in the US; the projected depth of the channel is 32 ft; the depth of the harbor is 30 ft at mean low water with a tidal variation of approx 2 ft. The 1,320-ft wide harbor separates the port's 2 parallel piers; 11 berths are avail.

Small Craft Harbor. Launching ramps, charter boats, and pleasure craft docking. Jct US 49, 90. Adj is

> **Marine Life Oceanarium.** Dolphin and sea lion feedings, giant reef tank, underwater divers, touch pool. Also Aqua Stadium with exotic birds and Captain Crooked's SS *Gravity*. (Daily; closed Dec 25) US 90 at US 49, in Jones Memorial Park. ¢¢¢

Annual Events

Spring Pilgrimage. Tours of antebellum houses, gardens. Contact Biloxi Community Center for details. Phone 228/432-5836. Late Mar-early Apr.

Mississippi Deep-Sea Fishing Rodeo. Small Craft Harbor. Anglers from US, Canada, and Latin America compete in various types of sportfishing. Phone 228/388-2271 or 228/863-2713. Early July.

Motels/Motor Lodges

★★ **BEST WESTERN BEACH VIEW INN.** *2922 W Beach Blvd (39501).* 228/864-4650; fax 228/863-6867; res 800/528-1234; toll-free 800/748-8969. 150 rms, 5 story. Mid-Feb-Mar, mid-May-Labor Day: S, D $75-$95; each addl $6; suites $130-$150; under 16 free; higher rates wknds; lower rates rest of yr. Crib free. TV; cable. Pool. Bar 10-6 am. Ck-out noon. Meeting rms. Overlooks harbor. Cr cds: A, C, D, DS, MC, V.

⬛🐾🏊🎣🔲🐾🏃

★★ **HOLIDAY INN.** *1600 E Beach Blvd (39501).* 228/864-4310; fax 228/865-0525; res 800/465-4329; toll-free 800/441-0887. 229 rms, 2-5 story. May-Labor Day: S, D $73-$120; each addl $5; under 19 free; lower rates rest of yr. Crib free. TV; cable. Pool; wading pool, poolside serv. Restaurant 6 am-10 pm. Bar 4 pm-1 am. Ck-out noon. Coin lndry. Meeting rms. In-rm modem link. Bellhops. Game rm. Opp beach. Cr cds: A, D, DS, JCB, MC, V.

⬛🐾🏊🎣🔲🐾

Hotel

★★★ **GRAND CASINO OF MISS GULFPORT.** *3215 W Beach Blvd*

(39501). 228/870-7777; fax 228/870-7220. www.grandcasinos.com. 381 rms, 18 story, 26 suites. Feb, May-Aug: S, D $99; each addl $10; suites $279; under 17 free; lower rates rest of yr. Crib avail. Valet parking avail. Indoor/outdoor pools, lap pool, whirlpool. TV; cable (premium), VCR avail. Complimentary coffee in rms. Restaurant. Bar. Ck-out noon, ck-in noon. Conference center, meeting rms. Business servs avail. Bellhops. Concierge. Dry cleaning. Gift shop. Salon/barber. Exercise rm, sauna, steam rm. Golf. Tennis, 2 courts. Beach access. Supervised children's activities. Video games. Cr cds: A, D, DS, MC, V.

⬛🐾🏊🎣🔲🏃🔲🐾

B&B/Small Inn

★ **RED CREEK INN, VINEYARD & RACING STABLE.** *7416 Red Creek Rd (39560), approx 5 mi W on US 90, N on Menge Ave to Red Creek Rd.* 228/452-3080; fax 228/452-4450; toll-free 800/729-9670. Email info@redcreek inn.com; www.redcreekinn.com. 5 rms, 3 story. No rm phones. S, D $49-$99. Complimentary continental bkfst, coffee in rms. Ck-out, ck-in by arrangement. Business servs avail. Lawn games. French Colonial house (1899) with 6 fireplaces, antique furnishings; 64-ft front porch. Situated on 11 acres of magnolia trees and ancient live oaks. Totally nonsmoking. Cr cds: A, DS, MC, V.

🔲🐾

Restaurants

★★★ **VRAZEL'S.** *3206 W Beach Blvd (US 90) (39501).* 228/863-2229. Email wvrazel@aol.com; www.gcww. com/vrazels/. Specializes in steak, fresh seafood, veal. Hrs: 11 am-2 pm, 5-10 pm; Sat from 5 pm. Closed Sun; hols. Res accepted. Wine list. Lunch á la carte entreés: $5.95-$13.95; dinner á la carte entreés: $12.95-$18.95. Elegant dining rm with views of gardens, beach. Cr cds: A, DS, MC, V.

⬛🔲

★ **WHITE CAP SEAFOOD RESTAURANT.** *1411 28th Ave (39501).* 228/863-4652. Specializes in seafood. Oyster bar. Hrs: 10:30 am-9 pm; Fri, Sat to 10 pm. Closed Tues; Jan 1, Thanksgiving; also last 2 wks in Dec. Bar. Lunch $4.95-$5.95; dinner $10-$15. Child's menu. On pier. Nautical decor. Family-owned. Cr cds: DS, MC, V.

Hattiesburg (G-4)

Founded 1882 **Pop** 41,882 **Elev** 161 ft
Area code 601
Web www.hattiesburg-adp.org
Information Area Development Partnership-Chamber Division, 1 Convention Center, PO Box 751, 39403; 800/238-4288

Once known as Twin Forks and Gordonville, the settlement was renamed by an early settler in honor of his wife, Hattie. When railroads were routed through Hattiesburg during the late 19th century, the town began to thrive. Unlike other towns that came and went with the lumber boom of the 1920s, Hattiesburg was able to diversify its economic base with a number of industries. The University of Southern Mississippi makes the town the educational center of the southern sector of the state.

Hotels

★★ **COMFORT INN.** *6595 Hwy 49 N (39401). 601/268-2170; fax 601/268-1820; res 800/228-5150. Email gm.ms084@choicehotels.com; www.choicehotels.com.* 119 rms, 2 story. S, D $50-$64; each addl $6; suites $90-$100; under 18 free. Crib free. Pet accepted, some restrictions. TV; cable (premium). Pool. Complimentary full bkfst. Restaurant 6 am-9:30 pm. Bar 5 pm-midnight; entertainment Fri, Sat. Ck-out noon. Coin lndry. Meeting rms. Business servs avail. Valet serv. Golf privileges. Cr cds: A, DS, MC, V.

★★ **HAMPTON INN.** *4301 Hardy St (39401). 601/264-8080; fax 601/264-9916; toll-free 800/426-7866. Email hattiesburg-gm@rfsmgmt.com; www.hampton-inn.com* 155 units, 2 story. S $55-$75; D $63-$75; under 18 free.

Crib free. TV; cable. Pool. Complimentary continental bkfst. Ck-out noon. Meeting rm. Business servs avail. In-rm modem link. Health club privileges. Cr cds: A, DS, MC, V.

★★ **HOLIDAY INN.** *6563 US 49 (39401), off I-59 Exit 67A. 601/268-2850; fax 601/268-2823; toll-free 800/465-4329. Email hbgunsales@cooper hotels.com.* 128 rms, 2 story. S, D $62.99; each addl $6; under 18 free. Crib free. TV; cable. Pool; whirlpool. Restaurant 6:30 am-2 pm, 5-10 pm. Bar 4:30 pm-midnight; entertainment. Ck-out noon. Meeting rms. Business servs avail. Lighted tennis. Some refrigerators. Cr cds: A, DS, MC, V.

Restaurants

★★ **CHESTERFIELD'S.** *2507 Hardy St (39401). 601/582-2778.* Specializes in beef, steak, seafood. Hrs: 11 am-10:30 pm; Fri, Sat to 11 pm; Sun to 10 pm. Closed Thanksgiving, Dec 25. Bar. Lunch, dinner $4.25-$14.95. Child's menu. Cr cds: A, D, DS, MC, V.

★★ **CRESCENT CITY GRILL.** *3810 Hardy St (39402). 601/264-0657. www.nsrg.com.* Specializes in steak, pasta, seafood. Hrs: 11 am-10 pm; Fri, Sat to 11 pm. Closed Thanksgiving, Dec 25. Bar. Lunch, dinner $12-$20. Child's menu. Casual, elegant dining. Local original art. Cr cds: A, DS, MC, V.

★★ **ROCKET CITY DINER.** *4700 Hardy St #AA (39402), at the Arbor in Turtle Creek Shopping Center. 601/264-7893.* Specializes in hamburgers, country-fried steak. Hrs: 11 am-10 pm; Fri, Sat to 11 pm; Sun to 9 pm. Closed Dec 25. Bkfst $3.50-$10.95; lunch, dinner $3.50-$10.95. Child's menu. 1950s atmosphere. Cr cds: A, DS, MC, V.

Holly Springs

(A-4) *See also Memphis, TN*

Founded 1835 **Pop** 7,261 **Elev** 609 ft
Area code 662 **Zip** 38635
Information Chamber of Commerce,
154 S Memphis; 662/252-2943

Holly Springs crowns the ridge along
which a Native American trail once
led from the Mississippi to the tribal
home of the Chickasaw Nation.
William Randolph, descendant of
Virginia's famed John Randolph, is
credited with founding the town.

Wealth from cotton went into buy-
ing more and more land, driving up
real estate prices. Soon lawyers, who
were needed to cope with squabbles
over land and deeds, outnumbered
all other professionals. The town
skipped the frontier stage as Georgian and Greek Revival mansions
rose instead of log cabins.

Holly Springs suffered 61 raids during the Civil War; the most devastating was by a Southern force led by
Confederate General Van Dorn in
1862; the Confederates destroyed
General Grant's supply base, delaying
the fall of Vicksburg by a year.

Annual Events

Pilgrimage. Historic houses and gardens open to visitors. Phone
662/252-2943. Mid-Apr.

Kudzu Festival. Arts and crafts, carnival, live music, barbeque. Late July.

Jackson

(E-3) *See also Mendenhall*

Founded 1821 **Pop** 196,637
Elev 294 ft **Area code** 601
Web www.visitjackson.com

Information Chamber of Commerce,
201 S President St, 39205; 601/948-
7575; or the Convention & Visitors
Bureau, PO Box 1450, 39215;
601/960-1891 or 800/354-7695

The beautiful site of Jackson, along
the bluffs above the Pearl River, was
selected as a perfect location for
commerce by a young French Canadian trader. Although Louis LeFleur
succeeded in his aim and set up a
trading post after his exploratory
voyage up the Pearl from the Gulf of
Mexico, the city has throughout its
existence been a center of government, rather than business.

It is impossible to separate the
town's history from its role as state
capital; it was designated such as
soon as the state's boundaries had
expanded sufficiently, by the ceding
of Native American lands, to make
Jackson the state's geographical center. The first session of the legislature
held in the town convened in January 1822. By then the city had
already been named for Andrew Jackson, idol of Mississippi, and laid out
in a checkerboard pattern in accor-
dance with Thomas Jefferson's rec-
ommendation to Governor Claiborne
17 years earlier. Evidence still remains
of the original plan, which reserved
every other square as a park or green.

There were attempts in 1829 to
move the capital to Clinton and in
the following year to Port Gibson,
but these were averted by a legislative act of 1832 that named Jackson
as the capital until 1850—by which
time it had a permanent stature.
Andrew Jackson addressed the legislature in what is now the Old Capitol in 1840, the year after its
completion, and a Mississippi Convention assembled to consider Henry
Clay's last compromise in 1850. The
building was the scene of the Secession Convention in January 1861.

Jackson was the junction of two
great railroads by the time of the
Civil War; it played an important role
as Confederate capital of Mississippi
until it was besieged in 1863, when
the capital was removed and the city
destroyed. All that was recorded in
Jackson of the state's turbulent politics and government went up in
smoke when General Sherman's army
reduced the city to ashes, bringing it
the ironic nickname, "Chimneyville."

The so-called "Black and Tan" convention that met at Jackson in January 1868, was the first political
organization in Mississippi with
black representation. It framed a constitution under which Mississippi
lived for 22 years, giving blacks the
franchise and enabling a few to
attain high political office. In the

same year, the governor was ejected from his office, and the carpetbaggers reigned until 1876. Jefferson Davis made his last public appearance in Jackson in 1884.

With the coming of the 20th century and half a dozen railroads connecting Jackson with the whole South, the population doubled within five years. Further growth came with the discovery of natural gas fields in 1930. The Ross Barnett Reservoir, covering 31,000 acres in central Mississippi, created tourist and recreational attractions as well as residential and industrial sites in the greater Jackson area.

What to See and Do

Battlefield Park. Site of US Civil War battle; original cannon and trenches. Porter St between Langley Ave & Terry Rd.

Davis Planetarium. Programs change quarterly; 230-seat auditorium. (Daily; closed hols) 201 E Pascagoula St. Phone 601/960-1550. ¢¢

Governor's Mansion. (1842) Restored to original plan and Greek Revival style; antiques and period furnishings. Grounds occupy entire blk and feature gardens, gazebos; tours. (Tues-Fri, mornings only; closed during official state functions) 300 E Capitol St, between N Congress & N West Sts. Phone 601/359-3175. **FREE**

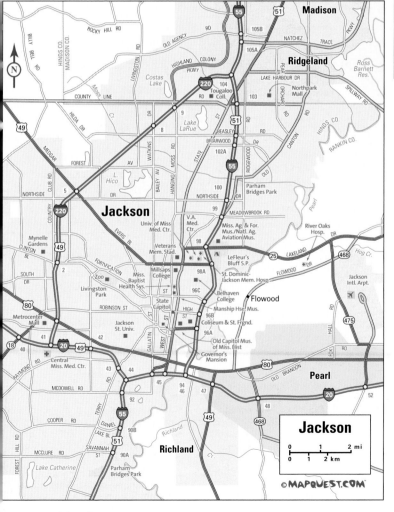

© MAPQUEST.COM

Jackson Zoological Park. More than 400 mammals, birds, and reptiles in naturalized habitats. (Daily; closed Jan 1, Dec 25) 2918 W Capitol St. Phone 601/352-2580. ¢¢

Manship House. Restored Gothic Revival cottage (ca 1855), was residence of Charles Henry Manship, mayor of Jackson during the US Civil War. Period furnishings; fine examples of wood graining and marbling. (Tues-Sat; closed hols) 420 E Fortification St. Phone 601/961-4724. **FREE**

Mississippi Agriculture & Forestry Museum and National Agricultural Aviation Museum. Complex, covering 39 acres, incl museum exhibit center, forest trail, 1920s living history town, and farm. Picnicking. (Daily; closed Jan 1, Dec 25) 1 mi NE on I-55, Exit 98 at Lakeland Dr. Phone 601/713-3365 or 800/844-8687. ¢¢

Mississippi Museum of Art. Exhibitions of 19th- and 20th-century works by local, regional, national, and intl artists. Special exhibitions, sculpture garden, hands-on children's gallery, restaurant, gallery programs, films, instruction, sales gallery. (Tues-Sun; closed hols) 201 E Pascagoula. Phone 601/960-1515. ¢¢

Mississippi Petrified Forest. Surface erosion exposed giant (up to 6 ft in diameter) petrified logs that were deposited in Mississippi area as driftwood by a prehistoric river. Self-guided nature trail. Museum at visitor center has dioramas; wood, gem, mineral, fossil displays; ultraviolet (black light) room. Picknicking, camping, gift shop. (Daily; closed Dec 25) 11 mi N on US 49, 1½ mi W via access road. Phone 601/879-8189. ¢¢

Mississippi Sports Hall of Fame and Museum. A variety of interactive exhibits can be found here such as touch-screen television kiosks that access archival sports footage. Through interactive technology, visitors can play championship golf courses, soccer, or pitch horseshoes. (Tues-Sun) 11152 Lakeland Dr. Phone 601/982-8264 or 800/280-FAME. ¢¢

Municipal Art Gallery. Changing exhibits in a variety of media displayed in antebellum house. (Tues-Sat, also Sun afternoons; closed hols; Fri of Thanksgiving wk; also Aug) 839 N State St. Phone 601/960-1582. **FREE**

Museum of Natural Science. Collections, designed for research and education, cover Mississippi's vertebrates, invertebrates, plants, and fossils. Exhibits and aquariums depict ecological story of region; educational programs and workshops offered for all ages. Professional library. Division of Mississippi Department of Wildlife Conservation. (Mon-Sat; closed hols) 2148 Riverside Dr. Phone 601/354-7303. **FREE**

Mynelle Gardens. A 5-acre display garden with thousands of azaleas, camellias, daylilies, flowering trees, and perennials; reflecting pools and statuary; Asian garden, miniature flower gardens, and an all-white garden. Turn-of-the-century Westbrook House is open for viewing. Changing art and photography exhibits. Gift shop, picnicking. (Daily; closed hols) 4736 Clinton Blvd, 2 blks off MS 220. Phone 601/960-1894. ¢

The Oaks House Museum. (1846) Greek Revival cottage, built of hand-hewn timber by James H. Boyd, former mayor of Jackson, was occupied by General Sherman during the siege of 1863. Period furniture, garden. (Tues-Sat; closed Jan 1, Thanksgiving, Dec 25) 823 N Jefferson St. Phone 601/353-9339. ¢ **Old Capitol.** Houses State Historical Museum. Exhibits tracing state history housed in restored Greek Revival bldg that was state capitol from 1839-1903; collection of Jefferson Davis memorabilia. Monthly exhibits. (Daily; closed hols) E end of Capitol St at State St. Phone 601/359-6920. **FREE** Adj are

Confederate Monument. (1891) Built with money raised by women of Mississippi and by legislative appropriations.

Archives and History Building. Houses state archives and history collections, research library. Phone 601/359-6850.

Ross R. Barnett Reservoir. Reservoir (43 mi in length) created by damming Pearl River. Swimming, waterskiing, fishing, boating; picnicking, camping. Standard fees. (Daily) 7 mi N on I-55, 3 mi E on Natchez Trace Pkwy. Phone 601/354-3448 or 601/856-6574.

Smith Robertson Museum. History and culture of African American Mississippians from Africa to present; large collection of photos, books, documents, art and crafts. (Mon-Fri, Sat mornings, Sun afternoons; closed hols) 528 Bloom St. Phone 601/960-1457. ¢

State Capitol. (1903) Impeccably restored in 1979, the lavish, beaux-arts capitol bldg was patterned after the national capitol in Washington. Houses legislature and governor's office. Tours (Mon-Fri). 400 High St. Phone 601/359-3114. **FREE**

Annual Events

Dixie National Livestock Show. Mississippi Coliseum. Late Jan-mid Feb. Rodeo 2nd wk Feb.

National Cutting Horse Association Show. Mississippi Coliseum. Entries from across the US participate in amateur to professional rider competitions. Late Mar.

Mississippi State Fair. State Fairgrounds, Jefferson St. Agricultural and industrial exhibits and contests; midway, entertainment. Phone 601/961-4000. Oct.

Motels/Motor Lodges

★ **BEST VALUE INN & SUITES.** *5035 I-55 N (39206), 601/982-1011; fax 601/982-1011; res 601/982-1011.* 133 rms, 2 story. S $46-$50; D $48-$54; each addl $5; suites $70-$100; under 17 free. Crib free. Pet accepted. TV; cable (premium). Pool. Restaurant 6 am-9 pm; closed Sat, Sun. Bar 5 pm-midnight. Ck-out noon. Coin lndry. Meeting rms. Business servs avail. In-rm modem link. Valet serv. Cr cds: A, DS, MC, V.

★ **CABOT LODGE MILLSAPS.** *2375 N State St (39202). 601/948-8650; fax 601/948-8650; toll-free 800/874-4737.* 205 rms, 6 story. S $53-71; D $61-$77; each addl $8; under 12 free; wkend rates. TV. Pool; wading pool. Complimentary continental bkfst. Ck-out noon. Coin lndry. Meeting rms. Business servs avail. In-rm modem links. Bellhops. Opp University Medical Center. Cr cds: A, C, D, DS, MC, V.

★★ **ECONO LODGE.** *2450 US 80 W (39204). 601/353-0340; fax 601/353-0340; toll-free 800/638-7949.* 40 rms. S $39-$59; D $45-$70; each addl $5; under 12 free. Crib $5. TV; cable. Complimentary continental bkfst. Restaurant nearby. Ck-out 11 am. Business servs avail. Cr cds: A, D, DS, JCB, MC, V.

★★ **HOLIDAY INN EXPRESS HOTEL.** *310 Greymont Ave (39202), I-55N, Exit 96C W. 601/948-4466; fax 601/352-9368; res 800/465-4329. Email wijackson@gte.net.* 110 rms, 5 story. S $43.95-$55.95; D $50.95-$55.95; each addl $7; under 18 free. Crib free. TV; cable (premium). Complimentary continental bkfst. Restaurant opp 11 am-9 pm. Ck-out noon. Meeting rms. Business servs avail. Some wet bars. Cr cds: A, C, D, DS, JCB, MC, V.

★ **LA QUINTA INN.** *150 Angle Dr (39204), I-20W, Exit 43S. 601/373-6110; fax 601/373-6115.* 101 rms, 2-3 story. S $51; D $57; suites $69-$81; each addl $6; under 18 free. Crib free. Pet accepted. TV; cable. Pool. Ck-out noon. Business servs avail. In-rm modem link. Valet serv. Airport transportation. Cr cds: A, C, D, DS, MC, V.

★★ **RESIDENCE INN BY MARRIOTT.** *881 E River Pl (39202), I-55N, Exit 96B E. 601/355-3599; fax 601/355-5127; res 800/331-3131.* 120 kit suites, 2 story. S, D $85-$149; wkly, monthly rates. Crib free. TV; cable (premium). Pool. Playground. Complimentary continental bkfst. Ck-out noon. Coin lndry. Meeting rms. Business servs avail. In-rm modem link. Health club privileges. Fireplaces. Some private patios, balconies. Cr cds: A, C, D, DS, MC, V.

Hotels

★★★ **EDISON WALTHALL.** *225 E Capitol St (39201). 601/948-6161; fax 601/948-0088; toll-free 800/932-6161.* 208 rms, 8 story. S $69-$75; D $79-$85; each addl $8; suites $90-$185; under 18 free. Crib free. Pet accepted. TV; cable. Pool; whirlpool. Restaurant 6:30 am-10 pm; Sat, Sun from 7 am. Bar from 4 pm; pianist Mon-Fri. Ck-out noon. Meeting rms. Business servs avail. In-rm modem link. Gift shop. Barber. Free covered parking. Free airport transportation. Exercise equipt. Cr cds: A, C, D, DS, MC, V.

★★★ **HILTON CONFERENCE CENTER.** *1001 County Line Rd (39211). 601/957-2800; fax 601/957-3191; res 800/445-8667; toll-free 888/263-0524.* 300 rms, 14 story. S $85-$115; D $95-$125; each addl $10; suites $255-$350; under 18 free; wkend rates. Crib free. TV; cable. Pool; whirlpool. Restaurants 6 am-10 pm. Bar 11-1 am; entertainment. Ck-out 1 pm. Convention facilities. Business center. Concierge. Barber, beauty shop. Free airport, railroad station, bus depot transportation. Tennis privileges. 18-hole golf privileges, driving range. Health club privileges. Bathrm phones, refrigerators. Luxury level. Cr cds: A, C, D, DS, ER, MC, V.

B&B/Small Inn

★★★ **MILLSAPS BUIE HOUSE.** *625 N State St (39202). 601/352-0221; fax 601/352-0221; res 800/874-0221; toll-free 800/784-0221. Email mbuiehouse@aol.com; www.milsapsbuiehouse.com.* 11 rms, 3 story, 1 suite. S $90; D $105. Valet parking avail. TV; cable. Complimentary full bkfst, newspaper. Restaurant. Bar. Ck-out 11 am, ck-in 2 pm. Meeting rm. Business center. Dry cleaning. Exercise privileges. Golf, 18 holes. Tennis, 6 courts. Cr cds: A, D, DS, MC, V.

Restaurants

★★ **DENNERY'S.** *330 Greymont Ave (39202). 601/354-2527.* Specializes in seafood, beef. Own baking. Hrs: 11 am-10 pm. Closed Sun; hols. Res accepted. Lunch $7-$10; dinner $11.50-$21.50. Child's menu. Parking. Grecian theme. Family-owned. Cr cds: A, D, DS, MC, V.

★★★ **NICK'S.** *1501 Lakeland Dr (39216). 601/981-8017. www.nicksrest.bellsouth.net.* Specializes in seafood, beef, veal. Own desserts. Hrs: 11 am-2 pm, 6-10 pm; Fri to 10:30 pm; Sat 6-10:30 pm. Closed Sun; hols. Bar. Wine list. Lunch $7-$13; dinner $14-$25. Child's menu.

Entertainment. Parking. Cr cds: A, C, D, MC, V.

★★ **POETS.** *1855 Lakeland Dr (55645). 601/982-9711.* Specializes in scampi, shrimp, crabmeat. Hrs: 11 am-2 pm, 4 pm-2 am; Sat 6 pm-2 am. Closed Sun; major hols. Bar. Lunch, dinner á la carte entrées: $3.25-$14.95. Parking. Antique bar, fixtures. Stained glass; Tiffany lamps. Tin ceiling. Cr cds: A, D, V.

★★ **PRIMOS RESTAURANT AT NORTHGATE.** *4330 N State St (39206). 601/982-2064.* Specializes in salads, seafood, steak. Hrs: 11 am-10 pm. Closed Sun. Res accepted. Bar. Lunch $6.50-$15.50. Complete meals: $4.95-$15.50; dinner $6.50-$15.50. Child's menu. Parking. Country French decor. Cr cds: A, MC, V.

★★ **TICO'S STEAK HOUSE.** *1536 E County Line Rd (39157). 601/956-1030.* Specializes in steak, fresh seafood. Own desserts. Hrs: 4:30-10:30 pm; Fri, Sat to 11 pm. Closed Sun; hols. Res accepted Fri, Sat. Bar. Dinner $8.95-$19.50. Parking. Lodge style. Beamed ceilings; fireplace. Cr cds: A, D, DS, MC, V.

Unrated Dining Spot

COCK OF THE WALK. *121 Madison Landing (39236), 15 mi N via I-55, Natchez Trace Exit to Ross Barnett Reservoir. 601/856-5500. www.thevirtualmenu.com/cockofthewalk.* Specializes in catfish, pickles, mustard greens. Hrs: 5-9 pm; Fri, Sat to 10 pm; Sun from 11:30 am. Closed Thanksgiving; Dec 24, 25. Bar. Dinner a la carte entrees: $8.95-$15.95. Child's menu. Parking. Rustic decor. Cr cds: A, C, D, DS, MC, V.

Kosciusko

(D-4) *See also Louisville*

Pop 6,986 **Elev** 488 ft **Area code** 662
Zip 39090
Web www.kopower.com/coc/coc.htm
Information Kosciusko-Attala Chamber of Commerce, 301 E Jefferson, PO Box 696; 662/289-2981

What to See and Do

Holmes County State Park. Approx 450-acre park has 2 lakes. Swimming beach, fishing, boating (rentals); nature trails, archery range, picnicking (shelters), playground, skating rink (call for schedule), coin laundry. Camping (water, electric hookups), cabins. Standard fees. 25 mi W on MS 12, then S on US 51, between US 51 & I-55. Phone 662/653-3351.

Kosciusko Museum-Information Center. Museum features information on the area, Natchez Trace Pkwy, and Polish general Tadeusz Kosciuszko; revolving displays. (Daily; closed Dec 25) Contact Chamber of Commerce. 1½ mi S via S Huntington St, Natchez Trace Pkwy Exit. **FREE**

Annual Event

Central Mississippi Fair. Central Mississippi Fairgrounds. Phone 662/289-2981. July.

Laurel

(F-4) *See also Hattiesburg*

Settled 1882 **Pop** 18,827 **Elev** 246 ft
Area code 601
Web www.jonseda.com
Information Jones County Chamber of Commerce, PO Box 527, 39441; 601/428-0574

Motel/Motor Lodge

★★ **RAMADA INN.** *1105 Sawmill Rd (39440). 601/649-9100; fax 601/* 649-6045; res 800/272-6232. 207 rms, 1-4 story. S $44; D $49; each addl $5; studio rms $50-$100; under 18 free. Crib free. TV; cable. Pool; poolside serv. Restaurant 6 am-10 pm; Sun to 9 pm. Bar 11-1 am; entertainment, Tues-Sat. Ck-out 1 pm. Meeting rms. Business servs avail. Valet serv. Some refrigerators. Cr cds: A, C, D, DS, MC, V.

Restaurant

★★ **PARKER HOUSE.** *3115 Audobon Dr (33940). 601/649-0261.* French menu. Specializes in seafood, steak, stuffed mushrooms. Hrs: 6-9 pm; Fri, Sat to 9:30 pm. Closed Sun, Mon; major hols. Res accepted. Bar. Dinner a la carte entrees: $6.95-$19.95. Child's menu. Parking. Cr cds: A, D, MC, V.

Louisville (D-5)

Pop 7,169 **Elev** 525 ft **Area code** 662
Zip 39339 **Web** www.coclwc.com
Information Louisville-Winston County Chamber of Commerce, 311 W Park, PO Box 551; 662/773-3921

Resort

★★ **LAKE TIAK OKHATA.** *213 Smyth Lake Rd (39339), ¼ mi off MS 15 Bypass S. 662/773-7853; fax 662/773-4555; toll-free 888/845-6151.* 80 rms, 2 story; duplex cottages. S $44-$75; D $49-$75; each addl $4; kit. cottages $45; wkly rates. Crib $5. TV in hotel rms, lobby; cable (premium). Dining rm 6 am-10 pm. Snack bar. Ck-out 11 am. Grocery 1 mi. Meeting rms. Business servs avail. Tennis. Private beach; swimming classes (summer), waterslide, lifeguard; boating (ramps, rentals), pedal boats. Nature trails. Picnic tables. 400 acre pine forest; 5 lakes. Cr cds: A, C, D, DS, MC, V.

McComb (G-3)

Founded 1872 **Pop** 11,591 **Elev** 460 ft
Area code 601 **Zip** 39649
Information Chamber of Commerce,
617 Delaware Ave, PO Box 83;
601/684-2291 or 800/399-4404

Annual Event

Lighted Azalea Trail. In keeping with
the Japanese tradition of lighting
cherry blossoms, McComb citizens
illuminate their azaleas; arts festival,
music programs. Two wks mid-Mar.

Mendenhall

(F-3) *See also Jackson*

Pop 2,463 **Elev** 323 ft **Area code** 601
Zip 39114

What to See and Do

Bienville National Forest. This central Mississippi tract of 178,374 acres
has numerous forest management
demonstration areas of second-
growth pine and hardwood. Swimming, boating; hiking, bridle trails,
picknicking, camping. Ranger District office is located in Forest. For
information, contact District Ranger,
Bienville Ranger District, 3473 Hwy
35S, Forest 39074. NW on US 49 to
MS 13, then N. Phone 601/469-3811.
Two major recreation areas are

> **Shongelo.** A 5-acre lake. Swimming
> (fee), bathhouse, fishing; picnick-
> ing, camping (fee). 22 mi E & N
> via MS 540, 35.

> **Marathon.** A 58-acre lake. Swim-
> ming (fee), fishing, boating; pic-
> nicking, camping (fee). 47 mi NE
> via MS 540, 18, 501, forest service
> roads.

D'Lo Water Park. Park incl 85 acres.
Swimming, bathhouse, fishing,
canoeing (rentals); nature trails,
lighted playing fields, picnicking,
camping (hookups; fee). (Daily;
closed Jan 1, Thanksgiving, Dec 25) 3
mi NW via US 49. Phone 601/847-
4310. **FREE**

Meridian (E-5)

Settled 1831 **Pop** 41,036 **Elev** 333 ft
Area code 601
Web www.cybertron.com/city.mdn
Information East Mississippi Develop-
ment Corporation, 1915 Front St,
Union Station, 39302; 601/693-1306
or 800/748-9970

Founded at the junction of two railroads, Meridian is now an industrial,
agricultural, and retailing center in
the heart of the South's finest tim-
ber-growing country.

What to See and Do

Bienville National Forest. (see
MENDENHALL) 45 mi W off I-20.

Clarkco State Park. Park covering
815 acres situated on 65-acre lake.
Swimming beach, waterskiing, fishing, boating (ramp, rentals); nature
trail, lighted tennis, picnicking (shelters), playground, playing field,
lodge, coin laundry. Primitive and
improved camping, cabins (each
with lake pier). Standard fees. 18 mi
S off US 45. Phone 601/776-6651.

Jimmie Rodgers Museum. Fashioned
after an old train depot, the museum
houses souvenirs and memorabilia of
the "Father of Country Music," incl a
rare Martin 00045 guitar. (Daily;
closed Jan 1, Thanksgiving, Dec 25)
19th St & 41st Ave, in Highland
Park. Phone 601/485-1808. ¢

Annual Events

Arts in the Park. Concerts, plays, art
shows, children's programs. First
wkend Apr.

Jimmie Rodgers Memorial Festival.
Country and western music. Last
wkend May.

Mississippi-Alabama State Fair. Agricultural exhibits, carnival. Oct.

Motels/Motor Lodges

★★ **BAYMONT INN.** *1400 Roebuck
Dr (39301). 601/693-2300; fax 601/
485-2534; res 800/301-0200.* 102 rms,
3 story. S $32.95-$37.95; D $35.95-
$40.95; under 18 free. Crib free. TV;
cable. Pool. Restaurant adj open 24

hrs. Ck-out noon. Meeting rms. Business servs avail. In-rm modem link. Cr cds: A, C, D, DS, MC, V.

★★ **BEST WESTERN MERIDIAN.** *2219 S Frontage Rd (39301), at jct I-20, I-59.* 601/693-3210; fax 601/ 693-3210; res 800/528-1234. 120 rms, 2 story. S $42-$53; D $47-$57; each addl $5; under 12 free. Crib free. TV; cable. Pool. Restaurant 6 am-10 pm; Sun to 3 pm. Bar 4 pm-1 am; closed Sun; entertainment. Ck-out noon. Meeting rms. Sundries. Cr cds: A, C, D, DS, MC, V.

★★ **HOLIDAY INN.** *1401 Roebuck Dr (39301), US 45 at jct I-20, I-59.* 601/693-4521; fax 601/693-4521; toll-free 800/465-4329. 172 rms, 1-2 story. S, D $49-$54; under 12 free. Crib free. Pet accepted. TV; cable (premium). Pool. Playground. Coffee in rms. Ck-out noon. Coin lndry. Meeting rms. Business servs avail. In-rm modem link. Valet serv. Cr cds: A, C, D, DS, JCB, MC, V.

★ **HOWARD JOHNSON INN.** *110 Hwy 80 E (39301), 2 mi E, Exit 154 at I-59, I-20.* 601/483-8281; fax 601/ 485-2015; res 800/446-4656. Email *502@hotelcendant.com.* 142 rms, 2 story. S $45-$54; D $47-$58; each addl $4; suites $95-$250; under 18 free. Crib free. TV. Indoor pool; whirlpool. Restaurant 6 am-10 pm. Bar 11-1 am; entertainment exc Sun. Ck-out noon. Coin lndry. Meeting rms. Business servs avail. Sundries. Private patios, balconies. Cr cds: A, C, D, DS, MC, V.

★★ **RAMADA LIMITED.** *2915 St. Paul St (39301).* 601/485-2722; fax 601/485-3960; res 800/272-6232; toll-free 877/219-9498. www.ramada.com. 50 units, 2 story. S $48.98; D $52.98; each addl $5; under 12 free. Crib free. TV; cable. Pool; whirlpool. Ck-out noon. Business servs avail. Exercise equipt; sauna. Cr cds: A, C, D, DS, JCB, MC, V.

Restaurant

★★ **WEIDMANN'S.** *210 22nd Ave (39301).* 601/693-1751. Email weid

manns@aol.com. Specializes in crab Belvedere, trout almondine. Hrs: 7 am-9:30 pm; Sun to 2 pm. Closed hols. Bar. Bkfst $2.85-$5; lunch $5-$10; dinner $8-$16. Child's menu. Cr cds: A, C, D, DS, MC.

Natchez (F-1)

Settled 1716 **Pop** 19,460 **Elev** 215 ft
Area code 601 **Zip** 39120
Web www.natchez.ms.us

Information Convention and Visitors Bureau; 640 S Canal, Box C, PO Box 1485; 601/446-6345 or 800/647-6724

Natchez lives in the enchantment of the Old South, a plantation atmosphere where everything seems beautiful and romantic. Greek Revival mansions, manicured gardens and lawns, tree-shaded streets, and southern hospitality abound in this museum of the antebellum South.

Natchez, named for a Native American tribe, is also a manufacturing town with a history of trapping, trading, hunting, and farming. French, Spanish, English, Confederate, and US flags have flown over this town, one of the oldest in the Mississippi Valley. Vestiges of the Spanish influence can still be seen along South Wall Street, near Washington Street, a charming neighborhood once restricted to the Spanish dons. The city's modern stores and buildings serve to emphasize how lovingly the citizens of Natchez have preserved their past.

What to See and Do

✪ **Canal Street Depot.** Houses official Natchez Pilgrimage Tour and Tourist Headquarters. (Daily) Information on historic Natchez and the surrounding area. Offers tours (fee) of 15 antebellum mansions and tickets for spring, fall, and Christmas pilgrimages (see ANNUAL EVENTS). Corner of Canal & State St.

Dunleith. (ca 1856) National Historic Landmark. Restored antebellum, Greek-revival mansion completely surrounded by colonnaded galleries. Estate incl 40 acres of green pastures and wooded bayous within Natchez. French and English antiques. (Daily; closed Thanksgiving, Dec 25) Guest rms (see INNS). Tours. 84 Homochitto St. Phone 601/446-8500 or 800/433-2445 (exc MS). ¢¢

Emerald Mound. This 8-acre Mississippian mound, the second largest in the US, dates roughly from AD 1250-1600. Unlike earlier peoples, who constructed mounds to cover tombs and burials, the Mississippians (ancestors of the Natchez, Creek, and Choctaw) built mounds to support temples and ceremonial bldgs. When DeSoto passed through this area in the 1540s the flat-topped temple mounds were still in use. (Daily) 2680 Natchez Trace Pkwy. Phone 601/680-4025. **FREE**

Lady Luck Riverboat Casino. On riverfront, 21 Silver St. Phone 601/445-0605 or 800/722-5825.

Longwood. Enormous, Italianate detailed "octagon house" crowned with an onion dome. Under construction at start of US Civil War, interiors were never completed above first floor; ca 1840 furnishings. Owned and operated by the Pilgrimage Garden Club. (Daily; days vary during Pilgrimages) (See ANNUAL EVENTS) Lower Woodville Rd. ¢¢

Magnolia Hall. (1858) Last great mansion to be erected in city before outbreak of US Civil War, house is an outstanding example of Greek Revival architecture; period antiques; costume museum. (Daily) S Pearl at Washington. Phone 601/442-6672. ¢¢

Melrose Plantation. The National Park Service oversees this historic mansion and grounds, and tells the plantation story from a more national perspective. House open for guided tours only; self-guided tours of slave quarters. (Daily) 1 Melrose Ave, off Hwy 61. Phone 601/446-5790.

Monmouth. (ca 1818) Registered as a National Historic Landmark, the monumental, Greek Revival house, and auxiliary bldgs, once owned by Mexican War hero Gen. John Anthony Quitman, have been completely restored; antique furnishings; extensive gardens. Guest rms (see INNS). Tours (daily; closed Dec 25). 36 Melrose Ave. Phone 601/442-5852 or 800/828-4531. ¢¢

Mount Locust. Earliest inn on the Trace; restored to 1810s appearance. Interpretive program. (Feb-Nov, daily; grounds only, Dec-Jan) 2680 Natchez Trace Pkwy. Phone 601/680-4025. **FREE**

Annual Events

Pilgrimages. Headquarters, Canal Street Depot. Tours of antebellum houses sponsored by the Natchez Pilgrimage Assn (daily). Also Confederate Pageant at City Auditorium (Mon, Wed, Fri, Sat). Contact PO Box 347 or phone 800/647-6742 for details. Mar-early Apr; Fall Pilgrimage mid-Oct; Christmas Dec.

Great Mississippi River Balloon Race Weekend. Oct.

Seasonal Event

Natchez Opera Festival. Entire month of May.

Motels/Motor Lodges

★ **PARKWAY INN.** *271 D'Evereaux Dr (39120). 601/442-3686; fax 601/446-9998; toll-free 800/465-4329.* 139 rms, 2 story. S $47-$70; D $53-$76; each addl $6; under 18 free. Crib free. TV; cable. Pool. Restaurant 6 am-8:30 pm. Ck-out noon. Meeting rm. Business servs avail. In-rm modem link. Cr cds: A, C, D, DS, JCB, MC, V.
[D] [≈] [≥] [🐾] [SC]

★ **PRENTISS INN.** *45 Sergeant Prentiss Dr (39120), US 61, at jct US 65, 84, 98. 601/442-1691; fax 601/445-5895; res 800/541-1720.* 131 units, 1-2 story. S $41-$53; D $41-$61; each addl $5; suites $60-$75; under 12 free. TV; cable, VCR avail. Pool. Ck-out noon. Meeting rms. Business center. In-rm modem link. Cr cds: A, C, D, DS, MC, V.
[D] [≈] [≥] [🐾] [SC] [🚶]

★★ **RAMADA INN.** *130 John R. Junkin Dr (39120), at Mississippi River Bridge. 601/446-6311; fax 601/446-6321; res 800/272-6232; toll-free 800/256-6311.* 162 rms, 1-3 story. No elvtr. S $48-$60; D $48-$70; each addl $5; suites $140; under 18 free. Crib free. Pet accepted, some restrictions. TV; cable (premium), VCR avail. Pool; wading pool, poolside serv. Restaurant 6 am-10 pm. Rm serv. Bar; entertainment Fri, Sat. Ck-out 1 pm. Coin lndry. Meeting rms. Business servs avail. In-rm modem link. Sundries. Airport, bus depot transportation. Some refrigerators. On hilltop overlooking Mississippi River. Cr cds: A, C, D, DS, MC, V.

🅳 ◨ 📫 🛏 🟰 ⏃ 🔥

Hotels

★★ **ISLE OF CAPRI CASINO & HOTEL.** *645 S Canal St (39120).* 601/445-0605; fax 601/442-9823; toll-free 800/722-5825. 147 units, 6 story. S $55-$65; D $69; each addl $5; suites $155; under 18 free. Crib free. TV; cable. Pool; whirlpool, poolside serv. Restaurant 6:30 am-2 pm. Ck-out 1 pm. Meeting rms. Business servs avail. Casino. Cr cds: A, DS, MC, V.

🅳 🛏 🟰 ⏃ 🔥

★★★ **RADISSON NATCHEZ EOLA HOTEL.** *110 N Pearl St (39120).* 601/445-6000; fax 601/446-5310; res 800/333-3333. Email eolahotl@telepak. net. 125 rms, 7 story. S, D $75-$195; suites $120-$225. Crib free. Pet accepted. TV; cable. Restaurant 7 am-2 pm, 5-9 pm. Bar 5:30 pm-midnight. Ck-out 11 am. Meeting rms. Balconies; many with view of river. Classic architecture; antique furniture. Cr cds: A, C, D, DS, ER, JCB, MC, V.

🅳 ⏃ 🔥 ◨

B&Bs/Small Inns

★★★ **BRIARS BED & BREAKFAST.** *31 Irving Ln (39120).* 601/446-9654; fax 601/445-6037; toll-free 800/634-1818. Email www.thebriarsinn@bk bank.com; www.thebriarsinn.com. 12 rms, 2 story, 3 suites. S $145; D $150; each addl $35; suites $230. Parking lot. Pool. TV; cable (premium). Complimentary full bkfst, coffee in rms, newspaper, toll-free calls. Restaurant. Bar. Business center. Gift shop. Exercise privileges. Golf. Tennis, 12 courts. Bike rentals. Hiking trail. Picnic facilities. Cr cds: A, MC, V.

🅳 📫 🛎 🟰 🏃 ⏃ 🔥 ◨

★★ **THE BURN ANTEBELLUM BED & BREAKFAST INN C. 1834.** *712 N Union St. (39120).* 601/442-1344; fax 601/445-0606; res 601/442-1344; toll-free 800/654-8859. Email theburn@usa.com; www.theburnbnb.

com. 5 rms, 3 story, 3 suites. Mar-May, Sep-Dec: S, D $125; suites $180; lower rates rest of yr. Parking lot. Pool. TV; cable. Complimentary full bkfst, coffee in rms, newspaper. Restaurant nearby. Ck-out 11 am, ck-in 2 pm. Meeting rm. Business center. Coin lndry. Gift shop. Golf. Tennis. Cr cds: A, DS, MC, V.

🅳 🛎 ⏃ 🟰 🏃 ⏃ 🔥 🏃

★★★ **DUNLEITH ANTEBELLUM HOME.** *84 Homochitto St (39120).* 601/446-8500; fax 601/442-8554; toll-free 800/433-2445. www.dunleith plantation.com. 11 rms, 2 story. S, D $95-$140; each addl $15. Closed Easter, Thanksgiving, Dec 24-25. Children over 18 yrs only. TV; cable (premium). Complimentary full bkfst. Ck-out 11 am, ck-in 1-6 pm. Balconies. Antebellum mansion (ca 1856) on 40 acres; formal gardens, courtyard. Greek-revival architecture; rms individually decorated; antique furnishings; fireplaces. Cr cds: A, DS, MC, V.

★ **LINDEN.** *1 Linden Pl (39120).* 601/445-5472; fax 601/442-7548; toll-free 800/254-6336. www.natchezms. com/linden. 7 rms, 2 story. No rm phones. S, D $90-$120; each addl $30. Children over 10 yrs only. Complimentary full bkfst. Ck-out 11 am, ck-in 1 pm. Business servs avail. Antebellum house (ca 1800); antique furnishings; set among mossy oaks, cedars, and magnolias. Free tour of house. Cr cds: A, DS, MC, V.

🅳 🏃 ⏃

★★★ **MONMOUTH PLANTATION.** *36 Melrose Ave (39120).* 601/442-5852; fax 601/446-7762; res 800/828-4531. Email luxury@ monmouth plantation.com; www.monmouth plantation.com. 15 rms, 2 story, 16 suites. Mar-May, Oct: S, D $160; each addl $35; suites $195; lower rates rest of yr. Parking lot. TV; cable (premium). Complimentary full bkfst, newspaper. Restaurant. Bar. Ck-out 11 am, ck-in 3 pm. Meeting rm. Business center. Dry cleaning. Gift shop. Golf, 18 holes. Tennis, 8 courts. Bike rentals. Picnic facilities. Cr cds: A, C, D, DS, MC, V.

📫 🏃 ⏃ 🟰 🔥 🏃

Restaurants

★★ **CARRIAGE HOUSE.** *401 High St (39120).* 601/445-5151. Specializes in Southern fried chicken, ham. Hrs: 11 am-2 pm. Closed Jan 1, July 4. Res accepted. Bar. Lunch $3.50-$10.95. On grounds of Stanton Hall. Owned by the Pilgrimage Garden Club. Cr cds: A, DS, MC, V.
D

★ **COCK OF THE WALK.** *200 N Broadway (39120), on the Mississippi River.* 601/446-8920. Specializes in catfish. Hrs: 5-9 pm. Closed Sun; hols. Dinner complete meals: $9-$15.95. Child's menu. Parking. Rustic decor. Old train station on river. Cr cds: A, D, DS, MC, V.
D ⬛

Natchez Trace Parkway

One of the earliest "interstates," the Natchez Trace stretched from Natchez, Mississippi, to Nashville, Tennessee, and was the most heavily traveled road in the Old Southwest from approximately 1785-1820. Boatmen floated their products downriver to Natchez or New Orleans, sold them, and walked or rode home over the Natchez Trace. A "trace" is a trail or road. This one was shown on French maps as far back as 1733. It was still in use, to some extent, as late as the 1830s, though its importance diminished after the invention of the steam engine.

When completed, the Natchez Trace Parkway, operated by the National Park Service, will be a magnificent 445-mile-long road. At this writing, about 430 miles are paved and open, most of them in Mississippi; a continuous stretch of 341 miles is open between Jackson, MS and TN 100 south of Nashville, Tennessee. A 79-mile stretch is open west of Jackson, MS to near Natchez, MS.

The parkway crosses and recrosses the original trace, passing many points of historic interest, including Emerald Mound (see NATCHEZ).

The parkway headquarters and visitor center are five miles north of Tupelo, at jct US 45 Business (sign reads US 145) and the parkway. Interpretive facilities include a visitor center with exhibits depicting the history of the trace and an audiovisual program that tells the story of the trace (daily; closed Dec 25; free). Park Service personnel can furnish information on self-guided trails, wayside exhibits, interpretive programs, camping, and picnicking facilities along the parkway. For further information contact Superintendent, 2680 Natchez Trace Pkwy, Tupelo 38801; 662/680-4025 or 800/305-7417.

Ocean Springs

See also Biloxi, Gulfport, Pascagoula

Pop 14,658 **Elev** 20 ft **Area code** 228 **Zip** 39566
Web www.lillypr.com/oschamber
Information Chamber of Commerce, 1000 Washington Ave, PO Box 187; 228/875-4424

What to See and Do

Shearwater Pottery. Established in 1928. Displays incl thrown glazed ware by founder Peter Anderson and his son Jim; original paintings and block prints by Peter's brothers, James McConnell Anderson and Walter Anderson. (Mon-Sat and Sun afternoons; closed hols) 102 Shearwater Dr. Phone 228/875-7320. **FREE**

Annual Events

Garden and Home Pilgrimage. Late Mar or early Apr.

Anniversary of the Landing of d'Iberville. Pageant, street fair, and other activities commemorating the 1699 event. Last wkend Apr.

Restaurants

★★ **GERMAINE'S.** *1203 Bienville Blvd (US 90) (39564).* 228/875-4426. Email germaines@worldnet.att.net. Seafood menu. Specializes in crabmeat, stuffed mushrooms. Hrs: 11:30 am-2 pm, 6-10 pm; Sun to 2:30 pm. Closed Mon; major hols. Res accepted. Bar. Lunch, dinner $10-$21.95. Child's menu. Display of antique clocks. Changing exhibits of Gulf Coast art. Cr cds: A, C, D, DS, MC, V.

★★ **JOCELYN'S.** *Hwy 90E (39564). 228/875-1925.* Specializes in seafood. Hrs: 5-9 pm; Fri, Sat to 10:30 pm. Closed Sun, Mon. Bar. Dinner $10-$18. Child's menu. Renovated cottage (1890s). Casual dining. No cr cds aceppted.

Oxford (B-4)

Settled 1836 **Pop** 9,984 **Elev** 416 ft
Area code 662 **Zip** 38655
Web www.ci.oxford.ms.us
Information Oxford Tourism Council, PO Box 965; 662/234-4680 or 800/758-9177

Oxford was named for the English university city in an effort to lure the University of Mississippi to the site; in 1848 the university was opened. Today, "Ole Miss," with its forested, hilly 1,194-acre campus, dominates the area, and the town that boasted an opera house before the Civil War still reveres its role as a university town.

William Faulkner, Nobel Prize winning author, lived near the university at "Rowan Oak." Many landmarks of his fictional Yoknapatawpha County can be found in surrounding Lafayette County.

What to See and Do

🗙 **Rowan Oak.** Residence of William Faulkner from 1930-62; furnishings and memorabilia are as they were at the time of Faulkner's death. Maintained by the University of Mississippi. (Tues-Sun; closed school hols) Old Taylor Rd, 1½ mi SE. Phone 662/234-3284. **FREE**

Annual Event

Faulkner Conference. Center for Study of Southern Culture, University of Mississippi. Various programs celebrate the author's accomplishments. Phone 662/232-7282. Last wk July.

Motels/Motor Lodges

★ **DAYS INN.** *1101 Frontage Rd (38655). 662/234-9500; fax 662/236-2772; res 800/329-7466.* 100 rms, 2 story. S $45-$52, D $49-$60; each addl $5; under 12 free; higher rates college football games. Crib free. TV; cable. Pool. Complimentary coffee in rms. Restaurant 6 am-9 pm. Bar 2 pm-midnight; Thurs, Fri to 1 am. Ck-out noon. Meeting rms. Business servs avail. Cr cds: A, DS, MC, V.

★★ **DOWNTOWN INN.** *400 N Lamar Blvd (38655). 662/234-3031; fax 662/234-2834; toll-free 800/606-1497.* 123 rms, 2 story. S, D $63-$85; under 19 free. Crib free. TV; cable (premium), VCR avail. Pool. Restaurant 6 am-2 pm, 5-9 pm. Bar 4 pm-midnight. Ck-out 1 pm. Coin lndry. Meeting rms. Business servs avail. In-rm modem link. Valet serv. Free airport transportation. Cr cds: A, C, D, DS, ER, MC, V.

★★ **PORT PLACE INN AND SUITES.** *2201 Jackson Ave W (38655). 662/234-7013; fax 662/236-4378; toll-free 800/544-0084.* 116 rms, 2 story. S $49-$51; D $55-$57; each addl $6; suites $115; under 12 free; higher rates football wknds. Crib free. TV; cable. Pool. Ck-out noon. Business servs avail. Cr cds: A, C, D, DS, JCB, MC, V.

B&B/Small Inn

★★ **OLIVER-BRITT HOUSE INN & TEAROOM.** *512 Van Buren Ave (38655). 662/234-8043; fax 662/281-8065.* 5 rms, 2 story. No rm phones. S, D $45-$65; higher rates wkends. Pet accepted, some restrictions. TV; cable. Complimentary full bkfst. Restaurant nearby. Ck-out 11 am, ck-in 2 pm. Business servs avail. Restored manor house built 1905; some period furnishings. Cr cds: A, DS, MC, V.

Restaurant

★★ **DOWNTOWN GRILL.** *1115 Jackson Ave E (38655). 662/234-2659.* Specializes in catfish Lafitte, filet Paulette. Hrs: 10 am-2:30 pm, 5-9 pm; Thurs-Sat to 10 pm. Closed Sun; hols. Res accepted. Bar. Lunch $5.95-$9.95; dinner $11.95-$25.95. Entertainment: Thurs-Sat. Elegant dining. On Oxford Square. Cr cds: A, D, DS, V.

Pascagoula

(H-5) See also Biloxi, Ocean Springs; also see Mobile, AL

Pop 25,899 **Elev** 15 ft **Area code** 228 **Zip** 39567

Information Jackson County Chamber of Commerce, 825 Denny Ave, PO Box 480, 39568-0480; 228/762-3391

What to See and Do

Scranton Museum. Nautical, marine, and wetlands exhibits housed in restored shrimp boat. (Tues-Sat, Sun afternoons; closed hols) River Park at Pascagoula River. Phone 228/762-6017 or 228/938-6612. **FREE**

🌟 **Singing River.** Singing sound is best heard on late summer and autumn nights. The music seems to increase in volume, coming nearer until it appears to be underfoot. Scientists have said it could be made by fish, sand scraping the hard slate bottom, natural gas escaping from sand bed, or current sucked past a hidden cave. None of the explanations offered have been proven. Pascagoula River, 2 blks W of courthouse.

Annual Events

Mardi Gras. Month leading to Ash Wednesday.

Garden Club Pilgrimage. Tours of historic houses and gardens in town. Late Mar-early Apr.

River Jamboree. In Moss Point, N on MS 63. Arts and crafts, games. First Sat in May.

Jackson County Fair. Fairgrounds. Mid-Oct.

Motels/Motor Lodges

★ **DAYS INN.** *6700 Hwy 63 (39563), at I-10 Exit 69. 228/475-0077; fax 228/475-3783; res 800/325-2525.* 54 rms, 2 story. S, D $55.95-$70; each addl $5; under 12 free. Crib free. TV; cable. Pool. Complimentary continental bkfst. Restaurant adj 7 am-10 pm. Ck-out 11 am. Some refrigerators. Cr cds: A, C, D, DS, MC, V.

★★★ **LA FONT INN.** *2703 Denny Ave (39567). 228/762-7111; fax 228/934-4324; res 800/647-6077.* 192 rms, 2 story, 13 kits. S $61-$78; D $66-$78; each addl $5; suites $121-$148; under 14 free. Crib free. Pet accepted. TV; cable (premium). Pool; wading pool, whirlpool, poolside serv. Playground. Complimentary coffee in rms. Restaurant 6 am-10 pm. Bar 11 am-midnight. Ck-out 1 pm. Coin lndry. Meeting rms. Business servs avail. In-rm modem link. Bellhops. Valet serv. Sundries. Lighted tennis. 18-hole golf privileges. Exercise equipt; steam rm, sauna. Lawn games. Refrigerators. Cr cds: A, C, D, DS, MC, V.

Restaurants

★ **FILLETS.** *1911 Denny Ave (39567). 228/769-0280.* Specializes in seafood platter, po'boys. Hrs: 11 am-9 pm. Closed hols. Res accepted. Lunch, dinner $2-$13. Casual dining. Cr cds: A, C, D, DS, MC, V.

★★ **TIKI RESTAURANT, LOUNGE AND MARINA.** *3212 Mary Walker Dr (39553), 4 mi W off US 90. 228/497-1591.* Specializes in fresh seafood, steak. Hrs: 11 am-10 pm; Fri to midnight; Sat 3 pm-midnight. Closed Jan 1, Dec 24, 25. Res accepted. Bar. Lunch $4.50-$6.95; dinner $5.95-$20.95. Child's menu. Entertainment: Tues-Sun. On bayou. Family-owned. Cr cds: A, D, DS, MC, V.

Pass Christian

See also Gulfport

Settled 1704 **Pop** 5,557 **Elev** 10 ft
Area code 228 **Zip** 39571
Information Chamber of Commerce,
PO Box 307; 228/452-2252

The town was a resort before the Civil War and the site of the South's first yacht club, which was founded in 1849. It is Mrs. Jane Murphy Manders who is generally credited with the "bed sheet surrender" of Pass Christian on April 4, 1862; attempting to save the city from further shelling by the Union fleet after the Confederate forces evacuated, Mrs. Murphy waved a sheet from her doorway. Pass Christian has hosted six vacationing US presidents—Jackson, Taylor, Grant, Theodore Roosevelt, Wilson, and Truman. The world's largest oyster reef is offshore.

Annual Events

Mardi Gras. Carnival Ball and Parade. Sat, Sun before Shrove Tuesday.

Garden Club Pilgrimage. Visits to several historic houses and gardens in town. Information at Chamber of Commerce Bldg, Small Craft Harbor. Late Mar.

Blessing of the Fleet. Festival, boat decorations competition, band, entertainment. Last Sun May.

Seafood Festival. Entertainment. Mid-July.

Casino

★★ **CASINO MAGIC INN.** *711 Casino Magic Dr (39520), 9 mi W on US 90. 228/466-0891; fax 228/466-0870; toll-free 800/562-4425. www.casinomagic.com.* 201 rms, 4 story. S, D $65-$119; each addl $5; suites $175-$195; under 18 free; wkend rates; higher rates hols. Crib free. TV; cable. Heated pool; whirlpool. Complimentary coffee in rms. Restaurant adj 24 hrs. Ck-out 11 am. Meeting rms. Bellhops. Gift shop. Coin lndry. Some refrigerators. Cr cds: A, DS, MC, V.

Restaurant

★ **ANNIE'S.** *120 W Bayview (39571). 228/452-2062.* Specializes in seafood, steak, veal. Hrs: 11:30 am-10 pm; Sun to 9 pm. Closed Mon; also Dec. Res accepted. Bar. Lunch, dinner $4.50-$16.50. Child's menu. Mission bells from old Southern plantations displayed on patio. Family-owned. Cr cds: A, DS, MC, V.

Philadelphia

(D-4) *See also Louisville, Meridian*

Pop 6,758 **Elev** 424 ft **Area code** 601
Zip 39350
Information Philadelphia-Neshoba County Chamber of Commerce, 410 Poplar Ave, Suite 101, PO Box 51; 601/656-1742

Annual Events

Choctaw Indian Fair. Choctaw Indian Reservation, 8 mi W via MS 16. Entertainment, arts and crafts, cultural programs, princess pageant, music. Mid-July.

Neshoba County Fair. 8½ mi SW via MS 21S. Early Aug.

Shrimp boats, Pass Christian

Port Gibson

(F-2) *See also Vicksburg*

Settled 1788 **Pop** 1,810 **Elev** 120 ft
Area code 601 **Zip** 39150
Information Gibson-Claiborne
County Chamber of Commerce, PO
Box 491; 601/437-4351

Many antebellum houses and buildings remain in Port Gibson, lending support to the story that General Grant spared the town on his march to Vicksburg with the words: "It's too beautiful to burn."

The Samuel Gibson House (ca 1805), oldest existing structure in town, has been restored and now houses the Port Gibson-Claiborne County Chamber of Commerce and Visitor Information Center.

What to See and Do

⬛ **Antebellum houses.** Open yr-round by appointment; special schedule during Spring Pilgrimage. Phone 601/437-4351. ¢¢

Oak Square. (ca 1850) Restored 30-rm mansion with 6 fluted, Corinthian columns, each standing 22 ft tall. Antique furnishings from the 18th and 19th centuries. Extensive grounds, courtyard, gazebo. Guest rms avail (see INNS). Tours by appt. 1207 Church St, 1 mi off Natchez Trace Pkwy. Phone 601/437-4350 or 800/729-0240. ¢¢

Rosswood Plantation. (1857) Classic Greek Revival mansion designed by David Shroder, architect of Windsor, features columned galleries, 10 fireplaces, 15-ft ceilings, a winding stairway, and slave quarters in the basement. The 1st owner's diary has survived and offers details of antebellum life on a cotton plantation. The 14 rms are furnished with antiques. Guest rms avail (see INNS). (Tours Mar-Dec; closed hols) 9 mi S on US 61 to Lorman, then 2½ mi E on MS 552. Phone 800/533-5889. Tours ¢¢

Annual Event

Spring Pilgrimage. Tours of historic houses. Phone 601/437-4351 for dates. Early spring.

B&Bs/Small Inns

★★★ **CANE MOUNT PLANTATION.** *4003 MS 552 W (39096), 10 mi S on US 61, 8 mi W on MS 552. 601/877-3784; fax 601/877-2010; toll-free 800/423-0684. Email cmount@ vicksburg.com; www.canemount.com.* 6 rms, 2 suites. S $150; D $195; each addl $80; suites $225; under 12 free. Parking lot. Pool, whirlpool. TV; cable (DSS), VCR avail. Complimentary full bkfst, coffee in rms. Restaurant 6-10 pm. Bar. Meeting rms. Business servs avail. Golf, 9 holes. Tennis, 4 courts. Hiking trail. Picnic facilities. Cr cds: A, MC, V.

⬛ ⬛ ⬛ ⬛ ⬛ ⬛ ⬛ ⬛

★★ **OAK SQUARE COUNTRY INN.** *1207 Church St (39150). 601/437-4350; fax 601/437-5768; toll-free 800/729-0240.* 12 rms, 2 story. S, D $85-$120. TV; cable. Complimentary bkfst. Ck-out 11 am. Restored antebellum mansion (ca 1850) and guest house; antique furnishings. Courtyard, fountain, gazebo, massive oak trees. Free tour of mansion, grounds. Cr cds: A, DS, MC, V.

⬛ ⬛ ⬛ ⬛

★★ **ROSSWOOD PLANTATION.** *MS 552 (39096), 2½ mi E. 601/437-4215; fax 601/437-6888; toll-free 800/ 533-5889. Email whylander@aol.com; www.rosswood.net.* 4 rms, 2 story. S, D $115-$135. TV; VCR (movies). Heated pool; whirlpool. Complimentary full bkfst, coffee in rms. Ck-out 11 am, ck-in 2-5 pm. Landmark Greek-revival mansion (1857) on working Christmas tree plantation. Many antiques. Cr cds: A, DS, MC, V.

⬛ ⬛

Restaurant

★ **OLD DEPOT.** *1202 Market St (39150). 601/437-4711.* Specializes in steak, seafood, red beans and rice. Hrs: 11 am-2 pm, 5-9 pm; Sat from 5 pm. Closed Sun; hols. Res accepted Fri, Sat. Bar. Lunch, dinner $3.95-$15.75. Child's menu. Parking. Cr cds: A, C, DS, MC, V.

⬛ ⬛

Sardis (B-3)

Pop 2,128 **Elev** 379 ft **Area code** 662 **Zip** 38666

Information Chamber of Commerce, 114 W Lee St, PO Box 377; 662/487-3451

Motel/Motor Lodge

★★ **BEST WESTERN INN MOTEL AND RESTAURANT.** *410 E Lee St (38666), ⅛ mi W on MS 315 at I-55, Exit 252.* 662/487-2424; *fax* 662/487-2424; *toll-free* 800/328-2112. 79 rms, 2 story. S $35-$38; D $38-$50; each addl $6; under 12 free. Crib free. TV; cable (premium), VCR (movies). Pool; wading pool. Restaurant 6 am-10 pm. Bar 4 pm-midnight. Ck-out 11 am. Business servs avail. Some refrigerators. Cr cds: A, C, D, DS, MC, V.

D ≈ SC

Starkville

(C-5) *See also Columbus*

Founded 1831 **Pop** 18,458 **Elev** 374 ft **Area code** 662 **Zip** 39759
Web www.starkville.org

Information Visitors & Convention Council, 322 University Dr; 662/323-3322 or 800/649-8687

Starkville is the seat of Oktibbeha County and the home of Mississippi State University.

Motel/Motor Lodge

★★ **RAMADA INN.** *403 Hwy 12 E (39759), at Montgomery St, opp MSU.* 662/323-6161; *fax* 662/323-8073; *res* 800/272-6232. 173 rms, 2 story. S, D $55; each addl $6; under 18 free; higher rates football wkends. Crib free. Pet accepted. TV; cable (premium). Pool. Restaurant 6 am-2 pm, 5-10 pm. Bar 5 pm-midnight; closed Sun. Ck-out noon. Meeting rms.

Business servs avail. Cr cds: A, C, D, DS, MC, V.

D ◀ ⬤ ✦ ≈ ⬤ ⬤ ⬤

B&B/Small Inn

★★ **STATE HOUSE HOTEL.** *215 E Main St (39760), at Jackson St.* 662/323-2000; *fax* 662/323-3446; *toll-free* 800/722-1903. 43 units, 3 story, 9 suites. S $45-$70; D $55-$72; each addl $3-$10; suites $74-110; under 13 free; higher rates football wkends. Crib $8. TV, cable. Dining rm 6:30 am-2 pm, 6-9:30 pm. Ck-out noon, ck-in 2 pm. Refrigerators. Balconies. Antique furnishings; courtyard. Cr cds: A, C, D, DS, MC, V.

D ⬤ ⬤ SC

Restaurant

★★ **HARVEY'S.** *406 Hwy 12E (39759).* 662/323-1639. Specializes in steak, seafood, pasta. Hrs: 11 am-9:30 pm; Fri, Sat to 10 pm. Closed Sun; hols. Res accepted. Bar. Lunch $4.95-$9.95; dinner $5.95-$15.95. Child's menu. Cr cds: A, MC, V.

D ⬤

Tupelo (B-5)

Settled 1833 **Pop** 30,685 **Elev** 290 ft
Area code 662 **Zip** 38801
Web www.tupelo.net

Information Convention & Visitors Bureau, 399 E Main St, PO Drawer 47, 38802; 662/841-6521 or 800/533-0611

What to See and Do

Brices Cross Roads National Battlefield Site. One-acre site overlooks terrain where Confederate soldiers defeated an attacking Union force. Marker with texts and maps identifies landmarks. Adj cemetery is burial site of over 100 identified Confederate soldiers. (Daily) 17 mi N on US 45 to Baldwyn, then 6 mi W on MS 370. **FREE**

Elvis Presley Park and Museum. In park is small white frame house where Presley lived for the first 3 yrs of his life. Museum houses collection of Elvis memorabilia. Chapel (free). (Daily; bldgs closed Thanksgiving and Dec 25) 306 Elvis Presley Dr. Phone 662/841-1245. House ¢; Museum ¢¢

Natchez Trace Parkway Visitor Center. (see NATCHEZ TRACE PARKWAY) 5 mi N at jct Pkwy, US 45 Business.

Oren Dunn Museum of Tupelo. Displays incl NASA space equipment used in Apollo missions; Elvis Presley rm; reproductions of Western Union office, general store, train station, log cabin; US Civil War and Chickasaw items. (Daily; closed hols) 2 mi W via MS 6 at Ballard Park. Phone 662/841-6438. ¢

Tupelo National Battlefield. One-acre tract near area where Confederate line was formed to attack Union position. Marker with texts and maps explains battle. (Daily) 1 mi W on MS 6. **FREE**

Motels/Motor Lodges

★★ **COMFORT INN.** *1190 N Gloster St (38801). 662/842-5100; fax 662/844-0554; res 800/228-5150.* 83 rms, 5 story. S $50-$59; D $53-$65; each addl $4; under 18 free. Crib free. TV; cable (premium). Complimentary continental bkfst. Ck-out 11 am. Meeting rms. Business servs avail. In-rm modem link. Cr cds: A, C, D, DS, ER, MC, V.

[icons]

★★★ **EXECUTIVE INN.** *1011 N Gloster St (38801). 662/841-2222; fax 662/844-7836; toll-free 800/533-3220.* 115 rms, 5 story. S, D $62-$68; suites $170-$225; under 18 free. Crib free. TV; cable (premium). Indoor pool; whirlpool. Sauna. Restaurant 6 am-10 pm; Sat, Sun 7 am-2 pm. Rm serv 7 am-2 pm, 5-10 pm. Bar 4 pm-midnight; closed Sun. Ck-out noon. Meeting rms. Business servs avail. In-rm modem link. Bellhops. Cr cds: A, C, D, DS, MC, V.

[icons]

★★ **HOLIDAY INN.** *923 N Gloster St (38801), jct US 45, 78. 662/842-8811; fax 662/844-6884; res 800/465-4329; toll-free 800/800-6851.* 124 rms, 2 story. Feb-Aug: S $50; D $54; each addl $7; under 12 free; lower rates rest of yr. Pet accepted; $7/day. TV; cable (premium). Pool. Complimentary continental bkfst. Coin lndry. Meeting rms. Business servs avail. Cr cds: A, C, D, DS, MC, V.

[icons]

★★ **RAMADA INN.** *854 N Gloster St (38802), jct US 45, 78. 662/844-4111; fax 662/840-7960; res 800/228-2828.* 230 rms, 3 story. No elvtr. S $47; D $57; each addl $5; suites $115-$175; studio rms $55-$80; under 18 free. Crib free. TV; cable (premium), VCR avail. Pool; wading pool, poolside serv. Restaurant 6 am-10 pm. Bar 4 pm-midnight; entertainment. Ck-out 1 pm. Coin lndry. Convention facilities. Business center. In-rm modem link. Valet serv. Sundries. Free airport transportation. Exercise equipt. Cr cds: A, C, D, DS, MC, V.

[icons]

★ **RED ROOF INN.** *1500 McCullough Blvd (38804). 662/844-1904; fax 662/844-0139; res 800/733-7663.* 100 units, 2 story. S $38-$52; D $43-$56; each addl $5; under 16 free; wkly rates; higher rates special events. Crib free. TV; cable. Pool. Ck-out noon. Coin lndry. Business servs avail. In-rm modem link. Cr cds: A, C, D, DS, MC, V.

[icons]

B&B/Small Inn

★★ **MOCKINGBIRD INN BED & BREAKFAST.** *305 N Gloster St (38804). 662/841-0286; fax 662/840-4158.* 7 rms, 2 story. S, D $65-$125; each addl $10; wkend rates. Children over 10 yrs only. Pet accepted, some restrictions; $10. TV; cable. Complimentary full bkfst; afternoon refreshments. Restaurant opp 11 am-10 pm. Ck-out noon, ck-in 3-9 pm. Business servs avail. Built in 1925; porch, gazebo. Cr cds: A, DS, MC, V.

[icons]

Restaurants

★ **JEFFERSON PLACE.** *823 Jefferson St (38801). 662/844-8696. Email jeffersonplace@yahoo.com.* Specializes in steak, chicken, shrimp. Hrs: 11 am-midnight. Closed Sun; Thanksgiving; Dec 25. Bar. Lunch $3.95-$9.95; dinner $5.25-$14.95. Cr cds: A, DS, V.

[icon]

★★ **PAPA VANELLI'S.** *1302 N Gloster (38801). 662/844-4410. Email cheese@ebicom.net.* Specializes in pizza, pasta buffet. Hrs: 11 am-10 pm; Sun to 9 pm. Closed Dec 25. Bar. Lunch, dinner a la carte entrees: $4.95-$15.95. Child's menu. Family-owned. Cr cds: A, D, DS, MC, V.

D SC

Unrated Dining Spot

MALONE'S FISH & STEAK HOUSE. *1349 MS 41 (38801). 662/842-2747.* Specializes in steak, catfish. Salad bar. Hrs: 5-10 pm. Closed Sun, Mon; Thanksgiving; 2 wks late Dec. Dinner $3.95-$12.95. Child's menu. Cr cds: MC, V.

D

Vicksburg

E-2) *See also Port Gibson*

Settled 1790 **Pop** 20,908 **Elev** 200 ft
Area code 601 **Zip** 39180
Web www.vicksburg.org/cvb
Information Convention & Visitors Bureau, PO Box 110, 39181; 601/636-9421 or 800/221-3536

What to See and Do

Antebellum houses.

🔲 **Martha Vick House.** (1830) Built by the daughter of the founder of Vicksburg, Newit Vick. Greek Revival façade; restored original interior furnished with 18th- and 19th-century antiques; outstanding art collection. (Daily; closed hols) 1300 Grove St. Phone 601/638-7036. ¢¢

McRaven Home Civil War Tour Home. Heaviest-shelled house during Siege of Vicksburg; provides an architectural record of Vicksburg history, from frontier cottage (1797) to Empire (1836) and finally to elegant Greek Revival townhouse (1849); many original furnishings. Original brick walks surround the house; garden of live oaks, boxwood, magnolia, and many plants. Guided tours. (Mar-Nov, daily) 1445 Harrison St. Phone 601/636-1663. ¢¢

Cedar Grove. (1840) Elegant mansion shelled by Union gunboats in siege; restored, but a cannonball is still lodged in parlor wall; roof garden with view of Mississippi and Yazoo rivers; tea rm; many original furnishings. Over 4 acres of formal gardens; courtyards, fountains, gazebos. (Daily) Guest rms avail. 2200 Oak St. Phone 601/636-1000 or 800/862-1300. Guided tours ¢¢

Anchuca. (1830) Restored Greek Revival mansion furnished with period antiques and gas-burning chandeliers. Landscaped gardens, brick courtyard. (Daily; closed Dec 25) Guest rms (see INNS). 1010 First East St. Phone 601/661-0111. Guided tours ¢¢

Duff Green. (1856) Mansion of Paladian architecture shelled by Union forces during siege, then used as hospital for remainder of the war. Restored; antique furnishings. Guided tours. High tea and tour (by reservation). Guest rms avail (see INNS). (Daily) 1114 First East St. Phone 601/636-6968 or 800/992-0037. ¢¢

Biedenharn Museum of Coca-Cola Memorabilia. Bldg in which Coca-Cola was first bottled in 1894. Restored candy store, old-fashioned soda fountain, collection of Coca-Cola advertising and memorabilia. (Daily; closed hols) 1107 Washington St. Phone 601/638-6514. ¢

Old Court House Museum. (1858) Built with slave labor, this bldg offers a view of the Yazoo Canal from its hilltop position. Here Grant raised the US flag on July 4, 1863, signifying the end of fighting after 47 days. Courthouse now houses an extensive display of Americana: Confederate Rm contains weapons, documents on the siege of Vicksburg; also Pioneer Rm; Furniture Rm; Native American displays and objets d'art. (Daily; closed hols) Court Square, 1008 Cherry St. Phone 601/636-0741. ¢

Tourist Information Center. Furnishes free information, maps, and brochures on points of interest and historic houses. Guide service (fee). House (daily; closed Jan 1, Thanksgiving, Dec 25). For information contact

PO Box 110. Clay St at I-20. Phone 601/636-9421 or 800/221-3536.

⭐ **Vicksburg National Military Park & Cemetery.** This historic park, the site of Union siege lines and a brave Confederate defense, borders the eastern and northern sections of the city. A visitor center is at the park entrance, on Clay St at I-20. Museum; exhibits and audiovisual aids. Self-guided, 16-mi tour. (Daily; closed Dec 25) 3201 Clay St. Phone 601/636-0583. Per vehicle ¢¢ Within park is

> **Cairo Museum.** The Union ironclad USS *Cairo,* which sank in 1862, was raised in 1964 and subsequently was restored. An audiovisual program and more than 1,000 artifacts from the sunken gunboat can be viewed inside the museum. (Daily; closed Dec 25) 3201 Clay St. Phone 601/636-2199. **FREE**

Waterways Experiment Station. Principal research and testing laboratory of the US Army Corps of Engineers. Research ranges from hydraulics and soils to wetlands, and from concrete and military vehicles to environmental relationships. River, harbor, and flood control projects are studied on scale models, some with wave and tide-making machines, others with model towboats. Guided tours (Mon-Fri, mid-morning-early afternoon; closed hols); also self-guided tours. Visitor center (daily). 2 mi S of I-20 on Halls Ferry Rd. Phone 601/634-2502. **FREE**

Annual Events

Spring Pilgrimage. Twelve antebellum houses are open to the public at this time. Three tours daily. Late Mar-early Apr.

Siege Reenactment. Five hundred persons reenact the siege of Vicksburg. Memorial Day wkend.

Motels/Motor Lodges

⭐⭐ **BATTLEFIELD INN.** *4137 I-20 N Frontage Rd (39183), Exit 4B.* 601/638-5811; fax 601/638-9249; toll-free 800/359-9363. Email btlfdinn@ vicksburg.com. 117 rms, 2 story. S $35-$57; D $45-$67; each addl $5; under 16 free. Crib free. Pet accepted. TV; cable (premium). Pool. Complimentary bkfst buffet. Restaurant 6:30-9:30 am, 5-9 pm. Bar 5-11 pm; entertainment. Ck-out 12:30 pm. Meeting rms. Business

servs. In-rm modem link. Bellhops. Airport transportation. Some refrigerators. Cr cds: A, C, D, DS, MC, V.

⭐ **DAYS INN.** *2 Pemberton Blvd (39180).* 601/634-1622; fax 601/638-4337; res 800/329-7466. 86 units, 2 story, 20 suites. June-Aug: S $45-$50; D $50-$55; each addl $5; suites $55-$60; under 12 free; lower rates rest of yr. Crib free. TV; cable. Pool. Restaurant adj 6 am-midnight. Ck-out 11 am. Business servs avail. Cr cds: A, C, D, DS, MC, V.

⭐⭐ **HOLIDAY INN.** *3330 Clay St (39180).* 601/636-4551; fax 601/636-4552; res 800/465-4329; toll-free 800/847-0732. 173 rms, 2 story. S, D $65-$72; each addl $7; under 18 free. Crib free. Pet accepted. TV; cable (premium). Indoor pool. Sauna. Restaurant 6 am-10 pm. Bar 3 pm-midnight. Ck-out noon. Coin lndry. Meeting rms. Business servs avail. In-rm modem link. Bellhops. Game rm. Cr cds: A, DS, MC, V.

⭐⭐ **QUALITY INN.** *2390 S Frontage Rd (39180), at I-20.* 601/634-8607; fax 601/634-6053; toll-free 800/228-5151. 70 rms, 2 story. S $40-$50; D $45-$55; each addl $10; under 18 free. Crib $10. TV; cable. Pool; whirlpool. Sauna. Continental bkfst. Ck-out 11 am. Business servs avail. Refrigerators. Cr cds: A, D, DS, MC, V.

⭐ **SUPER 8.** *4127 I-20 Frontage Rd (39180).* 601/638-5077; fax 601/638-5077; res 800/800-8000. 62 rms, 2 story. S $45.88; D $52.88-$58.88; each addl $4; under 12 free; wkly rates. Crib free. TV; cable. Pool. Restaurant nearby. Ck-out 11 am. Business servs avail. Cr cds: A, C, D, DS, MC, V.

Hotel

⭐⭐⭐ **CEDAR GROVE MANSION INN.** *2200 Oak St (39180).* 601/636-1000; fax 601/634-6126; toll-free 800/862-1300. Email info@cedargroveinn. com; www.cedargroveinn.com. 29 rms, 3 story, 10 suites. Mar-May, Sep-Oct: S, D $130; suites $175; lower rates rest of yr. Crib avail. Pet accepted, some restrictions. Parking lot. Pool. TV; cable (premium), VCR avail, CD avail. Complimentary full bkfst, coffee in rms, newspaper. Restaurant, closed Mon. Bar. Meeting rms. Business center. Bellhops. Dry cleaning, coin lndry. Gift shop. Exercise privileges. Golf. Tennis. Hiking trail. Picnic facilities. Cr cds: A, DS, MC, V.

B&Bs/Small Inns

★★★ **ANCHUCA.** *1010 1st E St (39180). 601/661-0111; fax 601/610-0420; res 888/686-0111; toll-free 800/469-2597.* 6 rms, 2 story. S, D $85-$300; each addl $20. Crib free. TV; cable (premium). Pool; whirlpool. Complimentary bkfst. Ck-out noon, ck-in 2 pm. Business servs avail. Greek-revival house (1830). Gas-lit chandeliers, period antiques, and artifacts. Tour of house. Cr cds: MC, V.

★★★ **ANNABELLE BED AND BREAKFAST.** *501 Speed St (39180), in Historic River View Garden District. 601/638-2000; fax 601/636-5054; toll-free 800/791-2000. Email annabelle@ vicksburg.com; www.annabellebnb.com.* 8 rms, 2 story, 1 suite. Mar-Oct: S $85; D $95; each addl $25; suites $125; lower rates rest of yr. Parking lot. Pool. TV; cable (premium), CD avail. Complimentary full bkfst, newspaper, toll-free calls. Restaurant. Ck-out 11 am, ck-in 2 pm. Business center. Concierge. Gift shop. Golf. Tennis, 24 courts. Picnic facilities. Cr cds: A, DS, MC, V.

★★ **CORNERS BED & BREAKFAST INN.** *601 Klein St (39180). 601/636-7421; fax 601/636-7232; toll-free 800/444-7421.* 15 rms, 2 story. S $95; D $105; each addl $20; suites $120. TV; cable. Complimentary full bkfst. Restaurant nearby. Ck-out 11 am, ck-in 2 pm. Business servs avail. 1 blk from river. Built 1872 as a wedding gift. Antiques; extensive gardens. Totally nonsmoking. Cr cds: A, C, D, DS, MC, V.

★★★ **DUFF GREEN MANSION.** *1114 E 1st St (39181). 601/638-6662; fax 601/661-0079; toll-free 800/992-0037.* 7 units, 3 story. Mar-Nov: S, D $65-$160; each addl $10; suites $120-$160; under 5 free; wkly plan; lower rates rest of yr. Pet accepted. TV; cable, VCR avail. Pool; whirlpool. Complimentary full bkfst. Restaurant nearby. Ck-out 11 am, ck-in 3 pm. Business center. Paladian mansion (1856), used as both Confederate and Union hospital during Civil war, was shelled during siege; completely restored, many antiques. Cr cds: A, C, D, DS, MC, V.

Restaurants

★★ **CEDAR GROVE.** *2200 Oak St (39180). 601/636-1000. www.cedar groveinn.com.* Specializes in prime rib, filet mignon, New Orleans-style cooking. Hrs: 6-9 pm. Closed Mon. Res required. Bar. Dinner $16.95-$24.95. Parking. Split-level dining rm in antebellum mansion (1840). Cr cds: A, C, D, DS, MC, V.

★★ **EDDIE MONSOUR'S.** *127 Country Club Dr (39180). 601/638-1571.* Specializes in steak, seafood. Salad bar. Hrs: 11 am-2 pm, 5:30-10 pm; Sun to 2 pm. Closed hols. Res accepted. Bar. Lunch $5-$6; dinner $8.50-$25. Child's menu. Parking. Country French decor. Cr cds: A, MC, V.

★★ **MAXWELL'S.** *4207 E Clay St (39180). 601/636-1344.* Specializes in seafood, pasta, prime rib. Salad bar. Hrs: 11 am-2 pm, 4-10 pm; Sat from 4 pm. Closed Sun; hols. Bar. Lunch $5.50-$8.75. Buffet: $6.50; dinner $10.95-$24.95. Child's menu. Parking. Cr cds: A, D, DS, MC, V.

★ **WALNUT HILLS ROUND TABLES.** *1214 Adams St (39183). 601/638-4910.* Specializes in Southern cooking, fried chicken. Hrs: 11 am-9 pm; Sun to 2 pm. Closed Sat. Bar. Lunch, dinner á la carte entrées: $5.95-$15.95. Child's menu. Parking. Built 1880. Cr cds: A, C, D, DS, MC, V.

Woodville

(G-1) *See also Natchez*

Founded 1811 **Pop** 1,393 **Elev** 410 ft
Area code 601 **Zip** 39669
Information Woodville Civic Club,
PO Box 1055; 601/888-3998

What to See and Do

★ **Rosemont Plantation.** (ca 1810)
The home of Jefferson Davis and his
family. His parents, Samuel and Jane
Davis, moved to Woodville and built
the house when the boy was 2 yrs
old. The Confederate president grew
up here and returned to visit his
family throughout his life. Many
family furnishings remain, incl a
spinning wheel that belonged to
Jane Davis. Original working atmosphere of the 300-acre plantation.
Five generations of the Davis family
are buried here. (Mar-mid-Dec, Mon-
Fri) 1 mi E on MS 24 (Main St). ¢¢

Yazoo City

(D-3) *See also Jackson*

Founded 1823 **Pop** 12,427 **Elev** 120 ft
Area code 662 **Zip** 39194
Information Yazoo County Chamber
of Commerce, 212 E Broadway St, PO
Box 172; 662/746-1273

What to See and Do

Yazoo Historical Museum. Exhibits
cover history of Yazoo County from
prehistoric time to present; US Civil
War artifacts; fossils. Tours. (Mon-Fri;
closed hols, Dec 26) Triangle Cultural
Center, 332 N Main St. Phone
662/746-2273. **FREE**

NORTH CAROLINA

N orth Carolina, besides being a wonderful place for a vacation, is a cross section of America—a state of magnificent variety with three distinctive regions: the coast, the heartland, and the mountains. Its elevation ranges from sea level to 6,684 feet atop Mount Mitchell in the Black Mountain Range of the Appalachians. It has descendants of English, German, Scottish, Irish, and African immigrants. It has Quakers, Moravians, Episcopalians, and Calvinists. It produces two-thirds of our flue-cured tobacco, as well as cotton, peanuts, and vegetables on its farms. Fabrics, furniture, and many other products are made in its factories. It also has one of the finest state university systems in the nation with campuses at Chapel Hill, Raleigh, Greensboro, Charlotte, Asheville, and Wilmington.

In 1585, the first English settlement was unsuccessfully started on Roanoke Island. Another attempt at settlement was made in 1587—but the colony disappeared, leaving only the crudely scratched word "CROATOAN" on a tree—perhaps referring to the Croatan Indians who may have killed the colonists or absorbed them into their own culture, leaving behind one of history's great mysteries. Here, in the Great Smoky Mountains, lived the Cherokee before the government drove them westward to Oklahoma

Population: 6,628,637
Area: 48,843 square miles
Elevation: 0-6,684 feet
Peak: Mount Mitchell (Yancey County)
Entered Union: Twelfth of original 13 states (November 21, 1789)
Capital: Raleigh
Motto: To be rather than to seem
Nickname: Tar Heel State, Old North State
Flower: American Dogwood
Bird: Cardinal
Tree: Pine
Fair: October 12-21, 2001, in Raleigh
Time Zone: Eastern

The Great Smoky Mountains

over the Trail of Tears, on which one-third of them died. Descendants of many members of this tribe, who hid in the inaccessible rocky coves and forests, still live here. Some "mountain people," isolated, independent, still singing songs dating back to Elizabethan England, also live here. Few North Carolinians owned slaves, very few owned many, and, early on, the state accepted free blacks (in 1860 there were 30,463) as a part of the community.

Citizens take pride in being called "Tar Heels." During the Civil War, North Carolinians returning from the front were taunted by a troop from another state who had "retreated" a good deal earlier. The Carolinians declared that Jefferson Davis had decided to bring up all the tar from North Carolina to use on the heels of the other regiment to make them "stick better in the next fight." General Lee, hearing of the incident, said, "God bless the Tar Heel boys."

Individual and democratic from the beginning, this state refused to ratify the Constitution until the Bill of Rights had been added. Its western citizens strongly supported the Union in 1860. It did not join the Confederate States of America until after Fort Sumter had been fired upon and Lincoln had called for volunteers. Its independence was then challenged, and it furnished one-fifth of the soldiers of the Southern armies even though its population was only one-ninth of the Confederacy's. Eighty-four engagements (most of them small) were fought on its soil. Jealous of its rights, North Carolina resisted the authority of Confederate Army officers from Virginia and loudly protested many of the policies of Jefferson Davis; but its 125,000 men fought furiously, and 40,000 of them died for what they believed was right. For years after the Civil War, North Carolina was a poverty-stricken state, although it suffered less from the inroads of carpetbaggers than did many of its neighbors.

The state seems designed for vacationers. Beautiful mountains and flowering plants, lake and ocean swimming and boating, hunting and fishing, superb golf courses, old towns, festivals, pageantry, and parks are a few of the state's many attractions.

When to Go/Climate

North Carolina has the most varied climate of any state on the east coast. Subtropical temperatures on the coast are contrasted by a medium continental climate in the western mountain areas. Fall is hurricane season along the coast; winter in the western mountains can be snowy and cold. Fall foliage is magnificent in Sep and Oct; Mar and Apr are marked by blooming dogwood and azaleas.

AVERAGE HIGH/LOW TEMPERATURES (°F)

CAPE HATTERAS

Jan 52/37	**May** 74/60	**Sep** 81/68
Feb 53/38	**June** 81/68	**Oct** 72/58
Mar 60/44	**July** 85/72	**Nov** 65/49
Apr 67/51	**Aug** 85/72	**Dec** 57/41

RALEIGH

Jan 49/29	**May** 79/55	**Sep** 81/61
Feb 53/31	**June** 85/64	**Oct** 72/48
Mar 62/39	**July** 88/68	**Nov** 63/40
Apr 72/46	**Aug** 87/68	**Dec** 53/32

Parks and Recreation Finder

Directions to and information about the parks and recreation areas below are given under their respective town/city sections. Please refer to those sections for details.

NATIONAL PARK AND RECREATION AREAS

Key to abbreviations. I.H.S. = International Historic Site; I.P.M. = International Peace Memorial; N.B. = National Battlefield; N.B.P. = National Battlefield Park; N.B.C. = National Battlefield and Cemetery; N.C.A. = National Conservation Area; N.E.M. = National Expansion Memorial; N.F. = National Forest; N.G. = National Grassland; N.H.P. = National Historical Park; N.H.C. = National Heritage Corridor; N.H.S. = National Historic Site; N.L. = National Lakeshore; N.M. = National Monument; N.M.P. = National Military Park; N.Mem. = National Memorial; N.P. = National Park; N.Pres. = National Preserve; N.R.A. = National Recreational Area; N.R.R. = National Recreational River; N.Riv. = National River; N.S. = National Seashore; N.S.R. = National Scenic Riverway; N.S.T. = National Scenic Trail; N.Sc. = National Scientific Reserve; N.V.M. = National Volcanic Monument.

Place Name	Listed Under
Cape Hatteras N.S.	same
Cape Lookout N.S.	BEAUFORT
Carl Sandburg Home N.H.S.	HENDERSONVILLE
Croatan N.F.	NEW BERN
Fort Raleigh N.H.S.	same
Great Smoky Mountains N.P.	same
Guilford Courthouse N.M.P.	GREENSBORO
Moores Creek N.B.	WILMINGTON
Nantahala N.F.	FRANKLIN
Pisgah N.F.	BREVARD
Wright Brothers N.Mem.	KILL DEVIL HILLS

STATE PARK AND RECREATION AREAS

Key to abbreviations. I.P. = Interstate Park; S.A.P. = State Archaeological Park; S.B. = State Beach; S.C.A. = State Conservation Area; S.C.P. = State Conservation Park; S.Cp. = State Campground; S.F. = State Forest; S.G. = State Garden; S.H.A. = State Historic Area; S.H.P. = State Historic Park; S.H.S. = State Historic Site; S.M.P. = State Marine Park; S.N.A. = State Natural Area; S.P. = State Park; S.P.C. = State Public Campground; S.R. = State Reserve; S.R.A. = State Recreation Area; S.Res. = State Reservoir; S.Res.P. = State Resort Park; S.R.P. = State Rustic Park.

Place Name	Listed Under
Alamance Battleground S.H.S.	BURLINGTON
Bath S.H.S.	WASHINGTON
Bennett Place S.H.S.	DURHAM
Bentonville Battleground S.H.S.	DUNN
Brunswick Town-Fort Anderson S.H.S.	SOUTHPORT
Carolina Beach S.P.	WILMINGTON
Charlotte Hawkins Brown Memorial S.H.S.	GREENSBORO
Cliffs of the Neuse S.P.	GOLDSBORO
CSS *Neuse* S.H.S.	KINSTON
Duke Homestead S.H.S.	DURHAM
Duke Power S.P.	STATESVILLE
Falls Lake S.R.A.	RALEIGH
Fort Dobbs S.H.S.	STATESVILLE
Fort Fisher S.H.S.	SOUTHPORT
Fort Macon S.P.	MOREHEAD CITY
Governor Charles B. Aycock Birthplace S.H.S.	GOLDSBORO

CALENDAR HIGHLIGHTS

April

North Carolina Azalea Festival (Wilmington). Garden and home tours, horse show, celebrity entertainers, pageants, parade, street fair. Phone 910/763-0905.

Greater Greensboro Chrysler Classic Golf Tournament (Greensboro). Top golfers compete for more than $1.8 million on PGA circuit. For more information, contact Convention & Visitors Bureau, 336/274-2282 or 800/344-2282.

Springfest (Charlotte). Three-day festival in uptown, offers food, live entertainment.

May

Gliding Spectacular (Nags Head, Outer Banks). Hang gliding competition, novice through advanced. Spectacular flying and fun events. Phone 252/441-4124.

Artsplosure Spring & Arts Festival (Raleigh). Moore Sq and City Market. Citywide celebration of the arts. Showcase for regional dance, music, theater performances by nationally known artists; outdoor arts and crafts show; children's activities. Phone 919/832-8699.

June

Rogallo Kite Festival (Nags Head, Outer Banks). Competition for home-built kites; stunt kite performances, demonstrations; kite auction. Phone 252/441-4124.

"Singing on the Mountain" (Linville). On the slopes of Grandfather Mt. All-day program of modern and traditional gospel music featuring top groups and nationally known speakers. Concessions or bring your own food.

July

Mountain Dance and Folk Festival (Asheville). Civic Center. Folk songs and ballads. Finest of its kind for devotees of the 5-string banjo, gut-string fiddle, clogging, and smooth dancing. Phone 828/258-6107 or 800/257-5583.

September

CenterFest (Durham). Downtown. Two-day event with over 250 artists and craftsmen; musicians, jugglers, and clowns; continuous entertainment from 3 stages. Phone 919/560-2722.

Bull Durham Blues Festival (Durham). Historic Durham Athletic Park. Celebrates the blues with performances held at the location where *Bull Durham* was filmed. Phone 919/683-1709.

October

Southern Highland Craft Guild Fair (Asheville). Civic Center. More than 175 craftsmen from 9 Southern states exhibit and demonstrate their skills. Folk and contemporary entertainment daily. Phone 828/298-7928.

State Fair (Raleigh). State Fairgrounds. Phone 919/733-2145 or 919/821-7400.

Hanging Rock S.P.	WINSTON-SALEM
Historic Halifax S.H.S.	ROANOKE RAPIDS
Holmes S.F.	HENDERSONVILLE
House in the Horseshoe S.H.S.	SANFORD
Elizabeth II S.H.S.	MANTEO
James K. Polk Memorial S.H.S.	CHARLOTTE
Jones Lake S.P.	LUMBERTON
Kerr Reservoir	HENDERSON
Merchant's Millpond S.P.	EDENTON
Morrow Mountain S.P.	ALBEMARLE
Mount Jefferson S.P.	JEFFERSON
Mount Mitchell S.P.	LITTLE SWITZERLAND
Pilot Mountain S.P.	PILOT MOUNTAIN
Raven Rock S.P.	SANFORD
Reed Gold Mine S.H.S.	CONCORD (CABURRUS COUNTY)
Somerset Place S.H.S.	EDENTON
Stone Mountain S.P.	WILKESBORO
Town Creek Indian Mound S.H.S.	ALBEMARLE
William B. Umstead S.P.	RALEIGH
Zebulon B. Vance Birthplace S.H.S.	ASHEVILLE

Water-related activities, hiking, riding, various other sports, picnicking and visitor centers, as well as camping, are avail in many of these areas. Parks are open daily: June-Aug, 8 am-9 pm; Apr-May and Sep to 8 pm; Mar and Oct to 7 pm; Nov-Feb to 6 pm. Most parks have picnicking and hiking. Swimming ($3; 6-12, $2; under 3 free) and concessions open Memorial Day-Labor Day. Admission and parking free (exc reservoirs; $4); canoe and boat rentals ($3/hr first hr, $1/hr thereafter); fishing. Campgrounds: open all yr, limited facilities in winter; family of 6 for $12/day; hookups $5 more; primitive sites $8/day; youth group tent camping $1/person ($8 min). Senior citizen discounts offered. Dogs on leash only. Campgrounds are on first come, first served basis; res are allowed for minimum of 7 days, max of 14 days; write the Park Superintendent.

Information, incl a comprehensive brochure, may be obtained from the Division of Parks & Recreation, Dept of Environment, Health and Natural Resources, 1615 MSC Raleigh 27699-1615; 919/733-7275 or 919/733-4181.

SKI AREAS

Place Name	Listed Under
Appalachian Ski Mountain	BLOWING ROCK
Cataloochee Ski Area	MAGGIE VALLEY
Fairfield Sapphire Valley Ski Area	CASHIERS
Scaly Mountain Ski Area	HIGHLANDS
Ski Beech	BANNER ELK
Sugar Mountain Ski Area	BANNER ELK
Wolf Laurel Ski Resort	ASHEVILLE

FISHING AND HUNTING

Nonresident fishing license $30; daily license $10; 3-day license $15. Nonresident 6-day and basic hunting license $50. Nonresident trapping license $100. Nonresident comprehensive fishing license (incl basic fishing, trout, and trout waters on gamelands) $30; 3-day license $15; daily license $10. Waterfowl stamp (mandatory) $5.

For latest regulations contact License Section, Wildlife Resources Commission, Archdale Bldg, 512 N Salisbury St, Raleigh 27604-1188; 919/662-4370.

Driving Information

Safety belts are mandatory for all persons in front seat of vehicle. Children under 6 yrs must be in an approved child passenger restraint system anywhere in vehicle; ages 3-6 may use a regulation safety belt; children under 3 yrs must use an approved child passenger restraint system. For further information phone 919/733-7952.

INTERSTATE HIGHWAY SYSTEM

The following alphabetical listing of North Carolina towns in *Mobil Travel Guide* shows that these cities are within 10 miles of the indicated Interstate highways. A highway map should, however, be checked for the nearest exit.

Highway Number	Cities/Towns within 10 miles
Interstate 26	Asheville, Columbus, Hendersonville, Tryon.
Interstate 40	Asheville, Burlington, Durham, Greensboro, Hickory, Maggie Valley, Marion, Morganton, Raleigh, Statesville, Waynesville, Wilmington, Winston-Salem.
Interstate 77	Charlotte, Cornelius, Dobson, Statesville.
Interstate 85	Burlington, Charlotte, Concord, Durham, Gastonia, Greensboro, Henderson, High Point, Lexington, Salisbury.
Interstate 95	Dunn, Fayetteville, Lumberton, Roanoke Rapids, Rocky Mount, Smithfield, Wilson.

Additional Visitor Information

The North Carolina Gazetteer, by William S. Powell (University of North Carolina Press, Chapel Hill, 1968) lists over 20,000 entries that will enable the reader to find any place in the state, as well as information about size, history, and derivation of name. The Travel and Tourism Division, 301 N. Wilmington Raleigh 27601, 800/VISIT-NC, has free travel information, incl brochures.

North Carolina Welcome Center locations are: I-85 N, Box 156, Norlina 27563; I-85 S, Box 830, Kings Mt 28086; I-95 North, Box 52, Roanoke Rapids 27870; I-40, Box 809, Waynesville 28786; I-95 S, Box 518, Rowland 28383; I-26, Box 249, Columbus 28722; I-77 N, Box 1066, Dobson 27017; and I-77 S, Box 410724, Charlotte 28241-0724.

The Coastal Plains area of North Carolina is perhaps the state's most unique region. Take Highway 64 east from Raleigh to the Fort Raleigh National Historic Site, a restored fort where the first English colonists attempted to settle in 1585, but mysteriously disappeared, earning Fort Raleigh the name "The Lost Colony." From here, continue east to historic Manteo and visit the Elizabethan Gardens and the Elizabeth II State Historic Site, a living history site representing the English colonists of 400 years ago. From Manteo, take a quick detour north on Highway 12 to the Wright Brothers National Monument, where the brothers made their historic first flight on Dec 17, 1903, then return south on Highway 12 along the Cape Hatteras National Seashore, through villages and towns like Nags Head, Hatteras, and Ocracoke (which was rumored to have been the headquarters for the pirate Blackbeard). Return to Raleigh via Highway 70. **(Approx 450 mi)**

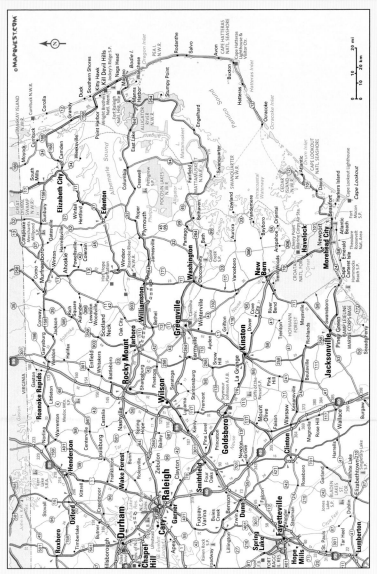

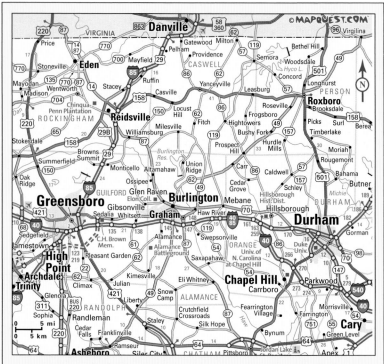

Located in north central North Carolina, just below the Virginia state line and running between Durham and Greensboro, the "Colonial Heritage Byway" provides an impressive tour of 18th and 19th century state history. Near Durham, visit the Bennett Place State Historic Site, where Confederate General Johnston surrendered to Union General Sherman on April 26, 1865. Also along the way are Hillsborough, once the summer capital of the state; the grave of North Carolina's third governor, Thomas Burke; a glimpse of Piedmont farms and rural life; mid 1800s general stores still in use today; and towns like Milton, which were booming communities prior to the Civil War. Just outside of Greensboro, visit the Charlotte Hawkins Brown Memorial State Historic Site, which honors African-American educational achievements in North Carolina. **(Approx 180 mi)**

Ahoskie (B-7)

Pop 4,391 **Elev** 53 ft **Area code** 252
Zip 27910

Motels/Motor Lodges

★ **AHOSKIE INN.** *Interchange 561 & 11 (27910), jct NC 11 and 561.* 252/ 332-4165; fax 252/332-1632; toll-free 800/582-3220. 98 rms, 2 story. S $47; D $56; each addl $10; suites $161; under 18 free. TV; cable (premium). Indoor pool. Coffee in rms. Restaurant 6 am-2 pm, 5:30-9 pm. Bar; entertainment Sat. Ck-out noon. Meeting rms. Business servs avail. In-rm modem link. Valet serv. Lawn games Cr cds: A, C, D, DS, MC, V.

🅳 ⬆ ➿ 📶 🔥

★ **TOMAHAWK MOTEL INC.** *601 Academy St N (27910).* 252/332-3194; fax 252/332-3194. 58 rms. S $34.85; D $44.85. TV; cable. Restaurant opp 6 am-8:30 pm. Ck-out 11 am. Business servs avail. Cr cds: A, C, D, DS, MC, V.

🔥 🆂🅲

Restaurant

★ **WHITLEY'S BARBECUE.** *NC 11 N (27855), 1¼ mi S on NC 11 (Beech-wood Blvd).* 252/398-4884. Specializes in seafood, chicken, pork. Own desserts. Hrs: 11 am-9 pm; Sun buffet noon-4 pm. Closed Mon; July 4; Christmas wk. Res accepted. Wine, beer. Lunch, dinner $5-$15. Sun brunch buffet: $10.95-$12.95. Parking. Family dining. Family-owned since 1963. Cr cds: DS, MC, V.

Albemarle

(C-4) *See also Concord*

Founded 1857 **Pop** 14,939 **Elev** 455 ft
Area code 704 **Zip** 28001
Information Stanly County Chamber of Commerce, 116 E North St, PO Box 909, 28002; 704/982-8116

Albemarle is in the gently rolling hills of the Uwharrie Mountains, in the Piedmont section of the state. It manufactures textiles, aircraft tires, automotive parts, and aluminum.

Motel/Motor Lodge

★★ **COMFORT INN.** *735 Hwy 24/27 Bypass (28001).* 704/983-6990; fax 704/983-5597; res 800/228-5150. 80 rms, 2 story. S $59.95-$69.95; D $63.95-$74.95; each addl $6; under 18 free; higher rates during races. Crib free. TV; cable (premium). Complimentary continental bkfst. Restaurant nearby. Ck-out noon. Meeting rms. Business servs avail. Pool. Some refrigerators. Cr cds: A, C, D, DS, ER, JCB, MC, V.

🅳 ⬆ ➿ 🐟 📶 🔥

Asheboro

(C-5) *See also Greensboro, High Point, Lexington*

Founded 1779 **Pop** 16,362 **Elev** 844 ft
Area code 336 **Zip** 27203
Web chamber.asheboro.com
Information Randolph Tourism Development Authority, 317 E Dixie Dr, PO Box 4774; 336/626-0364 or 800/626-2672

Annual Event

Asheboro Fall Festival. Arts, crafts, food, parade, music, entertainment. First wkend Oct.

Motel/Motor Lodge

★ **DAYS INN.** *999 Albemarle Rd (27203), at jct NC 49, US 220 Bypass.* 336/629-2101; fax 336/626-7944; res 800/222-0519; toll-free 800/329-7466. 136 rms, 2 story. S $46-$80; D $64-$78; each addl $4; suites $125. Crib free. TV; cable (premium). Pool. Ck-out 11 am. Meeting rms. Business servs avail. Valet serv. Health club privileges. Cr cds: A, C, D, DS, MC, V.

🅳 ➿ 📶 🔥 🆂🅲

Asheville

(C-2) *See also Maggie Valley, Waynesville*

Settled 1794 **Pop** 61,607 **Elev** 2,134 ft
Area code 828
Web www.ashevillechamber.org
Information Convention & Visitors Bureau, 151 Haywood St, PO Box 1010, 28802-1010; 828/258-6101 or 800/257-1300

Thomas Wolfe came from Asheville, the seat of Buncombe County, as did the expression "bunkum" (nonsense). A local congressman, when asked why he had been so evasive during a masterful oration in which he said nothing, replied, "I did it for Buncombe." Wolfe wrote often of his hill-rimmed home, shrewdly observant of the people and life of Asheville.

Asheville is a vacation headquarters in the Blue Ridge Mountains, as well as a marketing and industrial city. It is the North Carolina city nearest Great Smoky Mountains National Park (see) and attracts many of the park's visitors with its annual mountain fetes, local handicrafts, and summer theaters. It is the headquarters for the Uwharrie National Forest, Pisgah National Forest (see BREVARD), Nantahala National Forest (see FRANKLIN), and Croatan National Forest (see NEW BERN). The Blue Ridge Parkway brings many travelers to Asheville on their way south from the Shenandoah Valley of Virginia.

For further information about Croatan, Nantahala, Pisgah, and Uwharrie national forests contact the US Forest Service, 828/257-4202.

What to See and Do

Asheville Community Theatre. Comedies, musicals, and dramas performed throughout yr. 35 E Walnut St. Phone 828/254-1320 for schedule. ¢¢¢-¢¢¢¢

✪ **Biltmore Estate.** The 8,000-acre country estate incl 75 acres of formal gardens, numerous varieties of azaleas and roses, and the 250-rm chateau (85 rms are open for viewing), which is the largest house ever built in the New World. George W.

Vanderbilt commissioned Richard Morris Hunt to design the house, which was begun in 1890 and finished in 1895. Materials and furnishings were brought from many parts of Europe and Asia; a private railroad was built to transport them to the site. Life here was lived in the grand manner. Vanderbilt employed Gifford Pinchot, later Governor of Pennsylvania and famous for forestry and conservation achievements, to manage his forests. Biltmore was the site of the first US forestry school. Much of the original estate is now part of Pisgah National Forest. Tours of the estate incl gardens, conservatory, and winery facilities; tasting. Three restaurants on grounds. (Daily; closed Thanksgiving, Dec 25) Guidebook (fee) is recommended. S on US 25, 3 blks N of I-40 Exit 50. Phone 828/255-1700 or 800/543-2961. ¢¢¢¢

Biltmore Homespun Shops. At the turn of the century, Mrs George W. Vanderbilt opened a school to keep alive the skills of hand-dyeing, spinning, and hand-weaving wool into cloth. The business still has the old machinery and handlooms. An antique automobile museum and the North Carolina Homespun Museum are in an 11-acre park adj Grove Park Inn Resort. (Apr-Oct, daily; rest of yr, Mon-Sat; closed Jan 1, Thanksgiving, Dec 25) Grovewood Rd, near Macon Ave, 2 mi NE. Phone 828/253-7651. **FREE**

Botanical Gardens of Asheville. A 10-acre tract with thousands of flowers, trees, and shrubs native to southern Appalachia; 125-yr-old "dog trot" log cabin. (Daily) On campus of Univ of North Carolina. Phone 828/252-5190. **FREE**

Chimney Rock Park. Towering granite monolith Chimney Rock affords 75-mi view; 3 hiking trails lead to 404-ft Hickory Nut Falls, Moonshiner's Cave, Devil's Head balancing rock, Nature's Showerbath. Trails, stairs, and catwalks, picnic areas, playground, nature center, observation lounge with snack bar, gift shop. Twenty-six-story elevator shaft through granite. (Daily, weather permitting; closed Jan 1, Dec 25) 25 mi SE on US 74, just past jct US 64, NC 9. Phone 828/625-9611 or 800/277-9611. ¢¢

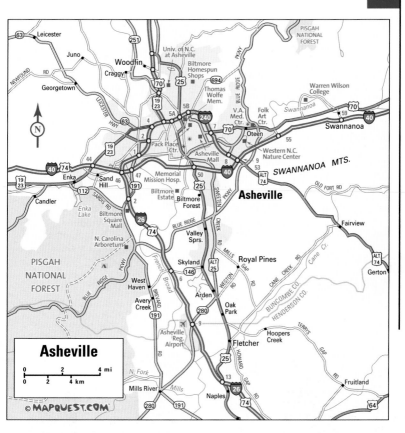

Asheville

0   2   4 mi
0   2   4 km

© MAPQUEST.COM

Folk Art Center. Home of the Southern Highland Craft Guild. Stone and timber structure; home of Blue Ridge Pkwy info center; craft exhibits, demonstrations, workshops, related programs. (Daily; closed Jan 1, Thanksgiving, Dec 25) 5 mi E on US 70, then ½ mi N on the Blue Ridge Pkwy to Milepost 382. Phone 828/298-7928. (See ANNUAL EVENTS) **FREE**

Graves of Thomas Wolfe (1900-38) and O. Henry (William Sydney Porter) (1862-1910). Riverside Cemetery. Entrance on Birch St off Pearson Dr.

Mount Mitchell State Park. (see LITTLE SWITZERLAND) 27 mi NE on Blue Ridge Pkwy, then 5 mi N on NC 128.

Pack Place Education, Arts, and Science Center. This 92,000-sq-ft complex features multiple museums and exhibit galleries as well as a state-of-the-art theater. A permanent exhibit entitled "Here Is the Square..." describes the history of Asheville. Restaurant (lunch only); gift shop. (Tues-Sat, also some Sun afternoons; closed Jan 1, Thanksgiving, Dec 24-25) 2 S Pack Square. Phone 828/257-4500 for general info. Incl

Asheville Art Museum. Permanent collection and changing exhibits. Phone 828/253-3227. ¢¢

Colburn Gem and Mineral Museum. Displays of 1,000 minerals from around the world; incl info on mineral locations in the state. Phone 828/254-7162. ¢¢

Diana Wortham Theatre. This 500-seat theater hosts local, regional, and national companies. Phone 828/257-4530 for box office info.

The Health Adventure. Extensive collection of imaginative, educational exhibits on the human body; incl a talking transparent woman, a bicycle-pedaling skeleton, and opportunity to hear sound of your own heartbeat. Also on premises is Creative PlaySpace, a special exhibit for young children. Phone 828/254-6373. ¢¢

YMI Cultural Center. Galleries featuring permanent and rotating exhibts on African American art. Phone 828/252-4614. ¢¢

River Rafting. Nantahala Outdoor Center. Offers various trips on the Nantahala, French Broad, Ocee, Nolichucky, and Chattooga rivers ranging from 1½ to 6 hrs. Contact 1377 US 19W, Bryson City 28713-9114. Phone 800/232-7238 for info and res. ¢¢¢¢

Thomas Wolfe Memorial. The state maintains the Wolfe boardinghouse as a literary shrine, restored and furnished to appear as it did in 1916. In Asheville it is known as the Old Kentucky Home. In *Look Homeward, Angel* it was referred to as "Dixieland"; Asheville was "Altamont." Visitor center with exhibit. (Apr-Oct, daily; rest of yr, Tues-Sun; closed hols) 48 Spruce St, between Woodfin & Walnut Sts. Phone 828/253-8304. ¢

Western North Carolina Nature Center. Live animals, children's petting barnyard, natural history exhibits, nature trail, educational programs. (Memorial Day-Labor Day, daily; rest of yr, Tues-Sat and Sun afternoons) Gashes Creek Rd, 3 mi E on NC 81. Phone 828/298-5600. ¢

Wolf Laurel Ski Resort. Quad, double chairlifts, Mitey-mite; patrol, school, rentals, snow making; restaurant. Longest run ¾ mi; vertical drop 700 ft. (Mid-Dec-mid-Mar, daily) 27 mi N off US 23. Phone 828/689-4111. ¢¢¢¢

Zebulon B. Vance Birthplace State Historic Site. Log house (reconstructed 1961) and outbldgs on site where Civil War governor of North Carolina grew up. Honors Vance family, which was deeply involved with early history of state. Visitor center, exhibits. Picnic area. (Apr-Oct, daily; rest of yr, Tues-Sun; closed hols) 9 mi N on US 19/23, exit New-Stock Rd, then 6 mi N on Reems Creek Rd in Weaverville. Phone 828/645-6706. **FREE**

Annual Events

Shindig-on-the-Green. College & Spruce Sts. In front of City Hall. Mountain fiddling, dulcimer players, singing, square dancing. Phone 828/258-6109. Sat eves, July-Labor Day exc last wkend July.

Mountain Dance and Folk Festival. Civic Center. Folk songs and ballads. Finest of its kind for devotees of the 5-string banjo, gut-string fiddle, clogging, and smooth dancing. Phone 828/258-6107. July 4 wkend.

Southern Highland Craft Guild Fair. Civic Center, Haywood St, just off I-240. More than 175 craftsmen from 9 Southern states exhibit and demonstrate their skills. Folk and contemporary entertainment daily. Phone 828/298-7928. Third wkend July, 3rd wkend Oct.

World Gee Haw Whimmy Diddle Competition. Folk Art Center. Competitions, demonstrations, storytelling, music, dance. Early Aug.

Seasonal Event

Shakespeare in the Park. Montford Park Players. Phone 828/254-4540. Wkends early June-late Aug.

Motels/Motor Lodges

★ **AMERICAN COURT.** *85 Merrimon Ave (28801). 828/253-4427; fax 828/253-2507; toll-free 800/233-3582. Email tom@americancourt.com; www. americancourt.com.* 22 rms, 1 story. June-Oct: S $59; D $79; each addl $5; lower rates rest of yr. Parking lot. Pool. TV; cable. Restaurant nearby. Ck-out 11 am, ck-in 2 pm. Fax servs avail. Coin lndry. Golf, 18 holes. Tennis, 2 courts. Cr cds: A, D, DS, MC, V.

★★ **BEST WESTERN ASHEVILLE BILTMORE.** *22 Woodfin St (28801), 1 blk off I-240 at Merrimon Ave Exit. 828/253-1851; fax 704/252-9205.* 150 rms, 5 story. June-Oct: S, D $65-$89; under 18 free; lower rates rest of yr. Crib free. TV; cable (premium). Heated pool. Complimentary coffee in rms. Restaurant 6:30-10 am; Sat, Sun 7-11 am. Bar 5 pm-1 am. Ck-out noon. Meeting rm. Business servs avail. In-rm modem link. Exercise equipt. Health club privileges. Cr cds: A, D, DS, MC, V.

★★ **FOREST MANOR INN.** *866 Hendersonville Rd (28803), on US 25, 1 mi S of I-40 Exit 50. 828/274-3531; fax 828/274-3036; res 800/866-3531.*

Email forestmanorinn@aol.com; www.
forestmanorinn.com. 21 rms, 1 story.
July-Aug, Oct: S, D $149; lower rates
rest of yr. Crib avail, fee. Parking lot.
Pool. TV; cable, VCR avail. Complimentary continental bkfst. Restaurant. Ck-out 11 am, ck-in 3 pm. Fax
servs avail. Concierge. Exercise privileges. Golf. Tennis, 40 courts. Downhill skiing. Cr cds: A, DS, MC, V.

★★ **HAMPTON INN.** 1 Rocky Ridge
Rd (28806), jct I-26 and NC 191. 828/
667-2022; fax 828/665-9680; toll-free
800/426-7866. 121 rms, 5 story. June-
Oct: S $69-$119; D $79-$119; suites
$145; under 18 free. Crib free. TV;
cable (premium). Indoor pool; whirlpool. Complimentary continental
bkfst, coffee in rms. Ck-out noon.
Meeting rms. Business servs avail. In-
rm modem link. Free airport transportation. Exercise equipt; sauna.
Refrigerator in suites. Cr cds: A, C, D,
DS, MC, V.

★★ **HAMPTON INN.** 204 Tunnel Rd
(28805), I-240 Exit 6 and 7, US 70 to
Tunnel Rd. 828/255-9220; fax 828/
254-4303; toll-free 800/426-7866. 120
rms, 5 story. June-Oct: S $69-$119; D
$79-$119; suites $95-$225; under 18
free; higher rates special events;
lower rates rest of yr. Crib free. TV;
cable (premium). Indoor pool; whirlpool. Complimentary continental
bkfst, coffee in rms. Restaurant
nearby. Ck-out noon. Meeting rms.
Business servs avail. Exercise equipt;
sauna. Refrigerators, microwaves
avail. Cr cds: A, C, D, DS, MC, V.

★★ **HOLIDAY INN.** 1 Holiday Inn
Dr (28806). 828/254-3211; fax 828/
285-2688; res 800/733-3211. www.
sunspree.com. 277 rms, 5 story. May-
Oct: S, D $89-$135; each addl $12;
suites $195-$275; family rates; ski,
golf plans; lower rates rest of yr. Crib
free. TV; cable (premium). 2 pools, 1
heated; wading pool. Supervised children's activities (May-Oct); ages 3-15.
Playground. Restaurant 6:30 am-10
pm. Bar. Ck-out noon. Convention
facilities. Business servs avail. Gift
shop. Bellhops. Valet serv. Indoor
and outdoor tennis, pro. 18-hole
golf, pro, putting green. Exercise
equipt. Health club privileges. Refrig-

erators; some wet bars; microwaves
avail. Private patios, balconies. Near
shopping center. Cr cds: A, C, D, DS,
ER, JCB, MC, V.

★ **HOWARD JOHNSON BILTMORE
INN.** 190 Hendersonville Rd (28803).
828/274-2300; fax 828/274-2304; res
800/446-4656. 68 rms, 2 story. Apr-
Oct: S $54-$149; D $64-$149; each
addl $8; higher rates: special events
wkends and autumn foliage; lower
rates rest of yr. Crib free. TV; cable
(premium). Pool. Restaurant 6:30
am-1:30 pm, 5:30-8:30 pm; Sat, Sun
from 7 am. Ck-out noon. Meeting
rms. Business servs avail. Private
patios, balconies. Cr cds: A, D, DS,
MC, V.

★★ **MOUNTAIN SPRINGS CAB-
INS.** US 151 (28715), I-40 W to Exit
44, 5 mi S on US 151. 828/665-1004;
fax 828/667-1581. Email mtnsprings@
ioa.com. 15 kit. cottages, 1-2 story. S,
D $90-$165; each addl $20. Crib free.
TV, cable. Ck-out 10 am. Lawn
games. Microwaves. Picnic tables,
outdoor grills. On mountain stream.
Cr cds: MC, V.

★★ **QUALITY INN BILTMORE.** 115
Hendersonville Rd (28803). 828/274-
1800; fax 828/274-5960. 160 rms, 5
story, 20 suites. Apr-Oct: S, D $95-
$107; each addl $8; suites $110-$150;
under 18 free; lower rates rest of yr.
Crib free. TV; cable (premium). Pool.
Complimentary coffee in rms.
Restaurant 6:30 am-10 pm. Bar 5-11
pm. Ck-out noon. Meeting rms. Business servs avail. Bellhops. Valet serv.
Health club privileges. Some refrigerators. Cr cds: A, D, DS, MC, V.

★ **RED ROOF INN.** 16 Crowell Rd
(28806), I-40 Exit 44. 828/667-9803;
fax 828/667-9810; res 800/733-7663.
109 rms, 3 story. May-Oct: S $65.99;
D $69.99; under 18 free; lower rates
rest of yr. Pet accepted, some restrictions. TV; cable (premium). Complimentary coffee in lobby. Restaurant
opp open 24 hrs. Ck-out noon. Business servs avail. Cr cds: A, C, D, DS,
MC, V.

Hotels

★ **BEST INNS.** *1435 Tunnel Rd (28805). 828/298-4000; fax 828/298-4000; res 800/237-8466. Email bie01100@mindspring.com.* 84 rms, 3 story. June-Oct: S $58; D $73; each addl $7; under 18 free; lower rates rest of yr. Crib avail. Pet accepted, some restrictions. Parking lot. Pool. TV; cable (premium). Complimentary continental bkfst, toll-free calls. Restaurant. Ck-out 1 pm, ck-in 2 pm. Fax servs avail. Golf. Cr cds: A, D, DS, MC, V.

★★★ **HAYWOOD PARK.** *1 Battery Park Ave (28801). 828/252-2522; fax 828/253-0481; res 800/228-2522. Email hotel@haywoodpark.com.* 33 suites, 4 story. S $130-$245; D $155-$295; each addl $15; under 18 free. TV; cable (premium), VCR. Complimentary continental bkfst. Restaurant 11 am-9:30 pm. Bar. Ck-out noon. Meeting rms. Business servs avail. In-rm modem link. Shopping arcade. Free valet parking. Exercise equipt; sauna. Bathrm phones, refrigerators; some in-rm whirlpools. Cr cds: A, C, D, DS, MC, V.

★★★ **RENAISSANCE ASHEVILLE HOTEL.** *One Thomas Wolfe Plaza (28801). 828/252-8211; fax 828/254-1374; res 800/468-3571.* 281 rms, 12 story. Apr-mid-Nov: S $89-$119; D $99-$139; each addl $10; suites $165-$225; under 18 free; lower rates rest of yr. Crib free. TV; cable (premium), VCR avail. Pool. Restaurant 6:30 am-10 pm. Bar 11-1 am. Ck-out noon. Convention facilities. Business servs avail. In-rm modem link. Concierge. Gift shop. Exercise equipt. Game rm. Minibars; refrigerators avail. Cr cds: A, C, D, DS, JCB, MC, V.

Resorts

GROVE PARK INN RESORT. *290 Macon Ave (28804). 828/252-2711; fax 828/253-7053; toll-free 800/438-5800.*

www.groveparkinn.com. Unrated due to renovation. 510 rms, 6-11 story. Apr-Dec: S, D $125-$230; each addl $25; suites $450; under 16 free; golf plans; lower rates rest of yr. Crib free. TV; cable (premium), VCR avail. 2 heated pools, 1 indoor; whirlpool, lifeguard. Supervised children's activities; ages 3-16. Restaurants 6:30 am-midnight. Bar from 11 am; entertainment. Ck-out 11 am, ck-in 4 pm. Convention facilities. Business center. Bellhops. Valet serv. Shopping arcade. 9 lighted tennis courts, 3 indoor. Golf, greens fee $75 (incl cart), nine holes $37.50, putting green. Rec rm. Exercise rm; sauna. Raquetball and squash courts. Massage. Luxury level. Cr cds: A, C, D, DS, JCB, MC, V.

Ashville skyline

★ **PISGAH INN.** *Blue Ridge Pkwy (28786), Enka-Candler Exit off I-40, S on US 19/23 4 mi to Candler, left on NC 151, 9 mi to Ranch. 828/235-8228; fax 828/648-9719.* 48 units. May-Oct: AP: S $55-$125/person, $300-$700/wk; D $55-$85/person, $300-$475/wk; family rates. Closed rest of yr. Crib free. TV. Heated pool. Playground. Dining rm: bkfst 8 am, lunch 12:30 pm, dinner 5:30 pm. Ck-out 11 am, ck-in 2 pm. Coin lndry. Meeting rms. Gift shop. Airport, bus depot transportation. Tennis. Hiking trails. Rec rm. Lawn games. Entertainment. Cr cds: A, DS, MC, V.

B&Bs/Small Inns

★★ **ADAMS CAIRN BRAE BED & BREAKFAST.** *217 Patton Mt Rd (28804). 828/252-9219. Email info@ cairnbrae.com, www.cairnbrae.com.* 3 rms, 1 with shower only, 2 story, 2 suites. No rm phones. S $85-$100; D $95-$120; each addl $20; suites $120. Children over 10 yrs only. TV in sitting rm; cable (premium). Complimentary full bkfst; afternoon refreshments. Ck-out 11 am, ck-in 3 pm. Rec rm. Picnic tables. Situated along mountainside. Totally nonsmoking. Cr cds: DS, MC, V.

★★ **ALBEMARLE INN.** *86 Edgemont Rd (28801). 828/255-0027; fax 828/236-3397; toll-free 800/621-7435. www.albemarleinn.com.* 11 rms, 3 story. S, D $95-$170; each addl $25. Children over 14 yrs only. TV; cable. Pool. Complimentary full bkfst; afternoon refreshments. Ck-out 11 am, ck-in 3 pm. Greek Revival mansion built 1909; many antiques. Totally nonsmoking. Cr cds: DS, MC, V.

★★ **APPLEWOOD MANOR INN.** *62 Cumberland Circle (28801), 1 mi N on I-240, Exit 4-C. 828/254-2244; fax 828/254-0899; res 828/254-2244; toll-free 800/442-2197. Email johan. verheis@gte.net.* 4 rms, 2 with shower only, 1 kit. cottage, 2 story. No rm phones. S $90-$110; D $95-$115; each addl $20; kit. cottage $105-$110; hols (2-day min). Children over 12 yrs only. TV in kit. cottage; cable. Complimentary full bkfst; afternoon refreshments. Ck-out 11 am, ck-in 3-7 pm. Business servs avail. Lawn games. Many fireplaces. Many balconies. Colonial turn-of-the-century home built in 1910; antiques. Totally nonsmoking. Cr cds: MC, V.

★★★ **BEAUFORT HOUSE.** *61 N Liberty St (28801). 828/254-8334; fax 828/251-2082; toll-free 800/261-2221. www.beauforthouse.com.* 11 rms, 1 shower only, 3 story, 1 suite. Apr-Dec: S, D $95-$185; suite $195; call ahead for wkend rates (2-day min); lower rates rest of yr. Children over 10 yrs only. TV; cable; VCR (movies). Complimentary full bkfst. Restaurant nearby. Ck-out 11 am, ck-in 3-7 pm.

Exercise equipt. Many in-rm whirlpools, fireplaces. Built in 1894. Victorian decor; antiques. Totally nonsmoking. Cr cds: A, MC, V.

★★★ **CEDAR CREST.** *674 Biltmore Ave (28803). 828/252-1389; fax 828/253-7667; toll-free 800/252-0310. Email stay@cedarcrestvictorianinn.com; www.cedarcrestvictorianinn.com.* 9 rms, 3 story, 2 cottage suites. S, D $130-$170; each addl $20; suites $130-$220. Children over 10 yrs only. Complimentary full bkfst. Ck-out 11 am, ck-in 3-10 pm. Business servs avail. Lawn games. Balconies. Historic inn (1890); antiques. Flower gardens. Cr cds: A, D, DS, MC, V.

★ **CORNER OAK MANOR.** *53 St. Dunstans Rd (28803). 828/253-3525; fax 828/253-3525; toll-free 888/633-3525.* 4 rms, 2 story, 1 kit. unit. No rm phones. S $75; D $100-$115; kit. unit $145. Children over 12 yrs only. Complimentary full bkfst. Ck-out 11 am, ck-in 3 pm. Whirlpool on terrace. Picnic tables. English Tudor home (1920); antiques. Totally nonsmoking. Cr cds: A, DS, MC, V.

★★ **FLINT STREET INNS.** *116 Flint St (28801). 828/253-6723; fax 828/254-6685; toll-free 800/234-8172. Email flintstreetinn@cs.com; www. flintstreetinns.com.* 8 rms, 2 story. S $75; D $110; each addl $25; under 14 free. Parking lot. TV; cable. Complimentary full bkfst, coffee in rms, newspaper. Restaurant nearby. Ck-out 11 am, ck-in noon. Business center. Golf. Cr cds: A, DS, MC, V.

★★★ **LION AND THE ROSE.** *276 Montford Ave (28801). 828/255-7673; fax 828/285-9810; toll-free 800/546-6988. Email info@lion-rose.com; www. lion-rose.com.* 4 rms, 3 story, 1 suite. Apr-Dec: S $125; D $145; suites $245; lower rates rest of yr. Parking lot. TV; cable; VCR avail. Complimentary full bkfst, coffee in rms, newspaper, toll-free calls. Restaurant nearby. Ck-out 8 am, ck-in 3 pm. Internet dock/port avail. Concierge. Exercise privileges. Golf. Tennis. Cr cds: A, DS, MC, V.

★★ **THE OLD REYNOLDS MANSION.** *100 Reynolds Hts (28804). 828/254-0496; toll-free 800/709-0496. www.oldreynoldsmansion.com.* 10 rms, 3 story, 1 suite. July-Aug, Oct: S $99; D $135; suites $135; lower rates rest of yr. Parking lot. TV; cable, VCR avail. Complimentary full bkfst. Ck-out 11 am, ck-in 3 pm. Golf. Downhill skiing. Cr cds: A, DS, MC, V.

★★★ **OWLS NEST.** *2630 Smokey Park Hwy (28715), W on I-40, Exit 37. 828/665-8325; fax 828/667-2539; res 800/665-8868. Email owlsnest@circle. net; www.circle.net/owlsnest.* 4 rms, 3 story, 1 suite. Apr-Dec: S $100; D $110; each addl $25; suites $175; lower rates rest of yr. Parking lot. TV; cable (premium), VCR avail, CD avail. Complimentary full bkfst, newspaper. Restaurant nearby. Bar. Meeting rm. Business center. Concierge. Gift shop. Exercise equipt, whirlpool. Golf, 18 holes. Downhill skiing. Hiking trail. Picnic facilities. Cr cds: A, DS, MC, V.

★★★★ **RICHMOND HILL INN.** *87 Richmond Hill Dr (28806), I-240 Exit 4A to Hwy 19/23N, Exit Hwy 251, W to Riverside Dr, then S to Pearson Bridge Rd, then W to Richmond Hill Dr. 828/ 252-7313; fax 828/252-8726; toll-free 800/545-9238. Email info@richmond hillinn.com; www.richmondhillinn.com.* Romance isn't hard to come by at this beautiful bed and breakfast nestled on nine acres in the Blue Ridge Mountains. A Queen Anne-style mansion, originally built in 1889, five cottages, and a garden pavilion house 36 rooms, all including complimentary afternoon tea and a full breakfast. Partake in a genuinely Victorian recreation and shoot wickets on the manicured croquet lawn. 33 rooms, 3 story, 3 suites. Oct: S, D $295; each addl $30; suites $450; under 8 free; lower rates rest of yr. Crib avail. Valet parking avail. TV; cable. Complimentary full bkfst, coffee in rms, newspaper, toll-free calls. Restaurant 6-10 pm. Ck-out 11 am, ck-in 3 pm. Business servs avail. Concierge. Dry cleaning. Gift shop. Exercise equipt. Golf. Tennis. Hiking trail. Cr cds: A, MC, V.

All Suite

★★ **COMFORT SUITES.** *890 Brevard Rd (28806), I-26 Exit 2. 828/665-4000; fax 828/665-9082; res 800/228-5150; toll-free 800/622-4005. Email ashevilladmin@crownam.com; www.ashevillenccomfort.com.* 125 rms, 5 story, 125 suites. June-July, Oct: S, D $119; suites $119; under 18 free; lower rates rest of yr. Pet accepted, some restrictions, fee. Parking lot. Pool. TV; cable (premium). Complimentary continental bkfst, coffee in rms, newspaper, toll-free calls. Restaurant nearby. Ck-out noon, ck-in 3 pm. Meeting rms. Business servs avail. Dry cleaning, coin lndry. Free airport transportation. Exercise equipt. Golf. Downhill skiing. Cr cds: A, C, D, DS, ER, JCB, MC, V.

Restaurants

★★★ **23 PAGE.** *1 Battery Park Ave. 828/252-3685. www.23page.com.* Specializes in seafood, desserts, pasta. Hrs: 5:30-9:30 pm. Closed hols. Res accepted. Bar. Wine list. Dinner a la carte entrees: $15.95-$28.95. Child's menu. Intimate dining. Cr cds: A, D, DS, MC, V.

★★ **FINE FRIENDS.** *946 Merrimon Ave (28804), in Northland Shopping Center. 828/253-6649.* Specializes in seafood, beef, pasta. Own desserts. Hrs: 11:30 am-9 pm; Fri, Sat to 10 pm; Sun brunch 11 am-3:30 pm. Closed Thanksgiving, Dec 24, 25. Res accepted. Bar. Lunch $5.95-$10.95; dinner $10.95-$16.95. Sun brunch $6-$8. Child's menu. Cr cds: A, D, DS, MC, V.

★★★ **GABRIELLE'S.** *87 Richmond Hill Dr. 828/252-7313. www.richmond hillinn.com.* Specializes in fresh fish, game, beef. Own pasta. Hrs: 6-9:30 pm. Res accepted. Wine list. Dinner $25-$42. Child's menu. Entertainment: pianist Thurs-Mon. Valet parking. Jacket. Formal dining. Cr cds: A, MC, V.

★★ **GREENERY.** *148 Tunnel Rd (28803). 828/253-2809.* African menu. Specializes in Maryland crabcakes, mountain trout. Hrs: 5-10 pm.

Closed Jan, Feb. Res accepted. Bar. Dinner $14.95-$24.95. Cr cds: A, MC, V.

D

★★★ GROVE PARK INN RESORT.
290 Macon Ave. 828/252-2711. www. groveparkinn.com. Specializes in Lone Star ostrich au poivre, double breast of free range chicken, mixed grill of American wild game. Hrs: 6-9 pm. Closed Sun, Mon. Res accepted. Wine list. Dinner $21-$36. Complete meals: $58. Entertainment: piano Tues-Sat. Valet parking. Jacket. Formal dining in elegant setting with mountain views. Cr cds: A, D, DS, MC, V.

D

★★ THE MARKET PLACE RESTAURANT & WINE BAR.
20 Wall St (28801). 828/252-4162. Email tmp@main.nc.us; www.marketplace-restaurant.com. Specializes in seafood, veal, lamb. Hrs: 6-9:30 pm. Closed Sun; hols. Res accepted. Bar. Dinner a la carte entrees: $12.50-$27.95. Child's menu. 3 formal dining areas. Cr cds: A, D, MC, V.

D

★ MCGUFFEY'S GRILL & BAR.
1853 Hendersonville Rd (28803). 828/252-0956. Eastern European menu. Specializes in beef, seafood, chicken. Hrs: 11 am-10:30 pm; Sun brunch to 4 pm. Closed Thanksgiving, Dec 25. Bar. Lunch $4.99-$8.99; dinner $6.99-$15. Sun brunch $4.99-$10.99. Cr cds: A, D, DS, MC, V.

D SC ⊟

★★ VINCENZO'S.
10 N Market St (28801). 828/254-4698. Email vin-piano@aol.com. Specializes in veal, pasta, seafood. Hrs: 5:30-10 pm; Fri, Sat to 11 pm; Sun to 9 pm. Closed hols. Res accepted. Bar. Dinner $9-$27. Child's menu. Entertainment. Cr cds: A, D, DS, MC, V.

★★ WINDMILL EUROPEAN GRILL.
85 Tunnel Rd (28805), at Innsbruck Mall. 828/253-5285. Specializes in beef, chicken, seafood. Hrs: 5:30-10 pm; Sun to 9 pm. Closed Mon; Jan 1, Dec 25. Res accepted. Bar. Dinner $10.99-$21.99. Cr cds: A, D, MC, V.

D ⊟

Unrated Dining Spot

MOUNTAIN SMOKE HOUSE. *802 Fairview Rd (28803). 828/253-4871.* Specializes in barbecued chopped pork, herb-smoked chicken, barbecued ribs. Hrs: 11:45 am-9 pm; Fri, Sat to 10 pm; June-Nov hrs vary. Closed Sun, Mon. Res accepted. Bar. Lunch, dinner $7.95-$16.95. Child's menu. Entertainment: bluegrass band, clogging. Casual, family atmosphere. Cr cds: A, D, DS, MC, V.

D SC

Atlantic Beach

(see Morehead City)

Banner Elk

See also Blowing Rock, Boone, Linville

Pop 933 **Elev** 3,739 ft **Area code** 828 **Zip** 28604 **Web** www.banner-elk.com **Information** Chamber of Commerce, PO Box 335; 828/898-5605

Motel/Motor Lodge

★ PINNACLE INN.
301 Pinnacle Inn Rd (28604), off NC 184. 828/387-2231; fax 828/387-3745; toll-free 800/405-7888. Email pinaclehoa@skybest. com. 242 kits, 3 story. No elvtr. Mid-Nov-mid-Mar: kit. units $75-$170; lower rates rest of yr. Crib $5. TV; cable. Indoor pool; whirlpool. Sauna. Free supervised children's activities (mid-June-mid-Sep). Restaurant nearby. Ck-out 10 am. Coin lndry. Meeting rms. Business servs avail. Tennis. Downhill ski ½ mi. Game rm. Fireplaces. Balconies. Picnic tables, grills. Cr cds: MC, V.

D 🐾 ⚡ 🏂 ⛷ 🏊 ➖ 🔥

Hotel

★★ HOLIDAY INN.
1615 Tynecastle Hwy (NC 184) (28604), 1 mi S on NC 184 between NC 194 and NC 105. 828/898-4571; fax 828/898-8437; res 800/HOLIDAY; toll-free 877/877-4553. Email stephwhite@skybest.com; www. holidayinnbannerelk.com. 101 rms, 2

story. Dec-Feb, June-Aug, Oct: S, D $139; lower rates rest of yr. Crib avail, fee. Parking lot. Pool, whirlpool. TV; cable. Complimentary coffee in rms. Restaurant. Ck-out 11 am, ck-in 3 pm. Meeting rms. Fax servs avail. Coin lndry. Exercise equipt. Golf. Downhill skiing. Picnic facilities. Cr cds: A, D, DS, MC, V.

B&B/Small Inn

★★ **ARCHER'S MOUNTAIN INN.** *2489 Beech Mt Pkwy (28604). 828/ 898-9004; fax 828/898-9007; toll-free 888/827-6155. www.archersinn.com.* 15 rms, 2 story. Mid-Dec-mid-Mar: S, D $75-$200; each addl $10; lower rates rest of yr. Crib free. TV; cable, VCR some rms. Complimentary full bkfst, coffee in rms. Restaurant (see also JACKALOPE'S VIEW). Swimming privileges. Ck-out 11 am, ck-in 3 pm. Tennis privileges. Golf privileges. Downhill ski 2 mi. Fireplaces; many refrigerators. Many balconies. Rustic decor. Cr cds: DS, MC, V.

Restaurant

★★ **JACKALOPE'S VIEW.** *2489 Beech Mt Pkwy. 828/898-9004. www.archersinn.com.* Specializes in steak, seafood, wild game. Own baking. Hrs: 5-9 pm; Fri, Sat to 9:30 pm. Closed Mon. Res accepted. Bar. Dinner $10-$20. Child's menu. Floor-to-ceiling windows overlook mountains, patio; artwork by local artists. Cr cds: DS, MC, V.

Beaufort

(D-7) *See also Morehead City*

Pop 3,808 **Elev** 7 ft **Area code** 252 **Zip** 28516 **Web** www.sunnync.com

Information Carteret County Tourism Development Bureau, PO Box 1406, Morehead City 28557; 252/726-8148 or 800/SUNNY-NC

Beaufort, dating from the colonial era, is a seaport with more than 125 historic houses and sites.

What to See and Do

Beaufort Historic Site. Old Burying Ground, 1829 restored Old Jail, restored houses (1767-1830), courthouse (ca 1796), apothecary shop, art gallery, and gift shop. Obtain additional info, self-guided walking tour map from Beaufort Historical Assn, Inc, 138 Turner St, PO Box 1709. (Mon-Sat; closed hols) Phone 252/728-5225. Admission to 6 bldgs open to the public ¢¢

Cape Lookout National Seashore. This unit of the National Park System, on the outer banks of North Carolina, extends 55 mi S from Ocracoke Inlet and incl unspoiled barrier islands. There are no roads or bridges; access is by boat only (fee). Ferries from Beaufort, Harkers Island, Davis, Atlantic, and Ocracoke (Apr-Nov). Excellent fishing and shell collecting; primitive camping; interpretive programs (seasonal). Lighthouse (1859) at Cape Lookout is still operational. Phone 252/728-2250.

North Carolina Maritime Museum and Watercraft Center. Natural and maritime history exhibits, field trips; special programs in maritime and coastal natural history. (Daily; closed Jan 1, Thanksgiving, Dec 25) 315 Front St. Phone 252/728-7317. **FREE**

Annual Events

Beaufort by the Sea Music Festival. Late Apr.

Old Homes Tour and Antiques Show. Private homes and historic public bldgs; Carteret County Militia; bus tours and tours of old burying ground; historical crafts. Sponsored by the Beaufort Historical Assn, Inc, PO Box 1709. Phone 919/728-5225. Last wkend June.

B&Bs/Small Inns

★★ **THE CEDARS INN.** *305 Front St (28516). 252/728-7036; fax 252/ 728-1685. www.cedarsinn.com.* 6 rms, 2 story, 5 suites. Apr-Oct: S, D $125; each addl $25; suites $165; under 10 free; lower rates rest of yr. Parking lot. TV; cable. Complimentary full bkfst, newspaper. Restaurant. Bar. Ck-out 11 am, ck-in 3 pm. Meeting rm. Business servs avail. Concierge. Gift shop. Exercise privileges. Golf, 18 holes. Beach access. Bike rentals. Picnic facilities. Cr cds: A, D, DS, MC, V.

★★ **DELAMAR INN.** *217 Turner St (28516). 919/728-4300; toll-free 800/ 349-5823. www.bbonline.com/nc/ delamarinn*3 rms, 2 with shower only, 2 story. No rm phones. May-Sep: D $82-$120; lower rates rest of yr. Children over 10 yrs only. Complimentary continental bkfst; afternoon refreshments. Restaurant nearby. Ck-out 11 am, ck-in 1 pm. Business servs avail. Built 1865; first and 2 floor porches. Many antiques. Totally nonsmoking. Cr cds: MC, V.

★★ **PECAN TREE INN.** *116 Queen St (28516). 252/728-6733. Email pecantreeinn@coastalnet.com; www. pecantree.com.* 7 rms, 2 story, 2 suites. Apr-Oct: S $135; D $145; each addl $15; suites $145; lower rates rest of yr. Parking lot. TV; cable. Complimentary continental bkfst, newspaper. Restaurant. Ck-out 11 am, ck-in 2 pm. Concierge. Gift shop. Whirlpool. Golf. Bike rentals. Picnic facilities. Cr cds: A, DS, MC, V.

Restaurant

★★ **LOUGHRY'S LANDING.** *510 Front St (28516), on the waterfront. 252/728-7541. www.loughryslanding. com.* Specializes in fresh local seafood, pasta. Hrs: 11:30 am-8:30 pm; winter hrs vary. Closed Jan-mid-Mar. Bar. Lunch a la carte entrees: $3.75-$7.95; dinner a la carte entrees: $8.75-$15.95. Child's menu. Overlooks harbor. Cr cds: A, D, DS, MC, V.

Blowing Rock

(B-3) *See also Banner Elk, Boone, Linville*

Founded 1889 **Pop** 1,257
Elev 4,000 ft **Area code** 828
Zip 28605
Web www.blowingrock.com/northcarolina

Information Chamber of Commerce, PO Box 406; 828/295-7851 or 800/295-7851

Annual Event

Tour of Homes. Fourth Fri July.

Motels/Motor Lodges

★ **ALPINE VILLAGE INN.** *297 Sunset Dr (28605). 828/295-7206. Email alpinev@boone.net; www.alpine-village-inn.com.* 15 rms, 1 story, 1 suite. June-Oct: S, D $85; each addl $6; suites $125; under 12 free; lower rates rest of yr. Crib avail, fee. Parking lot. TV; cable, VCR avail. Restaurant nearby. Ck-out 11 am, ck-in 2 pm. Golf. Tennis. Downhill skiing. Hiking trail. Cr cds: A, DS, MC, V.

★★ **BLOWING ROCK INN.** *788 N Main St (28605), ¼ mi N on US 221/321 Business. 828/295-7921.* 24 rms. July-Nov: S, D $69-$84; each addl $5; lower rates early-mid-Nov, Apr-May; also 1-bedrm villas avail. Closed Dec-Mar. TV; cable. Heated pool. Complimentary coffee on porch. Restaurant nearby. Ck-out 11 am. Picnic tables. Cr cds: A, DS, MC, V.

★★ **CLIFF DWELLERS INN.** *116 Lakeview Ter (28605), 1 mi S, Blue Ridge Pkwy Exit for US 321, across from Shoppes on the Pkwy. 828/295-3121; fax 828/295-3121; toll-free 800/322-7380. Email cliffdwellers@boone.net.* 20 rms, 3 story, 3 suites, 2 kit. units. No elvtr. Mid-May-early Nov: S, D $95-$115; each addl $5; suites, kit. units $155-$245; under 12 free; lower rates rest of yr. Closed Dec-Apr exc wkends, Christmas hol. Crib $5. TV; cable. Heated pool; whirlpool. Complimentary coffee in rms. Restaurant nearby. Ck-out 11 am. Refrigerators; microwaves avail. Balconies. View of mountains. Cr cds: C, D, MC, V.

Resorts

★★★ **CHETOLA RESORT AT BLOWING ROCK.** *N Main St (28605). 828/295-5500; fax 828/295-5529; res 800/243-8652. Email info@chetola.com; www.chetola.com.* 118 rms, 3 story, 5 suites. June-Aug,

Oct: S, D $160; each addl $10; suites $220; under 12 free; lower rates rest of yr. Crib avail. Parking lot. Indoor pool, whirlpool. TV; cable, VCR avail. Complimentary coffee in rms, toll-free calls. Restaurant. Bar. Ck-out 11 am, ck-in 3 pm. Meeting rms. Business center. Bellhops. Concierge. Dry cleaning. Gift shop. Exercise equipt, sauna. Golf. Tennis, 3 courts. Downhill skiing. Bike rentals. Supervised children's activities. Hiking trail. Picnic facilities. Video games. Cr cds: A, DS, MC, V.

D ⬇ 🐾 🏊 🏋 🎿 🚶 ⛷ 🛶 🔥 SC 🚶

★★★ **HOUND EARS CLUB.** *PO Box 188 (28605), 7 mi W, ½ mi off NC 105. 828/963-4321; fax 828/963-8030. Email houndears@boone.net.* 29 rms in lodge and club house, 2 story. MAP, mid-June-Oct: S $150; D $270; each addl $48; suites $290-$330; under 11, $55; lower rates rest of yr. Serv charge 17%. TV; cable (premium), VCR avail. Heated pool; poolside serv, lifeguard. Free supervised children's activities (June-Sep); ages 8-16. Dining rm 7-10 am, noon-2:30 pm, 6:30-9:30 pm (res required). Bar; entertainment. Ck-out 11 am, ck-in 1:30 pm. Meeting rms. Business servs avail. Bellhops. Valet serv. 6 tennis courts, pro. 18-hole golf, greens fee $38, pro. Exercise equipt; sauna. Cr cds: A, MC, V.

D ⬇ 🎿 🏋 🏊 🏊 🛶 🔥

B&Bs/Small Inns

★★ **CRIPPEN'S COUNTRY INN.** *239 Sunset Dr (28605). 828/295-3487; fax 828/295-0388. www.crippens.com.* 8 rms, 2 with shower only, 3 story, 1 guest house. May-Dec: S, D $129; each addl $25; guest house $159; hols (2-day min); lower rates rest of yr. TV in common rm; cable (premium). Complimentary continental bkfst. Restaurant (see also CRIPPEN'S). Rm serv 6-10 pm. Ck-out 11 am, ck-in 3 pm. Business servs avail. Built in 1931. Totally nonsmoking. Cr cds: A, DS, MC, V.

🛶 🔥

★ **HOMESTEAD INN.** *153 Morris St (28605). 828/295-9559; fax 828/295-9551. Email homesteadinn@prodigy.net; www.homestead-inn.com.* 15 rms, 1 story. June-Oct: S $54; D $69; each addl $5; suites $109; lower rates rest of yr. Crib avail. Parking lot. TV;

cable (premium), VCR avail. Complimentary coffee in rms, newspaper, toll-free calls. Restaurant nearby. Ck-out 11 am, ck-in 2 pm. Business servs avail. Golf. Tennis. Downhill skiing. Hiking trail. Picnic facilities. Cr cds: A, DS, MC, V.

D ⬇ 🎿 🏊 🏋 🚶 ⛷ 🛶 🔥

★★★ **INN AT RAGGED GARDENS.** *203 Sunset (28605). 828/295-9703. Email innkeeper@ragged-gardens.com; www.ragged-gardens.com.* 5 rms, 3 story, 7 suites. D $155; each addl $25; suites $195. Parking lot. TV; cable (premium), VCR avail. Complimentary full bkfst, coffee in rms, newspaper, toll-free calls. Restaurant nearby. Ck-out 11 am, ck-in 3 pm. Meeting rm. Concierge. Golf. Tennis. Downhill skiing. Cr cds: MC, V.

🏊 🏋 🏊 🛶 🔥

★★ **MAPLE LODGE.** *152 Sunset Dr (28605). 828/295-3331; fax 828/295-9986. Email mobilguest@maplelodge.net; www.maplelodge.net.* 10 rms, 2 story, 1 suite. May-Oct: S $90; D $140; each addl $20; suites $170; lower rates rest of yr. Parking lot. TV; cable, VCR avail. Complimentary full bkfst, newspaper. Restaurant nearby. Ck-out 11 am, ck-in 3 pm. Meeting rms. Business servs avail. Concierge. Gift shop. Golf, 18 holes. Tennis. Downhill skiing. Hiking trail. Cr cds: A, D, DS, MC, V.

🏊 🏋 🏊 🛶 🔥

★★★ **MEADOWBROOK INN.** *Main St (28605). 704/295-4300; fax 704/295-4300; res 800/456-5456. www.meadowbrook-inn.com.* 61 rms, 2-3 story. S, D $119-$139; each addl $10; suites $139-$259; under 12 free; ski plans. TV; cable, VCR avail. Indoor pool; whirlpool. Complimentary continental bkfst. Dining rm 6-9 pm. Bar. Ck-out 11 am, ck-in 3 pm. Meeting rms. Business servs avail. Downhill ski 3 mi. Exercise equipt. European-style country inn. Cr cds: A, D, DS, MC, V.

D 🏊 🏊 🚶 🛶 🔥 SC

Restaurants

★★ **BEST CELLAR.** *US 321 and Blowing Rock Rd (28605), behind Food Lion Shopping Center. 828/295-3466.* Specializes in roast duckling, Sterling Silver beef, banana cream pie. Hrs: 5:30-9:30 pm; Fri, Sat to 10 pm.

Closed Sun; Tues, Wed (Dec-Apr). Res accepted. Dinner $15.95-$21.95. Valet parking. Rustic decor; pine floor, stone walls, 3 fireplaces. Cr cds: A, MC, V.

[D] [≥]

★★★ **CRIPPEN'S.** *239 Sunset Dr. 828/295-3487. www.crippens.com.* Specializes in grilled Maine lobster, grilled North Carolina ostrich, horseradish-encrusted salmon. Own pasta. Hrs: 6-10 pm; Fri, Sat from 5 pm. Closed Mon; hols; Super Bowl Sun. Res accepted. Bar. Dinner $16.95-$33. Child's menu. Parking. Semi-formal, spacious dining area. Cr cds: A, MC, V.

[D]

★★ **RIVERWOOD.** *7179 Valley Blvd (28605), ½ mi S of Blue Ridge Pkwy. 828/295-4162. www.riverwood.com.* Specializes in stuffed rainbow trout, marinated beef tenderloin. Own desserts. Hrs: 5-9 pm; Sat 4:30-10 pm. Closed Sun, Mon. Res accepted. Bar. Dinner $13.95-$23.95. Cr cds: C, DS, MC, V.

[D]

★★ **TWIG'S.** *US 321 Bypass (28605). 828/295-5050.* Specializes in crab cakes, lamb, fresh seafood. Hrs: 5:30-9:30 pm; Fri, Sat to 10 pm. Closed Mon; Dec 24-25. Res accepted. Bar. Dinner $13.95-$21.95. Porch dining (summer). Cr cds: A, DS, MC, V.

[D] [≥]

Blue Ridge Parkway

(see Virginia)

Boone

(B-3) *See also Banner Elk, Blowing Rock, Linville*

Settled 1772 **Pop** 12,915 **Elev** 3,266 ft
Area code 828 **Zip** 28607
Web www.boonechamber.com

Information Convention & Visitors Bureau, 208 Howard St, 28607-4032; 828/262-3516 or 800/852-9506; or North Carolina High Country Host, 1700 Blowing Rock Rd; 828/264-1299 or 800/438-7500

Seasonal Events

Horn in the West. Daniel Boone Amphitheatre, 1 mi E off US 421. Outdoor drama depicts Daniel Boone and settlers of the mountain during the American Revolution. Tues-Sun eves. Contact PO Box 295; 828/264-2120. Mid-June-mid-Aug.

An Appalachian Summer. Appalachian State Univ. Concerts, drama, art exhibits. Phone 800/841-2787.

Motels/Motor Lodges

★ **GREYSTONE LODGE.** *RR 6 Box 46 (28607), 3 mi S on NC 105. 828/264-4133; fax 828/262-0101; res 800/560-5942.* 101 rms, 4 story. Mid-June-late Oct, late Dec-Feb: S, D $52-$89; each addl $3; under 18 free; lower rates rest of yr. Crib free. TV; cable (premium). Indoor pool. Complimentary continental bkfst. Restaurant nearby. Ck-out 11 am. Business servs avail. Downhill/x-country ski 8 mi. Game rm. Cr cds: A, C, D, DS, MC, V.

[D] [≥] [≈] [≥] [≈] [SC]

★★ **HAMPTON INN.** *1075 Hwy 105 (28607). 828/264-0077; fax 828/264-4600; res 800/426-7866. Email boold02@hi-hotel.com.* 95 rms, 5 story. June-Oct: S, D $89-$119; under 18 free; golf plan; lower rates rest of yr. Crib free. TV; cable (premium), VCR avail. Indoor pool. Complimentary continental bkfst. Restaurant adj 11 am-10 pm. Ck-out 11 am. Meeting rms. Business servs avail. Health club privileges. Cr cds: A, D, DS, JCB, MC, V.

[D] [♣] [⛄] [🛏] [≈] [🏃] [⛷] [≥] [≈]

★★ **HOLIDAY INN EXPRESS.** *1855 Blowing Rock Rd (28607). 828/264-2451; fax 828/265-3861; res 888/733-6867; toll-free 800/465-4329. Email holidayinn@boone.mail.net; www.holiday-inn.com.* 138 rms, 2 story. June-Oct, ski season: S, D $69-$109; each addl $8; under 18 free; lower rates rest of yr. Crib free. TV; cable (premium), VCR avail. Heated pool. Complimentary continental bkfst, coffee in rms. Ck-out 11 am. Coin lndry. Meeting rms. Business servs avail. In-rm modem link. Exercise equipt. Downhill ski 5 mi. Cr cds: A, C, D, DS, JCB, MC, V.

🅳 ⛷ ☁ 🏂 🔅 🔥 SC

Hotel

★★ **QUALITY INN & CONVENTION CENTER.** *949 Blowing Rock Rd (28607), 1 mi S at jct US 321, NC 105. 828/262-0020; fax 828/262-0020; res 800/903-8209. www.qualityinnboone. com.* 132 rms, 7 story. Mid-June-mid-Nov: S $90; D $95; each addl $8; suites $90-$165; under 18 free; ski, golf packages; higher rates late Dec-Feb; lower rates rest of yr. TV; cable (premium). Indoor pool. Restaurant 7 am-2 pm, 5:30-10 pm. Bar 5 pm-1 am. Ck-out 11 am. Guest lndry. Meeting rms. Business servs avail. Golf privileges. Downhill ski 8 mi; x-country ski 9 mi. Exercise equipt. Health club privileges. Refrigerator in suites. Cr cds: A, C, D, DS, ER, JCB, MC, V.

🅳 ⛷ 🏋 🛬 ☁ 🏂 🔅 🔥 SC

B&B/Small Inn

★★★ **LOVILL HOUSE INN.** *404 Old Bristol Rd (28607), off US 421N. 828/264-4204; res 800/849-9466. Email innkeeper@lovillhouseinn.com; www.lovillhouseinn.com.* 6 rms, 2 story. May-Oct: S, D $145; each addl $20; suites $195; children $20; under 12 free; lower rates rest of yr. Parking lot. TV; cable (premium), VCR avail, CD avail. Complimentary full bkfst, coffee in rms, newspaper, toll-free calls. Restaurant nearby. Ck-out noon, ck-in 3 pm. Meeting rm. Business servs avail. Exercise privileges. Golf. Tennis, 4 courts. Downhill skiing. Bike rentals. Hiking trail. Picnic facilities. Cr cds: MC, V.

🔅 🔥 ⛷ 🏋 🔅 🏂 ☁ 🔥 SC

Restaurants

★ **DAN'L BOONE INN.** *130 Hardin St (28607), at jct US 421 and US 321. 828/264-8657.* Specializes in fried chicken. Hrs: 11:30 am-9 pm; Sat, Sun from 8 am; Nov-May from 5 pm. Closed Dec 24, 25. Bkfst $6.95; lunch, dinner $11.95. In one of oldest bldgs

in Boone; country atmosphere. Family-owned. Cr cds: A, DS, MC, V.

🅳

★★ **MAKOTO.** *2124 Blowing Rock Rd (28607). 828/264-7976.* Specializes in seafood, beef, poultry. Sushi bar Fri, Sat. Hrs: 11 am-9 pm; Fri, Sat to 9:30 pm. Closed Thanksgiving, Dec 25. Lunch complete meals: $3.95-$9.95; dinner complete meals: $8.50-$22.95. 15% serv chg. Child's menu. Tableside preparation. Cr cds: A, D, DS, MC, V.

🅳

Brevard

(C-2) *See also Asheville, Hendersonville*

Settled 1861 **Pop** 5,388 **Elev** 2,230 ft **Area code** 828 **Zip** 28712

Information Chamber of Commerce, PO Box 589; 828/883-3700 or 800/648-4523

Annual Events

Festival of the Arts. Music, crafts, art, sporting events. Second wk July.

Twilight Tour on Main. Horse and buggy rides, entertainment, refreshments. First Sat Dec.

Seasonal Event

Summer Festival of Music. Brevard Music Center. Whittington-Pfhol Auditorium. More than 50 programs presented, incl symphonic, choral, chamber, recital; musical comedy and operatic performances; guest artists. Mon-Sat eves; Sun afternoons. Contact Box 312; 828/884-2019 or 828/884-2011. Late June-early Aug.

Motels/Motor Lodges

★ **IMPERIAL MOTOR LODGE.** *US 64 and 276 N (28712), ½ mi N on US 64, 276. 828/884-2887; fax 828/883-9811; toll-free 800/869-3335.* 95 rms, 1-2 story. June-Oct: S, D $45-$85; each addl $5; under 12 free; lower rates rest of yr. Crib $5. TV; cable (premium). Pool. Complimentary continental bkfst. Restaurant opp 6 am-midnight. Ck-out 11:30 am. Refrigerators. Grill. Cr cds: A, C, D, DS, MC, V.

🅳 🔅 🔥 🛬 ☁ 🏂 🔥

★ **SUNSET MOTEL.** *415 S Broad St (28712). 828/884-9106; fax 828/883-4919.* 15 rms, 1 story, 3 suites. June-Oct: S $50; D $60; each addl $5; suites $55; lower rates rest of yr. Crib avail. Pet accepted. Parking lot. TV; cable. Ck-out 11 am, ck-in 2 pm. Exercise privileges. Golf. Tennis, 4 courts. Hiking trail. Cr cds: A, C, D, DS, MC, V.

Bryson City

(C-1) *See also Cherokee, Franklin, Waynesville*

Pop 1,145 **Elev** 1,736 ft
Area code 828 **Zip** 28713
Web www.greatsmokies.com
Information Chamber of Commerce, PO Box 509; 828/488-3681 or 800/867-9246

Motel/Motor Lodge

★ **BUDGET HOST INN.** *5280 Ela Rd N (28713). 828/488-2284; fax 828/488-2284.* 21 rms, 1 cottage. No rm phones. Mid-June-Oct: S, D $68; kit. cottage $160; lower rates May-mid-June. Closed rest of yr. TV; cable. Pool. Coffee in rms. Ck-out 11 am. Cr cds: DS, MC, V.

B&Bs/Small Inns

★★ **THE CHALET INN.** *285 Lone Oak Dr (28789), 14 mi E on US 74/441. 828/586-0251; res 800/789-8024. Email paradisefound@chaletinn.com; www.chaletinn.com.* 4 rms, 3 story, 2 suites. June-Aug, Oct: S, D $115; each addl $20; suites $160; lower rates rest of yr. Parking lot. TV; cable, CD avail. Complimentary full bkfst, toll-free calls. Restaurant nearby. Ck-out 10:30 am, ck-in 3 pm. Concierge. Golf. Tennis. Hiking trail. Picnic facilities. Cr cds: MC, V.

★ **FOLKESTONE INN BED & BREAKFAST.** *101 Folkestone Rd (28713). 828/488-2730; fax 828/488-0722; toll-free 888/812-3385. Email innkeeper@folkestone.com; www.folkestone.com.* 10 rms, 3 story. June-Oct: S $93; D $99; each addl $12; under 6 free; lower rates rest of yr. Parking lot. TV; cable, CD avail. Complimentary full bkfst. Ck-out 11 am, ck-in 3 pm. Concierge. Golf, 18 holes. Tennis, 2 courts. Hiking trail. Picnic facilities. Cr cds: A, DS, MC, V.

★★ **HEMLOCK INN.** *911 Galbriath Creek Rd (28713), 3 mi NE, 1 mi N of US 19. 828/488-2885; fax 828/488-8985. Email hemlock@dnet.net; www.innbook.com/hemlock/html.* 22 rms, 1 story, 3 suites. S $150; D $140; each addl $39; suites $239; children $20. Crib avail. Parking lot. TV; cable, CD avail. Complimentary full bkfst, newspaper. Restaurant. Ck-out 11 am, ck-in 1 pm. Gift shop. Golf, 18 holes. Tennis, 3 courts. Hiking trail. Cr cds: DS, MC, V.

Burlington

(B-5) *See also Greensboro, High Point*

Settled ca 1700 **Pop** 39,498
Elev 656 ft **Area code** 336
Web wwwburlington-area-nc.org
Information Burlington/Alamance County Convention & Visitors Bureau, PO Drawer 519, 27216; 336/570-1444 or 800/637-3804

Annual Events

Antiques Fair. Three-day event where antiques are sold and auctioned. Mar.

Hospice League Horizons Balloon Fest. Hot-air-balloon race, air show, parachuting, music. Phone 800/637-3804. May.

Seasonal Event

The Sword of Peace Summer Outdoor Drama. 18 mi SW via I-85, Liberty-49S Exit, then NC 49S and NC 1005 to Snow Camp. Repertory outdoor theater (eves) and summer arts festival; 150-yr-old and 200-yr-old bldgs converted into museums, craft gallery, and cane mill. Thurs-Sat. Contact PO Box 535, Snow Camp 27349; 910/376-6948 or 800/726-5115. Late June-late Aug.

Motels/Motor Lodges

★★ **COMFORT INN.** *I-85 & SR 49 (27215), I-85, Exit 145. 336/227-3681; fax 336/570-0900.* 127 rms, 2 story. S $57-$88; D $61-$88; each addl $4; under 18 free; higher rates Furniture Market. Crib free. Pet accepted, some restrictions. TV; cable (premium). Pool; wading pool. Complimentary continental bkfst, coffee in rms. Restaurant adj 11 am-11 pm. Ck-out noon. Coin lndry. Meeting rms. Business servs avail. Valet serv. Some refrigerators; microwaves avail. Cr cds: A, C, D, DS, JCB, MC, V.
🄳 🤚 🌊 🖼️ 🔥 SC

★★ **HAMPTON INN.** *2701 Kirkpatrick Rd (27215), I-85, Exit 141. 336/584-4447; fax 336/721-1325.* 116 rms, 4 story. S $60-$65; D $65-$70; suites $92; under 18 free; higher rates Furniture Market (Apr and Oct). Crib free. TV; cable (premium). Pool; whirlpool. Complimentary continental bkfst. Restaurant adj 5-10 pm. Ck-out noon. Meeting rms. Business servs avail. Exercise equipt; sauna. Cr cds: A, D, DS, MC, V.
🄳 🌊 🧍 🖼️ 🔥 SC

★ **KIRKS MOTOR COURT.** *1155 N Church St (27217). 336/228-1383; fax 336/228-9786.* 102 rms, 1-2 story, 14 kits. S $28-$36; D $36-$44; each addl $6; kit. units $245-$285/wk; under 12 free. Crib $4. TV; cable. Pool; wading pool. Restaurant nearby. Ck-out 11 am. Meeting rms. Business servs avail. Valet serv. Sundries. Cr cds: MC, V.
🄳 🌊 🖼️ 🔥

★★ **RAMADA INN.** *2703 Ramada Rd (27215), at jct I-85. 336/227-5541; fax 910/570-2701; toll-free 800/272-6232.* 138 rms, 2 story. S $59; D $65; each addl $6; under 18 free; higher rates: Furniture Market, special events. Crib free. TV; cable (premium). Pool. Restaurant 6 am-2 pm. Bar 5-10 pm; closed Sun. Ck-out noon. Convention facilities. Business servs avail. Health club privileges. Cr cds: A, C, D, DS, MC, V.
🄳 🌊 🧍 🖼️ 🔥 SC

★ **RED ROOF INN.** *2133 W Hanford Rd (27215), I-85 Exit 145. 336/227-1270; fax 336/227-1702; toll-free 800/329-7466.* 122 rms, 2 story. S $44; D $49; each addl $5; under 12 free. Crib avail. TV. Pool. Complimentary continental bkfst. Restaurant adj 6 am-11 pm; Fri, Sat to 1 am. Ck-out noon. Meeting rms. Business servs avail. Valet serv. Health club privileges. Cr cds: A, C, D, DS, ER, JCB, MC, V.
🄳 🌊 🖼️ 🔥 SC

Restaurant

★ **HURSEY'S PIG PICKIN' BAR-B-Q.** *1834 S Church St (27215). 336/226-1694.* Specializes in woodcooked pit barbecue. Hrs: 11 am-9 pm. Closed Sun; Dec 25. Lunch, dinner $3.50-$7.50. Child's menu. Rustic decor. Family-owned since 1949. Cr cds: MC, V.
🄳 🔧

Burnsville

(C-2) *See also Asheville, Little Switzerland*

Pop 1,482 **Elev** 2,814 ft
Area code 828 **Zip** 28714
Web www.yanceychamber.com
Information Yancey County Chamber of Commerce, 106 W Main St; 828/682-7413 or 800/948-1632

A Ranger District office of the Pisgah National Forest (see BREVARD) is located here.

Annual Events

Mount Mitchell Crafts Fair. Town Square. First Fri and Sat Aug.
Old Time Days. Town Square. Early Oct.

B&B/Small Inn

★★ **NU WRAY INN.** *102 Town Sq (28714). 828/682-2329; fax 828/682-1113; toll-free 800/368-9729. Email nuwrayinn@aol.com;www.nuwrayinn.com.* 25 rms, 3 story, 5 suites. July-Aug, Oct: S $75; D $85; each addl $10; suites $90; lower rates rest of yr. Crib avail. Street parking. TV; cable. Complimentary full bkfst, newspaper. Restaurant, closed Wed. Ck-in 3 pm. Meeting rms. Fax servs avail. Exercise privileges. Downhill skiing. Hiking trail. Picnic facilities. Cr cds: A, DS, MC, V.
🄳 🐾 ♿ 🌊 🧍 🖼️ 🔥

Buxton (Outer Banks)

Pop 3,250 **Elev** 10 ft **Area code** 252 **Zip** 27920

This town is on Hatteras Island, part of the Outer Banks (see). It is surrounded by Cape Hatteras National Seashore (see).

Motels/Motor Lodges

★ **CAPE HATTERAS MOTEL.** *NC 12 (27920). 252/995-5611; fax 252/995-4303; toll-free 800/995-0711. Email chmotel@pinn.net; www.cape hatterasmotel.com.* 6 rms, 3 story, 30 suites. June-Aug: S, D $130; suites $225; lower rates rest of yr. Crib avail, fee. Parking lot. Pool, whirlpool. TV; cable (premium). Restaurant nearby. Ck-out 10 am, ck-in 3 pm. Coin lndry. Golf. Tennis, 2 courts. Beach access. Cr cds: A, DS, MC, V.

★★ **COMFORT INN.** *NC 12 and Old Lighthouse Rd (27920), near Cape Hatteras Lighthouse. 252/995-6100; fax 252/995-5444; toll-free 800/432-1441.* 60 rms, 2 story. Mid-June-mid-Sep: S, D $92-$125; each addl $5; under 18 free; lower rates rest of yr. Crib free. TV; cable (premium). Pool. Complimentary continental bkfst. Restaurant nearby. Ck-out 11 am. Business servs avail. In-rm modem link. Guest lndry. Refrigerators, microwaves. Near beach. Cr cds: A, D, DS, MC, V.

★ **FALCON MOTEL.** *Hwy 12 (27920). 252/995-5968; fax 252/995-7803; res 800/635-6911. www.outer-banks.com/falconmotel.* 30 rms, 5 kits. No rm phones. Memorial Day-Labor Day: S, D $63-$75; kits. $70-$90; under 6 free; wkly rates; lower rates Labor Day-mid-Dec. Closed rest of yr. Crib free. TV; cable (premium). Pool. Restaurant opp 6:30-11 am, 5-9:30 pm. Ck-out 11 am. Refrigerators avail. Picnic tables. Bicycles avail. Near ocean. Cr cds: A, DS, MC, V.

Restaurant

★ **TIDES.** *NC 12 (27920). 252/995-5988.* Specializes in seafood, steak. Hrs: 6 am-9 pm. Closed Dec-Mar. Wine, beer. Bkfst $2.50-$5.50; lunch $7.50-$18.50; dinner $7.50-$18.50. Nautical decor. Cr cds: MC, V.

Cape Hatteras National Seashore

See also Buxton, Hatteras, Kill Devil Hills, Nags Head, Ocracoke

(Enter from Cedar Island or Swan Quarter toll ferry. Res advised. Free ferry from Ocracoke Island to Hatteras Island)

This thin strand stretches for 75 miles along the Outer Banks (see), threaded between the windy, pounding Atlantic and shallow Pamlico Sound. Nags Head (see) is the northern limit of the recreational area, which has three sections (separated by inlets): Bodie (pronounced *body*), Hatteras (largest of the barrier islands), and Ocracoke (see), the most picturesque. Bounded on three sides by the park, but separate from it, are the villages of Rodanthe, Waves, Salvo, Avon, Buxton, Frisco, Hatteras, and Ocracoke. Although the area is noted for long expanses of sand beaches, wildflowers bloom most of the year. There are also stands of yaupon (holly), loblolly pine, and live oak. Several freshwater ponds are found on Bodie, Hatteras, and Ocracoke Islands. Many migratory and nonmigratory waterfowl winter here, incl gadwalls, greater snow and Canada geese, loons, grebes, and herons.

There is an information station at Whalebone Junction (Memorial Day-Labor Day, daily), S of Nags Head. Near Bodie Island Lighthouse is a bird observation platform, a nature trail, and a visitor center (Good Friday-Columbus Day, daily) with natural history exhibits. There are also visitor centers with history exhibits at Ocra-

Lighthouse on Cape Hatteras

coke (same hours), Bodie Island Lighthouse (same hours), and the Cape Hatteras Lighthouse at Buxton (daily; closed December 25).

Sportfishing, boating, sailing, swimming (recommended only at protected beaches); picnicking and camping (fee), also waterfowl hunting in season under regulation.

For further information contact the Superintendent, Rte 1, Box 675, Manteo 27954; or phone the Hatteras Island Visitor Center, 252/995-4474.

Cashiers

See also Franklin, Highlands

Pop 1,200 **Elev** 3,486 ft
Area code 828 **Zip** 28717
Web www.cashiers-nc.com
Information Cashiers Area Chamber of Commerce, PO Box 238; 828/743-5191

High in the Blue Ridge Mountains, this well-known summer resort area offers scenic drives on twisting mountain roads, hiking trails, views, waterfalls, lake sports, fishing, and other recreational activities.

Motels/Motor Lodges

★ **LAURELWOOD MOUNTAIN INN.** *58 Hwy 107 N (28717). 828/743-9939; fax 828/743-5300; toll-free 800/346-6846. www.laurelwood mountianinn.com.* 22 rms, 10 with shower only, 3 A/C, 1-2 story. May-Oct: S, D $62-$135; under 12 free; wkly rates; wkends, hols (2-day min); lower rates rest of yr. Crib free. TV; cable. Complimentary coffee in rms. Restaurant opp 6:30 am-10 pm. Ck-out 11 am. Playground. Refrigerators; some in-rm whirlpools, microwaves. Some balconies. Picnic tables, grills. Cr cds: A, D, DS, MC.

★ **THE OAKMONT LODGE.** *173 Oakmont St (28717), ½ mi N of jct US 64. 828/743-2298. Email oakmont lodge@earthlink.net.* 19 rms, 1 story, 1 suite. May-Oct: S, D $67; each addl $5; suites $95; children $5; under 18 free; lower rates rest of yr. Pet accepted, fee. Street parking. TV; cable. Complimentary coffee in rms, toll-free calls. Restaurant 11:30 am-10 pm, closed Mon. Ck-out 11 am, ck-in 3 pm. Golf. Picnic facilities. Cr cds: MC, V.

Resorts

★★★ **FAIRFIELD SAPPHIRE VALLEY.** *70 Sapphire Valley Rd (28774), 3 mi E. 828/743-3441; fax 828/743-2641; toll-free 800/533-8268. www.skisapphire.com.* 25 rms, 1 story, 15 suites. Apr-Oct: S, D $90; suites $110; lower rates rest of yr. Crib avail, fee. Parking lot. Indoor/outdoor pools, children's pool, whirlpool. TV; cable. Complimentary newspaper, toll-free calls. Restaurant 11 am-9 pm. Bar. Ck-out 10 am, ck-in 4 pm. Meeting rms. Business center. Salon/barber. Exercise equipt, sauna, steam rm. Golf, 18 holes. Tennis, 8 courts. Downhill skiing. Beach access. Bike rentals. Supervised children's activities. Hiking trail. Picnic facilities. Cr cds: A, C, D, DS, MC, V.

★★★ **HIGH HAMPTON INN AND COUNTRY CLUB.** *Hwy 107 S (28717), 2 mi S on NC 107. 828/743-2411; fax 828/743-5991; toll-free 800/334-2551. www.highhamptoninn.com.* 34 rms in 3-story inn, 15 cottages, 37 golf villas. No A/C. AP, July-Aug: S $94-$103; D $164-$198; each addl $57; golf villas (3-day min) $206-$385; wkly rates; golf, tennis plans; higher rates July-Aug. Closed late Nov-Apr. Crib free. Pet accepted, some restrictions. TV rm; cable. Supervised children's activities (June-Labor Day); ages 3-12. Complimentary afternoon refreshments. Dining rm 7-9:30 am, noon-2:15 pm, 6:30-8:15 pm. Box lunches, buffets. Ck-out 1 pm, ck-in 3 pm. Coin lndry. Business servs avail. Valet serv. Gift shop. Airport transportation. Sports dir. Tennis. 18-hole golf, greens fee $29, pro, 2 putting greens, driving range. Exercise equipt. Boats, dockage. Archery. Trail guides. Bicycle rentals. Outdoor, indoor games. Soc dir; entertainment, movies. Rec rm, library. Lawn games. Kennels. 1,400-acre mountain estate, 2 lakes. Cr cds: A, DS, MC, V.

B&Bs/Small Inns

★★★ **THE GREYSTONE INN.**
Greystone Ln (28747), 8 mi E on US 64. 828/966-4700; fax 828/862-5689. Email greystone@citcom.net; www. greystoneinn.com. 33 rms, 3 story, 17 A/C. May-Oct: S, D $280-$430; each addl $85; family rates; lower rates Apr, Nov, Dec. Open wkends Jan-Mar. Crib free. TV; cable (premium), VCR. Pool. Supervised children's activities (June-Aug); ages 5-14. Complimentary full bkfst; afternoon refreshments. Restaurant adj 8-10 am, 6:30-9:30 pm. Ck-out noon, ck-in 3 pm. Business servs avail. Concierge serv. Tennis, pro. 18-hole golf, greens fee $45, putting green, driving range. Massage. Refrigerators, minibars. Balconies. Picnic tables. On swimming beach. Cr cds: A, DS, MC, V.

★★★ **INNISFREE VICTORIAN INN.** *7 Lakeside Knoll (28736), 6 mi N on NC 107. 828/743-2946. www. innisfreeinn.com.* 10 rms, 1 and 2 story. No A/C. Some rm phones. June-Oct: S, D $150-$290; lower rates rest of yr. Adults only. TV in some rms; cable. Complimentary full bkfst; afternoon refreshments, complimentary coffee in rms. Ck-out 11 am, ck-

in 2:30 pm. Business servs avail. Bellhops. Concierge serv. Tennis privileges. Golf privileges. Game rm. Refrigerators, minibars; some fireplaces. Balconies. 1 blk from Lake Glenville. Built 1989 in Victorian style and furnished with antiques. Totally nonsmoking. Cr cds: A, DS, MC, V.

Cedar Island

Pop 333 (est) **Elev** 7 ft **Area code** 252 **Zip** 28520

There is daily ferry service from Cedar Island to Ocracoke (see).

Motel/Motor Lodge

★ **DRIFTWOOD MOTEL & RESTAURANT.** *NC 12 (28520), on NC 12 N at Cedar Island-Ocracoke Ferry Terminal. 252/225-4861; fax 252/225-1113. Email deg@clis.com; www.clis.com/deg.* 37 rms, 1 story. S $45; D $55; each addl $4; under 11 free. Crib avail. Pet accepted. Street parking. TV; cable (premium). Restaurant 5-9 pm. Ck-out noon, ck-in noon. Meeting rm. Business servs avail. Concierge. Gift shop. Beach access. Hiking trail. Picnic facilities. Cr cds: A, DS, MC, V.

Chapel Hill

(C-5) *See also Durham, Raleigh*

Founded 1793 **Pop** 38,719 **Elev** 487 ft **Area code** 919
Web www.chapelhillcarrboro.org
Information Chapel Hill-Carrboro Chamber of Commerce, 104 S Estes Dr, PO Box 2897, 27515; 919/967-7075

The community of Chapel Hill is centered around the University of North Carolina, the oldest state university in the United States. This school has been a leader in American education for more than 170 years and is now part of a "research triangle," together with Duke University at Durham and North Carolina State University at Raleigh. Despite heavy losses of faculty and students to the Civil War, the school remained open until the years of Reconstruction, 1870-75. During the next decade the university was reborn.

What to See and Do

Chapel of the Cross. (1842-48) Antebellum Gothic Revival Episcopal church. (Sun-Fri) 304 E Franklin St, adj to Morehead Planetarium. Phone 919/929-2193.

Horace Williams House. Historic house is home to the Chapel Hill Preservation Society; changing art exhibits, chamber music concerts. Guided tours. (Mon-Fri, also Sun afternoons; closed hols and first 2 wks Aug) 610 Rosemary St. Phone 919/942-7818. **FREE**

North Carolina Botanical Garden. Approx 600 acres; variety of trees and plants of southeastern US; wildflower areas, herb gardens. Nature trails (daily). (Mid-Mar-mid-Nov, daily; rest of yr, Mon-Fri) Old Mason Farm Rd and US 15/501 Bypass. Phone 919/962-0522. **FREE**

University of North Carolina at Chapel Hill. (1795) Approx 24,000 students. This institution, the first state univ in the country, is on a 720-acre campus and has more than 200 bldgs. On campus are

Coker Arboretum. Covers 5 acres. Extensive collection of ornamental plants and shrubs. Cameron Ave & Raleigh St.

Davie Poplar. Ancient ivy-covered tree named for the "father of the university," William Richardson Davie; more than 200 yrs old. N of Old Well.

Kenan Stadium. (1927) Seats 52,000; in wooded natural bowl. Behind Bell Tower.

Memorial Hall. (1930) White columns front this structure dedicated to war dead, honored alumni, and university benefactors. James K. Polk, class of 1818, has a commemorative tablet here. He graduated first in his class and became the 11th President of the US. Opp New West.

Morehead-Patterson Memorial Bell Tower. (1930) A 172-ft Italian Renaissance campanile; concert chimes. The 12 bells range in weight from 300 lbs to almost 2 tons. Popular tunes are rung daily.

Morehead Planetarium. Offers indoor star gazing, art gallery with permanent and changing exhibits, scientific exhibits; rare Zeiss instrument. Shows (daily; closed Dec 24, 25). Rose garden has mammoth sundial showing time around the world. E Franklin St. Phone 919/549-6863. Shows ¢¢

Old East. Oldest state university bldg in the country; cornerstone laid in 1793. Matched by Old West (1823). Still being used as a residence hall. E of Old Well.

Old Well. Long the unofficial symbol of the Univ, this well was the only source of water here for nearly a century. The present "Greek temple" structure dates from 1897. Cameron Ave in center of campus.

Paul Green Theater. (1978) Play-Makers Repertory Company. Named for one of the first dramatic arts students at the Univ. Green is known as the father of American outdoor drama. (Sep-May) Phone 919/962-1630.

Playmakers Theater. (1851) Greek Revival temple was designed as a combination library and ballrm.

South (Main) Building. Cornerstone laid in 1798 but bldg not completed until 1814, during which time the boys lived inside the roofless walls in little huts. Future President James K. Polk lived here from 1814-18. Opp Old Well.

Wilson Library. Houses special collections. Incl North Carolina Collection Gallery; historic rms, texts, and artifacts. Also here is the Southern Historical Collection, featuring manuscripts, rare books, and photographs. (Daily) Phone 919/962-0114.

Motels/Motor Lodges

★★ **BEST WESTERN UNIVERSITY INN.** NC 54 (27515), 2 mi E on NC 54, ¼ mi E of US 15/501 Bypass. 919/932-3000; fax 919/968-6513; res 800/528-1234. www.bestwestern.com/ universityinnchapelhill. 84 rms, 1-2 story. S, D $75-$110. Crib $5. TV;

cable (premium), VCR avail (movies). Pool. Complimentary continental bkfst. Ck-out noon. Business servs avail. Health club privileges. Refrigerators avail. Cr cds: A, D, DS, MC, V.

★★ **HAMPTON INN.** *1740 US 15/501 (27514). 919/968-3000; fax 919/929-0322; res 800/426-7866. Email chck5ch@aol.com; www.hampton innchapelhill.com.* 122 rms, 2 story. Apr-June, Sep-Nov: S, D $89; lower rates rest of yr. Crib avail. Parking lot. Pool, lap pool, whirlpool. TV; cable (DSS). Complimentary continental bkfst, coffee in rms, newspaper, toll-free calls. Restaurant. Meeting rm. Business servs avail. Dry cleaning. Exercise privileges. Golf, 18 holes. Tennis, 2 courts. Picnic facilities. Cr cds: A, D, DS, MC, V.

Hotels

★★★ **THE CAROLINA INN.** *211 Pittsboro St (27516), on Univ of North Carolina's campus. 919/933-2001; fax 919/962-3400; res 800/222-8733; toll-free 800/962-8519. Email information@ carolinainn.com; www.carolinainn.com.* 177 rms, 3 story, 7 suites. S, D $164; each addl $10; suites $269; under 17 free. Crib avail. Valet parking avail. TV; cable (DSS), VCR avail. Complimentary newspaper, toll-free calls. Restaurant 6:30 am-10 pm. Bar. Ck-out noon, ck-in 3 pm. Meeting rms. Business center. Bellhops. Concierge. Dry cleaning, coin lndry. Gift shop. Exercise privileges. Golf. Video games. Cr cds: A, C, D, DS, ER, JCB, MC, V.

★★ **HOLIDAY INN-CHAPEL HILL.** *1301 N Fordham Blvd (27514), 2 mi S of I-40 Exit 270 on 15501S, at Eastgate Shopping Center. 919/929-2171; fax 919/929-5736; toll-free 800/465-4329. Email hichapelhill@aol.com; www. holidayinnchapelhill.com.* 135 rms, 2 story, 4 suites. S, D $89; suites $139; under 15 free. Crib avail. Parking lot. Pool. TV; cable (premium). Complimentary coffee in rms, newspaper, toll-free calls. Restaurant 6:30 am-9 pm. Bar. Ck-out noon, ck-in 3 pm. Meeting rms. Business servs avail. Concierge. Dry cleaning, coin lndry.

Exercise equipt. Golf. Tennis, 6 courts. Video games. Cr cds: A, C, D, DS, ER, JCB, MC, V.

★★★ **SHERATON HOTEL.** *1 Europa Dr (27514). 919/968-4900; fax 919/968-3520; toll-free 800/843-6664. www.sheraton.com.* 168 rms, 4 story. S, D $169; each addl $10; suites $195-$275; under 16 free. Crib $10. TV; cable (premium). Pool. Restaurant 6:30 am-2 pm, 4-10 pm. Bar 4 pm-1 am. Meeting rms. Business servs avail. Concierge. Gift shop. Exercise equipt. Health club privileges. Private patios, balconies. Cr cds: A, C, D, DS, MC, V.

★★★ **THE SIENA HOTEL.** *1505 E Franklin St (27514). 919/929-4000; fax 919/968-8527; toll-free 800/223-7379. www.sienahotel.com.* 68 rms, 4 story, 12 suites. Mar-May, Sep-Nov: S, D $169; each addl $10; suites $250; under 17 free; lower rates rest of yr. Crib avail. Pet accepted, fee. Valet parking avail. TV; cable (premium), VCR avail. Complimentary full bkfst, newspaper, toll-free calls. Restaurant 6:30 am-10 pm. Bar. Ck-out noon, ck-in 4 pm. Meeting rms. Business center. Bellhops. Concierge. Dry cleaning. Exercise privileges. Golf, 18 holes. Tennis, 2 courts. Video games. Cr cds: A, C, D, ER, JCB, MC, V.

B&Bs/Small Inns

★★★★★ **THE FEARRINGTON HOUSE.** *2000 Fearrington Village Center (27312), 8 mi S on US 15/501. 919/542-2121; fax 919/542-4202. Email fhouse@fearrington.com; www. fearrington.com.* This 31-room inn is the anchor of a charming village eight miles from Chapel Hill. Exploring shops at Village Center, boating on Jordan Lake, or lounging on the porch staring at surrounding pastures will fill a relaxing day. English gardens circle the antique and art-filled rooms, all with courtyard, park, or Village Center views, and the restaurant's garden-inspired menu requires a visit. 16 rms, 2 story, 15 suites. Apr-May, Sep-Nov: S $150; D $200; each addl $25; suites $290; lower rates rest of yr. Parking lot. Pool, lap pool, children's pool, whirlpool. TV; cable (premium), VCR avail, CD avail. Complimentary full bkfst, newspaper, toll-free calls. Restaurant 6-9 pm, closed Mon. 24-hr rm serv. Bar. Ck-out noon, ck-in 3 pm. Meeting rms. Business center. Concierge. Dry cleaning. Gift shop. Salon/barber. Exercise equipt. Golf. Tennis, 2 courts. Bike rentals. Picnic facilities. Cr cds: A, MC, V.

D 🕯 🏃 🛏 🎿 🏃 🛶 🔥 🏃

★ **INN AT BINGHAM SCHOOL.** *6720 Mebane Oaks Rd (27514), 12 mi W on NC 54. 919/563-5583; fax 919/563-9826; toll-free 800/566-5583. www.chapel-hill-inn.com.* 5 rms, 2 with shower only, 2 story. S $70-$120; D $80-$130; each addl $15; suites $130; under 3 free. TV. Complimentary full bkfst. Restaurant nearby. Ck-out 11 am, ck-in 3 pm. A combination of Greek and Federal styles; antiques. Cr cds: A, DS, MC, V.

🐾 🏃 🛶 🛶 🔥

Restaurants

★★ **AURORA.** *1350 Raleigh Rd (27514), Carr Mill Shopping Center. 919/942-2400. Email aurora restaurant@mindspring.com; www. aurorarestaurant.com.* Own pasta. Menu changes daily. Hrs: 11:30 am-10 pm; Sat from 5:30 pm; Sun 5:30-9 pm. Closed hols. Res accepted. Bar. Lunch $3.95-$8.95; dinner $8.95-$17.95. In renovated textile mill. Cr cds: A, DS, MC, V.

D SC 📋

★★★ **CAROLINA CROSS-ROADS.** *211 Pittsboro St. 919/918-2777. www.citysearch.com/rdu/carolinainn.* Specializes in white shrimp and grits, grilled pork rib chop. Hrs: 6:30 am-10 pm. Res accepted. Bar. Wine list. Bkfst $6.95-$11.95; lunch a la carte entrees: $6.50-$12.50. Buffet: $8.95; dinner a la carte entrees: $15-$24. Child's menu. Entertainment: pianist Fri. Valet parking. French country decor; prints, plants. Cr cds: A, C, D, DS, ER, MC, V.

D

★★★★ **THE FEARRINGTON HOUSE.** *2000 Fearrington Village Center. 919/542-2121. Email fhouse@*

fearrington.com; www.fearrington.com. The garden-inspired menu at this quaint, countryside restaurant and inn is no surprise given its surrounding, English gardens and location on rolling farmland dating back to the 1700s. Executive chef Cory Mattson creates elevated, homestyle dishes with fresh garden ingredients and a Southern twist, such as confit of duck with moonshine-sugarcane glaze, huckleberry-sauternes sauce, and Watauga cheddar macaroni and cheese. Specializes in roast duck breast, rice paper-wrapped yellowfin tuna, maple glazed smoked quail. Own baking. Hrs: 6-9 pm; Sun to 8 pm. Closed Mon. Res required. Wine list. Dinner complete meals: $59. Cr cds: A, MC, V.

D

★★★ **IL PALIO.** *1505 E Franklin St. 919/929-4000. www.sienahotel.com.* Specializes in osso buco. Own pasta. Hrs: 6:30 am-10 pm; Sun brunch 11:30 am-2 pm. Res accepted. Bar. Wine cellar. Bkfst $7.50-$10; lunch $7.50-$18; dinner $17.95-$24. Sun brunch $16.95. Mediterranean decor with Northern Italian emphasis; much artwork, wall ornamentation, flower arrangements. Cr cds: A, D, DS, MC, V.

D

★★ **LA RESIDENCE.** *202 W Rosemary St (27516). 919/967-2506. Email larez2@juno.com; www. aresidence.citysearch.com.* Continental menu. Specializes in local seafood, duckling, wild game. Hrs: 6-9:30 pm. Closed Sun; July 4, Dec 24, 25. Res accepted. Bar. Dinner a la carte entrees: $15.95-$24.95. Cr cds: A, D, MC, V.

D 📋

★ **SQUID'S.** *1201 N Fordham Blvd (US 15/501 Bypass) (27514). 919/942-8757.* Specializes in fresh seafood. Hrs: 5-9:30 pm; Fri, Sat to 10 pm; Sun, Mon to 9 pm. Closed Jan 1, Thanksgiving, Dec 24, 25. Bar. Dinner $9-$15. Child's menu. Oyster bar. Cr cds: A, D, DS, MC, V.

D SC 📋

Charlotte

(C-4) *See also Gastonia; also see Rock Hill, SC*

Settled 1748 **Pop** 395,934 **Elev** 700 ft
Area code 704
Web www.charlottecvb.org
Information Convention & Visitors Bureau, 122 E Stonewall St, 28202; 704/331-2700 or 800/231-4636

The Carolinas' largest metropolis, Charlotte grew quickly as a regional retail, financial, and distribution center and became the nation's leader in the textile industry. General Cornwallis occupied the town for a short time in 1780 but met such determined resistance that he called it a "hornet's nest," a name that has been applied with pride on the city seal and by several local groups. Gold was discovered here in 1799, and the region around Charlotte was the nation's major gold producer until the California gold rush in 1848. There was a US Mint here between 1837-61. The last Confederate Cabinet meeting was held here in 1865.

Chiefly agricultural and dependent on slave labor in antebellum days, the region took eagerly to industry after Appomattox. Abundant water power for electricity from the Catawba River has been a principal reason for its rapid growth. Today, Charlotte is among the largest banking centers in the country.

Transportation

Charlotte/Douglas International Airport. Information 704/359-4013; lost and found 704/359-4012.

Car Rental Agencies. See IMPORTANT TOLL-FREE NUMBERS.

Public Transportation. Buses (Charlotte Transit System), phone 704/336-3366.

Rail Passenger Service. Amtrak 800/872-7245.

What to See and Do

Charlotte Coliseum. This 23,000-seat arena hosts various sports events as well as family shows and concerts. 100 Paul Buck Blvd. Phone 704/357-4700 for schedule information.

The Charlotte Museum of History and Alexander Homesite. Incl Hezekiah Alexander House (1774), oldest dwelling still standing in Mecklenburg County; 2-story springhouse; working log kitchen. Tours (fee). (Tues-Fri, also Sat and Sun afternoons; closed hols) 3500 Shamrock Dr. Phone 704/568-1774. **FREE**

Discovery Place. Hands-on science museum features aquarium; also science circus, life center, rain forest, collections gallery; Omnimax theater; Space Voyager Planetarium; major traveling exhibits. (Daily; closed Thanksgiving, Dec 25) 301 N Tryon St. Phone 704/372-6261 or 800/935-0553. ¢¢¢

James K. Polk Memorial State Historic Site. Replica of log cabin and outbldgs at birthsite of 11th President of the US. Visitor center with exhibits, film. Guided tour. (Apr-Nov, Mon-Sat, also Sun afternoons; rest of yr, Tues-Sat, also Sun afternoons; closed hols) 308 S Polk St, in Pineville (1½ mi S of Exit 65B on I-485). Phone 704/889-7145. **FREE**

Latta Plantation Park. Approx 1,000-acre nature preserve on Mt Island Lake. Interpretive Center, Carolina Raptor Center, Audubon Sanctuary, Equestrian Center (fees for each). Canoe access, fishing; bridle paths, hiking trails, picnicking. (Daily) 5225 Sample Rd, Huntersville 28078. Phone 704/875-1391. **FREE** Also here is

Latta Place. (ca 1800) Restored Federal-style plantation house, original storehouse, log slave house replica; barns, farm animals; kitchen garden, cotton field. (Tues-Sun; closed hols) Phone 704/875-2312. ¢

Mint Museum of Art. First Branch US Mint operated here 1837-61 and 1867-1913, and in 1933 it was chartered as an art museum. Collections incl European and American art from Renaissance to contemporary; fine pottery and porcelain collection; maps; period costumes; survey collection of pre-Columbian and African artifacts; exhibition of coins. (Tues-Sun; closed Jan 1, Thanksgiving, Dec 25) 2730 Randolph Rd. Phone 704/337-2000. ¢¢

Mint Museum of Craft & Design. 220 N Tryon St. Phone 704/337-2000.

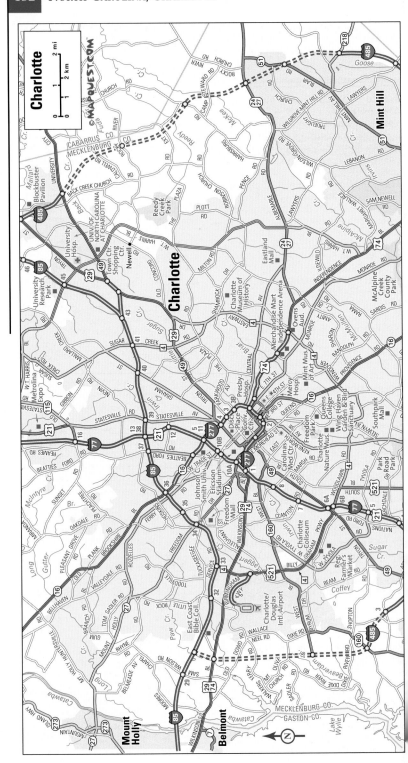

Nature Museum. Live Animal Rm, nature trail, puppet theater; earth science hall. (Daily; closed Thanksgiving, Dec 25) 1658 Sterling Rd. Phone 704/372-6261. ¢

Ovens Auditorium. Shows by touring Broadway companies (fall-late spring); musicals; symphony. 2700 E Independence Blvd, 5 mi E on US 74. Phone 704/372-3600 for schedule.

Paramount's Carowinds. Hundred-acre family theme park has over 40 rides, shows, and attractions incl 12-acre water entertainment complex WaterWorks; Animation Station children's area; DROP ZONE stunt tower; rollercoasters. Thirteen-thousand-seat Paladium Amphitheater hosts special events. Campground (all yr). (June-late Aug, daily; Mar-May and Sep-Oct, wkends) 14523 Carowinds Bvld. Phone 704/588-2600, 803/548-5300, or 800/888-4386. ¢¢¢¢¢

Professional sports.

　NBA (Charlotte Hornets). Charlotte Coliseum. 100 Paul Buck Blvd. Phone 704/357-0252.

　NFL (Carolina Panthers). Ericsson Stadium. 800 S Mint St. Phone 704/358-7000.

Spirit Square Center for the Arts. Exhibitions by well-known contemporary artists; studio art classes (fee); performances (fee). Parking fee. 345 N College St. Phone 704/372-9664; 704/372-1000 (box office).

University of North Carolina at Charlotte. (1946) 15,000 students. Beautiful landscaping and blooming plants (Mar-Nov); rhododendron garden (blooms Apr-May); ornamental garden, public greenhouse with rainforest and orchid collection. Sculpture garden. Rare Book Rm and panoramic view of campus, 10th floor of library (Mon-Fri; closed hols). Walking tour guide and map. 9201 University Blvd. Phone 704/547-4286.

Annual Events

Springfest. Three-day festival in uptown, offers food, live entertainment. Last wkend Apr.

Festival in the Park. Freedom Park. Arts and crafts, entertainment. Phone 704/338-1060. Six days mid-Sep.

Seasonal Events

Symphony. 201 S College St. Charlotte Symphony Orchestra, Inc. Phone 704/332-6136. Performs yr-round.

Theatre Charlotte. 501 Queens Rd. Classic and Broadway plays. Features 6 productions a yr on alternate months beginning in Sep. Phone 704/376-3777 Thurs-Sat eves. 1-704-376-3777.

Opera. 345 N College St. Opera Carolina. Phone 704/332-7177. Oct-Apr. 1-704-332-7177.

Auto racing. Charlotte Motor Speedway. 5555 Concord Parkway in South Harrisburg. Phone 704/455-3200. Coca-Cola 600 Winston Cup stock car race (Memorial Day wkend); Mello Yello 500 Winston Cup stock car race (early Oct); Spring AutoFair car show and flea market (mid-Apr); Fall AutoFair (mid-Sep).

Motels/Motor Lodges

★★ **COMFORT INN AIRPORT.** *4040 S I-85 (28208), Exit 32 (Little Rock Rd), near Douglas Intl Airport. 704/394-4111; fax 704/394-4117; res 800/228-5150; toll-free 800/392-4005.* 118 rms, 2 story. S $65; D $75; each addl $5; under 18 free; higher rates stock car races. Crib free. TV; cable (premium). Pool. Complimentary continental bkfst. Bar 5-11 pm. Ck-out 11 am. Meeting rms. Business servs avail. Free airport transportation. Exercise equipt. Refrigerators, microwaves avail. Cr cds: A, DS, MC, V.

　🄳 🛏 🕅 ✈ 🔥

★★ **COMFORT INN UNCC.** *5111 N Service Rd, I-85 Exit 41 (28269). 704/598-0007; fax 704/319-2683; res 800/228-5150; toll-free 800/882-3835.* 87 rms, 2 story. Mar-Oct: S $53; D $59; each addl $10; suites $69; under 12 free; lower rates rest of yr. Crib avail. TV; cable (premium). Restaurant 7 am-11 pm. Ck-out 11 am, ck-in 2 pm. Meeting rm. Golf. Cr cds: A, C, D, DS, ER, JCB, MC, V.

　🕅 🖂 🕅 SC

★★ **COURTYARD BY MARRIOTT.** *800 Arrowood Rd (28217), I-77 Exit 3. 704/527-5055; fax 704/525-5848; toll-free 800/228-9290.* 146 rms, 3 story. S, D $89-$99; wkend rates; under 6 free. Crib free. TV; cable (premium).

Pool; whirlpool. Coffee in rms. Bar 5-10 pm. Ck-out noon. Coin lndry. Meeting rms. Business servs avail. Valet serv. Exercise equipt. Some refrigerators. Private patios, balconies. Cr cds: A, D, DS, MC, V.

⊡ ⋈ 🏃 🔄 🔥 SC

★★ COURTYARD BY MARRIOTT. 333 W W.T. Harris Blvd (28262), I-85 N, Exit 45-A. 704/549-4888; fax 704/549-4946; toll-free 800/321-2211. 152 rms, 4 story. S $99; D $109; suites $109; under 12 free; wkend rates; higher rates special events. Crib free. TV; cable (premium). Pool; whirlpool. Complimentary coffee in rms. Bar. Ck-out noon. Coin lndry. Meeting rms. Business servs avail. In-rm modem link. Exercise equipt. Refrigerator in suites. Near Univ of NC. Cr cds: A, C, D, DS, MC, V.

⊡ ⋈ 🏃 🔄 🔥 SC

★★ FAIRFIELD INN BY MARRIOTT. 5415 N I-85 Service Rd (28262), I-85 Exit 41. 704/596-2999; fax 704/596-3329; toll-free 800/228-2800. 133 rms, 3 story. S, D $49; under 18 free; lower rates wkends; higher rates special events. Crib free. TV; cable (premium). Pool. Complimentary continental bkfst. Restaurant nearby. Ck-out noon. Business servs avail. Cr cds: A, D, DS, MC, V.

⊡ ⋈ 🔄 🔥 SC

★★ HAMPTON INN. 440 Griffith Rd (28217), approx 6 mi S via I-77, Tyvola Rd Exit 5. 704/525-0747; fax 704/522-0968; res 800/426-7866. Email cltn01@hi-hotel.com. 161 rms, 4 story. S $72; D $80-$85; under 18 free. Crib free. TV; cable (premium). Pool. Complimentary continental bkfst. Ck-out noon. Meeting rms. Business servs avail. Valet serv. Airport transportation. Exercise equipt; sauna. Microwaves avail. Cr cds: A, D, DS, MC, V.

⊡ ⋈ 🏃 🔄 🔥

★★ HOLIDAY INN. 2707 Little Rock Rd (28214). 704/394-4301; fax 704/394-1844; toll-free 800/647STAY. 215 rms, 4 story. S $69; D $69-$79; suites $109; under 18 free; higher rates race wkends. Crib avail. TV; cable (premium). Complimentary continental bkfst, coffee in rms. Restaurant 6 am-11 pm. Rm serv 7 am-10:30 pm. Bar 2 pm-1 am; entertainment Fri, Sat. Ck-out noon. Meeting rms. Business servs avail. Bellhops. Free airport transportation. Exercise equipt; sauna. Heated pool. Game rm. In-rm whirlpool, refrigerator, microwave in suites. Cr cds: A, C, D, DS, MC, V.

⊡ ⋈ 🏃 ✈ 🔄 🔥 SC

★ INNKEEPER COLISEUM. 305 Archdale Dr (28217). 704/525-3033; fax 704/525-3033; toll-free 800/822-9899. 69 rms, 2 story. S $45.99; D $45.99-$55.99; each addl $5; under 16 free; higher rates special events. Crib free. TV; cable (premium). Pool. Complimentary continental bkfst. Restaurant nearby. Ck-out noon. Business servs avail. Microwaves avail. Cr cds: A, C, D, DS, MC, V.

⊡ ⋈ 🔄 🔥 SC

★ LA QUINTA INN. 7900 Nations Ford Rd (28217), S via I-77 to Exit 4. 704/522-7110; fax 704/521-9778; toll-free 800/687-6667. www.laquinta.com. 118 rms, 3 story. S, D $66-$74; each addl $7; under 18 free; higher rates: auto race wkends, special events. Crib free. Pet accepted, some restrictions. TV; cable (premium). Heated pool. Continental bkfst. Restaurant adj open 24 hrs. Ck-out noon. Business servs avail. Valet serv. Health club privileges. Microwaves avail. Cr cds: A, C, D, DS, MC, V.

⊡ 🐾 ⋈ 🔄 🔥 SC

★ RED ROOF INN. 131 Red Roof Dr (28217), I-77 S to Exit 4 (Nations Ford Rd). 704/529-1020; fax 704/529-1054. 115 rms, 3 story. S $36-$41; D $41-$47; up to 5, $59; under 18 free. Crib free. Pet accepted, some restrictions. TV; cable (premium). Complimentary coffee in lobby. Ck-out noon. Business servs avail. Health club privileges. Cr cds: A, D, DS, JCB, MC, V.

⊡ 🐾 🏃 🔄 🔥

★ RODEWAY INN. 1416 W Sugar Creek Rd (28262). 704/597-5074; fax 704/597-5074; toll-free 800/638-7949. 56 rms, 2 story. S $40.95-$48.95; D $46.95-$54.95; each addl $5; higher rates special events; under 12 free. Crib free. TV; cable (premium). Pool. Complimentary continental bkfst. Restaurant adj open 24 hrs. Ck-out 11 am. Cr cds: A, C, D, DS, MC, V.

⊡ ⋈ 🔄 🔥 SC

Hotels

★★★ ADAM'S MARK. 555 S McDowell St (28204), at jct US 74 and

equ
gan
MC
D

★★
630
Sout
704
stor
wke
(pre
serv
10:3
pm-
out
facil
rms.
ter.
Exer
saun
privi
wave
patio
Cr c
DS,
D

★★
HAM
HOT
Yorkn
(282(
Grah
seum
704/
free 8
wynd
164 r
$129;
undei
lot. P
plime
Restau
noon,
ness s
airpor
equip
courts
DS, M
D

All S

★★★
Tryon
704/5
Email
embas
suites.
$179;

US 77. 704/372-4100; fax 704/348-4646; res 800/444-2326. 615 rms, 18 story. S, D $99-$155; each addl $15; suites $125-$450; under 18 free. Crib free. TV; cable (premium). Heated pools, 1 indoor; whirlpool. Restaurant (see also BRAVO). Bars 11-1 am; entertainment. Ck-out noon. Convention facilities. Concierge. Gift shop. Exercise equipt; sauna. Health club privileges. Racquetball courts. Wet bar in some suites. Opp park. Cr cds: A, C, D, DS, JCB, MC, V.

★★★ **DOUBLETREE HOTEL.** *895 W Trade St (28202). 704/347-0070; fax 704/347-0267; toll-free 800/222-8733. Email hotel@cltwc.doubletree. com; www.doubletree.com.* 183 rms, 8 story, 4 suites. Mar-May, Oct: Crib avail. Parking garage. Pool, whirlpool. TV; cable (premium). Complimentary coffee in rms, newspaper. Restaurant 6:30 am-10 pm. Bar. Ck-out noon, ck-in 3 pm. Meeting rms. Bellhops. Dry cleaning. Exercise equipt, sauna. Golf. Cr cds: A, C, D, DS, JCB, MC, V.

★★ **DUNHILL.** *237 N Tryon St (28202). 704/332-4141; fax 704/376-4117; toll-free 800/354-4141. Email dunhillhtl@hotmail.com.* 60 rms, 10 story. S, D $99-$300; wkend rates; higher rates special events. Crib free. TV; cable (premium). Restaurant 6:30 am-10:30 pm. Bar. Ck-out noon. Meeting rms. Business servs avail. In-rm modem link. Concierge. Free garage parking. Health club privileges. Refrigerators. European-style hotel built in 1929; 18th-century furnishings, original artwork. Cr cds: A, D, DS, MC, V.

★★ **FOUR POINTS HOTEL SHERATON.** *201 S McDowell St (28204). 704/372-7550; fax 704/333-6737; toll-free 800/325-3535.* 191 rms, 11 story, 2 suites. Mar-July, Oct-Nov: S, D $300; each addl $30; suites $600; under 17 free; lower rates rest of yr. Crib avail. Parking garage. Pool. TV; cable (DSS), VCR avail, CD avail. Complimentary continental bkfst, coffee in rms, newspaper, toll-free calls. Restaurant 6:30 am-10:30 pm. Bar. Ck-out noon, ck-in 3 pm. Meeting rms. Business servs avail. Bellhops. Concierge. Dry cleaning. Free airport transportation. Exer-

cise equipt. Golf. Tennis. Cr cds: A, C, D, DS, MC, V.

★★★ **HILTON AT UNIVERSITY PLACE.** *8629 J. M. Keynes Dr (28262), off I-85, Exit 45A (Harris Blvd). 704/547-7444; fax 704/549-9708; res 800/445-8667. www.hilton.com.* 243 rms, 12 story. S, D $89-$179; each addl $15; wkend rates. Crib $15. Pet accepted; $50. TV; cable. Pool; poolside serv. Restaurant 6:30 am-10 pm. Bar 11-2 am. Ck-out noon. Meeting rms. Business servs avail. In-rm modem link. Exercise equipt. Microwaves avail. Cr cds: A, D, DS, MC, V.

★★★ **HILTON CHARLOTTE AND TOWERS.** *222 E 3rd St (28202). 704/377-1500; fax 704/377-4143.* 407 rms, 22 story. S $175, D $195; each addl $25; suites $195-$600; under 18 free; wkend rates. Crib free. Garage parking; valet $18. TV; cable (premium), VCR avail. Pool privileges. Restaurant 6:30 am-11 pm. Bar 11-1:30 am. Ck-out noon. Convention facilities. Business center. In-rm modem link. Shopping arcade. Airport transportation. Tennis privileges. Golf privileges. Health club privileges. Minibars; some bathrm phones; refrigerators avail. Wet bar in suites. Luxury level. Cr cds: A, C, D, DS, JCB, MC, V.

★★★ **HILTON HOTEL EXECUTIVE PARK.** *5624 Westpark Dr (28217), I-77 Exit 5. 704/527-8000; fax 704/529-5963; toll-free 800/445-8667.* 178 rms, 7 story, 32 suites. Apr-May, July-Oct: S $149; D $159; suites $189; lower rates rest of yr. Crib avail. Pet accepted, some restrictions, fee. Valet parking avail. Pool, children's pool, whirlpool. TV; cable (DSS), VCR avail. Complimentary coffee in rms, newspaper, toll-free calls. Restaurant 6 am-11 pm. Bar. Ck-out 11 am, ck-in 3 pm. Meeting rms. Business center. Bellhops. Dry cleaning, coin lndry. Free airport transportation. Exercise privileges. Golf. Tennis. Bike rentals. Hiking trail. Picnic facilities. Cr cds: A, C, D, DS, ER, JCB, MC, V.

whirlpool. TV; cable (premium), VCR avail. Complimentary full bkfst, coffee in rms, newspaper. Restaurant. Meeting rms. Business servs avail. Dry cleaning, coin lndry. Free airport transportation. Exercise privileges. Golf, 18 holes. Picnic facilities. Cr cds: A, C, D, DS, JCB, MC, V.

D ◉ 👖 ⛱ 🏋 🔄 🔥

Restaurants

★★★ **BISTRO 100.** *100 N Tryon St (28202). 704/344-0515. www.bistro 100restaurant.com.* Bistro menu. Specializes in wood roasted specialties beef, chicken, seafood. Hrs: 11:30 am-10 pm; Fri, Sat to 11 pm; Sun 1-9 pm. Closed hols. Res accepted. Wine, beer. Lunch $7.95-$14.95; dinner $10.95-$21.95. Brunch $7.95-$14.95. Child's menu. Entertainment. Cr cds: A, D, DS, MC, V.

D ⊒

★★★ **BRAVO.** *555 S McDowell St. 704/372-5440.* Specializes in fresh seafood, pasta, chicken. Hrs: 5:30-10 pm; Fri, Sat to 10:30 pm; Sun brunch 10 am-2 pm. Res accepted. Bar. Dinner $15.25-$24.50. Sun brunch $18.95. Entertainment: singing waiters. Italian decor. Cr cds: A, D, DS, MC, V.

⊒

★★ **GUYTANO'S.** *200 E Bland St (28203). 704/375-6700. www. guytanos.com.* Specializes in sea bass chili herb spiced, spiedini of jumbo shrimp. Hrs: 6-10 pm; Fri, Sat to midnight. Closed hols. Wine, beer. Dinner $14-$29. Child's menu. Entertainment. Cr cds: A, MC, V.

D ⊒

★★ **HEREFORD BARN STEAK HOUSE.** *4320 N I-85 (28206), on Service Rd between Sugar Creek Rd and Graham St. 704/596-0854.* Specializes in steak, prime rib, chicken. Hrs: 5-10 pm; Fri, Sat to 11 pm. Closed Sun, Mon; hols. Dinner $9.95-$29.95. Child's menu. Country-barn decor; farm implements; fireplace. Family-owned. Cr cds: A, D, DS, MC, V.

SC ⊒

★★★ **LA BIBLIOTHEQUE.** *1901 Roxborough Rd (28211), in Roxborough Office Bldg. 704/365-5000. www.la bibliotheque.com.* Eclectic menu. Specializes in seafood, beef, veal. Hrs:

11:30 am-10 pm; Sat from 5:30 pm. Closed Sun; Jan 1, Thanksgiving, Dec 25. Res accepted. Lunch a la carte entrees: $7.95-$11.95; dinner a la carte entrees: $14-$35. Entertainment: pianist Tues-Sat. Jacket (dinner). Terrace dining. Traditional decor; oil paintings. Cr cds: A, D, DS, MC, V.

D ⊒

★★★ **LAMP LIGHTER.** *1065 E Morehead St (28204). 704/372-5343.* Specializes in fresh seafood, wild game, ostrich. Own baking. Hrs: 5:30-10 pm; Fri, Sat to 10:30 pm; Sun to 9:30 pm. Closed Jan 1, Thanksgiving, Dec 25. Res accepted. Bar. Wine list. Dinner $15.95-$29.95. Valet parking. Jacket. In Spanish-colonial house built 1926. Cr cds: A, D, DS, MC, V.

D ⊒

★★★★ **LA VECCHIA'S.** *225 E 6th St (28202). 704/370-6776. Email charlavecchia@msn.com.* Seafood menu. Specializes in sesame seared yellow fin tuna, pan seared Chilean sea bass. Hrs: 5:30-10 pm; Fri, Sat to 11 pm. Closed Sun. Res accepted. Wine, beer. Dinner $18-$26. Child's menu. Entertainment: jazz Fri, Sat. Cr cds: A, D, MC, V.

D ⊒

★★ **MCNINCH HOUSE.** *511 N Church St (28202). 704/332-6159.* Specializes in rack of lamb, crab cakes, white chocolate mousse with macadamia nuts. Hrs: 6:30-9 pm. Closed Mon, Sun; hols. Res required. Bar. Dinner complete meal: $78. 20% serv chg. Valet parking. In 100-yr-old Victorian house. Cr cds: A, MC, V.

★★★ **PASTIS.** *2000 South Blvd (28203). 704/333-1928.* Specializes in salmon, osso buco, lamb tiara. Hrs: 11 am-2 pm, 6-11 pm. Closed Sun, Mon. Res accepted. Wine, beer. Lunch $7.50-$12.50; dinner $16-$18.50. Entertainment. Cr cds: A, D, DS, MC, V.

D ⊒

★★★ **PATOU BISTRO.** *2400 Park Rd Suite M (28203). 704/376-2233.* Specializes in seafood waterzooi, snails in roquefort sauce, confit of duck. Hrs: 11:30 am-10 pm; Fri to 11 pm; Sat 5-11 pm; Mon to 2 pm. Closed Sun; hols. Res accepted. Bar. Wine cellar. Lunch $5-$9; dinner

$10-$18. Parking. Bistro decor; black/white photos. Cr cds: A, DS, MC, V.

[D] [symbol]

★ **RANCH HOUSE.** *5614 Wilkinson Blvd (28208). 704/399-5411.* Specializes in steak, seafood, chicken. Hrs: 5-11 pm. Closed Sun; hols. Dinner $9.75-$20.75. Child's menu. Western decor. Family-owned. Cr cds: A, D, DS, MC, V.

[D] [symbol]

★ ★ ★ **SMOKY'S GRILL.** *2200 Rexford Rd. 704/364-8220.* Specializes in fresh seafood, regional cuisine. Own baking. Hrs: 6:30 am-10:30 pm; Sat, Sun from 7 am. Res accepted. Bar. Wine list. Bkfst $2.50-$9.95; lunch $4.95-$14.95; dinner $15.95-$27.95. Sun brunch $16.95-$29.95. Child's menu. Entertainment: pianist. Valet parking. English club decor. Cr cds: A, D, DS, MC, V.

[D] [symbol]

★ ★ ★ **TOWNHOUSE.** *1011 Providence Rd (28270). 704/335-1546. Email townhouse2@aol.com.* Specializes in fowl, beef, seafood. Own baking, pasta. Hrs: 6-10 pm. Closed Sun; hols. Res accepted. Bar. Wine list. Dinner $19.50-$30. 18th-century English decor. Cr cds: A, D, DS, MC, V.

[D] [symbol]

Cherokee

See also Bryson City, Maggie Valley, Waynesville

Pop 8,519 **Elev** 1,991 ft
Area code 828 **Zip** 28719
Web www.cherokee-nc.co

Information Cherokee Travel and Promotion, PO Box 460; 828/497-9195 or 800/438-1601

Seasonal Event

Unto These Hills. Mountainside Theater. On US 441, ½ mi from jct US 19. Kermit Hunter drama re-creating the history of Cherokee Nation from 1540-1838; in natural amphitheater. Mon-Sat eves. Phone 828/497-2111. Mid-June-late Aug.

Motels/Motor Lodges

★ ★ **BEST WESTERN.** *441 N & Aquoni Rd (28719). 828/497-2020; fax 828/497-3903; toll-free 800/528-1234.* 152 rms, 2 story. Late May-Oct: S, D $85; each addl $6; under 12 free; lower rates rest of yr. Crib free. TV; cable (premium). Pool; wading pool. Restaurant 7 am-9 pm. Ck-out 11 am. Coin lndry. Meeting rms. Business servs avail. Sundries. Cr cds: A, C, D, DS, MC, V.

[D] [symbol] [symbol] [symbol] [SC]

★ ★ **COMFORT INN.** *US 19 S (28719), ½ mi W of jct US 441 and 19. 828/497-2411; fax 828/497-6555; res 800/228-5150.* 87 rms, 2 story. Late May-Oct: S, D $59-$109; each addl $8; under 18 free; lower rates Apr-late May and Nov-Dec. Closed rest of yr. Crib $2. TV; cable (premium). Pool; whirlpool. Complimentary continental bkfst. Restaurant nearby. Ck-out 11 am. Meeting rm. Business servs avail. Some refrigerators. On river. Cr cds: A, C, D, DS, MC, V.

[D] [symbol] [symbol] [symbol] [symbol] [symbol]

★ **COOL WATERS MOTEL.** *US Hwy 19 N (28719), 1½ mi E. 828/497-3855; fax 828/497-3855.* 50 rms. Mid-June-Oct: S, D $42-$70; lower rates rest of yr. Crib $3. TV; cable. Pool; wading pool. Restaurant opp 6:30 am-9 pm. Ck-out 11 am. Tennis. Some patios. Picnic tables, grills. On stream; trout pond. Cr cds: DS, MC, V.

[symbol] [symbol] [symbol] [symbol] [symbol]

★ **CRAIG'S MOTEL.** *Hwy 19 (28719). 828/497-3821; fax 828/497-3821; res 800/550-6869; toll-free 800/560-6869.* 30 rms. S, D $49-$63; each addl $5; higher rates: hols, wkends, fall foliage season. TV; cable (premium). Pool. Playground. Restaurant 7 am-10 pm. Ck-out 11 am. On stream; picnic tables nearby. Cr cds: A, DS, MC, V.

[D] [symbol] [symbol] [symbol] [symbol]

★ **DAYS INN.** *US 19 N (28719). 828/497-9171; fax 828/497-3424; res 800/329-7466.* 58 rms, 2 story. June-Oct: S, D $119; each addl $5; under 12 free; lower rates rest of yr. Crib avail. Parking lot. Pool, children's pool. TV; cable (premium). Complimentary coffee in rms, newspaper, toll-free calls. Restaurant nearby. Ck-out 11 am, ck-in 2 pm. Fax servs avail. Golf. Cr cds: A, C, D, DS, JCB, MC, V.

★★ **HOLIDAY INN CHEROKEE.** *PO Box 1929 (28719), 1 mi W. 828/ 497-9181; fax 828/497-5973; res 800/HOLIDAY. Email guestser@wnc.net.* 154 rms, 2 story. Mid-June-Oct: S, D $66-$100; each addl $6; under 19 free; lower rates rest of yr. Crib free. TV; cable (premium). 2 pools, 1 indoor; wading pool, whirlpool. Sauna. Playground. Coffee in rms. Restaurant 7-11 am, 5-9 pm. Ck-out 11 am. Coin lndry. Meeting rm. Sundries. Gift shop. Game rm. Cr cds: A, C, D, DS, ER, JCB, MC, V.

★ **PIONEER MOTEL AND COT- TAGES.** *Hwy 19 S (28719). 828/497- 2271.* 21 rms, 6 kit. cottages. Mid-June-Labor Day, Oct: S, D $48- $68; each addl $5; cottages $75-$150; under 12 free; lower rates Apr-mid- June, Sep. Closed rest of yr. Crib free. TV; cable (premium). Pool. Complimentary coffee in lobby. Restaurant nearby. Ck-out 11 am. At river. Cr cds: A, DS, MC, V.

Cherryville

See also Gastonia, Shelby

Founded 1881 **Pop** 4,756 **Elev** 960 ft **Area code** 704 **Zip** 28021
Information Chamber of Commerce, 301 E Main St, PO Box 305; 704/435- 3451 or 704/435-4200

Customs of Cherryville's original German settlers still live on in this town nestled in the rolling hills of the Piedmont.

Annual Event

Shooting in the New Year. Old rite to bring fertility to fruit trees and for good luck in the coming yr. Men chant blessings and fire black powder muzzleloaders as they go from home to home New Year's Eve until dusk, Jan 1.

Concord (Cabarrus County)

(C-4) *See also Albemarle, Charlotte*

Pop 27,347 **Elev** 704 ft **Area code** 704 **Zip** 28026
Information Chamber of Commerce, 23 Union St N, PO Box 1029; 704/782-4111

Concord was founded by Scottish-Irish and German-Dutch settlers and received its name when the two factions settled a dispute regarding the location of the county seat. An early textile area in the South, Concord continues to lead in dyeing, finishing, and weaving of hosiery and knitted textiles.

What to See and Do

Reed Gold Mine State Historic Site. First documented discovery of gold in the US (1799) occurred here. Panning area (Apr-Oct, daily; fee); underground mine tours, history trail; working machinery, demonstrations, exhibits, visitor center; film; picnicking. (Apr-Oct, Mon-Sat, also Sun afternoons; rest of yr, Tues-Sat, also Sun afternoons) 10 mi SE on US 601 and NC 200 to Georgeville, then 2 mi S on NC 1100. Phone 704/786- 8337. **FREE**

Motels/Motor Lodges

★ **COLONIAL INN.** *1325 Concord Pkwy N (28025), ¾ mi NW on US 29/601 Concord Exit. 704/782-2146; fax 704/786-9856.* 65 rms, 1 story. S $44; D $49. Crib avail, fee. Pet accepted, fee. Pool. TV; cable (premium). Complimentary newspaper. Restaurant 6 am-10 pm. Ck-out 11 am, ck-in 2 pm. Meeting rm. Fax servs avail. Golf. Cr cds: A, DS, MC, V.

★★ **COMFORT INN.** *3100 Clover- leaf Pkwy (28081). 704/786-3100; fax 704/784-3114; toll-free 800/638-7949.* 71 rms, 2 story. S, D $58.95; each addl $5; suites $72.95; under 18 free; higher rates: auto races, horse shows. Crib $5. TV; cable (premium), VCR avail (movies). Pool. Complimentary continental bkfst, coffee in rms. Restaurant adj 11 am-11 pm. Ck-out 11 am. Coin lndry. Meeting rms. Business servs avail. Health club privileges. Many refrigerators. Cr cds: A, C, D, DS, ER, JCB, MC, V.

Cornelius

See also Charlotte, Statesville

Founded 1893 **Pop** 2,581 **Elev** 831 ft
Area code 704 **Zip** 28031
Web www.lakenorman.org
Information North Mecklenburg Chamber & Visitors Center, PO Box 760; 704/892-1922

A dispute between two cotton companies in Davidson during the late 1800s led to one of the firms relocating south of the city limits and establishing a new town. Originally called Liverpool, the community changed its name to Cornelius in honor of an investor.

What to See and Do

Lake Norman. The state's largest freshwater lake (32,510 acres); created by Cowans Ford Dam, a Duke Power project on the Catawba River. Eight public access areas. NW of town. Phone 704/382-8587.

Annual Event

LakeFest. County Park. Entertainment, dog show, Art in the Park, concessions. KidzFest, petting zoo, magic shows, face painting. Phone 704/892-1922. Second wkend mid-Sep.

Motels/Motor Lodges

★★ **BEST WESTERN LAKE NORMAN.** *19608 Liverpool Pkwy (28031). 704/896-0660; fax 704/896-8633; res 800/528-1234.* 80 rms, 4 story, 10 suites. S $65.95; D $72.95; each addl $7; suites $89.95-$99.95; under 15 free; higher rates special events. Crib free. TV; cable (premium), VCR avail (movies $6). Pool. Complimentary continental bkfst. Restaurant nearby. Ck-out 11 am. Meeting rms. Business servs avail. Exercise equipt. Refrigera-

tors, microwaves avail. Cr cds: A, DS, MC, V.

★★ **COMFORT INN LAKE NORMAN.** *20740 Torrence Chapel Rd (28031), 1 mi W on I-77, Exit 28. 704/892-3500; fax 704/892-6473; toll-free 800/848-9751.* 90 rms, 2-3 story. S, D $71.95; suites $125-$175; under 18 free; wkend, hol, wkly rates; higher rates special events. Crib free. TV; cable (premium), VCR avail (movies). Pool. Complimentary continental bkfst, coffee in rms. Restaurant nearby. Ck-out 11 am. Coin lndry. Meeting rm. Business servs avail. Health club privileges. Refrigerators. Microwaves avail. Cr cds: A, C, D, DS, ER, JCB, MC, V.

★★ **HAMPTON INN.** *19501 Statesville Rd (28031), I-77 Exit 28. 704/892-9900; fax 704/896-7488; toll-free 800/426-7866.* 117 rms, 5 story. S, D $74-$79; under 18 free; higher rates wkends, special events. Crib free. TV; cable (premium). Pool. Complimentary continental bkfst. Restaurant adj 6 am-10 pm. Ck-out noon. Meeting rm. Business servs avail. Exercise equipt. Some refrigerators. Cr cds: A, C, D, DS, ER, JCB, MC, V.

★★ **LAKE NORMAN HOLIDAY INN.** *19901 Holiday Ln (28031), jct NC 73 and I-77 Exit 28. 704/892-9120; fax 704/892-3854; toll-free 800/465-4329.* 119 rms, 2 story. S, D $84; under 18 free; higher rates special events. Crib free. Pet accepted; $25. TV; cable (premium). Pool. Complimentary coffee in rms. Restaurant 6 am-10 pm. Bar 4:30 pm-midnight. Ck-out 11 am. Coin lndry. Meeting rms. Exercise equipt. Some refrigerators, microwaves. Cr cds: A, C, D, DS, JCB, MC, V.

Hotel

★★ **HOLIDAY INN EXPRESS.** *14135 Statesville Rd (28078), 5 mi S on I-77, Exit 23. 704/875-1165; fax 704/875-1894; res 800/465-4329. Email hunex@aol.com; www.hiexpress. com.* 44 rms, 2 story, 16 suites. Apr-Oct: S $79; D $84; each addl $5;

suites $84; under 16 free; lower rates rest of yr. Crib avail. Parking lot. Pool. TV; cable (premium), VCR avail. Complimentary continental bkfst, coffee in rms, newspaper, toll-free calls. Restaurant nearby. Ck-out 11 am, ck-in 2 pm. Meeting rm. Fax servs avail. Dry cleaning. Exercise equipt. Golf. Cr cds: A, C, D, DS, JCB, MC, V.

[D] [†] [≈] [↗] [⊠] [♨] [SC]

B&B/Small Inn

★★ **DAVIDSON VILLAGE INN.** *117 Depot St (28036), 1 mi N on I-77, Exit 30. 704/892-8044; fax 704/896-2184; toll-free 800/892-0796. Email info@ davidsoninn.com; www.davidsoninn. com.* 18 rms, 3 story, 4 suites. S, D $100-$110; suites $115-$125; under 16 free; wkends, hols (2-day min); higher rates special events. Crib free. TV; cable (premium), VCR avail. Complimentary continental bkfst. Restaurant adj 11 am-10 pm. Ck-out 11 am, ck-in 3 pm. Business servs avail. Valet serv. Health club privileges. Refrigerator, microwave, wet bar in suites; microwaves avail. Cr cds: A, DS, MC, V.

[D] [↯] [↗] [♨] [✦]

Restaurants

★ **CAPTAIN'S GALLEY.** *105 Statesville Rd # J (28078), 2 mi S on I-77, Exit 23. 704/875-6038.* Specializes in seafood. Own baking. Hrs: 11 am-9 pm; Fri to 10 pm; Sat noon-10 pm. Closed Sun; hols. Lunch $3.75-$10; dinner $4.95-$16. Child's menu. Nautical decor; wall murals. Family-owned since 1978. Cr cds: MC, V.

[D] [SC] [⊟]

★★ **KOBE JAPANESE HOUSE OF STEAK & SEAFOOD.** *20465 Chartwell Center Dr (28031). 704/896-7778.* Specializes in teppanyaki preparation, Kobe beef, seafood. Sushi bar. Hrs: 11:30 am-10 pm; Fri, Sat to 11 pm; Sat, Sun from 5 pm; early-bird dinner Mon-Fri 5-6 pm. Closed Thanksgiving, Dec 25. Res accepted. Bar. Lunch $5.95-$14.95; dinner $9.95-$24.95. 15% serv chg. Child's menu. Japanese decor. Cr cds: A, D, DS, MC, V.

[D]

Dunn

(C-6) *See also Fayetteville, Goldsboro*

Pop 8,336 **Elev** 213 ft **Area code** 910 **Zip** 28334

What to See and Do

Bentonville Battleground State Historic Site. Biggest battle on North Carolina soil, Mar 19-21, 1865. It was the last organized attempt to stop Gen William Tecumseh Sherman after he left Atlanta. A month later, the rebel cause was lost; Lee surrendered at Appomattox Apr 9; Lincoln was shot Apr 14; and Johnston surrendered Apr 26. The restored Harper House was used as a hospital to treat wounded of both sides. Reconstructed and original trenches; history trail with exhibits. Picnic area. Visitor center, audiovisual show. (Apr-Oct, daily; rest of yr, Tues-Sun; closed hols) 15 mi E via NC 55 to Newton Grove, 3 mi N via US 701 to NC 1008, then 3 mi E. Phone 910/594-0789. **FREE**

Motels/Motor Lodges

★★ **BEST WESTERN.** *603 Springbranch Rd (28334), I-95, Exit 72. 910/892-2162; fax 910/892-3010; toll-free 800/528-1234.* 142 rms, 2 story. S, D $29.99-$52.99; family rates. Crib $5. Pet accepted. TV; cable (premium). Pool. Restaurant 5-10 am, 5:30-9:30 pm. Ck-out 11 am. Business servs avail. Cr cds: A, C, D, DS, MC, V.

[D] [≈] [↗] [⊠] [♨] [SC]

★ **ECONO LODGE.** *1125 E Broad St (28334). 910/892-1293; fax 910/891-1038; res 800/053-2666.* 105 rms, 2 story. May-Sep: S $39.95-$54.95; D $44.95-$65.95; under 18 free; higher rates special events; lower rates rest of yr. Pet accepted. TV; cable (premium). Complimentary continental bkfst. Restaurant 5-10 pm. Ck-out 11 am. Meeting rm. Business servs avail. Pool. Some refrigerators. Cr cds: A, C, D, DS, MC, V.

[D] [≈] [↗] [⊠] [♨]

★★ **RAMADA INN.** *1011 E Cumberland St (28334), I-95 Exit 73. 910/892-8101; fax 910/892-2836; res 800/272-6232.* 100 rms, 2 story. S $39-

$59; D $49-$69; each addl $6; under 18 free. Crib free. Pet accepted. TV; cable (premium). Pool. Restaurant 6:30 am-2 pm, 5-9 pm. Ck-out noon. Meeting rms. Business servs avail. In-rm modem link. Valet serv. Some refrigerators. Cr cds: A, C, D, DS, MC, V.

Durham

(C-5) *See also Chapel Hill, Raleigh*

Founded 1853 **Pop** 136,611
Elev 406 ft **Area code** 919
Web dcvb.durham.nc.us

Information Convention & Visitors Bureau, 101 E Morgan St, 27701; 800/772-2855

Durham's sparkle has brought it near-top national ranking in numerous livability studies. Known for excellence in medicine, education, research, and industry, Durham is also a recreational and cultural center in the rolling Piedmont region.

In 1924, an endowment from James B. Duke, head of the American Tobacco Company, helped establish Duke University as a leader among the nation's institutions of higher learning. North Carolina Central University makes its home here. In the 1950s, Durham County was chosen as the site of Research Triangle Park, a planned scientific research center that includes the Environmental Protection Agency, the National Institute for Environmental Health Sciences, IBM Corporation, the Glaxo Wellcome Company, and others. Duke University Medical Center, Durham Regional Hospital, and several other outstanding medical institutions here have earned Durham the title "City of Medicine, USA."

What to See and Do

Bennett Place State Historic Site. Site of signing (Apr 26, 1865) of surrender of Confederate General Johnston to Union General Sherman, one of the last and most significant of the Confederate surrenders. Reconstructed Bennett homestead. Picnick-ing. Visitor center, exhibits, audiovisual show. (Apr-Oct, daily; rest of yr, Tues-Sun; closed hols) Just SW of jct I-85 Exit 173 & US 70. Phone 919/383-4345. **FREE**

Duke Homestead State Historic Site. (1852) Ancestral home of Duke family; first Duke tobacco factory; curing barn; outbldgs; farm crops. Tobacco Museum, exhibits, film; furnishings of period. Tours. (Apr-Oct, daily; rest of yr, Tues-Sun; closed hols) 2828 Duke Homestead Rd, ½ mi N of jct I-85, Guess Rd. Phone 919/477-5498. **FREE**

Duke University. (1838) 10,000 students. Two campuses, E and W, on 8,000 acres. Incl original Trinity College. The W Campus, occupied since 1930, is the showplace of the univ. 919/684-8111. On campus are

Art Museum. (Tues-Sun; closed hols) E Campus, off W Main St. Phone 919/684-5135. **FREE**

Duke Chapel. Beautiful Gothic-style chapel with a carillon of 50 bells in its 210-ft tower; 5,000-pipe Flentrop organ. (Daily) Chapel Dr to main quadrangle. Phone 919/684-2572.

Duke Libraries. Most comprehensive in the South, with more than 4 million volumes and 7 million manuscripts. Large Confederate imprint collection; Walt Whitman manuscripts. Phone 919/684-3009.

Duke Medical Center. Research and teaching complex. Treats more than ½ million patients annually. Phone 919/684-8111 for information.

Duke's Wallace Wade Stadium. (33,941 capacity) And the 8,564-seat Cameron Indoor Stadium. Home of the Duke Blue Devils.

Sarah P. Duke Gardens. Fifty-five acres of landscaped gardens, pine forest. Continuous display. (Daily) Main entrance on Anderson St. Phone 919/684-3698. **FREE**

Historic Stagville Center. State-owned historic property, once part of the Bennehan-Cameron plantation; several historic 18th- and 19th-century plantation bldgs on 71 acres of land. (Mon-Fri; closed hols) 7 mi NE via Roxboro Rd and Old Oxford Hwy. Phone 919/620-0120. **FREE**

North Carolina Museum of Life and Science. North Carolina wildlife; hands-on science exhibits; aerospace, weather, and geology collections; train ride; farmyard; science park; discovery rms; Butterfly House. Picnic area. (Daily; closed Jan 1, Thanksgiving, Dec 25) 433 Murray Ave. Phone 919/220-5429. ¢¢¢

West Point on the Eno. A 371-acre park along the scenic Eno River; restored farmhouse (1850); working gristmill; museum of photography; blacksmith shop. Fishing, boating; picnicking, hiking, environmental programs (fee). Park (daily). Mill, farmhouse, museum (Mar-Dec, Sat and Sun). I-85, Duke St Exit then 3½ mi N. Phone 919/471-1623. **FREE**

Duke Chapel

Annual Events

CenterFest. Downtown. Two-day event with over 250 artists and craftsmen; musicians, jugglers, and clowns; continuous entertainment from 3 stages. Phone 919/560-2722. Sep.

Bull Durham Blues Festival. Historic Durham Athletic Park. Celebrates the blues with performances held at the location where *Bull Durham* was filmed. Phone 919/683-1709. Wkend mid-Sep.

Seasonal Event

American Dance Festival. Page Auditorium and Reynolds Industries Theater, Duke Univ, W Campus. Six wks of performances by the finest of both major and emerging modern dance companies from the US and abroad. Contact the Festival at PO Box 6097, College Station 22708; 919/684-6402. June-July.

Motels/Motor Lodges

★★ **BEST WESTERN SKYLAND INN.** *I-85 N or S Exit 170 (27705), jct I-85 Exit 170 and US 70W.* 919/383-2508; fax 919/383-7316; res 800/528-1234. 31 rms. S, D $58-$72; each addl $10; under 12 free. Crib $10. Pet accepted. TV; cable (premium). Pool. Playground. Coffee in rms. Complimentary continental bkfst. Ck-out noon. Business servs avail. Refrigerators. Picnic tables, grills. Cr cds: A, C, D, DS, ER, JCB, MC, V.
🄳 ➰ ⌚ ≈ 🛅 🚫 🐾

★★ **COMFORT INN UNIVERSITY.** *3508 Mt Moriah Rd (27707).* 919/490-4949; fax 919/419-0535. 138 rms, 4 story, 18 suites. S, D $69-$75; each addl $6; suites $119-$149; under 16 free; higher rates special events. Crib free. TV; cable (premium). Pool; whirlpool. Complimentary continental bkfst, coffee in lobby. Restaurant nearby. Ck-out noon. Coin lndry. Meeting rms. Business servs avail. Exercise equipt; sauna. Cr cds: A, D, DS, MC, V.
🄳 ⌚ ≈ 🛅 🚭 🔥

★★ **COURTYARD BY MARRIOTT.** *1815 Front St (27705).* 919/309-1500; fax 919/383-8189. 146 rms, 4 story. Apr-Nov: S $79.97-$109.95; D $89.95-$119.95; each addl $10; suites $109.95-$169.95; under 18 free; package plans; higher rates special events; lower rates rest of yr. Crib free. TV; cable (premium). Complimentary coffee in rms. Restaurant nearby. Ck-out noon. Meeting rms. Business servs avail. In-rm modem link. Sundries. Coin lndry. Exercise equipt. Health club privileges. Pool. Refrigerator in suites. Some balconies. Cr cds: A, D, DS, MC, V.
🄳 ≈ 🛅 🚭 🐾

★ **RED ROOF INN.** *1915 N Pointe Dr (27705), I-85 Exit 175.* 919/471-9882; fax 919/477-0512. 120 rms, 3 story. S $47.99-$61.99; D $50.99-$63.99. Crib free. Pet accepted, some restrictions. TV; cable (premium). Complimentary coffee in lobby.

Restaurant nearby. Ck-out noon. Business servs avail. Cr cds: A, C, D, DS, MC, V.

★★★ **REGAL UNIVERSITY HOTEL.** *2800 Campus Walk Ave (27705).* 919/383-8575; fax 919/383-8495; toll-free 800/222-8888. Email *regaluni@gte.net.* 315 rms, 4 story. S, D $99-$185; each addl $15; suites $190-$375; under 18 free. Crib $10. TV; cable (premium). Complimentary continental bkfst. Coffee in rms. Heated pool; whirlpool, poolside serv. Restaurant 6:30 am-2 pm, 5-10:30 pm. Bar 11:30 am-midnight. Ck-out 11 am. Meeting rms. Business servs avail. Bellhops. Concierge. Free airport transportation. Exercise equipt. Refrigerator in suites; microwaves avail. Luxury level. Cr cds: A, D, DS, MC, V.

Hotels

★★ **DOUBLETREE GUEST SUITES.** *2515 Meridian Pkwy (27713), 1 blk N of I-40 Exit 278, near Research Triangle Park.* 919/361-4660; fax 919/361-2256; res 800/222-8733; toll-free 800/365-9876. Email *dtgsrdu@aol.com.* 203 suites, 7 story. Suites $144-$175; under 18 free; wkend rates. Crib free. TV; cable (premium), VCR avail. 2 heated pools, 1 indoor; whirlpool. Complimentary coffee in rms. Restaurant 6:30 am-10 pm. Bar 11 am-midnight. Ck-out noon. Coin lndry. Meeting rms. Business center. Free airport transportation. Lighted tennis. Sauna. Refrigerators; microwaves avail. Private patios, balconies. Small lake adj; paddleboat rentals. Cr cds: A, C, D, DS, JCB, MC, V.

★★ **DURHAM FAIRFIELD INN.** *3710 Hillsborough Rd (27705).* 919/382-3388; fax 919/382-3388; res 800/228-2800. 135 rms, 3 story. S, D $119; under 18 free. Crib avail. Parking lot. Pool. TV; cable. Complimentary continental bkfst, toll-free calls. Restaurant nearby. Ck-out noon, ck-in 3 pm. Dry cleaning. Cr cds: A, C, D, DS, MC, V.

★★ **HILTON DURHAM.** *3838 Hillsborough (27705).* 919/383-8033; fax 919/383-4287; res 800/445-8667. Email *hiltondurh@aol.com.* 194 rms, 6 story. S $79-$139; D $79-$149; each addl $10; suites $129-$349; family rates. Crib free. TV; cable (premium). Pool; whirlpool. Coffee in rms. Restaurant 6 am-10 pm. Bar 2 pm-1 am; Sun to 11 pm. Ck-out noon. Meeting rms. Business center. In-rm modem link. Exercise equipt; sauna. Health club privileges. Some bathrm phones. Cr cds: A, C, D, DS, MC, V.

★★★ **MARRIOTT.** *201 Foster St (27701).* 919/768-6000; fax 919/768-6037. 187 rms, 10 story. S, D $79-$149; suites $199-$209. Crib free. TV; cable (premium). Swimming privileges. Coffee in rms. Restaurant 6:30-10:30 am, 11:30 am-2 pm, 5-10 pm. Bar 2 pm-midnight. Ck-out noon. Meeting rms. Business center. Gift shop. Exercise equipt. Health club privileges. Cr cds: A, C, D, DS, ER, JCB, MC, V.

★★ **MARRIOTT AT RESEARCH TRIANGLE PARK.** *4700 Guardian Dr (27703).* 919/941-6200; fax 919/941-6229; res 800/228-8290. www. marriott.com. 220 rms, 6 story, 4 suites. Sep-Nov: S, D $159; suites $250; lower rates rest of yr. Crib avail. Parking lot. Indoor pool, whirlpool. TV; cable (premium). Complimentary coffee in rms, newspaper. Restaurant 7 am-11 pm. Bar. Meeting rms. Business center. Bellhops. Concierge. Dry cleaning. Gift shop. Free airport transportation. Exercise privileges, sauna. Golf. Tennis. Cr cds: A, C, D, DS, ER, JCB, MC, V.

★★★ **SHERATON IMPERIAL HOTEL & CONVENTION CENTER.** *4700 Emperor Blvd (27703), 1 blk S of I-40 Exit 282.* 919/941-5050; fax 919/941-5156; res 800/325-3535. www. sheratonrtp.com. 312 rms, 10 story, 19 suites. Feb-Apr, Sep-Nov: S, D $195; suites $200; lower rates rest of yr. Crib avail. Valet parking avail. Pool. TV; cable (premium), VCR avail. Complimentary coffee in rms, newspaper, toll-free calls. Restaurant. Bar. Ck-out noon, ck-in 3 pm. Conference center, meeting rms. Business center. Bellhops. Concierge. Dry cleaning. Gift shop. Free airport transportation.

Exercise rm. Golf. Tennis, 2 courts. Cr cds: A, D, DS, MC, V.

★ ★ ★ ★ **WASHINGTON DUKE INN & GOLF CLUB.** *3001 Cameron Blvd (27706), on Duke Univ campus, 20 min from Raleigh/Durham Airport. 919/490-0999; fax 919/493-0015; toll-free 800/443-3853. www.washington dukeinn.com.* This inn and golf club offers 164 rooms and seven suites with charming, English-country decor. The 18-hole championship golf course was designed by Robert Trent Jones, and nongolfers will enjoy the outdoor pool overlooking the 9th fairway and Duke Faculty Club's 10 tennis courts. Dine indoors at the Fairview Restaurant or request an outdoor table-with-a-view at Terrace-On-The-Green. 171 rms, 5 story. S, D $170-$315; each addl $20; suites $435-$725; under 17 free; golf plans. Crib free. TV; cable (premium), VCR avail. Heated pool. Complimentary coffee in lobby. Restaurant 7 am-10 pm. Bar 11:30 am-midnight; Sun brunch, 2 sittings: 11:30 am and 1:30 pm. Ck-out noon. Meeting rms. Business center. In-rm modem link. Concierge. Gift shop. Airport transportation. Lighted tennis, pro. 18-hole golf, greens fee $55-$80, pro, putting green, driving range. Health club privileges. Refrigerators avail. Cr cds: A, DS, MC, V.

★ ★ **WYNDHAM GARDEN HOTEL.** *4620 S Miami Blvd (27703), 10 mi SE on I-40, Exit 281, near Research Triangle Park. 919/941-6066; fax 919/941-6363; res 800/972-0264; toll-free 800/528-1234.* 172 rms, 7 story. S, D $129-$159; each addl $10; suites $160-$210; under 16 free; wkend rates. Crib free. TV; cable (premium). Pool; whirlpool. Complimentary coffee in rms. Restaurant 6:30-10 am, 11 am-2:30 pm, 5-10 pm; Sat 7 am-2:30 pm, 5-10 pm. Bar 5 pm-midnight; Fri, Sat to 11 pm. Ck-out noon. Meeting rms. Business servs avail. In-rm modem link. Free airport transportation. Exercise equipt. Some refrigerators, microwaves. Cr cds: A, C, D, DS, MC, V.

B&Bs/Small Inns

★ ★ **ARROWHEAD INN BED & BREAKFAST.** *106 Mason Rd (27712),* US 501, 7 mi N of I-85. 919/477-8430; fax 919/471-9538; toll-free 800/528-2207. Email info@arrowheadinn.com; www.arrowhead.com. 6 rms, 2 story, 2 suites. Mar-June, Sep-Nov: S $110; D $145; each addl $20; suites $215; lower rates rest of yr. Crib avail. Parking lot. TV; cable, VCR avail, CD avail. Complimentary full bkfst, coffee in rms, newspaper, toll-free calls. Ck-out 11 am, ck-in 3 pm. Meeting rms. Business center. Concierge. Gift shop. Whirlpool. Golf, 18 holes. Tennis, 3 courts. Hiking trail. Picnic facilities. Cr cds: A, D, DS, MC, V.

★ **HILLSBOROUGH HOUSE INN.** *209 E Tryon St (27278), 15 mi W on I-85. 919/644-1600; fax 919/644-1308; toll-free 800/616-1660. www.citysearch. com/rdu/hillsboroughinn.* 6 rms, 2 story. No rm phones. S, D $95-$125; suite $200. Children over 10 yrs only. TV in sitting rm; cable (premium). Pool. Complimentary bkfst. Restaurant nearby. Ck-out 11 am, ck-in 3 pm. Portions of this large frame house date to 1790; decor incl work by local artists. On 7 acres. Totally nonsmoking. Cr cds: A, DS, MC, V.

All Suite

★ ★ **HAWTHORN SUITES.** *300 Meredith Dr (27713), I-40 Exit 278. 919/361-1234; fax 919/361-1213; toll-free 800/527-1133. Email hshotel@bell south.net; www.hawthorn.com.* 3 story, 100 suites. May: S $145; D $180; suites $180; lower rates rest of yr. Crib avail. Pet accepted, some restrictions, fee. Parking lot. Lap pool. TV; cable. Complimentary full bkfst, coffee in rms, newspaper, toll-free calls. Restaurant nearby. Ck-out noon, ck-in 3 pm. Meeting rms. Dry cleaning, coin lndry. Free airport transportation. Exercise privileges. Golf. Cr cds: A, C, D, DS, MC, V.

Restaurants

★ **BULLOCK'S BBQ.** *3330 Quebec (27705). 919/383-3211.* Specializes in barbecued pork, seafood, chicken. Hrs: 11:30 am-8 pm. Closed Sun, Mon; 2 wks July, 1 wk Christmas. Lunch, dinner $5-$9. Child's menu.

Family-owned for over 50 yrs. No cr cds accepted.

D ⌐

★★ **CAFE PARIZADE.** *2200 W Main St (27705). 919/286-9712. Email foodpassion@mindspring.com; www. parizade.com.* Specializes in angel hair pasta, lump crab meat risotto. Hrs: 11:30 am-2:30 pm, 5:30-10 pm; Fri, Sat 11 pm; Sun to 9 pm. Res accepted. Wine, beer. Lunch $5.95-$9.50; dinner $9.50-$28. Entertainment. Cr cds: A, D, DS, MC, V.

D

★★★ **FAIRVIEW.** *3001 Cameron Blvd. 919/493-6699. Email wdi@ netmar.com; www.washingtondukeinn. com.* Specializes in seasonal seafood, pan-seared veal chops, game. Own desserts. Hrs: 7 am-10 pm; Sun brunch sittings 11:30 am and 1:30 pm. Res accepted. Bar. Wine cellar. Bkfst $7.95-$12.95; lunch $7.95-$20.95; dinner $16.95-$32. Sun brunch $18.95. Child's menu. Entertainment: pianist Thurs-Sat, Sun brunch. Valet parking. Formal atmosphere; view of grounds and 18th green. Cr cds: A, D, DS, MC, V.

D

★★★ **FOUR SQUARE.** *2701 Chapel Hill Rd (27707). 919/401-9877. Email ffoursquare@aol.com.* Contemporary menu. Hrs: 5:30-10 pm; Fri, Sat to 11 pm. Closed Sun. Res accepted. Wine, beer. Dinner $16-$29. Entertainment. Victorian house built in 1908. Cr cds: A, D, MC, V.

D

★★★ **MAGNOLIA GRILL.** *1002 9th St (27705). 919/286-3609.* Specializes in seasonal cuisine. Hrs: 6-9:30 pm; Fri, Sat 5:30-10 pm. Closed Sun, Mon; hols. Res accepted. Bar. Wine list. Dinner a la carte entrees: $13-$21. Local artwork on display. Cr cds: MC, V.

D

★★ **PAPA'S GRILL.** *1821 Hillandale Rd (27705), in Loehmann's Plaza at Croasdaile. 919/383-8502. www.papas-grill.citysearch.com.* Specializes in chicken, lamb, beef. Own baking. Hrs: 11:30 am-10 pm; Fri to 10:30 pm; Sat 5-10:30 pm. Closed Thanksgiving, Dec 25. Res accepted. Bar.

Lunch $5.95-$10.95; dinner $7.50-$26.95. Cr cds: A, D, DS, MC, V.

D ⌐

★★ **PARIZADE.** *2200 W Main St (27705). 919/286-9712. www.parizade. com.* Specializes in beef, chicken, duck. Hrs: 11:30 am-10 pm; Fri to 11 pm; Sat 5:30-11 pm; Sun 5:30-9 pm. Closed Dec 25. Res accepted. Bar. Lunch $5.95-$10.95; dinner $8.95-$25. Semiformal dining in Mediterranean atmosphere. Cr cds: A, D, DS, MC, V.

★ **PIE WORKS.** *607 Broad St (27707). 919/286-6670.* Italian menu. Specializes in pasta. Hrs: 11 am-10 pm; Fri, Sat to 11 pm. Closed hols. Wine, beer. Lunch $4.99-$20.99; dinner $7.99-$20.99. Child's menu. Entertainment. Cr cds: A, C, D, DS, ER, MC, V.

D

★★ **TAVERNA NIKOS.** *905 W Main (27701). 919/682-0043. www.taverna nikos.citysearch.com.* Specializes in lamb steak, grilled salmon, mamoussaka. Hrs: 11 am-3 pm, 5-10 pm. Closed Sun. Res accepted. Wine, beer. Lunch $4.50-$9; dinner $8.50-$16. Entertainment. Cr cds: A, C, D, MC, V.

D

Edenton (B-7)

Settled 1658 **Pop** 5,268 **Elev** 16 ft
Area code 252 **Zip** 27932
Web www.edenton.com

Information Chamber of Commerce, 116 E King St, PO Box 245; 252/482-3400; or Historic Edenton, 108 N Broad St, PO Box 474, 252/482-2637

This is one of the oldest communities in North Carolina and was the capital of the colony for more than 22 years. The women of Edenton staged their own Revolutionary tea party on October 25, 1774, signing a resolution protesting British injustice. A bronze teapot, at the west side of the Courthouse Green, commemorates the event.

The seat of Chowan County, Edenton is now an important industrial town and marketing place. It is a charming town with the graciousness of the Old South and many houses and bldgs that date back to the 1700s. Joseph Hewes, a signer of the Declaration of Independence, lived here.

What to See and Do

Historic Edenton. Tour of historic properties, which may be seen individually or as a group; allow 2½ to 3 hrs for complete tour. (Apr-Dec, daily; rest of yr, Tues-Sun; closed hols; also day after Thanksgiving, 3 days at Christmas) Phone 252/482-2637. ¢¢

Chowan County Courthouse. (1767) A fine example of Georgian architecture, in continuous use since built. E King & Court Sts.

Cupola House. (1758) Considered an outstanding example of Jacobean architecture. Formal garden restored from 1769 map of Edenton. W Water & S Broad Sts.

Historic Edenton Visitor Center. Audiovisual program (free), exhibits, visitor info, gift shop, tickets for guided tours of Historic Edenton. 108 N Broad St.

James Iredell House. (1800/1827) Home of early attorney general of North Carolina who was appointed by George Washington to first US Supreme Court. E Church St.

St. Paul's Episcopal Church. (1736) A charming church with many old gravestones in its yard; 3 colonial governors are buried here. W Church & Broad Sts.

Merchant's Millpond State Park. This 2,900-acre swamp forest is dominated by massive gum and cypress trees. Pond fishing, canoeing (rentals); nature trails, picnicking, developed and primitive camping. Interpretive program. Standard fees. Contact Superintendent, Rte 1, Box 141-A, Gatesville 27938. 25 mi N on NC 32, 5 mi N of Gatesville on SR 1403. Phone 252/357-1191.

B&Bs/Small Inns

★★ **CAPTAIN'S QUARTERS INN.** *202 W Queen St (27932). 252/482-8945; toll-free 800/482-8945. Email captqtrinn@coastalnet.com; www. captainsquartersinn.com.* 8 rms, 2 story. S $55-$65; D $80-$95; suites $80. Children over 8 yrs only. TV; cable, VCR avail. Complimentary full bkfst. Restaurant nearby. Ck-out 11 am, ck-in 3-10 pm. Golf privileges. Tennis privileges. Bicycles avail. Built in 1907; antiques. Totally nonsmoking. Cr cds: MC, V.

D ⛷ 🏃 🖼 🔥

★ **GOVERNOR EDEN INN.** *304 N Broad St (27932). 252/482-2072; fax 252/482-3613. Email govedeninn@aol. com.* 4 rms, 2 story. S $70; D $90. Parking lot. TV; cable. Complimentary full bkfst, newspaper. Restaurant. Ck-out 11 am, ck-in 3 pm. Internet access avail. Golf. Tennis, 4 courts. Cr cds: A, MC, V.

🏃 🖼 🏃 🖼 🔥

★★★ **LORDS PROPRIETORS INN.** *300 N Broad St (27932). 252/482-3641; fax 252/482-2432; toll-free 800/348-8933. Email stay@edentoninn.com; www.edentoninn.com.* 20 rms in 3 bldgs, 2 story. MAP: S, D $185-$235; each addl $20, lower rates Sun-Mon. TV; cable (premium), VCR (movies). Pool privileges. Ck-out 11 am, ck-in 1 pm. Meeting rm. Business servs avail. Gift shop. Library. Three adj restored homes furnished with antiques. Cr cds: A, DS, MC, V.

D 🖼 🖼 🔥

★★ **TRESTLE HOUSE INN.** *632 Soundside Rd (27932), 4 mi S on NC 32, turn right on Soundside Rd. 919/482-2282; fax 919/482-7003; res 800/645-8466. Email thinn@coastalnet.com; www.edenton.com/trestlehouse.* 5 rms, 2 story. No rm phones. S $60-$70; D $80-$100; each addl $15; wkly rates. TV; cable, VCR avail (movies). Complimentary full bkfst; afternoon refreshments. Ck-out 11 am, ck-in 2 pm. Business servs avail. Tennis privileges. 18-hole golf privileges. Picnic tables. Private lake fed by Albermarle Sound. Some antiques. Totally nonsmoking. Cr cds: A, MC, V.

🐟 🏃 🖼 🖼 🔥 SC

Elizabeth City

(B-8)

Settled ca 1665 **Pop** 18,472 **Elev** 18 ft **Area code** 252 **Zip** 27909 **Web** www.elizcity.com

Information Elizabeth City Area Chamber of Commerce, 502 E

Ehringhaus St, PO Box 426; 252/335-4365

A town with a freshwater harbor on the Pasquotank River and accessible to the ocean, Elizabeth City has seen seafaring activity since the middle of the 17th century. The town was chartered in 1793 at the narrows of the river as Redding, and renamed Elizabeth City in 1801. The Dismal Swamp Canal, dug in 1793, provided a critical north-south transportation route and brought prosperity to Elizabeth City. Shipyards, warehouses, fisheries, tanneries, sawmills, and other industries flourished along with commission merchants, artisans, and navigators; trading occured with Norfolk, the West Indies, New England, New York, and Charleston.

Although captured in the Civil War, Elizabeth City sustained minor damage. Today, many antebellum homes still stand alongside the historic homes and commercial buildings of the late 19th and early 20th centuries, a testament to the vitality of the community. Wood, agriculture, small specialty industries, and the United States Coast Guard contribute to the area's steady economic growth. The town also welcomes boating traffic from the Intracoastal Waterway, and is a coveted location for sportfishing and hunting. It serves as a gateway to Nags Head and Cape Hatteras National Seashore (see).

Annual Events

RiverSpree. Water events, arts, crafts, live entertainment. Late May.

Albemarle Craftsman's Fair. Late Oct.

Historic Ghostwalk. Historic homes tour with skits. Late Oct.

Mistletoe Show. Crafts, wood carvings. Second wkend Nov.

Motels/Motor Lodges

★★ **COMFORT INN.** *306 S Hughes Blvd (27909). 252/338-8900; fax 252/338-6420; toll-free 800/638-7949.* 80 rms, 5 story, 28 suites. S, D $55-$95; each addl $8; suites $65-$105; under 18 free; higher rates hol wkends. Crib free. TV; cable (premium), VCR avail (movies). Pool. Complimentary continental bkfst. Restaurant nearby. Ck-out 11 am.

Business servs avail. In-rm modem link. Refrigerator in suites. Cr cds: A, C, D, DS, MC, V.
[D] [≈] [≋] [🏃] [SC]

★★ **HAMPTON INN.** *402 Halstead Blvd (27909). 252/333-1800; fax 252/333-1801; res 800/426-7866.* 101 rms, 5 story, 10 suites. S, D $56-$80; suites $85-$120; under 18 free. Crib free. TV; cable. Complimentary continental bkfst, coffee in rms. Restaurant nearby 6:30 am-10 pm. Ck-out 11 am. Meeting rms. Business servs avail. In-rm modem link. Valet serv. Sundries. Health club privileges. Pool. Some in-rm whirlpools; refrigerator in suites. Cr cds: A, D, DS, MC, V.
[D] [≈] [≋] [🏃] [SC]

★★ **HOLIDAY INN.** *522 S Hughes Blvd (27909). 252/338-3951; fax 252/338-6225.* 158 rms, 2 story. S $60-$75; D $65-$75; each addl $6; under 19 free. Crib free. TV; cable (premium). Pool. Complimentary continental bkfst, coffee in rms. Restaurant 6:30-10 am, 5-10 pm. Rm serv (dinner only). Bar 5 pm-midnight. Ck-out noon. Coin lndry. Meeting rms. Business servs avail. In-rm modem link. Exercise equipt. Health club privileges. Cr cds: A, C, D, DS, JCB, MC, V.
[D] [≈] [🏃] [≋] [🏃] [SC]

Restaurant

★ **MARINA.** *Camden Causeway (27909), ½ mi E on US 158. 252/335-7307.* Specializes in steak, seafood. Hrs: 5-10 pm; Sun 11 am-9 pm. Closed Mon; Jan 1, Thanksgiving, Dec 25. Lunch, dinner $5-$14.95. Child's menu. Overlooks Pasquotank River. Cr cds: MC, V.
[D] [≋]

Fayetteville

(D-5) *See also Goldsboro*

Founded 1739 **Pop** 75,695 **Elev** 102 ft
Area code 910 **Web** www.facvb.com

Information Convention & Visitors Bureau, 245 Person St, 28301; 910/483-5311 or 800/255-8217

In 1783 the towns of Cross Creek and Campbellton merged and were renamed Fayetteville for the Marquis de Lafayette, becoming the first US city to thus honor him. It was the site of North Carolina's Constitutional Convention in 1787 and the capital of the state from 1789-93. By 1831 it had become a busy commercial city.

Fayetteville is the state's farthest inland port, at the head of navigation on the Cape Fear River, with an 8-foot-deep channel connecting it to the Intracoastal Waterway. Fayetteville State University (1867) and Methodist College (1956) are located here. In 1985, Fayetteville received the All-America City Award. Today, it's a center for retail, manufacturing, and conventions, as well as the home of Fort Bragg and Pope Air Force Base.

What to See and Do

Cape Fear Botanical Garden. On 85 acres overlooking Cross Creek and the Cape Fear River. Wildflowers, oaks, native plants. Nature trails. (Mid-Dec-mid-Feb, Mon-Sat; rest of yr, daily; closed hols) 536 N Eastern Blvd. Phone 910/486-0221. ¢

First Presbyterian Church. Classic Southern Colonial-style architecture and whale-oil chandeliers. Among contributors to the original bldg (destroyed by fire in 1831) were James Monroe and John Quincy Adams. Tours (by appt only). Bow & Ann Sts. Phone 910/483-0121.

Fort Bragg and Pope AFB. 10 mi NW on NC 24. Here are

82nd Airborne Div War Memorial Museum. Weapons, relics of WWI, WWII, and Vietnam; library; gift shop. (Tues-Sun; closed Jan 1, Dec 25) Ardennes St. Phone 910/432-3443. **FREE**

John F. Kennedy Special Warfare Museum. Guerrilla warfare weapons. (Tues-Sun; closed hols) Ardennes St. (Bldg. #D-2502). Phone 910/432-1533. **FREE**

Parachute Jumps. Phone 910/396-6366 for schedule information.

Museum of the Cape Fear. Retraces the regional cultural history from prehistoric Indian artifacts through 20th century. A branch of the North Carolina Museum of History. (Tues-Sun; closed hols) 801 Arsenal Ave. Phone 910/486-1330. **FREE**

Annual Events

Dogwood Festival. Late Apr.

Pope AFB/Fort Bragg Joint Open House & Air Show. Aerial demonstrations, aircraft and equipment displays, military drill team performances. Phone 910/394-4183. Aug or Sep.

Motels/Motor Lodges

★★ **CLARION PLAZA HOTEL.** *1965 Cedar Creek Rd (28301), I-95 Exit 49.* 910/323-8282; fax 910/323-4039; toll-free 800/253-7808. 168 rms, 4 story. S, D $59-$69; each addl $6; suites $69-$79; under 18 free; golf plans. Crib free. TV; cable (premium). Indoor/outdoor pool; whirlpool. Complimentary bkfst buffet, coffee in rms. Restaurant 6 am-2 pm, 5-9 pm. Bar. Ck-out noon. Meeting rms. Business center. Exercise equipt; sauna, steam rm. Some private patios. Luxury level. Cr cds: A, C, D, DS, JCB, MC, V.

⬛ 🏊 ⛷ 🔜 🧖 SC 🏃

★★ **COMFORT INN.** *1957 Cedar Creek Rd (28301).* 910/323-8333; fax 910/323-3946; res 800/228-5150; toll-free 800/621-6596. 120 rms, 2 story. Jan-Feb, Apr-Sep: S $75; D $80; each addl $6; under 18 free; lower rates rest of yr. Crib avail. Pet accepted, some restrictions. Parking lot. Pool. TV; cable (premium). Complimentary full bkfst, coffee in rms, newspaper, toll-free calls. Restaurant. Ck-out noon, ck-in 3 pm. Meeting rm. Business servs avail. Dry cleaning. Gift shop. Exercise equipt. Golf, 18 holes. Tennis, 2 courts. Cr cds: A, C, D, DS, ER, JCB, MC, V.

⬛ 🐾 ⛷ 🎿 🔜 ⛷ 🔜 🧖

★★ **COMFORT INN CROSS CREEK.** *1922 Skibo Rd (28314), off US 401 Bypass.* 910/867-1777; fax 910/867-0325; res 800/228-5150; toll-free 800/537-2268. 176 rms, 4 story. S, D $50-$69; each addl $6; suites $75-$135; under 16 free. Crib free. TV; cable (premium). Pool. Complimentary continental bkfst. Restaurant nearby. Coin lndry. Ck-out noon. Business servs avail. Health club privileges. Bathrm phone, refrigerator in suites. Cr cds: A, C, D, DS, ER, JCB, MC, V.

⬛ 🏊 ⛷ 🔜 🧖

★ **DAYS INN.** *2065 Cedar Creek Rd (28301). 910/483-6191; fax 910/483-4113; res 800/621-6594; toll-free 800/329-7466.* 122 rms, 2 story. S $39-$49; D $45-$55; each addl $6; under 12 free. Crib free. TV; cable (premium). Pool. Complimentary continental bkfst. Restaurant 24 hrs. Ck-out 11 am. Meeting rms. Business servs avail. Game rm. Cr cds: A, C, D, DS, ER, JCB, MC, V.

[D] [≈] [≥‡] [🔥] [SC]

★ **ECONO LODGE.** *1952 Cedar Creek Rd (28306), jct NC 210 and US 53; I-95 Exit 49. 910/433-2100; fax 910/433-2009.* 150 rms, 2 story. S $46.95-$54.95; D $49.95-$59.95; each addl $5; under 18 free. Crib free. TV; cable (premium). Pool. Complimentary continental bkfst. Restaurant nearby. Ck-out noon. Business servs avail. Cr cds: A, D, DS, MC, V.

[D] [≈] [≥‡] [🔥]

★★ **FAIRFIELD INN CROSS CREEK.** *562 Cross Creek Mall (28303). 910/487-1400; fax 910/487-1400; res 800/228-2800.* 134 rms, 3 story. S $49-$69; D $55.95-$69.95; each addl $6; under 18 free. Crib free. TV; cable (premium). Pool. Complimentary continental bkfst. Restaurant nearby. Ck-out noon. Business servs avail. In-rm modem link. Valet serv. Cr cds: A, C, D, DS, MC, V.

[D] [≈] [≥‡] [🔥]

★★ **HAMPTON INN.** *1922 Cedar Creek Rd (28301), at I-95 Exit 49. 910/323-0011; fax 910/323-8764.* 122 rms, 2 story. S $59; D $65; under 18 free. Crib free. TV; cable (premium). Pool. Complimentary continental bkfst. Restaurant nearby. Ck-out noon. Business servs avail. In-rm modem link. Valet serv. Cr cds: A, DS, MC, V.

[D] [≈] [≥‡] [🔥] [SC]

★★ **HOLIDAY INN.** *1944 Cedar Creek Rd (28301), I-95 Exit 49. 336/323-1600; fax 910/323-0691; toll-free 800/465-4329.* 198 rms, 2 story. Mar-Nov: S, D $69-$109; each addl $5; kits. $89-$125; under 12 free; lower rates rest of yr. Crib free. TV; cable (premium). Indoor pool; whirlpool. Complimentary coffee in rms. Restaurant 6:30 am-2 pm, 5-10 pm. Bar. Ck-out noon. Coin lndry. Meeting rms. Business servs avail. In-rm modem link. Bellhops. Free airport transporta-tion. Exercise equipt. Game rm. Cr cds: A, C, D, DS, ER, JCB, MC, V.

[D] [≈] [🛪] [≥‡] [🔥] [SC]

★★ **HOLIDAY INN EXPRESS.** *1706 Skibo Rd (28303). 910/867-6777; fax 910/864-9541; res 800/HOLIDAY; toll-free 877/867-6777. Email hiexpressnc@aol.com.* 54 rms, 4 story, 28 suites. Mar-Aug: S $58-$88; D $62-$92; each addl $6; suites $60-$95; under 17 free; package plans; lower rates rest of yr. Crib free. TV; cable (premium), VCR avail (movies). Complimentary continental bkfst, coffee in rms. Restaurant adj 6 am-midnight. Ck-out 11 am. Meeting rms. Business servs avail. In-rm modem link. Pool. Many refrigerators, microwaves. Cr cds: A, C, D, DS, ER, JCB, MC, V.

[D] [≈] [🛪] [≥‡] [🔥]

★ **HOWARD JOHNSON.** *218 Eastern Blvd (28301). 910/483-1113; fax 910/483-3366; toll-free 800/446-4656.* 134 units, 2 story, 12 kits. S, D $35.95-$49.95; kit. units avail; wkly rates. TV; cable. Pool. Complimentary coffee. Restaurant 11 am-9 pm. Ck-out noon. Business servs avail. In-rm modem link. Bathrm phones. Cr cds: A, C, D, DS, MC, V.

[D] [≈] [≥‡] [🔥] [SC]

★★ **QUALITY INN AMBASSADOR.** *I-95 Bus Rte (28306), jct I-95 Business, US 301S. 910/485-8135; fax 910/485-8682; res 800/228-5151; toll-free 800/828-2346.* 59 rms, 1 story, 3 suites. Mar-Oct: S $70; each addl $6; under 18 free; lower rates rest of yr. Crib avail, fee. Street parking. Pool. TV; cable. Complimentary coffee in rms, newspaper, toll-free calls. Restaurant 6 am-9 pm. Ck-out noon, ck-in noon. Meeting rm. Business servs avail. Bellhops. Dry cleaning. Golf. Tennis. Picnic facilities. Cr cds: A, C, D, DS, ER, JCB, MC, V.

[🛏] [🎾] [≈] [🛪] [≥‡] [🔥]

Conference Center

★★ **HOLIDAY INN BORDEAUX.** *1707 Owen Dr (28304). 910/323-0111; fax 910/484-9444; res 800/465-4329; toll-free 800/325-0211. Email hotel4u@fayettevillenc.com; www.fayettevillenc.com/bordeaux.* 289 rms, 9 story, 7 suites. Mar-Oct: S, D $88; suites $85; under 16 free; lower rates rest of yr. Crib avail. Pet accepted, fee. Valet parking avail. Pool. TV; cable (DSS). Complimentary continental bkfst, coffee in rms, newspaper, toll-free calls. Restaurant 6 am-10 pm. Bar. Ck-out 11 am, ck-in 3 pm. Conference center, meeting rms. Business center. Bellhops. Concierge. Dry cleaning, coin lndry. Free airport transportation. Exercise privileges. Golf, 18 holes. Tennis, 3 courts. Bike rentals. Supervised children's activities. Hiking trail. Picnic facilities. Video games. Cr cds: A, C, D, DS, JCB, MC, V.

Restaurants

★ **CANTON STATION.** *301 N McPherson Church Rd (28303).* *910/864-5555.* Specializes in seafood, pork, chicken. Hrs: 11:30 am-10 pm. Res accepted. Bar. Lunch $3.50-$5.15. Buffet: $5.15; dinner $7.10-$14.95. Buffet: $7.10. Chinese decor. Cr cds: A, DS, MC, V.

★★ **DE LAFAYETTE.** *6112 Cliffdale Rd (28314).* *910/868-4600.* Specializes in French and Creole cooking. Hrs: 5-10 pm. Closed Sun, Mon; hols. Res accepted. Bar. Dinner a la carte entrees: $12-$26. Entertainment: piano; jazz quartet Fri. Formal dining rms with views of lake. French decor. Cr cds: A, C, D, DS, MC, V.

★★ **TRIO CAFE.** *201 S McPherson Church Rd (28303).* *910/868-2443.* *www.sayscope.com.* Specializes in steaks, fresh pasta, fresh seafood. Hrs: 11:30 am-10 pm; Sun to 3 pm. Closed Dec 25. Res accepted. Bar. Lunch, dinner a la carte entrees: $8.50-$24.50. Parking. Open kitchen. Art Deco decor. Cr cds: A, D, DS, MC, V.

Fontana Dam

See also Bryson City

Founded 1947 **Pop** 130 (est)
Elev 2,900 ft **Area code** 704
Zip 28733

At the southwest corner of Great Smoky Mountains National Park, this village was originally built for the construction crew that worked on the Fontana Dam project. The 480-foot dam is crossed by the Appalachian Trail. The region is now a resort area, with swimming, fishing, boating, hiking, and horseback riding centering around Fontana Lake, 30 miles long.

Fort Raleigh National Historic Site

See also Cape Hatteras National Seashore, Kill Devil Hills, Nags Head; Outer Banks

(Off US 64, 3 mi N of Manteo)

The first English colony in America was attempted here on Roanoke Island in 1585. Virginia Dare, born here August 18, 1587, was the first child of English parents born in what is now the United States.

Governor John White left the island for England a few days after Virginia's birth, intending to return shortly with supplies. He was detained by the war with Spain and did not get back until August, 1590. The colony had disappeared, leaving behind only the mysterious word "CROATOAN" cut into a tree or post.

What happened to the colonists is unknown, though some believe that the present-day Lumbee Indians of Robeson County descend from them. Fort Raleigh has been excavated and the fort built by the colonists reconstructed. The Lindsay Warren Visitor Center has relics, an audiovisual program, and exhibits. Park and Visitor Center (daily; closed Dec 25). For further information, contact Fort Raleigh National Historic Site, Rte 1, Box 675, Manteo 27954; 252/473-5772. **FREE**

Seasonal Event

***The Lost Colony* Outdoor Drama.** Waterside Theater, 3 mi NW of Manteo on US 64/264. Outdoor drama by Pulitzer Prize winner Paul Green about the first English colony established in the New World, whose curious disappearance remains a mystery to this day. Sun-Fri eves. Res advised. Contact 1409 US 64, Manteo 27954; 919/473-3414 or 800/488-5012. Mid-June-late Aug.

Franklin (Macon County)

(C-1) *See also Cashiers, Highlands*

Pop 2,873 **Elev** 2,133 ft
Area code 828 **Zip** 28734
Web www.franklin-chamber.com
Information Chamber of Commerce, 425 Porter St; 828/524-3161 or 800/336-7829

Home of the Cowee Valley ruby mines, Franklin attracts rockhounds who often find interesting gems in surface mines. Franklin is surrounded by waterfalls, mountain lakes, and streams that offer excellent fishing for trout and bass, or boating, tubing, and swimming. Around the county are 420,000 acres of the Nantahala National Forest, which offers hiking trails, camping, and fishing. A Ranger District office is located here. The Appalachian Trail bisects the western part of the county through Standing Indian Wildlife Management area and over Wayah Bald Mountain.

Annual Events

Macon County Gemboree. Jewelry and gem exhibits, ruby mining, field trips. Late July.

Macon County Fair. Mid-Sep.

Motels/Motor Lodges

★ **COUNTRY INN TOWN - MOTEL.** *668 E Main St (28734). 828/524-4451; fax 828/524-0703; toll-free 800/233-7555.* 46 rms. S $34-$37; D $42-$45; each addl $5; under 12 free; higher rates fall foliage season. Crib $5. TV; cable. Pool. Ck-out 11 am. Sundries. Health club privileges. On Little Tennessee River. Cr cds: A, DS, MC, V.

★ **DAYS INN.** *1320 E Main St (28734), US 441/23N, 1 mi N. 828/524-6491; fax 704/369-9636; res 800/329-7466.* 41 rms. May-Oct: S, D $54-$95; each addl $5; higher rates: Gemboree, Labor Day wkend, Oct; lower rates rest of yr. Pet accepted. TV; cable (premium). Pool. Complimentary continental bkfst. Restaurant opp 7 am-11 pm. Business servs avail. Microwaves avail. Scenic view of mountains. Cr cds: A, C, D, DS, MC, V.

B&B/Small Inn

★ **HERITAGE INN BED & BREAKFAST.** *43 Heritage Hollow Dr (28734), ½ mi W off N Main St. 828/524-4150; res 888/524-4150. Email heritage@ smnet.net; www.heritageinnbb.com.* 5 rms, 2 story, 1 suite. Apr-Nov: S $65; D $75; each addl $10; suites $105; under 12 free; lower rates rest of yr. Parking lot. TV; cable, VCR avail, CD avail. Complimentary full bkfst, coffee in rms. Ck-out 11 am, ck-in 2 pm. Meeting rm. Gift shop. Golf. Downhill skiing. Hiking trail. Cr cds: A, D, MC, V.

Restaurants

★★ **FROG & OWL KITCHEN.** *46 E Main St (28734). 828/349-4112.* Eclectic menu. Specializes in duck, fresh seafood, pasta. Hrs: 11 am-3 pm. Closed Sun. Lunch $5-$7. Intimate dining. Family-owned. Cr cds: MC, V.

★ **GAZEBO CAFE.** *44 Heritage Hollow (28734). 828/524-8783. Email kknec74931@aol.com.* Specializes in deli and specialty sandwiches, soups. Own pasta. Hrs: 10:30 am-8 pm; Sat-Mon to 4 pm. Closed hols; late Oct-May. Lunch, dinner $3.95-$5.95. Child's menu. Cr cds: MC, V.

Gastonia

(C-3) *See also Charlotte*

Pop 54,732 **Elev** 816 ft **Area code** 704
Web www.gaston.org
Information Gaston County Travel and Tourism, 2551 Pembroke, PO Box 2339, 28054; 704/867-2170 or 800/849-9994

This is an industrial town in the Piedmont, turning out textiles, textile machinery and supplies. In addition, Gastonia produces chain saws, plastics, oil seals, lithium, automotive parts, trucks, and truck parts.

Motel/Motor Lodge

★★ **HAMPTON INN GASTONIA.**
1859 Remount Rd (28054), I-85 Exit New Hope Rd. 704/866-9090; fax 704/866-7070; res 800/426-7866. 109 rms, 5 story. S, D $64-$71; under 12 free. Crib free. TV; cable (premium). Pool. Complimentary continental bkfst, coffee in rms. Restaurant adj open 24 hrs. Ck-out noon. Meeting rm. Cr cds: A, C, D, DS, MC, V.
⊡ ⇌ 🛠 ⊠ 🔥

Goldsboro (C-6)

Established 1847 **Pop** 40,709
Elev 121 ft **Area code** 919
Web www.goldsboro.com
Information Wayne County Chamber of Commerce, PO Box 1107, 27533-1107; 919/734-2241

Center of the bright-leaf tobacco belt, Goldsboro is also the seat of Wayne County and home of Seymour Johnson Air Force Base. Poultry production and tobacco warehousing and processing are important industries. There are also many food, wood product, and textile plants here.

Motels/Motor Lodges

★★ **BEST WESTERN GOLDS-BORO.** *801 US 70 Bypass E (27534). 919/735-7911; fax 919/735-5030; res 800/528-1234. www.bestwestern.com.* 113 rms, 2 story, 3 suites. S $61; D $66; each addl $5; suites $96; under

12 free. Crib avail. Pet accepted, some restrictions, fee. Parking lot. Pool. TV; cable (premium). Complimentary continental bkfst, coffee in rms, newspaper, toll-free calls. Restaurant. Bar. Meeting rms. Business servs avail. Coin lndry. Exercise privileges. Golf. Tennis. Cr cds: A, C, D, DS, JCB, MC, V.
⊡ ⇌ 🛠 🏃 ⊠ 🏃 ⊠ 🔥

★★ **DAYS INN.** *2000 Wayne Memorial Dr (27534). 919/734-9471; fax 919/736-2623; res 800/329-7466.* 121 rms, 2 story. S $46-$52; D $49-$54; each addl $4. Crib free. Pet accepted. TV; cable. Pool. Restaurant 6 am-9 pm; Sun to 4 pm. Ck-out 11 am. Business servs avail. Sundries. Exercise equipt. Health club privileges. Some refrigerators, microwaves. Cr cds: A, DS, MC, V.
⊡ ⇌ 🏃 🏃 ⊠ 🏃 ⊠ 🔥

★★ **HAMPTON INN - GOLDS-BORO.** *905 N Spence Ave (27534). 919/778-1800; fax 919/778-5891; res 800/426-7866.* 111 rms, 4 story. S, D $58-$68; each addl $6; suites $141; under 18 free. Crib free. TV; cable (premium). Pool. Complimentary continental bkfst, coffee in rms. Restaurant adj 9 am-midnight. Ck-out noon. Meeting rms. Business servs avail. In-rm modem link. Coin lndry. Exercise equipt. Some refrigerators. Cr cds: A, DS, MC, V.
⊡ ⊠ 🏃 ⊠ 🔥

★★ **HOLIDAY INN EXPRESS.** *909 N Spence Ave (27534). 919/751-1999; fax 919/751-1506; toll-free 800/465-4329.* 122 rms, 5 story. S, D $60-$75; each addl $6; suites $100-$140; under 18 free. TV; cable (premium). Pool. Complimentary continental bkfst, coffee in rms. Restaurant adj. Ck-out noon. Sundries. Business servs avail. In-rm modem link. Exercise equipt. Health club privileges. Cr cds: A, C, D, DS, JCB, MC, V.
⊡ ⊠ 🏃 ⊠ 🔥 **SC**

★★ **QUALITY INN & SUITES.** *708 Us Hwy 70 (27534), 1½ mi NE on US 13, 70 Bypass. 919/735-7901; fax 919/734-2946; res 800/228-5151.* 108 rms, 2 story. S $58-$78; D $64-$78; each addl $6; suites $99-$135; under 12 free. Pet accepted. TV; cable (premium). Pool. Restaurant 6-9 am, 5-10 pm. Bar 5-11 pm; wkends to 1 am. Ck-out noon. Meeting rms. Business servs avail. In-rm modem link. Exercise equipt. Health club privileges. Cr cds: A, D, DS, MC, V.

★★ RAMADA INN. *808 W Grantham St (27530), jct US 70 and US 117s. 919/736-4590; fax 919/735-3218.* 128 rms, 2 story. S $39-$74; D $43-$79; suites from $85; under 18 free. Crib free. Pet accepted. TV; cable (premium). Pool. Restaurant 5 am-10 pm. Bar 5 pm-2 am; entertainment Fri, Sat. Ck-out noon. Coin lndry. Meeting rms. Business servs avail. In-rm modem link. Valet serv. Sundries. Health club privileges. Game rm. Some refrigerators, microwaves. Picnic table. Cr cds: A, C, D, DS, JCB, MC, V.

Restaurant

★ CAPTAIN BOB'S SEAFOOD. *430 N Berkeley Blvd (27534), across from Eastgate Shopping Center. 919/778-8332.* Specializes in seafood, chargrilled steak. Salad bar. Hrs: 11 am-9 pm; Fri to 9:30 pm; Sat 4-9:30 pm; Sun 11 am-8 pm. Closed Mon; Thanksgiving, Dec 25. Res accepted Tues-Fri. Lunch $3.99-$5.25; dinner $5.95-$9.25. Child's menu. Nautical decor. Cr cds: MC, V.

Great Smoky Mountains National Park

See also Bryson City, Cherokee, Fontana Dam, Maggie Valley

(50 mi W of Asheville off US 19)

The Appalachian Mountains, product of a slow upthrusting of ancient sediments that took place more than 200 million years ago, stand tall and regal in this 800-square-mile area. Red spruce, basswood, eastern hemlock, yellow birch, white ash, cucumber trees, silverbells, Fraser fir, tulip poplar, red maple, and Fraser magnolias tower above hundreds of other species of flowering plants. Perhaps the most spectacular of these are the purple rhododendron, mountain laurel, and flame azalea, in bloom from early June to mid-July.

The moist climate has helped make this a rich wilderness. From early spring to late fall the "coves" (as the open valleys surrounded by peaks are called) and forest floors are covered with a succession of flowers with colorful variety. Summer brings heavy showers, days that are warm (although 15° to 20° cooler than in the valleys below), and cool nights. Autumn is breathtaking as the deciduous trees change color. Winter brings snow, occasionally heavy, and fog over the mountains. Winter is a very good time to visit the park; but be aware of temporary road closures.

Half in North Carolina and half in Tennessee, with the Appalachian Trail following the state line along the ridge for 70 miles, this is a place to hike. In the lowlands are the cabins, barns, and mills of the mountain people whose ancestors came years ago from England and Scotland. It is also a place to see the descendants of the once mighty Cherokee Nation, whose ancestors hid in the mountains from the soldiers in the winter of 1838-39 to avoid being driven over the Trail of Tears to Oklahoma. This is the tribe of Sequoyah, the brilliant chief who invented a written alphabet for the Cherokee people.

Stop first at one of the three visitor centers: Oconaluftee Center in North Carolina, two miles north of Cherokee on Newfound Gap Road, designated US 441 outside of park (daily; closed Dec 25; phone 423/436-1200); Sugarlands, in Tennessee, two miles southwest of Gatlinburg (daily; closed Dec 25; phone 423/436-1200); or Cades Cove, in Tennessee, ten miles SW of Townsend (daily, closed Dec 25; phone 423/436-1200). All have exhibits and information about the park. There are hundreds of miles of foot trails and bridle paths. Camping is popular; ask at any visitor center for locations and regulations. There are developed campgrounds (fee). For reservations at Elkmont, Cades Cove, or Smokemont phone 800/365-CAMP; reservations are not taken for other sites.

The views from Newfound Gap and the observation tower at Clingmans Dome (closed in winter) are spectacular. Cades Cove is an outdoor museum reflecting the life of the original mountain people, about 25 miles west of Sugarlands. It has log cabins and barns. Park naturalists conduct campfire programs and hikes during the summer. There are also self-guided nature trails. LeConte Lodge, reached only by foot or horseback, is an accommodation within the park; phone 423/429-5704 (late Mar-mid-Nov).

Fishing is permitted with a TN or NC state fishing license. Obtain list of regulations at visitor centers and campgrounds. The park is a wildlife sanctuary; any disturbance of plant or animal life is forbidden. Dogs and cats are not permitted on trails but may be brought in if kept on leash or other physical restrictive controls. Never feed, tease, or frighten bears; always give them a wide berth, as they can inflict serious injury. Watch bears from car with the windows closed. Park (daily). For the disabled, there is an all-access trail, the Sugarland Valley Nature Trail, equipped with special interpretive exhibits. Accessibility information is available at the visitor centers. **FREE**

For information contact the Superintendent, Great Smoky Mountains National Park, 107 Park Headquarters Rd, Gatlinburg, TN 37738; 423/436-1200.

Greensboro

(C-5) *See also Burlington, High Point*

Founded 1808 **Pop** 183,521
Elev 841 ft **Area code** 336
Web www.greensboronc.org
Information Greensboro Area Convention & Visitors Bureau, 317 S Greene St, 27401; 336/274-2282 or 800/344-2282

William Sydney Porter (O. Henry) was born and raised near Greensboro, a diversified Piedmont industrial city whose products are typical of North Carolina: textiles, cigarettes, machinery, and electronic components. It was settled by Quakers, Germans, and the Scotch-Irish with a zeal for political, religious, and economic freedom. Men from this region fought in the Revolution and the War of 1812, and turned to the Confederacy in 1861. It was in Greensboro, the rebel supply depot, that Jefferson Davis met General Johnston after Richmond fell in 1865 and agreed on surrender terms. Today it is an educational, manufacturing, and distribution center.

What to See and Do

Charlotte Hawkins Brown Memorial State Historic Site. North Carolina's first state historic site, honoring the achievements of African-American education in the state. In 1902, C.H. Brown, granddaughter of former slaves, founded Palmer Memorial Institute, which became one of the finest preparatory schools for blacks in the nation. Guided tours of historic campus (several bldgs being restored), visitor center, audiovisual program. Picnicking. (Apr-Oct, daily; rest of yr, Tues-Sun; closed hols) 10 mi E on I-85 to Exit 135, then ½ mi W on US 70. Phone 336/449-4846. **FREE**

✪ **Chinqua-Penn Plantation.** English-style country house, extensive formal and rose gardens; 27 rms contain furnishings, art objects from around the world; no pets; picnic area. (Mar-Dec, Tues-Sat, also Sun afternoons; closed July 4, Thanksgiving, Dec 25) 20 mi N on US 29, Exit Hwy 14, 3 mi NW on Wentworth Rd. Phone 336/349-4576. **¢¢**

Greensboro Historical Museum. Housed in 19th-century church; exhibits on first Lady Dolley Madison, author O. Henry; military history, incl Revolutionary Battle of Guilford Courthouse; 1960s lunch counter sit-ins; decorative arts; vintage autos; period furnishings. (Tues-Sun; closed hols) 130 Summit Ave. Phone 336/373-2043. **FREE**

Hagan-Stone Park. Swimming, fishing; hiking, picnicking, playground, camping (hookups, dump station). Park (all yr). Some fees. Pets on leash only. 6 mi S on US 421, then 2 mi W on Hagan-Stone Park Rd. Phone 336/674-0472.

Natural Science Center of Greensboro, Inc. Natural science museum with zoo, trails, and indoor exhibits incl geology, paleontology, aquarium, herpetarium, and science and technology. Kid's Alley, an exploratorium for young children. Planetarium shows; inquire for schedule. Some fees. (Daily; closed hols) 4301 Lawndale Dr. Phone 336/288-3769. ¢¢

University of North Carolina at Greensboro. (1891) 13,000 students. 1000 Spring Garden St. Phone 336/334-5243 (admissions) or 336/334-5000 (main). On campus is

Weatherspoon Art Gallery. Permanent collection of over 4,000 contemporary paintings, graphic arts, sculpture. (Tues-Sun; closed hols) Anne and Benjamin Cone Bldg. Phone 336/334-5770. **FREE**

Annual Event

Greater Greensboro Chrysler Classic Golf Tournament. Top golfers compete for more than $2.2 million on PGA circuit. Mid-late Apr.

Motels/Motor Lodges

★★ **AMERISUITES.** *1619 Stanley Rd (27407). 336/852-1443; fax 336/854-9339; toll-free 800/833-1516. www.amerisuites.com.* 126 suites, 6 story. S, D $80-$109; each addl $5; under 12 free; wkend rates; golf plans; higher rates special events. Crib free. TV; cable (premium), VCR. Complimentary continental bkfst, coffee in rms. Restaurant nearby. Ck-out 11 am. Meeting rms. Business center. In-rm modem link. Free airport, railroad station transportation. Golf privileges. Exercise equipt. Heated pool. Refrigerators, microwaves, wet bars. Cr cds: A, DS, MC, V.
✈ D ⚄ ⚄ 🏊 ⚄ 🏃 SC

★★ **COMFORT INN.** *2001 Veasley St (27407). 336/294-6220; fax 336/294-6220; res 800/228-5150.* 123 rms, 2 story. S $57-$62; D $62-$65; each addl $5; under 16 free; higher rates special events. Crib free. TV; cable (premium). Pool. Complimentary continental bkfst. Ck-out noon. Meeting rm. Business servs avail. Health club privileges. Some refrigerators. Cr cds: A, C, D, DS, ER, JCB, MC, V.
D ⚄ 🏃 ⚄ ⚄ 🏊

★ **DAYS INN CENTRAL.** *120 Seneca Rd (27406), I-85 and S Elm. 336/275-9571; fax 336/275-9572; res*

800/329-7466. Email dayseneca@yahoo.com. 122 rms, 2 story. S $45-$58; D $48-$64; each addl $6; family rates. Crib free. TV; cable. Pool; wading pool. Playground. Complimentary continental bkfst. Ck-out 11 am. Cr cds: A, C, D, DS, MC, V.
D ⚄ ⚄ 🏊

★★ **FAIRFIELD INN BY MARRIOTT.** *2003 Athena Ct (27407). 336/294-9922; fax 336/294-9922; toll-free 800/228-2800.* 135 rms, 3 story. S $49.95; D $54.95; each addl $3; under 18 free. Crib free. TV; cable (premium). Pool. Complimentary continental bkfst. Restaurant nearby. Ck-out noon. Business servs avail. Cr cds: A, D, DS, MC, V.
D ⚄ ⚄ 🏊 SC

★ **GREENSBORO TRAVELODGE.** *2112 W Meadowview (27403). 336/292-2020; fax 336/852-3476; res 800/578-7878.* 108 rms, 2 story. S, D $49-$64; each addl $5; under 17 free; higher rates golf tournament. Crib free. TV; cable (premium). Pool. Complimentary coffee in rms. Restaurant adj 11 am-10 pm. Ck-out noon. Meeting rms. Business servs avail. Cr cds: A, DS, MC, V.
⚄ 🏊

★★ **HAMPTON INN FOUR SEASONS.** *2004 Veasley St (27407). 336/854-8600; fax 910/854-8741; toll-free 800/426-7866.* 121 rms, 2 story. S $59; D $65-$73; under 18 free. Crib free. Pet accepted, some restrictions. TV; cable (premium). Pool. Complimentary continental bkfst. Meeting rm. Business servs avail. Cr cds: A, C, D, DS, JCB, MC, V.
D 🐾 ⚄ ⚄ 🏊 SC

★★ **PARK LANE HOTEL.** *3005 High Point Rd (27403). 336/294-4565; fax 336/294-0572; res 800/942-6556.* 161 rms, 4 story. S $70-$80; D $76-$86; each addl $10; suites $130; under 16 free. Crib free. TV; cable (premium). Pool. Complimentary continental bkfst. Restaurant 6-10 am, 5-9:30 pm; wkends 7-11 am. Bar 4:30-10 pm. Ck-out noon. Coin lndry. Meeting rms. Business servs avail. In-rm modem link. Sundries. Free airport transportation. Exercise equipt; sauna. Health club privileges. Some in-rm whirlpools; refrigerator, wet bar in suites; microwaves avail. Cr cds: A, C, D, DS, MC, V.

[D] [icons]

★★ **RAMADA INN-AIRPORT.** *7067 Albert Pick Rd (27409), near Piedmont Triad Airport. 336/668-2431; fax 910/668-7012.* 170 rms, 2 story. S, D $74-$78; each addl $8; higher rates special events. Crib free. TV; cable (premium). Pool; poolside serv. Sauna. Restaurant 7-10 am, 11:30 am-2 pm, 5-10 pm; Sat 7-10 am, 5-10 pm; Sun 7-10 am. Bar 4 pm-midnight. Ck-out noon. Meeting rms. Business servs avail. Bellhops. Valet serv. Free airport transportation. Cr cds: A, D, DS, MC, V.

[D] [icons]

Hotels

★★★ **BILTMORE.** *111 W Washington St (27401). 336/272-3474; fax 336/275-2523; toll-free 800/332-0303. Email biltmorenc@aol.com.* 25 rms. S, D $75-$110; under 18 free. Crib free. TV; cable (premium). Complimentary continental bkfst. Ck-out noon. Meeting rm. Business center. Concierge. Airport transportation. Refrigerators, wet bars. Built 1895. Cr cds: A, C, D, DS, ER, JCB, MC, V.

[icons]

★★★ **EMBASSY SUITES HOTEL.** *204 Centreport Dr (27409), near Piedmont Triad Airport. 336/668-4535; fax 336/668-3901.* 221 suites, 7 story. Suites $79-$214; under 16 free. Crib free. TV; cable (premium), VCR avail. Indoor pool; whirlpool. Complimentary full bkfst. Restaurant 6 am-10 pm. Bar 4 pm-midnight. Ck-out noon. Coin lndry. Meeting rms. Business center. Gift shop. Free airport transportation. Exercise equipt; sauna. Game rm. Refrigerators, wet bars. Microwaves avail. Balconies. Atrium lobby; glass elevators. Cr cds: A, C, D, DS, JCB, MC, V.

[D] [icons] [SC]

★★★ **HILTON.** *304 N Greene St (27401). 336/379-8000; fax 336/275-2810; res 800/445-8667.* 281 rms, 11 story. S, D $109-$139; suites $185-$450; under 17 free; wkend rates. Crib free. TV; cable (premium). Indoor pool; whirlpool. Supervised children's activities; ages 6 months-15 yrs. Restaurant 6:30 am-10 pm. Bar 4 pm-1 am. Ck-out 11 am. Convention facilities. Covered parking. Exercise rm; sauna. Refrigerator in suites. Luxury level. Cr cds: A, C, D, DS, MC, V.

[D] [icons]

★★★ **MARRIOTT AIRPORT HOTEL.** *1 Marriott Dr (27409), I-40 Exit 210, at Piedmont Triad Airport. 336/852-6450; fax 336/665-6522; res 800/468-3571.* 299 rms. S, D $114; suites $175-$250; under 16 free. Crib free. TV; cable (premium). Indoor/outdoor pool; whirlpool, poolside serv. Restaurant 6 am-10 pm. Bar 11:30-2 am. Ck-out noon. Coin lndry. Convention facilities. Business servs avail. In-rm modem link. Gift shop. Free airport transportation. Lighted tennis. Exercise equipt. Lawn games. Luxury level. Cr cds: A, C, D, DS, ER, JCB, MC, V.

[D] [icons]

★★★ **SHERATON GREENSBORO HOTEL AT FOUR SEASONS.** *3121 High Point Rd (27407), I-40 Exit 217A in Four Seasons Mall. 336/292-9161; fax 292/292-1407; toll-free 800/242-6556. www.kourycenter.com.* 986 rms, 28 story. S $130-$140; D $140-$150; each addl $10; under 18 free; higher rates special events. Crib free. TV; cable (premium). Indoor/outdoor pool; whirlpool, wading pool, poolside serv. Restaurants 6 am-midnight. Bars 11-1 am, Sun from 1 pm; entertainment. Ck-out noon. Convention facilities. Business center. Bellhops. Valet serv. Gift shop. Free airport transportation. Golf privileges. Racquetball courts. Exercise equipt; sauna. Cr cds: A, C, D, DS, JCB, MC, V.

[D] [icons]

Restaurant

★★★ **GATE CITY CHOP HOUSE.** *106 S Holden St (27407). 336/294-9977.* Specializes in Angus beef, grilled fish, chops. Salad bar. Hrs: 11:30 am-10 pm; Sat 4:30-10:30 pm. Closed Sun; hols. Res accepted. Bar. Wine list. Lunch $5.95-$8.95; dinner $13.95-$31.95. Child's menu. Five dining areas; circular oak bar. Cr cds: A, D, DS, MC, V.

[D]

Greenville

(C-7) *See also Washington, Williamston*

Founded 1786 **Pop** 44,972 **Elev** 55 ft
Area code 252
Web ci.greenville.nc.us
Information Greenville-Pitt County
Convention and Visitors Bureau, 525
S Evans St, PO Box 8027, 27835-
8027; 252/752-8044 or 800/537-5564

An educational, cultural, commercial, and medical center, Greenville is
one of the towns named for General
Nathanael Greene, a hero of the
American Revolutionary War.

Motel/Motor Lodge

★ **SUPER 8 MOTEL.** *1004 S Memorial Dr (27834).* 252/758-8888; fax
252/758-0523; res 800/800-8000. 48
rms, 2 story. S $52; D $55; each addl
$3; under 12 free. Crib avail. Parking
lot. TV; cable (premium). Complimentary continental bkfst. Restaurant nearby. Ck-out 11 am, ck-in 2
pm. Business servs avail. Free airport
transportation. Golf. Tennis. Cr cds:
A, C, D, DS, MC, V.

Hotels

★★ **FAIRFIELD INN.** *821 S Memorial Dr (27834).* 252/758-5544; fax
252/758-1416; res 800/228-2800.
www.fairfieldinn.com. 113 rms, 2
story. June-Aug: S $55; D $61; each
addl $6; under 17 free; lower rates
rest of yr. Crib avail. Parking lot.
Pool. TV; cable (premium), VCR
avail. Complimentary continental
bkfst, newspaper. Restaurant nearby.
Ck-out noon, ck-in 3 pm. Meeting
rm. Business center. Dry cleaning.
Free airport transportation. Exercise
privileges. Golf. Picnic facilities. Cr
cds: A, C, D, DS, JCB, MC, V.

★★ **HAMPTON INN.** *3439 S Memorial Dr (27834).* 252/355-2521; fax
252/355-0262; res 800/426-7866.
Email grnmm01@hi-hotel.com. 121
rms, 2 story. S $55; D $61; under 18
free. Crib avail. Parking lot. Pool. TV;
cable (premium). Complimentary
continental bkfst, coffee in rms,

newspaper, toll-free calls. Ck-out
noon, ck-in 4 pm. Meeting rm. Dry
cleaning. Free airport transportation.
Exercise privileges. Golf. Cr cds: A, C,
D, DS, MC, V.

★★★ **HILTON INN.** *207 SW
Greenville Blvd (27834).* 252/355-
5000; fax 252/355-5099; res 800/
HILTONS. Email rtucker@greenvillenc.
com; www.hilton.com. 141 rms, 6
story. S, D $89-$114; each addl $10;
suites $175-$275; under 18 free. Crib
free. TV; cable (premium). Pool;
whirlpool, poolside serv. Coffee
in rms. Restaurant 6:30 am-10:30
pm. Bar 11-2 am. Ck-out noon.
Meeting rms. Business center. In-rm
modem link. Airport transportation.
Exercise equipt. Refrigerator in suites.
Cr cds: A, DS, MC, V.

★★ **RAMADA PLAZA.** *203 W
Greenville Blvd (27834).* 252/355-
8300; fax 252/756-3553; res 800/228-
2828; toll-free 800/272-6232. 192 rms,
4 story. S, D $54-$84; each addl $6;
suites $100-$120; under 12 free. Crib
free. TV; cable (premium). Pool.
Restaurant 6:30-9:30 am, 11:30 am-
1:30 pm, 6-9 pm. Bar 5 pm-2 am;
entertainment. Ck-out noon. Meeting rms. Business servs avail. Exercise
equipt. Cr cds: A, C, D, DS, JCB,
MC, V.

Restaurants

★★ **BEEF BARN.** *400 St Andrews Dr
(27834).* 252/756-1161. Specializes in
beef, steak, seafood. Salad bar. Hrs:
11:30 am-9:30 pm; Fri to 10 pm; Sat
5-10 pm. Closed hols. Res accepted.
Bar. Lunch $4.25-$7.25; dinner
$8.95-$25.95. Child's menu.
Antiques. Family-owned. Cr cds: A,
D, DS, MC, V.

★ **PARKER'S BAR-B-QUE.** *3109
Memorial Dr (27834).* 252/756-2388.
Specializes in pork barbecue, fried
chicken. Hrs: 9 am-9 pm. Closed
Thanksgiving, Dec 25; 1 wk mid-
June. Res accepted. Lunch, dinner
$5.50-$8.50. Child's menu. Family-
owned. No cr cds accepted.

Hatteras (Outer Banks)

Pop 1,660 **Elev** 2 ft **Area code** 252 **Zip** 27943

This Hatteras Island fishing village on the Outer Banks (see) was settled, it is said, by shipwrecked sailors from Devon, England. The Devon accent is indeed heard here and on the islands of Ocracoke and Manteo. There are ferries south to Ocracoke (see).

Motels/Motor Lodges

★ **HATTERAS MARLIN MOTEL.** *NC 12 (27943). 252/986-2141; fax 252/986-2436.* 32 rms, 2 story, 5 kits. May-early Sep: S $48, D $54; each addl $5; kit. units $58; under 6 free; lower rates rest of yr. Crib free. TV; cable. Pool. Restaurant nearby. Ck-out 11 am. Business servs avail. Sun deck. Picnic tables. Cr cds: MC, V.
⊡ ☀ ⌦ ☼

★ **SEA GULL MOTEL.** *NC 12 (27943). 252/986-2550; fax 252/986-2525. www.seagullhatteras.com.* 45 rms, 1-2 story, 10 kits. Mid-May-mid-Sep: S, D $60-$90; each addl $5; kit. units $70-$100; under 5 free. Closed Dec-Feb. Crib $5. TV; cable. Pool; wading pool. Restaurant opp 6 am-9 pm. Ck-out 11 am. Many microwaves, refrigerators. Picnic tables. Grills. Beach adj. Cr cds: DS, MC, V.
⊡ ☀ ⌦ ☒ ☼

Resort

★★ **HOLIDAY INN EXPRESS.** *58822 NC 12 (27943). 252/986-1110; fax 252/986-1131; res 800/465-4329; toll-free 800/361-1590. Email holexphatt@thrvb.com.* 72 rms, 2 story, 32 suites. May-Labor Day: S, D $69-$149; suites $89-$169; under 18 free; hols (3-day min); lower rates rest of yr. Crib free. TV; cable (premium). Complimentary continental bkfst. Restaurant nearby. Ck-out 11 am. Business servs avail. In-rm modem link. Guest lndry. Pool. Refrigerators, microwaves. Balcony with suites. On beach. Cr cds: A, DS, MC, V.
⊡ ☀ ⌦ ✈ ☒ ☼ SC

Henderson (B-6)

Founded 1840 **Pop** 15,655 **Elev** 509 ft **Area code** 252 **Zip** 27536
Web www.kerrlake-nc.com
Information Vance County Tourism Department, 943 K-West Andrews Ave; 252/438-2222

Annual Events

Governor's Cup Regatta. Kerr Lake. Two days mid-June.

Parade of Lights on Water. Kerr Lake. Fireworks, entertainment. Labor Day wkend.

Seasonal Event

Tobacco auctions. Held at 7 warehouses. Inquire at Chamber of Commerce. Sep-Nov.

Motels/Motor Lodges

★ **HOWARD JOHNSON EXPRESS INN.** *200 Parham Rd (27536), Parham Rd at jct US 1, 158 & I-85. 252/492-7001; fax 252/438-2389; res 800/654-2000.* 98 rms, 2 story. S $49-$60; D $54-$66; each addl $6; under 18 free. Crib free. TV; cable (premium). Pool. Complimentary continental bkfst. Ck-out noon. Meeting rms. Business servs avail. In-rm modem link. Sundries. Balconies; some private patios. Cr cds: A, C, D, DS, MC, V.
⊡ ☀ ⌦ ☒ ☼

★★ **QUALITY INN.** *I-85 & Parham Rd (27536), 1¼ mi N on US 1, 158 at jct I-85 Exit 215. 252/492-1126; fax 252/492-2575.* 156 rms, 2 story. S $48-$61; D $49-$84; each addl $6; under 19 free. Pet accepted. TV; cable (premium). Pool; wading pool. Complimentary continental bkfst, coffee in rms. Bar 11 am-11 pm. Ck-out 11 am. Meeting rms. Business servs avail. In-rm modem link. Sundries. Cr cds: A, C, D, DS, MC, V.
⊡ ☀ ⌦ ☒ ☼ SC

Hendersonville

(C-2) *See also Asheville, Brevard*

Pop 7,284 **Elev** 2,146 ft
Area code 828
Web www.hendersonvillenc.org
Information Chamber of Commerce, 330 N King St, 28792; 828/692-1413

What to See and Do

⭐ **Carl Sandburg Home National Historic Site.** (Connemara) The famous poet's 264-acre farm residence is maintained as it was when Sandburg and his family lived here from 1945 until his death in 1967. On grounds are house and bldgs for animals as well as a visitor center. For further info contact the Superintendent, Flat Rock 28731. (Daily; closed Dec 25) 1928 Little River Rd, 3 mi S on US 25, in Flat Rock. Phone 828/693-4178. Tours ¢¢

Holmes State Forest. Managed forest designed to facilitate better understanding of the value of forests in our lives. Features "talking trees" with recorded narration about site and forest history. Picnicking. Camping (res required). For res or info contact Rte 4, Box 308. (Mid-Mar-Nov, Tues-Sun) SW on Crab Creek Rd. Phone 828/692-0100. **FREE**

Jump-Off Rock. Panoramic view from atop Jump-Off Mt. 5th Ave, 6 mi W.

Annual Event

North Carolina Apple Festival. Labor Day wkend.

Seasonal Event

Flat Rock Playhouse. 3½ mi S on US 25 in Flat Rock. Outstanding professional theater since 1939; State Theater of North Carolina since 1961. Vagabond Players offer 8 Broadway and London productions in 15 wks. Wed-Sat eves; Thurs, Sat, Sun matinees. For res phone 828/693-0731. Late May-early Sep.

Motel/Motor Lodge

⭐⭐ **COMFORT INN.** *206 Mitchell Dr (28792). 828/693-8800; fax 828/ 693-8800; res 800/228-5150; toll-free*
800/882-3843. 85 rms, 2 story. June-Oct: S $55.95; D $69; each addl $10; under 18 free; higher rates wkends; lower rates rest of yr. Crib free. Pet accepted. TV; cable, VCR. Pool. Complimentary continental bkfst, coffee in rms. Restaurant nearby. Ck-out 11 am. Meeting rm. Business servs avail. In-rm modem link. Refrigerators, microwaves avail. Cr cds: A, D, DS, MC, V.

🄳 🐾 ⛱ 🆓 🖎 🔥

Hotels

⭐⭐ **HAMPTON INN.** *155 Sugarloaf Rd (28792). 828/697-2333; fax 828/ 693-5280; res 800/426-7866. Email hamptoninn@a-o.com.* 117 rms, 4 story, 2 suites. June-Oct: S $92; D $97; suites $140; lower rates rest of yr. Crib avail. Parking lot. Pool. TV; cable (premium). Complimentary continental bkfst, coffee in rms, newspaper, toll-free calls. Ck-out 11 am, ck-in 2 pm. Business center. Dry cleaning. Golf, 18 holes. Tennis, 5 courts. Cr cds: A, C, D, DS, MC, V.

🄳 🛉 🆓 ⛱ 🖎 🔥 🏃

⭐⭐ **QUALITY INN.** *201 Sugarloaf Rd (28792), at jct I-26 & US 64. 828/692-7231; fax 828/693-9905; toll-free 800/581-4745. Email info@quality inn-suiteshvl.com; www.qualityinn-suites hvl.com.* 133 rms, 2 story, 16 suites. May-Oct: S, D $89; each addl $6; suites $159; under 18 free; lower rates rest of yr. Crib avail. Parking lot. Indoor pool, whirlpool. TV; cable (premium). Complimentary coffee in rms, newspaper, toll-free calls. Restaurant 6:30 am-9 pm. Bar. Ck-out 11 am, ck-in 3 pm. Meeting rms. Business servs avail. Bellhops. Dry cleaning, coin lndry. Free airport transportation. Exercise equipt, sauna. Golf. Tennis. Hiking trail. Picnic facilities. Cr cds: A, D, DS, JCB, MC, V.

🄳 🛉 🆓 ⛱ 🕺 🆓 🖎 🔥 **SC**

Resort

⭐⭐ **HIGHLAND LAKE INN.** *PO Box 1026 (28731), I-26 Exit 22, then W on Upward Rd to Highland Lake Rd. 828/693-6812; fax 828/696-8951; toll-free 800/762-1376. Email dgrup@ highlandlake.com; www.highlandlake inn.com.* 36 rms, 2 story, 2 suites.

Apr-Oct: S, D $205; each addl $15; suites $205; lower rates rest of yr. Crib avail. Parking lot. Pool, children's pool, lifeguard. TV; cable (DSS), VCR avail. Complimentary continental bkfst, coffee in rms, newspaper. Restaurant. Bar. Meeting rms. Business center. Coin lndry. Gift shop. Golf. Tennis, 2 courts. Downhill skiing. Bike rentals. Supervised children's activities. Hiking trail. Picnic facilities. Cr cds: A, DS, MC, V.

⊡ 🛌 🐾 🍴 🕯 🍽 🔨 🗓 🔥 🎿

B&Bs/Small Inns

★★★ **CHALET CLUB.** *532 Washburn Rd (28746), 13 mi NE on US 64, then 8 mi E on US 64/74. 828/625-9315; fax 828/625-9373; res 800/336-3309. www.chaletclub.com.* 21 rms, 1-2 story, 7 cottages. Apr, June-Aug, Oct, AP: S, D $84-$90; cottages $87-$92; golf plans; package plans; lower rates rest of yr. Crib free. TV in common rm. Ck-out 11 am, ck-in varies. Coin lndry. Tennis privileges. Exercise equipt. Pool. Refrigerators, fireplaces. Built in 1927. Cr cds: MC, V.

⊡ 🍴 🍽 🕯 🔥

★★ **ECHO MOUNTAIN INN.** *2849 Laurel Park Hwy (28739). 828/693-9626; fax 828/697-2047; toll-free 800/324-6466. Email info@echoinn.com; www.echoinn.com.* 37 units, 2 story, 8 kits. May-Oct: S, D $75-$175; kit. suites $95-$135; each addl $10; lower rates rest of yr. Crib $10. TV; cable. Pool. Complimentary continental bkfst. Restaurant 5-9:30 pm; closed Sun, Mon. Bar. Ck-out 11 am, ck-in 2 pm. Meeting rm. Business servs avail. On mountain top. Built 1896; stone and frame structure. Totally nonsmoking. Cr cds: A, DS, MC, V.

⊡ 🍽 🗓 🔥

★★ **LAKE LURE INN.** *Hwy 64 & 74A (28746), 13 mi NE on US 64, 8 mi E on US 64/74A. 704/625-2525; fax 704/625-9655; toll-free 800/277-5873. Email lakelureinn@wncguide.com; www.wncguide.com/rutherford/lakelureinn.* 50 rms, 3 story. Mid-Mar-Nov: S, D $109-$150; each addl $10; under 12 free; lower rates rest of yr. Crib free. TV; cable (premium). Pool. Complimentary continental bkfst. Dining rm 11 am-2 pm, 5-9 pm; Sun 11 am-2:30 pm. Bar. Ck-out 11 am, ck-in 3 pm. Business servs avail. Golf privileges. On lake; view of Blue Ridge

Mts. Mediterranean-style hostelry (1927). Cr cds: A, D, DS, MC, V.

⊡ 🛌 🍴 🗓 🔥 SC

★★★ **LODGE ON LAKE LURE BED & BREAKFAST.** *361 Charlotte Dr (28746), 13 mi NE on US 64, then 8 mi E on US 64/74. 828/625-2789; fax 828/625-2421; toll-free 800/733-2785.* 14 rms, 7 with shower only, 2 story. No rm phones. Apr-mid-Nov: S, D $99-$149; each addl $15; wkends (2-day min); lower rates rest of yr. Crib free. TV; cable, VCR avail (movies). Complimentary full bkfst; afternoon refreshments. Restaurant nearby. Ck-out 11 am. Business servs avail. Concierge serv. Tennis privileges. 18-hole golf privileges. Picnic tables, grills. On lake. Built in 1930. Totally nonsmoking. Cr cds: A, DS, MC, V.

🕯 🍴 🛷 🍴 🗓 🔥

★★ **THE WAVERLY INN.** *783 N Main St (28792). 828/693-9193; fax 828/692-1010; toll-free 800/537-8195. Email waverlyinn@ioa.com; www waverlyinn.com.* 14 rms, 3 story, 1 suite. June-Oct: S $90; D $159; each addl $20; suites $195; under 11 free; lower rates rest of yr. Parking lot. TV; cable, VCR avail, CD avail. Complimentary full bkfst, newspaper, toll-free calls. Restaurant. Ck-out 11 am, ck-in 1 pm. Business center. Gift shop. Exercise privileges. Golf. Tennis, 2 courts. Cr cds: A, C, D, DS, MC, V.

🍴 🍴 🍴 🗓 🔥 🔨

★★ **WOODFIELD.** *2905 Greenville Hwy US 25 (28731), 3 mi S on US 25. 828/693-6016; fax 828/693-0437; toll-free 800/533-6016. Email wood1@chettah.com.* 17 rms, 3 story. S, D $89-$149. Complimentary full bkfst. Ck-out 11 am. Tennis. Nature trail. Built 1852; antiques. Cr cds: A, C, D, DS, ER, JCB, MC, V.

⊡ 🍴 🗓 🔥

Restaurants

★★★ **EXPRESSIONS.** *114 N Main St (28792). 828/693-8516.* Specializes in beef, crab cakes, fish. Hrs: 6-9 pm; Fri, Sat to 9:30 pm. Closed Sun; most major hols; mid-Jan-mid-Feb. Res accepted. Bar. Wine cellar. Dinner $13.95-$24.50. Child's menu. Fine dining in subdued atmosphere. Cr cds: D, MC, V.

⊡

★★★ **SINBAD.** *202 S Washington St (28739). 828/696-2039. www.sinbad restaurant.com.* Specializes in Lebanese, Greek, Indian dishes. Hrs: 11:30 am-10 pm. Closed Sun, Mon; also Jan 1, Thanksgiving, Dec 25. Res accepted. Bar. Wine cellar. Lunch $3.95-$6.95; dinner $11.95-$19.95. Parking. Traditional Middle East decor. Cr cds: A, DS, MC, V.

D

Hickory

(C-3) *See also Statesville*

Pop 28,301 **Elev** 1,163 ft
Area code 828
Information Catawba County Chamber of Commerce, 470 US 70 SW, PO Box 1828, 28603; 828/328-6111

What to See and Do

Arts Center of Catawba Valley. 243 3rd Ave NE. Here are

Catawba Science Center. Interactive exhibits feature life, earth, medical, and physical sciences. Also changing exhibits. (Tues-Sun; closed hols) Phone 828/322-8169. ¢

Hickory Museum of Art. American realist 19th- and 20th-century art, incl works by Gilbert Stuart; Hudson River School, Thos. Cole to Homer Martin; American Impressionists; European, Asian, and pre-Columbian pieces; changing exhibits quarterly. (Tues-Sun; closed Easter, Dec 25) Phone 828/327-8576. **FREE**

Bunker Hill Covered Bridge. One of only 2 remaining covered bridges in state. Built in 1895, it spans Lyle's Creek. Nature trail, picnicking. On US 70, approx 10 mi E. Phone 828/465-0383.

Seasonal Event

Auto racing. Hickory Motor Speedway. 4 mi E on US 70. Stock car racing. For schedule, prices phone 828/464-3655. Mid-Mar-early Oct.

Motels/Motor Lodges

★★ **HAMPTON INN HICKORY.** *1520 13th Ave Dr SE (28602). 828/323-1150; fax 828/324-8979; res 800/426-7866. Email hckpc01@twave. com.* 119 rms, 2 story. S $62-$65; D $68-$71; under 18 free. Crib free. TV; cable. Pool. Complimentary continental bkfst. Restaurant adj 6 am-8 pm. Ck-out noon. Business servs avail. In-rm modem link. Cr cds: A, C, D, DS, JCB, MC, V.

D ⌧ ⌧ ⌧ ⌧

★★★ **HOLIDAY INN SELECT.** *1385 Lenoir Rhyne Blvd SE (28602), I-40 Exit 125. 828/323-1000; fax 828/322-4275; res 800/HOLIDAY; toll-free 800/366-5010. Email hcknc@twave.net.* 200 rms, 2 story. S, D $89-$109; under 19 free. Crib $6. TV; cable (premium). Indoor pool; whirlpool. Complimentary coffee in rms. Restaurant 6 am-11 pm. Bar 4:30 pm-1 am; Sun to midnight. Ck-out noon. Coin lndry. Meeting rms. Business servs avail. In-rm modem link. Valet serv. Exercise equipt; sauna. Some refrigerators. Balconies. Cr cds: A, C, D, DS, JCB, MC, V.

D ⌧ ⌧ ⌧ ⌧ ⌧ ⌧ ⌧ ⌧

★ **RED ROOF INN.** *1184 Lenoir Rhyne Blvd (28602). 828/323-1500; fax 828/323-1509; res 800/733-7663.* 108 rms, 2 story. S $38-$48; D $45-$55; each addl $7; under 18 free. Crib free. Pet accepted, some restrictions. TV. Complimentary coffee in lobby. Restaurant adj. Ck-out noon. In-rm modem link. Cr cds: A, DS, MC, V.

D ⌧ ⌧

★ **SLEEP INN.** *1179 13th Ave Dr SE (28602). 828/323-1140; fax 828/324-6203; res 800/753-3746.* 100 rms, 3 story. May-Aug, Oct: S $89; D $129; each addl $7; under 18 free; lower rates rest of yr. Parking lot. TV; cable. Complimentary continental bkfst, newspaper, toll-free calls. Restaurant. Ck-out 11 am, ck-in 3 pm. Fax servs avail. Dry cleaning, coin lndry. Golf. Cr cds: A, C, D, DS, ER, JCB, MC, V.

⌧ ⌧ ⌧ SC

B&B/Small Inn

★★ **HICKORY BED & BREAKFAST.** *464 7th SW St (28602). 828/324-0548; fax 828/324-7434; toll-free*

800/654-2961. 4 rms, 2 story. Rm phones avail. S, D $85-$105. Children over 12 yrs only. TV in sitting rm. Pool. Complimentary full bkfst. Ck-out 11 am, ck-in 4 pm. Built in 1908; Georgian-style architecture; antiques. Totally nonsmoking. Cr cds: A, DS, MC, V.

All Suite

★★ **COMFORT SUITES.** *1125 13th Dr SE (28602), off I-40 Exit 125. 828/323-1211; fax 828/322-4395; res 800/517-4000; toll-free 800/742-7026.,* 2 story, 116 suites. S $72; D $82; each addl $10; under 18 free. Crib avail. Parking lot. Pool. TV; cable (premium). Complimentary full bkfst, coffee in rms, newspaper, toll-free calls. Restaurant nearby. Ck-out 11 am, ck-in 3 pm. Meeting rm. Business servs avail. Dry cleaning, coin lndry. Golf. Tennis. Picnic facilities. Cr cds: A, C, D, DS, MC, V.

Restaurants

★★ **1859 CAFE.** *443 2nd Ave SW (28602). 828/322-1859.* Specializes in fresh seafood, prime beef, pasta. Hrs: 5:30-10 pm. Closed Sun; hols. Res accepted. Bar. Dinner $14.50-$22.95. Entertainment: Fri, Sat. Three dining rms in converted house. Cr cds: A, D, DS, MC, V.

★★★ **VINTAGE HOUSE.** *271 3rd Ave NW (28601). 828/324-1210. Email vintagehouse@twave.net.* Specializes in osso buco, mountain trout with lobster, lump crab cakes. Hrs: 6-9 pm; Fri, Sat to 10 pm. Closed Sun; also hols. Res accepted. Bar. Wine cellar. Dinner $15-$20. Child's menu. Parking. Cr cds: A, MC, V.

Highlands

See also Cashiers, Franklin

Pop 948 **Elev** 3,835 ft **Area code** 828 **Zip** 28741

Information Chamber of Commerce, PO Box 404; 828/526-2112

Motel/Motor Lodge

★★ **MOUNTAIN HIGH MOTEL.** *200 Main St (28741). 828/526-2790; fax 828/526-2750.* 55 rms, 1-2 story. June-Labor Day, Oct: S, D $93-$175; under 18 free; higher rates: wkends, hols; lower rates rest of yr. Crib $5. Pet accepted. TV; cable (premium). Complimentary continental bkfst. Restaurant opp 7:15 am-9:30 pm. Ck-out noon. Meeting rms. Business servs avail. Downhill ski 7 mi. Some bathrm phones, in-rm whirlpools, refrigerators, fireplaces; microwaves avail. Balconies. Picnic tables. Cr cds: A, DS, MC, V.

B&B/Small Inn

★★ **HIGHLANDS INN AND KELSEY PLACE RESTAURANT.** *4th & E Main St (28741). 828/526-9380; fax 828/526-9380; res 800/964-6955.* 30 rms, 3 story. Apr-Nov: S, D $89-$99; suites $99-$125; wkly rates. Closed rest of yr. TV; cable. Complimentary continental bkfst. Ck-out 11 am, ck-in 4 pm. Balconies. Built in 1880; antiques. Cr cds: A, MC, V.

All Suite

★★ **HIGHLANDS SUITE HOTEL.** *205 Main St (28741). 828/526-4502; fax 828/526-4840; toll-free 800/221-5078. Email mtnhi@gte.net; www. highlandssuitehotel.com.* 28 rms, 2 story. May-Oct: S, D $206; each addl $10; under 15 free; lower rates rest of yr. Parking garage. TV; cable (DSS), VCR avail. Complimentary continental bkfst, coffee in rms. Restaurant nearby. Ck-out noon, ck-in 3:30 pm. Fax servs avail. Golf. Hiking trail. Cr cds: A, DS, MC, V.

Restaurants

★★ **NICK'S.** *NC 28 at Satulah Rd (28741), 4 blks S on NC 28. 828/526-2706.* Specializes in veal, prime rib, seafood. Hrs: 11 am-10 pm. Closed Wed; Jan-Feb. Res accepted. Lunch $5.95-$11.95; dinner $10.95-$29.95. Child's menu. Cr cds: MC, V.

★★ ON THE VERANDAH. *1536 Franklin Rd (28741), at Sequoyah Lake. 828/526-2338. Email otv1@ontheverandah.com; www.ontheverandah.com.* Specializes in pasta, seafood. Hrs: 6-10 pm; Sun brunch from 11 am. Closed Jan-Mar. Res accepted. Dinner $15.50-$25. Sun brunch $18. Entertainment: pianist. Vaulted ceiling; contemporary rustic decor. Cr cds: DS, MC, V.

High Point

(C-4) *See also Burlington, Greensboro, Lexington*

Founded 1859 **Pop** 69,496 **Elev** 939 ft
Area code 336
Web www.highpoint.org
Information Convention and Visitors Bureau, 300 S Main St, PO Box 2273, 27261; 336/884-5255 or 800/720-5255

What to See and Do

Furniture Discovery Center. Nation's only museum of modern day furniture manufacturing. Hands-on displays; miniatures; hall of fame; special exhibits. (Apr-Oct, daily; rest of yr, Tues-Sun; closed hols) 101 W Green Dr. Phone 336/887-3876. ¢¢

Peterson Doll and Miniature Museum. Collection of more than 2,000 dolls and related artifacts from around the world, some dating back to the 15th century. (Apr-Oct, daily; Nov-Mar, Tues-Sun; closed hols) Main & Green Sts. Phone 336/885-3655 or 336/887-3876. ¢¢

World's Largest Chest of Drawers. Bldg designed to look like a 19th-century dresser; symbolizes city's position as a furniture center. Built in 1926. 508 N Hamilton St. Phone 336/883-2016. **FREE**

Annual Events

Gas Boat Drag Championships. Oak Hollow Lake. One of several World Series Championship races. Phone 336/883-2016. Fourth wkend July.

Day in the Park. City Lake Park. Arts and crafts, rides, entertainment. Phone 336/889-2787. Late Sep.

Seasonal Event

North Carolina Shakespeare Festival. 220 E Commerce Ave, High Point Theatre. Season incl three productions and *A Christmas Carol.* Phone 336/841-6273 or 336/841-2273. Aug-Oct and Dec.

Motel/Motor Lodge

★★ RAMADA INN. *236 S Main St (27260). 336/886-7011; fax 336/886-5595; toll-free 800/272-6232.* 165 rms, 2-6 story. S, D $62-$68; each addl $10; suites $115-$135; under 18 free; higher rates Furniture Market. Crib free. Pet accepted. TV; cable (premium). Pool. Restaurant 7 am-2 pm, 5-10 pm. Bar 5-11 pm. Ck-out noon. Coin lndry. Meeting rms. Business servs avail. Barber. Many poolside rms with balcony. Cr cds: A, C, D, DS, MC, V.

Hotel

★★★ RADISSON HIGH POINT. *135 S Main St (27260). 336/889-8888; fax 336/889-8870; res 800/333-3333. Email lcrater@boykin.com; www.radisson.com/highpointnc.* 232 rms, 8 story, 10 suites. Mar-Apr, Sep-Oct: S $300; D $325; each addl $10; suites $175; under 12 free; lower rates rest of yr. Crib avail. Parking garage. Indoor pool, whirlpool. TV; cable (DSS), VCR avail. Complimentary coffee in rms, newspaper, toll-free calls. Restaurant 6:30 am-10 pm. Bar. Ck-out 11 am, ck-in 3 pm. Meeting rms. Business center. Bellhops. Dry cleaning. Free airport transportation. Exercise privileges. Golf. Tennis, 10 courts. Downhill skiing. Cr cds: A, C, D, DS, ER, JCB, MC, V.

B&B/Small Inn

★★ BOULDIN HOUSE BED AND BREAKFAST. *4332 Archdale Rd (27263), 2 mi S on I-85, Exit 111. 336/431-4909; fax 336/431-4914; res 800/739-1816. Email lmiller582@aol.com; www.bbonline.com/nc/bouldin.* 4 rms. No rm phones. S, D $85-$110; each addl $25; higher rates Furniture Market. Children over 12 yrs only. TV in common rm; cable, VCR avail (movies). Complimentary full bkfst, coffee in rms. Ck-out 11 am, ck-in 5-7 pm. Business servs avail. Fireplaces. Grills. Built in 1918. Totally non-smoking. Cr cds: A, DS, MC, V.

Restaurant

★★ **J BASUL NOBLE'S.** *101 S Main St (27260). 336/889-3354. www.nobles restaurant.com.* Specializes in beef, veal, seafood. Hrs: 5:30-10 pm; Fri, Sat to 11 pm. Closed Sun; major hols. Res accepted. Bar. Dinner a la carte entrees: $10.95-$24.95. Entertainment: jazz combo Thurs-Sat. Cr cds: A, MC, V.

Jacksonville (D-7)

Pop 30,013 **Elev** 15 ft **Area code** 910

Motel/Motor Lodge

★★ **HAMPTON INN JACK-SONVILLE.** *474 Western Blvd (28546). 910/347-6500; fax 910/347-6858; res 800/426-7866. hamptoninn. com.* 120 rms, 2 story. S, D $63-$78; higher rates wkends. Crib free. TV; cable (premium). Pool. Complimentary continental bkfst. Restaurant adj 11 am-11 pm. Ck-out noon. Coin lndry. Meeting rms. Business servs avail. In-rm modem link. Sundries. Health club privileges. Cr cds: A, DS, MC, V.

Hotel

★★ **HOLIDAY INN EXPRESS.** *2115 Hwy 17 N (28546). 910/347-1900; fax 910/347-7593; res 800/465-4329. Email jxhiacct@shanerhotels.com.* 118 rms, 4 story. S, D $69; each addl $5; suites $74. Crib avail. Parking lot. Pool. TV; cable. Complimentary continental bkfst, coffee in rms, newspaper. Restaurant nearby. Ck-out 11 am, ck-in 3 pm. Meeting rm. Business servs avail. Dry cleaning, coin lndry. Exercise privileges. Golf. Tennis. Cr cds: A, C, D, DS, JCB, MC, V.

Jefferson
(B-3) *See also Boone*

Founded 1800 **Pop** 1,300
Elev 2,960 ft **Area code** 336
Zip 28640
Web www.ashechamber.com
Information Ashe County Chamber of Commerce, PO Box 31, West Jefferson 28694; 336/246-9550

Motel/Motor Lodge

★★ **BEST WESTERN ELDRETH INN.** *829 E Main St (28640), US 221 & NC 88. 336/246-8845; fax 336/246-9109; res 800/528-1234; toll-free 800/022-1882.* 48 rms, 1-2 story. Mid-May-Dec: S $56-$67; D $60-$74; each addl $6; lower rates rest of yr. Crib free. TV; cable. Restaurant 6 am-9 pm; Sun to 3 pm. Ck-out 11 am. Meeting rms. Exercise equipt; sauna. Some refrigerators, microwaves. Cr cds: A, C, D, DS, MC, V.

B&B/Small Inn

★★★ **GLENDALE SPRINGS INN.** *PO Box 117 7414 Hwy 16 (28629), 8 mi SE on NC 16. 336/982-2103; fax 336/982-2103; res 336/982-2103; toll-free 800/287-1206.* 9 rms, 2 story, 1 guest house. No rm phones. S, D $85-$115; each addl $10; guest house $115. TV; cable, VCR avail (movies). Complimentary full bkfst. Restaurant 11 am-2 pm, 5-9 pm. Ck-out 11 am, ck-in 2 pm. Business servs avail. 18-hole golf privileges. Some in-rm whirlpools. Built in 1898; Victorian décor. Totally nonsmoking. Cr cds: A, D, DS, MC, V.

Kill Devil Hills (Outer Banks)
See also Manteo, Nags Head

Pop 4,238 **Elev** 20 ft **Area code** 252
Zip 27948 **Web** www.outer-banks. com/visitor-info
Information Dare County Tourist Bureau, 704 US 64/264, PO Box 399,

Manteo 27954; 252/473-2138 or 800/446-6262

Although the name Kitty Hawk is usually associated with the Wright Brothers, their early flying experiments took place on and near these dunes on the Outer Banks (see).

What to See and Do

☒ **Wright Brothers National Memorial.** Field where first powered flight took place, Dec 17, 1903, is marked showing takeoff point and landing places. The living quarters and hangar bldgs used by the Wrights during their experiments have been reconstructed. The visitor center has reproductions of 1902 glider and 1903 flyer with exhibits on story of their invention. 3,000-ft airstrip. (Daily; closed Dec 25) Off US 158, between Mileposts 7 & 8. Phone 252/441-7430. ¢¢

Motels/Motor Lodges

★ **BEACH HAVEN MOTEL.** *4104 Virginia Dare Trail (27949), NC 12 milepost 4. 252/261-4785; res 888/ 559-0506. www.beachhavenmotel.com.* 6 rms. Early July-Labor Day: S, D $69-$112; each addl $6; wknd rates; higher rates hols (3-day min); lower rates Apr-June and Sep-Oct. Closed rest of yr. Crib free. TV; cable. Complimentary coffee in rms. Restaurant nearby. Ck-out 10 am. Coin lndry. Refrigerators, microwaves. Swimming beach. Grills. Cr cds: A, MC, V.
🐾 ⊠ 🐾 SC

★★ **BEST WESTERN OCEAN REEF SUITES.** *107 Virginia Dare Tr (27948). 252/441-1611; fax 252/441-1482; res 800/528-1234. www.best western.com/oceanreefsuites.* 70 kit. suites, 5 story. May-Sep: kit. suites (up to 6) $154-$190; each addl $10; under 17 free; lower rates rest of yr. Crib $5. TV; cable, VCR avail (movies). Heated pool; whirlpool. Restaurant 7 am-9 pm. Ck-out 11 am. Business servs avail. Exercise equipt; sauna, steam rm. Private patios, balconies. Cr cds: A, C, D, DS, ER, MC, V.
D 🐾 ⚒ ≈ 🕴 ⊠ 🐾

★★ **COMFORT INN.** *401 N Virginia Dare Tr (27948), NC 12 Milepost 8.*

252/480-2600; fax 252/480-2873; res 800/854-5286; toll-free 800/638-7949. 121 rms, 3 story. Memorial Day-Labor Day: S, D $117-$180; each addl $5; under 18 free; lower rates rest of yr. Crib free. TV; cable (premium). Pool. Complimentary continental bkfst, coffee in rms. Ck-out 11 am. Coin lndry. Business servs avail. Some refrigerators. Balconies. On ocean; swimming beach. Cr cds: A, C, D, DS, MC, V.
D 🐾 ≈ ⊠ 🐾 SC

★ **DAYS INN - OCEANFRONT.** *101 N Virginia Dare Tr (27948), NC 12 milepost 8.5. 252/441-7211; fax 919/441-8080.* 52 units, 2 story, 15 kits. Mid-June-early Sep: S, D $90-$105; each addl $5; kit. units $125-$160; higher rates: hols, wkends; lower rates mid-Sep-mid-June. Crib free. TV; cable (premium). Pool. Complimentary continental bkfst. Ck-out 11 am. Business servs avail. In-rm modem link. Refrigerators. On swimming beach. Volleyball. Cr cds: A, D, DS, JCB, MC, V.
🐾 ≈ ⊠ 🐾

★★ **HOLIDAY INN.** *1601 Virginia Dare Tr (27948), on NC 12 between Mileposts 9 and 10. 252/441-6333; fax 252/441-7779; res 800/465-4329; toll-free 800/843-1249.* 105 rms, 4 story. May-Sep: S, D $139-$190; each addl $10; under 19 free; lower rates rest of yr. Crib free. TV; cable. Pool; whirlpool, wading pool. Restaurant 7-11 am, 5:30-9 pm. Bar 5:30 pm-1:30 am; entertainment. Ck-out 11 am. Coin lndry. Meeting rms. Business servs avail. In-rm modem link. Refrigerators, microwaves. Private patios, balconies. Oceanfront deck. On beach; many oceanfront rms. Cr cds: A, C, D, DS, MC, V.
D 🐾 ⚒ ≈ 🕴 ⊠ 🐾

★★ **NAGS HEAD BEACH.** *804 N Virginia Dare Tr (27948). 252/441-0411; fax 252/441-7811; res 800/338-7761.* 96 rms, 4 story. Mid-June-early Sep: S, D $78-$100; under 18 free; higher rates hol wkends; lower rates rest of yr. Crib free. Pet accepted. TV; cable (premium). Pool. Complimentary continental bkfst. Ck-out 11 am. Refrigerators. Many balconies. Cr cds: A, D, DS, MC, V.
D 🐾 🐾 ≈ ⊠ 🐾 SC

Resort

★★ RAMADA INN OUTER BANKS RESORT & CONFERENCE CENTER.
1701 S Virginia Dare Tr (27948), Milepost 9.5, NC 12. 252/441-2151; fax 252/441-1830; res 800/228-2828; toll-free 800/635-1824. www.ramada innnagshead.com. 172 rms, 5 story. June-Aug: S, D $229; each addl $10; under 17 free; lower rates rest of yr. Crib avail. Pet accepted, some restrictions, fee. Parking lot. Indoor pool, whirlpool. TV; cable, VCR avail. Complimentary coffee in rms, toll-free calls. Restaurant 7 am. Bar. Ck-out 11 am, ck-in 4 pm. Meeting rms. Business servs avail. Bellhops. Exercise privileges. Golf. Tennis. Beach access. Bike rentals. Picnic facilities. Cr cds: A, C, D, DS, ER, JCB, MC, V.

B&B/Small Inn

★ CYPRESS HOUSE B & B. *500 N Virginia Dare Tr (27948), on NC 12, Milepost 8. 252/441-6127; fax 252/441-2009; toll-free 800/554-2764. Email cypresshse@aol.com; www.cypress houseinn.com.* 6 rms, 2 story. No rm phones. June-Aug: S, D $110; lower rates Apr-May and Sep-Oct. Closed rest of yr. Children over 13 yrs only. TV; cable. Complimentary continental bkfst. Ck-out 11 am, ck-in 3 pm. Sitting rm. Near swimming beach. Totally nonsmoking. Cr cds: A, DS, MC, V.

Restaurants

★★ FLYING FISH CAFE. *2003 Croatan Hwy (27948). 252/441-6894. Email gwp3@earthlink.net.* Specializes in seafood prepared Mediterranean style, pasta. Own baking. Hrs: 11:30 am-10 pm; Sat, Sun from 5 pm; early-bird dinner 5-6 pm. Res accepted. Bar. Lunch $3.95-$6.95; dinner $9.95-$17.95. Child's menu. Parking. Cr cds: A, DS, MC, V.

★ JOLLY ROGER. *1836 N Virginia Dare Tr (27948), on NC 12 between Mileposts 6.5 and 7. 252/441-6530. Email mardud@beachlink.com.* Specializes in seafood, pasta, beef. Hrs: 6-1 am. Bar. Bkfst $1.50-$8; lunch $2-$8; dinner $7.95-$29.95. Cr cds: A, D, DS, MC, V.

★★ PORT O' CALL. *504 Virginia Dare Tr (27948). 252/441-8001. Email portocall@aginet.com.* Specializes in seafood, beef, pasta. Hrs: 5-10 pm. Closed Jan-mid-Mar. Res accepted. Bar. Dinner $9.95-$34.95. Child's menu. Turn-of-the-century Victorian decor. Gift shop, antiques, art gallery. Cr cds: A, DS, MC, V.

Kinston (C-7)

Pop 25,295 **Elev** 44 ft **Area code** 252 **Zip** 28501

Motels/Motor Lodges

★★ BEST WESTERN RIVERVIEW.
208 E New Bern Rd (28504). 252/527-4155; fax 252/527-2900; toll-free 800/528-1234. www.holiday.com. 100 rms, 2 story. S, D $47-$69; each addl $5. Crib free. TV; cable (premium). Pool; wading pool. Restaurant 6 am-2 pm, 5:30-10 pm. Bar 5 pm-1 am. Ck-out noon. Meeting rms. Business center. In-rm modem link. Cr cds: A, C, D, DS, JCB, MC, V.

★★ COMFORT INN. *200 W New Bern Rd (28504). 252/527-3200; fax 252/527-3200; res 800/228-5150.* 60 rms, 2 story. Apr-Sep: S, D $52-$60; each addl $5; suites $65; under 18 free; lower rates rest of yr. Crib $5. TV; cable (premium); VCR avail. Pool. Complimentary continental bkfst, coffee in rms. Restaurant nearby. Ck-out noon. Meeting rms. Business center. Exercise equipt; sauna. Refrigerators, microwaves. Cr cds: A, D, DS, JCB, MC, V.

★★ HAMPTON INN. *1382 NC 258 S (28501). 252/523-1400; fax 252/523-1326; res 800/250-5370.* 123 rms, 4 story. June-late Sep: S $54-$59; D $59-$64; under 17 free; lower rates rest of yr. Crib free. Pet accepted. TV; cable (premium). Pool. Complimentary continental bkfst. Ck-out noon. Meeting rms. Business servs avail.

Some refrigerators. Cr cds: A, C, D, DS, MC, V.

Kitty Hawk (Outer Banks)

(see Kill Devil Hills)

Laurinburg

(D-5) *See also Pinehurst, Southern Pines*

Settled (ca 1700) **Pop** 11,643 **Elev** 227 ft **Area code** 910 **Web** www.ncseorg/scotland.html

Information Laurinburg-Scotland County Area Chamber of Commerce, 606 Atkinson St, PO Box 1025, 28353; 910/276-7420

Motels/Motor Lodges

★★ **COMFORT INN.** *1705 US 401 S (28352), 1 mi S of US 74 on US 15/401.* 910/277-7788; fax 910/277-7229; res 800/228-5150. 80 rms, 2 story. S $59-$99; D $59-$110; each addl $8; under 18 free; family rates; higher rates: special events, Rockingham Races. Crib free. TV; cable (premium), VCR avail. Pool. Complimentary continental bkfst. Restaurant adj 5:30-9:30 pm. Ck-out noon. Meeting rms. Business servs avail. Sundries. Exercise equipt. Some in-rm whirlpools, refrigerators. Cr cds: A, C, D, DS, JCB, MC, V.

★ **PINE ACRES LODGE.** *11860 McCall Rd (28352), US 15, 401 S Bypass.* 910/276-1531; fax 910/277-1481; toll-free 800/348-8242. 74 rms. S, D $22.50-$40; each addl $6. TV; cable (premium). Pool; wading pool. Complimentary continental bkfst. Restaurant nearby. Ck-out 11 am. Refrigerators. Cr cds: A, C, D, DS, MC, V.

Restaurant

★ **CHAMPS.** *1500 US 401 S (28352).* 910/276-4386. Specializes in sandwiches, seafood, beef. Salad bar. Hrs: 4 pm-12:30 am; Wed to 11 pm. Closed Sun, Mon; Easter, July 4, Dec 25. Res accepted. Bar. Dinner $9-$19.95. Child's menu. Decorated with ACC colleges memorabilia. Cr cds: A, D, DS, MC, V.

Lenoir

(C-3) *See also Blowing Rock*

Pop 14,192 **Elev** 1,182 ft **Area code** 828 **Zip** 28645

Motel/Motor Lodge

★★ **RAMADA LIMITED.** *142 Wilkesboro Blvd SE (28645).* 828/758-4403; fax 878/758-1349; res 800/2RAMADA. 100 rms, 2 story. S, D $55-$65; each addl $10; under 19 free. Crib free. TV. Pool. Complimentary continental bkfst. Ck-out 11 am. Meeting rms. Cr cds: A, C, D, DS, JCB, MC, V.

Lexington

(C-4) *See also Asheboro, High Point, Winston-Salem*

Settled 1750 **Pop** 16,581 **Elev** 809 ft **Area code** 336 **Zip** 27292

Information Chamber of Commerce, 16 E Center St, PO Box C, 27293; 336/248-5929

In 1775, settlers learned of the battle of Lexington in Massachusetts and decided to name this town for it. Local industry is diversified and includes furniture making, textiles and clothing, food processing, electronics, ceramics, machinery, and fiberglass. Native to the area is traditional pork barbecue, which can be found in many local restaurants.

What to See and Do

High Rock Lake. Its 300-mi shoreline is a center for water sports in the piedmont. 10 mi SW on US 70 or S on NC 8.

Old Davidson County Courthouse. (1858) Greek Revival bldg facing the town square; old courtrm houses museum of local history. (Tues-Fri, also Sun afternoons; closed hols) Center of city. Phone 336/242-2035. **FREE**

Linville

See also Banner Elk, Blowing Rock, Boone

Pop 244 (est) **Elev** 3,669 ft
Area code 828 **Zip** 28646

Linville is in the heart of a ruggedly beautiful resort area. Several miles to the south, just off the Blue Ridge Parkway, is scenic Linville Falls, cascading down the steep Linville Gorge, designated a national wilderness. Visible from vantage points in this area are the mysterious Brown Mountain lights.

What to See and Do

★ **Grandfather Mountain.** (5,964 ft) Highest peak in the Blue Ridge, with spectacular views, rugged rock formations; 1-mi-high swinging bridge; bald eagles, deer, cougars, black bears, bear cubs, and others in natural habitats. Hiking trails, picnic areas. Museum with exhibits on local animals, birds, flowers, geology; restaurant; gift shop. (Daily; winter, open weather permitting; closed Thanksgiving, Dec 25) 2 mi NE via US 221, 1 mi S of jct Blue Ridge Pkwy & US 221. Phone 828/733-4337. ¢¢¢

Annual Events

Grandfather Mountain Nature Photography Weekend. Grandfather Mt. Nationally known photographers give illustrated lectures; nature photography contest; picnic dinner. Preregistration required. Late May-early June.

"Singing on the Mountain." On the slopes of Grandfather Mt. All-day program of modern and traditional gospel music featuring top groups and nationally known speakers. Concessions or bring your own food. Fourth Sun June.

Grandfather Mountain Highland Games. MacRae Meadows, on US 221 at Grandfather Mt. Gathering of members of over 100 Scottish clans and societies to view or participate in traditional Scottish sports, track-and-field events, mountain marathon; highland dancing, piping, and drumming; ceremonies and pageantry. Mid-July.

Resort

★★★★ **ESEEOLA LODGE.** *175 Linville Ave (28646), US 221 & NC 105, 2 mi W of Blue Ridge Pkwy. 828/733-4311; fax 828/733-3227; toll-free 800/742-6717. Email reservations@eseeola.com; www.eseeola.com.* The fresh mountain air alone demands return visits to this 24-room haven in the Blue Ridge Mountains. Open since 1892, the lodge welcomes guests mid-May through October for hiking the high country or enjoying the eight Har-tru tennis courts and 18-hole championship course at Linville Golf Club. Rates include breakfast and dinner prepared by chef John Hofland who specializes in southern-influenced, international cuisine. 19 rms, 2 story, 5 suites. July-Oct: S, D $325; each addl $60; suites $425; lower rates rest of yr. Crib avail. Parking lot. Pool, lifeguard. TV; cable (premium). Complimentary full bkfst, coffee in rms,

Mile High Swinging Bridge, Grandfather Mountain

newspaper, toll-free calls. Restaurant. Bar. Ck-out 11 am, ck-in 4 pm. Business center. Bellhops. Concierge. Exercise rm. Golf, 18 holes. Tennis, 8 courts. Supervised children's activities. Hiking trail. Picnic facilities. Cr cds: MC, V.

Little Switzerland

See also Burnsville, Linville, Morganton

Founded 1910 **Pop** 200 (est)
Elev 3,500 ft **Area code** 828
Zip 28749 **Web** www.mitchell-county.com/north-carolina

Information Mitchell County Chamber of Commerce, Rte 1, Box 796, Spruce Pine 28777; 828/765-9483 or 800/227-3912

Hotels

★★★ **CHALET SWITZERLAND INN.** *226A Blue Ridge Pkwy (28749), Blue Ridge Pkwy at Milepost 334. 828/765-2153; fax 828/765-0049; toll-free 800/654-4026. Email swissinn@wnclink.com; www.switzerlandinn.com.* 57 rms, 2 story, 8 suites. Sep-Oct: S $100; D $130; each addl $15; suites $130; children $5; under 12 free; lower rates rest of yr. Pet accepted, some restrictions. Parking lot. Pool. TV; cable. Complimentary full bkfst, coffee in rms, newspaper, toll-free calls. Restaurant 7:30 am-9:30 pm. Bar. Ck-out 11 am, ck-in 3 pm. Meeting rms. Business center. Gift shop. Golf. Tennis, 2 courts. Supervised children's activities. Hiking trail. Picnic facilities. Cr cds: A, MC, V.

★ **PINEBRIDGE INN.** *101 Pinebridge Ave (28777), 3 mi S on NC 226, off Summit St. 828/765-5543; fax 828/765-5544; toll-free 800/356-5059. Email thomas@m-y.net; www.pinebridgeinn.com.* 44 rms, 3 story, 1 suite. S, D $67; each addl $10; suites $84; under 12 free. Crib avail, fee. Parking lot. TV; cable. Complimentary continental bkfst, coffee in rms, newspaper, toll-free calls. Restaurant nearby. Ck-out 2 pm, ck-in noon. Meeting rms.

Business servs avail. Gift shop. Exercise privileges, sauna, steam rm. Golf. Tennis. Downhill skiing. Hiking trail. Picnic facilities. Cr cds: A, DS, MC, V.

B&Bs/Small Inns

★ **ALPINE INN.** *PO Box 477 (28749), Blue Ridge Pkwy Milepost 334, then S on NC 226A. 828/765-5380; res 828/765-5380.* 13 rms, 3 story, 1 suite. July-Aug, Oct: S $40; D $52; suites $65; lower rates rest of yr. Street parking. TV; cable. Ck-out noon, ck-in 1 pm. Golf, 18 holes. Cr cds: DS, MC, V.

★★ **BIG LYNN LODGE.** *NC 226A (28749), 1½ mi W on NC 226A. 828/765-4257; fax 828/765-0301; toll-free 800/654-5232. Email biglynn@m-y.net; www.biglynnlodge.com.* 38 rms, 2 story, 4 suites. July-Aug, Oct: S $75; D $85; each addl $23; suites $129; under 5 free; lower rates rest of yr. Crib avail. Parking lot. TV; cable. Complimentary full bkfst. Restaurant. Ck-out 11 am, ck-in 3 pm. Business servs avail. Coin lndry. Gift shop. Golf. Downhill skiing. Hiking trail. Cr cds: MC, V.

Lumberton (D-5)

Founded 1787 **Pop** 18,601 **Elev** 137 ft
Area code 910 **Zip** 28358
Web www.I95travel.org

Information Visitors Bureau, 3431 Lackey St, 28358; 910/739-9999 or 800/359-6971

Annual Event

Scottish Highland Games. Celebration of Scottish heritage with music; dancing; competitions; children's events. Phone 910/843-5000. First wkend Oct.

Motels/Motor Lodges

★★ **COMFORT INN.** *3070 Roberts Ave (28360). 910/739-4800; fax 910/738-5299.* 65 rms, 2 story. S

$49.95-$65; D $52.95-$65; each addl $5; suites $75-$85; under 18 free; higher rates special events. Crib $5. TV; cable (premium), VCR avail (movies). Complimentary continental bkfst, coffee in rms. Restaurant nearby. Ck-out 11 am. Business servs avail. In-rm modem link. Exercise equipt. Pool. Refrigerators, microwaves. Cr cds: A, DS, MC, V.

★★ COMFORT SUITES. *215 Wintergreen Dr (28358). 910/739-8800; fax 910/739-0027; res 800/228-5150.* 93 suites, 4 story. Suites $65-$95; each addl $5; under 18 free. Crib free. TV; cable (premium), VCR avail. Pool. Complimentary continental bkfst, coffee in rms. Restaurant nearby. Ck-out 11 am. Coin lndry. Meeting rms. Business servs avail. In-rm modem link. Exercise equipt; sauna. Health club privileges. Refrigerators; microwaves avail. Cr cds: A, C, D, DS, MC, V.

★★ COUNTRY INN AND SUITES. *3621 Dawn Dr (28358). 910/738-2481; fax 910/738-8260; res 800/456-4000; toll-free 800/524-9999. www.countryinn.com.* 53 rms, 4 story, 10 suites. June-Sep: S $45.95-$65.95; D $50.95-$80.95; each addl $7; suites $65.95-$85.95; under 12 free; higher rates special events; lower rates rest of yr. Crib $7. TV; cable (premium). Complimentary continental bkfst, coffee in rms. Restaurant nearby. Ck-out noon. Business servs avail. In-rm modem link. Sundries. Coin lndry. Exercise equipt. Pool. Refrigerator, microwave in suites. Cr cds: A, C, D, DS, MC, V.

★★ HOLIDAY INN. *5201 Fayetteville Rd (28358). 910/671-1166; fax 910/671-1166; toll-free 800/465-4329.* 108 rms, 2 story. S, D $55-$70; each addl $6; under 18 free. Crib free. TV; cable (premium). Pool. Restaurant open 24 hrs. Ck-out noon. Meeting rms. Business servs avail. In-rm modem link. Health club privileges. Cr cds: A, D, DS, MC, V.

★★ QUALITY INN AND SUITES. *3608 Kahn Dr (28358). 910/738-8261; fax 910/671-9075; res 800/228-5151.* 120 rms, 2 story. Late Apr-mid-Sep: S,

D $49.95-$65; each addl $6; suites $65-$79; under 17 free; higher rates special events; lower rates rest of yr. Crib free. Pet accepted. TV; cable. Pool. Complimentary continental bkfst. Restaurant 6 am-10 pm. Bar 5 pm-midnight. Ck-out noon. Meeting rms. Business servs avail. Health club privileges. Refrigerator, microwave in suites. Cr cds: A, D, DS, MC, V.

Hotels

★★ FAIRFIELD INN. *3361 Lacket St (28360). 910/739-8444; fax 910/739-8466; res 800/288-2800.* 100 rms, 3 story, 5 suites. June-Aug: S, D $99; under 18 free; lower rates rest of yr. Crib avail. Parking lot. Pool. TV; cable (premium). Complimentary continental bkfst, newspaper, toll-free calls. Restaurant nearby. Ck-out 11 am, ck-in 2 pm. Fax servs avail. Exercise privileges. Cr cds: A, C, D, DS, MC, V.

★★ HAMPTON INN. *201 Wintergreen Dr (28358). 910/738-3332; fax 910/739-8641; res 800/426-7866.* 66 rms, 2 story, 2 suites. June-Aug: S, D $119; suites $133; under 18 free; lower rates rest of yr. Crib avail. Parking lot. Pool. TV; cable (premium). Complimentary continental bkfst, coffee in rms, newspaper, toll-free calls. Restaurant nearby. Ck-out 11 am, ck-in 2 pm. Business center. Dry cleaning, coin lndry. Exercise privileges. Golf. Cr cds: A, C, D, DS, MC, V.

Restaurant

★★ JOHN'S. *4880 Kahn Dr (28358). 910/738-4709.* Specializes in beef, seafood, prime rib. Hrs: 5:30-10 pm. Closed Sun, Mon; hols. Res accepted. Bar. Dinner $10.50-$22.95. Cr cds: A, D, DS, MC, V.

Maggie Valley

See also Asheville, Cherokee, Waynesville

Pop 185 **Elev** 3,020 ft **Area code** 828
Zip 28751
Web www.maggivalley.com/chamber
Information CVB Chamber of Commerce, 2487 Soco Rd, PO Box 87; 828/926-1686 or 800/785-8259

Annual Events

International Folk Festival. Premier folk groups from over 10 countries demonstrate their cultural heritage through lively music and costumed dance. Phone 828/452-2997. Eleven days late July.

Clogging Hall of Fame. World-class cloggers from all across US compete. Oct.

Motels/Motor Lodges

★★ **BEST WESTERN MOUNTAIN BROOK.** *3811 Soco Rd PO Box 565 (28751), on US 19.* 828/926-3962; *res* 800/528-1234. 48 rms, 2 story. May-Oct: S, D $49-$99; each addl $8; under 12 free; ski plans; higher rates special events; lower rates rest of yr. Crib free. TV; cable (premium). Pool; whirlpool. Complimentary continental bkfst, coffee in rms. Restaurant adj 7:30 am-8 pm. Ck-out 11 am. Meeting rms. Business servs avail. Sundries. 18-hole golf privileges, greens fee $50, putting green, driving range. Refrigerators, microwaves. Picnic tables. Cr cds: A, D, DS, MC, V.

🄳 🐾 🏕 🏊 🏋 🏂 🔥

★ **CARDINAL INN.** *3735 Soco Rd (28751), on US 19.* 828/926-0422; *fax* 828/926-2570; *toll-free* 800/826-0422. *Email* berg@primeline.com; *www.the cardinalinn.com.* 10 rms, 1 story. July, Oct: S, D $100; each addl $5; suites $110; under 6 free; lower rates rest of yr. Crib avail. Parking lot. TV; cable (premium), VCR avail. Complimentary toll-free calls. Restaurant. Ck-out 11 am, ck-in 11 pm. Business center. Golf, 18 holes. Downhill skiing. Hiking trail. Picnic facilities. Cr cds: A, DS, MC, V.

🄳 🏂 🏋 🎿 🚣 🏊 🔥 🏃

★★ **COMFORT INN.** *3282 Soco Rd (28751), on US 19.* 828/926-9106; *fax* 828/926-9106; *res* 800/228-5150. 68 rms, 2 story. June-Oct: S $55-$99; D $65-$99; each addl $10; under 18 free; lower rates rest of yr. Crib free. TV; cable (premium). Pool. Complimentary continental bkfst, coffee. Restaurant opp 7 am-10 pm. Ck-out 11 am. Whirlpool in some suites. Cr cds: A, D, DS, JCB, MC, V.

🄳 🐾 🏕 🏊 🏂 🔥

★★ **JOHNATHAN CREEK INN AND VILLAS.** *4324 Soco Rd (28751), on US 19.* 828/926-1232; *fax* 828/926-9751; *toll-free* 800/577-7812. *Email* jeff@jonathancreekinn.com; *www. jonathancreekinn.com.* 32 rms, 2 story, 10 suites. June-Oct: S $89; D $99; each addl $5; suites $109; under 17 free; lower rates rest of yr. Crib avail. Parking lot. Indoor pool, whirlpool. TV; cable. Complimentary coffee in rms, newspaper, toll-free calls. Restaurant. Ck-out 11 am, ck-in 2 pm. Fax servs avail. Coin lndry. Gift shop. Golf. Downhill skiing. Supervised children's activities. Hiking trail. Picnic facilities. Video games. Cr cds: A, DS, MC, V.

🄳 🐾 🏂 🏋 🚣 🎿 🏊 🔥 SC

★ **RIVERLET MOTEL.** *4102 Soco Rd (28751), 4½ mi W on US 19.* 828/926-1900; *toll-free* 800/691-9952. *Email* donnal@riverlet.com; *www.riverlet.com.* 21 rms, 2 story. May-Oct: S, D $45; each addl $7; children $7; under 10 free; lower rates rest of yr. Crib avail. Parking lot. Pool. TV; cable (premium). Complimentary toll-free calls. Restaurant 7 am-11 pm. Ck-out 11 am, ck-in 1 pm. Meeting rm. Fax servs avail. Golf. Downhill skiing. Supervised children's activities. Hiking trail. Picnic facilities. Cr cds: DS, MC, V.

🄳 🐾 🏂 🏋 🚣 🎿 🏊 🔥

★ **ROCKY WATERS.** *4898 Soco Rd (28751), 1½ mi W on US 19, 3 mi E of Blue Ridge Pkwy, Soco Exit.* 828/926-1585; *toll-free* 888/224-4882. 30 rms, 1 story. June-July, Oct: S $58; D $85; each addl $8; lower rates rest of yr. Crib avail. Parking lot. Indoor/outdoor pools. TV; cable. Restaurant nearby. Ck-out 11 am, ck-in 1 pm. Golf. Hiking trail. Picnic facilities. Cr cds: A, DS, MC, V.

🐾 🏂 🏋 🚣 🏊 🔥

★ **STONY CREEK.** *4494 Soco Rd (28751). 828/926-1996; toll-free 800/ 926-1196. Email mandyh@brinet.com; www.smokymountainsnc.com/stony creek.htm.* 19 rms, 2 story. July-Aug, Oct: S, D $90; lower rates rest of yr. Crib avail. Parking lot. TV; cable (premium). Restaurant. Ck-out 11 am, ck-in noon. Golf, 18 holes. Downhill skiing. Picnic facilities. Cr cds: MC, V.
⊡ ⬚ ⬚ ⬚ ⬚ ⬚

Guest Ranch

★★★ **CATALOOCHEE SKI AREA.** *119 Ranch Dr (28751), 3 mi NE of US 19. 828/926-0285; fax 828/926-9249; toll-free 800/868-1401.* 15 rms in two 2-story lodges, 11 cabins, 2 suites. No A/C. July, Aug, Oct, and Dec: S $125-$140; D $130-$250; each addl $55-$60; suites, kit. cottages $190-$210; lower rates rest of yr. Crib free. Serv charge 17%. Supervised children's activities (June-Aug); ages 6-16. Box lunches, cookouts. Beer, wine, setups. Ck-out 11 am, ck-in 3 pm. Business servs avail. Tennis. Downhill ski 1 mi. Whirlpool. Lawn games. Card rm. Mountain music entertainment. Fireplace in lobby, cottages, some rms. 5,000-ft elevation. 1,000-acre working ranch; Appalachian stone barn (1870) remodeled to ranch house. Cr cds: A, MC, V.
⊡ ⬚ ⬚ ⬚ ⬚ ⬚ ⬚ ⬚

Restaurant

★★ **J. ARTHUR'S.** *2843 Soco Rd (28751), on US 19S. 828/926-1817.* Specializes in steak, fresh seafood. Own desserts. Hrs: 5-9:30 pm. Closed Thanksgiving, Dec 25. Bar. Dinner $9.25-$24.95. Child's menu. Loft dining area. Cr cds: A, MC, V.
⊡ ⬚

Manteo

See also Kill Devil Hills, Nags Head

Pop 991 **Elev** 5 ft **Area code** 252 **Zip** 27954 **Web** www.outer-banks.com/visitor-info
Information Dare County Tourist Bureau, 704 US 64/264, PO Box 399; 252/473-2138 or 800/446-6262

Seasonal Event

The Lost Colony. Drama by Paul Green (see FORT RALEIGH NATIONAL HISTORIC SITE).

B&B/Small Inn

★★★ **TRANQUIL HOUSE INN.** *405 Queen Elizabeth St (27954). 252/ 473-1404; fax 252/473-1526; toll-free 800/458-7069. Email djust1587@aol. com.* 25 rms, 3 story. Memorial Day-Labor Day: S, D $129-$179; suites $179; wkly rates; lower rates rest of yr. Crib $10. TV; cable (premium). Complimentary continental bkfst; afternoon refreshments. Restaurant 5-10 pm. Ck-out 11 am, ck-in 3 pm. Business servs avail. Bicycles. Built in style of a 19th-century Outer Banks inn; cypress woodwork, beveled glass doors, observation tower. On bay; overlooks marina. Cr cds: A, DS, MC, V.
⊡ ⬚ ⬚ ⬚ ⬚

Restaurants

★★ **CLARA'S SEAFOOD GRILL.** *Queen Elizabeth Ave (27954), on the waterfront. 252/473-1727. Email 3@ beachlink.com.* Specializes in fresh seafood, beef, pasta. Hrs: 11:30 am-9 pm; summer hrs vary. Closed Thanksgiving, Dec 25; Jan. Bar. Lunch, dinner $3.95-$17.95. Child's menu. Three dining rms with view of bay. Art Deco decor. Cr cds: A, DS, MC, V.
⊡ ⬚

★★ **QUEEN ANNE'S REVENGE.** *1064 Old Wharf Rd (27981), S on NC 345. 252/473-5466.* Specializes in fresh seafood. Hrs: 5-9 pm. Closed Tues in Oct-June; Dec 24, 25. Wine, beer. Dinner $13-$25. Child's menu. Artwork. Cr cds: A, D, DS, MC, V.
⊡ ⬚

Marion

(B-3) *See also Little Switzerland, Morganton*

Founded 1843 **Pop** 4,765 **Elev** 1,395 ft **Area code** 704 **Zip** 28752

Permits for the Linville Gorge Wilderness of the Pisgah National Forest (see BREVARD) can be obtained at the Grandfather Ranger District Office (Rte 1 Box 110A; 704/652-2144), located here.

What to See and Do

Linville Caverns. Beneath Humpback Mt. Half-hr guided tours. Gift shop. (Mar-Nov, daily; rest of yr, wkends only) 17 mi N on US 221. Phone 704/756-4171. ¢¢

Morehead City

(D-7) *See also Beaufort*

Founded 1857 **Pop** 6,046 **Elev** 16 ft
Area code 252 **Zip** 28557
Web www.sunnync.com

Information Carteret County Tourism Development Bureau, PO Box 1406; 252/726-8148 or 800/SUNNY-NC

Annual Events

Big Rock Blue Marlin Tournament. Largest tournament of its kind on the East Coast. Fishing for blue marlin; cash awards; registration required. Phone 252/247-3575. Six days early June.

Atlantic Beach King Mackerel Tournament. Phone 252/247-2334. Mid-Sep.

North Carolina Seafood Festival. Seafood, arts and crafts, music. Phone 252/726-NCSF. First wkend Oct.

Motels/Motor Lodges

★★ **BEST WESTERN BUCCANEER.** *2806 Arendell St (28557). 252/726-3115; fax 252/726-3864; res 800/528-1234; toll-free 800/682-4982.* 91 rms, 3 story. May-Aug: S, D $65-$92; each addl $5; under 18 free; lower rates rest of yr. Crib free. TV; cable (premium). Pool. Complimentary full bkfst. Restaurant adj 6 am-10 pm. Ck-out noon. Meeting rms. Business servs avail. Refrigerators; some in-rm whirlpools. Cr cds: A, C, D, DS, MC, V.

★★ **COMFORT INN.** *3100 Arendell St (28557). 252/247-3434; fax 252/247-4411; res 800/228-5150; toll-free 800/422-5404. Email comfort@moreheadhotels.com; www.moreheadhotels.com.* 101 rms, 2 story. Apr-Aug: S $50-$95; D $55-$100; each addl $5; under 18 free; lower rates rest of yr. Crib $5. TV; cable (premium), VCR avail. Pool. Complimentary continental bkfst. Restaurant adj 6 am-11 pm. Ck-out 11 am. Meeting rm. Business servs avail. Some refrigerators. Cr cds: A, DS, MC, V.

★★ **CRYSTAL COAST.** *109 Salterpath Rd (28512), 3 mi W on NC 58. 252/726-2544; fax 252/726-6570; res 800/733-7888.* 114 rms, 5 story. May-Aug: S, D $129-$189; each addl $10; under 18 free; golf plans; lower rates rest of yr. Crib free. TV; cable (premium). Pool; wading pool. Restaurant 7 am-1 pm, 5:30-9 pm. Bar 5-10 pm. Ck-out 11 am. Meeting rms. Business servs avail. In-rm modem link. Tennis privileges. Golf privileges. Private patios, balconies. Picnic tables. On beach. Cr cds: A, C, D, DS, JCB, MC, V.

★ **DAYS INN AND SUITES.** *602 W Fort Macon Rd (28512), S on Atlantic Beach Bridge, then ½ mi W on Fort Macon Rd (NC 58). 252/247-6400; fax 252/247-2264; res 800/329-7466; toll-free 800/972-3297.* 90 rms, 2 story. May-Sep: S, D $84-$135; under 12 free; package plans; lower rates rest of yr. Crib free. TV; cable. Pool. Complimentary continental bkfst. Restaurant nearby. Ck-out noon. Coin lndry. Business servs avail. In-rm modem link. Refrigerators; microwaves avail. Balconies. Picnic tables. Ocean nearby. Cr cds: A, DS, MC, V.

★ **ECONO LODGE.** *3410 Bridges St (28557). 252/247-2940; fax 252/247-0746.* 56 rms, 2 story. June-Aug: S, D $48-$85; each addl $5; under 19 free; wkly rates; lower rates rest of yr. Crib $5. TV; cable (premium). Pool; wading pool. Complimentary continental bkfst. Restaurant nearby. Ck-out 11 am. Meeting rms. Business servs avail. In-rm modem link. Cr cds: A, D, DS, MC, V.

★ **SEAHAWK MOTOR LODGE.**
*Salter Path Rd (28512), S on US 70,
then W on NC 58. 252/726-4146; toll-
free 800/682-6898. www.insiders.com/
crystalcoast/wwwads/seahawk.* 36 rms,
2 story. May-Labor Day: S, D $97-
$120; kit. cottages $130; villas
$1,600/wk; under 16 free; 3-day min
hol wkends; lower rates rest of yr.
TV; cable (premium). Pool. Restaurant 7:30 am-2 pm. Ck-out 11 am.
Refrigerators. Some balconies, patios.
On ocean; swimming beach. Cr cds:
MC, V.

★ **WINDJAMMER INN.** *Salter Path
Rd (28512), S on US 70, then 3 mi W
on NC 58. 252/247-7123; fax 252/
247-0133; toll-free 800/233-6466.
Email fleming@nternet.net; www.
windjammerinn.com.* 45 rms, 5 story.
May-Sep: S, D $92-$125; under 12
free; wkly rates; lower rates rest of yr.
Crib free. TV; cable (premium). Pool.
Complimentary coffee in lobby.
Restaurant nearby. Ck-out 11 am.
Bathrm phones, refrigerators. Bal-
conies. On beach. Cr cds: A, DS,
MC, V.

Hotels

★★ **HAMPTON INN.** *4035 Arendell
St (28557). 252/240-2300; fax 252/240-
2311; toll-free 800/467-9375. Email
gm.hampton@tectonhospitality.com.*
110 rms, 4 story, 9 suites. May-Aug:
S $114; D $124; suites $140; under
18 free; lower rates rest of yr. Crib
avail. Parking lot. Pool. TV; cable,
VCR avail. Complimentary continental bkfst, coffee in rms, newspaper,
toll-free calls. Restaurant. Meeting
rms. Business servs avail. Dry cleaning. Exercise privileges. Golf. Cr cds:
A, C, D, DS, MC, V.

★★★ **SHERATON.** *2717 W Fort
Macon Rd (28512), 3 mi W on NC 58.
252/240-1155; fax 919/240-1452.* 200
rms, 9 story. Mid-May-Labor Day: S,
D $135-$165; each addl $15; suites
$210-$235; under 18 free; lower rates
rest of yr. Crib free. TV; cable (premium). Indoor/outdoor pool; whirlpool, poolside serv. Supervised
children's activities (Memorial Day-
Labor Day). Complimentary coffee in
rms. Restaurant 6:30 am-2 pm, 5-
10:30 pm. Bar 5 pm-2 am; entertain-

ment. Ck-out noon. Meeting rms.
Business servs avail. Gift shop. Exercise equipt. Refrigerators. microwaves. Balconies. On ocean. Cr cds:
A, C, D, DS, ER, JCB, MC, V.

B&Bs/Small Inns

★★ **EMERALD ISLE INN AND BED
& BREAKFAST.** *502 Ocean Dr
(28594), 13 mi S US 58. 252/354-3222;
fax 252/354-3222. Email adetwiller@
coastalnet.com; www4.coastalnet.com/
emeraldisleinn.* 4 rms, 2 story. Mid-
May-Labor Day: S, D, suites $125-
$160; each addl $15; under 6 free;
lower rates rest of yr. Complimentary
full bkfst. Restaurant nearby. Ck-out
11 am, ck-in 3 pm. On Bogue Banks.
Totally nonsmoking. Cr cds: A, DS,
MC, V.

★★ **HARBOR LIGHT GUEST
HOUSE.** *332 Live Oak Dr (28584), 20
mi S on NC 24/58. 252/393-6868; fax
252/393-6868; toll-free 800/624-8439.
www.bbhost.com/harborlightgh.* 3 story,
7 suites. S, D $140; each addl $40;
suites $140; under 16 free. Street
parking. Indoor pool, whirlpool. TV;
cable, VCR avail, CD avail. Complimentary full bkfst, coffee in rms,
newspaper, toll-free calls. Restaurant
nearby. Ck-out 11 am, ck-in 3 pm.
Business center. Concierge. Exercise
privileges. Golf. Tennis, 4 courts.
Beach access. Hiking trail. Cr cds: A,
MC, V.

Restaurants

★★ **ANCHOR INN.** *109 N 28th St
(28557). 252/726-2156. www.anchor.
inn.com.* Specializes in black Angus
beef, fresh local seafood, chicken.
Hrs: 7 am-9 pm. Closed Dec 24, 25.
Res accepted. Bar. Bkfst $3-$7; dinner
$8.95-$27. Child's menu. Rattan furniture, ceiling fans, paintings. Cr cds:
A, D, DS, MC, V.

★ **CAPTAIN BILL'S WATERFRONT.**
701 Evans St (28557). 252/726-2166.
Specializes in seafood, pie. Hrs: 11
am-9 pm; Fri, Sat to 10 pm. Lunch
$4.95-$18.95; dinner $6.95-$18.95.
Child's menu. On Bogue Sound;

overlooks fishing fleet. Gift shop. Cr cds: DS, MC, V.

[D] [SC] [⊟]

★ **MRS. WILLIS.** *3114 Bridges St (28557). 252/726-3741.* Specializes in fresh seafood, beef. Hrs: 11 am-10 pm; Sat from 5 pm. Closed Dec 24-30. Res accepted. Bar. Lunch $3-$5; dinner $5-$20. Child's menu. Parking. Three dining rms. Family-owned. Cr cds: A, DS, MC, V.

[D] [⊟]

★ **SANITARY FISH MARKET.** *501 Evans St (28557). 252/247-3111. www.sanitaryfishmarket.com.* Specializes in fresh seafood, steaks, and chicken. Hrs: 11 am-8 pm; May-Sep to 9 pm. Closed Dec-Jan. Lunch $4.50-$21.95; dinner $7.95-$21.95. Child's menu. Overlooks water, fishing fleet, state port. Family-owned. Cr cds: DS, MC, V.

[D] [⊟]

Morganton

See also Little Switzerland, Marion

Pop 15,085 **Elev** 1,182 ft
Area code 828 **Zip** 28655
Web www.hci.net/~bcttc
Information Burke County Travel & Tourism, 102 E Union St, Courthouse Sq; 828/433-6793

What to See and Do

Boating, fishing, swimming. Lake James. 8 mi W on NC 126. **Lake Rhodhiss.** 10 mi E off US 70.

Boat tours. Tours of Lake James on 38-ft pontoon *Harbor Queen*. Departs Mountain Harbor Marina. Phone 828/584-0666. ¢¢¢

Annual Events

Waldensian Celebration of the Glorious Return. On I-40, Exit 112 in Valdese. Commemoration of the end of persecution during the reign of Louis XIV; ethnic games, arts and crafts, dances, food. Phone 828/879-2129. Mid-Aug.

Historic Morganton Festival. Downtown. Arts, crafts, ethnic foods,

band concert. Phone 828/438-5280. Mid-Sep.

Seasonal Event

From This Day Forward. Church St, Valdese. Outdoor historical drama depicting hardships of the Waldenses and their struggle for religious freedom. Phone 800/743-8398. Thurs-Sun eves. Mid-July-mid-Aug.

Motel/Motor Lodge

★ **SLEEP INN.** *2400 A S Sterling St (28655). 828/433-9000; fax 828/433-9000; toll-free 800/638-7949.* 61 rms, shower only, 2 story. S $49; D $55; each addl $6; under 18 free; higher rates wkends. Crib free. TV; cable (premium). Swimming privileges. Complimentary continental bkfst, coffee in rms. Restaurant adj 6 am-10 pm. Ck-out 11 am. In-rm modem link. Valet serv. Refrigerators avail. Cr cds: A, C, D, DS, JCB, MC, V.

[D] [⇘] [⊟] [♨] [SC]

Hotel

★★ **HOLIDAY INN.** *2400 S Sterling St (28655), 1 mi SE on NC 18, at I-40. 828/437-0171; fax 828/437-1639; res 800/465-4329.* Email nikkicarswell@hotmail.com. 135 rms, 2 story. Oct: S, D $8900; lower rates rest of yr. Crib avail. Parking lot. Pool. TV; cable. Complimentary full bkfst, coffee in rms, newspaper, toll-free calls. Restaurant 6 am-10 pm. Bar. Ck-out noon, ck-in 3 pm. Meeting rms. Business center. Dry cleaning. Exercise privileges. Golf. Tennis, 3 courts. Downhill skiing. Bike rentals. Hiking trail. Picnic facilities. Cr cds: A, D, DS, JCB, MC, V.

[D] [♪] [✦] [⚐] [♨] [↻] [⇘] [♁] [⊟] [♨] [SC] [♁]

B&B/Small Inn

★ **RICHMOND INN BED & BREAKFAST.** *51 Pine Ave (28777), E on US 19. 828/765-6993; fax 828/765-7224; toll-free 877/765-6993.* Email innkeepr richmond@aol.com; www.richmond-inn.com. 8 rms, 2 story, 2 suites. S, D $75; each addl $15; suites $110; under 6 free. Parking lot. TV; cable (premium), VCR avail, CD avail. Complimentary full bkfst, newspaper, toll-free calls. Restaurant nearby.

Business center. Gift shop. Exercise privileges, whirlpool. Golf. Tennis, 4 courts. Downhill skiing. Bike rentals. Supervised children's activities. Hiking trail. Picnic facilities. Cr cds: A, D, DS, MC, V.

🅳 ⬧ ⬧ ⬧ ⬧ ⬧ ⬧ ⬧ ⬧ ⬧ ⬧

Nags Head (Outer Banks)

(B-8) *See also Kill Devil Hills, Manteo*

Pop 1,838 **Elev** 10 ft **Area code** 252 **Zip** 27959 **Web** www.outer-banks. com/visitor-info

Information Dare County Tourist Bureau, 704 US 64/264, PO Box 399, Manteo 27954; 252/473-2138 or 800/446-6262

Annual Events

Gliding Spectacular. Hang gliding competition, novice through advanced. Spectacular flying and fun events. Phone 252/441-4124. Second wkend May.

Rogallo Kite Festival. Competition for homebuilt kites; stunt kite performances, demonstrations; kite auction. Phone 252/441-4124. First wkend June.

Motels/Motor Lodges

★ **BEACON MOTOR LODGE.** *2617 S Virgina Dare Tr (27959), on the oceanfront at milepost 11. 252/441-5501; fax 919/441-2178; toll-free 800/441-4804.* 47 rms, 1-2 story, 20 kits. Late May-early Sep: S, D $80-$100; each addl $10; suites $700-$800/wk; kit. units $650/wk; kit. cottages $700-$1,000/wk; higher rates hols, wkends; lower rates mid-Mar-late May, early Sep-Oct. Closed rest of yr. Crib $3. TV; cable (premium). Pool; 2 wading pools. Playground. Restaurant nearby. Ck-out 11 am. Coin lndry. Business servs avail. In-rm modem link. Refrigerators, microwaves. Picnic tables, grill. Sun deck. Beach. Cr cds: A, D, DS, MC, V.

🅳 ⬧ ⬧ ⬧ ⬧ ⬧

★ **BLUE HERON MOTEL.** *6811 Virginia Dare Tr (27959). 252/441-7447.* 30 rms, 3 story. June-Aug: S, D $106; each addl $5; children $5; under 1 free; lower rates rest of yr. Crib avail, fee. Parking lot. Indoor/outdoor pools, lap pool, whirlpool. TV; cable. Complimentary coffee in rms, newspaper. Restaurant nearby. Ck-out 11 am, ck-in 4 pm. Golf. Beach access. Picnic facilities. Cr cds: DS, MC, V.

🅳 ⬧ ⬧ ⬧ ⬧

★★ **COMFORT INN.** *8031 Old Oregon Inlet Rd (27959). 252/441-6315; fax 252/441-6315; res 800/334-3302.* 105 rms, 7 story. June-Labor Day S, D $128-$170; each addl $10; under 17 free; higher rates hols (3-day min); lower rates rest of yr. Crib free. TV; cable. Pool; wading pool. Complimentary continental bkfst. Restaurant nearby. Ck-out 11 am. Meeting rms. Business servs avail. Refrigerators, microwaves. Ocean view balconies. Swimming beach. Cr cds: A, D, DS, MC, V.

🅳 ⬧ ⬧ ⬧ ⬧ SC

★★ **ISLANDER MOTEL.** *7001 Virginia Dare Tr (27959), on US 158 Business, near milepost 16. 252/441-6229; fax 252/480-3883. www.islander motel.com.* 24 rms, 3 story. June-Aug: S, D $118; each addl $10; lower rates rest of yr. Crib avail. Parking lot. Pool. TV; cable. Restaurant nearby. Ck-out 11 am, ck-in 3 pm. Fax servs avail. Coin lndry. Golf. Beach access. Cr cds: A, MC, V.

⬧ ⬧ ⬧ ⬧ ⬧ ⬧

★★ **QUALITY INN.** *7123 S Virginia Dare Tr (27959), 3½ mi S on US 158 Business at milepost 16.5. 252/441-7191; fax 919/441-1961; toll-free 800/440-4386.* 111 rms, 1-3 story. Memorial Day-Labor Day: S, D $90-$150; each addl $10; under 18 free; lower rates rest of yr. Crib free. TV; cable (premium), VCR avail (movies). Pool; wading pool. Ck-out 11 am. Business servs avail. Most rms with balcony overlook ocean. Some rms across street. Cr cds: A, C, D, DS, JCB, MC, V.

🅳 ⬧ ⬧ ⬧ ⬧ ⬧ ⬧

★★ **SEA FOAM MOTEL.** *7111 S Virginia Dare Tr (27959). 252/441-7320; fax 252/441-7324. www.sea foam.com.* 51 rms, 2 story, 18 kits., three 2-bedrm kit. cottages, 1 apt. Late May-early Sep: D $77-$95; each addl $5; kit. units $525-$630/wk; kit.

cottages $725/wk; apt. $675/wk; under 12 free; lower rates Mar-Memorial Day, Labor Day-mid-Dec. Closed rest of yr. Crib $5. TV; cable (premium). Pool. Playground. Restaurant adj 5-10 pm. Ck-out 11 am. Airport transportation. Lawn games. Refrigerators. Some private patios, balconies. Picnic tables, grills. Playground. Beach. Cr cds: A, MC, V.

★★ **SURF SIDE MOTEL.** *6701 S Virginia Dare Tr (27959), milepost 16.*

252/441-2105; fax 252/441-2456; toll-free 800/552-7873. Email surfside@pinn.net; www.insiders.com/outerbanks/wwwads/surfside/. 76 rms, 5 story, 14 suites. Mid-June-early Sep: S, D $104-$139; each addl $10; suites $229; kit. units $169-$209; under 13 free; higher rates hol wkends; lower rates rest of yr. Crib $5. TV; cable. 2 pools, 1 indoor; whirlpool. Complimentary continental bkfst. Restaurant nearby. Ck-out 11 am. Coin lndry. Meeting rms. Business servs avail. Game rm.

Refrigerators, microwaves. Balconies. On beach. Cr cds: A, DS, MC, V.

D 🐾 🏖 🕴 🛏 🐾 SC

Hotel

★★ **NAGS HEAD INN.** *4701 S Virginia Dare Tr (27959). 252/441-0454; fax 252/441-0454; toll-free 800/327-8881. Email nhi@interpath.com; www.nagsheadinn.com.* 99 rms, 5 story, 1 suite. May-Sep: S, D $190; each addl $10; suites $230; under 11 free; lower rates rest of yr. Crib avail, fee. Parking garage. Indoor pool, whirlpool. TV; cable (premium). Complimentary toll-free calls. Restaurant nearby. Ck-out 11 am, ck-in 4 pm. Meeting rm. Business servs avail. Golf. Beach access. Cr cds: A, DS, MC, V.

D 🐾 🕴 🏖 🛏 🔥

B&B/Small Inn

★★★ **FIRST COLONY INN.** *6720 S Virginia Dare Tr (27959). 252/441-2343; fax 919/441-9234; toll-free 800/368-9390.* 26 rms, 3 story, 4 kits. Memorial Day-Labor Day: S, D $145-$275; each addl $30; lower rates rest of yr. Crib free. TV; cable, VCR avail (free movies). Pool. Complimentary full bkfst; afternoon refreshments; coffee in rms. Restaurant nearby. Ck-out 11 am, ck-in 3 pm. Business servs avail. In-rm modem link. Concierge serv. Picnic tables, grills. Two-story veranda; overlooks ocean. On 5 acres of landscaped grounds. Totally non-smoking. Cr cds: A, C, D, DS, MC, V.

D 🐾 🏖 🕴 🛏 🐾

Restaurants

★★ **OWENS'.** *7114 S Virginia Dare Tr (27959). 252/441-7309. www.owensrestaurant.com.* Specializes in crab cakes, grilled fish, whole Maine lobster. Hrs: 5-9 pm. Closed Jan-mid-Mar. Bar. Dinner $13.95-$18.95. Child's menu. Entertainment: jazz in summer. Parking. Historic artifacts of US Lifesaving Service (forerunner of US Coast Guard) on display; uniforms, log books, photographs. Family-owned. Cr cds: A, DS, MC, V.

D ⊐

★★ **PENGUIN ISLE.** *6708 S Croatan Hwy (US 158) (27959), Milepost 16. 252/441-2637. www.penguinisle.com.*

Specializes in seafood, black Angus beef. Hrs: 4:30-10 pm; early-bird dinner to 6 pm. Closed Dec 24, 25. Bar. Dinner $9.95-$22.95. Child's menu. Entertainment: Thurs-Sat. Nautical decor. View of sound. Cr cds: A, DS, MC, V.

D ⊐

★★ **WINDMILL POINT.** *US 158 (27959), at Milepost 16. 252/441-1535.* Specializes in seafood, veal, pasta. Hrs: 4-10 pm. Features memorabilia of SS United States. Bar. Dinner $13.95-$20.95. Child's menu. Cr cds: A, D, DS, MC, V.

D

New Bern

(D-7) *See also Kinston*

Settled 1710 **Pop** 17,363 **Elev** 15 ft
Area code 252
Web www4.coastalnet.com/cvb
Information Visitor Information Center, 314 S Front St, PO Box 1413, 28560; 252/637-9400 or 800/437-5767

The first settlers in this, one of North Carolina's earliest towns, were Germans and Swiss seeking political and religious freedom in the New World. The name Bern came from the city in Switzerland. Many Georgian and Federal-style buildings give New Bern an architectural ambiance unique in North Carolina. Many of these homes can be visited during April and October.

Swimming, boating, and freshwater and saltwater fishing can be enjoyed on the Neuse and Trent rivers. A Ranger District office of the Croatan National Forest is located here.

What to See and Do

New Bern Firemen's Museum. Antique firefighting equipment, relics, and pictures, 1917 double-size ladder trucks and engines, 1913 pumper. (Daily; closed hols) 410 Hancock St, off US 17, 70 Business. Phone 252/636-4087. ¢

★**Tryon Palace Historic Sites and Gardens.** Built in 1767-70 by the Royal Governor, William Tryon, this "most beautiful building in the colonial Americas" burned by accident in 1798 and lay in ruins until rebuilt between 1952-59. It served as the colonial and first state capitol. Reconstruction, furnishings, and 18th-century English gardens are beautiful and authentic. Docent-guided tours (daily; closed hols). Also self-guided garden tours. Combination ticket incl admission to all historic sites and gardens that are part of the Tryon Palace. 610 Pollock St, S end of George St, 1 blk S of US 17, 70 Business, NC 55. Phone 800/767-1560. Combination ticket ¢¢¢¢ On grounds are

Dixon-Stevenson House. (ca 1830) Early Federal architecture reflects maritime history of the area in its interior woodwork and widow's walk. Furnished in Federal and Empire antiques.

John Wright Stanly House. (ca 1780) Georgian-style house, furnished with 18th-century American antiques. Elegant interior woodwork. Formal gardens typical of the period.

New Bern Academy. (ca 1810) Four blks from Tryon Palace complex, in the historic residential district. Major surviving landmark of an educational institution founded in the 1760s, the Academy is restored as a self-guided museum of New Bern Civil War history, early education, and local architecture. Phone 252/514-4874.

Motels/Motor Lodges

★★ **COMFORT SUITES RIVER-FRONT PARK.** 218 E Front St (28560). 252/636-0022; fax 252/636-0051; res 800/228-5150. 100 rms, 4 story. Apr-Oct: S $69-$104; D $74-$129; under 18 free; lower rates rest of yr. Crib free. TV; cable (premium), VCR avail. Pool; whirlpool. Complimentary continental bkfst, coffee in rms. Restaurant nearby. Ck-out noon. Meeting rms. Business servs avail. Tennis privileges. Health club privileges. Refrigerators, microwaves. Cr cds: A, D, DS, JCB, MC, V.

★★ **HAMPTON INN.** 200 Hotel Dr (28562). 252/637-2111; fax 252/637-2000; res 800/426-7066; toll-free

800/448-8288. Email jaipark@mailcity. 101 rms, 4 story. S, D $57-$80; under 18 free; higher rates wkends. Crib free. TV; cable (premium). Pool. Complimentary continental bkfst, coffee in rms. Restaurant nearby. Ck-out noon. Meeting rms. Business servs avail. In-rm modem link. Exercise equipt. Health club privileges. Cr cds: A, C, D, DS, MC, V.

Hotel

★★★ **SHERATON HOTEL & MARINA.** 100 Middle St (28563). 252/638-3585; fax 252/638-8112; res 800/326-3745. www.sheratonnewbern. com. 172 rms, 5 story. S, D $95-$135; each addl $10; suites $195; under 17 free. Crib free. Pet accepted. TV; cable (premium). Pool. Coffee in rms. Restaurant 6:30 am-2 pm, 5-10 pm. Bar noon-2 am; entertainment Fri, Sat. Ck-out noon. Meeting rms. Business center. In-rm modem link. Free airport transportation. Golf privileges. Exercise equipt. Health club privileges. Refrigerators. Balconies. On river; marina facilities. Cr cds: A, C, D, DS, MC, V.

B&Bs/Small Inns

★★ **AERIE INN BED & BREAKFAST.** 509 Pollock St (28562). 252/636-5553; fax 252/514-2157; toll-free 800/849-5553. Email aeriebb@coastal net.com; www.aerieinn.com. 7 rms, 2 story. S $60; D $89-99; each addl $20; under 6 free. TV; cable. Complimentary full bkfst. Ck-out 11 am, ck-in 3 pm. Business servs avail. Airport transportation. Health club privileges. Victorian house built in 1880; antiques. One blk E of Tryon Palace. Cr cds: A, DS, MC, V.

★★ **HARMONY HOUSE INN.** 215 Pollock St (28560). 252/636-3810; fax 252/636-3810; toll-free 800/636-3113. Email harmony@cconnect.net; www. harmonyhouseinn.com. 7 rms, 2 story, 3 suites. S $79; D $109; each addl $20; suites $150. Crib avail. Parking lot. TV; cable. Complimentary full bkfst. Restaurant. Ck-out 11 am, ck-in 3 pm. Meeting rms. Business center. Gift shop. Exercise privileges. Golf, 18 holes. Cr cds: DS, MC, V.

★ **INN AT ORIENTAL.** *508 Church St (28571), approx 25 mi E on NC 55. 252/249-1078; fax 252/248-1201; toll-free 800/485-7174.* 8 rms, 2 story. No rm phones. May-Nov: S, D $75-$110; each addl $15; lower rates rest of yr. Complimentary full bkfst. Restaurant nearby. Ck-out 11 am, ck-in 3 pm. Built in 1840; antiques. Totally non-smoking. Cr cds: A, MC, V.

★★ **KINGS ARMS BED AND BREAKFAST INN.** *212 Pollock St (28560). 919/638-4409; fax 919/638-2191; toll-free 800/872-9306.* 8 rms, 3 story. S, D $60-$90; each addl $10; under 10 free. TV; cable. Complimentary full bkfst; afternoon refreshments. Ck-out 11 am, ck-in 3 pm. Business servs avail. In-rm modem link. Valet serv. Airport transportation. Tennis privileges. Golf privileges. In restored house (ca 1848); antiques, canopied beds. Cr cds: A, MC, V.

★ **NEW BERN HOUSE INN.** *709 Broad St (28560). 252/636-2250; toll-free 800/842-7688.* 7 rms, 3 story. S $68; D $88. Children over 12 yrs only. TV in sitting rm; cable. Complimentary full bkfst. Restaurant nearby. Ck-out 11 am, ck-in 2 pm. Free airport transportation. Colonial Revival house (1923); porch. Totally nonsmoking. Cr cds: A, MC, V.

Restaurants

★ **FRED & CLAIRE'S.** *247 Craven St (28560). 252/638-5426.* Specializes in casserole dishes, quiche, soups. Hrs: 11 am-7 pm; Fri to 8 pm; Sat to 3 pm. Closed Sun; hols. Res accepted. Wine, beer. Lunch $1.50-$7.25; dinner $5.95-$9.95. Housed in historic building (1870). Casual dining. No cr cds accepted.

★★★ **HARVEY MANSION.** *221 S Front St (28560). 252/638-3205. www.innplace.com.* Specializes in seafood, beef, veal. Hrs: 6-9 pm; Fri, Sat to 9:30 pm. Closed Mon; Dec 24, 25. Res accepted. Bar. Dinner $12.95-

$25.95. In 18th-century mansion near confluence of Trent and Neuse Rivers. Cr cds: A, DS, MC, V.

★★★ **HENDERSON HOUSE.** *216 Pollock St (28560). 252/637-4784.* Specializes in veal, Angus beef, seafood. Hrs: 6-9 pm. Closed Sun, Mon. Res accepted. Dinner $17.95-$28.95. Restored house built in 1810. Cr cds: A, MC, V.

Ocracoke (Outer Banks)

See also Buxton

Pop 658 (est) **Elev** 6 ft **Area code** 252 **Zip** 27960

One of the visitor centers for Cape Hatteras National Seashore (see) is here.

What to See and Do

Cedar Island to Ocracoke Ferry Service. (Winter and summer, daily) **Swan Quarter to Ocracoke.** (All yr, daily) Ferries are crowded; there may be a wait. Res are recommended; they may be made up to 1 yr in advance by phone or in person at the ferry terminal. Res are void if vehicle is not in loading lane at least 30 min before departure. Phone 252/928-3841 (Ocracoke), 252/225-3551 (Cedar Island), 252/926-1111 (Swan Quarter), or 800/BY-FERRY.

Ocracoke to Hatteras Ferry. Northward across Hatteras Inlet.

Motels/Motor Lodges

★ **BLUFF SHOAL.** *306 NC Hwy 12 (27960). 252/928-4301; toll-free 800/292-2304.* 8 rms, 1 story, 1 suite. June-Aug, Oct: S $85; D $95; each addl $8; under 11 free; lower rates rest of yr. Crib avail. Parking lot. TV; cable (premium). Complimentary coffee in rms. Restaurant nearby. Ck-out 11 am, ck-in 2 pm. Hiking trail. Picnic facilities. Cr cds: DS, MC, V.

★ **OCRACOKE ISLAND INN.** *100 Lighthouse Rd (27960), on NC 12. 252/928-4351; fax 252/928-4352; toll-*

free 877/456-3466. 35 rms, 2-3 story, 4 suites. No elvtr. Early May-late Sep: D $49-$99; each addl $5; suites $80-$100 (3-day min); cottages $675/wk; lower rates rest of yr. Crib free. Pet accepted. TV; cable (premium). Heated pool. Restaurant 7-11 am, 5-8:30 pm. Ck-out 11 am. Free airport transportation. Private patios. Near beach. Built in 1901; antiques. Cr cds: A, DS, MC, V.

Biking in the Outer Banks

★ **PONY ISLAND MOTEL.** *NC 12 (27960).* 252/928-4411; fax 252/928-2522. 50 rms, 9 kits. Memorial Day-Labor Day: S, D $80-$95; each addl $5; kit. units, suites $85-$140; cottages $700-$850/wk; lower rates rest of yr. TV; cable (premium). Pool. Restaurant adj 7-11 am, 5-9 pm. Ck-out 11 am. Business servs avail. Picnic tables, grills. Bicycle rentals. Cr cds: DS, MC, V.

Resort

★★ **THE ANCHORAGE INN.** *NC 12 (27960).* 252/928-1101; fax 252/928-6322. Email info@theanchorage inn.com; www.theanchorageinn.com. 35 rms, 4 story. May-Oct: S, D $89-$115; higher rates special events; lower rates rest of yr. Crib $5. Pet accepted. TV; cable (premium). Pool. Complimentary continental bkfst. Ck-out 11 am. Business servs avail. Balconies. Picnic tables, grill. Marina. Cr cds: A, DS, MC, V.

B&Bs/Small Inns

★★ **BERKLEY MANOR BED & BREAKFAST.** *NC 12 (27960), near S Ferry Docks.* 252/928-5911; toll-free 800/832-1223. Email berkley@beachlink.com; www.berkleymanor.com. 12 rms, 2 story. June-Sep: S, D $135; suites $195; under 15 free; lower rates rest of yr. Parking lot. TV; cable (premium). Complimentary full bkfst, newspaper. Restaurant nearby. Ck-out 11 am, ck-in 3 pm. Meeting rm. Fax servs avail. Exercise privileges. Beach access. Bike rentals. Hiking trail. Picnic facilities. Cr cds: A, DS, MC, V.

★ **BOYETTE HOUSE.** *NC 12 (27960), 1½ blks from Harbor in Village.* 252/928-4261; fax 252/928-4901; toll-free 800/928-4261. www.boyettehouse.com. 22 rms, 3 story, 2 suites. May-Oct: S $60; D $65; each addl $8; suites $160; children $4; under 11 free; lower rates rest of yr. Crib avail. TV; cable (premium). Complimentary coffee in rms. Restaurant nearby. Ck-out 11 am, ck-in 2 pm. Business servs avail. Free airport transportation. Exercise equipt, steam rm, whirlpool. Cr cds: DS, MC, V.

Restaurants

★★ **BACK PORCH.** *110 Back Rd (27960).* 252/928-6401. Specializes in crab cakes, fresh fish. Hrs: 5-9:30 pm. Closed Dec-Mar. Wine, beer. Dinner $7.95-$19.50. Child's menu. Porch dining. Cr cds: MC, V.

★ **ISLAND INN.** *NC 12 (27960).* 252/928-7821. www.ocracokeislandinn.com. Specializes in clam chowder, prime rib. Hrs: 7 am-9 pm. Closed Dec-Feb. Bkfst $2.95-$8.95; lunch $8.95-$15.95; dinner $8.95-$15.95.

Child's menu. Nautical decor. Cr cds: DS, MC, V.

[D] [⊣]

Outer Banks

Web www.outer-banks.com/chamber

Information Chamber of Commerce, PO Box 1757, Kill Devil Hills 27948; 252/441-8144

The Outer Banks are a chain of narrow, sandy islands stretching 175 miles from Cape Lookout to Back Bay, Virginia. Parts of the chain are 30 miles from the mainland. Cape Hatteras is about 75 miles from the southern end. The islands may be reached by bridge from Point Harbor and Manteo or by ferry from Cedar Island and Swan Quarter to Ocracoke (see).

The following Outer Banks areas are included in the *Mobil Travel Guide*. For information on any one of them, see the individual alphabetical listing: Buxton, Cape Hatteras National Seashore, Hatteras, Kill Devil Hills, Nags Head, Ocracoke.

Resort

★ ★ ★ **SANDERLING INN RESORT & SPA.** *1461 Duck Rd (27949). 252/ 261-4111; fax 252/261-1638; toll-free 800/701-4111. Emailcomments@ sanderlinginn.com; www.sanderlinginn. com.* 93 rms, 3 story, 12 suites. Apr-Oct: S, D $299; each addl $37; suites $421; under 4 free; lower rates rest of yr. Crib avail. Parking lot. Indoor/outdoor pools, lap pool, whirlpool. TV; cable (premium), VCR avail. Complimentary continental bkfst, coffee in rms, newspaper. Restaurant 8 am-9 pm. Bar. Ck-out 11 am, ck-in 4 pm. Meeting rms. Business center. Bellhops. Concierge. Dry cleaning. Gift shop. Exercise rm, sauna, steam rm. Golf, 18 holes. Tennis, 2 courts. Beach access. Bike rentals. Hiking trail. Cr cds: A, D, DS, MC, V.

[D] [↻] [⌖] [⅀] [📷] [⅀] [⌖] [↻] [≊] [🔥] [⌖]

Pilot Mountain

Pop 1,181 **Elev** 1,152 ft
Area code 336 **Zip** 27041

Hotel

★ ★ **RAMADA INN.** *Jct US 52 & NC 268, PO Box 668 (27041). 336/368- 2237; fax 336/368-1212; res 800/272- 6232. Email knobcity@advi.net.* 68 rms, 2 story. Apr-Oct: S $60; D $65; each addl $5; suites $63; under 17 free; lower rates rest of yr. Crib avail. Parking lot. Pool. TV; cable (premium). Complimentary continental bkfst. Restaurant 6:30 am-9 pm. Ck-out noon, ck-in 1 pm. Meeting rms. Business center. Dry cleaning. Exercise equipt. Golf, 18 holes. Tennis, 2 courts. Cr cds: A, C, D, DS, MC, V.

[D] [↻] [⌖] [≊] [⌖] [≊] [📷] [SC] [⌖]

Pinehurst

(C-5) *See also Southern Pines*

Founded 1895 **Pop** 5,103 **Elev** 529 ft
Area code 910 **Zip** 28374
Web www.homeofgolf.com

Information Convention & Visitors Bureau, PO Box 2270, Southern Pines 28388; 910/692-3330 or 800/346-5362

A famous year-round resort village, Pinehurst preserves an era steeped both in tradition and golfing excellence. Its New England style was designed over 100 years ago by the firm of Frederick Law Olmsted, which also designed New York's Central Park and landscaped Asheville's Biltmore Estate. Handsome estates and other residences, mostly styled in Georgian Colonial, dot the village. The Pinehurst Resort and Country Club has eight 18-hole golf courses, a 200-acre lake, 24 tennis courts, and other recreational facilities that are open to members as well as to guests staying there.

Motel/Motor Lodge

★ ★ **COMFORT INN PINEHURST.** *9801 US Hwy 15-501 (28374). 910/215-5500; fax 910/215-5535; res 800/228-5150; toll-free 800/831-0541.*

Email cipi@carolina.net. 80 rms, 2 story. Mid-Feb-Nov: S $78; D $84; each addl $6; suites $118-$125; under 18 free; lower rates rest of yr. Crib free. TV; cable (premium). Pool. Complimentary continental bkfst. Restaurant nearby. Ck-out noon. Meeting rms. Valet serv. Coin lndry. Exercise equipt. Health club privileges. Some refrigerators. Cr cds: A, C, D, DS, MC, V.

B&Bs/Small Inns

★★ **MAGNOLIA.** 65 Magnolia Rd (28374), jct Magnolia & Chinquapin Rds. 910/295-6900; fax 910/215-0858; toll-free 800/526-5562. Email magnolia@pinehurst.net; www.the magnoliainn.com. 11 rms, 3 story. Feb-Nov: S $120; D $195; lower rates rest of yr. Parking lot. Pool. TV; cable. Complimentary full bkfst. Restaurant 6-9:30 pm. Bar. Ck-out noon, ck-in 4 pm. Business center. Dry cleaning. Golf. Tennis, 10 courts. Cr cds: A, MC, V.

★ **PINE CREST INN.** Dogwood Rd (28370). 910/295-6121; fax 910/295-4880; toll-free 800/371-2545. Email frontdesk@pinecrestinnpinehurst.com; www.pinecrestinnpinehurst.com. 40 rms, 3 story. MAP, Mar-May and early Sep-Nov: S $85-$115; D $140-$180; under 12 free; lower rates rest of yr. Crib free. TV; cable (premium). Dining rm 7-9 am, 7-9 pm. Bar Wed-Sat. Ck-out noon, ck-in 2 pm. Tennis privileges. 18-hole golf privileges. Health club privileges. Golf decor and artifacts in lobby. Cr cds: A, DS, MC, V.

★★★★ **PINEHURST.** Carolina Vista Dr (28374). 910/295-6811; fax 910/295-1339; toll-free 800/487-4653. For those seeking world-class recreation, this is the mecca for golf. Recent refurbishments and renovations have given both the lodging and sports facilities a new luster. The main Carolina Hotel offers a traditional resort experience while the Holly Inn, a smaller, more historic building, is intimate and artful. Non golfers will appreciate the lush setting and many alternative recre-

ations. 549 rms, 4 story. S $179-$1,125, D $320-$817. Cribs. TV, cable. Pool. Restaurants. Exercise rm. Business center. 8 golf courses. 24 tennis courts. Concierge. Valet. 200-acre lake and marina. Cr cds: A, DS, MC, V.

Raleigh

(C-6) See also Chapel Hill, Durham

Founded 1792 **Pop** 207,951
Elev 363 ft **Area code** 919
Web www.raleighcvb.org

Information Greater Raleigh Convention & Visitors Bureau, One Hannover Sq, 421 Fayetteville St Mall, Suite 1505, PO Box 1879, 27602-1879; 919/834-5900 or 800/849-8499

The capital of North Carolina, Raleigh is also known as a center of education and high-technology research. It still retains the flavor of a relaxed residential town with two centuries of history. Fine residences coexist with apartment houses and modern shopping centers; rural areas with meadows and plowed fields can be found within a few miles.

Named for Sir Walter Raleigh, the town was laid out in 1792, following a resolution by the North Carolina General Assembly that an "unalterable seat of government" should be established within ten miles of Isaac Hunter's tavern. The founders were able to find a site just four miles from the tavern. The site was laid off in a square. Lots within and just outside the city were sold as residences, which helped finance the capitol building and the governor's residence. Both structures were subsequently destroyed (the capitol by fire in 1831, the governor's residence by Union troops during the Civil War). Their replacements remain standing today. Fortunately, many of the lovely homes and gardens of the antebellum period have survived.

Like much of North Carolina, Raleigh was sprinkled with Union sympathizers until Fort Sumter was fired upon. Lincoln's call for volunteers was regarded as an insult, and

North Carolina joined the Confederacy. Raleigh surrendered quietly to General Sherman in April, 1865. During Reconstruction, carpetbaggers and scalawags controlled the Assembly, voted themselves exorbitant salaries, set up a bar in the capitol, and left permanent nicks in the capitol steps from the whiskey barrels rolled up for the thirsty legislators.

Located within 15 miles of Raleigh is the Research Triangle Park, a 6,800-acre research and development center with more than 50 companies. Complementing these facilities are the resources of three major universities that form the triangle region—North Carolina State University, Duke University in Durham, and the University of North Carolina at Chapel Hill.

What to See and Do

Capital Area Visitor Center. Info center; brochures. Tours may be scheduled to the State Capitol, the North Carolina Executive Mansion, the State Legislative Bldg, historic sites, and other attractions. (Daily; closed hols) 301 N Blount St. Phone 919/733-3456. **FREE**

Falls Lake State Recreation Area. Man-made lake built as a reservoir and for flood control. Approx 38,000 acres of land and water offer swimming beach, waterskiing, fishing, boating (ramps); hiking, picnicking (shelters), playground. Three state recreation areas in vicinity. 12 mi N via NC 50. Phone 919/676-1027. Per vehicle ¢¢

J.C. Raulston Arboretum at NC State University. Eight acres of gardens featuring more than 5,000 diverse trees and shrubs from around the world. (Daily) 4301 Beryl Rd. Phone 919/515-3132. **FREE**

Mordecai Historic Park. Preserved plantation home (1785 and 1826) with many original furnishings, noted for its neoclassical architecture; early Raleigh office bldg, St. Mark's chapel, Badger-Iredell Law Office, 1830s herb garden. Also house in which Andrew Johnson, 17th president of the US, was born. Guided tours. (Wed-Mon; closed hols) Mimosa St & Wake Forest Rd. Phone 919/834-4844. ¢¢

North Carolina Museum of Art. European and American painting and sculpture; Egyptian, Greek, Roman, African, and pre-Columbian objects; Judaica collection; changing exhibits. Amphitheatre. Restaurant. (Tues-Sun; closed hols) 2110 Blue Ridge Rd. Phone 919/839-6262. **FREE**

North Carolina Museum of History. Four innovative exhibits convey the state's history. Gift shop; auditorium. (Tues-Sun) 5 E Edenton St. Phone 919/715-0200. **FREE**

Pullen Park. Scenic 72-acre park in the heart of downtown featuring 1911 carousel, train ride, paddle boats, indoor aquatic center, ball fields, tennis courts, playground, and picnic shelters. (Daily) 520 Ashe Ave. Phone 919/831-6468. Admission **FREE**; Rides ¢

State Capitol. (1840) A simple, stately Greek Revival style bldg. Statues of honored sons and daughters decorate the grounds. The old legislative chambers, in use until 1963, have been restored to their 1840s appearance, as have the old state library rm and the state geologist's office. (Daily; closed Jan 1, Thanksgiving, late Dec) Capitol Square. Phone 919/733-4994 or 919/733-3456. **FREE**

State Legislative Building. First bldg constructed to house a state general assembly (1963); designed by Edward Durell Stone in a blend of modern and classical styles. Tours of chambers may incl view of legislators at work. (Daily; closed Jan 1, Thanksgiving, Dec 25) Corner of Salisbury & Jones Sts. Phone 919/733-7928. **FREE**

State Museum of Natural Sciences. Exhibits depict natural history of state; "Freshwater Wetlands" exhibit. (Daily; closed hols) 11 W Jones St. Phone 919/733-7450 or 877/4NATSCI. **FREE**

William B. Umstead State Park. On 5,377 acres with a 55-acre lake. Fishing, boating; hiking, riding, picnicking, camping (Mar-mid-Dec, Thurs-Sun). Nature study. **Reedy Creek Section,** 10 mi NW off I-40. Approx 1,800 acres. Fishing; hiking, riding, picnicking. Nature study. Hrs vary. Standard fees for boat rentals and camping. Crabtree Creek Section, 10 mi NW on US 70. Phone 919/571-4170 (Reedy Creek).

Annual Events

Artsplosure Spring Arts Festival. Moore Square and City Market. City-wide celebration of the arts. Showcase for regional dance, music, theater performances by nationally known artists; outdoor arts and crafts show; children's activities. For further info phone 919/832-8699. Mid-May.

State Fair. State Fairgrounds. 5 mi W on US 1, then 1 mi W on NC 54. For further info contact 1025 Blue Ridge Blvd, 27607; 919/733-2145 or 919/821-7400. Mid-Oct.

Motels/Motor Lodges

★★ **COMFORT INN NORTH.** *2910 Capital Blvd (27604). 919/878-9550; fax 919/876-5457. www.citysearch. com/rdu.comfortinnnorth.* 149 rms, 2-4 story. S $54-$59; D $64-$69; each addl $5; kit. suite $89-$94; higher rates state fair. Crib free. TV; cable (premium). Pool. Complimentary continental bkfst. Restaurant nearby. Ck-out noon. Coin lndry. Meeting rms. Business servs avail. Some refrigerators. Cr cds: A, C, D, DS, ER, JCB, MC, V.
🄳 🏊 🖎 🔥 SC

★★ **COMFORT INN SOUTH.** *1602 Mechanical Blvd (27529). 919/779-7888; fax 919/779-4603; res 800/970-5432; toll-free 800/638-7949.* 60 rms, 2 story. S $59-$89; each addl $5; suites $89-$99; under 12 free. Crib $7. TV; cable (premium); VCR avail. Pool. Complimentary continental bkfst, coffee in rms. Restaurant opp 11 am-10 pm. Ck-out 11 am. Meeting rms. Exercise equipt; sauna. Microwaves; refrigerators. Cr cds: A, D, DS, MC, V.
🄳 🏊 🏃 🖎 🔥 SC

★★ **COURTYARD BY MARRIOTT.** *2001 Hospitality Ct (27560). 919/467-9444; fax 919/467-9332.* 152 rms, 4 story. S $109-$115; D $119-$125; each addl $10; suites $125-$135; under 18 free; higher rates special events. Crib free. TV; cable (premium). Complimentary coffee in rms. Restaurant 6-10 am, 5-10 pm. Bar. Ck-out noon. Meeting rms. Business servs avail. In-rm modem link. Valet serv. Sundries. Coin lndry. Free airport transportation. Exercise equipt. Pool; whirlpool. Refrigerator,

microwave in suites. Some balconies. Cr cds: A, D, DS, JCB, MC, V.
🄳 🏊 🏃 🖎 🔥

★★ **THE CRABTREE SUMMIT HOTEL.** *3908 Arrow Dr (27612). 919/782-6868; fax 919/881-9340; res 800/521-7521. www.crabtreesummit hotel.com.* 88 rms, 4 story, 7 suites. S, D $98-$150; suites $125-$150; wkend rates. Crib free. TV; cable (premium). Pool. Complimentary full bkfst. Restaurant nearby. Ck-out noon. Meeting rms. Business servs avail. In-rm modem link. Free airport, railroad station, bus depot transportation. Exercise equipt. Refrigerators, wet bars. Cr cds: A, C, D, DS, MC, V.
🄳 🏊 🏃 🖎 🔥

★ **DAYS INN.** *3901 S Wilmington St (27603). 919/772-8900; fax 919/772-1536; res 800/329-7466.* 103 rms, 3 story. S, D $49-$79; each addl $5; under 12 free. Crib free. TV; cable (premium). Pool. Complimentary continental bkfst, coffee in rms. Restaurant adj open 24 hrs. Ck-out 11 am. Business servs avail. Some refrigerators, microwaves. Cr cds: A, C, D, DS, MC, V.
🄳 🏊 🖎 🔥

★★ **HAMPTON INN.** *1001 Wake Towne Dr (27609). 919/828-1813; fax 919/834-2672; toll-free 800/426-7866. www.hampton-inn.com.* 130 rms, 5 story. S $65-$75; D $70-$80; under 18 free; wkend rates. Crib free. TV; cable (premium). Pool. Complimentary continental bkfst, coffee in rms. Restaurant nearby. Ck-out noon. Meeting rm. Business servs avail. In-rm modem link. Valet serv. Sundries. Health club privileges. Cr cds: A, C, D, DS, MC, V.
🄳 🏊 🖎 🔥 SC

★★ **HAMPTON INN - CRABTREE.** *6209 Glenwood Ave (27612). 919/782-1112; fax 919/782-9119; res 800/426-7866.* 141 rms, 6 story, 17 suites. S $80-$84; D $85-$89; suites $99-$149; under 18 free; wkend rates; higher rates special events. Crib free. TV; cable (premium). Complimentary continental bkfst. Restaurant adj 11 am-11 pm. Ck-out noon. Meeting rms. Business servs avail. In-rm modem link. Free airport transportation. Exercise equipt; sauna. Pool. Some in-rm whirlpools, wet bars; bathroom phone, refrigerator, microwave in suites. Some balconies. Cr cds: A, C, D, DS, JCB, MC, V.

★★ **HAMPTON INN RALEIGH DURHAM AIRPORT.** *1010 Airport Blvd (27560), approx 10 mi W on NC 54. 919/462-1620; fax 919/462-3217; res 800/HAMPTON.* 102 rms, 4 story. S, D $89-$99; under 18 free. Crib free. TV; cable (premium). Pool. Complimentary continental bkfst. Restaurant nearby. Ck-out noon. Business servs avail. Free airport transportation. Health club privileges. Cr cds: A, D, DS, MC, V.

★★ **NORTH RALEIGH COURT-YARD BY MARRIOTT.** *1041 Wake Towne Dr (27609). 919/821-3400; fax 919/821-1209; res 800/321-2211.* 153 rms, 4 story, 13 suites. S $65-$99; D $109; suites $85-$122; under 12 free; wkend rates. Crib free. TV; cable (premium), VCR avail. Pool; whirlpool. Complimentary coffee in rms. Restaurant 6:30-10 am; Sat, Sun 7 am-noon. Bar 4-11 pm. Ck-out noon. Coin lndry. Meeting rms. In-rm modem link. Valet serv. Exercise equipt. Health club privileges. Refrigerator in suites; microwaves avail. Some balconies. Cr cds: A, C, D, DS, JCB, MC, V.

★★ **PLANTATION INN RESORT.** *6401 Capital Blvd (27616), 9 mi NE on US 1. 919/876-1411; fax 919/790-7093; toll-free 800/992-9662.* 94 rms, 2 story. S, D $59-$79; suites $75-$100. Crib free. TV; cable (premium), VCR avail. Pool; wading pool, poolside serv. Playground. Complimentary continental bkfst. Restaurant 6:30-10:30 am, 11:30 am-2:30 pm, 5-11 pm. Ck-out noon. Meeting rms. Business servs avail. In-rm modem link. Bellhops. Airport transportation. Putting green. Health club privileges. Some refrigerators. Picnic tables. Greek Revival detailing. Cr cds: A, C, D, MC, V.

★ **RED ROOF INN.** *3520 Maitland Dr (27610). 919/231-0200; fax 919/231-0228; toll-free 800/843-7663.* 115 rms, 3 story. S $41.99-$46.99; D $50.99; each addl $5; under 18 free. Crib $5. Pet accepted. TV; cable (premium). Complimentary coffee in lobby. Restaurant adj 6 am-10 pm.

Ck-out noon. Health club privileges. Cr cds: A, C, D, DS, MC, V.

★ **RED ROOF INN OF NORTH RALEIGH.** *3201 Wake Forest Rd (27609). 919/878-9310; fax 919/790-1451; res 800/716-6406.* 148 rms, 2 story. S, D $45.99-$59.99; under 18 free. Crib free. Pet accepted, some restrictions; $25 deposit. TV; cable (premium). Pool. Complimentary continental bkfst. Restaurant adj open 24 hrs. Ck-out 11 am. Meeting rm. Picnic tables, grill. Cr cds: A, D, DS, MC, V.

★★ **RESIDENCE INN BY MAR-RIOTT.** *1000 Navaho Dr (27609). 919/878-6100; fax 919/876-4117; res 800/331-3131.* 144 kit. suites, 1-2 story. S, D $119-$154; wkly, monthly rates. Crib free. Pet accepted, some restrictions; $200. TV; cable (premium). Heated pool; whirlpool. Complimentary continental bkfst. Coffee in rms. Ck-out noon. Coin lndry. Meeting rm. Business servs avail. In-rm modem link. Valet serv. Health club privileges. Refrigerators, microwaves; some bathrm phones. Private patios, balconies. Picnic tables, grills. Cr cds: A, C, D, DS, ER, JCB, MC, V.

★★★ **VELVET CLOAK INN.** *1505 Hillsborough St (27605), in university area, W of downtown. 919/828-0333; fax 919/828-9943; toll-free 800/334-4372. Email ernestiner@prodigy.net; www.thevelvetcloakinn.citysearch.com.* 164 rms, 4 story, 8 suites. S $107; D $117; each addl $10; suites $350. Crib avail. Parking lot. Indoor pool. TV; cable (premium), VCR avail. Complimentary newspaper, toll-free calls. Restaurant 6:50 am-8 pm (See CHARTER ROOM). Bar. Ck-out 11 am, ck-in 4 pm. Meeting rms. Business servs avail. Bellhops. Free airport transportation. Exercise privileges. Golf, 18 holes. Tennis, 2 courts. Cr cds: A, C, D, DS, ER, JCB, MC, V.

Hotels

★★ **BROWNSTONE HOTEL.** *1707 Hillsborough St (27605). 919/828-0811; fax 919/834-0904; toll-free 800/331-7919. Email brownstone@aol.com;*

www.brownstone.com. 192 rms, 9 story. S, D $69-$125; each addl $10. Crib free. TV; cable (premium). Pool. Coffee in rms. Restaurant 6:30 am-2 pm; Sat, Sun 7 am-3 pm. Bar 5-11 pm; closed Sun. Ck-out 1 pm. Meeting rms. Business servs avail. Free airport transportation. Balconies. Cr cds: A, DS, MC, V.

★★ FAIRFIELD INN BY MARRIOTT. 2641 Appliance Ct (27610). 919/856-9800; fax 919/856-9800; res 800/228-2800. www.fairfieldinn.com. 131 rms, 3 story. May-Sep, Dec: S, D $59; lower rates rest of yr. Crib avail, fee. Parking lot. Pool. TV; cable (premium). Complimentary continental bkfst, newspaper. Restaurant nearby. Ck-out noon, ck-in 6 pm. Business servs avail. Dry cleaning. Cr cds: A, D, DS, MC, V.

★★ FOUR POINTS HOTEL RALEIGH. 4501 Creedmoor Rd (27612). 919/787-7111; fax 919/783-0024; res 800/325-3535. Email jproctor@fourpointsraleigh.com. 317 rms, 4-10 story. S $65-$130; D $95-$140; each addl $10; suites $110-$160; under 18 free; wkend rates. Crib free. TV; cable (premium), VCR avail. Indoor pool. Restaurant 6:30 am-10:30 pm; Sat, Sun from 7:30 pm. Bar 4 pm-midnight. Ck-out noon. Convention facilities. Business center. In-rm modem link. Concierge. Gift shop. Free airport transportation. Exercise equipt. Health club privileges. Luxury level. Cr cds: A, C, D, DS, ER, JCB, MC, V.

★★★ HILTON NORTH RALEIGH. 3415 Wake Forest Rd (27609). 919/872-2323; fax 919/876-0890; toll-free 800/445-8667. 338 units, 6 story. S $99-$160; D $109-$170; each addl $10; suites $135-$450; wkend rates. Crib free. TV; cable (premium), VCR avail. Indoor pool; whirlpool. Restaurant 6:30 am-10 pm. Bars 11-2 am; entertainment. Ck-out noon. Convention facilities. Business center. In-rm modem link. Gift shop. Free airport transportation. Exercise equipt. Luxury level. Cr cds: A, DS, MC, V.

★★ HOLIDAY INN. 320 Hillsborough St (27603). 919/832-0501; fax 919/833-1631; res 800/HOLIDAY; toll-free 800/465-4329. Email dosral@lodgian.com; www.holiday-inn.com. 201 rms, 20 story, 1 suite. Apr-Oct: S, D $99; suites $149; lower rates rest of yr. Crib avail. Pet accepted, some restrictions, fee. Pool. TV; cable (premium). Complimentary coffee in rms, newspaper, toll-free calls. Restaurant 6 am-10 pm. Bar. Ck-out noon, ck-in 3 pm. Meeting rms. Business servs avail. Dry cleaning, coin lndry. Exercise equipt. Golf, 18 holes. Video games. Cr cds: A, C, D, DS, JCB, MC, V.

★★ HOLIDAY INN. 4100 Glenwood Ave (27612). 919/782-8600; fax 919/782-7213; res 800/HOLIDAY. Email bglisson@boykin.com; www.holidayinncrabtree.com. 176 rms, 12 story. Feb-Mar, Oct-Nov: S, D $129; each addl $10; under 10 free; lower rates rest of yr. Crib avail, fee. Pet accepted, some restrictions, fee. Parking lot. Pool. TV; cable (premium). Complimentary coffee in rms, toll-free calls. Restaurant. Bar. Ck-out noon. Meeting rms. Business center. Dry cleaning. Free airport transportation. Exercise equipt, sauna. Golf. Video games. Cr cds: A, C, D, DS, MC, V.

★★ HOMEWOOD SUITES. 5400 Homewood Dr (27612). 919/785-1131; fax 919/781-3119; res 800/ALLHOME. Email hwsuites@intrex.net. 137 suites, 7 story. S, D $89-$169; wkends, hols (2-day min). Crib free. TV; cable (premium). Complimentary full bkfst, coffee in rms. Restaurant adj 11 am-9 pm. Ck-out noon. Meeting rms. Business servs avail. In-rm modem link. Shopping arcade. Coin lndry. Free airport transportation. Exercise equipt. Pool. Refrigerators, microwaves. Some balconies. Cr cds: A, D, DS, MC, V.

★★★ MARRIOTT. 4500 Marriott Dr (27612), on US 70W opp Crabtree Valley Mall. 919/781-7000; fax 919/781-3059; res 800/228-9290. www.marriott.com. 372 rms, 6 story, 4 suites. S, D $149. Crib avail. Parking lot. Indoor/outdoor pools; whirlpool. TV; cable (premium). Complimentary coffee in rms, newspaper, toll-free calls. Restaurant 6:30 am-

11 pm. Bar. Ck-out 11 am, ck-in 4 pm. Conference center, meeting rms. Business center. Bellhops. Concierge. Dry cleaning, coin lndry. Gift shop. Free airport transportation. Exercise equipt. Golf. Cr cds: A, C, D, DS, MC, V.

B&B/Small Inn

★★ **OAKWOOD INN BED & BREAKFAST.** *411 N Bloodworth St (27604). 919/832-9712; fax 919/836-9263; res 919/832-9712; toll-free 800/267-9712. Email oakwoodbb@aol.com; www.members.aol.com/oakwoodbb.* 6 rms, 2 story. S $75-$120; D $85-$130. TV, cable. Complimentary full bkfst; afternoon refreshments. Ck-out 11:30 am, ck-in 3 pm. Meeting rm. In-rm modem link. Fireplaces. Historic district; built 1871. Cr cds: A, DS, MC, V.

All Suites

★★★ **EMBASSY SUITES HOTEL.** *4700 Creedmoor Rd (27612). 919/881-0000; fax 919/782-7225; res 800/362-2779. www.embassysuitesraleigh.com.* 9 story, 225 suites. Feb-Dec: S, D $189; each addl $10 suites $189; under 18 free; lower rates rest of yr. Crib avail. Parking garage. Indoor pool, whirlpool. TV; cable (DSS), VCR avail. Complimentary full bkfst, coffee in rms, newspaper, toll-free calls. Restaurant 11 am-10 pm. Bar. Ck-out noon, ck-in 3 pm. Meeting rms. Business servs avail. Bellhops. Dry cleaning, coin lndry. Gift shop. Free airport transportation. Exercise privileges, sauna, steam rm. Golf. Tennis. Supervised children's activities. Hiking trail. Picnic facilities. Video games. Cr cds: A, C, D, DS, JCB, MC, V.

★★ **QUALITY SUITES HOTEL.** *4400 Capital Blvd (27604). 919/876-2211; fax 919/790-1352; res 800/221-2222. www.qualitysuites.citysearch. com.* 3 story, 114 suites. Suites $75; under 18 free. Crib avail. Pet accepted, some restrictions, fee. Parking lot. Pool. TV; cable, VCR avail. Complimentary full bkfst, coffee in rms, newspaper, toll-free calls. Restaurant. Bar. Ck-out noon, ck-in 3 pm. Meeting rms. Business center. Dry cleaning. Exercise equipt. Golf.

Tennis. Cr cds: A, C, D, DS, ER, JCB, MC, V.

Restaurants

★★ **42 STREET OYSTER BAR & SEAFOOD.** *508 W Jones St (27603). 919/831-2811. www.citysearch.com.* Specializes in fresh fish, beef, chicken. Hrs: 11:30 am-11 pm; Sat from 5 pm; Sun 5-10 pm. Closed Jan 1, Thanksgiving, Dec 24, 25. Res accepted. Bar. Lunch $5.95-$10.95; dinner $10.95-$49.95. Child's menu. Entertainment: R&B, jazz bands Thurs-Sat. Oyster bar. Nautical decor. Cr cds: A, D, MC, V.

★★★★ **ANGUS BARN.** *9401 Glenwood Ave (27612), 12½ mi NW on US 70. 919/787-3505. Email angusbarn@aol.com; www.angusbarn.com.* Specializes in prime rib, charcoal-broiled steak, seafood. Own baking. Hrs: 5-11 pm; Sun to 10 pm. Closed Jan 1, Thanksgiving, Dec 24, 25. Res accepted Sun-Fri. Bar. Wine list. Dinner $14.95-$47.95. Child's menu. Valet parking. Farm decor; fireplaces. Colt revolver display. Family-owned. Cr cds: A, D, DS, MC, V.

★★ **CASA CARBONE RISTORANTE.** *6019-A Glenwood Ave (27612). 919/781-8750.* Specializes in veal, pasta. Own desserts. Hrs: 5-10 pm; Sun 4-9 pm. Closed Mon; hols. Dinner $7-$15. Child's menu. Mediterranean decor. Cr cds: A, C, D, DS, MC, V.

★★★ **CHARTER ROOM.** *1505 Hillsborough St. 919/828-0333.* Specializes in chicken, steak, seafood. Hrs: 11 am-10 pm. Res accepted. Bar. Wine list. Bkfst $2-$10; lunch $6.95-$13.95; dinner $7.95-$27.95. Sun brunch $12.95. Child's menu. Valet parking. Cr cds: A, D, DS, MC, V.

★ **COURTNEY'S.** *407 E Six Forks Rd (27609). 919/834-3613.* Specializes in omelettes. Hrs: 7 am-2:30 pm. Closed Thanksgiving, Dec 25. Bkfst $5.50-$6.95; lunch $5.50-$6.95. Child's menu. Cr cds: MC, V.

★★ **IRREGARDLESS CAFE.** *901 W Morgan (27603). 919/833-9920. www.*

citysearch.com. Specializes in chicken, seafood, vegetarian dishes. Hrs: 11:30 am-9:30 pm; Fri to 10:30 pm; Sat 5:30-11:30 pm; Sun brunch 10 am-2 pm. Bar. Lunch $4-$8; dinner $8-$16. Sun brunch $7.95-$9.75. Entertainment: jazz, folk, classical musicians. Cr cds: A, D, DS, MC, V. [D]

★ **JEAN CLAUDE'S CAFE.** *6112 Falls of Neuse Rd (27609), in North Ridge Shopping Center. 919/872-6224. www.jeanclaudes.com.* Specializes in beef tenderloin, salmon in puff pastry, rack of lamb. Hrs: 11 am-9 pm; Fri, Sat to 9:30 pm. Closed Sun, Mon; hols. Wine, beer. Lunch $4.95-$8.99; dinner $8-$24. Child's menu. Two dining rms with French decor. Cr cds: A, MC, V. [D]

★ **LAS MARGARITAS.** *231 Timber Dr (27529), 20 mi E on US 70, in Timber Crossing Shopping Center. 919/662-1030.* Specializes in fajitas, seafood, margaritas. Hrs: 11 am-10 pm; Fri, Sat to 11 pm; Sat, Sun from noon. Closed hols. Res accepted. Bar. Lunch $3.75-$5.95; dinner $6.10-$9.25. Child's menu. Parking. Contemporary atmosphere. Cr cds: A, DS, MC, V. [D] [⌣]

★★ **PEKING GARDEN.** *126 Millbrook Rd (27609), in Colony Shopping Center. 919/848-4663.* Specializes in Chinese cuisine. Hrs: 11:30 am-10 pm. Bar. Lunch a la carte entrees: $4.95-$10; dinner a la carte entrees: $7.95-$20. Modern decor with Chinese accents. Cr cds: A, DS, MC, V. [D] [⌣]

★★★ **SIMPSON'S.** *5625 Creedmoor Rd (27612), in Creedmore Crossing Shopping Center. 919/783-8818. www.simpsonsrestaurant.com.* Specializes in grilled fish, steak, prime rib. Hrs: 5-10 pm; Fri, Sat to 11 pm. Closed Sun; hols. Res accepted. Bar. Dinner $9.95-$45.95. Child's menu. Entertainment: pianist wkdays; jazz wkends. Formal dining in spacious surroundings. Cr cds: A, C, D, DS, MC, V. [D] [⌣]

★★ **VINNIE'S STEAKHOUSE.** *7440 Six Forks Rd (27615). 919/847-7319.* Specializes in steak, seafood. Hrs: 5-11 pm; Sun to 10 pm. Closed hols. Bar. Dinner a la carte entrees: $15-$55. Club decor. Cr cds: A, D, MC, V. [D] [⌣]

★★ **WINSTON'S GRILLE.** *6401 Falls of Neuse Rd (27615), in Sutton Square Shopping Center. 919/790-0700.* Specializes in beef, seafood, pasta. Hrs: 11 am-10 pm; Fri, Sat to 11 pm; Sun brunch to 3 pm. Closed hols. Res accepted. Bar. Lunch a la carte entrees: $4.95-$9.95; dinner a la carte entrees: $9.95-$22.95. Sun brunch $4.95-$10.95. Child's menu. Cr cds: A, D, DS, MC, V. [D] [⌣]

Roanoke Rapids

(B-6)

Pop 15,722 **Elev** 170 ft **Area code** 252 **Zip** 27870 **Web** www.visithalifax.com

Information Halifax County Tourism Development Authority, PO Box 144; 252/535-1687 or 800/522-4282

Motels/Motor Lodges

★★ **COMFORT INN.** *I-95 N & Rte 46 (27870), at I-95 Exit 176. 252/537-1011; fax 252/537-9258; toll-free 800/832-8375.* 100 rms, 2 story. S, D $48-$60; each addl $5; under 18 free. Crib free. TV; cable (premium). Pool. Complimentary continental bkfst. Restaurant 6:30 am-9 pm. Ck-out 11 am. Business servs avail. Gift shop. Cr cds: A, C, D, DS, MC, V. [D] [⇌] [⌐] [↖] [SC]

★★ **HAMPTON INN.** *1914 Weldon Rd (27870), I-95 Exit 173. 252/537-7555; fax 252/537-9852; toll-free 800/426-7866.* 124 rms, 2 story. S $58-$70; D $65-$75; under 18 free. Crib free. TV; cable (premium). Pool. Complimentary continental bkfst, coffee in rms. Restaurant adj 6 am-10 pm. Ck-out noon. Meeting rms. Business servs avail. In-rm modem link. Health club privileges. Picnic tables, grills. Cr cds: A, C, D, DS, MC, V. [D] [⇌] [⌐] [↖] [SC]

★★ **HAMPTON INN.** *1914 Julian R. Allsbrook Hwy (27870). 252/537-7555; fax 252/537-9852; toll-free 800/HAMP-*

TON. www.hampton-inn.com. 124 rms, 2 story. S, D $75; under 18 free. Crib avail. Parking lot. Pool. TV; cable (premium). Complimentary continental bkfst, coffee in rms, newspaper, toll-free calls. Restaurant nearby. Ck-out noon, ck-in 3 pm. Meeting rms. Business servs avail. Exercise privileges. Golf, 18 holes. Tennis, 4 courts. Cr cds: A, D, DS, MC, V.

🅳 🏋 📠 ☁ 🛌 🦶 🐾 SC

Robbinsville

See also Bryson City, Fontana Dam

Pop 709 **Elev** 2,064 ft **Area code** 828 **Zip** 28771

B&Bs/Small Inns

★ **TAPOCO LODGE.** *Rte 72 Box A-1 (28771), 15 mi N on US 129. 828/498-2435; toll-free 800/822-5083. www. tapocolodge.com.* 6 rms, 3 story, 1 suite. S $69; D $79; each addl $10; suites $125. Crib avail. Parking lot. Pool, children's pool. TV; cable (premium). Complimentary coffee in rms. Restaurant 8 am-7 pm. Ck-out 10 am, ck-in 3 pm. Meeting rms. Business servs avail. Gift shop. Tennis. Supervised children's activities. Hiking trail. Cr cds: A, DS, MC, V.

🐾 📠 ☁ 🛌 🦶 🦶

★★ **SNOWBIRD MOUNTAIN LODGE.** *275 Santeetlah Rd (28771), 12 mi NW, off US 129. 828/479-3433; fax 828/479-3473; toll-free 800/941-9290.* 22 rms, 2 story. No A/C. No rm phones. Mid-Apr-early Nov: D $125-$200. Closed rest of yr. Children over 12 yrs only. Dining rm (by res only) 8-9:30 am, 6-8 pm. Setups. Ck-out 10 am, ck-in 1 pm. Hiking trails. Lawn games. 100 acres atop mountain; stone lodge with great room; adj to Joyce Kilmer Memorial Forest. Cr cds: MC, V.

🅳 🐾 🦶 🛌 🦶 🦶

Rocky Mount

(B-6) *See also Wilson*

Settled 1840 **Pop** 48,997 **Elev** 120 ft **Area code** 252

Information Chamber of Commerce, 2501 Sunset Ave, PO Box 392, 27802

Seasonal Event

Tobacco auctions. Numerous warehouses. Inquire locally. Aug-mid-Nov.

Motels/Motor Lodges

★ **CARLETON HOUSE INN.** *215 N Church St (27804). 252/977-0410; fax 252/985-2115.* 42 rms, 2 story. S $42-$49; D $49-$56; suites $75; under 16 free. Crib free. TV; cable (premium). Pool. Coffee in rms. Restaurant 6:30 am-9 pm; Sat 7 am-noon, 5-10 pm; Sun 7:30-10:30 am, 11:30 am-2 pm, 5-8 pm. Ck-out noon. Meeting rm. Business servs avail. Sundries. Health club privileges. Cr cds: A, MC, V.

☁ 🛌 🦶 SC

★★ **FAIRFIELD INN BY MAR-RIOTT.** *1200 Benvenue Rd (27804). 919/972-9400; fax 919/972-9400; res 800/228-2800. www.fairfieldinn.com.* 104 rms, 3 story. D $55.95-$62.95; under 18 free. Crib free. TV; cable (premium). Pool. Complimentary continental bkfst. Ck-out noon. Business servs avail. In-rm modem link. Cr cds: A, D, DS, MC, V.

🅳 ☁ 🛌 🦶 SC

★★ **HOLIDAY INN DORTCHES.** *I-95; 5350 Dortches Blvd (27804). 252/937-6300; fax 252/937-6312; res 888/937-4938; toll-free 800/465-4329.* 154 rms, 2 story. S, D $61.95-$67.95; under 18 free. Crib free. TV; cable (premium). Pool. Complimentary coffee in rms. Restaurant 6 am-2 pm, 4:30-10 pm. Ck-out noon. Meeting rms. Business servs avail. Coin lndry. Health club privileges. Some refrigerators. Cr cds: A, D, DS, MC, V.

🅳 ☁ 🛌 🦶 SC

★★ **HOLIDAY INN ROCKY MOUNT.** *651 Winstead Ave (27804), 1 mi E of I-95, Exit 138. 252/937-6888; fax 252/937-4788; toll-free 888/832-9231.* 171 rms, 4 story. S, D $75-$90; each addl $6; suites $99-$125; under 12 free. Crib free. TV; cable (premium). Pool. Restaurant 6:30-11 am, 11:30 am-10 pm. Bar. Ck-out noon. Meeting rms. Business servs avail. Bellhops. Exercise equipt. Refrigerator in suites. Cr cds: A, C, D, DS, JCB, MC, V.

🅳 ☁ 🛌 🦶 🦶

Hotel

★★ **HAMPTON INN.** *530 N Winstead Ave (27804). 252/937-6333; fax 252/937-4333; res 800/HAMPTON; toll-free 800/426-7866. Email rwinc01@hi-hotel.com.* 117 rms, 4 story, 7 suites. July-Sep: S, D $68; suites $99; under 18 free; lower rates rest of yr. Crib avail. Parking lot. Pool, whirlpool. TV; cable (premium). Complimentary continental bkfst, coffee in rms, newspaper, toll-free calls. Restaurant. Ck-out noon, ck-in 3 pm. Meeting rms. Business center. Dry cleaning. Golf. Picnic facilities. Cr cds: A, D, DS, MC, V.

Salisbury

(C-4) *See also Concord, Lexington, Statesville*

Founded 1753 **Pop** 23,087 **Elev** 746 ft **Area code** 704 **Zip** 28144
Web www.visitsalisburync.com.

Information Rowan County Convention & Visitors Bureau, PO Box 4044, 28145; 704/638-3100 or 800/332-2343. Visit the Visitor Information Center at 132 E Innes for brochures, maps and audio tape tours

Motels/Motor Lodges

★★ **HAMPTON INN.** *1001 Klumack Rd (28147), I-85 Exit 75. 704/637-8000; fax 704/639-9995; toll-free 800/426-7866.* 121 rms, 4 story. S $59; D $64; suites $95; under 18 free; higher rates: Furniture Market, auto racing events. Crib free. Pet accepted, some restrictions. TV; cable (premium). Pool. Complimentary continental bkfst. Restaurant adj 11 am-11 pm. Ck-out noon. Meeting rms. Business servs avail. Health club privileges. Refrigerator in suites. Cr cds: A, C, D, DS, MC, V.

★★ **HOLIDAY INN.** *530 Jake Alexander Blvd (28147), I-85 Exit 75. 704/638-0311; fax 704/637-9152; res 800/465-4329.* 181 rms, 3 story. S $63-$88; D $67-$90; each addl $6; suites $95-$125; under 18 free;

higher rates special events. Crib free. TV; cable (premium). Indoor/outdoor pool. Restaurant 7 am-2 pm, 6-9 pm. Bar 5 pm-1 am; Sat from 6 pm; entertainment Fri, Sat. Ck-out noon. Business servs avail. Bellhops. Valet serv. Exercise equipt. Refrigerator avail in suites. Cr cds: A, C, D, DS, JCB, MC, V.

Sanford (C-5)

Pop 14,475 **Elev** 375 ft **Area code** 919 **Zip** 27330

Motels/Motor Lodges

★★ **COMFORT INN.** *1403 N Horner Blvd (27330). 919/774-6411; fax 919/774-7018; toll-free 800/424-6423.* 122 rms, 2 story. S $50-$56; D $54-$60; suites $85-$105; under 18 free. Crib free. TV; cable (premium). Pool. Complimentary full bkfst. Restaurant nearby. Meeting rms. Coin lndry. Exercise equipt; sauna. Some refrigerators. Cr cds: A, C, D, DS, MC, V.

★ **PALOMINO MOTEL.** *1508 Westover Dr (27331), 2½ mi on US 1, US 15/501 Bypass. 919/776-7531; fax 919/776-9670; toll-free 800/641-6060.* 92 rms. S $34-$42; D $44-$48; each addl $2; suites $108. Crib $5. Pet accepted. TV; cable (premium). Pool; whirlpool. Playground. Restaurant 6 am-9 pm. Bar 4-11 pm. Ck-out noon. Meeting rms. Golf privileges. Exercise equipt; sauna. Picnic tables, grill. Cr cds: A, D, DS, MC, V.

Shelby

See also Gastonia

Pop 14,669 **Elev** 853 ft **Area code** 704
Web www.co.cleveland.nc.us

Information Cleveland County Economic Development, 311 E Marion St, PO Box 1210, 28151; 704/484-4999 or 800/480-8687

Seat of Cleveland County, this town in the Piedmont boasts of diversified industry and agriculture. It is named for Colonel Isaac Shelby, hero of the Battle of Kings Mountain in the Revolutionary War. (See KINGS MOUNTAIN NATIONAL MILITARY PARK, SC.) The town celebrates its heritage and culture with special events, fairs, and historic preservation.

What to See and Do

Central Shelby Historic District Walking Tour. Two-hr self-guided tour encompasses much of original area established in 1841. Features 38 architecturally significant structures ca 1850s. Phone 704/481-1842 for info.

Motel/Motor Lodge

★ **DAYS INN.** *1431 W Dixon Blvd (28152). 704/482-6721; fax 704/480-1423; toll-free 800/892-3845.* 97 rms, 2 story. S $50; D $54; each addl $5; under 12 free. Crib free. TV; cable (premium). Pool. Complimentary continental bkfst. Restaurant 11 am-2 pm, 5-9 pm. Ck-out noon. Meeting rms. Cr cds: A, D, DS, MC, V.
🄳 ⛱ 🔆 🔥 SC

Smithfield

(C-6) *See also Dunn, Goldsboro, Raleigh*

Pop 7,540 **Elev** 153 ft **Area code** 919 **Zip** 27577

Motels/Motor Lodges

★★ **COMFORT INN.** *1705 Industrial Park Dr (27576), approx 5 mi N on US 301. 919/965-5200; fax 919/965-5200; res 800/228-5150. www.comfortinn.com.* 73 rms, 2 story, 7 suites. Mar-Apr, June-Aug, Dec: S $81; D $85; each addl $5; suites $85; under 16 free; lower rates rest of yr. Crib avail, fee. Parking lot. TV; cable (premium), VCR avail. Complimentary continental bkfst, newspaper. Restaurant 7 am-9 pm. Ck-out 11 am, ck-in 1 pm. Fax servs avail. Salon/barber. Exercise privileges, whirlpool. Golf. Cr cds: A, D, DS, MC, V.
🄳 🏋 🏃 🔆 🔥

★ **MASTERS ECONOMY INN.** *318 US Hwy 70 E (33316). 919/965-3771; fax 919/965-5565; toll-free 800/633-3434. www.masters-inns.com.* 119 rms, 2 story. S $31.95, D $35.95; each addl $4; under 18 free. Crib $6. TV; cable (premium). Pool. Ck-out noon. Meeting rms. Business servs avail. Cr cds: A, D, DS, MC, V.
🄳 ⛱ 🔆 🔥 SC

South Brunswick Islands

See also Southport; also see Myrtle Beach, SC

Web www.weblync.com/sbi_chamber
Information Chamber of Commerce, PO Box 1380, Shallotte 28459; 910/754-6644 or 800/426-6644

The South Brunswick Islands offer wide, gently sloping beaches and beautiful scenery. Located just 50 miles from the Gulf Stream, the region has a subtropical climate and mild temperatures. Resort activities are plentiful and include fishing, swimming, tennis, and golf. Shallotte is the hub of the area that includes Holden, Ocean Isle, and Sunset beaches. The islands are reached by bridges across the Intracoastal Waterway.

Annual Events

A Day at the Docks. Holden Beach. Blessing of the fleet, arts and crafts, bobble race. Late Mar.

King Classic King Mackerel Tournament. Holden Beach. Early Sep.

North Carolina Oyster Festival. In Shallotte. Arts and crafts, music, sports, oyster-shucking contest. Third wkend Oct.

Resort

★★ **THE WINDS OCEANFRONT INN & SUITES.** *310 E 1st St (28469), 1½ mi N of jct NC 904 & E 1st St. 910/579-6275; fax 910/579-2884; toll-free 800/334-3581. Email info@ thewinds.com; www.thewinds.com.* 72 units, 4 story, 45 suites, 58 kit. units,

6 houses (1-4 bedrm). No elvtr. Early June-late Aug: S, D $114-$207; each addl $15; suites, kits. $164-$412; houses $481-$544; under 18 free; lower rates rest of yr. Crib $5. TV; cable. Pool; whirlpool, poolside serv. Complimentary bkfst buffet, coffee in rms. Ck-out 11 am. Coin lndry. Meeting rms. Business servs avail. In-rm modem link. Tennis privileges. 18-hole golf privileges, pro, putting green, driving range. Exercise equipt. Rec rm. Lawn games. Bicycle rental. Refrigerators, wet bars. Balconies. Picnic tables, grills. On beach. Cr cds: A, C, D, DS, ER, JCB, MC, V.

Southern Pines

(C-5) *See also Pinehurst*

Pop 9,129 **Elev** 512 ft **Area code** 910
Zip 28387
Web www.homeofgolf.com
Information Convention & Visitors Bureau, PO Box 2270, 28388; 910/692-3330 or800/346-5362

Annual Event

House and Garden Tour. Conducted by Southern Pines Garden Club. Mid-Apr.

Motel/Motor Lodge

★★ **HAMPTON INN.** *1675 US 1S (28387). 910/692-9266; fax 910/692-9298.* 126 rms, 2 story. Mar-May, Sep-Nov: S, D $64-$89; under 18 free; golf plan; higher rates: wkends, special events; lower rates rest of yr. Crib free. TV; cable (premium), VCR avail. Pool. Complimentary continental bkfst, coffee in rms. Restaurant nearby. Ck-out noon. Coin lndry. Meeting rm. Business servs avail. Valet serv. Golf privileges. Health club privileges. Cr cds: A, D, DS, MC, V.

Hotel

★★ **HOLIDAY INN.** *US 1 at Morganton Rd Exit (28387). 910/692-8585; fax 910/692-5213; res 800/465-4329;* toll-free 800/262-5737. Email holiday@ pinehurst.net; www.pinehurst.net/~ holiday. 150 rms, 2 story, 8 suites. Mar-May, Sep-Oct: S $89; D $99; suites $140; under 17 free; lower rates rest of yr. Crib avail. Parking lot. Pool. TV; cable (premium). Complimentary coffee in rms, newspaper, toll-free calls. Restaurant 6:30 am-9:30 pm. Bar. Ck-out noon, ck-in 3 pm. Meeting rms. Business center. Dry cleaning. Free airport transportation. Exercise privileges. Golf. Tennis, 4 courts. Cr cds: A, C, D, DS, ER, JCB, MC, V.

Resorts

★★★ **MID PINES INN AND GOLF CLUB.** *1010 Midland Rd (28387). 910/692-2114; fax 910/692-4615; toll-free 800/323-2114.* 112 rms in 3-story hotel, 6 golf villas, 10 lakeside villas. Mar-May, Sep-Nov: S, D $140-$210; each addl $10; under 12 free; golf, tennis plans; lower rates rest of yr. TV; cable, VCR avail. Pool. Coffee in rms. Dining rm (public by res) 6:30-9 am, noon-2:30 pm, 6:30-8:30 pm. Box lunches; snack bar. Rm serv in hotel. Bar 11 am-11 pm. Ck-out 11 am, ck-in 2 pm. Meeting rms. Business center. Airport transportation. Lighted tennis. 18-hole golf, greens fee $70-$140, pro lessons, putting green. Health club privileges. Lawn games. Rec rm. Minibars; some refrigerators. Cr cds: A, DS, MC, V.

★★★ **PINE NEEDLES LODGE.** *1005 Midland Rd (28387), on NC 2, 1 mi W of jct US 1. 910/692-7111; fax 910/692-5349; toll-free 800/747-7272. Email info@rossresorts.com; www.ross resorts.com.* 71 rms in 10 lodges, 2 story. Mid-Mar-mid-June and mid-Sep-mid-Nov: S, D $135-$230/person; under 4 free; golf plans; lower rates rest of yr. Crib free. TV; cable (premium). Heated pool; poolside serv. Complimentary coffee in rms. Dining rm 7-9 am, 11:30 am-2:30 pm, 7-8:30 pm. Box lunches. Snack bar. Picnics. Bar noon-11 pm. Ck-out 11 am, ck-in 2 pm. Meeting rms. Business servs avail. In-rm modem link. Bellhops. Valet serv. Lighted grass tennis. 18-hole golf, greens fee $70-$100, pro, putting green, driving range. Health club privileges. Bicycles (rentals). Lawn games. Rec rm. Game rm. Some refrigerators. Balconies. Family-owned golf resort with course designed in 1927 by renowned golf course architect Donald Ross. Cr cds: A, MC, V.

Restaurants

★★ LA TERRACE. *270 SW Broad St (28387). 910/692-5622.* French menu. Specializes in seafood, lamb, Angus beef. Hrs: 11:30 am-9 pm; Sat 6-10 pm. Closed Sun; Jan 1, Dec 25. Res accepted. Lunch a la carte entrees: $7.25-$9.75; dinner a la carte entrees: $13.50-$25.95. Intimate dining in formal atmosphere. Cr cds: MC, V.

★ SQUIRE'S PUB. *1720 US 1S (28387). 910/695-1161.* Specializes in fish and chips, shepherd's pie, Welsh rabbit. Hrs: 11 am-10 pm. Closed Sun; Thanksgiving, Dec 24 and 25. Bar. Lunch $4.95-$10.95; dinner $4.95-$15.95. Child's menu. English decor. Cr cds: DS, MC, V.

★ VITO'S RISTORANTE. *615 SE Broad St (28387), off US 1. 910/692-7815.* Specializes in veal, chicken. Hrs: 5-9:30 pm. Closed Sun; hols. Dinner $5-$15. Child's menu. Italian decor. No cr cds accepted.

Southport

(E-6) *See also South Brunswick Islands, Wilmington*

Founded 1792 **Pop** 2,369 **Elev** 22 ft
Area code 910 **Zip** 28461
Web www.southport.net/chamberpage.html
Information Southport-Oak Island Area Chamber of Commerce, 4841 Long Beach Rd SE; 910/457-6964 or 800/457-6964

Annual Events

Robert Ruark Chili Cook Off. Easter wkend.

"Old Baby" lighthouse

US Open King Mackerel Tournament. First wkend Oct.

B&Bs/Small Inns

★★ LOIS JANE'S RIVERVIEW INN. *106 W Bay St (28461). 910/457-6701; fax 910/457-6701.* 4 rms, 2 share bath, 2 story. No rm phones. May-Sep: S, D $75-$100; lower rates rest of yr. TV; cable. Complimentary full bkfst; refreshments. Restaurant opp 11:30 am-9 pm. Ck-out 11 am, ck-in 3 pm. Built in 1892; antiques. Cr cds: MC, V.

★★ THEODOSIA'S BED & BREAK-FAST. *2 Keelson Row Harbour Village (28461),* take Bald Head Island Ferry to facility. *910/457-6563; fax 910/457-6055; res 800/656-1812.* Email garrett@theodosias.com. 10 rms, 7 with shower only, 3 story, 1 suite, 1 guest house. Mar-Oct: S $135-$180; D $150-$195; each addl $25; suites $185; guest house $150; under 5 free; wkends, hols (2-3 day min); lower rates rest of yr. TV; cable (premium), VCR avail. Complimentary full bkfst. Restaurant adj 7 am-10 pm. Ck-out 11:30 am, ck-in 3 pm. Valet serv. Free ferry transportation. Lighted tennis. 18-hole golf, greens fee $50, pro, putting green, driving range. Pool privileges. In-rm whirlpool in suite. Balconies. Antiques. Totally nonsmoking. Cr cds: DS, ER, MC, V.

Restaurant

★ **SANDFIDDLER SEAFOOD RESTAURANT.** *1643 N Howe St (28461), near jct NC 87. 910/457-6588.* Seafood menu. Specializes in seafood, prime rib. Hrs: 11 am-8:30 pm; Sat from 5 pm; Sun from 11:30 am. Closed hols. Lunch $2.95-$14.95; dinner $4.95-$26.95. Child's menu. Nautical decor. Cr cds: MC, V.

[D] [⟶]

Statesville

(C-4) *See also Cornelius, Hickory, Salisbury*

Founded 1789 **Pop** 17,567 **Elev** 923 ft
Area code 704 **Zip** 28677
Information Greater Statesville Chamber of Commerce, 115 E Front St, PO Box 1064, 28687; 704/873-2892

Statesville is a community of many small, diversified industries, including furniture, apparel, metalworking, and textiles. Iredell County, of which Statesville is the seat, is known for its dairy and beef cattle.

Annual Events

Carolina Dogwood Festival. Apr.

Tar Heel Classic Horse Show. Early May.

Iredell County Fair. One wk beginning Labor Day.

National Balloon Rally. Third wkend Sep.

Motels/Motor Lodges

★★ **FAIRFIELD INN STATESVILLE.** *1505 E Broad St (28625). 704/878-2091; fax 704/873-1368. Email fistatesville@hudsonhotels.com.* 117 rms, 2 story. S $56; D $61; each addl $5; under 17 free. Crib free. TV; cable. Pool. Complimentary continental bkfst. Restaurant nearby. Ck-out noon. Business servs avail. Cr cds: A, C, D, DS, MC, V.

[D] [⟶] [≋] [🔥]

★★ **HAMPTON INN.** *715 Sullivan Rd (28677). 704/878-2721; fax 704/873-6694; toll-free 800/426-7866.* 122 rms, 2 story. S $59-$69; D $64-$74; under 18 free; higher rates: wkends, special events. Crib free. TV; cable (premium), VCR avail. Pool. Complimentary continental bkfst. Ck-out 11 am. Meeting rm. Business servs avail. In-rm modem link. Cr cds: A, C, D, DS, MC, V.

[D] [≋] [⟶] [🔥] [SC]

★★ **HOLIDAY INN.** *1215 Gardner Bagnal Blvd (28677). 704/878-9691; fax 704/873-6927; toll-free 800/465-4329.* 134 rms, 2 story. S, D $77-$84; under 18 free; higher rates special events. Crib free. TV; cable (premium). Pool. Coffee in rms. Restaurant 6:30 am-2 pm, 5-9 pm. Bar 5 pm-2 am. Ck-out noon. Meeting rms. Business servs avail. In-rm modem link. Guest lndry. Exercise equipt. Cr cds: A, C, D, DS, JCB, MC, V.

[D] [≋] [🏃] [⟶] [🔥] [SC]

★ **RED ROOF INN.** *1508 E Broad St (28625). 704/878-2051; fax 704/872-3885; toll-free 800/843-7663.* 115 rms, 3 story. S $42.99-$45.99; D $49.99-$58.99; each addl $5; under 18 free. Crib free. TV; cable. Complimentary coffee in lobby. Restaurant nearby. Ck-out noon. Cr cds: A, C, DS, MC, V.

[D] [⟶] [🔥] [SC]

B&B/Small Inn

★★★ **HIDDEN CRYSTAL.** *471 Sulphur Springs Rd (28636), 17 mi NW on US 64. 828/632-0063; fax 828/632-3562; toll-free 800/439-1639.* 12 rms, 2 share bath, 2 story. S, D $75-$115; each addl $15; suites $160. Crib free. TV; cable. Pool. Complimentary full bkfst. Restaurant 11:30 am-2 pm, 5-9 pm; Sun 11 am-2 pm. Ck-out 10:30 am, ck-in 2 pm. Business servs avail. Colonial house built in 1930s. Totally nonsmoking. Cr cds: A, C, D, MC, V.

[D] [⚓] [≋] [🏃] [🎿] [⟶] [🔥]

Tryon

See also Hendersonville

Pop 1,680 **Elev** 1,085 ft
Area code 828 **Zip** 28782

Information Polk County Travel & Tourism, Visitor Information, 425 N Trade St; 828/859-8300 or 800/440-7848

On the southern slope of the Blue Ridge Mountains in the "thermal belt," almost at the South Carolina border, Tryon was named for Royal Governor William Tryon, who held office during the Revolution. The Fine Arts Center is the focal point for much of the cultural life of the community.

What to See and Do

Foothills Equestrian Nature Center (FENCE). Three-hundred-acre nature preserve has 5 mi of riding and hiking trails; wildlife programs; bird and nature walks. Host to many equestrian events. (Daily) 500 Hunting Country Rd. Phone 828/859-9021. **FREE**

White Oak Mountain. Scenic drive around the mountain. Turn off onto Houston Rd at Columbus and take dirt road, which winds around mountain.

Annual Events

Steeplechase Races. Third wkend Apr.
Blue Ridge Barbecue. Music festival, arts and crafts. June.

Motel/Motor Lodge

★★★ **PINE CREST INN.** *200 Pine Crest Ln (28782). 828/859-9135; fax 828/859-9135; toll-free 800/633-3001. Email info@pinecrestinn.com; www. pinecrestinn.com.* 30 rms, 2 story, 5 suites. S, D $160; each addl $35; suites $200; under 12 free. Crib avail. Parking lot. Pool. TV; cable (premium), VCR avail. Complimentary continental bkfst, newspaper. Restaurant 6-10 pm, closed Sun. Bar. Ck-out 11 am, ck-in 3 pm. Meeting rms. Business center. Concierge. Dry cleaning. Exercise privileges. Golf. Tennis, 3 courts. Hiking trail. Cr cds: A, DS, MC, V.

[D] [icons]

Restaurant

★★★ **PINE CREST INN.** *85 Pine Crest Ln. 828/859-9135. www.pine crestinn.com.* Specializes in crab cakes, rack of lamb, creme brulee. Hrs: 8 am-8:30 pm; Fri, Sat to 9:30 pm. Closed Sun. Res accepted. Bar. Wine cellar. Bkfst $5-$10; dinner $17-$26. Elegant, rustic decor in the style of a Colonial tavern; heavy pine tables, beamed ceiling, stone fireplace. Cr cds: A, DS, MC, V.

[D]

Warsaw

Pop 2,859 **Elev** 160 ft **Area code** 910 **Zip** 28398

What to See and Do

Duplin Wine Cellars. Largest winery in state. Videotape, tour, winetasting, retail outlet. (Mon-Sat; closed hols) 2 mi S via US 117; off I-40 Exit 380. Phone 910/289-3888. **FREE**

Motel/Motor Lodge

★ **COUNTRY SQUIRE REST & VINTAG.** *748 NC Hwy 24-50 (28398). 910/296-1727; fax 910/296-1431; res 910/296-7727. Email csquire@intrstar. net.* 12 rms. S $58; D $65; each addl $15; under 12 free; wknd rates. TV. Complimentary continental bkfst. Restaurant 11:30 am-2 pm, 5:30-10 pm; Fri, Sat from 5:30 pm. Ck-out 11 am. Golf privileges. English gardens; gazebos. Cr cds: A, D, MC, V.

[D] [icons]

Restaurant

★★ **COUNTRY SQUIRE.** *748 NC 24 50 (28398). 910/296-1727.* Specializes in beef, poultry. Hrs: 11:30 am-10 pm; Fri to 11 pm; Sat 5:30-11 pm; Sun from noon. Closed Thanksgiving, Dec 24, 25. Res accepted. Bar. Lunch $3.50-$12.75; dinner $10.95-$34.95. Child's menu. Five dining rms with historical themes. Gardens. Cr cds: A, MC, V.

[D] [SC] [icon]

Washington

(C-7) *See also Greenville*

Founded 1776 **Pop** 9,075 **Elev** 14 ft **Area code** 252 **Zip** 27889
Information Chamber of Commerce, PO Box 665; 252/946-9168

First American village named for the first president, Washington was rebuilt on the ashes left by evacuating Union troops in April 1864. The rebels lost the town in March 1862, and, because it was an important saltwater port, tried to retake it for two years. Evidence of the shelling and burning can be seen in the stone foundations on Water Street. Water sports, including sailing, yachting, fishing, and swimming, are popular.

Annual Event

Washington Summer Festival. Beach music street dance, ski show, arts and crafts, children's rides. Three days last full wkend July.

Motels/Motor Lodges

★★ **COMFORT INN.** *1636 Carolina Ave (27889), US 17N. 252/946-4444; fax 252/946-2563; res 800/228-5150; toll-free 800/424-6423.* 56 rms, 2 story. S, D $55; each addl $5; under 18 free. Crib free. TV; cable (premium). Pool. Complimentary continental bkfst. Restaurant adj 6 am-10 pm. Ck-out noon. Business servs avail. In-rm modem link. Exercise equipt. Refrigerators avail. Cr cds: A, C, D, DS, JCB, MC, V.

🅓 ⇌ 🏋 ⇙ 🔥 SC

★ **DAYS INN.** *916 Carolina Ave (27889). 252/946-6141; fax 252/946-6167; toll-free 800/329-7466.* 72 rms, 2 story. S $38-$65; D $42-$75; each addl $5; under 12 free. Crib free. TV; cable (premium). Pool. Bar 4 pm-2 am; entertainment wknds. Ck-out 11 am. Business servs avail. In-rm modem link. Cr cds: A, C, D, DS, JCB, MC, V.

🅓 ⇌ ⇙ 🔥 SC

B&Bs/Small Inns

★★ **PAMLICO HOUSE BED & BREAKFAST.** *400 E Main St (27889). 252/946-7184; fax 252/946-9944; toll-free 800/948-8507. Email pamlico house@coastalnet.com; www.pamlico house.com.* 4 rms, 2 story. S $65-$75; D $75-$85; each addl $15. Children over 6 yrs only. TV; cable. Complimentary full bkfst. Ck-out 11 am, ck-in 3 pm. Former rector's house

(1906); antiques, library. Cr cds: A, DS, MC, V.

⇙ 🔥

★★ **RIVER FOREST MANOR.** *738 E Main St (27810), approx 30 mi E on US 264 at marina on Intracoastal Waterway. 252/943-2151; fax 252/ 943-6628; toll-free 800/346-2151.* 11 rms, 2 story. S, D $50-$85. TV; cable (premium). Pool; whirlpool. Complimentary continental bkfst. Restaurant (see also RIVER FOREST MANOR). Ck-out 11 am, ck-in 2 pm. Business servs avail. Gift shop. Airport transportation. Tennis. View of river. 1899 bldg, antique furnishings. Golf carts avail for touring town. Cr cds: A, MC, V.

🅓 🏋 ⇌ 🔥 🐾

Restaurant

★★ **RIVER FOREST MANOR.** *738 E Main St. 252/943-2151. Email marina@belhavennc.com; www.river forestmanor.com.* Specializes in crabmeat casserole, pickled sausages, oyster fritters. Salad bar. Hrs: 6-9 pm. Bar. Dinner buffet: $15.95. Classical Greek Revival house built 1899. Cr cds: A, MC, V.

🅓 ⇙

Waynesville

(C-2) *See also Asheville, Cherokee, Maggie Valley*

Pop 6,758 **Elev** 2,644 ft
Area code 828 **Zip** 28786
Information Visitor & Lodging Information, 1233 N Main St, Suite I-40; 800/334-9036

Motels/Motor Lodges

★ **THE LODGE.** *909 Russ Ave (28786). 828/452-0353; fax 828/452-3329; toll-free 888/213-2666.* 40 rms, 2 story. June-Oct: S $47; D $70; each addl $5; under 18 free; lower rates rest of yr. Crib free. TV; cable (premium). Pool. Complimentary continental bkfst. Restaurant nearby. Ck-out 11 am. Cr cds: A, C, D, DS, MC, V.

🅓 ⇌ ⇙ 🔥

★ **PARKWAY INN.** *2093 W Dell-wood Rd (28786). 828/926-1841; fax 828/926-6093; toll-free 800/537-6397. Email ffueltz@asap-com.com; www. smokeymountains.net/parkwayinn.html.* 30 rms, 1 story. June-July, Sep-Oct: S, D $53; each addl $5; under 11 free; lower rates rest of yr. Crib avail, fee. Pet accepted, some restrictions, fee. Parking lot. TV; cable. Complimentary coffee in rms, newspaper, toll-free calls. Restaurant. Ck-out 11 am, ck-in 1 pm. Golf. Cr cds: DS, MC, V.
D 🐾 🛅 🔜 🔥

Resort

★★★ **WAYNESVVILLE COUNTRY CLUB.** *176 Country Club (28786), 1½ mi W on US 23/74 bypass off I-40. 828/456-3551; fax 828/456-3555; toll-free 800/627-6250.* 94 rms, eight 1-bedrm cottages, 1-2 story. May-Oct: S $110-$155; D $148-$184; cottages $184-$220; each addl $50; lower rates rest of yr. TV; cable. Pool. Dining rm 7-9:15 am, 10 am-4 pm, 6:30-8:30 pm. Bar 4-10 pm; entertainment Tues, Wed, Fri, Sat. Ck-out noon. Meeting rms. Business servs avail. Bellhops. Airport transportation. Tennis. Golf, greens fee $13-$23, pro. Downhill ski 20 mi. Balconies. Cr cds: A, MC, V.
D 🏊 🛅 🐾 🍽 🔥

B&Bs/Small Inns

★★ **BALSAM MOUNTAIN INN.** *Seven Springs Dr (28707), 7 mi W on US 74W Balsam Exit. 828/456-9498; fax 828/452-1405; toll-free 800/224-9498. Email merrily@dnet.net; www. aski.net/ncmark/balsam.htm.* 50 rms, 21 with shower only, 3 story, 8 suites. No A/C. No rm phones. June-Oct, winter wkends: S, D $95; each addl $15; suites $115-$150; wkend, hol rates (2-day min); lower rates rest of yr. Crib free. Complimentary coffee in library. Dining rm 8-9:30 am, 6-7:30 pm; Sun noon-2 pm; wkend hrs vary. Ck-out 11 am, ck-in 3 pm. Meeting rm. Business servs avail. Gift shop. Restored, turn-of-the-century inn nestled on scenic mountainside. Near Great Smoky Mountain Scenic Railway. Cr cds: DS, MC, V.
D 🔜 🐾 SC

★ **GRANDVIEW LODGE.** *466 Lickstone Rd (28786). 828/456-5212; fax 828/452-5432; toll-free 800/255-7826. Email innkeeper@grandviewlodgenc. com; www.grandviewlodgenc.com.* 9 rms, 1 story. June-Aug, Oct: S $85; D $115; each addl $30; suites $120; children $20; under 12 free; lower rates rest of yr. Parking lot. TV; cable, VCR avail, CD avail. Complimentary full bkfst, newspaper, toll-free calls. Restaurant 8:30 am-7 pm. Ck-out 10 am, ck-in 1 pm. Meeting rm. Golf. Tennis. Downhill skiing. Cr cds: MC, V.
🏊 🎿 🐾 🔜 🔥

★★★ **OLD STONE.** *109 Dolan Rd (28786). 828/456-3333; toll-free 800/432-8499. www.oldstoneinn.com.* 15 rms, 1 story, 2 suites. June-Oct: S $83; D $98; each addl $39; suites $139; lower rates rest of yr. Parking lot. TV; cable (premium), VCR avail. Complimentary full bkfst, newspaper, toll-free calls. Restaurant 6-10 pm, closed Sun. Bar. Ck-out 11 am, ck-in 3 pm. Meeting rm. Business center. Concierge. Gift shop. Exercise privileges. Golf. Tennis, 8 courts. Downhill skiing. Hiking trail. Picnic facilities. Cr cds: A, DS, MC, V.
🛅 🐾 🏊 🛅 🐾 🎿 🐾 🔜 🐾 🎿

★★★★ **THE SWAG COUNTRY INN.** *2300 Swag Rd (28786), W on US 19, then 2.3 mi N on US 276 to Hemphill Rd, then left for 4 mi, follow sign up private driveway. 828/926-0430; fax 828/926-2036; res 828/926-0430; toll-free 800/789-7672. Email swaginnkeeper@aol.com.* The name of this seasonal country inn (open May through November) refers to its mountain-ridge location 5,000 feet up in the Smoky Mountains. Built of hand-hewn logs, the rooms and cabins have a rustic decor of early American antiques and handmade quilts and rugs. The 250-acre property is quietly majestic, the perfect destination for group gatherings or even a romantic retreat. 16 rms, 1-2 story, 3 cabins. AP, mid-May-Oct: S, D $235-$490; each addl $80; higher rates: wkends, hols (2-3-day min), fall foliage. Closed rest of yr. Children over 7 yrs only. Coffee, tea in rms. Dining rm (public by res), 2 sittings: noon and 7 pm. Ck-out 11 am, ck-in 3 pm. Business servs avail. Gift shop. Underground racquetball court. Badminton, croquet court. Sauna. Whirlpool. Massage. Fireplaces. Balconies. Library, video collection. Swimming pond with swinging bridge. Walking trails. Cr cds: A, DS, MC, V.

⬛ ⬛ ⬛ ⬛ ⬛

★★★ **WINDSONG: A MOUNTAIN INN.** *459 Rockcliffe Ln (28721), I-40, Exit 24, then 3 mi N on NC 209, then 2½ mi W on Riverside Dr, then 1 mi N on Ferguson Cove Loop. 828/627-6111; fax 828/627-8080. Email russ@ windsongbb.com; www.windsongbb. com.* 5 rms, 2 story, 2 suites. June-Oct: D $145; each addl $20; suites $170; children $10; lower rates rest of yr. Parking lot. Pool, whirlpool. TV; cable (DSS); VCR avail. Complimentary full bkfst. Ck-out 11 am, ck-in 3 pm. Fax servs avail. Gift shop. Golf. Tennis. Downhill skiing. Hiking trail. Picnic facilities. Cr cds: A, DS, JCB, MC, V.

⬛ ⬛ ⬛ ⬛ ⬛ ⬛ ⬛ ⬛ ⬛ SC

★★★ **YELLOW HOUSE ON PLOT CREEK ROAD.** *89 Oakview Dr (28786). 828/452-0991; fax 828/452-1140; toll-free 800/563-1236. Email yelhouse@asap-com.com; www.the yellowhouse.com.* 2 rms, 3 story, 4 suites. Oct: S, D $135; each addl $20; suites $175; under 12 free; lower rates rest of yr. Parking lot. Pool, whirlpool. TV; cable (DSS); VCR avail. Complimentary full bkfst, coffee in rms, newspaper, toll-free calls. Restaurant. Ck-out 11 am, ck-in 2 pm. Meeting rm. Business servs avail. Gift shop. Exercise privileges. Golf, 18 holes. Tennis, 3 courts. Downhill skiing. Bike rentals. Hiking trail. Picnic facilities. Cr cds: MC, V.

⬛ ⬛ ⬛ ⬛ ⬛ ⬛ ⬛ ⬛ ⬛ ⬛

Wilkesboro

(B-3) *See also Jefferson*

Settled 1779 **Pop** 2,573 **Elev** 1,042 ft **Area code** 336 **Zip** 28697

Motel/Motor Lodge

★★ **ADDISON INN.** *US 421 N (28697), 2 mi N on US 421. 336/838-1000; fax 336/667-7458; toll-free 800/672-7218. Email addisonmi@ aol.com.* 115 rms, 2 story. S $53.99-$56.99; D $58.99-$61.99; each addl $5; under 18 free; higher rates special

events. Crib free. TV; cable (premium). Pool. Coffee in lobby. Complimentary continental bkfst. Restaurant adj 6 am-11 pm; Fri, Sat to 1 am. Ck-out 11 am. Meeting rm. Business servs avail. Health club privileges. Some refrigerators. Cr cds: A, DS, MC, V.

⬛ ⬛ ⬛ ⬛ ⬛ ⬛ ⬛

Williamston

(C-7) *See also Washington*

Pop 5,503 **Elev** 80 ft **Area code** 252 **Zip** 27892

What to See and Do

Hope Plantation. Two-hr guided tour of Georgian plantation house (ca 1800) built by Governor David Stone. Period furnishings; outbldgs; gardens. (Mon-Sat, also Sun afternoons) US 13 to Windsor, then 4 mi W on NC 308. Phone 252/794-3140. ¢¢¢ Incl in admission is

King-Bazemore House. (1763) Tour of this unique Colonial-style house with gambrel roof, dormer windows, and solid brick ends. Period furnishings; outbldgs; gardens.

Motels/Motor Lodges

★★ **COMFORT INN.** *100 East Blvd (27892), jct US 17 and US 13/64. 252/792-8400; fax 252/809-4800; toll-free 800/827-8400.* 59 rms, 2 story. S $56; D $60; each addl $5; suites $60-$64; under 18 free. Crib free. Pet accepted. TV; cable (premium). Complimentary continental bkfst. Restaurant nearby. Ck-out noon. Business servs avail. Exercise equipt. Cr cds: A, C, D, DS, ER, JCB, MC, V.

⬛ ⬛ ⬛ ⬛ ⬛ SC

★★ **HOLIDAY INN.** *101 East Blvd (27892), 1 mi S on US 17. 252/792-3184; fax 252/792-9003; toll-free 800/792-3101. Email holidayinn@ williamstonnc.com.* 100 rms, 2 story. S, D $59-$65; each addl $5; under 18 free. Crib free. Pet accepted. TV; cable (premium). Pool. Restaurant 6 am-9 pm. Bar 5 pm-midnight. Ck-out noon. Meeting rms. Business servs avail. In-rm modem link. Cr cds: A, D, DS, MC, V.

⬚🔧🔲🛏️🚹🛗🗑️🔥

Wilmington

(E-6) *See also Southport, Wrightsville Beach*

Settled 1732 **Pop** 55,530 **Elev** 25 ft
Area code 910 **Web** www.cape-fear.nc.us
Information Cape Fear Coast Convention & Visitors Bureau, 24 N 3rd St, 28401; 910/341-4030 or 800/222-4757

What to See and Do

Battleship *North Carolina*. WWII vessel moored on W bank of Cape Fear River. Tour of museum, gun turrets, galley, bridge, sick bay, engine rm, wheelhouse. (Daily) Jct of US 74/76, 17 & 421. Phone 910/251-5797. ¢¢¢

Bellamy Mansion Museum of History and Design Arts. Restored 1859 landmark home has exhibits featuring history, restoration, southern architecture, and regional design arts. Tours. (Wed-Sun) 5th & Market Sts. Phone 910/251-3700. ¢¢

Burgwin-Wright House. (1770) Restored colonial town house built on foundation of abandoned town jail. British General Cornwallis had his headquarters here during Apr, 1781. Eighteenth-century furnishings and garden. Tours. (Tues-Sat; closed hols; also Jan and wk of Dec 25) 224 Market St, at 3rd St. Phone 910/762-0570. ¢¢

Cape Fear Museum. Interprets social and natural history of Lower Cape Fear. Changing exhibits. (Tues-Sun; closed hols) 814 Market St. Phone 910/341-7413. ¢

Carolina Beach State Park. This 700-acre park is a naturalist's delight; the rare Venus flytrap as well as 5 other species of insect-eating plants grow here. Fishing, boating (ramps, marina); picnicking, concession, nature and hiking trails, camping (dump station). Naturalist program. Standard fees. 1010 Masion Borro State Park Rd. Phone 910/458-8206 or 910/458-7770 (marina).

Sightseeing cruises.

Henrietta II **Paddlewheel Riverboat Cruises.** One-and-a-half-hr narrated sightseeing cruise down Cape Fear River to North Carolina State Port. (June-Aug, 2 cruises Tues-Sun; Apr-May, Sep-Oct, 1 cruise Tues-Sun) Dinner cruises (Apr-Dec, Fri and Sat; June-Aug, Wed-Sat). 113B Dock St. Phone 910/343-1611 or 800/676-0162. ¢¢

Captain J.N. Maffitt **River Cruises.** Five-mi narrated sightseeing cruise covering Wilmington's harbor life and points of interest. Also "river taxi" service (addl fee) from Battleship *North Carolina*. (May-Sep, daily) 113B Dock St. Phone 910/343-1611 or 800/676-0162. ¢¢

St. John's Museum of Art. Collection of Mary Cassatt prints; paintings and works on paper, Jugtown Pottery, sculpture. Changing exhibits; lectures; educational programs. (Tues-Sun; closed hols) 114 Orange St. Phone 910/763-0281. ¢

Wilmington Railroad Museum. Exhibits on railroading past and present, centering on the Atlantic Coast Line and other Southeastern rail lines. HO scale regional history exhibit on 2nd floor; outside are ACL steam locomotive and caboose for on-board viewing. (Daily; closed Jan 1, Thanksgiving, Dec 25) 501 Nutt St. Phone 910/763-2634. ¢¢

Annual Events

North Carolina Azalea Festival. Garden and home tours, horse show, celebrity entertainers, pageants, parade, street fair. Early Apr.

Riverfest. Arts and crafts, music, dancing and entertainment; boat rides; raft regatta; street fair. Phone 910/452-6862. First full wkend Oct.

Motels/Motor Lodges

★ ★ **COURTYARD BY MARRIOTT.** *151 Van Campen Dr (28403), near New Hanover Regional Airport. 910/395-8224; fax 910/452-5569; toll-free 800/321-2211. www.marriott.com.* 128 rms, 2 story. Mid-May-mid-Oct: S, D $79-$119; suites $99-$159; under 18 free; wkends (2-day min); higher rates special events; lower rates rest of yr. Crib free. TV; cable (premium). Complimentary coffee in rms. Restaurant 6:30-10 am; Sat, Sun 7-11

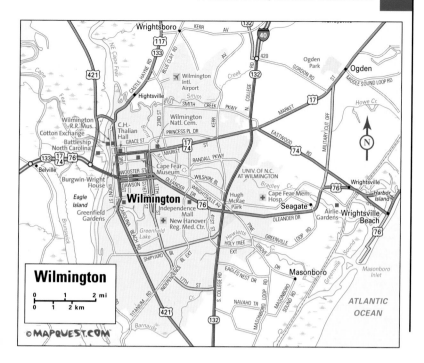

Wilmington

0   1   2 mi
0   1   2 km

© MAPQUEST.COM

am. Bar 5-11 pm. Ck-out noon. Meeting rms. Business servs avail. In-rm modem link. Valet serv. Coin lndry. Exercise equipt. Pool; whirlpool. Some bathrm phones, in-rm whirlpools, refrigerators, microwaves, wet bars. Some balconies. Cr cds: A, D, DS, MC, V.

★ **DAYS INN.** *5040 Market St (28405). 910/799-6300; fax 910/791-7414; toll-free 800/329-7466.* 122 rms, 2 story. S $42-$85; D $48-$85; each addl $4; under 12 free; family rates; higher rates: Azalea Festival, Riverfest, summer hols, wkends. Crib free. TV; cable (premium). Pool. Restaurant 6 am-8:45 pm. Ck-out 11 am. Business servs avail. Sundries. Picnic tables, grills. Cr cds: A, C, D, DS, JCB, MC, V.

★★ **DOCKSIDER OCEANFRONT INN.** *202 N NC Rte 421 - Oceanfront (28449), 20 mi S on US 421. 910/458-4200; fax 910/458-6468; toll-free 800/815-8636. Email reservations@ docksiderinn.com; www.docksiderinn. com.* 34 rms, 3 story. May-Sep: D $160; lower rates rest of yr. Crib

avail. Parking lot. Pool. TV; cable (premium). Complimentary coffee in rms, toll-free calls. Restaurant. Ck-out 11 am, ck-in 2 pm. Business center. Bellhops. Concierge. Gift shop. Golf. Tennis, 14 courts. Beach access. Bike rentals. Hiking trail. Picnic facilities. Cr cds: A, C, D, DS, MC, V.

★★ **FAIRFIELD INN.** *306 S College Rd (28403). 910/392-6767; fax 910/392-2144; toll-free 800/228-2800.* 134 rms, 3 story. Apr-Sep: S, D $57.95-$95.95; each addl $3; under 18 free; lower rates rest of yr. Crib free. TV; cable (premium). Pool. Complimentary continental bkfst. Restaurant nearby. Ck-out noon. Meeting rms. Business servs avail. Cr cds: A, C, D, DS, MC, V.

★ **FOUR POINTS HOTEL.** *5032 Market St (28405). 910/392-1101; fax 910/397-0698; res 800/833-4721.* 124 rms, 5 story. S, D $59-$109; each addl $10; suites $85-$250; under 18 free; wkend rates; higher rates: Azalea Festival, Memorial Day, July 4, Labor Day. Crib free. TV; cable (premium). Indoor pool; whirlpool. Restaurant 6 am-2 pm, 5-10 pm. Bar. Ck-out noon. Meeting rms. Business servs avail. Bellhops. Exercise equipt; sauna. Refrigerator in suites. Microwaves avail. Cr cds: A, C, D, DS, MC, V.

D ⛱ 🏃 ⛵ 🔥 SC

★ ★ **HAMPTON INN.** *5107 Market St (28405). 910/395-5045; fax 910/799-1974; res 800/426-7866. Email ilmmk01@hi-hotel.com.* 118 rms, 2 story. Apr-Sep: S $99; D $119; under 18 free; lower rates rest of yr. Crib avail. Parking lot. Pool. TV; cable (premium). Complimentary continental bkfst, coffee in rms, newspaper, toll-free calls. Restaurant nearby. Ck-out noon, ck-in 3 pm. Meeting rm. Business servs avail. Dry cleaning. Free airport transportation. Exercise privileges. Golf. Tennis. Cr cds: A, C, D, DS, MC, V.

D 🏌 ⛳ ⛱ 🏃 ⛵ 🔥 SC

★ **HOWARD JOHNSON EXPRESS INN.** *3901 Market St (28403). 910/343-1727; fax 910/343-1727; res 800/654-2000.* 80 rms, 1 story. Apr-Aug: S, D $49.95; each addl $8; lower rates rest of yr. Crib avail. Parking lot. TV; cable. Complimentary continental bkfst, coffee in rms, newspaper, toll-free calls. Restaurant nearby. Business servs avail. Exercise equipt. Cr cds: A, C, D, DS, ER, JCB, MC, V.

D ⛵ 🔥 SC

★ ★ **RAMADA INN CONFERENCE CENTER.** *5001 Market St (28405). 910/799-1730; fax 910/799-1730; res 800/272-6232; toll-free 800/433-7144.* 100 rms, 2 story. Apr-Sep: S, D $44-$125; under 18 free; golf plans; lower rates rest of yr. Crib free. TV; cable (premium). Pool. Complimentary full bkfst Mon-Fri. Restaurant 6 am-2 pm, 5-10 pm. Bar 5 pm-2 am; entertainment. Ck-out noon. Meeting rms. Business servs avail. Free airport transportation. Some refrigerators. Cr cds: A, C, D, DS, MC, V.

D ⛱ ✈ ⛵ 🔥 SC

★ **SLEEP INN.** *5225 Market St (28405). 910/313-6665; fax 910/313-2679. www.choicehotels.com.* 104 rms, 3 story. S, D $59-$89; under 18 free; hols (2-day min). Crib free. TV; cable (premium), VCR avail. Complimentary continental bkfst. Restaurant nearby. Ck-out 11 am. Meeting rms. Business servs avail. In-rm modem

link. Valet serv. Exercise equipt. Pool. Cr cds: A, C, D, DS, JCB, MC, V.

D ⛱ 🏃 ⛵ 🔥 SC

Hotels

★ ★ **COMFORT INN.** *151 S College Rd (28403). 910/791-4841; fax 910/790-9100; res 800/221-2222.* 146 rms, 6 story. S, D $55-$120; each addl $7; suites $125; under 18 free. Crib free. TV; cable (premium). Pool. Complimentary continental bkfst. Restaurant nearby. Ck-out noon. Meeting rms. Business servs avail. Valet serv. Cr cds: A, DS, MC, V.

D ⛱ 🏃 🔥

★ ★ ★ **HILTON WILMINGTON RIVERSIDE.** *301 N Water St (28412). 910/763-5900; fax 910/343-6148; res 800/445-8667. www.wilmingtonhilton.com.* 178 rms, 9 story. S, D $99-$179; each addl $10; suites $179-$340; under 18 free. Crib free. Pet accepted. TV; cable (premium). Pool; whirlpool. Complimentary coffee in rms. Restaurant 6:30 am-10:30 pm. Bar 4 pm-midnight. Ck-out noon. Meeting rms. Business servs avail. In-rm modem link. Gift shop. Free airport transporation. Exercise equipt. Boat dock. Luxury level. Cr cds: A, C, D, DS, MC, V.

D 🐾 ⛱ 🏃 ⛵ 🔥 🏃

★ ★ **HOLIDAY INN.** *160 Vancampen Blvd (28403). 910/392-3227; fax 910/395-9907.* 131 rms, 5 story. S, D $99-$139; each addl $10; suites $119-$159; under 19 free. Crib free. TV; cable (premium). Pool. Complimentary continental bkfst. Restaurant nearby. Ck-out noon. Meeting rms. Business servs avail. Coin lndry. Exercise equipt. Refrigerator in suites; microwaves avail. Cr cds: A, C, D, DS, ER, JCB, MC, V.

D 🐾 ⛱ 🏃 ⛵ 🔥 🏃

★ ★ **HOLIDAY INN.** *4903 Market St (28405). 910/799-1440; fax 910/799-2683; res 800/HOLIDAY; toll-free 800/782-9061. Email howdenr@bellsouth.net; www.holiday-inn.com/wilmingtonnc.* 224 rms, 2 story, 24 suites. Apr-Sep: S, D $109; suites $129; under 18 free; lower rates rest of yr. Crib avail. Parking lot. Pool, lap pool. TV; cable (premium), VCR avail. Complimentary full bkfst, coffee in rms, newspaper, toll-free calls. Restaurant. Bar. Meeting rms. Business center. Bellhops.

Concierge. Dry cleaning, coin lndry. Free airport transportation. Exercise rm, sauna. Golf. Tennis, 5 courts. Supervised children's activities. Picnic facilities. Cr cds: A, D, DS, MC, V.

B&Bs/Small Inns

★★ **CATHERINE'S INN.** *410 S Front St (28401). 910/251-0863; fax 910/772-9550; res 910/251-0863; toll-free 800/476-0723. Email catheri@ wilmington.net.* 5 rms, 2 story. S $75-$87.50; D $85-$110; each addl $20. Children over 10 yrs only. TV; cable (premium). Complimentary full bkfst. Restaurant nearby. Ck-out 11 am, ck-in 3-6 pm. Built in 1883; antiques. Totally nonsmoking. Cr cds: A, MC, V.

★★ **THE CURRAN HOUSE B&B.** *312 S Third St. (28401). 910/763-6603; fax 910/763-5116; toll-free 800/763-6603.* 3 rms, 2 story. Mar-Oct: S, D $119; lower rates rest of yr. Parking lot. TV; cable, VCR avail. Complimentary full bkfst, newspaper, toll-free calls. Restaurant nearby. Ck-out 11 am, ck-in 3 pm. Business center. Free airport transportation. Golf. Tennis, 2 courts. Cr cds: A, MC, V.

★★ **FRONT STREET INN.** *215 S Front St (28401). 910/762-6442; fax 910/762-8991. Email jay@frontstreet inn.com.* 9 rms, 2 story. S, D $89-$165; under 16 free; wkly rates. Crib free. TV; cable (premium), VCR avail. Complimentary continental bkfst, coffee in rms. Restaurant nearby. Ck-out 11 am, ck-in 4 pm. Business servs avail. In-rm modem link. Exercise equipt. Game rm. Refrigerators; microwaves avail. Balconies. Brick bldg (1923) that once housed Salvation Army. Cr cds: A, C, D, DS, MC, V.

★★★ **THE GRAYSTONE INN.** *100 S Third St (28401). 910/763-2000; fax 910/763-5555; toll-free 888/763-4773. Email reservations@graystone inn.com; www.graystoneinn.com.* 7 rms, 3 story, 2 suites. Mar-Nov: S, D $223; each addl $25; suites $274; under 12 free; lower rates rest of yr.

Street parking. TV; cable (premium), VCR avail. Complimentary full bkfst, newspaper, toll-free calls. Restaurant. Ck-out 11 am, ck-in 4 pm. Meeting rm. Business servs avail. Concierge. Exercise equipt. Golf. Tennis, 6 courts. Cr cds: A, C, D, DS, MC, V.

★★★ **ROSEHILL INN BED & BREAKFAST.** *114 S 3rd St (28401). 910/815-0250; fax 910/815-0350; toll-free 800/815-0250. Email rosehill@ rosehill.com; www.rosehill.com.* 7 rms, 2 story. Mar-Oct: S, D $129-$195; each addl $25; package plans; higher rates special events; lower rates rest of yr. Street parking. TV; cable (premium), VCR avail. Complimentary full bkfst. Ck-out 11 am, ck-in 3 pm. Business servs avail. Dry cleaning. Golf. Tennis, 5 courts. Cr cds: A, DS, MC, V.

★★ **TAYLOR HOUSE INN BED AND BREAKFAST.** *14 N 7th St (28401). 910/763-7581; toll-free 800/382-9982. Email taylorhousebb@aol. com; www.bbonline.com/nc/taylor.* 5 rms, 2 story. Mar-Oct: S $110; D $140; each addl $15; suites $225; children $15; lower rates rest of yr. Crib avail. Street parking. TV; cable, VCR avail. Complimentary full bkfst, coffee in rms, newspaper, toll-free calls. Restaurant nearby. Ck-out 10:30 am, ck-in 4 pm. Free airport transportation. Golf, 18 holes. Tennis, 10 courts. Bike rentals. Cr cds: MC, V.

★★★ **THE VERANDAS.** *202 Nun St (28401). 910/251-2212; fax 910/251-8932. Email verandas4@aol.com; www.verandas.com.* 8 rms, 3 story. Mar-Oct: S, D $190; lower rates rest of yr. Parking lot. TV; cable, VCR avail. Complimentary full bkfst, newspaper. Restaurant 11 am-11 pm. Ck-out 11 am, ck-in 4 pm. Business servs avail. Exercise privileges. Golf. Tennis. Cr cds: A, DS, MC, V.

★★ **THE WORTH HOUSE.** *412 S 3rd St (28401). 910/762-8562; fax 910/763-2173; toll-free 800/340-8559. Email worthhouse@aol.com; www.worth house.com.* 5 rms, 3 story, 2 suites. Mar-Oct: S $125; D $135; each addl

$25; suites $150; children $15; lower rates rest of yr. Street parking. TV; cable, VCR avail. Complimentary full bkfst, newspaper, toll-free calls. Restaurant nearby. Ck-out 11 am, ck-in 4 pm. Business servs avail. Free airport transportation. Golf. Tennis, 4 courts. Cr cds: A, DS, MC, V.

All Suites

★★★ DARLINGS BY THE SEA - OCEANFRONT WHIRLPOOL SUITES. *329 Atlantic Ave - Oceanfront (28449), 15 mi S on US 421. 910/458-8887; fax 910/458-0849; res 800/383-8111. Email reservations@darlings bythesea.com; www.darlingsbythesea. com.* 3 story, 5 suites. May-Sep: D $239; lower rates rest of yr. Parking lot. TV; cable (DSS), VCR avail, CD avail. Complimentary full bkfst, coffee in rms, toll-free calls. Restaurant. Ck-out 11 am, ck-in 2 pm. Business center. Bellhops. Concierge. Gift shop. Exercise equipt, whirlpool. Golf. Tennis, 14 courts. Beach access. Bike rentals. Hiking trail. Picnic facilities. Cr cds: A, C, D, DS, MC, V.

★★★ THE INN AT ST. THOMAS COURT. *101 S 2nd St (28401). 910/343-1800; fax 910/251-1149; res 800/525-0909. Email theinnatst thomas@cs.com; www.innatstthomas court.com.* 3 story, 40 suites. Apr-Nov: S, D $129; each addl $10; suites $129; children $10; under 12 free; lower rates rest of yr. Parking lot. TV; cable (premium), VCR avail. Complimentary continental bkfst, coffee in rms, newspaper, toll-free calls. Restaurant 11:30 am-11 pm, closed Mon. Bar. Ck-out 11 am, ck-in 3 pm. Meeting rms. Business center. Concierge. Dry cleaning, coin lndry. Whirlpool. Golf. Tennis, 5 courts. Picnic facilities. Cr cds: A, D, DS, MC, V.

Restaurants

★ CAFFE PHOENIX. *9 S Front St (28401). 910/343-1395. Email caffe phx@aol.com.* Specializes in pasta, grilled seafood. Hrs: 7:30 am-10 pm; Fri, Sat to 11 pm; Sun from 11:30 am. Closed hols. Bar. Bkfst $6-$8; lunch $6-$8; dinner $13-$25. Child's

menu. Casual decor. Cr cds: A, D, DS, MC, V.

★ COTTAGE. *1 N Lake Park Blvd (28428), 15 mi S on US 421. 910/458-4383.* Specializes in mix and match pasta, seafood, appetizers. Hrs: 11:30 am-10 pm. Closed Sun; hols; Dec 26. Res accepted. Bar. Lunch $4.95-$8.95; dinner $7.50-$18.95. Child's menu. Street parking. In old restored beach cottage. Cr cds: A, DS, MC, V.

★ DRAGON GARDEN. *341-52 S College Rd (28403), Univ Commons. 910/452-0708.* Specializes in Hunan, Szechuan, and Mandarin dishes. Hrs: 11 am-9 pm; Fri, Sat to 10:30 pm. Closed Thanksgiving, Dec 24, 25. Res accepted. Bar. Lunch $4-$6; dinner $5-$12. Chinese decor with many artifacts. Cr cds: A, DS, MC, V.

★ EDDIE ROMANELLI'S. *5400 Oleander Dr (28403). 910/799-7000.* Specializes in marinated steak, prime rib, pasta. Hrs: 11:30 am-11 pm; Sun from 11 am. Closed Thanksgiving, Dec 25. Bar. Lunch $3.95-$7.95; dinner $8.95-$18.95. Child's menu. Parking. Beamed ceiling with skylight. Cr cds: A, MC, V.

★★ ELIJAH'S. *2 Ann St (28401). 910/343-1448.* Specializes in chowder, hot crab dip. Hrs: 11:30 am-10 pm; Fri, Sat to 11 pm; Sun brunch to 3 pm. Closed Jan 1, Thanksgiving, Dec 25. Bar. Lunch $5.95-$9.95; dinner $9.95-$22.95. Sun brunch $4.95-$7.95. Child's menu. Entertainment: pianist Sun brunch. View of river. Nautical decor; former maritime museum. Cr cds: A, D, DS, MC, V.

★ FREDDIE'S. *111 K Ave (28449), 15 mi S on US 421. 910/458-5979.* Specializes in 4-layer lasagna, Freddie's special chop, chicken cacciatore. Hrs: 5-10 pm; early-bird dinner to 6 pm. Closed Mon; Jan 1, Thanksgiving, Dec 25. Bar. Dinner $8.95-$18.95. Child's menu. Street parking. Murals. Cr cds: A, MC, V.

★★ HARVEST MOON. *5704 Oleander Dr (28403). 910/792-0172. www. beachline.com.* Specializes in beef,

seafood. Hrs: 5:30-10 pm; Fri, Sat to 10:30 pm. Closed Sun; hols. Res accepted. Bar. Dinner $10.95-$22.95. Child's menu. Mediterranean decor. Cr cds: A, DS, MC, V.
[D]

★★ **HIERONYMUS SEAFOOD.** *5035 Market St (28405). 910/392-6313.* Specializes in seafood, prime rib, chicken. Hrs: 4-9:30 pm; Fri, Sat to 10 pm. Closed Jan 1, Thanksgiving, Dec 24, 25. Res accepted. Bar. Lunch $3.95-$10.95; dinner $4.95-$18.95. Child's menu. Oyster bar in lounge. Nautical decor. Cr cds: A, D, MC, V.
[D] [⊟]

★★ **MARKET STREET CASUAL DINING.** *6309 Market St (28405). 910/395-2488.* Specializes in grilled seafood, steak, pasta. Hrs: 5-11 pm. Closed Thanksgiving, Dec 25, Super Bowl Sun. Bar. Dinner $4.95-$14.95. Cr cds: A, DS, MC, V.
[D] [⊟]

★ **OH! BRIAN'S.** *4311 Oleander Dr (28403). 910/791-1477.* Specializes in ribs, chicken, salads. Hrs: 11 am-10 pm; Fri, Sat to 11 pm. Closed Thanksgiving, Dec 25. Res accepted Sun-Thurs. Bar. Lunch $3.95-$6.95; dinner $4.95-$16.95. Child's menu. Atrium. Cr cds: A, D, MC, V.
[D] [⊟]

★★ **PILOT HOUSE.** *2 Ann St (28401), Chandler's Wharf on Waterfront. 910/343-0200.* Specializes in crab melt sandwich, Caribbean fudge pie. Own bread. Hrs: 11:30 am-10 pm; Fri, Sat to 11 pm; Sun brunch to 3 pm. Closed Jan 1, Dec 24, 25. Res accepted. Lunch a la carte entrees: $2.95-$9.95; dinner a la carte entrees: $10.95-$24.95. Sun brunch $19.95. Child's menu. Parking. Located in restored area of waterfront; built in 1870. Cr cds: A, D, DS, MC, V.
[D] [⊟]

★★ **PORT CITY CHOP HOUSE.** *1981 Eastwood Rd (28405). 910/256-4955.* Specializes in Angus beef, grilled fish, lamb chops. Hrs: 11:30 am-10:30 pm. Closed Sun; Thanksgiving, Dec 25. Res accepted. Bar. Lunch $5-$10; dinner $13.95-$33.95. Child's menu. Contemporary decor

with brick and light woods; open kitchen area. Cr cds: A, D, DS, MC, V.
[D] [⊟]

★ **RUCKERJOHN'S.** *5511 Carolina Beach Rd (28412), on US 421. 910/452-1212.* Specializes in beef, pasta, seafood. Hrs: 11 am-10 pm; Fri, Sat to 11 pm. Closed Thanksgiving, Dec 25. Bar. Lunch $4.50-$6.50; dinner $5.95-$14.95. Child's menu. Casual, friendly atmosphere. Cr cds: A, MC, V.
[D] [⊟]

★★ **VINNIE'S.** *1900 Eastwood Rd (28403), in Lumina Station. 910/256-0995. www.vinnies.com.* Specializes in prime rib, seafood. Own pasta. Hrs: 5-10 pm; Fri, Sat to 11 pm. Closed Jan 1, Dec 25. Bar. Dinner $10.95-$49.95. Entertainment: Thurs-Sat. Semiformal club decor; mahogany woodwork, framed caricatures. Cr cds: A, MC, V.
[D] [SC] [⊟]

★ **WATER STREET.** *5 S Water St (28401). 910/343-0042.* Specializes in seafood, sandwiches, soups. Hrs: 11:30 am-9 pm; Fri, Sat to midnight. Closed Thanksgiving, Dec 25. Res accepted. Bar. Lunch $4.95-$9.95; dinner $7.95-$15.95. Entertainment: Wed-Sun. Riverfront dining in old warehouse. Cr cds: A, MC, V.
[D] [⊟]

Unrated Dining Spot

DOXEY'S MARKET & CAFE. *1319 Military Cut-off Rd (28403). 910/256-9952.* Specializes in soups, salads, sandwiches. Salad bar. Hrs: 9 am-7 pm. Closed Sun; hols. Lunch, dinner $3-$7. Cr cds: A, DS, MC, V.
[D]

Wilson

(C-6) *See also Rocky Mount*

Pop 36,930 **Elev** 145 ft **Area code** 252

Motels/Motor Lodges

★★ **BEST WESTERN LASAM-MANA.** *817 A Ward Blvd (27893). 252/237-8700; fax 252/237-8092; res*

800/528-1234. 78 rms, 2 story, 4 suites. July-Oct: S, D $64; each addl $5; suites $125; under 12 free; lower rates rest of yr. Crib avail, fee. Pool. TV; cable (DSS), VCR avail. Complimentary continental bkfst, coffee in rms, newspaper, toll-free calls. Restaurant. Ck-out 11 am, ck-in noon. Meeting rm. Business center. Dry cleaning. Exercise privileges. Golf. Tennis. Cr cds: A, C, D, DS, MC, V.

★★ **HAMPTON INN.** *1801 S Tarboro St (27893), 6 mi E of I-95, Exit 121. 252/291-2323; fax 252/291-7696; res 800/426-7866.* 99 rms, 2 story, 1 suite. S $66; D $71; under 18 free. Crib avail. Parking lot. Pool. TV; cable (premium), VCR avail. Complimentary continental bkfst, coffee in rms, newspaper, toll-free calls. Restaurant. Ck-out 2 pm, ck-in 11 pm. Meeting rm. Business center. Dry cleaning. Exercise privileges, sauna, steam rm. Golf, 18 holes. Tennis, 3 courts. Picnic facilities. Cr cds: A, C, D, MC, V.

★★ **HOLIDAY INN.** *1815 Hwy 301 S (22033). 252/243-5111; fax 252/291-9697; res 800/329-7466; toll-free 800/465-4329.* 100 rms, 2 story. S, D $51.14; each addl $5; under 12 free. Crib free. Pet accepted, some restrictions; $10. TV; cable (premium). Pool. Complimentary continental bkfst, coffee in rms. Bar. Ck-out noon. Meeting rms. Business servs avail. Cr cds: A, C, D, DS, JCB, MC, V.

★ **MICROTEL INN.** *5013 Hayes Pl (27896). 252/234-0444; fax 252/234-0065; res 888/771-7171.* 62 rms, 2 story. S $39.95-$54.95; D $41.95-$56.95; suites $64.94-$84.95; under 18 free; golf plans. TV; cable (premium). Complimentary coffee in lobby. Restaurant nearby. Ck-out 11 am. Business servs avail. In-rm modem link. Coin lndry. Cr cds: A, D, DS, JCB, MC, V.

Hotel

★★ **COMFORT INN.** *4941 US 264 W (28403). 252/291-6400; fax 252/291-7744; toll-free 800/228-5150.*

Email comfortnc@aol.com. 76 rms, 2 story, 24 suites. Mar-Nov: S $65; D $69; each addl $10; suites $125; under 18 free; lower rates rest of yr. Crib avail. Parking lot. Pool. TV; cable (premium). Complimentary continental bkfst, coffee in rms, newspaper, toll-free calls. Restaurant 6 am-9 pm. Ck-out 11 am, ck-in 2 pm. Meeting rms. Business servs avail. Dry cleaning. Golf. Cr cds: A, C, D, DS, MC, V.

B&B/Small Inn

★★ **MISS BETTY'S B&B INN.** *600 W Nash St (27873). 252/243-4447; fax 252/243-4447; res 800/258-2058. Email missbettysbnb@coastalnet.com; www.missbettysbnb.com.* 10 rms, 2 story, 3 suites. Suites $80. Parking lot. TV; cable (premium), VCR avail. Complimentary full bkfst, newspaper, toll-free calls. Restaurant, closed Sun. Ck-out 11 am, ck-in 3 pm. Business center. Coin lndry. Golf. Tennis. Picnic facilities. Video games. Cr cds: A, C, D, DS, MC, V.

Winston-Salem

(B-4) *See also Greensboro, High Point, Lexington*

Founded Salem: 1766; Winston: 1849; combined as Winston-Salem: 1913 **Pop** 143,485 **Elev** 912 ft
Area code 336

Information Convention and Visitors Bureau, PO Box 1409, 27102; 336/777-3796 or 800/331-7018

First in industry in the Carolinas and one of the South's chief cities, Winston-Salem is a combination of two communities. Salem, with the traditions of its Moravian founders and Winston, an industrial center, matured together. Tobacco markets, large banks, and arts and crafts galleries contribute to this thriving community.

What to See and Do

Hanging Rock State Park. Approx 6,200 acres in Sauratown Mts. Lake swimming, bathhouse, fishing, boating (rentals); nature trails, picnicking, concession, tent and trailer sites, 6 family cabins (Mar-Nov, by res only). Observation tower. Standard fees. 32 mi N, between NC 66 & 89 near Danbury. Phone 336/593-8480.

Historic Bethabara Park. Site of first Moravian settlement in North Carolina (1753); restored bldgs incl Gemeinhaus (1788), Potter's House (1782), Buttner House (1803); reconstructed palisade fort (1756-63); stabilized archaeological foundations of original settlement and God's Acre (graveyard); reconstructed community gardens (1759). Visitor center; exhibits, slide show. Nature trails. Picnicking. (Apr-Nov, daily; walking tour all yr) 2147 Bethabara Rd. Phone 336/924-8191. **FREE**

Historic Old Salem. (1766) Restoration of a planned community which Moravians, with their Old World skills, made the 18th-century trade and cultural center of North Carolina's Piedmont. Many of the sturdy structures built for practical living have been restored and furnished with original or period pieces. Early crafts are demonstrated throughout the town. Here also is an original Tannenberg organ in working condition. A number of houses are privately occupied. Nine houses plus outbldgs are open to the public. Tours (self-guided) start at Visitor Center on Old Salem Rd. Special events are held during the yr. (Daily; no tours Thanksgiving, Dec 24-25) S of business district on Old Salem Rd. Phone 336/721-7300. Ticket to all bldgs (exc museum) ¢¢¢ In the old village are

> **Museum of Early Southern Decorative Arts.** Twenty-one period rms and 6 galleries (1690-1820), with decorative arts of Maryland, Virginia, Georgia, Kentucky, Tennessee, and the Carolinas. (Daily; closed Thanksgiving, Dec 24-25) 924 S Main St. Phone 336/721-7360. Museum ¢¢¢; Combination ticket incl Old Salem ¢¢¢¢¢
>
> **Salem Academy and College.** (1772) 1,100 women. When founded by the Moravians, it was the only school of its kind for women in the South. The Fine Arts Center offers art exhibits, lectures, films, concerts, and plays (mid-

Sep-mid-May, daily; eves during special events; some fees). Campus tours on request. Church St, on Salem Sq in Old Salem. Phone 336/721-2702.

Reynolda House, Museum of American Art. On estate of the late R. J. Reynolds of the tobacco dynasty. American paintings, original furniture, art objects, costume collection. Adj is Reynolda Gardens, 125 acres of open fields and naturalized woodlands; formal gardens, greenhouse. (Tues-Sat, also Sun afternoons; closed Jan 1, Thanksgiving, Dec 25) Approx 2 mi N on University Pkwy, then ½ mi E on Coliseum Dr then N on Reynolda Rd. 2250 Reynolda Rd. Phone 336/725-5325. ¢¢

R.J. Reynolds Tobacco Company, Whitaker Park Cigarette Plant. Guided tours (Mon-Fri; closed hols) 1100 Reynolds Blvd. Phone 336/741-5718. **FREE**

SciWorks. Hands-on exhibits of physical and natural sciences; planetarium; 31-acre outdoor environmental park and nature trails. (Daily; closed hols) 400 W Hanes Mill Rd at US 52N. Phone 336/767-6730. ¢¢

Southeastern Center for Contemporary Art. Exhibits by contemporary artists from across the country with accompanying educational programs. (Tues-Sat; closed hols) 750 Marguerite Dr. Phone 336/725-1904. ¢¢

Salem Moravian settlement

Tanglewood Park. Swimming, fishing, boating (paddleboats, canoes); horseback riding, golf, miniature golf, tennis, nature trail, picnicking, playgrounds, camping (fee), accommodations. Deer park. Steeplechase (early May). (Daily) 12 mi SW off I-40, in Clemmons (Exit 182). Phone 336/778-6300. Per vehicle ¢

Wake Forest University. (1834) 5,600 students. On campus are Fine Arts Center, Museum of Anthropology; also Reynolda Village, a complex of shops, offices, and restaurants. Bowman Gray School of Medicine is on Medical Center Blvd. 1834 Wake Forest Rd. Phone 336/759-5000 or 336/758-5000.

Motels/Motor Lodges

★★ **COURTYARD BY MARRIOTT.** *3111 University Pkwy (27105). 336/727-1277; fax 336/722-8219; res 800/321-2211.* 124 rms, 2 story. S, D $75; under 18 free; higher rates graduation (May). Crib free. TV; cable (premium). Pool; whirlpool. Complimentary coffee in lobby. Restuarant nearby. Ck-out noon. Coin lndry. Business servs avail. Exercise equipt. Health club privileges. Cr cds: A, DS, MC, V.

D ⌨ 🏊 🏋 🛟 🐾 SC

★ **DAYS INN.** *3330 Silas Creek Pkwy (27103), I-40 Wake Forest Exit. 336/760-4770; fax 336/760-1085; toll-free 800/329-7466.* 135 rms, 5 story. S $52-$54; D $57-$60; each addl $5; under 17 free. Crib free. TV; cable (premium). Pool; whirlpool. Complimentary continental bkfst. Ck-out noon. Meeting rms. Business servs avail. Health club privileges. Cr cds: A, D, DS, MC, V.

D ⌨ 🛟 🐾 SC

★★ **HAMPTON INN.** *5719 University Pkwy (27105). 336/767-9009; fax 336/661-0448; toll-free 800/HAMPTON.* 117 rms, 2 story. S $60-$65; D $65-$70; under 18 free. Crib free. TV; cable (premium). Pool. Complimentary continental bkfst. Restaurant adj 6 am-10 pm. Ck-out noon. Meeting rms. Business servs avail. In-rm modem link. Cr cds: A, C, D, DS, MC, V.

D ⌨ 🏋 🛟 🐾

★★ **HAMPTON INN.** *1990 Hampton Inn Ct (27103), I-40 Exit 189, at*

Stradford Rd. 336/760-1660; fax 336/768-9168; res 800/HAMPTON. 131 rms, 5 story. S, D $63-$120; each addl $6; under 18 free; higher rates special events. TV; cable (premium). Pool. Complimentary continental bkfst. Ck-out noon. Meeting rms. Business servs avail. Exercise equipt. Some refrigerators. Minibars. Cr cds: A, D, DS, MC, V.

D 🐾 ⌨ 🏋 🛟 🐾 🐾

★★ **RESIDENCE INN BY MARRIOTT.** *7835 N Point Blvd (27106). 336/759-0777; fax 336/759-9671; toll-free 800/331-3131.* 88 kit. suites, 2 story. S, D $89-$129; under 18 free; wkly rates. Crib free. Pet accepted; $75-$150. TV; cable (premium). Heated pool; whirlpool. Complimentary continental bkfst, coffee in rms. Ck-out noon. Coin lndry. Valet serv. Health club privileges. Refrigerators, microwaves. Picnic tables, grills. Cr cds: A, C, D, DS, JCB, MC, V.

D 🐾 ⌨ 🐾 🐾 SC

Hotels

★★ **ADAM'S MARK PLAZA.** *425 N Cherry St (27101). 336/725-3500; fax 336/721-2240; toll-free 800/444-2326. www.adamsmark.com.* 605 rms, 17 story. S, D $79-$180; suites $275-$550; under 18 free; wkend rates. Crib free. Garage $6. TV; cable (premium), VCR avail. Indoor pool; poolside serv. Restaurants 6:30 am-11 pm. Rm serv 24 hrs. Bar 11:30-1 am; entertainment Fri-Sat. Ck-out 1 pm. Convention facilities. Business servs avail. In-rm modem link. Concierge. Gift shop. Exercise equipt; sauna. Health club privileges. Game rm. Refrigerator in suites. Local art displayed. Luxury level. Cr cds: A, C, D, DS, MC, V.

D ⌨ 🏋 🛟 🐾 SC

★★ **HOLIDAY INN SELECT.** *5790 University Pkwy (27105). 336/767-9595; fax 336/744-1888; toll-free 800/553-9595.* 150 rms, 6 story. S, D $86; suites $99; under 18 free; wkend rates; higher rates. Crib free. TV; cable (premium), VCR avail. Pool. Restaurant 6:30 am-2 pm, 5:30-10 pm. Bar; entertainment. Ck-out noon. Meeting rms. Business servs avail. Exercise equipt. Health club privileges. Some refrigerators, minibars. Cr cds: A, D, DS, MC, V.

D ⌨ 🏋 🛟 🛟 🐾 🏋

B&Bs/Small Inns

★★ **AUGUSTUS T ZEVELY.** *803 S Main St (27101). 336/748-9299; fax 336/721-2211; toll-free 800/928-9299. Email ctheall@dddcompany.com; www. winston-salem-inn.com/philadelphia.* 12 rms, 3 story, 1 suite. S $92; D $104; each addl $15; suites $205. Pet accepted, some restrictions. Parking lot. TV; cable (premium). Complimentary full bkfst, toll-free calls. Restaurant 11 am-9 pm, closed Sun. Ck-out 11 am, ck-in 3 pm. Meeting rms. Business servs avail. Concierge. Dry cleaning. Exercise privileges, steam rm, whirlpool. Golf. Tennis, 8 courts. Hiking trail. Cr cds: A, MC, V.

★★★ **BROOKSTOWN INN.** *200 Brookstown Ave (27101). 336/725-1120; fax 336/773-0147; toll-free 800/845-4262.* 71 units, 4 story. S $90-$125; D, suites $105-$135; each addl $20; under 12 free. Crib free. TV; cable (premium). Complimentary continental bkfst; afternoon refreshments. Coffee in rms. Ck-out noon, ck-in 2 pm. Business servs avail. In-rm modem link. Exercise equipt. Health club privileges. Restored brick cotton mill (1837); antiques, handmade quilts. Cr cds: A, D, MC, V.

★★ **COLONEL LUDLOW INN.** *434 Summit and W 5th (27101). 336/777-1887; fax 336/777-0518; toll-free 800/301-1887. Emailinnkeeper@bbinn.com; www.bbinn.com.* 9 rms, 2 story. S $89; D $169; suites $209. Parking lot. TV; cable (premium), VCR avail, CD avail. Complimentary full bkfst, coffee in rms, newspaper. Restaurant. Bar. Ck-out 11:30 am, ck-in 3 pm. Meeting rm. Business servs avail. Concierge. Dry cleaning. Exercise equipt, whirlpool. Golf. Tennis, 10 courts. Cr cds: A, DS, MC, V.

★★ **TANGLEWOOD PARK.** *434 Summit and W 5th (27012), 12 mi SW on US 158, I-40 Exit 182, in Tanglewood Park. 336/778-6300; fax 336/778-6379.* 18 rms in lodge, 10 rms in manor house, 2 story. S $35-$95; D $45-$107. Crib $3. TV. Pool; wading pool, lifeguard. Complimentary continental bkfst. Ck-out noon, ck-in 2 pm. Meeting rms. Tennis. Golf. Facilities of Tanglewood Park avail. Cr cds: MC, V.

Restaurants

★★ **OLD SALEM TAVERN.** *736 S Main St (27101). 336/748-8585. Email salemtavern@aol.com.* Specializes in roast duck, rack of lamb. Hrs: 11:30 am-9 pm; Sun to 2 pm. Closed first 2 wks Jan, Dec 25. Lunch $4.75-$7.50; dinner $13-$20. Child's menu. Cr cds: A, MC, V.

★★ **RYAN'S STEAK CHOPS & SEAFOOD.** *719 Coliseum Dr (27106). 336/724-6132. www.ryansrestaurant. com.* Specializes in beef, seafood. Own soup, some desserts. Hrs: 5-10 pm; Fri, Sat to 10:30 pm. Closed Sun; Jan 1, Thanksgiving, Dec 24, 25. Res accepted. Bar. Dinner $15.25-$34.95. Wooded setting. Cr cds: A, D, MC, V.

★★ **STALEY'S CHARCOAL STEAK HOUSE.** *2000 Reynolda Rd (27106). 336/723-8631.* Scandanavian menu. Specializes in prime rib, shish kebab. Hrs: 5-10 pm; Fri, Sat to 11 pm. Closed Sun; hols. Res accepted. Dinner $11.95-$39.95. Child's menu. Fountain at entrance. Cr cds: A, D, DS, MC, V.

★★ **VINEYARD.** *120 Reynolda Village (27106). 336/748-0269.* Specializes in beef, seafood, vegetarian dishes. Hrs: 5-10 pm. Closed Sun; hols. Bar. Dinner $10-$19. Child's menu. Entertainment: Wed-Sat. Casual, contemporary atmosphere. Cr cds: A, D, MC, V.

★★ **ZEVELY HOUSE.** *901 W 4th St (27101). 336/725-6666.* Specializes in potato cakes with smoked salmon and caviar, chicken pie, mixed grill. Hrs: 5:30-9 pm; Sun brunch 11 am-2 pm. Closed Mon; hols. Res accepted. Bar. Dinner $12.95-$21. Sun brunch $6.95-$11. Child's menu. Antiques, fireplace in older brick house. Cr cds: A, MC, V.

Wrightsville Beach

(E-6) *See also Wilmington*

Pop 2,937 **Elev** 7 ft **Area code** 910
Zip 28480

Motels/Motor Lodges

★ **ONE SOUTH LUMINA.** *1 S Lumina Ave (28480). 910/256-9100; fax 910/509-1639; toll-free 800/421-3255.* 17 kit. suites, 3 story. Memorial Day-Labor Day: D $145-$210; each addl $10; wkly rates; lower rates rest of yr. TV; cable. Pool. Coffee in rms. Restaurant nearby. Ck-out 11 am. Guest lndry. Microwaves. Balconies. On swimming beach. Cr cds: A, DS, MC, V.
🅳 ⬛ ⬛ 🏃 ⬛ ⬛ ⬛

★ **SILVER GULL MOTEL.** *20 E Salisbury St (28480). 910/256-3728; fax 910/256-2909; res 910/256-2388; toll-free 800/842-8894.* 32 kit. units, 3 story. June-Labor Day: S, D $135-$220; each addl $7; lower rates rest of yr. Crib $7. TV; cable. Ck-out 11 am. Coin lndry. Balconies. On ocean. Cr cds: A, D, DS, MC, V.
🅳 ⬛ ⬛ ⬛

★★ **SURF MOTEL.** *711 S Lumina Ave (28480). 910/256-2275; fax 910/256-1206.* 45 kit. suites, 4 story. Late May-early Sep: S, D $150-$215; each addl $10; wkly rates; wkend rates; lower rates rest of yr. Crib $10. TV; cable. Pool. Coffee in rms. Restaurant adj 11 am-10 pm. Ck-out 11:30 am. Coin lndry. Balconies. Swimming beach. Cr cds: A, C, D, DS, MC, V.
🅳 ⬛ ⬛ ⬛ ⬛ **SC**

★ **WATERWAY LODGE.** *7246 Wrightsville Ave (28403). 910/256-3771; fax 910/256-6916; toll-free 800/677-3771.* 42 units, 4 story. May-Sep: S, D $90-$115; each addl $10; kits. $100-$130; under 12 free; wkly rates; higher rates wkends (2-day min); lower rates rest of yr. Crib free. Pet accepted; $15. TV; cable (premium). Pool. Coffee in rms. Restaurant opp 11 am-10 pm. Ck-out 11:30 am. Business servs avail. Refrigerators, microwaves Cr cds: A, DS, MC, V.
⬛ ⬛ ⬛ ⬛ **SC**

Hotel

★★ **LANDFALL PARK HAMPTON INN.** *1989 Eastwood Rd (28403), 4 mi E on US 74. 910/256-9600; fax 910/256-1996; res 800/426-7866; toll-free 877/256-9600. Email indpkntl@bell south.net.* 120 rms, 4 story, 30 kit. suites. May-Sep: S, D $119; suites $169-$349; under 18 free; wkly rates; golf plans; wkends (2-day min); higher rates special events; lower rates rest of yr. Crib free. Pet accepted; $25. TV; cable (premium). Complimentary continental bkfst. Restaurant adj 11 am-11 pm. Bar 4:30-10 pm. Ck-out 11 am. Coin lndry. Meeting rms. Business servs avail. In-rm modem link. Concierge. Gift shop. 18-hole golf privileges, greens fee $75, pro, putting green, driving range. Exercise equipt. Pool; poolside serv. Some in-rm whirlpools, fireplaces; refrigerator, microwave, wet bar in kit. suites. Picnic tables, grills. Cr cds: A, D, DS, MC, V.
🅳 ⬛ ⬛ ⬛ ⬛ 🏃 ⬛ ⬛ ⬛

Resort

★★★ **BLOCKADE RUNNER RESORT & HOTEL.** *275 Waynick Blvd (28480), ¼ mi S on US 76. 910/256-2251; fax 910/256-2251; res 800/541-1161; toll-free 800/722-5809. Email brftdesk@wilmington.net; www. blockade-runner.com.* 147 rms, 7 story, 3 suites. May-Aug: S, D $320; each addl $25; suites $375; under 11 free; lower rates rest of yr. Crib avail. Valet parking avail. Pool, whirlpool. TV; cable. Complimentary coffee in rms, newspaper, toll-free calls. Restaurant 6:30 am-10 pm. Bar. Ck-out 11:30 am, ck-in 3 pm. Meeting rms. Business servs avail. Bellhops. Gift shop. Free airport transportation. Exercise equipt, sauna. Golf. Tennis. Beach access. Bike rentals. Supervised children's activities. Cr cds: A, C, D, DS, MC, V.
🅳 ⬛ ⬛ ⬛ ⬛ 🏃 ⬛ ⬛ ⬛

B&B/Small Inn

★ **THE COTTAGE.** *225 S Lumina Ave (28480). 910/256-2251; fax 910/256-5502; toll-free 800/541-1161. Email brftdsk@wilmington.net; www. blockade-runner.com.* 3 rms, 2 story, 5 suites. May-Aug: S, D $290; each addl $25; suites $320; under 12 free;

lower rates rest of yr. Crib avail. Valet parking avail. Pool, whirlpool. TV; cable. Complimentary toll-free calls. Restaurant 6:30 am-8 pm. Ck-out 11:30 am, ck-in 3 pm. Meeting rm. Fax servs avail. Gift shop. Free airport transportation. Exercise privileges, sauna. Golf. Tennis. Beach access. Bike rentals. Supervised children's activities. Cr cds: A, C, D, DS, MC, V.

D 🐾 🛏 🌅 ≋ 🧍 ⬇ 🔥

Restaurants

★★ **BRIDGE TENDER.** *1414 Airle Rd (28480), at Wrightsville Beach Bridge.* 910/256-4519. Specializes in seafood, beef. Hrs: 11:30 am-2 pm, 5:30-10 pm; Fri to 11 pm; Sat 5-11 pm. Closed Sun; Jan 1, Thanksgiving, Dec 25. Bar. Lunch $5.95-$8.95; dinner $13.95-$23.95. View of waterway, marina. Cr cds: A, C, D, DS, MC, V.

D 🖨

★ **DOCKSIDE.** *1308 Airlie Rd (28480).* 910/256-2752. Seafood menu. Specializes in grilled seafood, pasta. Hrs: 11 am-9:30 pm; Fri, Sat to 10 pm. Closed Thanksgiving, Dec 24, 25. Bar. Lunch $1.75-$9.95; dinner $7.95-$17.95. Casual dining. Overlooks dock, waterway; docking facilities. Cr cds: DS, MC, V.

D 🖨

★★ **KING NEPTUNE.** *11 N Lumina Ave on US 76 (28480).* 910/256-2525. Specializes in prime rib, seafood. Hrs: 5-10 pm. Closed Thanksgiving, Dec 25. Bar. Dinner $9.95-$20.95. Child's menu. Caribbean decor. Cr cds: A, MC, V.

SC 🖨

★★ **OCEANIC.** *703 S Lumina Ave (28480).* 910/256-5551. Specializes in seafood. Hrs: 11:30 am-11 pm; Sun 10 am-10 pm; winter hrs vary. Closed Jan 1, Thanksgiving, Dec 25. Bar. Lunch $4.95-$10.95; dinner $10.95-$21.95. Sun brunch $4.75-$9.95. Child's menu. Parking. Panoramic view of ocean. Cr cds: A, D, MC, V.

D 🖨

★★ **OCEAN TERRACE.** *275 Waynick Blvd.* 910/256-2251. *www.blockaderunner.com.* Specializes in seafood, pasta. Hrs: 6:30 am-10 pm. Closed

wk of Dec 25. Res accepted. Bar. Bkfst $10.95; lunch $7-$14; dinner $15-$32. Sun brunch $14.95. Child's menu. Entertainment: pianist Fri, Sat; jazz Sun brunch. Parking. Cr cds: A, D, DS, MC, V.

D 🖨

★★ **RIALTO.** *530 Causeway Dr (28480), in the Landing Shopping Center.* 910/256-1099. Specializes in seafood, pasta. Hrs: 5:30-10 pm; Fri, Sat to 10:30 pm. Closed Jan 1, Thanksgiving, Dec 25. Bar. Dinner $9.50-$18. Child's menu. Cr cds: A, D, DS, MC, V.

D 🖨

SOUTH CAROLINA

In South Carolina, the modern age has neither masked the romance of the Old South nor overshadowed the powerful events of colonial and Confederate times. This state's turbulent and romantic history tells a story that remains deeply ingrained in the history of the United States.

Spanish explorers made the first attempt to settle in present-day South Carolina in 1526, less than 35 years after the Europeans discovered America. A severe winter, hostile natives, and disease proved too much for the Spanish to overcome, and the settlement was abandoned. A group of French Huguenots, led by Jean Ribaut, landed near the site of present-day Parris Island Marine Corps Base in 1562. The French colony might have been a success, had not Ribaut's return to the colony from France on business been delayed. The remaining colonists, fearing they had been abandoned, built a craft and sailed for home. Light winds stranded their boat at sea, and they faced the danger of starvation until a passing English ship rescued them.

Population: 3,497,800
Area: 30,207 square miles
Elevation: 0-3,560 feet
Peak: Sassafras Mountain (Pickens County)
Entered Union: Eighth of original 13 states (May 23, 1788)
Capital: Columbia
Motto: Prepared in mind and resources; While I breathe, I hope
Nickname: Palmetto State
Flower: Carolina Yellow Jessamine
Bird: Carolina Wren
Tree: Palmetto
Fair: October 4-14, 2001, in Columbia
Time Zone: Eastern
Website: www.prt.state.sc.us/sc

The task of settlement fell to the English, whose challenge to Spanish control of the New World eventually met with success. A land grant from England's King Charles II gave the Carolinas to eight English noblemen (still known today as the "Lords Proprietors"). In 1670, the English arrived at Albemarle Point and established Charles Towne, the first successful European settlement in the Carolinas.

During the Revolutionary War, almost 200 battles and skirmishes were fought in South Carolina. The first overt act of revolution occurred at Fort Charlotte on July 12, 1775; this was the first British property seized by American Revolutionary forces. On December 20, 1860, South Carolina became the first state to secede from the Union. The initial clash of the Civil War also occurred on South Carolina soil; the bombardment of Fort Sumter in 1861 resulted in its seizure by Confederate forces, which maintained possession until the evacuation of Charleston in 1865. Bloodied, impoverished, and blackened by the fires of General Sherman's march to the sea, South Carolina emerged from the difficult Reconstruction days and was readmitted to the Union in 1868.

For most of the period since the Civil War, South Carolina has had economic problems, but in recent years these have eased as industry has been attracted by hospitable communities and favorable tax rates. From town to town, throughout the state, diversified industries have brought with them greater prosperity. Power projects have been created by damming the Santee, Saluda, Savannah, and other rivers. Four atomic energy plants provide commercial energy. Tourism, the state's second-largest industry, continues to grow.

A temperate climate makes South Carolina an attractive all-year resort. The cool upland western area merges into a subtropical seacoast. South Carolina is a major producer of tobacco, cotton, pine lumber, corn, oats, sweet potatoes, soybeans, peanuts, peaches, melons, beef cattle, and hogs.

When to Go/Climate

South Carolina enjoys a moderate climate. Summers, however, especially in the low country and along the coast, can be uncomfortably hot and humid. The barrier islands and upcountry elevations provide summer havens from the blistering heat. Early spring and late fall are good times to visit, with comfortable temperatures and moderate rainfall.

AVERAGE HIGH/LOW TEMPERATURES (°F)

CHARLESTON

Jan 56/41	**May** 80/66	**Sep** 83/71
Feb 59/43	**June** 85/72	**Oct** 75/61
Mar 65/50	**July** 88/75	**Nov** 67/52
Apr 73/58	**Aug** 87/75	**Dec** 60/45

GREENVILLE

Jan 50/30	**May** 80/56	**Sep** 81/61
Feb 54/32	**June** 86/64	**Oct** 72/49
Mar 64/40	**July** 88/68	**Nov** 63/41
Apr 72/48	**Aug** 87/67	**Dec** 53/33

Parks and Recreation Finder

Directions to and information about the parks and recreation areas below are given under their respective town/city sections. Please refer to those sections for details.

NATIONAL PARK AND RECREATION AREAS

Key to abbreviations. I.H.S. = International Historic Site; I.P.M. = International Peace Memorial; N.B. = National Battlefield; N.B.P. = National Battlefield Park; N.B.C. = National Battlefield and Cemetery; N.C.A. = National Conservation Area; N.E.M. = National Expansion Memorial; N.F. = National Forest; N.G. = National Grassland; N.H.P. = National Historical Park; N.H.C. = National Heritage Corridor; N.H.S. = National Historic Site; N.L. = National Lakeshore; N.M. = National Monument; N.M.P. = National Military Park; N.Mem. = National Memorial; N.P. = National Park; N.Pres. = National Preserve; N.R.A. = National Recreational Area; N.R.R. = National Recreational River; N.Riv. = National River; N.S. = National Seashore; N.S.R. = National Scenic Riverway; N.S.T. = National Scenic Trail; N.Sc. = National Scientific Reserve; N.V.M. = National Volcanic Monument.

Place Name	Listed Under
Congaree Swamp N.M.	COLUMBIA
Cowpens N.B.	GAFFNEY
Fort Sumter N.M.	same
Francis Marion N.F.	CHARLESTON
Kings Mountain N.M.P.	same
Ninety Six N.H.S.	GREENWOOD
Sumter N.F.	same

STATE PARK AND RECREATION AREAS

Key to abbreviations. I.P. = Interstate Park; S.A.P. = State Archaeological Park; S.B. = State Beach; S.C.A. = State Conservation Area; S.C.P. = State Conservation Park; S.Cp. = State Campground; S.F. = State Forest; S.G. = State Garden; S.H.A. = State Historic Area; S.H.P. = State Historic Park; S.H.S. = State Historic Site; S.M.P. = State Marine Park; S.N.A. = State Natural Area; S.P. = State Park; S.P.C. = State Public Campground; S.R. = State Reserve; S.R.A. = State Recreation Area; S.Res. = State Reservoir; S.Res.P. = State Resort Park; S.R.P. = State Rustic Park.

Place Name	Listed Under
Aiken S.P.	AIKEN
Andrew Jackson S.P.	ROCK HILL
Baker Creek S.P.	GREENWOOD
Barnwell S.P.	ALLENDALE
Caesar's Head S.P.	GREENVILLE
Cheraw S.P.	CHERAW
Chester S.P.	CHESTER
Colleton S.P.	WALTERBORO
Croft S.P.	SPARTANBURG
Dreher Island S.P.	NEWBERRY
Edisto Beach S.P.	CHARLESTON
Hampton Plantation S.P.	GEORGETOWN
Hickory Knob Resort S.Res.P.	GREENWOOD
Hunting Island S.P.	BEAUFORT
Huntington Beach S.P.	GEORGETOWN
Kings Mountain S.P.	KINGS MOUNTAIN NATIONAL MILITARY PARK
Lake Greenwood S.P.	GREENWOOD
Lake Hartwell S.P.	ANDERSON
Lake Wateree S.P.	CAMDEN
Landsford Canal S.P.	ROCK HILL
Lee S.P.	HARTSVILLE
Little Pee Dee S.P.	DILLON
Lynches River S.P.	FLORENCE
Myrtle Beach S.P.	MYRTLE BEACH
N.R. Goodale S.P.	CAMDEN
Oconee S.P.	CLEMSON
Old Dorchester S.P.	CHARLESTON
Paris Mountain S.P.	GREENVILLE
Poinsett S.P.	SUMTER
River Bridge S.P.	ALLENDALE
Sadlers Creek S.P.	ANDERSON
Santee S.P.	SANTEE
Sesquicentennial S.P.	COLUMBIA
Table Rock S.P.	GREENVILLE
Woods Bay S.P.	FLORENCE

Water-related activities, hiking, various other sports, picnicking, and visitor centers, as well as camping, are available in many of these areas. Cabins are located at Barnwell, Cheraw, Devils Fork, Dreher Island, Edisto Beach, Givhans Ferry, Hickory Knob Resort, Hunting Island, Keowee-Toxaway, Myrtle Beach, Oconee, Poinsett, Santee, and Table Rock. No pets in cabins. Cabin reservations made at individual parks. Camping: 14-day maximum; reservations accepted only at Calhoun Falls, Devils Fork, Dreher Island, Edisto Beach, Hunting Island, Huntington Beach, Lake Hartwell, Myrtle Beach, Oconee, Santee, and Table

Rock; $10-$20/night; pets on leash only. Not all state parks are open every day; hours of operation also vary. Contact Columbia office or individual park before making final trip plans. Daily parking fee at major coastal parks in summer, $3-$15. Swimming fee at inland parks with supervised areas & bathhouses (early June-late Aug), $2; age 3-12, $1.50; ocean swimming free. Fees subject to change. For cabin rates and further information contact Department of Parks, Recreation & Tourism, Edgar A. Brown Bldg, 1205 Pendleton St, Columbia 29201; 803/734-0156 or 888/88-PARKS.

FISHING AND HUNTING

There is no closed fishing season; well-stocked lakes and rivers are close at hand in all parts of the state. Surf casting and deep-sea fishing can be enjoyed all along the Atlantic shore. Mountain streams offer trout fishing. Nonresident

CALENDAR HIGHLIGHTS

MARCH

Triple Crown (Aiken). Three events; trials (Aiken Training Track), steeplechase (Clark Field), harness race (Aiken Mile Track). For more information, phone Aiken Chamber of Commerce 803/641-1111.

Family Circle Magazine Cup Tennis Tournament (Hilton Head Island). Sea Pines Racquet Club. Phone 843/363-3500.

MAY

Spoleto Festival USA (Charleston). Internationally acclaimed counterpart to the arts festival in Spoleto, Italy, founded by Gian Carlo Menotti; incl opera, ballet, dance, visual arts, theater, chamber music, jazz, symphonic, and choral performances and much more. Piccolo Spoleto, running concurrent with the main festival, has performances by local and regional artists. Phone 843/722-2764.

JUNE

Sun Fun Festival (Myrtle Beach). More than 60 seaside entertainment events, incl parades. Contact Chamber of Commerce, 843/626-7444 or 800/356-3016.

JULY

Freedom Weekend Aloft (Greenville). More than 200 balloonists compete. Phone 864/232-3700.

SEPTEMBER

Southern 500 (Darlington). Darlington Raceway. Five hundred-mi stock car classic; also beauty pageant; "Southern 500" Festival parade; golf tournament. Preceded by 2 days of trials. For tickets, phone 843/395-8499.

Hilton Head Island Celebrity Golf Tournament (Hilton Head Island). Palmetto Hall, Indigo Run, and Sea Pines Plantation. Phone 843/842-7711.

OCTOBER

Fall Tour of Homes and Gardens (Beaufort). Contact Historic Beaufort Foundation, 843/524-3163 or 800/638-3525.

South Carolina State Fair (Columbia). Fairgrounds. Agricultural, floral, home, craft, livestock, and commercial exhibits. Entertainment, shows, carnival. Phone 803/799-3387.

NOVEMBER

Colonial Cup International Steeplechase (Camden). Springdale Race Course. Phone 803/432-6513.

freshwater license: $35; 7-day nonresident license: $11. Saltwater stamp: $5.50. No license or permit required of children under 16. Fees subject to change.

Quail, dove, wild turkey, white-tailed deer, rabbit, squirrel, and fox are all legal quarry. Nonresident annual license: $100; ten-day (consecutive) license: $50; 3-day (consecutive) license: $25; wildlife management area permit: $76. Nonresident big game permit for deer, turkey, and bear: $89. State duck stamp: $5.50. Fees subject to change. For further hunting and fishing information contact South Carolina Department of Natural Resources, PO Box 167, Columbia 29202; 803/734-3888 (general information) or 803/734-3886 (wildlife and freshwater fisheries).

Driving Information

Safety belts are mandatory for all persons anywhere in vehicle. Children must be in an approved safety seat or wear a safety belt. For further information phone 803/737-8340.

INTERSTATE HIGHWAY SYSTEM

The following alphabetical listing of South Carolina towns in *Mobil Travel Guide* shows that these cities are within 10 miles of the indicated Interstate highways. A highway map should, however, be checked for the nearest exit.

Highway Number	Cities/Towns within 10 miles
Interstate 20	Aiken, Camden, Columbia, Darlington, Florence.
Interstate 26	Charleston, Clinton, Columbia, Newberry, Orangeburg, Spartanburg.
Interstate 77	Columbia, Rock Hill.
Interstate 85	Anderson, Clemson, Gaffney, Greenville, Spartanburg.
Interstate 95	Darlington, Dillon, Florence, Hardeeville, Santee, Walterboro.

Additional Visitor Information

For additional information on South Carolina contact the Department of Parks, Recreation & Tourism, 1205 Pendleton St, Columbia 29201; 803/734-0122 or 888/88-PARKS (Toll-Free).

There are 10 travel information centers in South Carolina; visitors will find the information provided at these stops useful for planning travel and making lodging reservations in the state. Their locations are: at the eastern end of the state, on I-95 on the SC/NC border; in the eastern coastal region on US 17 on SC/NC border; in the southern section on US 301 on the SC/GA border, and on I-95 on SC/GA border; in midstate center on the southbound side of I-95 near Santee; on the southwestern side on I-20 on the SC/GA border; in the western part of the state on I-85 on the SC/GA border; located in the northwestern part of the state are centers on I-85 on the SC/NC border and on I-26 on the SC/NC border; in the northern part of the state on I-77 on the SC/NC border, and also at the State House Tour and Information Center located in Columbia.

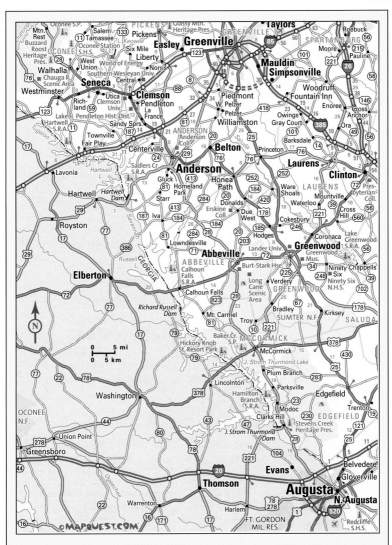

The Savannah River National Scenic Highway stretches more than 100 miles, from the intersection of South Carolina Route 28 and US Route 21 at the South Carolina border to the intersection of South Carolina Routes 24 and 11 in Oconee County. The scenic drive winds along the river, past J. Strom Thurmond Lake, Richard B. Russell Lake, and Lake Hartwell. Some highlights along the way are: Dorn Mill in McCormick, Mack Art Gallery in the Old Keturah Hotel, and the Anderson County Museum. Also near the highway are the Abbeville Opera House, Pendleton's Farmer's Society Hall, and the Ashtabula & Woodburn Plantation. **(Approx 100 mi)**

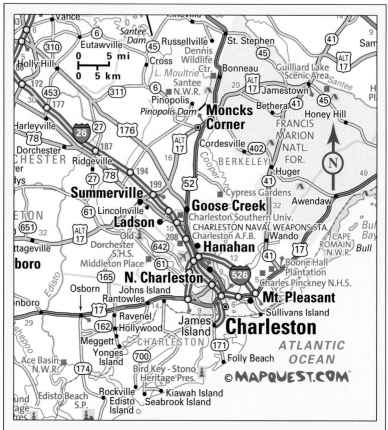

Just outside Charleston, South Carolina, Route 61 is a winding road canopied by ancient oaks and dripping moss. It leads to Middleton Gardens, Magnolia Plantation, and Drayton Hall. Then take ALT 17 to Jamestown, passing Old Santee Canal State Park, and return to Charleston via Highway 41 through the Francis Marion National Forest. **(Approx 80 mi)**

Aiken

(E-3) *See also Allendale, Orangeburg*

Founded 1834 **Pop** 19,872 **Elev** 476 ft
Area code 803
Web www.chamber.aiken.net
Information Chamber of Commerce,
121 Richland Ave E, PO Box 892,
29802; 803/641-1111

Annual Events

Triple Crown. Three events: trials
(Aiken Training Track), steeplechase
(Clark Field), harness race (Aiken
Mile Track). Three consecutive Sat
Mar.

Lobster Race. Aiken restaurants provide seafood fare. Festivities incl lobster races, beach music, and other
activities. Phone 803/648-4981. May.

Seasonal Event

Polo games. Whitney Field. Sun
afternoons. Feb-July and Sep-Nov.

Motel/Motor Lodge

★ ★ **THE INN OF AIKEN.** *110
Frontage Rd (29801), at jct SC 19, I-20
Exit 18. 803/502-0000; fax 803/502-
0005.* 110 units, 2 story. S, D $49-
$53; each addl $6; under 18 free;
higher rates Masters Golf Tournament. Crib free. Pet accepted, some
restrictions. TV; cable (premium),
VCR avail. Pool; wading pool.
Restaurant 6:30-9:30 am, 6-10 pm;
closed Sun. Bar 5-10 pm. Ck-out
noon. Meeting rms. Business servs
avail. Refrigerators, microwaves avail.
Cr cds: A, C, D, DS, MC, V.

B&B/Small Inn

★ ★ ★ **WILLCOX INN.** *100 Colleton
Ave and Whiskey Rd (29801). 803/649-
1377; fax 803/643-0971; toll-free
800/368-1047. www.willcoxinn.com.*
30 rms, 3 story, 6 suites. Apr: S, D
$100; each addl $15; suites $125;
under 17 free; lower rates rest of yr.
Crib avail. Parking lot. TV; cable.
Complimentary continental bkfst,
coffee in rms, newspaper. Restaurant
7 am-9 pm. Bar. Ck-out noon, ck-in 3
pm. Meeting rms. Business servs

avail. Dry cleaning. Golf, 18 holes.
Tennis. Cr cds: A, C, D, DS, MC, V.

Allendale

(F-3) *See also Aiken, Orangeburg, Walterboro*

Pop 4,410 **Elev** 191 ft **Area code** 803
Zip 29810
Information Chamber of Commerce,
PO Box 517; 803/584-0082

Moved six miles in 1872 to its present
site to be on the old Port Royal Railroad line, Allendale is an agricultural
town with access to the lush hunting
and fishing areas of the Savannah
River Valley. More than 130 commercial farms with an average size in
excess of 1,000 acres—the largest in
the state—surround the town.

Anderson

(D-2) *See also Clemson, Greenville,
Greenwood*

Founded 1826 **Pop** 26,184 **Elev** 770 ft
Area code 864
Information Anderson Area Chamber
of Commerce, 706 E Greenville St,
PO Box 1568, 29622; 864/226-3454

Annual Event
Anderson County Fair. Mid-Sep.

Motels/Motor Lodges

★ ★ **HOLIDAY INN.** *3025 N Main St
(29621), I-85 Exit 19A, on US 76.
864/226-6051; fax 864/964-9145.* 130
rms, 2 story. S $59-$64; D $65-$70;
each addl $6; under 18 free; higher
rates Clemson Univ football games.
Crib free. Pet accepted, some restrictions. TV; cable. Pool. Complimentary coffee in rms. Restaurant 6:30
am-10 pm. Bar 5 pm-midnight. Ck-
out noon. Coin lndry. Meeting rms.
Business servs avail. In-rm modem
link. Valet serv. Health club privi-

leges. Refrigerators, microwaves avail. Cr cds: A, D, DS, MC, V.

★ **LA QUINTA INN.** *3430 N Main St (29621). 864/225-3721; fax 864/225-7789; toll-free 800/687-6667.* 100 rms, 2 story. S $58-$65; D $64-$71; each addl $7; under 18 free. Crib free. TV; cable. Pool. Complimentary continental bkfst. Ck-out noon. Meeting rms. Business servs avail. In-rm modem link. Cr cds: A, C, D, DS, JCB, MC, V.

★ **SUPER 8 MOTEL.** *3302 Cinema Ave (29621). 864/225-8384; fax 864/225-8384.* 62 rms, 3 story. No elvtr. S $34.88-$38.88; D $40.88-$48.88; each addl after 3, $4; under 12 free; higher rates: Clemson football wkends, special events. TV. Complimentary coffee. Restaurant nearby. Ck-out 11 am. Cr cds: A, C, D, DS, MC, V.

Beaufort

(G-4) *See also Charleston, Hardeeville, Hilton Head Island, Kiawah Island, Walterboro*

Founded 1710 **Pop** 9,576 **Elev** 11 ft
Area code 843 **Zip** 29902
Web www.beaufortsc.org

Information Greater Beaufort Chamber of Commerce, 1106 Carteret St, PO Box 910, 29901-0910; 843/524-3163

What to See and Do

Parris Island. Famous US Marine Corps Recruit Depot. Visitor center in Bldg 283; Museum in War Memorial Bldg. Ribaut Monument is memorial to Jean Ribaut, French Huguenot founder of Charlesfort (1562); Iwo Jima monument; monument to Spanish settlement of Santa Elena (1521). Historic driving and narrated bus tours depart from visitor center (Sat-Wed, 1pm, res required at least 24 hrs in advance). (Daily) 10 mi S. Phone 843/525-3650. **FREE**

St. Helena's Episcopal Church. (1712) Still in use; tombstones from surrounding burial ground became operating tables when church was used as hospital during Civil War. Sil-

ver Communion set in church was donated in 1734 by Capt John Bull in memory of his wife, who was captured by Native Americans. (Mon-Sat) 507 Newcastle St, at North St. Phone 843/522-1712.

US Naval Hospital. On grounds are ruins of Fort Frederick (1731), one of largest "tabby" (cement and oyster shell) forts in US. 4 mi S on SC 802, between Beaufort & Port Royal, an early French settlement.

Verdier House. (ca 1790) Federal period house once known as the Lafayette Bldg; the Marquis de Lafayette is said to have spoken here from the piazza in 1825. (Mon-Sat; closed Thanksgiving, Dec 25) 801 Bay St. Phone 843/524-6334. ¢¢

Annual Events

Beaufort Water Festival. Along waterfront at harbor. Incl parade, water show, boat races; concerts, dance. Phone 843/524-0600. Mid-July.

Fall Tour of Homes and Gardens. Contact Historic Beaufort Foundation, PO Box 11, 29901; 843/524-6334. Late Oct.

Beaufort Shrimp Festival. Waterfront. Bridge Run, shrimp recipe tastings, frogmore stew contest, Bless'en de Fleet. Phone 843/524-3163. Mid-Oct.

Motels/Motor Lodges

★★ **HOLIDAY INN.** *2001 Boundary St Hwy 21 & Ribaut Rd. (29902). 843/524-2144; fax 843/524-2144; toll-free 800/465-4329.* 152 rms, 4 story. S, D $74; each addl $8; under 19 free. Crib free. TV; cable (premium). Pool. Coffee in rms. Restaurant 6:30 am-2 pm, 5:30-9 pm. Bar 5-11 pm; Sat to midnight. Meeting rms. Business servs avail. In-rm modem link. Valet serv Mon-Fri. Golf privileges. Refrigerators, microwaves avail. Cr cds: A, C, D, DS, JCB, MC, V.

Hotel

★★ **BEST WESTERN-SEA ISLAND INN.** *1015 Bay St (29902), in Historic District. 843/522-2090; fax 843/521-4858; toll-free 800/528-1234. www.beautifulbeaufort.com.* 43 rms, 2 story. Mar-Nov: S, D $109; each addl $10;

under 12 free; lower rates rest of yr. Crib avail. Parking lot. Pool. TV; cable (premium). Complimentary continental bkfst, newspaper. Restaurant nearby. Ck-out 11 am, ck-in 3 pm. Business servs avail. Exercise equipt. Golf. Bike rentals. Cr cds: A, C, D, DS, MC, V.

🍴 🏊 🏋 🛏 🐾 SC

B&Bs/Small Inns

★★★ **BEAUFORT INN & RESTAURANT.** *809 Port Republic St (29902). 843/521-9000; fax 843/521-9500. Email bftinn@hargray.com; www. beaufortinn.com.* 11 rms, 3 story, 4 suites. Mar-May, Oct-Nov: D $160; each addl $20; suites $195; children $20; under 8 free; lower rates rest of yr. Crib avail. Parking lot. TV; cable (premium), VCR avail. Complimentary full bkfst, coffee in rms, newspaper, toll-free calls. Restaurant. Bar. Meeting rms. Business servs avail. Concierge. Dry cleaning. Golf. Bike rentals. Cr cds: A, DS, MC, V.

🅳 🏋 🍴 🐾 🛏 🐾

★★★★ **RHETT HOUSE INN.** *1009 Craven St (29902), at New Castle St. 843/524-9030; fax 843/524-1310; toll-free 888/480-9530. Email rhetthse@ hargray.com; www.rhetthouseinn.com.* A film site for several popular movies, this 17-room, white-pillared bed-and-breakfast is wrapped in spacious verandas where guests can relax and take in lush garden surroundings. The beautifully restored, 1820 plantation house is meticulously maintained, filled with antiques, oriental rugs, fresh flowers, and fireplaces. The property borders the Intracoastal Waterway offering plenty of outdoor recreations. 17 rms, 3 story. S, D $125-$225; each addl $25. Children over 5 yrs only. TV; VCR avail. Swimming privileges. Complimentary full bkfst; continental bkfst avail in rms; afternoon refreshments. Ck-out 11 am, ck-in 3 pm. Business servs avail. Tennis privileges, pro. 18-hole golf privileges. Health club privileges. Some fireplaces. Bicycles. Cr cds: A, DS, MC, V.

🅳 🏋 🍴 🐾 🛏 🐾

★★ **TWO SUNS INN BED & BREAKFAST.** *1705 Bay St (29902), in Historic District. 843/522-1122; fax 843/522-1122; toll-free 800/532-4244. Email twosuns@islc.net; www.twosuns inn.com.* 6 rms, 3 story. S $130; D $160; each addl $25. Parking lot. TV; cable, VCR avail. Complimentary full bkfst. Restaurant nearby. Ck-out noon, ck-in 3 pm. Meeting rm. Business servs avail. Gift shop. Golf. Tennis, 4 courts. Bike rentals. Cr cds: A, D, DS, MC, V.

🅳 🏋 🎿 🛏 🐾

Restaurant

★★★ **BEAUFORT INN.** *809 Port Republic St. 843/521-9000. www. beaufortinn.com.* Specializes in fresh seafood, veal, game. Hrs: 6-9:30 pm. Closed Dec 24, 25. Res accepted. Wine list. Dinner $17.95-$26.95. Cr cds: A, DS, MC, V.

🅳

Bennettsville

(D-5) *See also Cheraw, Darlington, Dillon, Florence, Hartsville*

Founded 1819 **Pop** 9,345 **Elev** 150 ft
Area code 803 **Zip** 29512
Information Marlboro County Chamber of Commerce, 300 W Main St, PO Box 458; 803/479-3941

Near the geographic center of the Carolinas, Bennettsville radiates highway spokes in every direction. Founded by Welsh settlers, and now the seat of Marlboro County, it has diversified industry including paper and electrical products, textiles, and farm equipment. Agriculture is still important; cotton is the leading crop.

Camden

(E-4) *See also Columbia, Sumter*

Settled 1732 **Pop** 6,696 **Elev** 213 ft
Area code 803 **Zip** 29020
Web www.camden-sc.org
Information Kershaw County Chamber of Commerce and Visitor Center, 724 S Broad St, PO Box 605; 803/432-2525 or 800/968-4037

The oldest inland town in the state, Camden was named after Lord Camden, defender of colonial rights. During the Revolution, General Cornwallis occupied Camden and made it the principal British garrison in the state and the interior command post for the South. Although several battles were fought in and near the town, including the Battle of Camden, the town was never recaptured by the Americans. Instead, it was evacuated and burned by the British in 1781. Camden contributed six generals to the Confederate cause and served as a storehouse, a hospital for the wounded, and a haven of refuge until captured by General Sherman in 1865.

Today, Camden is famous for its history and equestrian sports—horseback riding, horse shows, hunt meets, polo, and steeplechase races. There are 200 miles of bridle paths in the area and three race tracks; Springdale Course is an extremely difficult and exciting steeplechase run.

Annual Events

Carolina Downhome Blues Festival & Fine Arts. Center of Kershaw County. Phone 803/425-7676. Mid-Oct.

Revolutionary War Field Days. Broad St. Historic Camden Revolutionary War Site. Two-day Revolutionary War encampment, festivities, battle re-enactments. Phone 803/432-9841. First wkend in Nov.

Horse racing. Springdale Race Course. 200 Knights Hill Rd. Phone 803/432-6513. Carolina Cup Steeplechase, early Apr. Colonial Cup Intl Steeplechase, mid-Nov.

Motels/Motor Lodges

★★ **COLONY INN.** *2020 W Dekalb St (29020). 803/432-5508; fax 803/432-0920; res 803/432-5508; toll-free 800/356-9801.* 53 rms, 2 story. S $45-$55; D $55; each addl $3. Crib $5. Pet accepted, some restrictions $10. TV; cable. Pool. Restaurant 5:30-11 am. Ck-out 11 am. Valet serv. Cr cds: A, C, D, DS, MC, V.

★★ **HOLIDAY INN OF CAMDEN.** *850 US 1 (29078), 3 mi S. 803/438-9441; fax 803/438-5784.* 117 rms, 2 story. S $59-$89; D $64-$94; each addl $5; under 18 free. Crib free. TV; cable (premium). Pool; wading pool. Complimentary full bkfst. Coffee in rms. Restaurant 6:30-9:30 am, 5-10 pm. Bar 5 pm-midnight. Ck-out 11 am. Meeting rms. Business servs avail. In-rm modem link. Valet serv. Health club privileges. Some in-rm whirlpools; refrigerators, microwaves avail. Cr cds: C, D, JCB, MC, V.

★★ **THE INN AT CAMDEN.** *928 US 1 S (29078). 803/438-4961; fax 803/438-4961; toll-free 877/843-4667.* 84 rms, 2 story. S $48; D $53; each addl $5; under 18 free. Crib free. TV; cable. Pool. Restaurant adj 6 am-11 pm; Fri, Sat to 1 am. Ck-out noon. Meeting rm. Microwaves avail. Cr cds: A, C, D, DS, MC, V.

B&B/Small Inn

★★ **GREENLEAF INN.** *1310 Broad St (29020). 803/425-1806; fax 803/425-5853; toll-free 800/437-5874.* 11 rms, 2 story. S $55-$65; D $65-$75; each addl $10; suite $65-$75; under 12 free. TV; cable (premium). Complimentary continental bkfst. Dining rm 6-10 pm; closed Wed, Sun. Ck-out 11 am, ck-in 2 pm. Health club privileges. Built in 1810. Cr cds: A, MC, V.

Restaurants

★★ **LILIFREDS OF CAMDEN.** *8425 Main St (29128). 803/432-7063.* Specializes in fresh seafood, black Angus beef. Hrs: 6-10 pm. Closed Sun-Tues; hols. Res accepted. Dinner $13.95-$21.95. Rustic decor. Cr cds: MC, V.

★★ **LUCY'S.** *1043 Broad St (29020). 803/432-9096.* Specializes in seafood, veal, beef. Own bread. Menu changes seasonally. Hrs: 11:30 am-2 pm, 5:30-9 pm; Tues from 5:30 pm. Closed Sun, Mon; Jan 1, Dec 25. Res accepted. Bar. Lunch $5.95-$8.95; dinner $10.95-$21.95. Historic antique bar. Cr cds: A, MC, V.

★★ **MILL POND.** *84 Boykin Mill Rd (29128), S on US 521, S on SC 261. 803/424-0261.* Specializes in seafood, Angus beef. Hrs: 5-10 pm; Fri, Sat to 11 pm. Closed Sun, Mon; Jan 1, Dec

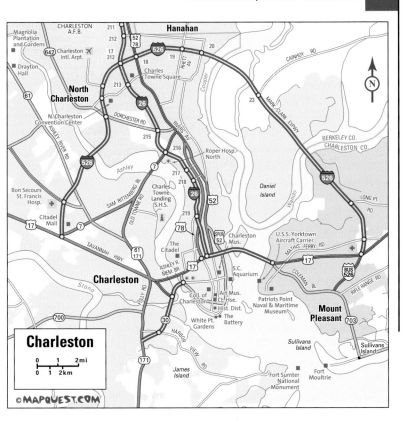

Charleston

```
0    1    2mi
0  1  2km
```

©MAPQUEST.COM

25; also 1st wk July. Res accepted. Bar. Dinner $17.95-$28.95. Rustic country decor. Brick fireplace. Cr cds: MC, V.

Charleston

(F-4) *See also Beaufort, Kiawah Island, Walterboro*

Founded 1670 **Pop** 80,414 **Elev** 9 ft
Area code 843
Web www.charlestoncvb.com
Information Visitor Reception and Transportation Center, 375 Meeting St, PO Box 975, 29402; 843/853-8000 or 800/868-8118

This aristocratic and storied American city lives up to its reputation for cultivated manners. Charleston's homes, historic shrines, old churches, lovely gardens, winding streets, and intricate iron lace gateways exude charm and dignity.

Charleston enjoys international and coastal commerce in the fine harbor formed, according to local opinion, where the "Ashley and Cooper rivers unite to form the Atlantic Ocean." The strategic harbor, inlets, and sea islands provide recreational retreats.

The Charleston of today is the survivor of siege, flood, hurricane, and epidemic. Capital of the province until 1786, its history and that of South Carolina are almost the same. Charleston received colonists from the Old World and sent them into the wilderness. The city served as the personification of Europe's luxury and culture in the New World.

The first permanent settlement in the Carolinas, Charles Towne, as it was first called, was established as a tiny colony, westward across the Ashley River, by Anthony Ashley Cooper, Earl of Shaftesbury. At the same time, he established the only American nobility in history, with barons, landgraves (dukes), and caciques (earls), each owning great plantations.

This nobility lasted less than 50 years, but it was the foundation for an aristocratic tradition that still exists, even though the rice and indigo that made the early Charleston people rich are gone. Colonists from Barbados, England, and Ireland came to enlarge the settlement in 1670, and by 1680 the colony moved across the river to become a city-state. Although many of the colonists went on to the Carolina Lowcountry and established grand plantations, every year on the traditional date of May 10, the planters and their families moved back to Charleston to escape the mosquitoes and malarial heat. From spring to frost, these planters created a season of dancing, sport, musicales, theater, and socials. Commerce and plantations provided the prosperity on which the city's cosmopolitan graces were based. Charleston founded the first playhouse designed solely for presentation of drama, the first museum, the first public school in the colony, the first municipal college in America, and the first fire insurance company on the continent. (It was a victim the next year of a fire that destroyed half the city.) The city became famous throughout the world as "a flourishing capital of wealth and ease."

The First Provincial Congress of South Carolina met in Charleston in 1775 and prepared the city to repulse a British attack on June 28, 1776. But in 1780 the city was captured and for two and a half years was occupied by the enemy. Charleston was almost the last point in the state to be cleared of British troops. With peace came great prosperity, but rivalry between the small farmers of the interior and the merchants and plantation owners of the Lowlands resulted in removal of the capital to Columbia.

The convention that authored the Ordinance of Secession came to Charleston to pass that declaration; the Civil War then began with the bombardment of Fort Sumter by Fort Johnson. A long siege followed, including the gallant defense of Fort Sumter (1863-65), blockade running, the first submarine warfare, evacua-

tion after Sherman had demolished Columbia, and, finally, bombardment of the city by the Union Army.

What to See and Do

Aiken-Rhett House. (1817) Home of Governor William Aiken (1833-87). Enlarged in Greek Revival style (1833-36); subsequent additions (1858) created some of the finest rms in Charleston, incl a Rococo Revival art gallery. Many original furnishings from 1833. (Daily; closed hols) 48 Elizabeth St, corner of Judith St. Phone 843/724-8481. ¢¢¢; Combination ticket ¢¢¢¢ incl Nathaniel Russell House.

Boat trips.

　Fort Sumter Tours. Tour (2¼ hrs) through Charleston harbor to Fort Sumter (see). (Daily; closed Dec 25) Also 1½ hr Charleston harbor tour, 3-hr *Spirit of Charleston* dinner cruise. Municipal Marina, Lockwood Blvd & Patriots Point, Mt Pleasant. Phone 843/722-1691. ¢¢¢¢ Dinner cruise ¢¢¢¢

　Gray Line Water Tours. Tours (approx 2 hrs) of harbor, US Naval Base, view of forts, other points of interest. For info, res contact PO Box 861, 29402-0861. City Municipal Marina, Lockwood Blvd. Phone 843/722-1112. ¢¢¢

Boone Hall Plantation. (1681) A 738-acre estate with 9 original slave houses and ginhouse (ca 1750), pecan grove, ½-mi "Avenue of Oaks." Several rms in the house are open to the public. (Daily; closed Thanksgiving, Dec 25) 8 mi N off US 17 on Long Point Rd in Mt Pleasant. Phone 843/884-4371. Children ¢¢; Adults ¢¢¢

Chamber of Commerce. Bldg was once the South Carolina Railway Warehouse, home of one of the nation's first steam locomotives. Organized in 1773, the Chamber of Commerce is one of the oldest city commercial organizations in the country. Also houses the Charleston Area Convention & Visitors Bureau. 81 Mary St. Phone 843/577-2510.

Charles Towne Landing. Unusual 664-acre park on site of state's first permanent English settlement (1670). Reconstructed fortifications in original settlement area; replica of *Adventure*, 17th-century trading vessel; 1670 experimental crop garden; formal gardens; nature trails; Colonial

Village; 20-acre animal forest. Also featured is a 30-min movie, *Carolina*. Tram tours and bicycle rentals. Picnicking, playground; restaurant. (Daily; closed Dec 24, 25) 1500 Old Town Rd, on SC 171. Phone 843-852-4200. ¢¢

Cypress Gardens. Consists of 163 acres with giant cypresses, blackwater swamp, azaleas and camellias, dogwoods, daffodils. Boat trips. Picnic area. Free parking. Gift shop. (Daily; closed Thanksgiving, Dec 25) 24 mi N off US 52, between Goose Creek & Moncks Corner. Phone 843/553-0515. ¢¢

Drayton Hall. One of the oldest surviving pre-Revolutionary War plantation houses (1738) in the area, this Georgian Palladian house is surrounded by live oaks and is located on the Ashley River. Held in the Drayton family for 7 generations, the mansion has been maintained in virtually its original condition. A National Trust for Historic Preservation property. Tours (hrly, exc Mar and Apr tours begin every ½ hour). (Daily; closed Jan 1, Thanksgiving, Dec 25) Children under 6 are free. 9 mi NW via SC 61 (Old Ashley River Rd). Phone 843/766-0188. ¢¢

Edisto Beach State Park. Approx 1,200 acres. One-and-a-half mi of beach; shell collecting is very good here. Ocean swimming, fishing; nature trail, picnic area (shelters), gift shop, camping (higher fees Apr-Labor Day), cabins. Standard fees. 21 mi W on US 17, then 29 mi S on SC 174. Phone 843/869-2756.

Folly Beach County Park. Approx 4,000 ft of ocean frontage and 2,000 ft of river frontage. There is a 600-ft section of beach for swimming (Apr-Sep); lifeguards. Dressing areas, outdoor showers; picnic areas; concessions; shelter. (Daily) S via SC 171 on W end of Folly Island. Phone 843/588-2426. Per vehicle ¢¢

Fort Sumter National Monument. (see).

Francis Beidler Forest. National Audubon Society Sanctuary. Boardwalk 1½ mi into the center of a beautiful blackwater swamp; close-up view of one of the largest stands of old-growth bald cypress and tupelo gum forest in the world. Self-guided tour. Visitor center, slide show.

Canoe trips, night walks (in season, by res only; fee). (Tues-Sun; closed hols) No pets, food facilities, or camping. Four Holes Swamp. 40 mi NW via I-26W to Exit 187, then S on SC 27 to US 78, then W to US 178, follow signs. Phone 843/462-2150. ¢¢

Francis Marion National Forest. Early colonial settlements, plantations; lakes, moss-hung oaks, flowering trees, and shrubs on 250,000 acres. Boating, fishing; camping, picnicking, hiking, horseback riding, motorcycling, rifle ranges, hunting. Fees may be charged at recreation sites. Headquarters are in Columbia (Mon-Fri). (Daily) NE via US 17 & 17A, SC 41. Phone 843/336-3248.

Hampton Park. Historic park with camellias and azaleas in spring, roses in summer; 1-mi nature trail; Charleston's mounted horse patrol stables. Rutledge Ave & Cleveland St. Phone 843/724-7321. **FREE**

Joseph Manigault House. (1803) Outstanding example of Adam-style architecture. Features Charleston antiques, silver; curving staircase. (Daily; closed hols) Combination ticket (addl fee) incl Heyward-Washington House and the Charleston Museum. 350 Meeting St. Phone 843/723-2926. ¢¢

Kahal Kadosh Beth Elohim. (1840) Founded in 1749; first Reform Jewish congregation in America (1824). Museum. Gift shop. (Mon-Fri mornings; closed Jewish hols) 90 Hasell St. Phone 843/723-1090. **Donation**

★ **Magnolia Plantation and Gardens.** Internationally famous gardens are America's oldest (ca 1680); now covering 50 acres with camellias, azaleas, magnolias, and hundreds of other flowering species. Azaleas best mid-Mar-Apr; camellias best mid-Nov-Mar. Also on grounds is a 125-acre waterfowl refuge; trilevel observation tower, 16th-century maze, 18th-century herb garden; biblical gardens; topiary; nature trails; petting zoo; canoe and bicycle rentals; picnicking. Gift shop, snack shop; orientation theater. Plantation home and local art gallery (addl fee). (Daily) 10 mi NW on SC 61. Phone 843/571-1266. ¢¢¢¢ Through Magnolia Plantation, enter

Audubon Swamp Garden. Boardwalks, bridges, and dikes make this

60-acre blackwater cypress and tupelo swamp accessible to visitors. Home to all local species of wildlife, this colorful area is planted with hundreds of varieties of local and exotic flowering shrubs. (Daily) Phone 843/571-1266. ¢¢

Medical University of South Carolina. (1824) 2,200 students. Oldest medical school in the South. 171 Ashley Ave. Phone 843/792-3621. On campus is

    Waring Historical Medical Library & Macaulay Museum of Dental History. (Mon-Fri; closed hols) Phone 843/792-2288. **FREE**

Middleton Place Gardens, House & Stableyards. Once home of Arthur Middleton, signer of the Declaration of Independence, Middleton Place encompasses America's oldest landscaped gardens, the Plantation Stableyards, and the restored House Museum. The gardens, laid out in 1741, highlight ornamental butterfly lakes, sweeping terraces, and a wide variety of flora and fauna. The Stableyards feature numerous craftspeople demonstrating skills necessary for a self-sufficient 18th-century plantation. Special events incl Starlight Pops (May), Spoleto Finale (mid-June), Plantation Days (Nov), and Plantation Christmas (Dec). (Daily) 14 mi NW on SC 61. Phone 843/556-6020. ¢¢¢¢

Old Dorchester State Park. Congregationalists from Massachusetts established a village in 1696 at the head of the Ashley River. It grew as a trading center until 1752, when there was a general exodus of Congregationalists to Georgia in a search for plentiful land and a better climate. By 1780 the once thriving town was occupied by the British and had only 40 houses and a church. In late 1781, Col Wade Hampton advanced against Dorchester. The British did not wait for the attack but instead destroyed the town and retreated to Charleston. Remains of the church tower and Fort Dorchester may be seen; 97-acre area has been partially excavated. Fishing; picknicking. Drawings, artifacts in interpretive bldg. (Daily) Children under 15, handicapped, and SC residents 65+ are free. 19 mi NW on SC 642. Phone 843/873-1740. ¢

Palmetto Islands County Park. Nature oriented park in tropical setting. Natural swimming facility with sand bottom, fishing supplies, canoe trails; bicycle paths, marsh boardwalks, picnicking, and grills throughout park. Two-acre pond. Pedal boat, canoe, and bicycle rentals. BigToy Playground. Fifty-ft observation tower with play area. Interpretive trails; concession. (Daily; closed Jan 1, Thanksgiving, Dec 24-25) N on US 17, ½ mi past Snee Farm, then left on Long Point Rd. Phone 843/884-0832. ¢

Patriots Point Naval and Maritime Museum. Home of the WWII aircraft carrier *Yorktown;* also submarine *Clamagore,* destroyer *Laffey,* Coast Guard cutter *Ingham,* and the Medal of Honor Museum. Vintage military aircraft and weapons on display. Living and working areas of ships tour. Gift shop. (Daily) Located on Charleston Harbor, in Mt Pleasant (at foot of Cooper River Bridges). Children under 6 and disabled are free. Phone 843/884-2727. Children ¢¢¢; Adults ¢¢¢¢

Sightseeing tours.

Gray Line bus tours. For info, contact PO Box 219, 29402-0219. Phone 843/722-4444.

Old South Carriage Company. Offers narrated, horse-drawn carriage tours of Old

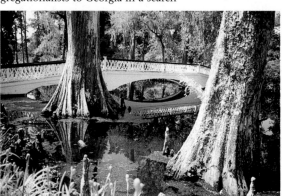

Swamp Garden foot bridge, Magnolia Plantation

Charleston (1 hr). (Daily; closed Thanksgiving, Dec 25) 14 Hayne St. Phone 843/577-0042. Adults ¢¢¢¢; Children ¢¢¢

Palmetto Carriage Tours. One-hr tour through Old Charleston by horse- and mule-drawn carriages. Tours originate at Rainbow Market. (Daily; closed Dec 25). Children under 4 are free. 40 N Market St. Phone 843/723-8145. Adults ¢¢¢¢; Children 4-11 ¢¢

St. John's Lutheran Church. (1817) Congregation established in 1742. Steeple, wrought-iron gates, churchyard fence, graves of interest. Interior restored. Pastor John Bachman (1815-74), who coauthored *Quadrupeds of America* with Audubon, is buried beneath the altar in the church nave. (Mon-Fri; also Sun worship) Archdale & Clifford Sts. Phone 843/723-2426.

St. Mary's Church. (1838) Mother church for Catholic dioceses of Carolinas and Georgia. Congregation established in 1789. Stained-glass windows, paintings. (Daily) 89 Hasell St, between King & Meeting Sts. Phone 843/722-7696.

The Charleston Museum. (1773) Oldest museum in US. Cultural, historical, natural history collections; children's "Discovery Me" rm; decorative arts exhibits. (Daily; closed hols) Combination ticket (addl fee) incl Heyward-Washington House and Joseph Manigault House. 360 Meeting St, at John St. Phone 843/722-2996. ¢¢

The Citadel, Military College of South Carolina. (1842) 2,000 uniformed cadets. Originally located near city's pre-Revolutionary War rampart, the college moved to its present site in 1922. Dress parades (academic yr, Fri). Moultrie & Rutledge aves, near Hampton Park. Phone on campus is 843/953-5006.

The Citadel Archives Museum. Exhibits depict history of the South Carolina Corps of Cadets at The Citadel. (Academic yr, afternoons) Phone 843/953-6846. **FREE**

Unitarian Church. (1772) Second oldest church in the city; under restoration. Fan tracery ceiling; interior modeled after Henry VII Chapel, Westminster Abbey. (Mon-Fri) 8 Archdale St. Phone 843/723-4617.

Walking tour of Old Charleston.

✠ **White Point Gardens.** View of harbor, city, Fort Sumter National Monument (see), and Fort Moultrie. Murray Blvd & E Battery, at foot of peninsula. Walk N on E Battery ½ blk to

Edmondston-Alston House. (ca 1825) Built by wealthy merchant and wharf owner, remodeled by next owner, an important rice planter, beginning in 1838; Greek Revival style. Uninterrupted view across harbor. Documents, engravings, portraits, original furnishings, elaborate woodwork. Guided tours (Daily; closed Jan 1, Thanksgiving, Dec 25). Phone 843/722-7171. ¢¢ Continue N on E Battery (which becomes E Bay St) 8 blks, past Rainbow Row (14 houses dating from the mid-18th century, each painted a different color) to Broad St and the

Old Exchange & Provost Dungeon. (1771) Built by the British with material brought from England, this was the last bldg constructed by them on colonial soil in Charleston prior to the Revolutionary War; served as an exchange and a customs house. Used as a prison during the Revolutionary War. Original seawall of Charleston preserved in dungeon. Extensively restored; site of many important historical events. (Daily) 122 E Bay St. Phone 843/727-2165. ¢¢ Follow Broad St to Church St and turn S; walk past Catfish Row (made famous by *Porgy and Bess*) to

Heyward-Washington House. (1772) Once owned by Thomas Heyward Jr, signer of Declaration of Independence and host to George Washington during his visit in 1791. Period pieces of exquisite design and craftsmanship; Charleston-made furniture; house is a classic example of a Georgian town house. Garden laid out with shrubs, plants that grew in city in Washington's time; carriage house, kitchen. (Daily; closed hols) Combination ticket (addl fee) incl the Charleston Museum and Joseph Manigault House. 87 Church St. Phone 843/722-0354. ¢¢ Walk N on Church St to

Huguenot Church. (1845) Third bldg on this site; rebuilt on site of earlier structure burned in 1796. Congregation founded 1681. Only church in US using Calvinist Huguenot liturgy; services were in French until 1928. 136 Church St, at Queen St. Phone 843/722-4385. Continue N to

St. Philip's Church. (1838) Episcopal. Lofty steeple held mariner's light, was target for Union guns. Late Georgian architecture. Third bldg used by St. Philip's parish. First Anglican parish (1670) S of Virginia. John C. Calhoun and other notables buried in churchyard. 146 Church St. Phone 843/722-7734. From here walk N to Cumberland St then W to

The Powder Magazine. (ca 1710) Part of city's original fortifications, oldest public bldg remaining. Used in Revolutionary War. Walls of this 8-gabled structure are 32 inches thick. Now houses historic colonial museum. (Mon-Sat, also Sun afternoons; closed Jan 1, Thanksgiving, Dec 25) 79 Cumberland St. Phone 843/805-6730. **FREE** Walk W to Meeting St, then 1 blk S to

Gibbes Museum of Art. Permanent collection of American paintings, miniatures, Japanese wood block prints; changing exhibits. (Tues-Sat, also Sun afternoons; closed hols) 135 Meeting St. Phone 843/722-2706. ¢¢-¢¢¢ Walk S to

City Hall Art Gallery. (1801) On the site of colonial marketplace, first housed Bank of United States; became City Hall in 1818. Superb picture gallery on 2nd floor resulted from custom of commissioning artists to paint famous visitors; incl portrait of Washington by John Trumbull, considered one of the best of the general in his later yrs; painting of President Monroe by Samuel F.B. Morse. Tours. (Mon-Fri; closed hols) 80 Broad St, at Meeting St. Phone 843/724-3799. **FREE** On next blk is

St. Michael's Church. (1752) Steeple rises 186 ft; tower has 4-faced clock in operation since 1764. Steeple bells were captured by the British, returned after the Revolution, sent to Columbia during the Civil War, and partly destroyed by fire there. Later they were sent back to England, recast in the original molds, and returned in 1867. (Mon-Fri; closed hols and periodically for maintenance) Meeting & Broad Sts. Phone 843/723-0603. 2 blks S is

Nathaniel Russell House. (1808) Home of wealthy merchant; example of Adam-style architecture; free-flying staircase, oval drawing rms, period furnishings. (Daily; closed Dec 25) 51 Meeting St. Phone 843/724-8481. (¢¢; combination ticket ¢¢¢) incl Aiken-Rhett House, Nearby are

Sword Gates. Gates represent one of the best examples of wrought-iron art, with 2 spears joining at center of broadsword to form cross. (Private) 32 Legare St.

Annual Events

Southeastern Wildlife Exposition. Eighteen downtown historical locations. More than 500 exhibitors display wildlife art, carvings, antique collections, and crafts for sale. Phone 843/723-1748. Mid-Feb.

Festival of Houses & Gardens. Many of the city's finest private residences (ca 1710-1850) and gardens are open to visitors. Afternoon and candlelight tours; res recommended. Phone 843/722-3405. Mid-Mar-mid-Apr.

Family Circle Magazine Cup Tennis Tournament. Daniel Island. Phone 843/363-3500. Mid-Mar.

Spoleto Festival USA. Internationally acclaimed counterpart to the arts festival in Spoleto, Italy, founded by Gian Carlo Menotti; incl opera, ballet, dance, visual arts, theater, chamber music, jazz, symphonic and choral performances, and much more. Piccolo Spoleto, running concurrent with the main festival, has performances by local and regional artists. Phone 843/722-2764. May 25-June 10.

Fall House & Garden Candlelight Tours. Evening tours of privately owned houses and gardens in the Historic District (fee). Phone 843/722-4630. Late Sep-late Oct.

Additional Visitor Information

The Charleston Visitor Reception and Transportation Center, 375 Meeting St, has information on other points of interest, tours, campsites, fishing trips, cultural, special and annual events, maps, and self-guided walking tour of the city. (Daily; closed Jan 1, Thanksgiving, Dec 25) Contact PO Box 975, 29402; 843/853-8000. For city bus service information phone SCE & G at 843/747-0922; for DASH, Downtown Area Shuttle, phone 803/577-6970, Ext 500.

Forever Charleston, a multimedia presentation about the city, is shown every half hr at the Visitor Center.

Motels/Motor Lodges

★★ BEST WESTERN-KING CHARLES INN. *237 Meeting St (29401).* 843/723-7451; fax 843/723-2041. www.charlestownmanagement.com. 91 rms, 3 story. Mar-Oct: S, D $99-$199; each addl $10; under 12 free; higher rates wkends; lower rates rest of yr. Crib free. TV; cable. Pool. Restaurant nearby. Ck-out noon. Business servs avail. Bellhops. Valet serv. Cr cds: A, D, DS, MC, V.
D 🏃 ☁ 🛉 🏂 ➘ 🔥

★ DAYS INN. *2998 W Montague Ave (29418), near Intl Airport.* 843/747-4101; fax 843/566-0378. 147 rms, 2 story. S $45-$65; D $50-$72; each addl $6; under 12 free. Crib free. Pet accepted; $6. TV; cable (premium). Pool. Playground. Restaurant 6 am-9 pm. Ck-out noon. Coin lndry. Business servs avail. Some refrigerators, microwaves. Cr cds: A, D, DS, MC, V.
D 🐾 🏃 ☁ 🛉 ➘ 🔥

★★ HAMPTON INN & SUITES. *1104 Isle of Palms Connector (29464), at Hwy 17N.* 843/856-3900; fax 843/881-6277. Email chsmpolons@hotel.com. 121 rms, 3 story, 40 kit. suites. S $79-$109; D $89-$119; kit. suites $99-$139; higher rates hols. Crib free. TV; cable (premium), VCR (movies) avail in suites. Restaurant adj 6 am-10 pm. Ck-out noon. Meeting rms. Business servs avail. In-rm modem link. Sundries. Gift shop. Guest lndry. Exercise equipt. Pool. Refrigerator, microwave, wet bar in suites. Cr cds: A, C, D, DS, MC, V.
D ☁ 🛉 ✈ ➘ 🔥

★★ HAMPTON INN HISTORIC DISTRICT. *345 Meeting St (29403).* 843/723-4000; fax 843/722-3725; res 800/426-7866. Email hotel@chshd.com; www.hamptoninn.com. 171 rms, 5 story. Mid-Feb-early Nov: S $99; D

$109; suites $150; under 18 free; higher rates wkends, special events; lower rates rest of yr. Crib free. Garage $9. TV; cable (premium). Pool. Complimentary continental bkfst. Restaurant nearby. Ck-out noon. Meeting rms. Business servs avail. In-rm modem link. Bellhops. Concierge. Valet serv. Health club privileges. Some refrigerators; microwaves avail. Cr cds: A, C, D, DS, JCB, MC, V.
D ☁ 🛉 ➘ 🔥

★★★ HAMPTON INN RIVERSIDE. *11 Ashley Pointe Dr (29407).* 843/556-5200; fax 843/571-5499. 177 rms, 4 story. S $75-$99; D $85-$115; under 18 free; higher rates wkends, special events. Crib free. Pet accepted. TV; cable (premium). Pool. Complimentary continental bkfst. Restaurant adj 11 am-11 pm. Ck-out noon. Coin lndry. Meeting rm. Business servs avail. In-rm modem link. Valet serv. Golf privileges. Health club privileges. Opp Ashley River; marina. Cr cds: A, C, D, DS, MC, V.
D ☁ ➘ 🔥 🎣

★ KNIGHTS INN. *2355 Aviation Ave (29406).* 843/744-4900; fax 843/745-0668; res 800/722-7220. 242 rms, 2 story, 31 kits. S $29.95-$45; D $35-$45; each addl $3; suites $75; kit. units $55. Crib $3. TV; cable (premium). 2 pools. Complimentary continental bkfst. Ck-out noon. Coin lndry. Business servs avail. Airport transportation. Some refrigerators, microwaves. Lawn games. Cr cds: A, D, DS, MC, V.
☁ 🛉 ➘ 🔥

★ LA QUINTA. *2499 La Quinta Ln (29420), at I-26N Exit 209.* 843/797-8181; fax 803/569-1608; res 800/687-6667. 122 rms, 2 suites, 2 story. S $60-$70; D $70-$80; each addl $10; suites $90-$100; under 18 free; higher rates wkends. Crib free. Pet accepted. TV; cable (premium). Pool. Complimentary continental bkfst. Restaurant adj 6 am-11 pm. Ck-out noon. Business servs avail. In-rm modem link. Valet serv. Refrigerators, microwaves avail. Picnic tables, grill. Cr cds: A, D, DS, MC, V.
D 🐾 🏃 🧊 ☁ 🛉 ➘ 🔥

★★ RAMADA INN COLISEUM/CONVENTION CENTER. *2934 W Montague Ave @ I-26 (29418), 7 mi*

NW at I-26. 843/744-8281; fax 843/744-6230; res 800/2RAMADA. Email irenemorrison@mindspring.com; www.charlestownmanagement.com/ric. 154 rms, 2 story. Mar-Oct: S $69; D $79; each addl $10; lower rates rest of yr. Crib avail, fee. Parking lot. Pool. TV; cable (premium), VCR avail. Complimentary coffee in rms, newspaper, toll-free calls. Restaurant 5 am-9 pm, closed Sun. Bar. Ck-out noon, ck-in 3 pm. Meeting rms. Business servs avail. Dry cleaning, coin lndry. Free airport transportation. Exercise privileges. Golf. Tennis, 6 courts. Picnic facilities. Video games. Cr cds: A, C, D, DS, MC, V.

★ **RED ROOF INN.** *7480 Northwoods Blvd (29406), I-26 to Exit 209. 843/572-9100; fax 843/572-0061; toll-free 800/843-7663. Email i0142@ redroof.com.* 109 rms, 2 story. S $39-$51; D $44-$57; each addl $7; under 18 free. Crib free. Pet accepted, some restrictions. TV; cable (premium). Complimentary coffee in lobby. Restaurant nearby. Ck-out noon. Microwaves, refrigerators avail. Cr cds: A, DS, MC, V.

★★ **SHEM CREEK INN.** *1401 Shrimp Boat Ln (87501), approx 5 mi E on US 17/701, S on US Business 17 to Mt Pleasant. 843/881-1000; fax 843/849-6969; toll-free 800/523-4951.* 50 rms, 2 story. Mid-Feb-Nov: S, D $89-$175; under 18 free; higher rates special events; lower rates rest of yr. Crib free. TV; cable. Pool. Complimentary continental bkfst, coffee in rms. Restaurant adj 4:30 am-10 pm. Ck-out 11 am. Meeting rms. Business servs avail. Health club privileges. Refrigerators, microwaves avail. Cr cds: A, C, D, DS, MC, V.

★★★ **TOWN AND COUNTRY INN.** *2008 Savannah Hwy (29407). 843/571-1000; fax 843/766-9444; toll-free 800/334-6660. Email towncntry@ aol.com.* 124 rms, 2 story. 20 kits. Mar-Nov: S $69; D $89; each addl $7; suites $109-$189; kit. units $7 addl; under 18 free; lower rates rest of yr. Crib free. TV; cable (premium). 2 pools, 1 indoor; whirlpool. Restaurant 6:30 am-10 pm. Bar 3 pm-midnight. Ck-out noon. Coin lndry. Meeting rms. Business servs avail. In-

rm modem link. Valet serv. Golf privileges, pro. Exercise equipt; sauna. Racquetball court. Some refrigerators. Cr cds: A, C, D, DS, MC, V.

Hotels

★★ **BEST WESTERN.** *7401 Northwoods Blvd (29406), NW on I-26. 843/572-2200; fax 843/863-8316; res 800/528-1234. www.bwcharleston.com.* 195 rms, 4 story, 2 suites. Crib avail. Parking lot. Indoor/outdoor pools, whirlpool. TV; cable (DSS). Complimentary full bkfst, coffee in rms, newspaper, toll-free calls. Restaurant 5-9 pm. Bar. Ck-out 11 am, ck-in 3 pm. Meeting rms. Business center. Bellhops. Concierge. Dry cleaning, coin lndry. Exercise privileges. Golf. Tennis. Cr cds: A, C, D, DS, MC, V.

★★★ **BOARDWALK INN.** *5757 Palm Blvd (29451). 843/886-6000; fax 843/886-2916; toll-free 800/845-8880. www.wilddunes.com.* 93 rms, 5 story, 9 suites. June-Sep: S, D $129-$199; suites $250-$325; under 18 free; wkends, hols (3-day min); lower rates rest of yr. Crib free. TV; cable (premium), VCR avail (movies). Complimentary coffee in rms. Restaurant 6:30 am-11 pm. Bar 11 am-midnight. Ck-out 11 am. Meeting rms. Business center. In-rm modem link. Concierge. Gift shop. Beauty shop. Lighted tennis, pro. Golf, greens fee $39-$145, pro, putting green, driving range. Exercise rm; sauna. Massage. Indoor pool; wading pool, poolside serv. Playground. Supervised children's activities (June-Sep); ages 3-12. Lawn games. Refrigerators, minibars. Balconies. On beach. Cr cds: A, D, DS, MC, V.

★★★★ **CHARLESTON PLACE HOTEL.** *205 Market St (29401), between Hazel and Market Sts, 20 min from airport. 843/722-4900; fax 843/722-0728; res 800/611-5545. Email pstracey@orientx.net.* The elegant fountain entrance and romantic appeal of this 18th-century-style hotel fits in perfectly to this town's timeless magic. The 320-room property includes 40 suites and 80 top-floor, club-level rooms with private concierge service and various enhanced services. Chef Bob Waggoner creates inspired, southern cuisine at the Charleston Grill or guests can try Palmetto Cafe for a more casual meal. 440 rms, 8 story. S $295; D $315; each addl $20; suites $375-$2,000; under 18 free. Crib free. Garage $9, valet parking $13. TV; cable (premium). Indoor/outdoor pool; whirlpool, poolside serv. Supervised children's activities (June-Aug). Restaurants 6:30 am-10 pm (see CHARLESTON GRILL). Rm serv 24 hrs. Bar 11:30-1 am; entertainment. Ck-out noon. Convention facilities. Business center. In-rm modem link. Concierge. Shopping arcade. Tennis privileges. Golf privileges. Exercise rm; sauna. Massage. Some balconies. Luxury level. Cr cds: A, C, D, DS, MC, V.

★★★ **EMBASSY SUITES HISTORIC CHAS.** *337 Meeting St (29403). 843/723-6900; fax 843/723-6938; res 800/362-2779. Email hotel sales@charleston.net.* 153 suites, 5 story. Mid-Mar-early June, late Sep-late Nov: S, D $169-$269; each addl $10; under 18 free; higher rates Southeastern Wildlife Exposition, Bridge Run; lower rates rest of yr. Crib free. Valet parking $11; garage $9. TV; cable (premium). Complimentary full bkfst. Restaurant nearby. Bar 4-11 pm. Ck-out noon. Meeting rms. Business servs avail. In-rm modem link. Gift shop. Coin lndry. Exercise equipt. Pool. Refrigerators, microwaves, wet bars; some in-rm whirlpools. Cr cds: A, C, D, DS, ER, JCB, MC, V.

★★★ **HARBOURVIEW INN.** *2 Vendue Range (29401). 843/853-8439; fax 843/853-4034; toll-free 888/853-8439. Email visscher@bigfoot.com; www. harbourviewcharleston.com.* 47 rms, 4 story, 5 suites. Mar-Nov: S, D $199; each addl $20; suites $269; under 17 free; lower rates rest of yr. Crib avail. Valet parking avail. TV; cable (premium). Complimentary continental bkfst, newspaper, toll-free calls. Restaurant nearby. Ck-out noon, ck-in 3 pm. Business servs avail. Bellhops. Concierge. Dry cleaning. Whirlpool. Golf. Cr cds: A, C, D, DS, MC, V.

★★ **HOLIDAY INN.** *301 Savannah Hwy (29407). 843/556-7100; fax 843/556-6176; res 800/465-4329. Email kathykkm@aol.com; www.holiday-inn. com/chs-riverview.* 181 rms, 14 story, 4 suites. Mar-Oct: S, D $149; each addl $10; suites $250; under 18 free; lower rates rest of yr. Crib avail. Pet accepted. Parking lot. Pool. TV; cable (DSS). Complimentary coffee in rms, newspaper. Restaurant 6:30 am-10 pm. Bar. Ck-out noon, ck-in 3 pm. Meeting rm. Business servs avail. Bellhops. Dry cleaning, coin lndry. Exercise privileges. Golf. Tennis, 5 courts. Video games. Cr cds: A, C, D, DS, JCB, MC, V.

★ **LANDS INN.** *25 S Savannah Hwy (29414). 843/763-8885; fax 843/556-9536.* 57 rms, 2 story. Mar-Oct: S $59-$69; D $69-$79; each addl $10; under 16 free; higher rates wkends; lower rates rest of yr. Crib free. Pet accepted; $10. TV; cable. Complimentary continental bkfst. Restaurant nearby. Rm serv open 24 hrs. Ck-out 11 am. Business servs avail. Pool. On river. Cr cds: A, DS, MC, V.

★★★ **THE MILLS HOUSE.** *115 Meeting St (29401), at Queen St. 843/577-2400; fax 843/722-2112; res 800/465-4329; toll-free 800/874-9600. Email jedwards@bristolhotels.com; www.millshouse.com.* 195 rms, 7 story, 20 suites. Mar-May, Sep-Oct: S, D $279; suites $329; lower rates rest of yr. Crib avail. Valet parking avail. Pool. TV; cable (premium). Complimentary coffee in rms, newspaper, toll-free calls. Restaurant. Bar. Ck-out 11 am, ck-in 3 pm. Meeting rms. Business center. Bellhops. Concierge. Dry cleaning. Gift shop. Exercise privileges. Golf. Tennis. Beach access. Picnic facilities. Cr cds: A, C, D, DS, JCB, MC, V.

★★ **QUALITY SUITES CONVENTION CENTER.** *5225 N Arco Ln (29418). 843/747-7300; fax 843/747-6324; res 800/228-5150. www. charlestonqualitysuites.com.* 5 story, 168 suites. Mar-May: S, D $129; each addl $10; under 18 free; lower rates rest of yr. Crib avail. Parking lot. Pool, whirlpool. TV; cable, VCR avail. Complimentary full bkfst, coffee in rms, newspaper, toll-free calls. Restaurant 6 am-9 pm. Bar. Ck-out 11 am, ck-in 3 pm. Meeting rms. Business servs avail. Dry cleaning, coin lndry. Gift shop. Free airport transportation. Exercise equipt. Golf. Cr cds: A, D, DS, JCB, MC, V.

★★★ **RADISSON HOTEL CHARLESTON AIRPORT.** *5991 Rivers Ave (29406), jct Aviation Ave and I-26. 843/744-2501; fax 843/744-2501; res 800/333-3333. Email rhi_ncha@radisson.com; www.radisson. com.* 159 rms, 8 story. S $79; D $89; each addl $10; under 17 free. Crib avail. Parking lot. Indoor pool, whirlpool. TV; cable. Complimentary coffee in rms, newspaper, toll-free calls. Restaurant 6 am-10:30 pm. Bar. Ck-out noon, ck-in 3 pm. Meeting rms. Business center. Bellhops. Dry cleaning. Free airport transportation. Exercise privileges. Golf. Tennis. Cr cds: A, C, D, DS, ER, JCB, MC, V.

★★★ **SHERATON NORTH CHARLESTON.** *4770 Goer Dr (29406), 8 mi W on I-26 Exit Montague Ave. 843/747-1900; fax 843/744-6108; res 800/325-3535; toll-free 888/ 747-1900. www.charleston.net/com/ sheraton.* 295 rms, 8 story. Mar-May, Sep-Oct: S $149; D $159; each addl $15; suites $325; under 17 free; lower rates rest of yr. Crib avail. Pet accepted, some restrictions, fee. Parking lot. Indoor/outdoor pools, whirlpool. TV; cable (DSS). Complimentary coffee in rms, newspaper. Restaurant 6 am-10 pm. Bar. Ck-out noon, ck-in 4 pm. Conference center. Business servs avail. Bellhops. Concierge. Dry cleaning, coin lndry. Gift shop. Free airport transportation. Exercise privileges. Golf. Cr cds: A, C, D, DS, MC, V.

★★★ **WESTIN FRANCIS MARION.** *387 King St (29403). 843/722-0600; fax 843/723-4633; res 800/WESTIN1. www.westin.com.* 226 rms, 12 story. Mar-June, Oct: D $219; each addl $20; suites $179; lower rates rest of yr. Crib avail. Valet parking avail. TV; cable (premium), VCR avail. Complimentary coffee in rms, newspaper, toll-free calls. Restaurant. 24-hr rm serv. Bar. Ck-out noon, ck-in 4 pm. Meeting rms. Business center. Bellhops. Concierge. Dry cleaning. Gift

shop. Exercise equipt. Golf. Cr cds: A, C, D, DS, MC, V.

★★★★ **WOODLANDS RESORT & INN.** *125 Parsons Rd (29483), approx 20 mi N on I-26, Exit 199A, 2 mi W on US 17A, N on SC 165 to Parsons Rd. 843/875-2600; fax 843/875-2603; toll-free 800/774-9999. Email reservations@woodlandsinn.com; www. woodlandsinn.com.* Just north of Charleston in Carolina Low country sits this English, country-house inn surrounded by 42 private, wooded acres. All 19 rooms include special touches such as an iced split of Perrier-Jouet champagne upon arrival and house-made chocolates at bedtime. Spend the days walking the grounds, getting pampered at the spa, lounging by the pool, or visiting nearby historic attractions and golf courses. 19 rms, 3 story, 9 suites. Mar-May, Sep-Oct: S, D $295; suites $350; lower rates rest of yr. Crib avail. Pet accepted, some restrictions. Valet parking avail. Pool. TV; cable (premium), VCR avail, CD avail. Complimentary newspaper. Restaurant 7 am-9 pm. 24-hr rm serv. Bar. Ck-out noon, ck-in 3 pm. Meeting rms. Business servs avail. Bellhops. Concierge. Dry cleaning. Gift shop. Exercise privileges. Golf. Tennis, 2 courts. Bike rentals. Hiking trail. Cr cds: A, D, DS, MC, V.

Resorts

★★★ **HILTON CHARLESTON HARBOR RESORT.** *20 Patriots Point Rd (29464). 843/856-0028; fax 843/ 856-8333; res 800/HILTONS; toll-free 888/856-0028. Email tom_starling@ hilton.com.* 125 rms, 4 story, 6 suites. Mar-Oct: S $150; D $180; each addl $20; suites $375; lower rates rest of yr. Crib avail. Valet parking avail. Pool, whirlpool. TV; cable (premium). Complimentary coffee in rms. Restaurant 6:30 am-10:30 pm. Bar. Ck-out noon, ck-in 4 pm. Meeting rms. Business servs avail. Bellhops. Concierge. Dry cleaning. Exercise privileges. Golf, 18 holes. Tennis, 6 courts. Picnic facilities. Cr cds: A, C, D, DS, ER, JCB, MC, V.

★★★ **SEABROOK ISLAND.** *1002 Landfall Way (29455), 23 mi SE off US*

17. 843/768-2500; fax 843/768-4922; toll-free 800/845-2475. Email resort@ charleston.net; www.seabrookresort.com. 170 kit. villas, 1-2 story. Mid-Mar-mid Aug: 1-bedrm $165-$240; 2-bedrm $205-$315; 3-bedrm $230-$375; package plans; lower rates rest of yr. Crib $5. TV; cable, VCR avail. 7 pools; wading pool, lifeguard. Supervised children's activities (Memorial Day-Labor Day). Dining rm 7 am-9 pm. Bar from 11 am. Ck-out 11 am, ck-in 4 pm. Business center. Grocery. Convention facilities. Tennis, pro. 36-hole golf, greens fee $55-$100, pro, putting green, driving range. Private beach. Sailboat. Deep sea fishing. Bicycles. Horseback riding. Exercise equipt. Health club privileges. Entertainment. Game rm. Refrigerators, microwaves; some fireplaces. Private patios, balconies. Sunset cruises avail. Cr cds: A, D, DS, MC, V.

★★★★ **WILD DUNES RESORT.**
5757 Palm Blvd (29451), E on US 17, N on SC 703. 843/886-6000; fax 843/ 886-2916; res 843/886-2260; toll-free 800/845-8880. Email reservations@ wilddunes.com; www.wilddunes.com. 84 rms, 5 story, 9 suites. June-Aug: D $230; suites $349; lower rates rest of yr. Crib avail. Valet parking avail. Pool, lap pool, children's pool, lifeguard. TV; cable, VCR avail. Complimentary coffee in rms, newspaper, toll-free calls. Restaurant. Bar. Ck-out 11 am, ck-in 4 pm. Meeting rms. Business center. Bellhops. Concierge. Gift shop. Salon/barber. Exercise rm, sauna, steam rm. Golf. Tennis, 17 courts. Beach access. Bike rentals. Supervised children's activities. Video games. Cr cds: A, D, DS, MC, V.

B&Bs/Small Inns

★★★ **ANCHORAGE INN.** *26 Vendue Range (29401), in Historic District. 843/723-8300; fax 843/723-9543; toll-free 800/421-2952. www.insiders.com.* 17 rms, 2 story, 2 suites. Mid-Mar-mid-June, Sep-Nov: D $125-$199; suites $255; lower rates rest of yr. Garage parking $6/day. TV; cable (premium). Complimentary continental bkfst; afternoon refreshments. Restaurant nearby. Ck-out 11 am,

ck-in 3 pm. Business servs avail. Concierge serv. Antiques. Library/sitting rm. Renovated antebellum warehouse adj to harbor, Waterfront Park; individually decorated rms. Cr cds: A, MC, V.

★★ **THE ASHLEY INN B&B.** *201 Ashley Ave (29403). 843/723-1848; fax 843/579-9060; toll-free 800/581-6658. www.charleston-sc-inns.com.* 6 rms, 5 with shower only, 1 suite, 3 story. Early Mar-Nov: S, D $98-$150; suite $160; lower rates rest of yr. Children over 10 yrs only. TV; cable (premium). Complimentary full bkfst; afternoon refreshments. Ck-out 10 am, ck-in 3 pm. Business servs avail. Bicycles. Built 1832; antiques. Garden with fish pond, fountain. Totally nonsmoking. Cr cds: A, DS, MC, V.

★★★ **BARKSDALE HOUSE INN.**
27 George St (29401), in Historic District. 843/577-4800; fax 843/853-0482; toll-free 888/577-4980. www. barksdalehouse.com. 14 rms, 3 story. Mar-Oct: S, D $80-$195; each addl $10; lower rates rest of yr. Children over 10 yrs only. TV; cable (premium). Complimentary continental bkfst; afternoon refreshments. Restaurant nearby. Ck-out 11 am, ck-in 3 pm. Business servs avail. Health club privileges. Townhouse built in 1778; porches, courtyard in rear. Cr cds: MC, V.

★★★ **BATTERY CARRIAGE HOUSE INN.** *20 S Battery St (73401). 843/727-3100; fax 843/727-3130; toll-free 800/775-5575. www.charleston-inns.com.* 11 rms, 4 with shower only, 2 story. Mar-mid-June, mid-Sep-mid-Nov: S, D $149-$199; each addl $15; higher rates wkends (2-day min); lower rates rest of yr. Children over 12 yrs only. TV; cable (premium). Complimentary continental bkfst, coffee in rms. Ck-out noon, ck-in 3 pm. Concierge serv. Street parking. On Battery Park, harbor. Cr cds: A, DS, MC, V.

★★ **CANNONBORO INN BED AND BREAKFAST.** *184 Ashley Ave (29403). 843/723-8572; fax 843/723-8007; res 800/235-8039. Email*

cannon@cchat.com; www.cchat.com.
cannon. 7 rms, 4 with shower only, 2
story, 1 suite. Early Mar-Nov: S, D $98-
$155; each addl $25; suite $180; lower
rates rest of yr. Children over 10 yrs
only. TV. Complimentary full bkfst;
afternoon refreshments. Restaurant
nearby. Ck-out 10 am, ck-in 3 pm.
Business servs avail. Refrigerators avail.
Bicycles. Second-story porch. Some
Victorian furnishings; antiques. Totally
nonsmoking. Cr cds: A, DS, MC, V.

★★★ **INDIGO INN.** *1 Maiden Ln
(29401). 843/577-5900; fax 843/577-
0378; toll-free 800/845-7639. Email
indigoinn@awod.com; www.aesir.com/
indigoinn.* 40 rms, 3 story. Mar-May,
Sep-Nov: S, D $195; each addl $20;
lower rates rest of yr. Crib avail, fee.
Pet accepted, some restrictions, fee.
Parking lot. TV; cable (premium).
Complimentary continental bkfst,
newspaper, toll-free calls. Restaurant
nearby. Business center. Concierge.
Dry cleaning. Golf, 18 holes. Tennis,
4 courts. Cr cds: A, D, DS, MC, V.

★★★ **JOHN RUTLEDGE HOUSE
INN.** *116 Broad St (29401). 843/723-
7999; fax 843/720-2615; toll-free 800/
476-9741. www.charminginns.com.* 19
rms, 2-3 story, 3 suites. Mid-Mar-mid-
June, mid-Sep-Oct: S $180-$240; D
$200-$260; each addl $20; suites
$310; under 12 free; lower rates rest
of yr. Crib free. TV; cable (premium).
Complimentary continental bkfst;
afternoon refreshments. Restaurant
nearby. Ck-out noon, ck-in 4 pm.
Business servs avail. In-rm modem
link. Valet serv. Concierge serv. Health
club privileges. Stocked refrigerators,
fireplaces. Cr cds: A, DS, MC, V.

★ **KING GEORGE IV INN.** *32
George St (29401). 843/723-9339; fax
843/723-7749; toll-free 888/723-1667.*
10 rms, 5 with shower only, 2 share
bath, 4 suites. No elvtr. Mid-
Feb-early June, Oct-Nov: S, D $89-
$139; each addl $10; suites
$135-$155; wkends (2-day min);
lower rates rest of yr. TV. Complimentary continental bkfst, coffee in rms.
Restaurant nearby. Ck-out 11 am, ck-
in 1-6 pm. Refrigerators, fireplaces.
Built in 1790s; Federal style. Totally
nonsmoking. Cr cds: A, MC, V.

★★★ **KINGS COURTYARD INN.**
*198 King St (29401). 843/723-7000;
fax 843/720-2608; toll-free 800/845-
6119. Email kci@charminginns.com;
www.charminginns.com.* 37 rms, 3
story, 4 suites. Mar-June, Sep-Nov: S
$155; D $175; each addl $20; suites
$240; under 12 free; lower rates rest
of yr. Crib avail. Parking lot. TV;
cable (premium). Complimentary
continental bkfst, newspaper, toll-free
calls. Restaurant 7 am-10 pm. Ck-out
noon, ck-in 3 pm. Meeting rms. Business servs avail. Concierge. Dry cleaning. Exercise privileges, whirlpool.
Golf. Tennis. Cr cds: A, D, DS, MC, V.

★★ **LAUREL HILL PLANTATION
B&B.** *8913 N SC 17 PO Box 190
(29458), 30 mi N on SC 17. 843/887-
3708; fax 843/887-3878; res 888/843-
3708; toll-free 888/887-3708. Email
laurelhill@prodigy.net; www.bbonline.
com/sc/laurelhi.* 4 rms, 3 story. No
elvtrs. No rm phones. Feb-May, Sep-
Oct: S, D $95-$115; each addl $15;
lower rates rest of yr. TV in some
rms. Complimentary full bkfst. Ck-
out 11 am, ck-in 4-7 pm. On creek.
Totally nonsmoking. Cr cds: A, C, D,
DS, MC, V.

★★★ **THE LODGE ALLEY INN.**
*195 E Bay (29402). 843/722-1611; fax
843/577-7497; toll-free 800/845-1004.
Email alleyinn@bellsouth.net; www.
lodgealleyinn.com.* 95 rms, 4 story, 50
kit. units. Mid-Mar-early June, early
Sep-early Nov: S, D $145-$179; each
addl $15; kit. suites $155-$349;
under 12 free; package plans; lower
rates rest of yr. Crib free. TV; cable
(premium). Complimentary coffee;
refreshments. Dining rm 7-10:30 am,
11:30 am-2:30 pm, 6-10 pm; Sun to
2:30 pm. Rm serv to 10:30 am. Bar
11:30 am-midnight; closed Sun;
entertainment spring, fall. Ck-out
noon, ck-in 4 pm. Business servs
avail. Valet serv. Health club privileges. Refrigerators, minibars; some
fireplaces. Some balconies. Built in
1773; antiques. Courtyard gardens
with fountain. Cr cds: A, MC, V.

★★★ **MAISON DU PRE.** *317 E Bay
St (29401). 843/723-8691; fax 843/
723-3722; toll-free 800/844-4667.* 15
rms, 1-3 story, 1 kit. Early Feb-mid-
June, Sep-mid-Nov: S, D $98-$165;

suites $160-$200; carriage house with kit. $160; lower rates rest of yr. Crib free. TV; cable. Complimentary continental bkfst. Ck-out noon, ck-in 2 pm. Built in 1804. Composed of 3 single Charleston houses and 2 carriage houses with porches. Three fountains. Cr cds: DS, MC, V.
⬛⬛⬛

★★★ **MEETING STREET INN.** *173 Meeting St (29401), in heart of Downtown Historic District. 843/723-1882; toll-free 800/842-8022. Email meetingstinn@cchat.com.* 56 rms, 4 story. Mid-Mar-early June, mid-Sep-Oct: S, D $109-$210; each addl $10; under 13 free; lower rates rest of yr. Crib free. Parking $6. TV; cable (premium). Whirlpool. Complimentary continental bkfst; afternoon refreshments. Bar noon-11 pm, closed Sun. Ck-out noon, ck-in 3 pm. Business servs avail. Health club privileges. Walking tours. Refrigerators avail. Courtyard with fountain. Opp Old City Market. Cr cds: A, D, DS, MC, V.
⬛⬛⬛

★★ **MIDDLETON INN.** *4290 Ashley River Rd (29414), 14 mi W. 843/556-0500; fax 803/556-0500; toll-free 800/543-4774.* 55 rms, 2-3 story. S, D $99-$169; each addl $20. Crib free. TV; cable. Pool. Coffee in rms. Complimentary bkfst. Meeting rms. Business servs avail. Tennis. Golf privileges. Kayak, swamp tours. Refrigerators, fireplaces. On 7,000 acres overlooking river, former rice fields; free admission to nearby Middleton Place Gardens. Cr cds: A, MC, V.
⬛⬛⬛⬛⬛⬛SC

★★★ **PLANTERS INN.** *112 N Market St (29401). 843/722-2345; fax 843/577-2125; res 800/845-7082. Email reservations@plantersinn.com.* 56 rms, 4 story, 6 suites. Mid-March-mid-June, mid-Sep-mid-Nov: S, D $160-$250; suites $300-$450; lower rates rest of yr. Crib free. TV; cable (premium). Complimentary continental bkfst; afternoon refreshments. Restaurant (see PENINSULA GRILL). Ck-out noon, ck-in 3 pm. Meeting rm. Business servs avail. In-rm modem link. Concierge serv. Health club privileges. Massage. Many antiques. Cr cds: A, D, DS, MC, V.
⬛⬛⬛⬛

★★ **RUTLEDGE VICTORIAN GUESTHOUSE.** *114 Rutledge Ave (29401). 843/722-7551; fax 843/727-0065; toll-free 888/722-7553. Email normlyn@prodigy.net; www.bbonline. com/sc/rutledge.* 10 rms, 3 story, 1 suite. Mar-June, Sep-Nov: S $139; D $169; each addl $35; suites $199; lower rates rest of yr. Parking lot. TV; cable (premium). Complimentary continental bkfst, newspaper, toll-free calls. Restaurant nearby. Ck-out 11 am, ck-in 2 pm. Business servs avail. Concierge. Exercise privileges. Golf. Tennis. Bike rentals. Picnic facilities. Cr cds: A, DS, MC, V.
⬛⬛⬛⬛⬛SC

★★★ **VENDUE INN.** *19 Vendue Range (29401). 843/577-7970; fax 843/577-2913; toll-free 800/845-7900. Email vendueinnresv@aol.com; www. vendueinn.com.* 22 rms, 3 story, 23 suites. Mar-Jun, Sep-Oct: S $160; D $170; each addl $15; suites $295; under 10 free; lower rates rest of yr. Crib avail, fee. Valet parking avail. TV; cable (premium). Complimentary full bkfst, newspaper, toll-free calls. Restaurant, closed Sun. Bar. Meeting rms. Business servs avail. Concierge. Dry cleaning. Golf. Tennis. Bike rentals. Supervised children's activities. Picnic facilities. Cr cds: A, D, DS, MC, V.
⬛⬛⬛⬛⬛⬛⬛

★★★ **VICTORIA HOUSE INN.** *208 King St (29401). 843/720-2944; fax 843/720-2930; toll-free 800/933-5464. www.charminginns.com.* 18 rms, 3 story, 4 suites. Mar-mid-June, Sep-Nov: S $165; D $185; each addl $20; suites $235; under 12 free; lower rates rest of yr. Crib free. TV; cable (premium). Complimentary continental bkfst; afternoon refreshments. Restaurant adj 8 am-3 pm. Ck-out noon, ck-in 3 pm. Business servs avail. In-rm modem link. Concierge serv. Health club privileges. Massage. Refrigerators. Romanesque Period-style building (1889). Cr cds: D, DS, MC, V.
⬛⬛SC

★★★ **WENTWORTH MANSION.** *149 Wentworth St (29401). 843/853-1896; fax 843/720-5290; toll-free 888/466-1886. Email wentworthmansion@aol.com; www.wentworthmansion.com.* 14 rms, 5 story, 7 suites. Mar-Jun,

Sep-Nov: S, D $295; each addl $50; suites $395; under 12 free; lower rates rest of yr. Crib avail. Parking lot. TV; cable (premium), VCR avail, CD avail. Complimentary continental bkfst, newspaper, toll-free calls. Restaurant 7:30 am-10:30 pm. Bar. Ck-out noon, ck-in 4 pm. Meeting rms. Business servs avail. Concierge. Dry cleaning. Gift shop. Free airport transportation. Exercise privileges. Golf. Tennis. Cr cds: A, D, DS, MC, V.

All Suite

★★★ DOUBLETREE GUEST SUITES HISTORIC CHARLESTON.
181 Church St (29401). 843/577-2644; fax 843/577-2697; res 800/222-8733; toll-free 877/408-8733. Email hotel@ chscs.doubletree.com; www.doubletree. com. 17 rms, 5 story, 165 suites. Feb-Nov: S, D $259; each addl $8; suites $259; under 16 free; lower rates rest of yr. Crib avail. Valet parking avail. TV; cable (DSS), VCR avail. Complimentary coffee in rms, newspaper, toll-free calls. Restaurant. Bar. Ck-out noon, ck-in 4 pm. Meeting rms. Business servs avail. Bellhops. Concierge. Dry cleaning, coin lndry. Gift shop. Exercise equipt. Golf, 18 holes. Bike rentals. Video games. Cr cds: A, C, D, DS, MC, V.

Restaurants

★★ 82 QUEEN.
82 Queen St (29401). 843/722-4428. www.82queen. com. Specializes in seafood, regional Low Country dishes. Hrs: 11:30 am-10 pm; Fri, Sat to 10:30 pm. Res accepted. Bar. Lunch $6.50-$10.95; dinner $16-$22. Located in 1800s bldg. Cr cds: A, DS, MC, V.

★★ ANSON.
12 Anson St (29401). 843/577-0551. www.ansonrestaurant. com. Specializes in fresh seafood, chops. Hrs: 5:30-11 pm. Res accepted. Bar. Dinner a la carte entrees: $14.95-$24.95. Bilevel dining. Decor reminiscent of Low Country plantation homes. Cr cds: A, D, DS, MC, V.

★ AW SHUCKS.
70 State St (29401). 843/723-1151. Specializes in seafood. Salad bar. Hrs: 11 am-10 pm; Fri, Sat to 11 pm. Closed Thanksgiving, Dec

Historic charm of Charleston

25. Bar. Lunch $5.99-$9.99; dinner $9.99-$14.99. Casual rustic decor. Cr cds: A, D, DS, MC, V.

★★★ BARBADOES ROOM.
115 Meeting St. 843/577-2400. Specializes in seafood. Own baking. Hrs: 6:30 am-10 pm. Res accepted. Bar. Wine list. Bkfst $5.95-$8.95. Buffet: $8.95; lunch $5.95-$9.95; dinner $14.95-$24.95. Sun brunch $16.95. Entertainment: pianist. Valet parking. Cr cds: A, D, DS, MC, V.

★★ BEAUMONT'S CAFE.
12 Cumberland St (29401). 843/577-5500. www.beaumonts.com. Specializes in bouillabaisse, fois gras, duck. Hrs: 11 am-3 pm, 5-11 pm. Closed Dec 25; Sun in Aug. Res accepted. Bar. Lunch $5.25-$12.95; dinner $6.95-$21.75. View of courtyard. Cr cds: A, D, DS, MC, V.

★★ BLOSSOM CAFE.
171 E Bay St (29401). 843/722-9200. www. magnolias-blossom.com. Specializes in oak-roasted salmon, pizzas cooked in wood-burning oven. Hrs: 11:30 am-11 pm; Fri, Sat to midnight; Sun 10 am-2:30 pm, 4-10 pm. Closed Jan 1, Dec 25. Res accepted. Bar. Lunch, dinner $6.25-$21.95. Child's menu. Modern decor. Cr cds: A, D, DS, MC, V.

★★ CAROLINA'S.
10 Exchange St (29401). 843/724-3800. www.carolinas rest.com. Specializes in grilled

seafood, pasta, regional cuisine. Own baking. Hrs: 5-10 pm. Res accepted. Bar. Dinner $7.95-$25.95. Cr cds: A, D, DS, MC, V.

D ⊣

★★★★ **CHARLESTON GRILL.** *130 Market St. 843/577-4522. www. charlestongrill.com.* At the Charleston Place hotel, this warm, jazz-filled dining room is home to chef Bob Waggoner's detailed, creative cuisine. Dishes are a fusion between California freshness, French technique, and Carolina "low country" ideals. Local products and traditional Southern ingredients are combined in unexpected ways as in lobster tempura, lemon grits, and fried, green tomatoes in yellow-tomato-tarragon butter. Specializes in game, beef, fresh local seafood. Own baking, soups. Hrs: 6-10 pm; Fri, Sat to 11 pm. Res accepted. Bar. Wine cellar. Dinner a la carte entrees: $16-$29. Entertainment: jazz trio. Valet parking. Cr cds: A, D, DS, MC, V.

D

★★★★ **THE DINING ROOM AT WOODLANDS.** *125 Parsons Rd. 843/875-2600. www.realischataux.com.* This resort is a true oasis. Nestled in a Charleston suburb known for its healthy spa environment, the property exceeds expectations with the highest level of fine dining, exquisite architecture and decor and impeccable service. Chef Ken Vedrinski offers one of the best dining experiences in all the Carolinas with painstakingly selected ingredients and masterfully created, world-class cuisine peppered with Southern influences. Specializes in seafood, lamb, beef. Hrs: 7 am-9:30 pm. Res accepted. Bar. Wine cellar. Bkfst $4.75-$18; lunch $7-$18; dinner complete meals: $48-$65. Valet parking. Jacket (dinner). Cr cds: A, D, DS, MC, V.

D SC

★★★ **ELLIOTT'S ON THE SQUARE.** *387 King St (29403), Francis Marion Westin Hotel. 843/724-8888.* Specializes in fresh seafood. Hrs: 6:30 am-10 pm; Fri, Sat to 11 pm. Res accepted. Bar. Bkfst $3.95-$7.95; lunch $5.95-$11.50; dinner $17-$19.95. Valet parking. Art Deco decor. Cr cds: A, D, DS, MC, V.

D

★★★ **FULTON FIVE.** *5 Fulton St (29401). 843/853-5555.* Specializes in risotto, antipasto spoleto, lemon sherbet with Campari. Own baking. Hrs: 5:30-11 pm; Fri, Sat to midnight. Closed Sun; also late Aug-1st wk Sep. Res accepted. Bar. Wine cellar. Dinner $12-$24. Street parking. Intimate atmosphere. European decor. Cr cds: A, DS, MC, V.

D

★★ **GARIBALDI'S.** *49 S Market St (29401). 843/723-7153.* Specializes in fresh seafood, pasta, veal. Own desserts. Hrs: 5:30-10:30 pm. Closed Dec 25. Dinner $7.95-19.95. Bistro atmosphere. In center of historic Charleston Market. Cr cds: A, MC, V.

★★ **IDLEWILDS.** *976 Houston Northcutt Blvd (29464). 843/881-4511.* Specializes in rack of lamb, seafood, shrimp 'n grits. Hrs: 11:30 am-3 pm, 5:30-10 pm; Fri, Sat to 11 pm. Closed Dec 25. Res accepted. Wine, beer. Lunch $5.25-$7.95; dinner $10.95-$18.50. Child's menu. Entertainment. Cr cds: A, DS, MC, V.

D ⊣

★★ **J BISTRO.** *819 Coleman Blvd (29464). 843/971-7778.* Specializes in pork chops, seafood. Hrs: 5-10 pm; Sun brunch 10:30 am-2:30 pm. Closed Mon; hols. Bar. Dinner $6-$18. Sun brunch $12. Two-level dining area. Casual decor. Cr cds: A, MC, V.

⊣

★★★ **MAGNOLIAS.** *185 E Bay St (29401). 843/577-7771. www. magnolias-blossom.com.* Specializes in pan-fried chicken livers, spicy shrimp and sausage, veal meatloaf. Hrs: 11:30 am-10 pm; Fri, Sat to 11 pm. Closed Jan 1, Dec 25. Res accepted. Bar. Lunch $7.50-$17.50; dinner $8.25-$21.95. Contemporary decor within historic structure; overlooks Lodge Alley. Cr cds: A, DS, MC, V.

D

★★★ **MCCRADY'S TAVERN.** *2 Unity Alley (29401). 843/577-0025.* Specializes in seafood, pasta, veal. Hrs: 5:30-10 pm. Closed Sun; hols. Bar. Dinner $7.95-$19. Historic tavern (1778). Cr cds: A, MC, V.

★ **ONE-EYED PARROT.** *1130 Ocean Blvd (29451), E on US 17B to SC 703,*

then S. 843/886-4360. Specializes in seafood, beef. Hrs: 5-10 pm; Fri, Sat to 11 pm. Closed Thanksgiving, Dec 25. Bar. Dinner $6.95-$16.99. Child's menu. Entertainment: Fri-Sun. Terrace dining, second floor dining rm overlooking ocean. Cr cds: A, D, DS, MC, V.
⊟

★ **PAPILLON.** *32 N Market St (29401). 843/723-6510.* Specializes in pasta calzones, pizza baked in wood-burning oven. Own pastries. Hrs: 11 am-11 pm. Lunch $5.95-$8.95. Buffet: $5.95; dinner $8.95-$12.95. Trattoria atmosphere. Cr cds: A, D, DS, MC, V.
D ⊟

★★★ **PENINSULA GRILL.** *121 N Market St. 843/723-0700.* Specializes in wild mushroom grits, pistachio-crusted sea bass, benne seed-crusted rack of New Zealand lamb. Own pastries. Hrs: 5:30-10 pm; Fri, Sat to 11 pm. Res accepted. Bar. Wine cellar. Dinner $15-$27. Child's menu. Elegant atmosphere reminiscent of 1940s supper club. Cr cds: A, D, DS, MC, V.
D

★★ **POOGAN'S PORCH.** *72 Queen St (29401), in Historic District. 843/577-2337.* Specializes in Cajun shrimp, bread pudding, shrimp Creole. Hrs: 11:30 am-2:30 pm, 5:30-10 pm; Sun 10:30 am-2:30 pm, 5:30-9:30 pm. Res accepted. Bar. Lunch $4.95-$7.95; dinner $9.95-$17.95. Restored house (1891). Intimate dining. Garden rm; fireplace. Cr cds: A, MC, V.

★★ **SARACEN.** *141 E Bay St (29401). 843/723-6242.* Specializes in fresh seafood, beef, pork. Own baking. Hrs: 6-10 pm. Closed Sun, Mon; hols. Res accepted. Bar. Dinner $11-$25. Child's menu. Entertainment: jazz Fri, Sat (seasonal). Street, garage parking. Former bank bldg (1853) combines Moorish, Persian, Hindu, and Gothic architecture. On National Register of Historic Places. Cr cds: A, C, DS, MC, V.
D ⊟

★★ **SERMET'S CORNER.** *276 King St (29401). 843/853-7775.* Specializes in citrus-crusted salmon, pork tenderloin, grilled calamari. Hrs: 11 am-3 pm, 4-11 pm; Fri, Sat from 4 pm; Sun to 10 pm. Res accepted. Bar. Lunch $7.75-$9; dinner $11-$17.

Child's menu. Street parking. Cr cds: A, MC, V.

★★ **SLIGHTLY NORTH OF BROAD.** *192 E Bay St (29401). 843/723-3424.* Specializes in seafood, pasta, beef. Hrs: 11:30 am-3 pm, 5:30-10 pm; Fri to 10:30 pm; Sat 5:30-11 pm; Sun from 5:30 pm. Closed hols. Bar. Lunch a la carte entrees: $6.75-$10.95; dinner a la carte entrees: $8.50-$18.95. Child's menu. Open kitchen. Cr cds: A, D, DS, MC, V.
D

★★ **SLIGHTLY UP THE CREEK.** *130 Mill St (29464). 843/884-5005.* Specializes in grilled barbecue tuna, fried oysters in golden ginger citrus sauce. Hrs: 5:30-10 pm. Closed Jan 1, Dec 25. Res accepted. Bar. Dinner $6.50-$18.50. Child's menu. Parking. Cr cds: A, D, DS, MC, V.
D

Unrated Dining Spot

LOUIS'. *200 Meeting St at Pinckney (29401). 843/853-2550. www.louis restaurant.com.* Specializes in crab cakes. Hrs: 6-11 pm. Res accepted. Bar. Dinner $18-$24. Child's menu. Valet parking. Cr cds: D, DS, MC, V.
D

Cheraw

See also Bennettsville, Camden, Darlington, Florence, Hartsville

Settled 1740 **Pop** 5,505 **Elev** 150 ft
Area code 843 **Zip** 29520
Information Chamber of Commerce, 221 Market St; 843/537-8425 or 843/537-7681

Profiting in commerce from both Carolinas, Cheraw grew rapidly when the Pee Dee River was opened for traffic. It is said that the town owes its many trees to an ordinance that required every person seen intoxicated in public to go out into the woods and fetch a tree for planting within the town.

Annual Event

Spring Festival. Family Fun Run; tours; arts and crafts shows; Confederate reenactments; entertainment, trolley rides, car show. Phone 843/537-8420. Early Apr.

Motel/Motor Lodge

★ **INN CHERAW.** *321 2nd St (29520). 843/537-2011; fax 843/537-0227; toll-free 800/535-8709.* 50 rms, 2 story. S $36-$60; D $40-$65; each addl $5; kit. units $45-$60; under 6 free; golf plans; higher rates NASCAR races. Crib free. Pet accepted, some restrictions. TV; cable (premium), VCR. Complimentary continental bkfst, coffee in rms. Restaurant adj 11 am-9 pm. Ck-out 11 am. Meeting rms. Valet serv. Refrigerators; microwaves avail. Cr cds: A, D, DS, MC, V.

D 🐾 ⛵ 🐾 SC

B&B/Small Inn

★★ **SPEARS GUEST HOUSE.** *228 Huger St (29520). 843/537-1094; fax 843/537-0302; res 888/424-3729.* 4 rms, 1 story. S, D $67; each addl $15. Crib avail, fee. Parking lot. Pool. TV; cable (premium), VCR avail, CD avail. Complimentary continental bkfst, coffee in rms, newspaper. Restaurant nearby. Ck-out noon, ck-in 3 pm. Business center. Dry cleaning. Free airport transportation. Golf, 18 holes. Tennis, 2 courts. Cr cds: A, MC, V.

🎿 🏌 ⛵ ⛵ 🔥 🚶

Chester

(D-3) *See also Rock Hill*

Settled 1755 **Pop** 7,158 **Elev** 485 ft
Area code 803 **Zip** 29706
Information Chester County Chamber of Commerce, 109 Gadsden St, PO Box 489; 803/581-4142

Seat of Chester County, this town was named by settlers from Pennsylvania. Aaron Burr, guarded here in 1807 while under arrest for treason, broke away and climbed a high rock. After haranguing a surprised crowd, he was recaptured.

What to See and Do

Chester State Park. Approx 500 acres. Lake fishing, boating; nature trail, picnicking (shelters), recreation bldg, camping (hookups, dump station). Equestrian show ring. Standard fees. 3 mi SW on SC 72. Phone 803/385-2680.

Clemson

(D-2) *See also Anderson, Greenville*

Founded 1889 **Pop** 11,096 **Elev** 850 ft
Area code 864 **Zip** 29631
Web www.clemsonchamber.org
Information Clemson Area Chamber of Commerce, PO Box 1622, 29633; 864/654-1200 or 800/542-0746

Home of Clemson University, this community also hosts vacationers attracted to the huge lake that the Hartwell Dam has formed on the Savannah River.

What to See and Do

Clemson University. (1889) 17,000 students. Named for Thomas G. Clemson, son-in-law of John C. Calhoun, who bequeathed the bulk of his estate, Fort Hill, for establishment of a scientific college. 11 mi NW of I-85 at jct US 76, SC 93. Phone 864/656-3311 or 864/656-2061. On this 1,400-acre campus are

Fort Hill. (1803) Mansion on 1,100 acres acquired by Calhoun during his first term as vice president. House has many original furnishings belonging to Calhoun, Clemson. (Daily; closed hols) Phone 864/656-2475. **FREE**

Hanover House. (1716) This French Huguenot house was moved here from its original site near Pinopolis to prevent submersion by Lake Moultrie. (Wkends) Phone 864/656-2241. **FREE**

State Botanical Gardens. This 250-acre area incl azalea and camelia trails, ornamental plantings, large collection of shrubs; dwarf conifer flower and turf display gardens; wildflower pioneer and bog garden is labeled in Braille. (Daily) E side of campus. Phone 864/656-3405. **FREE**

Annual Event

Clemson Fest. Entertainment, arts and crafts, children's activities. Boat parade and contest precedes fireworks display. Phone 864/646-6110. July 4.

Motels/Motor Lodges

★★ **HOLIDAY INN.** *894 Tiger Blvd (29631), 1½ mi E on US 123.* 864/654-4450; fax 864/654-8451; toll-free 888/442-0422. 220 rms, 2 story. S, D $57-$63; each addl $5; suites $129; under 19 free; higher rates football wkends. Crib free. Pet accepted. TV; cable (premium). Pool. Coffee in rms. Restaurant 6:30 am-2 pm, 5:30-8:30 pm. Bar 4 pm-midnight; closed Sun. Ck-out noon. Coin lndry. Meeting rms. Business servs avail. In-rm modem link. Valet serv. Golf privileges. Health club privileges. On lake. Cr cds: A, C, D, DS, JCB, MC, V.

★★ **RAMADA INN.** *US 76 and 123 (29633).* 864/654-7501; fax 864/654-7301. 149 rms, 4 story. S $49-$58; D $54-$65; suites $125-$150; under 18 free; wkend rates; higher rates football wkends, special events. Crib free. TV; cable (premium). Indoor pool; whirlpool. Sauna. Restaurant 6:30 am-2 pm, 5-10 pm. Bar Mon-Sat. Ck-out 11 am. Meeting rms. Valet serv. Golf privileges. Some refrigerators. Cr cds: A, C, D, DS, JCB, MC, V.

Hotel

★★ **COMFORT INN.** *1305 Tiger Blvd (29631).* 864/653-3600; fax 864/654-3123; res 800/228-5150. Email cicclemson@aol.com. 104 rms, 4 story, 18 suites. Sep-Nov: S $69; D $75; each addl $6; suites $125; under 18 free; lower rates rest of yr. Crib avail. Parking lot. Pool. TV; cable (premium). Complimentary continental bkfst, coffee in rms, newspaper. Restaurant nearby. Ck-in 4 pm. Meeting rms. Business servs avail. Dry cleaning, coin lndry. Exercise privileges, sauna. Golf. Tennis. Cr cds: A, D, DS, MC, V.

B&B/Small Inn

★★ **SUNRISE FARM BED & BREAKFAST INN.** *325 Sunrise Dr (29676), 1 mi E of SC 130.* 864/944-0121; fax 864/944-6195; toll-free 888/991-0121. Email sfbb@bellsouth.net; www.bbonline.com/sc/sunrisefarm. 4 rms, 1 story, 1 suite. S, D $85; each addl $10; suites $150; children $10. Crib avail. Pet accepted, some restrictions. Parking lot. TV; cable (premium), VCR avail, CD avail. Complimentary full bkfst, coffee in rms, newspaper, toll-free calls. Restaurant nearby. Ck-out 11 am, ck-in 3 pm. Business center. Coin lndry. Golf. Downhill skiing. Beach access. Hiking trail. Picnic facilities. Cr cds: MC, V.

Clinton

(D-3) *See also Greenville, Greenwood, Newberry, Spartanburg*

Pop 7,987 **Elev** 680 ft **Area code** 864 **Zip** 29325

Information Laurens County Chamber of Commerce, PO Box 248, Laurens 29360; 864/833-2716

In 1865, Clinton was "a mudhole surrounded by barrooms," according to the young Reverend William Jacobs, who not only rid the town of barrooms but founded a library, orphanage, high school, and Presbyterian College (1880). A young attorney by the name of Henry Clinton Young was hired by the townspeople to help lay out the streets, hence the town came to be named for his middle name.

Motels/Motor Lodges

★ **DAYS INN.** *12374 US 56 N (29325), Exit 52.* 864/833-6600; fax 864/833-6600; toll-free 800/329-7466. 59 rms, 2 story. S $42-$45; D $49-$50; each addl $5; suites $80; under 17 free. Crib free. Pet accepted. TV; cable (premium). Pool. Complimentary continental bkfst. Restaurant adj 6:30 am-10 pm. Ck-out 11 am. Coin lndry. Meeting rms. Exercise equipt; sauna. Some refrigerators, microwaves. Cr cds: A, C, D, DS, MC, V.

★★ **RAMADA INN.** *US 56 and I-26 (29325), Exit 52.* 864/833-4900; fax

864/833-4916; toll-free 877/CLINTON. Email ramadaclintonsc@aol.com. 102 rms, 2 story. S, D $65. TV; cable (premium). Pool. Restaurant 6:30 am-2 pm, 5-9 pm; Sat 6:30-10 am, 5-9 pm; Sun to 2 pm. Bar 5 pm-midnight. Ck-out noon. Lndry facilities. Meeting rms. Business servs avail. Sundries. Exericise equipt. Refrigerators avail. Cr cds: A, D, DS, MC, V.

D ⇌ 🏋 🔧 🖳 🐾

Columbia

(E-4) *See also Camden, Newberry, Orangeburg, Sumter*

Founded 1786 **Pop** 98,052 **Elev** 213 ft
Area code 803
Web www.columbiasc.net
Information Columbia Metropolitan Visitors Center, 1012 Gervais St, 29201; 803/254-0479 or 800/264-4884

The broad-boulevarded capital of South Carolina is not only the state's political and governmental capital, but also its wholesale and retail trade center. Located within three miles of the geographic center of the state, Columbia was laid out as the capital as a compromise between the contending Up Country and Low Country farmers. The city rarely departs from a checkerboard pattern; the streets are sometimes 150 feet wide, planned that way originally to discourage malaria.

The General Assembly met for the first time in the State House in Columbia on January 4, 1790. George Washington was a guest here during his Southern tour the next year. On December 17, 1860, a convention assembled in Columbia's First Baptist Church and drew up the Ordinance of Secession, setting off a chain of events that terminated, for the city, on February 17, 1865, when General William T. Sherman's troops occupied Columbia and reduced it to ashes. An area of 84 blocks and 1,386 buildings was destroyed; on Main Street only the unfinished new statehouse and the home of the French consul were spared. From these ashes, a city of stately buildings has risen.

The economy of the city is based on trade, industry, finance, and government.

Since 1801, when the South Carolina College, now the University of South Carolina, was established here, the city has been an educational center; today it is the site of nine schools of higher education.

Columbia is the headquarters for the Francis Marion National Forest (see CHARLESTON) and the Sumter National Forest (see GREENWOOD).

What to See and Do

Columbia Museum of Art. Galleries house Renaissance paintings from the collection of Samuel H. Kress; 19th- and 20th-century American, emphasizing the Southeast, and European paintings; changing exhibitions drawn from permanent collection and from objects on loan. Concerts, films, lectures, and special events accenting exhibitions. (Tues-Sun; closed hols) Main & Hampton Sts. Phone 803/799-2810. ¢¢

Confederate Relic Room and Museum. Relic collection from the Colonial period through the space age with special emphasis on South Carolina's Confederate period. (Mon-Fri, also 1st Sat of month) 920 Sumter St. Phone 803/898-8095. **FREE**

Congaree Swamp National Monument. Old-growth, bottomland hardwood forest, approximately 22,200 acres. Trees and waters teem with wildlife. Fishing, canoeing; hiking trails, boardwalks, public contact station, primitive camping (by permit). (Daily; closed Dec 25) 20 mi SE off SC 48. Phone 803/776-4396. **FREE**

First Baptist Church. (1859) First Secession Convention, which marked the beginning of the Civil War, met here Dec 17, 1860. (Sun-Fri; closed hols) 1306 Hampton St. Phone 803/256-4251.

First Presbyterian Church. (1853) First congregation organized in Columbia (1795); President Woodrow Wilson's parents are buried in churchyard. (Daily) 1324 Marion St, at Lady St. Phone 803/799-9062.

Fort Jackson. The most active entry training center for US Army, with 16,000 soldiers assigned. Museum on

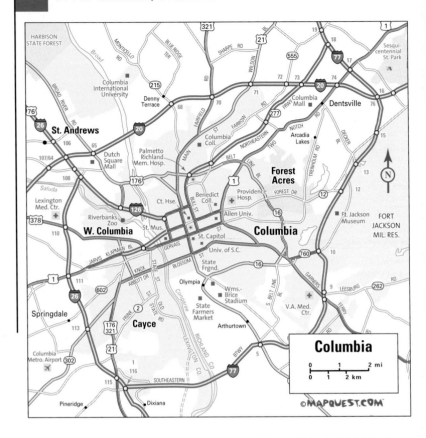

Jackson Blvd has displays on history of fort and of today's army. (Tues-Sat; closed hols) E edge of city, between I-20 & US 76. Phone 803/751-7419 or 803/751-7355. **FREE**

Governor's Mansion. (1855) Built as officers' quarters for Arsenal Academy. Tours (Tues-Thurs). Res required. 800 Richland St. Phone 803/737-1710. **FREE**

Hampton-Preston Mansion. (1818) Purchased by Wade Hampton I; occupied by the Hamptons and the family of his daughter, Mrs. John Preston. In February 1865, it served as headquarters for Union General J.A. Logan. Many Hampton family furnishings and decorative arts of the antebellum period. (Tues-Sat; closed hols) 1615 Blanding St. Phone 803/252-1770. ¢¢

Lake Murray. Lake is 41 mi long, with 520-mi shoreline; impounded by Saluda Dam for hydroelectric purposes. Swimming, waterskiing, boating, fishing, picnicking, camping (fee). Marina in White Rock, 17 mi

NW; phone 803/749-1554. 15 mi NW via I-26, Irmo Exit. Phone 803/781-5940 for further info.

Lexington County Museum Complex. Historic restoration from mid-1800s; depicts life of area farmer. Period country furnishings, textiles, decorative arts. Spinning and weaving demonstrations. (Tues-Sun; closed hols) 10 mi W via US 378 at Fox St in Lexington. Phone 803/359-8369. ¢

Riverbanks Zoological Park & Botanical Garden. Exhibits of animals in nonrestrictive natural habitat areas; aquarium-reptile complex with diving demonstrations; birdhouse with daily rainstorm; demonstrations at Riverbanks Farm; penguin and sea lion feedings. (Daily; closed Thanksgiving, Dec 25) 500 Wildlife Pkwy. Phone 803/779-8717. ¢¢¢

Robert Mills Historic House (1823) & Park. One of a few residences designed by Robert Mills, Federal architect and designer of the Washington Monument; mantels, art, furnishings of Regency period.

(Tues-Sun; closed hols) 1616 Blanding St. Phone 803/252-1770. ¢¢

Sesquicentennial State Park. On 1,445 acres. Log house (1756). Interpretive center. Lake swimming, bathhouse, boating (rentals), fishing; nature and exercise trails, picnicking (shelters), playground, recreation bldg, camping (hookups, dump station). Swimming and boating (Memorial Day-Labor Day). Standard fees. 13 mi NE on US 1. Phone 803/788-2706.

South Carolina Archives Building. Historical and genealogical research facility with documents dating from 1671; changing exhibits. Research rm (Tues-Sat, also Sun afternoons; closed hols). Tours (by appt). 8301 Parklane Rd. Phone 803/896-6100. **FREE**

South Carolina State Museum. Located in world's first fully electric textile mill (1894); exhibits on art, natural history, cultural history, and science and technology with emphasis on contributions by South Carolinians; numerous hands-on exhibits; dioramas. Incl is a center dedicated to Nobel Prize winner Charles Townes, who helped develop the laser. Gift shop. (Mon-Sat, also Sun afternoons; closed hols) 301 Gervais St. Phone 803/898-4921. ¢¢

Town Theatre. One of the oldest (since 1919) community theater groups in the US. Broadway plays and musicals. Tours (by appt). Performances (late Sep-late May; also summer show). 1012 Sumter St. Phone 803/799-2510 for tour schedule and ticket info.

Trinity Cathedral. (1846) Episcopal. Reproduction of Yorkminster, England; the oldest church bldg in Columbia and one of the largest Episcopal congregations in the US. Hiram Powers baptismal font, box pews, English stained glass. Three Wade Hamptons (a politically prominent South Carolina family) are buried in the churchyard; graves of 7 governors and 6 bishops are also here. In 1977 it became the Cathedral Parish of the Episcopal Diocese of Upper South Carolina. (Spring and fall, Mon-Fri, limited hrs) 1100 Sumter St, at Senate St, opp statehouse. Phone 803/771-7300. **FREE**

University of South Carolina. (1801) 26,000 students. Located downtown.

For campus tour info stop at the Univ of South Carolina Visitor Center. (Mon-Sat) Pendleton & Assemby Sts. Phone 803/777-0169 (exc SC) or 800/922-9755. Points of interest incl

Carolina Coliseum. Houses Gamecock Basketball and other sports events, concerts, exhibitions, trade shows, circuses, and other entertainment. Assembly & Blossom Sts.

Koger Center for the Arts. Contemporary structure houses center for the performing arts. Diverse musical, theatrical, and dance programs. Assembly & Greene Sts.

McKissick Museum. Houses Bernard M. Baruch Silver Gallery with antique European silver, J. Harry Howard gemstone collection, Laurence L. Smith Mineral Library, Catawba Native American pottery collection, Southern Folk Art, historical collections, Art Gallery, Education Museum, Broadcasting Archives. (Daily; closed hols, also Dec 24) At the head of the Horseshoe. Phone 803/777-7251. **FREE**

The Horseshoe. Original campus area. Ten of the 11 bldgs on the quadrangle date back to the 19th century and are listed in the National Register of Historic Places. Monument erected in 1827 was designed by Robert Mills. Off Sumter St.

Woodrow Wilson Boyhood Home. (1872) Built by Wilson's father; items associated with Wilson's family and career. (Tues-Sun; closed hols) 1705 Hampton St. Phone 803/252-1770. ¢¢

Annual Event

South Carolina State Fair. Fairgrounds, 1200 Rosewood Dr. Agricultural, floral, home, craft, livestock, and commercial exhibits. Entertainment, shows, carnival. Phone 803/799-3387. Oct.

Motels/Motor Lodges

★★ **AMERISUITES.** *7525 Two Notch Rd (29223), at I-20. 803/736-6666; fax 803/788-6011; res 800/833-1516.* 112 suites, 6 story. S, D $69-$109; each addl $5; under 16 free; wkend rates. Crib free. TV; cable (premium), VCR. Pool. Complimentary continental bkfst. Coffee in rms. Restaurant nearby. Ck-out noon. Meeting rms. Business center. Valet serv. Exercise equipt. Refrigerators, microwaves. Cr cds: A, D, DS, MC, V.

⊡ 🕿 📶 ⇌ 🏃 🔽 🐾 🏃

★★ **BAYMONT INN & SUITES.**
1538 Horseshoe Dr (29223), Exit 74 to Horseshoe Dr. 803/736-6400; fax 803/788-7875; toll-free 800/301-0200. 102 rms, 3 story. S $35.95-$43.95; D $42.95-$49.95. Crib free. TV; cable (premium). Pool. Complimentary continental bkfst. Coffee in rms. Restaurant adj open 24 hrs. Ck-out noon. Coin lndry. Meeting rm. Business servs avail. In-rm modem link. Valet serv. Microwaves avail. Cr cds: A, C, D, DS, MC, V.

⊡ ⇌ 🏃 🔽 🔥

★★ **COLUMBIA COURTYARD NW.**
347 Zimalcrest Dr (24210). 803/731-2300; fax 803/722-6465; res 800/321-2211. 149 units, 3 story. S $84; suites $98; wkend rates. Crib free. TV; cable (premium). Pool; whirlpool. Coffee in rms. Restaurant 6:30-10 am; wkends 7-11 am. Bar 5-10 pm (Mon-Sat). Ck-out noon. Coin lndry. Meeting rms. Business servs avail. In-rm modem link. Valet serv. Exercise equipt. Refrigerators avail. Cr cds: A, C, D, DS, JCB, MC, V.

⊡ ⇌ 🏃 🔽 🔥

★ **COLUMBIA WEST TRAVELODGE.** *2210 Bush River Rd (29210), at I-20.* 803/798-9665; fax 803/731-9642; res 800/578-7878. www.travellodgecolumbia.com. 108 rms, 3 story. S $49.95; D $54.95; each addl $5; under 18 free. Crib free. Pet accepted. TV; cable (premium). Pool. Coffee in rms. Restaurant opp 6 am-10 pm. Ck-out 11 am. Meeting rms. Business servs avail. Valet serv. Guest lndry. Health club privileges. Refrigerators, microwaves avail. Cr cds: A, D, DS, MC, V.

⊡ 🕿 ⇌ 🏃 🔽 🐾

★★ **HAMPTON INN.** *1094 Chris Dr (29169).* 803/791-8940; fax 803/739-2291. 121 rms, 4 story. S, D $57-$71; under 18 free. Crib free. TV; cable (premium). Pool. Complimentary continental bkfst. Business servs avail. In-rm modem link. Cr cds: A, D, DS, MC, V.

⊡ 🕿 📶 ⇌ 🏃 🔽 🐾

★★ **HAMPTON INN.** *1551 Barbara Dr (29223).* 803/865-8000; fax 803/

865-8046; res 800/426-7866. Email caene01@hihotel.com. 111 rms, 5 story, 18 suites. Late-May-Aug: S $68; D $73; suites $92-$97; under 18 free; higher rates special events; lower rates rest of yr. Crib free. TV; cable (premium), VCR avail. Complimentary continental bkfst. Coffee in rms. Restaurant opp 11 am-11 pm. Ck-out noon. Meeting rm. Business servs avail. In-rm modem link. Exercise equipt. Pool. Health club privileges. Some in-rm whirlpools; refrigerator, microwave, wet bar in suites. Cr cds: A, D, DS, MC, V.

⊡ ⇌ 🏃 🔽 🐾 🏃

★★ **HOLIDAY INN NORTHEAST.**
7510 Two Notch Rd (29223), at I-20. 803/736-3000; fax 803/736-6399; toll-free 800/465-4329. 253 rms, 2 story. S, D $69; each addl $6; under 12 free; wkend rates. Crib free. Pet accepted. TV; cable (premium). Indoor/outdoor pool; whirlpool, poolside serv. Complimentary bkfst. Restaurant 6:30-10:30 am, 5-10 pm. Bar 5 pm- midnight. Ck-out 11 am. Coin lndry. Meeting rms. Business servs avail. In-rm modem link. Sauna. Health club privileges. Game rm. Courtyard. Cr cds: A, C, D, DS, MC, V.

⊡ 🐕 ⇌ 🔽 🐾 SC

★ **LA QUINTA INN.** *1335 Garner Ln (29210).* 803/798-9590; fax 803/731-5574; res 800/531-5900. 120 rms, 2 story. S $53; D $59; each addl $6; under 18 free. Crib free. TV; cable (premium). Pool. Complimentary continental bkfst. Restaurant adj 4-11 pm. Ck-out noon. Meeting rms. Business servs avail. Valet serv. Cr cds: A, C, D, DS, MC, V.

⊡ ⇌ 🏃 🔽 🔽 🐾

★★ **RAMADA LIMITED NORTH-WEST.** *773 Saint Andrews Rd (29210), I-26 Exit 106.* 803/772-7275; fax 803/750-1877; toll-free 800/465-4329. 101 rms, 2 story. S, D $50-$65; family rates. Crib free. TV; cable (premium). Pool. Complimentary continental bkfst. Restaurant adj 10:30 am-10 pm. Ck-out noon. Meeting rms. Business servs avail. Valet serv. Health club privileges. Cr cds: A, C, D, DS, JCB, MC, V.

⊡ ⇌ 🔽 🐾 SC

★★ **RAMADA PLAZA.** *8105 Two Notch Rd (29223), at I-77.* 803/736-5600; fax 803/736-1241. 187 units, 6 story. S $66.75; D $74.25; suites

$112.50-$142.50; under 18 free; golf plan. Crib $6. Pet accepted, some restrictions. TV; cable. Pool; whirlpool. Coffee in rms. Restaurant 6:30 am-10 pm. Bar 6:30-10 pm. Ck-out noon. Convention facilities. Business servs avail. In-rm modem link. Bellhops. Valet serv. 18-hole golf privileges. Exercise equipt; sauna. Refrigerator, microwave in suites. Cr cds: A, D, DS, MC, V.

★ **RED ROOF INN.** *7580 Two Notch Rd (29223), at I-20 Two Notch Rd Exit. 803/736-0850; fax 803/736-4270; toll-free 800/843-7663.* 108 rms, 2 story. S $40.99; D $46.99; each addl $6; under 18 free. Crib free. TV; cable (premium). Complimentary coffee in lobby. Restaurant adj 6 am-10 pm. Business servs avail. In-rm modem link. Cr cds: A, C, D, DS, MC, V.

State Capitol

★★ **RESIDENCE INN BY MAR-RIOTT.** *150 Stoneridge Dr (29210), off I-126 Greystone Blvd Exit. 803/779-7000; fax 803/779-0408; res 800/331-3131. www.residenceinn.com.* 128 kit. suites, 2 story. S $99; D $109-$134; family rates. Crib free. Pet accepted, some restrictions. TV; cable (premium). Pool; whirlpool. Complimentary continental bkfst. Coffee in rms. Ck-out noon. Coin lndry. Meeting rms. Business servs avail. In-rm modem link. Valet serv. Exercise equipt. Microwaves; some fireplaces. Some grills. Cr cds: A, D, DS, MC, V.

★★★ **THE WHITNEY HOTEL.** *700 Woodrow St (29205). 803/252-0849; fax 803/771-0495; toll-free 800/637-4008. www.robin.hodgeameristar.com.* 74 kit. suites, 7 story. 1-bedrm $119; 2-bedrm $139. TV; cable (premium). Pool. Complimentary continental bkfst. Restaurant nearby. Ck-out noon. Meeting rms. Business servs avail. Valet serv. Free airport transportation. Health club privileges. Microwaves. Balconies. In residential area. Cr cds: A, C, D, DS, MC, V.

Hotels

★★ **ADAM'S MARK HOTEL & RESORTS.** *1200 Hampton St (29201). 803/771-7000; fax 803/254-2911; res 800/444-2326. Email xprice@adams mark.com.* 301 rms, 13 story. S $129; D $139; each addl $10; suites $225-$450; under 18 free; wkend rates. Crib free. Pet accepted; $50 deposit. TV; cable. Indoor pool; whirlpool. Restaurants 6 am-midnight. Bar 11:30-1 am. Ck-out noon. Convention facilities. Business servs avail. In-rm modem link. Airport transportation. Exercise equipt. Some refrigerators. Some balconies. Cr cds: A, C, D, DS, MC, V.

★★ **COLUMBIA SHERATON.** *2100 Bush River Rd (29210). 803/731-0300; fax 803/731-2839; res 800/325-3535.* 237 rms, 5 story. S $109; D $119; each addl $10; suites $129-$350; under 17 free. Crib free. TV; cable (premium). 2 pools, 1 indoor; whirlpool. Coffee in rms. Restaurant 6:30 am-10:30 pm. Bars; entertainment. Meeting rms. Business center. In-rm modem link. Gift shop. Free airport transportation. Exercise equipt; sauna. Some refrigerators; bathrm phone in suites. Some balconies. Luxury level. Cr cds: A, C, D, DS, ER, MC, V.

★★★ EMBASSY SUITES HOTEL.
200 Stoneridge Dr (29210), on I-126 at Greystone Blvd Exit. 803/252-8700; fax 803/256-8749; res 800/EMBASSY. 214 suites, 7 story. S $99-$139; D $109-$149; under 17 free; wkend rates. Crib free. TV; cable (premium). Indoor pool; whirlpool. Complimentary full bkfst, coffee in rms. Restaurant 11 am-10 pm; Fri, Sat to 11 pm. Bar 2-11 pm; Fri, Sat to midnight. Ck-out noon. Coin lndry. Meeting rms. Business servs avail. In-rm modem link. Gift shop. Free airport transportation. Exercise equipt; sauna. Microwaves, refrigerators. Atrium lobby; glass-enclosed elvtr. Cr cds: A, C, D, DS, JCB, MC, V.

D ⟠ 🏋 🖼 🐾 🚶

B&Bs/Small Inns

★★★ CLAUSSEN'S INN.
2003 Greene St (29205). 803/765-0440; fax 803/799-7924; toll-free 800/622-3382. 29 units, 2 story. S $100-$115; D, suites $115-$130; each addl $10; under 12 free. Crib free. TV; cable (premium). Complimentary continental bkfst; afternoon refreshments. Ck-out noon, ck-in 3 pm. Meeting rms. Health club privileges. Whirlpool. Refrigerators avail. Private patios. In renovated bakery (1928). Cr cds: A, MC, V.

D 🖼 🐾 SC

★★★ RICHLAND STREET BED & BREAKFAST.
1425 Richland St (29201). 803/779-7001; fax 803/256-3725; toll-free 800/779-7011. 8 rms, 2 story, 1 suite. S $79-$110; D $79-$130; each addl $10; suite $140. Children over 12 yrs only. TV; cable. Complimentary continental bkfst; afternoon refreshments. Restaurant nearby. Ck-out 11 am, ck-in 4 pm. Health club privileges. Modern building (1992) in Victorian style. Totally nonsmoking. Cr cds: A, MC, V.

D 🐾 🏋 🏃 🖼 🐾

Restaurants

★★ AL'S UPSTAIRS.
304 Meeting St (29169), 1 mi W on US 1, in National Register Bldg. 803/794-7404. Specializes in veal, pasta, fresh fish. Hrs: 5-10 pm. Closed Sun; hols. Res accepted. Bar. Dinner $11.95-$19.95. Parking. Overlooks river. Views of Columbia's skyline. Cr cds: A, DS, MC, V.

★★ BLUE MARLIN.
1200 Lincoln St (29201). 803/799-3838. www.blue marlinfood.com. Seafood menu. Specializes in shrimp and grits, oyster skillet bienville, blackened catfish. Own pastries. Hrs: 11:30 am-10 pm; Fri, Sat to 11 pm. Closed Jan 1, Dec 25. Bar. Lunch $5.95-$7.45; dinner $9.95-$14.95. Child's menu. Nautical decor in former passenger train station. Cr cds: A, DS, MC, V.

D ⟦🐾

★★ GARIBALDI'S.
2013 Greene St (29205). 803/771-8888. www. garibaldi@logicsouth.com. Specializes in fresh seafood, steak, pasta. Hrs: 5:30-10:30 pm; Fri, Sat to 11 pm. Res accepted. Bar. Dinner a la carte entrees: $6.95-$21.95. Valet parking. Art Deco furnishings. Cr cds: A, MC, V.

D ⟦🐾

★★ HAMPTON STREET VINE-YARD.
1207 Hampton St (29201). 803/252-0850. Specializes in seafood, veal, duck. Own desserts. Hrs: 11:30 am-2 pm, 6-10 pm; Sat from 6 pm. Closed Sun; Jan 1, July 4, Dec 25. Res accepted. Bar. Lunch $6.25-$8.75; dinner $12.50-$18.75. Street parking. In historic Sylvan Bldg (1871). Bistro atmosphere. French posters adorn walls. Cr cds: A, D, MC, V.

★★ HENNESSY'S.
1649 Main St (29201). 803/799-8280. Email henn1649@aol.com; www.surfsc.com/ hennessys. Specializes in steak, poultry, fresh seafood. Hrs: 11:30 am-2:30 pm, 6-9:30 pm; Fri to 10 pm; Sat 6-10 pm. Closed Sun; hols. Res accepted. Bar. Lunch $4.95-$8.95; dinner $12.95-$23.95. Converted hardware store. Cr cds: A, D, MC, V.

D

★★ RISTORANTE DIVINO.
803 Gervais St (29201). 803/799-4550. Specializes in seafood, pasta, veal. Hrs: 6-10 pm. Closed Sun, Mon; Jan 1, Dec 25. Res accepted. Dinner $12.95-$17.75. Casual, intimate dining. Cr cds: A, MC, V.

D

★★ VISTA BREWING & BISTRO.
936 Gervais St (29201). 803/799-2739. Specializes in lobster ravioli with saffron sauce, herb-encrusted salmon, honey-roasted pork loin. Hrs: 11:30 am-11 pm. Closed Sun; Dec 25. Res accepted. Bar. Lunch $5.95-$6.95; din-

ner $14.95-$17.50. Entertainment: jazz Tues. Casual decor. Brewing equipt on view. Cr cds: A, D, DS, MC, V.

D ⊟

Darlington

(D-5) *See also Cheraw, Florence; also see Bennettsville, Hartsville*

Founded 1798 **Pop** 7,311 **Elev** 157 ft
Area code 843 **Zip** 29532
Information Greater Darlington Chamber of Commerce, PO Box 274; 843/393-2641

What to See and Do

NMPA Stock Car Hall of Fame/Joe Weatherly Stock Car Museum. Museum is said to house largest collection of race cars in the world. Major automotive companies have displays tracing the evolution of the racing stock car and accessories from 1950-present; cars, engines, and trophies of famous drivers. (Daily; closed Dec 25) 1 mi W on SC 34 at Darlington Raceway, the oldest superspeedway in the country. Phone 843/395-8821. ¢¢

Annual Events

TranSouth Financial 400. Darlington Raceway. Late-model stock car race. Late Mar.

Southern 500. Darlington Raceway. Five-hundred-mi stock car classic; also beauty pageant, "Southern 500" Festival parade; golf tournament. Preceded by 2 days of trials. Labor Day wkend.

Dillon

(D-5) *See also Bennettsville, Darlington, Florence*

Settled 1887 **Pop** 6,829 **Elev** 115 ft
Area code 843 **Zip** 29536

B&B/Small Inn

★★★ **ABINGDON MANOR.** *307 Church St (29565), S on I-95, Exit 181, 6 mi E. 843/752-5090; fax 843/752-*

6034; toll-free 888/752-5090. Email abingdon@southtech.net; www. abingdonmanor.com. 4 rms, 2 story, 1 suite. S, D $120; suites $160; under 12 free. Parking lot. TV; cable, VCR avail, CD avail. Complimentary full bkfst, coffee in rms, toll-free calls. Restaurant. Bar. Meeting rms. Business servs avail. Concierge. Dry cleaning. Free airport transportation. Whirlpool. Golf. Tennis. Bike rentals. Hiking trail. Picnic facilities. Cr cds: A, DS, JCB, MC, V.

🐾 🛠 🏊 ⛳ 🗲 🔥

Florence

(E-5) *See also Darlington, Dillon, Hartsville*

Settled 1890 **Pop** 29,813 **Elev** 149 ft
Area code 843
Information Greater Florence Chamber of Commerce, 610 W Palmetto St, PO Box 948, 29503; 843/665-0515

Annual Event

Arts Alive. Francis Marion University. Arts, crafts, music, dance, theater, demonstrations, exhibits. Phone 843/661-1225. Apr.

Motels/Motor Lodges

★★ **COMFORT INN.** *1916 W Lucas St (29502), jct I-95 and US 52. 843/ 665-4558; fax 843/665-4558; toll-free 800/228-5150.* 162 rms, 2 story. S $49; D $59; each addl $6; under 18 free. Crib free. TV; cable (premium). Pool; whirlpool. Complimentary continental bkfst. Coffee in rms. Restaurant adj. Ck-out 11 am. Meeting rms. Exercise equipt. Some in-rm whirlpools; refrigerators, microwaves avail. Cr cds: A, D, DS, MC, V.

D ⊠ 🛠 🗲 🔥 SC

★ **DAYS INN NORTH.** *2111 W Lucas St (29501), jct I-95 and US 52. 843/665-4444; fax 843/665-4444; toll-free 800/489-4344.* 103 rms, 2 story. S, D $38-$75; under 12 free; higher rates: race wkends, hols. Crib free. Pet accepted, some restrictions. TV; cable (premium). Pool; whirlpool. Complimentary continental bkfst. Restaurant adj 6 am-midnight. Ck-out 11 am.

Meeting rms. Business servs avail. Exercise equipt; sauna. Some in-rm whirlpools, refrigerators, microwaves. Cr cds: A, C, D, DS, MC, V.

D ◑ ⬛ 🏋 🖃 🐾 SC

★★ **RAMADA INN.** *2038 W Lucas St (29501). 843/669-4241; fax 843/665-8883; res 800/272-6232. www.imichotels.com.* 173 rms, 2 story, 6 suites. S $64; D $69; each addl $5; suites $150; under 18 free. Crib avail. Pet accepted, some restrictions. Parking lot. Pool, whirlpool. TV; cable (premium). Complimentary full bkfst, coffee in rms, newspaper, toll-free calls. Restaurant 6 am-10 pm. Bar. Ck-out noon, ck-in 3 pm. Meeting rms. Business servs avail. Dry cleaning. Exercise equipt, sauna. Golf. Tennis, 4 courts. Cr cds: A, C, D, DS, ER, JCB, MC, V.

D ◑ 🏐 🕴 🏋 🖃 🐾

★ **RED ROOF INN.** *2690 David H. McLeod Blvd (29501). 843/678-9000; fax 843/667-1267; res 800/843-7663.* 112 rms, 2 story. S $36.99; D $43.99-$52.99; each addl $5; under 18 free; higher rates special events. Crib free. Pet accepted. TV; cable (premium). Complimentary coffee in lobby. Restaurant adj open 24 hrs. Ck-out noon. Business servs avail. Cr cds: A, D, DS, MC, V.

D ◑ 🏋 🖃 🐾

★★ **TRAVELERS INN.** *1914 W Lucas St (29501), jct I-95 and US 52 Exit 164. 843/665-2575; fax 843/661-0700; toll-free 800/847-7666.* 143 rms, 2 story, 24 suites. Mar-Apr, Jul-Aug: S $36; D $48; each addl $7; suites $52; under 18 free; lower rates rest of yr. Parking lot. Pool, whirlpool. TV; cable (premium). Complimentary toll-free calls. Restaurant. Bar. Ck-out 11 am, ck-in 1 pm. Exercise equipt. Golf, 18 holes. Cr cds: A, C, D, DS, MC, V.

D ◑ 🕴 🖃 🏋 🖃 🐾

Fort Sumter National Monument

See also Charleston, Kiawah Island

On an island in Charleston harbor. Accessible by private boat or by Fort Sumter tour boat, leaving City Marina, Lockwood Boulevard, Charleston (see), and from Patriots Point Naval Museum, Mount Pleasant.

The national monument includes Fort Sumter, located three miles southeast of Charleston at the harbor entrance, and Fort Moultrie, located one mile east of Fort Sumter on Sullivan's Island. Fort Moultrie is reached via US 17 to SC 703; turn right and follow signs. Fort Moultrie was originally built in 1776, of sand and palmetto logs. Colonel William Moultrie's forces drove British ships from Charleston Harbor at Fort Moultrie in June 1776. The present Fort Moultrie was completed in 1809 and was garrisoned by Union forces in late 1860, when these forces were moved to Fort Sumter.

South Carolina, first state to secede, passed its Ordinance of Secession December 20, 1860. Surrender of Fort Sumter was demanded on April 11, 1861. This demand was refused by Major Robert Anderson, in command of Union forces at the fort. At 4:30 am, April 12, Confederate firing began, and the fort was surrendered after 34 hours of intense bombardment. This attack compelled President Lincoln to call for 75,000 volunteers to put down the rebellion, thus beginning the Civil War. Fort Sumter and Fort Moultrie have been modified through the years. Both were active through World War II.

Fort Moultrie has been restored by the National Park Service; Visitor Center has an audiovisual program depicting the evolution of seacoast defense. Self-guided tour. (Daily; closed Dec 25) ¢

Fort Sumter's ruins have been partially excavated, and a museum has been established. (Daily; closed Dec 25) Contact the Superintendent, 1214 Middle St, Sullivan's Island 29482; 843/883-3123 or 843-883-3124. Daily tour boat (fee). **FREE**

Gaffney

(D-3) *See also Rock Hill, Spartanburg; also see Charlotte, NC*

Settled 1803 **Pop** 13,145 **Elev** 779 ft
Area code 864 **Zip** 29340

Information Cherokee County Chamber of Commerce, 225 S Limestone St; 864/489-5721

Annual Event

South Carolina Peach Festival. Arts and crafts, sports events, entertainment. Mid-July.

Motels/Motor Lodges

★★ **COMFORT INN.** *143 Corona Dr (29341), Exit 92. 864/487-4200; fax 864/487-4637.* 83 rms, 2 story. S $62; D $68; each addl $5; under 18 free; higher rates special events. Crib free. TV; cable (premium). Pool. Complimentary continental bkfst. Ck-out 11 am. Meeting rms. Exercise equipt. Refrigerators, microwaves. Cr cds: A, DS, MC, V.

⌨ D 🏃 ✍ SC 🏋

Georgetown

(F-5) *See also Myrtle Beach*

Founded 1729 **Pop** 9,517 **Elev** 10 ft
Area code 843 **Zip** 29440
Web tidelands.com
Information Georgetown County Chamber of Commerce, PO Box 1776, 29442; 843/546-8436 or 800/777-7705

What to See and Do

Brookgreen Gardens. On site of former rice and indigo plantations; more than 500 pieces of American sculpture in garden; boxwood, massive moss-hung oaks, native plants; wildlife park with native animals. Picnicking. (Daily; closed Dec 25) 18 mi N on US 17, 3 mi S of Murrells Inlet. Phone 803/237-4218. ¢¢¢

Captain Sandy's Plantation Tours. Leaves from Harborwalk Seaport. Phone 803/527-4106 for schedule. ¢¢¢¢

Motels/Motor Lodges

★★ **CLARION CAROLINIAN INN.** *706 Church St (29440). 843/546-5191; fax 843/546-1514; res 800/252-7466; toll-free 800/722-4667.* 89 rms, 1-2 story. May-Aug: S $48-$75; D $54-$75; each addl $10; under 18 free; higher rates hols; lower rates rest of yr. Crib $5. TV; cable (premium). Pool. Complimentary continental bkfst. Restaurant 4-9 pm; closed Sun. Ck-out 11 am. Meeting rms. Business servs avail. In-rm modem link. Cr cds: A, DS, MC, V.

⌨ ✍ 🏋 D SC

B&Bs/Small Inns

★★★ **ALEXANDRA'S INN.** *620 Prince St (29440). 843/527-0233; fax 843/520-0718; toll-free 888/557-0233. Email www.alexandrasinn.com; www. alexinn@sccoast.net.* 6 rms, 2 with shower only, 1-2 story, 1 guest house. S, D $95-$135; guest house $135; guest house 3-day min. TV; cable (premium), VCR avail. Complimentary full bkfst. Restaurant nearby. Ck-out 11 am, ck-in 3-7 pm. Business servs avail. Pool. Some in-rm whirlpools, fireplaces. Built in 1880; Greek Revival. Totally nonsmoking. Cr cds: A, MC, V.

D 🕐 ⌨ 🏃 🎿 ✍ 🏋

★★ **SEAVIEW INN.** *414 Myrtle Ave (29585), N on US 17. 843/237-4253; fax 843/237-7909. Email www.seaview inn.net1seaview@gte.net.* 20 rms, 14 air-cooled, all share bath, 2 story. No rm phones. Mid-Apr-Oct, AP: S $109-$135; D $168-$220; each addl $50; wkly rates. Closed rest of yr. Children over 3 yrs only. Ck-out 11 am, ck-in noon. Built in 1930s. On beach; view of ocean. Cr cds: A, MC, V.

D 🕐 🏃 🎿 ✍ 🏋

★★ **THE SHAW HOUSE B&B.** *613 Cypress Court (29440). 843/546-9663. Email jeshaw@sccoast.net.* 3 rms, 2 story. Mar-Jun: S $60; D $80; each addl $20; children $20; under 10 free; lower rates rest of yr. Parking lot. TV; cable (premium). Complimentary full bkfst, newspaper. Restaurant nearby. Ck-out 11 am, ck-in 1 pm. Meeting rm. Business servs avail. Coin lndry. Exercise privileges. Beach access. Bike rentals. Picnic facilities. Cr cds: A, MC, V.

🕐 🏃 🎿 ✍ 🏋 SC

Restaurants

★★ **COMMUNITY HOUSE.** *10555 Ocean Hwy (29585), 20 mi S on US*

17S. 843/237-8353. Specializes in fresh local seafood, veal, pasta. Own baking, pasta. Hrs: 6-10 pm. Closed Sun. Res accepted. Bar. Wine list. Dinner $10.95-$21.95. Child's menu. In old schoolhouse bldg (1932). Country decor. Cr cds: D, MC, V.
[D]

★★ **RICE PADDY.** *819 Front St (29440). 843/546-2021.* Specializes in seafood, lamb, veal. Hrs: 11:30 am-2:30 pm, 6-10 pm. Closed Sun. Res accepted. Bar. Wine list. Lunch $5.50-$9.95; dinner $15.95-$23.95. Local art displayed. Overlooks Sampit River. Cr cds: A, D, MC, V.
[D] [⊟]

★★ **RIVER ROOM.** *801 Front St (29440). 843/527-4110.* Specializes in grilled local fish, crab cakes, shrimp and grits. Own desserts. Hrs: 11 am-2:30 pm, 5-10 pm. Closed Sun; Jan 1, Thanksgiving, Dec 24, 25. Bar. Lunch $4.75-$11.95; dinner $9.95-$19.95. Child's menu. Restored dry goods store (1880s). View of river. Cr cds: A, MC, V.
[D] [⊟]

Unrated Dining Spot

SYD AND LUTHER'S. *713 Front St (29442). 843/527-3106.* Menu changes daily. Hrs: 11 am-9 pm. Closed hols. Res accepted. Wine, beer. Lunch $5.95-$7.95; dinner $14.95-$28. Child's menu. Entertainment. Cr cds: A, DS, MC, V.
[D]

Greenville

(D-2) *See also Anderson, Clemson, Clinton, Spartanburg*

Founded 1797 **Pop** 58,282 **Elev** 966 ft
Area code 864
Web greatergreenville.com
Information Convention & Visitors Center, 206 S Main St, City Hall Bldg, PO Box 10527, 29603; 864/233-0461 or 800/717-0023

Annual Event

Freedom Weekend Aloft. More than 200 balloonists compete. Phone 864/232-3700. May 25-28.

Motels/Motor Lodges

★★ **COURTYARD BY MARRIOTT.** *70 Orchard Park Dr (29615). 864/234-0300; fax 864/234-0296; res 800/321-2211.* 146 rms, 3 story. S, D $89.95; suites $99.95. Crib free. TV; cable (premium). Heated pool; whirlpool. Complimentary coffee in rms. Restaurant 6:30-10:30 am; Sat, Sun 7-11 am. Coin lndry. Meeting rms. Business servs avail. Valet serv. Exercise equipt. Refrigerator, microwave in suites. Cr cds: A, D, DS, JCB, MC, V.
[D] [🐾] [⚷] [≈] [🏋] [≋] [🔥]

★ **DAYS INN.** *831 Congaree Rd (29607). 864/288-6221; fax 864/288-2778.* 124 rms, 5 story. S, D $59-$69; each addl $5; under 18 free; higher rates special events. Crib free. TV; cable (premium). Pool. Complimentary continental bkfst. Restaurant nearby. Ck-out 11 am. Meeting rms. In-rm modem link. Health club privileges. Cr cds: A, C, D, DS, MC, V.
[D] [≈] [🏋] [≋] [🔥]

★★ **FAIRFIELD INN BY MARRIOTT.** *60 Roper Mountain Rd (29607), I-385 Exit 37. 864/297-9996; fax 864/297-9965; toll-free 800/228-2800.* 132 rms, 3 story. S, D $56; under 18 free. Crib free. TV; cable (premium). Pool. Complimentary continental bkfst. Restaurant nearby. Ck-out noon. Business servs avail. In-rm modem link. Health club privileges. Cr cds: A, D, DS, MC, V.
[D] [≈] [≋] [🔥] [SC]

★★ **HAMPTON INN.** *246 Congaree Rd (29607), off I-385. 864/288-1200; fax 864/288-5667.* 123 rms, 4 story. S $59-$67; D $69-$75; under 18 free. Crib free. TV; cable (premium). Pool. Complimentary continental bkfst. Ck-out noon. Meeting rm. Business servs avail. In-rm modem link. Health club privileges. Cr cds: A, C, D, DS, JCB, MC, V.
[D] [≈] [🏋] [🏋] [≋] [🔥]

★★ **HOLIDAY INN.** *4295 Augusta Rd (29605), I-85 Exit 46-A. 864/277-8921; fax 864/299-6066; res 800/HOLIDAY.* 154 rms, 5 story. S, D $74; suites $79; under 18 free; higher rates special events. Crib free. TV; cable (premium). Pool. Complimentary coffee in rms. Restaurant 7 am-2 pm, 5-10 pm. Bar 4 pm-midnight. Ck-out noon. Meeting rms. Business servs avail. In-rm modem link. Bellhops.

Valet serv. Free airport transportation. Golf privileges. Cr cds: A, D, DS, MC, V.

★ **LA QUINTA INN.** *31 Old Country Rd (29607).* 864/297-3500; fax 864/458-9818. 122 rms, 2 story. S $57; D $63; under 18 free. Crib free. Pet accepted. TV; cable (premium). Pool. Complimentary continental bkfst. Restaurant adj 6 am-10 pm. Ck-out noon. Coin lndry. Business servs avail. Valet serv. Cr cds: A, C, D, DS, MC, V.

★★ **QUALITY INN.** *50 Orchard Park Dr (29615).* 864/297-9000; fax 864/297-8292. www.conradusa.com. 147 rms, 2 story. S $49; D $58; each addl $6; suites $75; under 18 free; higher rates Textile Show. Crib $6. TV; cable. Pool. Complimentary continental bkfst, coffee in rms. Ck-out noon. Meeting rms. Valet serv. Health club privileges. Cr cds: A, D, DS, JCB, MC, V.

★ **SUPER 8.** *1515 Hwy 101 S (29651).* 864/848-1626; fax 864/848-3092; res 800/800-8000. www.super8.com. 61 rms, 2 story, 6 suites. S $45; D $45-$50; suites $80-$90; under 12 free; higher rates special events. Crib free. TV; cable (premium). Complimentary continental bkfst. Restaurant nearby. Ck-out 11 am. Business servs avail. In-rm modem link. Pool. Some refrigerators, microwaves. Cr cds: A, D, DS, MC, V.

Hotels

★★★ **CROWNE PLAZA.** *851 Congaree Rd (29607).* 864/297-6300; fax 864/234-0747; res 800/227-6963. 208 rms, 6 story. S $119.95; D $129.95; each addl $10; under 18 free; wkend rates. TV; cable (premium). Indoor pool; whirlpool, poolside serv. Coffee in rms. Restaurant 6:30 am-10 pm. Bar 11-2 am; closed Sun. Ck-out noon. Meeting rms. Business servs avail. In-rm modem link. Free airport transportation. Exercise equipt. Some refrigerators. Cr cds: A, D, DS, MC, V.

★★★ **EMBASSY SUITES.** *670 Verdae Blvd (29607), I-85 Exit 48B.* 864/676-9090; fax 864/676-0669; toll-free 800/362-2779. www.embassysuites.com. 268 suites, 9 story. S $129; D $139; each addl $10; under 18 free; wkend rates. Crib free. TV; cable (premium). 2 pools, 1 indoor; whirlpool. Complimentary full bkfst. Coffee in rms. Restaurant 11 am-10 pm. Bar 11 am-midnight. Coin lndry. Convention facilities. Business center. In-rm modem link. Gift shop. Free airport transportation. Tennis privileges. 18-hole golf privileges, greens fee $44, pro, putting green, driving range. Exercise equipt; sauna. Refrigerators. Cr cds: A, D, DS, MC, V.

★★★ **HILTON GREENVILLE.** *45 W Orchard Park Dr (29615).* 864/232-4747; fax 864/235-6248; res 800/445-8667. www.greenvillesc.hilton.com. 250 rms, 9 story, 6 suites. S, D $159; each addl $20; suites $350. Crib avail. Parking lot. Indoor/outdoor pools, lap pool, whirlpool. TV; cable (premium). Complimentary coffee in rms, newspaper, toll-free calls. Restaurant 6:30 am-11 pm. Bar. Ck-out noon, ck-in 3 pm. Conference center, meeting rms. Business center. Concierge. Dry cleaning. Free airport transportation. Exercise privileges. sauna. Golf. Tennis, 6 courts. Cr cds: A, C, D, DS, JCB, MC, V.

★★★ **HYATT REGENCY.** *220 N Main St (29601).* 864/235-1234; fax 864/232-7584; toll-free 800/233-1234. 327 rms, 8 story. S $135; D $160; each addl $25; suites $195-$500; under 18 free; wkend rates. Crib free. Covered parking $5; valet $9. TV; cable (premium). Pool; whirlpool, poolside serv. Restaurants 6:30 am-11 pm. Bar; closed Sun. Ck-out noon. Convention facilities. Business center. In-rm modem link. Shopping arcade. Free airport transportation. Indoor tennis privileges. Golf privileges. Exercise equipt. Health club privileges. Cr cds: A, C, D, DS, JCB, MC, V.

★★★ **MARRIOTT.** *1 Parkway E (29615), near Greenville/Spartanburg Airport.* 864/297-0300; fax 864/281-0801. 204 rms, 7 story. S, D $129;

each addl $10; under 18 free; higher rates Textile Show. Crib free. TV; cable (premium), VCR avail. 2 pools, 1 indoor; whirlpool, poolside serv. Coffee in rms. Restaurant 6:30 am-10 pm. Bar 3:30 pm-1 am; Sat to midnight; closed Sun; entertainment. Ck-out noon. Convention facilities. Business center. In-rm modem link. Concierge. Free airport transportation. Tennis privileges. 18-hole golf privileges. Exercise equipt; sauna. Luxury level. Cr cds: A, D, DS, JCB, MC, V.

All Suite

★★ **GUESTHOUSE SUITES PLUS.** *48 McPrice Ct (29615). 864/297-0099; fax 864/288-8203; res 800/214-8373; toll-free 800/214-8378. www. guesthouse.net.* 2 story, 96 suites. S $99; D $119. Crib avail. Pet accepted, fee. Parking lot. Pool, whirlpool. TV; cable (premium). Complimentary continental bkfst, coffee in rms, newspaper, toll-free calls. Restaurant nearby. Ck-out noon, ck-in 3 pm. Meeting rm. Dry cleaning, coin lndry. Exercise privileges. Golf. Cr cds: A, C, D, DS, JCB, MC, V.

Restaurants

★ **BISTRO EUROPA.** *219 N Main St (29601). 864/467-9975. Email bistro eur@aol.com.* Specializes in pepper-crusted tenderloin, Bistro catch. Hrs: 11:30 am-2:30 pm, 5-10:30 pm. Closed Sun; hols. Bar. Lunch $6.95-$8.95; dinner $6.95-$18.95. Bistro decor. Cr cds: A, D, DS, ER, MC, V.

★★ **OPEN HEARTH.** *2801 Wade Hampton Blvd (29687), 5 mi N on US 29. 864/244-2665.* Specializes in aged steak, fresh seafood. Hrs: 5:30-10 pm. Closed Sun; hols. Res accepted. Bar. Dinner $9.95-$25.95. Child's menu. Family-owned. Cr cds: A, D, DS, MC, V.

★★★ **RESTAURANT YAGOTO.** *500 Congaree Rd (29607), in Nippon Center Yagoto. 864/288-8471. www.yagoto. com.* Specializes in sushi, sashimi. Sushi bar. Hrs: 6-9:30 pm. Closed Sun; hols. Res accepted. Bar. Wine cellar. Dinner a la carte entrees: $13-$28. Complete meals: $34.50-$39. Tatami rm. Housed in Japanese cultural center. Tours and tea ceremonies avail by appt. Cr cds: A, D, DS, MC, V.

★★★ **SEVEN OAKS.** *104 Broadus Ave (29601). 864/232-1895.* Specializes in fresh seafood, lamb, beef. Own baking. Hrs: 6-9:30 pm. Closed Sun; hols. Res accepted. Wine cellar. Dinner a la carte entrees: $16.95-$26. Beautifully restored 1895 mansion; 8 fireplaces. Cr cds: A, D, DS, MC, V.

★★★ **STAX'S PEPPERMILL.** *30 Orchard Park Dr (29615). 864/288-9320. www.staxs.com.* Specializes in lamb, beef, fresh fish. Own baking. Hrs: 5:30-10 pm. Closed Sun; hols. Res accepted. Bar. Wine list. Dinner $14-$31.50. Entertainment: Wed-Sat. Tableside preparation. Cr cds: A, DS, MC, V.

★★ **VINCE PERONE'S.** *1 E Antrim Dr (29607). 864/239-2100.* Specializes in fresh seafood, pasta. Hrs: 11 am-10 pm. Closed hols. Lunch $4.95-$7.99; dinner $8.99-$17.99. Child's menu. Cr cds: A, D, DS, MC, V.

Greenwood

(E-2) *See also Clinton, Newberry*

Settled 1830 **Pop** 20,807 **Elev** 665 ft
Area code 864
Information Chamber of Commerce, PO Box 980, 29648; 864/223-8431

Annual Event

South Carolina Festival of Flowers. Arts and crafts, photography display, musical groups, golf and tennis tournaments, theater, water show, Railroad Historical Exhibit, flower shows, Park Seed Flower Day. Phone 864/223-8411. Third wkend June.

Motels/Motor Lodges

★★ **COMFORT INN.** *1215 NE Hwy 72 Bypass (29649). 864/223-2838; fax 864/942-0119; res 800/221-2222.* 83 rms, 2 story. S $52-$60; D $57-$71;

suites $100; under 12 free. Crib free. TV; cable (premium). Pool; whirlpool. Complimentary continental bkfst, coffee in rms. Restaurant nearby. Ck-out noon. Meeting rms. Business servs avail. Valet serv. Exercise equipt. Refrigerators, microwaves. Cr cds: A, C, D, DS, ER, JCB, MC, V.

★★ **EXTENDED STAY GREENWOOD INN.** *919 Montague Ave (29649), US 25N and SC 72 Bypass.* 864/223-3979; fax 864/223-3297; toll-free 800/575-0133. 100 rms, 2 story. S $35-$44; D $40-$49; each addl $5. TV; cable (premium). Pool. Complimentary bkfst. Bar 5 am-10 pm. Ck-out 11 am. Meeting rms. Business servs avail. In-rm modem link. Cr cds: A, C, D, DS, MC, V.

★★ **RAMADA INN.** *1014 Montague Ave (29649).* 864/223-4231; fax 864/223-6911. 100 rms, 2 story. S, D $65; each addl $6; under 19 free. Crib free. TV; cable (premium). Pool. Complimentary coffee in lobby. Restaurant 6-9 am, 6-9 pm; Sat, Sun 7-10 am. Bar 6-10 pm; closed Sun. Ck-out noon. Coin lndry. Meeting rms. Business servs avail. In-rm modem link. Valet serv. Cr cds: A, C, D, DS, MC, V.

B&Bs/Small Inns

★★ **BELMONT INN.** *104 E Pickens St (29620), E on SC 72.* 864/459-9625; fax 864/459-9625; res 844/459-9625; toll-free 877/459-8118. Email Belmont Inn@nctel.net. 25 rms, 3 story. S, D $69-$99; higher rates wkends. Crib free. TV, cable (premium). Complimentary continental bkfst. Dining rm 5:30-9 pm. Bar 4:30 pm-midnight. Ck-out noon, ck-in 3 pm. Business servs avail. Historic bldg (1903); restored. Period reproduction; antique furnishings. Cr cds: A, D, DS, MC, V.

★★★ **INN ON THE SQUARE.** *104 Court St (29646), at Main St.* 864/223-4488; fax 864/223-7067; toll-free 800/231-9109. www.innonthesquare.com. 48 rms, 3 story. S, D $72-$80. Crib $15. TV; cable (premium). Pool.

Complimentary full bkfst; afternoon refreshments. Dining rm 6:30-10 am, 11:30 am-2 pm, 5:30-10 pm; wkend hrs vary. Ck-out 11 am, ck-in 2 pm. Business servs avail. Atrium. Rms furnished with 18th-century reproductions. Cr cds: A, D, DS, MC, V.

Restaurant

★ **BLAZER'S.** *US 221 E & SC 72 E (29649), 8 mi E on SC 72.* 864/388-7999. Specializes in fresh seafood, steak, ribs. Hrs: 11-6 am; Sat to midnight. Closed Sun; hols. Bar. Dinner $7.95-$14.95. Child's menu. Overlooks Lake Greenwood. Cr cds: A, D, DS, MC, V.

Hardeeville

(G-3) *See also Beaufort, Hilton Head Island*

Pop 1,583 **Elev** 80 ft **Area code** 843 **Zip** 29927

Motel/Motor Lodge

★ **SCOTTISH INN.** *Hwy 17 & I-95 (29927), at I-95 Exit 5.* 843/784-2151; fax 843/784-3026; toll-free 800/800-8000. 100 rms, 2 story. S $28.95; D $35.86; each addl $5. Crib free. TV; cable. Pool. Coffee in lobby. Ck-out 11 am. Coin lndry. Cr cds: A, C, D, DS, MC, V.

Hotel

★ **HOWARD JOHNSON INN.** *I-95 and US 17 (29927).* 843/784-2271; fax 843/784-5334; toll-free 800/654-2000. 120 rms, 2 story. Apr, Jul, Oct, Dec: S $39.95; D $58.95; each addl $5; under 16 free; lower rates rest of yr. Pet accepted, fee. Parking lot. Pool. TV; cable. Complimentary continental bkfst, coffee in rms. Restaurant. Ck-out 11 am, ck-in noon. Business center. Coin lndry. Cr cds: A, C, D, DS, MC, V.

Hartsville

(D-4) *See also Bennettsville, Camden, Cheraw, Darlington, Florence*

Settled 1760 **Pop** 8,372 **Elev** 200 ft
Area code 843 **Zip** 29550
Web www.hartsvillesc.com
Information Chamber of Commerce, 214 N 5th St, PO Box 578, 29551; 843/332-6401

Hilton Head Island

(G-4) *See also Beaufort, Hardeeville*

Pop 23,694 **Elev** 15 ft **Area code** 843
Web www.hiltonheadisland.org
Information Chamber of Commerce, PO Box 5647, 29938; 843/785-3673

This year-round resort island, the development of which began in 1956, is reached by a bridge on US 278. The island is bordered by one of the few remaining unpolluted marine estuaries on the East Coast and is the largest sea island between New Jersey and Florida. Its growth was rapid; there are 12 miles of beaches and the climate is delightful. There are numerous golf courses and tennis courts, swimming, miles of bicycle paths, horseback riding, four nature preserves, and deep-sea, sound, and dockside fishing. The facilities also include nine marinas and a paved 3,700-foot airstrip with parallel taxiway. There are more than 3,000 hotel and motel rooms, more than 6,000 homes/villas/condos on the rental market, more than 200 restaurants, and 28 shopping centers. For the less athletic, there are many art galleries and numerous sporting and cultural events.

Annual Events

Springfest. Food, wine, and seafood festivals. Sports events. Concerts, shows, and house tours. Phone 843/686-4944. Mar.

MCI Heritage Classic. Harbour Town Golf Links. Top PGA golfers. Phone 843/671-2448. Mid-Apr.

Hilton Head Island Celebrity Golf Tournament. Palmetto Hall, Indigo Run, and Sea Pines Plantation. Phone 843/842-7711. Late-Aug-early-Sep.

St. Luke's Tour of Homes. Tour of distinctive contemporary houses. Phone 843/785-4099. Oct.

Motels/Motor Lodges

★★ **BEST WESTERN INN AT HILTON HEAD.** *40 Waterside Dr (29928). 843/842-8888; fax 843/842-5948; toll-free 888/813-2560.* 92 rms, 3 story. Mar-early Sep: S $85; D $90; each addl $5; under 19 free; lower rates rest of yr. Crib free. TV; cable (premium). Complimentary continental bkfst. Restaurant adj 11-2 am. Ck-out 11 am. Business servs avail. In-rm modem link. Valet serv. Health club privileges. Pool. Refrigerators avail. Cr cds: A, C, D, DS, JCB, MC, V.
D ⊠ ⊠ 🐾 SC

★★ **FAIRFIELD INN.** *9 Marina Side Dr (29928). 843/842-4800; fax 843/842-4800; toll-free 800/833-6334.* 119 rms, 3 story, 14 suites. Apr-mid-Sep: S $66; D $73; suites $83-$89; under 18 free; golf plans; higher rates wkends; lower rates rest of yr. Crib free. TV; cable. Heated pool. Complimentary continental bkfst. Restaurant nearby. Ck-out 11 am. Business servs avail. In-rm modem link. Golf privileges. Miniature golf adj. Health club privileges. Refrigerator in suites. Picnic tables, grills. Cr cds: A, C, D, DS, MC, V.
D ⊠ ⊠ 🐾 SC 🔧

★★ **HAMPTON INN.** *1 Dillon Rd (29926). 843/681-7900; fax 843/681-4330; res 800/426-7866. www.hampton-inn.net.* 124 rms, 2 story, 20 suites, 12 kit. units. Mar-Sep: S $79-$99; D $84-$104; suites, kit. units $94-$124; under 18 free; lower rates rest of yr. Crib free. TV; cable (premium). Pool. Complimentary continental bkfst. Restaurant nearby. Ck-out noon. Coin lndry. Meeting rms. Business servs avail. In-rm modem link. Free airport transportation. Tennis privileges, pro. 18-hole golf privileges. Exercise equipt. Some refrigerators, microwaves. Cr cds: A, C, D, DS, JCB, MC, V.
D 🐕 ⚓ ⊠ 🎿 🎱 ✈ ⊠ 🐾 ⛷ 🔧

★ **RED ROOF INN-HILTON HEAD.** *5 Regency Pkwy (29928), off US 278. 843/686-6808; fax 843/842-3352.* 112

rms, 2 story. June-Sep: S, D $64.99-$69.99; suites $89.99-$139.99; family rates; wknd rates; higher rates hols; lower rates rest of yr. Crib free. TV; cable (premium). Pool. Restaurant adj 5-10 pm. Ck-out noon. Business servs avail. Some refrigerators, microwaves. Cr cds: A, C, D, DS, MC, V.

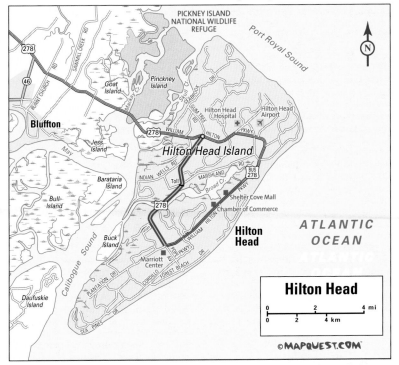

Hotels

★★ **HOLIDAY INN.** *1 S Forest Beach Dr (29938). 843/785-5126; fax 843/785-6678; res 800/845-7018; toll-free 800/423-9897. www.hihiltonhead.com.* 201 rms, 5 story. Jun-Sep: S, D $229; each addl $10; under 18 free; lower rates rest of yr. Crib avail. Valet parking avail. Pool, children's pool. TV; cable. Complimentary coffee in rms, toll-free calls. Restaurant 7 am-9 pm. Bar. Ck-out 11 am, ck-in 4 pm. Meeting rms. Business center. Bellhops. Concierge. Dry cleaning, coin lndry. Gift shop. Exercise privileges. Golf. Tennis. Beach access. Bike rentals. Supervised children's activities. Cr cds: A, C, D, DS, MC, V.

★★ **RESIDENCE INN BY MARRIOTT.** *12 Park Ln (29928), off US 278. 843/686-5700; fax 843/686-3952; toll-free 877/247-3431. Email residence@hardgray.com.* 156 kit. suites, 3 story. Mar-Nov: S, D $119-$169; under 18 free; family rates; golf plans; lower rates rest of yr. Crib free. TV; cable (premium). Pool; whirlpool. Complimentary continental bkfst. Restaurant adj 5-1 am. Ck-out noon. Coin lndry. Business servs avail. Free airport transportation. Lighted tennis. Golf privileges. Bicycles. Fireplaces, microwaves. Private patios, balconies. Picnic tables. Cr cds: A, D, DS, MC, V.

Resorts

★★★ **CROWNE PLAZA RESORT.** *130 Shipyard Dr (29928), in Shipyard Plantation. 843/842-2400; fax 843/785-8463; toll-free 800/334-1881. Email info@crowneplazaresort.com; www.crowneplazaresort.com.* 316 rms, 5 story, 24 suites. Mar-Oct: S, D $339; suites $525; under 18 free; lower rates rest of yr. Crib avail, fee. Valet parking avail. Indoor/outdoor pools, children's pool, whirlpool. TV; cable (premium). Complimentary coffee in rms, newspaper, toll-free calls. Restaurant 7 am-10 pm. Bar. Ck-out noon, ck-in 4 pm. Conference center, meeting rms. Business center. Bellhops. Concierge. Dry cleaning, coin lndry. Gift shop. Exercise rm, sauna. Golf. Tennis, 16 courts. Beach access. Bike rentals. Supervised children's activities. Hiking trail. Picnic facilities. Video games. Cr cds: A, D, DS, MC, V.

★ ★ ★ **DISNEY HILTON HEAD ISLAND RESORT.** *22 Harborside Ln (29928). 843/341-4000; fax 843/341-4130; toll-free 800/800-9100.* 102 kit. units, 2 story. Mid-June-mid-Aug: S, D $175-$490; golf plans; lower rates rest of yr. Crib free. TV; cable (premium); VCR (movies). Heated pools; wading pool, whirlpool, poolside serv, lifeguard. Supervised children's activities, ages 3-16. Restaurant nearby. Ck-out 11 am, ck-in 4 pm. Gift, grocery shop. Guest lndry. Concierge. Valet serv. Lighted tennis, pro. Three 18-hole golf courses, putting green, driving range. Boats. Bicycle rental. Exercise equipt. Lawn games. Microwaves. Balconies. Fishing pier. Cr cds: A, D, DS, MC, V.

★ ★ ★ **HILTON OCEANFRONT RESORT.** *23 Ocean Lane (29928), on Palmetto Dunes. 843/842-8000; fax 843/341-8033; res 800/HILTONS; toll-free 800/845-8001. Email hiltonhh@ hargray.com; www.hiltonheadhilton. com.* 291 rms, 5 story, 32 suites. Jun-Aug: S, D $254; each addl $20; suites $450; under 18 free; lower rates rest of yr. Crib avail. Valet parking avail. Pool, lap pool, children's pool, whirlpool. TV; cable (premium). Complimentary coffee in rms, newspaper, toll-free calls. Restaurant 7 am-10 pm. Bar. Ck-out 11 am, ck-in 4 pm. Conference center, meeting rms. Business center. Bellhops. Concierge. Dry cleaning, coin lndry. Gift shop. Exercise equipt, sauna. Golf. Tennis, 25 courts. Beach access. Bike rentals. Supervised children's activities. Hiking trail. Picnic facilities. Video games. Cr cds: A, C, D, DS, ER, JCB, MC.

★ ★ ★ **HYATT REGENCY.** *1 Hyatt Cir at Palmetto Dunes (29928), on US 278.*

843/785-1234; fax 843/842-4695; res 800/233-1234. www.hyatt.com. 474 rms, 10 story, 31 suites. Apr-Oct: S, D $275; each addl $25; suites $750; under 18 free; lower rates rest of yr. Crib avail. Valet parking avail. Indoor/outdoor pools, lap pool, children's pool, whirlpool. TV; cable, VCR avail. Complimentary coffee in rms, newspaper. Restaurant. Bar. Conference center, meeting rms. Business center. Bellhops. Concierge. Dry cleaning. Gift shop. Salon/barber. Free airport transportation. Exercise equipt, sauna. Golf. Tennis, 25 courts. Beach access. Bike rentals. Supervised children's activities. Cr cds: A, C, D, DS, JCB, MC, V.

★ ★ ★ **PALMETTO DUNES RESORT.** *William Hilton Pkwy (29938), 7 mi SE of Byrnes Bridge, off US 278. 843/785-7300; fax 843/686-2877; toll-free 800/845-6130. Email www.reservations@palmettodunesresort. com; www.palmettodunesresort.com.* 400 rms. Apr, Jun-Aug: Crib avail. Parking garage. Indoor/outdoor pools, lap pool, children's pool, whirlpool. TV; cable. Restaurant. Ck-out 10 am, ck-in 4 pm. Conference center, meeting rms. Fax servs avail. Dry cleaning. Golf. Tennis, 25 courts. Beach access. Bike rentals. Supervised children's activities. Hiking trail. Cr cds: A, C, D, DS, MC, V.

★ ★ ★ **SEA PINES PLANTATION.** *32 Green Wood Dr (29928). 843/785-3333; fax 843/842-1475; toll-free 800/ 732-7463. www.seapines.com.* 400 kit. suites in villas, 1-5 story, 60 houses. June-Aug: 1-4 bedrm units $145-$300; wkly rates; golf, tennis packages; lower rates rest of yr. TV; cable, VCR. Pools, wading pools, poolside serv. Playgrounds. Supervised children's activities (June-Aug); ages 4-12. Restaurants 6:30 am-10 pm. Snack bars. Cookouts. Bars. Ck-out 10 am, ck-in 4 pm. Guest lndry. Grocery, package store. Convention facilities. Business center. Bellhops. Concierge. Sports dir. Lighted tennis, pro. Three 18-hole golf courses, greens fee $65-$180, putting green, driving range. Exercise rm. Sailboat instruction, charter boats, jet skis, windsurfing. Bicycles. Entertainment. Microwaves; some fireplaces. Screened porch in some houses and villas. On 5,000 acres; 605-acre forest, wildlife preserve. Cr cds: A, DS, MC, V.

★★★ **THE WESTIN RESORT.** *2 Grasslawn Ave (29928). 843/681-4000; fax 843/681-1087; res 800/WESTIN1. www.westin.com.* 412 rms, 5 story; 99 villas (2-, 3-, and 4-bedrm). Late Mar-early Nov: S, D $250-$350; suites from $355; villas $280-$325; under 18 free; tennis, golf plans; lower rates rest of yr. Serv charge $6/day. TV; cable (premium), VCR avail. 3 pools, 1 indoor; whirlpool, poolside serv. Playground. Supervised children's activities (Memorial Day-Labor Day, hols). Dining rm 6 am-10 pm. Rm serv 24 hrs. Bars 3 pm-2 am; entertainment (seasonal). Ck-out noon, ck-in 4 pm. Meeting rms. Business center. In-rm modem link. Concierge. Valet parking. Free airport transportation. Tennis, pro. Golf, greens fee (incl cart) $60-$90, putting green, driving range. Lawn games. Exercise rm; sauna, steam rm. Massage. Bathrm phones, refrigerators. Cr cds: A, C, D, DS, ER, JCB, MC, V.

B&B/Small Inn

★★★ **MAIN STREET INN.** *2200 Main St (29926). 843/681-3001; fax 843/681-5541; res 800/471-3001. Email mainstreetinn@digitel.net; www. mainstreetinn.com.* 29 rms, 3 story, 4 suites. Mar-Dec: S $210; D $185; suites $350; lower rates rest of yr. Parking lot. Pool, lap pool, whirlpool. TV; cable. Complimentary continental bkfst, coffee in rms, newspaper. Restaurant. Bar. Meeting rm. Business servs avail. Concierge. Golf, 18 holes. Bike rentals. Cr cds: A, DS, MC, V.

Restaurants

★★ **ALEXANDER'S.** *76 Queens Folly Rd (29928), in Palmetto Dunes Area. 843/785-4999.* Specializes in fresh local seafood, steak, lamb. Own desserts. Hrs: 5-10 pm. Res accepted. Bar. Dinner a la carte entrees: $16-$23.95. Child's menu. Parking. Garden rm decor. Overlooks lagoon. Cr cds: A, D, DS, MC, V.

★★ **CAFE EUROPA.** *Lighthouse in Harbour Town (29928). 843/671-3399.* Specializes in baked shrimp Daufuskie. Own pastries. Hrs: 9 am-2:30 pm, 5:30-9 pm. Closed Nov-mid-Feb. Res accepted. Bkfst $6-$8; lunch $6-$10; dinner $14-$20. Child's menu. Parking. Cr cds: A, MC, V.

★★★ **CHARLIE'S L'ETOILE VERTE.** *807 William Hilton Pkwy #1000 (29928). 843/785-9277.* Specializes in salmon in parmesan crust, rack of lamb, grilled pompano with mango vinaigrette. Own baking. Menu changes daily. Hrs: 11:30 am-2 pm, 6-9 pm. Closed Sun, Mon; hols. Res accepted (dinner). Bar. Wine cellar. Lunch $7.50-$10; dinner $19-$27. Bright, eclectic decor with French artwork on walls. Fresh flowers. Cr cds: A, D, DS, MC, V.

★ **DAMON'S, THE PLACE FOR RIBS.** *Hwy 278, Bldg B (29928). 843/785-6677. www.damons.com.* Specializes in barbecued ribs, onion loaf, steak. Hrs: 11 am-10 pm; Fri, Sat to 11 pm. Bar. Lunch $4.95-$13.99; dinner $6.99-$15.99. Child's menu. Parking. Casual atmosphere. Cr cds: A, D, DS, MC, V.

★★★ **GASLIGHT 2000.** *Park Plaza (29928), in Park Plaza Shopping Center. 843/785-5814. www.hiltonhead. com.* Specializes in quenelles of snapper, Dover sole, beef Wellington. Own baking. Hrs: 6-10 pm. Closed Sun. Res accepted. Dinner $19.50-$26. Parking. Cr cds: A, MC, V.

★★★ **HARBOURMASTER'S.** *Shelter Cove Harbour (29938). 843/785-3030.* Specializes in potato-crusted grouper, blackened tuna mango chutney, rack of lamb. Hrs: 5-10 pm. Closed Sun; Dec 25; also Jan. Res accepted. Bar. Wine cellar. Dinner $14.95-$24.95. Parking. Tableside preparation. View of yacht harbor. Cr cds: A, D, DS, MC, V.

★★ **HEMINGWAY'S.** *1 Hyatt Circle. 843/785-1234. www.hyattregency.com.* Specializes in fresh seafood, steak. Hrs: 5-10 pm. Res accepted. Bar. Dinner $18-$26. Entertainment: exc Mon. Valet parking. Cr cds: A, D, DS, MC, V.

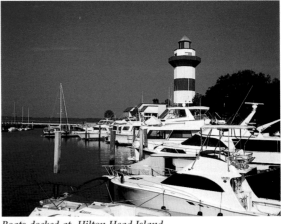

Boats docked at Hilton Head Island

★★ **HOF-BRAUHAUS.** *Pope Ave and Executive Park (29928).* 843/785-3663. Specializes in roast young duckling, sauerbraten, Wienerschnitzel. Hrs: 5-10 pm. Res accepted. Bar. Dinner $9.95-$17.25. 15% serv chg. Child's menu. Festive German decor. Stained-glass windows. Stein and mug collection. Cr cds: A, D, MC, V.

★ **HUDSON'S ON THE DOCKS.** *1 Hudson Rd (29926), 1 mi N off US 278.* 843/342-3636. Specializes in fresh seafood, live Maine lobster. Hrs: 11 am-10 pm. Closed hols. Bar. Lunch $5.95-$11.95; dinner $12.95-$21.95. Child's menu. Entertainment: magician (Memorial Day-Labor Day). Parking. Gift shop. On Intracoastal Waterway; near boat docks. Cr cds: A, C, D, MC, V.

★ **KINGFISHER SEAFOOD AND STEAK HOUSE.** *18 Harbourside Ln (29928), off US 278, on Shelter Cove Harbour.* 843/785-4442. Email *kingfisher@hargray.com; www.hilton headdlc.com/kingfish.htm.* Specializes in seafood. Hrs: 4:30-10 pm; winter hours vary. Closed Dec 25. Res accepted. Bar. Dinner $11-$21.95. Child's menu. Entertainment: guitarist in season. Parking. Windows overlook harbor and marshes. Cr cds: A, D, MC, V.

★★ **LITTLE VENICE.** *Shelter Cove (29928).* 843/785-3300. Specializes in veal chop, zuppa di pesce, chicken a la Florentina. Hrs: noon-2:30 pm, 5-10 pm. Closed Dec 25; also Jan. Res accepted. Bar. Lunch $6.95-$7.95; dinner $13.95-$19.95. Parking. Trattoria atmosphere. Overlooks marina. Cr cds: A, D, DS, MC, V.

★ **LONGHORN STEAK HOUSE.** *841 US 278 A (29928), in South Island Sq.* 843/686-4056. Specializes in steak, salmon, chili. Hrs: 11:15 am-10 pm; Fri to 10:30 pm; Sat to 10:30 pm; Sun from noon. Closed Thanksgiving, Dec 25. Bar. Lunch $6.25-$9.99; dinner $7.95-$18.99. Child's menu. Country Western decor. Cr cds: A, D, DS, MC, V.

★★ **NENO IL TOSCANO.** *105 Festival Center (29928).* 843/342-2400. Specializes in pasta, beef, chicken. Own baking. Hrs: 11:30 am-2 pm, 6-10 pm; Sat from 6 pm. Closed Sun; Jan 1, Easter, Dec 25. Res accepted. Bar. Lunch $8.95-$9.95; dinner $13.95-$24.95. European decor with 2-level dining area. Marble and mahogany bar. Cr cds: A, MC, V.

★★ **OLD OYSTER FACTORY.** *101 Marshland Rd (29928).* 843/681-6040. Specializes in fresh seafood, local oysters, steak. Hrs: 5-10 pm. Closed Thanksgiving, Dec 25. Bar. Dinner $9.95-$21.95. Child's menu. Entertainment: guitarist; vocalist in season. Parking. Overlooks creek, marshes. Cr cds: A, D, DS, MC, V.

★ **REILLEY'S.** *7D Greenwood Dr (29928), in Gallery of Shops.* 843/842-4414. Specializes in cottage pie, corned beef and cabbage, fish and chips. Own ice cream. Hrs: 11:30 am-11 pm. Closed Dec 25. Bar. Lunch, dinner $5.95-$19.95. Sun brunch $5.75-$8.95. Child's menu. Casual

dining. Irish pub atmosphere. Sports memorabilia. Cr cds: A, MC, V.
[D] [≛]

★★ **SCOTT'S FISH MARKET.** *Shelter Cove Harbour (29928). 843/785-7575.* Specializes in fresh local seafood. Hrs: 4:30-10 pm. Closed Sun; hols; also Jan. Bar. Dinner $15-$20. Parking. Nautical decor; view of harbor. Cr cds: A, D, DS, MC, V.
[D]

Unrated Dining Spot

KOKOPELLI. *Orleans Plaza (29928). 843/785-2343.* Specializes in Southwest and Mexican dishes. Own baking, pasta. Hrs: 5-10 pm. Closed Thanksgiving, Dec 25; also Super Bowl Sun. Res accepted. Bar. Dinner $10.95-$24.95. Parking. Cr cds: A, MC, V.
[D]

Kiawah Island

See also Beaufort, Charleston

Pop 718 **Area code** 843 **Web** kiawah-island.com

Information Visitor Center, 22 Beachwalker Dr, 29455; 843/768-5116 or -843/768-5117

Kiawah Island (pronounced KEE-a-wah) is one of the richest natural environments in the Middle Atlantic states. The island is a model for maintaining the ecological balance while allowing human habitation. Named for the Native Americans who once hunted and fished here, the island is separated from the mainland by the Kiawah River and a mile-wide salt marsh.

Extensive environmental study has helped to preserve nature while also providing for human needs. Separate resort areas and private residential neighborhoods have been planned to provide a minimum of automobile traffic and leave much of the island untouched. The Kiawah Island Resort offers activities like golf, tennis, and nature programs that take advantage of the island's natural beauty.

Resort

★★★ **KIAWAH ISLAND RESORT.** *12 Kiawah Beach Dr (29455), at W end of Kiawah Island. 843/768-2121; fax 843/768-9339; toll-free 800/654-2924.* 610 rms, 3 story, 460 villas and houses (1-4 bedrms). Mar-Nov: S, D $135-$225; villas $175-$500; under 18 free; wkly rates; package plans; lower rates rest of yr. Crib free. TV; cable (premium). 7 pools, 1 heated; wading pool, poolside serv, lifeguard. Playground. Supervised children's activities (Easter-Labor Day); ages 3-19. Coffee in rms. Dining rms 6:30 am-11 pm. Snack bar, picnics. Bar 11-1 am; entertainment (in season). Ck-out noon, ck-in 4 pm. Grocery. Package store 3 mi. Meeting rms. Business center. Bellhops. Valet serv. Concierge. Gift shop. Lighted tennis, pro. Four 18-hole golf courses, greens fee $105-$185, pro, driving range. Swimming beach; boats. Canoe trips. Bicycle rentals. Nature walks. Exercise rm. Lawn games. Rec rm. Game rm. Many wet bars, microwaves. On ocean; marina. Cr cds: A, C, D, DS, MC, V.
[≛] [⟆] [≊] [⟰] [⟲] [⟱] [⟳] [SC] [⟴]

Restaurant

★★★ **OLD POST OFFICE RESTAURANT.** *1442 SC 174 (29438). 843/869-2339.* Specializes in seafood. Own baking. Hrs: 6-10 pm. Closed Sun; hols. Res accepted. Bar. Wine cellar. Dinner $17-$20. Former post office bldg; old mail boxes in entry. Local artwork on walls. Cr cds: MC, V.
[D] [≛]

Kings Mountain National Military Park

See also Gaffney, Rock Hill, Spartanburg; also see Charlotte, NC

(20 mi NE of Gaffney off I-85, near Grover, NC)

On these 3,950 rugged acres, a fierce attack by Carolina, Georgia, and Virginia frontiersmen in October 1780 broke up Britain's southern campaign. The mountain men and other patriots were faced with the invasion of their homes by advancing Tories. After traveling more than 200 miles, the Americans surrounded and attacked Cornwallis's left wing, which was encamped atop Kings Mountain spur and under the command of Major Patrick Ferguson. Although untrained in formal warfare, American patriots killed, wounded, or captured Ferguson's entire force of 1,104 Tories. Twenty-eight patriots were killed and 62 were wounded. The battle led to renewed American resistance and American victory at Yorktown. Near the center of the park is the battlefield ridge, with several monuments, including the Centennial Monument, dedicated in 1880, and the US Monument, erected in 1909. The visitor center has exhibits and a film. Self-guided trail leads to main features of battlefield. (Daily; closed Jan 1, Thanksgiving, Dec 25) Contact Superintendent, PO Box 40, Kings Mountain, NC 28086; 864/936-7921. **FREE**

King's Mountain State Park on SC 161, adj to S edge of national military park, has 6,141 acres of scenic drives; living history farm; two lakes. Swimming, fishing, boating; nature, hiking, and bridle trails, carpet golf, picnicking (shelters), store, camping. Interpretive center. Standard fees. Phone 803/222-3209.

Myrtle Beach

(E-5) *See also Georgetown*

Pop 24,848 **Elev** 30 ft **Area code** 843 **Web** www.myrtlebeachlive.com

Information Myrtle Beach Area Chamber of Commerce, 1200 N Oak St, PO Box 2115, 29578; 843/626-7444 or 800/356-3016

With the Gulf Stream only a few miles offshore and dunes to shelter miles of white sand, Myrtle Beach is one of the most popular seaside resorts on the Atlantic coast. Swimming, fishing, golf, tennis, and boardwalk amusements combine to lure millions of vacationers each summer. The many myrtle trees in the area give this resort its name.

What to See and Do

✪ **"The Grand Strand."** Sixty mi of beach from the North Carolina border S to Georgetown. Fishing; camping, golf, tennis, amusement parks.

Myrtle Beach State Park. Approx 300 acres. Ocean and pool swimming, surf fishing (supplies avail); nature trail, picnicking (shelters), playground, stores, camping, cabins. Interpretive center. Standard fees (higher rates Apr-Sep). 3 mi S on US 17 Business. Phone 843/238-5325.

Annual Event

Sun Fun Festival. More than 60 seaside entertainment events, incl parades. First wk June.

Motels/Motor Lodges

★★ **BEST WESTERN DAYTON HOUSE.** *2400 N Ocean Blvd (29577). 843/448-2441; fax 843/448-5957; res 800/258-7963.* 323 kit. units, 5-16 story. June-Aug: S, D $89-$159; each addl $10; under 12 free; wkly rates; golf plans; higher rates wkends; lower rates rest of yr. Crib $5. TV; cable (premium). Heated indoor/outdoor pool; whirlpools. Complimentary coffee in lobby. Restaurant adj 6-11 am. Ck-out 11 am. Coin lndry. Golf privileges. Exercise equipt; sauna. Refrigerators, microwaves. Balconies. On beach. Cr cds: A, C, D, DS, MC, V.

★★ **CARIBBEAN RESORTS & VILLAS.** *3000 N Ocean Blvd (29577), at 30th Ave N. 843/448-7181; fax 843/448-3224. Email caribr@sccoast.net; www.caribbeanresort.com.* 278 rms, 5-14 story, 38 kits., 195 kit. suites. Early June-late Aug: D $79-$122; each addl $6; kit. units $84-$123; kit. suites $153; wkly rates; golf plans; higher rates hols, special events; lower rates rest of yr. Crib free. TV; cable (premium). Supervised children's activities (mid-June-early Sept); ages 5-13. Heated pool; whirlpool. Coffee in lobby. Restaurant adj 6 am-10 pm. Ck-out 11 am. Guest lndry. Business servs avail. Golf privileges. Lawn games. Game rm. Refrigerators. Balconies. On beach. Cr cds: A, C, D, DS, MC, V.

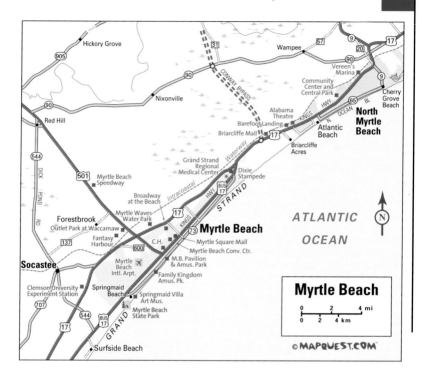

Myrtle Beach

0 2 4 mi
0 2 4 km

© MAPQUEST.COM

★★ **CHESTERFIELD INN.** *700 N Ocean Blvd (29577). 843/448-3177; fax 843/626-4736; toll-free 800/392-3869.* 32 inn rms, 26 motel rms, 3 story, 6 kits. Mid-June-late Aug, MAP: D $123-$145; each addl $31; kit. units $107; family rates; golf plans; lower rates Feb-mid-June, late Aug-Dec. Closed rest of yr. Crib free. TV; cable. Pool. Complimentary coffee in lobby. Restaurant 7:30-10 am, 5:30-7:30 pm. Ck-out 11 am. Golf privileges. Refrigerators. Balconies. On beach. Cr cds: A, DS, MC, V.

★★ **FAIRFIELD INN BY MAR-RIOTT.** *1350 Paradise Circle (29577). 843/444-8097; fax 843/444-8394; res 800/228-2800. Email ffib@sccoast.net.* 111 rms, 4 story. Mid-June-Sep: S $85-$105; D $93-$113; summer wkends, hols (2-4 day min); higher rates bike week; lower rates rest of yr. Crib free. TV; cable (premium). Complimentary continental bkfst. Restaurant nearby. Ck-out noon. Meeting rm. Business servs avail. In-rm modem link. Valet serv. Sundries. Golf privileges. Health club privileges. Heated pool; whirlpool. Some in-rm whirlpools. Cr cds: A, D, DS, MC, V.

★★ **HAMPTON INN.** *1140 Celebrity Circle (29577). 843/916-0600; fax 843/946-6308; toll-free 888/916-2001. www.hamptoninn.com.* 141 rms, 8 story. June-Aug: S $109; D $119-$299; under 14 free; higher rates wkends, hols; lower rates rest of yr. Crib free. TV; cable (premium). Complimentary continental bkfst, coffee in rms. Restaurant adj 11 am-10 pm. Bar 4:30-10:30 pm. Ck-out 11 am. Meeting rms. Business center. In-rm modem link. Free airport transportation. Exercise equipt; sauna. 2 pools, 1 indoor; whirlpool. Refrigerators, microwaves; some in-rm whirlpools. Some balconies. Cr cds: A, D, DS, MC, V.

★★ **HAMPTON INN NORTH-WOOD.** *620 75th Ave N (29572). 843/497-0077; fax 843/497-8845; res 800/426-7866.* 122 rms, 5 story, 20 suites. June-Labor Day: S $109-$129; D $119-$159; suites $149-$219; golf plans; lower rates rest of yr. Crib free.

TV; cable (premium), VCR avail. Indoor pool; whirlpool. Complimentary continental bkfst, coffee in rms. Restaurant adj 11-1 am. Ck-out 11 am. Meeting rms. Business servs avail. In-rm modem link. Coin lndry. Exercise equipt; sauna. Refrigerators, microwaves; some in-rm whirlpools; wet bar in suites. Cr cds: A, C, D, DS, JCB, MC, V.

⬛ 〰 🏃 ⬛ 🔥

★★★ **HOLIDAY INN.** *415 S Ocean Blvd (29577). 843/448-4481; fax 843/448-0086; res 800/HOLIDAY; toll-free 800/845-0313. Email holiday1@sccoast.net.* 306 rms, 8 story. Mid-May-Aug: S, D $99-$149; each addl $10; under 18 free; lower rates rest of yr. Crib free. TV; cable (premium). 2 pools, 1 indoor; whirlpool, poolside serv. Supervised children's activities (Memorial Day-Labor Day); ages 3-12. Coffee in rms. Restaurant 6 am-10 pm. Bars 1 pm-midnight; entertainment. Ck-out 11 am. Coin lndry. Convention facilities. Gift shop. Tennis privileges. Golf privileges. Exercise equipt; sauna. Game rm. On beach. Cr cds: A, D, DS, JCB, MC, V.

⬛ ⛵ 〰 🏃 ✈ ⬛ 🏃 🔥

★★ **LA QUINTA INN AND SUITES.** *1561 21st Ave N (29577). 843/916-8801; fax 843/916-8701; toll-free 800/687-6667.* 128 rms, 4 story. Memorial Day-Labor Day: S, D $135-$153; each addl $7; suites $153; under 18 free; lower rates rest of yr. Crib free. Pet accepted, some restrictions. TV; cable (premium). Complimentary continental bkfst, coffee in rms. Restaurant nearby. Rm serv 11 am-10 pm. Ck-out noon. Meeting rm. Business servs avail. Guest lndry. Exercise equipt. Heated pool; whirlpool. Some refrigerators, microwaves. Cr cds: A, C, D, DS, MC, V.

⬛ ⛵ 〰 🏃 ⬛ 🔥 SC

★ **THE OCEANFRONT VIKING MOTEL.** *1811 S Ocean Blvd (29577). 843/448-4355; fax 843/448-6174; res 800/334-4876. Email info@viking motel.com; www.vikingmotel.com.* 75 rms, 5 story. July: S $85; D $96; each addl $8; suites $127; under 12 free; lower rates rest of yr. Crib avail. Parking lot. Pool, children's pool. TV; cable. Ck-out 11 am, ck-in 3 pm. Fax servs avail. Coin lndry. Golf. Tennis,

6 courts. Beach access. Cr cds: A, C, D, DS, MC, V.

⬛ 🏃 🏊 〰 ✈ 🔥

★ **PALM CREST.** *701 S Ocean Blvd (29577). 843/448-7141; fax 843/444-4799; toll-free 800/487-9233. Email palmcrest1@aol.com; www.palmcrest motel.com.* 29 rms, 3 story, 12 suites. June-Aug: S $64; D $86; each addl $10; suites $128; under 18 free; lower rates rest of yr. Crib avail, fee. Pet accepted. Parking lot. Pool, children's pool. TV; cable. Complimentary toll-free calls. Restaurant nearby. Ck-out 11 am, ck-in 2 pm. Fax servs avail. Bellhops. Coin lndry. Free airport transportation. Golf. Beach access. Picnic facilities. Cr cds: DS, MC, V.

⛵ ⬛ 🏃 〰 ✈ ⬛ 🔥

★★ **PAN AMERICAN RESORT.** *5300 N Ocean Blvd (29577). 843/449-7411; fax 843/449-6031; res 800/845-4501. Email panam@sccoast.net; www.panamericanresort.com.* 80 rms, 6 story, 5 suites. May-Sep: S, D $124; each addl $8; suites $150; under 14 free; lower rates rest of yr. Crib avail. TV; cable. Restaurant 7 am-11 pm. Ck-out 11 am, ck-in 2 pm. Meeting rm. Golf. Tennis, 3 courts. Cr cds: A, DS, MC, V.

🏃 🔥 🔥

★★ **SEA ISLAND INN ON THE BEACH.** *6000 N Ocean Blvd (29577). 843/449-6406; fax 843/449-4102; toll-free 800/548-0767. Email seaisland@sccoast.net.* 112 units, 5 story, 46 kits. Early June-late Aug: D $118-$133; each addl $10; kit. units $124-$139; under 12 free; MAP avail; lower rates rest of yr. Crib free. TV; cable (premium). Heated pool; 2 wading pools. Restaurant 7:30-10 am, 5:30-8 pm. Ck-out 11 am. Meeting rms. Bellhops. Valet serv. Free airport transportation. Tennis privileges. Golf privileges. Refrigerators; some microwaves. Balconies. On ocean; swimming beach. Cr cds: A, DS, MC, V.

⬛ 🏃 🏃 〰 🏃 🏃 ⬛ 🔥

★★ **ST. JOHN'S INN.** *6803 N Ocean Blvd (29572). 843/449-5251; fax 843/449-3306; toll-free 800/845-0624.* 90 rms, 3 story, 28 kits. June-Labor Day: D $95; each addl $5; kit. units $102; under 12 free; golf plan; higher rates hols; lower rates rest of yr. Crib avail. Pet accepted, some restrictions. TV; cable. Pool; whirlpool. Restaurant 7-

11 am. Ck-out 11 am. Meeting rm. Lawn games. Refrigerators. Private patios, balconies. Bathrm phones. Beach opp. Cr cds: A, DS, MC, V.

★ **SUPER 8 MOTEL.** *1591 N US 17 (29582). 843/249-7339; fax 843/249-7339; res 888/249-8819; toll-free 800/ 800-8000. Email dsam53@aol.com.* 61 rms, 2 story. June-Aug: S $65; D $70; each addl $5; suites $80-$85; under 12 free; higher rates: hols, special events; lower rates rest of yr. Crib free. TV; cable (premium). Complimentary continental bkfst. Restaurant adj 11 am-10 pm. Ckout 11 am. Business servs avail. In-rm modem link. Exercise equipt. Indoor pool; whirlpool. Some refrigerators, microwaves. Cr cds: A, C, D, DS, MC, V.

★ **SURF AND DUNES MOTOR INN.** *2201 S Ocean Blvd (29578). 843/448-1755; fax 843/444-9360; toll-free 800/845-2109.* 129 units, 3-7 story, 80 kits. Mid-May-late Oct: S, D $36-$109; each addl $5; kit. units $50-$125; under 18 free; package plans; higher rates: Easter wk, all hol wkends in season; lower rates rest of yr. Crib free. TV; cable (premium). 3 pools, 1 indoor; whirlpool. Playground. Restaurant nearby. Ck-out 11 am. Coin lndry. Business servs avail. Lighted tennis. Golf privileges. Exercise equipt; sauna. Game rm. Lawn games. Refrigerators, microwaves. Some balconies. On beach. Cr cds: A, DS, MC, V.

Hotels

★★ **BEACH COLONY RESORT.** *5308 N Ocean Blvd (29577). 843/449-4010; fax 843/449-2810; toll-free 800/ 222-2141. Email bhcolony@socoast.net.* 222 kit. suites, 22 story. Mid-June-mid-Aug: 1-bedrm $162; 2-bedrm $1,700/wk; 3-bedrm $1,940/wk; 4-bedrm $2,230/wk; lower rates rest of

yr. Crib free. TV; cable. 3 pools, 1 indoor; wading pool, whirlpools, poolside serv. Free supervised children's activities (Memorial Day-Labor Day); ages 6-12. Restaurant (see FUSCO'S). Bar 5 pm-1 am. Ck-out 11 am. Coin lndry. Meeting rms. Free covered parking. Tennis privileges. Golf privileges. Exercise equipt; sauna. Microwaves. Balconies. On ocean, beach. Cr cds: A, C, D, DS, MC, V.

Golfing on Myrtle Beach

★★ **THE BREAKERS RESORT.** *2006 N Ocean Blvd (29577). 843/626-5000; fax 843/626-5001; toll-free 800/ 845-0688. Email info@breakers.com.* 398 units in 4 bldgs, 11, 15, 18 story, 98 kit. suites, 77 kits. June-Aug: D $103-$116; each addl $8; 1-, 2-bedrm kit. suites $137-$202; kit. units $108-$129; under 16 free; wkly rates; golf, tennis plans; lower rates rest of yr. Crib free. TV; cable. 3 pools, 1 indoor/outdoor; wading pool, whirlpool, poolside serv. Free supervised children's activities (June-Labor Day); ages 6-14. Restaurant 7-11 am, 5:30-9 pm. Bar 5 pm-2 am; entertainment. Ck-out 11 am. Coin lndry. Meeting rms. Free airport transportation. Tennis privileges. Golf privileges. Deep sea fishing. Exercise equipt; sauna. Refrigerators; microwaves avail. Private patios; balconies. On ocean. Cr cds: A, C, D, DS, MC, V.

★★ **CARAVELLE RESORT.** *6900 N Ocean Blvd (29572). 843/918-8000; fax 843/918-8199; toll-free 800/845-0893. Email cvell@socoast.net.* 360

rms, 4-15 story, 220 villas, 1-3 bedrm. June-Aug: S, D $90-$126; suites $107-$158; villas $98-$268; lower rates rest of yr. Crib free. TV; cable. 8 pools, 2 indoor; whirlpool, poolside serv. Free supervised children's activities (Memorial Day-Labor Day); ages 4-16. Restaurant 7-10 am, 6-9 pm. Ck-out 11 am. Coin lndry. Meeting rms. Business servs avail. Bellhops. Free airport, bus depot transportation. Golf privileges. Exercise equipt; sauna. Rec rm. Refrigerators, microwaves. Balconies. On beach. Cr cds: A, MC, V.

★★ **DUNES VILLAGE RESORT.** *5200 N Ocean Blvd (29578), at 52nd Ave. 843/449-5275; fax 843/449-5275; toll-free 800/648-3539.* 93 rms, 8 story. Mid-June-mid-Aug: D $115; each addl $8; kit. apts $129; under 14 free; wkly rates; lower rates rest of yr. Crib free. TV; cable, VCR avail (movies). 2 pools, 1 indoor; whirlpool. Restaurant 7-10 am, also noon-2 pm June-Aug. Ck-out 11 am. Guest lndry. Tennis. Golf privileges. Exercise equipt. Refrigerators; microwaves avail. Balconies. On beach. Cr cds: DS, MC, V.

★★ **MYRTLE BEACH MARTINIQUE RESORT.** *7100 N Ocean Blvd (29577). 843/449-4441; fax 843/497-3041; toll-free 888/385-8930. www.mbmartinique.com.* 203 units, 17 story, 92 kits. Mid-June-late Aug: D $139; each addl $10; suites $167-$386; kit. units $149; under 18 free; lower rates rest of yr. Crib free. TV; cable (premium). 2 pools, 1 indoor; whirlpool, poolside serv. Supervised children's activities (mid-June-mid-Aug); ages 5-12. Complimentary coffee in rms. Restaurant 7 am-2 pm, 5-9 pm. Bar 4 pm-2 am; entertainment in season. Ck-out 11 am. Free lndry facilities. Meeting rms. Business servs avail. Golf privileges. Exercise equipt; sauna. Refrigerators, microwaves. Balconies. On ocean, beach. Cr cds: A, C, D, DS, MC, V.

★★ **OCEAN DUNES RESORT AND VILLAS.** *201 75th Ave N (29578). 843/449-7441; fax 843/449-5036; toll-free 800/845-0635. Email sands@sand sresort.com* 138 rms, 8-15 story, 10 townhouses, 45 villas (2-bedrm), 165

tower suites (1-bedrm). Mid-June-mid-Aug: S, D $126-$140; villas $228; suites $138; townhouses $292; advance deposit required for 1-day stay; golf plan; lower rates rest of yr. Crib free. TV; cable. 5 pools, 1 indoor, 1 heated; whirlpool, poolside serv. Free supervised children's activities (Memorial Day-Labor Day); ages 5-12. Restaurant 7-10 am, 6-10 pm. Bar 4 pm-1 am; entertainment. Ck-out 11 am. Coin lndry. Convention facilities. Business servs avail. In-rm modem link. Concierge. Gift shop. Beauty shop. Free airport transportation. Tennis privileges. Golf privileges, pro shop. Exercise rm; steam rm. Game rm. Refrigerators; microwaves avail. Balconies. On beach. Cr cds: A, D, DS, MC, V.

★ **OCEAN FOREST PLAZA.** *5523 N Ocean Blvd (29577). 843/497-0044; fax 843/497-3051; toll-free 800/522-0818. www.oceanforest.com.* 190 kit. suites, 23 story. Memorial Day-Labor Day: 1-bedrm $82-$139; 2-bedrm $139-$229; under 18 free; wkly rates; golf plans; higher rates hols; lower rates rest of yr. Crib free. TV; cable. 2 pools, 1 indoor; whirlpool, steam rm, poolside serv. Sauna. Supervised children's activities (Memorial Day-Labor Day); ages 5-12. Restaurant 7 am-2 pm. Bar 5-11 pm. Ck-out 11 am. Meeting rms. Gift shop. Golf privileges. Game rm. Microwaves. Balconies. Opp beach. Cr cds: A, C, D, DS, MC, V.

★★ **SEA MIST RESORT.** *1200 S Ocean Blvd (29578). 843/448-1551; fax 803/448-5858; res 800/732-6478. Email seamist@sccoast.net.* 827 rms, 2-16 story, 552 kits. Mid-June-late Aug: S, D $80.50-$133; each addl $6; kit. units $99.50-$145; 2-4 bedrm suites $875-$3,250/wk; under 15 free; golf plans; lower rates rest of yr. Crib $7. TV; cable (premium). 1 indoor/outdoor; wading pools, whirlpool. Playground. Supervised children's activities (mid-June-mid-Aug); ages 4-12. Restaurant 5-10 am. No rm serv. Ck-out 11 am. Coin lndry. Convention facilities. Business servs avail. Gift shop. Lighted tennis. Golf privileges. Sauna, steam rm. Game rm. Children's water park. Many refrigerators. Some private patios, balconies.

Picnic tables, grills. On beach. Cr cds: A, DS, MC, V.

Resorts

★★ COMPASS COVE OCEAN-FRONT RESORT. *2311 S Ocean Blvd (29577). 843/448-8373; fax 843/448-5444; toll-free 800/228-9894. Email info@compasscove.com; www.compass cove.com.* 467 rms, 16 story, 350 suites. Jul-Aug: S $132; D $163; each addl $8; suites $163; under 16 free; lower rates rest of yr. Crib avail. Parking garage. Indoor/outdoor pools, lap pool, children's pool, whirlpool. TV; cable (premium). Restaurant 7 am-9 pm. Bar. Ck-out 11 am, ck-in 3 pm. Conference center, meeting rm. Business servs avail. Dry cleaning, coin lndry. Free airport transportation. Exercise privileges, sauna. Golf. Beach access. Bike rentals. Supervised children's activities. Picnic facilities. Video games. Cr cds: A, C, D, DS, MC, V.

★★★ EMBASSY SUITES KINGSTON PLANTATION. *9800 Lake Dr (29572). 843/449-0006; fax 843/497-1017; res 800/362-2779; toll-free 800/876-0010. Email kpres@sccoast.net; www.kingstonplantation. com.* 255 rms, 20 story, 255 suites. June-Aug: S, D $289; each addl $20; suites $289; under 18 free; lower rates rest of yr. Crib avail. Valet parking avail. Indoor/outdoor pools, lap pool, children's pool, lifeguard, whirlpool. TV; cable. Complimentary coffee in rms, newspaper, toll-free calls. Restaurant 6 am-11 pm. Bar. Ck-out noon, ck-in 4 pm. Conference center, meeting rms. Business center. Bellhops. Concierge. Dry cleaning. Gift shop. Salon/barber. Exercise rm, sauna. Golf, 18 holes. Tennis, 9 courts. Beach access. Supervised children's activities. Hiking trail. Cr cds: A, C, D, DS, JCB, MC, V.

★★ FOUR POINTS SHERATON MYRTLE BEACH. *2701 S Ocean Blvd (29577). 843/448-2518; fax 843/448-1506; toll-free 800/992-1055. Email sheraton@sccoast.net.* 214 rms, 16 story, 9 suites. June-Aug: S, D $175; each addl $10; suites $250; under 17 free; lower rates rest of yr. Crib avail. Parking garage. Indoor/outdoor pools, lap pool, whirlpool. TV; cable (premium), VCR avail. Complimentary coffee in rms, newspaper, toll-free calls. Restaurant 6:30 am-10 pm. Bar. Ck-out 11 am, ck-in 3 pm. Meeting rms. Business center. Bellhops. Concierge. Dry cleaning, coin lndry. Gift shop. Free airport transportation. Exercise equipt, sauna. Golf. Tennis. Beach access. Supervised children's activities. Picnic facilities. Video games. Cr cds: A, C, D, DS, ER, MC, V.

B&Bs/Small Inns

★★ BRUSTMAN HOUSE BED AND BREAKFAST. *400 25th Ave S (29577). 843/448-7699; fax 843/626-2478; toll-free 800/448-7699. Email wcbrustman@att.net; www.brustman house.com.* 4 rms, 2 story, 1 suite. Apr-Sep: S $90; D $95; each addl $20; suites $110; children $10; under 12 free; lower rates rest of yr. Parking lot. TV; cable (premium), VCR avail. Complimentary full bkfst, newspaper, toll-free calls. Restaurant nearby. Ck-out 11 am, ck-in 2 pm. Meeting rm. Business center. Free airport transportation. Exercise privileges, whirlpool. Golf. Beach access. Bike rentals. Picnic facilities. Cr cds: A, MC, V.

★★★ THE CYPRESS INN. *16 Elm St (29526). 834/248-8199; fax 843/248-0329; toll-free 800/575-5307. www.acypressinn.com.* 12 rms, 3 story. May-Sep: S, D $175; lower rates rest of yr. Parking lot. TV; cable, VCR avail. Complimentary full bkfst, newspaper, toll-free calls. Restaurant. Ck-out 11 am, ck-in 4 pm. Meeting rm. Business center. Concierge. Dry cleaning. Gift shop. Salon/barber. Exercise privileges. Golf, 18 holes. Tennis, 6 courts. Bike rentals. Cr cds: A, D, DS, MC, V.

★★ SERENDIPITY, AN INN. *407 71st Ave N (29572). 843/449-5268; fax 843/449-3998; toll-free 800/762-3229. Email serendipity-inn@worldnet. att.net; www.serendipityinn.com.* 14 rms, 2 story, 2 suites, 6 kits. June-

Aug: S, D $77-$99; suites $129; kits. $99-$129; lower rates rest of yr. Crib free. TV; cable. Heated pool; whirlpool. Complimentary continental bkfst. Restaurant adj 6 am-2 pm, 5-10 pm. Ck-out 11 am, ck-in 2 pm. Golf privileges. Lawn games. Refrigerators; microwaves avail. Balconies. Picnic tables, grills. Library/sitting rm; antiques. Beach nearby. Cr cds: A, DS, MC, V.

🏃 🏖 ♿

All Suite

★★ **BEACH COVE RESORT.** *4800 S Ocean Blvd (29582). 843/918-9000; fax 843/918-8399; toll-free 800/244-8826. Email bchcove@sccoast.net; www. beachcove.com.*, 16 story, 330 suites. Jun-Aug: S, D $150; each addl $10; suites $150; under 18 free; lower rates rest of yr. Crib avail, fee. Parking garage. Indoor/outdoor pools, children's pool, whirlpool. TV; cable. Restaurant 6:30 am-8 pm. Bar. Ck-out 11 am, ck-in 3 pm. Meeting rms. Business servs avail. Bellhops. Concierge. Dry cleaning, coin lndry. Gift shop. Free airport transportation. Exercise privileges, sauna. Golf. Tennis, 5 courts. Beach access. Bike rentals. Supervised children's activities. Picnic facilities. Cr cds: A, D, DS, MC, V.

D 🍴 ♿ 🏃 🎣 🏖 🎿 🛒 🎨 SC

Restaurants

★ **CAGNEY'S OLD PLACE.** *9911 N Kings Hwy (29577), US 17. 843/449-3824.* Specializes in seafood, chicken, prime rib. Hrs: 5-11 pm. Closed Sun; also mid-Dec-2nd wk Feb. Bar. Dinner $11.95-$18.95. Entertainment: wkends. Nostalgic decor. Cr cds: A, D, DS, MC, V.

D ♿

★★ **CAPTAIN DAVE'S DOCKSIDE.** *US 17 Business (29576), 12 mi S. 843/651-5850. www.webs4you.com/dockside.* Specializes in fresh seafood, aged beef. Hrs: 11:30 am-2:30 pm, 5-10 pm. Bar. Lunch $5.95-$15.95; dinner $12-$25. Child's menu. Nautical decor. View of marsh. Cr cds: D, MC, V.

D SC ♿

★★ **COLLECTORS CAFE.** *7726 N Kings Hwy (29572). 843/449-9370.* Specializes in pan-sauteed crab cakes, grilled filet of beef, Cajun-spiced shrimp. Hrs: noon-midnight. Closed Sun; hols. Res accepted. Bar. Dinner $14.95-$21.95. Child's menu. Parking. International art on walls. Cr cds: A, D, DS, MC, V.

D ♿

★ **DAMON'S THE PLACE FOR RIBS.** *4810 US 17S (29582), approx 15 mi N, in Barefoot Landing Shopping Center. 843/272-5107. www.ribsribs ribs.com.* Specializes in barbecued ribs, prime rib, steak. Hrs: 11 am-10 pm; Fri, Sat to 11 pm. Closed Dec 25. Bar. Lunch $4.50-$6.99; dinner $8.50-$19.99. Child's menu. Overlooks lagoon. Cr cds: A, DS, MC, V.

D ♿

★★ **FUSCO'S.** *5308 N Ocean Blvd. 843/449-4010.* Specializes in seafood, pasta, veal. Own baking. Hrs: 7-10 am, 11 am-2 pm, 4-10 pm. Closed 1st wk Jan. Res accepted. Bar. Bkfst $4.50-$5.45; lunch, dinner $12.95-$21.95. Child's menu. Casual atmosphere. Overlooks pool, ocean. Cr cds: A, D, DS, MC, V.

D SC

★★ **JOE'S BAR AND GRILL.** *810 Conway Ave (29582), approx 15 mi N on US 17. 843/272-4666. www.dine joes.com.* Specializes in steak au poivre, veal Marsala, lobster tail. Hrs: 5-10 pm. Closed Thanksgiving, Dec 25. Res accepted. Bar. Dinner $13.95-$25.95. Child's menu. Overlooks marsh. Cr cds: A, D, MC, V.

D SC ♿

★ **LONGHORN STEAKHOUSE.** *7604 N Kings Hwy (29572), US 17. 843/449-7013.* Specializes in choice steaks, seafood. Salad bar. Hrs: 5-10 pm; Sun to 9 pm; early-bird dinner 5-6 pm. Closed Thanksgiving; also 1 wk in Dec. Bar. Dinner $10.95-$36.95. Child's menu. Western decor. Family-owned. Cr cds: A, D, DS, MC, V.

D ♿

★★ **NICK'S ON 61ST.** *503 61st Ave (29577). 843/449-1716.* Specializes in Chinese chicken salad, triple mocha torte. Hrs: 11 am-3 pm; 5-10 pm. Closed Sun. Bar. Bkfst $5.95-$9.95; lunch $5.95-$9.95; dinner $12.95-$15.95. French bistro atmosphere. Cr cds: A, MC, V.

D ♿

★★ **OAK HARBOUR.** *1407 13th Ave N (29582), 16 mi N, at Vereen's*

Marina. *843/249-4737.* Specializes in prime rib, fresh seafood, veal. Hrs: 5-9 pm; Fri, Sat to 10 pm. Closed Thanksgiving, Dec 25. Res accepted. Bar. Dinner $13.95-$19.25. Child's menu. Overlooks marina. Cr cds: A, D, MC, V.

[D] [symbols]

★ **ROSA LINDA'S CAFE.** *4713 US 17 S (29582), approx 6 mi N. 843/272-6823.* Mexican menu. Specializes in fajitas, pasta, pizza. Hrs: 3-10 pm; Fri-Sun from noon. Closed Dec, Jan. Bar. Lunch $3.95-$6.95; dinner $6.50-$14.50. Child's menu. Mexican, Italian atmosphere. Cr cds: A, D, DS, MC, V.

[D] [symbols]

★★ **SEA CAPTAIN'S HOUSE.** *3000 N Ocean Blvd (29577). 843/448-8082.* Specializes in fresh seafood, steaks, homemade pies. Hrs: 6-10:30 am, 11:30 am-2 pm, 5-10 pm. Bkfst $4.50-$8.95; lunch, dinner $5.50-$29. Child's menu. Sea captain's house design. Flowering shrubs. Ocean view. Cr cds: A, D, MC, V.

[D] [symbols]

★★ **TONY'S.** *1407 US 17 (29582), 15 mi N. 843/249-1314.* Specializes in pasta, pizza, seafood, veal. Hrs: 5-10 pm. Closed Dec-Jan; also Sun Sep-May. Bar. Dinner $8.95-$29.50. Child's menu. Contemporary Mediterranean decor. Family-owned. Cr cds: A, C, D, DS, MC, V.

[D] [symbols]

Newberry

(E-3) *See also Clinton, Columbia, Greenwood*

Pop 10,542 **Elev** 500 ft **Area code** 803 **Zip** 29108

Motel/Motor Lodge

★★ **BEST WESTERN INN.** *11701 SC 34 (29108), jct I-26, Exit 74. 803/276-5850; fax 803/276-9851.* 116 rms, 1-2 story. S $37.95; D $42.95-$47.95; each addl $5; under 12 free. Crib free. TV, cable (premium). Pool. Complimentary continental bkfst. Bar 6 pm-midnight. Ck-out 11 am.

Meeting rms. Business servs avail. Exercise equipt. Cr cds: A, C, D, DS, MC, V.

[D] [symbols]

Orangeburg

(E-4) *See also Aiken, Santee*

Settled 1730s **Pop** 13,739 **Elev** 245 ft **Area code** 803 **Zip** 29115
Information Orangeburg County Chamber of Commerce, 1570 John C. Calhoun Dr, Box 328, 29116-0328; 803/534-6821

Named for the Prince of Orange, this community is the seat of Orangeburg County, one of the most prosperous farm areas in the state. Manufacturing plants for wood products, ball bearings, textiles, textile equipment, chemicals, hand tools, and lawn mowers are all located within the county.

What to See and Do

Edisto Memorial Gardens. City-owned 110-acre site. Seasonal flowers bloom all yr; more than 3,200 rose bushes, camellias, azaleas; also many flowering trees. Gardens (daily). Wetlands boardwalk park. Tennis courts, picnic areas, shelters nearby, playground. S on US 301, within city limits, alongside N Edisto River. Phone 803/533-6020. **FREE**

South Carolina State University. (1896) 5,000 students. 300 College St NE. Phone 803/536-7000. On campus is

I.P. Stanback Museum and Planetarium. Museum has changing exhibits (Sep-May, Mon-Fri; closed hols). Planetarium shows (Oct-Apr, 2nd and 4th Sun; closed hols). Phone 803/536-7174 for res. ¢

Annual Event

Orangeburg County Fair. Fairgrounds. Late Sep-early Oct.

Motel/Motor Lodge

★ **DAYS INN.** *3691 St. Matthews Rd (29115), on US 601N. 803/531-2590; fax 803/531-2829; toll-free 800/ 329-*

7466. 75 rms. S $45-$50; D $50-$60; each addl $7; under 12 free. Crib free. TV; cable (premium). Pool. Complimentary continental bkfst. Ck-out 11 am. Some refrigerators; microwaves avail. Cr cds: A, C, D, DS, MC, V.

D ⇌ ⇥ ⌖ SC

★★ **HOLIDAY INN.** *1415 John C. Calhoun Dr (29115).* 803/531-4600; fax 803/516-0187. Email gm.sc206@— hotel. 160 rms, 2 story. S $68-$78; D $76-$86; each addl $8; under 19 free. Crib free. Pet accepted. TV; cable (premium). Heated pool. Restaurant 6:30 am-2 pm, 5:30-9 pm; Sat, Sun from 7 am. Bar; closed Sun. Ck-out noon. Meeting rms. Business servs avail. In-rm modem link. Valet serv. Cr cds: A, D, DS, MC, V.

D ⌖ ⌖ ⇌ ⌿ ⇥ ⌖

Rock Hill

(D-4) *See also Chester, Gaffney; also see Charlotte, NC*

Founded 1852 **Pop** 41,643 **Elev** 667 ft **Area code** 803 **Web** www.yccvb.com

Information York County Convention & Visitors Bureau, 201 E Main St, PO Box 11377, 29731; 803/329-5200 or; 800/866-5200

Both a college and an industrial town, Rock Hill takes its name from the flint rock that had to be cut through when a railroad was being built through town.

What to See and Do

Andrew Jackson State Park. Approx 360 acres. Lake fishing, boating (rentals); nature trail, picnicking (shelters), playground, camping, recreation bldg, outdoor amphitheater. Log house museum contains documents, exhibits of Jackson lore. One-rm school with exhibits. Standard fees. 9 mi N on US 521. Phone 803/285-3344.

Kings Mountain State Park. (See KINGS MOUNTAIN NATIONAL MILITARY PARK).

Winthrop University. (1886) 5,000 students. Coeducational; 100 undergraduate and graduate programs. Concerts, lectures, sports, plays; art galleries. Large lake and recreational area. Oakland Ave. Phone 803/323-2236.

Annual Event

"Come-See-Me." Art shows, tour of houses, entertainment, road race, concerts. Ten days early Apr.

Motels/Motor Lodges

★★ **COMFORT INN.** *3725 Ave of the Carolinas (29708), N on I-77, Exit 90.* 803/548-5200; fax 803/548-6692; toll-free 800/228-5150. Email ft.mill071@rfsmgmt.com. 155 rms, 4 story. S $65-$95; D $75-$105; suites, kit. unit $130-$160; under 18 free; higher rates race weekends. Crib free. TV; cable (premium). Pool. Complimentary continental bkfst. Restaurant adj 6 am-10 pm. Ck-out 11 am. Meeting rms. In-rm modem link. Valet serv. Exercise equipt. Refrigerator in suites. Cr cds: A, C, D, DS, ER, JCB, MC, V.

D ⇌ ⌿ ⇥ ⌖ SC

★★ **COUNTRY INN AND SUITES.** *865 Patriot Pkwy (29730).* 803/329-5151; fax 803/329-5811; res 800/456-4000. www.countryinns.com. 43 rms, 3 story, 6 suites. S, D $69; suites $99; under 18 free; higher rates special events. Crib free. TV; cable (premium). Complimentary continental bkfst, coffee in rms. Restaurant nearby. Ck-out noon. Meeting rms. Business servs avail. In-rm modem link. Exercise equipt. Pool. Refrigerators, microwaves. Wet bar in suites. Cr cds: A, D, DS, MC, V.

D ⌖ ⌿ ⇌ ⌿ ⌿ ⇥ ⌖

★ **DAYS INN SOUTH.** *3482 Carowinds Blvd (29715), approx 5 mi N on I-77 Exit 90.* 803/548-8000; fax 803/548-6058; res 800/329-7466. Email daysinn@charlotte.infi.net; www.the.daysinn.com/ftmill00806. 119 rms, 2 story. Jun-Aug: Crib avail. Pet accepted, fee. Parking lot. Pool. TV; cable (premium). Complimentary continental bkfst, newspaper. Restaurant. Ck-out 11 am, ck-in 3 pm. Business servs avail. Golf. Cr cds: A, C, D, DS, JCB, MC, V.

D ⌖ ⌿ ⇌ ⇥ ⌖

★★ **HAMPTON INN.** *2111 Tabor Dr (29730).* 803/325-1100; fax 803/325-7814; res 800/HAMPTONS. Email rhhampton@rhtc.net. 162 rms, 5 story,

33 suites. S $75; D $79; suites $99-$149; under 18 free; higher rates special events. Crib avail. TV; cable (premium), VCR avail. Complimentary continental bkfst, coffee in rms. Restaurant nearby. Ck-out 11 am. Meeting rms. Business center. In-rm modem link. Coin lndry. Exercise equipt; sauna. Pool. Refrigerator, microwave in suites. Cr cds: A, C, D, DS, MC, V.

★★ **HOLIDAY INN.** *2640 N Cherry Rd (29730), jct I-77, US 21N.* 803/329-1122; fax 803/329-1072; toll-free 877/256-7399. 125 rms, 2 story. S, D $79; each addl $5; suites $95-$150; under 18 free. Crib free. Pet accepted, some restrictions; deposit. TV, cable (premium). Pool. Coffee in rms. Restaurant 6:30 am-10 pm. Bar 11-2 am, Sat to midnight. Ck-out noon. Coin lndry. Business servs avail. In-rm modem link. Airport transportation. Cr cds: A, D, MC, V.

Hotels

★ **ECONO LODGE.** *962 Riverview Rd (29730), I-77 Exit 82B.* 803/329-3232; fax 803/329-3232; res 800/553-2666. 105 rms, 2 story. Mar-Sep: S $40.95; D $44.95; each addl $6; under 16 free; lower rates rest of yr. Crib avail. Pet accepted, some restrictions, fee. Street parking. TV; cable (DSS), VCR avail. Complimentary continental bkfst, coffee in rms, newspaper, toll-free calls. Restaurant. Ck-out 11 am, ck-in 2 pm. Business servs avail. Exercise privileges. Golf, 18 holes. Tennis, 3 courts. Cr cds: A, C, D, DS, ER, JCB, MC.

★★ **RAMADA HOTEL CAROWINDS.** *225 Carowinds Blvd (29715), I-77 Carowinds Exit.* 803/548-2400; fax 803/548-6382; toll-free 800/237-8753. 208 rms, 11 story. S, D $71-$85; each addl $10; under 18 free; higher rates race wkends. Crib free. Pet accepted. TV; cable (premium). Pool. Complimentary bkfst. Restaurant 6:30 am-2 pm, 5-10 pm; Fri, Sat to 11 pm. Bar 4:30-11 pm. Ck-out noon. Coin lndry. Meeting rms. Business center. In-rm modem link. Free airport transportation.

Exercise equipt. Tennis. Cr cds: A, D, DS, MC, V.

B&B/Small Inn

★★ **EAST MAIN GUEST HOUSE.** *600 E Main St (29730).* 803/366-1161; fax 803/366-1210. Email mamawmel@ yahoo.com; www.bline.com/sc/east main. 3 rms. D $79; each addl $15; suites $89; under 12 free. Crib avail, fee. Parking lot. TV; cable, VCR avail, CD avail. Complimentary full bkfst. Restaurant. Ck-out noon, ck-in 3 pm. Business servs avail. Golf. Tennis, 6 courts. Picnic facilities. Cr cds: MC, V.

Restaurant

★ **TAM'S TAVERN.** *1027 Oakland Ave (29732).* 803/329-2226. Specializes in seafood, beef. Hrs: 11 am-3 pm, 5-10 pm; Fri, Sat to 10:30 pm. Closed Sun; hols. Res accepted. Bar. Lunch $4.95-$6.95; dinner $5.95-$16.95. Child's menu. Parking. Cr cds: A, D, DS, MC, V.

Santee

See also Orangeburg

Pop 638 **Elev** 250 ft **Area code** 803 **Zip** 29142
Web www.santeecoopercountry.org
Information Santee-Cooper Country, PO Drawer 40; 803/854-2131 or 800/227-8510 outside SC

Motels/Motor Lodges

★★ **BEST WESTERN INN.** *SC 6 (29142), I-95 Exit 98 E.* 803/854-3089; fax 803/854-3093; res 800/528-1234. 108 rms. S $50-$60; D $50-$65; under 12 free. Crib $4. TV; cable (premium). Heated pool. Complimentary continental bkfst. Restaurant 5-9:30 pm. Ck-out 11 am. Business servs avail. Some in-rm whirlpools. 18-hole golf privileges. Cr cds: A, D, DS, MC, V.

★ **DAYS INN.** *9074 Old #6 Hwy (29142). 803/854-2175; fax 803/854-2835; toll-free 800/329-7466.* 119 rms, 2 story. S $30-$50; D $40-$60; each addl $6; under 12 free; golf plans. Crib free. Pet accepted, some restrictions; $6. TV; cable (premium). Pool. Playground. Complimentary full bkfst. Restaurant 6-10 am, 5-9 pm. Ck-out noon. Guest lndry. Business servs avail. 18-hole golf privileges. Refrigerators avail. Cr cds: A, C, D, DS, MC, V.

🐕 ➳ 🏖 🔥 **SC** 🍴

Spartanburg

(D-3) *See also Clinton, Gaffney, Greenville*

Founded 1785 **Pop** 43,467 **Elev** 816 ft
Area code 864
Information Convention & Visitors Bureau, 105 N Pine St, PO Box 1636, 29304; 864/594-5050

Annual Event

Piedmont Interstate Fair. Art exhibit, livestock and flower shows, needlecraft and food displays; auto race. Phone 864/582-7042. Second full wk Oct.

Motels/Motor Lodges

★★ **COMFORT INN.** *2070 New Cut Rd (29303). 864/576-2992; fax 864/576-2992; toll-free 800/638-7949.* 99 rms, 2 story. S $45-$55; D $55-$85; each addl $6; suites $125; under 18 free. Crib free. TV; cable. Pool. Complimentary continental bkfst. Ck-out 11 am. Refrigerators, microwaves avail. Cr cds: A, C, D, DS, ER, JCB, MC, V.

🅳 ➳ 🏖 🔥 **SC**

★ **DAYS INN.** *1000 Hearon Circle (29303), jct I-85 and I-585. 864/503-9048; fax 864/503-0576.* 138 rms, 2-3 story. No elvtr. S $58-$64; D $64-$68; each addl $7. Crib free. TV. Pool. Coffee in rms. Restaurant 6-10:30 am. Bar 5 pm-2 am; entertainment exc Sun. Ck-out noon. Meeting rms. Business servs avail. Bellhops. Valet serv. Cr cds: A, D, DS, MC, V.

🅳 🐶 ➳ 🏃 🏋 🏖 🔥

★★ **HAMPTON INN.** *4930 College Dr (29301). 864/576-6080; fax 864/587-8901; toll-free 800/426-7866.* 110 rms, 2 story. S $55-$57; D $60-$62; under 18 free. Crib free. TV; cable. Pool. Complimentary continental bkfst. Ck-out noon. Meeting rm. Business servs avail. Cr cds: A, C, D, DS, MC, V.

🅳 ➳ 🏖 🐾 **SC**

Hotels

★★ **QUALITY HOTEL INN AND CONFERENCE CENTER.** *7136 Asheville Hwy (29303). 864/503-0780; fax 864/503-0780; toll-free 800/221-2222. Email quality169@msn.com; www.choicehotels,com.* 136 rms, 6 story, 3 suites. Apr, Oct: S $99; D $109; each addl $5; suites $145; under 18 free; lower rates rest of yr. Crib avail. Pet accepted, some restrictions. Parking lot. Pool. TV; cable (premium), VCR avail. Complimentary full bkfst, coffee in rms, newspaper, toll-free calls. Restaurant. Bar. Ck-out noon, ck-in 3 pm. Meeting rms. Business center. Dry cleaning. Free airport transportation. Exercise privileges. Golf, 18 holes. Tennis. Cr cds: A, C, D, DS, JCB, MC, V.

🅳 🐶 🍴 🏋 ➳ 🏃 🏖 🐾 🏃

★★ **RAMADA INN.** *200 International Dr (29303), jct I-26 and I-85 Exit 71. 864/576-5220; fax 864/574-1243; res 800/272-6232; toll-free 800/972-7511. www.ramada.com.* 223 rms, 3 story, 1 suite. S, D $89; suites $150; under 18 free. Crib avail. Pet accepted, some restrictions, fee. Parking lot. Indoor pool, children's pool, whirlpool. TV; cable (premium), VCR avail. Complimentary continental bkfst, coffee in rms, newspaper, toll-free calls. Restaurant 6:30 am-10 pm. Bar. Ck-out 11 am, ck-in 3 pm. Meeting rms. Fax servs avail. Dry cleaning, coin lndry. Free airport transportation. Exercise privileges, sauna. Golf. Tennis, 10 courts. Supervised children's activities. Cr cds: A, D, DS, MC, V.

🅳 🐶 🍴 🏋 ➳ 🏃 🏖 🐾

Sumter

(E-4) *See also Camden, Columbia*

Settled 1785 **Pop** 36,933 **Elev** 173 ft
Area code 803
Web www.sumter.sc.us
Information Convention & Visitors
Bureau, 32 E Calhoun St, PO Box
1449, 29150; 803/778-5434 or
800/688-4748

Long the center of a prosperous agricultural area, Sumter has, in recent
years, become an industrial center.
Both the city and county are named
for General Thomas Sumter, the
"fighting gamecock" of the Revolutionary War. As a tourism spot,
Sumter offers a unique contrast of
antebellum mansions and modern
facilities. Shaw Air Force Base, headquarters of the 9th Air Force and the
363rd Tactical Fighter Wing, is
nearby.

Poinsett State Park. Approx 1,000
acres of mountains, swamps. Named
for Joel Poinsett, who introduced the
poinsettia (which originated in Mexico) to the US. Spanish moss, mountain laurel, rhododendron. Lake
swimming, fishing, boating (rentals);
hiking and nature trails, picnicking
(shelters), playground, primitive and
improved camping (dump station),
cabins, nature center, programs.
Standard fees. 18 mi SW via SC 763,
261. Phone 803/494-8177.

Swan Lake Iris Gardens. Covers 150
acres; Kaempferi and Japanese iris;
seasonal plantings, nature trails;
ancient cypress, oak, and pine trees;
45-acre lake with all 8 species of
swan. Picnicking, playground. (Daily)
Home to the Iris Festival held every
May. (See ANNUAL EVENTS) W Liberty St. **FREE**

Annual Events

Sumter Iris Festival. Fireworks display, parade, art show, golf and tennis tournaments, barbecue cook-off,
local talent exhibition, square dance,
iris gardens display. Late May.

Fall Fiesta of Arts. Swan Lake Gardens.
Features visual and performing arts,
concerts, and choral groups. Phone
803/436-2258. Third wkend Oct.

Motels/Motor Lodges

★★ **HOLIDAY INN.** *2390 Broad St
(29150). 803/469-9001; fax 803/469-
9070; toll-free 800/465-4329.* 124 rms,
2 story. S, D $59-$79; each addl $6;
under 19 free. Crib free. TV; cable
(premium). Pool. Complimentary
bkfst buffet. Coffee in rms. Restaurant 6-9 am, 5:30-10 pm; Sat, Sun
6:30-10 am, 5:30-10 pm. Ck-out
noon. Meeting rms. Business center.
In-rm modem link. Valet serv. Tennis
privileges. Exercise equipt. Microwaves avail. Cr cds: A, C, D, DS, JCB,
MC, V.

⬛ 🏌 🏊 🎿 ⛷ SC 🚶

★ **TRAVELERS INN.** *Hwy 521 &
76/378 Broad St (29151). 803/469-
9210; fax 803/469-4306; toll-free
800/304-6389.* 104 rms. S $32.95; D
$35.95-$40.95; each addl $5; higher
rates: hol wkends, special events.
Crib free. TV; cable (premium). Pool.
Complimentary continental bkfst.
Ck-out 11 am. Cr cds: A, C, D, DS,
MC, V.

⬛ 🏊 🎿 🔥

Hotel

★★ **RAMADA INN.** *226 N Washington St (29151), on US 76/378/521.
803/775-2323; fax 803/773-9500; res
800/272-6232; toll-free 800/457-6884.
Email ramadagolf@aol.com; www.
ramadagolf.com.* 126 rms, 3 story.
Mar-Apr, Jun-Aug: S $69; D $76;
each addl $7; under 18 free; lower
rates rest of yr. Crib avail. Pet
accepted, some restrictions, fee. Parking lot. Pool. TV; cable (premium).
Complimentary full bkfst, coffee in
rms, newspaper, toll-free calls.
Restaurant. Bar. Ck-out noon, ck-in 3
pm. Meeting rms. Business center.
Dry cleaning, coin lndry. Exercise
privileges. Golf. Tennis, 20 courts.
Downhill skiing. Hiking trail. Picnic
facilities. Cr cds: A, C, D, DS, JCB,
MC, V.

⬛ 🐾 🏌 🎿 ⛷ 🎾 🏌 🏊 🎿 🚶

B&Bs/Small Inns

★★ **BED AND BREAKFAST OF
SUMTER.** *6 Park Ave (29150). 803/
773-2903; fax 803/775-6943; toll-free
888/786-8372. www.bbonline.com/
sc/sumter.* 4 rms, 2 story. S $70; D

$80. Parking lot. TV; cable. Complimentary full bkfst, coffee in rms, newspaper, toll-free calls. Restaurant. Ck-out 10 am, ck-in 3 pm. Business servs avail. Exercise privileges. Tennis, 2 courts. Supervised children's activities. Cr cds: DS, MC, V.

★★★ **MAGNOLIA HOUSE BED & BREAKFAST.** *230 Church St (29150). 803/775-6694; toll-free 888/666-0296. Email magnoliahouse@sumter.net; www.bbonline.com/sc/magnolia.* 3 rms, 2 story, 1 suite. Apr-Sep: S $85; D $95; each addl $15; suites $145; children $10; under 15 free; lower rates rest of yr. Pet accepted, some restrictions. Parking lot. TV; cable. Complimentary full bkfst. Restaurant. Ck-out 11 am, ck-in 3 pm. Internet access avail. Exercise privileges. Golf. Tennis, 3 courts. Cr cds: A, DS, MC, V.

Walterboro

(F-4) *See also Beaufort, Charleston*

Settled 1784 **Pop** 5,492 **Elev** 69 ft
Area code 843 **Zip** 29488
Web www.pride-net.com

Information Walterboro-Colleton Chamber of Commerce, 109 Benson St, PO Box 426; 843/549-9595

Settled in 1784 by Charleston plantation owners as a summer resort area, Walterboro has retained its charm of yesterday despite its growth. The town boasts a casual pace and rural lifestyle where people can enjoy fishing and hunting, early-19th-century architectural designs, plantations, and beach and recreational facilities.

Annual Events

Mount Carmel Herb Festival. Mt Carmel Rd. Features weed walks, herb walks, cook with herbs, herb gardening; sale of herbs, soaps, candles; music. Phone 843/538-3505. Mar.

Rice Festival. Entertainment, parade, arts and crafts; street dances, soapbox derby. Phone 803/549-1079. Last full wkend Apr.

Edisto Riverfest. Colleton State Park. Canoe and kayak trips, river rafting,

music, displays and workshops. For info contact SC Dept of Parks, Recreation, and Tourism, 1205 Pendleton St, Columbia 29201; 803/734-0156. June.

Motels/Motor Lodges

★ **ECONO LODGE.** *1145 Snider's Hwy (29488), I-95 and SC 63. 843/538-3830; fax 843/538-3341; res 800/553-2666. www.econolodgelowcountry.com.* 100 rms, 1-2 story. S, D $32.95-$65; each addl $5; under 18 free. Crib free. TV, cable (premium). Complimentary continental bkfst. Coffee in rms. Restaurant opp open 6 am-11 pm. Ck-out 11 am. Cr cds: A, D, DS, MC, V.

★ **TOWN AND COUNTRY INN.** *97 Downs Ln (29488), jct SC 63, I-95 Exit 53. 843/538-5911; fax 843/538-5911; res 800/757-1237.* 96 rms, 2 story. S $26.95-$29.95; D $36.95; each addl $4; under 18 free. Crib free. Pet accepted. TV; cable. Pool. Playground. Complimentary continental bkfst. Restaurant 6 am-10 pm. Ck-out 11 am. Business servs avail. Private patios, balconies. Cr cds: A, C, D, DS, MC, V.

Hotel

★★ **HOLIDAY INN.** *518 Sniders HW (29488). 843/538-5473; fax 843/538-5473; res 800/465-4329. Email rbwsshma@h-m-a.net.* 171 rms, 2 story. Apr-Oct: S, D $75; under 18 free; lower rates rest of yr. Crib avail. Pet accepted, fee. Parking lot. Pool, children's pool. TV; cable (premium). Complimentary coffee in rms, toll-free calls. Restaurant 6:30 am-9 pm, closed Sat. Ck-out noon, ck-in 2 pm. Meeting rms. Business servs avail. Dry cleaning. Golf, 18 holes. Tennis, 2 courts. Cr cds: A, D, DS, JCB, MC, V.

TENNESSEE

Handsomely rugged and rough-hewn, Tennessee reveals itself most characteristically in a 480-mile stretch from Mountain City at its northeastern boundary, southwest to Memphis and the Mississippi River, with its twisting western shore. In a place of individualistic, strong-minded people, history and legend blend into folklore based on the feats of Davy Crockett, Daniel Boone, Andrew Jackson, and Sam Houston. It is a state of mountain ballads and big-city ballet, of water-powered mills and atomic energy plants.

Population: 4,877,185
Area: 42,244 square miles
Elevation: 182-6,643 feet
Peak: Clingmans Dome (Sevier County)
Entered Union: June 1, 1796 (16th state)
Capital: Nashville
Nickname: Volunteer State
Flower: Iris
Bird: Mockingbird
Tree: Tulip Poplar
Fair: September 7-16, 2001, in Nashville
Time Zone: Eastern and Central

The state's economy and its basic patterns of life and leisure were electrified in the 1930s by the Tennessee Valley Authority (TVA), that depression-born, often denounced and often praised grand-scale public power, flood control, and navigation project. TVA harnessed rampaging rivers, saved cities from the annual plague of floods, created a broad system for navigation, and produced inexpensive power and a treasury of recreational facilities. TVA altered the mainstream of the state's economy, achieving a dramatic switch from agriculture to industry. Cheap power, of course, sparked that revolution. Today, Tennessee has manufacturing payrolls in excess of farm income. Chemicals, textiles, foods, apparel, tourism, healthcare, printing and publishing, metalworking, and lumber products are its chief industries.

Farms and forests still produce more than 50 different crops, but the emphasis is changing from cotton and tobacco to livestock. With more than 200 species of trees, Tennessee is the nation's hardwood producing center. Mining is also a leading industry in Tennessee, with limestone the major product. The state also ranks high in the production of zinc, pyrite, ball clay, phosphate rock, and marble.

In 1541, it is believed, the explorer DeSoto planted the flag of Spain on the banks of the Mississippi near what is now Memphis. Although French traders explored the Tennessee Valley, it was their English counterparts who came over the mountain ranges, settling among the Cherokee and establishing a claim to the area. By the end of the 17th century the Tennessee region was a territory of North Carolina. With the construction of Fort Loudoun (1756), the first Anglo-American fort garrisoned west of the Alleghenies, settlement began. The first permanent colonies were established near the Watauga River in 1769 and 1771 and are known as the Watauga settlements.

The free-spirited settlers in the outlying regions found themselves far from the seat of their formal government in eastern North Carolina. Dissatisfied and insecure, they formed the independent state of Franklin in 1784. But formal recognition of the independent state was never to come. After four chaotic years, the federal government took over and in 1790 established "The Territory of the United States South of the River Ohio." Tennessee was admitted to the Union six years later. Among the first representatives it sent to Washington was a raw backwoodsman named Andrew Jackson.

During the War of 1812, Tennessee riflemen volunteered in such great numbers that Tennessee was henceforth called the "Volunteer State," and Andrew Jackson emerged from the war a national hero.

Although there was strong abolitionist sentiment in parts of the state, Tennessee finally seceded in 1861 and became a battleground; some of the bloodiest battles of the war, including Shiloh, Stones River, Missionary Ridge, Fort Donelson, and the Battle of Franklin, were fought within the state's boundaries. In 1866, shortly after former Tennessee governor Andrew Johnson became president, the state was accepted back into the Union.

When to Go/Climate

Tennessee usually experiences cool winters and warm summers. There is little variation in temperatures from north to south, however temperatures do drop from west to east due to the rise in elevation. There is occasionally significant snowfall in the eastern mountains. The following temperature chart offers a representative sampling of high/low temperatures in the state.

AVERAGE HIGH/LOW TEMPERATURES (°F)

KNOXVILLE

Jan 46/26	**May** 78/53	**Sep** 81/59
Feb 51/29	**June** 85/62	**Oct** 71/46
Mar 61/37	**July** 87/66	**Nov** 60/38
Apr 70/45	**Aug** 87/65	**Dec** 50/30

MEMPHIS

Jan 49/31	**May** 81/61	**Sep** 84/65
Feb 54/35	**June** 89/69	**Oct** 74/52
Mar 63/43	**July** 92/73	**Nov** 62/43
Apr 73/52	**Aug** 91/71	**Dec** 53/35

Parks and Recreation Finder

Directions to and information about the parks and recreation areas below are given under their respective town/city sections. Please refer to those sections for details.

NATIONAL PARK AND RECREATION AREAS

Key to abbreviations. I.H.S. = International Historic Site; I.P.M. = International Peace Memorial; N.B. = National Battlefield; N.B.P. = National Battlefield Park; N.B.C. = National Battlefield and Cemetery; N.C.A. = National Conservation Area; N.E.M. = National Expansion Memorial; N.F. = National Forest; N.G. = National Grassland; N.H.P. = National Historical Park; N.H.C. = National Heritage Corridor; N.H.S. = National Historic Site; N.L. = National Lakeshore; N.M. = National Monument; N.M.P. = National Military Park; N.Mem. = National Memorial; N.P. = National Park; N.Pres. = National Preserve; N.R.A. = National Recreational Area; N.R.R. = National Recreational River; N.Riv. = National River; N.S. = National Seashore; N.S.R. = National Scenic Riverway; N.S.T. = National Scenic Trail; N.Sc. = National Scientific Reserve; N.V.M. = National Volcanic Monument.

Place Name	Listed Under
Andrew Johnson N.H.S.	same
Big South Fork N.R.A.	JAMESTOWN
Cherokee N.F.	same
Fort Donelson N.B.C.	same
Great Smoky Mountains N.P.	same
Shiloh N.M.P.	same
Stones River N.B.	MURFREESBORO

CALENDAR HIGHLIGHTS

APRIL

Dogwood Arts Festival (Knoxville). Arts and crafts exhibits and shows; over 80 public and private gardens on display; music; parades; sporting events; more than 60 miles of marked dogwood trails or auto or free bus tours; special children's and senior citizen activities. Phone 423/637-4561.

MAY

Memphis in May International Festival (Memphis). Month-long celebration of the cultural and artistic heritage of Memphis. Major events occur weekends, but activities are held daily. Incl The Beale St Music Festival, World Championship Barbecue Cooking Contest, and Sunset Symphony. Phone 901/525-4611.

JUNE

International Country Music Fan Fair (Nashville). Country music fans have opportunity to mix and mingle with their favorite stars. Autograph sessions, special concerts. Phone 615/889-7503.

Riverbend Festival (Chattanooga). Music and sporting events, children's activities, fireworks display. Phone 423/265-4112.

AUGUST

Tennessee Walking Horse National Celebration (Shelbyville). More than 2,100 horses participate. Events conclude with crowning ceremonies for world grand champion walking horse. Phone 931/684-5915.

SEPTEMBER

Labor Day Fest (Memphis). Beale St. Memphis musicians perform rhythm and blues, jazz, country, and rock at clubs and restaurants throughout the historic district. Phone 901/526-0110.

Tennessee State Fair (Nashville). Phone 615/862-8980.

Tennessee Valley Fair (Knoxville). Chilhowee Park. Entertainment; livestock and agricultural shows; contests, exhibits, fireworks, and carnival rides. Phone 423/637-5840.

Mid-South Fair and Exposition (Memphis). Mid-South Fairgrounds. Agricultural, commercial, industrial exhibits; rides and concerts. Largest rodeo E of the Mississippi. Phone 901/274-8800.

OCTOBER

National Storytelling Festival (Johnson City). Three-day gathering from across the nation features some of the country's best storytellers. Phone 423/753-2171.

Fall Color Cruise & Folk Festival (Chattanooga). Riverboat trips, arts and crafts, entertainment. Phone 706/275-8778.

NOVEMBER

A Country Christmas (Nashville). Opryland Hotel. Offers events ranging from a musical stage show to an art, antique, and craft show. Phone 615/871-7637.

STATE PARK AND RECREATION AREAS

Key to abbreviations. I.P. = Interstate Park; S.A.P. = State Archaeological Park; S.B. = State Beach; S.C.A. = State Conservation Area; S.C.P. = State Conservation Park; S.Cp. = State Campground; S.F. = State Forest; S.G. = State Garden; S.H.A. = State Historic Area; S.H.P. = State Historic Park; S.H.S. = State Historic

Site; S.M.P. = State Marine Park; S.N.A. = State Natural Area; S.P. = State Park; S.P.C. = State Public Campground; S.R. = State Reserve; S.R.A. = State Recreation Area; S.Res. = State Reservoir; S.Res.P. = State Resort Park; S.R.P. = State Rustic Park.

Place Name	Listed Under
Bledsoe Creek S.P.	GALLATIN
Booker T. Washington S.P.	CHATTANOOGA
Burgess Falls S.N.A.	COOKEVILLE
Carter S.N.A.	MONTEAGLE
Cedars of Lebanon S.P.	LEBANON
Chickasaw S.R.P.	JACKSON
Cove Lake S.P.	CARYVILLE
Cumberland Mountain S.P.	CROSSVILLE
David Crockett S.P.	LAWRENCEBURG
Davy Crockett Birthplace S.P.	GREENVILLE
Dunbar Cave S.N.A.	CLARKSVILLE
Edgar Evins S.P.	COOKEVILLE
Fall Creek Falls S.Res.P.	McMINNVILLE
Fort Pillow S.H.A.	COVINGTON
Frozen Head S.P.	OAK RIDGE
Harrison Bay S.P.	CHATTANOOGA
Henry Horton S.Res.P.	LEWISBURG
Indian Mountain S.P.	JELLICO
Meeman-Shelby Forest S.P.	MEMPHIS
Montgomery Bell S.Res.P.	DICKSON
Natchez Trace S.Res.P.	same
Nathan Bedford Forrest S.P.	PARIS
Old Stone Fort S.A.P.	MANCHESTER
Panther Creek S.P.	MORRISTOWN
Paris Landing S.P.	PARIS
Pickett S.R.P.	JAMESTOWN
Pickwick Landing S.Res.P.	SAVANNAH
Port Royal S.H.A.	CLARKSVILLE
Radnor Lake S.N.A.	NASHVILLE
Reelfoot Lake S.P.	TIPTONVILLE
Roan Mountain S.P.	ELIZABETHTON
Rock Island S.R.P.	McMINNVILLE
South Cumberland S.P.	MONTEAGLE
Standing Stone S.P.	CELINA
Sycamore Shoals S.H.A.	ELIZABETHTON
T.O. Fuller S.P.	MEMPHIS
Warriors' Path S.P.	KINGSPORT

Water-related activities, hiking, riding, various other sports, picnicking and visitor centers, as well as camping, are available in many of these areas. Most state parks have supervised swimming (June-Labor Day, $1.50-$2.25), golf in resort parks (18 holes, $19; 9 holes, $10), boating ($2.25-$3/hr), fishing and tent camping (1-2 persons, one must be over 17 yrs: $6-$14/day, each addl over 7 yrs, 50; 2-wk max). Cabins, rustic to very modern, are available in several parks (daily, $50-$135; reservations should be made at park of choice; 1-night deposit required; $5 surcharge added for 1-night-only rental). Reservations for camping at some parks. There is also camping in Cherokee National Forest and Great Smoky Mtns National Park (see both). For further information, contact the Tennessee Dept of Environment & Conservation, Bureau of State Parks, 401

Church St, 7th floor, Nashville 37243-0446; 615/532-0001, 800/421-6683, or 888/TN-PARKS.

SKI AREA

Place Name	Listed Under
Ober Gatlinburg Ski Resort	GATLINBURG

FISHING AND HUNTING

There are more than 30 different kinds of fish in the state's mountain streams and lakes, incl striped, largemouth, smallmouth, and white bass, rainbow trout, walleye, muskie, crappie, and catfish. Nonresident licenses: 3-day all species, $20.50; 10-day all species, $30.50; 3-day, no trout $10.50; 10-day, no trout $15.50; annual, no trout $26; annual, all species $51.

   Within the constraints of season and limits, everything from squirrel and deer to wild boar can be hunted. Nonresident licenses: 7-day small game and water fowl, $30.50; annual small game and water fowl, $56; 7-day all game, $105.50; annual all game, $156. For detailed information, contact the Tennessee Wildlife Resources Agency, Ellington Agricultural Center, PO Box 40747, Nashville 37204; 615/781-6500.

Driving Information

Safety belts are mandatory for all persons in front seat of vehicle. Children under 4 yrs must be in a child/passenger restraint system meeting Federal Motor Vehicle Safety Standards. Phone 615/741-3073.

INTERSTATE HIGHWAY SYSTEM

The following alphabetical listing of Tennessee towns and parks in *Mobil Travel Guide* shows that these cities are within 10 miles of the indicated Interstate highways. A highway map should be checked, however, for the nearest exit.

Highway Number	Cities/Towns within 10 miles
Interstate 24	Chattanooga, Clarksville, Manchester, Monteagle, Murfreesboro, Nashville.
Interstate 40	Cherokee Natl Forest, Cookeville, Crossville, Dickson, Hurricane Mills, Jackson, Knoxville, Lebanon, Lenoir City, Memphis, Nashville, Natchez Trace State Resort Park, Oak Ridge, Sevierville.
Interstate 65	Columbia, Franklin, Lewisburg, Nashville.
Interstate 75	Caryville, Chattanooga, Cleveland, Jellico, Knoxville, Lenoir City, Sweetwater.
Interstate 81	Kingsport, Morristown.

Additional Visitor Information

The Department of Tourist Development, 320 6th Ave N, 5th floor, Rachel Jackson Bldg, Nashville 37243, publishes a state map and a Tennessee vacation guide magazine highlighting attractions, historic sites, and major events and will provide information on vacationing in Tennessee. Phone 615/741-2158.

   The TVA and the US Army Corps of Engineers have transformed muddy rivers into lovely lakes, making Tennessee home to the "Great Lakes of the South" with more than 29 big lakes in the public province. Also, TVA has developed Land Between The Lakes (see under KENTUCKY), a giant national recreation area spanning the Kentucky-Tennessee border.

   There are 13 welcome centers in Tennessee; visitors may find the information and brochures helpful in their state travels. These centers operate yr-round; they are located on interstate highway entrances to the state.

While a major city with a hub airport all its own, Memphis could also be considered a major side trip for Nashville visitors, via I-40. Visitors to Memphis won't want to miss Beale Street, Graceland, the National Civil Rights Museum, and Sun Studio. **(Approx 430 mi)**

East Tennessee's legendary Smoky Mountains are a major draw for scenic driving, camping, hiking, and lake and river recreation in and around Great Smoky Mountains National Park. The mountain region has a down-home appeal due, in large part, to its cultural history of Appalachian music and crafts. Knoxville is casually considered the capital of eastern Tennessee. The most highly interpreted and developed mountain town is Gatlinburg, a stone's throw from Dollywood outside Pigeon Forge. From Nashville it's quite a long haul along I-40 before turning off at Knoxville on US 441. **(Approx 450 mi)**

Andrew Johnson National Historic Site

See also Greeneville

(Monument Ave, College & Depot Sts in Greeneville)

The tailor shop, two houses, and the burial place of the 17th president of the United States are preserved. Apprenticed to a tailor during his youth, Andrew Johnson came to Greeneville from his native Raleigh, NC, in 1826. After years of service in local, state, and federal governments, Senator Johnson chose to remain loyal to the Union when Tennessee seceded. After serving as military governor of Tennessee, Johnson was elected vice president in 1864. On April 15, 1865, he became president following the assassination of Abraham Lincoln. Continued opposition to the radical program of Reconstruction led to his impeachment in 1868. Acquitted by the Senate, he continued to serve as president until 1869. In 1875, Andrew Johnson became the only former president to be elected to the US Senate.

What to See and Do

Grave and monument. An eagle-capped marker sits over the President's grave. Members of his immediate family are also buried in what is now a national cemetery. (Daily) Monument Ave.

Park area. Camping (mid-Mar-Oct) nearby at Kinser Park, phone 423/639-5912, or call US Forest Service, 423/638-4109. For further information about the Historic Site contact Superintendent, PO Box 1088, Greeneville 37744. Phone 423/638-3551.

Visitor Center. The visitor center houses the Johnson tailor shop, preserved with some original furnishings and tools of the craft, as well as a museum with exhibits and memorabilia relating to Johnson's career. (Daily; closed Jan 1, Thanksgiving, Dec 25) Opp is the Johnson house (1830s-1851), occupied during his career as a tailor and as a congressman. Depot & College Sts. **FREE**

Johnson Homestead. Occupied by Johnson family from 1851-75, except during US Civil War and presidential yrs, the house is restored and furnished with amily heirlooms. (Daily; closed Jan 1, Thanksgiving, Dec 25) Tickets at Visitor Center. Main St. ¢

Caryville (E-6)

Pop 1,751 **Elev** 1,095 ft
Area code 423 **Zip** 37714

What to See and Do

Cove Lake State Park. Approx 1,500 acres incl 300-acre Cove Lake, where hundreds of Canada geese winter. Pool, wading pool, lifeguard, fishing, boat rentals; nature trails, programs, picnicking, concession, restaurant, playground, game courts, camping, tent and trailer sites. Standard fees. N, off US 25W. Phone 423/566-9701.

Motels/Motor Lodges

★ ★ **BUDGET HOST INN.** *115 Woods Ave, PO Box 16 (37714), I-75 Exit 134. 423/562-9595; fax 423/566-0515; res 800/283-4678. Email bhinn@hotmail. com; www.members.xoom.com/bhinn.* 22 rms, 2 story. June-Aug: S, D $44; lower rates rest of yr. Crib avail, fee. Pet accepted, some restrictions, fee. Parking lot. TV; cable. Ck-out 10:30 am, ck-in 11 am. Business servs avail. Dry cleaning. Golf, 18 holes. Tennis, 4 courts. Hiking trail. Picnic facilities. Cr cds: A, C, D, DS, MC, V.

★ **DAYS INN.** *221 Colonial Ln (37769), approx 10 mi S on I-75 Exit 129. 423/426-2816; fax 423/426-4626; res 800/329-7466.* 60 rms, 2 story. Mar-Oct: S $45-$65; D $55-$69; each addl $5; under 12 free; higher rates special events; lower rates rest of yr. Crib free. TV; cable (premium). Pool. Complimentary continental bkfst. Restaurant nearby.

Ck-out 11 am. Sundries. Cr cds: A, C, D, DS, MC, V.

★★ **HAMPTON INN.** *4459 Veterans Memorial Hwy (37714). 423/562-9888; fax 423/562-7474; toll-free 800/426-7866.* 64 rms, 2 story. May-Sep: S, D $64-$74; each addl $10; suites $89-$99; under 16 free; family, wkly rates; package plans; higher rates special events; lower rates rest of yr. Crib free. TV; cable (premium), VCR avail. Complimentary coffee in rms, full bkfst. Restaurant nearby. Ck-out 11 am. Meeting rms. Business servs avail. In-rm modem link. Sundries. Coin lndry. Golf privileges. Exercise equipt. Heated pool; whirlpool. Some bathrm phones, refrigerators, microwaves, fireplaces. Picnic tables, grills. Cr cds: A, C, D, DS, MC, V.

★ **LAKE VIEW INN.** *276 John McGhee Blvd (37714), at US 25W, I-75 Exit 134. 423/562-9456; fax 423/562-2596; res 800/431-6887.* 92 rms, 2 story. No elvtr. S, D $29-$49; each addl $5; under 16 free. Crib $3. TV; cable. Pool. Ck-out 11:30 am. Coin lndry. Business servs avail. Some refrigerators, microwaves. Cr cds: A, C, D, MC, V.

★ **SUPER 8.** *200 John McGhee Blvd (37714), TN 63, I-75 Exit 134. 433/562-8476; fax 423/562-8870; res 800/800-8000.* 98 rms, 2 story. S, D $35-$50; each addl $5. Crib free. Pet accepted; $5. TV; cable (premium). Pool; wading pool. Playground. Complimentary continental bkfst. Ck-out noon. Meeting rms. Business servs avail. Cr cds: A, DS, MC, V.

Celina (E-5)

Pop 1,493 **Elev** 562 ft **Area code** 931 **Zip** 38551

Located in the scenic Upper Cumberland section of Tennessee, Celina is the location of the first law office of revered statesman Cordell Hull.

Involved in both agriculture (especially cattle raising and truck farming) and industry (notably work clothes and denim sportswear), Celina is also noted for its nearby recreational facilities.

Resort

★ **CEDAR HILL RESORT.** *2371 Cedar Hill Rd (38551), 3½ mi N on TN 53. 931/243-3201; toll-free 800/872-8393. Email rproberts@twlakes.net; www.cedarhillresort.com.* June-Aug: S, D $52; each addl $6; lower rates rest of yr. Pet accepted, fee. Parking lot. Pool, lifeguard. TV; cable (DSS). Restaurant 6 am-9 pm. Ck-out 10 am, ck-in 3 pm. Concierge. Gift shop. Tennis, 4 courts. Supervised children's activities. Hiking trail. Picnic facilities. Cr cds: MC, V.

Chattanooga (F-5)

Settled 1835 **Pop** 152,466 **Elev** 685 ft **Area code** 423

Web www.chattanooga.net/cvb

Information Chattanooga Area Convention & Visitors Bureau, 2 Broad St, 37402; 423/756-8687 or 800/322-3344

Walled in on three sides by the Appalachian Mountains and the Cumberland Plateau, Chattanooga is a diversified city. It is the birthplace of miniature golf and the site of the first Coca-Cola bottling plant, and has the steepest passenger incline railway in the country.

It's a city celebrated in song and heralded in history. The Cherokees called it *Tsatanugi* (rock coming to a point), describing Lookout Mountain, which stands like a sentinel over the city. They called the creek here "Chickamauga" (river of blood).

Cherokee Chief John Ross founded the city. One of the starting points of the tragic "Trail of Tears" was from Chattanooga; Native Americans from three states were herded by Federal troops and forced to march in bitter winter to distant

Oklahoma. The Battle of Chickamauga in the fall of 1863 was one of
the turning points of the Civil War.
It ended when Union forces over-
powered entrenched Confederate
forces on Missionary Ridge; there
were more than 34,500 casualties.
Sherman's march to the sea began
immediately thereafter.

Chattanooga emerged as an important industrial city at the end of the
Civil War, when soldiers from both
sides returned to stake their futures
in this commercially strategic city.
Only 1,500 persons lived in Chattanooga at the war's end, but by
1880 the city had 77 industries.

In 1878, Adolph S. Ochs moved to
Chattanooga from Knoxville, purchased the *Chattanooga Times* and
made it one of the state's most influ-
ential newspapers. Although he later
went on to publish the *New York
Times,* Ochs retained control of the
Chattanooga journal until his death
in 1935.

Sparked by the Tennessee Valley
Authority, the city's greatest period
of growth began in the 1930s. In
the past few years, millions of dollars have been spent along Chattanooga's riverfront, making it a
popular visitor destination.

What to See and Do

Booker T. Washington State Park.
More than 350 acres on Chickamauga Lake. Swimming pools, fishing, boating (rentals, launch); nature
trail, picnicking, playground, lodge.
Some facilities seasonal. Standard
fees. 13 mi NE on TN 58. Phone
423/894-4955.

**Chattanooga African American His-
tory Museum.** Educational institution that portrays African American
contributions to the growth of Chattanooga and the nation. (Daily) 200
Martin Luther King Blvd. Phone
423/266-8658. ¢¢

Chattanooga Choo-Choo. Converted
1909 train station with hotel and
restaurants. Formal gardens, fountains, pools, turn-of-the-century
shops, gaslights, trolley ride (fee),
model railroad (fee). Terminal Station, 1400 Market St. Phone
423/266-5000 or 800/872-2529.

Chester Frost Park. Swimming, sand
beach, bathhouse, fishing, boating
(ramps); hiking, picnicking, conces-

sions, camping (fee; electricity,
water). Islands in park are accessible
by causeways. 2318 Gold Point Circle; 17 mi NE off I-75 exit 4, then TN
153 to Hixson Pike, N to Gold Point
Circle, on W shore of Chickamauga
Lake. Phone 423/842-0177. **FREE**

**Chickamauga and Chattanooga
National Military Park.** (see under
GEORGIA)

Creative Discovery Museum. Encour-
ages children to learn about their
world hands-on through creativity
and individual achievement. Exhibit
areas incl Artist's Studio, Inventor's
Workshop, Musician's Studio, and
Scientist's Field Laboratory. (May-
Aug, daily; rest of yr, Tues-Sun) 321
Chestnut St. Phone 423/756-2738.
¢¢¢

Harrison Bay State Park. More than
1,200 acres on Chickamauga Lake.
Swimming pool, fishing, boating
(ramp, rentals, marina); picnicking,
playground, snack bar, restaurant,
camp store (all seasonal). Camping.
Recreation building (seasonal). Standard fees. 11 mi NE off TN 58. Phone
423/344-6214 or 423/344-2272.

Houston Museum of Decorative Arts.
Glass, porcelain, pottery, music
boxes, dolls, collection of pitchers;
country-style furniture. (Daily; closed
hols) 201 High St, in Bluff View Art
District. Phone 423/267-7176. ¢¢

Hunter Museum of Art. Paintings,
sculpture, glass, drawings; permanent
collection of major American artists;
changing exhibits. Gift shop. (Tues-
Sun; closed hols) 10 Bluff View, in
Bluff View Art District. Phone
423/267-0968. ¢¢

**International Towing and Recovery
Hall of Fame and Museum.** Antique
vehicles on display; history of wreck-
ers and tow trucks. (Daily) 401 Broad
St. Phone 423/267-3132. ¢¢

🔲 **Lookout Mountain.** Mountain towers more than 2,120 ft above the city,
offering clear-day views of Tennessee,
Georgia, North Carolina, South Carolina, and Alabama. During the US
Civil War, the "Battle Above the
Clouds" was fought on the slope. S
of town via Ochs Hwy & Scenic Hwy.

Lookout Mountain Incline Railway.
World's steepest passenger incline
railway climbs Lookout Mt to
2,100-ft altitude; near top, grade is
at 72.7° angle; passengers ride
glass-roofed cars; Smoky Mts (200

mi away) can be seen from Upper Station observation deck. Round-trip approx 30 min. (Daily; closed Dec 25) Lower station at 3917 St. Elmo Ave. Phone 423/821-4224. ¢¢¢

Point Park. View of Chattanooga and Moccasin Bend from observatory. Monuments, plaques, museum tell story of battle. Visitor Center. Part of Chickamauga and Chattanooga National Military Park (see under GEORGIA). (Daily; closed Dec 25) Lookout Mt. Phone 423/821-7786. ¢

Cravens House. (1866) Oldest surviving structure on mountain, restored with period furnishings. Original house (1856), center of the "Battle Above the Clouds," was largely destroyed; present structure was erected on the original foundations in 1866. (Apr-Oct, daily) Golden Eagle Passport (see MAKING THE MOST OF YOUR TRIP). On Lookout Mt. Phone 423/821-7786. ¢

Ruby Falls-Lookout Mountain Caverns. Under the battlefield are twin caves with onyx formations, giant stalactites, and stalagmites of various hues; at 1,120 ft below surface Ruby Falls is a 145-ft waterfall inside Lookout Mountain Caverns. View of city from tower above entrance bldg. Guided tours. (Daily; closed Dec 25) Scenic Hwy TN 148, on Lookout Mt. Phone 423/821-2544. ¢¢

Rock City Gardens. Fourteen acres of mountaintop trails and vistas. Fairyland Caverns and Mother Goose Village, rock formations, swinging bridge, observation point. Restaurant; shops. (Daily; closed Dec 25) 2½ mi S on TN 58, on Lookout Mt. Phone 706/820-2531. ¢¢

Tennessee Wildlife Center at Reflection Riding. Park meant for leisurely driving offers winding 3-mi drive with vistas: historic sites, trees, wildflowers, shrubs, reflecting pools. Also wetland walkway, nature center, animal diorama, solar energy display, hiking trails, programs. (Daily) Garden Rd, 6 mi SW, near jct US 11/64, US 41 & US 72, on Lookout Mt. Phone 423/821-1160. ¢¢

Battles for Chattanooga Museum. Automated, 3-D display re-creates Civil War Battles of Chattanooga using 5,000 miniature soldiers, flashing lights, smoking cannons, and crackling rifles. Also here are dioramas of area history prior to Civil War. (Daily; closed Dec 25) 1110 E Brow Rd, adj to Point Park. Phone 706/820-2531. ¢¢

National Knife Museum. Permanent display of knives of every age and description; also changing exhibits. (Mon-Sat; closed hols) 7201 Shallowford Rd. Phone 423/892-5007. ¢

Nickajack Dam and Lake. TVA dam impounds lake with 192 mi of shoreline and 10,370 acres of water surface. Fishing, boat launch. Visitor lobby at navigation lock (daily). 25 mi W on US 41, 64, 72 or I-24. Phone 423/942-1633. **FREE**

Raccoon Mountain.

Raccoon Mountain Pumped Storage Plant. Raccoon Mountain is the largest of the TVA's rock-filled dams, measuring 230 ft high and 8,500 ft long. Water pumped from the Tennessee River flows from the reservoir atop the mountain to the powerhouse below. Cut 1,350 ft inside the mountain, the powerhouse chamber has 4 of the largest reversible pump turbines in the world. Visitor center and picnic area atop mountain (daylight hrs), fishing at base of mountain, overlooks with spectacular views of Tennessee River gorge and Chattanooga. 6 mi W. Phone 423/825-3100. **FREE**

Raccoon Mountain Caverns and Campground. Guided tours offer views of beautiful formations, stalagmites, and stalactites; also "wild" cave tours through undeveloped sections. Full-facility campground (fee). (Daily) Approx 5 mi W; exit 174 off I-24, 1 mi N on TN 41. Phone 423/821-9403 or 423/821-CAVE. Cave tour ¢¢¢

Raccoon Mountain Alpine Slide. Chairlift to top of mountain and personal-control sled ride (½ mi) to bottom. (Mid-May-Labor Day, daily; Mar-mid-May and early Sep-Nov, wkends only) Phone 423/825-5666. ¢¢

Grand Prix of Chattanooga. Three-quarter scale Formula cars race against clock on challenging ½-mi track; also go-carts. Must have valid driver's license. (Same days as Alpine Slide) Phone 423/825-5666. Per lap ¢¢

Signal Point. Mountain was used for signaling by Cherokees and later by Confederates. View of "Grand Canyon of the Tennessee" can be seen by looking almost straight down to the Tennessee River from Signal Point Military Park, off St. James Blvd. 9 mi N on Ridgeway Ave (US 127).

***Southern Bell* riverboat.** Sightseeing, breakfast, lunch, and dinner cruises on 500-passenger riverboat. (Apr-Dec, daily) 2 Riverfront Pkwy, Pier 2. Phone 423/266-4488 or 800/766-2784. ¢¢¢-¢¢¢¢

🔲 **Tennessee Aquarium.** First major freshwater life center in the country, focusing primarily on the natural habitats and wildlife of the Tennessee River and related ecosystems. Within this 130,000-sq-ft complex are more than 9,000 animals in their natural habitats. The Aquarium re-creates riverine habitats in 7 major freshwater tanks and 2 terrestial environments and is organized into 5 major galleries: **Appalachian Cove Forest** re-creates the mountain source of the Tennessee River; **Tennessee River Gallery** examines the river at midstream and compares the "original" river with the river as it now exists; **Discovery Falls** is a series of interactive displays and small tanks; **Mississipi Delta** explores the river as it slows to meet the sea; and **Rivers of the World** explores 6 of the world's great river systems. Highlight of the Aquarium is the 60-ft-high central canyon, designed to give visitors a sense of immersion into the river. (Daily; closed Thanksgiving, Dec 25). 1 Broad St, on the banks of the Tennessee River. Phone 423/265-0695 or 800/262-0695. ¢¢¢¢ Adj is

IMAX 3D Theater. Six-story movie screen. Discounted combination tickets with the Tennessee Aquarium are avail. (Daily) 201 Chestnut St. Phone 800/262-0695. ¢¢¢

Tennessee Valley Railroad. The South's largest operating historic railroad with steam locomotives, diesels, passenger coaches of various types.

Trains take passengers on a 6-mi ride, incl tunnel. Audiovisual show, displays; gift shop. (June-Labor Day, daily; Apr-May and Sep-mid-Nov, Mon-Fri) 4119 Cromwell Rd. Phone 423/894-8028. ¢¢¢

University of Tennessee at Chattanooga. (1886) 7,800 students. Fine Arts Center has Arena stage for entertainment and special events. Tours of campus by appt. 615 McCallie Ave. Phone 423/755-4662.

Annual Events

Kaleidoscope. Downtown at Ross's Landing. Creative festival for children incl interactive and educational activities. Phone 423/756-2212. Early May.

Riverbend Festival. Music and sporting events, children's activities, fireworks display. Phone 423/265-4112. Late June.

Seasonal Event

Theatrical, musical productions. **Tivoli Theater,** 709 Broad St. Variety of events, incl plays, concerts, opera; box office, phone 423/757-5042. **Chattanooga Theatre Centre,** 400 River St, box office, phone 423/267-8534. **Memorial Auditorium,** 399 McCallie Ave; box office, phone 423/756-5050. **Chattanooga Symphony and Opera Assn,** 25 concerts and 2 opera productions yrly, phone 423/267-8583. **Backstage Playhouse,** 3264 Brainerd Rd, dinner theater, phone 423/629-1565.

Motels/Motor Lodges

★★ **BEST INN.** *7717 Lee Hwy (37421). 423/894-5454; fax 423/499-9597; res 800/237-8466. Email best inn@yahoo.com; www.bestinn.com.* 64 rms, 2 story. Apr-Oct: S, D $68.95; each addl $5; suites $99.95; under 16 free; lower rates rest of yr. Crib avail. Pet accepted, some restrictions, fee. Parking lot. Pool. TV; cable (premium). Complimentary continental bkfst, coffee in rms, newspaper, toll-free calls. Restaurant. Fax servs avail. Cr cds: A, C, D, DS, ER, JCB, MC, V.

D 🔄 🏊 ⛵ 🐾 SC

★★ **BUDGET HOST INN.** *395 Main St (37347), 20 mi W on I-24, Exit 152. 423/837-7185; fax 423/837-7185; res 800/283-4678; toll-free 800/759-5804.*

65 rms, 2 story. May-Sep: S $50; D $60; each addl $5; under 12 free; lower rates rest of yr. Crib avail. Parking lot. Pool. TV; cable (DSS). Restaurant. Ck-out 11 am, ck-in 1 pm. Meeting rm. Business servs avail. Coin lndry. Golf. Cr cds: A, C, D, DS, MC, V.

◻ ⛉ ⇔ ⊠ 🔥

★ **DAYS INN AIRPORT.** *7725 Lee Hwy (37421). 423/899-2288; fax 423/899-2288; toll-free 800/453-4511. www.daysinn.com.* 80 rms, 2 story. June-Aug: S $48-$58; D $58-$78; each addl $5; under 12 free; lower rates rest of yr. Crib avail. Pet accepted, some restrictions; $5. TV; cable (premium). Indoor pool; whirlpool. Complimentary continental bkfst. Restaurant nearby. Ck-out 11 am. Microwaves avail. Cr cds: A, C, D, DS, ER, MC, V.

◻ ➚ ⇔ ⊠ 🔥 SC

★ **ECONO LODGE.** *1417 St. Thomas St (37412), I-75 Exit 1. 423/894-1417; fax 423/821-6840; toll-free 800/424-4777.* 89 rms, 2 story. S $29.95-$59.95; D $34.95-$59.95; each addl $5; under 12 free. Crib $4. Pet accepted, some restrictions. TV; cable (premium). Pool. Complimentary continental bkfst. Restaurant nearby. Ck-out 11 am. Cr cds: A, C, D, DS, MC, V.

◻ ➚ ⇔ ⊠ 🔥 SC

★★ **KING'S LODGE MOTEL.** *2400 Westside Dr (37404), 4 mi NE at jct US 41, I-24 East Ridge, 4th Ave Exit. 423/698-8944; fax 423/698-8949; toll-free 800/251-7702.* 138 rms, 2 story, 24 suites. S, D $40-$65; each addl $5; suites $60-$95; under 12 free. Crib free. Pet accepted, some restrictions. TV; cable (premium). Pool. Coffee in rms. Restaurant 7 am-11 pm. Rm serv. Bar 1 pm-3 am. Ck-out 11 am. Business servs avail. Refrigerators. Some balconies. Cr cds: A, C, D, DS, MC, V.

➚ ⚓ ⇔ ⊠ 🔥

★ **LA QUINTA INN.** *7015 Shallowford Rd (37421), at I-75. 423/855-0011; fax 423/499-5409; toll-free 800/687-6667.* 132 rms, 2 story. May-Oct: S $59-$66; D $65-$85; each addl $10; suites $92-$125; under 18 free; higher rates special events; lower rates rest of yr. Crib free. Pet

accepted, some restrictions. TV; cable (premium). Pool. Complimentary continental bkfst. Ck-out noon. Health club privileges. Some refrigerators; microwaves avail. Cr cds: A, C, D, DS, MC, V.

◻ ➚ ⇔ ⊠ 🔥 SC

★★★ **LOOKOUT MOUNTAIN INN.** *3800 Cummings Hwy (37419), I-24 Exit 174. 423/821-3531; fax 423/821-8403.* 162 rms, 2 story. S $64-$72; D $71-$79; each addl $7; suites from $81; under 19 free. Crib free. TV; cable (premium). Pool. Restaurant 6 am-10 pm. Bar 5 pm-midnight; entertainment. Ck-out 11 am. Meeting rms. Exercise equipt. Game rm. Volleyball, basketball. Picnic tables. Cr cds: A, C, D, DS, MC, V.

◻ ➚ ⚓ ⇔ ⛉ ⊠ 🔥

★ **RED ROOF INN.** *7014 Shallowford Rd (37421), I-75 Exit 5. 423/899-0143; fax 423/899-8384; toll-free 800/843-7663.* 112 rms, 2 story. June-July: S, D $43.99-$60.99; each addl $7; under 18 free; higher rates special events; lower rates rest of yr. Crib free. Pet accepted, some restrictions. TV; cable (premium). Complimentary coffee in lobby. Restaurant adj open 24 hrs. Ck-out noon. Cr cds: A, C, D, DS, MC, V.

◻ ➚ ⊠ 🔥

★ **SUPER 8 MOTEL.** *20 Birmingham Hwy (37419), I-24 Exit 174. 423/821-8880; fax 423/821-8880; toll-free 800/800-8000.* 74 rms, 3 story. Apr-Sep: S $42.88-$45.88; D $47.88-$55.88; each addl $5; under 12 free; lower rates rest of yr. Crib free. Pet accepted, some restrictions. TV; cable (premium). Complimentary coffee in lobby. Restaurant adj open 24 hrs. Ck-out 11 am. Coin lndry. Picnic tables. Cr cds: A, C, D, DS, MC, V.

◻ ➚ ⊠ 🔥 SC

Hotels

★★ **CHATTANOOGA CLARION HOTEL.** *407 Chesnut St (37402), at 4th St; US 27 Exit 1 C. 423/756-5150; fax 423/265-8708; res 800/252-7466. Email writeus@chattanoogaclarion.com; www.chattanoogaclarion.com.* 198 rms, 12 story, 3 suites. May-Oct: S $109; D $119; each addl $10; suites $199; under 18 free; lower rates rest of yr. Crib avail, fee. Valet parking avail.

Pool. TV; cable. Complimentary coffee in rms, toll-free calls. Restaurant 6 am-9 pm. Bar. Ck-out 11 am, ck-in 3 pm. Meeting rms. Business center. Bellhops. Concierge. Dry cleaning. Gift shop. Free airport transportation. Exercise equipt. Golf. Cr cds: A, C, D, DS, MC, V.

★★★ **CHATTANOOGA CHOO CHOO.** *1400 Market St (37402), 8 blks S in Terminal Station. 423/266-5000; fax 423/265-4635; res 800/872-2529. Email frontdesk@choochoo.com; www.choochoo.com.* 351 rms, 5 story, 10 suites. May-July, Sep-Oct: S, D $109; suites $175; lower rates rest of yr. Crib avail. Parking garage. Indoor/outdoor pools, whirlpool. TV; cable (premium), VCR avail. Complimentary coffee in rms, newspaper, toll-free calls. Restaurant 6 am-10 pm. Bar. Ck-out 11 am, ck-in 3 pm. Conference center, meeting rms. Business servs avail. Bellhops. Concierge. Dry cleaning. Gift shop. Free airport transportation. Exercise privileges. Golf, 18 holes. Tennis, 2 courts. Supervised children's activities. Picnic facilities. Cr cds: A, C, D, DS, JCB, MC, V.

★ **DAYS INN RIVERGATE.** *901 Carter St (37402), at Martin Luther King Blvd. 423/266-7331; fax 423/266-9357; res 800/329-7466. Email daysinnrivergate@excite.com.* 137 rms, 3 story. June-Aug: S $75; D $81; each addl $6; under 12 free; lower rates rest of yr. Crib avail. Parking lot. Pool. TV; cable (premium). Complimentary coffee in rms, newspaper, toll-free calls. Restaurant. Bar. Meeting rm. Business servs avail. Dry cleaning, coin lndry. Exercise equipt. Golf, 18 holes. Tennis, 6 courts. Bike rentals. Supervised children's activities. Hiking trail. Picnic facilities. Cr cds: A, D, DS, MC, V.

★★ **HAMPTON INN.** *7013 Shallowford Rd (37421), near Lovell Field Airport. 423/855-0095; fax 423/894-7600; toll-free 800/HAMPTON. Email chasfoi@hi-hotel.com; www.hamptoninn.com.* 167 rms, 2 story. June-Aug: S $76; D $79; under 12 free; lower rates rest of yr. Crib avail. Parking lot. Pool. TV; cable (premium). Complimentary continental bkfst, coffee in rms, newspaper,

toll-free calls. Restaurant nearby. Ck-out 11 am, ck-in 3 pm. Meeting rms. Business center. Dry cleaning, coin lndry. Free airport transportation. Exercise equipt. Golf, 18 holes. Tennis, 2 courts. Cr cds: A, D, DS, MC, V.

★★★ **MARRIOTT.** *2 Carter Plz (37402), adj convention center. 423/756-0002; fax 423/266-2254; toll-free 800/228-9290.* 343 rms, 16 story. S, D $65-$135; suites $150-$350; under 12 free; higher rates special events. Crib free. TV; cable, VCR avail. 2 pools, 1 indoor; whirlpool, poolside serv. Restaurant 6:30 am-11 pm. Bar; entertainment. Ck-out noon. Convention facilities. Business servs avail. Concierge. Shopping arcade. Garage parking. Exercise equipt; sauna. Game rm. Bathrm phones, refrigerators. Luxury level. Cr cds: A, C, D, DS, ER, MC, V.

★★★ **RADISSON READ HOUSE HOTEL.** *827 Broad St (37402), Martin Luther King Blvd and Broad St. 423/266-4121; fax 423/267-6447; res 800/333-3333. Email rhi-chat@radisson.com.* 238 rms, 10 story, 138 suites. S, D $108-$118; suites $118-$128; under 18 free. Crib free. TV; cable (premium). Pool. Restaurants 6:30 am-11 pm. Bar from 11 am. Ck-out noon. Meeting rms. Shopping arcade. Exercise equipt. Wet bars; some bathrm phones. Built to accommodate travelers on the Nashville/Chattanooga Railroad (1847). Cr cds: A, C, D, DS, MC, V.

B&Bs/Small Inns

★★★ **ADAMS HILBORNE MANSION.** *801 Vine St (37403). 423/265-5000; fax 423/265-5555; toll-free 888/IINNJOY. Email innjoy@worldnet.att.net; www.innjoy.com.* 11 rms, 3 story, 3 suites. Apr-Aug, Dec: S $115; D $125; each addl $35; suites $175; lower rates rest of yr. Parking lot. TV; cable, VCR avail. Complimentary full bkfst, newspaper. Restaurant five. 24-hr rm serv. Bar. Meeting rms. Business center. Concierge. Gift shop. Exercise privileges. Golf, 18 holes. Tennis, 3 courts. Hiking trail. Cr cds: A, D, MC, V.

★ ★ ★ **BLUFF VIEW INN.** *412 E 2nd St (37403). 423/265-5033. www. tennessee-inns.com/chattanooga/bluff-view-frame.html.* 16 rms in 3 bldgs, 2 story, 2 suites. S, D $100-$185; each addl $20; suites $200-$250. TV; cable. Complimentary full bkfst. Dining rm 11 am-10:30 pm. Ck-out noon, ck-in 3 pm. Balconies. Main house built 1928 on bluff overlooking river; antiques. Cr cds: A, DS, MC, V.

▧ 🔥

All Suite

★ ★ **COMFORT SUITES.** *7324 Shallowford Rd (37421), I-75 Exit 5. 423/892-1500; fax 423/892-0111; res 800/517-4000. www.comfortsuites. com/hotel/tn133.* 2 story, 62 suites. Apr, June-Aug, Oct: S $85; D $95; each addl $6; under 12 free; lower rates rest of yr. Crib avail. Parking lot. Indoor pool, whirlpool. TV; cable (premium), VCR avail. Complimentary continental bkfst, coffee in rms, newspaper, toll-free calls. Restaurant 6 am- 9 pm. Ck-out 11 am, ck-in 2 pm. Meeting rm. Business servs avail. Dry cleaning, coin lndry. Exercise equipt. Golf. Bike rentals. Cr cds: A, C, D, DS, MC, V.

🄳 ⚡ 🏋 ⚓ 👤 ✈ ▧ 🔥

Restaurants

★ ★ **212 MARKET.** *212 Market St (37402), adj to Tennessee Aquarium. 423/265-1212. Email rest@212market. com; www.212market.com.* Specializes in fresh seafood, steak, rack of lamb. Own baking. Hrs: 11 am-3 pm, 5-9:30 pm; Sat, Sun to 10 pm. Closed Jan 1, Dec 25. Res accepted. Bar. Wine list. Lunch $2.95-$10.50; dinner $9.75-$21.50. Sun brunch $6-$12. Child's menu. Southwestern decor, original art. Cr cds: A, D, DS, MC, V.

🄳 SC ⬛

★ **COUNTRY PLACE.** *7320 Shallowford Rd (37421), I-75 Exit 5. 423/855-1392.* Specializes in fried chicken, desserts. Salad bar. Hrs: 6:30 am-9 pm; Sun 8 am-8 pm. Closed Dec 25. Bkfst $2.79-$6.85; lunch, dinner $2.69-$8.75. Child's menu. Dining

rm features artwork and a miniature train. Cr cds: A, DS, MC, V.

🄳 SC ⬛

★ ★ **MOUNT VERNON.** *1707A Cummings Hwy (37409), 1½ mi SW on US 11, 41. 423/266-6591.* Specializes in fresh seafood, vegetables, desserts. Hrs: 11 am-9:30 pm; Sat from 4:30 pm; early-bird dinner 4:30-6:30 pm. Closed Sun; Dec 24-Jan 2. Lunch $4.25-$7.25; dinner $9.95-$13.95. Child's menu. Family-owned for 43 yrs. Cr cds: A, DS, MC, V.

🄳

Unrated Dining Spot

VINE STREET MARKET. *1313 Hanover St (37405). 423/266-8463.* Deli menu. Specializes in desserts. Menu recited. Hrs: 9 am-6 pm; Sat 10 am-4 pm. Closed Sun; some hols. Lunch a la carte entrees: $4-$8; dinner a la carte entrees: $11.50-$17.95. Child's menu.. Cr cds: A, MC, V.

🄳

Cherokee National Forest

See also Cleveland, Greeneville, Johnson City

(NE, SE & SW of Johnson City via US 23, 321, TN 91; E of Cleveland on US 64)

Slashed by river gorges and creased by rugged mountains, this 630,000-acre forest lies in two separate strips along the Tennessee-North Carolina boundary, northeast and southwest of Great Smoky Mountains National Park (see). A region of thick forests, streams, and waterfalls, the forest takes its name from the Native American tribe. There are more than 500 miles of hiking trails, including the Appalachian Trail. There are 29 campgrounds, 28 picnic areas, 8 swimming sites, and 13 boating sites. Hunting for game, including wild boar, deer, and turkey, is permitted under Tennessee game regulations. Fees may be charged at recreation sites. Contact Forest Supervisor, PO Box 2010, Cleveland 37320; 423/476-9700.

Clarksville

(E-3) *See also Hopkinsville, KY*

Founded 1784 **Pop** 75,494 **Elev** 543 ft
Area code 931
Information Clarksville/Montgomery
County Tourist Commission, 312
Madison St, PO Box 883, 37041;
931/647-2331

Clarksville, named for General
George Rogers Clark, has achieved a
balanced economy with many industries and heavy traffic in tobacco,
grain, and livestock. Clarksville has
long been considered one of the top
dark-fired tobacco markets in the
world. Natural gas and low-cost TVA
power have contributed to the
town's industrial development.
Clarksville is the home of Austin
Peay State University.

Annual Events

Old-Time Fiddlers Championship.
Late Mar.

Walking Horse Show. Fairgrounds.
Early June.

Motels/Motor Lodges

★ **DAYS INN.** *1100 Hwy 76; Connector Rd (37043), I-24 Exit 11. 931/358-
3194; fax 931/358-9869; toll-free
800/329-7466.* 84 rms, 2 story. S $36-
$50; D $45-$60; each addl $6; under
16 free. Crib free. Pet accepted. TV;
cable (premium). Pool. Complimentary continental bkfst. Restaurant adj
6 am-9 pm; wkends to 10 pm. Ck-
out 11 am. Business servs avail.
Microwaves avail. Cr cds: A, C, D,
DS, MC, V.
D ◆ ≈ ⊠ 🐾 SC

★ **ECONO LODGE INN.** *201 Holiday Rd (37040), I-24 Exit 4. 931/645-
6300; fax 931/645-5054; toll-free
800/553-2666.* 103 rms, 2 story. S $38-
$55; D $50-$69; each addl $6; under
12 free. Crib $6. TV; cable (premium),
VCR avail (movies). Pool. Complimentary continental bkfst. Restaurant
nearby. Ck-out 11 am. Coin lndry.
Meeting rm. Business servs avail. In-
rm modem link. Many microwaves;
some refrigerators, whirlpools. Cr cds:
A, C, D, DS, JCB, MC, V.
≈ ⊠ 🐾 SC

★★ **HAMPTON INN.** *190 Holiday
Rd (37040), I-24 Exit 4. 931/552-
2255; fax 931/552-4871.* 77 air-
cooled rms, 2 story. S $51-$59; D
$59-$63; under 18 free. Crib free. TV;
cable (premium). Pool; whirlpool.
Complimentary continental bkfst.
Restaurant nearby. Ck-out noon.
Coin lndry. Meeting rm. Sundries.
Exercise equipt. Some refrigerators,
microwaves Cr cds: A, D, DS, MC, V.
D 🛌 ≈ 🍴 ⊠ 🐾

★★ **QUALITY INN.** *803 N 2nd St
(37040), 1½ mi NW on US 41A, 79.
931/645-9084; fax 931/645-9084; toll-
free 800/228-5151.* 130 rms, 2 story. S
$45-$61; D $55-$61; each addl $6;
under 18 free. Crib free. Pet accepted,
some restrictions. TV; cable (premium). Indoor pool; whirlpool.
Sauna. Complimentary continental
bkfst. Bar 5-11 pm. Ck-out noon. Coin
lndry. Meeting rms. Business servs
avail. Valet serv. Microwave in suites.
Cr cds: A, C, D, DS, JCB, MC, V.
D ◆ ≈ ⊠ 🐾 SC

★★ **RIVERVIEW INN.** *50 College St
(37041). 931/552-3331; fax 931/647-
5005; toll-free 877/487-4837.* 154 rms,
7 story. S, D $54-$85; each addl $5;
under 18 free. Crib free. Pet accepted,
some restrictions. TV; cable (premium). Indoor pool. Restaurant 6
am-2 pm, 5-10 pm; Sat, Sun 7 am-2
pm. Bar from 5 pm. Ck-out noon.
Meeting rms. In-rm modem link.
Microwaves in suites. Cr cds: A, C, D,
DS, JCB, MC, V.
D ◆ ≈ ⊠ 🐾 SC

★ **TRAVELODGE.** *3075 Wilma
Rudolph Blvd (37040), US 79 & I-24
Exit 4. 931/645-1400; fax 931/645-
1096; toll-free 800/531-1900. Email
travel@knightwave.com.* 125 rms, 4
story. S, D $40-$50; under 18 free.
Crib free. Pet accepted. TV; cable
(premium). Heated pool; whirlpool.
Complimentary full bkfst, coffee in
rms. Restaurant 6 am-9 pm. Bar 5:30
pm-midnight. Ck-out noon. Meeting
rms. Business servs avail. Game rm.
Microwaves avail. Cr cds: A, C, D,
DS, MC, V.
D ◆ ≈ ⊠ 🐾 SC

Cleveland

(F-6) *See also Chattanooga*

Pop 30,354 **Elev** 920 ft **Area code** 423

Cleveland is the location of the Superintendent's office of the Cherokee National Forest (see).

Motels/Motor Lodges

★★ **BAYMONT INN & SUITES.** *107 Interstate Dr NW (37312). 423/339-1000; fax 423/339-2760; res 801/301-0200.* 83 rms, 3 story, 14 suites. S, D $63; each addl $7; under 18 free. Crib avail. Pet accepted, some restrictions. Pool. TV; cable (DSS), VCR avail. Complimentary continental bkfst, coffee in rms, newspaper, toll-free calls. Restaurant nearby. Ck-out noon, ck-in 3 pm. Meeting rm. Business servs avail. Dry cleaning, coin lndry. Golf, 18 holes. Cr cds: A, D, DS, MC, V.

★★ **HOLIDAY INN.** *2400 Executive Park Dr NW (37312), jct TN 60 and I-75 Exit 25. 423/472-1504; fax 423/479-5962.* 146 rms, 2 story. S $72-$80; D $70-$89; under 18 free; higher rates special events. Crib free. Pet accepted, some restrictions. TV; cable (premium). Pool. Restaurant 6 am-2 pm, 5-10 pm. Rm serv 7 am-9:30 pm. Ck-out noon. Meeting rms. Business servs avail. Sundries. Health club privileges. Cr cds: A, C, D, DS, JCB, MC, V.

★★ **QUALITY INN - CHALET.** *2595 Georgetown Rd NW (37311), jct TN 60 & I-75 Exit 25. 423/476-8511; fax 423/476-8511; toll-free 800/228-5151.* 97 rms, 2-3 story. No elvtr. May-Sep: S, D $56-$66; each addl $5; under 18 free; lower rates rest of yr. Crib $5. Pet accepted, some restrictions. TV; cable (premium). Pool; wading pool. Coffee in rms. Restaurant 11 am-10 pm. Ck-out noon. Coin lndry. Meeting rms. Some refrigerators; microwaves avail. Cr cds: A, C, D, DS, ER, MC, V.

Restaurant

★ **ROBLYN'S STEAK HOUSE.** *1422 25th St NW (37311), 2 blks E of I-75 Exit 25. 423/476-8808.* Specializes in steak, seafood. Salad bar. Hrs: 4-10 pm; Sun brunch 11 am-2 pm. Closed hols. Res accepted. Dinner $5-$15. Sun brunch $6.49. Child's menu. Parking. Family-owned. Cr cds: A, DS, MC, V.

Columbia

(E-4) *See also Franklin*

Settled 1807 **Pop** 28,583 **Elev** 637 ft **Area code** 931 **Zip** 38401

Information Maury County Convention & Visitors Bureau, #8 Public Square, 38401; 931/381-7176 or 888/852-1860

James K. Polk, 11th president of the United States, spent his boyhood in Columbia and returned here to open his first law office. The town is known for its many antebellum houses.

Annual Events

Mule Day. Liar's contest, auction, parade, mule pull, square dance, bluegrass night, pioneer craft festival, knife and coin show. First wkend Apr.

National Tennessee Walking Horse Jubilee. Maury County Park. Contact the park, Experiment Station Lane; 931/388-0303. Late May-early June.

Maury County Fair. Maury County Park Fairgrounds. Phone 931/388-0303. Late Aug-early Sep.

Majestic Middle Tennessee Fall Tour. Phone 931/381-4822. Last wkend Sep.

Plantation Christmas Tour of Homes. First wkend Dec.

Motels/Motor Lodges

★ **DAYS INN.** *1504 Nashville Hwy (38401). 931/381-3297; fax 931/381-8692; toll-free 800/329-7466.* 54 rms, 2 story. S, D $44-$55; each addl $4;

suite $70; under 13 free; wkend rates. Crib free. TV; cable (premium), VCR avail. Pool. Complimentary continental bkfst. Restaurant nearby. Ck-out 11 am. Meeting rm. Business servs avail. Cr cds: A, C, D, DS, ER, MC, V.

★★ **RAMADA INN.** *1208 Nashville Hwy (38401), 2½ mi N on US 31. 931/388-2720; fax 931/388-2360.* 155 rms, 2 story. S $42-$52; D $47-$57; each addl $5. Crib free. Pet accepted. TV; cable (premium), VCR avail. Pool. Restaurant 6 am-2 pm, 5-10 pm. Bar 4 pm-midnight. Ck-out noon. Meeting rms. Cr cds: A, DS, MC, V.

Restaurants

★★ **THE OLE LAMPLIGHTER.** *1000 Riverside Dr (38401). 931/381-3837. Email theole@edge.net.* Specializes in steak, seafood. Salad bar. Hrs: 4-10 pm. Closed hols; also 1st wk July. Res accepted. Bar. Dinner $8.95-$29.95. Child's menu. Rustic log building at river. Cr cds: A, D, DS, MC, V.

★ **RANCH HOUSE.** *900 Riverside Dr (38401). 931/381-2268.* Specializes in steak, fish. Hrs: 4-10 pm. Closed Sun, Mon. Res accepted. Dinner $6.95-$15.95. Child's menu. Overlooks river. Cr cds: A, D, DS, MC, V.

Cookeville (E-5)

Settled 1854 **Pop** 21,744 **Elev** 1,118 ft
Area code 931 **Zip** 38501
Web www.cookeville.com/chamber

Information Cookeville Area-Putnam County Chamber of Commerce, 302 S Jefferson Ave; 931/526-2211 or 800/264-5541

Motels/Motor Lodges

★★ **ALPINE LODGE & SUITES.** *2021 E Spring St. (38506), on US 70N at I-40 Exit 290. 931/526-3333; fax 931/528-9036; toll-free 800/213-2016.*

Burgess Falls

Email admin@alpinelodge.org; www. alpinelodge.org. 64 rms, 2 story, 24 suites. May-Sep: S $38; D $48; each addl $5; suites $62; under 17 free; lower rates rest of yr. Crib avail. Pet accepted, some restrictions, fee. Parking lot. Pool, children's pool. TV; cable (premium), VCR avail. Complimentary continental bkfst, coffee in rms, newspaper, toll-free calls. Restaurant 11 am-9 pm. Ck-out noon, ck-in 2 pm. Meeting rm. Fax servs avail. Coin lndry. Exercise equipt. Golf. Picnic facilities. Cr cds: A, C, D, DS, ER, JCB, MC, V.

★★ **BEST WESTERN.** *900 S Jefferson Ave (38501), ½ mi N of I-40 Sparta Rd Exit 287. 931/526-7115; fax 931/526-7115; toll-free 800/528-1234.* 76 rms, 3 story. S $30-$45; D $35-$47; suites $60-$100; each addl $4; under 12 free. Crib $6. Pet accepted. TV; cable. Pool. Complimentary continental bkfst. Restaurant adj 6 am-midnight. Ck-out noon. Meeting rms. Business servs avail. Exercise equipt. Cr cds: A, C, D, DS, JCB, MC, V.

★ **ECONO LODGE.** *1100 S Jefferson Ave (38506), I-40 Exit 287. 931/528-1040; fax 931/528-5227.* 71 air-cooled rms, 2 story. May-Oct: S $39.95-$49.95; D $44.95-$54.95;

each addl $5; suites $59.95-$69.95; under 10 free; lower rates rest of yr. Crib $5. Pet accepted; $5. TV; cable (premium). Pool. Complimentary continental bkfst. Ck-out 11 am. Business servs avail. Many refrigerators. Cr cds: A, D, DS, MC, V.

★★ **EXECUTIVE INN.** *897 S Jefferson Ave (38501), at jct TN 136 I-40, Exit 287. 931/526-9521; fax 931/528-2285; res 800/826-2791.* 83 rms, 2 story. S, D $35-$45; each addl $5. TV; cable (premium). Pool; wading pool. Continental bkfst. Restaurant 11 am-10 pm; Fri, Sat to 11 pm. Ck-out 11 am. Coin lndry. Meeting rm. Business servs avail. Cr cds: A, C, D, DS, ER, MC, V.

★★ **RAMADA LIMITED SUITES.** *1045 Interstate Dr (38501). 931/372-0086; fax 931/372-0030. www.tn directory.com/crsuites.* 60 rms, 3 story, 53 suites. S $54-$65; D $59-$70; each addl $5; suites $54-$70; under 18 free; higher rates special events. Crib free. TV; cable (premium). Indoor pool. Complimentary continental bkfst. Restaurant nearby. Ck-out 11 am. Coin lndry. Meeting rms. Business servs avail. In-rm modem link. Sundries. Exercise equipt. Refrigerators, minibars. Cr cds: A, D, DS, MC, V.

Hotel

★★★ **HOLIDAY INN.** *970 S Jefferson Ave (38501), at jct I-40 & TN 136, Exit 287. 931/526-7125; fax 931/526-7125. Email sales1@cooperhotels. com; www.holiday-inn.com/cookevilletn.* 197 rms, 2 story, 3 suites. June-Sep, Dec: S, D $74; suites $75; under 18 free; lower rates rest of yr. Crib avail. Pet accepted. Parking lot. Indoor/outdoor pools, whirlpool. TV; cable. Complimentary continental bkfst, coffee in rms, newspaper, toll-free calls. Restaurant 6 am-8:30 pm. Bar. Ck-out noon, ck-in 3 pm. Meeting rms. Bellhops. Dry cleaning, coin lndry. Exercise equipt. Golf. Cr cds: A, C, D, DS, JCB, MC, V.

Restaurant

★★ **NICK'S.** *895 S Jefferson Ave (38501), at jct I-40 & Sparta Hwy. 931/528-1434.* Specializes in charbroiled steak, seafood, ice cream pie. Hrs: 11 am-2 pm, 5-10 pm; Fri to 10:30 pm; Sat 5-10:30 pm; Sun 11 am-2:30 pm. Closed Mon. Bar. Lunch, dinner $5.95-$16.95. Parking. Cr cds: A, C, D, DS, MC, V.

Covington

(F-1) *See also Memphis*

Pop 7,487 **Elev** 339 ft **Area code** 901 **Zip** 38019

What to See and Do

Fort Pillow State Historic Area. This archaeologically significant area consists of 1,646 acres on the Chickasaw Bluffs, overlooking Mississippi River. It contains substantial remains of a large fort named for a Confederate general and 5 mi of earthworks. Fishing; wooded trails (15 mi), picnicking, tent and primitive camping. Visitor center (Mon-Fri), nature exhibits. (Daily; closed Dec 25) Standard fees. 33 mi NW via US 51N & TN 87W. Phone 901/738-5581.

Crossville

Pop 6,930 **Elev** 1,863 ft **Area code** 931 **Zip** 38555 **Information** Greater Cumberland County Chamber of Commerce, 108 S Main St, 38555; 931/484-8444

Annual Event

Cumberland County Fair. Exhibits; horse, cattle, and other animal shows; mule pulls; fiddlers' contest. Phone 931/484-9454. Late Aug.

Motels/Motor Lodges

★ **DAYS INN CROSSVILLE.** *105 Executive Dr (38555). 931/484-9691; fax 931/484-9691.* 61 rms, 2 story. Mid-May-Oct: S, D $50-$70; each addl $5; under 17 free; lower rates rest of yr. Crib free. Pet accepted, some restrictions. TV; cable (premium). Pool. Complimentary continental bkfst. Restaurant adj. Ck-out 11 am. Business servs avail. On river. Cr cds: A, C, D, DS, ER, MC, V.

★★ **HAMPTON INN CROSSVILLE.** *4038 Hwy 127 N (38555), I-40 Exit 317. 931/456-9338; fax 931/456-8758; res 800/426-7866. www. hampton-inn.com/hi/cross.* 60 rms, 3 story. Apr-Oct: S, D $69-$89; under 18 free; family rates; higher rates special events; lower rates rest of yr. Crib free. TV; cable (premium). Complimentary continental bkfst, coffee in rms. Restaurant adj open 24 hrs. Ckout 11 am. Meeting rms. Business servs avail. In-rm modem link. Exercise equipt. Indoor pool; whirlpool. Cr cds: A, C, D, ER, JCB, MC, V.

Resort

★★★ **FAIRFIELD GLADE RESORT.** *PO Box 1500 (38558), 10 mi N, 6 mi N off I-40 Peavine Rd (Exit 322). 931/484-7521; fax 931/484-3756; res 931/484-3723.* 100 rms, 67 villas. Mar-Oct: S, D $100; villas $110-$150; golf package plan; lower rates rest of yr. Crib free. TV; cable (premium). Indoor/outdoor pool; wading pool. Playground. Supervised children's activities (June-Aug); ages 5-12. Restaurants 7 am-10 pm. Snack bar. Private club. Ck-out 10 am, ck-in 4 pm. Grocery. Meeting rms. Business servs avail. Sports dir. Indoor and lighted tennis, pro. 18-hole golf, greens fee $50, putting green, driving range. Miniature golf. Private beach. Boats, motors, dock. Entertainment. Lawn games. Rec rm. Exercise rm. Private patios, balconies. Picnic tables, grills. Cr cds: A, D, DS, MC, V.

Cumberland Gap National Historical Park

(see Kentucky)

Dickson

(E-3) *See also Hurricane Mills, Nashville*

Founded 1873 **Pop** 8,791 **Elev** 794 ft **Area code** 615 **Zip** 37055
Web www.dickson.net/chamber
Information Chamber of Commerce, 119 US 70 E; 615/446-2349

Annual Event

Old-Timers' Day Festival. Parades, entertainment, and special events. First wkend May.

Dyersburg (E-2)

Pop 16,317 **Elev** 295 ft **Area code** 901 **Zip** 38024

Motels/Motor Lodges

★★ **COMFORT INN.** *815 Reelfoot Dr (38024), I-155 Exit 13. 901/285-6951; fax 901/285-6956; res 800/228-5150. Email cinndyersburg@mail.com.* 82 rms, 2 story. Mar-Sep: S $55-$59; D $60-$65; each addl $6; under 18 free; lower rates rest of yr. Crib $6. TV; cable. Pool. Complimentary continental bkfst. Ck-out 11 am. Coin lndry. Meeting rms. Exercise equipt. Some refrigerators; microwaves avail. Cr cds: A, C, D, DS, MC, V.

★★ **HOLIDAY INN.** *770 W Hwy 50 Bypass (54660), Exit 13 on I-155. 901/285-8601; fax 901/286-0494; toll-free 800/465-4329.* 106 rms, 2 story. S, D $59-$65; each addl $10; under 18 free. Crib free. TV; cable. Pool. Restaurant 6:30 am-2 pm, 5:30-10 pm. Ck-out noon. Meeting rms. Valet serv. Sundries. Cr cds: A, C, D, DS, JCB, MC, V.

🅓 ⊠ ⊠ ⚒ SC

Elizabethton

See also Johnson City

Pop 11,931 **Elev** 1,530 ft
Area code 423 **Zip** 37643
Information Elizabethton/Carter County Chamber of Commerce, 500 19E Bypass, PO Box 190, 37644; 423/547-3850 or 888/547-3852

Annual Events

Roan Mountain Wild Flower Tours & Bird Walks. Roan Mountain State Park. May.

Covered Bridge Celebration. Elk Ave Bridge, downtown. Arts and crafts festival, parade, antique show, ice-cream eating contest. Area country music stars and local talent perform. Six nights early June.

Rhododendron Festival. Roan Mountain State Park. Mid-late June.

Outdoor Drama. Sycamore Shoals State Historic Area. Depicts muster of Overmountain Men, who marched to King's Mt, SC, and defeated the British. Phone 423/543-5808. Mid-July.

Overmountain Victory Trail Celebration. Reenactment in period costume of original 200-mi march. Late Sep.

Fort Donelson National Battlefield and Cemetery

See also Clarksville

(1 mi W of Dover on US 79)

"Unconditional and immediate surrender!" demanded General Ulysses S. Grant when Confederate General Simon B. Buckner proposed a truce at Fort Donelson. Thus did Grant contribute to the long list of appropriate and pithy remarks for which American military men have become justly famous.

Nothing helped Grant so much during this four-day battle as weak generalship on the part of Confederate commanders John B. Floyd and Gideon J. Pillow. Although the Confederates repulsed an attack by Federal ironclad gunboats, the responsibility of surrendering the Confederate garrison of 15,000 was thrust upon Buckner on February 16, 1862. Grant's victory at Fort Donelson, coupled with the fall of Fort Henry ten days earlier, opened the Tennessee and Cumberland rivers into the heart of the Confederacy. In Grant, the people had a new hero. His laconic surrender message stirred the imagination, and he was quickly dubbed "Unconditional Surrender" Grant.

The fort walls, outer defenses, and river batteries still remain and are well-marked to give the story of the battle. A visitor center features a ten-minute slide program, museum, and touch exhibits (daily; closed Dec 25). A six-mile self-guided auto tour includes a visit to the fort, the cemetery, and the Dover Hotel, where General Buckner surrendered. The park is open year-round, dawn-dusk. Contact Superintendent, PO Box 434, Dover 37058; 931/232-5706. **FREE**

Franklin

(D-4) *See also Columbia, Nashville*

Founded 1799 **Pop** 20,098 **Elev** 648 ft
Area code 615 **Zip** 37064
Information Williamson County Chamber of Commerce, City Hall, PO Box 156, 37065-0156; 615/794-1225

What to See and Do

Carnton Plantation and McGavock Confederate Cemetery. Federal house (1826) modified in the 1840s to reflect Greek Revival style. Built by an early mayor of Nashville, house was a social and political center. At the end of the Battle of Franklin, which was fought nearby, 4 Confederate generals lay dead on the back porch. The nation's largest private Confederate cemetery is adj. (Daily; closed hols) 1345 Carnton Lane, 1 mi SE off US 431 (Lewisburg Pike). Phone 615/794-0903. ¢¢

Carter House. (1830) Served as the command post for the Union forces during the Battle of Franklin. Confederate museum has documents, uniforms, flags, guns, maps, Civil War prints. Guided tour of house and grounds, video presentation. (Daily; closed hols) 1140 Columbia Ave, on US 31. Phone 615/791-1861. ¢¢

⭐ **Heritage Trail.** Scenic drive along highway from Brentwood through Franklin to Spring Hill, an area that was, in the mid-1800s, plantation country. Southern culture is reflected in the drive's many antebellum and Victorian houses; Williamson County was 1 of the richest areas in Tennessee by the time of the Civil War. N & S on US 31.

Historic District. Earliest bldgs of Franklin, dating back to 1800; those along Main St are exceptional in their architectural designs and are part of a historic preservation project. Downtown area within 1st Ave S to 5th Ave S and N Margin St to S Margin St, centered around the Town Square and the Confederate Monument.

Annual Events

Heritage Foundation Town & Country Tour. Contact PO Box 723; 615/591-8500. First wkend May.

Carter House Christmas Candlelight Tour. Phone 615/791-1861. First wkend Dec.

Motels/Motor Lodges

⭐⭐ **BEST WESTERN FRANKLIN INN.** *1308 Murfreesboro Rd (37064), TN 96 at I-65 Exit 65. 615/790-0570; fax 615/790-0512; res 800/528-1234; toll-free 800/251-3200. Email stay@ bestwesternfranklin.com; www.best westernfranklin.com.* 142 rms, 2 story. Apr-Oct: S, D $80; under 18 free; lower rates rest of yr. Pet accepted, some restrictions. Parking lot. Pool.

TV; cable (premium). Complimentary continental bkfst, newspaper. Restaurant. Ck-out 11:30 am. Meeting rm. Business center. Coin lndry. Exercise equipt. Golf. Supervised children's activities. Picnic facilities. Cr cds: A, C, D, DS, MC, V.

D 🐾 🛁 🛎 🔜 🏋 SC 🏃

⭐ **SUPER 8 OF FRANKLIN.** *1307 Murfreesboro Rd (37064), TN 96 at I-65. 615/794-7591; fax 615/794-1042; toll-free 800/465-4329. www.marydir. com.* 100 rms, 2 story. May-Sep: S, D $58; each addl $5; under 16 free; lower rates rest of yr. Crib avail. Pet accepted, some restrictions, fee. Parking lot. Pool. TV; cable. Complimentary continental bkfst, coffee in rms, newspaper, toll-free calls. Restaurant. 24-hr rm serv. Meeting rms. Business center. Dry cleaning. Exercise privileges. Golf, 18 holes. Tennis, 2 courts. Picnic facilities. Cr cds: A, C, D, DS, MC, V.

D 🐾 🛎 🏋 🔜 🏋 🛏 🏃 SC 🏃

Gallatin

(E-4) *See also Nashville*

Founded 1802 **Pop** 18,794 **Elev** 526 ft **Area code** 615 **Zip** 37066

Information Chamber of Commerce, 118 W Main, PO Box 26; 615/452-4000

Annual Event

Sumner County Pilgrimage. Tour of historic houses. Contact Cragfont, 200 Cragfont Rd, Castalian Springs 37031. Phone 615/452-7070. Last Sat Apr.

Motel/Motor Lodge

⭐⭐ **SHONEY'S INN.** *221 W Main St (37066). 615/452-5433; fax 615/ 452-1665; res 800/222-2222.* 86 rms, 2 story. S $36-$45; D $45-$55; each addl $6; under 19 free; higher rates Fanfare. Crib free. TV; cable. Pool. Complimentary coffee in lobby. Restaurant adj 6 am-midnight; Fri, Sat to 2 am. Ck-out noon. Meeting rms. Business servs avail. Cr cds: A, DS, MC, V.

D 🔜 🛏 🏃

Hotel

★★★ **HOLIDAY INN.** *615 E Main St (37075), 2 mi E on US 31. 615/824-0022; fax 615/824-7977; res 800/465-4329. Email hihendvlle@aol.com.* 88 rms, 4 story, 5 suites. S, D $89; each addl $10; suites $129; under 18 free. Crib avail. Parking lot. Pool. TV; cable (premium), VCR avail. Complimentary full bkfst, coffee in rms, newspaper, toll-free calls. Restaurant. Bar. Meeting rms. Business servs avail. Bellhops. Dry cleaning, coin lndry. Gift shop. Exercise equipt. Golf, 18 holes. Tennis, 8 courts. Video games. Cr cds: A, C, D, DS, JCB, MC, V.

Gatlinburg

See also Pigeon Forge, Sevierville, Townsend

Pop 3,417 **Elev** 1,289 ft
Area code 865 **Zip** 37738
Web www.gatlinburg.com
Information Chamber of Commerce, 520 Parkway, PO Box 527; 423/430-4148 or 800/568-4748

Gatlinburg has retained most of its mountain quaintness while turning its attention to tapping into the stream of tourists that flows through the town en route to Great Smoky Mountains National Park, the country's most visited national park. The city has accommodations for 40,000 guests and a $22-million convention center. At the foot of Mount LeConte and at the head of the Pigeon River, Gatlinburg is noted for its many shops that make and sell mountain handicrafts—brooms, candles, candies, pottery, and furniture.

What to See and Do

Christus Gardens. Events from the life of Jesus portrayed in life-size dioramas; music and narration. Floral gardens in season. (Daily; closed Dec 25) 510 River Rd. Phone 865/436-5155. ¢¢¢

Craft shops. Along Main St and E along US 321 on Glades Rd.

Great Smoky Mountains National Park. (see)

Ober Gatlinburg Ski Resort. Double, 2 quad chairlifts; patrol, school, rentals, snowmaking; concession area, restaurant, bar. Longest run 5,000 ft; vertical drop 600 ft. (Dec-mid-Mar, daily) Also alpine slide, indoor ice-skating arena (daily; closed 2 wks Mar; fees); aerial tramway and sightseeing chairlift. Contact Ober Gatlinburg, Inc, 1001 Parkway. Ski Mountain Rd, on Mt Harrison. Phone 865/436-5423 or 800/251-9202 (Dec-Mar). ¢¢¢¢

Scenic rides.

Gatlinburg Space Needle. Glass-enclosed elevator to observation deck for view of the Smokies. (Daily) Airport Rd. Phone 865/436-4629. ¢¢

Sky Lift. Double chairlift ride up Crockett Mt to 2,300 ft. View of Smokies en route and from observation deck at summit; snack bar; gift shop. (Daily, weather permitting) 765 Parkway (US 441). Phone 865/436-4307. ¢¢

Sightseeing Chairlift-Ober Gatlinburg Ski Resort. Double chairlift operates to top of Mt Harrison. (Mar-Memorial Day, daily) Ski Mountain Rd, on Mt Harrison. ¢¢

Aerial Tramway-Ober Gatlinburg Ski Resort. Ten-min, 2-mi tram ride to top of Mt Harrison. (Daily; closed 2 wks Mar) 1001 Parkway. Phone 865/436-5423. ¢¢

Annual Events

Spring Wild Flower Pilgrimage. Late Apr.

Scottish Festival and Games. Bagpipe marching bands, highland dancing, sheep dog demonstrations. Third wkend May.

Dulcimer Harp Festival. In Cosby, 20 mi NE on US 321 to TN 32S. Dulcimer convention, folk music, crafts demonstrations, storytelling, workshops. Participants from throughout the Appalachian region. For information contact PO Box 8, Cosby 37722. Phone 865/487-5543. June 15-16, 2001.

Craftsmen's Fairs. Craft demonstrations, folk music. Late July-early Aug; also mid-Oct.

Seasonal Events

Sweet Fanny Adams Theater. 461 Parkway. Professional theater presenting musical comedies, Gay 90s revue, old-time sing-along. Mon-Sat, nightly. Res advisable. Phone 423/436-4039. Late Apr-Nov.

Smoky Mountain Lights. Winter celebration incl Yule log burnings, more than 2 million lights, and other special events. Late Nov-Feb. Citywide.

Motels/Motor Lodges

★ **ALTO MOTEL.** *404 Airport Rd (37738). 865/436-5175; fax 865/430-7342; toll-free 800/456-4336.* 21 rms, 2 story. Late May-Oct: S, D $60-$70; each addl $6; under 16 free; lower rates rest of yr. Crib free. TV; cable (premium). Pool; wading pool. Playground. Restaurant adj 7 am-11 pm. Ck-out 11 am. Downhill ski 1 mi. Refrigerators. Picnic tables, grills. Cr cds: A, DS, MC, V.
⊠ ⊠ ⊠

★★ **BENT CREEK GOLF RESORT.** *3919 E Parkway (37738), 11 mi E on US 321. 865/436-2875; fax 865/436-3257; toll-free 800/251-9336.* 108 rms, 3 story. No elvtr. Apr-Oct: S, D $99-$109; each addl $10; under 18 free; golf plans; lower rates rest of yr. Crib free. TV; cable (premium), VCR avail. Pool; wading pool. Playground. Restaurant 6:30 am-10 pm. Ck-out 11 am. Meeting rms. Business servs avail. 18-hole golf, greens fee $30, pro, putting green, driving range. Downhill ski 10½ mi. Health club privileges. Lawn games. Some refrigerators. Balconies. Cr cds: A, C, D, DS, MC, V.
⊠ ⊠ ⊠ ⊠ ⊠ SC

★★ **BEST WESTERN CROSS-ROADS.** *4440 Parkway (37738), at jct US 441 & TN 321. 865/436-5661; fax 865/436-6208; res 800/925-8889.* 78 rms, 2-4 story, 10 suites. May-Oct: S, D $49.50-$99.50; suites, kit. units $139.50-$150; lower rates rest of yr. Crib $6. TV; cable. Pool; wading pool. Ck-out 11 am. Coin lndry. Business servs avail. Downhill ski 2 mi. Some fireplaces. Covered patio. Cr cds: A, C, D, DS, MC, V.
⊠ ⊠ ⊠ ⊠ SC

★★ **BEST WESTERN FABULOUS CHALET.** *310 Cottage Dr (37738), at River Rd. 865/436-5151; fax 865/523-8363.* 75 rms, 2 story, 1 kit. S, D $70-$89.50; kit. unit $90-$109.50; under 18 free. Crib free. TV; cable. Pool; wading pool. Complimentary continental bkfst Apr-Oct. Coffee in rms. Restaurant nearby. Ck-out 11 am. Business servs avail. Refrigerators. Sun deck. Many rms overlook Little Pigeon River. Cr cds: A, D, DS, MC, V.
⊠ ⊠ ⊠ ⊠ ⊠ ⊠

★★ **BEST WESTERN NEWPORT INN.** *Cosby Hwy 32 (37822), I-40 Exit 435. 865/623-8713; fax 865/623-1804; res 800/251-4022.* 111 rms, 2 story. June-Oct: S $44-$59; D $54-$99; each addl $6; under 17 free; higher rates special events; lower rates rest of yr. Crib free. Pet accepted, some restrictions. TV; cable (premium). Complimentary full bkfst. Restaurant 6-10 am. Ck-out noon. Meeting rms. Business servs avail. Heated pool; wading pool, whirlpool. Some in-rm whirlpools. Cr cds: A, C, D, DS, MC, V.
⊠ ⊠ ⊠ ⊠ ⊠ SC

★ **BON AIR LODGE.** *950 Parkway (37738). 865/436-4857; fax 865/436-8942; toll-free 800/523-3919.* 74 rms, 3 story, 1 kit. chalet. Apr-Oct: S, D $43-$99; chalet $125-$175; higher rates special events; lower rates rest of yr. Crib free. Pet accepted. TV; cable. Pool. Restaurant nearby. Ck-out 11 am. Business servs avail. Downhill ski 1 mi. Refrigerators. Balconies. Cr cds: A, D, DS, MC, V.
⊠ ⊠ ⊠ ⊠ ⊠ SC

★★ **BROOKSIDE RESORT.** *463 E Parkway (37738), 3 blks E on US 321. 865/436-5611; fax 865/436-0039; toll-free 800/251-9597.* 216 rms in motel, cottages, 1-2 story, 30 kits. May-Nov: S $55-$110; D $70-$110; each addl $5; suites from $100; kit. units $55-$145; kit. cottages for 2-4, $60-$175; lower rates rest of yr. Crib free. TV; cable. Pool; wading pool, whirlpool. Playground. Restaurant opp 7 am-10 pm. Ck-out 11 am. Coin lndry. Meeting rm. Business servs avail. Downhill ski 6 mi. Lawn games. In-rm whirlpools, refrigerators, fireplaces. Picnic tables, grills. Spacious grounds. By mountain stream. Cr cds: A, C, D, MC, V.
⊠ ⊠ ⊠ ⊠ ⊠

★ **CREEKSIDE INN.** *239 Sycamore Ln (37738). 865/436-5977; toll-free 800/697-5977.* 42 rms, 4 story, 1 kit. Apr-Nov: S $50-$75; D $58-$98; each addl $4; kit. unit $78-$88; lower rates rest of yr. Crib $5. TV; cable. Pool; wading pool. Coffee in lobby. Restaurant nearby. Ck-out 11 am. Refrigerators. Picnic tables, grills. Porches overlook stream. Cr cds: A, C, D, DS, MC, V.

★ **DAYS INN.** *504 Airport Rd (37738). 865/436-9361; fax 865/436-6951; res 800/362-9522; toll-free 800/329-7466.* 217 rms, 5 story. S, D $39-$96; each addl $10; suites $85-$150; under 17 free. Crib free. TV; cable. 2 pools, 1 indoor; wading pool, whirlpool. Sauna. Playground. Restaurant 7 am-2 pm. Ck-out 11 am. Meeting rms. Business servs avail. In-rm modem link. Bellhops. Downhill/x-country ski 1 mi. Wet bar in suites. Picnic tables. On river. Cr cds: A, D, DS, MC, V.

★ **EAST SIDE MOTEL.** *315 E Parkway. 865/436-7569.* 29 rms, 2-3 story. No elvtr. June-Oct: S $45-$60; D $45-$65; each addl $5; lower rates mid-Mar-May, Nov. Closed rest of yr. Crib $5. TV; cable. Pool; wading pool. Playground. Complimentary coffee in rms. Restaurant nearby. Ck-out 11 am. Refrigerators. Picnic tables, grills. Cr cds: DS, MC, V.

★ **ECONO LODGE.** *405 Airport Rd (37738). 865/436-5836; res 800/933-8670.* 33 rms. 1-4 persons $42-$89.50; suites $79.50-$129.50. Crib free. TV; cable (premium). Pool. Complimentary coffee in rms. Restaurant adj 6 am-10 pm. Ck-out 11 am. Business servs avail. Refrigerators. Cr cds: A, C, D, DS, MC, V.

★★ **GILLETTE MOTEL.** *235 Airport Rd (37738), opp convention center. 865/436-5601; fax 865/430-5772; toll-free 800/437-0815.* 80 rms, 3 story, 1 kit. Late May-Oct: S, D $60-$75; each addl $10; kit. unit for 2-4, $85-$95; lower rates rest of yr. Crib $10. TV; cable. Pool. Complimentary coffee in rms. Restaurant nearby. Ck-out 11

am. Downhill ski 1 mi. Refrigerators. Balconies. Cr cds: A, C, D, DS, MC, V.

★★ **GREYSTONE LODGE.** *559 Parkway (37738). 865/436-5621; fax 865/430-4471; res 800/451-9202.* 257 rms, 2-5 story. June-Oct: S, D $69-$119; each addl $8; suites $99-$169; under 13 free; higher rates holidays; lower rates rest of yr. Crib free. TV; cable. Heated pool; wading pool. Complimentary continental bkfst. Ck-out 11 am. Coin lndry. Meeting rms. Business servs avail. Downhill ski 2 mi. Some fireplaces. Balconies. On river. Cr cds: A, C, D, DS, MC, V.

★★ **HAMPTON INN.** *967 Parkway (37738). 865/436-4878; fax 865/436-4088; toll-free 888/476-6597.* 96 rms, 4 story. S $67-$129; D $77-$129; each addl $5; under 18 free; golf plans; higher rates special events. Crib free. TV; cable (premium), VCR (movies). Heated pool; whirlpool. Complimentary continental bkfst. Restaurant adj 11 am-11 pm. Ck-out 11 am. Meeting rms. Business servs avail. Downhill ski ½ mi. Some refrigerators. Balconies. Cr cds: A, C, D, DS, MC, V.

★★★ **HOLIDAY INN.** *520 Airport Rd (37738). 865/436-9201; fax 865/436-7974; res 800/435-9201.* 402 rms, 2-8 story. May-Oct: S, D $69-$139; suites $150-$250; under 19 free; lower rates rest of yr. Crib free. Pet accepted. TV; cable (premium). 3 pools, 2 indoor; wading pool, whirlpools. Coffee in rms. Supervised children's activities (summer); ages 3-12. Restaurant 7 am-10 pm. Bar 5 pm-midnight. Ck-out 11 am. Coin lndry. Convention facilities. Business servs avail. Bellhops. Gift shop. Downhill ski 4 mi. Exercise equipt. Rec rm. Refrigerators. Picnic tables, grills. Cr cds: A, C, D, DS, JCB, MC, V.

★★ **JACK HUFF'S MOTOR LODGE.** *204 Cherokee Orchard Rd. 865/436-5171; toll-free 800/322-1817. Email jhuffs_2@aol.com; www.gatlinburg.com/jackhuffs.* 60 rms, 3 story. June-Oct: S, D $68-$83; each addl $5; lower rates rest of yr. Crib free. TV; cable. Pool; wading pool, whirlpool. Complimentary coffee. Restaurant nearby. Ck-out

11 am. Business servs avail. Downhill ski 4 mi. Cr cds: DS, MC, V.

★★ **JOHNSON'S INN.** *242 Bishop Ln (37738). 865/436-4881; fax 865/ 436-2582.* 80 rms, 1-4 story, 3 kits. June-Aug, Oct: S, D $59-$90; each addl $5; under 6 free; higher rates special events; lower rates rest of yr. TV; cable, VCR (movies). Pool; wading pool. Complimentary coffee. Restaurant nearby. Ck-out 11 am. Coin lndry. Business servs avail. Refrigerators, fireplaces. Cr cds: DS, MC, V.

★★ **LE CONTE VIEW.** *929 Parkway (37738). 865/436-5032; fax 865/436-7973; toll-free 800/842-5767.* 104 rms, 1-5 story. May-Oct: S, D $65-$105; each addl $7; suites $89-$141; under 18 free; fireplace units $14 addl; higher rates some hol wkends; lower rates rest of yr. Closed Dec 21-25. Crib $4. TV; cable. Indoor/outdoor pool; wading pool. Complimentary coffee in lobby. Restaurant nearby. Ck-out 11 am. Business servs avail. Downhill ski 1 mi. Refrigerators. Cr cds: A, C, D, DS, MC, V.

★★ **MIDTOWN LODGE.** *805 Parkway (37738). 865/436-5691; toll-free 800/633-2446.* 133 rms, 1-6 story, 13 kits. June-Oct: S, D $69.50-$99; suites $99.50-$129.50; kit cottages $99.50-$149.50; higher rates special events; lower rates rest of yr. Crib free. TV; cable. Pool; wading pool. Complimentary continental bkfst. Restaurant opp 7 am-11 pm. Ck-out 11 am. Business servs avail. Downhill ski 2 mi. Some refrigerators, fireplaces. Private patios, balconies. Cr cds: A, DS, MC, V.

★★ **OAK SQUARE.** *685 River Rd (37738). 865/436-7582; fax 865/430-7230.* 46 kit. suites, 4 story. Suites $55-$135; hol rates; ski plans; lower rates winter. Crib free. TV; cable. 2 pools, 1 indoor; whirlpool. Restaurant nearby. Ck-out 11 am. Meeting rm. Business servs avail. Downhill ski 1 mi. Fireplaces. Balconies. Opp river. Cr cds: MC, V.

★★ **RAMADA LIMITED.** *200 E Parkway (37738). 865/236-5043; fax 865/436-5043; res 800/933-8679.* 103 rms, 4 story. May-Oct: S, D up to 4 $84.50-$149.50; under 18 free; lower rates rest of yr. Crib $5. TV; cable. Pool; wading pool, whirlpool. Complimentary continental bkfst. Restaurant 7 am-2 pm. Ck-out 11 am. Coin lndry. Meeting rms. Business servs avail. Downhill ski 5 mi. Some fireplaces. Cr cds: A, D, DS, MC, V.

★★ **RIVER EDGE MOTOR LODGE.** *665 River Rd (37738). 865/436-9292; fax 865/436-3943; toll-free 800/544-2764.* 43 rms, 3 story. May-Oct: S, D $65-$135; each addl $5; higher rates: hols, Oct; lower rates rest of yr. Crib free. TV; cable. Pool; wading pool. Complimentary coffee in lobby. Restaurant nearby. Ck-out 11 am. Downhill ski 1 mi. Refrigerators; some fireplaces. Balconies. Cr cds: A, D, DS, MC, V.

★★ **RIVER TERRACE CREEK SIDE.** *125 LeConte Creek Rd (37738). 865/436-4865; fax 865/436-4089; toll-free 800/473-8319. Email rivert@river terrace.com.* 69 units, 1-3 story. Mid-May-early Jan: S, D $62-$99; each addl $10; suites $99-$179; lower rates rest of yr. TV; cable (premium). Pool; wading pool. Complimentary conti-

Deep Creek Mountains, Great Smoky Mountains National Park

nental bkfst. Restaurant adj 7 am-10 pm. Ck-out 11 am. Meeting rms. Business servs avail. Downhill ski 1 mi. Some in-rm whirlpools, fireplaces. Balconies. Cr cds: A, C, D, DS, MC, V.

🛇 🏊 🚫 🗋 🖑 SC

★ **ROCKY TOP VILLAGE INN.** *311 Airport Rd (37738). 865/436-7826; fax 865/436-7826; res 800/553-7738.* 84 rms, 3 story, 3 suites. June-Aug, Oct-Nov: S $45; D $61; each addl $5; suites $91; under 16 free; lower rates rest of yr. Crib avail. Parking garage. TV; cable. Complimentary toll-free calls. Restaurant. Meeting rm. Golf. Tennis, 8 courts. Downhill skiing. Hiking trail. Picnic facilities. Cr cds: A, C, D, DS, MC, V.

D 🛇 🏊 🚫 🖑 🚶 🗋 🖑

★★ **ROCKY WATERS MOTOR INN.** *333 Parkway (37738). 865/436-7861; fax 865/436-0241; toll-free 800/824-1111. Email rkywatrs@smoky-mtns. com; www.smoky-mtns.com.* 100 rms, 2-3 story. Early May-Oct: S, D $78-$83; each addl $5; lower rates rest of yr. Crib $2. TV; cable (premium), VCR (movies $3.50). 2 pools; wading pool, whirlpool. Coffee in lobby. Ck-out 11 am. Coin lndry. Meeting rm. Business servs avail. Downhill ski 2 mi. Refrigerators; some in-rm whirlpools, fireplaces. Private patios. Picnic tables. On river. Cr cds: A, C, D, DS, MC, V.

D 🛇 🏊 🚫 🗋 🖑 SC

★ **ROYAL TOWNHOUSE MOTOR INN.** *937 Parkway (37738), opp Civic Auditorium. 865/436-5818; fax 865/436-0411; toll-free 800/433-8792.* 81 rms, 3 story. Late May-Nov: S, D $59.95-$89.95; each addl $5; under 17 free; lower rates rest of yr. Crib $5. TV; cable. Pool; wading pool. Complimentary coffee in rms. Restaurant nearby. Ck-out 11 am. Meeting rms. Business servs avail. Downhill ski 1 mi. Some refrigerators, fireplaces. Cr cds: C, D, DS, MC, V.

🏊 🚫 🗋 🖑 SC

★ **SKYLAND MOTEL.** *223 E Parkway (37738), 1 blk E on US 321. 865/436-5821; fax 865/436-6876; toll-free 800/255-8738.* 56 rms, 1-2 story. May-Oct: S, D $59-$89; each addl $5; suites $95-$135; lower rates rest of yr. Crib $5. TV; cable. Pool. Complimen-

tary continental bkfst. Restaurant nearby. Ck-out 11 am. Downhill ski 5 mi. Refrigerators. Many balconies. Picnic tables. Cr cds: A, C, D, DS, MC, V.

D 🏊 🚫 🗋 🖑 SC

★ **SMOKYLAND MOTEL.** *727 Parkway (37738). 865/436-5191; fax 865/523-8363; res 800/933-8671.* 40 rms, 2 story. Memorial Day wkend-mid-Nov: S, D $79-$104; lower rates rest of yr. Crib $6. TV; cable. Pool; wading pool. Complimentary coffee in rms. Restaurant adj. Ck-out 11 am. Downhill ski 3 mi. Refrigerators; some fireplaces. Cr cds: A, D, DS, MC, V.

🏊 🚫 🗋 🖑 SC

★ **TRAVELODGE.** *610 Airport Rd (37738). 865/436-7851; fax 865/430-3580; toll-free 800/876-6888. Email travelodge@btitelecom.net.* 136 rms, 4 story, 15 suites. June-Oct: S, D $55-$88; each addl $6; suites $75-$150; under 17 free; higher rates hols; lower rates rest of yr. Crib free. TV; cable. 2 pools, 1 indoor; wading pool, whirlpool. Coffee in rms. Restaurant 7 am-2 pm. Ck-out 11 am. Coin lndry. Meeting rms. Business servs avail. Downhill/x-country ski 4 mi. Game rm. Refrigerators. Balconies. Picnic tables. On river. Cr cds: A, C, D, DS, MC, V.

D 🖑 🏊 🚶 🗋 🖑

Hotels

★★ **EDGEWATER HOTEL.** *402 River Rd (37738). 865/436-4151; fax 865/436-6947; res 800/865-9582. Email info@edgewater-hotel.com; www. edgewater-hotel.com.* 205 rms, 8 story. Apr-Oct: S, D $84-$129; each addl $5; suites $125-$175; under 16 free; lower rates rest of yr. Crib $5. TV; cable. Indoor/outdoor pool; whirlpool. Restaurant 7-11 am, 5-10 pm. Bar; entertainment. Ck-out 11 am. Meeting rms. Business servs avail. Downhill ski 1 mi. Some fireplaces. Balconies. On river. Cr cds: A, DS, MC, V.

🏊 🚫 🖑

★★★ **PARK VISTA HOTEL.** *705 Cherokee Orchard Rd (37738). 865/436-9211; fax 865/430-7533; toll-free 800/421-7275. Email prkvsta@ parkvista.com; www.parkvista.com.* 312

rms, 15 story. S, D $59-$129; suites $170-$400; under 17 free; higher rates special events. Crib free. TV; cable. Indoor pools; wading pool, whirlpool, poolside serv. Playground. Restaurant 6:30 am-2 pm, 5-10 pm. Rm serv 6:30 am-10:30 pm. Bar 4 pm-1 am. Ck-out 11 am. Coin lndry. Convention facilities. Business servs avail. Downhill ski 5 mi. Exercise equipt. Game rm. Balconies. Cr cds: A, C, D, DS, MC, V.

⬛ 🔅 🔅 🔅 🔅 🔅 🔅

★★ **QUALITY INN CONVENTION CENTER.** 938 Parkway (37738). 865/436-5607; fax 805/436-5607; res 800/228-5151; toll-free 800/933-8674. www.reaganresorts.com. 63 rms, 3 story. Apr-Nov: S, D $139; each addl $10; lower rates rest of yr. Crib avail, fee. Parking garage. Pool, children's pool. TV; cable. Complimentary full bkfst, coffee in rms. Toll-free calls. Restaurant nearby. Ck-out 11 am, ck-in 2 pm. Meeting rm. Golf. Tennis. Downhill skiing. Beach access. Supervised children's activities. Hiking trail. Picnic facilities. Cr cds: A, C, D, DS, JCB, MC, V.

🔅 🔅 🔅 🔅 🔅 🔅 🔅 🔅

B&Bs/Small Inns

★★ **BUCKHORN INN.** 2140 Tudor Mt Rd (37738), left on Buckhorn Rd, right on Tudor Mt Rd, off US 321N. 865/436-4668; fax 865/436-5009. 12 rms, 2 story. S $95-$250; D $105-$250; each addl $25; wkly rates; higher rates Oct. Complimentary full bkfst. Restaurant (public by res), 7:30 pm sitting. Ck-out 11 am, ck-in 3 pm. Porch overlooks Mt LeConte. Cr cds: A, DS, MC, V.

⬛ 🔅 🔅 🔅 🔅

★★★ **CHRISTOPHER PLACE, AN INTIMATE RESORT.** 1500 Pinnacles Way (37821), US 321 N to TN 32, 10 mi N on TN 32 to English Mt Rd. 865/623-6555; fax 865/613-4771; toll-free 800/595-9441. Email thebestinn@aol.com; www.christopherplace.com. 4 rms, 3 story, 4 suites. June-Oct: S, D $150; suites $250; lower rates rest of yr. Parking lot. Pool. TV; cable (premium), VCR avail. CD avail. Complimentary full bkfst, coffee in rms. Toll-free calls. Restaurant 7-10 pm. Ck-out 11 am, ck-in 3 pm. Meeting rm. Business center. Concierge. Coin lndry. Gift shop. Exercise equipt, sauna. Golf. Tennis. Downhill skiing.

Hiking trail. Picnic facilities. Video games. Cr cds: A, DS, MC, V.

⬛ 🔅 🔅 🔅 🔅 🔅 🔅 🔅 🔅

Restaurants

★ **BRASS LANTERN.** 710 Parkway (37738). 865/436-4168. Specializes in soup, ribs, chicken. Hrs: 11 am-10 pm; Sun from noon. Bar. Lunch, dinner $1.95-$14.95. Child's menu. Parking. Cr cds: A, D, DS, MC, V.

⬛ SC 🔅

★ **HEIDELBERG.** 148 N Parkway (37738). 865/430-3094. Specializes in sauerbraten, schnitzel, steak. Hrs: 5-10 pm; Fri, Sat noon-4 pm, 5-10 pm. Res accepted. Bar. Lunch à la carte entrées: $4.95-$13.95; dinner à la carte entrées: $8.95-$21.95. Child's menu. Parking. German music. Cr cds: A, D, DS, MC, V.

⬛

★★★ **MAXWELL'S BEEF AND SEAFOOD.** 1103 Parkway (37738). 865/436-3738. www.maxwells-inc.com. Specializes in fresh seafood, prime rib, pasta. Hrs: 4:30-10 pm; Fri, Sat 4-11 pm. Bar. Dinner $9.95-$36.95. Child's menu. Parking. Cr cds: A, C, DS, MC, V.

⬛ 🔅

★★ **OPEN HEARTH.** 1654 E Parkway (37738). 865/436-5648. Specializes in prime rib, steak, fresh seafood. Hrs: 4:30-10 pm; Fri, Sat to 11 pm. Bar. Dinner $12.95-$39.95. Child's menu. Entertainment: Fri, Sat. Parking. Family-owned. Cr cds: A, MC, V.

⬛ 🔅

★★ **PARK GRILL.** 1100 Parkway (37738). 865/436-2300. www.peddlerparkgrill.com. Specializes in trout, steak, vegetarian dishes. Hrs: 5-10 pm. Closed Dec 24. Bar. Dinner $8.95-$24.95. Child's menu. Parking. Located at entrance to Great Smoky Mountains National Park. Cr cds: A, D, DS, MC, V.

⬛ SC 🔅

★★ **THE PEDDLER.** 820 River Rd (37738). 865/436-5794. Specializes in steak. Salad bar. Own soups, desserts. Hrs: 5-10 pm; Sat from 4:30 pm. Closed Dec 25. Bar. Dinner $13.95-$29.95. Child's menu. Parking. Converted log cabin. Overlooks river. Cr cds: A, D, DS, MC, V.

⬛ SC 🔅

Great Smoky Mountains National Park

See also Gatlinburg

(44 mi SE of Knoxville via US 441)

Web www.nps.gov/grsm

The lofty peaks of the Appalachian Mountains stand tall and regal in this 800-square-mile area. They are products of a slow and powerful uplifting of ancient sediments that took place more than 200 million years ago. Red spruce, basswood, eastern hemlock, yellow birch, white ash, cucumber trees, silverbells, Fraser fir, tulip poplar, red maple, and Fraser magnolias tower above hundreds of other species of flowering plants. Perhaps the most spectacular of these are the purple rhododendron, mountain laurel, and flame azalea in bloom from early June to mid-July.

The moist, moderate climate has helped make this area a rich wilderness. From early spring to late fall the "coves" (open valleys surrounded by peaks) and forest floors are covered with a succession of flowers unmatched in the United States for colorful variety. Spring and summer bring heavy showers to the mountains, days that are warm, though 15°-20°F cooler than in the valleys below, and cool nights. Autumn is breathtaking as the deciduous trees change to almost every color in the spectrum. Winter brings snow, which is occasionally heavy, and fog over the mountains; while winter discourages many tourists, it can be a very good time to visit the park. (Some park roads, however, may be temporarily closed.)

A wonderful place to hike, half of the park is in North Carolina, while the other half is in Tennessee. The Appalachian Trail follows the state line for 70 miles along the high ridge of the park. The park preserves cabins, barns, and mills of the mountain people, whose ancestors came years ago from England and Scotland. It is also a place to see the descendants of the Cherokee Indian Nation, whose ancestors hid in the mountains from the soldiers during the winter of 1838-39 to avoid being driven over the "Trail of Tears" to Oklahoma. This is the tribe of Sequoya, a brilliant chief who invented a written alphabet for the Cherokee people.

Stop first at one of the three visitor centers: **Oconaluftee** (daily; closed Dec 25) in North Carolina, two miles north of Cherokee on Newfound Gap Road, designated US 441 outside of park; **Sugarlands** (daily; closed Dec 25) in Tennessee, two miles south of Gatlinburg; and **Cades Cove** (daily; closed Dec 25) in Tennessee, ten miles southwest of Townsend. Both have exhibits and information about the park. There are hundreds of miles of foot trails and bridle paths. Camping is popular; ask at any visitor center for locations, regulations. Developed campgrounds (inquire for fee) are available. Reservations may be made up to three months in advance by phoning 800/365-CAMP from mid-May-Oct for Elkmont, Cades Cove, and Smokemont; reservations not taken for other sites.

The views from Newfound Gap and the observation platform at Clingmans Dome (closed winter), about seven miles southwest, are spectacular. Cades Cove, about 25 miles west of Sugarlands, is an outdoor museum reflecting the life of the original mountain people. It has log cabins and barns. Park naturalists conduct campfire programs and hikes during summer. There are also self-guided nature trails. LeConte Lodge, reached only on foot or horseback, is a concession within the park (late Mar-mid-Nov).

Fishing is permitted with a Tennessee or North Carolina state fishing license. Obtain regulations at visitor centers and campgrounds. The park is a wildlife sanctuary; any disturbance of plant or animal life is forbidden. Dogs and cats are not permitted on trails, but may be brought in if kept on leash or under other physical restrictive controls. Never feed, tease, or frighten bears; always give them a wide berth, as they may inflict serious injury. Watch bears from a car with the windows closed. Park (daily). **FREE**

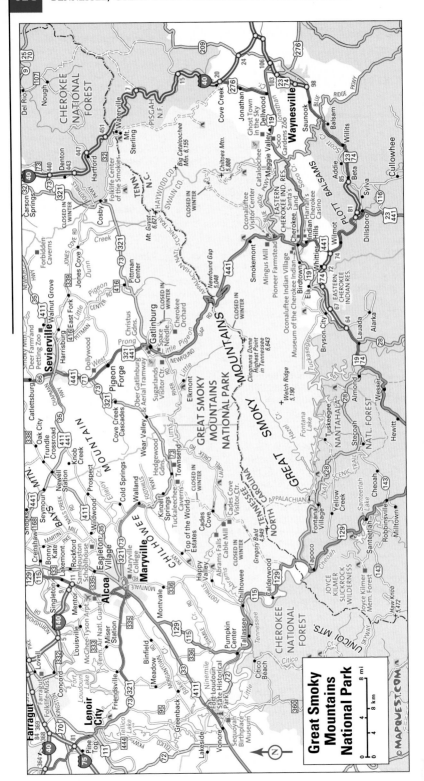

Great Smoky Mountains National Park

© MAPQUEST.COM

HARROGATE/TENNESSEE

CCInc Auto Tape Tours, a 90-minute cassette, offers a mile-by-mile self-guided tour of the park. It provides information on history, points of interest, and flora and fauna of the park. Available in Gatlinburg at motels and gift shops; in Cherokee, NC, at Raven Craft Shop on Main Street, and at Log Cabin Trading Post, across from the cinema. Tapes also may be purchased directly from CCInc, PO Box 227, 2 Elbrook Dr, Allendale, NJ 07401; 201/236-1666. ¢¢¢¢

For further information contact Superintendent, Great Smoky Mountains National Park, 107 Park Headquarters Rd, Gatlinburg 37738. Phone 423/436-1200. Lodging is available in the park at LeConte Lodge. Phone 423/429-5704.

Greeneville

Settled 1783 **Pop** 13,532 **Elev** 1,531 ft
Area code 423
Web www.greene.xtn.net/~gcp
Information Greene County Partnership, 115 Academy St, 37743; 423/638-4111

Motels/Motor Lodges

★ **CHARRAY INN.** *124 Serral Dr (37745).* 423/638-1331; fax 423/639-5289; toll-free 800/852-4682. 36 rms, 2 story. S, D $44-$60; each addl $4; under 16 free. Crib free. TV; cable (premium), VCR avail. Coffee in rms. Restaurant 6-11 am; Sat 7-11:30 am. Ck-out 11 am. Meeting rms. Business servs avail. In-rm modem link. Airport transportation. Refrigerators. Cr cds: A, C, D, DS, MC, V.

★ **DAYS INN.** *935 E Andrew Johnson Hwy (37745).* 423/639-2156; fax 423/639-2156; res 800/329-7466. 60 rms, 2 story. S, D $36-$120; each addl $6. Crib free. Pet accepted. TV; cable (premium). Complimentary continental bkfst. Restaurant nearby. Ck-out 11 am. Business servs avail. Cr cds: A, D, DS, MC, V.

★★ **HOLIDAY INN.** *1790 E Andrew Johnson Hwy (37745).* 423/639-4185; fax 423/639-7280; res 888/557-5007; toll-free 800/465-4329. 90 rms, 2 story. S, D $53-$65; under 18 free; higher rates special events. Crib free. TV; cable (premium). Pool. Restaurant 7 am-2 pm, 6-10 pm. Bar. Ck-out noon. Meeting rms. Business servs avail. Cr cds: A, C, D, DS, JCB, MC, V.

Restaurant

★★ **AUGUSTINO'S.** *3465 E Andrew Johnson Hwy (37745).* 423/639-5612. Specializes in fettuccine, prime rib. Hrs: 11 am-2 pm, 5-10 pm; Sat from 5 pm; Sun brunch to 2 pm. Closed hols. Lunch a la carte entrees: $3.75-$9; dinner a la carte entrees: $5.45-$33. Sun brunch $4.50-$9. Child's menu. Parking. Cr cds: A, DS, MC, V.

Harrogate (E-7)

Pop 2,657 **Elev** 1,300 ft
Area code 423 **Zip** 37752

What to See and Do

Abraham Lincoln Museum. Collection, one of the largest of its type in the world, contains more than 25,000 pieces of Lincolniana and items related to Civil War. Research center. (Daily; closed Easter, Thanksgiving, Dec 25) S on Cumberland Gap Pkwy, US 25E, on the Lincoln Memorial Univ campus. Phone 423/869-6235. ¢

Cumberland Gap National Historical Park. (See under KENTUCKY) 4 mi N on US 25E.

Motel/Motor Lodge

★★ **RAMADA INN CUMBERLAND GAP.** *Hwy 58 (37724), ½ mi E on US 25E.* 423/869-3631; fax 423/869-5953; res 800/272-6232. 147 rms, 4 story. S $54; D $60; each addl $6; under 19 free. Crib free. Pet accepted, some restrictions; $25. TV; cable (premium), VCR avail. Pool. Playground. Restaurant 6:30 am-2 pm, 5:30-9:30 pm. Bar 5 pm-midnight; closed Sun.

www.exxonmobiltravel.com

Ck-out noon. Coin lndry. Meeting rms. Valet serv. Sundries. Balconies. Cr cds: A, C, D, DS, MC, V.

Hurricane Mills

See also Dickson

Pop 40 (est) **Elev** 400 ft
Area code 931 **Zip** 37078
Web www.dogstar.waverly.net/hcchamber

Information Humphreys County Chamber of Commerce, 124 E Main St, PO Box 733, Waverly 37185; 931/296-4865

Motels/Motor Lodges

★★ **BEST WESTERN HURRICANE MILLS.** *15542 Hwy 13 S (37078), I-40 Exit 143. 931/296-4251; fax 931/296-9104; res 800/528-1231.* 89 rms, 2 story. May-Aug: S $50-$64; D $50-$70; each addl $4; under 12 free; higher rates special events; lower rates rest of yr. Crib $2. Pet accepted, some restrictions. TV; cable (premium), VCR avail (movies). Pool; whirlpool. Playground. Restaurant 6 am-9 pm. Ck-out 11 am. Coin lndry. Meeting rm. Some refrigerators; microwaves avail. Cr cds: A, D, DS, MC, V.

★ **DAYS INN.** *15415 Hwy 13 S (37078), off I-40 Exit 143. 931/296-7647; fax 931/296-5488; res 800/841-5813; toll-free 800/329-7466.* 78 rms, 2 story. S $40-$44; D $54-$64; each addl $5; higher rates special events. Crib free. Pet accepted. TV; cable (premium). Pool. Restaurant 6 am-10 pm. Ck-out noon. Meeting rm. Cr cds: A, C, D, DS, MC, V.

Jackson (D-1)

Founded 1822 **Pop** 48,949 **Elev** 401 ft
Area code 901

Information Jackson/Madison County Convention & Visitors Bureau, 400 S Highland, 38301; 901/425-8333 or 800/498-4748

Railroading is both the tradition and past livelihood of Jackson, home and burial place of John Luther "Casey" Jones, hero of ballad and legend. Because many of General Andrew Jackson's soldiers and many of his wife's relatives settled here, the town was named in his honor. Today Jackson is an industrial center of western Tennessee.

What to See and Do

Casey Jones Village. Complex of turn-of-the-century shops and bldgs centered around the life of one of America's most famous railroad heroes. 5 mi NW at US 45 Bypass & I-40. **FREE** In the village are

Casey Jones Home and Railroad Museum. The original house of the high-rolling engineer who, on Apr 30, 1900, climbed into the cab of "Old 382" on the Illinois Central Railroad and took his "farewell trip to that promised land"—and a place in American folklore. On display are personal effects of Jones and railroad memorabilia, incl railroad passes, timetables, bells and steam whistles; also steam locomotive of the type driven by Casey Jones and restored 1890s coach cars. (Daily; closed Easter, Thanksgiving, Dec 25) Phone 901/668-1222. ¢¢

Brooks Shaw & Son Old Country Store. Turn-of-the-century general store with more than 15,000 antiques on display; restaurant (see), ice-cream parlor, confectionery shop. (Daily; closed Easter, Thanksgiving, Dec 25) Phone 901/668-1223.

Motels/Motor Lodges

★★ **BAYMONT INN.** *2370 N Highland Ave (38305), at I-40 Exit 82A. 901/664-1800; fax 901/664-5456; res 800/301-0200.* 102 rms, 3 story. S $33.95-$41.95; D $41.95-$48.95; each addl $7; under 18 free. Crib free. TV; cable, VCR avail (movies). Pool. Complimentary continental bkfst, coffee in rms. Restaurant adj 11 am-10 pm. Ck-out noon. Meeting rm. Business servs avail. Cr cds: A, C, D, DS, MC, V.

★★ **BEST WESTERN INN.** *1849 Hwy 45 Bypass (38305), ½ mi S of I-40, Exit 80A.* 901/668-4222; fax 901/664-8536; toll-free 800/528-1234. 141 rms, 2 story. S $45-$52, D $49-$57; each addl $4; under 12 free. Crib $2. Pet accepted, some restrictions. TV; cable (premium). Pool; wading pool. Restaurant 6 am-10 pm. Bar 4 pm-1 am; entertainment exc Sun. Ck-out noon. Meeting rms. Business servs avail. Cr cds: A, C, D, DS, MC, V.

D 🔧 ⛵ 🏊 🐾 SC

★ **CASEY JONES STATION INN.** *1943 Hwy 45 Bypass (40475), I-40 Exit 80A, in Casey Jones Village.* 901/668-3636; fax 901/668-3636. 53 rms, 2 story. May-Aug: S, D $49.95-$59.95; each addl $5; suites $109.95; under 18 free; lower rates rest of yr. Crib $5. TV; cable (premium). Pool. Complimentary coffee in lobby. Restaurant adj 6 am-10 pm. Ck-out 11 am. Meeting rm. Restored authentic cabooses and railroad cars converted to sleeping rms. Cr cds: A, DS, MC, V.

D 🐶 ✈ 🎣 ⛵ 🏊 ⛵ 🔥

★ **DAYS INN.** *1919 US Hwy 45 Bypass (38305).* 901/668-3444; fax 901/668-7778; toll-free 800/329-7466. 120 rms, 3 story. S $31-$36; D $37-$44; each addl $4; under 17 free. Crib free. TV; cable. Pool. Ck-out noon. Business servs avail. Cr cds: A, C, D, DS, MC, V.

⛵ ⛵ 🔥 SC

★★ **FAIRFIELD INN.** *535 Wiley Parker Rd (38305), I-40 Exit 80A.* 901/668-1400; fax 901/668-1400; res 800/228-2800. www.fairfieldinn.com. 105 rms, 3 story. Mar-Oct: S, D $46.95-$61.95; under 18 free; lower rates rest of yr. Crib free. TV; cable (premium). Heated pool. Complimentary continental bkfst. Restaurant adj 7 am-11 pm. Ck-out noon. Business servs avail. Cr cds: A, D, DS, MC, V.

D ⛵ 🎣 ⛵ 🔥

★★★ **FOUR POINTS HOTEL SHERATON.** *2267 N Higland Ave (38305), 3 mi N on US 45 at I-40 Exit 82.* 901/668-1571; fax 901/664-8070; res 800/325-3535. Email sales@fourpointsjackson.com. 103 rms, 2 story, 35 suites. S, D $79-$98; each addl $6; suites $89-$99; under 18 free; wkend plans. Crib free. TV; cable (premium), VCR avail. Pool; poolside serv. Complimentary coffee in rms. Restaurant 6 am-10 pm. Bar; entertainment Sat. Ck-out noon. Valet serv. Health club privileges. Some refrigerators; bathrm phone in suites; microwaves avail. Some fireplaces, patios. English Tudor decor; antiques, paintings. Cr cds: A, C, D, DS, MC, V.

D 🎣 ⛵ 🎣 ⛵ 🔥 🚶 🎣

★★ **HAMPTON INN.** *1890 45 Bypass (38305).* 901/664-4312; fax 901/664-7894; toll-free 800/426-7866. 120 rms, 2 story. S $61-$65; under 18 free. Crib free. TV; cable (premium). Pool. Complimentary continental bkfst. Restaurant adj 6 am-midnight. Meeting rm. Business servs avail. Health club privileges. Cr cds: A, DS, MC, V.

🎣 ⛵ ⛵ 🔥

★★★ **HOLIDAY INN.** *541 Carriage House Dr (38305), I-40 Exit 80A.* 901/668-6000; fax 901/668-9516; toll-free 800/222-3297. 135 air-cooled rms, 5 story, 54 suites. S, D $75-$125; each addl $6; suites $85-$175; under 19 free; higher rates special events. Crib free. TV; cable (premium). Indoor pool. Restaurant 6 am-9 pm. Bar. Ck-out noon. Meeting rms. Business servs avail. In-rm modem link. Bellhops. Beauty shop. Valet serv. Health club privileges. Game rm. Refrigerators. Balconies overlooking atrium. Cr cds: A, C, D, DS, JCB, MC, V.

D ⛵ ⛵ 🔥 SC

★★ **QUALITY INN.** *2262 N Highland Ave (38305), at jct US 45, I-40, Exit 82A.* 901/668-1066; fax 901/660-6597; toll-free 800/228-5151. 88 rms, 2 story. May-Aug: S, D $38-$48; each addl $6; under 18 free; lower rates rest of yr. Crib $6. TV; cable (premium). Pool. Restaurant adj open 24 hrs. Ck-out noon. Coin lndry. Business servs avail. Microwaves avail. Cr cds: A, C, D, DS, JCB, MC, V.

⛵ ⛵ 🔥 SC

Hotel

★★ **COMFORT INN.** *1963 US 45 Bypass (38305), I-40 Exit 80A.* 901/668-4100; fax 901/664-6940; res 800/228-5150; toll-free 800/850-1131. Email comfortinndos@earthlink.net; www.comfortinn-jackson.com. 204 rms, 4 story, 1 suite. Mar, June-Sep: S $59; D $64; each addl $6; suites $87;

under 18 free; lower rates rest of yr. Crib avail. TV; cable (premium). Restaurant. Meeting rms. Cr cds: A, C, D, DS, JCB, MC, V.

Restaurant

★ **OLD COUNTRY STORE.** 56 *Casey Jones Ln (38305), I-40, Exit 80A, in Casey Jones Village. 901/668-1223. Email casey@aeneas.net; www.casey jonesvillage.com.* Specializes in Tennessee country ham, catfish, cobblers. Salad bar. Hrs: 6 am-10 pm. Closed Easter, Thanksgiving, Dec 25. Bkfst $1.49-$5.49. Buffet: $5.49; lunch $1.99-$9.99. Buffet: $5.99; dinner $6.99-$9.99. Entertainment: Fri, Sat. Parking. Turn-of-the-century decor. Family-owned. Cr cds: A, D, DS, MC, V.

Jamestown

(E-6) *See also Cookeville*

Pop 1,862 **Elev** 1,716 ft
Area code 931 **Zip** 38556

Once a hunting ground for Davy Crockett and later Sergeant Alvin C. York, Jamestown was also the home of Cordell Hull, FDR's secretary of state.

Annual Event

Rugby Pilgrimage. Tours of private historic houses in addition to bldgs open regularly. Contact Historic Rugby, Inc, PO Box 8, Rugby 37733. Phone 423/628-2441. First wkend Oct.

Jellico

(E-6) *See also Caryville*

Pop 2,447 **Elev** 982 ft **Area code** 423
Zip 37762

What to See and Do

Indian Mountain State Park. More than 200 acres. Swimming pool, fish-ing; hiking trail, picnicking, shelters, playgrounds, camping. Standard fees. 3 mi off I-75, Exit 160. Phone 423/784-7958.

Motel/Motor Lodge

★ **DAYS INN.** *I-75 US 25 W (37762), ¼ mi S on US 25W at jct I-75 Exit 160. 423/784-7281; fax 423/784-4529; toll-free 800/329-7466.* 126 rms, 2-3 story. No elvtr. S $39-$45; D $44-$55; each addl $5; under 18 free. Crib free. TV; cable (premium). Pool. Coffee in rms. Restaurant 6 am-9 pm. Ck-out 11 am. Cr cds: A, C, D, DS, JCB, MC, V.

Johnson City

(E-8) *See also Elizabethton, Kingsport*

Settled 1782 **Pop** 49,381 **Elev** 1,692 ft
Area code 423
Web www.johnsoncitytn.com
Information Chamber of Commerce, 603 E Market St, PO Box 180, 37605; 423/461-8000

Johnson City is a leading burley tobacco sales center, as well as a market and shipping point for Washington County's cattle, eggs, and alfalfa. Chemicals, textiles, building materials, electronics, and furniture are also produced in the town.

What to See and Do

Cherokee National Forest. (see) E on US 321; S on US 23/19W.

East Tennessee State University. (1911) 12,028 students. Campus has 63 bldgs on 366 acres; Slocumb Galleries, Memorial Center (sports), James H. Quillen College of Medicine (1974). Tours of campus. Lake & Stout Sts. Phone 423/929-4112. Also on campus is

> **Carroll Reece Museum.** Contemporary art and regional history exhibits; gallery tours; concert, film, and lecture series. (Daily; closed hols) Phone 423/439-4392. **FREE**

Hands On! Regional Museum. More than 20 hands-on exhibits designed for children of all ages. Traveling shows. (June-Aug, daily; rest of yr, Tues-Sun; closed hols) 315 E Main St. Phone 423/434-4263. ¢¢

✪ **Jonesborough.** Oldest town in Tennessee and the first capital of the state of Franklin. 6 mi W off US 11 E.

Historic District. Four-by-six-blk area through the heart of town reflecting 200 yrs of history. Private residences, commercial and public bldgs of Federal, Greek Revival, and Victorian styles; brick sidewalks, old-style lampposts, shops. Obtain walking tour brochures at Visitor Center, 117 Boone St. Phone 423/753-5961.

Jonesborough History Museum. Exhibits highlight history of Jonesborough from pioneer days to early 20th century. (Daily; closed hols) 117 Boone St, in Visitor Center. Phone 423/753-1015. ¢

Rocky Mount Historic Site & Overmountain Museum. Log house (ca 1770), territorial capitol under Governor William Blount from 1790-92, is restored to original simplicity with much 18th-century furniture; log kitchen, slave cabin, barn, blacksmith shop, smokehouse. Costumed interpreters reenact a day in the life of typical pioneer family; tour (1½ hrs) includes Cobb-Massengill house, kitchen, and slave cabin, as well as self-guided tour through the adj Museum of Overmountain History. (Memorial day-Labor Day, daily; rest of yr, Mon-Fri; closed Thanksgiving, Dec 21-Jan 5). Children under 6 are free. four mi NE on US 11E. Phone 423/538-7396. ¢¢-¢¢¢

Tipton-Haynes Historic Site. Site of the 1788 "Battle of the Lost State of Franklin." Six original bldgs and 4 reconstructions span American history from pre-colonial days through Civil War. Visitor center with museum display; gift shop. (Apr-Oct, Mon-Sat; rest of yr, Mon-Fri) Special programs, events. one mi off I-181 Exit 31, at S edge of town. Phone 423/926-3631. ¢¢

Whitewater rafting. Cherokee Adventures. Variety of guided whitewater rafting trips through the Nolichucky Canyon and along the Watauga and Russell Fork rivers. Mountain biking programs. (Mar-Oct) Contact 2000 Jonesborough Rd, Erwin 37650. 17 mi S on US 19/23, Exit 18, then 1 mi N on TN 81. Phone 423/743-7733 or 800/445-7238. ¢¢¢¢

Annual Events

Jonesborough Days. Six mi W, in Jonesborough. Incl parade, art show, crafts, old-time games, traditional music, square dancing and clogging, food. July 4th wknd.

Appalachian Fair. N, just off I-181 in Gray at fairgrounds. Regional fair featuring livestock, agriculture, youth exhibits, antique display; entertainment. Phone 423/477-3211. Aug 17-25, 2001.

National Storytelling Festival. Eight mi W in Jonesborough. Three-day gathering from across nation features some of the country's best storytellers. Phone 423/753-2171. First wknd Oct.

Christmas in Jonesborough. Six mi W. Tours of historic houses, tree decoration, workshops, old-time holiday events. Dec.

Motels/Motor Lodges

★ **DAYS INN.** *2312 Browns Mill Rd (37604).* 423/282-2211; fax 423/282-6111; toll-free 800/329-7466. 100 rms, 2 story. S $40-$45; D $45-$50; each

Fall Creek Falls, Fall Creek Falls State Resort Park

addl $5; under 12 free; higher rates special events. Pet accepted. TV; cable. Pool. Complimentary continental bkfst. Ck-out 11 am. Coin lndry. Meeting rm. Business servs avail. Cr cds: A, C, D, DS, MC, V.

★★ **FAIRFIELD INN.** *207 E Mountcastle Dr (37601). 423/282-3335; fax 423/282-3335; res 800/228-2800.* 132 rms, 3 story. S, D $39.95-$56.95; each addl $6-$9; under 18 free; higher rates special events. TV; cable (premium), VCR avail (movies). Pool. Complimentary continental bkfst, coffee in lobby. Restaurant adj 11 am-10 pm. Ck-out noon. Business servs avail. In-rm modem link. Health club privileges. Cr cds: A, D, DS, MC, V.

★★ **HAMPTON INN.** *508 N State of Franklin Rd (37604). 423/929-8000; fax 423/929-3336; res 800/426-7866.* 77 rms, 3 story. S $61-$66; D $66-$71; each addl $5; under 18 free; higher rates NASCAR races. Crib free. TV; cable (premium). Pool. Complimentary continental bkfst. Restaurant nearby. Ck-out noon. Meeting rms. Business servs avail. Health club privileges. Some refrigerators, minibars. Cr cds: A, D, DS, MC, V.

★ **SUPER 8.** *108 Wesley St (37601). 423/282-8818; fax 423/282-8818; res 800/800-8000.* 57 rms, 3 story, 1 suite. Mar-Oct: S $45; D $59; each addl $5; suites $90; lower rates rest of yr. Pet accepted, fee. TV; cable. Complimentary continental bkfst, toll-free calls. Restaurant. Ck-out 11 am, ck-in 3 pm. Coin lndry. Golf. Downhill skiing. Supervised children's activities. Hiking trail. Picnic facilities. Cr cds: A, D, DS, MC, V.

Hotels

★★★ **GARDEN PLAZA HOTEL.** *211 Mockingbird Ln (37604). 423/929-2000; fax 423/929-1783; toll-free 800/342-7336.* 181 rms, 5 story, 5 suites. S $85; D $95; each addl $10; suites $119; under 18 free. Crib avail. Pet accepted. Valet parking avail. Indoor/outdoor pools. TV; cable (DSS), VCR avail. Complimentary coffee in rms, newspaper. Restaurant. Bar. Ck-out noon, ck-in 3 pm. Meet-

ing rms. Business center. Bellhops. Concierge. Dry cleaning. Free airport transportation. Exercise privileges. Golf. Tennis. Downhill skiing. Cr cds: A, D, DS, MC, V.

★★★ **HOLIDAY INN - JOHNSON CITY.** *101 W Springbrook Dr (37604). 423/282-4611; fax 423/283-4869; res 800/465-4329. Email hi101@preferred. com; www.holiday-inn.com.* 205 rms, 6 story, 4 suites. June-Aug: S $99; D $105; each addl $6; suites $176; children $6; under 12 free; lower rates rest of yr. Crib avail. TV; cable (DSS), VCR avail. Restaurant 6 am-10 pm. Bar. Ck-out 11 am, ck-in 3 pm. Meeting rms. Cr cds: A, D, DS, JCB, MC, V.

★ **HOWARD JOHNSON PLAZA HOTEL.** *2406 N Roan St (37601). 423/282-2161; fax 423/282-2488; res 800/446-4656; toll-free 877/504-1007. Email fbullard@naxs.net; www. hojo.com.* 192 rms, 4 story, 4 suites. S, D $65; each addl $5; suites $130; under 12 free. Crib avail. Pet accepted, fee. Parking lot. Pool. TV; cable (premium), VCR avail. Complimentary coffee in rms, newspaper, toll-free calls. Restaurant 6 am-10 pm. Bar. Ck-out 11 am, ck-in 2 pm. Meeting rms. Business center. Bellhops. Dry cleaning, coin lndry. Gift shop. Free airport transportation. Exercise privileges. Golf. Tennis, 10 courts. Bike rentals. Hiking trail. Picnic facilities. Cr cds: A, C, D, DS, ER, MC, V.

Restaurants

★ **FIREHOUSE.** *627 W Walnut (37604). 423/929-7377. Email tom@ thefirehouse.com; www.thefirehouse. com.* Specializes in steak, ribs, barbecue beans. Own desserts. Hrs: 11 am-10 pm; Fri, Sat to 10:30 pm. Closed Easter, Thanksgiving, Dec 24, 25. Lunch $6-$8; dinner $7-$15. Child's menu. Parking. Converted fire hall (1930). Cr cds: A, D, DS, MC, V.

★ **MAKATO'S JAPANESE STEAKHOUSE.** *3021 Oakland Ave (37601). 423/282-4441.* Specializes in seafood, steak. Sushi bar. Hrs: 11 am-2 pm, 5-9 pm; Fri, Sat to 10 pm; Sun to 2:30 pm. Bar. Lunch complete meals:

$5.25-$11.43; dinner complete meals: $7.35-$35. Child's menu. Parking. Tableside cooking. Cr cds: A, D, DS, MC, V.

D

★ ★ ★ **PARSON'S TABLE.** *100 W Woodrow Ave (37659), W on US 11, 321.* 423/753-8002. Own baking. Hrs: 11:30 am-2 pm, 5:30-10 pm; Sun brunch to 2 pm. Closed Mon; Jan 1, Dec 24, 25. Res accepted. Lunch $6-$9; dinner $15-$25. Sun Brunch: $12.95. Child's menu. Parking. In historic district in 1870s church with loft and parsonage. Victorian decor. Cr cds: A, C, DS, MC, V.

D

★ ★ **PEERLESS.** *2531 N Roan St (37601).* 423/282-2351. Specializes in fresh seafood, steak, chicken. Hrs: 4-10 pm; Sat to 11 pm. Closed Sun; hols. Bar. Dinner a la carte entrees: $8.95-$15.95. Parking. Family-owned. Cr cds: A, C, D, DS, MC, V.

D SC

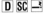

Kingsport

(E-8) See also Johnson City

Settled 1761 **Pop** 36,365 **Elev** 1,208 ft
Area code 423
Web www.kingsportchamber.org
Information Convention & Visitors Bureau, 151 E Main St, PO Box 1403, 37662; 423/392-8820 or 800/743-5282

Located at a natural gateway to the Southwest, this area saw the passage of the Great Indian Warrior & Trader Path and Island Road (1761), the first road built in Tennessee. The trail later became the Great Stage Road and was used for 150 years, marking the beginning of Daniel Boone's Wilderness Road. Kingsport was a little town on the Holston River, but it was converted to a planned industrial city during World War I. The first council-manager form of government in the state was installed in the town. The Eastman Chemical Company, the largest private employer in the state, is located in Kingsport.

Annual Event

Kingsport Fun Fest. Citywide. More than 100 events incl hot-air balloon races, sports events, entertainment. Phone 423/392-8800. Nine days late July.

Motels/Motor Lodges

★ ★ **COMFORT INN KINGSPORT.** *100 Indian Center Ct (37660), at TN 93 & US 11W.* 423/378-4418; fax 423/246-5249; res 800/228-5150. Email citn410@aol.com; www.comfortinn.com. 122 rms, 2 story. S, D $200; each addl $8; under 18 free. Crib avail. Pet accepted, fee. Parking lot. Pool, whirlpool. TV; cable (premium). Complimentary continental bkfst, coffee in rms, newspaper, toll-free calls. Restaurant nearby. Ck-out noon, ck-in 2 pm. Meeting rm. Business servs avail. Dry cleaning, coin lndry. Exercise privileges, sauna. Golf. Picnic facilities. Cr cds: A, C, D, DS, ER, JCB, MC, V.

D SC

★ **DAYS INN.** *805 Lynn Garden Dr (37660).* 423/246-7126; fax 423/247-8785; res 800/329-7466. 65 rms, 2 story. June-Oct: S, D $40-$125; each addl $6; under 13 free; higher rates special events; lower rates rest of yr. Crib free. TV; cable (premium), VCR avail. Complimentary coffee in rms. Restaurant 6 am-8 pm. Ck-out 11 am. Meeting rms. Business servs avail. Coin lndry. Pool. Refrigerators; microwaves avail. Cr cds: A, C, D, DS, JCB, MC, V.

D SC

★ **ECONO LODGE.** *1704 E Stone Dr (37660).* 423/245-0286; fax 423/245-2985; res 800/424-4777. 52 rms, 2 story. S, D $37-$55; each addl $4; under 18 free. Pet accepted, some restrictions. TV; cable (premium). Complimentary continental bkfst. Restaurant adj open 24 hrs. Ck-out 11 am. Business servs avail. Cr cds: A, C, D, DS, MC, V.

SC

★ ★ ★ **RAMADA INN.** *2005 Lamasa Dr (37660).* 423/245-0271; fax 423/245-7992; res 800/272-6232. Email Ramadainnkingsport@gal-tex. 198 rms, 2 story. S, D $66-$150; each addl $6; under 18 free. Crib free. TV; cable (premium). Pool. Restaurant 6 am-2 pm, 5-10 pm; Sat, Sun from 7 am. Rm serv 7 am-10 pm. Bar 5 pm-midnight. Ck-out noon. Meeting rms. Business servs avail. Sundries. Free airport transportation. Lighted tennis. Health club privileges. Cr cds: A, DS, MC, V.

Hotel

★★★ **MEADOWVIEW CONFERENCE CENTER.** *1901 Meadowview Pkwy (37660), I-181 Exit 52. 423/578-6600; fax 423/578-6630; res 800/228-9280; toll-free 800/820-5055. Email daemview@yahoo.com.* 195 rms, 7 story. Jan-Nov: S, D $59-$139; each addl $10; under 5 free; wkend rates; golf plans; higher rates special events; lower rates rest of yr. Crib free. Valet parking $3. TV; cable (premium), VCR avail. Complimentary coffee in rms. Restaurant 6:30 am-10 pm. Bar. Ck-out 1 pm. Meeting rms. Business center. In-rm modem link. Gift shop. Coin lndry. Free airport transportation. Lighted tennis. 18-hole golf, greens fee $28-$32, pro, putting green, driving range. Exercise equipt. Heated pool; whirlpool, poolside serv. Some bathrm phones, balconies; refrigerators, microwaves avail. Cr cds: A, C, D, DS, JCB, MC, V.

Restaurant

★★ **SKOBY'S.** *1001 Konnarock Rd (37664). 423/245-2761. www.skobys. com.* Specializes in steak, seafood. Salad bar. Own desserts. Hrs: 4:30-10 pm; Fri, Sat to 11 pm. Closed Sun; hols. Res accepted. Bar. Dinner a la carte entrees: $7-$25. Child's menu. Parking. Dining areas with varied themes. Family-owned. Cr cds: A, C, D, DS, MC, V.

Knoxville (E-7)

Settled 1791 **Pop** 165,121 **Elev** 936 ft
Area code 423
Web www.knoxville.org

Information Knox County Tourist Commission, 601 W Summitt Hill Dr, Suite 200B, Knoxville, TN, 37902-2011; 423/523-7263 or 800/727-8045

First capital of Tennessee, Knoxville today is the manufacturing center for the east Tennessee Valley. In its early days, Knoxville was a frontier outpost on the edge of the Cherokee nation, last stop on the way west. Headquarters of the Tennessee Valley Authority, marketplace for tobacco and livestock, Knoxville is also a diversified industrial city, a product of power plant rather than plantation and of the atomic age rather than the Old South (Oak Ridge is only 22 miles away). It is a gracious city with the University of Tennessee as a cultural center and dogwood-lined streets in its residential sections.

Founded by an American Revolution veteran from North Carolina and named after Secretary of War Henry Knox, Knoxville quickly became a provisioning place for westward-bound wagons. It was known for its whiskey and wild times. East Tennessee had many Union sympathizers; during the Civil War Knoxville was seized by Confederates and became headquarters for an army of occupation. In 1863, Southern troops withdrew to Chattanooga and a Union army moved in, only to be besieged by Confederates. While the battle for Knoxville saw large sections of the city destroyed, the Confederate attack was rebuffed, and Knoxville remained in Union hands for the rest of the war.

The postwar years brought many former Union soldiers, skilled Northern workmen, and investment capital to Knoxville. Within two decades its population more than tripled. During and since World War II it has enjoyed a similar period of industrial growth and commercial well-being. The University of Tennessee, Knoxville (1794) is located here.

What to See and Do

AKIMA East Tennessee Discovery Center & AKIMA Planetarium. Science center with exhibits on life, energy, transportation, minerals, fossils; incl aquarium and planetarium. (Mon-Fri, also Sat afternoons; closed hols) 516 N Beaman St, Chilhowee Park. Phone 423/594-1494. ¢¢

Beck Cultural Exchange Center- Museum of Black History and Culture. Research, preservation, and display of the achievements of Knoxville's black citizens from the early 1800s. Gallery features changing exhibits of local and regional artists. (Tues-Sat; closed hols) 1927 Dandridge Ave. Phone 423/524-8461. **FREE**

Confederate Memorial Hall. Antebellum mansion with Mediterranean-style gardens served as headquarters of Confederate General James Longstreet during siege of Knoxville. Maintained as a Confederate memorial, the 15-rm house is furnished with museum pieces, a collection of Southern and Civil War relics, library of Southern literature. (Tues-Fri) 3148 Kingston Pike SW. Phone 423/522-2371. ¢¢

Crescent Bend (Armstrong-Lockett House) and W. Perry Toms Memorial Gardens. (1834) Collections of American and English furniture; English silver (1640-1820); extensive terraced gardens. (Mar-Dec, Tues-Sun) 2728 Kingston Pike. Phone 423/637-3163. ¢¢

Governor William Blount Mansion. (1792) House of William Blount, Governor of the Southwest Territory and signer of the US Constitution, was the center of political and social activity in the territory. Restored to period of late 1700s with period furnishings, Blount memorabilia, 18th-century garden. Tennessee's 1st state constitution was drafted in the governor's office behind the mansion. (Mar-Oct, Tues-Sun; rest of yr, Tues-Fri; closed hols) 200 W Hill Ave. Phone 423/525-2375. ¢¢

Annual Events

Dogwood Arts Festival. More than 150 events and activities throughout the community incl arts and crafts exhibits and shows; over 80 public and private gardens on display; musical entertainment; parades; sporting events; more than 60 miles of marked dogwood trails for auto or free bus tours; special activities for children and senior citizens. Phone 423/637-4561. Mid-late Apr.

Tennessee Valley Fair. Chilhowee Park. Entertainment; livestock and agricultural shows; contests,

exhibits, fireworks, carnival rides. Phone 423/637-5840. Ten days early-mid-Sep.

Seasonal Event

Artfest. Citywide celebration with childrens' activities, entertainment, changing exhibits, art shows, professional and community theatricals. Phone 423/523-7543. Aug-Oct.

Motels/Motor Lodges

★★ **BAYMONT INN.** *11341 Campbell Lakes Dr (37922), I-40/75 Exit 373. 423/671-1010; fax 423/675-5039; toll-free 800/301-0200.* 100 rms, 3 story. S, D $63.95-$99.95; each addl $7; under 18 free; lower rates rest of yr. Crib free. Pet accepted, some restrictions. TV; cable (premium), VCR avail. Pool. Complimentary continental bkfst; coffee in rms. Restaurant adj 6 am-10 pm. Ck-out noon. Coin lndry. Meeting rms. Business servs avail. Exercise equipt; sauna. Some refrigerators; microwaves avail. Cr cds: A, C, D, DS, MC, V.

🄳 🐾 ➳ 🕉 🔾 🔾 SC

★★ **BEST WESTERN.** *420 N Peters Rd (37922). 865/539-0058; fax 865/539-4887; toll-free 800/348-2562.* 98 rms, 3 story, 23 suites. S, D $66-$72; each addl $6; suites $78-$125; under 18 free; wkend rates; higher rates special events. Crib free. TV; cable (premium). Pool. Complimentary continental bkfst, coffee in rms. Restaurant nearby. Ck-out 11 am. Meeting rms. Business servs avail. Valet serv. Health club privileges. Bathrm phone, refrigerator, wet bar in suites. Cr cds: A, C, D, DS, MC, V.

🄳 ➳ 🕉 🔾 🔾

★★ **BEST WESTERN HIGHWAY HOST.** *118 Merchants Rd NW (37912), I-75N Exit 108. 423/688-3141; fax 423/687-4645; res 800/826-4360; toll-free 800/446-4656. www.travelbase.com/destination/knoxville/bestwest-highway.* 213 rms, 6 story. S, D $59-$92; each addl $7; under 18 free; higher rates special events. Crib free. Pet accepted; $25 deposit. TV; cable (premium). Indoor pool; whirlpool. Complimentary coffee in rms. Restaurant open 24 hrs. Bar 11 am-midnight. Ck-out noon. Coin lndry.

Gift shop. Meeting rms. Business servs avail. Valet serv. Game rm. Microwaves avail. Balconies. Cr cds: A, C, D, DS, ER, MC, V.

[D] [🐕] [≈] [⛷] [🖐] [SC]

★★ **COMFORT INN.** *5334 Central Ave Pike (37912).* 423/688-1010; fax 423/687-4235; res 800/228-5150; toll-free 800/638-7949. 101 rms, 2 story. S $45-$70; D $55-$80; each addl $5; under 18 free. Crib $5. TV; cable (premium). Pool. Complimentary continental bkfst, coffee in rms. Restaurant nearby. Ck-out noon. Business servs avail. Health club privileges. Cr cds: A, C, D, DS, MC, V.

[≈] [⛷] [🖐] [SC]

★★ **COMFORT SUITES.** *811 N Campbell Sta Rd (32822).* 423/675-7585; fax 423/675-4442; res 800/228-5150. 59 rms, 2 story. Apr-Oct: suites $69-$109; under 18 free; higher rates special events; lower rates rest of yr. Crib free. TV; cable (premium). Complimentary continental bkfst, coffee in rms. Ck-out noon. Business center. Sundries. Coin lndry. Exercise equipt. Indoor pool; whirlpool. Refrigerators, microwaves; some in-rm whirlpools. Cr cds: A, C, D, DS, JCB, MC, V.

[D] [≈] [🏋] [⛷] [🖐] [SC] [🏃]

★★ **COURTYARD BY MARRIOTT.** *216 Langley Pl (37922).* 865/539-0600; fax 865/539-4488. 78 rms, 3 story. Apr-Oct: S, D $84-$104; each addl $10; under 12 free; higher rates Dogwood Arts Festival; lower rates rest of yr. Crib free. TV; cable (premium). Indoor pool. Complimentary coffee in rms. Restaurant 7-10 am. Ck-out noon. Meeting rms. Business servs avail. Sundries. Coin lndry. Exercise equipt. Some in-rm whirlpools; refrigerator, microwave in suites. Some balconies. Cr cds: A, D, DS, MC, V.

[D] [🐾] [🍴] [≈] [🏋] [🏃] [⛷] [🖐] [🏃]

★ **DAYS INN.** *1706 Cumberland Ave (37916), on Univ of TN campus.* 423/521-5000; fax 423/540-3866. 119 rms, 7 story. S, D $55-$65; each addl $5; under 12 free; higher rates special events. Crib free. Pet accepted; $15. TV; cable (premium). Ck-out 11 am. Complimentary continental bkfst. Meeting rms. Business servs avail. Cr cds: A, C, D, DS, JCB, MC, V.

[D] [🐕] [⛷] [🖐] [SC]

★ **DAYS INN WEST.** *326 Lovell Rd (37922), I-40 Exit 374.* 865/966-5801; fax 865/966-1755; res 800/329-7466. 112 rms, 2 story. June-Nov: S $65.00; D $75.00; each addl $6; under 13 free; lower rates rest of yr. Crib avail. Pet accepted, some restrictions, fee. Parking lot. Pool. TV; cable. Complimentary continental bkfst, newspaper. Restaurant nearby. Ck-out 11 am, ck-in 3 pm. Business servs avail. Coin lndry. Golf. Tennis. Cr cds: A, C, D, DS, JCB, MC, V.

[D] [🐕] [🎿] [🍴] [≈] [⛷] [🖐]

★★ **HAMPTON INN KNOXVILLE NORTH.** *117 Cedar Ln (37912), at I-75 & Merchants Rd.* 865/689-1011; fax 865/689-7917; res 800/426-7866. 130 rms, 3 story. May-Sep: S, D $60-$70; under 18 free; higher rates special events; lower rates rest of yr. Crib free. TV; cable (premium). Pool. Complimentary continental bkfst. Restaurant opp 6 am-10 pm. Ck-out 11 am. Business servs avail. Exercise equipt. Cr cds: A, DS, MC, V.

[≈] [🏋] [🖐]

★★ **HOLIDAY INN.** *1315 Kirby Rd (37909), jct I-40 & I-75.* 865/584-3911; fax 865/588-0920; toll-free 800/854-8315. 242 rms, 4 story. S, D $80-$119; under 18 free. Crib free. Pet accepted; $25. TV; cable (premium). Pool; whirlpool. Restaurant 6:30 am-10 pm. Bar 5 pm-1 am. Ck-out 11 am. Coin lndry. Meeting rms. Business servs avail. Free airport transportation. Health club privileges. Balconies. Picnic tables. Cr cds: A, C, D, DS, JCB, MC, V.

[D] [🐕] [≈] [🏋] [⛷] [🖐]

★ **HOWARD JOHNSON PLAZA.** *7621 Kingston Pike (37919).* 865/693-8111; fax 865/690-1031; res 800/446-4656. 162 rms, 4 story. S, D$58.50-$78.50; each addl $10; suites $100-$175; studio rms $65-$89.50; under 18 free. Crib free. Pet accepted, some restrictions; $10. TV; cable (premium). Pool. Restaurant 7 am-1 pm, 5-10 pm. Bar 4 pm-2 am; entertainment. Ck-out noon. Meeting rms. Business servs avail. Cr cds: A, C, D, DS, ER, JCB, MC, V.

[D] [🐕] [🎿] [🍴] [≈] [⛷] [🖐] [🏃]

★ **LA QUINTA INN.** *258 Peters Rd N (37923).* 423/690-9777; fax 423/531-8304; toll-free 800/687-6667. 130 rms, 3 story. S $60-$68; D $70-$78; each addl $10; under 18 free. Crib free. Pet accepted, some restrictions. TV; cable. Pool. Complimentary continental bkfst. Restaurant adj open 24 hrs. Ck-out noon. Coin lndry. Meeting rms. Business servs avail. Health club privileges. Microwaves avail. Cr cds: A, C, D, DS, MC, V.

D ⛏ ⛵ ⬛ ♨ SC

★ **LA QUINTA INN.** *5634 Merchant Center Blvd (37912). 423/687-8989; fax 423/687-9351; res 800/531-5900; toll-free 800/222-3297.* 123 rms, 5 story. S, D $49-$75; each addl $5; higher rates special events. Crib free. Pet accepted. TV; cable (premium). Pool. Complimentary continental bkfst, coffee in rms. Ck-out noon. Meeting rms. Health club privileges. Cr cds: A, C, D, DS, MC, V.

D ⛏ ⛵ ⬛ ♨ SC

★★ **RAMADA LIMITED SUITES.** *5317 Pratt Rd (37912), I-75 Exit 108. 865/687-9922; fax 865/687-1032.* 58 suites, 4 story. May-Aug: S, D $69-$99; each addl $5; under 18 free; wkend rates; higher rates special events; lower rates rest of yr. Crib free. TV; cable (premium), VCR avail. Complimentary continental bkfst, coffee in rms. Restaurant adj open 24 hrs. Ck-out noon. Meeting rms. Business center. In-rm modem link. Concierge. Sundries. Coin lndry. Exercise equipt. Indoor pool; whirlpool. Refrigerators, microwaves; some in-rm whirlpools. Cr cds: A, D, DS, MC, V.

D ⛵ 🕌 ⬛ ♨ 🏃

★ **RED ROOF INN.** *5640 Merchants Center Blvd (37912), at I-75 Exit 108. 865/689-7100; fax 865/689-7974.* 84 rms, 2 story. S $31-$52; D $36-$64; each addl $7; higher rates special events. Crib free. Pet accepted, some restrictions. TV; cable (premium). Ck-out noon. Business servs avail. Health club privileges. Cr cds: A, D, DS, MC, V.

D ⛏ 🐾 🕌 ⬛ ♨

★ **RED ROOF INN.** *209 Advantage Pl (77027), I-40/75 Exit 378. 423/691-1664; fax 423/691-7210; toll-free 800/843-7663. www.redroof.com.* 115 rms, 3 story. S, D $33.99-$69.99; each addl $9; under 18 free; higher rates: Dogwood Festival, special events; lower rates rest of yr. Crib free. TV; cable (premium). Compli-

mentary coffee in lobby. Restaurant adj 6 am-10 pm. Ck-out noon. Business servs avail. Health club privileges. Cr cds: A, C, D, DS, MC, V.

D ⬛ ♨ SC

★ **SUPER 8 MOTEL.** *6200 Papermill Rd (37919). 423/584-8511; fax 423/584-8511; res 800/800-8000.* 139 rms, 2-3 story. No elvtr. S $44-$75; D $54-$95; each addl $5; under 18 free. Crib free. Pet accepted, some restrictions. TV; cable (premium). Pool; wading pool, whirlpool. Complimentary continental bkfst. Ck-out 11 am. Meeting rm. Business servs avail. Exercise equipt. Coin lndry. Cr cds: A, C, D, DS, JCB, MC, V.

D 🐾 ⛵ 🕌 ⬛ ♨ SC

★★ **WYNDHAM GARDEN HOTEL.** *208 Market Place Ln (37922). 423/531-1900; fax 423/531-8807; res 800/996-3426; toll-free 800/258-2466.* 137 rms, 2 story, 16 kit. suites. S, D $84-$119; each addl $10; kit. suites $99-$129; under 16 free. Crib free. TV; cable (premium). Pool; whirlpool. Restaurant 6:30 am-10 pm. Ck-out noon. Coin lndry. Meeting rms. Business servs avail. Exercise equipt. Refrigerator, wet bar in suites. Balconies. Grills. Cr cds: A, C, D, DS, MC, V.

D ⛵ 🕌 ⬛ ♨ SC

Hotels

★★ **BUDGET INNS OF AMERICA.** *323 Cedarbluff Rd (37923). 865/693-7330; fax 865/693-7383.* 159 rms, 2 story, 10 suites. Apr-Sep: S $49; D $59; suites $79; lower rates rest of yr. Crib avail. Pet accepted, fee. Parking lot. Indoor pool, whirlpool. TV; cable. Restaurant 7 am-10 pm, closed Sun. 24-hr rm serv. Ck-out noon, ck-in noon. Meeting rms. Business center. Cr cds: A, D, DS, MC, V.

D ⛏ ⛵ ⬛ ♨ SC 🏃

★★★ **HILTON.** *501 Church Ave SW (37902), downtown. 423/523-2300; fax 865/525-6532; toll-free 800/445-8667. www.hilton.com.* 310 rms, 18 story, 7 suites. S, D $179; each addl $15; suites $325; under 18 free. Crib avail. Pet accepted, some restrictions, fee. Parking garage. Pool. TV; cable (premium). Complimentary coffee in rms, newspaper. Restaurant. Bar. Conference center, meeting rms. Business center. Bellhops. Dry cleaning. Gift shop. Exercise privileges. Golf. Tennis. Cr cds: A, C, D, DS, JCB, MC, V.

★★★ **HOLIDAY INN SELECT DOWNTOWN.** *525 Henley St (37902), at Convention Center. 423/522-2800; fax 423/523-0738; res 800/465-4329.* 293 rms, 11 story. S, D $93-$180; each addl $10; suites $261-$400; under 18 free; wkend rates; higher rates special events. TV; cable (premium), VCR avail. Indoor pool; whirlpool. Restaurant 6:30 am-1:30 pm, 6-10 pm; Sat, Sun from 7 am. Bar 5 pm-midnight. Ck-out 11 am. Coin lndry. Convention facilities. Business center. In-rm modem link. Exercise equipt; sauna. Refrigerator in suites. Luxury level. Cr cds: A, C, D, DS, JCB, MC, V.

★★★ **HYATT REGENCY.** *500 Hill Ave SE (37915). 865/637-1234; fax 865/637-1193; res 800/233-1234.* 385 rms, 11 story. S, D $130-$160; each addl $25; suites $175-$425; under 18 free; wkend rates; higher rates special events. Crib free. Pet accepted, some restrictions; $25. TV; cable (premium), VCR avail. Pool; poolside serv. Playground. Restaurants 6:30 am-midnight. Bar 4 pm-1 am. Ck-out noon. Convention facilities. Business center. Beauty shop. Gift shop. Airport transportation. Exercise equipt; sauna. Many balconies. Contemporary decor; 8-story lobby with atrium. On hill above Tennessee River. Cr cds: A, D, DS, MC, V.

★★★ **RADISSON HOTEL.** *401 Summit Hill Dr (37902). 423/522-2600; fax 423/523-7200; res 800/333-3333. Email radknox@esper.com.* 197 rms, 12 story. S $109-$119; D $119-$129; each addl $10; suites $175-$350; under 18 free; higher rates special events. Crib free. Pet accepted. TV; cable, VCR avail. Indoor pool. Restaurant 6 am-10 pm. Bar 4 pm-midnight. Ck-out noon. Meeting rms. Business servs avail. Gift shop. Exercise equipt. Microwaves avail. Cr cds: A, C, D, DS, ER, JCB, MC, V.

★★ **SIGNATURE INN.** *209 Market Place Ln (37922). 423/531-7444; fax*

865/531-7444; toll-free 800/822-5252. www.signaturesinns.com. 12 rms, 3 story, 3 suites. S, D $77; each addl $7; suites $92; under 12 free. Crib avail. Parking lot. Pool. TV; cable (premium), VCR avail. Complimentary continental bkfst, coffee in rms, newspaper, toll-free calls. Restaurant nearby. Ck-out noon, ck-in 3 pm. Meeting rms. Business center. Dry cleaning. Exercise privileges. Golf. Tennis. Cr cds: A, D, DS, MC, V.

Restaurants

★ **BUTCHER SHOP.** *806 World Fair Park Dr (37902). 865/637-0204.* Specializes in steak, seafood, chicken. Hrs: 5-10 pm; Sun from 4 pm. Closed hols. Res accepted. Bar. Dinner $13-$23. Child's menu. Parking. Option to select steak and cook it. Large, open charcoal grill in park. Cr cds: A, DS, MC, V.

★★ **CALHOUN'S.** *10020 Kingston Pike (37922). 865/673-3444.* Specializes in baby back ribs, prime rib, hickory-smoked pork. Hrs: 11 am-10 pm; Sat to 11 pm; Sun to 9:30 pm. Closed Thanksgiving, Dec 25. Res accepted. Bar. Lunch $6.50-$10; dinner $9.95-$19. Child's menu. Parking. Rustic decor. Antiques, farm implements. Cr cds: A, C, D, DS, MC, V.

★★ **CHEF BISTRO AND BAKERY.** *5003 Kingston Pike (37919). 423/584-1300. www.user.icx.net/~thechef.* Specializes in veal, lamb, steak. Hrs: 11 am-3:30 pm, 6-9 pm; Mon to 3:30 pm. Closed Sun; hols. Res accepted. Lunch $3.95-$10.95; dinner $12.95-$23.95. Bistro decor. Cr cds: A, MC, V.

★★ **CHESAPEAKE'S.** *500 N Henley St (37902). 423/673-3433.* Specializes in fresh seafood, Maine lobster. Hrs: 11 am-2:30 pm, 4:30-10 pm; Fri to 11 pm; Sat 4:30-11 pm; Sun 4:30-9:30 pm. Closed Jan 1, Thanksgiving, Dec 25. Res accepted. Bar. Lunch $5.95-$8.50; dinner $12.95-$24.95. Child's menu. Parking. Cr cds: A, C, D, DS, MC, V.

★★ **CHOP HOUSE.** *9700 Kingston Pike (37922). 865/531-2467. www.*

goldenpath.com/thechophouse. Specializes in pork chops, steak. Hrs: 11 am-10 pm; Fri, Sat to 11 pm. Closed Thanksgiving, Dec 25. Bar. Lunch, dinner $4.49-$22.99. Child's menu. Parking. Cr cds: A, D, DS, MC, V.

★★ **COPPER CELLAR.** *1807 Cumberland Ave (37916). 865/673-3411. Email aciaccia@utk.edu.* Specializes in fresh seafood, prime rib. Hrs: 11 am-10:30 pm; Thurs to 11 pm; Fri, Sat to 11:30 pm; Sun to 10 pm. Closed Thanksgiving, Dec 25. Bar. Lunch a la carte entrees: $4-$12; dinner a la carte entrees: $6.50-$26. Child's menu. Parking. Cr cds: A, D, DS, MC, V.

★★★ **COPPER CELLAR - CAPPUC-CINO'S.** *7316 Kingston Pike (37919). 865/673-3422.* Specializes in prime beef, fresh seafood. Hrs: 5-10 pm; Fri, Sat to 11 pm. Closed hols. Res accepted. Bar. Dinner $9.95-$24.95. Parking. Cr cds: A, C, D, DS, MC, V.

★★ **LITTON'S.** *2803 Essary Rd (37918). 865/688-0429.* Specializes in fresh seafood, steaks, desserts. Hrs: 11 am-9 pm; Fri, Sat to 10 pm. Closed Sun; hols. Lunch $5-$8; dinner $5-$15. Child's menu. Family-owned. Cr cds: A, MC, V.

★★ **MANDARIN HOUSE.** *314 J Merchants Dr (37912), I-75 N, Exit 108. 865/689-4800.* Specializes in duck, seafood. Hrs: 11 am-9:30 pm. Res accepted. Bar. Lunch $3.95-$5.25; dinner $7.95-$20. Contemporary decor. Cr cds: A, DS, MC, V.

★★ **MANDARIN HOUSE.** *8111 Gleason Dr (37919). 865/694-0350.* Hrs: 11 am-9:30 pm; Fri, Sat to 10 pm. Res accepted. Bar. Lunch $3.50-$5.25; dinner $5-$10. Parking. Cr cds: A, D, DS, MC, V.

★★ **NAPLES.** *5500 Kingston Pike (37919). 865/584-5033. Email bluper@aol.com.* Specializes in pasta, veal, seafood. Hrs: 11 am-2 pm, 5-10 pm; Fri to 11 pm; Sat 5-11 pm; Sun 5-10 pm. Closed July 4, Thanksgiving, Dec 24, 25. Res accepted. Bar. Lunch a la carte entrees: $5.99-$9.99; dinner a la carte entrees: $5.99-$15.95. Child's menu. Parking. Cr cds: A, C, D, DS, MC, V.

★★★ **THE ORANGERY.** *5412 Kingston Pike (37919). 865/588-2964.* French menu. Specializes in petite cotelettes d'agneau, boeuf Wellington, paella. Own baking. Hrs: 11:30 am-2:30 pm, 6-10 pm; Fri to 11 pm; Sat 6-11 pm. Closed Sun; hols. Res accepted. Bar. Lunch $5.95-$12.95; dinner $15-$30. Entertainment: pianist. European antiques. Atrium. Crystal chandeliers. Wine cellar dining area. Family-owned. Cr cds: A, D, MC, V.

★★★ **REGAS.** *318 N Gay St (37917), at Magnolia Ave. 865/637-9805. www.regasbrothers.com.* Specializes in clam chowder, prime rib, fresh seafood. Own baking. Hrs: 11 am-2:30 pm, 5-10 pm; Sat from 5 pm; early-bird dinner Mon-Sat 5 to 6:30 pm. Closed Sun; hols. Bar. Wine list. Lunch $6-$17; dinner $13-$25. Child's menu. Entertainment: Thurs-Sat. Dining rms individually decorated. Fireplaces. Original artwork. Family-owned. Cr cds: A, C, D, DS, MC, V.

Unrated Dining Spot

APPLE CAKE TEA ROOM. *11312 Station W Dr (37922), Exit 373. 865/966-7848.* Specializes in salads, sandwiches, soups. Hrs: 11 am-2:30 pm. Closed Sun; hols. Lunch a la carte entrées: $2.25-$6. Child's menu. Parking. Country antique decor. Fireplace. Artwork. Cr cds: MC, V.

Lawrenceburg

(F-3)

Founded 1815 **Pop** 10,412 **Elev** 890 ft
Area code 931 **Zip** 38464

What to See and Do

David Crockett State Park. This 1,000-acre area is located on the banks of Shoal Creek, where Crockett once operated a gristmill. Swimming pool, wading pool, bathhouse, fishing, boating (rentals); nature, bicycle trails, lighted tennis, picnicking, playground, concessions; park restaurant doubles as a dinner theater in summer (reservations required). Tent, trailer sites. Visitor center housed in water-powered gristmill (Memorial Day-Labor Day); amphitheater. Standard fees. W on US 64. Phone 931/762-9408.

Lebanon

(C-5) *See also Murfreesboro, Nashville*

Pop 15,208 **Elev** 531 ft **Area code** 615 **Zip** 37087

Information Lebanon/Wilson County Chamber of Commerce, 149 Public Square; 615/444-5503

Tall red cedars thrive in this area as they did in the Biblical lands of Lebanon. Thus the founding fathers named the city Lebanon. The dense cedar forest has been used for many industrial purposes including wood, paper, and pencils. Since 1842, Lebanon has been the home of Cumberland University.

Motels/Motor Lodges

★★ **BEST WESTERN EXECUTIVE INN.** *631 S Cumberland St (37087), I-40 Exit 238. 615/444-0505; fax 615/449-8516; toll-free 800/528-1234.* 125 rms, 2 story, 45 suites. May-Oct: S $45-$69; D $51-$69; each addl $5; suites $55-$89; under 12 free; lower rates rest of yr. Crib free. Pet accepted. TV; cable (premium). 2 pools, 1 indoor. Sauna. Restaurant adj 6 am-10:30 pm. Ck-out 11 am. Meeting rms. Business servs avail. Cr cds: A, C, D, DS, JCB, MC, V.

⬛ 🔧 ≋ 🔏 🐾 SC

★ **DAYS INN.** *914 Murfreesboro Rd (37090). 615/444-5635; fax 615/444-5635; res 800/329-7466.* 52 rms, 2 story. May-Oct: S $32-$67; D $42-

$70; each addl $5; under 18 free; higher rates special events; lower rates rest of yr. Crib free. Pet accepted; $5. TV; cable (premium). Pool. Complimentary continental bkfst. Restaurant nearby. Ck-out 11 am. Coin lndry. Business servs avail. Some refrigerators, microwaves. Cr cds: A, C, D, DS, MC, V.

⬛ 🔧 ≋ 🔏 🐾 🐾

★★ **HAMPTON INN.** *704 S Cumberland St (37087), I-40 Exit 238. 615/444-7400; fax 615/449-7969; res 800/426-7866.* 83 rms, 2 story, 4 suites. S, D $55-$90; suites $105-$125; under 18 free; higher rates special events. Crib free. Pet accepted, some restrictions. TV; cable. Pool; whirlpool. Complimentary continental bkfst. Restaurant nearby. Ck-out 11 am. Lndry facilities avail. Meeting rms. Business servs avail. Exercise equipt; sauna. Cr cds: A, D, DS, MC, V.

⬛ 🔧 🏋 🛟 ≋ 🏃 🐾 🐾

★ **SHONEYS INN.** *822 S Cumberland St (37087). 615/449-5781; fax 615/449-8201; res 800/222-2222.* 111 rms, 3 story, 10 suites. May-Sep: S $59; D $65; suites $72; under 12 free; lower rates rest of yr., fee. Pet accepted, some restrictions, fee. Parking lot. Indoor pool. TV; cable (DSS). Complimentary continental bkfst, coffee in rms, newspaper, toll-free calls. Ck-out noon, ck-in 3 pm. Meeting rm. Fax servs avail. Dry cleaning. Golf, 18 holes. Tennis, 2 courts. Cr cds: A, C, D, DS, ER, JCB, MC, V.

⬛ 🔧 🏌 🛟 🏃 ≋ 🐾 SC

Lenoir City

See also Knoxville, Sweetwater

Founded 1890 **Pop** 6,147 **Elev** 798 ft **Area code** 865 **Zip** 37771 **Web** www.loudoncounty.org

Information Loudon County Chamber of Commerce, PO Box 909, Loudon 37774; 865/458-2067

What to See and Do

Fort Loudoun Dam and Lake. This TVA dam, 4,190 ft long and 122 ft high, with a lock chamber to permit navigation of the river, transforms a 61-mi stretch of once unruly river into a placid lake extending to Knoxville. Fishing, boating on 14,600-acre lake. On US 11 at S end of city. Phone 865/986-3737. **FREE**

Tellico Dam and Lake. TVA dam on Little Tennessee River impounds 15,680-acre lake. Upper end of reservoir adjoins the Cherokee National Forest (see). Excellent fishing and boating with the Great Smoky Mts as backdrop. Summer pool, boat access sites; picnicking, camping. Approx 3 mi S off US 321. Phone 865/986-3737.

Motels/Motor Lodges

★ **DAYS INN.** *1110 Hwy 321 N (37771), at I-75 Exit 81. 865/986-2011; fax 865/986-6454; toll-free 800/526-4658.* 90 rms, 2 story. S $31-$34; D $41-$45; under 12 free. TV; cable. Pool; wading pool. Ck-out 11 am. Business servs avail. Some refrigerators. Cr cds: A, C, D, DS.

★ **KINGS INN.** *1031 Hwy 321 N (37771), 2 blks S of I-75 Exit 81. 865/986-9091.* 50 rms, 2 story. S $29-$41; D $39-$45; each addl $5; under 18 free. Crib $5. TV; cable. Pool. Restaurant opp 10 am-10 pm. Ck-out 11 am. Refrigerators. Cr cds: A, DS, MC, V.

Elvis Presley's grave, Memphis

B&Bs/Small Inns

★★★ **MASON PLACE BED AND BREAKFAST.** *600 Commerce St (37774), SW on I-75, Exit 72 or 76, off US 11. 865/458-3921; fax 865/458-6092. www.checkthenet.com/travel/mason.htm.* 5 rms, shower only, 2 story. No rm phones. S, D $96-$120; higher rates: Univ of Tennessee football games, hols. Children over 14 yrs only. TV; VCR in sitting rm. Pool. Complimentary full bkfst; afternoon refreshments. Restaurants nearby. Ck-out 11 am, ck-in 3 pm. Lawn games. Restored plantation house (1865) furnished with period antiques. Fireplaces. Cr cds: A, DS, MC, V.

★★★ **WHITESTONE COUNTRY INN.** *1200 Paint Rock Rd (37763), I-75 Exit 72, 8 mi W on TN 72. 865/376-0113; fax 865/376-4454. www.whitestones.com.* 11 rms, some with A/C, 2 story, 3 suites, 1 guest house. Rm phones in suites. S, D $85-$160; each addl $20; suites $125-$160; guest house $85-$125; under 12 free. Crib free. TV; VCR avail (movies). Complimentary full bkfst, coffee in rms. Restaurant 8 am-8 pm. Ck-out 11 am, ck-in 3 pm. Business servs avail. In-rm modem link. Gift shop. Tennis privileges. Exercise equipt; sauna. Game rm. Rec rm. Lawn games. In-rm whirlpools, fireplaces; some refrigerators, microwaves. Many balconies. Picnic tables, grills. On lake. On 275 acres; surrounded by wildlife refuge. Totally nonsmoking. Cr cds: A, DS, MC, V.

Lewisburg

(F-4) *See also Shelbyville*

Settled 1837 **Pop** 9,879 **Elev** 734 ft
Area code 931 **Zip** 37091
Information Marshall County Chamber of Commerce, 227 2nd Ave N; 931/359-3863

Named for Meriwether Lewis, of the Lewis and Clark expeditions, Lewisburg is largely linked to the dairy industry and is a trading and shipping center for the surrounding farms. Milk processing plants are supplemented by factories producing air conditioners, furniture, and pencils.

Manchester

(F-5) *See also Monteagle*

Pop 7,709 **Elev** 1,063 ft
Area code 931 **Zip** 37355
Information Chamber of Commerce, 110 E Main St; 931/728-7635

What to See and Do

Distillery tours.

George A. Dickel Distillery. Distillery built in 1870 and re-created in 1959 produces and matures Tennessee sour mash "whisky." Country store. Thirty-45-min guided tours (Mon-Fri; closed hols, Dec 24; also Friday before some hols) Approx 11 mi SW on TN 55 to Tullahoma, then N on US 41A, follow signs. Phone 931/857-3124. **FREE**

Jack Daniel Distillery. Nation's oldest registered distillery. One-hr and 20-min guided tours incl rustic grounds, limestone spring cave, old office. (Daily; closed Jan 1, Thanksgiving, Dec 25) 25 mi SW on TN 55, in Lynchburg. Phone 931/759-4221. **FREE**

Normandy Lake. Completed in 1976, the dam is 2,734 ft high and impounds a 3,160-acre lake. Controlled releases provide a scenic floatway (28 mi) below the dam with public access points along the way. Summer pool, excellent spring and fall fishing; picnicking, camping. 8 mi W; 2 mi upstream from Normandy.

Old Stone Fort State Archaeological Park. Park covering 600 acres surrounds earthen remains of a more than 2,000-year-old walled structure built along the bluffs of the Duck River. Fishing; picnicking, playground, camping, museum. Standard fees. 1½ mi W off I-24, Exit 110. Phone 931/723-5073.

Annual Event

Old Timer's Day. City Square. Parade, pet contest, entertainment, games, food. First Sat Oct.

Motels/Motor Lodges

★★ **AMBASSADOR INN AND LUXURY SUITES.** *925 Interstate Dr (37355), I-24 Exit 110.* 931/728-2200; fax 931/728-8376; toll-free 800/237-9228. 105 rms, 1-2 story. S from $45; each addl $5; suites $75-$100; under 12 free. Crib $5. TV; cable (premium), VCR avail. Pool. Complimentary continental bkfst. Restaurant adj 6 am-10 pm. Ck-out 11 am. Meeting rms. Exercise equipt. Refrigerators. Cr cds: A, C, D, DS, MC, V.
🄳 ⛐ 🐎 🖼 🐾 SC

★★ **EXPRESSWAY INN.** *126 Expressway Dr (37355), I-24 Exit 114.* 931/728-1001; fax 931/738-9949. 141 rms, 2 story. S, D $61-$70; each addl $5; suites $72-$84; under 18 free. Crib free. Pet accepted. TV; cable (premium), VCR avail. Pool. Restaurant 6 am-2 pm, 5-10 pm. Bar 5 pm-midnight. Ck-out noon. Free guest lndry. Meeting rms. Business servs avail. In-rm modem link. Some refrigerators, microwaves. Cr cds: A, C, D, DS, ER, MC, V.
🄳 🐾 ⛐ 🖼 🐾

★ **SUPER 8 MOTEL.** *2430 Hillsboro Blvd (37355), 1 mi S on US 41 at I-24 Exit 114.* 931/728-9720; fax 931/728-8529; toll-free 800/800-8000. 50 rms, 2 story. S $24-$36; D $31-$45; each addl $5; under 12 free; higher rates special events. Crib free. Pet accepted, some restrictions. TV; cable (premium). Pool. Complimentary continental bkfst. Ck-out 11 am. Cr cds: A, D, DS, MC, V.
🄳 🐾 ⛐ 🖼 🐾 SC

Restaurant

★ **OAK.** *947 Interstate Dr (37355), I-24 Exit 110.* 931/728-5777. Specializes in prime rib, lasagne. Salad bar. Hrs: 11 am-9 pm. Closed July 4, Dec 24, 25. Res accepted exc Sun. Lunch $4.69-$6.99; dinner $4.95-$12.95. Child's menu. Cr cds: A, D, DS, MC, V.
🄳 🖃

Maryville

(F-7) *See also Knoxville, Townsend*

Founded 1795 **Pop** 19,208 **Elev** 989 ft
Area code 423
Web www.chamber.blount.tn.us
Information Blount County Chamber of Commerce, 201 S Washington St, 37804; 423/983-2241 or 800/525-6843

Motel/Motor Lodge

★ **PRINCESS MOTEL.** *2614 US Hwy 411 S (37801), 2 mi S on US 129, 411.* 423/982-2490; fax 423/984-1675. 33 rms, 1-2 story. May-Oct: S $40-$50; D $50-$60; each addl $5; kit. units $210-$350/wk; under 12 free; higher rates special events; lower rates rest of yr. Crib $4. Pet accepted. TV; cable (premium). Pool. Restaurant adj open 24 hrs. Ck-out 11 am. Cr cds: A, C, D, DS, MC, V.

B&B/Small Inn

★★★★ **BLACKBERRY FARM.** *1471 W Millers Cove Rd (37886), 10 mi N on TN 321, first right after Foothills Parkway.* 423/984-8166; fax 423/983-5708. Email blkberryfrm@aol.com; www.blackberryhotel.com. The perfect blend of nature and luxury has attracted guests to this 1,100-acre, Smokey Mountain estate since the 1940s. Order a picnic lunch for an afternoon hike, fish for trout in a crystal-clear pond, or enlist the help of an experienced guide for a whitewater rafting excursion. Nightly rates for rooms, suites or private cottages include 3 gourmet meals and afternoon tea. 44 rms, 2 story. AP: S $295-$695; D $395-$795; hol plans. Children over 10 yrs only excluding hols. TV, cable. Heated pool. Dining rm 8-10:30 am, 6:30-8:30 pm. Ck-out noon, ck-in 4 pm. Business servs avail. Airport transportation. Valet serv. Concierge serv. Tennis. Golf privileges. Hiking. Hot air balloon rides. Whitewater rafting. Exercise rm. Game rm. Gift shop. Picnic tables. Private patios. Cr cds: A, DS, MC, V.

McMinnville (F-5)

Pop 11,194 **Elev** 976 ft **Area code** 931
Zip 37110 **Web** www.warrentn.com
Information McMinnville-Warren County Chamber of Commerce, 110 S Court Square, PO Box 574, 37111; 931/473-6611

Motel/Motor Lodge

★★ **COMFORT INN.** *508 Sunnyside Heights (37110).* 931/473-4446; fax 931/473-7753; res 800/228-5150. 61 rms, 3 story. May-Oct: S $90; D $95; each addl $5; lower rates rest of yr. Crib avail. TV; cable (premium). Restaurant nearby. Ck-out noon, ck-in 3 pm. Golf, 18 holes. Tennis, 2 courts. Cr cds: A, C, D, DS, MC, V.

B&B/Small Inn

★★ **FALCON MANOR BED AND BREAKFAST.** *2645 Faulkner Springs Rd (37110).* 931/668-4444; fax 931/815-4444. 5 rms, 1 with shower only, 2 story. No rm phones. S, D $105; each addl $10. Children over 11 yrs only. Premium cable TV in common rm; VCR. Complimentary full bkfst. Ck-out 11 am, ck-in 3 pm. Business servs avail. Gift shop. Lawn games. Microwaves avail. Fireplaces. Authentically restored Victorian mansion built in 1896. Totally non-smoking. Cr cds: A, DS, MC, V.

Memphis (E-1)

Settled 1819 **Pop** 610,337 **Elev** 264 ft
Area code 901
Web www.memphistravel.com

Information Convention & Visitors Bureau, 47 Union Ave, 38103; 901/543-5300

Memphis, on the Mississippi, is an old town with a new face. It is both "old South" and modern metropolis. The city has towering office buildings, flashy expressways, a $60 million civic center—and historic Beale Street, where W.C. Handy helped give birth to the blues.

General James Winchester is credited with naming the city for the Egyptian city Memphis, which means "place of good abode." The Nile-like Mississippi, of course, was the inspiration. Winchester, Andrew Jackson, and John Overton laid out the town on a land grant from North Carolina, selecting this site because of the high bluffs above the river and the natural harbor at the mouth of the Wolf River. The land deal was somewhat questionable, and General Jackson left under a barrage of criticism. River traffic quickly developed; stores, shops, and sawmills appeared, and Memphis became one of the busiest and most boisterous ports in America.

For a short time Memphis was the Confederate capital of the state, also serving as a military supply depot and stronghold for the Southern forces. In 1862, however, Northern troops seized the city after a river battle dominated by an armada of 30 Union ships and held it throughout the war. Plagued by yellow fever epidemics, an impoverished Memphis made a slow postwar recovery. But by 1892 the city was back on its feet, becoming the busiest inland cotton market and hardwood lumber center in the world.

Memphis dominates the flat, crop-rich, alluvial Mississippi Delta. It serves as hub of six railroads, port for millions of tons of river cargo annually, and home of over 1,100 manufacturing plants in the Memphis area. In national competition it has been acclaimed as the Cleanest City, the Safest City, and the Quietest City.

As much as one-third of the country's cotton crop is bought or sold in Memphis, known as the cotton center of the world, but the agricultural segment of the city's economy is highly diversified—corn, alfalfa, vegetables, soybeans, rice, livestock, and even fish farming. Memphis has the largest medical center in the South and more than a dozen institutions of higher learning, including the University of Memphis and Rhodes College. A city with a civic ballet, a symphony orchestra, an opera company, a repertory theater, art galleries, and College of Art, Memphis is also a major convention city and distribution center.

Throughout the world Memphis has become associated with the legendary Elvis Presley. Graceland, Presley's home, and Meditation Gardens, site of his grave, have become a destination for thousands of visitors annually. Each August, memorial celebrations are held citywide in honor of the "king of rock and roll."

Transportation

Memphis Intl Airport. Information 901/922-8000; lost and found 901/922-8050; weather 901/544-0399.

Car Rental Agencies. See IMPORTANT TOLL-FREE NUMBERS.

Public Transportation. Memphis Area Transit Authority, phone 901/274-6282.

Rail Passenger Service. Amtrak 800/872-7245.

What to See and Do

☒ **Beale Street.** Part of a 7-blk entertainment district stretching E from the Mississippi River bluffs with restaurants, shops, parks, and theaters. Statue of W.C. Handy in Handy Park. Downtown, off Riverside Dr. Phone 901/526-0110. Also on Beale St is

    W.C. Handy's Home. House where W.C. Handy wrote "Memphis Blues," "St. Louis Blues," and other classic tunes. Collection of Handy memorabilia. 352 Beale St. Phone 901/522-1556 for schedule. ¢

The Children's Museum of Memphis. Hands-on museum has created an interactive "kid-sized city" incl a bank, grocery store, and skyscraper, among others. Special workshops and exhibits. (Tues-Sun; closed hols) 2525 Central Ave. Phone 901/458-2678. ¢¢

Circuit Playhouse. Comedies, musicals, and dramas. 1705 Poplar Ave. Phone 901/726-4656.

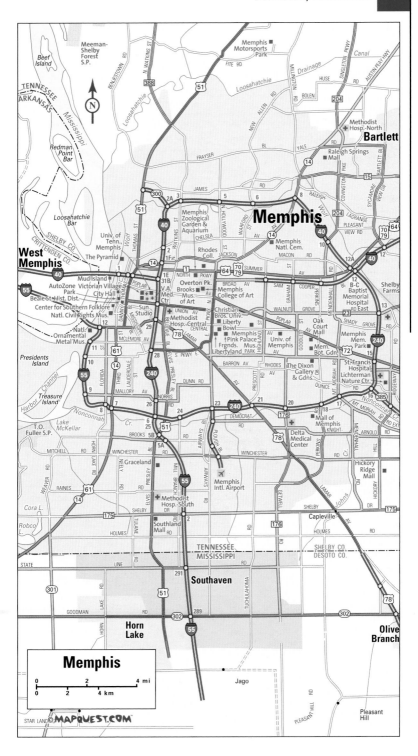

Memphis

0   2   4 mi
0   2   4 km

STAR LAND© MAPQUEST.COM

Crystal Shrine Grotto. Crystal cave made of natural rock, quartz, crystal, and semiprecious stones carved out of a hillside by naturalistic artist Dionicio Rodriguez in the late 1930s. Also scenes by the artist depicting life of Jesus and Biblical characters. (Daily) 5668 Poplar Ave, in Memorial Park Cemetery. Phone 901/767-8930. **FREE**

Dixon Gallery and Gardens. Museum surrounded by 17 acres of formal and woodland gardens with a camellia house and garden statuary; exhibition galleries display American and Impressionist art, British portraits and landscapes, English antique furnishings, 18th-century German porcelain. (Tues-Sun; closed hols) 4339 Park Ave. Phone 901/761-5250. ¢¢

Downtown Mall Trolley. Antique electric trolley loop runs up Main St and back in the Pinch Historic District providing transportation to hotels, Beale St, and attractions such as Pyramid Arena and the National Civil Rights Museum. (Daily) Phone 901/577-2648.

✪ **Graceland.** Elvis Presley home. Mansion tour incl main floor and lower level of house, trophy room, grounds, gravesite. Other attractions incl Automobile Museum, Presley's jet airplanes. (Daily; mansion tour, Nov-Feb, Mon, Wed-Sun; closed Jan 1, Thanksgiving, Dec 25; res recommended) Contact PO Box 16508, 38186-0508. 3734 Elvis Presley Blvd. Phone 901/332-3322 or 800/238-2000. ¢¢- ¢¢¢¢

Gray Line bus tours. Contact 5702 Summer Ave, 38106. Phone 901/384-3474.

Hunt-Phelan Home. Restored antebellum house with original furniture, some dating back to early 1608. (Apr-Aug, daily; rest of yr, Thurs-Mon; closed hols) 533 Beale St. Phone 901/344-3166 or 800/350-9009. ¢¢¢

Libertyland. Educational/historical amusement park with carnival rides, live shows, costumed characters, games, shops, food. (Mid-June-late Aug, Wed-Sun; May-mid-June and late Aug-Labor Day, wkends only) E Parkway at Mid-South Fairgrounds. Phone 901/274-1776. Admission/8-ride ticket ¢¢¢- ¢¢¢¢

Lichterman Nature Center. Wildlife sanctuary (65 acres) incl 12-acre lake, greenhouse, and hospital for wild animals. Hiking trails (3 mi), picnicking. (Tues-Sun; closed hols) 1680 Lynnfield. Phone 901/767-7322. ¢

Meeman-Shelby Forest State Park. A 12,500-acre park with 2 lakes bordering the Mississippi River. Swimming pool, fishing, boating; hiking and bridle trails, camping, cabins, nature center. Standard fees. 13 mi N via US 51, near Millington. Phone 901/876-5215.

Memphis Botanic Garden. Garden encompasses 96 acres; 20 formal gardens here incl the Japanese Garden of Tranquility, the Rose Garden, and the Wildflower Garden. (Daily; closed Jan 1, Thanksgiving, Dec 25) 750 Cherry Rd in Audubon Park. Phone 901/685-1566. ¢

Memphis Brooks Museum of Art. Paintings, drawings, sculpture, photographs, prints, and decorative arts from Renaissance to present. Permanent and changing exhibits. Guided tours, lectures, films, performing arts series. (Tues-Sun; closed Jan 1, Thanksgiving, Dec 25) In Overton Park, off Poplar Ave. Phone 901/544-6200. ¢¢

Memphis International Motorsports Park. Multiuse park features 4 tracks hosting a variety of racing events: drag, circle track, tractor pulls, motorcycle, go-cart, and 4-wheeler. (Mar-Nov; daily) N on I-240, 5500 Taylor Forge Dr. Phone 901/358-7223. ¢¢¢

Memphis Pink Palace Museum and Planetarium. Exhibits focus on natural and cultural history of the mid-South. Many facets of the region, incl insects, birds, mammals, geology, pioneer life, medical history, commerce, and the Civil War, can be explored; also changing exhibits and IMAX Theater. (Daily; closed hols) Planetarium has shows weekends and in summer (fee). 3050 Central Ave. Phone 901/320-6320. ¢¢¢

Memphis Zoo & Aquarium. More than 2,800 animals in naturalistic habitats such as Cat Country, Primate Canyon, Animals of the Night, and Once Upon a Farm. Tram, rides, cafe. (Daily; closed Thanksgiving, Dec 24, 25) Bounded by N Parkway, E Parkway & Poplar Ave. Phone 901/276-WILD. ¢¢¢

Mud Island. Fifty-acre island in the Mississippi is a unique park designed to showcase the character of the river. The River Walk is a 5-blk-long scale model of the Mississippi from Cairo, IL, to the Gulf of

Mexico; the River Museum features 18 galleries that chronicle the development of river music, art, lore, and history; also here are films, playground, river boat excursions, shops, restaurants, picnicking. Monorail to island at Front St Exit off I-40. Phone 901/576-7241. Also on island is

Memphis Belle. This B-17 bomber and her crew were the first to complete 25 missions over Nazi targets and return to the US during WWII. Named for the pilot's wartime sweetheart, the *Memphis Belle* was featured in a documentary by director William Wyler; film shown twice daily. Plane displayed under glass dome. 125 N Front St. ¢

★ National Civil Rights Museum. The nation's first civil rights museum honors the American civil rights movement and the people behind it, from colonial to present times. Exhibits, sound and light displays, audiovisual and visitor participation programs; auditorium and courtyard. (Mon, Wed-Sun; closed hols) 450 Mulberry St, at the Lorraine Motel, site of the 1968 assassination of Dr. Martin Luther King, Jr. Phone 901/521-9699. ¢¢

National Ornamental Metal Museum. Architectural and decorative metalwork. (Tues-Sun; closed hols) 374 Metal Museum Dr, on the river bluff. Phone 901/774-6380. ¢

Playhouse on the Square. Professional theater. 51 S Cooper, in Overton Sq. Phone 901/725-0776 or 901/726-4656 (ticket office). ¢¢¢¢

Pyramid Arena. This 32-story, 22,500-seat stainless steel and concrete pyramid, overlooking the Mississippi River is fashioned after the ancient Egyptian Great Pyramid of Cheops and is used as a multisports and entertainment arena. Tours (daily). Downtown Pinch Historic District, on the Wolf River at Auction St Bridge. Phone 901/521-9675. ¢¢

Rhodes College. (1848) 1,400 students. On campus is the 140-ft-high Richard Halliburton Memorial Tower, with 1st editions of Halliburton's books; memorabilia. Clough-Hanson Gallery has changing art exhibits (Mon-Fri; closed hols). Tours of campus. 2000 N Parkway at University St. Phone 901/843-3000.

River cruises.

Delta Queen, Mississippi Queen, and **American Queen.** Paddlewheelers offer 3- to 12-night cruises on the Mississippi, Ohio, Cumberland, and Tennessee rivers. For details, contact Delta Queen Steamboat Co, 30 Robin St Wharf, New Orleans, LA 70130-1890. Phone 800/543-1949.

Memphis Queen. Sightseeing, dinner cruises aboard Mississippi riverboat. (Sightseeing, Mar-Dec, daily; dinner cruises, May-Sep, Wed-Sun) Foot of Monroe at Riverside Dr. Phone 901/527-5694. ¢¢- ¢¢¢¢

★ Sun Studio. Legendary recording studio where Elvis Presley, Jerry Lee Lewis, Roy Orbison, Carl Perkins, and Johnny Cash made their 1st recordings. Tour (30 min; every ½ hr). (Daily; closed Jan 1, Thanksgiving, Dec 25) 706 Union Ave. Phone 901/521-0664. ¢¢

T.O. Fuller State Park. A 384-acre park where De Soto is believed to have crossed the Mississippi. Swimming pool, bathhouse; golf, picnicking, concessions, campsites (hookups). Standard fees. 10 mi S on US 61, then 4 mi W on Mitchell Rd. Phone 901/543-7581. In the park is

Chucalissa Archaeological Museum. Archaeological project of Univ of Memphis at site of Native American village founded about AD 900 and abandoned ca 1500. Native houses and temple have been reconstructed; archaeological exhibits. Museum displays artifacts and dioramas; 15-min slide program. (Daily; closed hols; no admittance to village area after 4:30 pm) 1987 Indian Village Dr. Phone 901/785-3160. ¢¢

Victorian Village. Eighteen landmark bldgs, either preserved or restored, range in style from Gothic Revival to neo-Classical. Within 1 mi of downtown area, 600 blk of Adams Ave. The 3 houses open to the public are

Magevney House. (1836) Restored house of pioneer schoolmaster Eugene Magevney. Oldest middle-class dwelling in the city, furnished with artifacts of the period. (Tues-Sat; closed hols) 198 Adams Ave. Phone 901/526-4464. **Donation.**

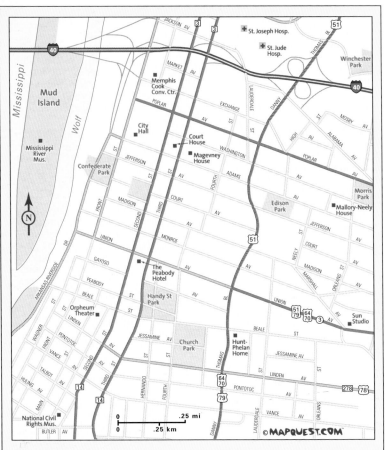

BEALE STREET

Beale Street is the "Home of the Blues," and any stroll down the city's historic street illustrates how the city celebrates its musical heritage. Start at the Mississippi River to see how the city came to be situated on this low bluff. Climb the gradual rise to the top where from the historic Orpheum Theater you can see Beale Street's commercial district splayed out before you. From the statue of the city's most famous resident, Elvis Presley (across from the supper club of the same name), four blocks are chock full of restaurants, nightclubs, and saloons among the shops. At night music emanates from nearly every doorway. Between 2nd and 3rd the "Walk of Fame" features musical notes embedded in the sidewalk with the names of famous blues artists. Be sure to stop at A.H. Schwab's, the old general store that has occupied this site since 1876. W.C. Handy Park is a popular site for outdoor centers and festivals, and Handy's birth home can be seen at the end of the strip. For a fitting end, schedule a detour to the Peabody Hotel on Union Street between 2nd and 3rd at 5 pm sharp to see the famous Peabody ducks (yes, ducks) make their ascent from the lobby fountain up the elevator to their penthouse suite.

Woodruff-Fontaine House. (1870) Restored and furnished 2nd Empire/Victorian mansion with antique textile/costume collection. Gift shop. (Daily; closed hols) 680 Adams Ave. Phone 901/526-1469. ¢¢

Mallory-Neely House. (1852) Preserved Italianate mansion (25 rms) with original furnishings. (Tues-Sun; closed hols) 652 Adams Ave. Phone 901/523-1484. ¢¢

Annual Events

Zydeco Festival. Beale St. Cajun-Creole and zydeco blues bands entertain in Beale St clubs. Early Feb.

Beale Street Music Festival. Beale St. Intl roster of musicians returns to Memphis for a musical family reunion. Part of the Memphis in May festivities. Early May.

Memphis in May International Festival. Month-long communitywide celebration focuses on cultural and artistic heritage of Memphis, featuring a different nation each yr. Major events occur weekends, but activities are held daily. Incl the Beale St Music Festival, World Championship Barbecue Cooking Contest, and Sunset Symphony. Phone 901/525-4611. May.

Carnival Memphis. Features parade, exhibits, salute to industry, and the Cottonmaker's Jubilee. Phone 901/278-0243. Ten days early June.

Elvis Presley International Tribute Week. More than 30 events take place throughout the city in honor of Presley and his music. Phone 901/332-3322. Aug.

Labor Day Fest. Beale St. Memphis musicians perform blues, jazz, rhythm and blues, country, and rock at clubs and restaurants throughout the historic district. Phone 901/526-0110. Early Sep.

Mid-South Fair and Exposition. Mid-South Fairgrounds, E Parkway S & Southern Ave. Agricultural, commercial, industrial exhibits; midway rides and concerts. Largest rodeo E of the Mississippi. Phone 901/274-8800. Late Sep-early Oct.

Seasonal Events

Outdoor concerts. Raoul Wallenberg Overton Park Shell, said to be the true birthplace of rock 'n' roll; Elvis Presley gave one of his first live performances here. Concerts feature local blues, rock, and jazz musicians; also theater, movies, and dance presentations. For schedule phone 901/274-6046. Late Mar-early Nov.

Theatre Memphis. 630 Perkins Extended. Internationally acclaimed community theater. Phone 901/682-8601. Mainstage offers 6-play season Sep-June; Little Theatre features 4-play season July-May.

Additional Visitor Information

For further information contact the Convention & Visitors Bureau, 47 Union Ave, 38103; phone 901/543-5300. Tourists may also inquire at the TN St Welcome Center located at 119 N Riverside Dr, phone 901/543-5333.

City Neighborhoods

Many of the restaurants, unrated dining establishments and some lodgings listed under Memphis incl neighborhoods as well as exact street addresses. Geographic descriptions of these areas are given.

Beale Street Area. Downtown area along 7 blks of Beale St from Riverside Dr on the W to Danny Thomas Blvd on the E.

Downtown. S of I-40, W of Danny Thomas Blvd (US 51), N of Calhoun Ave, and E of the Mississippi River. **E of Downtown:** E of US 51.

Overton Square. S of Poplar Ave, W of Cooper St, N of Union Ave, and E of McLean Blvd.

Motels/Motor Lodges

★★ **COMFORT INN.** *5877 Poplar Ave (38119), E of downtown. 901/767-6300; fax 901/767-0098; toll-free 800/228-5150.* 126 rms, 5 story. S, D $68-$79; each addl $6; under 18 free; higher rates special events. Crib free. Pet accepted, some restrictions, $20. TV; cable (premium). Pool. Complimentary continental bkfst. Ck-out noon. Meeting rms. Bellhops. Sundries. Free airport transportation. Exercise equipt. Cr cds: A, D, DS, MC, V.

★★ **COMFORT INN.** *2889 Austin Peay Hwy (38128), N of downtown. 901/386-0033; fax 901/386-0036; toll-free 800/638-7949.* 83 rms, 20 kit. suites. S, D $49-$67; each addl $5; kit. suites $70-$130; under 16 free. TV; cable (premium). Indoor pool; whirlpool. Complimentary continental bkfst. Restaurant nearby. Ck-out noon. Meeting rms. Business servs avail. Cr cds: A, C, D, DS, ER, MC, V.

D ☒ ☒ ☒ SC

★★ **COURTYARD BY MARRIOTT MEMPHIS PARK AVENUE.** *6015 Park Ave (38119), E of downtown. 901/761-0330; fax 901/682-8422; toll-free 800/321-2211.* 146 units, 3 story. S, D $86-$96; each addl $10; suites $102-$112; under 17 free. Crib free. TV; cable (premium), VCR avail. Heated pool; whirlpool. Complimentary coffee in rms. Restaurant 6:30-10 am. Bar 5-10 pm. Ck-out noon. Coin lndry. Meeting rms. Business servs avail. Valet serv. Sundries. Exercise equipt. Health club privileges. Refrigerator, microwaves avail. Cr cds: A, C, D, DS, MC, V.

D ☒ ☒ ☒ ☒ SC

★★ **HAMPTON INN.** *1180 Union Ave (38103), downtown. 901/276-1175; fax 901/276-4261.* 126 rms, 4 story. S $56-$64; D $64-$70; under 18 free. Crib free. TV; cable (premium), VCR avail. Pool. Complimentary continental bkfst. Restaurant nearby. Ck-out 11 am. Business servs avail. Sundries. Cr cds: A, C, D, DS, MC, V.

D ☒ ☒ ☒ SC

★ **RED ROOF INN.** *6055 Shelby Oaks Dr (38134), I-40 Exit 12, E of downtown. 901/388-6111; fax 901/388-6157; res 800/REDROOF.* 108 rms, 2 story. S $43.99; D $51.99; each addl $8; under 18 free; higher rates special events. Crib free. Pet accepted, some restrictions. TV; cable (premium). Complimentary coffee in lobby. Restaurant adj open 24 hrs. Ck-out noon. Microwaves avail. Cr cds: A, C, D, DS, MC, V.

D ☒ ☒ ☒

★ **RED ROOF INN MEMPHIS AIRPORT.** *3875 American Way (38118), E of downtown. 901/363-2335; fax 901/363-2335; toll-free 800/843-7663.* 109 rms, 3 story. S $38.99-$54.99; D $41.99-$49.99; each addl $8; under 18 free. Pet accepted. TV; cable (pre-mium). Complimentary coffee in lobby. Ck-out noon. Cr cds: A, C, D, DS, MC, V.

D ☒ ☒ ☒

★★ **RESIDENCE INN.** *6141 Old Poplar Pike (38119), E of downtown. 901/685-9595; fax 901/685-1636; res 800/331-3131.* 105 kit. suites, 4 story. Kit. suites $109-$154. Crib free. Pet accepted, some restrictions; $100-$200. TV; cable, (premium). Pool; whirlpool. Complimentary continental bkfst. Restaurant nearby. Ck-out noon. Coin lndry. Meeting rms. Business servs avail. Health club privileges. Microwaves. Private patios, balconies. Cr cds: A, DS, MC, V.

D ☒ ☒ ☒ ☒ ☒ ☒

★★★ **RIDGEWAY INN.** *5679 Poplar Ave (38119), at I-240, E of downtown. 901/766-4000; fax 901/763-1857; toll-free 800/822-3360.* 155 rms, 7 story. S, D $94-$129; each addl $10; suites $195-$295; under 12 free. Crib free. TV; cable (premium). Pool. Restaurant 6:30 am-11 pm; Fri, Sat to 1 am; Sun to 10 pm. Bar from 11 am; Fri, Sat to 1 am; Sun noon-10 pm. Ck-out noon. Meeting rm. Business servs avail. Free airport transportation. Exercise equipt. Health club privileges. Luxury level. Cr cds: A, C, D, DS, ER, MC, V.

D ☒ ☒ ☒ ☒ SC

★★ **STUDIO 6.** *4300 American Way (38118), E of downtown. 901/366-9333; fax 901/366-7835; toll-free 800/466-8356.* 120 kit. suites, 3 story. Kit. suites $69-$99; under 16 free. Crib free. Pet accepted. TV; cable (pre-mium). Pool; whirlpool. Complimentary continental bkfst; coffee in rms. Restaurant adj open 24 hrs. Ck-out noon. Coin lndry. Meeting rms. Business servs avail. Valet serv. Sundries. Free airport transportation. Microwaves. Cr cds: A, C, D, DS, MC, V.

D ☒ ☒ ☒ ☒ SC

★★ **WILSON WORLD HOTEL.** *2715 Cherry Rd (38130), E of downtown. 901/366-0000; fax 901/366-6361; toll-free 800/872-8366.* 178 rms, 4 story, 90 suites. S, D $79-$85; each addl $6; suites $89-$99; under 18 free. Crib free. TV; cable (premium). Indoor pool. Restaurant 6 am-2 pm, 5:30-10 pm. Bar from 5 pm; pianist exc Sat, Sun. Ck-out noon. Meeting rms. Business servs avail. Bellhops. Gift shop. Barber, beauty shop. Free airport transportation. Refrigerators, wet bars. Balconies. Cr cds: A, D, DS, MC, V.

🅳 ⊠ ⊠ 🐾 SC

Hotels

★★★ **ADAM'S MARK HOTEL - MEMPHIS.** *939 Ridge Lake Blvd (38120), E of downtown.* 901/684-6664; fax 901/762-7411; toll-free 800/444-2326. www.adamsmark.com. 403 rms, 27 story, 5 suites. S, D $119; suites $500; under 18 free. Crib avail. Valet parking avail. Pool, lap pool, whirlpool. TV; cable. Complimentary coffee in rms, newspaper. Restaurant. Bar. Conference center, meeting rms. Business center. Bellhops. Concierge. Dry cleaning, coin lndry. Gift shop. Free airport transportation. Exercise equipt. Golf. Tennis, 10 courts. Cr cds: A, C, D, DS, MC, V.

🅳 ⅀ ⅂ ⊠ 🏃 ⅄ ⊠ 🏃

★★★ **EMBASSY SUITES.** *1022 S Shady Grove Rd (38120), E of downtown.* 901/684-1777; fax 901/685-8185. 220 suites, 5 story. Suites $129-$149; under 12 free; wkend rates. Crib free. TV; cable (premium). Indoor pool; whirlpool. Complimentary full bkfst, coffee in rms. Restaurant 11 am-10 pm. Bar to 11 pm. Ck-out noon. Coin lndry. Convention facilities. Business servs avail. In-rm modem link. Gift shop. Free airport transportation. Exercise equipt; sauna. Game rm. Refrigerators. Cr cds: A, C, D, DS, MC, V.

🅳 ⊠ 🏃 ⊠ 🐾

★★★ **FOUR POINTS BY SHERATON.** *2240 Democrat Rd (38132), near intl airport, S of downtown.* 901/332-1130; fax 901/398-5206. 380 rms, 5 story. S $99-$114; D $109; each addl $10; suites $179-$450; under 18 free. Crib free. TV; cable. Pool; poolside serv. Restaurant 6 am-11 pm. Bars 3-11 pm. Fri, Sat to midnight, Sun 3:30-11 pm. Ck-out noon. Convention facilities. Business center. Free airport transportation. 2 lighted tennis courts. Exercise equipt; sauna. Wet bar in suites. Indoor courtyard. Cr cds: A, C, D, DS, ER, MC, V.

🅳 ⅂ ⊠ 🏃 ✈ ⊠ 🐾 SC 🏃

★★ **HOLIDAY INN MIDTOWN.** *1837 Union Ave (38104), in Overton Square.* 901/278-4100; fax 901/272-3810; res 800/holiday; toll-free 800/

465-4329. www.holidayinnmemphis.com. 167 rms, 8 story, 6 suites. Apr-Nov: S $80; D $75; each addl $6; suites $159; under 17 free; lower rates rest of yr. Crib avail, fee. Parking garage. Pool. TV; cable (premium). Complimentary coffee in rms, newspaper. Restaurant, closed Sun. Bar. Meeting rms. Business servs avail. Bellhops. Dry cleaning, coin lndry. Free airport transportation. Exercise privileges. Golf. Cr cds: A, C, D, DS, JCB, MC, V.

🅳 ⅂ ⊠ ⊠ 🐾 SC

★★★ **HOLIDAY INN SELECT.** *160 Union Ave (38103), at 2nd St, downtown.* 901/525-5491; fax 901/529-8950; toll-free 888/300-5491. 190 rms, 14 story. S, D $109-$129; each addl $10; suites $199; under 18 free. Crib free. TV; cable (premium). Pool. Restaurant 6 am-midnight. Bar 4 pm-midnight, Sat to 2 am. Ck-out 11 am. Meeting rms. Business center. In-rm modem link. Valet serv. Airport transportation. Exercise equipt. Wet bar in suites. Refrigerators. Cr cds: A, C, D, DS, ER, JCB, MC, V.

🅳 ⊠ 🏃 ⊠ 🐾 SC 🏃

★★★ **MARRIOTT.** *2625 Thousand Oaks Blvd (38118), SE of downtown; I-240, Exit 18.* 901/362-6200; fax 901/360-8836; toll-free 800/228-9290. 320 rms, 12 story. S $79-$146; D $79-$161; suites $200-$350; under 18 free. Crib free. Pet accepted. TV; cable (premium). 2 pools, 1 indoor; whirlpool. Restaurant 6:30 am-11 pm; wknds from 7 am. Bars 11-2 am. Ck-out noon. Convention facilities. Business servs avail. In-rm modem link. Concierge. Free airport transportation. Exercise equipt; sauna. Some bathrm phones, refrigerators. Luxury level. Cr cds: A, C, D, DS, ER, JCB, MC, V.

🅳 🐾 ⊠ 🏃 ⊠ 🐾 SC

★★★ **MARRIOTT DOWNTOWN.** *250 N Main St (32830), downtown.* 901/527-7300; fax 901/526-1561; toll-free 888/557-8740. www.crownplaza.com. 402 rms, 18 story. S $125-$155; D $125-$175; each addl $10; suites $250-$400; under 18 free. Crib free. Pet accepted, some restrictions. Valet parking $10, garage $5. TV; cable (premium). Indoor pool; whirlpool. Restaurant 6 am-11 pm. Bar 11-2 am. Ck-out noon. Convention facilities.

Business center. Concierge. Shopping arcade. Exercise equipt; sauna. Some refrigerators. Cr cds: A, C, D, DS, JCB, MC, V.

`D` 🛎 ≈ ⫻ ⊠ 🖐 `SC` ⫻

★★★ **PEABODY.** *149 Union Ave (38103), downtown. 901/529-4000; fax 901/529-3600; res 800/PEABODY; toll-free 800/732-2639. Email tblack@ peabodymemphis.com; www.peabody memphis.com.* 468 rms, 12 story, 15 suites. Mar-June, Sep-Oct: S $180; D $210; each addl $30; suites $725; under 18 free; lower rates rest of yr. Crib avail. Valet parking avail. Indoor pool, whirlpool. TV; cable (premium), VCR avail. Complimentary newspaper. Restaurant 6:30 am-10 pm (See CHEZ PHILIPPE). 24-hr rm serv. Bar. Ck-out 11 am, ck-in 4 pm. Conference center, meeting rms. Business center. Bellhops. Concierge. Dry cleaning. Gift shop. Salon/barber. Exercise rm, sauna, steam rm. Golf. Video games. Cr cds: A, C, D, DS, ER, JCB, MC, V.

`D` 🏋 ≈ ⫻ ⊠ 🔥 🖐 ⫻

★★★ **RADISSON.** *185 Union Ave (38103), downtown. 901/528-1800; fax 901/525-8509; res 800/333-3333. Email scardenas@memphisradisson.com.* 280 rms, 10 story. S, D $109-$119; each addl $10; suites $125-$245; under 18 free. Crib free. Garage/valet $5. TV; cable (premium). Pool; whirlpool. Restaurant 6-2 am. Bar 11 am-midnight. Ck-out noon. Convention facilities. Business servs avail. Gift shop. Exercise equipt; sauna. Near Beale St, Mud Island, and Pyramid. Cr cds: A, D, DS, MC, V.

`D` 🏃 ✈ ≈ ⫻ 🔥 ⊠ 🔥

★★★ **RADISSON INN MEMPHIS AIRPORT.** *2411 Winchester Rd (38116), at intl airport, S of downtown. 901/332-2370; fax 901/345-9398; res 800/333-3333; toll-free 800/365-2370. Email rsales@ionictech.com; www. radisson.com/memphistn_airport.* 207 rms, 3 story, 4 suites. S, D $139; suites $139. Crib avail. Parking lot. Pool. TV; cable (premium). Complimentary coffee in rms, newspaper. Restaurant 6 am-10 pm. Bar. Ck-out noon, ck-in 3 pm. Meeting rms. Business center. Bellhops. Dry cleaning. Free airport transportation. Exercise equipt. Golf. Tennis. Cr cds: A, C, D, DS, JCB, MC, V.

`D` 🏋 ✈ ≈ ⫻ ✈ ⊠ 🔥 ⫻

All Suite

★★ **FRENCH QUARTER SUITES INN.** *2144 Madison Ave (38104), in Overton Square. 901/728-4000; fax 901/278-1262; toll-free 800/843-0353. Email gmmem@lodgian.com; www. memphisfrenchquarter.com.* 4 story, 105 suites, suites $89; under 16 free. Parking lot. Pool. TV; cable (premium). Complimentary coffee in rms, newspaper, toll-free calls. Restaurant 5-10 pm. Bar. Ck-out noon, ck-in 4 pm. Meeting rms. Business center. Bellhops. Dry cleaning. Free airport transportation. Exercise privileges. Golf. Tennis. Video games. Cr cds: A, D, DS, MC, V.

`D` 🏋 📠 ≈ ⫻ ⫻ ⊠ 🖐 ⫻

Restaurants

★ **ALFRED'S.** *197 Beale St (38103), in Beale St area. 901/525-3711. www. alfredsonbeale.com.* Specializes in blackened catfish, barbecue ribs. Hrs: 10-3 am. Bar. Lunch $3.95-$4.95; dinner $4.99-$14.99. Entertainment: rock 'n roll Tues-Sun. Parking. Cr cds: A, C, DS, MC, V.

`D` ⫻

★★ **AUBERGINE.** *5007 Black Rd (38117), E of downtown. 901/767-7840.* Specializes in roasted breast of duck a l'orange, roasted thigh of chicken with escargot, warm chocolate pyramid cake. Hrs: 11:30 am-2 pm, 6-9:30 pm; Sat from 6 pm. Closed Sun, Mon; hols. Res accepted. Lunch a la carte entrees: $10; dinner a la carte entrees: $20-$25. Intimate dining. Cr cds: A, MC, V.

`D`

★ **AUTOMATIC SLIM'S TONGA CLUB.** *83 S 2nd St (38103), downtown. 901/525-7948.* Specializes in Argentinian-style churrasco, stacked tenderloin, hauchinango. Hrs: 11 am-2 pm, 5-11 pm; Sat from 5 pm Mon,Thurs. 11 am- 2 am 11 am-2:30 pm, 5-11 pm; Fri to 11 pm; Sat 5-11 pm. Closed Sun; Jan 1, July 4, Dec 25. Res accepted. Bar. Lunch $4.75-$8.95; dinner $12.95-$21.95. Child's menu. Entertainment: jazz Fri. Caribbean decor. Cr cds: A, D, MC, V.

`D` ⫻

★★ **BENIHANA OF TOKYO.** *912 Ridge Lake Blvd (38120), E of downtown. 901/683-7390.* Hrs: 11:30 am-2 pm, 5-10 pm; Fri, Sat to 11 pm.

Closed Sun. Res accepted. Bar. Lunch complete meals: $5.75-$13.50; dinner complete meals: $13-$28. Child's menu. Parking. Cr cds: A, MC, V.
[D] [≡]

★ **BOSCOS PIZZA KITCHEN AND BREWERY.** *7615 W Farmington (38138), E on US 72, at Poplar Ave, in Saddle Creek Shopping Plaza. 901/756-7310. www.boscobear.com.* Specializes in wood-burning oven pizza, pasta. Own beer brewery. Hrs: 11 am-10:30 pm; Fri, Sat to 12:30 am. Closed Thanksgiving, Dec 25. Bar. Lunch $3.95-$8.95; dinner $4.95-$14.95. Parking. Contemporary decor. Cr cds: A, C, D, DS, MC, V.
[D] [≡]

★ **BUCKLEY'S FINE FILET GRILL.** *5355 Poplar Ave (38119), at Estate Dr, E of downtown. 901/683-4538. Email buckleys2@wspice.com.* Specializes in filet steak, pasta. Hrs: 4-9:30 pm; Fri, Sat to 10:30 pm. Closed Thanksgiving, Dec 24, 25. Bar. Dinner $8.99-$17.49. Parking. Artwork and hanging plants create a friendly atmosphere in this local favorite. Cr cds: A, D, DS, MC, V.
[D] [≡]

★ **BUNTYN.** *4972 Park Ave (38117), E of downtown. 901/458-8776.* Specializes in meatloaf, chicken, beef

tips. Own baking. Hrs: 11 am-8 pm. Closed Sat, Sun; hols. Lunch, dinner $3.50-$6.80. Child's menu. Family-owned since 1920. Cr cds: D, DS, MC, V.
[SC]

★★★★ **CHEZ PHILIPPE.** *149 Union Ave. 901/529-4188.* Located off the luxurious lobby of The Peabody hotel, a 130-year-old, Mississippi-delta landmark, this classic-French restaurant is a gilded-nest of skillfully presented cuisine and refined, personable service. Chef Jose Gutierrez, who trained with such culinary geniuses as Paul Bocuse and Roger Petit, serves a Provence-influenced, seasonal menu in a regal setting of vaulted ceilings, faux-marble columns, and luxurious murals. Continental menu. Specializes in hush-puppies stuffed with shrimp Provencal, roasted rack of lamb. Hrs: 6-10 pm. Closed Sun, hols. Res accepted. Wine list. Dinner a la carte entrees: $25-$32. Jacket. Cr cds: A, D, DS, MC, V.
[D] [≡]

★★ **COOKER BAR AND GRILLE.** *6120 Poplar Ave (38119), E of downtown. 901/685-2800.* Specializes in meat loaf, pot roast, pasta. Hrs: 11 am-10:30 pm; Fri, Sat to 11:30 pm; Sun to 10 pm. Closed Thanksgiving, Dec 25. Bar. Lunch $2.95-$7.95; dinner $6.95-$14.95. Child's menu. Cr cds: A, D, MC, V.
[D] [≡]

★★★ **DUX.** *149 Union Ave. 901/529-4199.* Specializes in mesquite-grilled black Angus steak and seafood. Own baking. Hrs: 6:30-11:30 am, noon-2:30 pm; 5-10 pm; Fri to midnight; Sat noon-2:30 pm, 5:30-midnight; Sun 6:30-11:30 am, 5:30 pm-midnight. Res accepted. Bar. Wine list. Bkfst $3.95-$13.95; lunch $6.95-$14.95; dinner $5.95-$28.95. Child's menu. Valet parking. Cr cds: A, C, D, DS, MC, V.
[D] [≡]

★ **ERIKA'S.** *52 S 2nd St (38103), downtown. 901/526-5522.* Hrs: 11 am-2 pm; Fri, Sat 5:30-9:30 pm. Closed Sun,

Beale Street

Mon; hols. Lunch $4.95-$8.95; dinner $5-$11. Cr cds: A, C, D, DS, MC, V.

[D] [≡]

★★★ **ERLING JENSEN.** *1044 S Yates Rd (38119), E of downtown. 901/763-3700.* Specializes in game, fresh seafood, veal. Hrs: 5-10 pm. Closed hols. Res accepted. Wine cellar. Dinner $25-$32. Elegant atmosphere. Cr cds: A, D, DS, MC, V.

[D]

★★ **FOLK'S FOLLY.** *551 S Mendenhall Rd (38117), E of downtown. 901/762-8200. www.memphistravel.com/folksfolly.* Steak menu. Specializes in steak, seafood. Own desserts. Hrs: 6-10 pm; Fri, Sat to 11 pm; Sun to 9 pm. Closed hols; also Jan 2. Res accepted. Bar. Dinner à la carte entrées: $15.50-$36. Entertainment: pianist Mon-Sat. Valet parking. Private, intimate dining. Cr cds: A, D, MC, V.

[D] [≡]

★ **INDIA PALACE.** *1720 Poplar Ave (38104), in Overton Square. 901/278-1199.* Specializes in chicken Tikka massala, Palak paneer, Tandoori chicken. Own baking. Hrs: 11 am-2:30 pm, 5-10 pm; Sun from 5 pm. Closed Thanksgiving, Dec 25. Res accepted. Lunch buffet: $5.95; dinner $5.95-$10.95. Elephant and tiger murals. Indian decor. Cr cds: A, D, DS, MC, V.

[D] [≡]

★★★ **LA TOURELLE.** *2146 Monroe Ave (38104), near Overton Square. 901/726-5771. www.latourellememphis.com.* Specializes in rosemary-marinated rack of lamb, herb-coated veal chop, grilled mahi mahi. Own baking. Hrs: 6-9:30 pm; Sun brunch 11 am-2 pm. Closed Jan 1, Thanksgiving, Dec 25. Res accepted. Wine cellar. Dinner a la carte entrees: $21-$30. Complete meal: $50. Converted 1910 home. Intimate dining. Cr cds: MC, V.

[D]

★ **MELOS TAVERNA.** *2021 Madison Ave (38104), in Overton Square. 901/725-1863.* Specializes in lamb, moussaka. Hrs: 4:30-10:30 pm; Fri, Sat to 11 pm. Closed Sun, Mon; July 4, Thanksgiving, Dec 25. Res accepted. Bar. Dinner $8.75-$21. Parking. Greek artwork. Cr cds: A, C, D, DS, MC, V.

[D] [≡]

★★ **PAULETTE'S.** *2110 Madison Ave (38104), in Overton Square. 901/726-5128.* Specializes in filet Paulette, grilled salmon, crabcakes. Hrs: 11 am-10 pm; Fri, Sat to 11 pm; Sat, Sun brunch to 4 pm. Closed major hols. Res accepted. Bar. Lunch $6.95-$11.95; dinner $11.95-$21.95. Sun brunch $6.95-$12.95. Child's menu. Entertainment: pianist Fri-Sun. Parking. Cr cds: A, C, D, DS, MC, V.

[D] [≡]

★★ **THE PIER.** *100 Wagner Pl (38103), downtown. 901/526-7381.* Specializes in New England clam chowder, prime rib, fresh fish. Hrs: 5-10 pm. Closed hols; Super Bowl Sun. Res accepted. Dinner $11.95-$23.95. On river. Nautical decor. Cr cds: A, C, D, DS, MC, V.

[D] [≡]

★ **THE PUBLIC EYE.** *17 S Cooper (38104), in Overton Square. 901/726-4040.* Specializes in barbecued pork, ribs. Hrs: 11 am-9:30 pm; Fri, Sat to 11 pm. Closed Jan 1, Dec 25. Bar. Lunch $4-$7. Buffet: $5.95; dinner $5-$20. Child's menu. Parking. Cr cds: A, C, D, DS, MC, V.

[D] [≡]

★★★ **RAJI.** *712 W Brookhaven Cir (38117), E of downtown. 901/685-8723. Email rag.1@aol.com.* Specializes in tandoori game hens with corn and cumin tomato sauce, grilled scallops and lobster in lentil pastry with ginger-flavored beurre blanc. Hrs: Sittings: 7 pm, 9:30 pm. Closed Sun, Mon; hols. Res required. Bar. Wine list. Dinner $40. Several elegant dining rms in former residence. Cr cds: A, MC, V.

[D]

★★ **RONNIE GRISANTA AND SONS.** *2855 Poplar Ave (38111), E of downtown. 901/323-0007.* Specializes in grilled porterhouse steak with truffles, grilled tuna in puttanesca sauce, frutti di mare. Hrs: 5-11 pm. Closed Sun; hols; also 1st wk July. Bar. Dinner $9.95-$25.95. Child's menu. Parking. Italian artwork. Cr cds: A, MC, V.

[D] [≡]

★ **SAIGON LE.** *51 N Cleveland (38104), E of downtown. 901/276-5326.* Specializes in roasted wheat clute, Saigon egg roll, green shell mussels with French butter. Own baking. Hrs: 11 am-9 pm. Closed

Sun; Thanksgiving, Dec 25. Res accepted. Lunch $3.45-$3.95; dinner $6.45-$8.75. Casual dining. Cr cds: A, DS, MC, V.

⊡ ⊡

Unrated Dining Spots

BUTCHER SHOP. *101 S Front St (38103), downtown. 901/521-0856.* Steak menu. Salad bar. Hrs: 5-9:30 pm; Fri, Sat to 10:30 pm. Closed Jan 1, Thanksgiving, Dec 24, 25. Bar. Dinner $15-$21. Child's menu. Grill in dining room. Option to select and cook own steak. 1907 building. Cr cds: A, D, DS, MC, V.

⊡

RENDEZVOUS. *52 S 2nd St (38103), in Gen Washburn Alley, downtown. 901/523-2746.* Specializes in barbecued ribs. Hrs: 4:30-11 pm; Fri from 11:30 am; Sat from noon. Closed Sun, Mon; 2 wks late July, 2 wks late Dec. Bar. Lunch, dinner $3-$10. In 1890 downtown building; memorabilia, many antiques, collectibles; jukebox. Cr cds: A, C, D, DS, MC, V.

⊡

Monteagle

See also Manchester

Pop 1,138 **Elev** 1,927 ft
Area code 931 **Zip** 37356

Information Oliver's Smoke House Motor Lodge and Restaurant, US 64, US 41A, Box 579; 931/924-2091 or 800/489-2091

Seasonal Events

Sewanee Summer Music Center Concerts. Guerry Hall, Univ of the South. Four-day festival concludes season. Phone 931/598-1225 or 931/598-1286. Wkends, late June-early Aug.

Monteagle Chautauqua Assembly. Concerts, lectures, academic courses, art classes. Phone 931/924-2268. Early July-late Aug.

Motel/Motor Lodge

★★ **JIM OLIVER'S SMOKEHOUSE LODGE.** *850 Main St (37356), I-24 Exit 134. 931/924-2091; fax 931/924-3442; toll-free 800/489-2091. www. thesmokehouse.com.* 97 rms, 2 story. S $39-$69; D $49-$79; each addl $5; suites $75-$120; 1-2-bedrm cabins $99-$166; under 13 free. Crib $5. Pet accepted. TV; cable (premium). Pool. Playground. Restaurant 6 am-10 pm. Ck-out 11 am. Meeting rms. Business servs avail. Sundries. Tennis. Microwaves avail. Cr cds: A, DS, MC, V.

⊡ 🐾 ♨ 🏊 ≈ 🎣 🛶 🔥 SC

B&B/Small Inn

★★ **ADAMS EDGEWORTH INN.** *Monteagle Assembly Grounds (37356), I-24 Exit 134. 931/924-4000; fax 931/924-3236; toll-free 87RELAXINN. Email innjoy@blomand.net; www.1896-edgeworth-mountain-inn.com.* 12 rms, 4 story, 2 suites. May-Oct: S $95; D $125; each addl $25; suites $175; lower rates rest of yr. Crib avail, fee. Street parking. Pool, children's pool, lifeguard. TV; cable (premium), VCR avail, CD avail. Complimentary full bkfst. Restaurant. 24-hr rm serv. Meeting rms. Business center. Concierge. Gift shop. Exercise privileges. Golf, 18 holes. Tennis, 5 courts. Supervised children's activities. Hiking trail. Cr cds: A, MC, V.

⊡ ♨ 🏊 ≈ 🎣 🛶 🔥 🏃

Morristown (E-7)

Settled 1783 **Pop** 21,385 **Elev** 1,350 ft
Area code 423 **Zip** 37814

Information Chamber of Commerce, 825 W 1st North St, PO Box 9, 37815; 423/586-6382

Bounded by Clinch Mountain and the Great Smoky Mountains, Morristown is a major manufacturing center. Davy Crockett lived in the town from 1794-1809.

Motels/Motor Lodges

★ **DAYS INN.** *2512 E Andrew Johnson Hwy (37814), I-81 Exit 8. 423/587-2200; fax 423/587-9752; res 800/329-7466.* 65 rms, 2 story. S $38-$48; D $42-$52; each addl $5; under 12 free; higher rates special events. Crib free. Pet accepted, some restrictions. TV; cable (premium). Complimentary continental bkfst. Restaurant nearby. Ck-out 11 am. Business servs avail. In-rm modem link. Some in-rm whirlpools, refrigerators. Cr cds: A, C, D, DS, MC, V.

★ **SUPER 8.** *2430 E Andrew Johnson Hwy (37814), I-81 Exit 8. 423/586-8880; fax 423/585-0654.* 63 rms, 2 story. S $35-$40; D $39-$46; each addl $5; under 12 free; higher rates special events. Crib free. Pet accepted; $25. TV; cable (premium). Complimentary continental bkfst. Restaurant nearby. Ck-out 11 am. Meeting rms. Business servs avail. In-rm modem link. Health club privileges. Some in-rm whirlpools, refrigerators, microwaves. Cr cds: A, D, DS, MC, V.

Hotel

★★ **HOLIDAY INN.** *3304 W Andrew Johnson Hwy (37814). 423/581-8700; fax 423/581-7128; res 800/HOLIDAY. Email holiday@lcs.net.* 117 rms, 2 story, 12 suites. June-Oct: S $80; D $86; each addl $6; under 18 free; lower rates rest of yr. Crib avail. Parking lot. Pool. TV; cable (premium), VCR avail. Complimentary coffee in rms, newspaper, toll-free calls. Restaurant 6 am-10:30 pm. Bar. Ck-out noon, ck-in 2 pm. Meeting rms. Business servs avail. Dry cleaning. Exercise privileges. Golf, 18 holes. Cr cds: A, D, DS, JCB, MC, V.

Conference Center

★★ **HOLIDAY INN MORRISTOWN CONFERENCE CENTER I-81 EXIT 8.** *5435 S Davy Crockett Parkway (37815), 6 mi S at I-81 & US 25E Exit 8. 423/587-2400; fax 423/581-7344; res 800/465-4329. Email holidaym@usit.net.* 106 rms, 3 story, 5 suites. June-Oct: S $75; D $79; each addl $5; suites $99; under 18 free; lower rates rest of yr. Crib avail. Pet accepted, some restrictions. Parking lot. Pool, children's pool. TV; cable, VCR avail. Complimentary coffee in rms, newspaper, toll-free calls. Restaurant 6 am-9 pm. Ck-out noon, ck-in 3 pm. Meeting rms. Fax servs avail. Dry cleaning. Exercise equipt. Golf, 18 holes. Tennis, 4 courts. Cr cds: A, C, D, DS, JCB, MC, V.

Murfreesboro

(F-4) See also Lebanon, Nashville

Founded 1811 **Pop** 44,922 **Elev** 619 ft **Area code** 615

Information Rutherford County Chamber of Commerce, 501 Memorial Blvd, PO Box 864, 37133-0864; 615/893-6565

Murfreesboro lies in the geographic center of Tennessee. Because of this strategic location the town was almost named the state capital. The legislature did meet in Murfreesboro from 1819-26, but it never returned after convening in Nashville. The area is rich in Civil War history and is known as the "antique center of the South." Rutherford County is also noted for its production of cattle and prize-winning Tennessee walking horses.

Annual Events

Street Festival & Folkfest. Intl dancers, arts and crafts. Early May.

Uncle Dave Macon Days. Old-time music, dance, arts and crafts; 615/893-2369. Second wknd July.

International Grand Championship Walking Horse Show. Early Aug.

Motels/Motor Lodges

★★ **HAMPTON INN.** *2230 Old Fort Parkway (37129). 615/896-1172; fax 615/895-4277; toll-free 800/426-7866.* 119 rms, 2 story. S, D $59-$66; each addl $5; under 18 free. Crib free. Pet accepted, some restrictions. TV; cable, VCR avail. Pool. Complimentary continental bkfst. Restaurant adj open 24 hrs. Ck-out noon. Meeting rm. Business servs avail. Microwaves avail. Cr cds: A, C, D, DS, MC, V.

D ★ ≈ ≥ ☺ SC

★★ **HOLIDAY INN.** *1414 Princeton Pl (37076). 615/871-4545; fax 615/871-4545; res 615/465-4329.* 86 rms, 4 story. S, D $65-$85; each addl $10; under 18 free; higher rates Fanfare. Crib free. TV; cable (premium). Complimentary continental bkfst, coffee in rms. Restaurant adj 6 am-10 pm. Ck-out 11 am. Meeting rms. Business center. In-rm modem link. Sundries. Coin lndry. Exercise equipt. Pool; whirlpool. Some refrigerators; in-rm whirlpool, minibar, wet bar in suites. Cr cds: A, C, D, DS, MC, V.

D ★ ☆ ≈ ≥ ☺

★ **HOWARD JOHNSON.** *2424 S Church St (37127), at jct US 231 I-24. 615/896-5522; fax 615/890-0024; toll-free 800/446-4656.* 79 rms, 2 story. S $29.95-$69; D $34.95-$79; each addl $5; under 17 free; higher rates special events. Crib free. Pet accepted, some restrictions; $5. TV; cable (premium). Pool. Complimentary continental bkfst. Restaurant adj 11 am-8 pm. Ck-out 11 am. Coin lndry. Meeting rm. Business servs avail. Microwaves avail. Cr cds: A, C, D, DS, MC, V.

D ★ ≈ ≥ ☺ SC

★★ **RAMADA LIMITED.** *1855 S Church St (37130), I-24 Exit 81. 615/896-5080; fax 615/898-0261.* 80 rms, 2 story. Mar-Dec: S, D $39.95-$75; each addl $5; under 18 free; lower rates rest of yr. Crib free. Pet accepted. TV; cable (premium). Complimentary continental bkfst. Restaurant adj open 24 hrs. Ck-out noon. Meeting rms. Business servs avail. Sundries. Pool. Cr cds: A, DS, MC, V.

D ★ ☆ ☆ ≈ ☆ ≥ ☺

★★ **SHONEYS INN.** *1954 S Church St (37130). 615/896-6030; fax 615/896-6037; toll-free 800/222-2222.* 125 rms, 2 story. S, D $51-$57; each addl $6; under 18 free; higher rates special events. Crib free. TV; cable (premium). Pool. Complimentary coffee in lobby. Restaurant adj 6 am-11 pm. Ck-out noon. Meeting rms. Health club privileges. Some refrigerators. Cr cds: A, D, DS, MC, V.

D ≈ ≥ ☺ SC

Hotel

★★★ **GARDEN PLAZA HOTEL.** *1850 Old Fort Parkway (37129). 615/895-5555; fax 615/895-3557; toll-free 800/342-7336.* 165 rms, 5 story, 3 suites. Mar, May-June, Aug-Sep: S $94; D $99; suites $149; lower rates rest of yr. Crib avail. Pet accepted, some restrictions. Parking lot. Indoor/outdoor pools, whirlpool. TV; cable (DSS), VCR avail. Complimentary coffee in rms, newspaper. Restaurant. 24-hr rm serv. Bar. Meeting rms. Business center. Concierge. Exercise privileges. Golf. Tennis. Video games. Cr cds: A, D, DS, MC, V.

D ★ ☆ ☆ ≈ ☆ ≥ ☺ ☆

Restaurants

★ **DEMOS' STEAK AND SPAGHETTI HOUSE.** *1115 NW Broad St (37129). 615/895-3701.* Specializes in steak, spaghetti, seafood. Hrs: 11 am-10 pm; wkends to 11 pm. Closed Thanksgiving, Dec 24, 25. Bar. Lunch $3.95-$6.95; dinner $5.95-$12.95. Child's menu. Parking. Contemporary decor. Three dining areas. Cr cds: A, C, D, DS, MC, V.

D ≥

★★ **PARTHENON MEDITER-RANEAN.** *1935 S Church St (37130). 615/895-2665.* Specializes in veal scalloysina Athena, filet Diana, lamb chops. Hrs: 4-9:30 pm; Fri, Sat to 10:30 pm; Sun 11 am-9 pm. Closed hols. Res accepted. Bar. Lunch $5.95-$9.95; dinner $7.95-$21.95. Child's menu. Greek artwork. Cr cds: A, C, D, DS, MC, V.

D ≥

★ **SANTA FE STEAK CO.** *127 SE Broad St (37130). 615/890-3030.* Steak menu. Specializes in steak, barbecue ribs. Hrs: 11 am-10:30 pm; Fri, Sat to 11:30 pm. Bar. Lunch $4.29-$6.99; dinner $5.49-$14.99. Child's menu. Parking. Cr cds: A, C, D, DS, MC, V.

D ≥

Nashville

(E-4) *See also Franklin, Lebanon, Murfreesboro*

Settled 1779 **Pop** 488,374 **Elev** 440 ft
Area code 615
Web www.nashville.musiccity
usa.com/tour

Information Convention & Visitors Bureau, 161 4th Ave N, 37219; 615/259-4700

Commercial center and capital city, Nashville's heritage is part Andrew Jackson's Hermitage and part Grand Ole Opry. It is often referred to as the "Athens of the South" because of its 16 colleges and universities, religious publishing firms, and some 750 churches. To prove this point, it has the Parthenon, the only full-size replica of the Athenian architectural masterpiece.

The Nashville region's economy is diverse, and the area has benefitted from low unemployment, consistent job growth, and a broadening of the labor force. The city is a leader in publishing, finance and insurance, healthcare, music and entertainment, transportation technology, higher education, and tourism.

In recent years, millions of dollars in investment capital have been used for new buildings and vast expansion programs. This redevelopment has given the lovely old capital a new and airy setting. Throughout this bustle of commerce and construction, Nashville retains an Old South quality, proud of its gracious homes and its old traditions.

These traditions stem back to the days when a band of pioneers built a log stockade on the west bank of the Cumberland River in 1779, naming it Fort Nashborough. The Cumberland Compact established a governing body of 12 judges at this wilderness village. By an act of the North Carolina legislature, the name was changed to Nashville. Nearly 50 years after Tennessee became a state, Nashville was made the permanent capital.

During the Civil War, the city was taken by Union troops in March 1862. In December 1864, a Confederate force under General John Bell Hood moved to the hills south of the city in an attempt to recapture it. However, two Union counterattacks virtually wiped out the Confederate army.

Just as the Cumberland Compact of May 1780 was an innovation in government, so was a new charter which became effective in 1963, setting up Nashville and Davidson County under a single administration with a legislative body of 40 members.

Transportation

Nashville Intl Airport. Information 615/275-1675; lost and found 615/275-1675; weather 615/244-9393; cash machines, Main Terminal, entry level.

Car Rental Agencies. See IMPORTANT TOLL-FREE NUMBERS.

Public Transportation. Metro Transit Authority, phone 615/862-5950.

What to See and Do

Agricultural Museum. Former horse barn on historic estate. Oldest Agricultural Hall of Fame in US. Farm tools, equipment, and household items of 19th and early 20th centuries. (Mon-Fri; closed hols) Ellington Center, 6 mi S. Phone 615/837-5197. **FREE**

Belle Meade. (1853) Mansion and outbldgs were once part of 5,300-acre working plantation. At the turn of the 20th century, Belle Meade was considered the greatest thoroughbred breeding farm in the country. The 14-rm Greek Revival mansion contains Empire and Victorian furnishings and heirloom showcase with racing trophies and mementos. Also on grounds are Dunham Station log cabin (1793) and the Carriage House (1890s), containing one of the South's largest carriage collections. (Daily; closed Jan 1, Thanksgiving, Dec 25) Harding Rd & Leake Ave, 7 mi SW. Phone 615/356-0501 or 800/270-3991. ¢¢

Belmont Mansion. Built in the 1850s in the style of an Italian villa, this mansion, once considered one of the finest private residences in the US, has original marble statues, Venetian glass, gasoliers, mirrors, and paintings in the 15 rms open to public; gardens feature large collection of 19th-century garden ornaments and cast iron gazebos. (June-Aug, daily; rest of yr,

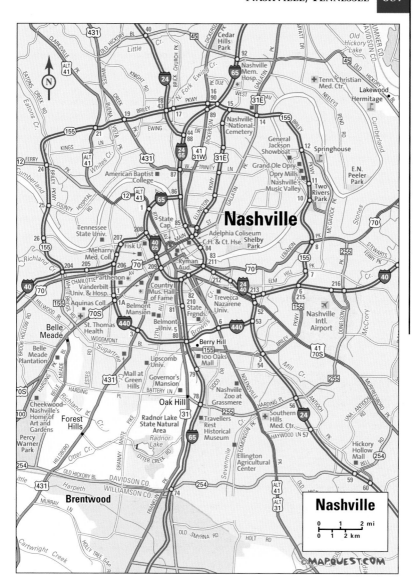

Nashville

0   1   2 mi
0 1 2 km

©MAPQUEST.COM

Tues-Sat; closed hols) 1900 Belmont Blvd, at Acklen Ave, on Belmont Univ campus. Phone 615/460-5459. ¢¢

Cheatham Lake, Lock, and Dam. Some recreation areas have swimming, fishing, boating (commercial docks); camping (fee; electricity addl). Camping closed Nov-Mar. Fees for some areas. 30 mi NW on TN 12, near Ashland City. Phone 615/792-5697 or 615/254-3734.

Cheekwood. Cultural center on 55 acres incl museum with permanent collection of 19th- and 20th-century American art; Botanic Hall with atrium of tropical flora and changing plant exhibits; public greenhouses featuring orchids, camellias, and plants from Central American cloud forests; and 5 major gardens specializing in dogwood, wildflowers, herbs, daffodils, roses, and tulips. (Daily; closed hols) 8 mi SW on Forrest Park Dr, next to Percy Warner Park. Phone 615/356-8000. ¢¢

Country Music Hall of Fame & Museum. Exhibits incl Elvis Presley's Cadillac, films, costumes, musical instruments, memorabilia of country music notables. Participatory exhibits. (Daily; closed Jan 1, Thanksgiving, Dec 25) 4 Music Square E. Phone 615/256-1639. ¢¢¢ Also incl is a visit to

RCA Studio B. Studio where music greats recorded. Major renovation has updated the studio's equipment to current standards for session and demo recording.

Country Music Wax Museum and Shopping Mall. More than 60 wax figures; original stage costumes and memorabilia. Record, western wear, crafts, and gift shops; restaurant, entertainment. (Daily; closed Thanksgiving, Dec 25) 2515 Mc Gavock Pike. Phone 615/883-3612. ¢¢¢

Cumberland Science Museum. Planetarium, live animal and science programs. (June-Aug, daily; rest of yr, Tues-Sun; closed hols) 800 Fort Negley Blvd, near Greer Stadium. Phone 615/862-5160. ¢¢¢

Grand Ole Opry

Fisk University. (1866) 900 students. A National Historic District with Jubilee Hall, a historic landmark. Carl Van Vechten Art Gallery houses Stieglitz Collection of modern art. Aaron Douglas Gallery houses collection of African art. 17th Ave N. Phone 615/329-8500.

Fort Nashborough. Patterned after the pioneer fort established several blocks from this site in 1779; replica is smaller and has fewer cabins. Stockaded walls, exhibits of pioneer implements. (Tues-Sun, weather permitting; closed hols) 170 1st Ave N,

at Church St, in N end of Riverfront Park. **FREE**

General Jackson. A 300-ft, 4-deck paddlewheel showboat on Cumberland River highlights a musical stage show in its Victorian Theater. Two-hr day cruises offer entertainment and optional food service; 3-hr night cruises offer entertainment and dinner. (All yr; addl cruises in summer) For schedule and departure times, contact Customer Service, 2802 Opryland Dr, 37214. Phone 615/889-6611. ¢¢¢¢

Grand Ole Opry. Live radio show featuring the best in country music is broadcast from the Grand Ole Opry House, the world's largest broadcast studio, which seats 4,400. The Opry has been broadcast wkends continuously since 1925. (Wkends all yr; also June-Aug, Tues matinees.) Res recommended. For information contact Opryland Customer Service, 2808 Opryland Dr, 37214. Phone 615/889-6611. ¢¢¢¢

Grand Ole Opry Tours. One-hr, 3-hr, and all-day bus tours incl houses of country music stars, Music Row, recording studios, backstage visit to Grand Ole Opry House. Contact 2810 Opryland Dr, 37214. Phone 615/889-9490. ¢¢¢¢

Gray Line bus tours. Contact 2416 Music Valley Dr, Suite 102, 37214. Phone 615/883-5555 or 800/251-1864.

⭐ **The Hermitage.** (1819; rebuilt after a fire in 1834) Greek Revival residence of President Andrew Jackson is furnished almost entirely with original family pieces, many of which were associated with Jackson's military career and yrs in the White House. Also on 660-acre estate are a garden with graves of Jackson and his wife, Rachel; 2 log cabins; a church; and visitor center and museum with biographical film on Jackson. (Daily; closed Thanksgiving, Dec 25, also 3rd wk Jan) 12 mi E off I-40 Exit 221A, follow sign. Phone 615/889-2941. ¢¢¢ Included in fee is

⭐ **Tulip Grove.** (1836) Greek Revival house of Andrew Jackson

Donelson, Mrs. Jackson's nephew, and President Jackson's private secretary. Interior has examples of 19th-century faux marbling.

J. Percy Priest Lake. Waterskiing, fishing, boating (ramps, commercial boat docks); picnicking, tent and trailer sites (fee). Visitor center near dam (Mon-Fri). Some areas closed Nov-Mar. 11 mi E off I-40. Phone 615/889-1975.

Museum of Beverage Containers and Advertising. More than 36,000 antique soda and beer cans form the largest collection of its kind. Also on display are thousands of period advertising pieces. (Daily; closed hols) 15 mi N on I-65 to Millersville, 1055 Ridgecrest Dr. Phone 615/859-5236. ¢

Museum of Tobacco Art & History. Houses exhibits tracing history of tobacco from Native Americans to present. On display are rare antique pipes, tobacco containers, snuff-boxes, cigar store figures, art, photographs. (Mon-Sat; closed hols) 800 Harrison St, at 8th Ave N. Phone 615/271-2291. **FREE**

Music Valley Wax Museum of the Stars. More than 50 lifelike wax figures of famous stars, dressed in authentic costumes. Also features Sidewalk of the Stars with hand and foot imprints of more than 250 stars. (Daily; closed Thanksgiving, Dec 25) 2515 McGavock Pike, NE via Briley Pkwy, Exit 12. Phone 615/883-3612. ¢¢

Nashville Toy Museum. Features unique displays of antique toys, including German and English bears from early 1900s, china dolls from 1850, and lead soldiers in battle dioramas. Train rm contains more than 250 toy and model locomotives and 2 train layouts depicting Tennessee in the 1930s and Britain at the turn of the century. (Daily; closed Thanksgiving, Dec 25) 2613-B McGavock Pike. Phone 615/883-8870. ¢¢

Old Hickory Lake. Several recreation areas around reservoir have swimming, fishing, boating (commercial docks); hiking, archery, picnicking. Tent and trailer sites (fee). (All yr; some areas closed Oct-Mar) 15 mi NE via US 31E, near Hendersonville. Phone 615/822-4846 or 615/847-2395.

Opryland Museums. Located just outside Opryland Park, in the Plaza area near the Grand Ole Opry House. **Minnie Pearl Museum** features 50 yrs of memorabilia; **Roy Acuff Museum** incll musical instruments; **Grand Ole Opry Museum** pays tribute to country stars with audiovisual and interactive devices. (Daily) **FREE**

The Parthenon. Replica of the Parthenon of Pericles' time was built in plaster for the Tennessee Centennial of 1897 and later reconstructed in concrete aggregate. As in the original, there is not a straight horizontal or vertical line and no 2 columns are placed the same distance apart. Houses 19th- and 20th-century artworks, changing art exhibits, replicas of Elgin Marbles, 42-ft statue of goddess Athena. (Apr-Sep, Tues-Sun; rest of yr, Tues-Sat; closed Jan 1, Dec 25) In Centennial Park, West End Ave & 25th Ave N. Phone 615/862-8431. ¢¢

Radnor Lake State Natural Area. A 1,100-acre environmental preserve with an 85-acre lake. Provides scenic, biological, and geological areas for hiking and nature study. (Daily) 7 mi S on US 31, then 1½ mi W on Otter Creek Rd. Phone 615/373-3467. **FREE**

Ryman Auditorium & Museum. Home of the Grand Ole Opry from 1943-74. Tour includes a visit to the stage and displays and exhibits detailing the Ryman's unique and varied history. (Daily; closed Jan 1, Thanksgiving, Dec 25) 116 5th Ave N. Phone 615/254-1445. ¢¢

Sam Davis Home. Described as "the most beautiful shrine to a private soldier in the US," this stately house and 168-acre working farm have been preserved as a memorial to Sam Davis, Confederate scout caught behind Union lines and tried as a spy. Offered his life if he revealed the name of his informer, Davis chose to die on the gallows. His boyhood home is restored and furnished with many original pieces; grounds incl kitchen, smokehouse, slave cabins, and family cemetery where Davis is buried. (Daily; closed Jan 1, Thanksgiving, Dec 25) 20 mi S off I-24 in Smyrna, at 1399 Sam Davis Rd. Phone 615/459-2341. ¢¢

State Capitol. (1845-59) Greek Revival structure with 80-ft tower rising above the city; columns grace the ends and sides. Architect William Strickland died before the bldg was completed and was buried within its walls. Of special interest are the grand stairway, library, legislative chambers, and murals in gubernatorial suite. (Mon-Fri; closed hols). Charlotte Ave between 6th & 7th Aves. Phone 615/741-1621.

Tennessee State Museum. Exhibits on life in Tennessee from early man through the early 1900s. (Tues-Sat; closed hols) James K. Polk State Bldg, 5th Ave between Union & Deaderick Sts. Phone 615/741-2692. **FREE**

The Upper Room Chapel and Museum. Chapel with polychrome wood carving of Leonardo da Vinci's "The Last Supper," said to be largest of its kind in world; also World Christian Fellowship Window. Museum contains various religious artifacts incl seasonal displays of 100 nativity scenes and Ukranian Easter eggs. (Mon-Fri; closed hols) 1908 Grand Ave. Phone 615/340-7207.

Travellers Rest Historic House. (1799) Restored Federal-style house of Judge John Overton. Maintained as a historical museum with period furniture, records, letters, the bldg reflects history and development of early Tennessee. Eleven-acre grounds with formal gardens, kitchen house, smokehouse. Gift shop. Allow at least 45 min for visit. (Tues-Sat, also Sun afternoons; closed Jan 1, Thanksgiving, Dec 25) I-65 Exit 78, S on US 31 (Franklin Rd), follow signs. Phone 615/832-8197. ¢¢

Vanderbilt University. (1873) 10,000 students. The 330-acre campus features 19th- and 20th-century architectural styles. Fine Arts Gallery has a permanent collection supplemented by traveling exhibits. Blair School of Music offers regular concerts. Tours avail. West End Ave & 21st Ave S. Phone 615/322-5000.

Annual Events

Running of the Iroquois Memorial Steeplechase. Old Hickory Blvd at entrance to Percy Warner Park. Natural amphitheater seats 100,000. Phone 615/322-7284. Second Sat May.

Music festivals. Nashville is host to many festivals, incl Summer Lights in Music City (late May-early June), the Intl Country Music Fan Fair with its Grand Master Old-Time Fiddling Championship (early June), Gospel Music Week (Apr), and Franklin Jazz Festival (Aug).

Tennessee State Fair. Fairgrounds, Wedgewood Ave & Rains. Contact Box 40208-Melrose Station, 37204. Phone 615/862-8980. Sep 8-17, 2001.

Longhorn Rodeo. Nashville Arena. Professional cowboys compete for world championship points. Phone 615/876-1016. Mid-Nov.

A Country Christmas. Opryland Hotel. Offers events ranging from a musical stage show to an art, antique, and craft show. Phone 615/871-7637.

Additional Visitor Information

The Nashville Convention and Visitors Bureau, 161 4th Ave N, 37219, has maps, brochures, lists of tour companies, and calendar of events; phone 615/259-4700. Advance reservations are strongly advised for the summer season (mid-May-mid-Sep) and all wkends. The Visitor Information Center is located in the glass tower of the Nashville Arena at 501 Broadway; phone 615/259-4747.

City Neighborhoods

Many of the restaurants, unrated dining establishments, and some lodgings listed under Nashville incl neighborhoods as well as exact street addresses. Geographic descriptions of these areas are given, followed by a table of restaurants arranged by neighborhood.

Downtown. S of Harrison St, W of I-24/65, N of McGavock St, and E of 12th Ave N. **S of Downtown:** S of McGavock St. **E of Downtown:** E of I-24/I-65. **W of Downtown:** W of I-40.

Music Row. Area incl 16th Ave S from West End Ave to Demonbreun St; Music Square E from South St to Demonbreun St; Music Square W from South St to Division St; and Division and Demonbreun Sts from 18th Ave S to I-40.

Opryland Area. S of McGavock Pike, W of Briley Pkwy (TN 155), and N and E of the Cumberland River.

Motels/Motor Lodges

★★ **BAYMONT INN AND SUITES.** *120 S Cartwright Ct (37072), 14 mi N* on I-65, Exit 97. 615/851-1891; fax 615/851-4513; toll-free 800/301-0200. 100 rms, 3 story, 32 suites. Apr-Oct: S, D $45.95-$60.95; each addl $7; suites $95.95-$122.95; under 18 free; lower rates rest of yr. Crib free. Pet accepted, some restrictions. TV; cable (premium). Pool. Complimentary continental bkfst. Restaurant adj 6 am-10 pm. Ck-out noon. Meeting rm. Business servs avail. Valet serv. Sundries. Exercise equipt. Cr cds: A, C, D, DS, MC, V.

🅓 🐟 ⇥ 🕇 🖼 🐾 SC

★★ **BAYMONT INN AND SUITES NASHVILLE WEST.** 5612 Lenox Ave (37209), I-40 Exit 204, W of downtown. 615/353-0700; fax 615/352-0361; res 800/301-0200. 110 rms, 3 story. S $59.95-$71.95; D $59.95-$79.95; each addl $7; under 18 free; higher rates special events. Crib free. TV; cable (premium). Pool. Complimentary continental bkfst, coffee in rms. Restaurant adj 6 am-11 pm. Ck-out noon. Meeting rms. Business servs avail. Sundries. Cr cds: A, D, DS, MC, V.

🅓 ⇥ 🖼 🐾

★★ **CLUBHOUSE INN AIRPORT.** 2435 Atrium Way (37214), E of downtown. 615/883-0500; fax 615/889-4827; res 800/258-2466. 135 rms, 3 story, 17 suites. Apr-Oct: S, D $79-$104; each addl $10; suites $109-$129; under 16 free; wkend rates; higher rates special events; lower rates rest of yr. TV; cable (premium), VCR avail. Heated pool; whirlpool. Complimentary full bkfst. Ck-out noon. Coin lndry. Meeting rms. Business servs avail. Valet serv. Free airport transportation. Health club privileges. Refrigerator. Balconies. Cr cds: A, C, D, DS, MC, V.

🅓 ⇥ 🕇 🖼 🐾 SC

★★★ **COURTYARD BY MARRIOTT AIRPORT.** 2508 Elm Hill Pike (37214), near airport, E of downtown. 615/883-9500; fax 615/883-0172; res 800/321-2211. 145 rms, 4 story. S, D $90-$120; wkend rates; higher rates special events. Crib free. TV; cable (premium), VCR avail. Pool; whirlpool. Complimentary coffee in rms. Restaurant 6-10 am; wkend hrs vary. Bar 5-11 pm. Ck-out noon. Coin lndry. Meeting rms. Business servs avail. Valet serv. Sundries. Free airport

transportation. Exercise equipt. Refrigerators avail. Some balconies. Cr cds: A, C, D, DS, JCB, MC, V.

🅓 🐟 ⇥ 🕇 🖼 🐾

★ **DAYS INN SUITES.** 809 Wren Rd (37072), 12 mi N on I-65, Rivergate Exit 96. 615/859-1771; fax 615/857-7512; res 800/329-7466. 46 rms, 3 story. No elvtr. May-Aug: S, D $49.95-$95.95; each addl $5; under 12 free; higher rates special events; lower rates rest of yr. TV; cable (premium). Complimentary continental bkfst. Restaurant nearby. Ck-out 11 am. Business servs avail. Cr cds: A, C, D, DS, JCB, MC, V.

🅓 🖼 🐾

★★ **DRURY INN.** 2306 Brick Church Pike (37207), I-65 Exit 87B, N of downtown. 615/226-9560; fax 615/226-9560; res 800/288-5050; toll-free 800/638-7949. 95 rms, 4 story. S $42.95-$54.95; D $48.95-$59.95; each addl $5; under 16 free; higher rates special events. Crib free. TV; cable (premium). Pool. Complimentary continental bkfst. Restaurant adj open 24 hrs. Ck-out noon. Business servs avail. Cr cds: A, C, D, DS, MC, V.

🅓 ⇥ 🖼 🐾 SC

★ **ECONO LODGE.** 2460 Music Valley Dr (37214), in Opryland area. 615/889-0090; res 800/553-2666. 86 rms, 3 story. May-Oct: S, D $69.95-$74.95; each addl $10; under 18 free; higher rates special events; lower rates rest of yr. Crib free. Pet accepted, some restrictions. TV; cable (premium). Pool. Complimentary coffee in lobby. Restaurant nearby. Ck-out noon. Gift shop. Cr cds: A, C, D, DS, MC, V.

🅓 🐟 ⇥ 🖼 🐾 SC

★ **FIDDLERS INN NORTH.** 2410 Music Valley Dr (37214), in Opryland area. 615/885-1440; fax 615/883-6477. Email jwhgroup@aol.com; www.musicvalleyhotels.com. 200 rms, 3 story, 2 suites. S, D $69; each addl $5; under 18 free. Parking lot. Pool. TV; cable (premium). Complimentary continental bkfst, toll-free calls. Business servs avail. Dry cleaning. Gift shop. Golf, 18 holes. Supervised children's activities. Cr cds: A, DS, MC, V.

🅓 🕇 ⇥ 🖼 🐾 SC

★ **GUESTHOUSE INN AND SUITES.** *1909 Hayes St (37203), downtown.* 615/329-1000; fax 615/329-1000; toll-free 800/777-4904. 108 rms, 7 story. Mar-Aug: S, D $64-$91; each addl $7; under 18 free; lower rates rest of yr. Crib free. TV; cable, VCR avail. Complimentary continental bkfst. Restaurant nearby. Ck-out noon. Coin lndry. Meeting rm. Business servs avail. Refrigerators, microwaves, wet bars. Cr cds: A, C, D, DS, MC, V.

D ☒ ♿ SC

★★ **HAMPTON INN.** *5630 Franklin Pike (37027), S on I-65, Exit 74B.* 615/373-2212; fax 615/370-9832; toll-free 800/426-7866. 114 air-cooled rms, 5 story. S, D $79-$89; under 18 free. Crib free. TV; cable (premium). Complimentary continental bkfst. Restaurant adj 6 am-midnight. Ck-out noon. Meeting rms. Business servs avail. Sundries. Health club privileges. Some refrigerators. Cr cds: A, C, D, DS, MC, V.

D ☒ ♿ SC

★★ **HAMPTON INN.** *202 Northgate Dr (37214), 13 mi N on I-65, Exit 97.* 615/851-2828; fax 615/851-2830. 61 rms, 3 story. June-mid-Sep: S $69-$74; D $74-$79; under 18 free; higher rates Fanfare; lower rates rest of yr. Crib free. TV; cable (premium). Complimentary continental bkfst. Restaurant nearby. Ck-out noon. Meeting rms. Business servs avail. In-rm modem link. Health club privileges. Pool. Some in-rm whirlpools, refrigerators, microwaves, wet bars. Cr cds: A, C, D, DS, MC, V.

D ✦ ⚡ ☒ ✈ ♿ ☒ ♨

★★ **HAMPTON INN AND SUITES AIRPORT.** *583 Donelson Pike (37214), near airport, E of downtown.* 615/885-4242; fax 615/885-6726; res 800/HAMPTON; toll-free 877/806-8159. 111 rms, 7 story, 31 kit. suites. S, D $89-$129; kit. suites $119-$129; under 18 free; higher rates special events. Crib free. Parking. TV; cable (premium), VCR. Pool. Complimentary continental bkfst, coffee in rms. Restaurant nearby. Ck-out noon. Meeting rms. Business servs avail. Gift shop. Free airport transportation. Exercise equipt. Some refrigerators. Cr cds: A, C, D, DS, MC, V.

D ☒ ✈ ✈ ☒ ♨

★★ **HAMPTON INN BRILEY PARKWAY, OPRYLAND.** *2350 Elm Hill Pike (37214), E of downtown.* 615/871-0222; fax 615/885-5325; res 800/426-7866. www.hampton.com. 120 rms, 3 story. S, D $73-$89; each addl $10; under 18 free. Crib free. TV; cable (premium). Pool. Complimentary continental bkfst. Restaurant adj open 24 hrs. Ck-out 11 am. Meeting rm. Business servs avail. In-rm modem link. Near airport. Cr cds: A, C, D, DS, MC, V.

D ☒ ☒ ♿ SC

★★ **HAMPTON INN HICKORY HOLLOW.** *210 Crossings Place (37013), E I-24, Exit 60, E of downtown.* 615/731-9911; fax 615/731-9912; res 800/426-7866. 86 rms, 4 story. S, D $70-$76; each addl $6; under 18 free; higher rates Fanfare. Crib $5. TV; cable (premium). Complimentary continental bkfst. Restaurant nearby. Ck-out noon. Meeting rms. Business servs avail. Free airport transportation. Exercise equipt. Health club privileges. Pool. Cr cds: A, C, D, DS, MC, V.

D ☒ ✈ ☒ ♿

✗ ★★★ **HILTON SUITES.** *9000 Overlook Blvd (37027), S on I-65 Exit 74B.* 615/370-0111; fax 615/370-0272; res 800/445-8667. www.hilton.com. 203 suites, 4 story. S, D $125-$165; each addl $20; family rates. Crib free. Pet accepted, some restrictions. TV; cable (premium), VCR (movies $2). Indoor pool; whirlpool. Complimentary full bkfst, coffee in rms. Restaurant 6-9:30 am, 11:30 am-1:30 pm, 5-10 pm; Sat, Sun 7-11 am, 5-10 pm. Rm serv from 5 pm. Bar 4 pm-midnight. Ck-out noon. Free guest lndry. Meeting rms. Business center. Gift shop. Exercise equipt. Rec rm. Refrigerators, microwaves, wet bars. Balconies. Cr cds: A, C, D, DS, ER, JCB, MC, V.

D ✦ ☒ ✈ ☒ ♿ SC ✈

★★ **HOLIDAY INN.** *2401 Brick Church Pike (37207), I-65 Exit 87, N of downtown.* 615/226-4600; fax 615/228-6412; toll-free 800/654-2000. 172 rms, 5 story. Apr-Oct: S, D $55-$80; under 18 free; higher rates special events; lower rates rest of yr. Crib free. TV; cable (premium). Pool. Ck-out 11 am. Coin lndry. Meeting rms. Business servs avail. In-rm modem link. Exercise equipt; sauna. Cr cds: A, C, D, DS, JCB, MC, V.

D ☒ ✈ ☒ ♿ SC

★★ **HOLIDAY INN.** *201 Crossings Pl (94010), E on I-24, Exit 60, E of downtown.* 615/731-2361; fax 615/731-6828; res 888/683-8883; toll-free 800/465-4329. Email ngt1@ msn.com. 139 rms, 5 story. S, D $79-$89; each addl $7; under 18 free; higher rates special events. Crib free. Pet accepted, some restrictions. TV; cable (premium). Complimentary coffee in rms. Restaurant 6-10 am, 4:30-10 pm; Sat, Sun 7-11 am, 4:30-10 pm. Bar. Ck-out noon. Meeting rms. Business servs avail. In-rm modem link. Sundries. Free airport transportation. Exercise equipt. Health club privileges. Pool. Refrigerators avail. Cr cds: A, C, D, DS, MC, V.

★★ **HOLIDAY INN.** *981 Murfreesboro Pike (37217), E of downtown.* 615/367-9150; fax 615/361-4465; res 800/465-4329. 210 rms, 2 story. S, D $65-$85; under 18 free; higher rates special events. Crib free. TV; cable (premium). Pool; whirlpool. Complimentary continental bkfst, coffee in rms. Restaurant adj 11 am-11 pm; wkends to midnight. Ck-out noon. Coin lndry. Meeting rms. Business servs avail. Bellhops. Valet serv. Free airport transportation. Cr cds: A, D, DS, MC, V.

★★ **HOLIDAY INN EXPRESS.** *1111 Airport Center Dr (37214), near airport, E of downtown.* 615/883-1366; fax 615/889-6867; toll-free 800/465-4329. 206 rms, 3 story. S, D $69-$99; each addl $8; under 18 free; higher rates special events. Crib free. TV; cable (premium). Pool. Complimentary continental bkfst. Restaurant nearby. Ck-out noon. Meeting rms. Business servs avail. Bellhops. Free airport transportation. Some balconies. Cr cds: A, C, D, DS, JCB, MC, V.

★★ **RAMADA INN & SUITES.** *2425 Atrium Way (37214), near Airport, E of downtown.* 615/883-5201; fax 615/883-5594; res 800/272-6232. www.ramadainnnashville.com. 120 suites, 3 story. S, D $83-129; under 18 free. Crib free. TV; cable (premium). Pool. Complimentary continental bkfst, coffee in rms. Ck-out noon. Coin lndry. Meeting rms. Business

servs avail. Valet serv. Free airport transportation. Refrigerators; microwaves avail. Cr cds: A, DS, MC, V.

★★ **RAMADA INN AIRPORT.** *709 Spence Ln (37217), SE of downtown.* 615/361-0102; fax 615/361-4765; res 800/288-2828; toll-free 888/361-9117. 228 rms, 2 story. S, D $50-$75; each addl $8; under 12 free. Crib free. TV; cable (premium). Pool. Restaurant 6 am-2 pm, 5-9:30 pm. Bar 4 pm-2 am; entertainment. Ck-out noon. Bellhops. Sundries. Coin lndry. Meeting rms. Business servs avail. In-rm modem link. Airport transportation. Cr cds: A, C, D, DS, MC, V.

★★ **RAMADA LIMITED.** *5770 Old Hickory Blvd (37076), 6 mi E on I-40, Exit 221B.* 615/889-8940; fax 615/821-4444; res 800/272-6232. Email 1967@hotel.cendant.com. 100 rms, 3 story. June-Aug: S $35-$55; D $40-$70; each addl $6; under 18 free; higher rates special events; lower rates rest of yr. Crib free. Pet accepted, some restrictions; $5. TV; cable. Pool. Complimentary continental bkfst. Restaurant nearby. Ck-out noon. Business servs avail. Microwaves avail. Cr cds: A, C, D, DS, MC, V.

★ **RED ROOF INN.** *510 Claridge Dr (37214), I-40 Exit 216, near airport, E of downtown.* 615/872-0735; fax 615/871-4647; toll-free 800/843-7663. 120 rms, 3 story. Mar-Sep: S $39.99-$49.99; D $45.99-$55.99; each addl $6; under 17 free; higher rates special events; lower rates rest of yr. Crib avail. Pet accepted, some restrictions. TV; cable (premium). Complimentary coffee in lobby. Restaurant nearby. Ck-out 11 am. Free airport transportation. Cr cds: A, C, D, DS, MC, V.

★ **RED ROOF INN.** *4271 Sidco Dr (37204), at jct I-65 & Harding Pl, S of downtown.* 615/832-0093; fax 615/832-0097. 85 rms, 3 story. Mar-Sep: S $44.99-$69.99; D $46.99-$69.99; each addl $8; under 18 free; lower rates rest of yr. Crib free. Pet accepted. TV; cable. Complimentary coffee in lobby. Restaurant nearby.

Ck-out 11 am. Business servs avail. Cr cds: A, C, D, DS, ER, JCB, MC, V.

★★★ **RESIDENCE INN BY MAR-RIOTT.** *2300 Elm Hill Pike (37214), near airport, E of downtown.* 615/889-8600; fax 615/871-4970; res 800/321-3131; toll-free 800/331-3131. *www. residenceinn.com.* 168 kit. suites, 2 story. Suites: 1-bedrm studio $109-$129; 2-bedrm penthouse $129-$159. Pet accepted; $150. TV; cable. Pool; whirlpool. Complimentary continental bkfst. Ck-out noon. Coin lndry. Meeting rms. Business servs avail. Refrigerators, microwaves; many fireplaces. Balconies. Cr cds: A, C, D, DS, JCB, MC, V.

★★ **SHONEY'S INN.** *1501 Demonbreun St (37203), in Music Row.* 615/255-9977; fax 615/242-6127; toll-free 800/222-2222. 147 rms, 3 story. S $62-$72; D $72-$79; each addl $6; suites $109-$119; under 19 free; higher rates special events. Crib free. TV; cable (premium). Pool. Complimentary coffee in lobby. Restaurant adj 6 am-midnight. Ck-out noon. Meeting rms. Business servs avail. Cr cds: A, C, D, DS, ER, MC, V.

★ **SUPER 8 MOTEL.** *412 Robertson Ave (37209), I-40 Exit 204, W of downtown.* 615/356-0888; fax 615/324-2138; toll-free 800/800-8000. 68 rms, 3 story. June-July: S $57-$60; D $65.88-$70.88; each addl $5; suites $75-$80; under 12 free; higher rates special events; lower rates rest of yr. Crib free. Pet accepted. TV; cable (premium). Complimentary continental bkfst. Restaurant adj open 24 hrs. Ck-out 11 am. Business servs avail. Cr cds: A, C, D, DS, MC, V.

★ **TRAVELER'S REST INN.** *107 Franklin Rd (37027), 1 blk W of I-65 Exits 74B.* 615/373-3033; fax 615/370-5709; toll-free 800/852-0618. 35 rms, 1-2 story, 2 kits. S $45-$52; D $52-$60; each addl $4; under 18 free. Crib $2. TV; cable (premium). Pool; wading pool. Complimentary continental bkfst, coffee in rms. Restaurant nearby. Ck-out noon. Coin lndry. Business servs avail. Some refrigerators. Picnic table. Cr cds: A, C, D, DS, MC, V.

★ **WILSON INN.** *600 Ermac Dr (37214), E of downtown.* 615/889-4466; fax 615/889-0484; res 800/945-7667. 110 rms, 5 story. S, D $55-$85; each addl $7; suites $70-$87; under 19 free; higher rates special events. Crib free. Pet accepted. TV; cable (premium). Complimentary continental bkfst. Restaurant adj open 24 hrs. Ck-out noon. Meeting rms. Business servs avail. Free airport transportation. Refrigerators; wet bar in suites; microwaves avail. Cr cds: A, C, D, DS, JCB, MC, V.

Hotels

★★ **CLARION HOTEL - AIRPORT/OPRYLAND AREA.** *733 Briley Parkway (37217), I-40 Exit 215, E of downtown.* 615/361-5900; fax 615/367-4468; res 800/252-7466; toll-free 888/881-7666. 200 rms, 12 story. Mar-Oct: S $99; D $109; each addl $10; under 17 free; lower rates rest of yr. Crib avail. Parking lot. Pool. TV; cable (premium). Complimentary coffee in rms, newspaper, toll-free calls. Restaurant. Bar. Ck-out noon, ck-in 2 pm. Meeting rms. Business center. Bellhops. Dry cleaning. Free airport transportation. Exercise equipt. Golf. Picnic facilities. Cr cds: A, C, D, DS, ER, JCB, MC, V.

★★★ **COURTYARD BY MARRIOTT.** *1901 W End Ave (37203), W of downtown.* 615/327-9900; fax 615/327-8127; res 800/321-2211; toll-free 800/228-9290. 136 rms, 7 story. S, D $85-$95; suites $125-$135; under 18 free; higher rates special events. Crib free. TV; cable (premium). Complimentary coffee in rms. Restaurant 6:30 am-11 am. Bar 4-11 pm. Ck-out noon. Coin lndry. Meeting rms. Business servs avail. Exercise equipt. Refrigerator, microwave in suites. Balconies. Cr cds: A, C, D, DS, JCB, MC, V.

★★★ **DOUBLETREE HOTEL NASHVILLE.** *315 4th Ave N (37219), downtown.* 615/244-8200; fax 615/747-4894; res 800/222-8733. *Email hotels@bnadu.doubletree.com; www.doubletree.com.* 332 rms, 9 story, 6 suites. S, D $139; each addl $20; suites $250; under 18 free. Crib avail. Pet accepted, some restrictions, fee.

Valet parking avail. Indoor pool. TV; cable (DSS), VCR avail, CD avail. Complimentary coffee in rms, newspaper, toll-free calls. Restaurant 6 am-midnight. Bar. Ck-out noon, ck-in 3 pm. Conference center, meeting rms. Business center. Bellhops. Concierge. Dry cleaning. Gift shop. Free airport transportation. Exercise equipt. Golf. Cr cds: A, D, DS, JCB, MC, V.

★★ **FAIRFIELD INN.** *211 Music City Circle (37110), in Opryland area. 615/872-8939; fax 615/872-7230; res 800/228-2800. Email chrish@lin-gate. com.* 109 rms, 3 story. S, D $79; suites $99. Crib avail. Parking lot. Indoor pool. TV; cable (premium). Complimentary continental bkfst, coffee in rms, newspaper, toll-free calls. Restaurant nearby. Ck-out noon, ck-in 3 pm. Business servs avail. Dry cleaning. Free airport transportation. Exercise equipt. Golf. Video games. Cr cds: A, D, DS, MC, V.

★★ **HAMPTON INN I65N.** *2407 Brick Church Pk (37207), I-65 Exit 87B, N of downtown. 615/226-3300; fax 615/226-0170; res 800/426-7866.* 125 rms, 5 story. June-Aug: S $64; D $79; under 17 free; lower rates rest of yr. Crib avail. Street parking. Pool. TV; cable (premium). Complimentary continental bkfst, coffee in rms. Restaurant nearby. Ck-out noon, ck-in 3 pm. Meeting rms. Business center. Concierge. Dry cleaning. Golf. Video games. Cr cds: A, D, DS, MC, V.

★★★ **HOLIDAY INN.** *760 Old Hickory Blvd (37027), I-65 Exit 74A. 615/373-2600; fax 615/377-3893; toll-free 800/465-4329. Email hibrent2@ pahmanagement.com; www.hotel-nashville.com/holidayinn/.* 246 rms, 8 story, 13 suites. Apr-June, Sep-Oct: S, D $129; suites $149; lower rates rest of yr. Crib avail. Parking lot. Pool, whirlpool. TV; cable (DSS). Complimentary coffee in rms, newspaper. Restaurant 6 am-8 pm. Bar. Ck-out noon, ck-in 3 pm. Meeting rms. Business servs avail. Bellhops. Concierge. Dry cleaning, coin lndry. Free airport transportation. Exercise privileges, sauna. Golf. Tennis, 4 courts. Supervised children's activities. Picnic

facilities. Video games. Cr cds: A, C, D, DS, ER, JCB, MC, V.

★★ **HOLIDAY INN VANDERBILT.** *2613 W End Ave (37203), W of downtown. 615/327-4707; fax 615/327-8034; res 800/465-4329.* 300 rms, 14 story. May-Nov: S, D $130-$142; each addl $10; suites $150-$200; under 18 free; holiday rates; higher rates Fan Fair, football games; lower rates rest of yr. Crib free. Pet accepted; deposit. TV; cable (premium), VCR avail. Complimentary coffee in rms. Restaurant 6 am-11 pm. Bar 2 pm-1 am; entertainment Fri, Sat. Ck-out noon. Meeting rms. Business center. In-rm modem link. Concierge. Gift shop. Coin lndry. Airport transportation. Exercise equipt. Pool. Balconies. Luxury level. Cr cds: A, C, D, DS, JCB, MC, V.

★★★ **LOEWS VANDERBILT PLAZA.** *2100 W End Ave (37203), downtown. 615/320-1700; fax 615/320-5019; res 800/235-6397; toll-free 800/336-3335. Email lowesvanderbilt@ loweshotels.com.* 340 rms, 12 story. S $164-$214; D $184-$234; each addl $20; suites $450-$800; under 18 free. Crib free. Pet accepted. Garage $8; valet parking $12. TV; cable (premium), VCR avail. Restaurants 6:30 am-10 pm. Rm serv to midnight; Fri, Sat to 1 am. Bars 3 pm-1 am; entertainment exc Sun. Ck-out noon. Convention facilities. Business center. In-rm modem link. Concierge. Shopping arcade. Barber, beauty shop. Exercise equipt. Minibars; microwaves avail. Luxury level. Cr cds: A, C, D, DS, ER, JCB, MC, V.

★★★ **MARRIOTT.** *600 Marriott Dr (32140), E of downtown. 615/889-9300; fax 615/889-9315; toll-free 800/228-9290.* 399 rms, 18 story. S, D $145-$160; suites $200-$350; under 18 free; wkend plans. TV; cable (premium), VCR avail. Indoor/outdoor pool; whirlpool, poolside serv. Restaurant 6 am-10:30 pm. Bar 11-2 am. Ck-out noon. Lndry facilities. Convention facilities. Business center. In-rm modem link. Free parking. Free airport transportation. Lighted tennis. Exercise equipt; sauna. Picnic tables, grills. Near Percy Priest Lake.

Luxury level. Cr cds: A, C, D, DS, ER, JCB, MC, V.

⊡ 🏄 ➴ 🏋 ✈ ⊠ 🔥 SC 🚶

★ ★ ★ **REGAL MAXWELL HOUSE.** *2025 Metro Center Blvd (37228), N of downtown.* 615/259-4343; fax 615/313-1327; res 800/222-8888; toll-free 800/457-4460. Email sales@maxwell househotel.com; www.maxwellhouse hotel.com. 285 rms, 10 story, 4 suites. Apr-June, Sep-Oct: S $169; D $179; each addl $20; suites $300; under 17 free; lower rates rest of yr. Crib avail. Pet accepted, some restrictions, fee. Parking lot. Pool, whirlpool. TV; cable. Complimentary coffee in rms, newspaper, toll-free calls. Restaurant. Bar. Ck-out noon, ck-in 3 pm. Conference center, meeting rms. Business center. Bellhops. Concierge. Dry cleaning, coin lndry. Gift shop. Exercise equipt, sauna, steam rm. Golf. Tennis, 2 courts. Video games. Cr cds: A, C, D, DS, MC, V.

⊡ 🏄 🏋 🦅 ➴ 🏋 ⊠ 🔥 SC 🚶

★ ★ ★ **RENAISSANCE.** *611 Commerce St (37203), downtown.* 615/255-8400; fax 615/255-8163; res 800/468-3571; toll-free 800/327-6618. www.renaissancehotels.com. 649 rms, 25 story, 24 suites. Mar-May, Sep-Nov: S $190; D $210; each addl $20; suites $450; under 17 free; lower rates rest of yr. Crib avail. Pet accepted, some restrictions. Valet parking avail. Indoor pool, whirlpool. TV; cable (premium), VCR avail. Complimentary coffee in rms, newspaper, toll-free calls. Restaurant 6 am-10 pm. 24-hr rm serv. Bar. Ck-out noon, ck-in 3 pm. Conference center, meeting rms. Business center. Bellhops. Concierge. Dry cleaning. Gift shop. Exercise privileges, sauna. Golf. Tennis. Video games. Cr cds: A, C, D, DS, JCB, MC, V.

⊡ 🏄 🏋 🦅 ➴ 🏋 ⊠ 🔥 SC 🚶

★ ★ ★ **SHERATON MUSIC CITY.** *777 McGavock Pike (37214), near airport, E of downtown.* 615/885-2200; fax 615/231-1134. Email mcity@ sheraton.com. 412 rms, 4 story. S, D $159-$179; each addl $15; suites $150-$550; under 18 free; wkend rates. Pet accepted. TV; cable (premium), VCR avail. Indoor/outdoor pools; wading pool, whirlpool. Restaurants 6 am-11 pm. Bar 11-3 am; entertainment. Ck-out noon. Convention facilities. Business cen-

ter. Concierge. Beauty shop. Gift shop. Free airport transportation. Lighted tennis. Golf privileges. Exercise rm; sauna. Bathrm phones; some refrigerators. Private balconies. On 23 landscaped acres on top of hill. Semiformal decor. Cr cds: A, C, D, DS, ER, MC, V.

⊡ 🏄 🦅 ⚡ ➴ 🏋 🏋 ⊠ 🔥 🚶

★ ★ ★ **SHERATON NASHVILLE DOWNTOWN.** *623 Union St (37219), opp Capitol, downtown.* 615/259-2000; fax 615/742-6056. 473 rms, 28 story. S, D $154-$184; each addl $20; under 18 free; wkend rates. Crib free. Garage $10; valet parking $14. TV; cable (premium), VCR avail. Indoor pool. Restaurant 6 am-10 pm. Rm serv to midnight. Bars 4 pm-midnight. Ck-out noon. Meeting rms. Business center. Concierge. Gift shop. Airport transportation. Exercise equipt. Luxury level. Cr cds: A, C, D, DS, ER, JCB, MC, V.

⊡ ➴ 🏋 ⊠ 🔥 🚶

★ ★ **SHONEY'S INN.** *100 Northcreek Blvd (37072), 13 mi N on I-65, Exit 97.* 615/851-1067; fax 615/851-6069; toll-free 800/222-2222. www.shoneys inn.com. 110 rms, 3 story. June-Aug: S $79; D $61; each addl $6; under 18 free; lower rates rest of yr. Crib avail. Pet accepted, some restrictions, fee. Parking lot. Pool. TV; cable (DSS). Complimentary continental bkfst, coffee in rms, newspaper, toll-free calls. Restaurant nearby. Ck-out noon, ck-in 3 pm. Meeting rm. Business servs avail. Dry cleaning. Golf. Tennis. Cr cds: A, C, D, DS, ER, JCB, MC, V.

⊡ 🏄 🏋 🦅 ➴ 🏋 ⊠ 🔥 SC

★ ★ **SHONEY'S INN/OPRYLAND AREA.** *2420 Music Valley Dr (37214), in Opryland area.* 615/885-4030; fax 615/391-0632; res 800/222-2222. 172 rms, 5 story, 13 suites. Apr-Oct: S $98; D $108; each addl $10; suites $135; under 18 free; lower rates rest of yr. Crib avail. Pet accepted, some restrictions. Parking garage. Indoor pool, whirlpool. TV; cable. Complimentary continental bkfst, coffee in rms, newspaper. Restaurant nearby. Bar. Ck-in 3 pm. Meeting rms. Business servs avail. Dry cleaning. Free airport transportation. Exercise privileges. Golf. Cr cds: A, C, D, DS, ER, JCB, MC, V.

⊡ 🏄 🏋 ➴ 🏋 ⊠ 🔥 SC

★ ★ ★ **UNION STATION.** *1001 Broadway (37203), downtown. 615/726-1001; fax 615/248-3554; toll-free 800/331-2123. www.citysearch. com.* 111 rms, 7 story, 13 suites. S $159; D $179; suites $209; under 18 free. Crib avail. Pet accepted, some restrictions. Valet parking avail. TV; cable (DSS). Complimentary coffee in rms, newspaper. Restaurant 11 am-11 pm. Bar. Ck-out noon, ck-in 3 pm. Meeting rms. Bellhops. Concierge. Dry cleaning. Exercise privileges. Cr cds: A, C, D, DS, ER, JCB, MC, V.

★ ★ **WESTIN HERMITAGE HOTEL.** *231 N 6th Ave (37219), downtown. 615/244-3121; fax 615/254-6909; res 800/251-1908.* 120 suites, 9 story. 1-bedrm suites $129-$189; 2-bedrm suites $250-$275; each addl $15; wkend rates. Valet parking $10. TV; cable (premium), VCR avail. Restaurant (see CAPITOL GRILLE). Bars 11 am-midnight. Ck-out noon. Meeting rms. Business center. Health club privileges. Bathrm phones, refrigerators, wet bars; microwaves avail. Hotel built in 1910 as a tribute to Beaux Arts classicism; fully restored to original elegance. Cr cds: A, C, D, DS, JCB, MC, V.

All Suites

★ ★ **AMERISUITES.** *202 Summit View Dr (37027), approx 9 mi S on I-65, Exit 74A. 615/661-9477; fax 615/661-9936; res 800/833-1516.* 126 kit. suites, 6 story. Mar-Oct: S, D $80-$150; each addl $10; under 18 free; higher rates special events; lower rates rest of yr. Crib free. Pet accepted, some restrictions; $10. TV; cable (premium), VCR (movies). Heated pool. Complimentary continental bkfst, coffee in rms. Restaurant nearby. Ck-out noon. Meeting rms. Business center. Valet serv. Sundries. Coin lndry. Exercise equipt. Refrigerators, microwaves. Cr cds: A, C, D, DS, ER, JCB, MC, V.

★ ★ **AMERISUITES OPRYLAND.** *220 Rudy's Circle (37214), in Opryland area. 615/872-0422; fax 615/872-9283; res 800/833-1516. Email locne@ primehospitality.com; www.amerisuites.*

com. 5 story, 125 suites. S $99; D $119; each addl $10; under 17 free. Crib avail. Parking lot. Pool. TV; cable (DSS), VCR avail. Complimentary continental bkfst, coffee in rms, newspaper, toll-free calls. Restaurant. Ck-out 11 am, ck-in 3 pm. Meeting rm. Business center. Dry cleaning, coin lndry. Free airport transportation. Exercise equipt. Golf, 18 holes. Tennis, 5 courts. Cr cds: A, C, D, DS, MC, V.

★ ★ ★ **DOUBLETREE GUEST SUITES.** *2424 Atrium Way (37214), near airport, E of downtown. 615/889-8889; fax 615/883-7779; toll-free 800/222-8733. Email dtgsnashville@aol. com; www.citysearch.doubletree.com.*, 3 story, 138 suites. Apr-June, Sep-Oct: S $139; D $149; each addl $10; suites $139; under 12 free; lower rates rest of yr. Parking lot. Indoor/outdoor pools. TV; cable (premium). Complimentary coffee in rms, newspaper. Restaurant. Bar. Meeting rms. Business servs avail. Bellhops. Dry cleaning, coin lndry. Free airport transportation. Exercise equipt. Golf. Cr cds: A, C, D, DS, ER, JCB, MC, V.

★ ★ ★ **EMBASSY SUITES.** *10 Century Blvd (37214), near airport, E of downtown. 615/871-0033; fax 615/883-9245; res 800/362-2779. Email hotel@bnana.embassysuites.com; www. embassynasshville.com.* 9 story, 296 suites. Mar-May, Oct: S $129; D $169; each addl $10; suites $169; under 17 free; lower rates rest of yr. Crib avail. Pet accepted, some restrictions, fee. Parking lot. Indoor pool, whirlpool. TV; cable (premium). Complimentary full bkfst, coffee in rms, newspaper, toll-free calls. Restaurant. Bar. Meeting rms. Business servs avail. Bellhops. Concierge. Dry cleaning, coin lndry. Gift shop. Free airport transportation. Exercise equipt, sauna. Golf, 18 holes. Tennis, 2 courts. Cr cds: A, C, D, DS, JCB, MC, V.

Conference Centers

★ ★ **CLUBHOUSE INN.** *920 Broadway (37203), downtown. 615/244-0150; fax 615/244-0445; res 800/258-2466.* 271 rms, 8 story, 13 suites. May-July: S, D $79; each addl $10;

suites $109; under 17 free; lower rates rest of yr. Crib avail, fee. Parking garage. Pool. TV; cable (premium). Complimentary full bkfst, toll-free calls. Restaurant noon-9 pm. Bar. Ck-out noon, ck-in 3 pm. Conference center, meeting rms. Business servs avail. Bellhops. Concierge. Dry cleaning. Gift shop. Exercise privileges. Cr cds: A, C, D, DS, MC, V.

⬛ ⬛ ⬛ ⬛ ⬛ ⬛

★★★ **OPRYLAND HOTEL.** 2802 Opryland Dr (37214), 5 mi NE of jct I-40 & Briley Parkway, in Opryland Area. 615/871-6853; fax 615/871-5077; res 615/883-2211. www.oprylandhotels.com. 2663 rms, 7 story, 220 suites. S, D $220; each addl $20; suites $950; under 18 free. Crib avail. Valet parking avail. Pool, lifeguard. TV; cable (premium), VCR avail. Complimentary coffee in rms. Restaurant 6 am-midnight. 24-hr rm serv. Bar. Ck-out 11 am, ck-in 3 pm. Conference center, meeting rms. Business center. Bellhops. Concierge. Dry cleaning. Gift shop. Salon/barber. Exercise equipt. Golf, 18 holes. Video games. Cr cds: A, C, D, DS, JCB, MC, V.

⬛ ⬛ ⬛ ⬛ ⬛ ⬛ ⬛ ⬛

Restaurants

★★ **101ST AIRBORNE.** 1362 A Murfreesboro Rd (37217), E of downtown. 615/361-4212. Specializes in steak, seafood, prime rib. Hrs: 11 am-2:30 pm, 4:30-10 pm; Fri, Sat 5-11 pm; Sun 4:30-10 pm; Sun brunch 9 am-2:30 pm. Res accepted. Bar. Lunch $5.95-$10.95; dinner $9.95-$24.95. Sun brunch $16.95. Child's menu. Entertainment: Fri, Sat. Parking. House dramatizes a headquarters operation for the 101st Airborne Division; World War II memorabilia. Cr cds: A, C, D, DS, MC, V.

⬛ ⬛

★★★ **ARTHUR'S.** 1001 Broadway. 615/255-1494. Email arthurs restaurant@att.net; www.arthurs restaurant.com. Specializes in seafood, lamb, flaming desserts. Own baking. Menu changes wkly. Hrs: 5:30-10 pm; Fri, Sat to 11 pm; Sun to 9 pm. Closed hols. Res accepted. Bar. Wine cellar. Dinner table d'hote: $55-$70. Valet parking. Jacket. In an Old World-style hotel converted from an 1897 train station. Cr cds: A, D, DS, MC, V.

⬛ ⬛

★★ **BELLE MEADE BRASSERIE.** 101 Page Rd (37205), W of downtown. 615/356-5450. Email chefrobt@bell south.net; www.bellemeadebrasserie.com. Specializes in seafood, pasta, homemade desserts. Hrs: 5-10 pm; Fri, Sat to 11 pm. Closed Sun; hols. Res accepted. Bar. Dinner a la carte entrees: $12-$24. Parking. Contemporary decor. Original art. Cr cds: A, DS, MC, V.

⬛ ⬛

★ **BLUEBIRD CAFE.** 4104 Hillsboro Rd (37215), S of downtown. 615/383-1461. Email bluebirdcafe@aol.com; www.bluebirdcafe.com. Specializes in Cajun catfish, chocolate chunk cheesecake. Hrs: 5:30-10 pm; Sun from 6 pm. Closed hols. Res accepted. Bar. Dinner $4-$9. Entertainment: popular performance club featuring songwriters and other entertainers. Parking. Cr cds: A, D, DS, MC, V.

⬛

★ **BOSCOS PIZZA KITCHEN AND BREWERY.** 1805 21st Ave S (37212), S of downtown. 615/385-0050. Email nashville@boscos.com; www.boscosbeer.com. Specializes in wood-burning oven pizza, pasta, fresh fish. Hrs: 11 am-11 pm; Fri, Sat to midnight; Sun brunch 11am-3 pm. Closed Thanksgiving, Dec 25. Res accepted. Bar. Lunch $3.95-$12.95; dinner $3.95-$15.95. Sun brunch $3.95-$8.95. Child's menu. Brewery on site. Cr cds: A, D, DS, MC, V.

⬛ ⬛

★★ **BOUNDRY.** 911 20th Ave S (37212), S of downtown. 615/321-3043. Email boundry@bellsouth.net; www.citysearch.com/nashville/boundry. Specializes in planked trout, grilled Tennessee ostrich, lobster, BLT pizza. Hrs: 5 pm-1 am; Fri, Sat to 2 am. Closed hols. Res accepted. Bar. Dinner $9.95-$23.50. Valet parking. Murals, artwork. Cr cds: A, D, DS, MC, V.

⬛ ⬛

★★★ **CAPITOL GRILLE.** 231 6th Ave N. 615/244-3121. www.capitol-grille.com. Specializes in sauteed red snapper, creme brulee Napoleon, soft-shell crawfish. Hrs: 6:30 am-2 pm, 5:30-10 pm; Sun brunch 11 am-2 pm. Res accepted. Bar. Wine list. Bkfst $3.50-$9.95; lunch $5.95-$8.95; dinner $16.50-$24.95. Sun brunch $24.95. Valet parking. Russian panel-

Nashville skyline

ing. Marble columns. Cr cds: A, D, DS, MC, V.

D

★★★ **CASABLANCA.** *1911 Broadway (37203), downtown. 615/327-8001.* Specializes in Moroccan spiced crab cakes, sauteed veal chops, Rick's bouillabaisse. Hrs: 5-10 pm. Closed Sun; hols. Res accepted. Bar. Wine cellar. Dinner a la carte entrees: $17-$25.50. Entertainment: piano Wed-Sat. Valet parking. Decor imitates theme of movie Casablanca. Cr cds: A, C, D, DS, MC, V.

D ⊸

★ **COCK OF THE WALK.** *2624 Music Valley Dr (37214), in Opryland Area. 615/889-1930.* Specializes in catfish, fried dill pickles, flipped cornbread. Hrs: 5-9 pm; Fri, Sat to 10 pm; Sun 11 am-9 pm. Closed Thanksgiving, Dec 24, 25; also Super Bowl Sun. Res accepted. Bar. Dinner $8.95-$12.50. Child's menu. Parking. Split-level dining in rustic atmosphere. Cr cds: A, D, MC, V.

D ⊸

★★★ **F. SCOTT'S.** *2210 Crestmoor Rd (37215), W of downtown. 615/269-5861. www.nashville.citysearch.com.* Specializes in seafood, lamb. Hrs: 5:30-10 pm; Fri, Sat to 11 pm. Closed most major hols. Res accepted. Bar. Wine list. Dinner a la carte entrees: $12.95-$24.95. Child's menu. Entertainment. Valet parking. Art Deco decor. Cr cds: A, D, DS, MC, V.

D ⊸

★ **GOTEN 2.** *209 10th Ave (37203), downtown. 615/251-4855.* Specializes in sushi, tempura, bento box. Hrs: 11 am-2:30 pm, 4:30 pm-midnight; Fri 4:30 pm-1 am; Sat 5 pm-1am. Closed Sun; Thanksgiving, Dec 25. Res accepted. Bar. Lunch, dinner $3.50-$14.50. Parking. Casual sushi bar in redeveloped historic building. Cr cds: A, D, DS, MC, V.

D ⊸

★★ **GREEN HILLS GRILLE.** *2122 Hillsboro Dr (37215), W of downtown. 615/383-6444. Email srnash@aol.com.* Specializes in lemon artichoke chicken, roasted chicken, barbecue ribs. Hrs: 11 am-10 pm; Thurs-Sat to 11 pm. Closed Thanksgiving, Dec 25. Bar. Lunch, dinner $5.95-$15.45. Child's menu. Valet parking. Southwestern decor. Cr cds: A, D, DS, MC, V.

D ⊸

★★ **J. ALEXANDER'S.** *73 White Bridge Rd (37205), W of downtown. 615/352-0981. www.jalexanders.com.* Specializes in prime rib, fresh seafood, salads. Hrs: 11 am-10 pm; Fri, Sat to 11 pm. Closed Thanksgiving, Dec 25. Bar. Lunch, dinner $4.95-$17.95. Child's menu. Parking. Glass window permits diners to observe salad preparation area. Cr cds: A, C, D, DS, MC, V.

D ⊸

★★ **JIMMY KELLY'S.** *217 Louise Ave (37203), W of downtown. 615/329-4349.* Specializes in hand-cut aged beef. Hrs: 5 pm-midnight. Closed Sun; hols. Res accepted. Bar. Dinner $12.75-$28.75. Child's menu. Valet parking. In renovated Victorian mansion (1911). Family-owned. Cr cds: A, DS, MC, V.

★ **LOVELESS CAFE.** *8400 Hwy 100 (37221), S of downtown.* 615/646-9700. *Email nsh@aol.com; www.city search.com/nas/lovelesscafe.com.* Specializes in scratch biscuits, fried chicken. Hrs: 8 am-2 pm, 5-9 pm; Sat, Sun 8 am-9 pm. Closed Jan 1, Thanksgiving, Dec 25. Res accepted. Bkfst $3.95-$9.95; lunch, dinner $5-$14.95. Child's menu. Parking. Private dining in rms that were previously motel rms. Family-owned. Cr cds: A, MC, V.

★ **MAD PLATTER.** *1239 6th Ave N (37208), N of downtown.* 615/242-2563. *www.madplatter.com.* Specializes in rack of lamb moutarde, chocolate Elvis. Hrs: 11 am-2 pm, 5:30-10 pm; Fri to 11 pm; Sat 5:30-11 pm; Sun 5-9 pm. Closed Mon; hols. Res required. Lunch $6.25-$11.95; dinner $18.50-$48. Building more than 100 yrs old. Cr cds: A, C, D, DS, MC, V.

★★★ **MARIO'S.** *2005 Broadway (37203), downtown.* 615/327-3232. Specializes in pastas, fresh seafood, veal. Hrs: 5:30-10:30 pm. Closed Sun; major hols. Res accepted. Bar. Wine cellars. Dinner a la carte entrees: $18-$26. Parking. Theater dining rm. Family-owned. Cr cds: A, D, DS, MC, V.

★★★ **MERCHANTS.** *401 Broadway (37203), downtown.* 615/254-1892. *www.merchantsrestaurant.com.* Specializes in fresh grilled meats and seafood. Own baking. Hrs: 10:30 am-2:30 pm, 5-10 pm; Fri to 11 pm; Sat noon-11 pm; Sun 5-9 pm; Sun brunch 10:30 am-2:30 pm. Res accepted. Bar. Wine cellar. Lunch à la carte entrées: $3.95-$10.95; dinner à la carte entrées: $9.95-$23.95. Sun brunch $5.95-$16.95. Entertainment: pianist. Valet parking. In historic building. Dining on 3 levels. Original wood floors. Cr cds: A, D, DS, MC, V.

★★★ **MERE BULLES.** *152 2nd Ave N (37201), downtown.* 615/256-1946.

Specializes in pasta, seafood, steak. Hrs: 11 am-2 pm; 5-10 pm; Fri, Sat 5-11 pm; Sun 10:30 am-2 pm, 5-9 pm. Closed Jan 1. Res accepted. Bar. Dinner $17.95-$32.95. Sun brunch $23.95. Entertainment. Local art on display. Cr cds: A, D, DS, MC, V.

★★ **MIDTOWN CAFE.** *102 19th Ave S (37203), S of downtown.* 615/320-7176. *www.midtowncafe.city search.com.* Specializes in fresh daily seafood. Hrs: 11 am-2:30 pm, 5-10 pm; Fri to 11 pm; Sat 5:30-11 pm; Sun 5-10 pm. Closed hols. Res accepted. Bar. Lunch $6.75-$10.95; dinner $11.25-$22.95. Child's menu. Valet parking. Intimate dining. Cr cds: A, D, DS, MC, V.

★ **MONELL'S.** *1235 6th Ave N (37208), in Germantown, N of downtown.* 615/248-4747. *www.capitolgrill. com.* Specializes in skillet-fried chicken, sweet potato casserole, chocolate pecan pie. Hrs: 10:30 am-2 pm; Thurs-Sat 5-8:30 pm; Sun 10:30 am-3 pm. Closed Dec 24, 25. Bkfst $8-$10; lunch $8-$10; dinner $10-$12. Parking. Family-style dining in 1870 historical home. Cr cds: MC, V.

★★ **NEW ORLEANS MANOR.** *1400 Murfreesboro Rd (37217), E of downtown.* 615/367-2777. Specializes in seafood, lobster, prime rib. Salad bar. Hrs: 5:30-9 pm; Sat from 5 pm. Closed Sun, Mon; Jan 1, Thanksgiving, Dec 24, 25. Res accepted. Dinner buffet: $31-$37. Child's menu. Parking. Scenic grounds. Colonial-type mansion built in 1930. Cr cds: A, D, DS, MC, V.

★★★ **THE OLD HICKORY STEAK-HOUSE.** *2800 Opryland Dr.* 615/889-1000. Menu changes seasonally. Hrs: 5-10 pm; Fri, Sat to 11 pm. Res accepted. Wine, beer. Dinner $17-$32. Entertainment: pianist. Cr cds: A, C, D, DS, MC, V.

★ **OLD SPAGHETTI FACTORY.** *160 2nd Ave N (37201), downtown.* 615/254-9010. *www.osf.com.* Specializes in spaghetti with a variety of sauces. Hrs: 11:30 am-2 pm, 5-10 pm; Fri 5-11 pm; Sat 11:30 am-11 pm; Sun 11:30 am-10 pm. Closed Thanksgiving, Dec 24, 25. Bar. Lunch complete meals: $3.25-$5.60; dinner complete meals: $5-$10. Child's menu. In converted warehouse (1869). Doorway arch from the Bank of London. Antiques. Cr cds: A, D, DS, MC, V.

D 🏃

★ ★ **PRIME CUT STEAKHOUSE.**
170 2nd Ave N (37201), downtown.
615/242-3083. www.primecut@mind
spring.com. Specializes in steak, marinated chicken, fresh fish. Hrs: 5-10 pm; Fri, Sat to 11 pm. Closed Thanksgiving, Dec 25. Res accepted. Bar. Dinner $15.95-$21.95. Child's menu. Entertainment: Fri, Sat. Option to cook own steak. Cr cds: A, D, DS, MC, V.

D 🏃

★ ★ **ROYAL THAI.** *204 Commerce St*
(37201), downtown. 615/255-0821.
Specializes in pad kra pao, pla sam rod, pad Thai. Hrs: 11 am-3 pm, 5-9 pm; Sat to 11 pm. Closed Jan 1, Dec 25. Res accepted. Bar. Lunch $4.95-$6.95; dinner $6.95-$19.95. Oriental decor. Family-owned. Cr cds: A, D, DS, MC, V.

D 🏃

★ ★ ★ **RUTH'S CHRIS STEAK-HOUSE.** *2100 W End Ave (37203), W*
of downtown. 615/320-0163. Specializes in filet, porterhouse, Maine lobster. Hrs: 5-10:30 pm; Sun to 9:30 pm. Closed hols. Res accepted. Bar. Dinner a la carte entrees: $12.95-$28.95. Valet parking. Cr cds: A, D, DS, MC, V.

D 🏃

★ **SEANACHIE.** *327 Broadway*
(37201), downtown. 615/726-2006.
www.seanachie.com. Specializes in boxty, beef and Guinness pie, Irish stew. Hrs: 11 am-midnight; Thurs to 1 am; Fri, Sat to 2 am; Sun to 10 pm. Closed Dec 25. Res accepted. Bar. Lunch, dinner $5.95-$14.95. Sun brunch $4.95-$14.95. Child's menu. Entertainment: Celtic music Tues-Sun. Irish decor and atmosphere. Cr cds: A, D, DS, MC, V.

D 🏃

★ **SITAR INDIAN RESTAURANT.**
116 21st Ave N (37203), N of downtown. 615/321-8889. Specializes in chicken tikka masala, lamb pasanda, karahai shrimp. Hrs: 11 am-2:30 pm,

5-10 pm; Sun noon-3 pm. Bar. Lunch $5.99-$7.99. Buffet: $5.99; dinner $6.95-$13.95. Indian artwork. Cr cds: A, D, DS, MC, V.

D SC 🏃

★ ★ **SOLE MIO.** *94 Peabody St*
(37210), downtown. 615/256-4013.
www.solemio.citysearch.com. Specializes in lasagne al forno, gnocchi sorrentino. Own pasta. Hrs: 11 am-9:30 pm; Fri, Sat to 11 pm. Closed Mon; most hols. Res accepted. Bar. Lunch a la carte entrees: $7-$18; dinner à la carte entrées: $7-$23. Brunch à la carte entrées: $8.95-$12. Entertainment: piano Fri, Sat. Parking. Cr cds: A, MC, V.

D 🏃

★ ★ ★ **SPERRY'S.** *5109 Harding Rd*
(37205), W of downtown. 615/353-0809. www.sperrys.com. Specializes in fresh seafood, steak. Salad bar. Own desserts, soups, sauces. Hrs: 5-10 pm; Fri to 11 pm; Sat to midnight. Closed major hols. Bar. Dinner à la carte entrées: $12.50-$28.50. Parking. Nautical and hunting decor. Cr cds: A, DS, MC, V.

D 🏃

★ ★ **STOCKYARD.** *901 2nd Ave N*
(37201), downtown. 615/255-6464.
Specializes in charcoal-grilled steak, fresh seafood, grilled chicken breast. Hrs: 5-10 pm; Fri, Sat to 11 pm. Closed Dec 25. Bar. Dinner $15-$50. Child's menu. Parking. Cr cds: A, D, DS, MC, V.

D 🏃

★ ★ **SUNSET GRILL.** *2001 A Belcourt Ave (37212), S of downtown.*
615/386-3663. Email sunsetgrill@
mindspring.com; www.sunsetgrill.com.
Specializes in fresh seafood, pasta, lamb. Hrs: 11-1:30 am; Sat 4:45 pm-1:30 am; Sun 4:45-11 pm. Res accepted. Bar. Lunch $5-$10; dinner $6-$24. Child's menu. Valet Parking. Five dining areas include a glass-enclosed patio. Original artwork. Cr cds: A, D, DS, MC, V.

D 🏃

★ **TIN ANGEL.** *3201 W End Ave*
(37212), W of downtown. 615/298-3444. Specializes in chicken quesadilla, Angel Louie spaghetti, meatloaf. Hrs: 11 am-10 pm; Fri to 11 pm; Sat 4:30-11 pm; Sun brunch

11 am-3 pm. Closed hols. Bar. Lunch a la carte entrees: $7-$12; dinner a la carte entrees: $8-$17. Sun brunch $7-$12. Valet parking. In historical building. Cr cds: A, D, DS, MC, V.

[D] [symbol]

★★ **TRACE.** *2000 Belcourt Ave (37212), S of downtown. 615/385-2200.* Specializes in lamb shank, tuna au poivre. Hrs: 4 pm-2:45 am. Closed Jan 1, Dec 25. Bar. Dinner $9-$21. Entertainment: Jazz Sun. Valet parking. Cr cds: A, DS, MC, V.

[D] [symbol]

★★★ **VALENTINO'S.** *1907 W End Ave (37203), W of downtown. 615/327-0148.* Specializes in chicken, seafood, pasta. Hrs: 11 am-2 pm, 5-10 pm. Closed Sun; hols. Res accepted. Bar. Lunch $5.95-$10.95; dinner $9.95-$22.95. Valet parking. Cr cds: A, C, D, DS, MC, V.

[D] [symbol]

★★★★ **THE WILD BOAR.** *2014 Broadway (37203), downtown. 615/329-1313. www.wboar.com.* Chef Guillaume Burlion's classic French credentials are a rare find in this southern town. The formal, medieval-style dining room hidden in an office building atrium is an exceptional backdrop for refined service, special-occasion ambiance and contemporary-French cuisine. Wine connoisseurs will be in heaven staring at the glassed-in cellar, choosing from the two-inch-thick list and sipping from sparkling, Riedel crystal. Specializes in fresh wild game, fresh seafood, souffles. Hrs: 6-10 pm. Closed Sun; hols. Res accepted. Bar. Wine cellar. Dinner $22.95-$34.95. Entertainment: pianist Fri, Sat. Valet parking. Cr cds: A, C, D, DS, MC, V.

[D]

★★ **ZOLA.** *3001 W End Ave (37203), W of downtown. 615/320-7778. www.zola.citysearch.com.* Specializes in fish, poultry, vegetarian entrees. Hrs: 5:30-10 pm; Fri, Sat to 11 pm. Closed Sun; most major hols. Res accepted. Dinner $10.50-$21.95. Cr cds: A, D, DS, MC, V.

[D]

Unrated Dining Spot

TOWN HOUSE TEA ROOM AND RESTAURANT. *165 8th Ave N (37203), downtown. 615/254-1277.*

Salad bar. Own baking, soups. Hrs: 8 am-2:30 pm. Closed Sat, Sun; hols. Bkfst $3.95-$7.95; lunch $3.45-$7.50. Buffet: $5.25. Historic 24-room mansion (1840s). Fireplaces. Oak floors. Antiques. Paintings. Cr cds: A, D, DS, MC, V.

[SC]

Natchez Trace State Resort Park

(40 mi NE of Jackson, off I-40)

Named for the pioneer trail that connected Nashville and Natchez, this 48,000-acre park is the largest recreation area in western Tennessee and the location of a pecan tree that is said to be the world's third largest. Four lakes provide swimming, fishing, boating (launch, rentals); nature trails, backpacking, picnicking, playground, recreation lodge. Tent and trailer sites, cabins, inn. Standard fees. Phone 901/968-8176.

Motels/Motor Lodges

★★ **BEST WESTERN CROSS-ROADS INN.** *21045 TN 22 N (38388), 8 mi W of park entrance, on TN 22 at I-40 Exit 108. 901/968-2532; fax 901/968-2082; toll-free 800/528-1234.* 40 rms. May-Oct: S $42-$50; D $48-$56; each addl $10; higher rates special events; lower rates rest of yr. Crib free. TV; cable (premium). Pool. Restaurant nearby. Ck-out 11 am. Cr cds: A, D, DS, MC, V.

[D] [symbols] [SC]

★★ **PIN OAK LODGE.** *567 Pin Oak Lodge Ln (38388). 901/968-8176; fax 901/968-6515; toll-free 800/250-8616.* 20 rms, 2 story, 18 kit. cottages. Mar-Nov: S, D $56-$62; each addl $6; kit. cottages $65-$70; under 16 free; lower rates rest of yr. Crib free. TV in motel rms. Pool; wading pool. Playground. Restaurant 7 am-9 pm. Ck-out 11 am. Meeting rms. Lighted tennis. Rec rm. Dock. Balconies. Picnic tables, grills. On lake. State-owned; all facilities of park avail. Cr cds: A, DS, MC, V.

[D] [symbols] [SC]

Oak Ridge

(E-6) *See also Knoxville*

Founded 1943 **Pop** 27,310 **Elev** 900 ft
Area code 423 **Zip** 37830
Web www.visit-or.org

Information Convention & Visitors
Bureau, 302 S Tulane Ave; 423/482-
7821 or 800/887-3429

Annual Event

Appalachian Music & Craft Festival.
Children's Museum of Oak Ridge.
Late Nov.

Motels/Motor Lodges

★★ **COMFORT INN.** *433 S Rutgers
Ave (37830). 865/481-8200; fax
865/483-6142; res 800/228-5150; toll-
free 800/553-7830. Email oakridge
admin@crownam.com; www.oakridgetn
comfortinn.com.* 122 rms, 5 story, 26
suites. S, D $71-$81; each addl $7;
suites $71-$91; under 18 free. Crib
free. Pet accepted. TV; cable. Pool.
Complimentary continental bkfst.
Restaurant nearby. Ck-out noon. Coin
lndry. Meeting rms. Business servs
avail. Health club privileges. Refrigerator in suites. Cr cds: A, DS, MC, V.

★ **DAYS INN.** *206 S Illinois Ave
(37830). 423/483-5615; fax 423/483-
5615; res 800/329-7466.* 80 rms, 2
story. S $43-$53; D $49-$59; each
addl $3; under 12 free. Crib free. Pet
accepted. TV; cable. Heated pool.
Playground. Complimentary continental bkfst. Restaurant adj 6:30 am-
midnight; Fri, Sat to 2 am. Ck-out 11
am. Meeting rms. Business servs
avail. Refrigerators. Cr cds: A, C, D,
DS, MC, V.

★★★ **GARDEN PLAZA HOTEL.**
*215 S Illinois Ave (37830). 423/481-
2468; fax 423/481-2474; toll-free
800/342-7336.* 168 rms, 5 story. S, D
$79-$99; each addl $7; suites $99-
$115; under 18 free. Crib free. TV;
cable (premium). Indoor/outdoor
pool; whirlpool, poolside serv. Coffee
in rms. Restaurant 6:30 am-2 pm, 5-
10 pm. Bar. Ck-out noon. Meeting
rms. Business center. Health club

privileges. Refrigerator, wet bar in
suites. Cr cds: A, C, D, DS, MC, V.

★★ **HAMPTON INN.** *208 S Illinois
Ave (37868). 423/482-7889; fax 423/
482-7493; res 800/426-7866.* 60 rms,
5 story. S, D $63-$89; each addl $7;
under 18 free. Crib free. TV; cable
(premium). Heated pool; whirlpool.
Complimentary continental bkfst.
Restaurant nearby. Ck-out 11 am.
Coin lndry. Meeting rms. Business
servs avail. In-rm modem link. Exercise equipt; sauna. Some refrigerators, microwaves. Cr cds: A, C, D, DS,
MC, V.

Paris

(E-3) *See also Land Between The Lakes,
KY*

Founded 1821 **Pop** 9,332 **Elev** 519 ft
Area code 901 **Zip** 38242

Information Paris-Henry County
Chamber of Commerce, PO Box 8;
901/642-3431 or 800/345-1103

Motels/Motor Lodges

★★ **BEST WESTERN TRAVELER'S
INN.** *1297 E Wood St (38242). 901/
642-8881; fax 901/644-2881; toll-free
800/528-1234.* 98 rms, 2 story. S $40-
$54; D $42-$57; each addl $5; under
12 free; wkly rates. Crib free. TV;
cable. Pool. Complimentary continental bkfst. Restaurant adj 6 am-
midnight. Private club; setups, beer.
Ck-out noon. Meeting rms. Cr cds: A,
C, D, DS, MC, V.

★ **TERRACE WOODS TRAVEL
LODGE.** *1190 N Market St (38242).
901/642-2642; fax 901/641-0172.* 19
rms, 1-2 story. S $29-$31; D $33-$35;
each addl $4; under 12 free. Crib $4.
TV; cable. Complimentary coffee in
lobby. Ck-out 11 am. Refrigerators,
microwaves. Cr cds: A, C, D, DS,
MC, V.

Restaurant

★ **PAULETTE'S.** *200 S Market St (38242). 901/644-3777.* Specializes in sandwiches, quiche. Hrs: 10:30 am-2 pm, 5-9 pm; Sun 11 am-2 pm, 5-9 pm. Closed Sat; hols. Res accepted. Lunch, dinner $1.95-$6.95. Child's menu. Casual dining. Cr cds: D, DS, MC, V.

D -\

Pigeon Forge

(F-7) *See also Gatlinburg, Sevierville*

Pop 3,027 **Elev** 1,031 ft
Area code 865 **Zip** 37863
Web www.pigeon-forge.tn.us
Information Dept of Tourism, 2450 Parkway, PO Box 1390, 37868-1390; 865/453-8574 or 800/251-9100

Located in the shadow of the Smokies, this resort town was named for the river on which it sits and the iron forge built in the early 1800s.

What to See and Do

Country music and comedy shows.

Country Tonite Theatre. (Mar-Dec, Tues-Sat) 2249 Parkway Blvd. Phone 865/453-2003 or 800/792-4308. ¢¢¢¢

Hillbilly Hoedown Music Theatre. (Feb-Dec) 2135 Parkway. Phone 865/428-5600. ¢¢¢¢

Memories Theatre. 2141 Parkway. Phone 865/428-7852 or 800/325-3078. ¢¢¢¢

Music Mansion Theatre. (Apr-Dec) 100 Music Rd. Phone 865/428-7469. ¢¢¢¢

Smoky Mountain Jubilee. 2115 Parkway. Phone 865/428-1836.

The Comedy Barn. 2775 Parkway. Phone 865/428-5222. ¢¢¢¢¢

Dollywood. Dolly Parton's entertainment park. More than 40 musical shows daily; over 30 rides and attractions and more than 70 shops and restaurants. (Mid April-end of Dec) 1 mi E on US 441, on Dollywood Lane. Phone 865/428-9488. ¢¢¢¢¢

Motels/Motor Lodges

★★ **AMERICANA INN.** *2825 Parkway (37863). 865/428-0172; fax*

865/428-7903. 170 rms, 4 story. S $40-$50; D $55-$75; higher rates hols, special events. Crib $10. TV. Heated pool; whirlpool. Restaurant 8 am-9 pm; closed Sun. Ck-out 11 am. Downhill ski 10 mi. Balconies. Cr cds: DS, MC, V.

D ⇥ ≈ ⊠ 🔥

★★ **BAYMONT INN AND SUITES.** *2179 Parkway (33701). 423/428-7305; fax 423/428-8977; res 800/896-2950; toll-free 800/428-3438.* 131 rms, 4 story. Apr-Dec: S, D $39.95-$99.95; suites $49.95-$109.95; higher rates special events; lower rates rest of yr. Crib free. Pet accepted. TV; cable (premium), VCR avail (movies). Heated pool. Complimentary continental bkfst. Restaurant adj 11 am-11 pm. Ck-out noon. Coin lndry. Meeting rms. Business servs avail. Downhill ski 10 mi. Refrigerator, microwave in suites. Cr cds: A, C, D, DS, MC, V.

D 🐾 ⇥ ≈ ⊠ 🔥 SC

★★ **BEST WESTERN PLAZA INN.** *3755 Parkway (37863). 865/453-5538; fax 865/654-5326; res 800/528-1234; toll-free 800/232-5656. Email info@ bwplazainn.com.* 201 rms, 3-5 story. S, D $69-$129. Crib $6. TV; cable. Indoor/outdoor pool; whirlpool. Complimentary continental bkfst. Restaurant opp 7 am-9 pm. Ck-out 11 am. Meeting rm. Business servs avail. Downhill ski 6 mi. Sauna. Game rm. Some in-rm whirlpools, refrigerators, fireplaces. Cr cds: A, D, DS, MC, V.

D 🐟 ⇥ ≈ ⊠ 🔥

★★ **BILMAR MOTOR INN.** *3786 Parkway (37863), on US 441. 865/453-5593; fax 865/428-8953.* 76 rms, 2-3 story. Late May-Labor Day, Oct: S, D $36-$85; each addl $5; lower rates Mar-mid-May, after Labor Day-Jan. Closed Jan-Feb. Crib $5. TV; cable. Heated pool. Complimentary continental bkfst, coffee in rms. Restaurant nearby. Ck-out 11 am. Business servs avail. Some in-rm whirlpools, refrigerators. Cr cds: DS, MC, V.

D 🐟 🛗 ≈ 🎣 ⊠ 🔥

★★ **BRIARSTONE INN.** *3626 Parkway (37868). 865/453-3050; fax 865/453-2564.* 57 rms, 3 story. No elvtr. July-Oct: S, D $32-$120; each addl $6; higher rates special events; lower rates rest of yr. TV; cable (premium). Pool; whirlpools. Coffee in rms. Restaurant adj 7 am-11 pm. Ck-

out 11 am. Business servs avail.
Refrigerators; some fireplaces. Cr cds:
A, DS, MC, V.

★ ★ **CAPRI MOTEL.** *4061 Parkway
(37863). 865/453-7147; fax 865/453-
7157; toll-free 800/528-4555.* 106 rms,
2 story. Apr-Dec: S $25-$105; D $25-
$145; under 18 free; hols (2-day
min); higher rates special events;
lower rates rest of yr. Crib free. TV;
cable (premium). Heated pool. Complimentary continental bkfst. Restaurant nearby. Ck-out 11 am. Meeting
rms. Business servs avail. Downhill
ski 5 mi. Many refrigerators. Cr cds:
A, DS, MC, V.

★ ★ **COLONIAL HOUSE.** *3545
Parkway (37863). 865/453-0717; fax
865/453-8412.* 63 rms, 3 story. Mar-
Nov: S, D $29-$99; each addl $5;
higher rates: hols, special events;
lower rates rest of yr. Crib $5. TV;
cable. Heated pool; wading pool.
Complimentary continental bkfst.
Ck-out 11 am. Downhill ski 7 mi.
Some in-rm whirlpools, fireplaces.
Some private patios, balconies. On
river. Cr cds: A, DS, MC, V.

★ ★ **CREEKSTONE INN.** *4034 S
River Rd (37868). 865/453-3557; fax
865/453-2564.* 172 rms, 5 story. July-
Oct: S $32-$114; D $38-$120; suites
$68-$162; under 18 free; lower rates
rest of yr. Crib $5. TV; cable. Pool.
Restaurant nearby. Ck-out 11 am.
Refrigerators. On Little Pigeon River.
Cr cds: A, DS, MC, V.

★ **DAYS INN.** *2760 Parkway (37863),
US 441. 865/453-4707; fax 865/428-
7928; res 800/645-3079; toll-free 800/
329-7466.* 144 rms, 3 story. May-Oct:
S $68-$88; D $78-$98; each addl $5;
under 17 free; higher rates: hols, special events; lower rates rest of yr. Crib
free. TV; cable. Heated pool. Complimentary coffee in lobby. Restaurant
adj 7 am-10 pm. Ck-out 11 am. Business servs avail. Downhill ski 7 mi.
Cr cds: A, C, D, DS, MC, V.

★ **ECONO LODGE.** *2440 Parkway
(37863). 865/428-1231; fax 865/453-
6879; res 800/632-6104.* 202 rms, 3
story. June-Oct: S, D $79-$89; under
18 free; higher rates: wkends, hols,
special events; lower rates rest of yr.
Crib free. TV. Pool; wading pool,
whirlpool. Complimentary continental bkfst. Restaurant nearby. Ck-out
11 am. Meeting rm. Business servs
avail. Downhill ski 10 mi. Picnic
tables. View of river, mountains. Cr
cds: A, C, D, DS, MC, V.

★ ★ **GRAND RESORT HOTEL AND
CONVENTION CENTER.** *3171 N
Parkway (37863). 865/453-1000; fax
865/428-3944; toll-free 800/362-1188.*
425 rms, 5 story. May-Oct: S, D $70-
$100; each addl $10; suites $80-$199;
under 12 free; higher rates special
events; lower rates rest of yr. Crib
free. Pet accepted. TV; cable. Pool;
whirlpool. Complimentary continental bkfst. Restaurant 7 am-9 pm. Ck-
out 11 am. Convention facilities.
Business servs avail. Gift shop.
Downhill ski 7 mi. Some fireplaces.
Cr cds: A, D, DS, MC, V.

★ **GREEN VALLEY MOTEL.** *4109
Parkway (37863). 865/453-9091; fax
865/428-9271; toll-free 800/892-1267.*
50 rms, 3 story. No elvtr. May-Oct: S,
D $48-$98; each addl $5; lower rates
rest of yr. Crib $5. TV; cable (pre-
mium), VCR (movies $3). Heated
pool. Ck-out 11 am. Downhill ski 7
mi. Refrigerators. Cr cds: MC, V.

★ ★ **HEARTLAND COUNTRY
RESORT.** *2385 Parkway (37863).
865/453-4106; fax 865/453-4106; res
800/843-6686.* 160 rms, 5 story. Late
May-early Nov: S, D $59-$119; each
addl $5; under 12 free; lower rates
rest of yr. Crib free. Pet accepted. TV;
cable. 2 pools, 1 indoor; whirlpool.
Continental bkfst. Ck-out 11 am.
Meeting rms. Business servs avail.
Sundries. Game rm. Balconies. Cr
cds: A, C, D, DS, MC, V.

★ ★ ★ **HOLIDAY INN RESORT.**
*3230 Parkway (37863), US 441.
865/428-2700; fax 865/428-2700; res
800/782-3119. Email hipftn@usit.net;
www.4lodging.com.* 210 rms, 5 story,
10 suites. May-Oct: S, D $59-$129;
suites $99-$199; under 18 free;
higher rates special events; lower

rates rest of yr. Crib free. TV. Indoor pool; whirlpool. Restaurant 7 am-10 pm. Ck-out 11 am. Coin lndry. Meeting rms. Business servs avail. In-rm modem link. Exercise equipt. Downhill ski 7 mi. Game rm. Some refrigerators. Cr cds: A, C, D, DS, JCB, MC, V.

⊡ ⊠ ⊠ ⊠ ⊠ ⊠ SC

★ **HOWARD JOHNSON.** *2826 Parkway (37868). 865/453-9151; fax 865/428-4141; res 800/654-2000; toll-free 800/453-6008.* 145 rms, 3 story. May-Oct: S, D $38.80-$88.80; each addl $6; studio rms $36.80-$88.80; kit. units $74.80-$140; under 18 free; higher rates special events; lower rates rest of yr. Crib free. TV; cable (premium). Pool; wading pool. Restaurant 7 am-noon. Ck-out 11 am. Coin lndry. Business servs avail. Downhill ski 10 mi. Some in-rm whirlpools. Cr cds: A, D, DS, ER, MC, V.

⊡ ⊠ ⊠ ⊠ ⊠ ⊠

★ **KNIGHTS INN MOTEL.** *2162 Parkway (31419). 865/428-3824; fax 865/428-2564; toll-free 800/523-3919.* 65 rms, 3 story. S, D $22-$102; under 18 free; higher rates: wkends, hols, special events. Crib $5. TV; cable (premium). Pool. Complimentary coffee in lobby. Restaurant opp 11 am-11 pm. Ck-out 11 am. Downhill ski 10 mi. Refrigerators. Cr cds: A, DS, MC, V.

⊠ ⊠ ⊠ ⊠ SC

★ **MAPLES MOTOR INN.** *2959 Parkway (37868), ½ mi N on US 441. 865/453-8883; res 888/453-8883.* 63 rms, 2 story. Mar-Dec: S $26-$85; D $36-$95; each addl $5; suites $79-$135; higher rates: some hols, special events. Closed rest of yr. Crib $5. TV; cable (premium). Pool. Complimentary coffee in lobby. Restaurant nearby. Ck-out 11 am. Some whirlpools, fireplaces. Picnic tables, grills. Cr cds: DS, MC, V.

⊡ ⊠ ⊠ ⊠

★★ **MCAFEE INN.** *3756 Parkway (37863). 865/453-3490; fax 865/429-5432; toll-free 800/925-4443.* 127 rms, 3 story. June-Aug, Oct: S, D $73-$119; higher rates: hols, special events; lower rates rest of yr. Crib $5. TV; cable (premium). Heated pool; wading pool, whirlpool. Complimentary continental bkfst, coffee in rms. Restaurant adj 7 am-9 pm. Ck-out 11 am. Business servs avail. Downhill ski 5

mi. Refrigerators; some in-rm whirlpools, wet bars. Some balconies. Picnic tables. Cr cds: A, C, D, DS, MC, V.

⊡ ⊠ ⊠ ⊠ ⊠ SC

★ **MOUNTAIN BREEZE MOTEL.** *2926 Parkway (37863). 865/453-2659; res 888/453-2659.* 71 rms. June-Oct: S, D $60-$95; kit. units $120; higher rates special events; lower rates rest of yr. Crib $4. TV; cable. Pool. Complimentary coffee in rms. Restaurant nearby. Ck-out 11 am. Refrigerators, microwaves. Cr cds: DS, MC, V.

⊡ ⊠ ⊠ ⊠ SC

★★ **NORMA DAN MOTEL.** *3864 Parkway (37863). 865/453-2403; fax 865/428-1948; toll-free 800/582-7866.* 86 rms, 3 story. S $28-$78; D $34-$88; kit. cottage $85-$134; under 18 free; wknds, hols (2-3-day min); higher rates special events. Crib free. TV; cable (premium). Heated pool; wading pool, whirlpool. Complimentary coffee in lobby. Restaurant opp 7 am-10 pm. Ck-out 11 am. Coin lndry. Meeting rms. Business servs avail. Downhill ski 7 mi. Many refrigerators. Balconies. Picnic tables. Cr cds: A, C, D, DS, MC, V.

⊡ ⊠ ⊠ ⊠ ⊠

★ **PARKVIEW MOTEL.** *2806 Parkway (37863). 865/453-5051; toll-free 800/239-9116.* 39 rms, 1-2 story. June-Oct: S, D $58-$90; higher rates some events; lower rates Mar-May, Nov-late Dec. Closed rest of yr. TV; cable. Heated pool. Complimentary coffee in lobby. Restaurant adj 7 am-10 pm. Ck-out 11 am. Cr cds: A, D, DS, MC, V.

⊡ ⊠ ⊠ ⊠

★★ **RAMADA INN.** *4010 Parkway (37862). 865/453-1823; fax 865/429-8462; toll-free 800/523-3919.* 123 rms, 3 story. No elvtr. Mid-May-Oct: S, D $29-$115; suites $49-$195; under 18 free; higher rates special events; lower rates rest of yr, under 18 free. TV; cable. Heated pool; whirlpool. Complimentary coffee in lobby. Restaurant nearby. Ck-out 11 am. Business servs avail. Downhill/x-country ski 7 mi. Refrigerators. Cr cds: A, D, DS, MC, V.

⊡ ⊠ ⊠ ⊠ ⊠ SC

★ **RIVERCHASE MOTEL.** *3709 Parkway (37863). 865/428-1299; fax 865/453-1678; res 888/754-3316.* 105 rms, 4 story. June-Oct: S, D

$60-$95; each addl $5; higher rates hol wkends; lower rates rest of yr. Crib $10. TV. Heated pool. Restaurant opp 7 am-10 pm. Ck-out 11 am. Downhill ski 7 mi. Miniature golf. Some in-rm whirlpools. Cr cds: A, DS, MC, V.

★ **RIVER PLACE INN.** *3223 Parkway (37863). 865/453-0801; toll-free 800/ 428-5590. www.riverplaceinnatpigeon forge.com.* 52 rms, 2 story. June-Aug, Oct: S $78.95; D $89.95; each addl $5; under 12 free; lower rates rest of yr. Parking lot. Pool, whirlpool. TV; cable. Restaurant 6:30 am-9:50 pm. Ck-out 11 am, ck-in 3 pm. Golf, 18 holes. Picnic facilities. Cr cds: DS, MC, V.

★★ **RIVERSIDE MOTOR LODGE.** *3575 Parkway (37863). 865/453-5555; fax 865/453-5555.* 56 kit. suites, 5 story. May-Oct: kit. suites $99-$150; each addl after 4, $5; under 16 free; lower rates rest of yr. TV; cable (premium). Indoor pool; whirlpool. Complimentary coffee in lobby. Restaurant nearby. Ck-out 11 am. Cr cds: A, DS, MC, V.

★ **RODEWAY INN MOUNTAIN SKIES.** *4236 Parkway (37863), on US 441. 865/453-3530; fax 865/453-3530; toll-free 800/523-3919.* 116 rms, 2-3 story. No elvtr. May-Oct: S, D $26-$108; suite $62-$138; family rates; higher rates special events; lower rates rest of yr. TV; cable. Pool. Ck-out 11 am. Downhill ski 10 mi. Refrigerators. Cr cds: A, C, D, DS, MC, V.

★ **TENNESSEE MOUNTAIN LODGE.** *3571 Parkway (37868). 865/ 453-4784; fax 865/453-3612; toll-free 800/446-1674.* 50 rms, 3 story. May-Oct: S, D $28-$60; each addl $5; higher rates special events; lower rates rest of yr. Crib $2. TV; cable. Heated pool; wading pool. Restaurant adj 7 am-9:30 pm. Ck-out 11 am. Business servs avail. Downhill ski 6 mi. Refrigerators. On river. Cr cds: A, DS, MC, V.

★ **TRAVELODGE.** *4025 Parkway (37863). 865/453-9081; fax 865/428-*

3240; *res 800/345-6799.* 181 rms, 2 story. May-mid-Nov: S, D $59-$125; each addl $9; golf package; higher rates: hols, football wkends, special events; lower rates rest of yr. Crib free. TV; cable. Indoor pool; wading pool, whirlpool. Playground. Ck-out 11 am. Meeting rms. Business servs avail. Downhill ski 10 mi. Cr cds: A, C, D, DS, MC, V.

★★ **VALLEY FORGE INN.** *2795 Parkway (37863). 865/453-7770; fax 865/429-3816; toll-free 800/544-8749.* 171 rms, 4 story. June-Aug, Oct: S, D $62.50-$92.50; suites $10-$50 addl; higher rates: wkends, hols, special events; lower rates rest of yr. Crib $4. TV; cable. 2 pools, 1 indoor; wading pool, whirlpool. Complimentary continental bkfst. Restaurant opp 6 am-9 pm. Ck-out 11 am. Coin lndry. Downhill ski 10 mi. Some in-rm whirlpools, refrigerators. Some balconies. On river. Cr cds: A, DS, MC, V.

B&Bs/Small Inns

★★ **DAY DREAMS COUNTRY INN.** *2720 Colonial Dr (37863). 865/428-0370; toll-free 800/377-1469. Email daydreams@sprynet.com; www.day dreamscountryinn.com.* 6 rms, 2 story. No rm phones. S $69-$109; D $79-$119; each addl $15; under 2 free. Crib free. TV; cable (premium), VCR avail (free movies). Complimentary full bkfst; afternoon refreshments. Restaurants nearby. Ck-out 11 am, ck-in 3 pm. Downhill/x-country ski 10 mi. Antiques. Screened-in porches. Totally nonsmoking. Cr cds: DS, MC, V.

★★ **HILTON'S BLUFF B&B INN.** *2654 Valley Hights Dr (37863), US 321S S to Valley Heights Dr. 865/428-9765; fax 865/428-8997; toll-free 800/441-4188. www.hiltonsbluff.com.* 10 rms, 2 story. S, D $129; each addl $20; under 9 free. Parking lot. TV; cable (premium), VCR avail, CD avail. Complimentary full bkfst, newspaper. Restaurant nearby. Ck-out 11 am, ck-in 3 pm. Meeting rm. Business servs avail. Golf. Tennis, 12 courts. Downhill skiing. Hiking trail. Picnic facilities. Cr cds: A, MC, V.

Restaurants

★ **APPLE TREE INN.** *3215 Parkway (37868), US 441.* 865/453-4961. Specializes in spoon bread. Soup, salad bar. Hrs: 6:30 am-10 pm. Closed Jan-mid-Mar. Res accepted. Bkfst $1.50-$5.29; lunch $1.50-$6.95; dinner $4.25-$11. Child's menu. Parking. Family-owned. Cr cds: A, MC, V.

★ **OLD MILL.** *164 Old Mill Ave (37863).* 865/429-3463. Specializes in prime rib, seafood, fried chicken. Hrs: 7 am-9 pm. Bkfst $5.25-$8.75; lunch $5.95-$8.95; dinner $9.99-$17.95. Child's menu. Parking. Art exhibits by local artists. Overlooks river. Cr cds: A, D, DS, MC, V.

Savannah (F-3)

Pop 6,547 **Elev** 436 ft **Area code** 901 **Zip** 38372

What to See and Do

Pickwick Landing Dam, Lock, and Lake. This TVA dam (113 ft high, 7,715 ft long) impounds a 53-mi-long lake with 496 miles of shoreline. Also a 1,000-ft-long navigation lock. Powerhouse visitor lobby. Navigation Museum at lock. (Daily) 14 mi S on TN 128. Phone 901/925-4346. **FREE** Adj is

Pickwick Landing State Resort Park. Approximately 1,400 acres adj to Pickwick Dam. Swimming pool, beach, fishing, boating (marina, launch, rentals); nature trails, golf, tennis, picnicking, playground, concession, cafe; camping, lodge (see). Standard fees. 15 mi S on TN 128 to TN 57. Phone 901/689-3129.

Motels/Motor Lodges

★★ **PICKWICK INN.** *TN 57 (38365), near Pickwick Dam, in state park.* 901/689-3135; fax 901/689-3606.

78 rms in 3-story lodge, 10 kit. cabins. Mar-Dec: S, D $58-$62; each addl $6; suites $175; kit. cabins (1-wk min) $540/wk; under 16 free; lower rates rest of yr. Crib free. TV; cable (premium). Pool; wading pool. Dining rm 7 am-8 pm. Ck-out 11 am. Meeting rms. Lighted tennis. 18-hole golf, pro, greens fee. Lawn games. Boat rentals. Lodge rms overlook lake; balconies. State-owned; all facilities of state park avail. Cr cds: A, D, DS, MC, V.

Sevierville

(F-7) *See also Gatlinburg, Pigeon Forge*

Founded 1795 **Pop** 7,178 **Elev** 903 ft **Area code** 865

Information Chamber of Commerce, 866 Winfield Dunn Pkwy, 37876; 865/453-6411

Motels/Motor Lodges

★★ **COMFORT INN.** *860 Winfield Dunn Parkway (37876).* 423/428-5519; fax 423/428-6700; res 800/441-0311. 95 air-cooled suites, 3 story. May-Oct: S, D $46-$159; each addl $5; under 18 free; golf plans; higher rates special events; lower rates rest of yr. Crib $7. TV; cable (premium). 2 pools, 1 indoor; wading pool, whirlpool. Complimentary continental bkfst. Complimentary coffee in rms. Restaurant nearby. Ck-out 11 am. Meeting rms. Business servs avail. Golf privileges. Downhill ski 16 mi. Refrigerators, wet bars. Balconies. Cr cds: A, C, D, DS, ER, MC, V.

★ **DAYS INN.** *1841 Parkway (37862).* 423/428-3353; fax 423/428-7613; res 800/590-4861. 100 rms, 4 story. Apr-Oct: S $58-$88; D $78-$98; each addl $5; under 17 free; higher rates special events; lower rates rest of yr. Crib free. TV; cable. Heated pool. Complimentary continental bkfst. Restaurant nearby. Ck-out 11 am. Business servs avail. Downhill ski 10 mi. Some refrigerators. Cr cds: A, C, D, DS, MC, V.

★ **DAYS INN.** *3402 Winfield Dunn Parkway (37764), I-40 Exit 407. 423/933-4500; fax 423/933-9799; res 800/304-3915; toll-free 800/329-7466.* 78 rms, 4 story. Apr-Oct: S, D $48-$88; each addl $5; under 17 free; higher rates special events; lower rates rest of yr. Crib free. TV; cable (premium). Complimentary continental bkfst. Restaurant opp 7 am-9 pm. Ck-out 11 am. Business servs avail. In-rm modem link. Heated pool. Some in-rm whirlpools. Balconies. Cr cds: A, C, D, DS, MC, V.
[D] 🏊 🖹 🐾 **SC**

★ **MIZE MOTEL.** *804 Parkway (37862). 423/453-4684; fax 423/453-0485; toll-free 800/239-9117.* 42 rms, 1-2 story, 4 kits. May-Oct: S, D $38.50-$82.50; each addl $5; kit. units $45-$125; higher rates special events; lower rates rest of yr. TV; cable (premium). Pool. Complimentary coffee. Restaurant nearby. Ck-out 11 am. Business servs avail. Picnic tables, grill. Cr cds: A, D, DS, MC, V.
[D] 🏊 🖹 🐾

★★ **OAK TREE LODGE.** *1620 Parkway (37862). 423/428-7500; fax 423/429-8603; toll-free 800/637-7002. www.pigeonforge.com.* 100 rms, 3 story, 22 suites. Mid-May-mid-Nov: S, D $59.50-$89.50; suites $79.50-$119.50; under 18 free; higher rates special events; lower rates rest of yr. Crib free. TV; cable. Heated pool. Complimentary continental bkfst. Complimentary coffee in rms. Restaurant nearby. Ck-out noon. Meeting rms. Business servs avail. Downhill/x-country ski 10 mi. Exercise equipt. Refrigerators. Balconies. Picnic tables, grills. Cr cds: A, D, DS, MC, V.
[D] 🔧 🛟 🏊 🍴 🖹 🐾 **SC**

★★ **QUALITY INN.** *3385 Winfield Dunn Parkway (37764), I-40 Exit 407, at TN 66. 423/933-7378; fax 423/933-9145; res 800/348-4652.* 78 rms, 3 story. May-Oct: S $58-$78; D $68-$98; each addl $5; suites $88-$128; under 17 free; higher rates: hols, car shows; lower rates rest of yr. TV; cable (premium). Indoor pool. Complimentary coffee in lobby. Restaurant adj 6 am-10 pm. Ck-out 11 am. Business servs avail. Downhill/x-country ski 20 mi. Balconies. Cr cds: A, C, D, DS, MC, V.
[D] 🛟 🏊 🖹 🐾 **SC**

B&B/Small Inn

★★ **LITTLE GREENBRIER LODGE.** *3685 Lyon Springs Rd (37862). 865/429-2500; fax 865/429-4093.* 10 rms, 8 with shower only, 2 share bath, 3 story. No rm phones. May-Dec: S $65; D $75-$110; lower rates rest of yr. Children over 12 yrs only. Cable TV in parlor. Complimentary full bkfst. Ck-out 11 am, ck-in 4 pm. Downhill ski 9 mi. Balconies. Antiques and Victorian decor in lodge built in 1939. Totally non-smoking. Cr cds: DS, MC, V.
🛟 🛠 🖹 🐾

Restaurant

★ **APPLEWOOD FARM HOUSE.** *240 Apple Valley Rd (37862). 865/428-1222.* Specializes in apple fritters, country ham, fried chicken. Hrs: 8 am-8:30 pm. Bkfst $4.25-$8.95; lunch $4.95-$7.95; dinner $11.95-$16.95. Child's menu. Parking. Grounds with gazebo. Apple trees along river. Cr cds: A, D, DS, MC, V.
[D]

Shelbyville (F-4)

Founded 1809 **Pop** 14,049 **Elev** 765 ft
Area code 931 **Zip** 37160
Web www.shelbyvilletn.com

Information Shelbyville & Bedford County Chamber of Commerce, 100 N Cannon Blvd; 931/684-3482 or 888/662-2525

Enshrined in the hearts and thoughts of every true citizen of Shelbyville is the Tennessee walking horse, that most noble of animals whose high-stepping dignity and high-level intelligence is annually celebrated here. There are 50 walking horse farms and training stables within a 14-mile radius of town; obtain maps at the Chamber of Commerce.

Annual Events

Spring Fun Show. Celebration grounds. Amateur and professional-class walking horses compete. Phone

931/684-5915.
Three days late
May.

**Tennessee Walking
Horse National
Celebration.** Outdoor arena at Celebration Grounds.
More than 2,100
horses participate.
Events conclude
with crowning ceremonies for world
grand champion
walking horse. For
tickets contact PO
Box 1010, 37162.
Phone 931/684-5915. Late Aug.

Bald Cypresses, Reelfoot Lake State Park

Motels/Motor Lodges

★ ★ **BEST WESTERN CELEBRATION INN.** *724 Madison St (37160).
931/684-2378; fax 931/685-4936; toll-free 800/528-1234.* 58 rms, 2 story. S
$60; D $70; each addl $8; suites $80-$100; higher rates special events. Crib
$3. TV; cable (premium), VCR avail.
Indoor pool. Complimentary continental bkfst. Restaurant nearby. Ck-out
noon. Coin lndry. Meeting rm. Exercise equipt. Cr cds: A, D, DS, MC, V.

★ **SUPER 8.** *317 N Cannon Blvd
(37160). 931/684-6050; fax 931/684-2714; res 800/800-8000; toll-free
800/622-0466. www.super8motel.com.*
76 rms, 2 story. S $49; D $55; each
addl $5; under 14 free. Crib avail,
fee. Pet accepted, some restrictions,
fee. Parking lot. Pool. TV; cable (premium). Complimentary continental
bkfst, newspaper, toll-free calls.
Restaurant. Meeting rm. Business
servs avail. Dry cleaning. Golf. Supervised children's activities. Cr cds: A,
C, D, DS, ER, JCB, MC, V.

Sweetwater

(F-6) *See also Lenoir City*

Pop 5,066 **Elev** 917 ft **Area code** 865
Zip 37874
Web www.monroecounty.com

Information Monroe County Chamber of Commerce Visitor Center,
4765 Hwy 68, Madisonville 37354;
865/442-9147 or 800/245-5428

What to See and Do

Lost Sea. Glass-bottom boats explore
the nation's largest underground lake
(4½ acres) in the Lost Sea Caverns.
Guided tours (1 hr). Temperature is
constant at 58°F. (Daily; closed Dec
25) 6 mi SE on TN 68. Phone
865/337-6616. ¢¢¢

**McMinn County Living Heritage
Museum.** The museum contains 26
exhibit areas with more than 6,000
items that reflect life in this region
during the time span from the
Cherokees to the Great Depression.
(Mon-Fri, Sat and Sun afternoons;
closed hols) 522 W Madison Ave, 13
mi S on US 11, in Athens. Phone
865/745-0329. ¢¢

Motels/Motor Lodges

★★ **BUDGET HOST INN.** *207 Hwy
68 (37874). 423/337-9357; fax
423/337-7436.* 61 rms, 2 story. Mar-Nov: S $29.95-$39.95; D $33.95-$43.95; each addl $7; under 10 free;
wkly rates; higher rates football
games; lower rates rest of yr. Crib $5.
Pet accepted; $3. TV; cable (premium), VCR avail (movies). Complimentary coffee in lobby. Restaurant
adj open 24 hrs. Ck-out 11 am. Coin
lndry. Some refrigerators, microwaves. Cr cds: A, D, DS, MC, V.

★★ **COMFORT INN.** *803 S Main St (37874), on US 11. 423/337-6646; fax 423/337-5409; toll-free 800/638-7949.* 60 rms, 2 story. S $32-$55; D $36-$55; each addl $4; under 18 free. Crib $5. Pet accepted; $5. TV; cable. Pool; wading pool. Complimentary continental bkfst. Restaurant nearby. Ck-out 11 am. Business servs avail. Pond, picnic area. Cr cds: A, C, D, DS, ER, MC, V.

[D] [≺] [⚓] [≈] [⌐] [🔥] [SC]

Restaurant

★ **DINNER BELL.** *576 Oakland Rd (37874), Exit 62. 423/337-5825.* Specializes in Southern cooking. Salad bar. Own cobblers. Hrs: 6 am-10 pm; Fri, Sat to 11 pm. Closed Dec 25. Res accepted. Bkfst $2.29-$4.79. Buffet: $3.99; lunch $1.69-$8.99. Buffet: $5.29; dinner $1.69-$8.99. Buffet: $6.29. Child's menu. Parking. Gift shop. Family-owned. Cr cds: A, D, MC, V.

[D] [SC] [⌐]

Tiptonville (E-2)

Pop 2,149 **Elev** 301 ft **Area code** 901 **Zip** 38079
Information Northwest Tennessee Tourism, PO Box 963, Martin 38237; 901/587-4213

Motels/Motor Lodges

★ **REELFOOT LAKE STATE PARK.** *TN 78 and TN 213 (38079), 8 mi N on TN 78, 3 mi E on TN 213. 901/253-7756; fax 901/253-8940.* 20 rms, 1-2 story. S, D $56; each addl $6; suites $75; under 16 free. Closed early Oct-Dec. TV; cable, VCR avail. Pool. Complimentary coffee in rms. Restaurant 7 am-8 pm. Ck-out 11 am. Meeting rms. Business servs avail. Tennis. Private patios. 3,500-ft landing strip. All facilities of Reelfoot Lake State Park avail; overlooks Reelfoot Lake. Cr cds: A, D, DS, MC, V.

[D] [⚓] [⛷] [≈] [🏃] [⛷] [🔥]

Restaurants

★ **BOYETTE'S DINING ROOM.** *Rte 1, Box 455 (Hwy 21) (38079), 2½ mi E on TN 21. 901/253-7307.* Specializes in catfish, country ham, fried chicken. Hrs: 11 am-9 pm. Closed Thanksgiving, Dec 24, 25. Res accepted. Lunch $2.50-$11; dinner $3.50-$11. Child's menu. Parking. On Reelfoot Lake. Family-owned. Cr cds: A, MC, V.

[D] [⌐]

Townsend

See also Gatlinburg, Maryville

Pop 329 **Elev** 1,036 ft **Area code** 865 **Zip** 37882
Web www.chamber.blount.tn.us/smo kymvb
Information Smoky Mountain Visitors Bureau, 7906 E Lamar Alexander Pkwy; 865/448-6134 or 800/525-6834

What to See and Do

Cades Cove. (see) 5 mi SE on TN 73, then 8 mi SW on unnumbered road in Great Smoky Mountains National Park.

Tuckaleechee Caverns. Cathedral-like main chamber is largest cavern room in eastern US; drapery formations, walkway over subterranean streams, flowstone falls; waterfalls tour. Temperature 58°F in caverns. Guided tours every 15-20 min (mid-Mar-mid-Nov, daily). 3 mi S, off US 321. Phone 865/448-2274. ¢¢¢

Motels/Motor Lodges

★★ **BEST WESTERN VALLEY INN.** *Hwy 321 (37882). 865/448-2237; fax 865/448-9957; res 800/528-1234; toll-free 800/292-4844. Email bestwestvv@aol.com.* 91 rms, 2 story, 39 suites. May-Oct: S, D $49.50-$89.50; each addl $5; suites $64.50-$125.50; lower rates rest of yr. Crib $5. Pet accepted. TV; cable (premium). 3 pools, 1 indoor; whirlpools. Complimentary continental bkfst, coffee in rms. Restaurant nearby. Ck-out 11 am. Meeting rms. Business servs avail. Lawn games. Refrigerators; some fireplaces; minibar in suites. Private patios, balconies. Covered picnic area, grill. Cr cds: A, C, D, DS, MC, V.

🅳 ⬆ ⬇ ⬇ 🔥

★ **FAMILY INNS OF AMERICA.**
7239 E Lamar Alexander Parkway (37882). 423/448-9100; fax 423/448-6140; toll-free 800/332-8282. 39 rms, 2 story, 7 suites, 8 kits. May-Oct: S $46-$63; D $48-$85; each addl $5; suites $79-$139; kit. units $54-$99; under 18 free; higher rates hols; lower rates rest of yr. TV; cable. Heated pool. Complimentary continental bkfst. Restaurant nearby. Ck-out 11 am. Business servs avail. Refrigerator in suites. Picnic tables. On river. Cr cds: A, D, DS, MC, V.

🅳 ⬆ ⬇ ⬇ 🔥 SC

★★ **HAMPTON INN.** *7824 E Lamar Alexander Parkway (37882). 423/448-9000; fax 423/448-9254. Email hampton@esper.com.* 54 rms, 2 story. Apr-Nov: S $39-$84; D $44-$89; under 18 free; higher rates special events; lower rates rest of yr. Crib free. TV; cable (premium). Pool. Complimentary continental bkfst, coffee in rms. Ck-out 11 am. Business servs avail. Refrigerators. Cr cds: A, C, D, DS, MC, V.

🅳 ⬇ ⬇ 🔥 SC

★★ **HIGHLAND MANOR MOTEL.**
7766 E Lamar Alexander Parkway (37882). 423/448-2211; fax 423/448-2312; toll-free 800/213-9462. www.highlandmanor.com. 50 rms, 2 story, 8 suites. May-Oct: S, D $49.50-$89.50; each addl $5; suites $59.50-$109.50; kit. units $89.50; family, wkly rates; golf plans; lower rates rest of yr. Crib $3. TV; cable (premium). Pool; wading pool. Complimentary continental bkfst. Restaurant opp 7 am-11 pm. Ck-out 11 am. Meeting rms. Business servs avail. 18-hole golf privileges, greens fee $32, pro. Exercise equipt. Refrigerators. Balconies. Picnic tables. Opp river. Cr cds: A, C, D, DS, MC, V.

🅳 ⬇ 🏊 ⬇ 🔥 SC

★★ **TALLEY HO INN.** *8314 TN 73 (37882), ¼ mi off US 321. 865/448-2465; fax 865/448-3913.* 46 rms, 2 story. June-Labor Day, Oct: S, D $42-$72; each addl $5; suites $79-$102; under 12 free; lower rates rest of yr.

Crib $5. TV; cable. Heated pool; wading pool. Restaurant 7 am-9 pm. Ck-out 11 am. Meeting rm. Business servs avail. Tennis. Many refrigerators. Private patios, balconies. Cr cds: A, D, DS, MC, V.

🅳 ⬆ 🏊 🏊 ⬇ ⬇ 🔥 🅟

B&B/Small Inn

★★★ **RICHMONT INN.** *220 Winterberry Ln (37882), Old Tuckaleechee Rd to Laurel Valley. 865/448-6751; fax 865/448-6480. Email richmontinn@worldnet. att.com; www.thesmokies.com/richmont_inn.* 12 rms, 3 story, 1 suite. No rm phones. S, D $95-$200; each addl $35. Children over 12 yrs only. Complimentary full bkfst, coffee in rms. Ck-out 10:30 am, ck-in 3 pm. Gift shop. Golf privileges. Exercise equipt. Lawn games. Built in style of Appalachian cantilever barn. Many antques. View of Rich Mountain. Totally nonsmoking. Cr cds: A, DS, MC, V.

🅳 🏋 🏊 ⬇ 🔥 🅟

Cottage Colony

★ **PIONEER CABINS AND GUEST FARM.** *253 Boat Gunnel Rd (37882). 865/448-6100; fax 865/448-9652. thesmokies.com/pioneer_cabins/.* 7 kit. cabins, 1-2 story. (2-day min): cabins $97.50-$130; each addl $10; wkly rates. Crib free. TV; VCR. Restaurant nearby. Ck-out 11 am, ck-in 3 pm. Grocery ¼ mi. Coin lndry. Hiking. Porches. Picnic tables, grills. On 47 private acres; fishing pond, petting farm. Cr cds: A, DS, MC, V.

🅳 ⬆ 🔥

Union City

(E-2) *See also Tiptonville*

Pop 10,513 **Elev** 337 ft **Area code** 901 **Zip** 38261

What to See and Do

Davy Crockett Cabin. Frontiersman's cabin is now a museum with period artifacts; grave of Crockett's mother is on grounds. (Memorial Day-Labor Day) 20 mi S on US 45W, in Rutherford. Phone 901/665-7166. ¢

ATTRACTION LIST

Attraction names are listed in alphabetical order followed by a symbol identifying their classification and then city. The symbols for classification are: [A] for Annual Events, [S] for Seasonal Events, and [W] for What to See and Do.

82nd Airborne Div War Memorial Museum [W] *Fayetteville, NC*
Abraham Lincoln Birthplace National Historic Site [W] *Elizabethtown, KY*
Abraham Lincoln Birthplace National Historic Site [W] *Hodgenville, KY*
Abraham Lincoln Museum [W] *Harrogate, TN*
Acadian Unit [W] *New Orleans, LA*
Acadian Village: A Museum of Acadian Heritage and Culture [W] *Lafayette, LA*
A Country Christmas [A] *Nashville, TN*
A Day at the Docks [A] *South Brunswick Islands, NC*
Adelina Patti's House and Courtyard [W] *New Orleans, LA*
Adventureland Theme Park [W] *Dothan, AL*
Aerial Tramway-Ober Gatlinburg Ski Resort [W] *Gatlinburg, TN*
A.G. Rhodes Memorial Hall [W] *Atlanta, GA*
Agricultural Museum [W] *Nashville, TN*
Agricultural Museum of Stuttgart [W] *Stuttgart, AR*
Aiken-Rhett House [W] *Charleston, SC*
AKIMA East Tennessee Discovery Center & AKIMA Planetarium [W] *Knoxville, TN*
Alabama Constitution Village [W] *Huntsville, AL*
Alabama Department of Archives and History [W] *Montgomery, AL*
Alabama Jubilee [A] *Decatur, AL*
Alabama Music Hall of Fame [W] *Florence, AL*
Alabama Music Hall of Fame [W] *Sheffield, AL*
Alabama National Fair [A] *Montgomery, AL*
Alabama Renaissance Faire [A] *Florence, AL*
Alabama Shakespeare Festival [W] *Montgomery, AL*
Alabama Sports Hall of Fame Museum [W] *Birmingham, AL*

Alabama State Docks [W] *Mobile, AL*
Alabama State University [W] *Montgomery, AL*
Albany Museum of Art [W] *Albany, GA*
Albemarle Craftsman's Fair [A] *Elizabeth City, NC*
Alben W. Barkley Monument [W] *Paducah, KY*
Alexander H. Stephens [W] *Washington, GA*
Alexandria Museum of Art [W] *Alexandria, LA*
Alice Walker: A Driving Tour [W] *Eatonton, GA*
Allatoona Lake [W] *Cartersville, GA*
Alliance Theatre Company [W] *Atlanta, GA*
American Adventures [W] *Marietta, GA*
American Dance Festival [S] *Durham, NC*
American Printing House for the Blind [W] *Louisville, KY*
American Rose Center [W] *Shreveport, LA*
American Saddle Horse Museum [W] *Lexington, KY*
Americus Historic Driving Tour [W] *Americus, GA*
Amicalola Falls State Park [W] *Dahlonega, GA*
An Appalachian Summer [S] *Boone, NC*
Anchuca [W] *Vicksburg, MS*
Andalusia Mardi Gras Parade [A] *New Iberia, LA*
Anderson County Fair [A] *Anderson, SC*
Andersonville Historic Fair [A] *Andersonville, GA*
Andersonville National Cemetery [W] *Andersonville, GA*
Andersonville National Historic Site [W] *Americus, GA*
Andersonville National Historic Site [W] *Andersonville, GA*
Andersonville Trail, The [W] *Perry, GA*
Andrew Jackson State Park [W] *Rock Hill, SC*

Andrew Low House [W] *Savannah, GA*

Angola Prison Rodeo [A] *St. Francisville, LA*

Anna Ruby Falls [W] *Dahlonega, GA*

Anna Ruby Falls [W] *Helen, GA*

Annie Miller's Swamp & Marsh Tours [W] *Houma, LA*

Anniston Museum of Natural History [W] *Anniston, AL*

Anniversary of the Landing of d'Iberville [A] *Ocean Springs, MS*

Antebellum houses [W] *Port Gibson, MS*

Antiques Fair [A] *Burlington, NC*

Antoine's [W] *New Orleans, LA*

Appalachian Celebration [A] *Morehead, KY*

Appalachian Fair [A] *Johnson City, TN*

Appalachian Music & Craft Festival [A] *Oak Ridge, TN*

Appalachian National Scenic Trail [W] *Dahlonega, GA*

Appalachian Wagon Train [A] *Chatsworth, GA*

Aquarium of the Americas [W] *New Orleans, LA*

Archives and History Building [W] *Jackson, MS*

Arkansas Air Museum [W] *Fayetteville, AR*

Arkansas All-Arabian Horse Show [A] *Little Rock & North Little Rock, AR*

Arkansas Alligator Farm & Petting Zoo [W] *Hot Springs & Hot Springs National Park, AR*

Arkansas Arts Center [W] *Little Rock & North Little Rock, AR*

Arkansas Entertainers Hall of Fame [W] *Pine Bluff, AR*

Arkansas Folk Festival [A] *Mountain View, AR*

Arkansas Horse Park [W] *Murfreesboro, AR*

Arkansas Museum of Natural Resources [W] *El Dorado, AR*

Arkansas-Oklahoma State Fair [A] *Fort Smith, AR*

Arkansas Post Museum [W] *Arkansas Post National Memorial, AR*

Arkansas Post National Memorial [W] *Dumas, AR*

Arkansas Post National Memorial [W] *Pine Bluff, AR*

Arkansas Repertory Theatre [W] *Little Rock & North Little Rock, AR*

Arkansas State Fair and Livestock Show [A] *Little Rock & North Little Rock, AR*

Arkansas State Fiddlers' Contest [A] *Mountain View, AR*

Arkansas State University [W] *Jonesboro, AR*

Arkansas Symphony Orchestra [W] *Little Rock & North Little Rock, AR*

Arkansas Territorial Restoration [W] *Little Rock & North Little Rock, AR*

Arlington [W] *Birmingham, AL*

Armored Vehicle Presentation [A] *Fort Knox, KY*

Artfest [S] *Knoxville, TN*

Art Museum [W] *Durham, NC*

Art Museum [W] *Lexington, KY*

Arts & Science Center for Southeast Arkansas [W] *Pine Bluff, AR*

Arts Alive [A] *Florence, SC*

Arts Center of Catawba Valley [W] *Hickory, NC*

Arts Center of the Ozarks [W] *Springdale, AR*

Arts Council of Spartanburg, The [W] *Spartanburg, SC*

Arts in the Park [A] *Meridian, MS*

Artsplosure Spring Arts Festival [A] *Raleigh, NC*

Asheboro Fall Festival [A] *Asheboro, NC*

Ashe County Cheese Factory [W] *Jefferson, NC*

Asheville Art Museum [W] *Asheville, NC*

Asheville Community Theatre [W] *Asheville, NC*

Ashland [W] *Lexington, KY*

Atchafalaya Basin Airboat tours [W] *Morgan City, LA*

Athenaeum, The [W] *Columbia, TN*

Athens State College [W] *Athens, AL*

Atlanta Botanical Garden [W] *Atlanta, GA*

Atlanta Cyclorama [W] *Atlanta, GA*

Atlanta Dogwood Festival [A] *Atlanta, GA*

Atlanta History Center [W] *Atlanta, GA*

Atlanta History Museum [W] *Atlanta, GA*

Atlanta State Farmers' Market [W] *Atlanta, GA*

Atlanta Steeplechase [A] *Atlanta, GA*

Atlantic Beach King Mackerel Tournament [A] *Morehead City, NC*

Attmore-Oliver House [W] *New Bern, NC*

Auburn University [W] *Auburn, AL*

Audubon Park and Zoological Garden [W] *New Orleans, LA*

Audubon Pilgrimage [A] *St. Francisville, LA*

Audubon Swamp Garden [W] *Charleston, SC*

Augusta Invitational Rowing Regatta [A] *Augusta, GA*

Augusta Museum of History [W] *Augusta, GA*

Augusta Opera Association [S] *Augusta, GA*

Augusta State University [W] *Augusta, GA*

Augusta Symphony Orchestra [S] *Augusta, GA*

Auto or streetcar tour of universities and Audubon Park [W] *New Orleans, LA*

Auto Racing [A] *Atlanta, GA*

Auto racing [S] *Charlotte, NC*

Auto racing [S] *Hickory, NC*

Auto tour [W] *Shiloh National Military Park, TN*

Auto tours [W] *Hot Springs & Hot Springs National Park, AR*

Auto tour to City Park and Lake Pontchartrain [W] *New Orleans, LA*

Auxiliary Theater [W] *Savannah, GA*

Ave Maria Grotto [W] *Cullman, AL*

Avery Island [W] *New Iberia, LA*

Azalea Dogwood Festival [A] *Dothan, AL*

Azalea Trail [A] *Lafayette, LA*

Azalea Trail Festival [S] *Mobile, AL*

Babyland General Hospital [W] *Helen, GA*

Baker Creek [W] *Greenwood, SC*

Bandstand and Peristyle, [W] *New Orleans, LA*

Barataria Preserve Unit [W] *New Orleans, LA*

Barber House [W] *Valdosta, GA*

Bardstown Historical Museum [W] *Bardstown, KY*

Barkley Dam, Lock, and Lake [W] *Cadiz, KY*

Barkley Lock and Dam [W] *Gilbertsville, KY*

Barren River Dam and Lake [W] *Glasgow, KY*

Barren River Lake State Resort Park [W] *Glasgow, KY*

Bathhouse Row [W] *Hot Springs & Hot Springs National Park, AR*

Bath House Show [W] *Hot Springs & Hot Springs National Park, AR*

Bath State Historic Site [W] *Washington, NC*

Battlefield Park [W] *Jackson, MS*

Battle-Friedman House [W] *Tuscaloosa, AL*

Battle of Pleasant Hill Re-Enactment [A] *Many, LA*

Battle Re-Enactment [A] *Fayetteville, AR*

Battles for Chattanooga Museum [W] *Chattanooga, TN*

Battleship *North Carolina* [W] *Wilmington, NC*

Battleship Memorial Park, USS *Alabama* [W] *Mobile, AL*

Baxter County Fair [A] *Mountain Home, AR*

Bay Fest [A] *Mobile, AL*

Bayou Folk Museum [W] *Natchitoches, LA*

Beach Music Festival [A] *Jekyll Island, GA*

Beale Street [W] *Memphis, TN*

Beale Street Music Festival [A] *Memphis, TN*

Bean Fest and Great Arkansas Championship Outhouse Race [A] *Mountain View, AR*

Bear Creek [W] *Russellville, AL*

Beaufort by the Sea Music Festival [A] *Beaufort, NC*

Beaufort Historic Site [W] *Beaufort, NC*

Beau Fort Plantation [W] *Natchitoches, LA*

Beaufort Shrimp Festival [A] *Beaufort, SC*

Beaufort Water Festival [A] *Beaufort, SC*

Beauregard-Keyes House and Garden [W] *New Orleans, LA*

"Beauvoir"—Jefferson Davis Home and Presidential Library [W] *Biloxi, MS*

Beaver Creek Wilderness [W] *Somerset, KY*

Beaver Lake [W] *Rogers, AR*

Beck Cultural Exchange Center-Museum of Black History and Culture [W] *Knoxville, TN*

Beech Bend Park [W] *Bowling Green, KY*

Behringer-Crawford Museum [W] *Covington (Cincinnati Airport Area), KY*

Bellamy Mansion Museum of History and Design Arts [W] *Wilmington, NC*

Bellarmine College [W] *Louisville, KY*

Belle Meade [W] *Nashville, TN*

Belle of Hot Springs. [W] *Hot Springs & Hot Springs National Park, AR*

Bellevue [W] *La Grange, GA*

Bellingrath Gardens and Home [W] *Mobile, AL*

BellSouth Golf Classic [A] *Atlanta, GA*

Bell Theatre (1939) [W] *Pineville, KY*

Belmont Mansion [W] *Nashville, TN*

Ben Hawes State Park [W] *Owensboro, KY*

Bennett's Mill Bridge [W] *Ashland, KY*

Bennett Place State Historic Site [W] *Durham, NC*

Bentonville Battleground State Historic Site [W] *Dunn, NC*

Berea Craft Festival [A] *Berea, KY*
Berman Museum [W] *Anniston, AL*
Bernheim Arboretum and Research Forest [W] *Shepherdsville, KY*
Bernheim Forest [W] *Bardstown, KY*
Berry College [W] *Rome, GA*
Bible Museum [W] *Eureka Springs, AR*
Bible Museum [W] *Monroe and West Monroe, LA*
Biedenharn Family House [W] *Monroe and West Monroe, LA*
Biedenharn Museum of Coca-Cola Memorabilia [W] *Vicksburg, MS*
Bienville National Forest [W] *Mendenhall, MS*
Bienville National Forest [W] *Meridian, MS*
Big Bone Lick State Park [W] *Walton, KY*
Big Oak [W] *Thomasville, GA*
Big River Arts & Crafts Festival [A] *Henderson, KY*
Big Rock Blue Marlin Tournament [A] *Morehead City, NC*
Big South Fork National River/Recreation Area [W] *Cumberland Falls State Resort Park, KY*
Big Spring International Park [W] *Huntsville, AL*
Big Spring Jam [A] *Huntsville, AL*
Biltmore Estate [A] *Asheville, NC*
Biltmore Homespun Shops [W] *Asheville, NC*
Birmingham Botanical Gardens [W] *Birmingham, AL*
Birmingham Civil Rights Institute [W] *Birmingham, AL*
Birmingham-Jefferson Convention Complex [W] *Birmingham, AL*
Birmingham Museum of Art [W] *Birmingham, AL*
Birmingham-Southern College [W] *Birmingham, AL*
Birmingham Zoo [W] *Birmingham, AL*
Birthplace of the Frog Exhibit [W] *Greenville, MS*
Black Gold Festival [A] *Hazard, KY*
Black Heritage Tour [W] *Selma, AL*
Blanchard Springs Caverns [W] *Mountain View, AR*
Blessing of the Fleet [A] *Biloxi, MS*
Blessing of the Fleet [A] *Mobile, AL*
Blessing of the Fleet [A] *Pass Christian, MS*
Blessing of the Shrimp Fleet [A] *Darien, GA*
Blessing of the Shrimp Fleet [A] *Houma, LA*
Bluegrass in the Park [A] *Henderson, KY*
Blue Grass Stakes [A] *Lexington, KY*
Blue-Gray Football Classic [A] *Montgomery, AL*

Blue Heron Mining Community [W] *Cumberland Falls State Resort Park, KY*
Blue Licks Battlefield State Park [W] *Maysville, KY*
Blue Mountain Lake [W] *Paris, AR*
Blue Ridge Barbecue [A] *Tryon, NC*
Blues Festival [A] *Baton Rouge, LA*
Blue Springs State Park [W] *Ozark, AL*
Blues to the Point—Two Rivers Blues Festival [A] *Carrollton, KY*
Bluff Hall [W] *Demopolis, AL*
Boating, fishing, swimming. Lake James [W] *Morganton, NC*
Boat tours [W] *Morganton, NC*
Boat trips [W] *Gulfport, MS*
Bobby Davis Memorial Park [W] *Hazard, KY*
Bobby Davis Park Museum [W] *Hazard, KY*
Bob Jones University [W] *Greenville, SC*
Bob Jones University Collection of Religious Art [W] *Greenville, SC*
Bonne Fete [A] *Baton Rouge, LA*
Bon Secour National Wildlife Refuge [W] *Gulf Shores, AL*
Booker T. Washington Monument [W] *Tuskegee, AL*
Booker T. Washington State Park [W] *Chattanooga, TN*
Boone County Heritage Museum [W] *Harrison, AR*
Boone Hall Plantation [W] *Charleston, SC*
Botanical Gardens of Asheville [W] *Asheville, NC*
Bouligny Plaza [W] *New Iberia, LA*
Bourbon County Fair [A] *Paris, KY*
Bragg-Mitchell Mansion [W] *Mobile, AL*
Brasstown Bald Mountain-Visitor Information Center [W] *Hiawassee, GA*
Breaks Interstate Park [W] *Pikeville, KY*
Brenau University [W] *Gainesville, GA*
Brices Cross Roads National Battlefield Site [W] *Tupelo, MS*
Brickfest [A] *Malvern, AR*
Brimstone Historical Society Museum [W] *Lake Charles, LA*
Bringhurst Park [W] *Alexandria, LA*
Brookgreen Gardens [W] *Georgetown, SC*
Brooks Shaw & Son Old Country Store [W] *Jackson, TN*
Brownell Memorial Park & Carillon Tower [W] *Morgan City, LA*
Brown-Pusey Community House [W] *Elizabethtown, KY*
Browns Crossing Craftsmen Fair [A] *Milledgeville, GA*

Brulatour Courtyard, [W] *New Orleans, LA*

Brunswick Town-Fort Anderson State Historic Site [W] *Southport, NC*

Bry Hall Art Gallery [W] *Monroe and West Monroe, LA*

Buccaneer State Park [W] *Pass Christian, MS*

Buckhorn Lake State Resort Park [W] *Hazard, KY*

Buck's Pocket State Park [W] *Guntersville, AL*

Bull Durham Blues Festival [A] *Durham, NC*

Bull Run Steam Plant [W] *Oak Ridge, TN*

Bull Shoals State Park [W] *Bull Shoals Lake Area, AR*

Bunker Hill Covered Bridge [W] *Hickory, NC*

Burgwin-Wright House [W] *Wilmington, NC*

Burns Park [W] *Little Rock & North Little Rock, AR*

Burritt Museum & Park [W] *Huntsville, AL*

Bussey Brake Reservoir [W] *Bastrop, LA*

Butts-Mehre Heritage Museum [W] *Athens, GA*

Cable News Network studio tour [W] *Atlanta, GA*

Cades Cove [W] *Townsend, TN*

Cadiz Public Use Area [W] *Cadiz, KY*

Cadron Settlement Park [W] *Conway, AR*

Caesar's Head [W] *Greenville, SC*

Cahawba [W] *Selma, AL*

Cahawba Festival [A] *Selma, AL*

Cairo Museum [W] *Vicksburg, MS*

Cajun Jack's [W] *Morgan City, LA*

Callaway Gardens [W] *Pine Mountain (Harris County), GA*

Callaway Plantation [W] *Washington, GA*

Calloway County Fair [A] *Murray, KY*

Camping [W] *Cumberland Gap National Historical Park, KY*

Canal Street Depot [W] *Natchez, MS*

Canoe trips [W] *London, KY*

Cape Fear Botanical Garden [W] *Fayetteville, NC*

Cape Fear Museum [W] *Wilmington, NC*

Cape Lookout National Seashore [W] *Beaufort, NC*

Capital Area Visitor Center [W] *Raleigh, NC*

Capital Expo Festival [A] *Frankfort, KY*

Capitol Arts Center [W] *Bowling Green, KY*

Capitol Grounds [W] *Baton Rouge, LA*

Capitoline Wolf Statue [W] *Rome, GA*

Captain J.N. Maffitt River Cruises [W] *Wilmington, NC*

Captain Sandy's Plantation Tours [W] *Georgetown, SC*

Cardome Centre [W] *Georgetown, KY*

Carlen House Museum [W] *Mobile, AL*

Carl Sandburg Home National Historic Site [W] *Hendersonville, NC*

Carnival Memphis [A] *Memphis, TN*

Carnton Plantation and McGavock Confederate Cemetery [W] *Franklin, TN*

Carolina Beach State Park [W] *Wilmington, NC*

Carolina Coliseum [W] *Columbia, SC*

Carolina Dogwood Festival [A] *Statesville, NC*

Carolina Downhome Blues Festival & Fine Arts [A] *Camden, SC*

Carolina Power & Light Company Visitors Center [W] *Southport, NC*

Carr Fork Lake [W] *Hazard, KY*

Carriage House [W] *Newport, AR*

Carroll Chimes Bell Tower [W] *Covington (Cincinnati Airport Area), KY*

Carroll County Fair [A] *Berryville, AR*

Carroll County Heritage Center [W] *Berryville, AR*

Carroll Reece Museum [W] *Johnson City, TN*

Carter Caves State Resort Park [W] *Olive Hill, KY*

Carter Display [W] *Americus, GA*

Carter House [W] *Franklin, TN*

Carter House Christmas Candlelight Tour [A] *Franklin, TN*

Carters Lake [W] *Chatsworth, GA*

Casa Faurie (Brennan's) [W] *New Orleans, LA*

Casey Jones Home and Railroad Museum [W] *Jackson, TN*

Casey Jones Railroad Museum [W] *Yazoo City, MS*

Casey Jones Village [W] *Jackson, TN*

Casinos [W] *Biloxi, MS*

Cataloochee Ski Area [W] *Maggie Valley, NC*

Catawba County Museum of History [W] *Hickory, NC*

Catawba Cultural Center [W] *Rock Hill, SC*

Catawba Science Center [W] *Hickory, NC*

Cathedral Basilica of the Assumption [W] *Covington (Cincinnati Airport Area), KY*

Cathedral Garden [W] *New Orleans, LA*

Cathedral of the Immaculate Conception [W] *Mobile, AL*

Cave Hill Cemetery [W] *Louisville, KY*

Cave Run Lake [W] *Morehead, KY*

Cave tours [W] *Mammoth Cave National Park, KY*

C. Bickham Dickson Park [W] *Shreveport, LA*

Cecil B. Day Butterfly Center [W] *Pine Mountain (Harris County), GA*

Cedar Creek [W] *Russellville, AL*

Cedar Grove [W] *Vicksburg, MS*

Cedar Island to Ocracoke Ferry Service [W] *Ocracoke (Outer Banks), NC*

Celebration of Traditional Music Festival [A] *Berea, KY*

Cemetery & Voodoo History Tour [W] *New Orleans, LA*

Centennial Olympic Park [W] *Atlanta, GA*

CenterFest [A] *Durham, NC*

Center for Cultural Arts [W] *Gadsden, AL*

Center of Banking [W] *New Orleans, LA*

Central Kentucky Steam and Gas Engine Show [A] *Paris, KY*

Central Mississippi Fair [A] *Kosciusko, MS*

Central Park [W] *Ashland, KY*

Central Shelby Historic District Walking Tour [W] *Shelby, NC*

CFMA Cajun Music and Food Festival [A] *Lake Charles, LA*

Chalmette Unit [W] *New Orleans, LA*

Chamber of Commerce [W] *Charleston, SC*

Chapel [W] *Tuskegee, AL*

Chapel of the Cross [W] *Chapel Hill, NC*

Charleston Museum, The [W] *Charleston, SC*

Charles Towne Landing [W] *Charleston, SC*

Charlotte Coliseum [W] *Charlotte, NC*

Charlotte Hawkins Brown Memorial State Historic Site [W] *Greensboro, NC*

Charlotte Museum of History and Alexander Homesite, The [W] *Charlotte, NC*

Chastain Memorial Park [W] *Atlanta, GA*

Chattahoochee National Forest [W] *Chatsworth, GA*

Chattahoochee National Forest [W] *Dahlonega, GA*

Chattahoochee Valley Art Museum [W] *La Grange, GA*

Chattanooga African American History Museum [W] *Chattanooga, TN*

Chattanooga Choo-Choo [W] *Chattanooga, TN*

Chattooga Wild and Scenic River [W] *Clayton, GA*

Cheaha State Park [W] *Talladega, AL*

Cheatham Lake, Lock, and Dam [W] *Nashville, TN*

Cheekwood [W] *Nashville, TN*

Chehaw Park [W] *Albany, GA*

Chehaw Wild Animal Park [W] *Albany, GA*

Chemin-a-Haut State Park [W] *Bastrop, LA*

Cherokee Dam and Lake [W] *Morristown, TN*

Cherokee National Forest [W] *Johnson City, TN*

Cherry Blossom Festival [A] *Macon, GA*

Chester Frost Park [W] *Chattanooga, TN*

Chester State Park [W] *Chester, SC*

Chewacla State Park [W] *Auburn, AL*

Chickamauga and Chattanooga National Military Park [W] *Chattanooga, TN*

Chickamauga and Chattanooga National Military Park [W] *Dalton, GA*

Chicot State Park [W] *Opelousas, LA*

Chief Paduke Statue [W] *Paducah, KY*

Chieftains Museum [W] *Rome, GA*

Children's Hands-on Museum [W] *Tuscaloosa, AL*

Children's Museum [W] *Rocky Mount, NC*

Children's Museum of Memphis, The [W] *Memphis, TN*

Chimney Rock Park [W] *Asheville, NC*

Chinqua-Penn Plantation [W] *Greensboro, NC*

Chitimacha Cultural Center [W] *Franklin, LA*

Chitimacha Cultural Center [W] *New Orleans, LA*

Choctaw Indian Fair [A] *Philadelphia, MS*

Chowan County Courthouse [W] *Edenton, NC*

Chretien Point Plantation [W] *Lafayette, LA*

Christ Episcopal Church [W] *Savannah, GA*

Christmas Festival of Lights [A] *Natchitoches, LA*

Christmas in Jonesborough [A] *Johnson City, TN*

Christmas in Savannah [A] *Savannah, GA*

Christmas on the River [A] *Baton Rouge, LA*

Christmas on the River [A] *Demopolis, AL*

Christmas Parade & Tour [A] *Bessemer, AL*
Christ of the Ozarks [W] *Eureka Springs, AR*
Christus Gardens [W] *Gatlinburg, TN*
Chucalissa Archaeological Museum [W] *Memphis, TN*
Churchill Downs [W] *Louisville, KY*
Churchill Weavers [W] *Berea, KY*
Church of St. Michael and All Angels, The [W] *Anniston, AL*
Church of the Holy Cross [W] *Sumter, SC*
Church-Waddel-Brumby House [W] *Athens, GA*
Circuit Playhouse [W] *Memphis, TN*
Citadel Archives Museum, The [W] *Charleston, SC*
Citadel, Military College of South Carolina, The [W] *Charleston, SC*
City Hall [W] *Macon, GA*
City Hall [W] *Savannah, GA*
City Hall Art Gallery [W] *Charleston, SC*
City Stages [A] *Birmingham, AL*
City Yacht Harbor, New Orleans Yacht Club, Southern Yacht Club [W] *New Orleans, LA*
Civil Rights Memorial [W] *Montgomery, AL*
Civil War fortifications [W] *Cumberland Gap National Historical Park, KY*
Civil War Reenactment/September Skirmish [A] *Decatur, AL*
Civil War Village of Andersonville [W] *Andersonville, GA*
Clarkco State Park [W] *Meridian, MS*
Clark County Fair [A] *Arkadelphia, AR*
Clarkson Covered Bridge [W] *Cullman, AL*
Claude D. Kelley State Park [W] *Atmore, AL*
Clemson Fest [A] *Clemson, SC*
Clemson University [W] *Clemson, SC*
Clinton Birthplace Home [W] *Hope, AR*
Clogging Hall of Fame [A] *Maggie Valley, NC*
Cloudmont Ski Resort [W] *Fort Payne, AL*
Coastal Alliance for the Arts [W] *St.Simons Island, GA*
Coca-Cola Airshow of the Ozarks [A] *Harrison, AR*
Coheelee Creek Covered Bridge [W] *Blakely, GA*
Coker Arboretum [W] *Chapel Hill, NC*
Colburn Gem and Mineral Museum [W] *Asheville, NC*
Coldwater Covered Bridge [W] *Anniston, AL*

Coleman's Crystal Mine [W] *Hot Springs & Hot Springs National Park, AR*
Colleton County Courthouse [W] *Walterboro, SC*
Colleton State Park [W] *Walterboro, SC*
Colonel Harland Sanders' Original Restaurant [W] *Corbin, KY*
Colonel Harland Sanders Museum [W] *Louisville, KY*
Colonial Park Cemetery [W] *Savannah, GA*
Columbia Museum of Art [W] *Columbia, SC*
Columbus Convention and Trade Center [W] *Columbus, GA*
Columbus Museum, The [W] *Columbus, GA*
Comedy Barn, The [W] *Pigeon Forge, TN*
"Come-See-Me" [A] *Rock Hill, SC*
Condé-Charlotte Museum House [W] *Mobile, AL*
Conecuh National Forest [W] *Evergreen, AL*
Confederate Cemetery [W] *Camden, AR*
Confederate Flag Pole [W] *Blakely, GA*
Confederate Memorial Hall [W] *Knoxville, TN*
Confederate Memorial Park [W] *Clanton, AL*
Confederate Monument [W] *Jackson, MS*
Confederate Museum [W] *New Orleans, LA*
Confederate Powder Works Chimney [W] *Augusta, GA*
Confederate Relic Room and Museum [W] *Columbia, SC*
Congaree Swamp National Monument [W] *Columbia, SC*
Congregation Mickve Israel [W] *Savannah, GA*
Consolidated Gold Mines [W] *Dahlonega, GA*
Constitution Square State Shrine [W] *Danville, KY*
Contraband Days [A] *Lake Charles, LA*
Converse Dalton Ferrell House [W] *Valdosta, GA*
Cook's Natural Science Museum [W] *Decatur, AL*
Corn Island Storytelling Festival [A] *Louisville, KY*
Cosmic Cavern [W] *Berryville, AR*
Cotile Recreation Area [W] *Alexandria, LA*
Cottage Plantation [W] *Baton Rouge, LA*
Cotton Exchange [W] *Augusta, GA*

Cotton Exchange [W] *Wilmington, NC*

Country by the Sea Music Festival [A] *Jekyll Island, GA*

Country Music Hall of Fame & Museum [W] *Nashville, TN*

Country Music Shows [S] *Eureka Springs, AR*

Country Music Wax Museum and Shopping Mall [W] *Nashville, TN*

Country Tonite Theatre [W] *Pigeon Forge, TN*

County Fair and Livestock Show [A] *Camden, AR*

County Fair and Livestock Show [A] *Malvern, AR*

Courthouse [W] *Richmond, KY*

Courthouse Museum [W] *Newport, AR*

Courthouse Square [W] *Blakely, GA*

Courthouse Square [W] *Washington, GA*

Court of Two Sisters [W] *New Orleans, LA*

Cove Lake Recreation Area [W] *Paris, AR*

Cove Lake State Park [W] *Caryville, TN*

Covered Bridge Celebration [A] *Elizabethton, TN*

Crackerland Tennis Tournament [A] *Athens, GA*

Craft shops [W] *Gatlinburg, TN*

Craftsmen's Fairs [A] *Gatlinburg, TN*

Craighead Forest Park [W] *Jonesboro, AR*

Crater of Diamonds State Park [W] *Murfreesboro, AR*

Cravens House [W] *Chattanooga, TN*

Crawford W. Long Medical Museum [W] *Commerce, GA*

Creative Discovery Museum [W] *Chattanooga, TN*

Creole Nature Trail National Scenic Byway [W] *Lake Charles, LA*

Crescent (Valdosta Garden Center), The [W] *Valdosta, GA*

Crescent Bend (Armstrong-Lockett House) and W. Perry Toms Memorial Gardens [W] *Knoxville, TN*

Crisson's Gold Mine [W] *Dahlonega, GA*

Croatan National Forest [W] *New Bern, NC*

Croft State Park [W] *Spartanburg, SC*

Crooked Creek Crawdad Days [A] *Harrison, AR*

Crowley's Ridge State Park [W] *Jonesboro, AR*

Crown Garden and Archives [W] *Dalton, GA*

Crystal Onyx Cave [W] *Cave City, KY*

Crystal Shrine Grotto [W] *Memphis, TN*

Cullman County Museum [W] *Cullman, AL*

Cumberland County Fair [A] *Crossville, TN*

Cumberland Falls State Resort Park [W] *Corbin, KY*

Cumberland Gap National Historical Park [W] *Harrogate, TN*

Cumberland Island National Seashore [W] *Brunswick, GA*

Cumberland Island National Seashore [W] *Jekyll Island, GA*

Cumberland Island National Seashore [W] *St.Simons Island, GA*

Cumberland River, [W] *Williamsburg, KY*

Cumberland Science Museum [W] *Nashville, TN*

Cupola House [W] *Edenton, NC*

Cypremort Point State Park [W] *Franklin, LA*

Cypress Gardens [W] *Charleston, SC*

Dahlonega Courthouse Gold Museum State Historic Site [W] *Dahlonega, GA*

Daisy International Air Gun Museum [W] *Rogers, AR*

Dale Hollow Lake State Resort Park [W] *Monticello, KY*

Daniel Boone's Grave [W] *Frankfort, KY*

Daniel Boone Festival [A] *Barbourville, KY*

Daniel Boone National Forest [W] *Barbourville, KY*

Daniel Boone National Forest [W] *Hazard, KY*

Daniel Boone National Forest [W] *London, KY*

Daniel Boone National Forest [W] *Williamsburg, KY*

Daniel Boone Pioneer Festival [A] *Winchester, KY*

Dan Nicholas Park [W] *Salisbury, NC*

Dauphin Island Campground [W] *Dauphin Island, AL*

Davenport House [W] *Savannah, GA*

David Crockett State Park [W] *Lawrenceburg, TN*

Davie Poplar [W] *Chapel Hill, NC*

Daviess County Fair [A] *Owensboro, KY*

Davis Planetarium [W] *Jackson, MS*

Davy Crockett Cabin [W] *Union City, TN*

Davy Crockett Days [A] *Union City, TN*

Day in the Park [A] *High Point, NC*

Decatur County Fall Festival and Fair [A] *Bainbridge, GA*

Decorative Arts Museum [W] *Little Rock & North Little Rock, AR*

DeGray Lake [W] *Arkadelphia, AR*

DeGray Lake Resort State Park [W] *Arkadelphia, AR*

DeKalb County VFW Agricultural Fair [A] *Fort Payne, AL*

Delta Blues and Heritage Festival [A] *Greenville, MS*

Delta Cultural Center [W] *Helena, AR*

Delta Jubilee [A] *Clarksdale, MS*

Delta National Forest [W] *Yazoo City, MS*

Delta Queen, Mississippi Queen, and *American Queen* [W] *Memphis, TN*

Denny Chimes [W] *Tuscaloosa, AL*

Department of Energy's Graphite Reactor, The [W] *Oak Ridge, TN*

Desha County Museum [W] *Dumas, AR*

DeSoto Caverns Park [W] *Birmingham, AL*

DeSoto Caverns Park [W] *Sylacauga, AL*

DeSoto State Park [W] *Fort Payne, AL*

Destrehan Plantation [W] *New Orleans, LA*

Devil's Den State Park [W] *Fayetteville, AR*

Devou Park [W] *Covington (Cincinnati Airport Area), KY*

Dexter Avenue King Memorial Baptist Church [W] *Montgomery, AL*

Dexter Harding House [W] *Pine Bluff, AR*

Diana Wortham Theatre [W] *Asheville, NC*

Discovery Place [W] *Charlotte, NC*

Dixie National Livestock Show [A] *Jackson, MS*

Dixon Gallery and Gardens [W] *Memphis, TN*

Dixon-Stevenson House [W] *New Bern, NC*

D'Lo Water Park [W] *Mendenhall, MS*

Dogwood Arts Festival [A] *Knoxville, TN*

Dogwood Festival [A] *Fayetteville, NC*

Dogwood Festival [A] *Hopkinsville, KY*

Dogwood Trail Celebration [A] *Paducah, KY*

Dollywood [W] *Pigeon Forge, TN*

Double-barreled cannon [W] *Athens, GA*

Douglas Dam and Lake [W] *Sevierville, TN*

Downtown Mall Trolley [W] *Memphis, TN*

Downtown Riverfront [W] *Baton Rouge, LA*

Drayton Hall [W] *Charleston, SC*

Dreher Island State Park [W] *Newberry, SC*

Dr. Josephus Hall House [W] *Salisbury, NC*

Dr. Thomas Walker State Historic Site [W] *Barbourville, KY*

Dryden Potteries [W] *Hot Springs & Hot Springs National Park, AR*

Dublin-Laurens Museum [W] *Dublin, GA*

Dueling Oaks, [W] *New Orleans, LA*

Duff Green [W] *Vicksburg, MS*

Duke's Wallace Wade Stadium [W] *Durham, NC*

Duke Chapel [W] *Durham, NC*

Duke Homestead State Historic Site [W] *Durham, NC*

Duke Libraries [W] *Durham, NC*

Duke Medical Center [W] *Durham, NC*

Duke Power State Park [W] *Statesville, NC*

Duke University [W] *Durham, NC*

Dulcimer Harp Festival [A] *Gatlinburg, TN*

Duncan Tavern Historic Shrine [W] *Paris, KY*

Dunleith [W] *Natchez, MS*

Duplin Wine Cellars [W] *Warsaw, NC*

Earl May Boat Basin and Park [W] *Bainbridge, GA*

East Carolina Village of Yesteryear [W] *Greenville, NC*

East Tennessee State University [W] *Johnson City, TN*

Ebenezer Baptist Church [W] *Atlanta, GA*

Edisto Beach State Park [W] *Charleston, SC*

Edisto Memorial Gardens [W] *Orangeburg, SC*

Edisto Riverfest [A] *Walterboro, SC*

Edmondston-Alston House [W] *Charleston, SC*

Egyptian Event [A] *Lexington, KY*

Eichold-Heustis Medical Museum [W] *Mobile, AL*

Eiffel Tower Day & Hot Air Balloon Festival [A] *Paris, TN*

Eighth Air Force Museum [W] *Bossier City, LA*

Elijah Clark [W] *Washington, GA*

Elizabethan Gardens [W] *Manteo, NC*

Elizabeth II State Historic Site [W] *Manteo, NC*

Elk River [W] *Florence, AL*

Ellis Library, Convocation Center, and Museum [W] *Jonesboro, AR*

Elsong Gardens & Conservatory [W] *Monroe and West Monroe, LA*

Elvis Presley International Tribute Week [A] *Memphis, TN*

Elvis Presley Park and Museum [W] *Tupelo, MS*

Emerald Mound [W] *Natchez, MS*

Emerald Village [W] *Little Switzerland, NC*

Emy-Lou Biedenharn Foundation [W] *Monroe and West Monroe, LA*

Energy Central [W] *Port Gibson, MS*

Enid Lake and Dam [W] *Sardis, MS*

ENSAT Center [W] *Athens, GA*

E.P. "Tom" Sawyer State Park [W] *Louisville, KY*

Etowah Indian Mounds Historic Site and Archaeological Area [W] *Cartersville, GA*

Eufaula National Wildlife Refuge [W] *Eufaula, AL*

Eufaula Pilgrimage [A] *Eufaula, AL*

Eureka Springs & North Arkansas Railway [W] *Eureka Springs, AR*

Eureka Springs Gardens [W] *Eureka Springs, AR*

Eureka Springs Historical Museum [W] *Eureka Springs, AR*

Eureka Springs Trolley [W] *Eureka Springs, AR*

Eutaw Springs Battlefield Site [W] *Santee, SC*

Evangeline Monument [W] *St. Martinville, LA*

Evangeline Oak [W] *St. Martinville, LA*

Exhibit Hall [W] *Savannah, GA*

Exploreum Museum of Science [W] *Mobile, AL*

Factors Walk [W] *Savannah, GA*

Fall Celebration [A] *Hiawassee, GA*

Fall Color Cruise & Folk Festival [A] *Chattanooga, TN*

Fall Fiesta of Arts [A] *Sumter, SC*

Fall House & Garden Candlelight Tours [A] *Charleston, SC*

Fall on the Flint Festival [A] *Albany, GA*

Falls Lake State Recreation Area [W] *Raleigh, NC*

Fall Tour of Homes and Gardens [A] *Beaufort, SC*

Family Circle Magazine Cup Tennis Tournament [A] *Charleston, SC*

Farmington [W] *Louisville, KY*

Fasching Karnival [S] *Helen, GA*

Faulkner Conference [A] *Oxford, MS*

Faulkner County Fair [A] *Conway, AR*

Fernbank Natural History Museum [W] *Atlanta, GA*

Fernbank Science Center [W] *Atlanta, GA*

Ferry Service. Southport to Fort Fisher [W] *Southport, NC*

Festival International de Louisiane [A] *Lafayette, LA*

Festival in the Park [A] *Charlotte, NC*

Festival of Arts [A] *Birmingham, AL*

Festival of Houses & Gardens [A] *Charleston, SC*

Festival of the Arts [A] *Brevard, NC*

Festival of the Bluegrass [A] *Lexington, KY*

Festival of the Singing River [A] *Florence, AL*

Festival of the Two Rivers [A] *Arkadelphia, AR*

Festivals Acadiens [A] *Lafayette, LA*

Filson Club, The [W] *Louisville, KY*

Fine Arts Center [W] *Fayetteville, AR*

First Baptist Church [W] *Columbia, SC*

First Creek [W] *Florence, AL*

First Presbyterian Church [W] *Columbia, SC*

First Presbyterian Church [W] *Fayetteville, NC*

First Presbyterian Church [W] *Port Gibson, MS*

First White House of the Confederacy [W] *Montgomery, AL*

Fishing [W] *Houma, LA*

Fishing and hunting [W] *Morgan City, LA*

Fishing, hunting [W] *Lake Charles, LA*

Fishing, water sports [W] *Monroe and West Monroe, LA*

Fish Trap Cut [W] *Dublin, GA*

Fishtrap Lake [W] *Pikeville, KY*

Fisk University [W] *Nashville, TN*

Flat Rock Playhouse [S] *Hendersonville, NC*

Float trips [W] *Harrison, AR*

Floral Clock [W] *Frankfort, KY*

Florence Marina State Park [W] *Lumpkin, GA*

Folk Art Center [W] *Asheville, NC*

Folly Beach County Park [W] *Charleston, SC*

Fontainebleau State Park [W] *Covington, LA*

Foothills Equestrian Nature Center (FENCE) [W] *Tryon, NC*

Forbidden Caverns [W] *Sevierville, TN*

Forkland Park [W] *Demopolis, AL*

Fort Benning [W] *Columbus, GA*

Fort Boonesborough State Park [W] *Winchester, KY*

Fort Bragg and Pope AFB [W] *Fayetteville, NC*

Fort Campbell [W] *Hopkinsville, KY*

Fort Condé Mobile Visitor Welcome Center [W] *Mobile, AL*

Fort Dobbs State Historic Site [W] *Statesville, NC*

Fort Fisher State Historic Site [W] *Southport, NC*

Fort Frederica National Monument [W] *Brunswick, GA*

Fort Frederica National Monument [W] *St.Simons Island, GA*

Fort Gaines [W] *Dauphin Island, AL*

Fort Hill [W] *Clemson, SC*

Fort Jackson [W] *Columbia, SC*

Fort Jesup State Commemorative Area [W] *Many, LA*

Fort King George State Historic Site [W] *Darien, GA*

Fort Lookout [W] *Camden, AR*

Fort Loudoun Dam and Lake [W] *Lenoir City, TN*

Fort McAllister Historic Park [W] *Savannah, GA*

Fort McPherson [W] *Atlanta, GA*

Fort Morgan [W] *Gulf Shores, AL*

Fort Morgan Museum [W] *Gulf Shores, AL*

Fort Morgan Park [W] *Gulf Shores, AL*

Fort Mountain State Park [W] *Chatsworth, GA*

Fort Nashborough [W] *Nashville, TN*

Fort Payne Opera House [W] *Fort Payne, AL*

Fort Pillow State Historic Area [W] *Covington, TN*

Fort Pulaski National Monument [W] *Savannah, GA*

Fort Pulaski National Monument [W] *Tybee Island, GA*

Fort Raleigh National Historic Site [W] *Manteo, NC*

Fort Smith Art Center [W] *Fort Smith, AR*

Fort Smith National Historic Site [W] *Fort Smith, AR*

Fort St Jean Baptiste State Commemorative Area [W] *Natchitoches, LA*

Fort Sumter National Monument [W] *Charleston, SC*

Fort Sumter Tours [W] *Charleston, SC*

Fort Toulouse/Jackson Park National Historic Landmark [W] *Montgomery, AL*

Fort Watson Battle Site and Indian Mound [W] *Santee, SC*

Fort Yargo State Park [W] *Winder, GA*

Foscue Creek Park [W] *Demopolis, AL*

Founder's Day [A] *Hodgenville, KY*

Founders Day [A] *Abraham Lincoln Birthplace National Historic Site, KY*

Founders Memorial Garden [W] *Athens, GA*

Foxfire Museum and Center [W] *Clayton, GA*

Fox Theatre [W] *Atlanta, GA*

Francis Beidler Forest [W] *Charleston, SC*

Francis Marion National Forest [W] *Charleston, SC*

Franklin D. Roosevelt State Park [W] *Pine Mountain (Harris County), GA*

Freedom Fest [A] *Murray, KY*

Freedom Weekend Aloft [A] *Greenville, SC*

French Market, [W] *New Orleans, LA*

French Quarter Festival [A] *New Orleans, LA*

Friendship Oak, The [W] *Pass Christian, MS*

Frog Fantasies [W] *Eureka Springs, AR*

From This Day Forward [S] *Morganton, NC*

Frontier Days [A] *Hope, AR*

Frozen Head State Park [W] *Oak Ridge, TN*

Frozen Niagara [W] *Mammoth Cave National Park, KY*

F. Scott and Zelda Fitzgerald Museum [W] *Montgomery, AL*

Ft Pike State Commemorative Area [W] *Slidell, LA*

Furniture Discovery Center [W] *High Point, NC*

Gadsden Museum of Fine Arts [W] *Gadsden, AL*

Gaineswood [W] *Demopolis, AL*

Gallier House Museum [W] *New Orleans, LA*

Gann Museum [W] *Benton, AR*

Garden and Home Pilgrimage [A] *Ocean Springs, MS*

Garden Club Pilgrimage [A] *Biloxi, MS*

Garden Club Pilgrimage [A] *Pascagoula, MS*

Garden Club Pilgrimage [A] *Pass Christian, MS*

Garden District,, The [W] *New Orleans, LA*

Gas Boat Drag Championships [A] *High Point, NC*

Gascoigne Bluff [W] *St. Simons Island, GA*

Gatlinburg Space Needle [W] *Gatlinburg, TN*

General Burnside State Park [W] *Somerset, KY*

General Butler State Resort Park [W] *Carrollton, KY*

General Coffee State Park [W] *Douglas, GA*

General Jackson [W] *Nashville, TN*

George A. Dickel Distillery [W] *Manchester, TN*

George Payne Cossar State Park [W] *Sardis, MS*

George Washington Carver Museum [W] *Tuskegee, AL*

Georgia Agrirama, 19th-Century Living History Museum [W] *Tifton, GA*

Georgia Capitol Museum [W] *Atlanta, GA*

Georgia College [W] *Milledgeville, GA*

Georgia Heritage Festival [A] *Savannah, GA*

Georgia Historical Society [W] *Savannah, GA*

Georgia Mountain Fair [A] *Hiawassee, GA*

Georgia Museum of Art [W] *Athens, GA*

Georgia Music Hall of Fame [W] *Macon, GA*

Georgia Renaissance Festival [S] *Atlanta, GA*

Georgia Sea Island Festival [A] *St.Simons Island, GA*

Georgia Southern University [W] *Statesboro, GA*

Georgia Southwestern College [W] *Americus, GA*

Georgia Sports Hall of Fame [W] *Macon, GA*

Georgia State Fair [A] *Macon, GA*

Georgia Veterans Memorial State Park [W] *Cordele, GA*

Germantown Museum [W] *Minden, LA*

Gertrude Herbert Institute of Art [W] *Augusta, GA*

Ghost Town in the Sky [W] *Maggie Valley, NC*

Gibbes Museum of Art [W] *Charleston, SC*

Glencairn Garden [W] *Rock Hill, SC*

Gliding Spectacular [A] *Nags Head (Outer Banks), NC*

Golden Isles [W] *Darien, GA*

Golden Isles Art Festival [A] *St.Simons Island, GA*

Golden Memorial State Park [W] *Philadelphia, MS*

Golden Pond Visitor Center [W] *Land Between the Lakes, KY*

Gold Miners' Camp [W] *Dahlonega, GA*

Gold Panning Competition [A] *Dahlonega, GA*

Gold Rush Days [A] *Dahlonega, GA*

Gorgas House [W] *Tuscaloosa, AL*

Governor's Cup Regatta [A] *Henderson, NC*

Governor's Derby Breakfast [A] *Frankfort, KY*

Governor's Mansion [W] *Baton Rouge, LA*

Governor's Mansion [W] *Columbia, SC*

Governor's Mansion [W] *Frankfort, KY*

Governor's Mansion [W] *Jackson, MS*

Governor William Blount Mansion [W] *Knoxville, TN*

Graceland [W] *Memphis, TN*

Grand Bois Inter Tribal [A] *Houma, LA*

Grand Circuit Meet [A] *Lexington, KY*

Grandfather Mountain [W] *Linville, NC*

Grandfather Mountain Highland Games [A] *Linville, NC*

Grandfather Mountain Nature Photography Weekend [A] *Linville, NC*

Grand Gulf Military Park [W] *Port Gibson, MS*

Grand Ole Opry [W] *Nashville, TN*

Grand Ole Opry Tours [W] *Nashville, TN*

Grand Opera House [W] *Macon, GA*

Grand Prix of Chattanooga [W] *Chattanooga, TN*

Grand Promenade, [W] *Hot Springs & Hot Springs National Park, AR*

"The Grand Strand" [W] *Myrtle Beach, SC*

Grant Park [W] *Atlanta, GA*

Grapevine Recreation Area [W] *Pikeville, KY*

Grave and monument [W] *Andrew Johnson National Historic Site, TN*

Graves of Thomas Wolfe(1900-1938) and O. Henry (William Sydney Porter) (1862-1910) [W] *Asheville, NC*

Gray Line bus tours [W] *Atlanta, GA*

Gray Line bus tours [W] *Charleston, SC*

Gray Line bus tours [W] *Memphis, TN*

Gray Line bus tours [W] *Nashville, TN*

Gray Line bus tours [W] *New Orleans, LA*

Gray Line bus tours [W] *Savannah, GA*

Gray Line City tours [W] *Mobile, AL*

Gray Line Water Tours [W] *Charleston, SC*

Grayson Lake State Park [W] *Olive Hill, KY*

Great Arkansas PigOut Festival [A] *Morrilton, AR*

Greater Baton Rouge Zoo [W] *Baton Rouge, LA*

Greater Greensboro Chrysler Classic Golf Tournament [A] *Greensboro, NC*

Greater Gulf State Fair [A] *Mobile, AL*

Great Mississippi River Balloon Race Weekend [A] *Natchez, MS*

Great Passion Play, The [S] *Eureka Springs, AR*

Great Smoky Mountains National Park [W] *Gatlinburg, TN*

Greenbo Lake State Resort Park [W] *Ashland, KY*

Greenfield Gardens [W] *Wilmington, NC*

Green-Meldrim House [W] *Savannah, GA*

Green River Lake State Park [W] *Campbellsville, KY*

Greensboro Historical Museum [W] *Greensboro, NC*

Green Street Historical District [W] *Gainesville, GA*

Green Street Station [W] *Gainesville, GA*

Greenville Museum of Art [W] *Greenville, NC*

Greenwood [W] *Baton Rouge, LA*

Grevemberg House [W] *Franklin, LA*

Greyhound racing. Mobile Greyhound Park [W] *Mobile, AL*

Greyhound racing. VictoryLand Track [W] *Montgomery, AL*

Guilford College [W] *Greensboro, NC*

Guilford Courthouse National Military Park [W] *Greensboro, NC*

Gulf Islands National Seashore [W] *Gulfport, MS*

Gulf State Park [W] *Gulf Shores, AL*

Guntersville Dam and Lake [W] *Guntersville, AL*

Hagan-Stone Park [W] *Greensboro, NC*

Hall of History Museum [W] *Bessemer, AL*

Hamel's Amusement Park [W] *Shreveport, LA*

Hammond Museum of Bells [W] *Eureka Springs, AR*

Hampton Park [W] *Charleston, SC*

Hampton Plantation State Park [W] *Georgetown, SC*

Hampton-Preston Mansion [W] *Columbia, SC*

Hands On! Regional Museum [W] *Johnson City, TN*

Hanging Rock State Park [W] *Winston-Salem, NC*

Hank Williams' grave [W] *Montgomery, AL*

Hank Williams, Sr Boyhood Home & Museum [W] *Greenville, AL*

Hanover House [W] *Clemson, SC*

Hardin County Fair [A] *Elizabethtown, KY*

Hardin Planetarium [W] *Bowling Green, KY*

Harness racing [S] *Lexington, KY*

Harold Kaminski House [W] *Georgetown, SC*

Harris House [W] *Augusta, GA*

Harrison Bay State Park [W] *Chattanooga, TN*

Harrodsburg Pottery and Craft Shop [W] *Harrodsburg, KY*

Hart House [W] *Eufaula, AL*

Hartsville Museum [W] *Hartsville, SC*

Hartwell Lake [W] *Toccoa, GA*

Harvest Festival [A] *Forrest City, AR*

Harvest Homecoming [A] *Harrison, AR*

Hay House [W] *Macon, GA*

H. B. Robinson Nuclear Information Center [W] *Hartsville, SC*

Headley-Whitney Museum [W] *Lexington, KY*

Headquarters House [W] *Fayetteville, AR*

Health Adventure, The [W] *Asheville, NC*

Heart of Georgia Tours [W] *Macon, GA*

Heflin House Museum [W] *Sardis, MS*

Helen Keller Days [A] *Florence, AL*

Helen Keller Festival [A] *Sheffield, AL*

Henderson State University Museum [W] *Arkadelphia, AR*

Hendrix College [W] *Conway, AR*

Henrietta II Paddlewheel Riverboat Cruises [W] *Wilmington, NC*

Hensley Settlement [W] *Cumberland Gap National Historical Park, KY*

Herb Harvest Fall Festival [A] *Mountain View, AR*

Heritage Foundation Town & Country Tour [A] *Franklin, TN*

Heritage Holidays [A] *Rome, GA*

Heritage Museum and Village [W] *Baton Rouge, LA*

Heritage Trail [W] *Franklin, TN*

Hermann-Grima Historic House [W] *New Orleans, LA*

Hermitage, The [W] *Nashville, TN*

Herrington Lake [W] *Danville, KY*

Heyward-Washington House [W] *Charleston, SC*

Hickory Knob Resort [W] *Greenwood, SC*

Hickory Museum of Art [W] *Hickory, NC*

High Hope Steeplechase [A] *Lexington, KY*

Highland Games and Gathering of Scottish Clans [A] *Glasgow, KY*

High Museum of Art [W] *Atlanta, GA*

High Rock Lake [W] *Lexington, NC*

Hillbilly Days Spring Festival [A] *Pikeville, KY*

Hillbilly Hoedown Music Theatre [W] *Pigeon Forge, TN*

Hilton Head Island Celebrity Golf Tournament [A] *Hilton Head Island, SC*

Historic [W] *Mammoth Cave National Park, KY*

Historic "Charpentier" [W] *Lake Charles, LA*

Historical Library [W] *Madisonville, KY*

Historic areas. Silk Stocking District [W] *Talladega, AL*

Historic Bethabara Park [W] *Winston-Salem, NC*

Historic Brattonsville [W] *Rock Hill, SC*

Historic buildings [W] *Dublin, GA*

Historic District [W] *Carrollton, KY*

Historic District [W] *Franklin, TN*

Historic District [W] *Johnson City, TN*

Historic districts [W] *Louisville, KY*

Historic Edenton [W] *Edenton, NC*

Historic Edenton Visitor Center [W] *Edenton, NC*

Historic Ghostwalk [A] *Elizabeth City, NC*

Historic Guided Trolley Tour [W] *Milledgeville, GA*

Historic Halifax State Historic Site [W] *Roanoke Rapids, NC*

Historic Houses [W] *Athens, GA*

Historic Main Street [W] *Winchester, KY*

Historic Mobile Tours [A] *Mobile, AL*

Historic Morganton Festival [A] *Morganton, NC*

Historic New Orleans Collection [W] *New Orleans, LA*

Historic New Orleans Custom House [W] *New Orleans, LA*

Historic Old Salem [W] *Winston-Salem, NC*

Historic Riverview at Hobson Grove [W] *Bowling Green, KY*

Historic Savannah Waterfront Area [W] *Savannah, GA*

Historic Selma Pilgrimage [A] *Selma, AL*

Historic Stagville Center [W] *Durham, NC*

Historic Washington [W] *Maysville, KY*

Hodges Gardens [W] *Many, LA*

Hofwyl-Broadfield Plantation State Historic Site [W] *Darien, GA*

Holiday Tour of Homes [A] *Madison, GA*

Holla Bend National Wildlife Refuge [W] *Russellville, AR*

Holmes County State Park [W] *Kosciusko, MS*

Holmes State Forest [W] *Hendersonville, NC*

Homemakers' Harvest Festival [A] *Clayton, GA*

Homeplace-1850, The [W] *Land Between the Lakes, KY*

Homes & Gardens Tour [A] *St.Simons Island, GA*

Homespun [A] *Athens, AL*

Hope Plantation [W] *Williamston, NC*

Hopkins County Fair [A] *Madisonville, KY*

Hopsewee Plantation [W] *Georgetown, SC*

Horace Williams House [W] *Chapel Hill, NC*

Horn in the West [S] *Boone, NC*

Horse Cave Theatre [W] *Horse Cave, KY*

Horse farms [W] *Lexington, KY*

Horse racing [A] *Camden, SC*

Horse racing [S] *Covington (Cincinnati Airport Area), KY*

Horse racing [S] *Lake Charles, LA*

Horse racing [S] *Louisville, KY*

Horse Racing. Ellis Park [S] *Henderson, KY*

Horse racing. Fair Grounds Racetrack [S] *New Orleans, LA*

Horseshoe, The [W] *Columbia, SC*

Horseshoe Bend National Military Park [W] *Alexander City, AL*

Horton House [W] *Jekyll Island, GA*

Horton Mill Covered Bridge [W] *Gadsden, AL*

Hospice League Horizons Balloon Fest [A] *Burlington, NC*

Hot Air Balloon Race & Festival [A] *Helen, GA*

Hot Springs Mountain Tower [W] *Hot Springs & Hot Springs National Park, AR*

Hot Springs National Park [W] *Arkadelphia, AR*

Hot Springs National Park [W] *Benton, AR*

Hot Springs National Park [W] *Malvern, AR*

Houmas House [W] *Baton Rouge, LA*

House and Garden Tour [A] *Southern Pines, NC*

House in the Horseshoe State Historic Site [W] *Sanford, NC*

House on Ellicott Hill, The [W] *Natchez, MS*

Houston Memorial Library and Museum [W] *Athens, AL*

Houston Museum of Decorative Arts [W] *Chattanooga, TN*

Huguenot Church [W] *Charleston, SC*

Hummel Planetarium and Space Theater [W] *Richmond, KY*

Hunter Museum of Art [W] *Chattanooga, TN*

Huntingdon College [W] *Montgomery, AL*

Hunt-Morgan House [W] *Lexington, KY*

Hunt-Phelan Home [W] *Memphis, TN*

Huntsville Depot Museum [W] *Huntsville, AL*

Huntsville Museum of Art [W] *Huntsville, AL*

Hurricane Creek Park [W] *Cullman, AL*

Hurricane Creek Public Use Area [W] *Cadiz, KY*

Ice Cream Social [A] *Berryville, AR*

Ida Cason Callaway Memorial Chapel, [W] *Pine Mountain (Harris County), GA*

IMAX 3D Theater [W] *Chattanooga, TN*

Imperial Calcasieu Museum [W] *Lake Charles, LA*

Indian Mound and Museum [W] *Florence, AL*

Indian Mounds [W] *Baton Rouge, LA*

Indian Mountain State Park [W] *Jellico, TN*

Indian Museum [W] *Blakely, GA*

Indian Springs State Park [W] *Eatonton, GA*

Indian Springs State Park [W] *Forsyth, GA*

Indian Summer Days [A] *Eufaula, AL*

International Bar-B-Q Festival [A] *Owensboro, KY*

International Folk Festival [A] *Maggie Valley, NC*

International Friendship Bell [W] *Oak Ridge, TN*

International Grand Championship Walking Horse Show [A] *Murfreesboro, TN*

International Motorsports Hall of Fame [W] *Talladega, AL*

International Towing and Recovery Hall of Fame and Museum [W] *Chattanooga, TN*

I.P. Stanback Museum and Planetarium [W] *Orangeburg, SC*

Iredell County Fair [A] *Statesville, NC*

Irvin S. Cobb Memorial [W] *Paducah, KY*

Isabel Anderson Comer Museum & Arts Center [W] *Sylacauga, AL*

Isleñ;o Center [W] *New Orleans, LA*

Isle of Capri Casino [W] *Bossier City, LA*

Ivy Green [W] *Florence, AL*

Ivy Green [W] *Sheffield, AL*

Jack Daniel Distillery [W] *Manchester, TN*

Jackson Brewery [W] *New Orleans, LA*

Jackson County Fair [A] *Pascagoula, MS*

Jackson Historic District [W] *Jackson, LA*

Jacksonport State Park [W] *Newport, AR*

Jackson Square, [W] *New Orleans, LA*

Jackson Zoological Park [W] *Jackson, MS*

James Iredell House [W] *Edenton, NC*

James K. Polk Memorial State Historic Site [W] *Charlotte, NC*

James Oglethorpe Monument [W] *Brunswick, GA*

Janssen Park [W] *Mena, AR*

Japanese Gardens [W] *Birmingham, AL*

Jarrell Plantation State Historic Site [W] *Forsyth, GA*

Jasmine Hill Gardens [W] *Montgomery, AL*

J.B. Speed Art Museum [W] *Louisville, KY*

J.C. Raulston Arboretum at NC State University [W] *Raleigh, NC*

Jean Lafitte National Historical Park and Preserve [W] *New Orleans, LA*

Jefferson County Courthouse [W] *Louisville, KY*

Jefferson County Historical Museum [W] *Pine Bluff, AR*

Jefferson Davis Monument State Shrine [W] *Hopkinsville, KY*

Jekyll Island Club Historic District [W] *Jekyll Island, GA*

Jenkins' Ferry State Historic Monument [W] *Malvern, AR*

Jenny Wiley State Resort Park [W] *Prestonsburg, KY*

Jenny Wiley Theatre [S] *Prestonsburg, KY*

Jim Beam American Outpost [W] *Bardstown, KY*

Jim Beam Stakes Race [A] *Covington (Cincinnati Airport Area), KY*

Jim Bowie Museum [W] *Opelousas, LA*

Jimmie Rodgers Memorial Festival [A] *Meridian, MS*

Jimmie Rodgers Museum [W] *Meridian, MS*

Jimmy Carter National Historic Site [W] *Americus, GA*

Joe Wheeler State Park [W] *Florence, AL*

John C. Stennis Space Center [W] *Gulfport, MS*

John C. Stennis Space Center [W] *Slidell, LA*

John F. Kennedy Special Warfare Museum [W] *Fayetteville, NC*

John James Audubon State Park [W] *Henderson, KY*

Johnson Homestead [W] *Andrew Johnson National Historic Site, TN*

John S. Sibley Horticultural Center [W] *Pine Mountain (Harris County), GA*

John Tanner State Park [W] *Carrollton, GA*

John W. Kyle State Park [W] *Sardis, MS*

John Wright Stanly House [W] *New Bern, NC*

Jonesborough [W] *Johnson City, TN*

Jonesborough Days [A] *Johnson City, TN*

Jonesborough History Museum [W] *Johnson City, TN*

Jones Lake State Park [W] *Lumberton, NC*

Jonquil Festival [A] *Hope, AR*

Josephine Tussaud Wax Museum [W] *Hot Springs & Hot Springs National Park, AR*

Joseph Manigault House [W] *Charleston, SC*

Joseph T. Smitherman Historic Building [W] *Selma, AL*

Joyce Kilmer-Slickrock Wilderness [W] *Robbinsville, NC*

J. Percy Priest Lake [W] *Nashville, TN*

J. Strom Thurmond Dam and Lake [W] *Washington, GA*

Jubilee City Fest [A] *Montgomery, AL*

Juliette Gordon Low Birthplace [W] *Savannah, GA*

Jump-Off Rock [W] *Hendersonville, NC*

Jungle Gardens [W] *New Iberia, LA*

Junior League Horse Show [A] *Lexington, KY*

Ka-Do-Ha Indian Village, The [W] *Murfreesboro, AR*

Kahal Kadosh Beth Elohim [W] *Charleston, SC*

Kaleidoscope [A] *Chattanooga, TN*

Kalmia Gardens of Coker College [W] *Hartsville, SC*

Kemper Williams Park [W] *Morgan City, LA*

Kenan Stadium [W] *Chapel Hill, NC*

Kenlake State Resort Park [W] *Cadiz, KY*

Kenlake State Resort Park [W] *Gilbertsville, KY*

Kenlake State Resort Park [W] *Murray, KY*

Kennesaw Civil War Museum [W] *Marietta, GA*

Kennesaw Mountain National Battlefield Park [W] *Atlanta, GA*

Kennesaw Mountain National Battlefield Park [W] *Cartersville, GA*

Kennesaw Mountain National Battlefield Park [W] *Marietta, GA*

Kent House [W] *Alexandria, LA*

Kentucky Action Park [W] *Cave City, KY*

Kentucky Apple Festival [A] *Prestonsburg, KY*

Kentucky Center for the Arts [W] *Louisville, KY*

Kentucky Dam [W] *Gilbertsville, KY*

Kentucky Dam Village State Resort Park [W] *Gilbertsville, KY*

Kentucky Derby [A] *Louisville, KY*

Kentucky Derby Festival [A] *Louisville, KY*

Kentucky Derby Museum [W] *Louisville, KY*

Kentucky Diamond Caverns [W] *Park City, KY*

Kentucky Down Under/Mammoth Onyx Cave [W] *Horse Cave, KY*

Kentucky Fair and Exposition Center [W] *Louisville, KY*

Kentucky Guild of Artists & Craftsmen's Fair [A] *Berea, KY*

Kentucky Hardwood Festival [A] *Morehead, KY*

Kentucky Heartland Festival [A] *Elizabethtown, KY*

Kentucky Highlands Museum [W] *Ashland, KY*

Kentucky History Museum [W] *Frankfort, KY*

Kentucky Horse Park [W] *Lexington, KY*

Kentucky Kingdom—The Thrill Park [W] *Louisville, KY*

Kentucky Library [W] *Bowling Green, KY*

Kentucky Military History Museum [W] *Frankfort, KY*

Kentucky Museum [W] *Bowling Green, KY*

Kentucky Scottish Weekend [A] *Carrollton, KY*

Kentucky State Fair [A] *Louisville, KY*

Kentucky State University [W] *Frankfort, KY*

Kentucky Vietnam Veterans Memorial [W] *Frankfort, KY*

Kerr Reservoir [W] *Henderson, NC*

Kettle Creek Battleground [W] *Washington, GA*

Kids Farm Education Center [W] *Danville, KY*

Kincaid Lake State Park [W] *Williamstown, KY*

King-Bazemore House [W] *Williamston, NC*

King Birthplace [W] *Atlanta, GA*

King Biscuit Blues Festival [A] *Helena, AR*

King Classic King Mackerel Tournament [A] *South Brunswick Islands, NC*

Kings Mountain State Park [W] *Rock Hill, SC*

Kingsport Fun Fest [A] *Kingsport, TN*

Kisatchie National Forests [W] *Alexandria, LA*

Kiwanis West Kentucky-McCracken County Fair [A] *Paducah, KY*

Koger Center for the Arts [W] *Columbia, SC*

Kolomoki Mounds State Park [W] *Blakely, GA*

Konriko Rice Mill and Company Store [W] *New Iberia, LA*

Kosciusko Museum-Information Center [W] *Kosciusko, MS*

Kudzu Festival [A] *Holly Springs, MS*

Labor Day Fest [A] *Memphis, TN*

Lady Luck Riverboat Casino [W] *Natchez, MS*

Lafayette Museum [W] *Lafayette, LA*

Lafayette Natural History Museum, Planetarium, and Nature Station [W] *Lafayette, LA*

Lafayette Square, [W] *New Orleans, LA*

"Lafitte's Blacksmith Shop" [W] *New Orleans, LA*

Lake Barkley State Resort Park [W] *Cadiz, KY*

Lake Bistineau State Park [W] *Minden, LA*

Lake Catherine State Park [W] *Hot Springs & Hot Springs National Park, AR*

Lake Catherine State Park [W] *Malvern, AR*

Lake Charles State Park [W] *Walnut Ridge, AR*

Lake Chatuge [W] *Hiawassee, GA*

Lake Chehaw [W] *Albany, GA*

Lake Chicot State Park [W] *Dumas, AR*

Lake Cumberland [W] *Somerset, KY*

Lake Cumberland State Resort Park [W] *Jamestown, KY*

Lake Dardanelle [W] *Russellville, AR*

Lake Dardanelle State Park [W] *Russellville, AR*

Lake End Park [W] *Morgan City, LA*

LakeFest [A] *Cornelius, NC*

Lake Fort Smith State Park [W] *Alma, AR*

Lake Frierson State Park [W] *Jonesboro, AR*

Lake Gaston [W] *Roanoke Rapids, NC*

Lake Greenwood [W] *Greenwood, SC*

Lake Guntersville State Park [W] *Guntersville, AL*

Lake Hickory [W] *Hickory, NC*

Lake Lanier Islands [W] *Buford, GA*

Lake Lanier Islands [W] *Gainesville, GA*

Lake Lurleen State Park [W] *Tuscaloosa, AL*

Lake Malone State Park [W] *Greenville, KY*

Lake Murray [W] *Columbia, SC*

Lake Norman [W] *Cornelius, NC*

Lake Oconee [W] *Eatonton, GA*

Lake Oconee [W] *Madison, GA*

Lake Ouachita State Park [W] *Hot Springs & Hot Springs National Park, AR*

Lakepoint Resort State Park [W] *Eufaula, AL*

Lake Pontchartrain [W] *New Orleans, LA*

Lake Pontchartrain Causeway, [W] *New Orleans, LA*

Lake Sinclair [W] *Milledgeville, GA*

Lake Tobesofkee [W] *Macon, GA*

Lake Walter F. George [W] *Lumpkin, GA*

Lake Winfield Scott [W] *Dahlonega, GA*

Lake Wylie [W] *Rock Hill, SC*

Land Between The Lakes [W] *Clarksville, TN*

Landmark Park [W] *Dothan, AL*

Landmarks of DeKalb Museum [W] *Fort Payne, AL*

Landsford Canal State Park [W] *Rock Hill, SC*

Lapham-Patterson House State Historic Site [W] *Thomasville, GA*

Latta Place [W] *Charlotte, NC*

Latta Plantation Park [W] *Charlotte, NC*

Laura S. Walker State Park [W] *Waycross, GA*

Laurel Grove Cemetery (South) [W] *Savannah, GA*

Laurel River Lake [W] *Corbin, KY*

Laurel Valley Village [W] *Thibodaux, LA*

Laurens Henry Cohn, Sr. Memorial Plant Arboretum [W] *Baton Rouge, LA*

Lay Dam [W] *Clanton, AL*

Leake-Ingham Building [W] *Camden, AR*

Lee Circle, [W] *New Orleans, LA*

Lee State Park [W] *Hartsville, SC*

Legend of Daniel Boone, The [S] *Harrodsburg, KY*

Lenoir-Rhyne College [W] *Hickory, NC*

Levee and docks [W] *New Orleans, LA*

Levi Jackson Wilderness Road State Park [W] *London, KY*

Lexington Cemetery [W] *Lexington, KY*

Lexington County Museum Complex [W] *Columbia, SC*

Liberty Hall [W] *Frankfort, KY*

Libertyland [W] *Memphis, TN*

Library [W] *Frankfort, KY*

Lichterman Nature Center [W] *Memphis, TN*

Lighted Azalea Trail [A] *McComb, MS*

Lincoln's Birthday [A] *Abraham Lincoln Birthplace National Historic Site, KY*

Lincoln's Boyhood Home [W] *Hodgenville, KY*

Lincoln Days Celebration [A] *Hodgenville, KY*

Lincoln Heritage House [W] *Elizabethtown, KY*

Lincoln Homestead State Park [W] *Bardstown, KY*

Lincoln Jamboree [W] *Hodgenville, KY*

Lincoln Museum [W] *Hodgenville, KY*

Lincoln Parish Museum [W] *Ruston, LA*

Lindsey Miniature Village [W] *Maggie Valley, NC*

Linville Caverns [W] *Marion, NC*

Little Bear Creek [W] *Russellville, AL*

Little Red River [W] *Greers Ferry Lake Area, AR*

Little River Days [A] *Hopkinsville, KY*

Little Rock Zoo [W] *Little Rock & North Little Rock, AR*

Little Round House [W] *Tuscaloosa, AL*

Little White House Historic Site [W] *Pine Mountain (Harris County), GA*

Lloyd Wildlife Management Area [W] *Williamstown, KY*

Lobster Race [A] *Aiken, SC*

Locust Grove [W] *Louisville, KY*

Logan County Museum [W] *Paris, AR*

Logoly State Park [W] *Magnolia, AR*

Long Beach Scenic Walkway [W] *Southport, NC*

Longfellow-Evangeline State Commemorative Area [W] *St. Martinville, LA*

Longhorn Rodeo [A] *Nashville, TN*

Longue Vue House & Gardens [W] *New Orleans, LA*

Longwood [W] *Natchez, MS*

Lookout Mountain [W] *Chattanooga, TN*

Lookout Mountain Incline Railway [W] *Chattanooga, TN*

Lost Sea [W] *Sweetwater, TN*

Louis Armstrong Park [W] *New Orleans, LA*

Louisiana Arts and Science Center Riverside [W] *Baton Rouge, LA*

Louisiana Crawfish Festival [A] *New Orleans, LA*

Louisiana Passion Play [S] *Ruston, LA*

Louisiana Peach Festival [A] *Ruston, LA*

Louisiana Purchase Gardens and Zoo [W] *Monroe and West Monroe, LA*

Louisiana Shrimp and Petroleum Festival and Fair [A] *Morgan City, LA*

Louisiana State Arboretum [W] *Opelousas, LA*

Louisiana State Exhibit Museum [W] *Shreveport, LA*

Louisiana State Fair [A] *Shreveport, LA*

Louisiana State Library [W] *Baton Rouge, LA*

Louisiana State Penitentiary Museum [W] *St. Francisville, LA*

Louisiana State University and Agricultural and Mechanical College [W] *Baton Rouge, LA*

Louisiana Tech University [W] *Ruston, LA*

Louisiana Yambilee [A] *Opelousas, LA*

Louisville Falls Fountain [W] *Louisville, KY*

Louisville Presbyterian Theological Seminary [W] *Louisville, KY*

Louisville Science Center [W] *Louisville, KY*

Louisville Slugger Museum & Bat Factory [W] *Louisville, KY*

Louisville Zoo [W] *Louisville, KY*

Lovelace Athletic Museum [W] *Auburn, AL*

Lover's Oak [W] *Brunswick, GA*

Lost Colony, The [S] *Manteo, NC*

Lost Colony, The Outdoor Drama [S] *Fort Raleigh National Historic Site, NC*

Lower Commerce Street Historic District [W] *Montgomery, AL*

Lowndes County Historical Society Museum [W] *Valdosta, GA*

Loyola University [W] *New Orleans, LA*

Lum & Abner Days [A] *Mena, AR*

Mack Memorial Library [W] *Greenville, SC*

Macon County Fair [A] *Franklin (Macon County), NC*

Macon County Gemboree [A] *Franklin (Macon County), NC*

Macon Historic District [W] *Macon, GA*

Macon Museum of Arts and Sciences & Mark Smith Planetarium [W] *Macon, GA*

Madame John's Legacy [W] *New Orleans, LA*

Madewood Plantation House [W] *Thibodaux, LA*

Madison County Fair & Horse Show [A] *Richmond, KY*

Madison County Nature Trail [W] *Huntsville, AL*

Madison-Morgan Cultural Center [W] *Madison, GA*

Magevney House [W] *Memphis, TN*

Magnolia Grove [W] *Demopolis, AL*

Magnolia Hall [W] *Natchez, MS*

Magnolia Mound Plantation [W] *Baton Rouge, LA*

Magnolia Plantation and Gardens [W] *Charleston, SC*

Maifest [A] *Covington (Cincinnati Airport Area), KY*

MainStrasse Village [W] *Covington (Cincinnati Airport Area), KY*

Main Theater [W] *Savannah, GA*

Maison Le Monnier [W] *New Orleans, LA*

Majestic Middle Tennessee Fall Tour [A] *Columbia, TN*

Malbis Greek Orthodox Church [W] *Mobile, AL*

Mallory-Neely House [W] *Memphis, TN*

Mammoth Cave Chair Lift and Guntown Mountain [W] *Cave City, KY*

Mammoth Cave National Park [W] *Cave City, KY*

Mammoth Cave National Park [W] *Park City, KY*

Manship House [W] *Jackson, MS*

Mansion, The [W] *Bardstown, KY*

Marathon [W] *Mendenhall, MS*

Mardi Gras [A] *Biloxi, MS*

Mardi Gras [A] *New Orleans, LA*

Mardi Gras [A] *Pascagoula, MS*

Mardi Gras [A] *Pass Christian, MS*

Mardi Gras Celebration [A] *Gulf Shores, AL*

Margaret Mitchell House [W] *Atlanta, GA*

Marigold Festival [A] *Athens, GA*

Marine Life Oceanarium [W] *Gulfport, MS*

Maritime Museum [W] *Southport, NC*

Market House [W] *Paducah, KY*

Market House Museum [W] *Paducah, KY*

Market House Theatre [W] *Paducah, KY*

Marshes of Glynn [W] *Brunswick, GA*

Martha Vick House [W] *Vicksburg, MS*

Martin Luther King's Birthday [A] *Abraham Lincoln Birthplace National Historic Site, KY*

Martin Luther King, Jr, National Historic Site [W] *Atlanta, GA*

Mary Miller Doll Museum [W] *Brunswick, GA*

Mary Todd Lincoln House [W] *Lexington, KY*

Mary Woods II. [W] *Newport, AR*

Mason County Museum [W] *Maysville, KY*

Massee Lane Gardens [W] *Perry, GA*

Masters Golf Tournament [A] *Augusta, GA*

Masur Museum of Art [W] *Monroe and West Monroe, LA*

Maury County Fair [A] *Columbia, TN*

Maxwell AFB [W] *Montgomery, AL*

Maynard Pioneer Museum & Park [W] *Pocahontas, AR*

McCollum-Chidester House [W] *Camden, AR*

McDowell House and Apothecary Shop [W] *Danville, KY*

McElreath Hall [W] *Atlanta, GA*

McHargue's Mill [W] *London, KY*

MCI Heritage Classic [A] *Hilton Head Island, SC*

McIlhenny Company [W] *New Iberia, LA*

McKissick Museum [W] *Columbia, SC*

McMinn County Living Heritage Museum [W] *Sweetwater, TN*

McRaven Home Civil War Tour Home [W] *Vicksburg, MS*

Meadow Garden [W] *Augusta, GA*

Medical University of South Carolina [W] *Charleston, SC*

Meeman-Shelby Forest State Park [W] *Memphis, TN*

Melrose Plantation [W] *Natchez, MS*

Melrose Plantation [W] *Natchitoches, LA*

Melrose Plantation Arts & Crafts Festival [A] *Natchitoches, LA*

Melton Hill Dam and Lake [W] *Oak Ridge, TN*

Memorial Hall [W] *Chapel Hill, NC*

Memorial Tower [W] *Baton Rouge, LA*

Memories Theatre [W] *Pigeon Forge, TN*

Memphis Belle [W] *Memphis, TN*

Memphis Botanic Garden [W] *Memphis, TN*

Memphis Brooks Museum of Art [W] *Memphis, TN*

Memphis in May International Festival [A] *Memphis, TN*

Memphis International Motorsports Park [W] *Memphis, TN*

Memphis Pink Palace Museum and Planetarium [W] *Memphis, TN*

Memphis Queen [W] *Memphis, TN*

Memphis Zoo & Aquarium [W] *Memphis, TN*

Mercer University [W] *Macon, GA*

Merchant's Millpond State Park [W] *Edenton, NC*

Merle Travis Tribute [A] *Mountain View, AR*

Mid-19th-Century Townhouse [W] *New Orleans, LA*

Mid-America Science Museum [W] *Hot Springs & Hot Springs National Park, AR*

Middleton Place Gardens, House & Stableyards [W] *Charleston, SC*

Mid-South Fair and Exposition [A] *Memphis, TN*

Milbank Historic House [W] *Jackson, LA*

Miles College [W] *Birmingham, AL*

Millwood Dam and Reservoir [W] *Ashdown, AR*

Millwood State Park [W] *Ashdown, AR*

Minor Clark State Fish Hatchery [W] *Morehead, KY*

Mint Museum of Art [W] *Charlotte, NC*

Mint Museum of Craft & Design [W] *Charlotte, NC*

Miracle Worker, The [S] *Sheffield, AL*

Miss Green Riverboat Trip [W] *Mammoth Cave National Park, KY*

Mississippi Agriculture & Forestry Museum and National Agricultural Aviation Museum [W] *Jackson, MS*

Mississippi-Alabama State Fair [A] *Meridian, MS*

Mississippi Deep-Sea Fishing Rodeo [A] *Gulfport, MS*

Mississippi Museum of Art [W] *Jackson, MS*

Mississippi Petrified Forest [W] *Jackson, MS*

Mississippi Sandhill Crane National Wildlife Refuge [W] *Pascagoula, MS*

Mississippi Sports Hall of Fame and Museum [W] *Jackson, MS*

Mississippi State Fair [A] *Jackson, MS*

Mississippi State University [W] *Starkville, MS*

Mistletoe Show [A] *Elizabeth City, NC*

Mobile Museum of Art [W] *Mobile, AL*

Monmouth [W] *Natchez, MS*

Monteagle Chautauqua Assembly [S] *Monteagle, TN*

Monte Sano State Park [W] *Huntsville, AL*

Montgomery Museum of Fine Arts [W] *Montgomery, AL*

Montgomery Zoo [W] *Montgomery, AL*

Moonwalk [W] *New Orleans, LA*

Moores Creek National Battlefield [W] *Wilmington, NC*

Mooresville [W] *Decatur, AL*

Mordecai Historic Park [W] *Raleigh, NC*

Morehead-Patterson Memorial Bell Tower [W] *Chapel Hill, NC*

Morehead Planetarium [W] *Chapel Hill, NC*

Morehead State University [W] *Morehead, KY*

Morgan Row [W] *Harrodsburg, KY*

Moro Bay State Park [W] *El Dorado, AR*

Morris Museum of Art [W] *Augusta, GA*

Mossy Creek Barnyard Festival [A] *Perry, GA*

Moundville Archaeological Park [W] *Tuscaloosa, AL*

Moundville Native American Festival [A] *Tuscaloosa, AL*

Mountain Arts Center [W] *Prestonsburg, KY*

Mountain Dance and Folk Festival [A] *Asheville, NC*

Mountain Laurel Festival [A] *Pineville, KY*

Mountain Life Museum [W] *London, KY*

Mount Carmel Herb Festival [A] *Walterboro, SC*

Mount Jefferson State Park [W] *Jefferson, NC*

Mount Locust [W] *Natchez, MS*

Mount Mitchell Crafts Fair [A] *Burnsville, NC*

Mount Mitchell State Park [W] *Asheville, NC*

Mount Mitchell State Park [W] *Little Switzerland, NC*

Mount Nebo State Park [W] *Russellville, AR*

Mr. Cason's Vegetable Garden [W] *Pine Mountain (Harris County), GA*

MSU Appalachian Collection [W] *Morehead, KY*

Mud Island [W] *Memphis, TN*

Mule Day [A] *Columbia, TN*

Municipal Art Gallery [W] *Jackson, MS*

Murphy House [W] *Montgomery, AL*

Murray's Mill [W] *Hickory, NC*

Musée Conti—Wax Museum of Louisiana Legends [W] *New Orleans, LA*

Museum of Automobiles [W] *Morrilton, AR*

Museum of Beverage Containers and Advertising [W] *Nashville, TN*

Museum of Coastal History [W] *St.Simons Island, GA*

Museum of Discovery [W] *Little Rock & North Little Rock, AR*

Museum of Early Southern Decorative Arts [W] *Winston-Salem, NC*

Museum of Geoscience [W] *Baton Rouge, LA*

Museum of Mobile [W] *Mobile, AL*

Museum of Natural History [W] *Monroe and West Monroe, LA*

Museum of Natural Science [W] *Baton Rouge, LA*

Museum of Natural Science [W] *Jackson, MS*

Museum of North Carolina Minerals [W] *Little Switzerland, NC*

Museum of the American Quilter's Society [W] *Paducah, KY*

Museum of the Cape Fear [W] *Fayetteville, NC*

Museum of the Hills & Fantasy Kingdom [W] *Helen, GA*
Museum of the Jimmy Carter Library [W] *Atlanta, GA*
Museum of Tobacco Art & History [W] *Nashville, TN*
Museum of York County [W] *Rock Hill, SC*
Museum of Zoology [W] *Monroe and West Monroe, LA*
Musical Explosion [A] *Athens, AL*
Music festivals [A] *Nashville, TN*
Music Mansion Theatre [W] *Pigeon Forge, TN*
Music Valley Wax Museum of the Stars [W] *Nashville, TN*
Mynelle Gardens [W] *Jackson, MS*
My Old Kentucky Dinner Train [W] *Bardstown, KY*
My Old Kentucky Home State Park [W] *Bardstown, KY*
Myrtle Beach State Park [W] *Myrtle Beach, SC*
Myrtles, The [W] *Baton Rouge, LA*
Mystic Caverns [W] *Harrison, AR*
Nacoochee Indian Mound [W] *Helen, GA*
Nashville Toy Museum [W] *Nashville, TN*
Natchez Opera Festival [S] *Natchez, MS*
Natchez Trace Parkway Visitor Center [W] *Tupelo, MS*
Natchitoches-Northwestern Folk Festival [A] *Natchitoches, LA*
Natchitoches Pilgrimage [A] *Natchitoches, LA*
Nathan Bedford Forrest State Park [W] *Paris, TN*
Nathaniel Russell House [W] *Charleston, SC*
National Balloon Rally [A] *Statesville, NC*
National Cemetery [W] *Alexandria, LA*
National Cemetery [W] *Shiloh National Military Park, TN*
National Civil Rights Museum [W] *Memphis, TN*
National Corvette Museum [W] *Bowling Green, KY*
National Cutting Horse Association Show [A] *Jackson, MS*
National D-Day Museum [W] *New Orleans, LA*
National Fish Hatchery & Aquarium [W] *Natchitoches, LA*
National Headquarters of Gulf States Paper Corporation [W] *Tuscaloosa, AL*
National Infantry Museum [W] *Columbus, GA*

National Invitational Explorer Canoe Race [A] *Batesville, AR*
National Knife Museum [W] *Chattanooga, TN*
National League baseball (Atlanta Braves) [W] *Atlanta, GA*
National Museum, Boy Scouts of America [W] *Murray, KY*
National Ornamental Metal Museum [W] *Memphis, TN*
National Peanut Festival [A] *Dothan, AL*
National Prisoner of War Museum [W] *Andersonville, GA*
National Science Center's Fort Discovery [W] *Augusta, GA*
National Shrimp Festival [A] *Gulf Shores, AL*
National Storytelling Festival [A] *Johnson City, TN*
National Tennessee Walking Horse Jubilee [A] *Columbia, TN*
National Wildlife Refuge [W] *Starkville, MS*
Natural Bridge of Alabama [W] *Hamilton, AL*
Natural Bridge State Resort Park [W] *Winchester, KY*
Natural Science Center of Greensboro, Inc [W] *Greensboro, NC*
Nature Museum [W] *Charlotte, NC*
Nature Station, The [W] *Land Between the Lakes, KY*
Navigation Pool (Lock) No 3 [W] *Pine Bluff, AR*
Navigation Pool (Lock) No 4 [W] *Pine Bluff, AR*
NBA (Atlanta Hawks) [W] *Atlanta, GA*
NBA (Charlotte Hornets) [W] *Charlotte, NC*
N.C. Transportation Museum [W] *Salisbury, NC*
Neshoba County Fair [A] *Philadelphia, MS*
New Bern Academy [W] *New Bern, NC*
New Bern Firemen's Museum [W] *New Bern, NC*
New Echota State Historic Site [W] *Calhoun, GA*
New Holy Land [W] *Eureka Springs, AR*
New Orleans Historic Voodoo Museum [W] *New Orleans, LA*
New Orleans Jazz and Heritage Festival [A] *New Orleans, LA*
New Orleans Museum of Art [W] *New Orleans, LA*
New Orleans Pharmacy Museum (*La Pharmacie Française*) [W] *New Orleans, LA*
New Orleans Unit [W] *New Orleans, LA*

NFL (Atlanta Falcons) [W] *Atlanta, GA*

NFL (Carolina Panthers) [W] *Charlotte, NC*

NFL (New Orleans Saints) [W] *New Orleans, LA*

Nibroc Festival [A] *Corbin, KY*

Nickajack Dam and Lake [W] *Chattanooga, TN*

Night In Old Savannah [A] *Savannah, GA*

Nimrod Lake [W] *Russellville, AR*

NMPA Stock Car Hall of Fame/Joe Weatherly Stock Car Museum [W] *Darlington, SC*

Noccalula Falls Park [W] *Gadsden, AL*

Norfork Lake [W] *Mountain Home, AR*

Norfork National Fish Hatchery [W] *Mountain Home, AR*

Normandy Lake [W] *Manchester, TN*

Norrell and No 2 Locks & Dams [W] *Dumas, AR*

North Carolina Apple Festival [A] *Hendersonville, NC*

North Carolina Aquarium/Fort Fisher [W] *Wilmington, NC*

North Carolina Aquarium on Roanoke Island [W] *Manteo, NC*

North Carolina Azalea Festival [A] *Wilmington, NC*

North Carolina Botanical Garden [W] *Chapel Hill, NC*

North Carolina Maritime Museum and Watercraft Center [W] *Beaufort, NC*

North Carolina Museum of Art [W] *Raleigh, NC*

North Carolina Museum of History [W] *Raleigh, NC*

North Carolina Museum of Life and Science [W] *Durham, NC*

North Carolina Oyster Festival [A] *South Brunswick Islands, NC*

North Carolina Seafood Festival [A] *Morehead City, NC*

North Carolina Shakespeare Festival [S] *High Point, NC*

Northeast Louisiana University [W] *Monroe and West Monroe, LA*

North Georgia College and State University [W] *Dahlonega, GA*

North Georgia Folk Festival [A] *Athens, GA*

North Louisiana Cotton Festival and Fair [A] *Bastrop, LA*

Northwest Arkansas Bluegrass Music Festival [A] *Harrison, AR*

Northwest Arkansas District Fair [A] *Harrison, AR*

Northwestern State University [W] *Natchitoches, LA*

Note [W] *Bull Shoals Lake Area, AR*

Nottoway Plantation [W] *Baton Rouge, LA*

O'Dell Pottery [W] *Ruston, LA*

Oak Alley Plantation [W] *New Orleans, LA*

Oak Hill and the Martha Berry Museum [W] *Rome, GA*

Oaklands [W] *Murfreesboro, TN*

Oaklawn Manor Plantation [W] *Franklin, LA*

Oakleigh [W] *Mobile, AL*

Oakley [W] *Baton Rouge, LA*

Oak Mountain State Park [W] *Birmingham, AL*

Oaks House Museum, The [W] *Jackson, MS*

Oak Square [W] *Port Gibson, MS*

Ober Gatlinburg Ski Resort [W] *Gatlinburg, TN*

Ocmulgee National Monument [W] *Macon, GA*

Ocracoke to Hatteras Ferry [W] *Ocracoke (Outer Banks), NC*

Okefenokee Heritage Center [W] *Waycross, GA*

Okefenokee National Wildife Refuge [W] *Okefenokee Swamp, GA*

Okefenokee Spring Fling [A] *Waycross, GA*

Okefenokee Swamp [W] *Waycross, GA*

Okefenokee Swamp Park [W] *Okefenokee Swamp, GA*

Oktibbeha County Heritage Museum [W] *Starkville, MS*

Oktoberfest [A] *Covington (Cincinnati Airport Area), KY*

Oktoberfest [S] *Helen, GA*

Old Alabama Town [W] *Montgomery, AL*

Old Cane Ridge Meeting House [W] *Paris, KY*

Old Cannonball House & Macon-Confederate Museum [W] *Macon, GA*

Old Capitol [W] *Jackson, MS*

Old Colleton County Jail [W] *Walterboro, SC*

Old Court House Museum [W] *Vicksburg, MS*

Old Davidson County Courthouse [W] *Lexington, NC*

Old Davidsonville State Park [W] *Pocahontas, AR*

Old Decatur & Albany historic districts [W] *Decatur, AL*

Old Depot Museum [W] *Selma, AL*

Old Dorchester State Park [W] *Charleston, SC*

Old East [W] *Chapel Hill, NC*

Oldenberg Brewery/Museum [W] *Covington (Cincinnati Airport Area), KY*

Old Exchange & Provost Dungeon [W] *Charleston, SC*

Old Fashioned Christmas at the Crossroads [A] *Perry, GA*

Old Fort Days Rodeo [A] *Fort Smith, AR*

Old Fort Harrod State Park [W] *Harrodsburg, KY*

Old Fort Museum [W] *Fort Smith, AR*

Old Fort River Festival [A] *Fort Smith, AR*

Old Governor's Mansion [W] *Baton Rouge, LA*

Old Governor's Mansion [W] *Frankfort, KY*

Old Governor's Mansion [W] *Milledgeville, GA*

Old Hickory Lake [W] *Lebanon, TN*

Old Hickory Lake [W] *Nashville, TN*

Old Homes Tour and Antiques Show [A] *Beaufort, NC*

Old Mill, The [W] *Little Rock & North Little Rock, AR*

Old Mud Meeting House [W] *Harrodsburg, KY*

Old Observatory, The [W] *Tuscaloosa, AL*

Old South Carriage Company [W] *Charleston, SC*

Old Spanish Arsenal museum, [W] *Baton Rouge, LA*

Old Spanish Fort and Museum [W] *Pascagoula, MS*

Old State Capitol [W] *Baton Rouge, LA*

Old State Capitol Building [W] *Frankfort, KY*

Old State House, The [W] *Little Rock & North Little Rock, AR*

Old Stone Church [W] *Winchester, KY*

Old Stone Fort State Archaeological Park [W] *Manchester, TN*

Old Stone House [W] *Salisbury, NC*

Old Tavern [W] *Hope, AR*

Old Tavern [W] *Tuscaloosa, AL*

Old Time Days [A] *Burnsville, NC*

Old-Time Fiddlers Championship [A] *Clarksville, TN*

Old Timer's Day [A] *Manchester, TN*

Old-Timers' Day Festival [A] *Dickson, TN*

Oldtown Bridge [W] *Ashland, KY*

Old Town Clock (1871) and Clocktower Museum, The [W] *Rome, GA*

Old Town Historic District [W] *Selma, AL*

Old US Mint, The [W] *New Orleans, LA*

Old Washington Historic State Park [W] *Hope, AR*

Old Well [W] *Chapel Hill, NC*

One-room schoolhouse [W] *Lumberton, NC*

Onyx Cave Park [W] *Eureka Springs, AR*

Opera [S] *Charlotte, NC*

Opera House [W] *Dothan, AL*

Opera House [W] *Lexington, KY*

Opera House [W] *Sumter, SC*

Opryland Museums [W] *Nashville, TN*

Orangeburg County Fair [A] *Orangeburg, SC*

Oren Dunn Museum of Tupelo [W] *Tupelo, MS*

Original Log Cabin [W] *Cadiz, KY*

Original Southwest Louisiana Zydeco Music Festival [A] *Opelousas, LA*

Orlando Brown House [W] *Frankfort, KY*

Orton Plantation Gardens [W] *Wilmington, NC*

Oscar Getz Museum of Whiskey History [W] *Bardstown, KY*

Other historic houses [W] *Athens, GA*

Otter Creek Park [W] *Louisville, KY*

Ouachita Baptist University [W] *Arkadelphia, AR*

Ouachita National Forests [W] *Hot Springs & Hot Springs National Park, AR*

Outdoor concerts [S] *Memphis, TN*

Outdoor Drama [A] *Elizabethton, TN*

Outdoor Greek Theater [W] *Baton Rouge, LA*

Ovens Auditorium [W] *Charlotte, NC*

Overmountain Victory Trail Celebration [A] *Elizabethton, TN*

Owensboro Area Museum of Science & History [W] *Owensboro, KY*

Owensboro Museum of Fine Art [W] *Owensboro, KY*

Owensboro Symphony Orchestra [S] *Owensboro, KY*

Owens-Thomas House [W] *Savannah, GA*

Ozark Folk Center State Park [W] *Mountain View, AR*

Ozark Folk Festival [A] *Eureka Springs, AR*

Ozark National Forest [W] *Russellville, AR*

Ozark Scottish Festival [A] *Batesville, AR*

Pack Place Education, Arts and Science Center [W] *Asheville, NC*

Palmetto Carriage Tours [W] *Charleston, SC*

Palmetto Islands County Park [W] *Charleston, SC*

Panoply of the Arts Festival [A] *Huntsville, AL*

Panther Creek State Park [W] *Morristown, TN*

Parachute Jumps [W] *Fayetteville, NC*

Parade of Lights on Water [A] *Henderson, NC*

Paramount's Carowinds [W] *Charlotte, NC*

Paramount Arts Center [W] *Ashland, KY*

Paris Landing State Park [W] *Paris, TN*

Paris Mountain [W] *Greenville, SC*

Park area [W] *Andrew Johnson National Historic Site, TN*

Park Headquarters and Visitor Center [W] *Hot Springs & Hot Springs National Park, AR*

Parks [W] *Atlanta, GA*

Parlange Plantation [W] *Baton Rouge, LA*

Parris Island [W] *Beaufort, SC*

Parthenon, The [W] *Nashville, TN*

Patriots Point Naval and Maritime Museum [W] *Charleston, SC*

Patton Museum of Cavalry and Armor [W] *Fort Knox, KY*

Paul Green Theater [W] *Chapel Hill, NC*

Paul M. Grist State Park [W] *Selma, AL*

Pea Ridge National Military Park [W] *Rogers, AR*

Pebble Hill Plantation [W] *Thomasville, GA*

Peel Mansion & Historic Gardens [W] *Bentonville, AR*

Pennyrile Forest State Resort Park [W] *Hopkinsville, KY*

Pennyrile Forest State Resort Park [W] *Madisonville, KY*

Pennyroyal Area Museum [W] *Hopkinsville, KY*

Pentagon Barracks [W] *Baton Rouge, LA*

Performing arts [S] *Louisville, KY*

Perryville Battlefield State Historic Site [W] *Danville, KY*

Peterson Doll and Miniature Museum [W] *High Point, NC*

Petit Jean State Park [W] *Conway, AR*

Petit Jean State Park [W] *Morrilton, AR*

Petit Jean State Park [W] *Russellville, AR*

Petit Paris Museum [W] *St. Martinville, LA*

Phillips County Museum [W] *Helena, AR*

Phoenix Fire Museum [W] *Mobile, AL*

Pickwick Landing Dam, Lock, and Lake [W] *Savannah, TN*

Pickwick Landing State Resort Park [W] *Savannah, TN*

Piedmont Art Gallery, The [W] *Maysville, KY*

Piedmont Interstate Fair [A] *Spartanburg, SC*

Piedmont Park [W] *Atlanta, GA*

Pike Pioneer Museum [W] *Troy, AL*

Pilgrimage [A] *Columbus, MS*

Pilgrimage [A] *Holly Springs, MS*

Pilgrimages [A] *Natchez, MS*

Pilot Mountain State Park [W] *Pilot Mountain, NC*

Pine Mountain State Resort Park [W] *Pineville, KY*

Pinnacle Mountain State Park [W] *Little Rock & North Little Rock, AR*

Pinnacle Overlook [W] *Cumberland Gap National Historical Park, KY*

Pioneer Days Festival [A] *Harrodsburg, KY*

Pioneer Playhouse [S] *Danville, KY*

Pioneer Playhouse Village-of-the-Arts [W] *Danville, KY*

Pioneer Village [W] *Pine Bluff, AR*

Pitot House [W] *New Orleans, LA*

Pivot Rock and Natural Bridge [W] *Eureka Springs, AR*

Plantation Christmas Tour of Homes [A] *Columbia, TN*

Plantations and historic buildings [W] *St. Francisville, LA*

Plantations and St Francisville [W] *Baton Rouge, LA*

Plaquemine Locks [W] *Baton Rouge, LA*

Players Bluegrass Downs [S] *Paducah, KY*

Playhouse on the Square [W] *Memphis, TN*

Playmakers Theater [W] *Chapel Hill, NC*

Pleasure Island Festival of Art [A] *Gulf Shores, AL*

Poage Landing Days Festival [A] *Ashland, KY*

Poets & Dreamers Garden [W] *Salisbury, NC*

Pogofest [A] *Waycross, GA*

Poinsett State Park [W] *Sumter, SC*

Point Mallard Park [W] *Decatur, AL*

Point Park [W] *Chattanooga, TN*

Poison Spring Battleground Historical Monument [W] *Camden, AR*

Polo games [S] *Aiken, SC*

Pontalba Building, [W] *New Orleans, LA*

Pope's Tavern [W] *Florence, AL*

Pope AFB/Fort Bragg Joint Open House & Air Show [A] *Fayetteville, NC*

Pope County Fair [A] *Russellville, AR*

Poplar Grove Plantation [W] *Wilmington, NC*

Portfest & State Catfish Cooking Contest [A] *Newport, AR*

Port Hudson State Commemorative Area [W] *Baton Rouge, LA*

Port of Gulfport [W] *Gulfport, MS*
Port of Lake Charles [W] *Lake Charles, LA*
Potts Tavern/Museum [W] *Russellville, AR*
Powder Magazine, The [W] *Charleston, SC*
Prairie Grove Battlefield State Park [W] *Fayetteville, AR*
Prater's Mill Country Fair [A] *Dalton, GA*
Presbyt&egrave:re, The [W] *New Orleans, LA*
Presbyt&egrave:re [W] *St. Martinville, LA*
Preservation Hall [W] *New Orleans, LA*
Princess Theatre [W] *Decatur, AL*
Private John Allen National Fish Hatchery [W] *Tupelo, MS*
Providence Canyon State Conservation Park [W] *Lumpkin, GA*
Providence Spring [W] *Andersonville, GA*
Public facilities [W] *Jekyll Island, GA*
Pullen Park [W] *Raleigh, NC*
Putnam County Dairy Festival [A] *Eatonton, GA*
Pyramid Arena [W] *Memphis, TN*
Quapaw Quarter Historic Neighborhoods [W] *Little Rock & North Little Rock, AR*
Queen Wilhelmina State Park [W] *Mena, AR*
Raccoon Mountain Alpine Slide [W] *Chattanooga, TN*
Raccoon Mountain Caverns and Campground [W] *Chattanooga, TN*
Raccoon Mountain Pumped Storage Plant [W] *Chattanooga, TN*
Racking Horse World Celebration [A] *Decatur, AL*
Radnor Lake State Natural Area [W] *Nashville, TN*
Raft trips. Southeastern Expeditions [W] *Clayton, GA*
Randolph County Fair [A] *Pocahontas, AR*
Rauch Memorial Planetarium [W] *Louisville, KY*
Raven Rock State Park [W] *Sanford, NC*
RCA Studio B [W] *Nashville, TN*
Rebecca's Doll House [W] *Monroe and West Monroe, LA*
Recreation areas [W] *New Orleans, LA*
Red Line Scenic Tour [W] *Paducah, KY*
Red Mountain Museum and Road Cut [W] *Birmingham, AL*
Red River Revel Arts Festival [A] *Shreveport, LA*

Red Top Mountain State Lodge Park [W] *Cartersville, GA*
Reed Bingham State Park [W] *Adel, GA*
Reed Gold Mine State Historic Site [W] *Concord (Cabarrus County), NC*
Reelfoot Lake [W] *Tiptonville, TN*
Reelfoot Lake State Park [W] *Tiptonville, TN*
Reenactment of the Battle of Selma [A] *Selma, AL*
Regional Museum [W] *Spartanburg, SC*
Regional Ogeechee Fair [A] *Statesboro, GA*
Renaissance Tower [W] *Florence, AL*
Resaca Confederate Cemetery [W] *Calhoun, GA*
Reservoirs [W] *Russellville, AL*
Revolutionary War Field Days [A] *Camden, SC*
Reynolda House, Museum of American Art [W] *Winston-Salem, NC*
Rhodes College [W] *Memphis, TN*
Rhododendron Festival [A] *Elizabethton, TN*
Rice Festival [A] *Walterboro, SC*
Richard B. Russell Scenic Highway [W] *Helen, GA*
Richards-DAR House [W] *Mobile, AL*
Rickwood Caverns State Park [W] *Birmingham, AL*
Rip van Winkle Gardens [W] *New Iberia, LA*
Riverbanks Zoological Park & Botanical Garden [W] *Columbia, SC*
Riverbend Festival [A] *Chattanooga, TN*
Riverboat cruises [W] *Covington (Cincinnati Airport Area), KY*
Riverboat excursion [W] *Louisville, KY*
River Cruises [W] *Little Rock & North Little Rock, AR*
River cruises [W] *New Orleans, LA*
Riverfest [A] *Covington (Cincinnati Airport Area), KY*
Riverfest [A] *Little Rock & North Little Rock, AR*
Riverfest [A] *Wilmington, NC*
Riverfest Weekend [A] *Columbus, GA*
Riverfront Streetcar Line [W] *New Orleans, LA*
River Jamboree [A] *Pascagoula, MS*
River rafting. Nantahala Outdoor Center [W] *Asheville, NC*
Riverside Arts Festival [A] *Bainbridge, GA*
RiverSpree [A] *Elizabeth City, NC*
Riverwalk [W] *Augusta, GA*
Riverwalk [W] *New Orleans, LA*

R.J. Reynolds Tobacco Company, Whitaker Park Cigarette Plant [W] *Winston-Salem, NC*

Road Atlanta [S] *Gainesville, GA*

Roan Mountain Wild Flower Tours & Bird Walks [A] *Elizabethton, TN*

Roanoke Rapids Lake [W] *Roanoke Rapids, NC*

Robert Mills Historic House (1823) & Park [W] *Columbia, SC*

Robert Ruark Chili Cook Off [A] *Southport, NC*

Robert Toombs House State Historic Site [W] *Washington, GA*

Robert W. Woodruff Arts Center [W] *Atlanta, GA*

Rock City Gardens [W] *Chattanooga, TN*

Rock Eagle Effigy [W] *Eatonton, GA*

Rocky Mount Historic Site & Overmountain Museum [W] *Johnson City, TN*

Rodeo of the Ozarks [A] *Springdale, AR*

Rogallo Kite Festival [A] *Nags Head (Outer Banks), NC*

Rogers Historical Museum (Hawkins House) [W] *Rogers, AR*

Rolex-Kentucky Event & Trade Fair [A] *Lexington, KY*

Rose Center [W] *Morristown, TN*

Rosedown [W] *Baton Rouge, LA*

Rose Festival [A] *Thomasville, GA*

Rose garden, [W] *New Orleans, LA*

Rosemont Plantation [W] *Woodville, MS*

Ross R. Barnett Reservoir [W] *Jackson, MS*

Rosswood Plantation [W] *Port Gibson, MS*

Rowan Oak [W] *Oxford, MS*

Royal Spring Park [W] *Georgetown, KY*

R.S. Barnwell Memorial Garden and Art Center [W] *Shreveport, LA*

Ruby Falls-Lookout Mountain Caverns [W] *Chattanooga, TN*

Ruffner Mountain Nature Center [W] *Birmingham, AL*

Rugby Pilgrimage [A] *Jamestown, TN*

Ruins of Windsor, The [W] *Port Gibson, MS*

Running of the Iroquois Memorial Steeplechase [A] *Nashville, TN*

Rural Life Museum [W] *Baton Rouge, LA*

R.W. Norton Art Gallery [W] *Shreveport, LA*

Ryman Auditorium & Museum [W] *Nashville, TN*

Sabine Free State Festival [A] *Many, LA*

Sacred Arts Center [W] *Eureka Springs, AR*

Salem Academy and College [W] *Winston-Salem, NC*

Sam Davis Home [W] *Nashville, TN*

Samford University [W] *Birmingham, AL*

Sam Houston Jones State Park [W] *Lake Charles, LA*

Sandy Creek Nature Center [W] *Athens, GA*

Sandy Creek Park [W] *Athens, GA*

San Francisco Plantation [W] *New Orleans, LA*

Santee National Wildlife Refuge [W] *Santee, SC*

Santee State Park [W] *Santee, SC*

Sarah P. Duke Gardens [W] *Durham, NC*

Sardis Lake and Dam [W] *Sardis, MS*

Saunders Memorial Museum [W] *Berryville, AR*

Saunders Memorial Muzzleloading and Frontier Gun Shoot & Handcrafters' Show [A] *Berryville, AR*

Savannah History Museum [W] *Savannah, GA*

Savannah National Wildlife Refuge [W] *Hardeeville, SC*

Savannah National Wildlife Refuge [W] *Savannah, GA*

Savannah Science Museum [W] *Savannah, GA*

Savannah Scottish Games & Highland Gathering [A] *Savannah, GA*

Savannah Tour of Homes & Gardens [A] *Savannah, GA*

Sawmill Days [A] *Many, LA*

Schmidt's Coca-Cola Museum [W] *Elizabethtown, KY*

Science Center [W] *Laurinburg, NC*

SciTrek-The Science and Technology Museum of Atlanta [W] *Atlanta, GA*

SciWorks [W] *Winston-Salem, NC*

Scott County Courthouse [W] *Georgetown, KY*

Scottish Festival and Games [A] *Gatlinburg, TN*

Scottish Highland Games [A] *Lumberton, NC*

Scranton Museum [W] *Pascagoula, MS*

Scully's [W] *Morgan City, LA*

Seafood Festival [A] *Biloxi, MS*

Seafood Festival [A] *Pass Christian, MS*

Seafood Festival [A] *Savannah, GA*

Seminole State Park [W] *Bainbridge, GA*

Senior Bowl Football Game [A] *Mobile, AL*

Sequoyah Caverns [W] *Fort Payne, AL*

Sesquicentennial State Park [W] *Columbia, SC*
Seth Lore and Irwinton Historic District [W] *Eufaula, AL*
Sewanee Summer Music Center Concerts [S] *Monteagle, TN*
Shadows-on-the-Teche [W] *New Iberia, LA*
Shaker Festival [A] *South Union, KY*
Shaker Museum [W] *South Union, KY*
Shaker Village of Pleasant Hill [W] *Harrodsburg, KY*
Shakespeare in the Park [S] *Asheville, NC*
Shaw House [W] *Southern Pines, NC*
Shearwater Pottery [W] *Ocean Springs, MS*
Sheltowee Trace Outfitters [W] *Cumberland Falls State Resort Park, KY*
Shiloh Historic District [W] *Springdale, AR*
Shiloh Museum [W] *Springdale, AR*
Shiloh National Military Park [W] *Savannah, TN*
Shindig-on-the-Green [A] *Asheville, NC*
Ships of the Sea Museum [W] *Savannah, GA*
Shongelo [W] *Mendenhall, MS*
Shooting in the New Year [A] *Cherryville, NC*
Shorter Mansion [W] *Eufaula, AL*
Sidney's Tours of Historic Macon [W] *Macon, GA*
Sidney Lanier Cottage [W] *Macon, GA*
Siege Re-enactment [A] *Vicksburg, MS*
Sightseeing Chairlift-Ober Gatlinburg Ski Resort [W] *Gatlinburg, TN*
Sightseeing tours [W] *Lexington, KY*
Signal Point [W] *Chattanooga, TN*
Simon Kenton Festival [A] *Maysville, KY*
"Singing on the Mountain" [A] *Linville, NC*
Singing River [W] *Pascagoula, MS*
Six Flags Over Georgia [W] *Atlanta, GA*
Sky Lift [W] *Gatlinburg, TN*
Slidell Cultural Center [W] *Slidell, LA*
Sloss Furnaces National Historic Landmark [W] *Birmingham, AL*
Small Craft Harbor [W] *Gulfport, MS*
Smith Robertson Museum [W] *Jackson, MS*
Smoky Mountain Deer Farm [W] *Sevierville, TN*
Smoky Mountain Jubilee [W] *Pigeon Forge, TN*
Smoky Mountain Lights [S] *Gatlinburg, TN*
Snyder Memorial Museum [W] *Bastrop, LA*

Soco Gardens Zoo [W] *Maggie Valley, NC*
South (Main) Building [W] *Chapel Hill, NC*
South Arkansas Arboretum [W] *El Dorado, AR*
South Carolina Archives Building [W] *Columbia, SC*
South Carolina Artisans Center [W] *Walterboro, SC*
South Carolina Festival of Flowers [A] *Greenwood, SC*
South Carolina Peach Festival [A] *Gaffney, SC*
South Carolina State Fair [A] *Columbia, SC*
South Carolina State Museum [W] *Columbia, SC*
South Carolina State University [W] *Orangeburg, SC*
Southdown Plantation House/Terrebonne Museum [W] *Houma, LA*
Southeastern Center for Contemporary Art [W] *Winston-Salem, NC*
Southeastern Wildlife Exposition [A] *Charleston, SC*
Southern 500 [A] *Darlington, SC*
Southern Arkansas University [W] *Magnolia, AR*
Southern Bell riverboat [W] *Chattanooga, TN*
Southern Forest World [W] *Waycross, GA*
Southern Garden Symposium [A] *St. Francisville, LA*
Southern Highland Craft Guild Fair [A] *Asheville, NC*
Southern Livestock Exposition and World Championship Rodeo [A] *Montgomery, AL*
Southern Regional Research Center [W] *New Orleans, LA*
Southern Wildlife Festival [A] *Decatur, AL*
Spalding Hall [W] *Bardstown, KY*
Spalding University [W] *Louisville, KY*
Spirit of America Festival [A] *Decatur, AL*
Spirit Square Center for the Arts [W] *Charlotte, NC*
Spoleto Festival USA [A] *Charleston, SC*
Sportsman Lake Park [W] *Cullman, AL*
Springer Opera House [W] *Columbus, GA*
Springfest [A] *Charlotte, NC*
Springfest [A] *Hilton Head Island, SC*
Spring Festival [A] *Cheraw, SC*
Spring Fiesta [A] *New Orleans, LA*
Spring Fun Show [A] *Shelbyville, TN*

Spring Pilgrimage [A] *Gulfport, MS*
Spring Pilgrimage [A] *Port Gibson, MS*
Spring Pilgrimage [A] *Vicksburg, MS*
Spring Tour of Historic Homes [A] *Eureka Springs, AR*
Spring Tour of Homes [A] *Athens, GA*
Spring Tour of Homes [A] *Madison, GA*
Spring Wild Flower Pilgrimage [A] *Gatlinburg, TN*
Squire Boone Rock [W] *Richmond, KY*
St. Andrews Presbyterian College [W] *Laurinburg, NC*
State Botanical Garden [W] *Athens, GA*
State Botanical Gardens [W] *Clemson, SC*
State Capitol [W] *Atlanta, GA*
State Capitol [W] *Baton Rouge, LA*
State Capitol [W] *Frankfort, KY*
State Capitol [W] *Jackson, MS*
State Capitol [W] *Little Rock & North Little Rock, AR*
State Capitol [W] *Montgomery, AL*
State Capitol [W] *Nashville, TN*
State Capitol [W] *Raleigh, NC*
State Fair [A] *Birmingham, AL*
State Fair [A] *Raleigh, NC*
State Legislative Building [W] *Raleigh, NC*
State Museum of Natural Sciences [W] *Raleigh, NC*
State University of West Georgia [W] *Carrollton, GA*
St Bernard State Park [W] *New Orleans, LA*
St. Charles Avenue Streetcar [W] *New Orleans, LA*
Steeplechase Races [A] *Tryon, NC*
Stephen C. Foster State Park [W] *Okefenokee Swamp, GA*
Stephen Foster, The Musical [S] *Bardstown, KY*
Sternwheeler Annual Regatta [A] *Maysville, KY*
St. Francis National Forests [W] *Helena, AR*
St. Helena's Episcopal Church [W] *Beaufort, SC*
St. John's Episcopal Church [W] *Montgomery, AL*
St. John's Lutheran Church [W] *Charleston, SC*
St. John's Museum of Art [W] *Wilmington, NC*
St. Joseph Proto-Cathedral [W] *Bardstown, KY*
St. Louis Cathedral [W] *New Orleans, LA*
St. Luke's Tour of Homes [A] *Hilton Head Island, SC*
St Martin of Tours Catholic Church [W] *St. Martinville, LA*
St. Mary's Church [W] *Charleston, SC*

St. Michael's Church [W] *Charleston, SC*
Stompin Ground [W] *Maggie Valley, NC*
Stone Mountain Park [W] *Atlanta, GA*
Stone Mountain State Park [W] *Wilkesboro, NC*
Stones River National Battlefield [W] *Murfreesboro, TN*
Stovall Covered Bridge over Chickamauga Creek [W] *Helen, GA*
St. Patrick's Day Parade [A] *Savannah, GA*
St. Patrick's Festival [A] *Dublin, GA*
St. Paul's Episcopal Church [W] *Augusta, GA*
St. Paul's Episcopal Church [W] *Edenton, NC*
St. Philip's Church [W] *Charleston, SC*
Strand Theatre, The [W] *Shreveport, LA*
Street Festival & Folkfest [A] *Murfreesboro, TN*
St. Simons Lighthouse [W] *St.Simons Island, GA*
St Tammany Art Association [W] *Covington, LA*
Studio Craftspeople of Berea, The [W] *Berea, KY*
Sturdivant Hall [W] *Selma, AL*
Sugar Bowl College Football Classic [A] *New Orleans, LA*
Sugar Cane Festival and Fair [A] *New Iberia, LA*
Sugar Creek Arts & Crafts Fair [A] *Bentonville, AR*
Summer Festival [A] *Paducah, KY*
Summer Festival of Music [S] *Brevard, NC*
Summerset [A] *Little Rock & North Little Rock, AR*
Summer Waves [W] *Jekyll Island, GA*
Sumner County Pilgrimage [A] *Gallatin, TN*
Sumter County Museum [W] *Sumter, SC*
Sumter Gallery of Art [W] *Sumter, SC*
Sumter Iris Festival [A] *Sumter, SC*
Sumter National Forest [W] *Newberry, SC*
Sunflower River Blues and Gospel Festival [A] *Clarksdale, MS*
Sun Fun Festival [A] *Myrtle Beach, SC*
Sunshine Festival [A] *St. Simons Island, GA*
Sun Studio [W] *Memphis, TN*
Superdome, The [W] *New Orleans, LA*
Suwannee Canal Recreation Area [W] *Okefenokee Swamp, GA*
Swamp Gardens and Wildlife Zoo [W] *Morgan City, LA*
Swan House [W] *Atlanta, GA*
Swan Lake Iris Gardens [W] *Sumter, SC*

Sweet Fanny Adams Theater [S] *Gatlinburg, TN*

Sword Gates [W] *Charleston, SC*

Sword of Peace Summer Outdoor Drama, The [S] *Burlington, NC*

Symphony [S] *Charlotte, NC*

Symphony Hall [W] *Atlanta, GA*

Table Rock [W] *Greenville, SC*

Tale Telling Festival [A] *Selma, AL*

Talimena Scenic Drive [W] *Mena, AR*

Talladega National Forest [W] *Talladega, AL*

Talladega Superspeedway [W] *Talladega, AL*

Talledega-Texaco Walk of Fame [W] *Talladega, AL*

Tammany Trace [W] *Covington, LA*

Tanglewood Park [W] *Winston-Salem, NC*

Tannehill State Historical Park [W] *Bessemer, AL*

Tar Heel Classic Horse Show [A] *Statesville, NC*

Taylor-Grady House [W] *Athens, GA*

Telfair Museum of Art [W] *Savannah, GA*

Tellico Dam and Lake [W] *Lenoir City, TN*

Tennessee Aquarium [W] *Chattanooga, TN*

Tennessee River Fiddler's Convention [A] *Florence, AL*

Tennessee State Fair [A] *Nashville, TN*

Tennessee State Museum [W] *Nashville, TN*

Tennessee Valley Fair [A] *Knoxville, TN*

Tennessee Valley Old Time Fiddler's Convention [A] *Athens, AL*

Tennessee Valley Railroad [W] *Chattanooga, TN*

Tennessee Walking Horse National Celebration [A] *Shelbyville, TN*

Tennessee Wildlife Center at Reflection Riding [W] *Chattanooga, TN*

Theater of the Stars [S] *Atlanta, GA*

Theatre Charlotte [S] *Charlotte, NC*

Theatre Memphis [S] *Memphis, TN*

Theatrical, musical productions [S] *Chattanooga, TN*

Thomas Bonner House [W] *Carrollton, GA*

Thomas County Museum of History [W] *Thomasville, GA*

Thomas Edison House [W] *Louisville, KY*

Thomasville Cultural Center [W] *Thomasville, GA*

Thomas Wolfe Memorial [W] *Asheville, NC*

Thorncrown Chapel [W] *Eureka Springs, AR*

Thoroughbred racing [S] *Bossier City, LA*

Thoroughbred racing [S] *Hot Springs & Hot Springs National Park, AR*

Thoroughbred racing [S] *Lafayette, LA*

Thoroughbred racing [S] *Lexington, KY*

Thronateeska Heritage Center [W] *Albany, GA*

Thunder on Water Festival [A] *Grenada, MS*

Tiger Cage [W] *Baton Rouge, LA*

Tiger Trail of Auburn, The [W] *Auburn, AL*

Tiny Town [W] *Hot Springs & Hot Springs National Park, AR*

Tipton-Haynes Historic Site [W] *Johnson City, TN*

Toad Suck Daze [A] *Conway, AR*

Toad Suck Ferry Lock and Dam [W] *Conway, AR*

Tobacco auctions [S] *Henderson, NC*

Tobacco auctions [S] *Rocky Mount, NC*

Tobacco Festival [A] *South Union, KY*

Toccoa Falls College [W] *Toccoa, GA*

T.O. Fuller State Park [W] *Memphis, TN*

Toledo Bend Dam and Reservoir [W] *Many, LA*

Toltec Mounds Archeological State Park [W] *Little Rock & North Little Rock, AR*

Tombigbee National Forest [W] *Louisville, MS*

Tombigbee National Forest [W] *Tupelo, MS*

Touchstone Wildlife & Art Museum [W] *Bossier City, LA*

Toulouse St Wharf [W] *New Orleans, LA*

Touring Savannah [W] *Savannah, GA*

Tourist Information Center [W] *Vicksburg, MS*

Tour of Homes [A] *Blowing Rock, NC*

Town Theatre [W] *Columbia, SC*

Toyota Motor Manufacturing, Kentucky, Inc [W] *Georgetown, KY*

Trace State Park [W] *Tupelo, MS*

Track Rock Gap [W] *Dahlonega, GA*

TranSouth Financial 400 [A] *Darlington, SC*

Transylvania University [W] *Lexington, KY*

Traveler's Rest State Historic Site [W] *Toccoa, GA*

Travellers Rest Historic House [W] *Nashville, TN*

Travertine [W] *Mammoth Cave National Park, KY*

Tree That Owns Itself [W] *Athens, GA*

Trinity Cathedral [W] *Columbia, SC*

Triple Crown [A] *Aiken, SC*

Tri-State Peak [W] *Cumberland Gap National Historical Park, KY*

Troy State University [W] *Troy, AL*

Trustees' Garden Site [W] *Savannah, GA*

Tryon Palace Historic Sites and Gardens [W] *New Bern, NC*

Tubman African American Museum [W] *Macon, GA*

Tuckaleechee Caverns [W] *Townsend, TN*

Tulane University [W] *New Orleans, LA*

Tulip Grove [W] *Nashville, TN*

Tullie Smith Farm [W] *Atlanta, GA*

Tupelo National Battlefield [W] *Tupelo, MS*

Turn-of-the-Century House [W] *Morgan City, LA*

Tuskegee Institute National Historic Site [W] *Tuskegee, AL*

Tuskegee National Forest [W] *Tuskegee, AL*

Twickenham Historic District [W] *Huntsville, AL*

Twilight Tour on Main [A] *Brevard, NC*

Two Open Hot Springs [W] *Hot Springs & Hot Springs National Park, AR*

Tybee Museum and Lighthouse [W] *Tybee Island, GA*

Uncle Dave Macon Days [A] *Murfreesboro, TN*

Uncle Remus Museum [W] *Eatonton, GA*

Underground Atlanta [W] *Atlanta, GA*

Unicoi State Park [W] *Helen, GA*

Union Art Gallery [W] *Baton Rouge, LA*

Union County Fair [A] *El Dorado, AR*

Unitarian Church [W] *Charleston, SC*

United States Bullion Depository [W] *Fort Knox, KY*

University Art Museum [W] *Lafayette, LA*

University Museum [W] *Fayetteville, AR*

University of Alabama [W] *Tuscaloosa, AL*

University of Alabama at Birmingham [W] *Birmingham, AL*

University of Arkansas [W] *Fayetteville, AR*

University of Georgia [W] *Athens, GA*

University of Kentucky [W] *Lexington, KY*

University of Louisville [W] *Louisville, KY*

University of New Orleans [W] *New Orleans, LA*

University of North Alabama [W] *Florence, AL*

University of North Carolina at Chapel Hill [W] *Chapel Hill, NC*

University of North Carolina at Charlotte [W] *Charlotte, NC*

University of North Carolina at Greensboro [W] *Greensboro, NC*

University of South Alabama [W] *Mobile, AL*

University of South Carolina [W] *Columbia, SC*

University of Southwestern Louisiana [W] *Lafayette, LA*

University of Tennessee at Chattanooga [W] *Chattanooga, TN*

University President's House [W] *Athens, GA*

Unto These Hills [S] *Cherokee, NC*

Upper Bear Creek [W] *Russellville, AL*

Upper Room Chapel and Museum, The [W] *Nashville, TN*

US 10K Classic and Family Sports Festival [A] *Marietta, GA*

US Customs House [W] *Savannah, GA*

US Naval Hospital [W] *Beaufort, SC*

US Open King Mackerel Tournament [A] *Southport, NC*

USS *Kidd.* [W] *Baton Rouge, LA*

US Space and Rocket Center [W] *Huntsville, AL*

Utzman-Chambers House [W] *Salisbury, NC*

Valley Fest [A] *Russellville, AR*

Vanderbilt University [W] *Nashville, TN*

"The Vanishing Glory" [W] *Vicksburg, MS*

Vann House State Historic Site [W] *Chatsworth, GA*

Vardell Art Gallery [W] *Laurinburg, NC*

Verdier House [W] *Beaufort, SC*

Vicksburg National Military Park & Cemetery [W] *Vicksburg, MS*

Victorian and Edwardian Houses [W] *Helena, AR*

Victorian Square [W] *Lexington, KY*

Victorian Village [W] *Memphis, TN*

Village Creek State Park [W] *Forrest City, AR*

Villa Marre [W] *Little Rock & North Little Rock, AR*

Violet City [W] *Mammoth Cave National Park, KY*

Visitor Center [W] *Andrew Johnson National Historic Site, TN*

Visitor Center [W] *Cumberland Gap National Historical Park, KY*

Visitor Center [W] *Shiloh National Military Park, TN*

Vogel State Park [W] *Dahlonega, GA*

Volksmarch [A] *Helen, GA*

Von Braun Center [W] *Huntsville, AL*

Vulcan [W] *Birmingham, AL*

Wake Forest University [W] *Winston-Salem, NC*

Waldensian Celebration of the Glorious Return [A] *Morganton, NC*

Walking Horse Show [A] *Clarksville, TN*

Walking tour [W] *Hot Springs & Hot Springs National Park, AR*

Walking tour in the Vieux Carré [W] *New Orleans, LA*

Walking Tour of Old Savannah Gardens [A] *Savannah, GA*

Walnut Grove Plantation [W] *Spartanburg, SC*

Walton Arts Center [W] *Fayetteville, AR*

War Eagle Cavern [W] *Rogers, AR*

War Eagle Mill [W] *Rogers, AR*

Warfield Concert Series [S] *Helena, AR*

Waring Historical Medical Library & Macaulay Museum of Dental History [W] *Charleston, SC*

War Memorial Park [W] *Little Rock & North Little Rock, AR*

Washington [W] *Opelousas, LA*

Washington Summer Festival [A] *Washington, NC*

Washington-Wilkes Historical Museum [W] *Washington, GA*

Watermelon Festival [A] *Cordele, GA*

Watermelon Festival [A] *Hope, AR*

Water Tower [W] *Louisville, KY*

Water Town USA [W] *Shreveport, LA*

Waterways Experiment Station [W] *Vicksburg, MS*

Waterworks Visual Arts Center [W] *Salisbury, NC*

Waveland State Historic Site [W] *Lexington, KY*

W.C. Handy's Home [W] *Memphis, TN*

W.C. Handy Blues & Barbecue Festival [A] *Henderson, KY*

W.C. Handy Home, Museum, and Library [W] *Florence, AL*

W.C. Handy Music Festival [A] *Florence, AL*

Weatherspoon Art Gallery [W] *Greensboro, NC*

Weiss Dam and Lake [W] *Gadsden, AL*

Wesleyan College [W] *Macon, GA*

West Baton Rouge Museum [W] *Baton Rouge, LA*

Western Kentucky State Fair [A] *Hopkinsville, KY*

Western Kentucky University [W] *Bowling Green, KY*

Western North Carolina Nature Center [W] *Asheville, NC*

Westgate Park [W] *Dothan, AL*

West Point Lake [W] *La Grange, GA*

West Point on the Eno [W] *Durham, NC*

Westville [W] *Lumpkin, GA*

Westville events [A] *Lumpkin, GA*

Weymouth Woods-Sandhills Nature Preserve [W] *Southern Pines, NC*

Wheeler Dam [W] *Florence, AL*

Wheeler Dam [W] *Florence, AL*

Wheeler National Wildlife Refuge [W] *Decatur, AL*

Whistle Stop Cafe, The [W] *Forsyth, GA*

White and Yellow Duck Tours [W] *Hot Springs & Hot Springs National Park, AR*

White Hall State Historic House [W] *Richmond, KY*

Whitehaven [W] *Paducah, KY*

White Oak Lake State Park [W] *Camden, AR*

White Oak Mountain [W] *Tryon, NC*

White Point Gardens [W] *Charleston, SC*

White River National Wildlife Refuge [W] *Dumas, AR*

White River National Wildlife Refuge [W] *Stuttgart, AR*

White River Water Carnival [A] *Batesville, AR*

White Rock Mountain Recreation Area [W] *Alma, AR*

White Water [W] *Marietta, GA*

Whitewater rafting. Cherokee Adventures [W] *Johnson City, TN*

W.H. Tupper General Merchandise Museum [W] *Jennings, LA*

Wickland [W] *Bardstown, KY*

Wickliffe Mounds [W] *Wickliffe, KY*

Wiederkehr Wine Cellars [W] *Alma, AR*

Wilderness canoeing [W] *Okefenokee Swamp, GA*

Wild River Country [W] *Little Rock & North Little Rock, AR*

Wildwood Festival [A] *Little Rock & North Little Rock, AR*

Wilkinson County Museum [W] *Woodville, MS*

Will-A-Way Recreation Area [W] *Winder, GA*

William B. Bankhead National Forest [W] *Cullman, AL*

William Breman Jewish Heritage Museum [W] *Atlanta, GA*

William B. Umstead State Park [W] *Raleigh, NC*

William Carl Gardner Visitor Center [W] *Greers Ferry Lake Area, AR*

William S. Webb Museum of Anthropology [W] *Lexington, KY*

William Weinman Mineral Museum [W] *Cartersville, GA*

William Whitley House Historic Site [W] *Mount Vernon, KY*

Will T. Murphy African American Museum [W] *Tuscaloosa, AL*

Wilmington Railroad Museum [W] *Wilmington, NC*

Wilson Dam [W] *Florence, AL*

Wilson Lake [W] *Florence, AL*

Wilson Library [W] *Chapel Hill, NC*

Wind Creek State Park [W] *Alexander City, AL*

Windy Hollow Recreation Area [W] *Owensboro, KY*

Winery tours. Chateau Elan Winery and Resort [W] *Buford, GA*

Wings Over The Prairie Festival [A] *Stuttgart, AR*

Winthrop University [W] *Rock Hill, SC*

Withrow Springs State Park [W] *Eureka Springs, AR*

Woldenberg Riverfront Park [W] *New Orleans, LA*

Wolf Creek Dam [W] *Jamestown, KY*

Wolf Laurel Ski Resort [W] *Asheville, NC*

Woodrow Wilson Boyhood Home [W] *Columbia, SC*

Woodruff-Fontaine House [W] *Memphis, TN*

Woodruff Museum of Civil War Naval History [W] *Columbus, GA*

Wooldridge Monuments [W] *Mayfield, KY*

Woolly Hollow State Park [W] *Conway, AR*

World's Biggest Fish Fry [A] *Paris, TN*

World's Largest Chest of Drawers [W] *High Point, NC*

World Gee Haw Whimmy Diddle Competition [A] *Asheville, NC*

World of Coca-Cola, The [W] *Atlanta, GA*

World Trade Center of New Orleans [W] *New Orleans, LA*

Wormsloe State Historic Site [W] *Savannah, GA*

Wren's Nest [W] *Atlanta, GA*

Wright Brothers National Memorial [W] *Kill Devil Hills (Outer Banks), NC*

Yazoo Historical Museum [W] *Yazoo City, MS*

Yeiser Arts Center [W] *Paducah, KY*

Yellow River Game Ranch [W] *Atlanta, GA*

YMI Cultural Center [W] *Asheville, NC*

Zachary Taylor National Cemetery [W] *Louisville, KY*

Zebulon B. Vance Birthplace State Historic Site [W] *Asheville, NC*

Zigler Museum [W] *Jennings, LA*

Zoo Atlanta [W] *Atlanta, GA*

Zooland Animal Park [W] *Gulf Shores, AL*

Zydeco Festival [A] *Memphis, TN*

LODGING LIST

Establishment names are listed in alphabetical order followed by a symbol identifying their classification and then city and state. The symbols for classification are: [AS] for All Suites, [BB] for B&Bs/Small Inns, [CAS] for Casinos, [CC] for Cottage Colonies, [CON] for Villas/Condos, [CONF] for Conference Centers, [EX] for Extended Stays, [HOT] for Hotels, [MOT] for Motels/Motor Lodges, [RAN] for Guest Ranches, and [RST] for Resorts

1810 WEST INN [BB] *Augusta, GA*
1823 HISTORIC ROSE HILL INN [BB] *Lexington, KY*
1842 INN [BB] *Macon, GA*
1876 INN [MOT] *Eureka Springs, AR*
1884 PATON HOUSE INN [BB] *Thomasville, GA*
1906 PATHWAY INN BED & BREAKFAST [BB] *Americus, GA*
4 POINTS HOTEL [MOT] *Wilmington, NC*
ABINGDON MANOR [BB] *Dillon, SC*
ADAMS CAIRN BRAE BED & BREAKFAST [BB] *Asheville, NC*
ADAMS EDGEWORTH INN [BB] *Monteagle, TN*
ADAMS HILBORNE MANSION [BB] *Chattanooga, TN*
ADAM'S MARK [HOT] *Charlotte, NC*
ADAMS MARK HOTEL [HOT] *Mobile, AL*
ADAM'S MARK HOTEL & RESORTS [HOT] *Columbia, SC*
ADAM'S MARK HOTEL - MEMPHIS [HOT] *Memphis, TN*
ADAM'S MARK PLAZA [HOT] *Winston-Salem, NC*
ADDISON INN [MOT] *Wilkesboro, NC*
AERIE INN BED & BREAKFAST [BB] *New Bern, NC*
AHOSKIE INN [MOT] *Ahoskie, NC*
ALBEMARLE INN [BB] *Asheville, NC*
ALEXANDRA'S INN [BB] *Georgetown, SC*
ALPEN DORF, THE [MOT] *Eureka Springs, AR*
ALPINE INN [BB] *Little Switzerland, NC*
ALPINE LODGE & SUITES [MOT] *Cookeville, TN*
ALPINE VILLAGE INN [MOT] *Blowing Rock, NC*
ALTO MOTEL [MOT] *Gatlinburg, TN*
AMBASSADOR HOTEL [MOT] *New Orleans, LA*
AMBASSADOR INN AND LUXURY SUITES [MOT] *Manchester, TN*
AMBERLEY SUITE HOTEL [MOT] *Norcross, GA*
AMELIA'S FIELD COUNTRY INN [BB] *Paris, KY*

AMERICANA INN [MOT] *Pigeon Forge, TN*
AMERICAN COURT [MOT] *Asheville, NC*
AMERICAN INN [MOT] *Buford, GA*
AMERISUITES [MOT] *Augusta, GA*
AMERISUITES [MOT] *Columbia, SC*
AMERISUITES [MOT] *Greensboro, NC*
AMERISUITES [MOT] *Little Rock & North Little Rock, AR*
AMERISUITES [AS] *Louisville, KY*
AMERISUITES [MOT] *Nashville, TN*
AMERISUITES GWINNETT MALL [MOT] *Norcross, GA*
AMERSUITES OPRYLAND [AS] *Nashville, TN*
ANCHORAGE INN [BB] *Charleston, SC*
ANCHORAGE INN [RST] *Ocracoke (Outer Banks), NC*
ANCHUCA [BB] *Vicksburg, MS*
ANNABELLE BED AND BREAKFAST [BB] *Vicksburg, MS*
ANSLEY INN [BB] *Atlanta, GA*
APPLEWOOD MANOR INN [BB] *Asheville, NC*
ARCHER'S MOUNTAIN [BB] *Banner Elk, NC*
ARKANSAS' EXCELSIOR [HOT] *Little Rock & North Little Rock, AR*
ARLINGTON RESORT HOTEL AND SPA [HOT] *Hot Springs & Hot Springs National Park, AR*
ARROWHEAD INN BED & BREAKFAST [BB] *Durham, NC*
ARSENIC & OLD LACE B&B INN [BB] *Eureka Springs, AR*
ASHLAND PLAZA HOTEL [HOT] *Ashland, KY*
ASHLEY INN B&B, THE [BB] *Charleston, SC*
ASPEN HOTEL AND SUITES [HOT] *Fort Smith, AR*
ATLANTA DOWNTOWN TRAVELODGE [MOT] *Atlanta, GA*
ATLANTA MARRIOTT NORCROSS [HOT] *Norcross, GA*
ATLANTA NORTHLAKE COURTYARD [MOT] *Atlanta, GA*

AUBURN UNIVERSITY HOTEL AND CONFERENCE CENTER [HOT] *Auburn, AL*

AUGUSTUS T ZEVELY [BB] *Winston-Salem, NC*

AUSTIN HOTEL & CONVENTION CENTER, THE [HOT] *Hot Springs & Hot Springs National Park, AR*

AVANELLE MOTOR LODGE [MOT] *Hot Springs & Hot Springs National Park, AR*

AZALEA INN BED & BREAKFAST [BB] *Augusta, GA*

BALLASTONE INN & TOWNHOUSE [BB] *Savannah, GA*

BALSAM MOUNTAIN INN [BB] *Waynesville, NC*

BARDSTOWN PARKVIEW MOTEL [MOT] *Bardstown, KY*

BARKSDALE HOUSE INN [BB] *Charleston, SC*

BARREN RIVER LAKE STATE RESORT PARK [RST] *Glasgow, KY*

BARROW HOUSE INN [BB] *St. Francisville, LA*

BASIN PARK [HOT] *Eureka Springs, AR*

BASTROP INN [MOT] *Bastrop, LA*

BATTERY CARRIAGE HOUSE INN [BB] *Charleston, SC*

BATTLEFIELD INN [MOT] *Vicksburg, MS*

BAYMONT INN [MOT] *Huntsville, AL*

BAYMONT INN [MOT] *Jackson, TN*

BAYMONT INN [MOT] *Knoxville, TN*

BAYMONT INN [MOT] *Meridian, MS*

BAYMONT INN [MOT] *Montgomery, AL*

BAYMONT INN & SUITES [MOT] *Birmingham, AL*

BAYMONT INN & SUITES [MOT] *Cleveland, TN*

BAYMONT INN & SUITES [MOT] *Columbia, SC*

BAYMONT INN & SUITES [MOT] *Savannah, GA*

BAYMONT INN AND SUITES [MOT] *Columbus, GA*

BAYMONT INN AND SUITES [MOT] *Nashville, TN*

BAYMONT INN AND SUITES [MOT] *Pigeon Forge, TN*

BAYMONT INN AND SUITES NASHVILLE WEST [MOT] *Nashville, TN*

BEACH COLONY RESORT [HOT] *Myrtle Beach, SC*

BEACH COVE RESORT [AS] *Myrtle Beach, SC*

BEACH HAVEN MOTEL [MOT] *Kill Devil Hills (Outer Banks), NC*

BEACON MOTOR LODGE [MOT] *Nags Head (Outer Banks), NC*

BEAUFORT HOUSE [BB] *Asheville, NC*

BEAUFORT INN & RESTAURANT [BB] *Beaufort, SC*

BEAUMONT INN [BB] *Harrodsburg, KY*

BEAU RIVAGE BY MIRAGE RESORTS [RST] *Biloxi, MS*

BEAVER LAKE LODGE - THE OZARKS [MOT] *Rogers, AR*

BED & BREAKFAST INN [BB] *Savannah, GA*

BED AND BREAKFAST AT SILLS INN [BB] *Lexington, KY*

BED AND BREAKFAST OF SUMTER [BB] *Sumter, SC*

BEL'ARCO [RST] *Bull Shoals Lake Area, AR*

BELMONT INN [BB] *Greenwood, SC*

BENT CREEK GOLF RESORT [MOT] *Gatlinburg, TN*

BENTLEY'S BED AND BREAKFAST [BB] *Atlanta, GA*

BERKLEY MANOR BED & BREAKFAST [BB] *Ocracoke (Outer Banks), NC*

BEST INN [MOT] *Chattanooga, TN*

BEST INN [MOT] *Marietta, GA*

BEST INNS [HOT] *Asheville, NC*

BEST VALUE INN & SUITES [MOT] *Jackson, MS*

BEST WESTERN [MOT] *Athens, AL*

BEST WESTERN [MOT] *Baton Rouge, LA*

BEST WESTERN [HOT] *Charleston, SC*

BEST WESTERN [MOT] *Cherokee, NC*

BEST WESTERN [MOT] *Conway, AR*

BEST WESTERN [MOT] *Cookeville, TN*

BEST WESTERN [MOT] *Demopolis, AL*

BEST WESTERN [MOT] *Dunn, NC*

BEST WESTERN [MOT] *Guntersville, AL*

BEST WESTERN [MOT] *Harrodsburg, KY*

BEST WESTERN [MOT] *Hopkinsville, KY*

BEST WESTERN [MOT] *Knoxville, TN*

BEST WESTERN [MOT] *La Grange, GA*

BEST WESTERN [MOT] *London, KY*

BEST WESTERN [MOT] *Louisville, KY*

BEST WESTERN [MOT] *Madisonville, KY*

BEST WESTERN [MOT] *Ruston, LA*

BEST WESTERN [MOT] *Stuttgart, AR*

BEST WESTERN ASHEVILLE BILT-MORE [MOT] *Asheville, NC*

BEST WESTERN BEACH VIEW INN [MOT] *Gulfport, MS*

BEST WESTERN BENTONVILLE INN [MOT] *Bentonville, AR*

BEST WESTERN BRADBURY INN [MOT] *Norcross, GA*

BEST WESTERN BRADBURY SUITES [MOT] *Marietta, GA*

BEST WESTERN BRUNSWICK INN [MOT] *Brunswick, GA*

BEST WESTERN BUCCANEER [MOT] *Morehead City, NC*

BEST WESTERN CARDINAL INN [MOT] *Elizabethtown, KY*

BEST WESTERN CARRIAGE INN [MOT] *Mountain Home, AR*

BEST WESTERN CELEBRATION INN [MOT] *Shelbyville, TN*

BEST WESTERN CHATEAU SUITE HOTEL [HOT] *Shreveport, LA*

BEST WESTERN COACHMAN'S INN [MOT] *Magnolia, AR*

BEST WESTERN COLONIAL INN [HOT] *Athens, GA*

BEST WESTERN COLUMBUS [MOT] *Columbus, GA*

BEST WESTERN CONTINENTAL INN [MOT] *Arkadelphia, AR*

BEST WESTERN CONTINENTAL INN [MOT] *Bowling Green, KY*

BEST WESTERN CROSSROADS [MOT] *Gatlinburg, TN*

BEST WESTERN CROSSROADS INN [MOT] *Natchez Trace State Resort Park, TN*

BEST WESTERN DAYTON HOUSE [MOT] *Myrtle Beach, SC*

BEST WESTERN DOTHAN INN & SUITES [MOT] *Dothan, AL*

BEST WESTERN DUNES INN [RST] *Tybee Island, GA*

BEST WESTERN ELDRETH INN [MOT] *Jefferson, NC*

BEST WESTERN EUFAULA INN [MOT] *Eufaula, AL*

BEST WESTERN EXECUTIVE INN [MOT] *Lebanon, TN*

BEST WESTERN FABULOUS CHALET [MOT] *Gatlinburg, TN*

BEST WESTERN FIDDLERS' INN [HOT] *Mountain View, AR*

BEST WESTERN FOREST MOTOR [MOT] *Franklin, LA*

BEST WESTERN FRANKLIN INN [MOT] *Franklin, TN*

BEST WESTERN GENERAL NELSON [MOT] *Bardstown, KY*

BEST WESTERN GOLDSBORO [MOT] *Goldsboro, NC*

BEST WESTERN GOVERNORS INN SUITES [AS] *Little Rock & North Little Rock, AR*

BEST WESTERN GRENADA [MOT] *Grenada, MS*

BEST WESTERN HIGHWAY HOST [MOT] *Knoxville, TN*

BEST WESTERN HILL TOP INN [MOT] *Forsyth, GA*

BEST WESTERN HORSESHOE INN [MOT] *Alexander City, AL*

BEST WESTERN HOTEL ACADIANA [MOT] *Lafayette, LA*

BEST WESTERN HURRICANE MILLS [MOT] *Hurricane Mills, TN*

BEST WESTERN INN [HOT] *Atlanta, GA*

BEST WESTERN INN [MOT] *Blytheville, AR*

BEST WESTERN INN [MOT] *Bowling Green, KY*

BEST WESTERN INN [MOT] *Corbin, KY*

BEST WESTERN INN [MOT] *Covington (Cincinnati Airport Area), KY*

BEST WESTERN INN [MOT] *Dalton, GA*

BEST WESTERN INN [MOT] *Forrest City, AR*

BEST WESTERN INN [MOT] *Jackson, TN*

BEST WESTERN INN [MOT] *Morrilton, AR*

BEST WESTERN INN [MOT] *Newberry, SC*

BEST WESTERN INN [MOT] *Santee, SC*

BEST WESTERN INN & SUITES [MOT] *Alexandria, LA*

BEST WESTERN INN & SUITES [HOT] *New Iberia, LA*

BEST WESTERN INN-TOWN HOTEL [HOT] *Little Rock & North Little Rock, AR*

BEST WESTERN INN AT HILTON HEAD [MOT] *Hilton Head Island, SC*

BEST WESTERN INN MOTEL AND REST [MOT] *Sardis, MS*

BEST WESTERN INN OF THE OZARKS [MOT] *Eureka Springs, AR*

BEST WESTERN-KING CHARLES INN [MOT] *Charleston, SC*

BEST WESTERN KING OF THE ROAD [MOT] *Valdosta, GA*

BEST WESTERN KINGS INN [MOT] *El Dorado, AR*

BEST WESTERN KINGS ROW INN [MOT] *Texarkana, AR*

BEST WESTERN LAKE NORMAN [MOT] *Cornelius, NC*

BEST WESTERN LAKE PARK INN [MOT] *Valdosta, GA*

BEST WESTERN LANDMARK HOTEL [HOT] *Metairie, LA*

BEST WESTERN-LANIER CENTER HOTEL [HOT] *Gainesville, GA*

BEST WESTERN LASAMMANA [MOT] *Wilson, NC*

BEST WESTERN MARINER INN [MOT] *Opelika, AL*

BEST WESTERN MERIDIAN [MOT] *Meridian, MS*

BEST WESTERN MOUNTAIN BROOK [MOT] *Maggie Valley, NC*

BEST WESTERN NEWPORT INN [MOT] *Gatlinburg, TN*

BEST WESTERN OCEAN REEF SUITES [MOT] *Kill Devil Hills (Outer Banks), NC*

BEST WESTERN OF HAMILTON [MOT] *Hamilton, AL*

BEST WESTERN OF HOPE [MOT] *Hope, AR*

BEST WESTERN ON THE BEACH [MOT] *Gulf Shores, AL*

BEST WESTERN PARK PLAZA [MOT] *Tuscaloosa, AL*

BEST WESTERN PARKSIDE INN
[MOT] *Frankfort, KY*

BEST WESTERN PLAZA INN [MOT]
Pigeon Forge, TN

BEST WESTERN REGENCY [MOT]
Lexington, KY

BEST WESTERN RICHMOND SUITES
[MOT] *Lake Charles, LA*

BEST WESTERN RICHMOND SUITES
OF SHREVEPORT [MOT]
Shreveport, LA

BEST WESTERN RIME GARDEN INN
[MOT] *Birmingham, AL*

BEST WESTERN RIVERSIDE INN
[MOT] *Anniston, AL*

BEST WESTERN RIVERSIDE [MOT]
Macon, GA

BEST WESTERN RIVERVIEW [MOT]
Kinston, NC

BEST WESTERN ROAD STAR INN
[MOT] *Richmond, KY*

BEST WESTERN SCENIC MOTORINN
[MOT] *Batesville, AR*

BEST WESTERN-SEA ISLAND INN
[HOT] *Beaufort, SC*

BEST WESTERN SKYLND INN [MOT]
Durham, NC

BEST WESTERN SOUTH [MOT]
Shepherdsville, KY

BEST WESTERN STATE HOUSE INN
[MOT] *Montgomery, AL*

BEST WESTERN TRADEWINDS INN
[MOT] *Fort Smith, AR*

BEST WESTERN TRAVELER'S INN
[MOT] *Paris, TN*

BEST WESTERN UNIVERSITY INN
[MOT] *Chapel Hill, NC*

BEST WESTERN VALLEY INN [MOT]
Townsend, TN

BEST WESTERN WINDSOR SUITES
[MOT] *Fayetteville, AR*

BEVERLY HILLS INN [BB] *Atlanta, GA*

BIENVILLE HOUSE HOTEL [MOT]
New Orleans, LA

BIG LYNN LODGE [BB] *Little
Switzerland, NC*

BILMAR MOTOR INN [MOT] *Pigeon
Forge, TN*

BILTMORE [HOT] *Greensboro, NC*

BLOCKADE RUNNER RESORT &
HOTEL [RST] *Wrightsville
Beach, NC*

BLOWING ROCK INN [MOT] *Blowing
Rock, NC*

BLUEGRASS INN [MOT] *Frankfort, KY*

BLUE HERON MOTEL [MOT] *Nags
Head (Outer Banks), NC*

BLUE PARADISE RESORT [CC]
Mountain Home, AR

BLUFF SHOAL [MOT] *Ocracoke (Outer
Banks), NC*

BLUFF VIEW INN [BB] *Chattanooga,
TN*

BOARDWALK INN [HOT] *Charleston,
SC*

BOMAR INN [MOT] *Athens, AL*

BON AIR LODGE [MOT] *Gatlinburg,
TN*

BOONE TAVERN HOTEL [HOT] *Berea,
KY*

BOULDIN HOUSE BED AND
BREAKFAST [BB] *High Point, NC*

BOURBON ORLEANS - A WYNDHAM
HISTORIC HOTEL [HOT] *New
Orleans, LA*

BOYETTE HOUSE [BB] *Ocracoke (Outer
Banks), NC*

BRADY INN BED AND BREAKFAST
[BB] *Madison, GA*

BRADY MOUNTAIN RESORT [MOT]
*Hot Springs & Hot Springs
National Park, AR*

BRASSTOWN VALLEY RESORT [RST]
Hiawassee, GA

BREAKERS INN [MOT] *Biloxi, MS*

BREAKERS RESORT, THE [HOT]
Myrtle Beach, SC

BRECKINRIDGE INN [MOT]
Louisville, KY

BRIARS BED & BREAKFAST [BB]
Natchez, MS

BRIARSTONE INN [MOT] *Pigeon
Forge, TN*

BRIDGEFORD HOUSE [BB] *Eureka
Springs, AR*

BROOKSIDE RESORT [MOT]
Gatlinburg, TN

BROOKSTOWN INN [BB] *Winston-
Salem, NC*

BROWNSTONE HOTEL [HOT]
Raleigh, NC

BRUNSWICK MANOR [BB] *Brunswick,
GA*

BRUSTMAN HOUSE BED AND
BREAKFAST [BB] *Myrtle Beach,
SC*

BUCKHORN INN [BB] *Gatlinburg, TN*

BUCKHORN LAKE STATE RESORT
PARK [RST] *Hazard, KY*

BUDGET HOST [MOT] *Cartersville,
GA*

BUDGET HOST INN [MOT] *Bryson
City, NC*

BUDGET HOST INN [MOT] *Caryville,
TN*

BUDGET HOST INN [MOT]
Chattanooga, TN

BUDGET HOST INN [MOT]
Sweetwater, TN

BUDGET HOST WESTGATE INN
[MOT] *London, KY*

BUDGET INN [MOT] *Greers Ferry Lake
Area, AR*

BUDGET INN'S OF AMERICA [HOT]
Knoxville, TN

BUENA VISTA RESORT [CC] *Hot
Springs & Hot Springs National
Park, AR*

BURN ANTEBELLUM BED &
BREAKFAST INN C. 1834, THE
[BB] *Natchez, MS*

BURNETT PLACE CIRCLE 1830 [BB]
Madison, GA
BURNS-SUTTON HOUSE INN [BB]
Helen, GA
CABOT LODGE MILLSAPS [MOT]
Jackson, MS
CALLAWAY GARDENS [RST] Pine
Mountain (Harris County), GA
CAMBERLEY BROWN [HOT]
Louisville, KY
CAMPBELL HOUSE INN [MOT]
Lexington, KY
CAMPBELL SUILLE LODGE [MOT]
Campbellsville, KY
CANE MOUNT PLANTATION [BB]
Port Gibson, MS
CANNONBORO INN BED AND
BREAKFAST [BB] Charleston, SC
CAPE HATTERAS MOTEL [MOT]
Buxton (Outer Banks), NC
CAPITAL HOTEL [HOT] Little Rock &
North Little Rock, AR
CAPRI MOTEL [MOT] Pigeon Forge,
TN
CAPTAIN'S QUARTERS INN [BB]
Edenton, NC
CARAVELLE RESORT [HOT] Myrtle
Beach, SC
CARDINAL INN [MOT] Maggie Valley,
NC
CARIBBEAN RESORTS & VILLAS
[MOT] Myrtle Beach, SC
CARLETON HOUSE INN [MOT] Rocky
Mount, NC
CAROLINA INN, THE [HOT] Chapel
Hill, NC
CARROLLTON INN [BB] Carrollton,
KY
CARTER CAVES STATE RESORT PARK
[RST] Olive Hill, KY
CASEY JONES STATION INN [MOT]
Jackson, TN
CASINO MAGIC INN [CAS] Pass
Christian, MS
CASTLE INN [MOT] Helen, GA
CATALOOCHEE SKI AREA [RST]
Maggie Valley, NC
CATHERINE'S INN [BB] Wilmington,
NC
CEDAR CREST [BB] Asheville, NC
CEDAR GROVE MANSION INN
[HOT] Vicksburg, MS
CEDAR HILL RESORT [RST] Celina,
TN
CEDARS INN, THE [BB] Beaufort, NC
CHALET CLUB [BB] Hendersonville,
NC
CHALET INN, THE [BB] Bryson City,
NC
CHALET SWITZERLAND INN [HOT]
Little Switzerland, NC
CHANTICLEER LODGE [MOT]
Chickamauga and Chattanooga
National Military Park, GA

CHARLESTON PLACE HOTEL [HOT]
Charleston, SC
CHARRAY INN [MOT] Greeneville, TN
CHARTER HOUSE INN [HOT]
Bainbridge, GA
CHASE SUITE HOTEL BY WOODFIN
[MOT] Baton Rouge, LA
CHATEAU LEMOYNE FRENCH
QUART [MOT] New Orleans, LA
CHATEAU MOTOR HOTEL [HOT]
New Orleans, LA
CHATEAU SONESTA [HOT] New
Orleans, LA
CHATTANOOGA CLARION HOTEL
[HOT] Chattanooga, TN
CHATTANOOGA CHOO CHOO
[HOT] Chattanooga, TN
CHESTERFIELD INN [MOT] Myrtle
Beach, SC
CHETOLA RESORT AT BLOWING
ROCK [RST] Blowing Rock, NC
CHIMES BED & BREAKFAST [BB] New
Orleans, LA
CHRISTOPHER PLACE, AN
INTIMATE RESORT [BB]
Gatlinburg, TN
CIVIC CENTER INN [MOT] Monroe
and West Monroe, LA
CLARION CAROLINIAN INN [MOT]
Georgetown, SC
CLARION HOTEL @ BEL AIR MALL
[HOT] Mobile, AL
CLARION HOTEL - AIRPORT /
OPRYLAND AREA [HOT]
Nashville, TN
CLARION HOTEL RIVERVIEW [HOT]
Covington (Cincinnati Airport
Area), KY
CLARION INN [MOT] Fayetteville, AR
CLARION ON THE LAKE [RST] Hot
Springs & Hot Springs National
Park, AR
CLARION PLAZA HOTEL [MOT]
Fayetteville, NC
CLARION RESORT BUCCANEER
[MOT] Jekyll Island, GA
CLAUSSEN'S INN [BB] Columbia, SC
CLIFF DWELLERS INN [MOT] Blowing
Rock, NC
CLOISTER, THE [RST] Sea Island, GA
CLUBHOUSE INN [MOT] Norcross,
GA
CLUBHOUSE INN [HOT] Savannah,
GA
CLUBHOUSE INN [RST] Nashville, TN
CLUBHOUSE INN AIRPORT [MOT]
Nashville, TN
CLUBHOUSE INN AND SUITES
VALDOSTA [MOT] Valdosta, GA
COHUTTA LODGE & CONFERENCE
CENTER [HOT] Chatsworth, GA
COLONEL LUDLOW INN [BB]
Winston-Salem, NC
COLONIAL HOUSE [MOT] Pigeon
Forge, TN

COLONIAL INN [MOT] *Concord (Cabarrus County), NC*
COLONIAL MANSION INN [MOT] *Eureka Springs, AR*
COLONY INN [MOT] *Camden, SC*
COLUMBIA COURTYARD NW [MOT] *Columbia, SC*
COLUMBIA SHERATON [HOT] *Columbia, SC*
COLUMBIA WEST TRAVELODGE [MOT] *Columbia, SC*
COLUMBINE BED AND BREAKFAST [BB] *Louisville, KY*
COMFORT INN [MOT] *Albemarle, NC*
COMFORT INN [MOT] *Biloxi, MS*
COMFORT INN [MOT] *Blytheville, AR*
COMFORT INN [MOT] *Brunswick, GA*
COMFORT INN [MOT] *Burlington, NC*
COMFORT INN [MOT] *Buxton (Outer Banks), NC*
COMFORT INN [MOT] *Carrollton, GA*
COMFORT INN [MOT] *Cartersville, GA*
COMFORT INN [MOT] *Cherokee, NC*
COMFORT INN [HOT] *Clemson, SC*
COMFORT INN [MOT] *Columbus, MS*
COMFORT INN [MOT] *Concord (Cabarrus County), NC*
COMFORT INN [MOT] *Conway, AR*
COMFORT INN [HOT] *Cordele, GA*
COMFORT INN [HOT] *Dothan, AL*
COMFORT INN [MOT] *Dyersburg, TN*
COMFORT INN [MOT] *El Dorado, AR*
COMFORT INN [MOT] *Elizabeth City, NC*
COMFORT INN [MOT] *Evergreen, AL*
COMFORT INN [MOT] *Fayetteville, NC*
COMFORT INN [MOT] *Florence, AL*
COMFORT INN [MOT] *Florence, SC*
COMFORT INN [MOT] *Gaffney, SC*
COMFORT INN [MOT] *Greensboro, NC*
COMFORT INN [MOT] *Greenwood, MS*
COMFORT INN [MOT] *Greenwood, SC*
COMFORT INN [MOT] *Grenada, MS*
COMFORT INN [MOT] *Harrison, AR*
COMFORT INN [HOT] *Hattiesburg, MS*
COMFORT INN [MOT] *Helen, GA*
COMFORT INN [MOT] *Hendersonville, NC*
COMFORT INN [HOT] *Jackson, TN*
COMFORT INN [MOT] *Kill Devil Hills (Outer Banks), NC*
COMFORT INN [MOT] *Kinston, NC*
COMFORT INN [MOT] *Knoxville, TN*
COMFORT INN [MOT] *Laurinburg, NC*
COMFORT INN [MOT] *Lexington, KY*
COMFORT INN [MOT] *Lumberton, NC*
COMFORT INN [MOT] *Macon, GA*
COMFORT INN [MOT] *Maggie Valley, NC*

COMFORT INN [MOT] *McMinnville, TN*
COMFORT INN [MOT] *Memphis, TN*
COMFORT INN [MOT] *Memphis, TN*
COMFORT INN [MOT] *Morehead City, NC*
COMFORT INN [MOT] *Nags Head (Outer Banks), NC*
COMFORT INN [MOT] *Natchitoches, LA*
COMFORT INN [MOT] *Oak Ridge, TN*
COMFORT INN [MOT] *Perry, GA*
COMFORT INN [MOT] *Roanoke Rapids, NC*
COMFORT INN [MOT] *Rock Hill, SC*
COMFORT INN [MOT] *Ruston, LA*
COMFORT INN [MOT] *Sanford, NC*
COMFORT INN [MOT] *Searcy, AR*
COMFORT INN [MOT] *Sevierville, TN*
COMFORT INN [MOT] *Smithfield, NC*
COMFORT INN [MOT] *Spartanburg, SC*
COMFORT INN [MOT] *Statesboro, GA*
COMFORT INN [MOT] *Sweetwater, TN*
COMFORT INN [MOT] *Tifton, GA*
COMFORT INN [MOT] *Tupelo, MS*
COMFORT INN [MOT] *Washington, NC*
COMFORT INN [MOT] *Williamston, NC*
COMFORT INN [HOT] *Wilmington, NC*
COMFORT INN [HOT] *Wilson, NC*
COMFORT INN AIRPORT [MOT] *Charlotte, NC*
COMFORT INN AND SUITES [MOT] *Jekyll Island, GA*
COMFORT INN ATRIUM GARDENS [MOT] *Elizabethtown, KY*
COMFORT INN BUCKHEAD [MOT] *Atlanta, GA*
COMFORT INN CENTRAL [MOT] *Birmingham, AL*
COMFORT INN CONFERENCE CTR [MOT] *Valdosta, GA*
COMFORT INN CROSS CREEK [MOT] *Fayetteville, NC*
COMFORT INN KINGSPORT [MOT] *Kingsport, TN*
COMFORT INN LAFAYETTE [HOT] *Lafayette, LA*
COMFORT INN LAKE NORMAN [MOT] *Cornelius, NC*
COMFORT INN NORTH [MOT] *Raleigh, NC*
COMFORT INN PINEHURST [MOT] *Pinehurst, NC*
COMFORT INN SOUTH [MOT] *Raleigh, NC*
COMFORT INN UNCC [MOT] *Charlotte, NC*
COMFORT INN UNIVERSITY [MOT] *Durham, NC*

COMFORT INN UNIVERSITY [MOT]
Huntsville, AL
COMFORT SUITES [AS] Asheville, NC
COMFORT SUITES [AS] Chattanooga,
TN
COMFORT SUITES [AS] Hickory, NC
COMFORT SUITES [MOT] Knoxville,
TN
COMFORT SUITES [HOT] London, KY
COMFORT SUITES [MOT] Louisville,
KY
COMFORT SUITES [MOT] Lumberton,
NC
COMFORT SUITES [AS] Montgomery,
AL
COMFORT SUITES MERRY ACRES
[MOT] Albany, GA
COMFORT SUITES RIVERFRONT
PARK [MOT] New Bern, NC
COMPASS COVE OCEANFRONT
RESORT [RST] Myrtle Beach, SC
COOL WATERS MOTEL [MOT]
Cherokee, NC
CORDELE CONFERENCE CENTER
[MOT] Cordele, GA
CORNER OAK MANOR [BB] Asheville,
NC
CORNERS BED & BREAKFAST INN
[BB] Vicksburg, MS
COTTAGE, THE [BB] Wrightsville
Beach, NC
COTTONWOOD INN MOTEL [MOT]
Pocahontas, AR
COUNTRY HEARTH INN [MOT]
Danville, KY
COUNTRY HEARTH INN ATLANTA
[HOT] Atlanta, GA
COUNTRY INN [MOT] Bastrop, LA
COUNTRYINN & SUITES BY
CARLSON [AS] Decatur, AL
COUNTRY INN AND SUITES [MOT]
Cadiz, KY
COUNTRY INN AND SUITES [MOT]
Lumberton, NC
COUNTRY INN AND SUITES [MOT]
Rock Hill, SC
COUNTRY INN TOWN - MOTEL
[MOT] Franklin (Macon County),
NC
COUNTRY SQUIRE REST & VINTAG
[MOT] Warsaw, NC
COURTYARD BY MARRIOTT [MOT]
Athens, GA
COURTYARD BY MARRIOTT [MOT]
Atlanta, GA
COURTYARD BY MARRIOTT [MOT]
Augusta, GA
COURTYARD BY MARRIOTT [MOT]
Birmingham, AL
COURTYARD BY MARRIOTT [MOT]
Charlotte, NC
COURTYARD BY MARRIOTT [MOT]
Charlotte, NC
COURTYARD BY MARRIOTT [MOT]
Columbus, GA

COURTYARD BY MARRIOTT [MOT]
Covington (Cincinnati Airport
Area), KY
COURTYARD BY MARRIOTT [MOT]
Durham, NC
COURTYARD BY MARRIOTT [MOT]
Greenville, SC
COURTYARD BY MARRIOTT [HOT]
Huntsville, AL
COURTYARD BY MARRIOTT [MOT]
Knoxville, TN
COURTYARD BY MARRIOTT [HOT]
Lexington, KY
COURTYARD BY MARRIOTT [MOT]
Little Rock & North Little Rock,
AR
COURTYARD BY MARRIOTT [MOT]
Louisville, KY
COURTYARD BY MARRIOTT [MOT]
Macon, GA
COURTYARD BY MARRIOTT [MOT]
Montgomery, AL
COURTYARD BY MARRIOTT [HOT]
Nashville, TN
COURTYARD BY MARRIOTT [MOT]
Norcross, GA
COURTYARD BY MARRIOTT [MOT]
Paducah, KY
COURTYARD BY MARRIOTT [MOT]
Raleigh, NC
COURTYARD BY MARRIOTT [MOT]
Savannah, GA
COURTYARD BY MARRIOTT [MOT]
Wilmington, NC
COURTYARD BY MARRIOTT [MOT]
Winston-Salem, NC
COURTYARD BY MARRIOTT
AIRPORT [MOT] Nashville, TN
COURTYARD BY MARRIOTT
MEMPHIS PARK AVENUE
[MOT] Memphis, TN
COURTYARD BY MARRIOTT SOUTH
[HOT] Atlanta Hartsfield Airport
Area, GA
COVENANAT COVE LODGE AND
MARINA [MOT] Guntersville,
AL
CRABTREE SUMMIT HOTEL, THE
[MOT] Raleigh, NC
CRAIG'S MOTEL [MOT] Cherokee, NC
CREEKSIDE INN [MOT] Gatlinburg,
TN
CREEKSTONE INN [MOT] Pigeon
Forge, TN
CRENSHAW HOUSE BED &
BREAKFAST [BB] Auburn, AL
CRESCENT COTTAGE INN [BB]
Eureka Springs, AR
CRIPPEN'S COUNTRY INN [BB]
Blowing Rock, NC
CROSS COUNTRY INN- GREATER
CINCINNATI [MOT] Covington
(Cincinnati Airport Area), KY
CROWNE PLAZA [HOT] Greenville, SC
CROWNE PLAZA [HOT] Macon, GA

CROWNE PLAZA RAVINIA [HOT] *Atlanta, GA*
CROWNE PLAZA RESORT [RST] *Hilton Head Island, SC*
CRYSTAL COAST [MOT] *Morehead City, NC*
CUMBERLAND FALLS STATE PARK [RST] *Cumberland Falls State Resort Park, KY*
CUMBERLAND LODGE [MOT] *Jamestown, KY*
CURRAN HOUSE B&B, THE [BB] *Wilmington, NC*
CYPRESS HOUSE B & B [BB] *Kill Devil Hills (Outer Banks), NC*
CYPRESS INN, THE [BB] *Myrtle Beach, SC*
DARLINGS BY THE SEA - OCEANFRONT WHIRLPOOL SUITES [AS] *Wilmington, NC*
DAUPHINE ORLEANS HOTEL [HOT] *New Orleans, LA*
DAVIDSON VILLAGE INN [BB] *Cornelius, NC*
DAVIS INN [MOT] *Pine Mountain (Harris County), GA*
DAY DREAMS COUNTRY INN [BB] *Pigeon Forge, TN*
DAYLIGHT INN [MOT] *Perry, GA*
DAYS INN [MOT] *Adel, GA*
DAYS INN [MOT] *Alexandria, LA*
DAYS INN [MOT] *Asheboro, NC*
DAYS INN [MOT] *Ashland, KY*
DAYS INN [MOT] *Augusta, GA*
DAYS INN [MOT] *Berea, KY*
DAYS INN [MOT] *Biloxi, MS*
DAYS INN [MOT] *Calhoun, GA*
DAYS INN [MOT] *Carrollton, KY*
DAYS INN [MOT] *Cartersville, GA*
DAYS INN [MOT] *Caryville, TN*
DAYS INN [MOT] *Cave City, KY*
DAYS INN [MOT] *Charleston, SC*
DAYS INN [MOT] *Cherokee, NC*
DAYS INN [MOT] *Clanton, AL*
DAYS INN [MOT] *Clarksville, TN*
DAYS INN [MOT] *Clinton, SC*
DAYS INN [MOT] *Columbia, TN*
DAYS INN [MOT] *Conway, AR*
DAYS INN [MOT] *Cullman, AL*
DAYS INN [MOT] *Danville, KY*
DAYS INN [MOT] *Demopolis, AL*
DAYS INN [MOT] *Douglas, GA*
DAYS INN [MOT] *Elizabethtown, KY*
DAYS INN [MOT] *Eureka Springs, AR*
DAYS INN [MOT] *Evergreen, AL*
DAYS INN [MOT] *Fayetteville, AR*
DAYS INN [MOT] *Fayetteville, NC*
DAYS INN [MOT] *Florence, AL*
DAYS INN [MOT] *Frankfort, KY*
DAYS INN [MOT] *Franklin (Macon County), NC*
DAYS INN [MOT] *Gatlinburg, TN*
DAYS INN [MOT] *Glasgow, KY*
DAYS INN [MOT] *Goldsboro, NC*
DAYS INN [MOT] *Greeneville, TN*
DAYS INN [MOT] *Greenville, SC*

DAYS INN [MOT] *Harrison, AR*
DAYS INN [MOT] *Henderson, KY*
DAYS INN [MOT] *Hurricane Mills, TN*
DAYS INN [MOT] *Jackson, TN*
DAYS INN [MOT] *Jellico, TN*
DAYS INN [MOT] *Johnson City, TN*
DAYS INN [MOT] *Jonesboro, AR*
DAYS INN [MOT] *Kingsport, TN*
DAYS INN [MOT] *Knoxville, TN*
DAYS INN [MOT] *Lebanon, TN*
DAYS INN [MOT] *Lenoir City, TN*
DAYS INN [MOT] *Lexington, KY*
DAYS INN [MOT] *Little Rock & North Little Rock, AR*
DAYS INN [MOT] *Madison, GA*
DAYS INN [MOT] *Madisonville, KY*
DAYS INN [HOT] *Mayfield, KY*
DAYS INN [MOT] *Milledgeville, GA*
DAYS INN [MOT] *Monroe and West Monroe, LA*
DAYS INN [MOT] *Montgomery, AL*
DAYS INN [MOT] *Morehead, KY*
DAYS INN [MOT] *Morristown, TN*
DAYS INN [MOT] *Murray, KY*
DAYS INN [MOT] *Nashville, TN*
DAYS INN [MOT] *Oak Ridge, TN*
DAYS INN [MOT] *Opelika, AL*
DAYS INN [MOT] *Orangeburg, SC*
DAYS INN [MOT] *Owensboro, KY*
DAYS INN [MOT] *Oxford, MS*
DAYS INN [MOT] *Paducah, KY*
DAYS INN [MOT] *Pascagoula, MS*
DAYS INN [MOT] *Pigeon Forge, TN*
DAYS INN [MOT] *Prestonsburg, KY*
DAYS INN [MOT] *Raleigh, NC*
DAYS INN [MOT] *Richmond, KY*
DAYS INN [MOT] *Rock Hill, SC*
DAYS INN [MOT] *Rome, GA*
DAYS INN [MOT] *Santee, SC*
DAYS INN [MOT] *Scottsboro, AL*
DAYS INN [MOT] *Sevierville, TN*
DAYS INN [MOT] *Sevierville, TN*
DAYS INN [MOT] *Shelby, NC*
DAYS INN [MOT] *Shreveport, LA*
DAYS INN [MOT] *Spartanburg, SC*
DAYS INN [MOT] *Springdale, AR*
DAYS INN [MOT] *St.Simons Island, GA*
DAYS INN [MOT] *Statesboro, GA*
DAYS INN [MOT] *Thomasville, GA*
DAYS INN [MOT] *Tifton, GA*
DAYS INN [MOT] *Vicksburg, MS*
DAYS INN [MOT] *Walton, KY*
DAYS INN [MOT] *Washington, NC*
DAYS INN [MOT] *Williamsburg, KY*
DAYS INN [MOT] *Williamstown, KY*
DAYS INN [MOT] *Wilmington, NC*
DAYS INN [MOT] *Winder, GA*
DAYS INN [MOT] *Winston-Salem, NC*
DAYS INN ABERCORN/SOUTHSIDE [MOT] *Savannah, GA*
DAYS INN AIRPORT [MOT] *Birmingham, AL*
DAYS INN AIRPORT [MOT] *Chattanooga, TN*

DAYS INN [MOT] *Grenada, MS*

DAYS INN AND SUITES [MOT] *Forrest City, AR*

DAYS INN AND SUITES [MOT] *Morehead City, NC*

DAYS INN ATLANTA DOWNTOWN [HOT] *Atlanta, GA*

DAYS INN CENTRAL [MOT] *Greensboro, NC*

DAYS INN CHARLOTTE SOUTH/PARAMOUNT'S CAROWINDS [MOT] *Rock Hill, SC*

DAYS INN COLLEGE PARK [MOT] *Atlanta Hartsfield Airport Area, GA*

DAYS INN CROSSVILLE [MOT] *Crossville, TN*

DAYS INN - DAYS SUITES [HOT] *Savannah, GA*

DAYS INN DOTHAN [MOT] *Dothan, AL*

DAYS INN HAMILTON RESORT [MOT] *Hot Springs & Hot Springs National Park, AR*

DAYS INN MOTEL [MOT] *Jasper, AL*

DAYS INN NORTH [MOT] *Florence, SC*

DAYS INN - OCEANFRONT [MOT] *Kill Devil Hills (Outer Banks), NC*

DAYS INN OF SOMERSET [MOT] *Somerset, KY*

DAYS INN RIVERGATE [HOT] *Chattanooga, TN*

DAYS INN SUITES [MOT] *Nashville, TN*

DAYS INN TOCCOA [MOT] *Toccoa, GA*

DAYS INN UNION CITY GA [MOT] *Atlanta, GA*

DAYS INN WEST [MOT] *Knoxville, TN*

DELAMAR INN [BB] *Beaufort, NC*

DELTA INN [MOT] *Helena, AR*

DENTON MOTEL AND SUITES [MOT] *Paducah, KY*

DISNEY HILTON HEAD ISLAND RESORT [RST] *Hilton Head Island, SC*

DOCKSIDER OCEANFRONT INN [MOT] *Wilmington, NC*

DOGWOOD INN INC [MOT] *Eureka Springs, AR*

DOGWOOD MOTEL [MOT] *Mountain View, AR*

DOUBLETREE [HOT] *Atlanta, GA*

DOUBLETREE GUEST SUITES [HOT] *Atlanta, GA*

DOUBLETREE GUEST SUITES [HOT] *Atlanta, GA*

DOUBLETREE GUEST SUITES [HOT] *Durham, NC*

DOUBLETREE GUEST SUITES [AS] *Nashville, TN*

DOUBLETREE GUEST SUITES HISTORIC CHARLESTON [AS] *Charleston, SC*

DOUBLETREE HOTEL [HOT] *Charlotte, NC*

DOUBLETREE HOTEL [HOT] *New Orleans, LA*

DOUBLETREE HOTEL LAKESIDE NEW ORLEANS [HOT] *Metairie, LA*

DOUBLETREE HOTEL NASHVILLE [HOT] *Nashville, TN*

DOWNTOWN INN [MOT] *Oxford, MS*

DRAWBRIDGE INN AND CONVENTION CENTER [HOT] *Covington (Cincinnati Airport Area), KY*

DRIFTWOOD MOTEL & RESTAURANT [MOT] *Cedar Island, NC*

DRURY INN [MOT] *Nashville, TN*

DRURY INN [MOT] *Paducah, KY*

DRURY INN-MOBILE [HOT] *Mobile, AL*

DUFF GREEN MANSION [BB] *Vicksburg, MS*

DUNES VILLAGE RESORT [HOT] *Myrtle Beach, SC*

DUNHILL [HOT] *Charlotte, NC*

DUNLAP HOUSE BED & BREAKFAST [BB] *Gainesville, GA*

DUNLEITH ANTEBELLUM HOME [BB] *Natchez, MS*

DURHAM FAIRFIELD INN [HOT] *Durham, NC*

EARLY AMERICAN MOTEL [MOT] *Kenlake State Resort Park, KY*

EAST BAY INN [BB] *Savannah, GA*

EAST MAIN GUEST HOUSE [BB] *Rock Hill, SC*

EAST SIDE MOTEL [MOT] *Gatlinburg, TN*

ECHO MOUNTAIN INN [BB] *Hendersonville, NC*

ECONO LODGE [MOT] *Chattanooga, TN*

ECONO LODGE [MOT] *Cookeville, TN*

ECONO LODGE [MOT] *Dunn, NC*

ECONO LODGE [MOT] *Fayetteville, NC*

ECONO LODGE [MOT] *Gatlinburg, TN*

ECONO LODGE [MOT] *Jackson, MS*

ECONO LODGE [MOT] *Kingsport, TN*

ECONO LODGE [MOT] *Montgomery, AL*

ECONO LODGE [MOT] *Morehead City, NC*

ECONO LODGE [MOT] *Mount Vernon, KY*

ECONO LODGE [MOT] *Nashville, TN*

ECONO LODGE [MOT] *Pigeon Forge, TN*

ECONO LODGE [HOT] *Rock Hill, SC*

ECONO LODGE [MOT] *Troy, AL*

ECONO LODGE [MOT] *Walterboro, SC*

ECONO LODGE [MOT] *Walton, KY*

ECONO LODGE INN [MOT]
Clarksville, TN
ECONO LODGE NORTHWEST [MOT]
Marietta, GA
ECONOMY INN [MOT] *Huntsville, AL*
EDGEWATER HOTEL [HOT]
Gatlinburg, TN
EDGEWATER INN [MOT] *Biloxi, MS*
EDISON WALTHALL [HOT] *Jackson,
MS*
EDWARDIAN INN [BB] *Helena, AR*
ELIZA THOMPSON HOUSE [BB]
Savannah, GA
EMBASSY SUITES [HOT] *Atlanta, GA*
EMBASSY SUITES [AS] *Baton Rouge,
LA*
EMBASSY SUITES [HOT] *Birmingham,
AL*
EMBASSY SUITES [AS] *Brunswick, GA*
EMBASSY SUITES [AS] *Charlotte, NC*
EMBASSY SUITES [AS] *Covington
(Cincinnati Airport Area), KY*
EMBASSY SUITES [HOT] *Greenville, SC*
EMBASSY SUITES [HOT] *Memphis, TN*
EMBASSY SUITES [AS] *Nashville, TN*
EMBASSY SUITES HISTORIC CHAS
[HOT] *Charleston, SC*
EMBASSY SUITES HOTEL [HOT]
Columbia, SC
EMBASSY SUITES HOTEL [HOT]
Greensboro, NC
EMBASSY SUITES HOTEL [AS]
Raleigh, NC
EMBASSY SUITES HOTEL ATLANTA
[HOT] *Atlanta, GA*
EMBASSY SUITES HOTEL NEW
ORLEANS [HOT] *New Orleans,
LA*
EMBASSY SUITES KINGSTON
PLANTATION [RST] *Myrtle
Beach, SC*
EMERALD ISLE INN AND BED &
BREAKFAST [BB] *Morehead City,
NC*
EMORY INN [MOT] *Atlanta, GA*
EMPRESS OF LITTLE ROCK [BB] *Little
Rock & North Little Rock, AR*
ESEEOLA LODGE [RST] *Linville, NC*
EUREKA MATTERHORN TOWERS
[MOT] *Eureka Springs, AR*
EVANS-CANTRELL HOUSE B&B, THE
[BB] *Perry, GA*
EXECUTIVE INN [MOT] *Cookeville,
TN*
EXECUTIVE INN [MOT] *Corinth, MS*
EXECUTIVE INN [MOT] *Springdale,
AR*
EXECUTIVE INN [MOT] *Tupelo, MS*
EXECUTIVE INN MOTOR HOTEL
[MOT] *Louisville, KY*
EXECUTIVE INN RIVERMONT
[MOT] *Owensboro, KY*
EXECUTIVE WEST [HOT] *Louisville,
KY*
EXPRESSWAY INN [MOT] *Manchester,
TN*

EXTENDED STAY GREENWOOD INN
[MOT] *Greenwood, SC*
FAIRFIELD BAY RESORT [RST] *Greers
Ferry Lake Area, AR*
FAIRFIELD GLADE RESORT [RST]
Crossville, TN
FAIRFIELD INN [MOT] *Atlanta, GA*
FAIRFIELD INN [MOT] *Bowling Green,
KY*
FAIRFIELD INN [MOT] *Covington
(Cincinnati Airport Area), KY*
FAIRFIELD INN [HOT] *Greenville, NC*
FAIRFIELD INN [MOT] *Hilton Head
Island, SC*
FAIRFIELD INN [MOT] *Jackson, TN*
FAIRFIELD INN [MOT] *Johnson City,
TN*
FAIRFIELD INN [HOT] *Lumberton, NC*
FAIRFIELD INN [HOT] *Nashville, TN*
FAIRFIELD INN [MOT] *Norcross, GA*
FAIRFIELD INN [MOT] *Savannah, GA*
FAIRFIELD INN [MOT] *Wilmington,
NC*
FAIRFIELD INN BY MARRIOTT
[MOT] *Ashland, KY*
FAIRFIELD INN BY MARRIOTT
[MOT] *Birmingham, AL*
FAIRFIELD INN BY MARRIOTT
[MOT] *Charlotte, NC*
FAIRFIELD INN BY MARRIOTT
[MOT] *Greensboro, NC*
FAIRFIELD INN BY MARRIOTT
[MOT] *Greenville, SC*
FAIRFIELD INN BY MARRIOTT
[MOT] *Louisville, KY*
FAIRFIELD INN BY MARRIOTT
[MOT] *Montgomery, AL*
FAIRFIELD INN BY MARRIOTT
[MOT] *Myrtle Beach, SC*
FAIRFIELD INN BY MARRIOTT [HOT]
Raleigh, NC
FAIRFIELD INN BY MARRIOTT
[MOT] *Rocky Mount, NC*
FAIRFIELD INN BY MARRIOTT
[MOT] *Shreveport, LA*
FAIRFIELD INN CROSS CREEK [MOT]
Fayetteville, NC
FAIRFIELD INN STATESVILLE [MOT]
Statesville, NC
FAIRFIELD PLACE BED & BREAKFAST
[BB] *Shreveport, LA*
FAIRFIELD SAPPHIRE VALLEY [RST]
Cashiers, NC
FAIRMONT [HOT] *New Orleans, LA*
FALCON MANOR BED AND
BREAKFAST [BB] *McMinnville,
TN*
FALCON MOTEL [MOT] *Buxton
(Outer Banks), NC*
FAMILY INNS OF AMERICA [MOT]
Townsend, TN
FEARRINGTON HOUSE [BB] *Chapel
Hill, NC*
FIDDLERS INN NORTH [MOT]
Nashville, TN

FIELDSTONE RESORT & MARINA [RST] *Hiawassee, GA*
FIRST COLONY INN [BB] *Nags Head (Outer Banks), NC*
FLEUR DE LIS BED & BREAKFAST [BB] *Natchitoches, LA*
FLINT STREETS INNS [BB] *Asheville, NC*
FOLEY HOUSE [BB] *Savannah, GA*
FOLKESTONE INN BED & BREAKFAST [BB] *Bryson City, NC*
FOREST MANOR INN [MOT] *Asheville, NC*
FORREST HILLS MOUNTAIN RESORT [RST] *Dahlonega, GA*
FORT PAYNE TRAVELODGE [MOT] *Fort Payne, AL*
FOUR POINTS BY SHERATON [HOT] *Memphis, TN*
FOUR POINTS HOTEL [MOT] *Fort Smith, AR*
FOUR POINTS HOTEL AND SUITES [MOT] *Louisville, KY*
FOUR POINTS HOTEL RALEIGH [HOT] *Raleigh, NC*
FOUR POINTS HOTEL SHERATON [HOT] *Charlotte, NC*
FOUR POINTS HOTEL SHERATON [MOT] *Jackson, TN*
FOUR POINTS SHERATON HOTEL [MOT] *Tuscaloosa, AL*
FOUR POINTS SHERATON MYRTLE BEACH OCEANFRONT HOTEL [RST] *Myrtle Beach, SC*
FOUR SEASONS ATLANTA [HOT] *Atlanta, GA*
FOUR SEASONS COUNTRY INN [BB] *Glasgow, KY*
FRENCHMAN HOTEL [BB] *New Orleans, LA*
FRENCH QUARTER COURTYARD HOTEL [MOT] *New Orleans, LA*
FRENCH QUARTER GUEST HOUSE [BB] *New Orleans, LA*
FRENCH QUARTER SUITES INN [AS] *Memphis, TN*
FRONT STREET INN [BB] *Wilmington, NC*
FULTON LANE INN [HOT] *Charleston, SC*
GALT HOUSE [HOT] *Louisville, KY*
GALT HOUSE HOTEL, THE [HOT] *Louisville, KY*
GARDEN PLAZA HOTEL [HOT] *Johnson City, TN*
GARDEN PLAZA HOTEL [HOT] *Murfreesboro, TN*
GARDEN PLAZA HOTEL [MOT] *Oak Ridge, TN*
GASLIGHT INN BED & BREAKFAST [BB] *Atlanta, GA*
GASTONIAN INN [BB] *Savannah, GA*
GASTON'S WHITE RIVER RESORT [RST] *Bull Shoals Lake Area, AR*

GENERAL BUTLER STATE RESORT PARK [RST] *Carrollton, KY*
GEORGIAN TERRACE [HOT] *Atlanta, GA*
GILLETTE MOTEL [MOT] *Gatlinburg, TN*
GIROD HOUSE [BB] *New Orleans, LA*
GLENDALE SPRINGS INN [BB] *Jefferson, NC*
GOODBREAD HOUSE B AND B [BB] *Coeur d'Alene, ID*
GOVERNOR EDEN INN [BB] *Edenton, NC*
GRACE HALL BED & BREAKFAST [BB] *Selma, AL*
GRAND CASINO HOTEL BILOXI [HOT] *Biloxi, MS*
GRAND CASINO OF MISS GULFPORT [HOT] *Gulfport, MS*
GRAND HYATT ATLANTA [HOT] *Atlanta, GA*
GRAND MANOR BED AND BREAKFAST INN [BB] *Thomasville, GA*
GRAND RESORT HOTEL AND CONVENTION CENTER [MOT] *Pigeon Forge, TN*
GRANDVIEW LODGE [BB] *Waynesville, NC*
GRATZ PARK INN [BB] *Lexington, KY*
GRAYSTONE INN, THE [BB] *Wilmington, NC*
GREENBO LAKE STATE RESORT [RST] *Ashland, KY*
GREENLEAF INN [BB] *Camden, SC*
GREENSBORO TRAVELODGE [MOT] *Greensboro, NC*
GREEN VALLEY MOTEL [MOT] *Pigeon Forge, TN*
GREENWOOD EXECUTIVE INN [MOT] *Bowling Green, KY*
GREYSTONE, THE [BB] *Cashiers, NC*
GREYSTONE LODGE [MOT] *Boone, NC*
GREYSTONE LODGE [MOT] *Gatlinburg, TN*
GRIDER HILL DOCK AND INDIAN CREEK LODGE [MOT] *Monticello, KY*
GROVE PARK INN RESORT [RST] *Asheville, NC*
GUEST HOUSE INN [MOT] *Thomasville, GA*
GUESTHOUSE INN AND SUITES [MOT] *Nashville, TN*
GUESTHOUSE INN I95 EXIT 94 [MOT] *Savannah, GA*
GUESTHOUSE SUITES [MOT] *Huntsville, AL*
GUESTHOUSE SUITES PLUS [AS] *Greenville, SC*
HAMPTON INN [MOT] *Albany, GA*
HAMPTON INN [HOT] *Anniston, AL*
HAMPTON INN [MOT] *Asheville, NC*
HAMPTON INN [MOT] *Asheville, NC*
HAMPTON INN [MOT] *Athens, AL*

HAMPTON INN [HOT] *Bardstown, KY*
HAMPTON INN [HOT] *Baton Rouge, LA*
HAMPTON INN [MOT] *Birmingham, AL*
HAMPTON INN [MOT] *Blytheville, AR*
HAMPTON INN [MOT] *Boone, NC*
HAMPTON INN [MOT] *Bowling Green, KY*
HAMPTON INN [MOT] *Burlington, NC*
HAMPTON INN [MOT] *Caryville, TN*
HAMPTON INN [MOT] *Chapel Hill, NC*
HAMPTON INN [MOT] *Charlotte, NC*
HAMPTON INN [HOT] *Chattanooga, TN*
HAMPTON INN [MOT] *Clarksdale, MS*
HAMPTON INN [MOT] *Clarksville, TN*
HAMPTON INN [MOT] *Columbia, SC*
HAMPTON INN [MOT] *Columbia, SC*
HAMPTON INN [MOT] *Cornelius, NC*
HAMPTON INN [MOT] *Covington (Cincinnati Airport Area), KY*
HAMPTON INN [MOT] *Elizabeth City, NC*
HAMPTON INN [MOT] *Elizabethtown, KY*
HAMPTON INN [MOT] *Fayetteville, NC*
HAMPTON INN [MOT] *Forsyth, GA*
HAMPTON INN [MOT] *Gatlinburg, TN*
HAMPTON INN [MOT] *Greenville, MS*
HAMPTON INN [HOT] *Greenville, NC*
HAMPTON INN [MOT] *Greenville, SC*
HAMPTON INN [MOT] *Greenwood, MS*
HAMPTON INN [MOT] *Gulf Shores, AL*
HAMPTON INN [HOT] *Hattiesburg, MS*
HAMPTON INN [HOT] *Hendersonville, NC*
HAMPTON INN [MOT] *Hilton Head Island, SC*
HAMPTON INN [MOT] *Hot Springs & Hot Springs National Park, AR*
HAMPTON INN [MOT] *Huntsville, AL*
HAMPTON INN [MOT] *Jackson, TN*
HAMPTON INN [MOT] *Johnson City, TN*
HAMPTON INN [MOT] *Kinston, NC*
HAMPTON INN [MOT] *Lebanon, TN*
HAMPTON INN [HOT] *Lexington, KY*
HAMPTON INN [HOT] *Little Rock & North Little Rock, AR*
HAMPTON INN [MOT] *London, KY*
HAMPTON INN [MOT] *Louisville, KY*
HAMPTON INN [HOT] *Lumberton, NC*
HAMPTON INN [MOT] *Macon, GA*
HAMPTON INN [MOT] *Marietta, GA*
HAMPTON INN [MOT] *Memphis, TN*

HAMPTON INN [HOT] *Montgomery, AL*
HAMPTON INN [HOT] *Morehead City, NC*
HAMPTON INN [MOT] *Murfreesboro, TN*
HAMPTON INN [MOT] *Myrtle Beach, SC*
HAMPTON INN [MOT] *Nashville, TN*
HAMPTON INN [MOT] *Nashville, TN*
HAMPTON INN [MOT] *New Bern, NC*
HAMPTON INN [MOT] *Oak Ridge, TN*
HAMPTON INN [MOT] *Raleigh, NC*
HAMPTON INN [MOT] *Roanoke Rapids, NC*
HAMPTON INN [MOT] *Roanoke Rapids, NC*
HAMPTON INN [MOT] *Rock Hill, SC*
HAMPTON INN [HOT] *Rocky Mount, NC*
HAMPTON INN [MOT] *Salisbury, NC*
HAMPTON INN [MOT] *Savannah, GA*
HAMPTON INN [MOT] *Scottsboro, AL*
HAMPTON INN [HOT] *Searcy, AR*
HAMPTON INN [MOT] *Southern Pines, NC*
HAMPTON INN [MOT] *Spartanburg, SC*
HAMPTON INN [MOT] *Springdale, AR*
HAMPTON INN [MOT] *Statesville, NC*
HAMPTON INN [MOT] *Townsend, TN*
HAMPTON INN [MOT] *Valdosta, GA*
HAMPTON INN [MOT] *Wilmington, NC*
HAMPTON INN [MOT] *Wilson, NC*
HAMPTON INN [MOT] *Winchester, KY*
HAMPTON INN [MOT] *Winston-Salem, NC*
HAMPTON INN [MOT] *Winston-Salem, NC*
HAMPTON INN & SUITES [MOT] *Charleston, SC*
HAMPTON INN & SUITES-CONVENTION CENTER LOCATION [HOT] *New Orleans, LA*
HAMPTON INN - GOLDSBORO [MOT] *Goldsboro, NC*
HAMPTON INN AIRPORT [MOT] *Atlanta Hartsfield Airport Area, GA*
HAMPTON INN AIRPORT FAIREXPO [MOT] *Louisville, KY*
HAMPTON INN AND SUITES AIRPORT [MOT] *Nashville, TN*
HAMPTON INN BIRMINGHAM-EAST [MOT] *Birmingham, AL*
HAMPTON INN BRILEY PARKWAY, OPRYLAND [MOT] *Nashville, TN*
HAMPTON INN BRUNSWICK [MOT] *Brunswick, GA*
HAMPTON INN BUCKHEAD [MOT] *Atlanta, GA*
HAMPTON INN [MOT] *Mobile, AL*

HAMPTON INN COLONNADE [MOT] *Birmingham, AL*
HAMPTON INN-COLUMBUS AIRPORT [HOT] *Columbus, GA*
HAMPTON INN - CRABTREE [MOT] *Raleigh, NC*
HAMPTON INN CROSSVILLE [MOT] *Crossville, TN*
HAMPTON INN FOUR SEASONS [MOT] *Greensboro, NC*
HAMPTON INN GASTONIA [MOT] *Gastonia, NC*
HAMPTON INN HICKORY [MOT] *Hickory, NC*
HAMPTON INN HICKORY HOLLOW [MOT] *Nashville, TN*
HAMPTON INN HISTORIC DISTRIC [MOT] *Charleston, SC*
HAMPTON INN HOTEL [MOT] *Savannah, GA*
HAMPTON INN I65N [HOT] *Nashville, TN*
HAMPTON INN JACKSONVILLE [MOT] *Jacksonville, NC*
HAMPTON INN KNOXVILLE NORTH [MOT] *Knoxville, TN*
HAMPTON INN NORTHWOOD [MOT] *Myrtle Beach, SC*
HAMPTON INN RALEIGH DURHAM AIRPORT [MOT] *Raleigh, NC*
HAMPTON INN RIVERFRONT (DOWNTOWN AREA) [HOT] *Covington (Cincinnati Airport Area), KY*
HAMPTON INN RIVERSIDE [MOT] *Charleston, SC*
HAMPTON INN UNIVERSITY [MOT] *Tuscaloosa, AL*
HARBOR LIGHT GUEST HOUSE [BB] *Morehead City, NC*
HARBOURVIEW INN [HOT] *Charleston, SC*
HARMONY HOUSE INN [BB] *New Bern, NC*
HATTERAS MARLIN MOTEL [MOT] *Hatteras (Outer Banks), NC*
HAWTHORN SUITES [AS] *Durham, NC*
HAWTHORN SUITES [MOT] *Little Rock & North Little Rock, AR*
HAWTHORN SUITES [MOT] *Marietta, GA*
HAWTHORN SUITES [MOT] *Norcross, GA*
HAYWOOD PARK [HOT] *Asheville, NC*
HEARTLAND COUNTRY RESORT [MOT] *Pigeon Forge, TN*
HEARTSTONE INN AND COTTAGES [BB] *Eureka Springs, AR*
HEIDI MOTEL [MOT] *Helen, GA*
HEMLOCK INN [BB] *Bryson City, NC*
HERITAGE INN BED & BREAKFAST [BB] *Franklin (Macon County), NC*

HERITAGE QUALITY MOTEL [MOT] *Dalton, GA*
HICKORY BED & BREAKFAST [BB] *Hickory, NC*
HIDDEN CRYSTAL [BB] *Statesville, NC*
HIGH HAMPTON INN AND COUNTRY CLUB [RST] *Cashiers, NC*
HIGHLAND LAKE INN [RST] *Hendersonville, NC*
HIGHLAND MANOR MOTEL [MOT] *Townsend, TN*
HIGHLANDS INN AND KELSEY PLACE RESTAURANT [BB] *Highlands, NC*
HIGHLANDS SUITE HOTEL [AS] *Highlands, NC*
HILLSBOROUGH HOUSE INN [BB] *Durham, NC*
HILTON [HOT] *Greensboro, NC*
HILTON [HOT] *Knoxville, TN*
HILTON [HOT] *Little Rock & North Little Rock, AR*
HILTON ATLANTA [HOT] *Atlanta, GA*
HILTON ATLANTA AIRPORT [HOT] *Atlanta Hartsfield Airport Area, GA*
HILTON ATLANTA NORTHEAST [HOT] *Norcross, GA*
HILTON AT UNIVERSITY PLACE [HOT] *Charlotte, NC*
HILTON BATON ROUGE [HOT] *Baton Rouge, LA*
HILTON CHARLESTON HARBOR RESORT [RST] *Charleston, SC*
HILTON CHARLOTTE AND TOWERS [HOT] *Charlotte, NC*
HILTON CONFERENCE CENTER [HOT] *Jackson, MS*
HILTON DURHAM [HOT] *Durham, NC*
HILTON GARDEN INN BEACHFRONT [MOT] *Gulf Shores, AL*
HILTON GREENVILLE [HOT] *Greenville, SC*
HILTON HOTEL [HOT] *Columbus, GA*
HILTON HOTEL EXECUTIVE PARK [HOT] *Charlotte, NC*
HILTON HUNTSVILLE [HOT] *Huntsville, AL*
HILTON INN [HOT] *Covington (Cincinnati Airport Area), KY*
HILTON INN [HOT] *Fayetteville, AR*
HILTON INN [HOT] *Greenville, NC*
HILTON INN NORTH RIVERFRONT [HOT] *Little Rock & North Little Rock, AR*
HILTON LAFAYETTE & TOWERS [HOT] *Lafayette, LA*
HILTON LAKE LANIER ISLANDS RESORT [RST] *Buford, GA*
HILTON NEW ORLEANS AIRPORT [HOT] *Kenner, LA*
HILTON NEW ORLEANS RIVERSIDE [HOT] *New Orleans, LA*

HILTON NORTH RALEIGH [HOT] *Raleigh, NC*
HILTON OCEANFRONT RESORT [RST] *Hilton Head Island, SC*
HILTON'S BLUFF B&B INN [BB] *Pigeon Forge, TN*
HILTON SUITES [HOT] *Lexington, KY*
HILTON SUITES [MOT] *Nashville, TN*
HILTON WILMINGTON RIVERSIDE [HOT] *Wilmington, NC*
HISTORIC FRENCH MARKET INN [MOT] *New Orleans, LA*
HISTORIC STATESBORO INN [BB] *Statesboro, GA*
HOLIDAY INN [BB] *Alexandria, LA*
HOLIDAY INN [MOT] *Anderson, SC*
HOLIDAY INN [MOT] *Anniston, AL*
HOLIDAY INN [MOT] *Asheville, NC*
HOLIDAY INN [MOT] *Augusta, GA*
HOLIDAY INN [HOT] *Banner Elk, NC*
HOLIDAY INN [MOT] *Bardstown, KY*
HOLIDAY INN [MOT] *Beaufort, SC*
HOLIDAY INN [MOT] *Biloxi, MS*
HOLIDAY INN [MOT] *Birmingham, AL*
HOLIDAY INN [MOT] *Blytheville, AR*
HOLIDAY INN [MOT] *Bossier City, LA*
HOLIDAY INN [MOT] *Bowling Green, KY*
HOLIDAY INN [MOT] *Cave City, KY*
HOLIDAY INN [HOT] *Charleston, SC*
HOLIDAY INN [MOT] *Charlotte, NC*
HOLIDAY INN [MOT] *Clemson, SC*
HOLIDAY INN [MOT] *Cleveland, MS*
HOLIDAY INN [MOT] *Cleveland, TN*
HOLIDAY INN [MOT] *Columbus, MS*
HOLIDAY INN [HOT] *Cookeville, TN*
HOLIDAY INN [MOT] *Covington, LA*
HOLIDAY INN [HOT] *Covington (Cincinnati Airport Area), KY*
HOLIDAY INN [MOT] *Covington (Cincinnati Airport Area), KY*
HOLIDAY INN [MOT] *Dalton, GA*
HOLIDAY INN [MOT] *Douglas, GA*
HOLIDAY INN [MOT] *Dublin, GA*
HOLIDAY INN [MOT] *Dyersburg, TN*
HOLIDAY INN [MOT] *Elizabeth City, NC*
HOLIDAY INN [MOT] *Fayetteville, NC*
HOLIDAY INN [MOT] *Forsyth, GA*
HOLIDAY INN [HOT] *Frankfort, KY*
HOLIDAY INN [MOT] *Gainesville, GA*
HOLIDAY INN [HOT] *Gallatin, TN*
HOLIDAY INN [MOT] *Gatlinburg, TN*
HOLIDAY INN [MOT] *Greeneville, TN*
HOLIDAY INN [MOT] *Greenville, MS*
HOLIDAY INN [MOT] *Greenville, SC*
HOLIDAY INN [MOT] *Grenada, MS*
HOLIDAY INN [MOT] *Gulfport, MS*
HOLIDAY INN [MOT] *Guntersville, AL*
HOLIDAY INN [HOT] *Hattiesburg, MS*
HOLIDAY INN [MOT] *Hazard, KY*
HOLIDAY INN [HOT] *Hilton Head Island, SC*
HOLIDAY INN [MOT] *Hopkinsville, KY*

HOLIDAY INN [HOT] *Kenner, LA*
HOLIDAY INN [MOT] *Kill Devil Hills (Outer Banks), NC*
HOLIDAY INN [MOT] *Knoxville, TN*
HOLIDAY INN [HOT] *Lexington, KY*
HOLIDAY INN [HOT] *Louisville, KY*
HOLIDAY INN [MOT] *Louisville, KY*
HOLIDAY INN [MOT] *Lumberton, NC*
HOLIDAY INN [HOT] *Marietta, GA*
HOLIDAY INN [MOT] *Meridian, MS*
HOLIDAY INN [MOT] *Milledgeville, GA*
HOLIDAY INN [MOT] *Monroe and West Monroe, LA*
HOLIDAY INN [MOT] *Montgomery, AL*
HOLIDAY INN [MOT] *Morehead, KY*
HOLIDAY INN [HOT] *Morganton, NC*
HOLIDAY INN [HOT] *Morristown, TN*
HOLIDAY INN [MOT] *Mountain Home, AR*
HOLIDAY INN [MOT] *Murfreesboro, TN*
HOLIDAY INN [MOT] *Myrtle Beach, SC*
HOLIDAY INN [HOT] *Nashville, TN*
HOLIDAY INN [MOT] *Nashville, TN*
HOLIDAY INN [MOT] *Nashville, TN*
HOLIDAY INN [MOT] *Nashville, TN*
HOLIDAY INN [MOT] *Nashville, TN*
HOLIDAY INN [HOT] *New Iberia, LA*
HOLIDAY INN [MOT] *Opelika, AL*
HOLIDAY INN [MOT] *Orangeburg, SC*
HOLIDAY INN [MOT] *Owensboro, KY*
HOLIDAY INN [MOT] *Prestonsburg, KY*
HOLIDAY INN [HOT] *Raleigh, NC*
HOLIDAY INN [HOT] *Raleigh, NC*
HOLIDAY INN [MOT] *Richmond, KY*
HOLIDAY INN [MOT] *Rock Hill, SC*
HOLIDAY INN [MOT] *Russellville, AR*
HOLIDAY INN [MOT] *Salisbury, NC*
HOLIDAY INN [MOT] *Selma, AL*
HOLIDAY INN [HOT] *Sheffield, AL*
HOLIDAY INN [HOT] *Southern Pines, NC*
HOLIDAY INN [HOT] *Springdale, AR*
HOLIDAY INN [MOT] *Statesville, NC*
HOLIDAY INN [MOT] *Sumter, SC*
HOLIDAY INN [MOT] *Tupelo, MS*
HOLIDAY INN [MOT] *Vicksburg, MS*
HOLIDAY INN [HOT] *Walterboro, SC*
HOLIDAY INN [MOT] *Waycross, GA*
HOLIDAY INN [MOT] *Williamston, NC*
HOLIDAY INN [HOT] *Wilmington, NC*
HOLIDAY INN [HOT] *Wilmington, NC*
HOLIDAY INN [MOT] *Wilson, NC*
HOLIDAY INN [MOT] *Winchester, KY*
HOLIDAY INN ATHENS [MOT] *Athens, GA*
HOLIDAY INN ATLANTA/ROSWELL [HOT] *Norcross, GA*
HOLIDAY INN ATLANTA DOWNTOWN [HOT] *Atlanta, GA*
HOLIDAY INN [MOT] *Jackson, TN*

HOLIDAY INN BEACH RESORT [MOT] *Jekyll Island, GA*

HOLIDAY INN BORDEAUX [MOT] *Fayetteville, NC*

HOLIDAY INN BUCKHEAD [HOT] *Atlanta, GA*

HOLIDAY INN CARTERSVILLE [MOT] *Cartersville, GA*

HOLIDAY INN-CHAPEL HILL [HOT] *Chapel Hill, NC*

HOLIDAY INN CHEROKEE [MOT] *Cherokee, NC*

HOLIDAY INN CITY CENTER [HOT] *Fort Smith, AR*

HOLIDAY INN DORTCHES [MOT] *Rocky Mount, NC*

HOLIDAY INN DOWNTOWN-SUPERDOME [HOT] *New Orleans, LA*

HOLIDAY INN EAST [MOT] *Montgomery, AL*

HOLIDAY INN EXPRESS [MOT] *Albany, GA*

HOLIDAY INN EXPRESS [MOT] *Athens, GA*

HOLIDAY INN EXPRESS [MOT] *Boone, NC*

HOLIDAY INN EXPRESS [MOT] *Carrollton, KY*

HOLIDAY INN EXPRESS [MOT] *Commerce, GA*

HOLIDAY INN EXPRESS [HOT] *Cornelius, NC*

HOLIDAY INN EXPRESS [MOT] *Fayetteville, NC*

HOLIDAY INN EXPRESS [MOT] *Goldsboro, NC*

HOLIDAY INN EXPRESS [HOT] *Gulf Shores, AL*

HOLIDAY INN EXPRESS [RST] *Hatteras (Outer Banks), NC*

HOLIDAY INN EXPRESS [HOT] *Jacksonville, NC*

HOLIDAY INN EXPRESS [HOT] *Jonesboro, AR*

HOLIDAY INN EXPRESS [MOT] *Lafayette, LA*

HOLIDAY INN EXPRESS [HOT] *London, KY*

HOLIDAY INN EXPRESS [MOT] *Macon, GA*

HOLIDAY INN EXPRESS [MOT] *Madison, GA*

HOLIDAY INN EXPRESS [MOT] *Nashville, TN*

HOLIDAY INN EXPRESS [MOT] *Nashville, TN*

HOLIDAY INN EXPRESS [MOT] *New Orleans, LA*

HOLIDAY INN EXPRESS [MOT] *Paducah, KY*

HOLIDAY INN EXPRESS HOTEL [MOT] *Jackson, MS*

HOLIDAY INN EXPRESS HOTEL & SUITES [HOT] *Bentonville, AR*

HOLIDAY INN EXPR HERMITAGE [MOT] *Murfreesboro, TN*

HOLIDAY INN FINANCIAL PLAZA [MOT] *Shreveport, LA*

HOLIDAY INN HOTEL AND SUITES [HOT] *Montgomery, AL*

HOLIDAY INN I10 BELGRATH [HOT] *Mobile, AL*

HOLIDAY INN - JOHNSON CITY [HOT] *Johnson City, TN*

HOLIDAY INN LEXINGTON NORTH [MOT] *Lexington, KY*

HOLIDAY INN LOUSIVILLE DWTN [HOT] *Louisville, KY*

HOLIDAY INN MACARTHUR DRIVE [HOT] *Alexandria, LA*

HOLIDAY INN METAIRIE [MOT] *Metairie, LA*

HOLIDAY INN MIDTOWN [HOT] *Memphis, TN*

HOLIDAY INN MORGAN CITY [MOT] *Morgan City, LA*

HOLIDAY INN MORRISTOWN CONFERENCE CTR I-81 EXIT 8 [MOT] *Morristown, TN*

HOLIDAY INN NEW ORLEANS VETERANS [HOT] *Metairie, LA*

HOLIDAY INN NORTHEAST [MOT] *Columbia, SC*

HOLIDAY INN OF CAMDEN [MOT] *Camden, SC*

HOLIDAY INN OF JENNINGS [MOT] *Jennings, LA*

HOLIDAY INN PERRY [MOT] *Perry, GA*

HOLIDAY INN RESEARCH PARK [HOT] *Huntsville, AL*

HOLIDAY INN RESORT [MOT] *Pigeon Forge, TN*

HOLIDAY INN ROCKY MOUNT [MOT] *Rocky Mount, NC*

HOLIDAY INN SELECT [HOT] *Atlanta, GA*

HOLIDAY INN SELECT [MOT] *Hickory, NC*

HOLIDAY INN SELECT [HOT] *Memphis, TN*

HOLIDAY INN SELECT [HOT] *Norcross, GA*

HOLIDAY INN SELECT [HOT] *Winston-Salem, NC*

HOLIDAY INN SELECT DOWNTOWN [HOT] *Knoxville, TN*

HOLIDAY INN SELECT-WEST [HOT] *Little Rock & North Little Rock, AR*

HOLIDAY INN SKYTOP [HOT] *Rome, GA*

HOLIDAY INN SOUTH [HOT] *Baton Rouge, LA*

HOLIDAY INN SOUTH [MOT] *Dothan, AL*

HOLIDAY INN SOUTH ON THE LAKE [HOT] *Birmingham, AL*

HOLIDAY INN SPACE CENTER [HOT] *Huntsville, AL*

HOLIDAY INN SUWANEE [MOT] *Buford, GA*

HOLIDAY INN TEXARKANA I30 [HOT] *Texarkana, AR*

HOLIDAY INN VANDERBILT [HOT] *Nashville, TN*

HOLIDAY INN WEST [MOT] *Dothan, AL*

HOLIDAY INN WEST I-565 [MOT] *Huntsville, AL*

HOLIDAY INN WHITE SANDS RESORT [MOT] *Gulf Shores, AL*

HOLIDAY INN WOODLAWN [HOT] *Charlotte, NC*

HOLIDAY MOTEL INC [MOT] *Berea, KY*

HOMESTEAD EXECUTIVE INN [MOT] *Florence, AL*

HOMESTEAD INN [BB] *Blowing Rock, NC*

HOMEWOOD SUITES [MOT] *Norcross, GA*

HOMEWOOD SUITES [HOT] *Raleigh, NC*

HOMEWOOD SUITES [MOT] *Savannah, GA*

HOMEWOOD SUITES BY HILTON [HOT] *Norcross, GA*

HOTEL CHATEAU DUPRE [HOT] *New Orleans, LA*

HOTEL DE LA MONNAIE [MOT] *New Orleans, LA*

HOTEL INTER-CONTINENTAL NEW ORLEANS [HOT] *New Orleans, LA*

HOTEL MAISON DE VILLE [HOT] *New Orleans, LA*

HOTEL MONTELEONE [HOT] *New Orleans, LA*

HOUND EARS CLUB [RST] *Blowing Rock, NC*

HOUSE ON BAYOU ROAD [BB] *New Orleans, LA*

HOUSTON INN [MOT] *Glasgow, KY*

HOWARD JOHNSON [MOT] *Adel, GA*

HOWARD JOHNSON [MOT] *Calhoun, GA*

HOWARD JOHNSON [MOT] *Fayetteville, NC*

HOWARD JOHNSON [MOT] *Murfreesboro, TN*

HOWARD JOHNSON [MOT] *Pigeon Forge, TN*

HOWARD JOHNSON [MOT] *Thibodaux, LA*

HOWARD JOHNSON BILTMORE INN [MOT] *Asheville, NC*

HOWARD JOHNSON EXPRESS INN [MOT] *Alexandria, LA*

HOWARD JOHNSON EXPRESS INN [MOT] *Henderson, NC*

HOWARD JOHNSON EXPRESS INN [MOT] *Wilmington, NC*

HOWARD JOHNSON HOTEL [HOT] *Atlanta Hartsfield Airport Area, GA*

HOWARD JOHNSON INN [HOT] *Hardeeville, SC*

HOWARD JOHNSON INN [MOT] *Meridian, MS*

HOWARD JOHNSON INN [MOT] *Paris, KY*

HOWARD JOHNSON INNS & SUITES [MOT] *Commerce, GA*

HOWARD JOHNSON PLAZA [MOT] *Knoxville, TN*

HOWARD JOHNSON PLAZA HOTEL [HOT] *Johnson City, TN*

HUNTER HOUSE BED & BREAKFAST [BB] *Tybee Island, GA*

HYATT CHARLOTTE [HOT] *Charlotte, NC*

HYATT REGENCY [HOT] *Atlanta, GA*

HYATT REGENCY [HOT] *Greenville, SC*

HYATT REGENCY [RST] *Hilton Head Island, SC*

HYATT REGENCY [HOT] *Knoxville, TN*

HYATT REGENCY [HOT] *New Orleans, LA*

HYATT REGENCY LEXINGTON [HOT] *Lexington, KY*

HYATT REGENCY LOUISVILLE [HOT] *Louisville, KY*

HYATT REGENCY SAVANNAH [HOT] *Savannah, GA*

HYATT REGENCY SUITES ATLANTA [HOT] *Marietta, GA*

IMPERIAL MOTOR LODGE [MOT] *Brevard, NC*

INDIGO INN [BB] *Charleston, SC*

INN AT BINGHAM SCHOOL [BB] *Chapel Hill, NC*

INN AT BLACKBERRY FARM [BB] *Maryville, TN*

INN AT CAMDEN (LUGOFF), THE [MOT] *Camden, SC*

INN AT CHATEAU ELAN [RST] *Buford, GA*

INN AT DOUGLAS, THE [MOT] *Douglas, GA*

INN AT MOUNTAIN VIEW [BB] *Mountain View, AR*

INN AT ORIENTAL [BB] *New Bern, NC*

INN AT RAGGED GARDENS [BB] *Blowing Rock, NC*

INN AT ROSE HALL [BB] *Eureka Springs, AR*

INN AT ST. THOMAS COURT, THE [AS] *Wilmington, NC*

INN AT THE MILL [MOT] *Fayetteville, AR*

INN CHERAW [MOT] *Cheraw, SC*

INNISFREE VICTORIAN INN [BB] *Cashiers, NC*

INNKEEPER COLISEUM [MOT] *Charlotte, NC*

INN OF AIKEN, THE [MOT] *Aiken, SC*
INN OF PINE BLUFF [MOT] *Pine Bluff, AR*
INN ON THE SQUARE [BB] *Greenwood, SC*
INTERNATIONAL HOUSE [HOT] *New Orleans, LA*
ISLANDER HOTEL [MOT] *Nags Head (Outer Banks), NC*
ISLAND INN [MOT] *St.Simons Island, GA*
ISLE OF CAPRI CASINO & HOTEL [CAS] *Bossier City, LA*
ISLE OFF CAPRI CASINO & HOTEL [HOT] *Natchez, MS*
JACK HUFF'S MOTOR LODGE [MOT] *Gatlinburg, TN*
JAILER'S INN BED AND BREAKFAST [BB] *Bardstown, KY*
JAMESON INN [MOT] *Alexander City, AL*
JAMESON INN [MOT] *Brunswick, GA*
JAMESON INN [MOT] *Calhoun, GA*
JAMESON INN [MOT] *Statesboro, GA*
JAMESON INN [MOT] *Washington, GA*
JAMESTOWN RESORT AND MARINA [RST] *Jamestown, KY*
JASPER INN [MOT] *Jasper, AL*
JEKYLL ISLAND CLUB MOTEL [MOT] *Jekyll Island, GA*
JENNY WILEY STATE RESORT PARK [RST] *Prestonsburg, KY*
JIM OLIVER'S SMOKEHOUSE LODGE [MOT] *Monteagle, TN*
JOE WHEELER STATE RESORT LODGE [RST] *Florence, AL*
JOHNATHAN CREEK INN AND VILLAS [MOT] *Maggie Valley, NC*
JOHN RUTLEDGE HOUSE INN [BB] *Charleston, SC*
JOHNSON'S INN [MOT] *Gatlinburg, TN*
JONESBORO HOLIDAY INN [MOT] *Jonesboro, AR*
JOY MOTEL [MOT] *Eureka Springs, AR*
J. R.'S EXECUTIVE INN [MOT] *Paducah, KY*
JW MARRIOTT HOTEL LENOX [HOT] *Atlanta, GA*
KASTLE INN MOTEL [MOT] *Mount Vernon, KY*
KEHOE HOUSE, THE [BB] *Savannah, GA*
KELLOGG CONFERENCE CENTER [BB] *Tuskegee, AL*
KENLAKE STATE RESORT PARK [RST] *Kenlake State Resort Park, KY*
KENTUCKY DAM MOTEL [RST] *Gilbertsville, KY*
KEY WEST INN [MOT] *Gadsden, AL*
KEY WEST INN [MOT] *Sheffield, AL*
KEY WEST INN CLANTON [MOT] *Clanton, AL*

KIAWAH ISLAND RESORT [RST] *Kiawah Island, SC*
KING & PRINCE BEACH RESORT [HOT] *St.Simons Island, GA*
KING GEORGE IV INN [BB] *Charleston, SC*
KING-KEITH HOUSE B&B [BB] *Atlanta, GA*
KINGS ARMS BED AND BREAKFAST INN [BB] *New Bern, NC*
KINGS COURTYARD INN [BB] *Charleston, SC*
KINGS INN [MOT] *Lenoir City, TN*
KING'S LODGE MOTEL [MOT] *Chattanooga, TN*
KIRKS MOTOR COURT [MOT] *Burlington, NC*
KNIGHTS INN [MOT] *Ashland, KY*
KNIGHTS INN [MOT] *Charleston, SC*
KNIGHTS INN [MOT] *Corbin, KY*
KNIGHTS INN [MOT] *Covington (Cincinnati Airport Area), KY*
KNIGHTS INN AUGUSTA [MOT] *Augusta, GA*
KNIGHTS INN MOTEL [MOT] *Pigeon Forge, TN*
KUNTICKY INN [MOT] *Cave City, KY*
LADY LUCK CASINO & ENTERTAINMENT RESORT [MOT] *Clarksdale, MS*
LAFAYETTE HOTEL, THE [HOT] *New Orleans, LA*
LAFITTE GUEST HOUSE [BB] *New Orleans, LA*
LA FONT INN [MOT] *Pascagoula, MS*
LAKE BARKLEY STATE RESORT PARK [RST] *Cadiz, KY*
LAKE CUMBERLAND STATE RESORT PARK [RST] *Jamestown, KY*
LAKE GUNTERSVILLE STATE PARK AND LODGE [RST] *Guntersville, AL*
LAKE HAMILTON RESORT [RST] *Hot Springs & Hot Springs National Park, AR*
LAKE LURE INN [BB] *Hendersonville, NC*
LAKE NORMAN HOLIDAY INN [MOT] *Cornelius, NC*
LAKEPOINT RESORT [RST] *Eufaula, AL*
LAKESHORE RESORT [MOT] *Greers Ferry Lake Area, AR*
LAKE TIAK OKHATA [RST] *Louisville, MS*
LAKE VIEW INN [MOT] *Caryville, TN*
LAKEVIEW MOTEL [MOT] *Campbellsville, KY*
LA MAISON DE CAMPAGNE [BB] *Lafayette, LA*
LAMOTHE HOUSE [BB] *New Orleans, LA*
LANDFALL PARK HAMPTON INN [HOT] *Wrightsville Beach, NC*
LANDMARK FRENCH QUARTER [HOT] *New Orleans, LA*

LANDMARK INN [MOT] *Pikeville, KY*
LANDMARK INN [MOT] *Somerset, KY*
LANDS INN [HOT] *Charleston, SC*
LA PLACE D'EVANGELINE [BB] *St. Martinville, LA*
LA QUINTA [MOT] *Charleston, SC*
LA QUINTA [MOT] *Metairie, LA*
LA QUINTA INN [MOT] *Anderson, SC*
LA QUINTA INN [MOT] *Baton Rouge, LA*
LA QUINTA INN [MOT] *Bossier City, LA*
LA QUINTA INN [MOT] *Charlotte, NC*
LA QUINTA INN [MOT] *Chattanooga, TN*
LA QUINTA INN [MOT] *Columbia, SC*
LA QUINTA INN [MOT] *Columbus, GA*
LA QUINTA INN [MOT] *Greenville, SC*
LA QUINTA INN [MOT] *Huntsville, AL*
LA QUINTA INN [MOT] *Jackson, MS*
LA QUINTA INN [MOT] *Jackson, MS*
LA QUINTA INN [MOT] *Kenner, LA*
LA QUINTA INN [MOT] *Knoxville, TN*
LA QUINTA INN [MOT] *Knoxville, TN*
LA QUINTA INN [MOT] *Lexington, KY*
LA QUINTA INN [MOT] *Little Rock & North Little Rock, AR*
LA QUINTA INN [MOT] *Marietta, GA*
LA QUINTA INN [MOT] *Mobile, AL*
LA QUINTA INN [MOT] *Montgomery, AL*
LA QUINTA INN [MOT] *Nashville, TN*
LA QUINTA INN [MOT] *Norcross, GA*
LA QUINTA INN [MOT] *Slidell, LA*
LA QUINTA INN & SUITES [MOT] *New Orleans, LA*
LA QUINTA INN AIRPORT [MOT] *Monroe and West Monroe, LA*
LA QUINTA INN AND SUITES [MOT] *Myrtle Beach, SC*
LA QUINTA INN AT OTTER CREEK [MOT] *Little Rock & North Little Rock, AR*
LA QUINTA MOTOR INN [MOT] *Birmingham, AL*
LA QUINTA MOTOR INN [MOT] *Lafayette, LA*
LAUREL HILL PLANTATION B&B [BB] *Charleston, SC*
LAURELWOOD MOUNTAIN INN [MOT] *Cashiers, NC*
LE CONTE VIEW [MOT] *Gatlinburg, TN*
LE MERIDIEN [HOT] *New Orleans, LA*
LENOX INN [MOT] *Atlanta, GA*
LE PAVILLON [HOT] *New Orleans, LA*
LE RICHELIEU IN THE FRENCH QUARTER [MOT] *New Orleans, LA*
LE ROSIER [BB] *New Iberia, LA*
LIGHTHOUSE RESORT MOTEL, THE [MOT] *Gulf Shores, AL*
LINDEN [BB] *Natchez, MS*

LION AND THE ROSE [BB] *Asheville, NC*
LITTLE GREENBRIER LODGE [BB] *Sevierville, TN*
LODGE, THE [MOT] *Waynesville, NC*
LODGE ALLEY INN, THE [BB] *Charleston, SC*
LODGE ON LAKE LURE BED & BREAKFAST [BB] *Hendersonville, NC*
LOEWS VANDERBILT PLAZA [HOT] *Nashville, TN*
LOIS JANE'S RIVERVIEW INN [BB] *Southport, NC*
LOOKOUT MOUNTAIN INN [MOT] *Chattanooga, TN*
LORDS PROPRIETORS INN [BB] *Edenton, NC*
LOVILL HOUSE INN [BB] *Boone, NC*
MADEWOOD PLANTATION HOUSE [BB] *Thibodaux, LA*
MAGNOLIA [BB] *Pinehurst, NC*
MAGNOLIA HILL B&B [BB] *Helena, AR*
MAGNOLIA HOUSE BED & BREAKFAST [BB] *Sumter, SC*
MAGNOLIA PLACA INN [BB] *Savannah, GA*
MAGNOLIA PLACE [BB] *Magnolia, AR*
MAIN STREET INN [BB] *Hilton Head Island, SC*
MAISON DU PRE [BB] *Charleston, SC*
MAISON DUPUY [HOT] *New Orleans, LA*
MALAGA INN [BB] *Mobile, AL*
MAMMOTH CAVE HOTEL [MOT] *Mammoth Cave National Park, KY*
MANOR HOUSE [BB] *Savannah, GA*
MAPLE LODGE [BB] *Blowing Rock, NC*
MAPLES MOTOR INN [MOT] *Pigeon Forge, TN*
MARGLAND BED AND BREAKFAST [BB] *Pine Bluff, AR*
MARIETTA CONFERENCE CENTER & RESORT [HOT] *Marietta, GA*
MARRIOTT [HOT] *Chattanooga, TN*
MARRIOTT [HOT] *Durham, NC*
MARRIOTT [HOT] *Greenville, SC*
MARRIOTT [HOT] *Huntsville, AL*
MARRIOTT [HOT] *Memphis, TN*
MARRIOTT [HOT] *Nashville, TN*
MARRIOTT [HOT] *Norcross, GA*
MARRIOTT [HOT] *Raleigh, NC*
MARRIOTT AIRPORT HOTEL [HOT] *Greensboro, NC*
MARRIOTT ATLANTA AIRPORT [HOT] *Atlanta Hartsfield Airport Area, GA*
MARRIOTT AT RESEARCH TRIANGLE PARK [HOT] *Durham, NC*
MARRIOTT DOWNTOWN [HOT] *Memphis, TN*
MARRIOTT EAST [HOT] *Louisville, KY*

MARRIOTT EVERGREEN CONFERENCE RESORT [HOT] *Atlanta, GA*

MARRIOTT GRAND HOTEL [RST] *Mobile, AL*

MARRIOTT GRIFFIN GATE RESORT [RST] *Lexington, KY*

MARRIOTT HOTEL [HOT] *Charlotte, NC*

MARRIOTT MARQUIS [HOT] *Atlanta, GA*

MARRIOTT NORTH CENTRAL [HOT] *Atlanta, GA*

MASON PLACE BED AND BREAKFAST [BB] *Lenoir City, TN*

MASTERS ECONOMY INN [MOT] *Little Rock & North Little Rock, AR*

MASTERS ECONOMY INN [MOT] *Smithfield, NC*

MAXWELL'S INN & CONFERENCE CENTER [HOT] *Ruston, LA*

MCAFEE INN [MOT] *Pigeon Forge, TN*

MEADOWBROOK INN [BB] *Blowing Rock, NC*

MEADOWVIEW CONFERENCE CENTER [HOT] *Kingsport, TN*

MEETING STREET INN [BB] *Charleston, SC*

MELHANA THE GRAND PLANTATION [RST] *Thomasville, GA*

MELROSE MANSION [BB] *New Orleans, LA*

MICROTEL [MOT] *Lexington, KY*

MICROTEL INN [MOT] *Wilson, NC*

MIDDLETON INN [MOT] *Charleston, SC*

MID PINES INN AND GOLF CLUB [RST] *Southern Pines, NC*

MIDTOWN LODGE [MOT] *Gatlinburg, TN*

MILBANK HISTORIC HOUSE [BB] *Jackson, LA*

MILLSAPS BUIE HOUSE [BB] *Jackson, MS*

MILLS HOUSE, THE [HOT] *Charleston, SC*

MISS BETTY'S B&B INN [BB] *Wilson, NC*

MIZE MOTEL [MOT] *Sevierville, TN*

MOCKINGBIRD INN BED & BREAKFAST [BB] *Tupelo, MS*

MONMOUTH PLANTATOON [BB] *Natchez, MS*

MORNINGSTAR RETREAT [BB] *Eureka Springs, AR*

MOTEL 6 [MOT] *Dothan, AL*

MOTEL 6 [MOT] *Little Rock & North Little Rock, AR*

MOTEL BIRMINGHAM [MOT] *Birmingham, AL*

MOUNTAIN BREEZE MOTEL [MOT] *Pigeon Forge, TN*

MOUNTAIN BROOK INN [HOT] *Birmingham, AL*

MOUNTAIN HIGH MOTEL [MOT] *Highlands, NC*

MOUNTAIN SPRINGS CABINS [MOT] *Asheville, NC*

MULBERRY INN, THE [HOT] *Savannah, GA*

MURRAY PLAZA COURT [MOT] *Murray, KY*

MYRTLE BEACH MARTINIQUE RESORT [HOT] *Myrtle Beach, SC*

NAGGS HEAD BEACH [MOT] *Kill Devil Hills (Outer Banks), NC*

NAGS HEAD INN [HOT] *Nags Head (Outer Banks), NC*

NASHVILLE MARRIOTT [HOT] *Nashville, TN*

NATURAL BRIDGE STATE PARK [RST] *Natural Bridge State Resort Park, KY*

NEW BERN HOUSE INN [BB] *New Bern, NC*

NEW FRIENDSHIP INN [MOT] *Bowling Green, KY*

NEW ORLEANS HOTEL [HOT] *Eureka Springs, AR*

NEW ORLEANS MARRIOTT [HOT] *New Orleans, LA*

NEW PERRY HOTEL-MOTEL [MOT] *Perry, GA*

NICHOLSON HOUSE [BB] *Athens, GA*

NORMA DAN MOTEL [MOT] *Pigeon Forge, TN*

NORTH RALEIGH COURTYARD [MOT] *Raleigh, NC*

NOTTOWAY PLANTATION RESTAURANT & INN [BB] *Baton Rouge, LA*

NU WRAY INN [BB] *Burnsville, NC*

OAKMONT LODGE, THE [MOT] *Cashiers, NC*

OAK SQUARE [MOT] *Gatlinburg, TN*

OAK SQUARE COUNTRY INN [BB] *Port Gibson, MS*

OAK TREE LODGE [MOT] *Sevierville, TN*

OAKWOOD INN BED & BREAKFAST [BB] *Raleigh, NC*

OCEAN DUNES RESORT AND VILLAS [HOT] *Myrtle Beach, SC*

OCEAN FOREST PLAZA [HOT] *Myrtle Beach, SC*

OCEANFRONT VIKING MOTEL, THE [MOT] *Myrtle Beach, SC*

OCRACOKE ISLAND INN [MOT] *Ocracoke (Outer Banks), NC*

OLD BARDSTOWN INN [MOT] *Bardstown, KY*

OLDE HARBOUR INN [BB] *Savannah, GA*

OLD LOUISVILLE INN [BB] *Louisville, KY*

OLD REYNOLDS MANSION, THE [BB] *Asheville, NC*

OLD STONE [BB] *Waynesville, NC*

OLD TALBOTT TAVERN, THE [BB]
  Bardstown, KY
OLIVER-BRITT HOUSE INN &
  TEAROOM [BB] *Oxford, MS*
OMNI CHARLOTTE HOTEL [HOT]
  Charlotte, NC
OMNI HOTEL [HOT] *Atlanta, GA*
OMNI ROYAL CRESCENT [HOT] *New
  Orleans, LA*
OMNI ROYAL ORLEANS [HOT] *New
  Orleans, LA*
ONE SOUTH LUMINA [MOT]
  Wrightsville Beach, NC
OPRYLAND HOTEL [MOT] *Nashville,
  TN*
OWLS NEST [BB] *Asheville, NC*
OZARK FOLK CENTER [MOT]
  Mountain View, AR
PALACE HOTEL & BATH HOUSE [AS]
  Eureka Springs, AR
PALM CREST [MOT] *Myrtle Beach, SC*
PALMETTO DUNES RESORT [RST]
  Hilton Head Island, SC
PALOMINO MOTEL [MOT] *Sanford,
  NC*
PAMLICO HOUSE BED & BREAKFAST
  [BB] *Washington, NC*
PAN AMERICAN RESORT [MOT]
  Myrtle Beach, SC
PARK HOTEL, THE [HOT] *Charlotte,
  NC*
PARK INN INTERNATIONAL [MOT]
  Newport, AR
PARK LANE HOTEL [MOT]
  Greensboro, NC
PARK MAMMOTH RESORT [RST] *Park
  City, KY*
PARK PLACE INN [MOT] *Jonesboro,
  AR*
PARKVIEW MOTEL [MOT] *Pigeon
  Forge, TN*
PARK VISTA HOTEL [HOT]
  Gatlinburg, TN
PARKWAY INN [MOT] *Natchez, MS*
PARKWAY INN [MOT] *Waynesville,
  NC*
PEABODY [HOT] *Memphis, TN*
PECAN TREE INN [BB] *Beaufort, NC*
PELHAM HOTEL [HOT] *New Orleans,
  LA*
PENNYRILE FOREST STATE RESORT
  PARK [RST] *Madisonville, KY*
PERDIDO BEACH RESORT [RST] *Gulf
  Shores, AL*
PETIT JEAN MOUNTAIN STATE PARK
  MATHER LODGE [MOT] *Petit
  Jean State Park, AR*
PICKWICK HOTEL AND
  CONFERENCE CENTER [HOT]
  Birmingham, AL
PICKWICK INN [HOT] *Savannah, TN*
PINE ACRES LODGE [MOT]
  Laurinburg, NC
PINEBRIDGE INN [HOT] *Little
  Switzerland, NC*
PINE CREST INN [BB] *Pinehurst, NC*

PINECREST MOTEL [MOT] *Waycross,
  GA*
PINEHURST RESORT AND COUNTRY
  CLUB [BB] *Pinehurst, NC*
PINE MOUNTAIN STATE RESORT
  PARK [RST] *Pineville, KY*
PINE NEEDLES LODGE [RST] *Southern
  Pines, NC*
PINNACLE INN [MOT] *Banner Elk,
  NC*
PIN OAK LODGE [MOT] *Natchez
  Trace State Resort Park, TN*
PIONEER CABINS AND GUEST FARM
  [CC] *Townsend, TN*
PIONEER MOTEL AND COTTAGES
  [MOT] *Cherokee, NC*
PISGAH INN [RST] *Asheville, NC*
PLANTATION INN RESORT [MOT]
  Raleigh, NC
PLANTERS INN [BB] *Charleston, SC*
PLAYERS ISLAND RIVERBOAT
  HOTEL AND CASINO [MOT]
  Lake Charles, LA
PONTCHARTRAIN HOTEL [HOT]
  New Orleans, LA
PONY ISLAND MOTEL [MOT]
  Ocracoke (Outer Banks), NC
PORT PLACE INN AND SUITES
  [MOT] *Oxford, MS*
PRENTISS INN [MOT] *Natchez, MS*
PRESIDENT'S QUARTERS INN, THE
  [BB] *Savannah, GA*
PRINCESS MOTEL [MOT] *Maryville,
  TN*
PROVINCIAL HOTEL [HOT] *New
  Orleans, LA*
PRYTANIA PARK HOTEL [HOT] *New
  Orleans, LA*
QUAIL RUN LODGE [MOT]
  Savannah, GA
QUALITY HOTEL & CONFERENCE
  CENTER [MOT] *Metairie, LA*
QUALITY HOTEL INN AND
  CONFERENCE CENTER [HOT]
  Spartanburg, SC
QUALITY INN [MOT] *Arkadelphia, AR*
QUALITY INN [MOT] *Auburn, AL*
QUALITY INN [MOT] *Biloxi, MS*
QUALITY INN [MOT] *Brunswick, GA*
QUALITY INN [MOT] *Cave City, KY*
QUALITY INN [MOT] *Clarksville, TN*
QUALITY INN [MOT] *Fort Payne, AL*
QUALITY INN [MOT] *Greenville, SC*
QUALITY INN [RST] *Gulf Shores, AL*
QUALITY INN [MOT] *Hammond, LA*
QUALITY INN [MOT] *Henderson, NC*
QUALITY INN [HOT] *Hendersonville,
  NC*
QUALITY INN [MOT] *Hot Springs &
  Hot Springs National Park, AR*
QUALITY INN [MOT] *Jackson, TN*
QUALITY INN [MOT] *Nags Head
  (Outer Banks), NC*
QUALITY INN [MOT] *Norcross, GA*
QUALITY INN [MOT] *Opelousas, LA*
PINE CREST INN [BB] *Tryon, NC*

QUALITY INN [MOT] *Paducah, KY*
QUALITY INN [MOT] *Perry, GA*
QUALITY INN [MOT] *Sevierville, TN*
QUALITY INN [MOT] *Vicksburg, MS*
QUALITY INN & CONVENTION
    CENTER [HOT] *Boone, NC*
QUALITY INN & SUITES [MOT]
    Goldsboro, NC
QUALITY INN AMBASSADOR [MOT]
    Fayetteville, NC
QUALITY INN AND SUITES [MOT]
    Lumberton, NC
QUALITY INN BILTMORE [MOT]
    Asheville, NC
QUALITY INN - CALHOUN [MOT]
    Calhoun, GA
QUALITY INN - CHALET [MOT]
    Cleveland, TN
QUALITY INN CONVENTION CTR
    [RST] *Gatlinburg, TN*
QUALITY INN MERRY ACRES [MOT]
    Albany, GA
QUALITY INN MIDTOWN [HOT]
    New Orleans, LA
QUALITY INN NORTHEAST [MOT]
    Atlanta, GA
QUALITY INN NORTHWEST [MOT]
    Lexington, KY
QUALITY INN SOUTH [MOT]
    Valdosta, GA
QUALITY SUITES [MOT] *Baton Rouge,
    LA*
QUALITY SUITES CONVENTION
    CENTER [HOT] *Charleston, SC*
QUALITY SUITES HOTEL [AS]
    Raleigh, NC
QUEEN AND CRESCENT HOTEL,
    THE [HOT] *New Orleans, LA*
QUEENS COURT [MOT] *St. Simons
    Island, GA*
QUEEN WILHELMINA LODGE [BB]
    Mena, AR
RADCLIFF INN [HOT] *Fort Knox, KY*
RADISSON [HOT] *Memphis, TN*
RADISSON [HOT] *New Orleans, LA*
RADISSON HIGH POINT [HOT] *High
    Point, NC*
RADISSON HOTEL [HOT]
    Birmingham, AL
RADISSON HOTEL [HOT] *Knoxville,
    TN*
RADISSON HOTEL AND
    CONFERENCE CENTER [HOT]
    Baton Rouge, LA
RADISSON HOTEL BENTLEY [HOT]
    Alexandria, LA
RADISSON HOTEL CHARLESTON
    AIRPORT [HOT] *Charleston, SC*
RADISSON INN [HOT] *Atlanta, GA*
RADISSON INN MEMPHIS AIRPORT
    [HOT] *Memphis, TN*
RADISSON NATCHEZ EOLA HOTEL
    [HOT] *Natchez, MS*
RADISSON NEW ORLEANS AIRPORT
    [HOT] *Kenner, LA*

RADISSON PLAZA HOTEL [HOT]
    Lexington, KY
RADISSON READ HOUSE HOTEL
    [HOT] *Chattanooga, TN*
RADISSON RIVERFRONT HOTEL
    AUGUSTA [HOT] *Augusta, GA*
RADISSON SUITE HOTEL [AS]
    Huntsville, AL
RADISSON SUITES INN [MOT]
    Augusta, GA
RAMADA [HOT] *New Orleans, LA*
RAMADA HOTEL CAROWINDS
    [HOT] *Rock Hill, SC*
RAMADA INN [MOT] *Albany, GA*
RAMADA INN [HOT] *Batesville, AR*
RAMADA INN [MOT] *Bentonville, AR*
RAMADA INN [MOT] *Bessemer, AL*
RAMADA INN [MOT] *Branson/Table
    Rock Lake Area, MO*
RAMADA INN [MOT] *Burlington, NC*
RAMADA INN [MOT] *Camden, AR*
RAMADA INN [MOT] *Clemson, SC*
RAMADA INN [MOT] *Clinton, SC*
RAMADA INN [MOT] *Columbia, TN*
RAMADA INN [MOT] *Conway, AR*
RAMADA INN [MOT] *Cullman, AL*
RAMADA INN [HOT] *Dothan, AL*
RAMADA INN [MOT] *Dunn, NC*
RAMADA INN [MOT] *Eufaula, AL*
RAMADA INN [MOT] *Fayetteville, AR*
RAMADA INN [MOT] *Florence, SC*
RAMADA INN [HOT] *Fort Smith, AR*
RAMADA INN [MOT] *Goldsboro, NC*
RAMADA INN [MOT] *Greenville, AL*
RAMADA INN [MOT] *Greenville, MS*
RAMADA INN [MOT] *Greenwood, SC*
RAMADA INN [MOT] *Harrison, AR*
RAMADA INN [MOT] *High Point, NC*
RAMADA INN [HOT] *Hot Springs &
    Hot Springs National Park, AR*
RAMADA INN [MOT] *Kingsport, TN*
RAMADA INN [MOT] *La Grange, GA*
RAMADA INN [MOT] *Laurel, MS*
RAMADA INN [MOT] *Little Rock &
    North Little Rock, AR*
RAMADA INN [MOT] *Montgomery, AL*
RAMADA INN [MOT] *Mountain
    Home, AR*
RAMADA INN [MOT] *Natchez, MS*
RAMADA INN [MOT] *Pigeon Forge,
    TN*
RAMADA INN [HOT] *Pilot Mountain,
    NC*
RAMADA INN [HOT] *Pine Bluff, AR*
RAMADA INN [HOT] *Prestonsburg, KY*
RAMADA INN [HOT] *Rogers, AR*
RAMADA INN [MOT] *Shreveport, LA*
RAMADA INN [HOT] *Slidell, LA*
RAMADA INN [HOT] *Spartanburg, SC*
RAMADA INN [MOT] *Starkville, MS*
RAMADA INN [HOT] *Statesboro, GA*
RAMADA INN [HOT] *Sumter, SC*
RAMADA INN [MOT] *Tifton, GA*
RAMADA INN [MOT] *Tupelo, MS*
RAMADA INN [MOT] *Tuscaloosa, AL*

RAMADA INN & CONFERENCE CTR. [MOT] *Lexington, KY*

RAMADA INN & SUITES [MOT] *Nashville, TN*

RAMADA INN AIRPORT [HOT] *Birmingham, AL*

RRAMADA INN-AIRPORT [MOT] *Greensboro, NC*

AMADA INN AIRPORT [MOT] *Nashville, TN*

RAMADA INN - CENTRAL ATLANTA [MOT] *Atlanta, GA*

RAMADA INN COLISEUM/ CONVENTION CENTER [MOT] *Charleston, SC*

RAMADA INN CONFERENCE CENTER [MOT] *Wilmington, NC*

RAMADA INN CUMBERLAND GAP [MOT] *Harrogate, TN*

RAMADA INN NORTH [MOT] *Lafayette, LA*

RAMADA INN ON THE RIVER [MOT] *Rome, GA*

RAMADA INN OUTER BANKS RESORT & CONFERENCE CENTER [RST] *Kill Devil Hills (Outer Banks), NC*

RAMADA INN - SIX FLAGS [MOT] *Atlanta, GA*

RAMADA LIMITED [MOT] *Cartersville, GA*

RAMADA LIMITED [MOT] *Gatlinburg, TN*

RAMADA LIMITED [MOT] *Lenoir, NC*

RAMADA LIMITED [MOT] *Meridian, MS*

RAMADA LIMITED [MOT] *Murfreesboro, TN*

RAMADA LIMITED [MOT] *Nashville, TN*

RAMADA LIMITED [MOT] *Perry, GA*

RAMADA LIMITED [MOT] *Valdosta, GA*

RAMADA LIMITED NORTHWEST [MOT] *Columbia, SC*

RAMADA LIMITED SUITES [MOT] *Cookeville, TN*

RAMADA LIMITED SUITES [MOT] *Knoxville, TN*

RAMADA ON CANAL [HOT] *New Orleans, LA*

RAMADA PLAZA [MOT] *Atlanta Hartsfield Airport Area, GA*

RAMADA PLAZA [MOT] *Columbia, SC*

RAMADA PLAZA [HOT] *Greenville, NC*

RAMADA PLAZA HOTEL [MOT] *Mobile, AL*

RAMADA SHOALS HOTEL AND CONFERENCE CENTER [MOT] *Sheffield, AL*

RASISSON ADMIRAL SEMMES HOTEL [HOT] *Mobile, AL*

RED APPLE INN [MOT] *Greers Ferry Lake Area, AR*

RED BUD VALLEY RESORT [CC] *Eureka Springs, AR*

RED CREEK INN, VINEYARD & RACING STABLE [BB] *Gulfport, MS*

RED MONT BY WINDHAM [HOT] *Birmingham, AL*

RED RAVEN INN [BB] *Bull Shoals Lake Area, AR*

RED ROOF INN [MOT] *Asheville, NC*

RED ROOF INN [MOT] *Burlington, NC*

RED ROOF INN [MOT] *Charleston, SC*

RED ROOF INN [MOT] *Charlotte, NC*

RED ROOF INN [MOT] *Chattanooga, TN*

RED ROOF INN [MOT] *Columbia, SC*

RED ROOF INN [MOT] *Durham, NC*

RED ROOF INN [MOT] *Florence, SC*

RED ROOF INN [MOT] *Hickory, NC*

RED ROOF INN [MOT] *Knoxville, TN*

RED ROOF INN [MOT] *Knoxville, TN*

RED ROOF INN [MOT] *Lafayette, LA*

RED ROOF INN [MOT] *Lexington, KY*

RED ROOF INN [MOT] *Little Rock & North Little Rock, AR*

RED ROOF INN [MOT] *Louisville, KY*

RED ROOF INN [MOT] *Memphis, TN*

RED ROOF INN [MOT] *Monroe and West Monroe, LA*

RED ROOF INN [MOT] *Nashville, TN*

RED ROOF INN [MOT] *Nashville, TN*

RED ROOF INN [MOT] *Norcross, GA*

RED ROOF INN [MOT] *Raleigh, NC*

RED ROOF INN [MOT] *Statesville, NC*

RED ROOF INN [MOT] *Tupelo, MS*

RED ROOF INN DRUID HILLS [MOT] *Atlanta, GA*

RED ROOF INN-HILTON HEAD [MOT] *Hilton Head Island, SC*

RED ROOF INN MEMPHIS AIRPORT [MOT] *Memphis, TN*

RED ROOF INN OF NORTH RALEIGH [MOT] *Raleigh, NC*

RED ROOF INNS [MOT] *Fayetteville, AR*

RED ROOF INN SOUTH [MOT] *Mobile, AL*

REELFOOT LAKE STATE PARK [MOT] *Tiptonville, TN*

REGAL INN & SUITES, THE [MOT] *Gulf Shores, AL*

REGAL MAXWELL HOUSE [HOT] *Nashville, TN*

REGAL UNIVERSITY HOTEL [MOT] *Durham, NC*

REGENCY INN [MOT] *Dumas, AR*

REGENCY SUITES [AS] *Atlanta, GA*

RENAISSANCE [HOT] *Nashville, TN*

RENAISSANCE ASHEVILLE HOTEL [HOT] *Asheville, NC*

RENAISSANCE ATLANTA HOTEL DOWNTOWN [HOT] *Atlanta, GA*

RENAISSANCE CONCOURSE HOTEL [HOT] *Atlanta Hartsfield Airport Area, GA*

RENAISSANCE PINEISLE RESORT [RST] *Buford, GA*

RENAISSANCE WAVERLY [HOT] *Atlanta, GA*

RESIDENCE INN [MOT] *Covington (Cincinnati Airport Area), KY*

RESIDENCE INN [MOT] *Louisville, KY*

RESIDENCE INN [MOT] *Memphis, TN*

RESIDENCE INN ATLANTA MARRIOTT DUNWOODY [MOT] *Atlanta, GA*

RESIDENCE INN BY MARRIOTT [MOT] *Birmingham, AL*

RESIDENCE INN BY MARRIOTT [AS] *Bossier City, LA*

RESIDENCE INN BY MARRIOTT [EX] *Charlotte, NC*

RESIDENCE INN BY MARRIOTT [MOT] *Columbia, SC*

RESIDENCE INN BY MARRIOTT [HOT] *Hilton Head Island, SC*

RESIDENCE INN BY MARRIOTT [MOT] *Jackson, MS*

RESIDENCE INN BY MARRIOTT [MOT] *Nashville, TN*

RESIDENCE INN BY MARRIOTT [MOT] *Raleigh, NC*

RESIDENCE INN BY MARRIOTT [MOT] *Winston-Salem, NC*

RHETT HOUSE INN AND FINE DINING [BB] *Beaufort, SC*

RICHLAND STREET BED & BREAKFAST [BB] *Columbia, SC*

RICHMOND HILL INN [BB] *Asheville, NC*

RICHMOND INN BED & BREAKFAST [BB] *Morganton, NC*

RICHMONT INN [BB] *Townsend, TN*

RIDGEWAY INN [MOT] *Memphis, TN*

RITZ-CARLTON [HOT] *Atlanta, GA*

RITZ-CARLTON BUCKHEAD [HOT] *Atlanta, GA*

RIVENDELL BED AND BREAKFAST [BB] *Athens, GA*

RIVERCHASE MOTEL [MOT] *Pigeon Forge, TN*

RIVER EDGE MOTOR LODGE [MOT] *Gatlinburg, TN*

RIVER FOREST MANOR [BB] *Washington, NC*

RIVERLET MOTEL & RESTAURANT [MOT] *Maggie Valley, NC*

RIVER PLACE INN [MOT] *Pigeon Forge, TN*

RIVERSIDE MOTOR LODGE [MOT] *Pigeon Forge, TN*

RIVER STREET INN [BB] *Savannah, GA*

RIVER TERRACE CREEK SIDE [MOT] *Gatlinburg, TN*

RIVERVIEW INN [MOT] *Clarksville, TN*

ROAD RUNNER INN [MOT] *Eureka Springs, AR*

ROCKY TOP VILLAGE INN [MOT] *Gatlinburg, TN*

ROCKY WATERS [MOT] *Maggie Valley, NC*

ROCKY WATERS MOTOR INN [MOT] *Gatlinburg, TN*

RODEWAY INN [MOT] *Alexandria, LA*

RODEWAY INN [MOT] *Charlotte, NC*

RODEWAY INN [MOT] *Macon, GA*

RODEWAY INN MOUNTAIN SKIES [MOT] *Pigeon Forge, TN*

ROSEDALE BED & BREAKFAST [BB] *Paris, KY*

ROSEHILL INN BED & BREAKFAST [BB] *Wilmington, NC*

ROSEMARY HALL & LOOKAWAY HALL [BB] *Augusta, GA*

ROSSWOOD PLANTATION [BB] *Port Gibson, MS*

ROUGH RIVER DAM STATE PARK RESORT [RST] *Rough River Dam State Resort Park, KY*

ROYAL SONESTA [HOT] *New Orleans, LA*

ROYAL TOWNHOUSE MOTOR INN [MOT] *Gatlinburg, TN*

RUE ROYAL INN [BB] *New Orleans, LA*

RUTLEDGE VICTORIAN GUESTHOUSE [BB] *Charleston, SC*

RYDER INN [MOT] *Natchitoches, LA*

SALALE LODGE [MOT] *Hiawassee, GA*

SAND DUNES RESORT AND VILLAS [HOT] *Myrtle Beach, SC*

SANDERLING INN RESORT & SPA [RST] *Outer Banks, NC*

SAVANNAH MARRIOTT RIVERFRONT [HOT] *Savannah, GA*

SCANDIA INN [BB] *Eureka Springs, AR*

SCOTTISH INN [MOT] *Hardeeville, SC*

SCOTTISH INN [MOT] *Henderson, KY*

SEABROOK ISLAND [RST] *Charleston, SC*

SEA FOAM MOTEL [MOT] *Nags Head (Outer Banks), NC*

SEA GATE INN [MOT] *St.Simons Island, GA*

SEA GULL MOTEL [MOT] *Hatteras (Outer Banks), NC*

SEAHAWK MOTOR LODGE [MOT] *Morehead City, NC*

SEA ISLAND INN ON THE BEACH [MOT] *Myrtle Beach, SC*

SEA MIST RESORT [HOT] *Myrtle Beach, SC*

SEA PALMS GOLF AND TENNIS RESORT [RST] *St.Simons Island, GA*

SEA PINES PLANTATION [RST] *Hilton Head Island, SC*

SEAVIEW INN [BB] *Georgetown, SC*

SEELBACH HILTON LOUISVILLE, THE [HOT] *Louisville, KY*

SERENBE BED & BREAKFAST [BB] *Atlanta, GA*

SERENDIPITY, AN INN [BB] *Myrtle Beach, SC*

SERENDIPITY COTTAGE [BB] *Thomasville, GA*

SEVENTEEN HUNDRED NINETY INN & RESTAURANT [BB] *Savannah, GA*

SHADY OAKS RESORT [CC] *Bull Shoals Lake Area, AR*

SHAKER TAVERN [BB] *South Union, KY*

SHAKER VILLAGE OF PLEASANT HILL [BB] *Harrodsburg, KY*

SHAW HOUSE B & B, THE [BB] *Georgetown, SC*

SHELLMONT INN [BB] *Atlanta, GA*

SHEM CREEK INN [MOT] *Charleston, SC*

SHERATON [HOT] *Morehead City, NC*

SHERATON AIRPORT PLAZA HOTEL [HOT] *Charlotte, NC*

SHERATON BIRMINGHAM HOTEL [HOT] *Birmingham, AL*

SHERATON BUCKHEAD ATLANTA [HOT] *Atlanta, GA*

SHERATON COLONY SQUARE [HOT] *Atlanta, GA*

SHERATON GATEWAY HOTEL [HOT] *Atlanta Hartsfield Airport Area, GA*

SHERATON GREENSBORO HOTEL AT FOUR SEASONS [HOT] *Greensboro, NC*

SHERATON HOTEL [HOT] *Atlanta, GA*

SHERATON HOTEL [HOT] *Augusta, GA*

SHERATON HOTEL [HOT] *Chapel Hill, NC*

SHERATON HOTEL & MARINA [HOT] *New Bern, NC*

SHERATON IMPERIAL HOTEL & CONVENTION CENTER [HOT] *Durham, NC*

SHERATON INN [HOT] *Columbus, GA*

SHERATON INN AIRPORT [HOT] *Huntsville, AL*

SHERATON MUSIC CITY [HOT] *Nashville, TN*

SHERATON NASHVILLE DOWNTOWN [HOT] *Nashville, TN*

SHERATON NEW ORLEANS HOTEL [HOT] *New Orleans, LA*

SHERATON NORTH CHARLESTON [HOT] *Charleston, SC*

SHERATON PERIMETER PARK SOUTH [HOT] *Birmingham, AL*

SHERATON PIERREMONT [HOT] *Shreveport, LA*

SHERATON SUITES GALLERIA ATLANTA [AS] *Atlanta, GA*

SHERATON SUITES LEXINGTON [AS] *Lexington, KY*

SHERATON SUITES LEXINGTON [HOT] *Lexington, KY*

SHONEY'S INN [MOT] *Baton Rouge, LA*

SHONEY'S INN [MOT] *Gallatin, TN*

SHONEY'S INN [MOT] *Georgetown, KY*

SHONEY'S INN [MOT] *Lexington, KY*

SHONEY'S INN [HOT] *Mobile, AL*

SHONEY'S INN [MOT] *Murray, KY*

SHONEY'S INN [MOT] *Nashville, TN*

SHONEY'S INN [HOT] *Nashville, TN*

SHONEY'S INN [MOT] *Toccoa, GA*

SHONEY'S INN [MOT] *Valdosta, GA*

SHONEYS INN [MOT] *Lebanon, TN*

SHONEYS INN [MOT] *Murfreesboro, TN*

SHONEY'S INN/OPRYLAND AREA [HOT] *Nashville, TN*

SHORECREST RESORT [CC] *Hot Springs & Hot Springs National Park, AR*

SIENA HOTEL, THE [HOT] *Chapel Hill, NC*

SIERRA SUITES HOTELS [HOT] *Atlanta, GA*

SIGNATURE INN [HOT] *Knoxville, TN*

SIGNATURE INN [MOT] *Louisville, KY*

SIGNATURE INN [MOT] *Louisville, KY*

SIGNATURE INN TURFWAY [MOT] *Covington (Cincinnati Airport Area), KY*

SILVER GULL MOTEL [MOT] *Wrightsville Beach, NC*

SILVER RUN CABINS [CC] *Bull Shoals Lake Area, AR*

SKYLAND MOTEL [MOT] *Gatlinburg, TN*

SLEEP INN [MOT] *Brunswick, GA*

SLEEP INN [MOT] *Hickory, NC*

SLEEP INN [MOT] *Morganton, NC*

SLEEP INN [MOT] *Tuscaloosa, AL*

SLEEP INN [MOT] *Wilmington, NC*

SMITH HOUSE, THE [BB] *Dahlonega, GA*

SMOKYLAND MOTEL [MOT] *Gatlinburg, TN*

SNOWBIRD MOUNTAIN LODGE [MOT] *Robbinsville, NC*

SOMERSET LODGE [MOT] *Somerset, KY*

SONIAT HOUSE HOTEL [BB] *New Orleans, LA*

SOUTHPARK SUITE HOTEL [HOT] *Charlotte, NC*

SPEARS GUEST HOUSE [BB] *Cheraw, SC*

SPENCER HOUSE INN BED & BREAKFAST [BB] *Coeur d'Alene, ID*

SPRINGS INN [MOT] *Lexington, KY*

ST. FRANCISVILLE INN [BB] *St. Francisville, LA*

ST. JOHN'S INN [MOT] *Myrtle Beach, SC*

ST. LOUIS HOTEL [HOT] *New Orleans, LA*

ST. PETER GUEST HOUSE [BB] *New Orleans, LA*

ST. SIMONS INN BY THE LIGHTHOUSE [BB] *St.Simons Island, GA*

STATE HOUSE HOTEL [BB] *Starkville, MS*

STONY CREEK [MOT] *Maggie Valley, NC*

STRATFORD HOUSE INN [MOT] *Monroe and West Monroe, LA*

STUDIO 6 [MOT] *Memphis, TN*

SUGARLOAF INN [RST] *Bull Shoals Lake Area, AR*

SUGAR MAGNOLIA [BB] *Atlanta, GA*

SUITE HOTEL AT UNDERGROUND [HOT] *Atlanta, GA*

SUMMERFIELD SUITES BY WYNDHAM [MOT] *Atlanta, GA*

SUMMERFIELD SUITES HOTEL [MOT] *Atlanta, GA*

SUMMERFIELD SUITES HOTEL [EX] *Charlotte, NC*

SUNRISE FARM BED & BREAKFAST INN [BB] *Clemson, SC*

SUNSET MOTEL [MOT] *Brevard, NC*

SUPER 8 [MOT] *Atlanta, GA*

SUPER 8 [MOT] *Bainbridge, GA*

SUPER 8 [MOT] *Caryville, TN*

SUPER 8 [MOT] *Greenville, SC*

SUPER 8 [MOT] *Hope, AR*

SUPER 8 [MOT] *Johnson City, TN*

SUPER 8 [MOT] *Morristown, TN*

SUPER 8 [MOT] *Paducah, KY*

SUPER 8 [MOT] *Richmond, KY*

SUPER 8 [MOT] *Shelbyville, TN*

SUPER 8 [MOT] *Vicksburg, MS*

SUPER 8 MOTEL [MOT] *Adel, GA*

SUPER 8 MOTEL [MOT] *Alexander City, AL*

SUPER 8 MOTEL [MOT] *Anderson, SC*

SUPER 8 MOTEL [MOT] *Cave City, KY*

SUPER 8 MOTEL [MOT] *Chattanooga, TN*

SUPER 8 MOTEL [MOT] *Cordele, GA*

SUPER 8 MOTEL [MOT] *Dahlonega, GA*

SUPER 8 MOTEL [MOT] *Danville, KY*

SUPER 8 MOTEL [MOT] *Fort Smith, AR*

SUPER 8 MOTEL [MOT] *Greenville, NC*

SUPER 8 MOTEL [MOT] *Harrison, AR*

SUPER 8 MOTEL [MOT] *Hazard, KY*

SUPER 8 MOTEL [MOT] *Hot Springs & Hot Springs National Park, AR*

SUPER 8 MOTEL [MOT] *Knoxville, TN*

SUPER 8 MOTEL [MOT] *Lexington, KY*

SUPER 8 MOTEL [MOT] *Louisville, KY*

SUPER 8 MOTEL [MOT] *Malvern, AR*

SUPER 8 MOTEL [MOT] *Manchester, TN*

SUPER 8 MOTEL [MOT] *Morehead, KY*

SUPER 8 MOTEL [MOT] *Myrtle Beach, SC*

SUPER 8 MOTEL [MOT] *Nashville, TN*

SUPER 8 MOTEL [MOT] *Savannah, GA*

SUPER 8 MOTEL [MOT] *Tuscaloosa, AL*

SUPER 8 MOTEL [MOT] *Williamsburg, KY*

SUPER 8 OF BENTONVILLE [MOT] *Bentonville, AR*

SUPER 8 OF FRANKLIN [MOT] *Franklin, TN*

SURF AND DUNES MOTOR INN [MOT] *Myrtle Beach, SC*

SURF MOTEL [MOT] *Wrightsville Beach, NC*

SURF SIDE MOTEL [MOT] *Nags Head (Outer Banks), NC*

SUSINA PLANTATION INN [BB] *Thomasville, GA*

SWAG COUNTRY INN, THE [BB] *Waynesville, NC*

SWISS HOTEL ATLANTA [HOT] *Atlanta, GA*

SWISS VILLAGE INN [MOT] *Eureka Springs, AR*

TALLEY HO INN [MOT] *Townsend, TN*

TALL PINES MOTOR INN [MOT] *Eureka Springs, AR*

TANGLEWOOD PARK [BB] *Winston-Salem, NC*

TANYARD SPRINGS [CC] *Petit Jean State Park, AR*

TAPOCO LODGE [BB] *Robbinsville, NC*

TARRER INN [BB] *Blakely, GA*

TAYLOR HOUSE INN BED AND BREAKFAST [BB] *Wilmington, NC*

TEAL POINT RESORT [RST] *Mountain Home, AR*

TENNESSEE MOUNTAIN LODGE [MOT] *Pigeon Forge, TN*

TERRACE WOODS TRAVEL LODGE [MOT] *Paris, TN*

THEODOSIA'S BED & BREAKFAST [BB] *Southport, NC*

THOMAS QUINN SUITES [AS] *Fort Smith, AR*

TOMAHAWK MOTEL INC [MOT] *Ahoskie, NC*

TOWN AND COUNTRY INN [MOT] *Charleston, SC*

TOWN AND COUNTRY INN [MOT] *Walterboro, SC*

TRADEWINDS MOTEL [MOT] *Eureka Springs, AR*

TRANQUIL HOUSE INN [BB] *Manteo, NC*

TRAVELERS INN [MOT] *Florence, SC*

TRAVELERS INN [MOT] *Sumter, SC*

TRAVELER'S REST INN [MOT] *Nashville, TN*

TRAVELODGE [MOT] *Athens, AL*

TRAVELODGE [MOT] *Clarksville, TN*

TRAVELODGE [MOT] *Gatlinburg, TN*

TRAVELODGE [MOT] *Louisville, KY*

TRAVELODGE [MOT] *Monroe and West Monroe, LA*
TRAVELODGE [MOT] *Perry, GA*
TRAVELODGE [MOT] *Pigeon Forge, TN*
TRAVELODGE [MOT] *Tuscaloosa, AL*
TRAVELODGE [MOT] *Valdosta, GA*
TRAVELODGE HOTEL WEST [MOT] *New Orleans, LA*
TRAVELODGE LAFAYETTE CENTER [MOT] *Lafayette, LA*
TRAVEL RITE INN [MOT] *Jasper, AL*
TRESTLE HOUSE INN [BB] *Edenton, NC*
TUTWILER HOTEL [HOT] *Birmingham, AL*
TWENTY-FOUR THIRTY-NINE FAIRFIELD [BB] *Shreveport, LA*
TWOSUNS INN BED & BREAKFAST [BB] *Beaufort, SC*
UNICOI LODGE AND CONFERENCE CENTER [MOT] *Helen, GA*
UNION STATION [HOT] *Nashville, TN*
VALLEY FORGE INN [MOT] *Pigeon Forge, TN*
VALLEY INN RESORT [MOT] *Pine Mountain (Harris County), GA*
VALU-LODGE [MOT] *Augusta, GA*
VELVET CLOAK INN [MOT] *Raleigh, NC*
VENDUE INN [BB] *Charleston, SC*
VERANDAS, THE [BB] *Wilmington, NC*
VICTORIA - A COUNTRY INN [BB] *Anniston, AL*
VICTORIA HOUSE INN [BB] *Charleston, SC*
VICTORIA INN [MOT] *Eureka Springs, AR*
VILLAGE INN [BB] *Jackson, LA*
VILLAS BY THE SEA [RST] *Jekyll Island, GA*
VINTAGE COMFORT BED AND BREAKFAST [BB] *Hot Springs & Hot Springs National Park, AR*
WASHINGTON DUKE INN [HOT] *Durham, NC*
WATERWAY LODGE [MOT] *Wrightsville Beach, NC*
W ATLANTA [HOT] *Atlanta, GA*
WAVERLY INN, THE [BB] *Hendersonville, NC*
WAYNESVVILLE COUNTRY CLUB [RST] *Waynesville, NC*
WENTWORTH MANSION [BB] *Charleston, SC*
WESTIN ATLANTA NORTH AT PERIMETER, THE [HOT] *Atlanta, GA*
WESTIN FRANCIS MARION WESTIN [HOT] *Charleston, SC*
WESTIN HERMITAGE HOTEL [HOT] *Nashville, TN*
WESTIN HOTEL [HOT] *Atlanta Hartsfield Airport Area, GA*

WESTIN PEACHTREE PLAZA [HOT] *Atlanta, GA*
WESTIN RESORT, THE [RST] *Hilton Head Island, SC*
W FRENCH QUARTER HOTEL [HOT] *New Orleans, LA*
WHITESTONE COUNTRY INN [BB] *Lenoir City, TN*
WHITLOCK, THE [BB] *Marietta, GA*
WHITNEY HOTEL, THE [MOT] *Columbia, SC*
WHITWORTH INN [BB] *Buford, GA*
W HOTEL NEW ORLEANS, THE [HOT] *New Orleans, LA*
WILD DUNES RESORT [RST] *Charleston, SC*
WILLCOX INN [BB] *Aiken, SC*
WILSON INN [MOT] *Jonesboro, AR*
WILSON INN [MOT] *Nashville, TN*
WILSON WORLD HOTEL [MOT] *Memphis, TN*
WINDJAMMER INN [MOT] *Morehead City, NC*
WINDS OCEANFRONT INN & SUITES, THE [RST] *South Brunswick Islands, NC*
WINDSONG A MOUNTAIN INN [BB] *Waynesville, NC*
WINDSOR COURT HOTEL [HOT] *New Orleans, LA*
WINDSOR HOTEL [MOT] *Americus, GA*
WINDSOR INN [MOT] *Marietta, GA*
WINDWOOD INN OF DEMOPOLIS [MOT] *Demopolis, AL*
WOODFIELD [BB] *Hendersonville, NC*
WOODHAVEN BED AND BREAKFAST [BB] *Louisville, KY*
WOODLANDS RESORT & INN [HOT] *Charleston, SC*
WORTH HOUSE, THE [BB] *Wilmington, NC*
WYNDHAM GARDEN HOTEL [HOT] *Charlotte, NC*
WYNDHAM GARDEN HOTEL [HOT] *Durham, NC*
WYNDHAM GARDEN HOTEL [MOT] *Knoxville, TN*
WYNDHAM GARDEN MARIETTA [MOT] *Marietta, GA*
WYNDHAM MIDTOWN ATLANTA [HOT] *Atlanta, GA*
WYNDHAM NEW ORLEANS [HOT] *New Orleans, LA*
WYNDHAM RIVERFRONT [HOT] *New Orleans, LA*
WYNDHAM VININGS HOTEL [MOT] *Atlanta, GA*
WYNFIELD INN [MOT] *Montgomery, AL*
WYNFREY HOTEL [HOT] *Birmingham, AL*
YELLOW HOUSE ON PLOT CREEK ROAD [BB] *Waynesville, NC*

RESTAURANT LIST

Establishment names are listed in alphabetical order followed by a symbol identifying their classification and then city and state. The symbols for classification are: [RES] for Restaurants and [URD] for Unrated Dining Spots.

101ST AIRBORNE [RES] *Nashville, TN*
103 WEST [RES] *Atlanta, GA*
1620 [RES] *Little Rock & North Little Rock, AR*
1848 HOUSE [RES] *Marietta, GA*
1859 CAFE [RES] *Hickory, NC*
212 MARKET [RES] *Chattanooga, TN*
23 PAGE [RES] *Asheville, NC*
42 STREET OYSTER BAR & SEAFOOD [RES] *Raleigh, NC*
45 SOUTH [RES] *Savannah, GA*
82 QUEEN [RES] *Charleston, SC*
ABBEY, THE [RES] *Atlanta, GA*
ABITA BREW PUB [RES] *Covington, LA*
ABRUZZI RISTORANTE [RES] *Atlanta, GA*
AGNES & MURIEL'S [RES] *Atlanta, GA*
A-LA LUCIE [RES] *Lexington, KY*
ALADDIN LEBANESE RESTAURANT [RES] *Lake Charles, LA*
ALEXANDER'S [RES] *Hilton Head Island, SC*
ALEX PATOUT [RES] *New Orleans, LA*
ALFRED'S [RES] *Memphis, TN*
ALLEGRO BISTRO [RES] *New Orleans, LA*
ALL STEAK [RES] *Cullman, AL*
ALOUETTE'S [RES] *Little Rock & North Little Rock, AR*
AL'S UPSTAIRS [RES] *Columbia, SC*
ANCHOR INN [RES] *Morehead City, NC*
ANDREA'S [RES] *Metairie, LA*
ANDRE'S HILLCREST [RES] *Little Rock & North Little Rock, AR*
ANDREW JAEGER'S HOUSE OF SEAFOOD [RES] *New Orleans, LA*
ANDREW'S [RES] *Bowling Green, KY*
ANGUS BARN [RES] *Raleigh, NC*
ANIS [RES] *Atlanta, GA*
ANNIE'S [RES] *Pass Christian, MS*
ANSON [RES] *Charleston, SC*
ANTHONY'S [RES] *Atlanta, GA*
ANTOINE'S [RES] *New Orleans, LA*
APPLE CAKE TEA ROOM [URD] *Knoxville, TN*
APPLE TREE INN [RES] *Pigeon Forge, TN*
APPLEWOOD FARM HOUSE [RES] *Sevierville, TN*

A. Q. CHICKEN HOUSE [RES] *Springdale, AR*
ARIA [RES] *Atlanta, GA*
ARMAN'S [RES] *Birmingham, AL*
ARNAUD'S [RES] *New Orleans, LA*
ARTESIA [RES] *Covington, LA*
ARTHUR'S [RES] *Nashville, TN*
ARUGULA [RES] *Atlanta, GA*
ASIATIQUE [RES] *Louisville, KY*
ATLANTA FISH MARKET [RES] *Atlanta, GA*
ATLANTA GRILL [RES] *Atlanta, GA*
AUBERGINE [RES] *Memphis, TN*
AUGUSTINO'S [RES] *Greeneville, TN*
AURORA [RES] *Chapel Hill, NC*
AUTOMATIC SLIM'S TONGA CLUB [RES] *Memphis, TN*
AW SHUCKS [RES] *Charleston, SC*
BABETTE'S CAFE [RES] *Atlanta, GA*
BACCHANALIA [RES] *Atlanta, GA*
BACCO [RES] *New Orleans, LA*
BACK PORCH [RES] *Ocracoke (Outer Banks), NC*
BANGKOK CUISINE [RES] *New Orleans, LA*
BARBADOES ROOM [RES] *Charleston, SC*
BAR NONE BAR-B-Q [RES] *Mountain View, AR*
BARTHOLOMEW'S FINE FOODS [RES] *Madisonville, KY*
BASIL'S MEDITERRANNEAN CAFE [RES] *Atlanta, GA*
BAYONA [RES] *New Orleans, LA*
BB RIVERBOATS [URD] *Covington (Cincinnati Airport Area), KY*
BEAUFORT INN [RES] *Beaufort, SC*
BEAUMONT'S CAFE [RES] *Charleston, SC*
BEEF BARN [RES] *Greenville, NC*
BEGUE'S [RES] *New Orleans, LA*
BELLA LUNA [RES] *New Orleans, LA*
BELLE MEADE BRASSERIE [RES] *Nashville, TN*
BENIHANA OF TOKYO [RES] *Memphis, TN*
BENNIE'S RED BARN [RES] *St.Simons Island, GA*
BENTLEY ROOM [RES] *Alexandria, LA*
BEST CELLAR [RES] *Blowing Rock, NC*
BETTY'S BAR-B-Q [RES] *Anniston, AL*
BISTRO 100 [RES] *Charlotte, NC*

BISTRO AT MAISON DE VILLE [RES] *New Orleans, LA*

BISTRO EUROPA [RES] *Greenville, SC*

BISTRO SAVANNAH [RES] *Savannah, GA*

BIZOU RESTAURANT [URD] *New Orleans, LA*

BLACKBEARD'S [RES] *Jekyll Island, GA*

BLAIR HOUSE [RES] *Lafayette, LA*

BLANCHE'S COURTYARD [RES] *St.Simons Island, GA*

BLAZER'S [RES] *Greenwood, SC*

BLOSSOM CAFE [RES] *Charleston, SC*

BLUDAU'S GOETCHIUS HOUSE [RES] *Columbus, GA*

BLUEBIRD CAFE [RES] *Nashville, TN*

BLUE MARLIN [RES] *Columbia, SC*

BLUE RIDGE GRILL [RES] *Atlanta, GA*

BOB SYKES BAR-B-QUE [URD] *Bessemer, AL*

BOHEMIA [RES] *Hot Springs & Hot Springs National Park, AR*

BOLTON'S LANDING [RES] *Glasgow, KY*

BOMBAY CAFE [RES] *Birmingham, AL*

BONE'S [RES] *Atlanta, GA*

BON TON CAFE [RES] *New Orleans, LA*

BOSCOS PIZZA KITCHEN AND BREWERY [RES] *Memphis, TN*

BOSCOS PIZZA KITCHEN AND BREWERY [RES] *Nashville, TN*

BOTTEGA [RES] *Birmingham, AL*

BOUDANZ [RES] *Gulf Shores, AL*

BOUNDRY [RES] *Nashville, TN*

BOWEN'S [RES] *Arkadelphia, AR*

BOYETTE'S DINING ROOM [RES] *Tiptonville, TN*

BRASSERIE LE COZE [RES] *Atlanta, GA*

BRASS LANTERN [RES] *Gatlinburg, TN*

BRASS LANTERN [RES] *Kenlake State Resort Park, KY*

BRAVO [RES] *Charlotte, NC*

BREAKFAST CLUB [RES] *Tybee Island, GA*

BREEZES [RES] *Buford, GA*

BRENNAN'S [RES] *New Orleans, LA*

BRIDGE TENDER [RES] *Wrightsville Beach, NC*

BRIGHT STAR [RES] *Bessemer, AL*

BRIGSTEN'S [RES] *New Orleans, LA*

BROGEN'S [RES] *St.Simons Island, GA*

BROUSSARD'S [RES] *New Orleans, LA*

BROWN'S [URD] *Benton, AR*

BROWNING'S [RES] *Little Rock & North Little Rock, AR*

BRUNO'S LITTLE ITALY [RES] *Little Rock & North Little Rock, AR*

BUBBA'S BARBECUE [RES] *Eureka Springs, AR*

BUCKHEAD DINER [RES] *Atlanta, GA*

BUCKLEY'S FINE FILET GRILL [RES] *Memphis, TN*

BUFFALO GRILL [URD] *Little Rock & North Little Rock, AR*

BULLOCH HOUSE [RES] *Pine Mountain (Harris County), GA*

BULLOCK'S BBQ [RES] *Durham, NC*

BUNTYN [RES] *Memphis, TN*

BUTCHER SHOP [RES] *Knoxville, TN*

BUTCHER SHOP [URD] *Memphis, TN*

CABIN, THE [RES] *Atlanta, GA*

CABIN [RES] *Baton Rouge, LA*

CAFE, THE [RES] *Atlanta, GA*

CAFE DU MONDE [URD] *New Orleans, LA*

CAFE EUROPA [RES] *Hilton Head Island, SC*

CAFE GIOVANNI [RES] *New Orleans, LA*

CAFE KLASER [RES] *Greers Ferry Lake Area, AR*

CAFE MARGAUX [RES] *Lake Charles, LA*

CAFE METRO [RES] *Louisville, KY*

CAFE MIMOSA [RES] *Louisville, KY*

CAFE PARIZADE [RES] *Durham, NC*

CAFE PONTALBA [RES] *New Orleans, LA*

CAFE ST. MORITZ [RES] *Little Rock & North Little Rock, AR*

CAFE TU TU TANGO [RES] *Atlanta, GA*

CAFE VERMILIONVILLE [RES] *Lafayette, LA*

CAFE VOLAGE [RES] *New Orleans, LA*

CAFFE PHOENIX [RES] *Wilmington, NC*

CAGNEY'S OLD PLACE [RES] *Myrtle Beach, SC*

CAJUN BOILERS [RES] *Hot Springs & Hot Springs National Park, AR*

CALHOUN'S [RES] *Knoxville, TN*

CALICO COUNTY [RES] *Fort Smith, AR*

CALVERTS [RES] *Augusta, GA*

CAMEAUX LOUISIANA [RES] *Atlanta, GA*

CAMELLIA GRILL [URD] *New Orleans, LA*

CAMILLE'S [RES] *Atlanta, GA*

CANOE [RES] *Atlanta, GA*

CANTON STATION [RES] *Fayetteville, NC*

CAPITOL GRILLE [RES] *Nashville, TN*

CAPTAIN BILL'S WATERFRONT [RES] *Morehead City, NC*

CAPTAIN BOB'S SEAFOOD [RES] *Goldsboro, NC*

CAPTAIN DAVE'S DOCKSIDE [RES] *Myrtle Beach, SC*

CAPTAIN JOE'S [RES] *Brunswick, GA*

CAPTAIN'S GALLEY [RES] *Cornelius, NC*

CAPTAIN'S HOUSE [RES] *Greers Ferry Lake Area, AR*

CARBO'S CAFE [RES] *Atlanta, GA*

CAROLINA CROSSROADS [RES] *Chapel Hill, NC*

CAROLINA'S [RES] *Charleston, SC*

CARRIAGE HOUSE [RES] *Natchez, MS*

CARROLLTON INN [RES] *Carrollton, KY*
CASABLANCA [RES] *Nashville, TN*
CASA CARBONE RISTORANTE [RES] *Raleigh, NC*
CASSINELLI 1700 [RES] *Little Rock & North Little Rock, AR*
CASSIS [RES] *Atlanta, GA*
C. C. COHEN [RES] *Paducah, KY*
CECIL'S PUBLIC HOUSE [RES] *Alexander City, AL*
CEDAR GROVE [RES] *Vicksburg, MS*
CENTRAL GROCERY [URD] *New Orleans, LA*
CHALET BRANDT [RES] *Baton Rouge, LA*
CHAMPS [RES] *Laurinburg, NC*
CHARLES SEAFOOD RESTAURANT [RES] *Tifton, GA*
CHARLESTON GRILL [RES] *Charleston, SC*
CHARLEY G'S SEAFOOD GRILL [RES] *Lafayette, LA*
CHARLIE'S L'ETOILE VERTE [RES] *Hilton Head Island, SC*
CHARLIE TRIPPER'S [RES] *Valdosta, GA*
CHARTER ROOM [RES] *Raleigh, NC*
CHART HOUSE [RES] *Savannah, GA*
CHATEAU [RES] *Monroe and West Monroe, LA*
CHATEAU ELAN'S LE CLOS [RES] *Buford, GA*
CHEF BISTRO AND BAKERY [RES] *Knoxville, TN*
CHELSEA [RES] *St.Simons Island, GA*
CHELSEA'S [RES] *Mountain Home, AR*
CHESAPEAKE'S [RES] *Knoxville, TN*
CHESTERFIELD'S [RES] *Hattiesburg, MS*
CHEZ NOUS CHARCUTERIE [URD] *New Orleans, LA*
CHEZ PHILIPPE [RES] *Memphis, TN*
CHINA DELIGHT [RES] *Greers Ferry Lake Area, AR*
CHINA GARDEN [RES] *Tifton, GA*
CHIP'S BARBECUE [RES] *Little Rock & North Little Rock, AR*
CHOP HOUSE [RES] *Knoxville, TN*
CHOPS [RES] *Atlanta, GA*
CHRISTIAN'S [RES] *New Orleans, LA*
CHRISTINO'S [URD] *New Orleans, LA*
CIRCLE SUSHI [RES] *Atlanta, GA*
CITY GRILL [RES] *Atlanta, GA*
CLARA'S SEAFOOD GRILL [RES] *Manteo, NC*
CLOISTER MAIN DINING ROOM [RES] *Sea Island, GA*
CLOVER GRILL [URD] *New Orleans, LA*
CLUB 178 [RES] *Bull Shoals Lake Area, AR*
COACH HOUSE [RES] *Lexington, KY*
COBB LANE [RES] *Birmingham, AL*

COCK OF THE WALK [URD] *Jackson, MS*
COCK OF THE WALK [RES] *Nashville, TN*
COCK OF THE WALK [RES] *Natchez, MS*
COHUTTA DINING ROOM [RES] *Chatsworth, GA*
COLBY'S [RES] *Owensboro, KY*
COLLECTORS CAFE [RES] *Myrtle Beach, SC*
COLONNADE, THE [RES] *Atlanta, GA*
COMMANDER'S PALACE [RES] *New Orleans, LA*
COMMUNITY HOUSE [RES] *Georgetown, SC*
CONNIE KANAKIS' CAFE [RES] *Birmingham, AL*
COOHILL'S [RES] *Atlanta, GA*
COOKER BAR AND GRILLE [RES] *Memphis, TN*
COPPER CELLAR [RES] *Knoxville, TN*
COPPER CELLAR - CAPPUCCINO'S [RES] *Knoxville, TN*
COTTAGE [RES] *Wilmington, NC*
COUNTRY'S NORTH [URD] *Columbus, GA*
COUNTRY GRILL [RES] *Williamstown, KY*
COUNTRY PLACE [RES] *Atlanta, GA*
COUNTRY PLACE [RES] *Chattanooga, TN*
COUNTRY SQUIRE [RES] *Warsaw, NC*
COURTNEY'S [RES] *Raleigh, NC*
COURT OF TWO SISTERS [RES] *New Orleans, LA*
COVES [RES] *Pinehurst, NC*
COY'S STEAK HOUSE [RES] *Hot Springs & Hot Springs National Park, AR*
CREEKSIDE [RES] *Campbellsville, KY*
CRESCENT CITY BREWHOUSE [RES] *New Orleans, LA*
CRESCENT CITY GRILL [RES] *Hattiesburg, MS*
CRIPPEN'S [RES] *Blowing Rock, NC*
CROZIER'S RESTAURANT FRANCAIS [RES] *Metairie, LA*
CRYSTAL GRILL [RES] *Greenwood, MS*
CUCO'S [RES] *Biloxi, MS*
CUCOS [RES] *Alexandria, LA*
DAILEY'S [RES] *Atlanta, GA*
DAJONEL'S [RES] *Baton Rouge, LA*
DAKOTA [RES] *Covington, LA*
DALTON DEPOT [RES] *Dalton, GA*
DAMON'S, THE PLACE FOR RIBS [RES] *Hilton Head Island, SC*
DAMON'S THE PLACE FOR RIBS [RES] *Myrtle Beach, SC*
DAN'L BOONE INN [RES] *Boone, NC*
DANTE'S DOWN THE HATCH [RES] *Atlanta, GA*
DAPHNE LODGE [RES] *Cordele, GA*
DARRYL'S 1815 [RES] *Louisville, KY*

DARRYL'S 1891 RESTAURANT AND TAVERN [RES] *Lexington, KY*

DEE FELICE CAFE [RES] *Covington (Cincinnati Airport Area), KY*

DE LAFAYETTE [RES] *Fayetteville, NC*

DELICIOUS TEMPTATIONS [URD] *Little Rock & North Little Rock, AR*

DELMONICO [RES] *New Orleans, LA*

DEMOS' STEAK AND SPAGHETTI HOUSE [RES] *Murfreesboro, TN*

DENNERY'S [RES] *Jackson, MS*

DE SHA'S GRILLE AND BAR [RES] *Lexington, KY*

DESIRE OYSTER BAR [RES] *New Orleans, LA*

DICK & HARRY'S [RES] *Norcross, GA*

DINING ROOM, THE [RES] *Atlanta, GA*

DINING ROOM AT WOODLANDS, THE [RES] *Charleston, SC*

DINNER BELL [RES] *Berea, KY*

DINNER BELL [URD] *Branson/Table Rock Lake Area, MO*

DINNER BELL [RES] *Sweetwater, TN*

DISH [RES] *Atlanta, GA*

DOCKSIDE [RES] *Wrightsville Beach, NC*

DOMINICK'S [RES] *Norcross, GA*

DOMINQUE'S [RES] *New Orleans, LA*

DON JUAN [RES] *Hot Springs & Hot Springs National Park, AR*

DON'S SEAFOOD [RES] *Shreveport, LA*

DON'S SEAFOOD & STEAK HOUSE [RES] *Baton Rouge, LA*

DON'S SEAFOOD & STEAK HOUSE [RES] *Lafayette, LA*

DOOKY CHASE [RES] *New Orleans, LA*

DOWNTOWN GRILL [RES] *Oxford, MS*

DOXEY'S MARKET & CAFE [URD] *Wilmington, NC*

DRAGON GARDEN [RES] *Wilmington, NC*

DRAGON PALACE [RES] *Ashland, KY*

DUDLEY'S [RES] *Lexington, KY*

DUSTY'S BARBECUE [RES] *Atlanta, GA*

DUX [RES] *Memphis, TN*

ECLIPSE DI LUNA [RES] *Atlanta, GA*

EDDIE MONSOUR'S [RES] *Vicksburg, MS*

EDDIE ROMANELLI'S [RES] *Wilmington, NC*

ELIJAH'S [RES] *Wilmington, NC*

ELIZABETH ON 37TH [RES] *Savannah, GA*

ELLIOTT'S ON THE SQUARE [RES] *Charleston, SC*

ELLIS V [RES] *Demopolis, AL*

EMBERS SEAFOOD GRILLE [RES] *Atlanta, GA*

EMERIL'S [RES] *New Orleans, LA*

ENCORE AT THE FOX [RES] *Atlanta, GA*

ENGLISH GRILL, THE [RES] *Louisville, KY*

ERIKA'S [RES] *Memphis, TN*

ERLING JENSEN [RES] *Memphis, TN*

EXPRESSIONS [RES] *Hendersonville, NC*

F. SCOTT'S [RES] *Nashville, TN*

FADED ROSE [RES] *Hot Springs & Hot Springs National Park, AR*

FADED ROSE [RES] *Little Rock & North Little Rock, AR*

FAIRVIEW [RES] *Durham, NC*

FAT MATT'S [URD] *Atlanta, GA*

FEARRINGTON HOUSE [RES] *Chapel Hill, NC*

FEELINGS CAFE [RES] *New Orleans, LA*

FERD GRISANTI [RES] *Louisville, KY*

FIESTA GRILL [RES] *Atlanta, GA*

FIFTH QUARTER STEAKHOUSE [RES] *Louisville, KY*

FILLETS [RES] *Pascagoula, MS*

FINE FRIENDS [RES] *Asheville, NC*

FIREHOUSE [RES] *Johnson City, TN*

FIVE HAPPINESS [RES] *New Orleans, LA*

FLYING FISH CAFE [RES] *Kill Devil Hills (Outer Banks), NC*

FOGCUTTER [RES] *Huntsville, AL*

FOLK'S FOLLY [RES] *Memphis, TN*

FOOD MERCHANT [RES] *Marietta, GA*

FOOD STUDIO [RES] *Atlanta, GA*

FORMOSA CHINESE RESTAURANT [RES] *Birmingham, AL*

FOUR SQUARE [RES] *Durham, NC*

FRATELLI DI NAPOLI [RES] *Atlanta, GA*

FRED & CLAIRE'S [RES] *New Bern, NC*

FREDDIE'S [RES] *Wilmington, NC*

FRED'S FISH HOUSE [RES] *Mountain Home, AR*

FRED'S HICKORY INN [RES] *Bentonville, AR*

FRENCH CONNECTION [RES] *Biloxi, MS*

FRENCH MARKET [RES] *New Orleans, LA*

FROG & OWL KITCHEN [RES] *Franklin (Macon County), NC*

FRONT PAGE CAFE [RES] *Jonesboro, AR*

FU LIN [RES] *Conway, AR*

FULTON FIVE [RES] *Charleston, SC*

FUSCO'S [RES] *Myrtle Beach, SC*

FUSION BISTRO [RES] *Covington, LA*

GABRIELLE [RES] *New Orleans, LA*

GABRIELLE'S [RES] *Asheville, NC*

GALATOIRE'S [RES] *New Orleans, LA*

GARIBALDI'S [RES] *Charleston, SC*

GARIBALDI'S [RES] *Columbia, SC*

GARIBALDI'S CAFE [RES] *Savannah, GA*

GASLIGHT 2000 [RES] *Hilton Head Island, SC*

GATE CITY CHOP HOUSE [RES]
Greensboro, NC
GAUTREAU'S [RES] *New Orleans, LA*
GAZEBO CAFE [RES] *Franklin (Macon
County), NC*
GEORGE'S STEAK PIT [RES] *Sheffield,
AL*
GEORGIA GRILLE [RES] *Atlanta, GA*
GEORGIA ROOM [RES] *Pine Mountain
(Harris County), GA*
GERARD'S DOWNTOWN [RES] *New
Orleans, LA*
GERMAINE'S [RES] *Ocean Springs, MS*
GIFT HORSE [RES] *Gulf Shores, AL*
GOLDEN CITY CHINESE
RESTAURANT [RES]
Birmingham, AL
GOLDEN DRAGON [RES] *Jennings, LA*
GOTEN 2 [RES] *Nashville, TN*
GRADY'S AMERICAN GRILL [RES]
Birmingham, AL
GRAFFITI'S [RES] *Little Rock & North
Little Rock, AR*
GRAND DINING ROOM [RES]
Americus, GA
GRAND DINING ROOM [RES] *Jekyll
Island, GA*
GRAND DINING ROOM, THE [RES]
Mobile, AL
GRAZIE A BISTRO [RES] *Marietta, GA*
GREEN BAMBOO [RES] *Elizabethtown,
KY*
GREENERY [RES] *Asheville, NC*
GREEN HILLS GRILLE [RES] *Nashville,
TN*
GRILL ROOM [RES] *New Orleans, LA*
GROVE PARK INN RESORT [RES]
Asheville, NC
GUYTANO'S [RES] *Charlotte, NC*
HALL'S ON THE RIVER [RES]
Winchester, KY
HAMILTON HOUSE [RES] *Hot Springs
& Hot Springs National Park, AR*
HAMPTON STREET VINEYARD [RES]
Columbia, SC
HANWORRI [URD] *Atlanta, GA*
HARBOURMASTER'S [RES] *Hilton
Head Island, SC*
HARLEQUIN STEAKS & SEAFOOD
[RES] *Lake Charles, LA*
HARRISON'S [RES] *Thomasville, GA*
HARRY BISSETTS [RES] *Athens, GA*
HARVEST MOON [RES] *Wilmington,
NC*
HARVEST RESTAURANT [RES]
Atlanta, GA
HARVEY MANSION [RES] *New Bern,
NC*
HARVEY'S [RES] *Columbus, MS*
HARVEY'S [RES] *Starkville, MS*
HAVELI [RES] *Atlanta, GA*
HAZEL'S FAMILY RESTAURANT [RES]
Gulf Shores, AL
HEIDELBERG [RES] *Gatlinburg, TN*

HEMINGWAY'S [RES] *Hilton Head
Island, SC*
HENDERSON HOUSE [RES] *New Bern,
NC*
HENNESSY'S [RES] *Columbia, SC*
HENSON'S CYPRESS INN [RES]
Tuscaloosa, AL
HEREFORD BARN STEAK HOUSE
[RES] *Charlotte, NC*
HIERONYMUS SEAFOOD [RES]
Wilmington, NC
HIGHLANDS [RES] *Birmingham, AL*
HI LIFE [RES] *Norcross, GA*
HOFBRAUHAUS [RES] *Helen, GA*
HOFBRAUHAUS [RES] *Hilton Head
Island, SC*
HOOK LINE & SINKER SEAFOOD
[RES] *Biloxi, MS*
HORSERADISH GRILL [RES] *Atlanta,
GA*
HOT SPRINGS BRAU-HOUSE [RES]
*Hot Springs & Hot Springs
National Park, AR*
HSU'S GOURMET CHINESE [RES]
Atlanta, GA
HUDSON'S ON THE DOCKS [RES]
Hilton Head Island, SC
HUNTER HOUSE [RES] *Tybee Island,
GA*
HURSEY'S PIG PICKIN' BAR-B-Q
[RES] *Burlington, NC*
HYLANDER STEAK AND RIB [RES]
Eureka Springs, AR
IDLEWILDS [RES] *Charleston, SC*
IL PALIO [RES] *Chapel Hill, NC*
I MONELLI [RES] *Lafayette, LA*
IMPASTATO'S [RES] *Metairie, LA*
IMPERIAL FEZ [RES] *Atlanta, GA*
INDIA PALACE [RES] *Memphis, TN*
INDIA PALACE [RES] *Metairie, LA*
INDIGO COASTAL GRILL [RES]
Atlanta, GA
IRREGARDLESS CAFE [RES] *Raleigh,
NC*
ISLAND INN [RES] *Ocracoke (Outer
Banks), NC*
JACKALOPE'S VIEW [RES] *Banner Elk,
NC*
J. ALEXANDER'S [RES] *Nashville, TN*
J ARTHUR'S [RES] *Maggie Valley, NC*
J BASUL NOBLE'S [RES] *High Point,
NC*
J BISTRO [RES] *Charleston, SC*
JEAN CLAUDE'S CAFE [RES] *Raleigh,
NC*
JEAN LAFITTE INN [RES] *Lake
Charles, LA*
JEFFERSON PLACE [RES] *Tupelo, MS*
JEREMIAH'S [RES] *Paducah, KY*
JERRY'S [RES] *Elizabethtown, KY*
JESSIE'S FAMILY RESTAURANT [RES]
Louisville, KY
J. H. MCCLINTOCK'S [RES] *Harrison,
AR*
JIM'S SEAFOOD [RES] *Frankfort, KY*

JIMMY KELLY'S [RES] *Nashville, TN*
JIM WHITE'S HALF SHELL [RES]
   Atlanta, GA
J. MAC'S [RES] *St.Simons Island, GA*
JOCELYN'S [RES] *Ocean Springs, MS*
JOE'S BAR AND GRILL [RES] *Myrtle
   Beach, SC*
JOHN'S [RES] *Lumberton, NC*
JOHNNY HARRIS [RES] *Savannah, GA*
JOLLY ROGER [RES] *Kill Devil Hills
   (Outer Banks), NC*
JONES CAFE [RES] *Pine Bluff, AR*
JP MULLDOONS [RES] *Valdosta, GA*
JUBAN'S [RES] *Baton Rouge, LA*
KAMOGAWA [URD] *Atlanta, GA*
KELSEY'S [RES] *New Orleans, LA*
KILLER CREEK CHOP HOUSE [RES]
   Norcross, GA
KINGFISHER SEAFOOD AND STEAK
   HOUSE [RES] *Hilton Head
   Island, SC*
KING NEPTUNE [RES] *Wrightsville
   Beach, NC*
KIRK KIRKLAND'S HITCHIN' POST
   [RES] *Gulf Shores, AL*
KOBE JAPANESE HOUSE OF STEAK &
   SEAFOOD [RES] *Cornelius, NC*
KOKOPELLI [URD] *Hilton Head Island,
   SC*
KOREANA II [RES] *Louisville, KY*
K-PAUL'S LOUISIANA KITCHEN [RES]
   New Orleans, LA
KREG'S CATFISH [RES] *Arkadelphia,
   AR*
KUNZ'S FOURTH AND MARKET
   [RES] *Louisville, KY*
KURTZ [RES] *Bardstown, KY*
LA BIBLIOTHEQUE [RES] *Charlotte,
   NC*
LAFITTE'S LANDING [RES] *Baton
   Rouge, LA*
LA FONDA [RES] *Lafayette, LA*
LA GAULOISE BISTRO [RES] *New
   Orleans, LA*
LA GROTTA [RES] *Atlanta, GA*
LA GROTTA RAVINIA [RES] *Atlanta,
   GA*
LA MADELEINE [URD] *New Orleans,
   LA*
LA MAISON [RES] *Augusta, GA*
LAMP LIGHTER [RES] *Charlotte, NC*
LANDING [RES] *Natchitoches, LA*
LA PAREE [RES] *Birmingham, AL*
LA PAZ RESTAURANTE-CANTINA
   [RES] *Atlanta, GA*
LA PLACE D'EVANGELINE [RES] *St.
   Martinville, LA*
LA PROVENCE [RES] *Covington, LA*
LA RESIDENCE [RES] *Chapel Hill, NC*
LA RIVIERA [RES] *Metairie, LA*
LA SCALA [RES] *Little Rock & North
   Little Rock, AR*
LAS MARGARITAS [RES] *Raleigh, NC*
LA STRADA [RES] *Marietta, GA*
LAST RESORT GRILL [RES] *Athens, GA*

LASYONE MEAT PIE KITCHEN [RES]
   Natchitoches, LA
LA TERRACE [RES] *Southern Pines, NC*
LATITUDE 31 [RES] *Jekyll Island, GA*
LA TOURELLE [RES] *Memphis, TN*
LA VECCHIA'S [RES] *Charlotte, NC*
LEMON GRASS [RES] *New Orleans, LA*
LE RELAIS [RES] *Louisville, KY*
LE ROSIER [RES] *New Iberia, LA*
LE SAINT AMOUR [RES] *Atlanta, GA*
LICKSKILLET FARM [RES] *Norcross,
   GA*
LIGHTHOUSE INN, THE [RES] *Fort
   Smith, AR*
LILIFREDS OF CAMDEN [RES]
   Camden, SC
LILLY'S [RES] *Louisville, KY*
LITTLE RIVER INN [RES] *New Iberia,
   LA*
LITTLE VENICE [RES] *Hilton Head
   Island, SC*
LITTON'S [RES] *Knoxville, TN*
LOMBARDI'S [RES] *Atlanta, GA*
LONGHORN STEAK HOUSE [RES]
   Hilton Head Island, SC
LONGHORN STEAKHOUSE [RES]
   Myrtle Beach, SC
LOUGHRY'S LANDING [RES]
   Beaufort, NC
LOUIS' [URD] *Charleston, SC*
LOUIS XVI [RES] *New Orleans, LA*
LOVELESS CAFE [RES] *Nashville, TN*
LUCY'S [RES] *Camden, SC*
LULU GRILLE [RES] *Memphis, TN*
LUNA SI [RES] *Atlanta, GA*
LYNN'S PARADISE CAFE [RES]
   Louisville, KY
MACARTHUR'S [RES] *Atlanta, GA*
MACELWEE'S SEAFOOD HOUSE
   [RES] *Tybee Island, GA*
MAD PLATTER [RES] *Nashville, TN*
MAGGIANO'S LITTLE ITALY [RES]
   Atlanta, GA
MAGNOLIA GRILL [RES] *Durham, NC*
MAGNOLIAS [RES] *Charleston, SC*
MAJOR GRUMBLES [RES] *Selma, AL*
MAKATO'S JAPANESE STEAKHOUSE
   [RES] *Johnson City, TN*
MAKOTO [RES] *Boone, NC*
MALONE'S [RES] *Columbus, GA*
MALONE'S [RES] *Lexington, KY*
MALONE'S FISH & STEAK HOUSE
   [URD] *Tupelo, MS*
MAMM GRISANTI [RES] *Louisville, KY*
MANDARIN HOUSE [RES] *Knoxville,
   TN*
MANDARIN HOUSE [RES] *Knoxville,
   TN*
MANSION, THE [RES] *Atlanta, GA*
MANSION AT GRIFFIN GATE [RES]
   Lexington, KY
MAPLE STREET MANSION [RES]
   Carrollton, GA
MARIAH'S [RES] *Bowling Green, KY*
MARINA [RES] *Elizabeth City, NC*

MARINERS SEAFOOD & STEAK HOUSE [RES] *Natchitoches, LA*
MARIO'S [RES] *Nashville, TN*
MARISOL [RES] *New Orleans, LA*
MARKET PLACE RESTAURANT & WINE BAR, THE [RES] *Asheville, NC*
MARKET STREET CASUAL DINING [RES] *Wilmington, NC*
MARTINIQUE [RES] *New Orleans, LA*
MARY MAC'S TEAROOM [RES] *Atlanta, GA*
MARY MAESTRI'S [RES] *Springdale, AR*
MARY MAHONEY'S OLD FRENCH HOUSE [RES] *Biloxi, MS*
MASTERSON'S [RES] *Louisville, KY*
MATTEO'S ITALIAN RESTAURANT [RES] *Brunswick, GA*
MAXIMO'S ITALIAN GRILL [RES] *New Orleans, LA*
MAXWELL'S [RES] *Vicksburg, MS*
MAXWELL'S BEEF AND SEAFOOD [RES] *Gatlinburg, TN*
MCCLARD'S BAR-B-Q [RES] *Hot Springs & Hot Springs National Park, AR*
MCCRADY'S TAVERN [RES] *Charleston, SC*
MCGUFFEY'S GRILL & BAR [RES] *Asheville, NC*
MCKENDRICK'S [RES] *Atlanta, GA*
MCKINNON'S LOUISIANE [RES] *Atlanta, GA*
MCNINCH HOUSE [RES] *Charlotte, NC*
MELOS TAVERNA [RES] *Memphis, TN*
MERCHANTS [RES] *Nashville, TN*
MERE BULLES [RES] *Nashville, TN*
METRO BISTRO [RES] *New Orleans, LA*
MICHAUL'S [RES] *New Orleans, LA*
MICK'S UNDERGROUND [RES] *Atlanta, GA*
MIDI SOUTH OF FRANCE [RES] *New Orleans, LA*
MIDTOWN CAFE [RES] *Nashville, TN*
MIKE ANDERSON'S [RES] *Baton Rouge, LA*
MIKE ANDERSON'S SEAFOOD [RES] *New Orleans, LA*
MIKEE'S SEAFOOD [RES] *Gulf Shores, AL*
MIKE FINK [RES] *Covington (Cincinnati Airport Area), KY*
MILLER'S CHICKEN AND STEAK HOUSE [RES] *Hot Springs & Hot Springs National Park, AR*
MILL POND [RES] *Camden, SC*
MI SPIA [RES] *Atlanta, GA*
MIYABI SEAFOOD & STEAK [RES] *St.Simons Island, GA*
MOLLIE'S [RES] *Hot Springs & Hot Springs National Park, AR*
MOM & DAD'S [RES] *Valdosta, GA*
MONELL'S [RES] *Nashville, TN*

MONSIEUR PATOU [RES] *Shreveport, LA*
MOONLITE BAR-B-Q [RES] *Owensboro, KY*
MORNING CALL [URD] *Metairie, LA*
MORRELL'S [RES] *Cartersville, GA*
MOSCA'S [RES] *New Orleans, LA*
MOSSY GROVE SCHOOLHOUSE [RES] *Troy, AL*
MOTHER'S [URD] *New Orleans, LA*
MOUNTAIN SMOKE HOUSE [URD] *Asheville, NC*
MOUNT VERNON [RES] *Chattanooga, TN*
MR B'S BISTRO [RES] *New Orleans, LA*
MR B'S CATFISH [RES] *Greers Ferry Lake Area, AR*
MRS. WILLIS [RES] *Morehead City, NC*
MRS WILKES' DINING ROOM [RES] *Savannah, GA*
MUMBO JUMBO [RES] *Atlanta, GA*
NAKATO JAPANESE RESTAURANT [RES] *Atlanta, GA*
NAPLES [RES] *Knoxville, TN*
NAPOLEAN HOUSE [RES] *New Orleans, LA*
NATALIA'S [RES] *Macon, GA*
NAVA [RES] *Atlanta, GA*
NENO IL TOSCANO [RES] *Hilton Head Island, SC*
NEW CHINA [RES] *Brunswick, GA*
NEW ORLEANS MANOR [RES] *Nashville, TN*
NEW PERRY [RES] *Perry, GA*
NICK'S [RES] *Cookeville, TN*
NICK'S [RES] *Highlands, NC*
NICK'S [RES] *Jackson, MS*
NICK'S ON 61ST [RES] *Myrtle Beach, SC*
NICKIEMOTO'S [RES] *Atlanta, GA*
NIKI'S WEST [RES] *Birmingham, AL*
NIKOLAI'S ROOF [RES] *Atlanta, GA*
NINO'S ITALIAN RESTAURANT [RES] *Atlanta, GA*
NOLA [RES] *New Orleans, LA*
NOODLE'S ITALIAN EATERY & GRILL [RES] *Auburn, AL*
OAK [RES] *Manchester, TN*
OAK HARBOUR [RES] *Myrtle Beach, SC*
OAK TREE VICTORIAN RESTAURANT [RES] *Pine Mountain (Harris County), GA*
OCEANIC [RES] *Wrightsville Beach, NC*
OCEAN TERRACE [RES] *Wrightsville Beach, NC*
O'CHARLEY'S [RES] *Biloxi, MS*
O'CHARLEY'S [RES] *Tuscaloosa, AL*
OH! BRIAN'S [RES] *Wilmington, NC*
OK CAFE [RES] *Atlanta, GA*
OLD COUNTRY STORE [RES] *Jackson, TN*
OLD DEPOT [RES] *Port Gibson, MS*
OLDE INN [RES] *Cordele, GA*

OLDE PINK HOUSE [RES] *Savannah, GA*

OLD HICKORY STEAKHOUSE, THE [RES] *Nashville, TN*

OLD MILL [RES] *Pigeon Forge, TN*

OLD OYSTER FACTORY [RES] *Hilton Head Island, SC*

OLD POST OFFICE RESTAURANT [RES] *Kiawah Island, SC*

OLD SALEM TAVERN [RES] *Winston-Salem, NC*

OLD SOUTH BAR-B-Q [RES] *Marietta, GA*

OLD SPAGHETTI FACTORY [RES] *Louisville, KY*

OLD SPAGHETTI FACTORY [RES] *Nashville, TN*

OLD TOWN PUB [RES] *Eureka Springs, AR*

OLE LAMPLIGHTER, THE [RES] *Columbia, TN*

OL' HEIDELBERG [RES] *Huntsville, AL*

OL' ROCKHOUSE [RES] *Harrison, AR*

ONE-EYED PARROT [RES] *Charleston, SC*

ON THE VERANDAH [RES] *Highlands, NC*

OPEN HEARTH [RES] *Gatlinburg, TN*

OPEN HEARTH [RES] *Greenville, SC*

ORANGERY, THE [RES] *Knoxville, TN*

ORIENTAL WOK [RES] *Covington (Cincinnati Airport Area), KY*

ORIGINAL OYSTER HOUSE [RES] *Gulf Shores, AL*

OUR PLACE [RES] *Blakely, GA*

OWENS' [RES] *Nags Head (Outer Banks), NC*

PALACE CAFE [RES] *New Orleans, LA*

PANO'S & PAUL'S [RES] *Atlanta, GA*

PAPALENO'S [RES] *Berea, KY*

PAPA'S GRILL [RES] *Durham, NC*

PAPA VANELLI'S [RES] *Tupelo, MS*

PAPILLON [RES] *Charleston, SC*

PARIZADE [RES] *Durham, NC*

PARK 75 AT THE FOUR SEASONS [RES] *Atlanta, GA*

PARKER HOUSE [RES] *Laurel, MS*

PARKER'S BAR-B-QUE [RES] *Greenville, NC*

PARK GRILL [RES] *Gatlinburg, TN*

PARSON'S TABLE [RES] *Johnson City, TN*

PARTHENON MEDITERRANEAN [RES] *Murfreesboro, TN*

PASTIS [RES] *Charlotte, NC*

PATOU BISTRO [RES] *Charlotte, NC*

PAT'S OF HENDERSON [RES] *Lake Charles, LA*

PATTI'S [RES] *Gilbertsville, KY*

PAULETTE'S [RES] *Memphis, TN*

PAULETTE'S [RES] *Paris, TN*

PEARL'S ELEGANT PELICAN [RES] *Savannah, GA*

PEDDLER, THE [RES] *Gatlinburg, TN*

PEERLESS [RES] *Johnson City, TN*

PEKING GARDEN [RES] *Lake Charles, LA*

PEKING GARDEN [RES] *Raleigh, NC*

PELICAN CLUB [RES] *New Orleans, LA*

PENGS PAVILLION [RES] *Calhoun, GA*

PENGUIN ISLE [RES] *Nags Head (Outer Banks), NC*

PENINSULA GRILL [RES] *Charleston, SC*

PERDIDO PASS [RES] *Gulf Shores, AL*

PERISTYLE [RES] *New Orleans, LA*

PETITE AUBERGE [RES] *Atlanta, GA*

PIER, THE [RES] *Memphis, TN*

PIER 4 [RES] *Mobile, AL*

PIE WORKS [RES] *Durham, NC*

PILLARS, THE [RES] *Mobile, AL*

PILOT HOUSE [RES] *Wilmington, NC*

PINE CREST INN [RES] *Tryon, NC*

PITTYPAT'S PORCH [RES] *Atlanta, GA*

PLACE [RES] *Baton Rouge, LA*

PLAZA [RES] *Eureka Springs, AR*

PLAZA RESTAURANT [RES] *Thomasville, GA*

PLEASANT PEASANT [RES] *Atlanta, GA*

POETS [RES] *Jackson, MS*

POOGAN'S PORCH [RES] *Charleston, SC*

POOR BOY'S RIVERSIDE INN [RES] *Lafayette, LA*

POOR RICHARD'S [RES] *Gainesville, GA*

PORT CITY CHOP HOUSE [RES] *Wilmington, NC*

PORT O' CALL [RES] *Kill Devil Hills (Outer Banks), NC*

PRALINE CONNECTION [RES] *New Orleans, LA*

PREJEANS [RES] *Lafayette, LA*

PRICCI [RES] *Atlanta, GA*

PRIME [RES] *Atlanta, GA*

PRIME CUT STEAKHOUSE [RES] *Nashville, TN*

PRIMOS RESTAURANT AT NORTHGATE [RES] *Jackson, MS*

PROVINO'S [RES] *Opelika, AL*

PUBLIC EYE, THE [RES] *Memphis, TN*

QUEEN ANNE'S REVENGE [RES] *Manteo, NC*

RAFFERTY'S [RES] *Lexington, KY*

RAJI [RES] *Memphis, TN*

RALPH & KACOO'S [RES] *Bossier City, LA*

RALPH & KACOO'S [RES] *Metairie, LA*

RANCH HOUSE [RES] *Charlotte, NC*

RANCH HOUSE [RES] *Columbia, TN*

RANDOLPH HALL [RES] *Baton Rouge, LA*

RANDOL'S [URD] *Lafayette, LA*

RAY'S ON THE RIVER [RES] *Atlanta, GA*

RED APPLE DINING ROOM [RES] *Greers Ferry Lake Area, AR*

RED FISH GRILL [RES] *New Orleans, LA*

REGAS [RES] *Knoxville, TN*

REGATTA SEAFOOD GRILLE [RES] *Lexington, KY*
REILLEY'S [RES] *Hilton Head Island, SC*
RENDEZVOUS [URD] *Memphis, TN*
RESTAURANT YAGOTO [RES] *Greenville, SC*
RIALTO [RES] *Wrightsville Beach, NC*
RIB ROOM [RES] *New Orleans, LA*
RICE PADDY [RES] *Georgetown, SC*
RISTORANTE DIVINO [RES] *Columbia, SC*
RIVER FOREST MANOR [RES] *Washington, NC*
RIVER HOUSE [RES] *Savannah, GA*
RIVER ROOM [RES] *Georgetown, SC*
RIVER'S END [RES] *Savannah, GA*
RIVERVIEW [RES] *Covington (Cincinnati Airport Area), KY*
RIVERWOOD [RES] *Blowing Rock, NC*
ROBIN'S [RES] *Lafayette, LA*
ROBLYN'S STEAK HOUSE [RES] *Cleveland, TN*
ROCK BOTTOM [RES] *Atlanta, GA*
ROCKET CITY DINER [RES] *Hattiesburg, MS*
RONNIE GRISANTA AND SONS [RES] *Memphis, TN*
ROONEY'S [RES] *St.Simons Island, GA*
ROSA LINDA'S CAFE [RES] *Myrtle Beach, SC*
ROSSI'S [RES] *Birmingham, AL*
ROUSSOS SEAFOOD [RES] *Mobile, AL*
ROYAL THAI [RES] *Nashville, TN*
RUBY TUESDAY [RES] *Owensboro, KY*
RUCKERJOHN'S [RES] *Wilmington, NC*
RUDOLPH'S [RES] *Gainesville, GA*
RUE BOURBON [RES] *New Orleans, LA*
RUTH'S CHRIS STEAK HOUSE [RES] *Atlanta, GA*
RUTH'S CHRIS STEAK HOUSE [RES] *Baton Rouge, LA*
RUTH'S CHRIS STEAK HOUSE [RES] *Lafayette, LA*
RUTH'S CHRIS STEAK HOUSE [RES] *Mobile, AL*
RUTH'S CHRIS STEAKHOUSE [RES] *Nashville, TN*
RYAN'S STEAK CHOPS & SEAFOOD [RES] *Winston-Salem, NC*
SAHARA [RES] *Montgomery, AL*
SAHARA STEAK HOUSE [RES] *Cave City, KY*
SAIGON LE [RES] *Memphis, TN*
SAL & JUDY'S [RES] *Slidell, LA*
SANDFIDDLER SEAFOOD RESTAURANT [RES] *Southport, NC*
SANITARY FISH MARKET [RES] *Morehead City, NC*
SANTA FE STEAK CO [RES] *Murfreesboro, TN*
SARACEN [RES] *Charleston, SC*

SCOTT'S FISH MARKET [RES] *Hilton Head Island, SC*
SEA CAPTAIN'S HOUSE [RES] *Myrtle Beach, SC*
SEANACHIE [RES] *Nashville, TN*
SEA-N-SUDS [RES] *Gulf Shores, AL*
SEASONS OF SAVANNAH [RES] *Savannah, GA*
SEEGER'S [RES] *Atlanta, GA*
SEOUL GARDEN [RES] *Atlanta, GA*
SERMET'S CORNER [RES] *Charleston, SC*
SEVEN OAKS [RES] *Greenville, SC*
SHALIMAR INDIAN CUISINE [RES] *New Orleans, LA*
SHERMAN'S [RES] *Greenville, MS*
SHILLING'S ON THE SQUARE [RES] *Marietta, GA*
SHRIMP FACTORY [RES] *Savannah, GA*
SIA'S [URD] *Norcross, GA*
SICHUAN GARDEN [RES] *Louisville, KY*
SIMP MCGHEE'S [RES] *Decatur, AL*
SIMPSON'S [RES] *Raleigh, NC*
SINBAD [RES] *Hendersonville, NC*
SIR LOIN'S INN [RES] *Little Rock & North Little Rock, AR*
SITAR INDIAN RESTAURANT [RES] *Nashville, TN*
SKOBY'S [RES] *Kingsport, TN*
SLIGHTLY NORTH OF BROAD [RES] *Charleston, SC*
SLIGHTLY UP THE CREEK [RES] *Charleston, SC*
SMITH HOUSE [RES] *Dahlonega, GA*
SMOKY'S GRILL [RES] *Charlotte, NC*
SNUG HARBOR JAZZ BISTRO [RES] *New Orleans, LA*
SOHO CAFE [RES] *Atlanta, GA*
SOLE MIO [RES] *Nashville, TN*
SOTO JAPANESE RESTAURANT [RES] *Atlanta, GA*
SOUTH BEACH GALLERY AT THE WATER [RES] *Covington (Cincinnati Airport Area), KY*
SOUTH CITY KITCHEN [RES] *Atlanta, GA*
SOUTHLAND [RES] *Sheffield, AL*
SOUTH OF FRANCE [RES] *Atlanta, GA*
SPAULE [RES] *Little Rock & North Little Rock, AR*
SPEEDY PIG BAR-B-Q [RES] *Russellville, AL*
SPERRY'S [RES] *Nashville, TN*
SQUID'S [RES] *Chapel Hill, NC*
SQUIRE'S PUB [RES] *Southern Pines, NC*
ST. FRANCISVILLE INN [RES] *St. Francisville, LA*
STALEY'S CHARCOAL STEAK HOUSE [RES] *Winston-Salem, NC*
STAX'S PEPPERMILL [RES] *Greenville, SC*

STEAMBOAT WAREHOUSE [RES]
Opelousas, LA
STOCKYARD [RES] Nashville, TN
STONE HEARTH [RES] Elizabethtown,
KY
SUBURB-A-NIGHT PIZZA [RES]
Atlanta, GA
SUNDOWN CAFE [RES] Atlanta, GA
SUNSET GRILL [RES] Nashville, TN
SUPERIOR GRILL [RES] Shreveport, LA
SYD AND LUTHER'S [URD]
Georgetown, SC
TALE OF THE TROUT [RES] Rogers, AR
TALLY-HO [RES] Selma, AL
TAM'S TAVERN [RES] Rock Hill, SC
TAVERNA NIKOS [RES] Durham, NC
THAD AND JOE'S [RES] Atlanta, GA
THAI CHILI [RES] Atlanta, GA
THAI SIAM [RES] Louisville, KY
THREE MONKEYS [RES] Hot Springs &
Hot Springs National Park, AR
TICO'S STEAK HOUSE [RES] Jackson,
MS
TIDES [RES] Buxton (Outer Banks), NC
TIKI RESTAURANT, LOUNGE AND
MARINA [RES] Pascagoula, MS
TIMOTHY'S [RES] Louisville, KY
TIN ANGEL [RES] Nashville, TN
TOMTOM [RES] Atlanta, GA
TONY MORAN'S PASTA E VINO [RES]
New Orleans, LA
TONY ROMA'S [RES] Lexington, KY
TONY'S [RES] Myrtle Beach, SC
TONY'S PIZZA [RES] Lake Charles, LA
TOULOUSE [RES] Atlanta, GA
TOWNHOUSE [RES] Charlotte, NC
TOWN HOUSE TEA ROOM AND
RESTAURANT [URD] Nashville,
TN
TRACE [RES] Nashville, TN
TREY YUEN [RES] Covington, LA
TREY YUEN [RES] Hammond, LA
TREY YUEN [RES] Tuscaloosa, AL
TRIO CAFE [RES] Fayetteville, NC
TRUSTEES' HOUSE AT PLEASANT
HILL [RES] Harrodsburg, KY
TUJAGUE'S [RES] New Orleans, LA
TWIG'S [RES] Blowing Rock, NC
UNCLE GAYLORD'S [RES] Fayetteville,
AR
UPPERLINE [RES] New Orleans, LA
UPTOWN CAFE [RES] Louisville, KY
VALENTINO'S [RES] Nashville, TN
VAN GOGH'S [RES] Norcross, GA
VARSITY [URD] Athens, GA
VARSITY, THE [URD] Atlanta, GA
VARSITY JR, THE [URD] Atlanta, GA
VENI VIDI VICI [RES] Atlanta, GA
VERANDA [RES] New Orleans, LA
VICTORIA, THE [RES] Anniston, AL
VICTORIAN SAMPLER [RES] Eureka
Springs, AR
VICTORIAN TEA ROOM [RES] Pine
Mountain (Harris County), GA
VILLA CHRISTINA [RES] Atlanta, GA

VILLAGE WHEEL [RES] Bull Shoals
Lake Area, AR
VINCENZO'S [RES] Asheville, NC
VINCENZO'S [RES] Louisville, KY
VINCE PERONE'S [RES] Greenville, SC
VINE STREET MARKET [URD]
Chattanooga, TN
VINEYARD [RES] Winston-Salem, NC
VININGS INN, THE [RES] Atlanta, GA
VINNIE'S [RES] Wilmington, NC
VINNIE'S STEAKHOUSE [RES] Raleigh,
NC
VINNY'S ON WINDWARD [RES]
Atlanta, GA
VINTAGE HOUSE [RES] Hickory, NC
VINTAGE YEAR [RES] Montgomery, AL
VISTA BREWING & BISTRO [RES]
Columbia, SC
VITO'S RISTORANTE [RES] Southern
Pines, NC
VRAZEL'S [RES] Gulfport, MS
WALNUT HILLS ROUND TABLES
[RES] Vicksburg, MS
WAR EAGLE MILL [URD] Rogers, AR
WAREHOUSE NO. 1 [RES] Monroe and
West Monroe, LA
WATER STREET [RES] Wilmington, NC
WAVERLY GRILL [RES] Atlanta, GA
WEIDMANN'S [RES] Meridian, MS
WHALER'S CATCH [RES] Paducah, KY
WHISTLE STOP CAFE [URD] Forsyth,
GA
WHITE CAP SEAFOOD RESTAURANT
[RES] Gulfport, MS
WHITLEY'S BARBECUE [RES] Ahoskie,
NC
WIEDERKEHR WINE CELLARS [RES]
Alma, AR
WILD BOAR, THE [RES] Nashville, TN
WILLIAMS SEAFOOD [RES] Savannah,
GA
WILSONS SEAFOOD [RES] Brunswick,
GA
WINDMILL EUROPEAN GRILL [RES]
Asheville, NC
WINDMILL POINT [RES] Nags Head
(Outer Banks), NC
WINSTON'S [RES] Birmingham, AL
WINSTON'S [RES] Louisville, KY
WINSTON'S GRILLE [RES] Raleigh,
NC
WOODSHED PIT BAR-B-QUE [RES]
Hopkinsville, KY
YEN JING CHINESE RESTAURANT
[RES] Atlanta, GA
ZACHRY'S SEAFOOD [RES] Jekyll
Island, GA
ZEKE'S LANDING [RES] Gulf Shores,
AL
ZEVELY HOUSE [RES] Winston-Salem,
NC
ZOCALO [RES] Atlanta, GA
ZOE BISTROT [RES] New Orleans, LA
ZOLA [RES] Nashville, TN

CITY INDEX

Mobil
Travel Guide®

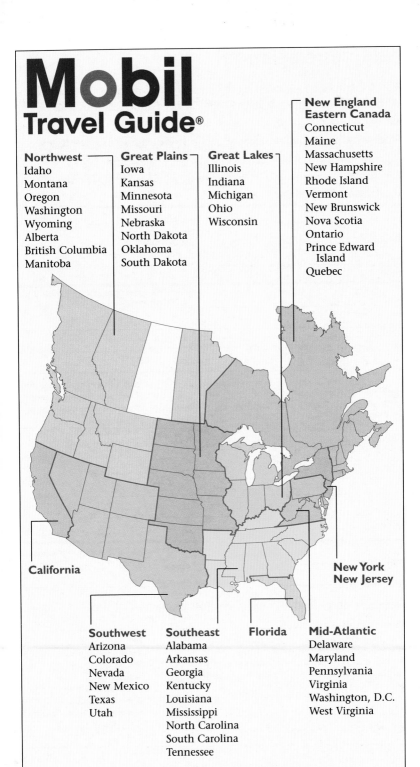

Northwest
Idaho
Montana
Oregon
Washington
Wyoming
Alberta
British Columbia
Manitoba

Great Plains
Iowa
Kansas
Minnesota
Missouri
Nebraska
North Dakota
Oklahoma
South Dakota

Great Lakes
Illinois
Indiana
Michigan
Ohio
Wisconsin

New England
Eastern Canada
Connecticut
Maine
Massachusetts
New Hampshire
Rhode Island
Vermont
New Brunswick
Nova Scotia
Ontario
Prince Edward
   Island
Quebec

California

New York
New Jersey

Southwest
Arizona
Colorado
Nevada
New Mexico
Texas
Utah

Southeast
Alabama
Arkansas
Georgia
Kentucky
Louisiana
Mississippi
North Carolina
South Carolina
Tennessee

Florida

Mid-Atlantic
Delaware
Maryland
Pennsylvania
Virginia
Washington, D.C.
West Virginia